Hampton-Brown EDGE

Reading, Writing & Language

PROGRAM AUTHORS

David W. Moore

Deborah J. Short

Michael W. Smith

Alfred W. Tatum

Literature Consultant

René Saldaña, Jr.

NATIONAL GEOGRAPHIC LEARNING | CENGAGE Learning

Acknowledgments

Grateful acknowledgment is given to the authors, artists, photographers, museums, publishers, and agents for permission to reprint copyrighted material. Every effort has been made to secure the appropriate permission. If any omissions have been made or if corrections are required, please contact the Publisher.

Photographic Credits

Cover: Ancient Eye, Arches National Park, Utah, USA, Marsel van Oosten. Photograph © Marsel van Oosten/ squiver.com.

Acknowledgments continue on page 1043.

For product information and technology assistance, contact us at
Customer & Sales Support, 888-915-3276

For permission to use material from this text or product, submit all requests online at **www.cengage.com/permissions**
Further permissions questions can be emailed to
permissionrequest@cengage.com

National Geographic Learning | Cengage Learning
1 Lower Ragsdale Drive
Building 1, Suite 200
Monterey, CA 93940

Cengage Learning is a leading provider of customized learning solutions with office locations around the globe, including Singapore, the United Kingdom, Australia, Mexico, Brazil, and Japan. Locate your local office at **www.cengage.com/global**.

Visit National Geographic Learning online at **ngl.cengage.com**
Visit our corporate website at **www.cengage.com**

Printed in the USA.
RR Donnelley, Willard, OH

ISBN: 978-12854-39594

Printed in the United States of America
15 16 17 18 19 20 21 22
10 9 8 7 6

CONTENTS AT A GLANCE

REVIEWERS

We gratefully acknowledge the many contributions of the following dedicated educators in creating a program that is not only pedagogically sound, but also appealing to and motivating for high school students.

LITERATURE CONSULTANT

Dr. René Saldaña, Jr., Ph.D.

Assistant Professor
Texas Tech University

Dr. Saldaña teaches English and education at the university level and is the author of *The Jumping Tree* (2001) and *Finding Our Way: Stories* (Random House/Wendy Lamb Books, 2003). More recently, several of his stories have appeared in anthologies such as *Face Relations*, *Guys Write for GUYS READ*, *Every Man for Himself*, and *Make Me Over*, and in magazines such as *Boy's Life* and *READ*.

Teacher Reviewers

Felisa Araujo-Rodriguez
English Teacher
Highlands HS
San Antonio, TX

Barbara Barbin
Former HS ESL Teacher
Aldine ISD
Houston, TX

Joseph Berkowitz
ESOL Chairperson
John A. Ferguson Sr. HS
Miami, FL

Dr. LaQuanda Brown-Avery
Instructional Assistant Principal
McNair MS
Decatur, GA

Troy Campbell
Teacher
Lifelong Education Charter
Los Angeles, CA

John Oliver Cox
English Language
Development Teacher
Coronado USD
Coronado, CA

Clairin DeMartini
Reading Coordinator
Clark County SD
Las Vegas, NV

Lori Kite Eli
High School Reading Teacher
Pasadena HS
Pasadena, TX

Debra Elkins
ESOL Teamleader/Teacher
George Bush HS
Fort Bend, IN

Lisa Fretzin
Reading Consultant
Niles North HS
Skokie, IL

Karen H. Gouede
Asst. Principal, ESL
John Browne HS
Flushing, NY

Alison Hyde
ESOL Teacher
Morton Ranch HS
Katy, TX

Patricia James
Reading Specialist
Brevard County
Melbourne Beach, FL

Dr. Anna Leibovich
ESL Teacher
Forest Hills HS
New York, NY

Donna D. Mussulman
Teacher
Belleville West HS
Belleville, IL

Rohini A. Parikh
Educator
Seward Park School
New York, NY

Sally Nan Ruskin
English/Reading Teacher
Braddock SHS
Miami, FL

Pamela Sholly
Teacher
Oceanside USD
Oceanside, CA

Dilmit Singh
Teacher/EL Coordinator
Granada Hills Charter HS
Granada Hills, CA

Amanda E. Stewart
Reading Teacher
Winter Park High School
Winter Park, FL

Beverly Troiano
ESL Teacher
Chicago Discovery Academy
Chicago, IL

Dr. Varavarnee Vaddhanayana
ESOL Coordinator
Clarkston HS
Clarkston, GA

Donna Reese Wallace
Reading Coach
Alternative Education
Orange County
Orlando, FL

Bonnie Woelfel
Reading Specialist
Escondido HS
Escondido, CA

Pian Y. Wong
English Teacher
High School of American Studies
New York, NY

Izumi Yoshioka
English Teacher
Washington Irving HS
New York, NY

Student Reviewers

We also gratefully acknowledge the high school students who read and reviewed selections and tested the Online Coach.

PROGRAM AUTHORS

David W. Moore, Ph.D.
Arizona State University

Dr. Moore taught high school in Arizona public schools before becoming a professor of education. He co-chaired the International Reading Association's Commission on Adolescent Literacy and is actively involved with several professional associations. His thirty-year publication record balances research reports, professional articles, book chapters, and books including *Developing Readers and Writers in the Content Areas, Teaching Adolescents Who Struggle with Reading,* and *Principled Practices for Adolescent Literacy.*

Deborah J. Short, Ph.D.
Center for Applied Linguistics

Dr. Short is a co-developer of the research-validated SIOP Model for sheltered instruction. She has directed scores of studies on English Language Learners and published scholarly articles in *TESOL Quarterly, The Journal of Educational Research, Language Teaching Research,* and many others. Dr. Short also co-wrote a policy report: *Double the Work: Challenges and Solutions to Acquiring Language and Academic Literacy for Adolescent English Language Learners.* She has conducted extensive research on secondary level newcomers programs and on long term English language learners.

Michael W. Smith, Ph.D.
Temple University

Dr. Michael Smith joined the ranks of college teachers after eleven years teaching high school English. He has won awards for his teaching both at the high school and college level. He contributed to the Common Core State Standards initiative by serving on the Aspects of Text Complexity working group. His research focuses on how readers read and talk about texts and what motivates adolescents' reading and writing both in and out of school. His books include *"Reading Don't Fix No Chevys": Literacy in the Lives of Young Men, Fresh Takes on Teaching Literary Elements: How to Teach What Really Matters About Character, Setting, Point of View, and Theme,* and *Oh, Yeah?! Putting Argument to Work Both in School and Out.*

Alfred W. Tatum, Ph.D.
Northern Illinois University

Dr. Tatum began his career as an eighth-grade teacher and reading specialist. He conducts research on the power of texts and literacy to reshape the life outcomes of striving readers. His research focuses on the literacy development of African American adolescent males. He has served on the National Advisory Reading Committee of the National Assessment of Educational Progress (NAEP). Dr. Tatum's books include *Reading for Their Life: (Re)Building the Textual Lineages of African American Adolescent Males* and *Teaching Reading to Black Adolescent Males: Closing the Achievement Gap.*

Genre Focus
Short Stories

Focus Strategy
Plan and Monitor

DOUBLE TAKE

EQ ESSENTIAL QUESTION:
When Do You Really Know Someone?

Man Holding African Masks, Cape Town, South Africa, Lavonne Bosman. Photograph ©Gallo Images/Alamy.

WRITING PROJECT

**Good Writing Trait
Focus and Unity**

UNIT 2

AGAINST THE
ODDS

EQ ESSENTIAL QUESTION:
How Do People Challenge Expectations?

A Man in a Wingsuit Leaps Off a Peak, Baffin Island, Canada, Krystle Wright. Photograph ©Krystle Wright.

WRITING PROJECT

Good Writing Trait
Voice and Style

THE TIES THAT BIND

EQ ESSENTIAL QUESTION:
What Tests a Person's Loyalty?

Selma to Montgomery March for Voting Rights, Alabama, USA, 1965, Matt Herron. Photograph ©1976 Matt Herron/ Take Stock/The Image Works.

WRITING PROJECT

Good Writing Trait
Development of Ideas

EXPRESS YOURSELF

EQ **ESSENTIAL QUESTION:**
What Does It Really Mean to Communicate?

Young Men Enjoying the Festival of Colors, Mathura, India, Poras Chaudhary. Photograph ©Poras Chaudhary/The Image Bank/Getty Images.

WRITING PROJECT

Good Writing Trait
Organization

MOMENT OF
TRUTH

EQ ESSENTIAL QUESTION:
What Do People Discover in a Moment of Truth?

A Papua Man Swims with a Whale Shark, Papua, New Guinea, Michael Aw. Photograph ©Michael Aw.

WRITING PROJECT

Good Writing Trait
Development of Ideas

RIGHTS
AND **RESPONSIBILITIES**

EQ ESSENTIAL QUESTION:
How Can We Balance Everyone's Rights?

Speaker at Speaker's Corner in Hyde Park, London, England, Will and Deni McIntyre. Photograph ©Will & Deni McIntyre/CORBIS.

WRITING PROJECT

Good Writing Trait
Focus and Unity

FOR WHAT IT'S WORTH

EQ ESSENTIAL QUESTION:
What Deserves Our Care and Respect?

Coal Miners Level an Appalachian Mountaintop, Kayford Mountain, West Virginia, USA, 2010, J. Henry Fair.
Photograph ©J. Henry Fair.

RESOURCES

Language and Learning Handbook
Language, Learning, Communication

Reading Handbook
Reading, Fluency, Vocabulary

Writing Handbook
Writing Process, Traits, Conventions

LITERATURE

Rhythm in Blue, 2004, Mark Buku. Oil on canvas, courtesy of Novica.com.

Poetry & Lyrics (continued)

Cartoon

INFORMATIONAL TEXTS

Article

Autobiography & Profile

Declarations

Diary

Essay

Expository

EQ **ESSENTIAL QUESTION:**

When Do You Really Know Someone?

She knows who she is because she knows who she isn't.

—NIKKI GIOVANNI

There is no truth, only perception.

—GUSTAVE FLAUBERT

Critical Viewing ▶
A man holds up two masks in Cape Town, South Africa. How do the masks hide the man? How do they reveal him?

DOUBLE
TAKE

EQ ESSENTIAL QUESTION:
When Do You Really Know Someone?

Study the Questions
Can you ever be sure that you really know another person? How well do you know your family, your friends, or your classmates? Look at these questions and see if you can answer them about a classmate. Then have your classmate answer the questions. When you are both done, compare your answers.

How Well Do You Know Someone?
Choose four of the following questions to answer. You can also come up with your own question.

1. What is your favorite (pick one): color, food, or sport?
2. What gift would you most like to receive?
3. What was the last movie you saw?
4. Would you rather ride a bike, ride a horse, or drive a car? Why?
5. If you had a choice to have a pet, what would it be?
6. If you had to do one of these, which would you rather do: wash dishes, mow the lawn, cook a meal, or vacuum the house?

Other question: _____

Source: Adapted from *Advocates for Youth*, http://www.advocatesforyouth.org

Analyze and Debate
1. What is something that you learned about your classmate that you didn't know? Which answer surprised you the most? Why?

2. Based on this information and your experience, what is the best way to get to know someone? By looking at their appearance? Judging their words? Evaluating their actions?

Discuss these questions with a group. Explain your opinions and give examples to support your ideas.

EQ ESSENTIAL QUESTION
In this unit, you will explore the **Essential Question** in class through reading, discussion, research, and writing. Keep thinking about the question outside of school, too.

① Plan a Project

Video or Sound Recording

In this unit, you'll create a video presentation or make a sound recording of a literary work that addresses the Essential Question. To get started, browse the Internet or the school library for poems, short stories, short essays, and other literary works. Consider

- what literary work you will choose
- whether to make a video or sound recording
- who will read or perform the literary work in your presentation.

Study Skills Start planning your recording. Use the forms on myNGconnect.com to plan your time and to prepare the content.

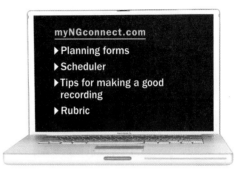

myNGconnect.com
▸ Planning forms
▸ Scheduler
▸ Tips for making a good recording
▸ Rubric

② Choose More to Read

These readings provide different answers to the Essential Question. Choose a book and online selections to read during the unit.

Farewell to Manzanar
by Jeanne Wakatsuki Houston and James D. Houston

The year was 1941. Japanese planes bombed U.S. territory. All Japanese Americans, including the Wakatsuki family, were forced to live in prison camps. Would they survive the prison camp? And even if they did, would their lives in the U.S. ever be the same?

▸ **NONFICTION**

The Metamorphosis
by Franz Kafka
adapted by Peter Kuper

Gregor Samsa does everything he can to support his family. But Gregor is treated like an insect. Then one morning he wakes to find he has become an insect! Will Gregor wake from his nightmare reality, or is he doomed to be an insect for the rest of his life?

▸ **GRAPHIC CLASSIC**

Stuck in Neutral
by Terry Trueman

What would it be like to see, hear, and understand, but not be able to talk, write, or even move? This is the life Shawn McDaniel leads. Shawn has cerebral palsy. His family loves him. They worry about him. But if he can't communicate, how can they really know him?

▸ **NOVEL**

myNGconnect.com

⊙ See statistics on how well parents and teens know each other.

⊙ Create a quiz for your friends and family to test how well they really know you.

⊙ Explore your ancestry and find out more about your family history.

USING READING STRATEGIES

Reading Strategy

When you read fiction or nonfiction, you can use strategies to understand different parts of the text. Reading strategies are tools for thinking that help you interact with the text and take control of your reading comprehension.

Reading Strategies

Plan and Monitor	Set a purpose before you read. Make predictions and then read on to confirm them. Figure out confusing text by rereading or reading on.
Visualize	Picture sensory details in your mind.
Make Connections	Connect what you read with what you have read or experienced.
Ask Questions	Ask about things you don't know. Look for clues in the text.
Make Inferences	Combine what you read with what you know to figure out what the author doesn't say directly.
Synthesize	Bring several ideas together to understand something new.
Determine Importance	Identify and summarize the most important ideas.

Reading Handbook, page 781

Now read how one student applied reading strategies with this selection. As you read, pay attention to the reading strategies you use.

DEMO TEXT

EYE OF THE BEHOLDER

What influences how you react when you meet a new person? What he looks like? How she's dressed? Who you're with? Where you are? Consider this example.

Subway Soloist

Some years ago, *The Washington Post* reported that on a chilly January weekday morning during the peak of the morning commute, a Caucasian man dressed in jeans, a long-sleeved T-shirt, and wearing a baseball cap stood beside a trash can in a Washington DC metro station. He opened his violin case, took out his violin, placed the open case on the floor in front of

Before I read, I can **plan and monitor**. I preview the title and headings. I predict the text will be about "stereotypes."

I can use details to **visualize**, or picture, the musician as he prepared to play in the busy metro station.

him, and began to play "Chaconne" from Johann Sebastian Bach's Partita No. 2 in D Minor. For the next forty-five minutes, he continued to play other classical pieces of music. During that time, more than 1000 passengers walked by him. Seven people stopped—for at least a minute—to listen, and about thirty hurriedly dropped money in his violin case. He made about $33. The musician was world-famous musician Joshua Bell. The violin he played cost about 3.5 million dollars. Prior to his subway performance, dressed in his typical attire of a black dress shirt and classic black pants, Bell had played at Symphony Hall in Boston to a full house. Some had paid more than $100 a ticket to hear him play.

*I can **make a connection** to the passengers. If I were on my way to work or school, I wouldn't have stopped either.*

Social Experiment

Obviously, Joshua Bell is not hard up for cash. He was participating in a social experiment conducted by *The Washington Post*. One of the purposes of the experiment was to figure out whether Bell would be recognized when placed in a completely different venue from the one in which he usually performs. The pieces he played were not popular pieces. In fact, Bell and the organizers of the experiment had deliberately chosen pieces that were not immediately familiar. They didn't want passengers drawn to the music because they recognized it. They wanted them to stop and listen because they recognized great music.

*I can **ask questions** about words in the text I don't know. I ask myself, What's a "venue"? I can use details in the text to help me. Now I know that a venue must be a place.*

Would Bell have attracted more attention had he been dressed less casually and been standing on the steps of the Lincoln Memorial during peak tourist season?

*Based on what I read and know, I can **infer** that Bell would have attracted more attention at the Washington Memorial.*

Stereotypes

A stereotype is a fixed idea about a particular person or group. People use stereotypes to simplify their worlds. It reduces the amount of thinking they have to do every time they encounter a new person. But stereotyping makes people ignore the differences between individuals. It makes us think things about people that are not true. Maybe if the people in the metro had known the guy standing next to garbage can was a world-famous musician, more would have stopped to listen. But instead, they saw just another street performer.

*I can **synthesize** from the details here that stereotyping is part of human nature.*

Now it's your turn. What stereotypes do you have? What do you think of when you read each of the following words?

judge, hero, victim, teenager, parent, heiress, garbage collector, dentist, politician

The truth is that everyone stereotypes. The trick is to recognize it when you're doing it. Everyone wants to be seen for who he or she really is. Let's try not to let stereotypes cloud our judgment.

*I can **determine what is important** by finding the main idea: Stereotypes cloud our judgment about people*

SHORT STORIES

One way to find out how stories work is to think about how you make sense of a little story like this one. Read "Partners."

Partners

The bell rang. Jada sighed, slowly moved from the lockers where she had been leaning, and headed down the hall to her chemistry class. Honors Chemistry! Jada couldn't believe that her mom was making her take the class just because Jada's counselor had said that she had real talent in science.

Jada had to admit that she liked science and that last year's class was a breeze, but come on, Honors Chemistry? She wouldn't know anyone in the class, and they probably wouldn't know anyone like *her*.

The good thing about being late is that it shortened the period a bit. The bad thing is that it made her seem like she was making a grand entrance. To make matters worse, the only two seats left in class were at the lab table at the very front of the room.

Jada sucked in her breath and walked in. Everyone's eyes were on her. She just knew it. They were staring at her coal black hair (freshly dyed), her black lipstick, her black fingernail polish, and her thrift-store black leather jacket. All she saw were polo shirts and khaki pants.

This can't get any worse, Jada thought. But at least she didn't get yelled at by the teacher. He was too busy talking to a new kid. A HUGE

new kid, maybe 6'4". He had to weigh at least 250 pounds. A football player, probably. She hated football players. They thought they were so great. That group of jocks that hung out by the cafeteria always made fun of her.

The new kid made his way over to her table with his head down. He had to squeeze into the seat, and his legs wouldn't fit under the lab table. He shot Jada a glance and blushed.

Mr. Martin, the teacher, began class with this announcement: "Okay, everyone. I know most of you know each other from last year's Honors Physical Science class." Jada sighed loudly. "But just take a minute and introduce yourself to the person sitting at your table. You'll be lab partners. You'll be working closely together all year."

Jada rolled her eyes and stared straight ahead. Then she heard a surprisingly soft voice from next to her. "Hi, I'm Robert. I'm new here." . . .

Reading Strategies

▶ Plan and Monitor
· Determine Importance
· Make Inferences
· Ask Questions
· Make Connections
· Synthesize
· Visualize

■ Connect Reading to Your Life

Rank the following six statements 1 to 6, with (1) showing what you think is *most likely* to happen as the story continues, and (6) showing what you think is *least likely* to happen.

Rank

_____ Robert deliberately sets up the first experiment wrong so that water spills all over Jada.

_____ The teacher assigns different partners to Jada and Robert.

_____ Robert tells the football players by the cafeteria to stop making fun of Jada.

_____ Jada and Robert have trouble on the first lab but start working together much better as the class goes on.

_____ Jada discovers that Robert likes the same metal bands she does, and they go to a concert together.

_____ Jada starts wearing polo shirts and khaki pants so she fits in better.

Compare your **predictions** with a partner. If your rankings are different, discuss how you decided which was most likely and which was least likely, using your own experience and the text of "Partners" as support.

Focus Strategy ▶ Plan and Monitor

The predictions you made are an important kind of planning. As you read, you'll be checking whether you're more or less sure of those predictions. That's called **monitoring**.

You plan and monitor all the time. Think of the last time you saw a horror movie. You probably made a prediction as to which character would be the first to die. As you watched, you might have changed your prediction or you might have become more sure of it.

■ Your Job as a Reader

Whenever you read a short story, pay attention to the title, the characters, the setting, and the conflict. Then make predictions based on that. Your plan for reading is, in part, to find out whether those predictions come true. Monitor your predictions by paying attention to new details and then seeing whether they fit your predictions or whether you have to revise them.

Academic Vocabulary
- **predict** *v.*, to tell in advance; **prediction** *n.*, statement of what someone thinks will happen
- **monitor** *v.*, to keep track of; to check

■ Unpack the Thinking Process

How you plan and monitor your reading depends on your knowledge of how different kinds of stories work and on your knowledge of how different kinds of people behave in various situations.

Characters and Conflicts

For example, we know that most stories (including the ones you watch on TV or in movies) involve a problem, or **conflict**. The conflicts can be **external**—problems caused by a person, by society, or even by nature. Conflicts can also be **internal**—problems caused by the character's own thoughts and feelings.

Conflicts always cause one or more of the characters to change in some way or another. In fact, there's even a special term for characters who change: **dynamic** characters. Characters who stay the same are **static**. The main character, or **protagonist**, is usually the one who changes the most. The character or characters causing the conflict—the **antagonist**—can change, too.

Experienced readers look for changes right from the start.

- If a character is lonely, look for events that might cause the character to become connected to others.
- If a character cares only about money, look for things that might teach the character that money isn't everything.
- A character who begins a story being happy about the success of others might become consumed by jealousy.

Stories involve movement and change. Picture a character's change like this.

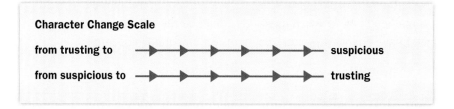

Character Change Scale

from trusting to ➔➔➔➔➔ suspicious

from suspicious to ➔➔➔➔➔ trusting

Elements of Literature

conflict *n.*, problem or struggle that drives a story's plot
dynamic *adj.*, active; full of energy
static *adj.*, not active; not moving or changing
protagonist *n.*, main character in the story
antagonist *n.*, opposing character in the story

Academic Vocabulary

- **external** *adj.*, outside; beyond
- **internal** *adj.*, inside; within

Sometimes characters influence those around them. Other times those people will influence the character. For example, you might predict that Robert may influence the football players in a positive way, but it's possible that they could influence him in a negative way. Because you can't be sure how characters will change, you have to monitor what's happening. You can be sure, however, that changes are likely.

Knowing how stories work isn't enough. You also have to apply what you know about the world. You probably applied what you know about students who remind you of Jada and Robert when you made your prediction. You probably also applied what you know about being new in school and taking a chemistry class.

■ Try an Experiment

Imagine that the story continues with Robert saying, "Um, I just started school here today. I'm nervous about this class. I didn't want to be in it. I don't think I'm very good in science. I hope I don't slow you down." Now rank these possible predictions again:

> _____ Robert deliberately sets up the first experiment wrong so that water spills all over Jada.
> _____ The teacher assigns different partners to Jada and Robert.
> _____ Robert tells the football players by the cafeteria to stop making fun of Jada.
> _____ Jada and Robert have trouble on the first lab, but start working together much better as the class goes on.
> _____ Jada discovers that Robert likes the same metal bands she does, and they go to a concert together.
> _____ Jada starts wearing polo shirts and khaki pants so she fits in better.

Think, Pair, Share Compare your predictions with a partner. Talk about how the new details affected your predictions. Then answer these questions:

1. Who is the protagonist in the story? How do you know?

2. What conflict does the protagonist face?

3. How are the characters likely to change? Draw a **Character Change Scale** for Jada and for Robert.

Monitor Comprehension

Conflict What purpose does conflict have in a story?

EQ When Do You Really Know Someone?
Watch for the moment when people show you who they are.

Make a Connection

Anticipation Guide Think about the people you know really well and how long it took you to get to know them. Then tell whether you agree or disagree with these statements.

ANTICIPATION GUIDE

Agree or Disagree

1. You can't really know someone who is different from you. _____

2. Your first impressions of a person are usually right. _____

3. Even the people you know well have secrets you know nothing about. _____

Learn Key Vocabulary

Study the Words Pronounce each word and learn its meaning. You may also want to look up the definitions in the Glossary.

● Academic Vocabulary

Key Words	Examples
characterize (**kair**-ik-tu-rīz) *verb* ▸ pages 15, 26	When you **characterize** someone, you describe the person's most important characteristics, or qualities. How would you **characterize** your best friend?
● **intensity** (in-**ten**-su-tē) *noun* ▸ page 19	To have **intensity** means to have a lot of feeling or strength. The woman's **intensity** on the basketball court made her a good player. *Synonym*: force; *Antonym*: weakness
lucid (**lü**-sid) *adjective* ▸ page 19	Sometimes the man talks crazy, but today he is **lucid** and sensible. *Synonym*: sane; *Antonym*: insane
obscure (ob-**skyur**) *verb* ▸ page 19	To **obscure** is to conceal or hide. The tall building across the street **obscured** the view outside my window. *Synonym*: block; *Antonym*: reveal
pathetic (pu-**the**-tik) *adjective* ▸ page 22	The person who has a **pathetic** look on her face appears to be miserable. *Synonyms*: sad, pitiful; *Antonyms*: funny, comical
● **perspective** (pur-**spek**-tiv) *noun* ▸ pages 29, 32, 33	Your **perspective** is your point of view or opinions about something. From your **perspective**, was the movie good or boring? *Synonym*: view
pretense (**prē**-tens) *noun* ▸ page 22	**Pretense** is the act of pretending. The fighter looked confident at the beginning of the fight, but that was just a **pretense**. He was actually afraid.
stigmatize (**stig**-mah-tīz) *verb* ▸ pages 29, 33	If you **stigmatize** someone, you label the person as bad and hurt the person's reputation. *Synonyms*: disgrace, shame; *Antonyms*: praise, honor

Practice the Words With a classmate, make a **Vocabulary Study Card** for each Key Vocabulary word. On one side of a note card, write the word. On the other side, define the word and use it in a sentence. After you have made a card for each word, use the cards to quiz your partner.

Before Reading The Moustache

short story by Robert Cormier

Reading Strategies

▶ **Plan and Monitor**
· Determine Importance
· Make Inferences
· Ask Questions
· Make Connections
· Synthesize
· Visualize

Analyze Conflict

In most short stories, the main character faces a **conflict**, or struggle.

1. In an **external conflict**, a character struggles against someone or something outside himself or herself. The conflict might be with another character or a group of people. It may even be a force of nature, such as a snowstorm.

2. In an **internal conflict**, a character struggles within himself or herself to make a hard decision or to overcome opposing feelings or desires.

Look Into the Text

The author sets up the conflict.

> I had to go to Lawnrest [Nursing Home] alone that afternoon. But first of all I had to stand inspection. My mother lined me up against the wall…. She frowned and started the routine.
> "That hair," she said….
> I sighed. I have discovered that it's better to sigh than argue.
> "And that moustache." She shook her head. "I still say a seventeen-year-old has no business wearing a moustache."
> "It's an experiment," I said….
> "It's costing you money, Mike," she said.
> "I know, I know."

Here are the causes of the conflict.

Is the conflict external or internal?

Focus Strategy ▶ Plan and Monitor

In most short stories, the **conflict** is resolved by the end of the story. As you read, make and confirm predictions about how the conflict will be resolved.

HOW TO MAKE AND CONFIRM PREDICTIONS

Focus Strategy

1. **Look for Clues** Notice clues about how the characters feel and what they think.

2. **Predict** Imagine that the characters are real. What would they do?

3. **Check It Out** Read on to see whether you were right. What evidence in the text confirms your prediction? Keep track on a chart like the one below.

Prediction	Did It Happen?	Evidence
I think Mike will keep his moustache.		

Robert Cormier
(1925–2000)

I take real people and put them in extraordinary situations.

Robert Cormier did not seem like an author who would create controversy, or argument. He never lived farther than three miles from his childhood home in Leominster, Massachusetts, and for many years, he was a popular columnist for a local newspaper. On most afternoons, he could be found in the area's public library.

However, controversy for Cormier began in 1974, when he published his novel *The Chocolate War.* The novel deals with bullying at a New England school in a realistic way. Soon some people were calling for the book to be banned from libraries and schools.

Despite this pressure, Cormier never backed down. "One of the

Robert Cormier worked as a radio reporter and newspaper editor before writing novels.

sentences that occurs all the time in letters I receive is: 'You tell it like it is.' And that's affirmation for me and keeps me going."

Cormier continued to write about the realities of growing up, with novels such as *I Am the Cheese* and stories such as "The Moustache." His stories reflect an amazing ability to focus on everyday American life and capture it from the perspective of teenagers, who see things that adults don't always see.

myNGconnect.com

🔊 Watch an interview with Robert Cormier.
🔊 Explore the psychology behind being a teenager.

The Moustache

by Robert Cormier

Curly, London, 1961, Peter Samuelson. Oil on board, private collection. The Bridgeman Art Library.

▲ Critical Viewing: Effect What is the mood, or feeling, of the young man in the painting? What creates this mood?

 Comprehension Coach

Set a Purpose
Read to find out how the teenage narrator responds to conflict.

At the last minute Annie couldn't go. She was <u>invaded</u> by one of those twenty-four-hour flu bugs that sent her to bed with a fever, <u>moaning</u> about the fact that she'd also have to break her date with Handsome Harry Arnold that night. We call him Handsome Harry because he's actually handsome, but he's also a nice guy, cool, and he doesn't treat me like Annie's kid brother, which I am, but like a regular person. Anyway, I had to go to Lawnrest alone that afternoon. But first of all I had to **stand inspection**. My mother lined me up against the wall. She stood there like a **one-man firing squad**, which is kind of funny because she's not like a man at all, she's very feminine, and we have this great relationship—I mean, I feel as if she really likes me. I realize that sounds strange, but I know guys whose mothers love them and cook special stuff for them and worry about them and all but there's something missing in their relationship.

Anyway. She <u>frowned</u> and started the <u>routine</u>.

"That hair," she said. Then admitted: "Well, at least you <u>combed</u> it."

I sighed. I have discovered that it's better to sigh than argue.

"And that moustache." She shook her head. "I still say a seventeen-year-old has no business wearing a moustache."

"It's an experiment," I said. "I just wanted to see if I could grow one." To tell the truth, I had proved my point about being able to grow a decent moustache, but I also had learned to like it.

"It's costing you money, Mike," she said.

"I know, I know."

The money was a reference to the movies. The Downtown Cinema has a special Friday night offer—half-price admission for high school couples, seventeen or younger. But the woman in the box office took one look at my moustache and charged me full price. Even when I showed her my

1 Make Predictions
What do you think Mike will do about his moustache? Keep track of your prediction on your chart.

In Other Words
stand inspection be looked over
one-man firing squad person ready to take aim

driver's license. She charged full admission for Cindy's ticket, too, which left me practically broke and unable to take Cindy out for a hamburger with the crowd afterward. That didn't help matters, because Cindy has been getting impatient recently about things like the fact that I don't own my own car and have to concentrate on my studies if I want to win that college scholarship, for instance. Cindy wasn't exactly crazy about the moustache, either.

Now it was my mother's turn to sigh.

"Look," I said, to cheer her up. "I'm thinking about shaving it off." Even though I wasn't. Another discovery: You can build a way of life on **postponement**. 2

"Your grandmother probably won't even recognize you," she said. And I saw the shadow fall across her face.

Let me tell you what the visit to Lawnrest was all about. My grandmother is seventy-three years old. She is a resident—which is supposed to be a better word than *patient*—at the Lawnrest Nursing Home. She used to make the

> **Your grandmother probably won't even recognize you.**

greatest turkey dressing in the world and was a nut about baseball and could even quote batting averages, for crying out loud. She always **rooted for** the losers. She was in love with the Mets until they started to win. Now she has arteriosclerosis, which the dictionary says is "a chronic disease **characterized** by abnormal thickening and hardening of the arterial walls." Which really means that she can't live at home anymore or even with us, and her memory has betrayed her as well as her body. She used to wander off and sometimes didn't recognize people. My mother visits her all the time, driving the thirty miles to Lawnrest almost every day. Because Annie was home for a semester break from college, we had decided to make a special Saturday visit. 3

2 **Conflict**
What do you predict will be the major conflict in the story? Explain.

3 **Access Vocabulary**
Arteriosclerosis is a medical term. Mike says the dictionary definition of this term. What else do you learn about the meaning of the term from this paragraph?

Key Vocabulary
characterize *v.*, to describe the quality or character of a person

In Other Words
postponement delay
rooted for cheered for

Now Annie was in bed, groaning theatrically—she's a drama major—but I told my mother I'd go, anyway. I hadn't seen my grandmother since she'd been admitted to Lawnrest. Besides, the place is located on the Southwest Turnpike, which meant I could **barrel along** in my father's new Le Mans. My ambition was to see the speedometer hit seventy-five. Ordinarily, I used the old station wagon, which can barely stagger up to fifty.

Frankly, I wasn't too crazy about visiting a nursing home. They reminded me of hospitals and hospitals turn me off. I mean, the smell of ether makes me nauseous, and I feel faint at the sight of blood. And as I approached Lawnrest—which is a terrible cemetery kind of name, to begin with—I was sorry I hadn't avoided the trip. Then I felt guilty about it. I'm loaded with **guilt complexes**. Like driving like a madman after promising my father to be careful. Like sitting in the parking lot, looking at the nursing home with dread and thinking how I'd rather be with Cindy. Then I thought of all the Christmas and birthday gifts my grandmother had given me and I got out of the car, guilty, as usual. **4**

Inside, I was surprised by the lack of hospital smell, although there was another odor or maybe the absence of an odor. The air was antiseptic, sterile. As if there was no atmosphere at all or I'd caught a cold suddenly and couldn't taste or smell.

4 Conflict
What do Mike's words reveal about his feelings? What is his internal conflict?

July Interior, 1964, Fairfield Porter. Oil on canvas, Hirshhorn Museum and Sculpture Garden, Smithsonian Institution, Washington, D.C.

▲ **Critical Viewing: Character** What details in this painting tell you what the woman's life might be like?

In Other Words
barrel along drive at a high speed
guilt complexes sad feelings about behaving badly in the past

Monitor Comprehension

Confirm Prediction
Do you still think your prediction is logical? Will Mike keep his moustache?

A nurse at the reception desk gave me directions—my grandmother was in East Three. I made my way down the tiled corridor and was glad to see that the walls were painted with cheerful colors like yellow and pink. A wheelchair suddenly shot around a corner, self-propelled by an old man, white-haired and toothless, who **cackled merrily** as he barely missed me. I jumped aside—here I was, almost getting wiped out by a two-mile-an-hour wheelchair after doing seventy-five on the pike. As I walked through the corridor seeking East Three, I couldn't help glancing into the rooms, and it was like some kind of wax museum—all these figures in various stances and attitudes, sitting in beds or chairs, standing at windows, as if they were frozen forever in these postures. To tell the truth, I began to hurry because I was getting depressed. **5** Finally, I saw a beautiful girl approaching, dressed in white, a nurse or an attendant, and I was so happy to see someone young, someone walking and acting normally, that I gave her a wide smile and a big hello and I must have looked like a kind of nut. Anyway, she looked right through me as if I were a window, which is about **par for the course** whenever I meet beautiful girls.

I finally found the room and saw my grandmother in bed. My grandmother looks like Ethel Barrymore. I never knew who Ethel Barrymore was until I saw a terrific movie, *None But the Lonely Heart,* on TV, starring Ethel Barrymore and Cary Grant. Both my grandmother and Ethel Barrymore have these great **craggy** faces like the side of a mountain and wonderful voices like syrup being poured. Slowly. **6** She was propped up in bed, pillows puffed behind her. Her hair had been combed out and fell upon her shoulders. For some reason, this flowing hair gave her an almost girlish appearance, despite its whiteness.

5 Conflict
What conflict is Mike experiencing? Is it internal or external? How can you tell?

6 Language
How does the author's language help you picture the face of Mike's grandmother?

In Other Words
cackled merrily laughed happily
par for the course what usually happens
craggy wrinkled, almost rocky looking

Cultural Background
Ethel Barrymore (1879–1959) was an award-winning actress. Several generations of the family became actors, including her great-niece, Drew Barrymore.

She saw me and smiled. Her eyes lit up and her eyebrows arched and she reached out her hands to me in greeting. "Mike, Mike," she said. And I breathed a sigh of relief. This was one of her good days. My mother had warned me that she might not know who I was at first.

I took her hands in mine. They were fragile. I could actually feel her bones, and it seemed as if they would break if I pressed too hard. Her skin was smooth, almost slippery, as if the years had worn away all the roughness the way the wind wears away the surfaces of stones.

"Mike, Mike, I didn't think you'd come," she said, so happy, and she was still Ethel Barrymore, that voice like a **caress**. "I've been waiting all this time." Before I could reply, she looked away, out the window. "See the birds? I've been watching them at the feeder. I love to see them come. Even the blue jays. The blue jays are like hawks—they take the food that the small birds should have. But the small birds, the chickadees, watch the blue jays and at least learn where the feeder is." **7**

She lapsed into silence, and I looked out the window. There was no feeder. No birds. There was only the parking lot and the sun **glinting** on car windshields.

She turned to me again, eyes bright. Radiant, really. Or was it a medicine brightness? "Ah, Mike. You look so grand, so grand. Is that a new coat?"

"Not really," I said. I'd been wearing my Uncle Jerry's old army-fatigue jacket for months, practically living in it, my mother said. But she insisted that I wear my raincoat for the visit. It was about a year old but looked new because I didn't wear it much. Nobody was wearing raincoats lately.

> I took her hands in mine.
> **They were fragile**

7 Make Predictions
What do you think Mike and his grandmother will talk about? Record your prediction on your chart.

In Other Words
caress soft touch
glinting reflecting brightly

"You always loved clothes, didn't you, Mike?" she said.

I was beginning to feel uneasy because she regarded me with such **intensity**. Those bright eyes. I wondered—are old people in places like this so lonesome, so abandoned that they go wild when someone visits? Or was she so happy because she was suddenly **lucid** and everything was sharp and clear? My mother had described those moments when my grandmother suddenly emerged from the fog that so often **obscured** her mind. I didn't know the answers, but it felt kind of spooky, getting such an emotional welcome from her.

"I remember the time you bought the new coat—the Chesterfield," she said, looking away again, as if watching the birds that weren't there. "That lovely coat with the velvet collar. Black, it was. Stylish. Remember that, Mike? It was hard times, but you could never resist the glitter."

I was about to protest—I had never heard of a Chesterfield, for crying out loud. But I stopped. Be patient with her, my mother had said. Humor her. Be gentle. **8**

Wind, 1995, Timothy Woodman. Oil on aluminum, private collection, courtesy Tibor de Nagy Gallery, New York.

 Critical Viewing: Conflict How does this sculpture reflect Mike's conflict? What mood does it communicate to you?

8 Conflict
Why does Mike stop himself from expressing his confusion?

Monitor Comprehension

Confirm Prediction
Did you change or keep your prediction as you read along? Explain.

Key Vocabulary
- **intensity** *n.*, a lot of feeling or strength
- **lucid** *adj.*, sensible and sane
- **obscure** *v.*, to conceal or hide

Cultural Background
A **Chesterfield** is a full-length wool overcoat. It is named for a 19th-century English nobleman, the Earl of Chesterfield.

What do you think will happen at the end of Mike's visit?

We were interrupted by an attendant who pushed a wheeled cart into the room. "Time for juices, dear," the woman said. She was the standard forty- or fifty-year-old woman: glasses, nothing hair, plump cheeks. Her manner was cheerful but a businesslike kind of cheerfulness. I'd hate to be called "dear" by someone getting paid to do it. "Orange or grape or cranberry, dear? Cranberry is good for the bones, you know."

My grandmother ignored the interruption. She didn't even bother to answer, having turned away at the woman's arrival, as if angry about her appearance.

The woman looked at me and winked. **A conspiratorial kind of wink.** It was kind of horrible. I didn't think people winked like that anymore. In fact, I hadn't seen a wink in years.

"She doesn't care much for juices," the woman said, talking to me as if my grandmother weren't even there. "But she loves her coffee. With lots of cream and two lumps of sugar. But this is juice time, not coffee time." Addressing my grandmother again, she said, "Orange or grape or cranberry, dear?"

"Tell her I want no juices, Mike," my grandmother **commanded regally**, her eyes still watching invisible birds.

The woman smiled, patience like a label on her face. "That's all right, dear. I'll just leave some cranberry for you. Drink it at your leisure. It's good for the bones." **9**

She wheeled herself out of the room. My grandmother was still absorbed in the view. Somewhere a toilet flushed. A wheelchair passed the doorway—probably that same old driver fleeing a hit-run accident. A television set exploded with sound somewhere, soap-opera voices filling the air. You can always tell soap-opera voices.

9 Conflict
What does the grandmother's reaction say about the kind of person she is?

In Other Words
A conspiratorial kind of wink. The sneaky look of someone who is plotting against another person.
commanded regally directed like a queen

I turned back to find my grandmother staring at me. Her hands cupped her face, her index fingers curled around her cheeks like parenthesis marks.

"But you know, Mike, looking back, I think you were right," she said, continuing our conversation as if there had been no interruption. "You always said, 'It's the things of the spirit that count, Meg.' The spirit! And so you bought the baby-grand piano—a baby grand in the middle of the Depression. A knock came on the door and it was the deliveryman. It took five of them to get it into the house." She leaned back, closing her eyes. "How I loved that piano, Mike. I was never that fine a player, but you loved to sit there in the parlor, on Sunday evenings, Ellie on your lap, listening to me play and sing." She hummed a bit, a fragment of melody I didn't recognize. Then she drifted into silence. Maybe she'd fallen asleep. My mother's name is Ellen, but everyone always calls her Ellie. "Take my hand, Mike," my grandmother said suddenly. Then I remembered—my grandfather's name was Michael. I had been named for him.

"Ah, Mike," she said, pressing my hands with all her feeble strength. "I thought I'd lost you forever. And here you are, back with me again. . . ."

Her expression scared me. I don't mean scared as if I were in danger but scared because of what could happen to her when she realized the mistake she had made. My mother always said I **favored** her side of the family. Thinking back to the pictures in the old family albums, I recalled my grandfather as tall and thin. Like me. But the resemblance ended there. He was thirty-five when he died, almost forty years ago. And he wore a moustache. I brought my hand to my face. I also wore a moustache now, of course. 🔟

Her expression scared me.

"I sit here these days, Mike," she said, her voice a lullaby, her hand still holding mine, "and I drift and dream. The days are fuzzy sometimes,

🔟 **Conflict**
What mistake does Mike's grandmother make about him?

In Other Words
favored looked like

Historical Background
The **Great Depression** was a period of financial disaster that lasted from October 1929 through most of the 1930s. Almost a quarter of American workers lost their jobs. Wages and prices fell, and many banks went out of business.

merging together. Sometimes it's like I'm not here at all but somewhere else altogether. And I always think of you. Those years we had. Not enough years, Mike, not enough. . . ."

Her voice was so sad, so mournful that I made sounds of sympathy, not words exactly but the kind of soothings that mothers murmur to their children when they awaken from bad dreams.

"And I think of that terrible night, Mike, that terrible night. Have you ever really forgiven me for that night?"

"Listen . . ." I began. I wanted to say: "Nana, this is Mike your grandson, not Mike your husband." **11**

"Sh . . . sh . . ." she whispered, placing a finger as long and cold as a candle against my lips. "Don't say anything. I've waited so long for this moment. To be here. With you. I wondered what I would say if suddenly you walked in that door like other people have done. I've thought and thought about it. And I finally made up my mind—I'd ask you to forgive me. I was too proud to ask before." Her fingers tried to mask her face. "But I'm not proud anymore, Mike." That great voice quivered and then grew strong again. "I hate you to see me this way—you always said I was beautiful. I didn't believe it. The Charity Ball when we led the grand march and you said I was the most beautiful girl there . . ."

"Nana," I said. I couldn't keep up the **pretense** any longer, adding one more burden to my load of guilt, leading her on this way, playing a **pathetic** game of make-believe with an old woman clinging to memories. She didn't seem to hear me. **12**

"But that other night, Mike. The terrible one. The terrible accusations I made. Even Ellie woke up and began to cry. I went to her and rocked her in my arms and you came into the room and said I was wrong. You were whispering, an awful whisper, not wanting to upset little Ellie but wanting to make me see the truth. And I didn't answer you, Mike. I was too proud.

11 Conflict/Make Predictions
How do you think Mike will respond to his grandmother's mistake?

12 Conflict
Why is Mike so upset?

Key Vocabulary
pretense *n.*, make-believe, pretending
pathetic *adj.*, pitiful, sad

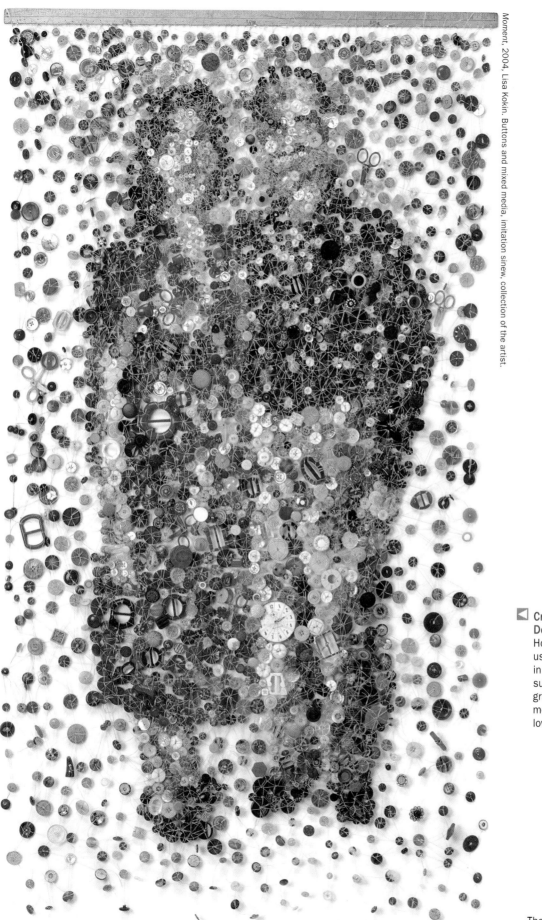

Moment, 2004, Lisa Kokin. Buttons and mixed media, imitation sinew, collection of the artist.

◁ **Critical Viewing: Design**
How does the use of buttons in this artwork suggest what the grandmother's memory of her loved ones is like?

I've even forgotten the name of the girl. I sit here, wondering now—was it Laura or Evelyn? I can't remember. Later, I learned that you were telling the truth all the time, Mike. That I'd been wrong . . ." Her eyes were brighter than ever as she looked at me now, but tear-bright, the tears gathering. "It was never the same after that night, was it, Mike? **The glitter was gone.** From you. From us. And then the accident . . . and I never had the chance to ask you to forgive me . . ."

My grandmother. My poor, poor grandmother. Old people aren't supposed to have those kinds of memories. You see their pictures in the family albums and that's what they are: pictures. They're not supposed to come to life. You drive out in your father's Le Mans doing seventy-five on the pike and all you're doing is visiting an old lady in a nursing home. **A duty call.** And then you find out that she's a person. She's *somebody*. She's my grandmother, all right, but she's also herself. Like my own mother and father. They exist outside of their relationship to me. I was scared again. I wanted to get out of there. **13**

"Mike, Mike," my grandmother said. "Say it, Mike."

I felt as if my cheeks would crack if I uttered a word.

"Say you forgive me, Mike. I've waited all these years . . ."

I was surprised at how strong her fingers were.

"Say, '*I forgive you, Meg.*'"

I said it. My voice sounded funny, as if I were talking in a huge tunnel. "I forgive you, Meg." **14**

Her eyes studied me. Her hands pressed mine. For the first time in my life, I saw love at work. Not movie love. Not Cindy's sparkling eyes when I tell her that we're going to the beach on a

I wanted to get
out of there.

13 Conflict
What does Mike realize that creates his internal conflict?

14 Confirm Predictions
Was your prediction logical? How did Mike respond to his grandmother's mistake?

In Other Words
The glitter was gone. The excitement had left.
A duty call. A commitment or requirement.

Sunday afternoon. But love like something alive and tender, asking nothing in return. She raised her face, and I knew what she wanted me to do. I bent and brushed my lips against her cheek. Her flesh was like a leaf in autumn, crisp and dry.

She closed her eyes and I stood up. The sun wasn't glinting on the cars any longer. Somebody had turned on another television set, and the voices were the show-off voices of the panel shows. At the same time you could still hear the soap-opera dialogue on the other television set.

I waited awhile. She seemed to be sleeping, her breathing serene and regular. I buttoned my raincoat. Suddenly she opened her eyes again and looked at me. Her eyes were still bright, but they merely stared at me. Without recognition or curiosity. Empty eyes. I smiled at her, but she didn't smile back. She made a kind of moaning sound and turned away on the bed, pulling the blankets around her.

I counted to twenty-five and then to fifty and did it all over again. I cleared my throat and coughed **tentatively**. She didn't move; she didn't respond. I wanted to say, "Nana, it's me." But I didn't. I thought of saying, "Meg, it's me." But I couldn't.

Finally I left. Just like that. I didn't say goodbye or anything. I stalked through the corridors, looking neither to the right nor the left, not caring whether that wild old man with the wheelchair ran me down or not.

On the Southwest Turnpike I did seventy-five—no, eighty—most of the way. I turned the radio up as loud as it could go. Rock music—anything to fill the air. **15** When I got home, my mother was vacuuming the living-room rug. She shut off the cleaner, and the silence was deafening. "Well, how was your grandmother?" she asked.

I told her she was fine. I told her a lot of things. How great Nana looked and how she seemed happy and had called me Mike. I wanted to ask her—

15 Conflict
Why do you think Mike needs "anything to fill the air"? What is his internal conflict?

In Other Words
tentatively softly, gently

hey, Mom, you and Dad really love each other, don't you? I mean—there's nothing to forgive between you, is there? But I didn't.

Instead I went upstairs and took out the electric razor Annie had given me for Christmas and shaved off my moustache. ❖

ANALYZE The Moustache

1. **Recall and Interpret** What does Mike decide to do about his moustache? What causes him to make this decision? Be sure to cite evidence from the text.

2. **Vocabulary** How would you **characterize** Mike? Using examples from the story, work with a partner to list three of Mike's qualities.

3. **Analyze Literature: Conflict** With a partner, use the following chart to summarize the conflicts that the characters experience.

What's the Conflict?	What's the Cause?	Is It External or Internal?
Mike wants to see his grandmother but doesn't like the nursing home.	The nursing home reminds him of hospitals.	external; Mike has a fear of hospitals and nursing homes.

4. **Focus Strategy Make and Confirm Predictions** Which of your predictions were most logical? Which weren't? Tell a partner what clues you used to make your predictions. Then compare your predictions with what really happened in the story.

Return to the Text

Reread and Write Look back at the last part of the story (pp. 20–26). What did Mike discover about people? Write a journal entry as if you are Mike after his visit to his grandmother.

GRANDMOTHER

BY SAMEENEH SHIRAZIE

I hadn't asked her much,
just how she felt,
and she told me all about her day,
and how she'd washed the sheets,
5   and how she could not understand
why the towel got so heavy
when it was wet.
She'd also sunned the mattresses,
such tired bones and so much to do,
10   and my eyes filled with tears
when I thought of how I was simply
going to say "Salaam" and walk away
and so many words would have been
trapped inside her.
15   I would have passed by as if
what lay between those bedclothes
was just old life
and not really my grandmother.

BEFORE READING **Who We Really Are**

news feature by Joshunda Sanders

Reading Strategies

▶ **Plan and Monitor**
- Determine Importance
- Make Inferences
- Ask Questions
- Make Connections
- Synthesize
- Visualize

Analyze Structure: News Feature

A **news feature**, or human interest story, is different from a **news story**, which reports just the facts about a current event. News features go into more detail about real people and their feelings, opinions, and problems.

Look Into the Text

The byline tells who wrote the story.

An interesting beginning makes readers want to read more.

Who We Really Are

BY JOSHUNDA SANDERS
CHRONICLE STAFF WRITER

Tamisha started her life with huge obstacles to overcome. She was exposed to drugs in utero and so sick that doctors didn't expect her to live. But when she was 4 days old, she went straight into foster care, where her foster mother nursed her back to health. Most people have heard stories about foster youth who are placed in one home after another, but Tamisha stayed in the same home her whole life. When she was 4 years old, her foster mother adopted her.

What is the purpose of the photo?

These are **facts** about a real person.

Focus Strategy ▶ Plan and Monitor

Previewing a news article will help you **set a purpose** for your reading.

HOW TO PREVIEW AND SET A PURPOSE

Focus Strategy

1. Look at the title and the subtitle. Read any subheads (the short titles above chunks of text).

2. Study the photos and the captions.

3. Look at other graphics, such as charts, tables, and graphs. What does the graphic show you?

4. Ask a question that gives you a personal reason to read. For example, "What does being a foster youth have to do with going to college?" is a good question that the selection might answer.

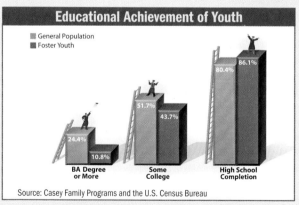

Educational Achievement of Youth

■ General Population
■ Foster Youth

- BA Degree or More: 24.4% / 10.8%
- Some College: 51.7% / 43.7%
- High School Completion: 80.4% / 86.1%

Source: Casey Family Programs and the U.S. Census Bureau

This bar chart gives more factual information about foster youth like Tamisha.

Connect Across Texts

In "The Moustache," Mike gains a new understanding about himself and others. Read this news feature about others who want to be seen for who they really are.

JOSHUNDA SANDERS

Who We Really Are

Tamisha started her life with huge obstacles to overcome. She was exposed to drugs **in utero** and so sick that doctors didn't expect her to live. But when she was 4 days old, she went straight into **foster care**, where her foster mother nursed her back to health. Most people have heard stories about foster youth who are placed in one home after another, but Tamisha stayed in the same home her whole life. When she was 4 years old, her foster mother **adopted her**. **1**

Today, she is a **giddy** 17-year-old with perfectly manicured nails. She loves to tell the story of how people used to call her the "miracle baby." But her expression turns more serious when she talks about people's perceptions of her. People always have questions, she says: "Don't you miss your family? Why not a black home? Why is your family white?"

Nationally, there are half a million youths in foster care. Many of them are **stigmatized** as hardened troublemakers. That attitude may keep some adults from adopting youths from foster care, and some foster youths see adoption as an undesirable option. But being adopted was "the best thing that could ever happen to me," Tamisha wrote in a 2004 exhibition at the Zeum children's museum. (The last names of the artists featured in the show were withheld at their request.)

That's what she tells prospective adoptive parents at seminars in San Mateo, California, where she now lives. By sharing her **perspective** on what it's like to be a former foster child through a videotape she made with Fostering Art—a local program that teaches foster youth about photography—Tamisha hopes to change some of the negative attitudes toward foster youth. **2**

"Just looking at the video we made . . . even me, coming from foster care and being adopted, it still touched me and it does every time," Tamisha said.

Fostering Art is an arts-based project that works with A Home Within, a nonprofit organization that has been

1 Preview
What does the introduction tell you?

2 Set a Purpose
Ask a question that gives you a personal reason to read the rest of this selection.

Key Vocabulary
   stigmatize *v.*, to label or mark as bad
 ● **perspective** *n.*, point of view

In Other Words
in utero before she was born
foster care a temporary, safe home
adopted her legally became her mother
giddy happy and carefree

In a photography workshop hosted by *National Geographic* magazine in San Francisco, teens from Fostering Art and other high school students showed their unique perspective on self and place. **3**

3 Elements of a News Feature
What do the photo and the caption tell you about this selection?

offering free **therapy** to foster youth for ten years. When A Home Within's founder, Toni Heineman, started the program, she was working with **a caseload** of young people who had been shuffled from therapist to therapist. It was taking a toll on them. Because "often, there's not a single person who is not being paid to care for them," Heineman created the Children's Psychotherapy Project that matched therapists who agreed to volunteer their services with one youth for as long as therapy would take. The project was so successful that the program has been duplicated in fourteen other cities nationwide.

In 2004, A Home Within started Fostering Art as another outlet for foster youth to express their feelings about the world they live in. "There will be some horrible story in *Newsweek* and then everyone is thinking about foster kids for a while," Heineman said, "but it's hard over time to understand

In Other Words
therapy counseling
a caseload several cases

what it's like to be raised by someone else's parents."

Fostering Art helps foster youth empower themselves. At the same time it educates the community about the day-to-day realities of foster care that are rarely seen. "Very often, we just don't think about who foster kids are," she said. "And if you can show people foster kids through art, they can stop and look at it, and it stays with them longer."

Plus, young people often asked her for a mental health approach that wasn't just "50 minutes sitting in a room talking to someone," Heineman added.

On a mustard yellow wall at Zeum, two white pages explain Fostering Art's mission: "We're special and unique. We are: foster kids . . . intelligent . . . human beings . . . not the people who

become outcasts of the world, hoodlums or drug dealers . . . people with a deeper understanding of the world because we've been through things many people haven't." 4

The exhibition provides a window into their world with photographs and a multimedia display that includes a videotape of the group as they read their poetry and thoughts about home, life, and who they are.

Each photographer has a sunken box containing their portraits and **artifacts**. Tamisha's box includes a picture of her smiling at the center, her braces still on. On the left side of the installation there's a cluster of photographs from her childhood; on the right, pictures of her now, with her family and friends.

"We're invisible to the media and

4 Elements of a News Feature
What do the words in quotation marks add to this selection?

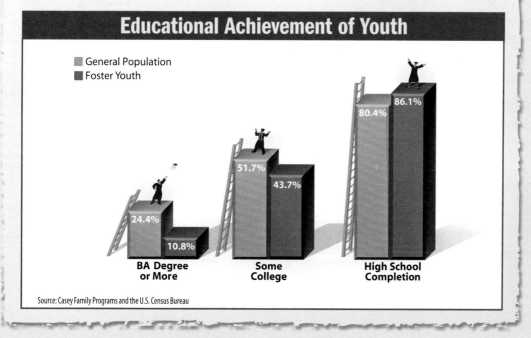

Educational Achievement of Youth

■ General Population
■ Foster Youth

| BA Degree or More | Some College | High School Completion |
| 24.4% / 10.8% | 51.7% / 43.7% | 80.4% / 86.1% |

Source: Casey Family Programs and the U.S. Census Bureau

◁ Interpret the Bar Graph
Do more or fewer foster youth complete high school compared to the general population?

In Other Words
artifacts objects people make

just about everybody else out there," writes Delpheanea, 16. No matter, she does well for herself and lists, beside her picture, a long group of positive accomplishments. She gets good grades, she's engaged, and she's only been late to class twice this year. And she also has, if she does say so herself, a beautiful smile.

"This group is a gateway to freedom, a way to express yourself without someone judging," another sheet reads. "Our hope for the show is to be a messenger, to tell people about ourselves and what we do, to tell our stories. We hope you will get to know who we really are." **5** ❖

5 Set a Purpose
What question did you ask to set a purpose for reading? What is your answer? How did your question affect your reading?

ANALYZE Who We Really Are

1. **Explain** What do you think the writer's main message is?

2. **Vocabulary** Did Tamisha's story change your **perspective** about foster youth? Why or why not?

3. **Analyze Structure: News Feature** What makes this a news feature and not a news story? Because it's a story. Though touch peoples

4. **Focus Strategy Preview and Set a Purpose** Tell your purpose for reading, whether you achieved your purpose, and how.

⤺ Return to the Text

Reread and Write What did you learn about foster youth? Write a paragraph with two or more points of information. Then explain what you would most want others to learn, and why.

EQ When Do You Really Know Someone?

Critical Thinking

EQ 1. **Interpret** Delpheanea says foster youth are "invisible to ... just about everybody." What does she mean? How do her words remind you of the different ways the attendant and Mike treated his grandmother?

2. **Analyze** Look again at your answers to the **Anticipation Guide** on page 10. How do you think Mike would respond to the statements? Tamisha? Explain.

EQ 3. **Compare** Compare the way Mike resolves his conflict over how his grandmother sees him with the way the foster youth resolve their conflict with how some people see them. Whose conflict is harder to live with, and why?

4. **Speculate** The Fostering Art program helps foster youth avoid being **stigmatized** by other people. How might the program be adapted to help older people like the grandmother in "The Moustache"?

EQ 5. **Imagine** How do you think Mike would answer the Essential Question? How do you think Tamisha would answer the same question? With a partner, role-play a conversation between Mike and Tamisha about the Essential Question.

Write About Literature

Make a Judgment Who do you think are treated better: the elderly or foster teens? Tell what you think in a paragraph. Reread both texts and look for examples of how people talk about and act toward each social group.

Key Vocabulary Review

Oral Review Work with a partner. Use these words to complete the paragraph.

characterize	obscure	pretense
intensity	pathetic	stigmatize
lucid	perspective	

Some people __(1)__ the elderly and young people in foster care with unfair labels. People who see only the negative traits of the elderly __(2)__ them as sad and __(3)__ creatures who can no longer think clearly. This view or __(4)__ is incorrect. Though illness may __(5)__ the minds of some old people, most of them are __(6)__ and live dignified lives with an __(7)__ that comes from the desire to live life to the fullest. As for foster youth, everyone should recognize their achievements and respect their individuality. No one should have to live under the __(8)__ of being someone he or she is not.

Writing Application Write a paragraph about an experience that gave you a new **perspective** on a person or group of people. Use at least four Key Vocabulary words.

Read with Ease: Phrasing

Assess your reading fluency with the passage in the Reading Handbook, p. 799. Then complete the self-check below.

1. I did/did not pause appropriately for punctuation and phrases.

2. My words correct per minute: _____ .

Write Complete Sentences

Sentences are the building blocks for most writing. In formal English, a sentence expresses a complete idea.

Annie is sick with the flu.

A sentence is complete if it has two parts. The part called the **subject** tells *whom* or *what* the sentence is about. The part called the **predicate** tells what the subject *does*, *has*, or *is*. Both the complete subject and the complete predicate may be one word or a phrase of several words.

Annie **is sick with the flu**.

Her brother Mike **helps**.

Look at each incomplete sentence. How was it fixed?

Incomplete Sentence	Complete Sentence
Visits his grandmother.	Mike visits his grandmother.
Ellen.	Ellen is Mike's mom.

Oral Practice (1–5) Look at the selections you just read. Find five complete sentences. Tell your partner what the subject and predicate are in each one.

Written Practice (6–10) Use each group of words to write a complete sentence.

6. goes to the nursing home to visit his grandmother
7. Mike the teenager
8. believes Mike is her husband, not her grandson
9. Mike's mother
10. is very patient

Express Ideas and Opinions

Pair Talk Share your ideas and feelings about the story with a partner. In your own words, tell about Mike's decisions and then tell what you think about them.

Analyze Setting

The **setting** of a story is the time and place in which events happen. An author communicates the setting in different ways:

Time	Place
• Past, present, or future • Season of year • Day of week • Time of day	• City or countryside • Nation or culture • Geographic feature or region • Specific building or room

Setting often affects the **plot**, or events, of a story and any conflicts the characters face. For example, the setting of "The Moustache" causes conflict for Mike. He hates the nursing home where his grandmother must now live. He thinks about staying home, even though he wants to see her. Mike would not have that same conflict if the story were set in his grandmother's house.

When you read a story, think about the setting. Ask yourself how the story would change if it were set in a different time or place.

With a group of students, brainstorm answers to the following questions.

1. What conflicts might you find in a story set in the 1800s in a city during a big snowstorm?
2. How might the conflicts change if the story were set today in the same place and with the same weather?

Prefixes

A **prefix** is a word part that comes at the beginning of a word and changes the word's meaning. The prefix *pre-* means "before." Use that knowledge to review the words below. Guess what they mean. Then confirm the definitions in the dictionary.

WORD	WHAT I THINK IT MEANS	DEFINITION
preview		
preheat		
premature		
predetermine		

Written Report

Social Studies: Biographical Sketch Jot down what you already know about a famous person you admire. Then list questions that would help you get to know that person better. Conduct research to answer the questions. For example:

myNGconnect.com

- Check out the Internet for a biography.
- Search the archives of a national newspaper or magazine.
- View videos about that person.

Write a short report to share with your class. Include the source of your information in your report.

🔖 **Writing Handbook**, p. 832

Write an Opinion Paragraph

A test may ask you to write a claim, or opinion, and support it with reasons. The prompt states a position on an issue and asks whether you agree or disagree.

❶ Unpack the Prompt Carefully read the prompt. Underline key words.

> **Writing Prompt**
>
> "School cafeterias and vending machines should not sell sugary soft drinks, candy, or other junk food to students."
>
> Do you agree or disagree? Write your claim, or opinion, and support it with at least two reasons.

❷ Plan Brainstorm reasons you agree or disagree. Then pick the best reasons.

> I disagree with the statement.
> 1. ~~We like fun foods. Don't take them away.~~
> 2. It won't stop us from drinking soda pop or eating candy. We'll bring them from home.
> 3. Schools shouldn't decide what we can and cannot drink or eat. Parents should decide.

❸ Draft Write your claim, or opinion, and reasons. Organize your paragraph like this.

> **Essay Organizer**
>
> Some people think that [Explain the topic of the paragraph.]. I think [State your claim clearly. Respond to the writing prompt.]. One reason I think this is that [Give your first reason. It may take several sentences.]. Another reason I think this is that [Give your second reason. It may take several sentences.]. In conclusion, [Restate your claim. Relate it to the writing prompt.].

❹ Edit and Proofread Reread your draft. Ask:

- Does my paragraph address the writing prompt?
- Did I give two or more reasons to support my ideas?
- Are my sentences complete?

🔖 **Writing Handbook**, p. 832

1

Inside a Hospital

Hospitals provide medical and surgical treatment for people who stay in the hospital for long periods of time or who just come in for an appointment. Often hospitals provide emergency care. Some hospitals specialize in treating certain illnesses, such as joint diseases or cancer.

Jobs in Hospitals

Hospitals have huge staffs of health care professionals. There are many job opportunities for people with various levels of training and experience.

2

Job	Responsibilities	Education/Training Required
Nursing Assistant **1**	• Helps patients dress, bathe, and eat • Checks patients' vital signs • Assists nurses in treatment of patients	• High school diploma • Certificate in training as a certified nursing assistant (CNA)
Registered Nurse **2**	• Records symptoms and patients' medical histories • Carries out instructions for patients' medication and care • Evaluates patients' progress	• College degree in nursing, associate's degree in nursing, or hospital diploma program • State licensing exam
Doctor **3**	• Diagnoses illnesses through examination, medical history, and tests • Treats patients' injuries and illnesses • Usually specializes in a field of medicine, such as surgery or internal medicine	• College degree • Four years of medical school • Three to eight years as an internist and a resident

Use Library Resources

Visit your school or local library to find the answers to your questions about a career in the medical field.

1. Choose a job from above or another job inside a hospital. Write two questions you have about the job. The questions could be about educational requirements, responsibilities, typical salaries, or any other general questions you have.

2. Trade your questions with a partner. Visit your school or local library and research the answers to your partner's questions.

3. Return your partner's questions. Talk about what you learned while trying to find the answers to each other's questions. Save the information in a professional career portfolio.

3

myNGconnect.com

◔ Learn more about jobs in hospitals.
◔ Download a form to evaluate whether you would like to work in this field.

🔖 **Language and Learning Handbook**, p. 750

Use Word Parts

Some words have parts that can help you know what they mean. For example, the word *unhappiness* has three parts—the prefix *un-*, the base word *happy*, and the suffix *-ness*. You know the meaning of *happy*, so if you know that *un-* means "not" and *-ness* means "the state of," you can figure out that *unhappiness* means "the state of not being happy."

The base word in *unhappiness* is one you probably recognize, but what about a word like *inaudible*? You may know that *in-* is a prefix that means "not," and *-ible* is a suffix that means "capable of," but what about *aud*? *Aud* is one of many English word parts that comes from Greek or Latin. It comes from the Latin word meaning "hear." If you know that, you can put together the pieces of *inaudible* to figure out that it means "not capable of being heard." Knowing common Greek and Latin roots will help you figure out many unfamiliar English words.

Make Meaning from Word Parts

Work with a partner to figure out the meaning of each of these words. Refer to the definitions to the right.

anthrop	human
meter	measure
ology	the study of
port	carry
re	back or again
therm	heat
tract	pull
trans	across

1. anthropology   **3.** transport

2. retract   **4.** thermometer

Put the Strategy to Use

When you come to a word you do not know, use this strategy to analyze its parts.

1. Look for a prefix or a suffix and cover it. Remember that the spelling of the root can change slightly.

2. Define the root.

3. Uncover the prefix or suffix and determine its meaning.

4. Put the meanings of the word parts together to define the whole word.

TRY IT ▶ Read the words below. Some of the word parts are in the box above, but others are not. Identify the word parts not shown in the box, research their meaning, and use the strategy to determine the meaning of each word.

▶ cardiology   contraction   transmit   anthropomorphic

▼ **Reading Handbook,** p. 781

EQ **When Do You Really Know Someone?**
Consider that there may be more to someone than you think.

Make a Connection

Quickwrite Sometimes we think we know someone, only to find out something new about him or her. For example, a new student may pretend it is no big deal to come to a new school yet be really nervous. Why do some people pretend to be what they are not? Share your thoughts in a brief paragraph.

Learn Key Vocabulary

Study the Words Pronounce each word and learn its meaning. You may also want to look up the definitions in the Glossary.

• Academic Vocabulary

Key Words	Examples
accusation (ak-yū-**za**-shun) *noun* ▶ pages 47, 53, 56, 64	Has anyone ever made an **accusation** about you by saying that you did something wrong? *Synonyms:* claim, blame; *Antonym:* praise
ambitious (am-**bi**-shus) *adjective* ▶ pages 42, 65	When you are **ambitious**, you have a strong desire for success. An **ambitious** person works hard to achieve big goals. *Synonym:* determined; *Antonym:* hesitant
assert (uh-**surt**) *verb* ▶ page 55	If you **assert** that something is true, you state it strongly and clearly. *Synonyms:* declare, state; *Antonym:* deny
discordant (dis-**kord**-nt) *adjective* ▶ page 49	Music that is **discordant** sounds harsh and unpleasant. I cover my ears when I hear **discordant** music.
expectation (ek-spek-**ta**-shun) *noun* ▶ pages 45, 56, 65	Have you ever had an **expectation**, or a belief that something will happen? Some students have the **expectation** that they will do well in every class.
• **inevitable** (in-**ev**-e-tuh-bul) *adjective* ▶ page 56	Something that is **inevitable** is sure to happen and unavoidable. It is **inevitable** that you will get wet if you walk in the rain without an umbrella or raincoat.
prodigy (**prah**-du-jē) *noun* ▶ page 42	A **prodigy** is an unusually talented child or a child genius. Wolfgang Amadeus Mozart, a **prodigy**, wrote a musical symphony when he was eight years old.
reproach (ri-**prōch**) *noun* ▶ pages 43, 58	A **reproach** is blame or disapproval. A person who is beyond **reproach** cannot be criticized for anything. *Synonym:* criticism; *Antonym:* praise

Practice the Words Work with a partner. Make a **Definition Map** for each Key Vocabulary word. Use a dictionary to find other forms of the word.

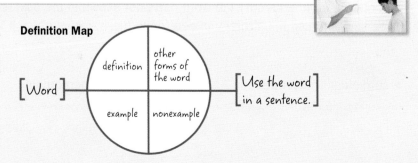

Definition Map

[Word] — definition / other forms of the word / example / nonexample — [Use the word in a sentence.]

Reading Strategies

▶ **Plan and Monitor**
· Determine Importance
· Make Inferences
· Ask Questions
· Make Connections
· Synthesize
· Visualize

Analyze Protagonist and Antagonist

When there is a conflict in a short story, often that conflict is between two characters who want different things. The main character is called the **protagonist**, and the opposing character is called the **antagonist**.

Look Into the Text

The author sets up the conflict with this event.

> Three days after watching *The Ed Sullivan Show,* my mother told me what my schedule would be for piano lessons and piano practice. She had talked to Mr. Chong, who lived on the first floor of our apartment building. Mr. Chong was a retired piano teacher and my mother had traded housecleaning services for weekly lessons and a piano for me to practice on every day, two hours a day, from four until six.
>
> When my mother told me this, I felt as though I had been sent to hell. I whined and then kicked my foot a little when I couldn't stand it anymore.

daughter—protagonist; mother—antagonist

How does the author show how the protagonist feels?

> "Why don't you like me the way I am? I'm *not* a genius! I can't play the piano. And even if I could, I wouldn't go on TV if you paid me a million dollars!" I cried.

Focus Strategy ▶ Plan and Monitor

When you monitor your reading, you check in with yourself to see if you are understanding. Look into the text above and find something that isn't clear to you. Then, use one of these strategies to clarify it, or make it clear.

HOW TO CLARIFY IDEAS

Focus Strategy

1. **Note Confusion** Stop reading when the selection is unclear, or confusing, to you.

2. **Reread** Go back to see whether you missed something important. Read slowly.

   NOT CLEAR: *Why does the daughter say she felt as if she had been sent to hell?*

   REREAD: ...my mother told me what my schedule would be for piano lessons...

3. **Read On** Keep reading. The author may give more information.

   READ ON: "Why don't you like me the way I am? I'm *not* a genius! I can't play the piano."

4. **Relate to Personal Experience** Use what you know to link ideas and clarify the meaning.

   CONNECTION: *Being pressured to be something you're not is really painful.*

The Writer and Her Experiences

Amy Tan
(1952–   )

A visit to China with her mother inspired Amy Tan to finish her first book *The Joy Luck Club*.

Amy Tan often finds inspiration for her work in her real-life experiences as the daughter of Chinese American immigrants. As a first-generation Chinese American, Tan felt alone and unsure of her identity. Was she Chinese? Was she American? After she wrote *The Joy Luck Club* (1989), she realized that she was not alone. She still hears from young adults today who say, "That's how I felt."

As a young adult, she read a book a day and was amazed by the power of words. "I grew up . . . with a love of language. Words were magic to me. You could say a word and it could conjure up all kinds of images or feelings or a chilly sensation . . ."

Tan took her love of language and explored the complicated emotions that occur between people from different cultures and generations in her first book, *The Joy Luck Club*. Since then, Tan has published several books, and her work has been translated into over thirty languages.

The experiences that Tan writes about were not always easy for her or her family, but she maintains a positive view of her role as a writer. "Writing is an extreme privilege," she says, "but it's also a gift. It's a gift to your self and it's a gift of giving a story to someone."

myNGconnect.com

🔍 Find out more about *The Joy Luck Club*.
🔍 See images of San Francisco's Chinatown.

Two Kinds by Amy Tan

Piano Room, 2000, Shuai Mei. Egg tempera on canvas, courtesy of Schoeni Art Gallery Ltd., Hong Kong.

▲ Critical Viewing Describe what is happening in this oil painting. How do you think each character feels about the music?

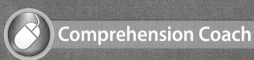

Comprehension Coach

My mother believed you could be anything you wanted to be in America. You could open a restaurant. You could work for the government and get good retirement. You could buy a house with almost no money down. You could become rich. You could become instantly famous.

"Of course you can be **prodigy**, too," my mother told me when I was nine. "You can be best anything. What does Auntie Lindo know? Her daughter, she is only best tricky."

America was where all my mother's hopes lay. She had come here in 1949 after losing everything in China: her mother and father, her family home, her first husband, and two daughters, twin baby girls. But she never looked back with regret. There were so many ways for things to get better.

We didn't immediately pick the right kind of prodigy. At first my mother thought I could be a Chinese Shirley Temple. We'd watch Shirley's old movies on TV as though they were training films. My mother would poke my arm and say, "*Ni kan*"—You watch. And I would see Shirley tapping her feet, or singing a sailor song, or pursing her lips into a very round O while saying, "Oh my goodness."

"*Ni kan*," said my mother as Shirley's eyes flooded with tears. "You already know how. Don't need talent for crying!"

Soon after my mother got this idea about Shirley Temple, she took me to a beauty training school in the Mission district and put me in the hands of a student who could barely hold the scissors without shaking. Instead of getting big fat curls, I emerged with an uneven mass of crinkly black fuzz. My mother dragged me off to the bathroom and tried to wet down my hair.

"You look like Negro Chinese," she **lamented**, as if I had done this on purpose.

The instructor of the beauty training school had to lop off these soggy

1 Language
Say or rewrite the mother's ideas in grammatically correct English.

2 Clarify Ideas
What is the mother trying to do? Reread the paragraph to clarify.

Key Vocabulary
ambitious *adj.*, having a strong desire for success
prodigy *n.*, unusually talented child, child genius

In Other Words
lamented moaned, cried

Cultural Background
Shirley Temple was a popular child movie star during the 1930s. She was famous for her curly hair and smile. In 1974, she became a United States ambassador to Ghana.

clumps to make my hair even again. "Peter Pan is very popular these days," the instructor assured my mother. I now had hair the length of a boy's, with straight-across bangs that hung at a slant two inches above my eyebrows. I liked the haircut and it made me actually look forward to my future fame.

In fact, in the beginning, I was just as excited as my mother, maybe even more so. I pictured this prodigy part of me as many different images, trying each one on for size. I was a dainty ballerina girl standing by the curtains, waiting to hear the right music that would send me floating on my tiptoes. I was like the Christ child lifted out of the straw manger, crying with **holy indignity**. I was Cinderella stepping from her pumpkin carriage with sparkly cartoon music filling the air. 3

In all of my imaginings, I was filled with a sense that I would soon become *perfect*. My mother and father would adore me. I would be beyond **reproach**. I would never feel the need to **sulk** for anything.

But sometimes the prodigy in me became impatient. "If you don't hurry up and get me out of here, I'm disappearing for good," it warned. "And then you'll always be nothing."

Every night after dinner, my mother and I would sit at the Formica kitchen table. She would present new tests, taking her examples from stories of amazing children she had read in *Ripley's Believe It or Not*, or *Good Housekeeping, Reader's Digest,* and a dozen other magazines she kept in a pile in our bathroom. My mother got these magazines from people whose houses she cleaned. And since she cleaned many houses each week, we had a great assortment. She would look through them all, searching for stories about remarkable children.

America was where all my mother's hopes lay.

3 Protagonist
How does the daughter first react to her mother's ambitious plans?

Key Vocabulary
reproach *n.,* blame

In Other Words
holy indignity no shame
sulk frown

Chinatown, 2002, Frank Rinna. Watercolor on paper, collection of the artist.

◀ **Critical Viewing: Design** What impression is created by the artist's choice of details and colors in this watercolor of Chinatown?

The first night she brought out a story about a three-year-old boy who knew the capitals of all the states and even most of the European countries. A teacher was quoted as saying the little boy could also pronounce the names of the foreign cities correctly.

"What's the capital of Finland?" my mother asked me, looking at the magazine story.

All I knew was the capital of California, because Sacramento was the name of the street we lived on in Chinatown. "Nairobi!" I guessed, saying the most foreign word I could think of. She checked to see if that was possibly one way to pronounce "Helsinki" before showing me the answer.

The tests got harder—multiplying numbers in my head, finding the queen of hearts in a deck of cards, trying to stand on my head without

Cultural Background

San Francisco's Chinatown is the second largest Chinese community in the United States. In this community, people can experience Chinese culture, food, and festivals.

using my hands, predicting the daily temperatures in Los Angeles, New York, and London.

One night I had to look at a page from the Bible for three minutes and then report everything I could remember. "Now Jehoshaphat had riches and honor in abundance and . . . that's all I remember, Ma," I said.

And after seeing my mother's disappointed face once again, something inside of me began to die. I hated the tests, the raised hopes and failed **expectations**. Before going to bed that night, I looked in the mirror above the bathroom sink and when I saw only my face staring back—and that it would always be this ordinary face—I began to cry. Such a sad, ugly girl! I made high-pitched noises like a crazed animal, trying to scratch out the face in the mirror. **4**

And then I saw what seemed to be the prodigy side of me—because I had never seen that face before. I looked at my reflection, blinking so I could see more clearly. The girl staring back at me was angry, powerful. This girl and I were the same. I had new thoughts, **willful thoughts**, or rather thoughts filled with lots of won'ts. I won't let her change me, I promised myself. I won't be what I'm not.

So now on nights when my mother presented her tests, I performed listlessly, my head propped on one arm. I pretended to be bored. And I was. I got so bored I started counting the **bellows** of the foghorns out on the bay while my mother **drilled** me in other areas. The sound was comforting and reminded me of the cow jumping over the moon. And the next day, I played a game with myself, seeing if my mother would give up on me before eight bellows. After awhile I usually counted only one, maybe two bellows at most. At last she was beginning to give up hope. **5**

> # The girl staring back at me was angry, powerful.

Key Vocabulary
expectation *n.*, belief that something will happen

In Other Words
willful thoughts stubborn ideas
bellows loud sounds
drilled tested

Predict

Do you think the mother will give up her plan to make her daughter a prodigy? Explain.

Two or three months had gone by without any mention of my being a prodigy again. And then one day my mother was watching *The Ed Sullivan Show* on TV. The TV was old and the sound kept shorting out. Every time my mother got halfway up from the sofa to adjust the set, the sound would go back on and Ed would be talking. As soon as she sat down, Ed would go silent again. She got up, the TV broke into loud piano music. She sat down. Silence. Up and down, back and forth, quiet and loud. It was like a stiff embraceless dance between her and the TV set. Finally she stood by the set with her hand on the sound dial. **6**

She seemed entranced by the music, a little frenzied piano piece with this mesmerizing quality, sort of quick passages and then teasing lilting ones before it returned to the quick playful parts.

"*Ni kan*," my mother said, calling me over with hurried hand gestures. "Look here."

I could see why my mother was fascinated by the music. It was being pounded out by a little Chinese girl, about nine years old, with a Peter Pan haircut. The girl had **the sauciness of a Shirley Temple**. She was proudly modest like a proper Chinese child. And she also did this fancy sweep of a curtsy, so that the fluffy skirt of her white dress cascaded slowly to the floor like the petals of a large carnation.

In spite of these warning signs, I wasn't worried. **7** Our family had no piano and we couldn't afford to buy one, let alone reams of sheet music and piano lessons. So I could be generous in my comments when my mother **bad-mouthed** the little girl on TV.

"Play note right, but doesn't sound good! No singing sound," complained my mother.

"What are you picking on her for?" I said carelessly. "She's pretty good.

6 Antagonist
What do the mother's repeated actions tell you about her character?

7 Clarify Ideas
Why isn't the daughter worried? Read on for more information.

In Other Words
the sauciness of a Shirley Temple
   the lively cuteness of Shirley Temple
bad-mouthed said negative things about, criticized

Cultural Background
The Ed Sullivan Show was a popular TV variety show from 1948–1971. It helped make performers such as Elvis Presley and the Beatles famous.

Maybe she's not the best, but she's trying hard." I knew almost immediately I would be sorry I said that.

"Just like you," she said. "Not the best. Because you not trying." She gave a little huff as she let go of the sound dial and sat down on the sofa. **8**

The little Chinese girl sat down also to play an encore of "Anitra's Dance" by Grieg. I remember the song, because later on I had to learn how to play it.

Three days after watching *The Ed Sullivan Show*, my mother told me what my schedule would be for piano lessons and piano practice. She had talked to Mr. Chong, who lived on the first floor of our apartment building. Mr. Chong was a retired piano teacher and my mother had traded housecleaning services for weekly lessons and a piano for me to practice on every day, two hours a day, from four until six.

When my mother told me this, I felt as though I had been sent to hell. I **whined** and then kicked my foot a little when I couldn't stand it anymore.

"Why don't you like me the way I am? I'm *not* a genius! I can't play the piano. And even if I could, I wouldn't go on TV if you paid me a million dollars!" I cried.

My mother slapped me. "Who ask you be genius?" she shouted. "Only ask you be your best. For you sake. You think I want you be genius? Hnnh! What for! Who ask you!"

"So ungrateful," I heard her mutter in Chinese. "If she had as much talent as she has temper, she would be famous now."

Mr. Chong, whom I secretly nicknamed Old Chong, was very strange, always tapping his fingers to the silent music of an invisible orchestra. He looked ancient in my eyes. He had lost most of the hair

Why don't you like me the way I am?

8 Conflict
What **accusation** does the mother make? Is she right? Explain.

Key Vocabulary
accusation *n.*, saying that another person has done something wrong

In Other Words
whined complained

on top of his head and he wore thick glasses and had eyes that always looked tired and sleepy. But he must have been younger than I thought, since he lived with his mother and was not yet married.

I met Old Lady Chong once and that was enough. She had this peculiar smell like a baby that had done something in its pants. And her fingers felt like a dead person's, like an old peach I once found in the back of the refrigerator; the skin just slid off the meat when I picked it up.

I soon found out why Old Chong had retired from teaching piano. He was deaf. "Like Beethoven!" he shouted to me. "We're both listening only in our head!" And he would start to conduct his frantic silent sonatas. **9**

Our lessons went like this. He would open the book and point to different things, explaining their purpose: "Key! Treble! Bass! No sharps or flats! So this is C major! Listen now and play after me!"

And then he would play the C scale a few times, a simple chord, and then, as if inspired by an old, unreachable itch, he gradually added more notes and running trills and a pounding bass until the music was really something quite grand.

I would play after him, the simple scale, the simple chord, and then I just played some nonsense that sounded like a cat running up and down on top of garbage cans. Old Chong smiled and applauded and then said, "Very good! But now you must learn to keep time!"

So that's how I discovered that Old Chong's eyes were too slow to keep up with the wrong notes I was playing. He went through the motions in half-time. To help me keep rhythm, he stood behind me, pushing down on my right shoulder for every beat. He balanced pennies on top of my wrists so I would keep them still as I slowly played scales and **arpeggios**. He had me curve my hand around an apple and keep that shape when playing chords. He marched stiffly to show me how to make each finger dance up and down, staccato like an obedient little soldier.

9 Clarify Ideas
What does it tell you about the narrator's mother that she didn't try to hire a better piano teacher?

In Other Words
arpeggios a series of chords

Historical Background
Beethoven (1770–1827) was a brilliant German composer who became deaf later in his life. He could not hear the music that he played.

Old Man, Chinatown, 2005, Andrew Neighbour. Digital painting, collection of the artist.

◀ Critical Viewing: Character
Does the man in the portrait reflect your impression of Old Chong? Why or why not?

He taught me all these things, and that was how I also learned I could be lazy and get away with mistakes, lots of mistakes. If I hit the wrong notes because I hadn't practiced enough, I never corrected myself. I just kept playing in rhythm. And Old Chong **kept conducting his own private reverie**.

So maybe I never really gave myself a fair chance. I did pick up the basics pretty quickly, and I might have become a good pianist at that young age. But I was so determined not to try, not to be anybody different that I learned to play only the most **ear-splitting** preludes, the most **discordant** hymns. 🔟

🔟 Protagonist
Why was the protagonist "so determined not to try"?

Key Vocabulary
discordant *adj.*, sounding harsh and unpleasant

In Other Words
kept conducting his own private reverie went on keeping time in his own private daydream
ear-splitting terrible-sounding

Over the next year, I practiced like this, dutifully in my own way. And then one day I heard my mother and her friend Lindo Jong both talking in a loud bragging tone of voice so others could hear. It was after church, and I was leaning against the brick wall wearing a dress with stiff white petticoats. Auntie Lindo's daughter, Waverly, who was about my age, was standing farther down the wall about five feet away. We had grown up together and shared all the closeness of two sisters **squabbling** over crayons and dolls. In other words, for the most part, we hated each other. I thought she was **snotty**. Waverly Jong had gained a certain amount of fame as "Chinatown's Littlest Chinese Chess Champion."

© Yong Jin Hao

▲ Critical Viewing:
Design
How do the chess pieces represent Jing-Mei's relationship with Waverly?

"She bring home too many trophy," lamented Auntie Lindo that Sunday. "All day she play chess. All day I have no time do nothing but dust off her winnings." She threw a scolding look at Waverly, who pretended not to see her.

"You lucky you don't have this problem," said Auntie Lindo with a sigh to my mother.

And my mother squared her shoulders and bragged: "Our problem worser than yours. If we ask Jing-Mei wash dish, she hear nothing but music. It's like you can't stop this natural talent."

And right then, I was determined to put a stop to her foolish pride. 11

A few weeks later, Old Chong and my mother **conspired** to have me play in a talent show which would be held in the church hall. By then, my parents had saved up enough to buy me a secondhand piano, a black Wurlitzer spinet with a scarred bench. It was the showpiece of our living room.

11 Clarify Ideas
This is an important sentence. Why is it important? If it is confusing, how can you clarify it?

In Other Words
squabbling fighting
snotty bossy, superior
conspired worked together

For the talent show, I was to play a piece called "Pleading Child" from Schumann's *Scenes from Childhood*. It was a simple, moody piece that sounded more difficult than it was. I was supposed to memorize the whole thing, playing the repeat parts twice to make the piece sound longer. But I **dawdled over** it, playing a few bars and then cheating, looking up to see what notes followed. I never really listened to what I was playing. I daydreamed about being somewhere else, about being someone else.

The part I liked to practice best was the fancy curtsy: right foot out, touch the rose on the carpet with a pointed foot, sweep to the side, left leg bends, look up and smile.

My parents invited all the couples from the Joy Luck Club to witness my debut. Auntie Lindo and Uncle Tin were there. Waverly and her two older brothers had also come. The first two rows were filled with children both younger and older than I was. The littlest ones got to go first. They recited simple nursery rhymes, squawked out tunes on miniature violins, twirled Hula Hoops, pranced in pink ballet tutus, and when they bowed or curtsied, the audience would sigh **in unison**, "Awww," and then clap enthusiastically. [12]

When my turn came, I was very confident. I remember my childish excitement. It was as if I knew, without a doubt, that the prodigy side of me really did exist. I had no fear whatsoever, no nervousness. I remember thinking to myself, This is it! This is it! I looked out over the audience, at my mother's blank face, my father's yawn, Auntie Lindo's stiff-lipped smile, Waverly's **sulky** expression. I had on a white dress layered with sheets of lace, and a pink bow in my Peter Pan haircut. As I sat down I envisioned people

> I daydreamed . . .
> about being
> someone else.

[12] **Antagonist**
What does it tell you about the parents that they invited all the couples from the Joy Luck Club to the performance?

In Other Words
dawdled over wasted time on
in unison at the same time, all together
sulky moody, unhappy

jumping to their feet and Ed Sullivan rushing up to introduce me to everyone on TV. [13]

And I started to play. It was so beautiful. I was so caught up in how lovely I looked that at first I didn't worry how I would sound. So it was a surprise to me when I hit the first wrong note and I realized something didn't sound quite right. And then I hit another and another followed that. A chill started at the top of my head and began to trickle down. Yet I couldn't stop playing, as though my hands **were bewitched**. I kept thinking my fingers would adjust themselves back, like a train switching to the right track. I played this strange jumble through two repeats, the sour notes staying with me all the way to the end.

When I stood up, I discovered my legs were shaking. Maybe I had just been nervous and the audience, like Old Chong, had seen me go through the right motions and had not heard anything wrong at all. I swept my right foot out, went down on my knee, looked up and smiled. The room was quiet, except for Old Chong, who was beaming and shouting, "Bravo! Bravo! Well done!" But then I saw my mother's face, her **stricken** face. The audience clapped weakly, and as I walked back to my chair, with my whole face quivering as I tried not to cry, I heard a little boy whisper loudly to his mother, "That was awful," and the mother whispered back, "Well, she certainly tried."

> ## I started to play. It was so beautiful.

And now I realized how many people were in the audience, the whole world it seemed. I was aware of eyes burning into my back. I felt the shame of my mother and father as they sat stiffly throughout the rest of the show. [14]

We could have escaped during intermission. Pride and some strange sense

[13] **Protagonist**
The protagonist seems to have changed her attitude. What caused her to change it?

[14] **Conflict**
How do the protagonist's feelings change during the recital?

In Other Words
were bewitched were under a magic spell, were enchanted
stricken horrified

of honor must have anchored my parents to their chairs. And so we watched it all: the eighteen-year-old boy with a fake mustache who did a magic show and juggled flaming hoops while riding a unicycle. The breasted girl with white makeup who sang from *Madama Butterfly* and got honorable mention. And the eleven-year-old boy who won first prize playing a tricky violin song that sounded like a busy bee.

After the show, the Hsus, the Jongs, and the St. Clairs from the Joy Luck Club came up to my mother and father.

"Lots of talented kids," Auntie Lindo said vaguely, smiling broadly.

"That was somethin' else," said my father, and I wondered if he was referring to me in a humorous way, or whether he even remembered what I had done.

Waverly looked at me and shrugged her shoulders. "You aren't a genius like me," she said matter-of-factly. And if I hadn't felt so bad, I would have pulled her braids and punched her stomach.

But my mother's expression was what devastated me: a quiet, blank look that said she had lost everything. I felt the same way, and it seemed as if everybody were now coming up, like **gawkers** at the scene of an accident, to see what parts were actually missing. When we got on the bus to go home, my father was humming the busy-bee tune and my mother was silent. I kept thinking she wanted to wait until we got home before shouting at me. But when my father unlocked the door to our apartment, my mother walked in and then went to the back, into the bedroom. No accusations. No blame. And in a way, I felt disappointed. I had been waiting for her to start shouting, so I could shout back and cry and blame her for all my **misery**. **15**

15 Clarify Ideas
Why does the mother keep silent? Use what you know to clarify the meaning.

In Other Words
gawkers people staring
misery suffering, distress

Monitor Comprehension

Confirm Prediction
How accurate was your prediction? Did you change your prediction as you read along?

I assumed my talent-show **fiasco** meant I never had to play the piano again. But two days later, after school, my mother came out of the kitchen and saw me watching TV.

"Four clock," she reminded me as if it were any other day. I was stunned, as though she were asking me to go through the talent-show torture again.

I wedged myself more tightly in front of the TV.

"Turn off TV," she called from the kitchen five minutes later.

I didn't **budge**. And then I decided. I didn't have to do what my mother said anymore. I wasn't her slave. This wasn't China. I had listened to her before and look what happened. She was the stupid one.

She came out from the kitchen and stood in the arched entryway of the living room. "Four clock," she said once again, louder.

"I'm not going to play anymore," I said **nonchalantly**. "Why should I? I'm not a genius."

She walked over and stood in front of the TV. I saw her chest was heaving up and down in an angry way.

"No!" I said, and I now felt stronger, as if my true self had finally emerged. So this was what had been inside me all along.

"No! I won't!" I screamed.

She yanked me by the arm, pulled me off the floor, snapped off the TV. She was frighteningly strong, half pulling, half carrying me toward the piano as I kicked the throw rugs under my feet. She lifted me up and onto the hard bench. I was sobbing by now, looking at her bitterly. Her chest was heaving even more and her mouth was open, smiling crazily as if she were pleased I was crying. **16**

"You want me to be someone that I'm not!" I sobbed. "I'll never be the kind of daughter you want me to be!"

16 Conflict
Why does the conflict between the mother and daughter become worse?

In Other Words
fiasco disaster
budge move
nonchalantly calmly, casually

"Only two kinds of daughters," she shouted in Chinese. "Those who are obedient and those who follow their own mind! Only one kind of daughter can live in this house. Obedient daughter!"

"Then I wish I wasn't your daughter. I wish you weren't my mother," I shouted. As I said these things I got scared. It felt like worms and toads and slimy things crawling out of my chest, but it also felt good, as if this awful side of me had surfaced, at last.

Mother Daughter, 2003, Cynthia Tom and Sue Tom. Mixed media on masonite, private collection of Diane Horowitz, San Francisco.

◁ Critical Viewing: Design
A mother and daughter created this art together. Does it reflect the mother and daughter in the story? Explain.

17 Clarify Ideas
Reread this paragraph. How does the daughter describe her feelings? What does she mean?

"Too late change this," said my mother shrilly.

And I could sense her anger rising to its breaking point. I wanted to see it spill over. And that's when I remembered the babies she had lost in China, the ones we never talked about. "Then I wish I'd never been born!" I shouted. "I wish I were dead! Like them."

It was as if I had said the magic words. Alakazam!—and her face went blank, her mouth closed, her arms went slack, and she backed out of the room, stunned, as if she were blowing away like a small brown leaf, thin, **brittle**, lifeless.

It was not the only disappointment my mother felt in me. In the years that followed, I failed her so many times, each time **asserting** my own will,

Key Vocabulary
assert v., to insist on, to state strongly and clearly

In Other Words
brittle breakable

my right to fall short of expectations. I didn't get straight As. I didn't become class president. I didn't get into Stanford. I dropped out of college.

For unlike my mother, I did not believe I could be anything I wanted to be. I could only be me.

And for all those years, we never talked about the disaster at the recital or my terrible accusations afterward at the piano bench. All that remained unchecked, like a betrayal that was now unspeakable. So I never found a way to ask her why she had hoped for something so large that failure was **inevitable**.

And even worse, I never asked her what frightened me the most: Why had she given up hope?

For after our struggle at the piano, she never mentioned my playing again. The lessons stopped. The lid to the piano was closed, shutting out the dust, my misery, and her dreams.

So she surprised me. A few years ago, she offered to give me the piano, for my thirtieth birthday. I had not played in all those years. I saw the offer as a sign of forgiveness, a tremendous burden removed. **18**

"Are you sure?" I asked shyly. "I mean, won't you and Dad miss it?"

"No, this your piano," she said firmly. "Always your piano. You only one can play."

"Well, I probably can't play anymore," I said. "It's been years."

"You pick up fast," said my mother, as if she knew this was certain. "You have natural talent. You could been genius if you want to."

"No I couldn't."

"You just not trying," said my mother. And she was neither angry nor sad. She said it as if to announce a fact that could never be disproved. "Take it," she said.

But I didn't at first. It was enough that she had offered it to me. And after that, every time I saw it in my parents' living room, standing in front of the

18 Antagonist
Did the mother truly forgive her daughter? Explain.

Key Vocabulary
● **inevitable** *adj.*, sure to happen, unavoidable

bay windows, it made me feel proud, as if it were a shiny trophy I had won back.

Last week I sent a **tuner** over to my parents' apartment and had the piano reconditioned, for purely sentimental reasons. My mother had died a few months before and I had been getting things in order for my father, a little bit at a time. I put the jewelry in special silk pouches. The sweaters she had knitted in yellow, pink, bright orange—all the colors I hated—I put those in moth-proof boxes. I found some old Chinese silk dresses, the kind with little slits up the sides. I rubbed the old silk against my skin, then wrapped them in tissue and decided to take them home with me. **19**

At the Piano, 1927, Marcel Gromaire. Oil on canvas, Musée d'Art Moderne de la Ville de Paris, Paris, France, The Bridgeman Art Library.

◁ Critical Viewing: Effect
What is the mood of this painting? How does that mood relate to the story?

19 Protagonist
What do the daughter's actions tell you about her feelings for her mother?

After I had the piano tuned, I opened the lid and touched the keys. It sounded even richer than I remembered. Really, it was a very good piano. Inside the bench were the same exercise notes with handwritten scales, the same secondhand music books with their covers held together with yellow tape.

I opened up the Schumann book to the dark little piece I had played at the recital. It was on the left-hand side of the page, "Pleading Child." It looked more difficult than I remembered. I played a few bars, surprised at how easily the notes came back to me.

In Other Words
tuner person who fixes a piano's sound

And for the first time, or so it seemed, I noticed the piece on the right-hand side. It was called "Perfectly Contented." I tried to play this one as well. It had a lighter melody but the same flowing rhythm and turned out to be quite easy. "Pleading Child" was shorter but slower; "Perfectly Contented" was longer, but faster. And after I played them both a few times, I realized they were two halves of the same song. ❖

ANALYZE Two Kinds

1. **Explain** How is the conflict between the mother and daughter settled? Be sure to cite evidence from the text.

2. **Vocabulary** Why does the mother **reproach** her daughter?

3. **Analyze Literature: Conflict** Complete the chart below. Then discuss with a partner how you think the two characters could have avoided conflict.

	Protagonist	Antagonist
What character wants		
How character feels		
How conflict is resolved		

4. **Focus Strategy Clarify Ideas** Find a passage that was hard for you to understand. How did you relate it to personal experience? Write a sentence about the meaning of the passage. Trade sentences with a partner to see if your sentences help clarify what is happening.

⟲ Return to the Text

Reread and Write Look back at the third part of the story, starting on p. 54. Pay attention to the daughter's feelings about her mother and what she has learned about her mother. Imagine the woman is your mother. Write a letter to the mother before she died.

WHY THE VIOLIN IS BETTER

by Hal Sirowitz

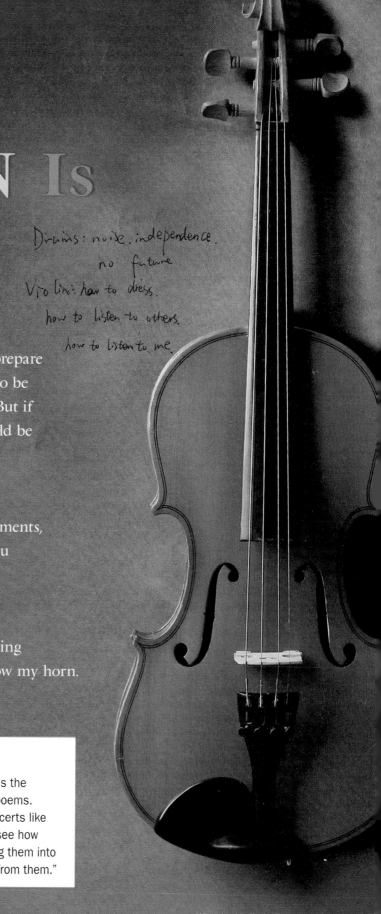

Drums: noise. independence.
no future
Violin: how to dress.
how to listen to others.
how to listen to me.

I don't know why you want to play
the drums, Mother said. They won't prepare
you for anything in life, except how to be
a garbage man, & bang cans around. But if
5   you keep studying the violin you could be
in an orchestra. It'll teach you how
to dress. You'll have to wear a suit
or a tuxedo. And you'll learn how
to play in harmony with other instruments,
10   like the trombone, which will help you
get along better with me. Because
quite frankly you've been living
in this house like you're the soloist,
making a lot of noise, but never stopping
15   for a moment to see if I wanted to blow my horn.

About the Poet

Hal Sirowitz (1949–) of New York is the
author of the popular "Mother Said" poems.
He has performed on MTV and at concerts like
Lollapalooza. He wants students "to see how
poetry can deepen their lives by taking them into
the head and eyes of those different from them."

BEFORE READING **Novel Musician**

profile of Amy Tan by Sharon Wootton

Reading Strategies

▶ **Plan and Monitor**
· Determine Importance
· Make Inferences
· Ask Questions
· Make Connections
· Synthesize
· Visualize

Analyze Structure: Profile

A **profile** is a short, lively character sketch of a real person. In the example below, the author writes a profile of Amy Tan. The details in a profile are factual. Sometimes the profile includes quotations from the subject—that is, the person whom the profile is about.

> **Look Into the Text**

Subject of profile

Most people know Amy Tan as the award-winning writer of *The Joy Luck Club* and *The Kitchen God's Wife*. What they don't know is that she sometimes moonlights as the leading vocalist for the Rock Bottom Remainders—a garage band made up of famous writers who secretly dream of being rock stars. Once a year, the band goes on tour across the United States to create a few laughs and to raise money for literacy-based charities.

Focus of the profile: her singing "career."

Lively, fun facts

Focus Strategy ▶ Plan and Monitor

A profile usually contains facts about the person that answer the "5Ws": **w**ho, **w**hat, **w**hen, **w**here, and **w**hy. To **clarify ideas**, ask these questions as you read.

HOW TO CLARIFY IDEAS

Focus Strategy

1. **Make a 5Ws Chart** To clarify a profile, make a **5Ws Chart** like the one shown.

Who?	Amy Tan
What?	
When?	
Where?	
Why?	

2. **Take Notes** Use the chart to answer the 5Ws. (You may have more than one note for each question.)

Connect Across Texts

"Two Kinds" reflects the serious side of author Amy Tan.
This profile shows another side of her that may surprise you.

Novel Musician

What You Don't Know About Amy Tan

by Sharon Wootton, *The Herald* (Washington)

Most people know Amy Tan as the award-winning writer of *The Joy Luck Club* and *The Kitchen God's Wife*. What they don't know is that she sometimes **moonlights** as the leading vocalist for the Rock Bottom **Remainders**—a garage band made up of famous writers who secretly dream of being rock stars. Once a year, the band goes on tour across the United States to create a few laughs and to raise money for literacy-based charities.

Wearing colorful wigs and costumes is part of the fun when Amy Tan sings with the Rock Bottom Remainders.

Amy Tan, Rock Star? 1

Best-selling horror novelist Stephen King and Tan "scare up" some creativity.

Tan's musical "career" started at age 5, when she practiced piano an hour a day. She was given an IQ test at age 6 and her parents were told that she was smart enough to be a doctor.

"Since my mother believed that the most important organ of the body was the brain, she decided I was going to be a neurosurgeon [and] then a concert pianist. There was, after all, no sense in taking all these lessons if you weren't going to make something of it."

1 Profile
Look at the subhead and the photos on this page. What do they tell you about Amy Tan?

In Other Words
moonlights works a second job
Remainders leftover things

Cultural Background
Literacy-based charities are organizations that help people learn to read and write. The Rock Bottom Remainders raise money for America Scores, a program that combines academic and athletics activities for children.

Two Kinds of Storytelling

The author sees the connection between music and creativity in terms of storytelling. "When I was practicing piano, what I always saw when I played the pieces were stories in my head," Tan said.

"The rock 'n' roll songs I like best are the ones with a definite story, often quite stupid stories, like the ones I'll be singing." (She's best known for her **off-key rendition** of Nancy Sinatra's classic, "These Boots Are Made for Walkin'.") "They're very dramatic, almost hysterical, and at best quite funny to watch."

Don't Quit Your Day Job

None of these literary giants is likely to quit writing to pursue a musical career, but they all enjoy **jamming** as part of the Rock Bottom Remainders. **2**

Author Name	Literary Achievement	Musical Contribution
Amy Tan	author of *The Joy Luck Club* and *The Kitchen God's Wife*	vocals
Dave Barry	nationally syndicated humor columnist	guitar and vocals
Stephen King	author of highly successful horror novels, including *Carrie*, *The Shining*, and *The Dark Tower* series	guitar and vocals
Scott Turow	attorney and author of best-selling legal thrillers, such as *Presumed Innocent* and *Ordinary Heroes*	vocals
James McBride	author of *The Color of Water*	saxophone

2 Clarify Ideas
How does the chart on this page help you clarify ideas about the band?

In Other Words
off-key rendition version that does not hit the right musical notes
jamming playing music for fun

"I will sing **my heart out** [and] with absolute seriousness that my career depends on it and everybody should have a good time. Mostly people think it's pretty hilarious. . . . Everyone [in the band] is so great about their lack of musical talent," Tan said. "We're a joke but we're actually not bad to dance to. My recommendation is for people to put on their '60s and '70s clothes and come and dance." ❖

ANALYZE Novel Musician

1. **Explain** What do you think the band's name means? Cite evidence from the text.

2. **Vocabulary** What kind of reaction would Amy Tan have if someone made an **accusation** that she lacked musical talent? Explain.

3. **Analyze Structure: Profile** What features make this selection a profile?

4. **Focus Strategy Clarify Ideas** With a partner, compare the answers you wrote on your **5Ws Chart**. What other facts did you discover in the profile?

Return to the Text

Reread and Write Reread the text to find two reasons that Amy Tan and her band go on tour. How do these reasons help you know Tan and the band members better?

In Other Words
my heart out with great enthusiasm

REFLECT AND ASSESS

▶ Two Kinds
▶ Why the Violin Is Better
▶ Novel Musician

EQ ## When Do You Really Know Someone?

Reading

Critical Thinking

1. **Compare** Compare the fictional mother in "Two Kinds" with Amy Tan's real mother, as she is described in "Novel Musician." What ambitions and **expectations** does each mother have for her daughter? Compare the two mothers' relationships with their grown-up daughters.

EQ 2. **Analyze** What, if anything, surprised you about the daughter's actions in "Two Kinds" and Amy Tan's in "Novel Musician"? How does each one reveal her "real self" through her actions?

EQ 3. **Interpret** On the basis of both stories, do you think Amy Tan believes that different generations can really understand each other? Explain.

4. **Draw Conclusions** The daughter in "Two Kinds" says that she never asked her mother the question that frightened her the most. What is that question? What do you think would be her mother's answer to the question?

EQ 5. **Evaluate** Which of the two selections—"Two Kinds" or "Novel Musician"—do you think tells you more about who Amy Tan really is? Explain. Support your answer with details from the text.

Writing

Write About Literature

Opinion Statement Everyone should be required to take music lessons as a child. Do you agree or disagree? Support your opinion with examples from both texts.

Vocabulary

Key Vocabulary Review

Oral Review Work with a partner. Use these words to complete the paragraph.

accusation	discordant	prodigy
ambitious	expectations	reproach
asserting	inevitable	

Rafael is an __(1)__ student and sets high __(2)__ for himself. He is so good at math that some people think he is a __(3)__ . He also sings in the school chorus for fun. Though he's not the best singer, he never hits a __(4)__ note. No one can make the __(5)__ that he's lazy, or __(6)__ him for not trying. Sometimes he is shy about __(7)__ his opinions in class. However, with his excellent grades, it's __(8)__ that he will go on to college.

Writing Application Write a paragraph about a time when you were **ambitious** about doing well in school or winning a game or contest. Use at least three Key Vocabulary words.

Fluency

Read with Ease: Expression

Assess your reading fluency with the passage in the Reading Handbook, p. 800. Then complete the self-check below.

1. My expression did/did not sound natural.

2. My words correct per minute: _____ .

"Reflect and Assess 65"

Reflect and Assess **65**

Make Subjects and Verbs Agree

The verb you use depends on your subject. These subjects and verbs go together. These verbs are forms of **be**.

I **am**	We **are**
You **are**	You **are**
He, she, or it **is**	They **are**

Action verbs have two forms in the present:

I **practice** a lot.   Mrs. Jones **practices** more.

Add **-s** to the action verb only when you talk about one other person, place, or thing. Find the subject in each sentence. How does the verb end?

The girl **plays** piano. She **practices** every day. She **performs** well.

Oral Practice (1–5) Choose from each column to make five sentences. Say them to a partner.

Example: The girl is on stage.

The girl	worries	every day.
The students	practices	on stage.
The man	is	before the show.
The mother	clap	a piano teacher.
The parents	perform	for more.

Written Practice (6–15) Write ten sentences about a show. Start with these sentences and choose the correct verb. Then tell what else happens.

The teacher (ask/asks) me to play the piano every day. I (practice/practices) after school. We (is/are) nervous about the show. We (play/plays) well and everyone claps. They (like/likes) the show.

Ask for and Give Information

Role Play Work with a partner to act out an interview with Amy Tan. One of you asks a question about something in the selections, and the other answers as Amy Tan would answer. Then reverse roles.

Analyze Characters and Plot

Most stories have both conflict and resolution. **Conflict** is a struggle between opposing forces. **Resolution** is the way that conflict ends.

For example, the mother and daughter in "Two Kinds" experience conflict about the daughter's future. The mother wants her to become a famous piano player, but the daughter plays badly and refuses to practice. The resolution occurs after the mother and daughter have an argument.

The map below shows the rising and falling action of the events in a story's plot.

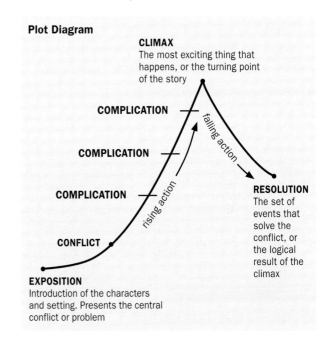

Plot Diagram

CLIMAX The most exciting thing that happens, or the turning point of the story

COMPLICATION

COMPLICATION

COMPLICATION

rising action

falling action

CONFLICT

RESOLUTION The set of events that solve the conflict, or the logical result of the climax

EXPOSITION Introduction of the characters and setting. Presents the central conflict or problem

With a partner, draw a map that outlines the plot in Amy Tan's "Two Kinds." List the conflict, the most important complications, the climax, and the resolution. Then tell how the characters' interactions complicate the plot and lead to the climax.

Vocabulary Study

Suffixes

A **suffix** is a word part that comes at the end of a word and changes the word's part of speech or meaning. For example, the suffix *-tion* turns a verb into a noun. Note that sometimes letters are added or dropped to make the new word. Copy the chart below, and then complete it. Then choose two verbs and new nouns and use them to tell a partner about Amy Tan.

VERB	SUFFIX	NEW NOUN	MEANING
expect	-tion	expectation	
accuse	-tion	accusation	
motivate	-tion		
correct	-tion		
complicate	-tion		

Listening / Speaking

Interview

Social Studies: Immigration to the United States
Interview an older person in your community who was born in another country.

1 **Plan the Interview** Request an appointment, and let the person know your interview topic. Write your questions. Ask about basic facts, such as *Where were you born*? and open-ended questions, such as *Tell me about your childhood.*

2 **Conduct the Interview** Start with the basic questions. Take notes on the person's answers.

Write a report based on your interview, and focus on what you learned about being an immigrant. Share your report with the class.

🔖 **Language and Learning Handbook,** p. 750

Writing

Writing a Narrative Paragraph

You can write a **narrative paragraph** about an **incident**, or an event that really happened.

1 **Choose an Incident** It could be one that taught you something about yourself or about another person. Write down some ideas and select one to write about.

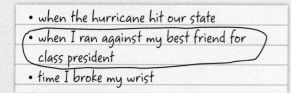

2 **Organize** Use a time line to organize important details for your story.

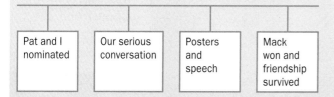

3 **Draft** Add interesting details, and write about the event in chronological order.

Model

> Pat and I had both been nominated for class president. We promised each other that we would remain friends no matter what happened. Both of us made dozens of posters and practiced our campaign speeches. On election day, another student, Mack, was elected class president. Pat and I were still friends. Friendship is much more important than winning an election.

4 **Edit and Proofread** Reread your narrative paragraph. Ask yourself:

- Does my paragraph clearly explain the incident?
- Do the subjects and verbs go together?

5 **Publish** Print your paragraph and share it with a friend.

🔖 **Writing Handbook,** p. 832

Oral Interpretation of Literature

When you have something important to say to someone you care about, think about using literature to add power to your message. For example, you could memorize and perform a poem that tells your mother how much she means to you. When a friend is discouraged, use a humorous passage from a story to cheer up him or her. Here is how to prepare and perform an oral interpretation for a special person.

I. Choose Your Selection

Find a selection that expresses the ideas or emotions you want to convey. It can be a poem, a personal narrative, or part of a short story or play. Make sure your selection has the following qualities:

- It is not difficult to understand.
- It has a strong effect on your emotions.
- It is short enough to speak in a reasonable time limit.

How can music support and enhance a performance?

2. Practice Speaking Your Selection

Practice the selection until you can say it well enough to achieve these goals:

- Show the emotions that the selection makes you feel.
- Speak the selection from memory or by seldomly using your notes.
- *If you are performing a poem*: Practice speaking the words in rhythm. Be sure you understand what the poem's images mean.
- *If you are performing prose*: Be aware of the author's organization, style, and the rhythm of the sentences. Decide where to pause for effect.
- If there is dialogue, decide how you will perform it.

3. Perform Your Selection

As you perform your selection, use these techniques:

- Speak the words clearly.
- Speak the selection with emotion and energy, so that your listeners can feel what you feel.
- Make eye contact with your listeners often.
- Use your voice, face, and body movements to add power to your words.

4. Evaluate a Partner's Oral Interpretation

To help perfect your oral interpretation, perform it for a classmate. Have him or her use the rubric to rate your performance. Then switch roles.

Oral Interpretation Rubric

Scale	Content of Literature	Speaker's Preparation	Speaker's Delivery
3 Great	• Grabbed my attention • Strongly affected my feelings	• Understood the selection completely • Used few or no notes	• Conveyed the rhythm of the poem or the pace of the prose very well • Made me feel the selection's emotions
2 Good	• Was interesting • Affected my feelings somewhat	• Understood the selection fairly well • Used a lot of notes	• Tried to convey the rhythm of the poem or the pace of the prose • Gave some sense of the selection's emotions
1 Needs Work	• Was not very interesting • Did not affect me	• Did not understand the selection • Had to read the selection	• Hesitated and was not smooth • Did not show selection's emotions

DO IT ▶ **When you are satisfied with your oral interpretation, perform it for a special audience!**

🪶 Language and Learning Handbook, p. 750

myNGconnect.com
🔵 Download the rubric.

PREPARE TO READ
▶ Skins
▶ One
▶ Nicole

EQ ## When Do You Really Know Someone?
Look beyond the stereotype.

Make a Connection

Brainstorm and Discuss A stereotype is an unfair statement or observation about a group of people. For example, some adults stereotype all teenagers as lazy. What other stereotypes do adults have about teenagers? With a small group of students, brainstorm a list. Then discuss how stereotypes can cause people to misunderstand each other.

Learn Key Vocabulary

Study the Words Pronounce each word and learn its meaning. You may also want to look up the definitions in the Glossary.

● Academic Vocabulary

Key Words	Examples
authenticity (aw-then-**ti**-su-tē) *noun* ▶ pages 97, 98, 99	If people check the **authenticity** of something, they see whether it is real, or genuine. The jeweler checked the **authenticity** of the stone to see whether it was a diamond or just glass.
compel (kum-**pel**) *verb* ▶ page 97	If you are **compelled** to do something, you feel you must do it. *Synonyms*: force, make; *Antonyms*: ask, request
● **discriminate** (dis-**kri**-mu-nāt) *verb* ▶ pages 95, 96	To **discriminate** means to treat someone differently because of prejudice. The freshmen were **discriminated** against just because they were the youngest students in school.
● **eliminate** (i-**li**-mu-nāt) *verb* ▶ pages 97, 99	He used extra soap to **eliminate** the stain. *Synonyms*: remove, get rid of; *Antonyms*: add, include
● **potential** (pu-**ten**-shul) *noun* ▶ pages 85, 91	**Potential** is natural ability. Ramón has the **potential** to be a great musician, but he needs to practice more often. *Synonym*: possibility; *Antonym*: inability
● **predominate** (pri-**dah**-mu-nāt) *verb* ▶ page 78	If one group of people **predominates** over another, it is more powerful than the second group. *Synonyms*: overrule, dominate; *Antonyms*: follow, submit
racism (**rā**-si-zum) *noun* ▶ pages 95, 96, 98	**Racism** is a belief that one race is better than another. For a long time because of **racism**, African Americans were denied the right to vote.
● **tension** (**ten**-shun) *noun* ▶ pages 83, 91	**Tension** is stress, strain, or anxiety. Did your **tension** go away when you turned in your term paper?

Practice the Words Work with a partner to make an **Expanded Meaning Map** for each Key Vocabulary word.

Expanded Meaning Map

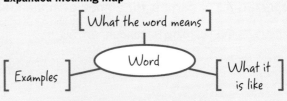

BEFORE READING Skins

short story by Joseph Bruchac

Reading Strategies

▶ **Plan and Monitor**
· Determine Importance
· Make Inferences
· Ask Questions
· Make Connections
· Synthesize
· Visualize

Analyze Character and Theme

The **theme** of a short story is a message or lesson about life in the story. To discover the theme, look for clues in the title of the story. Also think about the characters, their thoughts, and their conflicts.

Look Into the Text

Important characters

Character's thoughts

Skins

The first day I saw Jimmy T. Black, I thought he was a real Indian. Realer than me. I thought that even before I heard him tell the group of kids hanging around him that his middle initial stood for "Thorpe." Jim Thorpe was … the world's greatest [Native American] athlete…. [My] father was an Indian … [and my] mom is Swedish and as blonde as Brunhilde. Despite the hair coloring that I comb in every week or so, I know my classmates still see the old Mitchell Sabattis, would-be Native American. I tan up real dark in the summer, but during the winter my skin gets as pale as something you might find under a rock.

Details connected to title "Skins"

As you read, write the important clues in a **Theme Chart**. Use what you learn about the characters, title, conflicts, and events to understand the theme of the story.

What Important Characters Think, Say, and Do	Story Title and What It Suggests About the Story	Important Events and Conflicts	How Characters Learn from Experiences and How They Change

Focus Strategy ▶ Plan and Monitor

As you read "Skins," use these steps to unlock the meaning of unfamiliar words.

HOW TO CLARIFY VOCABULARY

Focus Strategy

1. **Look for familiar word parts.**

2. **Use what you know to make connections.** Look for clues in the sentence to help you find the meaning of the word.

3. **Compare words.** Look for parts they may have in common as well as how the words are used in the sentence.

It was one of our **pre-season** practices. *Pre-* means "before," so **pre-season** must mean "before the season."

Our pre-season practices were crucial, or **absolutely necessary**, to improving our team.

I know *un-* means "not" and **undefeated** means "not defeated." So when I see words like *unexpected* and *unremarkable*, I can guess what they mean.

Joseph Bruchac
(1942–)

A story can build a feeling of community and draw a person into a new experience.

Joseph Bruchac is a writer and a professional storyteller of Native American stories.

Growing up in the small town of Greenfield Center, New York, **Joseph Bruchac** spent a lot of time in his grandparents' general store, listening to the customers' stories. "In the fall and winter," he recalls, "I would sit around the wood stove and listen to the local farmers and lumberjacks tell tall tales."

Bruchac's grandparents raised him, and they were important influences in his life. His grandfather was an Abenaki Indian. His grandmother was an avid reader.

"It is because of her that I am always reading," Bruchac explains.

When Bruchac started a family of his own, he looked for stories from the Abenaki. "I wanted to share those stories with my sons," he says, "so I started to write them down."

Native American culture has been a constant source of inspiration for Bruchac. He has written more than seventy books, hundreds of poems and articles, and several plays. He also likes to write songs. He performs with his sister Marge and two adult sons as the Dawn Land Singers.

myNGconnect.com

🔾 **Find out more about the author.**
🔾 **Explore the world of the Abenaki people.**

SKINS

BY JOSEPH BRUCHAC

THE FIRST DAY I saw Jimmy T. Black, I thought he was a real
Indian. Realer than me. I thought that even before I heard him tell the group
of kids hanging around him that his middle initial stood for "Thorpe." Jim
Thorpe was the Sac and Fox guy who won the Olympics about a century ago
and was the world's greatest athlete. **1**

I'd heard a bunch of Jim Thorpe stories from Uncle Tommy Fox, who is
eighty-four years old and has packed more living into his life than most
people could experience in three centuries. Uncle Tommy knew Jim Thorpe.
He met him back in 1937 when Uncle Tommy went to Hollywood as a kid
and got lots of bit parts as anonymous Indian Number Two or Three who
spectacularly falls off his horse when the fair-haired cowboy hero fires his
six-shooter.

But this story isn't actually about Uncle Tommy, even though he is sort of
part of it. This happened the autumn when Uncle Tommy was away visiting
his grandchildren out in New Mexico. So I'll get back to Jimmy T and our
high school, which is, of course, where I first met him.

Long Pond Central High School is pretty big for the North Country.
It draws in students from all the little towns and **hamlets** around what we
laughingly call the major population center of Long Pond. Long Pond High
is big enough to have eleven-man football. Before our school was built, the
little regional high schools could barely scrape together a five-guy basketball
team. Now, with a hundred seniors, and even more kids in our junior class, we
have the whole range of sports, from football to girls' basketball. And because
there's not much else to do around here, we always get big crowds at all our
sporting events.

When you go to a high school in a town so small that if you blink, you'll
miss it, everyone knows who you are. Not just your name and your face.

1 Character
What does his reaction to Jimmy T tell us about the narrator?

In Other Words
hamlets small villages

Cultural Background
The Sac and Fox are a group of Native American people who lived in Canada, Michigan, Wisconsin, and Illinois.

They know everything about you, including stuff you wish they'd forget. That's especially true in school, where you've been with some of the same kids ever since preschool. **2** They remember the time when you were five and got **expelled** for a week because you bit a certain girl in the butt so hard you left toothmarks.

Another thing everyone remembers about me is my hair. It's long now and black as Jimmy T's. But everyone in school remembers that until sixth grade my hair was kind of dirty brown. That's what happens when your father was an Indian but your mom is Swedish and as blonde as Brunhilde. Despite the hair coloring that I comb in every week or so, I know my classmates still see the old Mitchell Sabattis, **would-be Native American**. I tan up real dark in the summer, but during the winter my skin gets as pale as something you might find under a rock. **3**

Summer is the big season for visitors up here. A few locals still work in the woods, but the logging business isn't what it used to be anymore. Our biggest industry is tourism. Tourism was what brought Jim Thorpe Black and three other new kids to our school. Their families moved here because of the

Songs of the Past, Allan Houser, bronze sculpture.

⬛ **Critical Viewing: Character** What personal qualities do you see in this sculpture? How do these qualities compare with Mitchell's characteristics?

2 **Clarify Vocabulary**
What does *preschool* mean? Think about each part of the word, and reread the sentence.

3 **Character and Theme**
How do you think Mitchell feels about his mixed heritage?

In Other Words
expelled sent home from school
would-be Native American a person who pretends to be a Native American

Cultural Background
In the mythology of Iceland and Germany, **Brunhilde** is a woman who guides the souls of dead soldiers to Valhalla, the great hall of the gods.

new Long Pond Northern Adirondack Interpretive Center. One new high schooler coming to a community as tight-knit as Long Pond makes waves. Four was a tsunami. **4**

When new kids come to a high school, there are two ways it can go. One is that everybody tries to get to know them. Two is that people hang back to check them out before making a move.

With Jimmy T it was approach *numero uno* all the way. Word had gotten out that this new kid was a star quarterback. Coach had mentioned it at one of our pre-season practices. He'd been all-league last year as a junior in a big city school. Scouts from Notre Dame and Syracuse were already interested. After decades of our being the **doormats of the North Country league**, this football season might be different. At a school like ours, a winning quarterback would be like Moses and Eminem rolled up into one. Long Pond kids flocked around Jimmy T the way bees swarm around honey. With his black hair, olive skin, and shiny teeth, Jimmy T had the stage presence of a pop idol.

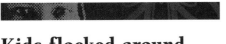

Kids flocked around Jimmy T the way bees swarm around honey.

"Doesn't he look like Enrique Iglesias?" one girl whispered to another as they pushed past me to get closer to him. **5**

To me, though, Jimmy T looked like that Indian guy in *Dances With Wolves*. The one who calls out at the end, "Dances With Wolves, you will always be my friend."

I know there are problems with that movie. Like that it is yet another one of those movies where the adopted white guy is even better at being an Indian than the real **skins**. Like that scene where he finds the buffalo herd before the Indians do? I mean, get real! But the one corny thought that went through my mind when I first saw Jimmy T, with his turquoise bracelets and

4 Clarify Vocabulary
What is a *tsunami*? Notice how the word is used in the sentence, and reread the sentence before it to determine the meaning.

5 Character and Theme
Why is Jimmy T so popular with the other students?

In Other Words
numero uno number one (in Spanish)
doormats of the North Country league worst team in the North Country league
skins Indians

that bone choker around his neck, was that I wanted to hear him yell that to me. "Mitchell Sabattis, you will always be my friend." Like I said, corny.

But while everyone else **made up to** Jimmy T, I hung back.

That's always been my way. Wait-and-See Sabattis, that's me. Even in sports. In basketball, I'm the guy who hangs back on the other team's fast break, so that when we get the ball again, I can take the pass down court and lay it up. And in football, I'm the same. I follow my blockers when I'm at tailback, or when I'm playing D-back, I play off my man enough so that the quarterback thinks he's not covered. When it comes to wild parties or doing crazy things, I'm the one who says, "Cool, but I'll catch you guys later." I spend all my spare time at Uncle Tommy's house, learning Indian stuff. Summers I work with him at the Indian Tourist Village. So I have this complicated **rep** as **a jock**, **a brainiac**, and sort of an outsider. 6

Which is how the three other new kids were being treated. Those White kids were getting the full-scale outsider treatment. I should explain, before you get the wrong idea, that their last name was **a misnomer**, because they weren't. They were black.

There had never been any black kids at our school before. It isn't that we're segregated. It is just that 99 percent of the African American population in New York State is outside the northern Adirondack Mountain region. African Americans who pass through are treated just like any other **flatlanders** with money to add to the local economy. But as far as living here, Dr. Franklin White, his wife Professor Efua Robinson White, their son Randolph, and their two daughters Coretta and Rosa, were the first.

Dr. White, with a Ph.D. in Ecological Science, was now the director of the just-built Northern Adirondack Interpretive Center. NAIC, for short. His wife was commuting to teach at Plattsburgh State, sixty miles away. They'd bought the biggest and newest house in town, on the point of the lake.

They'd even been the subject of a front page article in the *Long Pond Weekly*

6 **Character**
What do the details in this paragraph reveal about Mitchell's personality?

In Other Words
made up to acted very friendly toward
rep reputation
a jock an athlete
a brainiac a smart person
a misnomer an inappropriate name
flatlanders outsiders

Star. WELCOME THE WHITES was the banner headline, with a picture of their smiling faces beneath it. It is a measure of our local journalism that no irony was intended.

There hadn't been any article like that about Jimmy T's dad, the new Assistant Director. Their house, on the other side of Long Pond, wasn't even lakefront.

Randolph and his twin sisters were not smiling as they stood in the entrance to the school cafeteria that first day. People mumbled "Scuse me" as they slipped by, but no one made eye contact. No one shook hands. Maybe it was because no one knew what to say. Our images of African American teenagers up here **in the sticks** are what we get from TV, where rappers and gang-bangers **predominate**. What would the proper greeting be? "Yo, dog, whazzup?" or just a normal North Country "Hiya." Despite the fact that the White kids wore clothes so top-of-the-line that they might have been fashion models, everyone was avoiding them. It was obviously making Randolph and his sisters feel like four-day-old **road kill**. **7**

It made me want to yell, "What's wrong with everyone!"

Multicultural Patchwork, 2005, Elizabeth Rosen. Collage/mixed media, private collection.

▲ **Critical Viewing: Theme** Study the faces in the picture. What ideas do you think the collage expresses about people?

7 **Theme** What message do you think the author wants to convey in this paragraph?

Key Vocabulary
• **predominate** *v.*, to occur most often

In Other Words
in the sticks in the country
road kill body of an animal hit and killed by a car

I didn't, though. Instead I walked across the room, sort of in their direction, with my lunch tray in my hand. I didn't really intend to get involved. I could see now that Randolph was shorter than me by a good four inches, but he probably outweighed me. **8** Muscles bulged under his designer shirt. Although his jaw was clenched, his face was friendly and pleasant looking. His sisters were easy on the eyes, too. You'd look twice when they walked across a room. Though they were younger than their brother, they were almost my height, and I'm six-foot-three. The three Whites were black, but their skin color wasn't much darker than Uncle Tommy's.

Almost without realizing what I was doing, I did something that surprised myself. "Hey," I said. I held out my hand to Randolph.

He and his sisters jumped a little. They'd been so tense they hadn't even seen me come up to them. (Although I have been told that I have this way of sort of sneaking up on people without their noticing. Old Indian trick, as Uncle Tommy puts it.)

It only took Randolph half a second to recover his **poise**. "Hello," he said, cracking a small smile as he took my hand. His handshake was a surprise. It wasn't a **bone cruncher**, like jocks sometimes give each other when they meet. It was gentle, the way Indians shake hands.

"I'm Mitch Sabattis. Welcome to Wrong Pond," I said.

His smile got broader. It's the oldest joke we have up here, but under the circumstances it had a little more zip than usual.

"I'm pleased to meet you," he said. No "yo." No "dog." Perfectly **enunciated** standard English. "I'm Randolph. These are my two younger sisters, Rosa and Coretta." **9**

8 Clarify Vocabulary
Divide *outweighed* into its parts. Notice how it is used in the sentence. What does *outweighed* mean?

9 Character and Theme
How does meeting Randolph affect Mitchell's understanding of people?

In Other Words
poise calmness
bone cruncher crush or strong hold
enunciated pronounced

"Hello," they said, speaking and holding out their hands at the same time. Then, because they'd done it so perfectly **in sync**, like the start of a dance routine, they giggled.

Heads were turning in our direction. I'd **broken the ice** and survived. The lunch table we took filled up as other kids came over and introduced themselves. As we talked, I realized I'd be seeing a lot of Randolph. He was a football player, too. He'd played center at his old school. It wasn't the one Jimmy T went to, but they'd been in the same league.

"Is Jimmy T really a big-time QB?" Jacques Dennis asked.

"Yeah, he's as good as his clippings," Randolph said. The way he said it made me think there was something else he could have said, but he was **holding back**. I noticed, too, that the one time Jimmy T glanced over our way, it seemed as if a dirty look passed between him and Randolph.

I didn't ask Randolph about it. After all, we were just starting to get to know each other. I was looking forward to that. And his being a center made it even more likely that we'd be spending time together since I was the punter and place-kicker. Randolph had missed pre-season practice, but I got the feeling he'd do just fine. He couldn't do any worse than Jacques, who was our current center. Everybody knew that Jacques actually hated the position. Jacques loved D-tackle and we could use him there.

Rosa and Coretta were getting their share of attention, too. Nancy Post, who loves clothes **more than life itself**, was chatting the sisters up about accessorizing—whatever that means. Also, they were basketball players. With their height they'd really add something to our girls' team.

After the conversation was going good around the table, I excused myself.

"Later," I said to Randolph.

"I'll look forward to that," he responded. I could tell he meant it.

I still hadn't introduced myself to Jimmy T. **10** There seemed to be a little lull in the crowd around him where he was seated six tables down. But as soon

10 Character
Mitchell introduces himself to Randolph right away, but he still hasn't introduced himself to Jimmy T. What might explain this difference in behavior?

In Other Words
in sync together
broken the ice started a conversation
holding back not telling all he knew
more than life itself a lot

as I walked over, Jimmy T stood up and turned his back on me. The "Hiya" I was about to speak died on my lips. He made his way toward the door like he was late for an important appointment.

As small as Long Pond High is, I didn't see Jimmy T for the rest of the school day. It was almost as if he was trying to avoid me, although for the life of me I couldn't figure out why. Sure, there were some mutterings about how there was **bad blood** between him and Randolph. They'd played on different teams that were bitter rivals. 🔢 But I couldn't imagine that being friendly with Randolph would keep Jimmy T from talking to me. He must have heard I was Indian, too.

Even if I did have a blonde mother, I'd always been the only kid in Long

🔢 **Clarify Vocabulary**
Do you know what the word *rivals* means? Look for clues in the sentence and nearby sentences.

Citizenship, 2002, Rafael Lopez. Acrylic on woodboard, KQED Corporate Offices, courtesy of KQED Public Broadcasting.

🔺 **Critical Viewing: Design** Look closely. What image connects all the faces? What does this say to you about the people in the painting?

In Other Words
bad blood anger or hatred

Pond School who really identified himself as Indian. And I certainly wasn't the only one with Indian ancestry. There's plenty of Native blood in the mountains, but a lot of it is kept hidden. In the past, it was better not to be Indian. And it's not hard for people who are Indian to hide that fact. Just keeping quiet and cutting your hair short and dressing like everybody else is usually enough. A lot of people with Indian blood do just that. **12**

That was one of the reasons why I hoped Jimmy T would make an effort to get to know me. I admired him for the fact that he wasn't hiding who he was. He wasn't afraid to let the world know he was a real Indian. Realer than me, a guy who had to dye his brown hair black to make it more Indian.

He wasn't hiding who he was.

When I was little, I didn't think about it that much. My dad, who was as Indian-looking as Cochise, could always handle it with his good nature. People who started out hostile would end up buying him beers. Usually a few too many. They were surprised at how he could hold his booze, what with all they say about Indians not being able to drink without getting all crazy. I don't think my dad was even that drunk the night he died. After all, the tractor-trailer that hit his pickup skidded on the ice and crossed into his lane.

I started hanging out with Uncle Tommy after my mother and I got back from Sweden. Getting to know him, even though he wasn't really a relative, was like getting to know things about my dad that I'd never known before.

I remember the only time when Uncle Tommy asked me why I was hanging around him so much.

"My dad," I said, "never taught me how to be an Indian."

"Mitchell," Uncle Tommy said to me, "white men taught us how to be Indians. Before that, we were just people." **13**

12 Character and Theme
How do you think Mitchell feels about people who hide their heritage? Why?

13 Character and Theme
Why is Uncle Tommy's statement important? What does it show about him and Mitchell?

✓ Monitor Comprehension

Explain
How do the students at Mitchell's high school treat Jimmy T? How do they treat Randolph and his sisters? Reread to clarify.

Historical Background
Cochise was an Apache leader. In the 1860s, he and his people fought with the U.S. Army and settlers for control of native land in the Southwest.

"HEY CHIEF,"

Jacques Dennis said to me as I closed my locker.

"Hey," I said. "What's up?"

"It's all good," Jacques said. He was beaming. "Randolph is cool. A real center, hey? Yes!" He held up his right hand and I high-fived him, wondering as I did so if Randolph ever high-fived or simply insisted on a gentlemanly handshake.

Out on the field, Coach Carson pulled Randolph aside.

"Mitchell," Coach yelled. "Take a snap."

I dropped back and yelled, "Hike." A perfect spiral snap came whizzing back at me **like a bullet**.

"All right!" Coach Carson shouted, raising both fists. That surprised all of us. Coach doesn't usually show his feelings. But I understood. I'd love not having to chase balls snapped four feet over my head or six feet to my left. Jacques Dennis sucked at long snaps.

Jimmy T showed up just then. He was late, but Coach Carson didn't bawl him out. He just sent him over to work with the receivers. Before long it was obvious that Jimmy T could throw not just long balls and bullets, but also touch passes.

For the rest of practice, Coach Carson walked around humming a tune that sounded suspiciously like "Happy Days Are Here Again," and then catching himself at it and **clamming up**. His Long Pond Lumberjacks finally had a chance at a winning season.

I wasn't completely convinced. Maybe no one else had seen it, but I could still sense the tension building between Jimmy T and Randolph. The last half-hour of practice, Jimmy T was taking snaps from him. They were both so good that they got into a real rhythm after awhile. **14** That's the key, you know, that rhythm a center and a quarterback need to make everything come out right. I could tell that they both loved what they were doing so much that they'd

14 **Character and Theme**
The boys are rivals, but they practice together. What does that tell you about them?

Key Vocabulary
• **tension** *n.*, stress, strain, or anxiety

In Other Words
like a bullet very fast
clamming up keeping quiet

forgotten, for the moment at least, whatever bad blood was between them in the past. What worried me, though, was what would occur after practice.

But nothing bad happened. They just went to lockers at opposite ends of the room and ignored each other. In fact, after we hit the showers, while Jimmy T was toweling off his long hair, he finally said something to me, even though it was in a **guarded** voice.

"Nice job, kicker."

"Thanks," I replied.

It made me feel great to get that praise. For a half a second I wondered if maybe I should try to start a real conversation with him now. But I left it at that. It was better to hang back. No point in pushing my luck.

By the fourth week of school, we'd already had our first two games and won them both. I hadn't caught any passes yet, but I'd kicked eleven extra points and two field goals, which gives you an idea of just how well the Long Pond Lumberjacks were doing with Jimmy T as our quarterback and Randolph as our center. Whatever there was between them, they seemed to put it aside as soon as the whistle blew and we ran onto the field. They just concentrated on the game.

Concentrating on the game was hard for Jimmy T. His father was a Yeller. Different kinds of parents come to high school games. Some cheer a little too much for their kids. Even when they do something dumb, their parents call out "Great job!" Some just sit in the stands, watch politely, and cheer with the crowd. That was how Randolph's mom and dad acted. The worst are the Yellers. They don't stay in the stands. They walk up and down, as close to the field as they can get. They scream at referees, coaches, other players, and their own kids. **15**

Mr. Black was the worst Yeller I'd ever seen. He was tall and dark-haired like Jimmy. But he didn't wear his hair long or have Indian jewelry. Maybe he didn't want to call attention to himself at his job. But he surely called attention to himself during our first two games.

15 Clarify Vocabulary
What is a *Yeller*?
Look for examples in the paragraph.

In Other Words
guarded cautious

Jimmy hardly ever made a mistake. But the few times he did, Mr. Black bellowed at his son so hard that his face got beet red.

"Can't you take a snap?" he shouted, throwing his hat on the ground. "Didn't you see that open man? Come on, Jimmy. You're playing like you're asleep."

Jimmy tried to ignore it. But I noticed how flushed his face got when his father yelled. **16**

By now, I was spending a lot of my time with Randolph. We were both in advanced classes, so we saw each other almost every period. And, of course, there was football. I've always had a lot of acquaintances. You know the kind. You pass each other in the hall, give each other the high sign. But I'd never had any close friends my age. Randolph was getting to be one. He even invited me to dinner at his house. Jimmy T, on the other hand, I hardly even saw except on the field. He wasn't in any classes with me. His grades were just high enough to stay eligible for football.

I wished I could find the courage to really talk with Jimmy. It seemed to me that maybe he was doing what a lot of Indian kids do, not living up to his **potential** because he didn't want to play by *their* rules. But Jimmy seemed to be avoiding me and I didn't make it a point to seek him out.

During that dinner with Randolph's family, I got the shock of my life.

After saying grace, Mrs. White turned to me. "Do you speak any Abenaki, Mitchell?" she said.

I hadn't expected that.

"Some," I said. "My mom's not Indian, but she's been encouraging me to learn more."

During that dinner with Randolph's family, I got the shock of my life.

"That's very good," Mr. White said. "I've always been a race man myself. Young people should be proud of their history, proud of their race." **17**

16 Character
How do you think Jimmy T's actions at school differ from his actions at home?

17 Character
How would you describe Mr. and Mrs. White's personalities?

Key Vocabulary
• **potential** *n.*, natural ability

Cultural Background
Abenaki is part of an Algonquin family of Native American languages in New England and Northeast Canada.

"Plural, dear," Mrs. White said. "Races."

Across the table from me, Randolph looked like he was so amused that he was about to **bust a gut**. Coretta and Rosa were smiling at each other the way twins do when they're thinking exactly the same thing.

"Randolph," Mr. White said in a deep voice, "greet your friend in the language of your great-grandparents."

"*Osi yo ogi na li i,*" Randolph said in a language I'd never heard before. My mouth couldn't catch up to my mind.

"Huh?" was all I could say in return.

"That's 'Hello, my friend,' in Tsalagi, the Cherokee language," Mrs. White said. "Our family has Cherokee and Choctaw ancestors. Our great-great grandparents suffered through the Trail of Tears." **18**

"In Oklahoma," Mr. White rumbled, "the family name of White Path was shortened to White."

"Cherokee hair," Mrs. White said, reaching out to stroke the heads of her two daughters.

"Most African Americans," Mr. White said, "have some Indian ancestry. I expect you know that already, Mitchell. I'm afraid most white Americans are not about to accept that fact."

Even though Randolph **was clicking** as Jimmy T's center, there was tension between them. The day it came to a head at practice almost ruined our season. Coach Carson got an emergency call, so he went into the school to take it. We were on our own.

I heard Jimmy T say the "n" word. It shocked me so much that I turned around to see him staring at Randolph. Randolph was looking back at him.

Then Randolph shook his head. "Better than a faker, pal."

Jimmy T threw the football right at Randolph. The football thumped off Randolph's chest like a stick bouncing off a drum. It hit Jimmy T in the face, and blood spurted out of his nose. He lunged toward Randolph. I grabbed

18 Theme
How does the discovery of Randolph's heritage affect the way Mitchell thinks of him? Does it affect your thoughts about Randolph?

In Other Words
bust a gut laugh so hard his stomach might burst
was clicking was playing very well

Historical Background
The **Trail of Tears** is the route the Cherokee Indians took from 1838 to 1839, when they were forced to march from their home in western Georgia to a reservation in Oklahoma.

Jimmy, pinning his arms to his sides.

"Stop it," I hissed into his ear, pressing my cheek hard against his and getting my own face **smeared** with his blood. "You're better than this."

The tension went out of him. I slowly let go and stepped back. Jimmy T turned to look into my face. His eyes were filled with tears.

"No, I'm not," he whispered. He ran toward the school, holding his bloody nose. Randolph was still rooted to that same spot.

Three Red Linemen, © 1975, Ernie Barnes. Acrylic on canvas, collection of the artist.

ERNIE BARNES

△ **Critical Viewing: Effect** What effect does the artist create by exaggerating the shape of the football players and hiding their faces?

"It's okay," Randolph said. "I don't blame him. I blame his father." **19**

There was no time to find out what he meant just then. Coach Carson came back and I had to explain how Jimmy T got accidentally hit in the nose by the ball.

Later, in the locker room, Randolph explained what he'd meant.

"His father hates my dad," Randolph said, tying his shoes hard. "He thinks that *he* should have been the director of the center. He says that the only reason my father got the position was because of affirmative action." Randolph shook his head. "Dad won't talk about it, but Mom said he and Mr. Black were friends in graduate school. Now they're enemies who have to work together every day."

"So, you cool with Jimmy T now?" I asked.

19 Character
What do Jimmy T's tears and Randolph's comment about the father reveal about them?

In Other Words
smeared covered

Cultural Background
Affirmative action is a program that began in 1965 to help eliminate discrimination against women, African Americans, and other people who apply for jobs, college, and government contracts.

"Cool," Randolph said.

Sure enough, in practice the next day it was like nothing happened. Jimmy didn't apologize to Randolph, but they worked together like a center and quarterback should. And we kept winning football games.

One evening I was filling up my truck with gas at our one local station. It was the old beater Chevy I bought with some of the money I'd earned working summers at the Indian Village. Jimmy T's mother pulled up to the other pump.

I'd never seen Mrs. Black at games. She kept to herself and didn't go out much. Rumor was that she was sick. So it surprised me when this puffy-cheeked woman wearing dark eye shadow got out of her car and came up to me.

"You Mitchell Sabattis?" she said.

"Yes, ma'am?" I said.

"I'm Iris Black, Jimmy's mother."

She was so close to me that I could smell the alcohol on her breath. Her eyes were bright. My Dad's eyes used to get like that after a few beers.

"Pleased to meet you, Mrs. Black," I said.

She grabbed me so hard by the wrist that I almost dropped the gas cap.

"You have been so good to my son. You just do not know how important you are to him. He wishes he could be like you."

Mrs. Black leaned over and kissed me on my cheek. Then she got in her car and drove off.

Those surprises got me thinking about something Uncle Tommy told me. You never can tell what's in someone's heart by the way they look on the outside. [20]

What was really in Jimmy T's heart?

[20] **Character and Theme**
What do you think Uncle Tommy means by this?

Monitor Comprehension

Confirm Prediction
Did you logically predict what would happen to the tension between Randolph and Jimmy T? What happened?

THE SATURDAY AFTER I met Jimmy T's mom was the Big Creek game. We were down thirteen to zip. The Long Pond Lumberjacks had turned back into the Wrong Pond Flapjacks. Jimmy looked like he was moving in slow motion. He couldn't even *buy* a completed pass.

Like always, Jimmy's dad was on the sidelines yelling. He wasn't yelling at the referees or the other players at all. His whole attention was on Jimmy.

"You're a loser, kid, a loser" he bellowed like a wounded moose. "I always knew it. You're as weak as your mother."

After that Jimmy could barely make a clean hand-off. It was the worst first half of football I've ever been part of. Finally, and none too soon, it was halftime.

Jimmy sat with his head down in the locker room. **21** No one was talking to him. Not even Coach Carson. We had to be back on the field in five minutes. Coach motioned to the team.

"Let's go," he said. Jimmy didn't move.

Coach grabbed my arm before I could follow the rest of the team out the door. "Mitch," he whispered. "You're the only player with his head still in this game. Talk to him."

"Why me?" I said.

Coach looked up toward the sky in exasperation. "Jeezum, do you always have to go back and forth between being brilliant and brain-dead, Sabattis? Just do it."

From behind Coach's back, Randolph held up his hand and gave me the thumbs up sign. He believed in me, too, even if I didn't. **22**

Coach Carson shut the locker room door leaving the two of us alone.

"I never really said I was Indian," Jimmy T said, without looking up. "We moved around so much. Whenever I showed up at a new school wearing

21 Character
What details show Jimmy T's mood at halftime?

22 Character
The others want Mitchell to talk to Jimmy T. What does this show you about Mitchell's character?

this jewelry and with this hair, people assumed I was Native American. It was easier to just go along with it. But it's like Randolph said. I'm a phony. My real middle name is Tomas. There's no Indian blood in our family. We're Hungarian."

He slammed his fist against the locker next to him. I didn't say anything.

"Jeez," Jimmy T said. "My Dad is right." He looked across at me and I could see the pain in his eyes. "There's no way I can ever live up to his standards. He said it didn't matter how many football games I won, I was still a born loser."

I kept my mouth shut. Another lesson Uncle Tommy taught me. Never interrupt people when they're speaking from their heart.

Jimmy T took another deep breath. "I wish I really was Indian. I'm not real like you, Mitchell." He clenched his fists and looked down at his feet. "It's just so much easier to hide your real self."

"I know," I said.

Jimmy T hadn't avoided me because I wasn't real enough. He'd been afraid I'd see that he was playing a part. He'd become a pretend Indian to get away from the pain in his own life. But I didn't hate him for it. The real Indians I've known have done their share of trying to get away, too. Like Uncle Tommy told me, pain is part of the admission fee for being human. **23**

In that moment, I knew that we'd have our undefeated football season. Of course, I'm writing this after all that happened, so that's easy for me to say. But I really did know we'd go back out on the field with our hearts in the game and win.

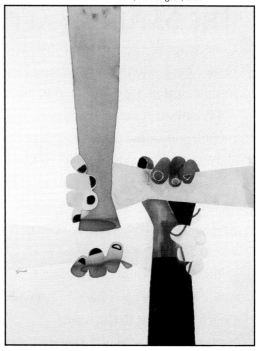

"Civilization is a method of living, an attitude of equal respect for all men," 1955, George Giusti. India ink and gouache on paper, Smithsonian American Art Museum, Washington, D.C.

▲ **Critical Viewing: Theme** Read the title of this drawing. How does it support the story?

23 **Character and Theme**
Why do you think Jimmy T pretends?

I also knew, as Jimmy T sat there with the look of a lost soul on his face, that there was only one thing I could say.

"Jimmy, I've got this friend. His name is Uncle Tommy Fox. When he comes back, I'm going to introduce you to him. But for right now, let me just tell you what I know *he'd* tell you."

I paused. Jimmy T lifted his head to look at me like a drowning person who hopes someone will throw him a life preserver.

"What?" Jimmy T said. "What would he say?"

I spoke, but I was hearing Uncle Tommy's voice, sharing a lesson that both Jimmy and I needed.

"Whoever you are is real enough. Underneath our skins, everyone's blood is red." ❖

ANALYZE Skins

1. **Explain** How does Mitchell help Jimmy T live up to his **potential**? Be sure to cite evidence from the text.

2. **Vocabulary** What is the source of **tension** between Jimmy T and Randolph?

3. **Analyze Character and Theme** Think about the theme of "Skins." Work with a partner and refer back to your **Theme Charts**. Use the clues from your charts to write a sentence about the life lesson you think the story teaches. Then share your sentence with the class.

4. **Focus Strategy Clarify Vocabulary** What words were you able to clarify as you read? Compare your strategies with a partner's strategies.

⮐ Return to the Text

Reread and Write What do the characters initially think about each other? Reread to find and record examples of the first impressions the characters have of each other. How did those impressions change? Using details in the story, describe how the characters show they are starting to know each other better.

One

by James Berry

Only one of me
and nobody can get a second one
from a photocopy machine.

Nobody has the fingerprints I have.
5 Nobody can cry my tears, or laugh my laugh
or have my expectancy when I wait.

But anybody can mimic my dance with my dog.
Anybody can howl how I sing out of tune.
And mirrors can show me multiplied
10 many times, say, dressed up in red
or dressed up in grey.

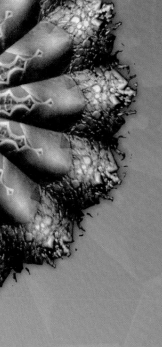

Nobody can get into my clothes for me
or feel my fall for me, or do my running.
Nobody hears my music for me, either.

15 I am just this one.
Nobody else makes the words
I shape with sound, when I talk.

But anybody can act how I stutter in a rage.
Anybody can copy echoes I make.
20 And mirrors can show me multiplied
many times, say, dressed up in green
or dressed up in blue.

About the Poet

James Berry (1926–) was born in Jamaica
and later lived in England. He gets his ideas for
his poems from his own feelings, from observing
people, places, and things, and from the sounds
of animals and music.

BEFORE READING Nicole

oral history by Rebecca Carroll and Nicole

Reading Strategies

▶ **Plan and Monitor**
· Determine Importance
· Make Inferences
· Ask Questions
· Make Connections
· Synthesize
· Visualize

Determine Viewpoint

In a **personal narrative**, a real person tells the story of events that actually happened to him or her. The writer speaks in the first person, using pronouns like *I* and *me*, and gives a **viewpoint**, or personal thoughts and feelings. A personal narrative usually captures the writer's **voice**, or what the person sounds like when speaking. In fact, a person may tell his or her narrative aloud to someone in an **oral history** or **interview** rather than write it down. "Nicole" is an oral history that was recorded by Rebecca Carroll.

Look Into the Text

First-person pronouns

Personal thoughts and feelings

Real events

My mother is white and my father is black. I don't consider myself biracial, or black, or white. I consider myself Nicole, although when we visit my white grandparents' house and there are other family members around like my cousin, it is he who is seen as the "good" child. He is pure white. I am the black sheep of the family, just like my mother is the black sheep of her family for dating my father. In society, I am made to feel like a black sheep for precisely that reason of my white mother and my black father getting together and having me, which was considered wrong at the time and still is in some people's minds. I am the walking representative of that wrongness.

Focus Strategy ▶ Plan and Monitor

Writers may give you clues to figure out what an unfamiliar word means. Look at the context, or the other words and sentences near the unfamiliar word. Using **context clues**, you can sometimes, but not always, determine the meaning.

HOW TO CLARIFY VOCABULARY

Focus Strategy

1. **Look for a Definition** A writer may define an unfamiliar word right after it appears.

   > Nicole doesn't consider herself to be black, white, or biracial, from two races.

2. **Look for a Synonym** A synonym is a word or phrase that means nearly the same thing as the unfamiliar word. It may be in a nearby sentence.

   > She knows precisely why her cousin is seen as the "good" child. He is exactly the image of what society thinks is good.

3. **Look for an Example** Sometimes a writer provides words that are an example of the word.

   > In the past, Nicole used defense mechanisms, such as fighting with others, to stand up for herself.

Nicole

Rebecca Carroll and Nicole

Connect Across Texts

In "Skins," three teenagers find out what makes people who they are. In this oral history, Nicole discusses how she wants people to see her.

My mother is white and my father is black.

I don't consider myself **biracial**, or black, or white. I consider myself Nicole, although when we visit my white grandparents' house and there are other family members around like my cousin, it is he who is seen as the "good" child. He is pure white. I am **the black sheep** of the family, just like my mother is the black sheep of her family for dating my father. In society, I am made to feel like a black sheep for precisely that reason of my white mother and my black father getting together and having me, which was considered wrong at the time and still is in some people's minds. I am the **walking representative** of that wrongness.

We all have the ability and the resources to be individuals, but when I walk down the street I am clearly identified as a black person and am **discriminated** against accordingly. I don't blame my parents and I don't blame people for their ignorance. **1** Nobody has done anything wrong here, but it's like having to work at a job I didn't apply for. I alone have to come up with the added strength to deal with **racism**, and that isn't something I bargained for when I came into this world. I don't draw from the loving union my parents had when they got together to make me; I draw from the love I have for and within myself. Basically, I'm the one who is going to be

1 Clarify Vocabulary
What is *ignorance*? Look for an example in the next sentence to help you determine the meaning.

Key Vocabulary
- **discriminate** *v.*, to treat differently because of prejudice
- **racism** *n.*, ill treatment of people on the basis of ancestry

In Other Words
biracial of two races
the black sheep a person who doesn't fit in or who is considered an outcast
walking representative living example

here in the end. I'm the one who is going to have to defend myself. I can tell my mother when I am discriminated against or whatever, but I'm the one who has to **look it square in the face**. **2**

I think when people act stupid they are holding themselves back and ultimately losing out. I'm the one winning in a situation where someone is acting stupid toward me. I have the advantage because when we **throw down**, in the final analysis I'm the one with the knowledge and the sense of self. The racist is the one who will forever have in his or her mind that I am bad and that they are good, which is a lie. It's just not true. Period. End of story. I get so tired of people believing in their heart of hearts that they can win or achieve anything by making someone feel inferior. I think that's how I have developed my defense mechanisms against racism; I just got so tired of hearing the rude remarks and having teachers and counselors tell me that there wasn't anything I could do about it. Because there most certainly is.

When I was younger, my teachers would tell me not to beat up these kids who were saying racist things to me because then they would win twice:

2 Determine Viewpoint
How does Nicole feel about dealing with racism?

© Stephan Daigle/Corbis

▲ Critical Viewing: Effect Compare this image with Nicole's description of herself. How does the image make you feel?

In Other Words
look it square in the face deal with it
throw down have a conflict

I would look like twice the animal they were telling me I was. What made me mad was that I didn't think they were winning at all, never mind once or twice, and I felt **compelled** to do them the favor of making that completely clear. My teachers would tell me just to walk away, that I would come off more powerful if I just walked away, which, **in retrospect**, I suppose was true, but it took me a long time to truly believe that. It's all well and good in theory, but it doesn't exactly **eliminate** the feeling of having a knife twisted around in your gut. Now, as I've grown older, I find that it is really important to just be focused and to stay as positive as I can. I do still get angry, though. I have a real temper. Emotions and theory don't really go hand in hand, so it

> # I find that it is **really important** to just **be focused** and to **stay as positive** as I can.

can be very difficult for me sometimes. But I have learned from my mistakes.

On the census checkoff lists that offer little boxes next to black, white, or other, I refuse to check just one box. I check them all off because I am all of those things. My mother told me that when I was born and she was filling out my birth certificate, the nurse asked her to write in *mulatto*, which my mother did not do. I think the word is incredibly negative and **degrading**. ▣ 3 It sounds like a sickness. The part of me that is black-identified doesn't fit into a category or a box. Society has such awful ideas about black people, and I don't want society to decide for me what it means to be black. When I think of being black, I think of kings and queens and history and beauty and **authenticity**.

3 Clarify Vocabulary
Do you know what *negative* means? Look for clues in this sentence and the one that follows.

You can call me black if you want to, you can call me *mulatto*, you can call me biracial, you can call me whatever you please, but I'll still be Nicole. Are you going to remember me as "that black girl"? No, you're going to

Key Vocabulary
compel *v.*, to urge forcefully, to cause to do
● **eliminate** *v.*, to remove, to get rid of
authenticity *n.*, realness, genuineness

In Other Words
in retrospect in thinking about the past
mulatto person of both white and African American ancestry (in Spanish)
degrading insulting

remember me as Nicole if you've taken the time to learn my name. And those who haven't taken the time, I don't care to be remembered by. It's Nicole today, it'll be Nicole tomorrow, and it'll be Nicole when I die. I don't care if you have something against black people, or if you have a problem with **interracial relationships**, or if you don't like biracial kids. I don't care. But if you are talking to me, call me by my name. 4 ❖

4 Determine Viewpoint
In your own words, sum up how Nicole feels about herself.

ANALYZE Nicole

1. **Paraphrase** Nicole talks about **racism** and ways that it affects her personally. Restate her message in your own words.

2. **Vocabulary** Nicole says that when she thinks of being black, she thinks of "kings and queens and history and beauty and **authenticity**." Describe what you think she means.

3. **Determine Viewpoint** Identify some details from the text that are features of a personal narrative. How do those features help express Nicole's viewpoint— her personal thoughts and feelings?

4. **Focus Strategy Clarify Vocabulary** Work with a partner to figure out the meaning of *census* (p. 97). Look for context clues such as a definition, a synonym, or an example. Write a definition for the word. Then check a dictionary to see whether your definition is right.

Return to the Text
Reread and Write How does Nicole want to be classified? Why? Write a paragraph to explain. Support your ideas with examples from the text.

In Other Words

interracial relationships friendships between people of different races

EQ When Do You Really Know Someone?

Critical Thinking

EQ 1. Analyze How well do you think Nicole (in "Nicole") and Mitchell (in "Skins") really know themselves? Use details from the text to support your answer.

2. Compare Compare the theme of "Skins" with the main idea of "Nicole." Are they the same or different? Support your opinion with details from both selections.

3. Interpret What is Jimmy T's attitude toward Mitchell in the beginning of the story? How does his attitude change by the end of the story?

4. Assess In your opinion, which selection gives a more believable picture of what life is like for biracial people? Why? Give examples from both selections.

EQ 5. Synthesize Both Mitchell and Nicole deal with their own **authenticity** as well as other people's perceptions. What do you think makes you who you are? How do your perceptions compare with Mitchell's and Nicole's?

Write About Literature

Personal Statement Uncle Tommy says, "You never can tell what's in someone's heart." Locate this and other insights Uncle Tommy shares about people. Elaborate on one such statement by relating it to your personal experience and an event in the story.

Key Vocabulary Review

Oral Review Work with a partner. Use these words to complete the paragraph.

authenticity	eliminate	racism
compelled	potential	tension
discriminated	predominate	

The United States is made up of ethnic, racial, and religious groups that work together yet preserve their true cultural __(1)__ . The Founders said everyone has a right to life, liberty, and happiness. Yet some accuse the Founders of __(2)__ because enslaved people and Native Americans were not given those rights. These prejudices have caused __(3)__ between groups. During the Civil Rights movement, people who were __(4)__ against felt __(5)__ to try to __(6)__ injustices, and they mostly succeeded. Even so, many Americans still believe that white Americans __(7)__ in business, industry, and government. In the end, individuals should be able to develop to their full __(8)__ .

Writing Application Write a paragraph describing ways to **eliminate** discrimination. Use at least four Key Vocabulary words.

Read with Ease: Intonation

Assess your reading fluency with the passage in the Reading Handbook, p. 801. Then complete the self-check below.

1. My intonation did/did not sound natural.

2. My words correct per minute: _____ .

Grammar

Fix Sentence Fragments

This group of words begins with a capital letter and ends with a period, just like a sentence.

Gets pale in the winter.

The group of words is not complete. It is a **sentence fragment**. The fragment needs a **subject**.

Mitchell gets pale in the winter.

Some fragments may need a **verb**.

Fragment: Jimmy T Black the star quarterback.
Sentence: Jimmy T Black **is** the star quarterback.

A fragment may need to become part of another sentence.

We play football. And still get good grades.
   sentence   fragment

We play football and still get good grades.

Oral Practice (1–5) Look at the selections you just read. Find five complete sentences. Break off a piece, and say it as a fragment. Ask your partner to change it back into a complete sentence.

Written Practice (6–10) Number your paper. Label each group of words with **S** for *Sentence* or **F** for *Fragment*. Write the fragments as complete sentences.

6. Big crowds at the games.
7. Jimmy T plays quarterback.
8. Uncle Tommy's house.
9. Color my hair darker.
10. Mitch introduced himself to Randolph.

Language Development

Engage in Discussion

Group Talk In groups, discuss the story characters and their actions. Did they always do the right thing? Share your ideas and opinions, too. Listen to what others have to say and ask them questions.

Literary Analysis

Characters: Static and Dynamic

In most stories, there are main characters and minor characters. The most important characters are the **main characters**. The other characters, or **minor characters**, interact with the main characters and keep the plot moving.

Characters in a story can be static or dynamic. A **static character** is one who remains the same throughout the story. A **dynamic character** is a main character who goes through changes throughout the story. These changes are often a result of the interactions among characters. The outcome of the interactions affects the story's plot.

In "Skins," Mitchell is a dynamic character because he changes his perception of Jimmy T and comes to a different understanding about other people. When Mitchell introduces himself to Randolph, their interaction causes a change. What change does this cause?

With a partner, use a chart to analyze the characters' interactions and explain how they affect the plot of "Skins."

CHARACTERS	INTERACTIONS	PLOT CHANGE
Mitchell and Randolph		
Randolph and Jimmy T		
Mrs. Black and Mitchell		

Greek and Latin Roots

Many English words include roots from the languages of Greek and Latin. Knowing what those roots mean can help you figure out the meaning of the English word. For example, if you know that *magni* means *large*, you can figure out that *magnify* means "make larger." For each word below, use the meaning of the root to determine the meaning of the word.

WORD	ROOT	ROOT MEANING	WORD MEANING
magnify	magni	large	make larger
dictate	dict	tell	
prescribe	scrib	write	

Oral Report

History: Affirmative Action Use the Internet and an encyclopedia to find out more about affirmative action.

1. **Find Answers to Questions** Look in your sources of information to answer the following questions:
   - What is the purpose of affirmative action?
   - What problems led to affirmative action?

2. **Jot Down Your Answers** Write the answers in your own words. That will help you make sure that you understand what the sources say.

3. **Present Your Report** Use the questions and answers to present your report to your class.

▼ **Language and Learning Handbook**, p. 761.

Focus and Unity

When you write, maintain focus and stick to one topic. Where does the writer change topics in the paragraph below?

Just OK

> Rosa Parks was an African American seamstress in Alabama, but there was more to her than someone who sewed clothes. One day in 1955 she refused to give up her seat on the bus to a white person. She had just finished a day of work and was tired. It was a long ride home. Her simple act compelled people to look beyond the stereotype of a quiet seamstress.

Here is how the writer fixed his mistake. Notice how the writer removes details that stray from the topic and then adds important information about the topic.

Much Better

> Rosa Parks was an African American seamstress in Alabama, but there was more to her than someone who sewed clothes. One day in 1955 she refused to give up her seat on the bus to a white person. ~~She had just finished a day of work and was tired. It was a long ride home.~~ At that time in Alabama, African Americans were required by law to give up their seat to a white person. Her simple act compelled people to look beyond the stereotype of a quiet seamstress.

Read the paragraph below. Decide where the writer changes topics. With a classmate, fix the paragraph.

> I have a lot of respect for my brother. Some of the kids at school thought that the new student, Arthur, was weird. No one wanted to be his lab partner in chemistry class. Our chemistry class is hard. We're studying the Periodic Table. My brother volunteered to be Arthur's lab partner.

▼ **Writing Handbook**, p. 841.

Yes
BY DENISE DUHAMEL

According to *Culture Shock:*
A Guide to Customs and Etiquette
of Filipinos, when my husband says yes,
he could also mean one of the following:

5   a.) *I don't know.*

b.) *If you say so.*

c.) *If it will please you.*

d.) *I hope I have said yes unenthusiastically enough*
    for you to realize I mean no.

10   You can imagine the confusion
surrounding our movie dates, the laundry,
who will take out the garbage
and when. I remind him
I'm an American, that all his yeses sound alike to me.

Modern art faces, Diana Ong ©Diana Ong/Ikon Image/age fotostock.

◁ **Critical Viewing: Effect** How do the images of the people in this painting illustrate the relationship of the people in the poem?

In Other Words
Etiquette Rules of Social Behavior
unenthusiastically unexcitedly, unhappily

15 I tell him here in America we have shrinks
 who can help him to be less of a people-pleaser.
 We have two-year-olds who love to scream "No!"
 when they don't get their way. I tell him,
 in America we have a popular book,

20 *When I Say No I Feel Guilty.*
 "Should I get you a copy?" I ask.
 He says yes, but I think he means
 "If it will please you," i.e., "I won't read it."
 "I'm trying," I tell him, "but you have to try too."

25 "Yes," he says, then makes *tampo,*
 a sulking that the book *Culture Shock* describes as
 "subliminal hostility . . . withdrawal of customary cheerfulness
 in the presence of the one who has displeased" him.
 The book says it's up to me to make things all right,

30 "to restore goodwill, not by talking the problem out,
 but by showing concern about the wounded person's
 well-being." Forget it, I think, even though I know
 if I'm not nice, *tampo* can quickly escalate into *nagdadabog*—
 foot stomping, grumbling, the slamming

35 of doors. Instead of talking to my husband, I storm off
 to talk to my porcelain Kwan Yin,
 the Chinese goddess of mercy
 that I bought on Canal Street years before
 my husband and I started dating.

40 "The real Kwan Yin is in Manila,"
 he tells me. "She's called Nuestra Señora de Guia.
 Her Asian features prove Christianity
 was in the Philippines before the Spanish arrived."
 My husband's telling me this

45 tells me he's sorry. Kwan Yin seems to wink,
 congratulating me—my short prayer worked.
 "Will you love me forever?" I ask,
 then study his lips, wondering if I'll be able to decipher
 what he means by his yes.

In Other Words

shrinks doctors
Guilty Bad, Sorry
i.e. in other words
subliminal hostility anger beneath the surface
Manila the capital city of the Philippines
Nuestra Señora de Guia Our Lady of Guidance

Cultural Background

Kwan Yin is the goddess of compassion in the Chinese Buddhist religion. Buddhists keep statues of Kwan Yin to honor her. She is sometimes identified with Christianity's Virgin Mary.

DOUBLE TAKE

EQ ESSENTIAL QUESTION:
When Do You Really Know Someone?

myNGconnect.com
🔊 Download the rubric.

EDGE LIBRARY

Present Your Project: Video or Sound Recording

It's time to record your reading or performance about the Essential Question for this unit: When Do You Really Know Someone?

1 Review and Complete Your Plan

As you complete your project, consider:

- how the literary work you found best addresses the Essential Question
- the recording format that best expresses how the literary work addresses the Essential Question

Divide up the tasks of choosing the literary work, reading aloud or performing in front of the camera, and recording the performance.

2 Make the Recording

Make your video or sound recording. Refer to the tips for making a good recording to ensure the quality.

3 Evaluate the Recording

Play the recording for your class. Use the online rubric to evaluate each of the video or sound recordings, including your own.

Reflect on Your Reading

Many of the characters in the stories in this unit learned more about themselves and other people.

Think back on your reading of the unit selections, including your choice of Edge Library books. Then, discuss the following with a partner or in a small group.

Genre Focus Compare and contrast the elements of a short story with the features of a magazine article. Give examples, using the selections in this unit.

Focus Strategy Choose a unit selection that some students would find difficult to read. On a note card, explain two reading strategies that would help students clarify their understanding of the selection. Trade cards with a partner, apply the strategies to a passage from the selection, and discuss how they helped.

EQ Respond to the Essential Question

Throughout this unit, you have been exploring the question "When do you really know someone?" Discuss this with a group. What have *you* decided? Support your response with evidence from your reading, discussions, research, and writing.

Write a Short Story

Writing Portfolio

Writing Mode
Narrative

Writing Trait Focus
Focus and Unity

Reflecting on turning points in your life can give you ideas for a compelling fictional story that others will relate to. For this project, you will write a short story about a character who faces a turning point in his or her own life.

Study Short Stories

Short stories are narratives about imaginary people, places, and events. Writers use vivid details and dialogue to bring the characters and conflicts to life.

❶ Connect Writing to Your Life

You have probably told a lot of stories in your life, both real and made up. Where did the ideas come from? Some of them probably came from your experiences or the experiences of people you know. Writing stories that are inspired by your own life is a great way to keep the memories forever while sharing them with others.

❷ Understand the Form

A short story usually has two or more characters, including a **protagonist**, or main character. The protagonist faces a conflict that is related to the **theme**, or central message, of the story. Rising action moves the plot forward, often leading to **complications** for the protagonist. He or she eventually reaches a **turning point**, or climax. After that, the conflict gets resolved in a way that relates back to the theme.

Plot Diagram

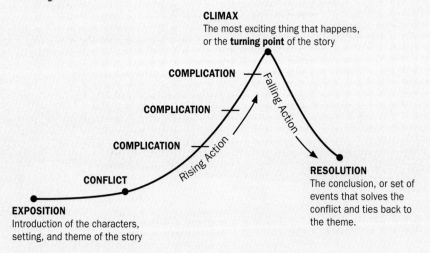

CLIMAX
The most exciting thing that happens, or the **turning point** of the story

COMPLICATION

COMPLICATION

COMPLICATION

Rising Action

Falling Action

CONFLICT

EXPOSITION
Introduction of the characters, setting, and theme of the story

RESOLUTION
The conclusion, or set of events that solves the conflict and ties back to the theme.

Along with dialogue, a writer may use **interior monologue**, passages that let readers "hear" the character's thoughts and insights. The writes reveals details about the character through these thoughts and uses them to develop the theme.

Now read a short story by a professional writer. Using the plot diagram and the margin notes, identify the theme and analyze the development of the character and plot.

❸ Analyze a Professional

As you read, look for the elements of the short story.

Mental Blocks

By Louise Jaffe

There were nine wooden blocks on the desk in front of Rissa. Each one had a letter on it. At first glance, the blocks looked like toys, but they spelled out a message: "Yes you can." Three simple words from Mr. B, the Reading Lab teacher. Yet there was nothing simple about reading, as far as Rissa was concerned.

For years, she had managed to get by in school, reading no better than a third-grader. She wasn't stupid; math came easily to her, and she loved science, which was mostly experiments and group work. Social studies and language arts were more of a challenge, but she always squeaked by. So what did it matter?

By high school, it mattered. The textbooks were thicker, the words were longer, and Rissa could no longer fake her way through class. That's how she had ended up in Reading Lab, where she now sat, staring at the blocks. Mr. B had just informed her she had *dyslexia*, a simple reading disorder. It was easy to overcome, he had reassured her. But it didn't sound easy—it sounded scary. *I'm not in control,* she thought. *I have a problem, and* it's *in control of me.*

Then Ted walked in. Ted Marino—tall, smart, and funny. *What's* he *doing here?* she gulped, her stomach lurching.

"Hey, Rissa," he said cheerfully. "Hey, Mr. B! So, what tricks you got up your sleeve for us today? I have a history test on Friday, and I'm having a really hard time getting through the reading. Too many words ending with *ism!*" he laughed. Then he turned to Rissa. "It isn't easy being as smart as everyone thinks you are, is it?"

So Ted had a reading disorder, too? Tall, smart, funny Ted? Yet he didn't seem to care. In fact, he was facing it head-on. He was taking control.

Suddenly the wooden words in front of Rissa started looking more like building blocks than road blocks. *Yeah, I can,* she thought.

The writer starts with a catchy beginning that introduces the **main character** and gives clues to the **setting** and **theme**.

In the exposition, the writer describes past events that lead up to a **conflict**.

The writer shows **rising action** and uses **interior monologue** to reveal details about the character and conflict.

The writer uses dialogue to lead to a **turning point**.

The conclusion provides a resolution that ties back to the **theme**, and the writer uses **interior monologue** again to reinforce the message.

✔ Prewrite

Now that you have analyzed the elements of a short story, make a Writing Plan. This will help you keep your theme clear in your mind and your story focused as you write.

❶ Choose Your Topic

Try these strategies to help you generate great ideas for your story:

- Use what you know. Think about interesting experiences that led to a turning point in your own life.
- Ask "what if" questions about your character to brainstorm what he or she is like. Put him or her in a different time and place than you were in when you had your experience. How would this change things?
- Use a Plot Diagram like the one on p. 106 to guide your brainstorming.

❷ Clarify the Audience, Theme, and Purpose

Determine your audience. Good writers know who is reading their work. Will young children, students in another school, or published writers read your short story? Understanding your audience can help you determine your word choices and style.

Think of what your story is mostly about. For example, the theme of "Mental Blocks" is that you can take control of your problems instead of letting them control you.

Finally, decide why you are writing this story. Is it to share something you have learned? To entertain? Make sure the details you include serve your purpose.

❸ Gather Supporting Details

To trap details about your theme, character, setting, and plot, use a graphic organizer such as the cluster map shown.

Prewriting Tip

Gather details based on the elements of a short story, but don't worry about coming up with just the right title, character names, and other minor details. For now, use whatever comes to mind, and revise it later.

❹ Organize the Plot and Details

After you gather your story details, organize them. A focused and unified story has a clear structure. It's easy for readers to follow because events and details flow well from one part of the story to another. Here is how the writer organized the events and details of the story "Guitar Lesson."

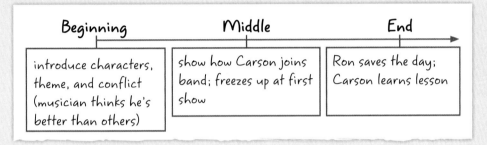

Beginning	Middle	End
introduce characters, theme, and conflict (musician thinks he's better than others)	show how Carson joins band; freezes up at first show	Ron saves the day; Carson learns lesson

❺ Finish Your Writing Plan

Make a Writing Plan like the one below to capture your story ideas.

Writing Plan

Title	Guitar Lesson
Audience	my classmates and teacher
Theme	too much pride can get you in trouble
Purpose	to entertain, to share insight about life
Time Frame	start today; due in 5 days
Beginning	Introduce characters and conflict: Teen guitar player tries out for bass player's band, doesn't take others seriously. Describe the setting: bass player's garage
Middle	Band plays together; use dialogue and interior monologue to show Carson's attitude, pride; doesn't think he needs to practice. Turning point: stage fright at show.
End	Resolution: rescued by Ron (bass player); Carson changes attitude, gains respect for Ron

Technology Tip

Send your Writing Plan as an e-mail attachment to two or three people whose opinions you trust. Ask them to give feedback by e-mail using the Comments feature in their word-processing program or by highlighting their feedback in a different color.

Reflect on Your Writing Plan

▶ Have you structured your story so that it includes rising action, a clear turning point, and a resolution that ties back to the theme? Have you included details that will give clues to the theme? Talk it over with a partner.

✔ Write a Draft

Use your Writing Plan as a guide to drafting your short story. Don't worry if you're still thinking over some details. You can make changes later.

❶ Keep Your Ideas Flowing

Even the best writers sometimes feel "blocked." Use these techniques to get ideas out of your head and onto the page.

- **Look Again** Take another look at your Writing Plan. Could you define your theme more clearly? Are important details missing from the descriptions of the characters or plot? Have you thought about how to use dialogue or interior monologue to reveal things about the characters?

- **Role Play** Bring ideas to life by asking friends to help you role-play your story's characters. Give your friends a brief description of each character and the conflict. Then, together, imagine what the characters would say and do. Think of ways to develop the plot so that it will hold the reader's attention. For example, use an unexpected turn of events to surprise your audience.

- **Freewrite** Sometimes writers get stuck trying to write a perfect first sentence. If you're stuck, just start writing about your characters and your idea and don't stop for five minutes. Don't think about punctuation or complete sentences. Write what comes to mind. Then, read what you wrote, and underline or circle the ideas, descriptions, or phrases that you like and can use in your story.

> **Technology Tip**
>
> Use Highlight from the Formatting toolbar on the computer to highlight parts of your draft that you aren't sure about or that you want to return to later. Remove the highlight after you revise your draft.

❷ Create a Compelling Beginning

A compelling, or strong, beginning makes readers want to keep reading. It can also make the rest of the writing flow. Here's an example:

OK

> Carson walked into the garage with his guitar, ready to try out for the band. Two other kids were there.

Better

> Carson swaggered into Ron Cruz's garage with his guitar slung over his shoulder. "I'm here for the band tryout," he announced. Ron played the bass—the boring stand-up kind—in the school orchestra. He was tuning it while another kid, Pauly, goofed around on the drums.

❸ Student Model

Read this draft to see how the student used the Writing Plan to get ideas down on paper. This first draft does not have to be perfect. As you will see, the student fixed the mistakes later.

Guitar Lesson

Carson swaggered into Ron Cruz's garage with his guitar slung over his shoulder. "I'm here for the band tryout," he announced. Ron played the bass—the boring stand-up kind—in the school orchestra. He was tuning it while another kid, Pauly, goofed around on the drums.

"I hope you're good. We have a gig in five days. Can you play 'Under the Moon' by The Nylon blends?"

Carson chuckled. *How old-school can you get?* he thought. *I've only known that song since I was, like, nine.* "Yeah, I think I can handle it," he said, trying to hide his sarcasm.

The drummer counted off the beat, the boys began to play. They sounded pretty good together and the bass blended well with Carson's guitar, which was red and shiny. There voices sounded decent, too. Carson belted out the lead. Ron sang backup. He had glasses and dark hair.

"That was great!" said Ron. It was almost noon. "You got the job. Here's the song list for the gig. We better practice so you can get used to playing with us."

Carson looked at the list. The songs were ancient classics by three of his dad's favorite Bands: the chargers Sloth-heads and dog's Day. "Nah, I don't need to practice. I've known how to play these songs forever."

Three days later, Carson stared out at the crowd that had gathered in front of the stage. Their were more people than he'd expected. Ron gave the signal, and Carson stepped up to the microphone. Suddenly, a wave of panic hit him. His throat tightened and his fingers froze.

Over his shoulder, he felt the glares of his bandmates. Then he heard the deep, twangy notes of Ron's bass. Ron was plucking it like an electric guitar instead of using his bow. It sounded funky, and the crowd loved it. He kept playing as if it was all part of the show, until Carson finally relaxed and jumped back in. Ron had saved him.

When the set ended, Carson walked offstage with a little less swagger in his step and a lot more respect for Ron.

Reflect on Your Draft

▶ Did you provide enough details? Do the characters, setting, and plot give clues to the theme? Do the events build to a turning point that supports the theme? Talk it over with a partner.

✔ Revise Your Draft

The word *revise* is made from word parts that mean "see again." Look at your draft with fresh eyes. You can then improve your story's focus and unity.

❶ Revise for Focus and Unity

Any kind of good writing has a **focus**—it has a central idea. In a short story, the focus is the theme, or message that you want readers to take away.

Good writing also has **unity**—that means that all of the parts are relevant to the central idea. In a short story, the dialogue and descriptive details about character, setting, and plot all give clues to the theme.

Don't expect to achieve focus and unity with your first draft. Every writer expects and needs to rewrite. Time spent revising helps you sharpen your focus. Cut out any ideas or details that stray from the theme or send a mixed message.

TRY IT ▶ With a partner, discuss which parts of the draft below seem unfocused. Think about where the details go off track.

Student Draft

> The drummer counted off the beat, the boys began to play. They sounded pretty good together and the bass blended well with Carson's guitar, which was red and shiny. There voices sounded decent, too. Carson belted out the lead. Ron sang backup. He had dark hair and glasses.
>
> "That was great!" said Ron. It was almost noon. "You got the job. Here's the song list for the gig. We better practice so you can get used to playing with us."

Now use the rubric to evaluate the focus and unity of your own draft. What score do you give your draft and why?

Focus and Unity

myNGconnect.com

 Rubric: Focus and Unity
 Evaluate and practice scoring other student stories.

	How clearly does the writing present a central message or theme?	How well does everything go together?
4 Wow!	The writing expresses a <u>clear</u> central message or theme.	**Everything** in the writing goes together. • Almost all details about the characters, setting, and plot give clues to the theme. • All details are relevant. • The resolution relates to the theme.
3 Ahh.	The writing expresses a <u>generally</u> clear central message or theme.	**Most** parts of the writing go together. • Most of the details about the characters, setting, and plot give clues to the theme. • Most details are relevant, but a few get in the way. • The resolution mostly relates to the theme.
2 Hmm.	The writing includes a central message or theme, but it is <u>not</u> clear.	**Some** parts of the writing go together. • Some of the details about the characters, setting, and plot give clues to the theme. • Some details are relevant, but others get in the way. • The resolution relates somewhat to the theme.
1 Huh?	The writing <u>does not</u> include a central message or theme.	The parts of the writing <u>do not</u> go together. • Few of the details about the characters, setting, and plot give clues to the theme. • Few details are relevant, while many get in the way. • The resolution does not relate to the theme.

❷ Revise Your Draft

You've now evaluated the focus and unity of your own draft. If you scored 3 or lower, how can you improve your work? Use the checklist below to revise your draft.

Revision Checklist

Ask Yourself	Check It Out	How to Make It Better
Is my story focused?	If your score is 3 or lower, revise.	☐ Decide on one insight, or bigger truth, to focus on and cut any others. ☐ Make sure the theme is clear.
Is my narrative unified?	If your score is 3 or lower, revise.	☐ Remove or replace any idea or detail that strays from the theme or makes the writing hard to follow. ☐ Add details about character, setting, and plot that make the theme clearer.
Does my plot have rising action, a turning point, and a clear resolution?	Find and mark the boundaries between these parts.	☐ Add any part that is missing.
Are the supporting details vivid and interesting?	Underline descriptive details. **Highlight** dialogue. Are there enough details to make the writing come alive?	☐ Add sensory details or dialogue. ☐ Add interior monologue to reveal your characters' thoughts and feelings.
Does the end of my story leave the reader with a greater understanding about the theme?	Read the conclusion aloud. Find a sentence that leaves readers with a clear message.	☐ If necessary, write a sentence that ties back to the theme.

🢒 **Writing Handbook,** p. 832

❸ Conduct a Peer Conference

Exchanging stories with a partner will help each of you revise your draft. Look for any part that:

- seems to be missing important details
- is difficult to understand
- seems very different from the rest of the writing

Discuss the draft with your partner. Focus on the items in the Revision Checklist. Use your partner's comments to make your story more engaging, more complete, and easier to understand.

❹ Make Revisions

Look at the revisions below and the peer-reviewer conversation on the right. Notice how the peer reviewer commented and asked questions. Notice how the writer used the comments and questions to revise the story.

Revised for Character and Theme

> Carson swaggered into Ron Cruz's garage with his guitar slung over his shoulder. "I'm here for the band tryout," he announced. Ron played the bass—the boring stand-up kind—in the school orchestra. He was tuning it while another kid, Pauly, goofed around on the drums. _Yep, these guys need me, thought Carson._ "Got an amp I can use?" he asked.
>
> "I hope you're good. We have a gig in five days. Can you play 'Under the Moon' by The Nylon blends?"
>
> "Sure, its over there," replied Ron.

Revised for Focus and Unity

> The drummer counted off the beat, the boys began to play. They sounded pretty good together and the bass blended _surprisingly_ well with Carson's _electric_ guitar ~~which was red and shiny.~~ There voices sounded decent, too. Carson belted out the lead _while_ Ron sang _a strong_ backup. ~~He had glasses and dark hair.~~
>
> "That was great!" said Ron. ~~It was almost noon.~~ "You got the job. Here's the song list for the gig. We better practice so you can get used to playing with us."

✔ Edit and Proofread Your Draft

Your revision should now be complete. Before you share it with others, find and fix any mistakes that you made.

❶ Capitalize Proper Nouns and Adjectives

Proper nouns are capitalized because they name specific people, places, and things. Common nouns, which are general, are not capitalized.

Common Noun	Proper Noun
band	The Road Bumps Band
country	Britain

Proper adjectives, which come from proper nouns, are also capitalized.

Proper Noun	Proper Adjective
Italy	Italian
America	American

TRY IT ▶ Copy the sentence. Fix the three capitalization errors. Use proofreader's marks.

> One of my dad's favorite Bands is a british rock band called broccolini.

❷ Punctuate Serial Commas Correctly

Use commas in a series of three or more items. There should be a comma after each item except the last one.

> Three great bands are The Chargers, Sloth-Heads, and Dog's Day.

TRY IT ▶ Copy the sentences. Add any necessary commas.

> 1. I can play the piano guitar and drums.
> 2. He enjoys music volunteering and sports.
> 3. Today we will study math science Spanish and history.

Proofreading Tip

If you are unsure of where to place a comma, look in a style manual for help and examples.

❸ Check Your Spelling

Homonyms are words that sound alike but have different meanings and spellings. Spell these homonyms correctly when you proofread.

Homonyms and Their Meanings	Examples
it's (contraction) = it is; it has	**It's** easy for you to play.
its (possessive adjective) = belonging to it	I play guitar. I like **its** sound.
there (adverb) = that place or position	A lot of people were **there**.
their (possessive adjective) = belonging to them	**Their** voices sounded decent.
they're (contraction) = they are	**They're** making progress.

Technology Tip

Learn how your word-processing program identifies errors. In Microsoft® Word, possible spelling errors are underlined with a red squiggly line. Possible grammar errors are underlined with a green squiggly line. These are both helpful features, but in the end *you* have to decide what is correct.

TRY IT ▶ Copy the sentences. Find and fix the four homonym errors.

> Their are two instruments with strings. There the guitar and the bass. Its easy to recognize the bass because of it's big size.

❹ Find and Fix Run-On Sentences

A run-on sentence consists of two or more sentences written incorrectly as one sentence. You can usually fix a run-on sentence by breaking it into two sentences. Insert end punctuation or, if there is a comma, replace it with end punctuation. Then start the second sentence with a capital letter. You can also fix a run-on by turning it into a compound sentence. Just insert a conjunction such as *and* after the comma.

> **Incorrect:** We started a band, it is called The Tuners.
> **Correct:** We started a band. **It** is called The Tuners.
> **OR**
> We started a band, **and** it is called The Tuners.

Sometimes you can fix a run-on sentence by replacing the comma with a semicolon.

> **Incorrect:** It's easy for you, you have talent.
> **Correct:** It's easy for you; you have talent.

TRY IT ▶ Copy the paragraph. Fix the run-on sentences.

> The drummer counted off the beat, the boys began to play. They sounded pretty good together, the bass blended well with Carson's guitar.

Reflect on Your Corrections

▶ Look back over the changes you made. Do you see a pattern? If there are things you keep missing, make a checklist of what to watch for in your writing.

🐦 **Writing Handbook**, p. 832

Here's the writer's revised and edited draft. How did the writer improve it?

Guitar Lesson

Carson swaggered into Ron Cruz's garage with his guitar slung over his shoulder. "I'm here for the band tryout," he announced. Ron played the bass—the boring stand-up kind—in the school orchestra. He was tuning it while another kid, Pauly, goofed around on the drums. *Yep, these guys need me*, thought Carson. "Got an amp I can use?" he asked.

"Sure, it's over there," replied Ron. "I hope you're good. We have a gig in five days. Can you play 'Under the Moon' by The Nylon Blends??"

The writer fixed **homonym** and **capitalization** errors.

Carson chuckled. *How old-school can you get?* he thought. *I've only known that song since I was, like, nine.* "Yeah, I think I can handle it," he said, trying to hide his sarcasm.

The drummer counted off the beat, and the boys began to play. They sounded pretty good together; the bass blended surprisingly well with Carson's electric guitar. Their voices sounded decent, too. Carson belted out the lead, while Ron sang a strong backup.

The writer fixed two **run-on sentences**, using a **conjunction** in one and a **semicolon** in the other.

"That was great!" said Ron. "You got the job. Here's the song list for the gig. We better practice so you can get used to playing with us."

The writer fixed more **homonym** errors.

Carson looked at the list. The songs were ancient classics by three of his dad's favorite bands: The Chargers, Sloth-heads, and Dog's Day. "Nah, I don't need to practice. I've known how to play these songs forever."

The writer added **serial commas** and fixed more **capitalization** errors.

Three days later, Carson stared out at the crowd that had gathered in front of the stage. There were more people than he'd expected. Ron gave the signal, and Carson stepped up to the front to play. Suddenly, a wave of panic hit him. His throat tightened and his fingers froze. *Pull it together! he told himself. What's going on?? You're better than this!*

The writer used **interior monologue** to reveal more about the character in a way that relates to the theme.

Over his shoulder, he felt the glares of his bandmates. Then he heard the deep, twangy notes of Ron's bass. Ron was plucking it like an electric guitar instead of using his bow. It sounded funky, and the crowd loved it. He kept playing as if it was all part of the show, until Carson finally relaxed and jumped back in. Ron had saved him.

When the set ended, Carson walked offstage with a little less swagger in his step and a lot more respect for Ron. "Thanks for rescuing me, Ron," he said. "Next time I think I'll practice."

The writer added **dialogue** at the end to show the message that the character took away.

✔ Publish and Present

You are now ready to publish and present your work. Print out your story or write a clean copy by hand. You may also want to present your work in a different way.

Alternative Presentations

Record a Reading of Your Story   Gather a group of students to help you record a reading of your story.

1 Plan How to Record   Decide how you will record it. Will you make an audio or videotape recording, copy it onto a CD or DVD to share with others, or create an audio file that can be uploaded onto a Web site? Be sure to check with your teacher to see what recording equipment is available. Follow school rules about sharing your work.

2 Cast the Characters   Assign roles to yourself and other students. You will need one student to read aloud each character's dialogue, plus one more reader to narrate the part in between. Make photocopies of your story. Ask the actors to highlight the lines they will read aloud.

3 Rehearse   Start with a "cold reading." This is when the actors first read aloud a text together. Don't worry if you occasionally make mistakes, such as reading the wrong line or skipping a line. Practice a few more times and you'll soon know each line by heart.

3 Perform   You can use your copies of the story when you perform. But don't hide behind them! Remember, people will hear, and perhaps view, your recorded performance. Read with expression and vary the tone of your voice.

Submit Your Writing to a School Newspaper or Magazine   Does your school have a newspaper or magazine? If so, you might try to publish your short story in it.

1 Meet the Requirements   Find out the rules for submitting writing to the school newspaper or magazine. For example, it may require writing of a certain length. Make the needed changes to your short story before submitting it.

2 Make Changes to Suit Your Audience   Remember that what you publish will have a bigger audience than just your teacher and classmates. If necessary, revise your story to make it better suited to the whole school.

3 Meet Deadlines   Most publications have a deadline after which they will not accept writings. Be sure to submit your story before the deadline.

📖 **Language and Learning Handbook**, p. 750

Technology Tip

When you read aloud, don't hurry! Make sure to pause for commas, periods, and paragraph breaks.

Reflect on Your Work

Think back on your writing experience.

▶ Which step in the process was the easiest? Which was the most difficult?

▶ What one thing would you most like to change about your finished story?

▶ What will you do differently next time?

☑ **In your portfolio, save a copy of your short story.**

EQ ESSENTIAL QUESTION:

How Do People Challenge Expectations?

You can't base your life on someone else's expectations.

—STEVIE WONDER

A ship in port is safe, but that is not what ships are built for.

—BENAZIR BHUTTO

Critical Viewing ▷
Jim Mitchell, wearing a special wingsuit, jumps off Ottawa Peak in the Canadian Arctic. How do risk-takers like Mitchell challenge expectations?

AGAINST THE
ODDS

EQ ESSENTIAL QUESTION:
How Do People Challenge Expectations?

Study the Photograph

What happens when people expect very little of you? Do you only do what they say you can? Do you try to do better than they expect? Wilma Rudolph was stricken with a crippling disease called polio when she was a child. No one thought she would walk normally again, let alone run fast. Yet she ended up winning three gold medals in track at the Olympics.

Wilma Rudolph takes the lead in a race at the 1960 Summer Olympic Games in Rome, Italy.
©Jerry Cooke

Analyze and Speculate

1. How do you think Wilma Rudolph felt about people's expectations for her?

2. What personal qualities do you think Rudolph displayed to help her challenge people's expectations?

Speculate about these questions with a partner. Explain your opinion, support your ideas with examples, and listen carefully to your partner's ideas.

EQ ESSENTIAL QUESTION

In this unit, you will explore the **Essential Question** in class through reading, discussion, research, and writing. Keep thinking about the question outside of school, too.

① Plan a Project

Press Conference

In this unit, you'll be holding a press conference, or a gathering of reporters to interview a famous person about issues that address the Essential Question. To get started, watch a few different press conferences on TV or on the Internet. Look for

- what types of questions the reporters ask
- how the famous person answers the questions
- how much time the press conference takes.

Study Skills Start planning your press conference. Use the forms on myNGconnect.com to plan your time and to prepare the content.

---

② Choose More to Read

These readings provide different answers to the Essential Question. Choose a book and online selections to read during the unit.

Spike Lee: By Any Means Necessary
by Jim Haskins

When Spike Lee decided to make movies, he knew he would have to break a few rules. Lee wanted to expose racial inequality in a way never done before. Lee created controversial films that inspired all races. And he did it by any means necessary.

▶ **NONFICTION**

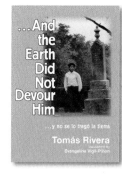

. . . And the Earth Did Not Devour Him
by Tomás Rivera

During the 1940s, 4 million Mexicans entered the United States hoping to find jobs. Many became farm workers. In this book, Tomás Rivera voices the anger, hopes, and fears of those Mexican migrant workers. You will remember this book long after you finish reading it.

▶ **NOVEL**

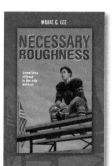

Necessary Roughness
by Marie G. Lee

Chan Kim is happy living in California. Then his family moves to Minnesota. Chan's family is the only Korean family in town. Chan joins the football team, but not everyone on the team accepts him. Then a tragic accident forces him to face the toughest challenge of all.

▶ **NOVEL**

myNGconnect.com

🔍 Read biographies of famous people who have challenged expectations.

🔍 Find out about students who overcame challenges.

Fiction tells a story that the author made up. Narrative *nonfiction* tells a story, too, but it is true—and based on facts. Read these true stories.

DEMO TEXT #1

I just watched a movie about the life of Rosa Parks. I started thinking about what I would put in a movie about my life. What stands out for me are the lessons I've learned about respecting people of all races.

It reminds me of when I was in middle school, and I'd read with Dad on Saturdays. Once, after he finished a book, he said, "This is something you need to know about." It was *Farewell to Manzanar*, a book about how the U.S. discriminated against Japanese Americans in the 1940s.

The thing is, Dad's Japanese American. Mom is white. To me that's no big deal, but as history shows, it's taken many people so long to see what seems perfectly obvious to me: We're all one race—the human race.

Still, I deal with these lessons, too. Once, two of my best friends, who happen to be the same race, wore the same color jacket to school. Someone spread a rumor that they were in a gang. That was so wrong, considering Calvin became valedictorian and Art volunteered at a literacy center.

I also think of a time when I took my little brother to the park. He was playing with a Korean American boy and an African American girl and having a great time. I thought, "Those kids don't seem to notice what color they are." I wonder why race matters to adults when kids don't care.

DEMO TEXT #2

I just watched a movie about the life of baseball player Roberto Clemente. I started thinking about what I would put in a movie about my life. I think I'll see the little moments that have taught me so much.

Like the time I was playing second base in the Little League division for 12- to 14-year olds. The bases were loaded in the last inning. I was only playing because the rules said that everyone had to play for at least two innings. There were two outs when an easy grounder came my way. I picked it up but panicked and threw it right past the first baseman. Two runs scored and we lost.

Flash ahead three years. I was playing baseball with older guys. One or two of them had even been scouted by the pros. Remembering my failures in Little League, I was nervous. I even thought about not playing. But there I was in center field. In my first inning a fly ball was hit my way, and I made a basket catch. One of the older guys yelled, "You looked like a Hall-of-Famer."

Or another little moment, like my first solo in choir. I was happy just being one of the group, but the director gave me a solo. I practiced a lot and thought I had things down, but as I left the safety of the choir to sing alone, my knees were shaking. The music started and it wasn't great, but it was OK. I found out I liked it, though.

Connect Reading to Your Life

Read this list of incidents, or events. Then decide which could be in Demo Text #1, Demo Text #2, both texts, or neither text.

_____ **1.** an incident about the author playing on a Little League team with an African American boy who's new in his neighborhood

_____ **2.** an incident about how the author's father won an important sales award

_____ **3.** an incident about the author getting to know a boy from India who had just moved into his neighborhood

_____ **4.** an incident about the author auditioning for a play for the first time

Reading Strategies
- Plan and Monitor
▶ **Determine Importance**
- Make Inferences
- Ask Questions
- Make Connections
- Synthesize
- Visualize

Focus Strategy ▶ Determine Importance

In order for you to make a decision about where each incident should go, you had to determine the **primary**, or most important, details in each **autobiography**. You added up these details to figure out the main point the author wanted to **emphasize** in each one.

You do that kind of adding up all the time in everyday conversation. If someone is telling you what his or her weekend was like, you listen to the **highlights** to get the whole picture. After hearing about the whole weekend, you might say, "It sounds as though you had a great time" or "Your weekend was even worse than mine." Sometimes, as in Demo Text #1, the author tells you the main point. Other times, as in Demo Text #2, they don't. When authors don't tell you their main point, it's up to you to figure it out.

Your Job as a Reader

Whenever you read narrative nonfiction, it's your job to think about why the author is choosing to tell you certain things. As you read about an incident, you have to ask yourself why the author chose to emphasize those particular details. As you move from one incident to the next, you have to ask yourself how the incidents are connected. That is, you have to ask what they add up to.

Elements of Literature
autobiography *n.*, story of a person's life or experiences written by that person

Academic Vocabulary
- **primary** *adj.*, main, chief, first in importance
- **emphasize** *v.*, to give special importance to, to stress; **emphasis** *n.*, special importance, force, stress
- **highlight** *n.*, main or most interesting part; **highlight** *v.*, to call attention to or to focus on

■ Unpack the Thinking Process

Think about your day. If you told someone all about everything you did, you'd have to go on for hours. Writers of narrative nonfiction face a similar problem. They know from their personal experience and their **research** more than anyone would read. So they choose their details carefully.

Development of Ideas

Authors select details and develop, or present, them in certain ways according to the message they want readers to remember. In Demo Text #1, the author tells you that he thinks it's important to respect people of all races. He uses two personal details to develop his ideas and make his message clear.

Now look at Demo Text #2. The author doesn't state his message at the beginning. You have to figure it out by looking at the personal details, which are presented as very short stories. By putting those details together, you can figure out the message that the author wants to convey.

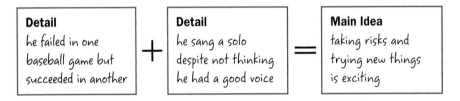

Detail		Detail		Main Idea
he failed in one baseball game but succeeded in another	+	he sang a solo despite not thinking he had a good voice	=	taking risks and trying new things is exciting

The author uses personal details to develop his message about taking risks.

Point of View

Authors also choose a particular perspective from which to tell their stories. The **point of view** for an autobiography is different from the point of view for a **biography**. In Demo Texts #1 and #2, the authors are telling their own life stories. Autobiographies, then, are told from the first-person point of view. The writer uses the pronouns *I* and *me*. Biographies are stories about a person's life written by *another* person. They are told from the third-person point of view, using pronouns such as *he* and *she*.

Elements of Literature

point of view *n.*, perspective from which a story is told

biography *n.*, story of a person's life or experiences written by another person

Academic Vocabulary

● **research** *n.*, gathering of facts about a subject, careful study, investigation; **research** *v.*, to gather facts about a subject

■ Try an Experiment

Read the following Demo Text. Look for important details and think about how the author presents them. Put those details together to determine the message that the author wanted to **communicate**.

Matthew Henson was born in Maryland on August 8, 1866. He faced many challenges in life. His parents died when he was a child. His relatives could not afford to keep him in school. In addition to poverty, Henson faced discrimination as an African American. But he never gave up. Between the ages of thirteen and nineteen, Henson worked on a sailing ship. He traveled the world and taught himself the languages of Russian and Inuit, mathematics, and navigation.

In 1887, Henson met Robert E. Peary. Peary hired Henson as a servant for an exploration trip to Nicaragua.

Peary learned that Henson was not only strong but smart. So, a few years later, he hired Henson to be on his exploration team. On April 6, 1909—after eighteen years of trying and failing—they succeeded in becoming the first people to reach the North Pole.

Peary became a national hero and received many honors. It was not until 1937, when he was 71 years old, that Henson was finally honored as an American hero. Henson said that he had felt inspired by Frederick Douglass to achieve something that would bring recognition to all African Americans.

Think, Pair, Share Work with a partner to use the primary details to determine the author's main idea.

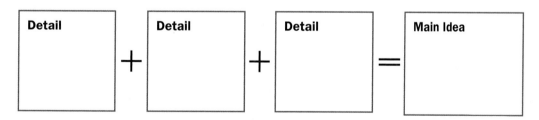

Then discuss how the author presented the details to develop his ideas. Share and compare your thoughts with the group.

Monitor Comprehension

Academic Vocabulary
- **communicate** *v.*, to transmit ideas or information; **communication** *n.*, act of transmitting ideas or information

Narrative Nonfiction
How is narrative nonfiction like and unlike a short story?

EQ How Do People Challenge Expectations?
Find out how people discover their potential.

Make a Connection

Anticipation Guide Tell whether you agree or disagree with these statements. After reading, see if you still feel the same way.

ANTICIPATION GUIDE	Agree or Disagree
1. Most people have expectations about others based on physical appearance.	_____
2. The more you expect from people, the more they achieve their potential.	_____
3. People will feel good about themselves if you don't expect too much from them.	_____

Learn Key Vocabulary

Study the Words Pronounce each word and learn its meaning. You may also want to look up the definitions in the Glossary.

• Academic Vocabulary

Key Words	Examples
contemplate (**kon**-tem-plāt) *verb* ▶ pages 135, 157	When you **contemplate** something, you think carefully about it. You should **contemplate** every move in a game of chess.
designate (**de**-zig-nāt) *verb* ▶ page 139	To **designate** is to point out or show. Signs **designate** the names of streets and highways.
disciplined (**di**-su-plund) *adjective* ▶ pages 155, 156	A **disciplined** person carefully controls his or her behavior. Tomas is very **disciplined** with his paycheck. He always saves 75 percent.
• **implement** (**im**-plu-ment) *verb* ▶ page 146	When you **implement** a plan, you perform all the stages of the plan. The mayor decided to **implement** the city evacuation plan as the hurricane moved closer.
• **innovative** (**i**-ne-vā-tiv) *adjective* ▶ pages 143, 152, 159	An **innovative** idea is new and original. Good companies ask designers to create **innovative** products that no other company has made. *Synonym:* creative; *Antonyms:* boring, unoriginal
perpetually (pur-**pe**-chü-we-lē) *adverb* ▶ page 134	**Perpetually** means always. Someone who is **perpetually** late is always late. *Synonym:* constantly; *Antonym:* never
procrastinate (prō-**kras**-te-nāt) *verb* ▶ page 155	If you **procrastinate**, you delay doing something. If your homework is due Monday, don't **procrastinate** until Sunday.
spontaneously (spon-**tā**-nē-us-lē) *adverb* ▶ page 148	To act **spontaneously** is to act suddenly, without a plan. Al **spontaneously** decided to go camping over the weekend.

Practice the Words Write four sentences. Use at least two Key Vocabulary words in each sentence.

Example: Because lazy people <u>procrastinate</u>, they <u>perpetually</u> need to hurry at the last minute.

BEFORE READING La Vida Robot

technology magazine article by Joshua Davis

Reading Strategies

- Plan and Monitor
- ▶ **Determine Importance**
- Make Inferences
- Ask Questions
- Make Connections
- Synthesize
- Visualize

Analyze Nonfiction Text Features

A technology article is one type of nonfiction. A technology writer may use a variety of **text features** such as section heads, diagrams, labels, photos, and captions. Such features help show what is important. They also can clarify the meaning of technical terms or add information to the main text.

Look Into the Text

A diagram is a picture or drawing. This diagram shows parts of the robot described in the text.

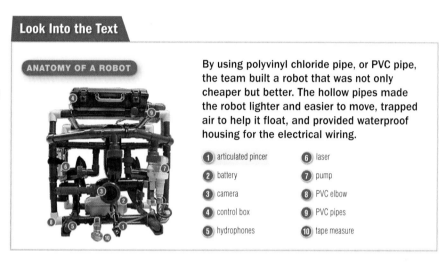

ANATOMY OF A ROBOT

By using polyvinyl chloride pipe, or PVC pipe, the team built a robot that was not only cheaper but better. The hollow pipes made the robot lighter and easier to move, trapped air to help it float, and provided waterproof housing for the electrical wiring.

A caption gives information or asks questions about the diagram. What does this caption do?

1. articulated pincer
2. battery
3. camera
4. control box
5. hydrophones
6. laser
7. pump
8. PVC elbow
9. PVC pipes
10. tape measure

Labels identify the different parts of the robot.

Focus Strategy ▶ Determine Importance

Section heads are words set off by themselves in large type. They usually divide an article according to its **main ideas** to show what each part is mostly about. The main ideas are supported by **details** that provide additional information. Look ahead to find the section heads in this article. As you read, use the strategy below to help you identify main ideas.

HOW TO IDENTIFY MAIN IDEAS AND DETAILS

Focus Strategy

1. **Turn Section Heads into Questions** The section head "The Team" can become "Who is on the team?"

2. **Collect Important Details** Collect details in a **Notetaking Chart** like the one shown here. After you read each section, review the details.

3. **Answer the Question** In this case, it is "Lorenzo, Cristian, Oscar, and Luis are on the team." This is the main idea of the section.

4. **Determine What's Important** Decide what is important to remember from each section.

Notetaking Chart

Section Question: Who is on the team?

Important Details:	Main Idea:
Lorenzo—rebuilt car engines; eager	Lorenzo is the mechanic.
Cristian—very smart, innovative	Cristian is the inventor.
Oscar—trained at ROTC; strong leader	Oscar is the team leader.
Luis—physically strong	Luis is the tether man.

This is the team.

I Want to Remember: each member's role

Joshua Davis

(1974–)

Some people are attracted to success. I'm not one of them. I spend most of my time thinking about my failures.

Joshua Davis knows what it means to overcome obstacles.

Success seems to come easily to some people, but not **Joshua Davis**. As an elementary school student, he shocked himself in his bathtub while building a model aircraft carrier. In high school he formed a rock band. At the first performance, he forgot the lyrics to the band's only song. "I was constantly getting knocked down and told I wasn't all that [good]," he recalls. Just getting by seemed like "a life or death fight."

But Davis continued to face challenges head on. The thin, 130-pounder entered an arm-wrestling competition. He placed fourth out of four. He trained and competed as an amateur sumo wrestler with similar results. In the process, however, Davis developed a writing career by selling accounts of his adventures to magazines. These stories are collected in his first book, *The Underdog: How I Survived the World's Most Outlandish Competitions*. This collection tracks Davis's attempts to measure up to the standards of others before finally learning to define success for himself.

Today, Davis is a contributing editor for *Wired* magazine, where "La Vida Robot" first appeared.

myNGconnect.com

🔊 Listen to a radio report about the students in "La Vida Robot."
🔊 Discover the world of underwater robotics.

La Vida Robot

How four underdogs from the mean streets of Phoenix took on the best from MIT in the national underwater bot championship

by Joshua Davis

The Team 1

The winter rain makes a mess of West Phoenix. It turns dirt yards into mud and forms reefs of garbage in the streets. Junk food wrappers, diapers, and Spanish-language magazines are swept into the gutters.

On West Roosevelt Avenue, security guards, squad cars, and a handful of cops watch teenagers file into the local high school. A sign reads: *Carl Hayden Community High School: The Pride's Inside.* There certainly isn't a lot of pride on the outside. The school buildings are mostly drab, late fifties-era boxes. The front lawn is nothing but brown scrub and patches of dirt. The class photos beside the principal's office tell the story of the past four decades. In 1965, the students were nearly all white, wearing blazers, ties, and long skirts. Now the school is 92 percent Hispanic. Drooping, baggy jeans and XXXL hoodies are the norm.

Across campus, in a second-floor windowless room, four students huddle around an odd, three-foot-tall frame constructed of PVC pipe. They have equipped it with propellers, cameras, lights, a laser, depth detectors, pumps, an underwater microphone, and an articulated pincer. At the top sits a black, waterproof briefcase containing a nest of **hacked processors, minuscule fans**, and LEDs. It's a cheap but astoundingly functional underwater robot capable of recording **sonar pings** and retrieving objects fifty feet below the surface.

The four teenagers who built it are all undocumented Mexican immigrants who came to this country through tunnels or hidden in the backseats of cars. They live in sheds and rooms without electricity. But over three days last summer, these kids from the desert proved they are among the smartest young underwater engineers in the country. 2

It was the end of June. Lorenzo Santillan, 16, sat in the front seat of the school van and looked out at the migrant farmworkers in the fields along Interstate 10. Lorenzo's

---

1 **Preview Text Features**
Section heads can help clarify the order in which things happen. Look at the section head on this page and the section heads on pages 139 and 148. How do they give you an overview of events?

2 **Identify Main Ideas/Details**
Unexpected details are often a signal of something important. What unexpected details are there on this page? List them in a **Notetaking Chart**.

In Other Words
hacked processors, minuscule fans old computer parts, tiny fans
sonar pings high-pitched sounds

Science Background
PVC (polyvinyl chloride) is an inexpensive, lightweight plastic that is often used for pipes in plumbing systems.

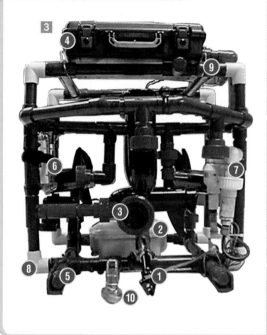

By using polyvinyl chloride pipe, or PVC pipe, the team built a robot that was not only cheaper but better. The hollow pipes made the robot lighter and easier to move, trapped air to help it float, and provided waterproof housing for the electrical wiring.

1 articulated pincer   6 laser

2 battery   7 pump

3 camera   8 PVC elbow

4 control box   9 PVC pipes

5 hydrophones   10 tape measure

◀ **Use Visuals to Access Text** Compare the diagram to the text. Which sentences describe the information in the diagram?

3 Text Features
Numbered labels are an important part of this text feature. What information do they give you?

face still had its baby fat, but he'd recently sprouted a moustache and had taken to wearing a fistful of gold rings, a gold chain, and a gold medallion of the Virgin Mary. The bling wasn't fooling anyone. His mother had been fired from her job as a hotel maid, and his father had trouble paying the rent as a gardener. They were **on the verge of eviction** for nonpayment of rent. He could see himself having to quit school to work in those fields. "What's a PWM cable?" 4 The sharp question from the van's driver, Allan Cameron, **snapped Lorenzo out of his reverie**. Cameron was the computer science teacher sponsoring Carl Hayden's robotics program. At 59, he had a neatly trimmed white beard, unkempt brown hair, and more energy than most men half his age. Together with his fellow science teacher

4 Language
Technology articles may include **acronyms**, or abbreviations made up of the initials of a technical term. Read on to find out what *PWM* stands for.

In Other Words
on the verge of eviction close to being kicked out
snapped Lorenzo out of his reverie focused Lorenzo's attention

Fredi Lajvardi, Cameron had put up flyers around the school a few months earlier, offering to sponsor anyone interested in competing in the third annual Marine Advanced Technology Education Center's Remotely Operated Vehicle (ROV) Competition. Lorenzo was one of the first to show up to the after-school meeting last spring.

Cameron hadn't expected many students to be interested,

LORENZO THE MECHANICS MAN

Lorenzo Santillan's knowledge of car engines gave him a head start at learning robot mechanics. 5

particularly not a kid like Lorenzo, who was failing most of his classes and **perpetually** looked like he was about to fall asleep. But Lorenzo didn't have much else to do after school. He didn't want to walk around the streets. He had tried that—he'd been a member of WBP 8th Street, a westside gang. When his friends started to get arrested for theft, he dropped out. He didn't want to go to jail.

That's why he decided to come to Cameron's meeting.

"PWM," Lorenzo replied automatically from the van's passenger seat. "Pulse width modulation. *Esto* controls analog circuits with digital output."

Over the past four months, Lorenzo **had flourished**, learning a new set of acronyms and raising his math grade from an F to an A. He had grown up rebuilding car engines with his brother and cousin. Now he was ready to build something of his own. The team had found its mechanics man. 6

5 Text Features
Photos and their captions often add information to a text. How does this photo add to your understanding of Lorenzo and his importance to the team?

6 Identify Main Ideas/Details
How can you tell that Lorenzo would be a good "mechanics man"? What information in the text supports this?

Monitor Comprehension

Summarize
Give two examples of life challenges Lorenzo faced.

Key Vocabulary
perpetually *adv.,* always

In Other Words
Esto It is the thing that (in Spanish)
had flourished had become more and more successful

Ever since his younger sister demanded her own room four years ago, Cristian Arcega had been living in a thirty-square-foot plywood shed attached to the side of his parents' trailer. He liked it there. It was his own space. He was free to **contemplate** the acceleration of a raindrop as it leaves the clouds above him. He could hear it hit the roof and slide toward the puddles on the street outside. He imagined that the puddles were oceans and that the underwater robot he was building at school can explore them.

Cameron and Ledge, as the students called Lajvardi, formed the robotics group for kids like Cristian. He was probably the smartest 16-year-old in West Phoenix—without even trying, he had one of the highest **GPAs** in the school district. His brains and diminutive stature (5 feet, 4 inches; 135 pounds) kept him apart at Carl Hayden. **7** That and the fact that students **socialized** based on Mexican geography: In the cafeteria, there were Guanajuato tables and Sonora tables. Cristian was from

CRISTIAN THE GENIUS

As a member of the robotics team, Cristian Arcega applied his intellect toward solving electrical and mechanical problems.

Mexicali, but he'd left Mexico in the back of a station wagon when he was 6. He thought of himself as part American, part Mexican, and he didn't know where to sit.

So he ate lunch in the storage room the teachers had **commandeered** for the underwater ROV club. Cristian devoted himself to solving thrust vector and power supply issues. The robot competition (sponsored in part by the Office of Naval Research and NASA) required students to build a **bot** that could survey a

7 Access Vocabulary
What does *diminutive* mean? Use context clues to determine the meaning.

sunken **mock-up** of a submarine—not easy stuff. The teachers had entered the club in the expert-level Explorer class instead of the beginner Ranger class. They **figured** their students would lose anyway, and there was more honor in losing to the college kids in the Explorer division than to the high schoolers in Ranger. Their real goal was to show the students that there were opportunities outside West Phoenix. The teachers wanted to give their kids hope.

Just getting them to the Santa Barbara contest in June with a robot would be an accomplishment, Cameron thought. He and Ledge had to gather a group of students who, in four months, could raise money, build a robot, and learn how to pilot it. They had no idea they were about to assemble the perfect team.

"We should use glass syntactic flotation foam," Cristian said excitedly at that first meeting. "It's got a really high compressive strength."

Cameron and Ledge looked at each other. Now they had their genius. **8**

Oscar Vazquez was a born leader. A senior, he'd been in **ROTC** since ninth grade and was planning on a career in the military. But when he called to schedule a recruitment meeting at the end of his junior year, the officer in charge told him he was **ineligible for military service**. Because he was undocumented—his parents had brought him to the United States from Mexico when he was 12—he couldn't join, wouldn't get any scholarships, and had to start figuring out what else to do

OSCAR THE LEADER **9**

The skills he learned in ROTC made Oscar Vazquez the perfect leader for the robotics team.

8 Identify Main Ideas/Details What is the important information about Cristian Arcega's contribution to the team? Locate information in the text that supports your answer. List it in your **Notetaking Chart**.

9 Text Features Labels on graphics give information to the reader at a glance. What does the label on this photo tell you?

In Other Words
mock-up model
figured believed
ROTC Reserve Officers Training Corps
ineligible for military service not allowed to join the military

with his life. Oscar felt **aimless** until he heard about the robot club from Ledge, who was teaching his senior biology seminar. Maybe, he thought, engineering could offer him a future.

ROTC had trained Oscar well: He knew how to motivate people. He made sure that everyone was in the room and focused when he phoned Frank Szwankowski, who sold industrial and scientific thermometers at Omega Engineering in Stamford, Connecticut. Szwankowski knew as much about thermometer applications as anyone in the United States. All day long, he talked to military contractors, industrial engineers, and environmental consultants. So he was momentarily confused when he heard Oscar's high-pitched Mexican accent on the other end of the line. The 17-year-old kid from the desert wanted advice on how to build a military-grade underwater ROV.

This was the second call Szwankowski had received from amateur roboticists in less than a month. 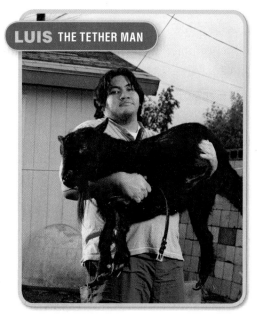 A few weeks earlier, some college oceanic engineering students

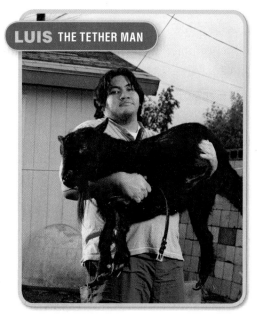

LUIS THE TETHER MAN

The team relied on Luis Aranda's strength to move their robot in and out of the water.

had called and said they were entering the national underwater ROV championships. Oscar said that his team, too, was competing and needed to learn as much as it could from the experts. Szwankowski was impressed. The other kids had simply asked him what they wanted and hung up. Oscar spent forty-five minutes on the phone **digging deeper and deeper into thermometer physics.**

Oscar began by explaining that his high school team was **taking on** college students from around the

10 Access Vocabulary
Do you know what a *roboticist* is? Look for a smaller word within the word. The base word *robot* gives you a clue that a roboticist has something to do with robots.

In Other Words
aimless without a goal in life
digging deeper and deeper into thermometer physics learning more and more about how thermometers work
taking on competing against

United States. He introduced his teammates: Cristian, the brainiac; Lorenzo, the *vato loco* who had a surprising **aptitude** for mechanics; and 18-year-old Luis Aranda, the fourth member of the crew. At 5 feet, 10 inches and 250 pounds, Luis looked like Chief from *One Flew Over the Cuckoo's Nest*. He was the tether man, responsible for the pickup and release of what would be a 100-pound robot.

Szwankowski was impressed by Oscar. He **launched into** an in-depth explanation of the technology, offering details as if he were letting them in on a little secret. "What you really want," he confided, "is a thermocouple with a cold junction compensator." He went over the **specifications** of the device and then paused. "You know," he said, "I think you can beat those guys from MIT. Because none of them know what I know about thermometers."

"You hear that?" Oscar said triumphantly when they hung up.

He looked at each team member pointedly. "We got people believing in us, so now we got to believe in ourselves."

The four boys built their robot out of common, everyday materials.

In Other Words
vato loco crazy, tough street guy (Spanish slang)
aptitude natural ability
launched into began
specifications technical details

Cultural Background
One Flew Over the Cuckoo's Nest is a famous novel by Ken Kesey that was also made into an Academy Award-winning movie. **Chief** is a tall, strong Native American character in the novel.

The Competition

11 Identify Main Ideas/Details
What do you expect to find out in this section? As you read it, fill out another **Notetaking Chart**.

Oscar helped persuade a handful of local businesses to donate money to the team. They raised a total of about $800. Now it was up to Cristian and Lorenzo to figure out what to do with the newfound resources.

They began by sending Luis to Home Depot to buy PVC pipe. Despite the donations, they were still on a tight budget. Cristian would have to keep dreaming about glass syntactic flotation foam; PVC pipe was the best they could afford. But PVC had benefits. The air inside the pipe would **create buoyancy** as well as provide a waterproof housing for wiring. Cristian calculated the volume of air inside the pipes and realized immediately that they'd need **ballast**. He proposed housing the battery system on board, in a heavy waterproof case.

It was a bold idea. If they didn't have to run a power line down to the bot, their tether could be much thinner, making the bot more mobile. Since the competition required that their bot run through a series of seven exploration tasks—from taking depth measurements to locating and retrieving acoustic pingers—**mobility was key**. Most of the other teams wouldn't even consider putting their power supplies in the water. A leak **could take the whole system down**. But if they couldn't figure out how to waterproof their case, Cristian argued, then they shouldn't be in an underwater contest.

12 Identify Main Ideas/Details
Why is Cristian's idea a "bold idea"? What examples in the text support your answer?

While other teams machined and welded metal frames, the guys broke out the rubber glue and began assembling the PVC pipe. They did the whole thing in one night and dubbed their new creation "Stinky." Lorenzo painted it garish shades of blue, red, and yellow to **designate** the functionality of specific pipes. Every inch of PVC had a clear purpose. It was the type of machine only an engineer would describe as beautiful.

Carl Hayden Community High School doesn't have a swimming pool, so one weekend in May, after about six weeks of work in the classroom, the team took Stinky to

---

Key Vocabulary
designate *v.*, to point out, show

In Other Words
create buoyancy make the pipe able to float
ballast weight to keep the robot from moving
mobility was key being able to move well was very important
could take the whole system down could stop the robot from moving

a scuba training pool in downtown Phoenix for its **baptism**. Luis hefted the machine up and gently placed it in the water. They powered it up. Cristian had hacked together off-the-shelf joysticks, a motherboard, motors, and an array of onboard finger-sized video cameras, which now sent flickering images to black-and-white monitors on a folding picnic table. Using five small electric trolling motors, the robot could spin and tilt in any direction. To move smoothly, two drivers had to coordinate their commands. The first thing they did was smash the robot into a wall.

"This is good, this is good," Oscar kept repeating, buying himself a few seconds to come up with a positive spin. "Did you see how hard it hit the wall? This thing's got power. Once we figure out how to drive it, we'll be the fastest team there."

By early June, as the contest neared, the team **had the hang of it**. Stinky now buzzed through the water, dodging all obstacles. The drivers, Cristian and Oscar, could make the bot hover, spin in place,

and angle up or down. They could send enough power to Stinky's small engines to pull Luis around the pool. They felt like they had a good shot at not placing last.

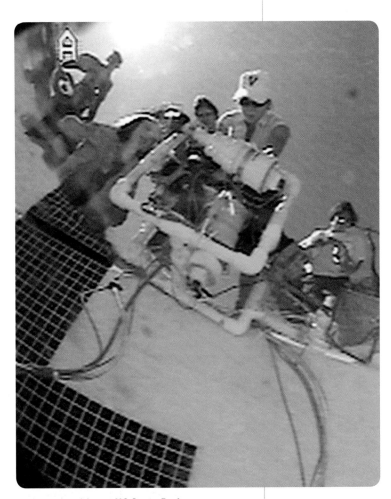

At the competition at UC Santa Barbara, a team from Virginia tests their ROV in the Olympic-size swimming pool.

13 Text Features
A photo and caption can help clarify text. How does this photo help you picture how the Carl Hayden team tested their ROV?

Monitor Comprehension

Summarize
How do the four boys prepare for the competition?

In Other Words
baptism first test in the water
had the hang of it knew how to do it

The team arrived at the Olympic-size UC Santa Barbara pool on a sunny Thursday afternoon. The pool was concealed under a black tarp—the contest organizers didn't want the students to get a peek at the layout of the mission. Students from cities across the country **milled around** the water's edge. The Carl Hayden teammates tried to hide their nervousness, but they were intimidated. Lorenzo had never seen so many white people in one place. He was also new to the ocean. He had seen it for the first time several months earlier on a school trip to San Diego. It still unnerved him to see so much water. He said it was "incredifying"—incredible and terrifying at the same time.

Even though Lorenzo had never heard of MIT, the team from Cambridge scared him, too. There were twelve of them—six ocean-engineering students, four mechanical engineers, and two computer science majors. Their robot was small, densely packed, and had a large ExxonMobil sticker emblazoned on the side. The largest corporation in the United States **had kicked in** $5,000. Other donations brought the MIT team's total budget to $11,000.

RESOURCES FOR THE COMPETITION

	MIT	Carl Hayden
Funding	$ 11,000	$ 800
Number of team members	12	4
Number of swimming pools	2	0

14

As Luis hoisted Stinky to the edge of the practice side of the pool, Cristian heard repressed snickering. It didn't give him a good feeling. He was proud of his robot, but he could see that it looked like a Geo Metro compared with the Lexuses and BMWs around the pool. **15** He had thought that Lorenzo's paint job was nice. Now it just looked clownish.

Things got worse when Luis lowered Stinky into the water. They noticed that the controls worked only **intermittently**. When they brought Stinky back onto the pool deck, there were a few drops of

14 Text Features
Charts sometimes summarize information in a memorable way. What does this chart help you understand more clearly?

15 Analogy
Writers often compare something unfamiliar with something familiar to help readers understand. This is called an **analogy**. Why does the author compare the robots to specific kinds of cars? How do the analogies help your understanding?

In Other Words
milled around crowded around
had kicked in had donated
intermittently sometimes

water in the waterproof briefcase that housed the control system. The case must have warped on the trip from Arizona in the back of Ledge's truck. If the water had touched the controls, the system would have shorted out and stopped working. Cristian knew that they were faced with two serious problems: bad wiring and a leak.

Someone had to be well rested for the contest, so Cristian and Luis slept that night. Oscar and Lorenzo stayed up **resoldering** the entire control system. It was nerve-racking work. The wires were slightly thicker than a human hair, and there were fifty of them. If the soldering iron got too close to a wire, it would melt and there'd be no time to rip the PVC and cable housing apart to fix it. One broken wire would destroy the whole system, forcing them to withdraw from the contest.

By two in the morning, Oscar's eyesight was blurring, but he kept

16 Text Features
What new information does the map present?

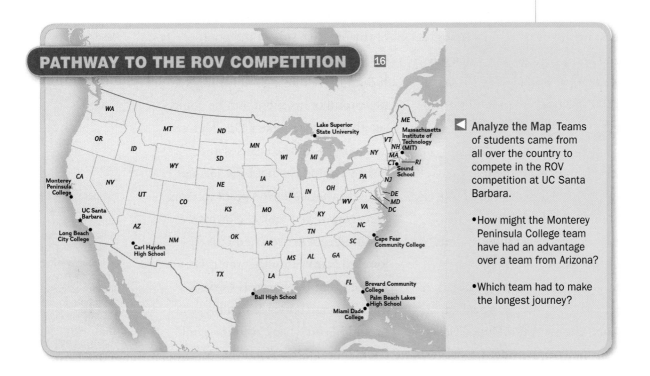

PATHWAY TO THE ROV COMPETITION 16

◀ **Analyze the Map** Teams of students came from all over the country to compete in the ROV competition at UC Santa Barbara.

• How might the Monterey Peninsula College team have had an advantage over a team from Arizona?

• Which team had to make the longest journey?

In Other Words
resoldering repairing the wires of

at it. Lorenzo held the wires in place while Oscar lowered the soldering gun. He dropped one last dab of **alloy** on the connection and sat back. Lorenzo flipped the power switch. Everything appeared to work again. 🔲17

On the day of the contest, the organizers purposely made it difficult to see what was happening under the water. A set of high-powered fans blew across the surface of the pool, obscuring the view below and forcing teams to navigate by instrumentation alone. The side effect was that no one had a good sense of how the other teams were doing.

One of seven tasks was to withdraw 500 milliliters of fluid from a container twelve feet below the surface. Its only opening was a small, half-inch pipe fitted with a one-way valve. Though the Carl Hayden team didn't know it, MIT had designed an **innovative** system of bladders and pumps to carry out this task. MIT's robot was supposed to land on the container, create a seal, and pump out the fluid.

On three test runs in Boston, the system worked fast and flawlessly.

MIT's ROV motored smoothly down and quickly located the five-gallon drum just outside the plastic submarine mock-up at the bottom of the pool. But as the robot hovered over the container, its protruding mechanical arm hit a piece of the submarine frame, blocking it from going any lower. They tried a different angle but still couldn't reach the drum. The bot wasn't small enough to slip past the gap between the frame and the drum, making their pump system useless. There was nothing they could do—they had to move on to the next assignment. 🔲18

When Stinky entered the water, it **careened wildly** as it dived toward the bottom. Luis stood at the pool's edge, **paying out** the tether cable. From the control tent, Cristian, Oscar, and Lorenzo monitored Stinky's descent on their videoscreens.

"*Vámonos*, Cristian, this is it!" Oscar said, pushing his control too far forward. They were nervous and overcompensated for each other's

🔲17 **Identify Main Ideas/Details**
What do the preparations on the night before the contest tell about the team? Add the details to your **Notetaking Chart**.

🔲18 **Identify Main Ideas/Details**
What do the details about the MIT robot add to the main idea of this section? Add them to your **Notetaking Chart**.

Key Vocabulary
- **innovative** *adj.*, new, original

In Other Words
alloy liquid metal
careened wildly moved quickly from side to side
paying out lengthening
Vámonos Let's go (in Spanish)

joystick movements, causing Stinky **to veer off course**. They settled down and knocked off the first two tasks. When they reached the submarine, they saw the drum and tried to steady the robot. Stinky had a bent copper proboscis, a bilge pump, and a dime-store balloon. They had to fit their long, quarter-inch-wide sampling tube into a half-inch pipe and then fill the balloon for exactly twenty seconds to get 500 milliliters. They had practiced dozens of times at the scuba pool in Phoenix, and it had taken them, on average, ten minutes to stab the proboscis into

MIT's ROV UNDERWATER TASK PERFORMANCE

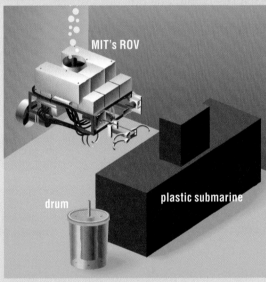

MIT's ROV moved toward the model submarine at the bottom of the pool.

The ROV's mechanical arm could not fit between the plastic submarine and the drum, so the ROV could not get low enough to sample the fluid in the drum.

In Other Words
to veer off course to move in the wrong direction

the narrow tube. Now they had thirty minutes total to complete all seven tasks on the checklist.

It was up to Oscar and Cristian. They readjusted their grip on the joysticks and leaned into the monitors. Stinky hovered in front of the submarine framing that had frustrated the MIT team. Because Stinky's copper pipe was eighteen inches long, it was able to reach the drum. The control tent was silent. Now that they were focused on the mission, both pilots relaxed and made **almost imperceptibly small movements** with their joysticks.

19 Text Features
How do the diagram and the text work together to give you a clearer understanding of Stinky?

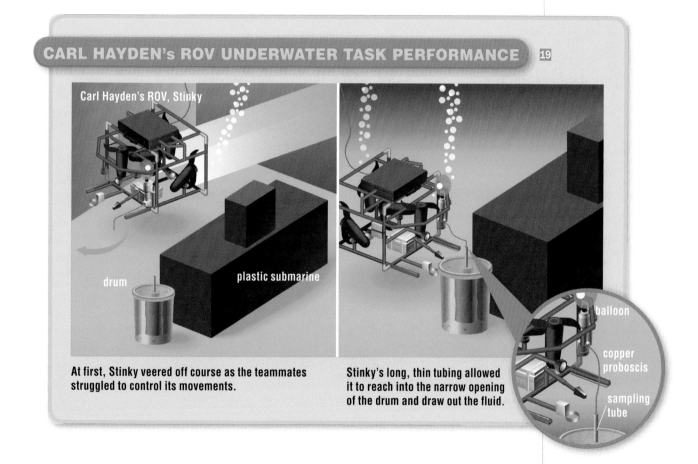

CARL HAYDEN's ROV UNDERWATER TASK PERFORMANCE **19**

Carl Hayden's ROV, Stinky

drum

plastic submarine

balloon

copper proboscis

sampling tube

At first, Stinky veered off course as the teammates struggled to control its movements.

Stinky's long, thin tubing allowed it to reach into the narrow opening of the drum and draw out the fluid.

In Other Words
almost imperceptibly small movements
barely visible movements

Monitor Comprehension

Summarize
Summarize what happens to the MIT robot during the task. Refer to the diagram and the text.

Oscar tapped the control forward while Cristian gave a short backward blast on the vertical propellers. As Stinky floated forward a half inch, its rear raised up and the sampling pipe sank perfectly into the drum. **20**

"*Díos mío*," Oscar whispered, not fully believing what he saw.

He looked at Lorenzo, who had already activated the pump and was counting out twenty seconds in a decidedly unscientific way.

"*Uno, dos, tres, quatro . . .* "

Oscar backed Stinky out of the sub. They spun the robot around, piloted it back to Luis at the edge of the pool, and looked at the judges, who stood in the control tent behind them.

"Can we make a little noise?" Cristian asked Pat Barrow, a NASA lab operations manager supervising the contest.

"Go on ahead," he replied.

Cristian started yelling, and all three ran out to hug Luis, who held the now-filled blue balloon. Luis stood there with a silly grin on his face while his friends danced around him.

It was a short celebration. They still had four more tasks. Luis attached Szwankowski's thermometer and quickly lowered the ROV back into the water. **21**

Tom Swean was the gruff 58-year-old head of the Navy's Ocean Engineering and Marine Systems program. He developed million-dollar autonomous underwater robots for the SEALs at the Office of Naval Research. He was not used to dealing with Mexican American teenagers sporting gold chains, fake diamond rings, and patchy, adolescent mustaches.

The Carl Hayden team stood nervously in front of him. He stared sullenly at them. This was the engineering review, and the results counted for more than half of the total possible points in the contest.

"How'd you make the laser range finder work?" Swean growled. MIT had admitted earlier that a laser would have been the most accurate way to measure distance underwater, but they'd concluded that it would have been difficult to **implement**.

20 Identify Main Ideas/Details Think about how the boys accomplished the task. What does that tell you about their ability to overcome challenges?

21 Text Features Why do you think the writer chose to break the text here?

Key Vocabulary
● **implement** *v.*, to perform, do

In Other Words
Díos Mío Oh my God (in Spanish)
Uno, dos, tres, quatro . . . One, two, three, four . . . (in Spanish)

Teacher Allan Cameron (center) proudly looks on as the Carl Hayden team competes in the underwater ROV competition.

"We used a helium neon laser, captured its phase shift with a photo sensor, and manually corrected by 30 percent to account for the index of refraction," Cristian answered rapidly, **keyed up on adrenaline**. Cameron **had peppered them with questions** on the drive to Santa Barbara, and Cristian was ready.

Swean raised a bushy, graying eyebrow. He asked about motor speed, and Lorenzo sketched out their combination of controllers and spike relays. Oscar answered the question about signal interference in the tether by describing how they'd experimented with a fifteen-meter cable before jumping up to one that was thirty-three meters.

"You're very comfortable with the metric system," Swean observed.

"I grew up in Mexico, sir," Oscar said.

Swean nodded. He eyed their rudimentary flip chart.

"Why don't you have a PowerPoint display?" he asked.

"PowerPoint is a distraction," Cristian replied. "People use it when they don't know what to say."

"And you know what to say?"

"Yes, sir."

22 Identify Main Ideas/Details
What does Swean's raised eyebrow tell you? What other details from this section support your idea? Add the details to your **Notetaking Chart**.

Monitor Comprehension

Summarize
What is the main idea of the section called "The Competition"? Refer to your **Notetaking Chart**.

In Other Words
keyed up on adrenaline full of energy
had peppered them with questions had asked them a lot of questions

The Results 23

In the lobby outside the review room, Cameron and Ledge waited anxiously for the kids. They expected them to come out shaken, but all four were smiling—convinced that they had answered Swean's questions perfectly. Cameron glanced nervously at Ledge. The kids were too confident. They couldn't have done that well.

Still, both teachers were in a good mood. They had learned that the team placed third out of eleven in the seven underwater exercises. Only MIT and Cape Fear Community College from North Carolina had done better. The overall winner would be determined by combining those results with the engineering interview and a review of each group's technical manual. Even if the team did poorly on the interview, Cameron and Ledge were now positive that they hadn't placed last.

"Congratulations, guys," Cameron said. "You officially don't suck."

The awards ceremony took place over dinner, and the Carl Hayden team was glad for that. They hadn't eaten well over the past two days, and even flavorless iceberg lettuce looked good to them. Their nerves had calmed. After the engineering interview, they decided that they had probably placed somewhere in the middle of the pack, maybe fourth or fifth overall. Privately, each of them was hoping for third.

The first award was a surprise: a judge's special prize that wasn't listed in the program. Bryce Merrill, the bearded, middle-aged recruiting manager for Oceaneering International, an industrial ROV design firm, was the announcer. He explained that the judges created this **spontaneously** to honor special achievement. He stood behind a podium on the temporary stage and glanced down at his notes. The contestants sat crowded around a dozen tables. Carl Hayden High School, he said, was that special team.

The guys trotted up to the stage, forcing smiles. It seemed obvious

23 Identify Main Ideas/Details What question would you create from this section head? Write it in a new **Notetaking Chart**.

Key Vocabulary
spontaneously *adv.,* suddenly and without a plan

Final Ranking	Explorer Class	Engineering Evaluation (80 points max)	Technical Report (25 points max)	Team Display (25 points max)	Mission Tasks	Total
1	Carl Hayden High School	53.17	20.25	13.5	32	118.92
2	MIT	44.67	17	8	48	117.67
3	Cape Fear Community College	45.83	19.25	8.5	40	113.58
4	Monterey Peninsula College	56.99	17	9	30	112.99
5	Brevard Community College	49.78	19.25	14.5	10	93.53
6	Lake Superior State University	51.48	17.5	9.5	10	88.48
7	Miami Dade College	46.32	18.75	12.5	10	87.57
8	Long Beach City College	45.18	18.5	7.5	10	81.18
9	Palm Beach Lakes High School	49.34	17.25	8.5	5	80.09
10	Sound School	31.50	14.5	9	15	70.00
11	Ball High School	44.04	11.25	3	10	68.29

that this was **a condescending pat on the back,** as if to say, "A for effort!" They didn't want to be "special"— they wanted third. It signaled to them that they'd missed it. 25

They returned to their seats, and Cameron and Ledge shook their hands.

"Good job, guys," Ledge said, trying to sound pleased. "You did well."

After a few small prizes were handed out (Terrific Tether Management, Perfect Pickup Tool), Merrill moved on to the final awards: Design Elegance, Technical Report, and Overall Winner. The MIT students shifted in their seats and stretched their legs. While they had been forced **to skip** the fluid sampling, they had completed more underwater tasks overall than Carl Hayden or Cape Fear. The Cape Fear team sat across the room, fidgeted with their napkins, and tried not to look nervous. The students from Monterey Peninsula College looked straight ahead. They placed fourth behind Carl Hayden in the underwater trials. They were the

24 **Text Features**
Study the chart. In which category did the Carl Hayden team have the greatest lead?

25 **Identify Main Ideas/Details**
What does the spontaneous award mean to the Carl Hayden team? What examples in the text support your answer? Record your ideas in your **Notetaking Chart.**

In Other Words
a condescending pat on the back false praise
to skip to miss

most likely third-place finishers. The guys from Phoenix glanced back at the buffet table and wondered if they could get more cake before the ceremony ended. 26

Then Merrill leaned into the microphone and said that the ROV named Stinky had captured the design award.

"What did he just say?" Lorenzo asked.

"Oh my God!" Ledge shouted. "Stand up!"

Before they could sit down again, Merrill told them that they had won the technical writing award.

"Us illiterate people from the desert?" Lorenzo thought. He looked at Cristian, who had been responsible for a large part of the writing. Cristian **was beaming**. To his analytical mind, there was no possibility that his team—a bunch of ESL students—could produce a better written report than kids from one of the country's top engineering schools.

They had just won two of the most important awards. All that was left was the grand prize. Cristian quickly **calculated the probability** of winning but couldn't believe what he was coming up with.

"And the overall winner for the Marine Technology ROV championship," Merrill continued, looking up at the crowd, "goes to Carl Hayden High School of Phoenix, Arizona!"

Cameron and Ledge hope to see all four kids go to college before they quit teaching, which means they're likely to keep working for a long time. Since the teenagers are undocumented, they don't qualify for federal loans. And though they've lived in Arizona for an average of eleven years, they would still have to pay out-of-state tuition, which can be as much as three times the in-state cost. They can't afford it. And they're not alone. Approximately 60,000 undocumented students graduate from United States high schools every year. 27

Oscar wipes the white gypsum dust from his face. It's a hot Tuesday afternoon in Phoenix, and he's hanging sheetrock.

26 **Identify Main Ideas/Details** What can you tell about the boys from this detail? What are their expectations at this point?

27 **Identify Main Ideas/Details** Unexpected details are often a clue to pay special attention. Why does the writer include information about college?

In Other Words
was beaming had a big smile
calculated the probability figured out the chance

He graduated from Carl Hayden last spring, and this is the best work he can find. He enjoys walking into the half-built homes and analyzing the engineering. He thinks it'll keep him sharp until he can save up enough money to study engineering at Arizona State University. It will cost him approximately $50,000 as an out-of-state student. That's a lot of sheetrocking.

Luis also graduated and works filing papers. Cristian and Lorenzo are now juniors. Their families can barely support themselves, let alone raise the money to send their kids to college.

When Oscar gets home from work that night, he watches the gypsum dust swirl down the sink drain when he washes his hands. He wonders what formulas define a vortex. On the other side of the neighborhood, Cristian lies on his bed and tries to picture the moisture in the clouds above. Rain isn't predicted anytime soon.

Epilogue [28]

First they whupped MIT and won a national underwater robot competition. Now the four underprivileged high school students from Phoenix's Carl Hayden Community High School have a better chance of paying for college—and their story may soon be a big-budget movie.

In the wake of the ROV competition, Phoenix school administrators set up a scholarship fund for Cristian Arcega, Lorenzo Santillan, Luis Aranda, and Oscar Vazquez. One month later, people had contributed more than $57,000. Meanwhile, John Wells, executive producer of *ER* and *The West Wing*, has signed on to produce a movie based on the story, financed by Warner Bros. "All this is way past incredifying," Santillan says. "I've got to bust out with a new word."

Meanwhile, the team's ranks have swelled to thirty. At a recent regional competition, the school's cheerleading squad even turned out to root for the robot crew. The team won and went on to win the Engineering Inspiration award at the nationals in Atlanta. But the high point was still the cheerleaders. "Cristian! Cristian!" they chanted while shaking their blue-and-gold pom-poms. That scene definitely belongs in the movie. ❖

[28] **Text Features/Identify Main Ideas**
A separate section head, **Epilogue**, introduces some final comments. What main idea would you expect in this section?

ANALYZE La Vida Robot

1. **Explain** How did the experience at the ROV competition affect each boy's life? Be sure to cite evidence from the text.

2. **Vocabulary** What was **innovative** about Stinky's design?

3. **Analyze Nonfiction Text Features** With a partner, list the photos and charts in "La Vida Robot" and state the purpose of each one.

Text Feature	Purpose
[Photo on p. 134]	[to show Lorenzo's interest in mechanics]

4. **Focus Strategy Identify Main Ideas and Details** Choose one of the **Notetaking Charts** you created for the selection and share it with a partner. Explain why you chose the details on your chart.

◗ Return to the Text

Reread and Write How do the boys challenge expectations? Reread to gather evidence that shows the expectations they had for themselves and the expectations other people had for them. Write a paragraph that explains how their actions led to their success.

Reading, Writing, and…Recreation?

news feature by Nancy C. Rodriguez

Reading Strategies

- Plan and Monitor
- ▶ **Determine Importance**
- Make Inferences
- Ask Questions
- Make Connections
- Synthesize
- Visualize

Analyze Development of Ideas

A newspaper or online news site contains many kinds of nonfiction, including news of the day's events, sports scores, and editorials. A **news feature** is a special report on a specific topic in the news or in daily life. Writers of good news features organize and develop their ideas by telling *who, what, where, when, why,* and *how* about the topic. (This kind of development is sometimes called the "five *Ws + H*.")

Look Into the Text

Why—tells why the topic of the feature is important

Reading, Writing, and…Recreation?

⌜ Why extracurricular activities give you "extra credit" toward success

by Nancy C. Rodriguez

Find something you like and get involved. But remember, school and grades come first. That's what students have to say about participating in extracurricular activities.

High school isn't just about going to classes, then heading home.

What—tells the topic of the news feature

⌜ It is also an opportunity for students to explore interests, take in new experiences, and get connected to their school. Or in the case of Courtney Otto, conquer a fear of public speaking.

Who—identifies those who are featured in the report

Focus Strategy ▶ Determine Importance

Main ideas are the most important ideas. Writers often put them in the title and support them with **details**. By noting details carefully, you can tell what is important.

HOW TO RELATE MAIN IDEAS AND DETAILS

Focus Strategy

1. Before you read, list the "five *Ws + H*"—*who, what, where, when, why,* and *how*.

2. As you read, identify each *W*. See if you can find another *why* in the text above.

3. State the main idea by telling **who** did **what**. If you can, also tell **when** and **where** and **why** they did it.

Who—students like Courtney Otto
What—participate in extracurricular activities
Why—gain "extra credit" toward success
Main Idea: Participation in extracurricular activities contributes to a student's success.

Connect Across Texts

In "La Vida Robot," four students lived up to their potential by building an award-winning robot. In this news feature, find out how other students explore their interests, overcome their fears, and aim for their future.

Reading, Writing, and . . . Recreation?

NANCY C. RODRIGUEZ

Why extracurricular activities give you "extra credit" toward success

Find something you like and get involved. But remember, school and grades come first. That's what students have to say about participating in extracurricular activities.

High school isn't just about going to classes, then heading home. It is also an opportunity for students to explore interests, take in new experiences, and get connected to their school. Or in the case of Courtney Otto, conquer a fear of public speaking.

Otto, who graduated from high school in May, joined the school's speech team in seventh grade, **confronting** her dislike of speaking before large groups.

Through her experience, Otto placed first in the state of Kentucky in public speaking and won the National Catholic Forensic League title in 2004, which helped her get accepted to Dartmouth College.

"For me, it's a challenge, which is something I enjoy," she said of being on the speech team. "A large part of it is just having the confidence. I can be **scared to death**, but I can get up and speak about things. I can share an opinion." **1**

Most schools offer athletics, band, and drama. But there also are a **plethora of** other clubs that focus on everything from

1 Development of Ideas
Which of the "five *W*s + *H*" questions does this paragraph answer? Explain.

Most schools offer extracurricular activities that relate to a wide variety of hobbies and interests.

In Other Words

confronting dealing with
scared to death extremely afraid
plethora of very large number of

foreign language and community service to skateboarding and chess. And many schools will let students start their own clubs if there is enough interest and a faculty member agrees to be the adviser.

Ashley Brown, a senior at Atherton High School, got involved with the Future Educators of America/Minority Teacher Recruitment club last year. Ashley, who wants to be a special-education teacher, said the club led her to another program that allows her to tutor students during school.

"I love doing it," she said. "It gives me a **sense of being** and makes me feel like I'm needed somewhere."

Being part of the club also gives her access to scholarships and information about teaching.

"It also helps you get respect with your other teachers because they see you like a mini one of them."

But being involved requires finding a balance between activities and schoolwork.

"It's definitely hard," said Taylor Distler, 15, a sophomore at St. Xavier

Joining a school team or club may contribute to your future success.

High School who is on the school's lacrosse team. "You've got to be kind of **disciplined** and manage your time."

Students say they find time for schoolwork during school, after school, and before practice or club meetings. Keisha Knight, 18, who graduated from Central High in May, said that students should begin working on assignments as soon as they get them, even if their deadline is sometime in the future.

"Don't **procrastinate**," she said. ❷ ❖

❷ **Relate Main Ideas/Details**
What is the main idea of the article? What details support the main idea?

Key Vocabulary
  disciplined *adj.*, self-controlled
  procrastinate *v.*, to wait, delay

In Other Words
  sense of being purpose

ANALYZE Reading, Writing, and . . . Recreation?

1. **Summarize** What reasons do students give for doing extracurricular activities?

2. **Vocabulary** Why does a student who participates in extracurricular activities need to be very **disciplined**?

3. **Analyze Development of Ideas** Think about the "five *W*s + *H*." Which of the questions do you think the writer considered most important for developing her ideas?

4. **Focus Strategy Relate Main Ideas/Details** How does Ashley Brown's experience support the main idea of the feature?

Return to the Text

Reread and Write Reread the quotations from Courtney Otto and Ashley Brown. What skills did the girls develop through their extracurricular activities that challenged expectations? Write a paragraph describing these skills and how they helped each girl.

EQ How Do People Challenge Expectations?

Critical Thinking

1. **Compare** Complete the **Anticipation Guide** on page 128 again as if you were one of the boys from "La Vida Robot." Are the new opinions similar to or different from your original opinions? Explain.

2. **Interpret** Oscar tells his teammates, "We got people believing in us, so now we got to believe in ourselves." How do the teenagers in both selections show that they believe in themselves? Give examples.

3. **Analyze** What do you think is the most powerful motivation for students to succeed? Support your answer with examples from both texts.

4. **Generalize** Do you think all extracurricular activities are equally useful for students? Explain and give examples.

EQ 5. **Synthesize** Do you think schools provide opportunities for all students to challenge expectations? Explain.

Writing
Write About Literature

Opinion Statement Do you believe that people do best what they enjoy doing? **Contemplate** this question and write your opinion. Support it with examples from both texts.

Key Vocabulary Review

Oral Review Work with a partner. Use these words to complete the paragraph.

contemplate   implement   procrastinate
designate   innovative   spontaneously
disciplined   perpetually

When some students __(1)__ whether to sign up for Science Club, they consider both the hard work and fun. Some students are so eager and enthusiastic, they do not __(2)__ but __(3)__ jump right in. Other students are more hesitant and __(4)__ hold back. Those who join enjoy solving problems with __(5)__ solutions. They proudly wear T-shirts that __(6)__ them as members of Science Club. They learn to be __(7)__ and carefully budget their time. Above all, they learn to __(8)__ their ideas and make them work.

Writing Application Write a flyer for an extracurricular activity that you are trying to get students to join. Use at least four Key Vocabulary words.

Fluency
Read with Ease: Phrasing

Assess your reading fluency with the passage in the Reading Handbook, p. 802. Then complete the self-check below.

1. I did/did not pause appropriately for punctuation and phrases.

2. My words correct per minute: _____.

INTEGRATE THE LANGUAGE ARTS

Use Subject Pronouns

A **subject pronoun** is used in the subject of a sentence.

- Use **I** when you talk about yourself.
- Use **we** when you talk about another person and yourself.
- Use **you** when you talk to one or more than one other person.
- Use **he**, **she**, **it**, and **they** when you talk about other people or things.

How do you know which to use?

Think about number:		Think about gender:		
One	**More Than One**	**Male**	**Female**	**Male and Female**
he she it	they we	he	she	they we

Oral Practice (1–5) Say each sentence with the correct subject pronoun.

1. Four students build a robot. ____ want to win.
2. Cristian writes the paper. ____ is a genius.
3. Cristian and I control the robot. ____ make it spin.
4. The robot is complete. ____ moves well.
5. The teachers work, too. ____ help the students.

Written Practice (6–10) Rewrite the paragraph using correct pronouns. Add three more sentences. Use subject pronouns.

Allan Cameron sponsors the robotics program. (He/It) needs to raise money for the contest. Four students form a team. (They/He) all have talent.

Describe a Process

Pair Talk Describe to a partner the process for how to do an everyday task. Use words like *first* and *next* to make your steps clear.

Analogy and Allusion

An **analogy** is a comparison that is used to describe or explain something. For example, to explain that Stinky looked cheap next to the other underwater robots, Davis compares Stinky to an economy car.

> [Stinky] looked like a Geo Metro compared with the Lexuses and BMWs around the pool.

An **allusion** is a reference to a famous person, event, or literary character. Davis uses this allusion to help you picture Luis:

> [He] looked like Chief from *One Flew Over the Cuckoo's Nest*.

Chief is a character in a novel who is known for his height and strength. Your knowledge about this character can help you picture Luis.

With a partner, use an analogy and an allusion to describe a person or object of your choice.

Technology Demonstration

Science: How-To Work in teams of four. Prepare an informal demonstration of how something works, such as downloading music or installing software.

1. **Prepare a Statement** Each team member should write down one step in the demonstration. Include useful diagrams or pictures.

2. **Practice Speaking** Each team member should practice giving clear explanations of materials and steps in the demonstration.

3. **Practice Questions and Answers** Each team member should ask the team a question. Everyone answers once.

4. **Perform the Demonstration** Show the demonstration to classmates. Include a real question-and-answer period.

Context Clues: Definitions

Authors sometimes include a word's definition in the text to clarify the word's meaning. These context clues are often set off by commas. For example, in "La Vida Robot," the text states:

> By using polyvinyl chloride pipe, or PVC pipe, the team built a robot that was not only cheaper but better.

Read the following sentences. Use the context clue to figure out the meaning of the underlined word.

1. Their underwater robot could record sonar pings, or high-pitched sounds.

2. The first flower in March is a harbinger, or sign, of spring.

Write a News Feature

Write a news feature about a music, science, art, or sports competition. Answer this question: "What motivates people to live up to their potential?"

1 **Prewrite** Write the "five Ws + H" in your notepad. As you take notes, pay attention to:

- **Accuracy** Get the facts. Don't guess.
- **Sequence** Keep events in time order.
- **Importance** Note only important details.
- **Focus** Stay on one interesting topic.

> **Who**—800 students, from every city high school; winner—11th-grade trumpeter Mark Johnson
> **What**—City-Wide Instrumental Music Competition
> **When**—Saturday and Sunday, April 11-12
> **Where**—C. L. Craig High School
> **Why**—College scholarship
> **How**—Interview question: "Why do you spend so many hours practicing?
> **Winner's Answer:** "Making music lifts me up like nothing else. I practice every day because I want to make the most beautiful music I possibly can."
> **Focus**—Motivation for success is love of music itself.

2 **Draft** Write your first draft. Use the "five Ws + H" as your guide.

3 **Revise** Ask yourself:

- Are all my facts accurate?
- Are the events ordered logically?
- Is the significance of the events clear?
- Have I wandered off the topic?

4 **Edit and Proofread** Ask yourself:

- Do I use subject pronouns correctly?
- Do I avoid confusion with pronouns?

5 **Publish** Type your final draft on a computer and print it out for your teacher.

📖 **Writing Handbook**, p. 832

1

Inside a Veterinary Clinic

Veterinary clinics provide care for dogs, cats, and other small animals. Doctors and assistants work together to perform medical exams and procedures. Many veterinary clinics also provide nonmedical services, such as grooming services and kennels where pet owners can leave their pets overnight.

Jobs in Veterinary Medicine

Most veterinary clinics employ a team of people who perform different tasks. One or more veterinarians supervise the team.

Job	Responsibilities	Education/Training Required
Veterinary Assistant 1	• Cleans kennels • Feeds and bathes animals • Gives medicine to animals	• High school diploma • On-the-job training
Veterinary Technician 2	• Prepares animals for surgery • Assists veterinarians during medical procedures and examinations • Conducts medical tests in laboratories	• Two-year program accredited by the American Veterinary Medical Association
Veterinarian 3	• Conducts medical exams • Diagnoses and treats sick or injured animals • Vaccinates animals against diseases	• Two years of preveterinary medicine and four years in a veterinary program • Two-year internship • License to practice veterinary medicine

2

Investigate the Job Market

Research the jobs available in veterinary medicine.

1. Visit the home page for the Association of American Veterinary Medical Colleges. Click on the link for "Jobs in Veterinary Medicine."

2. Browse the jobs available. Make a chart listing three different jobs. Include the following headings in your chart: Title, Responsibilities, Educational Requirements, Experience, and Salary.

3. Share your chart with a classmate who chose different jobs than you. Discuss which jobs seem the most interesting. Save the information in a professional career portfolio.

myNGconnect.com

🔊 **Learn more about veterinary medicine.**

🔊 **Download a form to evaluate whether you would like to work in this field.**

3

Use Context Clues

Suppose your friend is describing gnocchi to someone who is unfamiliar with Italian food. She says it's a lot like ravioli, and smaller than a meatball. She uses comparison and contrast clues to help the person understand what *gnocchi* is like.

You can also use **comparison clues** and **contrast clues** to figure out words you don't know. Comparison clues are often **synonyms**, while contrast clues are often **antonyms**.

> The dinner I cooked was ***delectable***, similar to the ***delicious*** meal my mom made the night before. **(synonym clue)**

> The price of the meal was ***exorbitant***, but the same meal at a different restaurant was much ***cheaper***. **(antonym clue)**

You can often identify synonym or antonym clues by signal words such as *like, or, another, also, as, likewise, but, unlike, yet,* and *instead*.

Explore Words and Context Clues

Work with a partner to determine the meanings of the highlighted words in the sentences on the right.

1. Copy the highlighted word from each sentence on the right.
2. Find the **synonym** or **antonym clue** for that word. Write it next to the highlighted word.
3. Determine the meaning of the highlighted word.

Put the Strategy to Work

When you see a word you don't know, use this strategy:

1. Look for signal words such as *or, like, also, as, unlike, yet,* or *instead*.
2. Look for familiar words or ideas in the surrounding text that may mean something similar or different.
3. Replace the unfamiliar word with the known one and see if it makes sense.

TRY IT ▶ Read the following sentence and use context clues to understand the meaning of the words in blue type. Then rewrite the sentence using words you do know to replace the words you didn't know.

> ▶ No compliments could undo the affront the chef felt when he received criticism instead of adulation.

1. Cooking dinner was **arduous**, but washing the dishes afterward was easy.

2. The chef was very **demure**, similar to his assistant who was very shy and quiet.

3. Unlike the quiet dining room, the cafeteria was **raucous**.

📖 Reading Handbook, p. 781

PREPARE TO READ

EQ How Do People Challenge Expectations?
Learn how people do "the impossible."

Make a Connection

Think-Pair-Share Automobile maker Henry Ford (1863–1947) has said, "If you think you can do a thing or think you can't do a thing, you're right." What do you think he meant? Discuss with a partner why you agree or disagree with Ford.

Learn Key Vocabulary

Study the Words Pronounce each word and learn its meaning. You may also want to look up the definitions in the Glossary.

• Academic Vocabulary

Key Words	Examples
• **consequence** (**kon**-su-kwens) noun ▶ page 182	A **consequence** is something that happens as a result of another action. If you never study, you may have to face a **consequence** such as bad grades.
contend (kun-**tend**) verb ▶ page 168	To **contend** is to say that you believe something is true. Many people **contend** that chicken soup is a cure for the common cold.
conviction (kun-**vik**-shun) noun ▶ pages 167, 182	A **conviction** is a strong belief. It is an American **conviction** that people should be allowed to choose their government's leaders.
dictate (dik-**tāt**) verb ▶ page 181	To **dictate** is to control or to determine. The school board can **dictate** what we're allowed to wear to school.
endeavor (in-**de**-vur) noun ▶ pages 176, 181, 183	An **endeavor** is a serious effort or try. Training for a marathon is her greatest **endeavor** so far.
momentous (mō-**men**-tus) adjective ▶ pages 167, 176	Most people believe that getting married is a **momentous** event. *Synonyms:* important, big; *Antonyms:* unimportant, small
profound (prō-**fownd**) adjective ▶ pages 174, 176	Something **profound** is filled with deep meaning. Poems sometimes express **profound** truths. *Synonym:* meaningful; *Antonym:* meaningless
transition (tran-**zi**-shun) noun ▶ page 179	A **transition** is a slow change. The **transition** from the teenage years to adulthood can be both difficult and joyful.

Practice the Words Work with a partner. Make a **Definition Map** for each Key Vocabulary word. Use a dictionary to find other forms of the word.

Definition Map

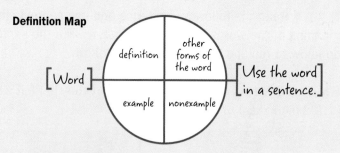

BEFORE READING **My Left Foot**

autobiography by Christy Brown

Reading Strategies

- Plan and Monitor
- ▶ **Determine Importance**
- Make Inferences
- Ask Questions
- Make Connections
- Synthesize
- Visualize

Analyze Development of Ideas

An **autobiography** is a type of nonfiction in which a real person tells his or her life story. The details that the writer chooses to share, and how he or she presents those details, help the reader know what is important to the writer.

Look Into the Text

The writer tells about real places and times.

The writer speaks in the first person.

> I was born in the Rotunda Hospital, on June 5th, 1932. There were nine children before me and twelve after me, so I myself belong to the middle group. Out of this total of twenty-two, seventeen lived, four died in infancy, leaving thirteen still to hold the family fort.
>
> Mine was a difficult birth, I am told. Both mother and son almost died.

Usually the writer tells about events in the order that they happened.

Focus Strategy ▶ Determine Importance

An autobiography includes all kinds of details, such as dates, names, and events. To focus on the big picture, you can **summarize**, or tell only the main ideas of a text. You make a **summary**, or a short restatement of the most important ideas. As you read "My Left Foot," use this strategy to summarize the main ideas.

HOW TO SUMMARIZE

Focus Strategy

1. **Think about** the title, the genre, and the author. This can help you name the topic of the text.

2. **Read a section** of the text and decide what it is mostly about.

3. **Note important details** such as the underlined words shown here. Use them to help you see the main ideas and details in your own words.

4. **Sum up the main ideas** as you read one or more paragraphs in the text. When you finish, write a one-paragraph summary of the selection using only the most important ideas. Your summary should make sense to someone who has not read the selection.

> I was born in the Rotunda Hospital, on June 5th, 1932. There were nine children before me and twelve after me, so I myself belong to the middle group. Out of this total of twenty-two, seventeen lived, four died in infancy, leaving thirteen still to hold the family fort.

Paragraph Summary

> Christy Brown was born in 1932. He was a middle child in a family of 13 children . . .

Christy Brown
(1932–1981)

Christy Brown was one of twenty-two children.

Nobody expected much from **Christy Brown** when he was a young child. He was born with cerebral palsy, a disease that can cause serious physical disabilities. Brown had difficulty controlling the movements of his body, and he could not speak. As a result, people labeled him a "half-wit." However, his family, especially his mother, never doubted his intelligence. "It is his body that is shattered, not his mind. I'm sure of that," his mother once said.

Brown's family worked patiently with him to discover what abilities he had. He could not communicate with anyone, so they did not know what he was thinking or whether he was able to learn. For a long time their efforts to interact with him seemed useless.

Brown's life changed when he was 5 years old. He says that he discovered "that thing that was to give my mind its chance of expressing itself." In 1955, Brown described this breakthrough in his autobiography, *My Left Foot*. He went on to write four novels and several books of poetry. He also became a successful painter.

In 1989, Brown's life story became the subject of the Academy Award–winning film *My Left Foot*.

myNGconnect.com

- Look at art by people with disabilities.
- Discover how machines help people with cerebral palsy communicate.

My Left Foot
by Christy Brown

Reread the title, look at the questions in the margins, and study the pictures. What can you tell about Christy Brown's life?

I was born in the Rotunda Hospital, on June 5th, 1932. There were nine children before me and twelve after me, so I myself belong to the middle group. Out of this total of twenty-two, seventeen lived, four died in infancy, leaving thirteen still **to hold the family fort**.

Mine was a difficult birth, I am told. Both mother and son almost died. A whole army of relations **queued up** outside the hospital until the small hours of the morning, waiting for news and praying furiously that it would be good.

After my birth, mother was sent **to recuperate** for some weeks and I was kept in the hospital while she was away. I remained there for some time, without name, for I wasn't baptized until my mother was well enough to bring me to church.

It was mother who first saw that there was something wrong with me. I was about four months old at the time. She noticed that my head had a habit of falling backwards whenever she tried to feed me. She attempted to correct this by placing her hand on the back of my neck to keep it steady. But when she took it away back it would drop again. That was the first warning sign. Then she became aware of other defects as I got older. She saw that my hands were clenched nearly all of the time and **were inclined to twine** behind my back; my mouth couldn't grasp the teat of the bottle because even at that early age my jaws would either lock together tightly, so that it was impossible for her to open them, or they would suddenly become limp and fall loose, dragging my whole mouth to one side. At six months I could not sit up without having a mountain of pillows around me; at twelve months it was the same. **1**

Very worried by this, mother told my father her fears, and they decided to seek medical advice without any further delay. I was a little over a year old

1 Summarize
Brown's mother suspected something was wrong with her son. What important details led to her suspicion?

In Other Words
to hold the family fort to keep the family alive
queued up stood in line
to recuperate to recover
were inclined to twine were likely to twist

when they began to take me to hospitals and clinics, convinced that there was something definitely wrong with me, something which they could not understand or name, but which was very real and disturbing.

Almost every doctor who saw and examined me labeled me a very interesting but also a hopeless case. Many told mother very gently that I was mentally defective and would remain so. That was **a hard blow to** a young mother who had already reared five healthy children. The doctors were so very sure of themselves that mother's faith in me seemed almost **an impertinence**. They assured her that nothing could be done for me.

She refused to accept this truth, the inevitable truth—as it then seemed—that I was beyond cure, beyond saving, even beyond hope. **2** She could not and would not believe that I was **an imbecile**, as the doctors told her. She had nothing in the world to go by, not a scrap of evidence to support her **conviction** that, though my body was crippled, my mind was not. In spite of all the doctors and specialists told her, she would not agree. I don't believe she knew why—she just knew without feeling **the smallest shade of doubt**.

Finding that the doctors could not help in any way beyond telling her not to place her trust in me, or, in other words, to forget I was a human creature, rather to regard me as just something to be fed and washed and then put away again, mother decided there and then to take matters into her own hands. I was *her* child, and therefore part of the family. No matter how dull and incapable I might grow up to be, she was determined to treat me **on the same plane** as the others, and not as the **"queer one"** in the back room who was never spoken of when there were visitors present. **3**

That was a **momentous** decision as far as my future life was concerned. It meant that I would always have my mother on my side to help me fight all the battles that were to come, and to inspire me with new strength when

2 Development of Ideas
What does this behavior say about the mother's character?

> Mine was a difficult birth, I am told.

3 Development of Ideas
As a writer, Christy Brown chose to include this information. What does it say about what is important to him?

Key Vocabulary
conviction *n.*, strong belief
momentous *adj.*, very important

In Other Words
a hard blow to a piece of very bad news for
an impertinence a sign of disrespect
an imbecile a person with little or no intelligence
the smallest shade of doubt any uncertainty
on the same plane in the same way
"queer one" unusual child

I was almost beaten. But it wasn't easy for her because now the relatives and friends had decided otherwise. They **contended** that I should be taken kindly, sympathetically, but not seriously. That would be a mistake. "For your own sake," they told her, "don't look to this boy as you would to the others; it would only **break your heart** in the end." Luckily for me, mother and father **held out against the lot of them**. But mother wasn't content just to say that I was not an idiot, she set out to prove it, not because of any rigid sense of duty, but out of love. That is why she was so successful. **4**

At this time she had the five other children to look after besides the "difficult one," though as yet it was not by any means a full house. There were my brothers, Jim, Tony, and Paddy, and my two sisters, Lily and Mona, all of them very young, just a year or so between each of them, so that they were almost exactly like steps of stairs.

4 Summarize
What advice do people give Brown's mother? Summarize it in your own words.

In 1989, Brown's autobiography was made into an award-winning movie starring Daniel Day-Lewis as Brown and Brenda Fricker as his mother.

Monitor Comprehension

Summarize
What has Brown's life been like up to this point?

Key Vocabulary
contend *v.*, to argue

In Other Words
break your heart hurt you
held out against the lot of them did not
   listen to what other people said

Predict
How do you think Brown's physical problems will make him feel?

Four years rolled by and I was now five, and still as helpless as a newly-born baby. While my father was out at bricklaying **earning our bread and butter** for us, mother was slowly, patiently pulling down the wall, brick by brick, that seemed to thrust itself between me and the other children, slowly, patiently **penetrating beyond** the thick curtain that hung over my mind, separating it from theirs. **5** It was hard, heartbreaking work, for often all she got from me in return was a vague smile and perhaps a faint gurgle. I could not speak or even mumble, nor could I sit up without support on my own, let alone take steps. But I wasn't **inert** or motionless. I seemed indeed to be **convulsed with movement**, wild, stiff, snakelike movement that never left me, except in sleep. My fingers twisted and twitched continually, my arms twined backwards and would often shoot out suddenly this way and that, and my head lolled and sagged sideways. I was a queer, crooked little fellow.

Mother tells me how one day she had been sitting with me for hours in an upstairs room, showing me pictures out of a great big storybook that I had got from Santa Claus last Christmas and telling me the names of the different animals and flowers that were in them, trying without success to get me to repeat them. This had gone on for hours while she talked and laughed with me. Then at the end of it she leaned over me and said gently into my ear:

"Did you like it, Chris? Did you like the bears and the monkeys and all the lovely flowers? Nod your head for yes, like a good boy." **6**

But I could make no sign that I had understood her. Her face was bent over mine, hopefully. Suddenly, **involuntarily**, my queer hand reached up and grasped one of the dark curls that fell in a thick cluster about her neck. Gently she loosened the clenched fingers, though some dark strands were still clutched between them.

5 Figurative Language
The wall and the curtain are imaginative, not real. What actually separates Brown from the other children? How is this thing like a wall or a curtain?

6 Development of Ideas
How did Brown's mother try to teach words to him? Why is this information important for the autobiography as a whole?

In Other Words
earning our bread and butter working to earn money to buy food
penetrating beyond passing through
inert unable to move
convulsed with movement very active
involuntarily without control

Then she turned away from my curious stare and left the room, crying. The door closed behind her. It all seemed hopeless. It looked as though there was **some justification** for my relatives' contention that I was an idiot and beyond help. **7**

They now spoke of **an institution**.

"Never!" said my mother almost fiercely, when this was suggested to her. "I know my boy is not an idiot. It is his body that is shattered, not his mind. I'm sure of that."

Sure? Yet inwardly, she prayed God would give her some proof of her faith. She knew it was one thing to believe but quite another thing to prove.

I was now five, and still I showed no real sign of intelligence. I showed no apparent interest in things except with my toes—more especially those of my left foot. Although my natural habits were clean I could not aid myself, but in this respect my father took care of me. I used to lie on my back all the time in the kitchen or, on bright warm days, out in the garden, a little bundle of crooked muscles and twisted nerves, surrounded by a family that loved me and hoped for me and that made me part of their own warmth and humanity. I was lonely, imprisoned in a world of my own, unable to communicate with others, cut off, separated from them as though a glass wall stood between my existence and theirs, thrusting me beyond the

I was lonely, imprisoned in a world of my own . . .

sphere of their lives and activities. I longed to run about and play with the rest, but I was unable to break loose from my **bondage.** **8**

7 **Access Vocabulary**
When the suffix *–tion* is added to a verb, it changes the verb to a noun. Based on your knowledge of the verb *contend*, what does the noun *contention* mean?

8 **Summarize**
Which sentence on this page do you think best summarizes Brown's condition? Why?

Monitor Comprehension

Confirm Prediction
How do Brown's physical problems make him feel? Did you change your prediction as you read?

In Other Words
some justification a good reason
an institution a place where severely disabled people are sent to live and to be cared for
bondage handicap

Then, suddenly, it happened! In a moment everything was changed, my future life molded into a definite shape, my mother's faith in me rewarded and her secret fear changed into open triumph.

It happened so quickly, so simply after all the years of waiting and uncertainty that I can see and feel the whole scene as if it had happened last week. It was the afternoon of a cold, gray December day. The streets outside glistened with snow; the white sparkling flakes stuck and melted on the windowpanes and hung on the boughs of the trees like molten silver. The wind howled dismally, whipping up little whirling columns of snow that rose and fell at every fresh **gust**. And over all, the dull, **murky** sky stretched like a dark **canopy**, a vast infinity of grayness.

Inside, all the family were gathered round the big kitchen fire that lit up the little room with a warm glow and made giant shadows dance on the walls and ceiling.

In a corner Mona and Paddy were sitting huddled together, a few torn **school primers** before them. They were writing down little sums on to an old chipped **slate**, using a bright piece of yellow chalk. I was close to them, propped up by a few pillows against the wall, watching.

It was the chalk that attracted me so much. It was a long, slender stick of vivid yellow. I had never seen anything like it before, and it showed up so well against the black surface of the slate that I was fascinated by it as much as if it had been a stick of gold. **9**

Suddenly I wanted desperately to do what my sister was doing. Then— without thinking or knowing exactly what I was doing, I reached out and took the stick of chalk out of my sister's hand—*with my left foot*.

I do not know why I used my left foot to do this. It is a puzzle to many people as well as to myself, for, although I had displayed a curious interest in

9 Development of Ideas
How does Brown make this scene come alive? Name two details that help you picture the room and why it was important to him.

In Other Words
gust breath of wind
murky difficult to see through
canopy covering like a roof
school primers textbooks
slate small blackboard

my toes at an early age, I had never attempted before this to use either of my feet in any way. They could have been as useless to me as were my hands. That day, however, my left foot, apparently **on its own volition**, reached out and very impolitely took the chalk out of my sister's hand.

I held it tightly between my toes, and, acting on an impulse, made a wild sort of scribble with it on the slate. Next moment I stopped, a bit dazed, surprised, looking down at the stick of yellow chalk stuck between my toes, not knowing what to do with it next, hardly knowing how it got there. Then I looked up and became aware that everyone had stopped talking and was staring at me silently. Nobody **stirred**. Mona, her black curls framing her chubby little face, stared at me with great big eyes and open mouth. Across the **open hearth**, his face lit by flames, sat my father, leaning forward, hands outspread on his knees, his shoulders tense. I felt the sweat break out on my forehead. **10**

My mother came in from the **pantry** with a steaming pot in her hand. She stopped midway between the table and the fire, feeling the tension flowing through the room. She followed their stare and saw me, in the corner. Her eyes looked from my face down to my foot, with the chalk gripped between my toes. She put down the pot.

Then she crossed over to me and knelt down beside me, as she had done so many times before.

> I felt the sweat break out on my forehead.

"I'll show you what to do with it, Chris," she said, very slowly and in a queer, jerky way, her face flushed as if with some inner excitement.

Taking another piece of chalk from Mona, she hesitated, then very deliberately drew, on the floor in front of me, the single letter "A."

10 Development of Ideas
Why does Brown go into so much detail about this moment?

In Other Words
on its own volition all by itself, automatically
stirred moved
open hearth fireplace
pantry food storage room

"Copy that," she said, looking steadily at me. "Copy it, Christy." [11]

I couldn't.

I looked about me, looked around at the faces that were turned towards me, tense, excited faces that were at that moment frozen, **immobile**, eager, waiting for a miracle **in their midst**.

[11] **Development of Ideas**
Why is this an important moment in the life of Brown's mother?

What Is Cerebral Palsy?

Cerebral palsy is a brain disorder that affects a person's control of body movements. Symptoms can be mild or severe. Some people have difficulty with tasks such as writing or using scissors. Others, like Christy Brown, are unable to walk or sit up on their own.

Doctors do not know exactly what causes cerebral palsy. However, they do know that it can develop either before birth or in the first few months of an infant's life. Early signs usually appear before 3 years of age. Infants with cerebral palsy are usually slow to reach important stages of development, such as learning to roll over, sit up, crawl, smile, or walk.

Currently there is no known cure for cerebral palsy; however, there are many treatments for the symptoms. These treatments, such as surgery, therapy, medications, and **leg braces**, allow many people who have the disorder to live near-normal lives.

Christy Brown learned to paint and write with his left foot. This allowed him to communicate with others.

In Other Words
immobile not moving
in their midst in the room
leg braces metal supports for the leg

The stillness was **profound**. The room was full of flame and shadow that danced before my eyes and **lulled my taut nerves** into a sort of waking sleep. I could hear the sound of the watertap dripping in the pantry, the loud ticking of the clock on the mantelshelf, and the soft hiss and crackle of the logs on the open hearth.

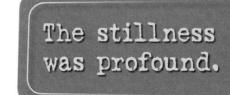

I tried again. I put out my foot and made a wild jerking stab with the chalk which produced a very crooked line and nothing more. Mother held the slate steady for me.

"Try again, Chris," she whispered in my ear.

Again.

I did. I stiffened my body and put my left foot out again, for the third time. I drew one side of the letter. I drew half the other side. Then the stick of chalk broke and I was left with a stump. I wanted to fling it away and give up. Then I felt my mother's hand on my shoulder. I tried once more. Out went my foot. I shook, I sweated and strained every muscle. My hands were so tightly clenched that my fingernails bit into the flesh. I set my teeth so hard that I nearly pierced my lower lip. Everything in the room swam till the faces around me were mere patches of white. But—I drew it—*the letter "A."* There it was on the floor before me. Shaky, with awkward, wobbly sides and a very uneven center line. But it *was* the letter "A." I looked up. I saw my mother's face for a moment, tears on her cheeks. Then my father stooped down and hoisted me on to his shoulder.

I had done it! It had started—the thing that was to give my mind its chance of expressing itself. True, I couldn't speak with my lips, but now I would speak through something more lasting than spoken words—written words. 12

That one letter, **scrawled** on the floor with a broken bit of yellow chalk

12 **Development of Ideas**
Brown says, "It had started." In your own words, tell what had started.

Key Vocabulary
profound *adj.*, filled with deep meaning

In Other Words
lulled my taut nerves caused me to relax
scrawled written poorly

gripped between my toes, was my road to a new world, my key to mental freedom. It was to provide a source of relaxation to the tense, taut thing that was me which **panted for expression** behind a twisted mouth.

Epilogue

That simple act awakened young Christy's determination to empower himself. With the help of his mother, some chalk, and his left foot, he **painstakingly** learned how to write each letter of the alphabet.

"Knowing the alphabet was half the battle won," he wrote, "for I was soon able to put letters together to form little words."

By the time Christy was six, he was able to spell out his full name. No sooner had he learned to write his first words, than he realized he wanted to do something bigger. He taught himself to read and paint. 🔢

"I was holding a paintbrush now, not a broken piece of chalk. But it meant the same thing—I had discovered a new way to communicate with the outside world, a new way to talk with my left foot."

The more he learned, the more he was determined to express himself. By the time he was seventeen, Christy knew he was destined to be a writer. He replaced his paintbrush with a pencil and began writing stories. He wrote Westerns, romance stories, and even mysteries.

Eventually he decided to share his life story. Christy Brown's autobiography, *My Left Foot,* became an international bestseller.

"There was something in me, some inner **urge** to speak, and I wanted to communicate it to others and make them understand it. I felt I had found something, something I had been looking for ever since I began to think and feel about myself. . . . It wasn't just about myself, but about all who had a life similar to my own, a life bounded and shut in on all sides by the high walls of a narrow, **suppressed life**. I felt that I had at last found a way of scaling those

🔢 **Text Features**
What is the purpose of the **Epilogue**? How can you tell that someone other than Brown wrote it?

In Other Words
panted for expression wanted to communicate
painstakingly very slowly and carefully
urge pressure, desire
suppressed life life prevented from developing

walls and breaking loose from the shadow of them, a way of taking my place in the sun and playing my part in the world. . . ."

From that time on, Christy Brown shared his work with the world. He continued writing and published several novels and poetry collections before he died in 1981. ❖

ANALYZE My Left Foot

1. **Retell** What **momentous** event inspired Christy Brown to title his autobiography "My Left Foot"? Cite evidence from the text by giving a few details of that event.

2. **Vocabulary** Do you think Brown would have succeeded in his **endeavors** without his mother's help? Explain.

3. **Analyze Development of Ideas** With a partner, list five events in Brown's life in the order in which they happened. Tell which event you think is the most important and why you think Brown included it.

4. **Focus Strategy Summarize** With a partner, write a summary that tells how Brown experienced the **profound** change in his life. Discuss what details to include and what to leave out. Share your summary with your class.

Return to the Text
Reread and Write Write a thank-you note from Brown to his mother. Reread to find two examples of times that she helped him challenge expectations. Include the examples in the thank-you note.

BEFORE READING Success Is a Mind-Set

interview from *Hewitt Magazine Online*

Reading Strategies

· Plan and Monitor
▶ **Determine Importance**
· Make Inferences
· Ask Questions
· Make Connections
· Synthesize
· Visualize

Relate Ideas

An **online magazine interview** is a kind of nonfiction where one person gets information from another person. The interview may take place in person or via e-mail. Then it is posted, or published, online. Like most interviews, it may be organized in a question-and-answer format.

Look Into the Text

The interviewer's question is in special print.

> **Q:** **Yours is an amazing success story. Why did you succeed when others in similar situations fail?**
>
> **A:** I'm always quick to point out that it's not just me; my brother is also very successful. We had, in our mother, someone who believed in us and was willing to make sacrifices on our behalf. She encouraged us to believe in ourselves. Success is a mind-set .

In this kind of organization, *Q* stands for question, *A* for answer.

The words of the person who is interviewed often relate to the title.

Focus Strategy ▶ Determine Importance

A good **summary** of a nonfiction selection is like a news report. The summary briefly tells the most important information.

HOW TO SUMMARIZE

Focus Strategy

A good way to understand and remember important ideas is to summarize them. To summarize "Success Is a Mind-Set," follow these steps.

1. Decide what each question-and-answer pair in the interview is mostly about.

Question	Answer
Why did you succeed?	Success is a mind-set.

2. Think about what the ideas mean to you.

3. Write each idea in your own words to form a summary.

> When I summarize what I read, I don't retell everything. I only give the most important details, including what's most important to me personally.

Connect Across Texts

In "My Left Foot," Christy Brown succeeded against the odds. In this interview, brain surgeon Benjamin Carson comments on people's potential.

Success Is a Mind-Set

interview from *Hewitt Magazine Online*

As a kid, Benjamin Carson was considered the "dummy" of his class, and he had a violent temper. "I was most likely to end up in jail, reform school, or the grave," he remembers. So how did he become a world-famous neurosurgeon?

Dr. Benjamin Carson is the director of pediatric neurosurgery at the Johns Hopkins Medical Institutions in Baltimore, Maryland. He is shown here discussing his work at an international press conference.

Ben was just 8 years old when his mother found out that the man she wed at 13 had another wife and five more children living across town. Sonja Carson filed for divorce and worked as **a domestic** to support Ben and his older brother. She observed her wealthy employers and shared insights with her sons. "This is how successful people behave," she'd say. "This is how they think. You boys can do it, too, and you can do it better!"

His mother's refusal to accept excuses for failure enabled Ben to make the **transition** from—in his own words—"the dumbest kid in fifth grade to one of the smartest kids in seventh grade." When he found his studies overwhelming, she'd say, "You weren't born to be a failure. You can do it."

Soon, the boy with poor grades and **low self-esteem** began thinking of himself as smart and acting accordingly. Academic awards and achievements followed. He received a scholarship to Yale and later went on to study medicine at the University of Michigan Medical School. **1**

1 Relate Ideas
What do you think the purpose of this introduction is? Is it effective? Explain.

Dr. Carson encourages young people to believe in themselves.

Key Vocabulary
transition *n.*, slow change

In Other Words
a domestic a maid
low self-esteem little belief in his abilities

Today, Dr. Carson performs about 400 surgeries each year, more than double the **caseload** of the average neurosurgeon. He's the author of three books and the cofounder, with his wife, Candy, of the Carson Scholars Fund, a nonprofit organization that recognizes and rewards academic achievement with college-assistance funds.

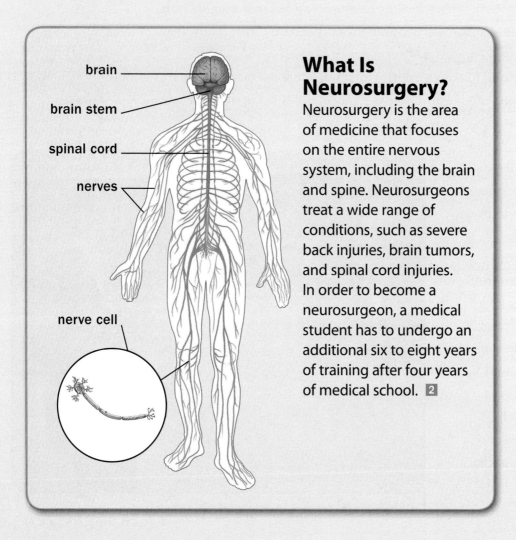

brain

brain stem

spinal cord

nerves

nerve cell

What Is Neurosurgery?

Neurosurgery is the area of medicine that focuses on the entire nervous system, including the brain and spine. Neurosurgeons treat a wide range of conditions, such as severe back injuries, brain tumors, and spinal cord injuries. In order to become a neurosurgeon, a medical student has to undergo an additional six to eight years of training after four years of medical school. **2**

2 Summarize
How does what you learn about neurosurgery affect your impression of Dr. Carson?

In Other Words
caseload amount of work

Q: Yours is an amazing success story. Why did you succeed when others in similar situations fail?

A: I'm always quick to point out that it's not just me; my brother is also very successful. We had, in our mother, someone who believed in us and was willing **to make sacrifices on our behalf**. She encouraged us to believe in ourselves. Success is **a mind-set**. If you have negative influences coming at you and you allow them to **dictate** your course in life, you'll never succeed. When you realize that the person with the greatest influence over what happens in your life is you, it makes a huge difference. Look at Walter Anderson, the CEO and publisher of *Parade* magazine. Growing up, his father didn't think reading was a worthwhile **endeavor**; he would beat him if he caught him reading. Instead of using that as an excuse for failure, Walter grew up to be the publisher of the largest-circulation magazine in the world. **3**

3 Summarize
What is this section mostly about? Summarize it in your own words.

Q: You've said, "Successful people don't have fewer problems, just different ways of looking at them." How so?

A: It all goes back to mind-set. How do you look at the problems you face—are they fences or are they hurdles? If you view them as fences, you allow them to contain you and they become excuses for inaction. But if you view problems as hurdles, then you have choices. You can go over them or under them or around them. It doesn't matter how you get by that hurdle; it just matters that you do. And each time you get by another hurdle, it strengthens you for the next one. In a corporate setting, it's essential that leaders not allow their employees to make excuses; eventually they'll stop constructing fences and start jumping hurdles. They learn to deal with and overcome their problems, and that leads to success. **4**

4 Relate Ideas/ Summarize
How can you tell that Dr. Carson's advice is for groups of people, not just for individuals? Summarize his advice to the group in this answer.

Key Vocabulary
dictate *v.*, to control, determine
endeavor *n.*, serious effort or try

In Other Words
to make sacrifices on our behalf to give up things for us
a mind-set a way of thinking, a belief

Q: In your most recent book, *The Big Picture*, you talk about understanding why to succeed. Can you explain?

A: People must want success for themselves, not because others demand it of them. Children are the best example. We say, "You need to study. You need to get A's." Soon they think they're doing it for Mom, Dad, or their teacher. They need to know they're doing it for themselves. They must understand that they have seventy to eighty years of life to live, the first twenty of which must be used to prepare. If they prepare, they'll have fifty years **to reap the benefits**. If they don't, they'll have fifty years to suffer the **consequences**. 5 ❖

5 **Summarize**
Think about what Dr. Carson means by "understanding why to succeed." Summarize his answer in a sentence.

ANALYZE Success Is a Mind-Set

1. **Explain** What **convictions** did Dr. Carson acquire from his mother? Be sure to cite evidence from the text.

2. **Vocabulary** According to Dr. Carson, what are the **consequences** of not wanting success for yourself?

3. **Relate Ideas** If you were interviewing Dr. Carson, what other question would you ask him, and why would you ask it?

4. **Focus Strategy Summarize** Create a summary of the questions and answers in the interview. Then compare it with a partner's summary. Discuss any differences and why each of you included the ideas you did.

Return to the Text
Reread and Write Do you agree or disagree with the idea that success is a mind-set? Reread to decide. Then explain your opinion in a paragraph.

Key Vocabulary
• **consequence** *n.*, result, effect

In Other Words
to reap the benefits to enjoy the rewards

EQ How Do People Challenge Expectations?

Reading

Critical Thinking

1. **Compare** Think about the ideas you discussed for the **Think-Pair-Share** on page 162. Compare your ideas with those of Christy Brown and Dr. Carson. Are your ideas similar or different? Explain.

EQ 2. **Analyze** How can family members help each other challenge other people's expectations of them? Give examples from both texts.

3. **Interpret** What is meant by the phrase "doing the impossible"? Explain, using examples from either text.

4. **Draw Conclusions** Why is attitude so important in achieving success? Support your answer with examples from both texts.

EQ 5. **Evaluate** In your opinion, are stories of successful people a good way to show other people how to challenge expectations? Explain.

Writing

Write About Literature

Opinion Statement Write a paragraph in which you agree or disagree with this opinion: Most people decide when they are young whether they can succeed. Use examples from both texts to support your opinion.

Vocabulary

Key Vocabulary Review

Oral Review Work with a partner. Use these words to complete the paragraph.

consequence	dictate	profound
contend	endeavor	transition
conviction	momentous	

> Though graduation is not a big deal at some schools, at my school it was a __(1)__ event. The mayor gave an inspiring speech that had many thoughtful and __(2)__ ideas in it. She said that success in life is a __(3)__, or result, of a positive attitude. Her parents never let poverty __(4)__ her choices in life. They had a powerful __(5)__ that she could succeed. Because of them, she worked hard at every __(6)__. She became active in efforts to improve the community, then finally decided to make the __(7)__ into politics. One student asked the mayor, "Do people have to be rich to succeed?" The mayor replied, "Not in my opinion. I __(8)__ that success is a matter of attitude, not money."

Writing Application Write an e-mail to a friend about one of your successful **endeavors**. Use at least four Key Vocabulary words.

Fluency

Read with Ease: Expression

Assess your reading fluency with the passage in the Reading Handbook, p. 803. Then complete the self-check below.

1. My expression did/did not sound natural.

2. My words correct per minute: _____.

Use Action Verbs in the Present Tense

An **action verb** tells what the subject does. **Present tense** action verbs tell what the subject does now or does often.

Dr. Benjamin Carson **works** as a surgeon.

Add **-s** to the action verb only when you talk about one other person, place, or thing.

His mother **believes** in him.

She **tells** him not to give up.

An action verb can have a **helping verb** and a main verb. The helping verbs **can**, **could**, **may**, or **might** come before the **main verb**.

I **could be** a doctor.

A doctor **can save** your life.

Never add **-s** to **can**, **could**, **may**, or **might**.

Oral Practice (1–5) Think about the selections you just read. Tell your partner five things that Dr. Carson or Christy Brown does. Use action verbs in the present tense.

Example: Dr. Carson performs many surgeries.

Written Practice (6–10) Choose the correct verb and rewrite the paragraph. Complete the last sentence about Christy Brown. Use verbs in the present tense.

Christy (stare/stares) at his mother. She (read/reads) Christy a book. Christy (take/takes) a piece of chalk. He (write/can write) a letter. His family...

Describe People and Actions

Pair Talk Describe one person in "My Left Foot" or in "Success Is a Mind-Set." Use words that tell how the person looks and what he or she does. Have your partner guess whom you are describing.

Author's Purpose, Text Structure, and Point of View

In "My Left Foot," Christy Brown wants to tell his life story. He uses **first-person point of view** and he chooses to organize his life story in **chronological order**—the order in which the events actually happened.

* As one event follows another, Brown changes and learns how to express himself.

* The chronological order suggests that Brown's purpose is to show that his life changed slowly, over a long period of time, and that the change was important to him.

With a partner, create a time line of Christy Brown's autobiography.

* Reread the selection.
* List the specific events in Brown's life.
* Find the events that are important.
* Write the important events on a time line.
* Use the time line to summarize the events.

Time Line

1930   1940   1950   1960   1970   1980   1990

Write an Analysis Answer these questions. Include examples from the text as evidence.

1. Did Christy Brown structure his ideas in a way that showed you what was important?
2. How did Christy Brown's use of the first person make the account of his life more believable?

Context Clues: Multiple-Meaning Words

To understand a word with more than one meaning, use the context to figure out which meaning the author intended. Read the following sentences and then work with a partner to determine the meaning of the underlined words. Then write a second sentence that uses a different meaning of the word.

1. The boxer hit the punching bag with great <u>power</u>.
2. Beautiful flowers grow along the <u>bank</u> of the river.
3. She spent two hours in front of the mirror trying to <u>style</u> her hair.

Summary of Events

Psychology: Living with Physical Challenges Some people succeed in life despite physical challenges. How do they challenge the expectations that society has of them? Research one of the following people online. Create a summary of the important events in the person's life and share it with your class.

myNGconnect.com

- 🌐 Helen Keller, writer and teacher
- 🌐 Christopher Reeve, actor
- 🌐 Stephen Hawking, scientist
- 🌐 Jim Abbott, baseball player

📖 **Writing Handbook**, p. 832

Voice and Style

When you write, you need to decide what **voice**, or way of saying things, you are going to use. This often depends on your particular audience. For example, you would not use the same **style** to write an essay for your English class as you would to write an e-mail to a friend. Does the writer use an appropriate voice in the school essay below?

Just OK

> I think Dr. Ben Carson is pretty cool. He kind of flunked out at first, but then he got it in gear and got good grades. He also got into the U. of Michigan to become a doctor. He didn't let anything knock him down. I wouldn't want to mess with him!

This essay shows the writer's opinion, but the language is inappropriate for an academic paper. The writer uses too much slang. Develop your own voice and style, but adjust for your audience.

Read how the writer improved the essay:

Much Better

> I admire Dr. Ben Carson. He didn't do well in school at first, but he turned his life around and got excellent grades. He also ended up getting into one of the country's best medical schools. He is a living example of how you can move beyond circumstances if you are hardworking and determined.

Now it's your turn to use the appropriate voice. Read this passage. Revise it in a more formal style.

> Christy Brown was born with a bad spine and couldn't walk or anything. It might have really stunk to be him, but he didn't let it get him down. He used the toes on his left foot to talk to people. How cool is that? Instead of doing nothing, he did lots of stuff like writing and painting.

After you rewrite the essay, check your work. Make more revisions if necessary:

- Is my voice appropriate for my audience?
- Did I keep the same ideas that were in the original essay?

📖 **Writing Handbook**, p. 832

Narrative Presentation

Have you ever done something someone thought you couldn't do? How did it make you feel? Tell an audience about a time when you challenged someone's expectations. A narrative presentation can bring this story to life. Here is how to prepare and perform a narrative of your own.

1. Plan Your Narrative Presentation

Think about a time when you did something others thought you couldn't. Then do the following:

- Write down as many details as you can. Include what happened, when and why it happened, and how you felt about it.
- Make sure the details you include are important to the story and follow chronological (time) order.
- Think of a message that someone could take from the experience. Do you want your message to inspire or educate?
- Use language that appeals to people's senses and emotions to describe details.

2. Practice Your Narrative Presentation

Polish your presentation skills by doing the following:

- Think of different ways to introduce the narrative; ask a friend which introduction is the most interesting and why.
- Use your voice and gestures to bring the narrative to life and to show time or mood changes.
- Practice until you are very familiar with your presentation and only have to glance at your notes.
- Be sure you don't finish too soon or speak for too long.

> How can this speaker's body language contribute to an effective presentation?

3. Give Your Narrative Presentation

Keep your presentation interesting by doing the following:

- Establish eye contact with members of your audience.
- Stay relaxed but focused on your message and purpose.
- Speak clearly and loudly.
- Use your notes as little as possible.
- Monitor your audience's interest as you speak. Do you need to make more eye contact? Use more energy? Adjust your speaking style, if needed.

4. Discuss and Rate the Narrative Presentation

Use the rubric to discuss and rate the narrative presentations, including your own.

Narrative Presentation Rubric

Scale	Content of Narrative Presentation	Student's Preparation	Student's Performance
3 Great	• Really addressed the topic • Inspired me	• Presented events in an easy-to-follow sequence • Showed a lot of attention to gathering descriptive details	• Spoke clearly and was easy to follow • Used facial expressions and gestures very well
2 Good	• Didn't really address the topic • Gave me a positive feeling	• Presented events in a sequence that was mostly easy to follow • Showed some attention to gathering details	• Spoke clearly most of the time and was usually easy to follow • Used facial expressions and gestures fairly well
1 Needs Work	• Didn't address the topic at all • Seemed uninspiring	• Presented events in a confusing sequence • Showed little attention to gathering details	• Was hard to hear and understand • Did not use facial expressions and gestures well

DO IT ▶ Now that you know how to do a narrative presentation, perform your narrative in front of an audience!

📘 Language and Learning Handbook, p. 750

myNGconnect.com
🔾 Download the rubric.

How Do People Challenge Expectations?

Find out why people challenge expectations.

Make a Connection

Quickwrite Do you agree or disagree with the following statements? Write down how you feel about the statements and tell why you feel that way.

- Most people are alike deep down inside.
- Some differences between people are too difficult to overcome.

Learn Key Vocabulary

Study the Words Pronounce each word and learn its meaning. You may also want to look up the definitions in the Glossary.

● Academic Vocabulary

Key Words	Examples
alienation (ā-lē-e-**nā**-shun) *noun* ▶ page 194	If you experience a feeling of **alienation**, you feel isolated and alone. *Synonyms:* isolation, distance; *Antonyms:* closeness, friendship
commiserate (ku-**mi**-zu-rāt) *verb* ▶ pages 198, 211	If you **commiserate** with somebody, you share their unhappiness. I **commiserate** with friends who have a lot of homework.
empathize (**em**-pu-thīz) *verb* ▶ pages 201, 206, 209	To **empathize** is to understand someone's feelings. I broke my arm last year, so I can **empathize** with what she's experiencing with her broken arm.
● **ethnicity** (eth-**ni**-se-tē) *noun* ▶ page 199	A person's **ethnicity** is the person's race, country of birth, religion, or family background. Her **ethnicity** is Mexican because she was born in Mexico.
● **integrate** (**in**-tu-grāt) *verb* ▶ page 202	To **integrate** is to mix people of all races. *Synonym:* unite; *Antonym:* separate
● **perception** (pur-**sep**-shun) *noun* ▶ pages 192, 210	A **perception** is an observation or feeling about something. My **perception** of the study guide is that it is really helpful.
segregation (se-gri-**gā**-shun) *noun* ▶ page 202	**Segregation** is the separation of people of different races. *Synonym:* separation; *Antonyms:* congregation, integration
tolerance (**to**-lu-runs) *noun* ▶ pages 193, 211, 213	**Tolerance** is respect for the beliefs, customs, and ways of life of people different from you. Our government has a **tolerance** for all religions.

Practice the Words Work with a partner. For each Key Vocabulary word, complete a **Word Square**.

Word Square

Definition: race, country of birth, religion, or family	Important Characteristics: a combination of many traits
Examples: Colombian, Jewish, African American	Nonexamples: male, female, child, adult

ethnicity

The Freedom Writers Diary

diary by The Freedom Writers with
Erin Gruwell

Reading Strategies

- Plan and Monitor
- ▶ **Determine Importance**
- Make Inferences
- Ask Questions
- Make Connections
- Synthesize
- Visualize

Relate Ideas

A **diary** is a kind of nonfiction in which a real person writes about daily life events that he or she considers important. The writer may also describe his or her feelings about the events. You might write a diary to record the everyday events of your life or to analyze your thoughts and feelings.

Look Into the Text

A diary includes a salutation like a letter.

These are real events.

> Dear Diary,
>
> We've been talking about the war in Bosnia and how similar some of the events are to the Holocaust. We have been reading about a young girl named Zlata, who many call the modern-day Anne Frank. Zlata and I seem to have a lot in common because while Zlata was living through a war in Sarajevo, I was living through a different kind of war—the L.A. riots. Ironically, Zlata and I were both eleven years old when our city was under siege. I can understand how afraid and scared she was to see her city go up in flames, because my city was on fire, too.

The writer uses a conversational style to describe her feelings about life events.

A diary entry often starts with a date and includes time-signal words like *first*, *next*, *meanwhile*, and *finally*. Why do you think these are important features of a diary?

Focus Strategy ▶ Determine Importance

Like most other nonfiction writers, diary writers give clues about which details they think are most important. When you read a diary entry, think about the writer's choice of details and why those details may be important. Use the strategies below to help you determine what is important in "The Freedom Writers Diary."

HOW TO DETERMINE WHAT'S IMPORTANT

Focus Strategy

Keep a **Reading Journal** to track your thoughts.

1. **Find the Main Idea** Write down what the selection is mainly about.

2. **Take Note of Important Details** Write down the ideas and information you think are important to remember.

3. **Summarize** Write down the most important ideas in your own words.

Reading Journal

This selection is mostly about ...	The important details include ...
similarities between life in Sarajevo and L.A.	Zlata and the writer were both eleven during the attacks.
The most important idea is ...	

The Writer and Her Experiences

Erin Gruwell
(1970–)

Erin Gruwell learned the meaning of success through her students.

When new teacher **Erin Gruwell** walked into her high school English class for the first time, she didn't know what to expect. Neither did her students. The class was filled with teenagers who had problems with learning or discipline. The other teachers called the teens "unteachable." However, the cautious attitude of both the teacher and students soon turned into a feeling of trust.

Gruwell asked her students to read about and relate their lives to those of other teenagers who faced difficult circumstances. As the students read, they wrote diaries describing the challenges in their own lives, as well as their thoughts and feelings about what they read.

In 1999, Gruwell and her students published their diary entries in the book *The Freedom Writers Diary*. A movie based on the book and starring Hilary Swank was released in early 2007.

Gruwell heads up the Freedom Writers Foundation, a service organization that educates teachers and students about the power of writing and how it can change violence and despair into tolerance and hope.

myNGconnect.com

🔊 Listen to excerpts from *The Freedom Writers Diary*.
🔊 View photos of Sarajevo before and after the Bosnian conflict.

The Freedom Writers Diary

by The Freedom Writers with Erin Gruwell

How a teacher and 150 teens used writing to change themselves and the world around them

Ms. Gruwell:

Dear Diary,

Tomorrow morning, my journey as an English teacher officially begins. Since first impressions are so important, I wonder what my students will think about me. Will they think I'm **out of touch** or too preppy? Or worse yet, that I'm too young to be taken seriously? Maybe I'll have them write a journal entry describing what their expectations are of me and the class. **1**

Even though I spent last year as a student teacher at Wilson High School, I'm still learning my way around the city. Long Beach is so different than the gated community I grew up in. Thanks to MTV dubbing Long Beach as the "gangsta-rap capital" with its depiction of guns and graffiti, my friends have a warped **perception** of the city, or L B C as the rappers refer to it. They think I should wear a bulletproof vest rather than pearls. Where I live in Newport Beach is a **utopia** compared to some of the neighborhoods seen in a Snoop Doggy Dogg video. Still, TV tends to **blow things out of proportion**.

The school is actually located in a safe neighborhood, just a few miles from the ocean. Its location and reputation make it desirable. So much so that a lot of the students that live in what they call the "'hood" take two or three buses just to get to school every day. Students come in from every corner of the city: Rich kids from the shore sit next to poor kids from the projects . . . there's every race, religion, and culture within the confines of the quad. But since the Rodney King riots, racial tension has spilled over into the school. **2**

Due to busing and an outbreak in gang activity, Wilson's traditional white, upper-class demographics have changed radically. African Americans, Latinos, and Asians now make up the majority of the student body.

As a student teacher last year, I was pretty naive. I wanted to see past color and culture, but I was immediately confronted by it when the first bell rang and a student named Sharaud sauntered in bouncing a basketball. He was a junior, a disciplinary transfer from Wilson's crosstown rival, and his

1 **Relate Ideas**
How does Ms. Gruwell feel the night before she starts her new job? Why do you think so?

2 **Relate Ideas**
In this paragraph and the one before it, how does the writer express both facts and personal feelings?

Key Vocabulary
● **perception** *n.*, observation or feeling

In Other Words
out of touch old-fashioned
utopia perfect place filled with peace and harmony
blow things out of proportion make things seem worse than they really are

reputation preceded him. Word was that he had threatened his previous English teacher with a gun (which I later found out was only a plastic water gun, but it had all the makings of a dramatic showdown). In those first few minutes, he made it brutally clear that he hated Wilson, he hated English, and he hated me. His sole purpose was to make his "preppy" student teacher cry. Little did he know that within a month, he'd be the one crying.

Sharaud became **the butt of a bad joke**. A classmate got tired of Sharaud's antics and drew a racial caricature of him with huge, exaggerated lips. As the drawing made its way around the class, the other students laughed hysterically. When Sharaud saw it, he looked as if he was going to cry. For the first time, **his tough facade began to crack**.

When I got a hold of the picture, I **went ballistic**. "This is the type of propaganda that the Nazis used during the Holocaust," I yelled. When a student timidly asked me, "What's the Holocaust?" I was shocked.

I asked, "How many of you have heard of the Holocaust?" Not a single person raised his hand. Then I asked, "How many of you have been shot at?" Nearly every hand went up.

I immediately decided to throw out my meticulously planned lessons and make **tolerance** the core of my curriculum. **3**

From that moment on, I would try to bring history to life by using new books, inviting guest speakers, and going on field trips. . . .

3 Determine What's Important Why do you think Ms. Gruwell reflects on a past event in her diary entry? Respond to the question in your **Reading Journal**.

> ## What Was the Holocaust?
>
> The Holocaust (1933–1945) was the organized mass murder of millions of European Jews and other groups viewed as inferior, or of less worth, by Germany's Nazi party. The groups in this chart were seen as unproductive members of society or as a threat to Nazi beliefs. It is unclear exactly how many people were victims of Nazi persecution, but most estimates are between 9 and 11 million.
>
> **The Holocaust in Numbers**
>
> | Group | Number Killed |
> |---|---|
> | European Jews | 6,000,000 |
> | Russian prisoners of war | 3,300,000 |
> | Non-Jewish Polish citizens | 1,900,000 |
> | Roma (gypsies) | 200,000 |
> | Disabled people | 200,000 |
> | Religious groups | 1,400 |
>
> Source: *Holocaust Encyclopedia*, United States Holocaust Memorial Museum

Monitor Comprehension

Explain
Why does Ms. Gruwell decide to make tolerance the theme of her English classes?

Key Vocabulary
tolerance *n.*, respect for different beliefs and ways of life

In Other Words
the butt of a bad joke the person who is the target of a mean joke
his tough facade began to crack he began to show his emotions
went ballistic became very angry

One Year Later . . .

Ms. Gruwell:

Dear Diary,

My class has become a dumping ground for disciplinary transfers, kids in rehab, or those on probation. But if Sharaud, who graduated in June, could turn his life around, there is hope for these new students yet. Ironically, "hope" is one of the few four-letter words not in their vocabulary.

When I asked one of my freshmen if he thought he'd graduate, he said, "Graduate? Hell, I don't even know if I'll make it to my sixteenth birthday!" To some of these kids, death seems more real than a diploma.

Their fatalistic attitude influenced my literature choices for this year. Since the incident with the racist note **segued into** a unit on tolerance, I'm going to revisit and expand on that theme. I've ordered four books about teens in crisis: *The Wave* by Todd Strasser; *Night* by Elie Wiesel; *Anne Frank: The Diary of a Young Girl*; and *Zlata's Diary: A Child's Life in Sarajevo*. The last two will be **the focal point** of the curriculum. 4

It's uncanny how many similarities my students have with Anne and Zlata. Since many of my students are fifteen, and Zlata is fifteen, and Anne Frank was fifteen when she died, I think the parallels between age, **alienation**, and teenage angst **will really hit home for them**.

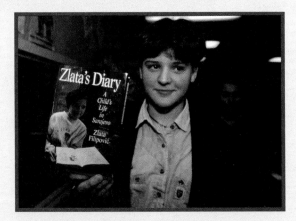

Zlata Filipović's diary about the Bosnian civil war was published In 1994. It became an international bestseller and was translated into 36 languages.

4 Relate Ideas/ Determine What's Important
Why do you think Ms.Gruwell feels that the choice of books is important enough to write about in her diary?

Key Vocabulary
alienation *n.,* feeling of being separate from others

In Other Words
Their fatalistic attitude Their belief that they have no control over their lives
segued into led to
the focal point the most important part
will really hit home for them will be meaningful to the students

Anne Frank's book was a natural choice, but I was really excited to discover the book by the young Bosnian writer, who critics are hailing as a "modern-day Anne Frank." *Scope* magazine's cover story about Zlata Filipović last spring inspired me to read her diary about war-torn Bosnia. Zlata began keeping a diary when she was ten. She called it "Mimmy"—similar to how Anne Frank called her diary "Kitty." Just as Anne's life changed dramatically under the Nazi occupation, so did Zlata's during the war in Sarajevo. Suddenly, Zlata's focus switched from her studies and watching MTV to the closing of her school and the destruction of the national library. As the war progressed, she experienced and **chronicled** food shortages, artillery shelling, and the death of children.

In 1991 at the age of eleven, as Zlata watched her once peaceful city erupt in war, my students witnessed Los Angeles literally burn in the wake of the Rodney King verdict; as Zlata dodged sniper fire in the streets where she once played, my students dodged stray bullets from drive-by shootings; as Zlata watched her friends killed by the senseless violence of war, my students watched friends get killed by senseless gang violence. In Sarajevo, Zlata described how soldiers used a "black crayon of war" to put an "S" on Serbs, a "C" on Croats, and an "M" on Muslims. I think my students could argue that they, too, have experienced a "black crayon" of sorts, labeling them with a "W" for white, a "B" for black, an "L" for Latino, and an "A" for Asian.

I think my students will be able to identify with the teen protagonists in all of the books I've selected. But since the books won't arrive for a while, I'm going to have them read short stories and plays that they'll be able to relate to. I think they'll be surprised how life mirrors art.

> To some of these kids, death seems more real than a diploma.

5 Determine What's Important
What is this section mainly about? What details are important to remember? Record them in your **Reading Journal**.

Monitor Comprehension

Summarize
Summarize how Ms. Gruwell's understanding of her students has changed in the time between her two diary entries.

In Other Words
chronicled wrote about

Historical Background
The Bosnian Conflict occurred during the 1990s among three groups of people—the Serbs, Croats, and Bosnians—for control of the country now called Bosnia and Herzegovina. Thousands of people died in "ethnic cleansing," the killing of people based on their nationality.

> Would Ms. Gruwell's students care that wartime conflict and intolerance had changed the lives of Anne Frank and Zlata Filipović—people they had never met? **6**

STUDENT DIARY ENTRY 36:

Dear Diary,

At first I asked Ms. G, "Why should I read books about people who don't look like me? People that I don't even know and that I am not going to understand because they don't understand me!" I thought I was a smart-ass for asking her this question. I thought to myself, "She's not going to give me an answer because this time I am right." She looked up and said very calmly, "How can you say that? You haven't even bothered to open the front cover. Try it, you never know. The book may come to life before your eyes."

> The book may come to life before your eyes.

So I started to read this book called *Anne Frank: The Diary of a Young Girl* because I wanted to prove Ms. G wrong. I wanted to show her that what she said was bull, and that her little technique was not going to work for me. I hate reading, and I hate her, for that matter.

To my surprise, I proved myself wrong because the book indeed came to life. At the end of the book, I was so mad that Anne died, because as she was dying, a part of me was dying with her. I cried when she cried, and just like her I wanted to know why the Germans were killing her people. Just like her, I knew the feeling of discrimination and to be **looked down upon** based on the way you look. Just like her, "I sometimes feel like a bird in a cage and just want to fly away." The first thing that came to my mind when I finished reading the book was the fact that Ms. G was right. I did find myself within the pages of the book, like she said I would. **7**

6 Access Vocabulary
The prefix *in-* means "not." Based on your understanding of the word *tolerance*, what does *intolerance* mean?

7 Relate Ideas/ Determine What's Important
This diary entry comes from a student. How can you tell that the writing is personal? How does the student show that Ms. Gruwell's choice of books was important? Write about it in your **Reading Journal.**

In Other Words
looked down upon judged

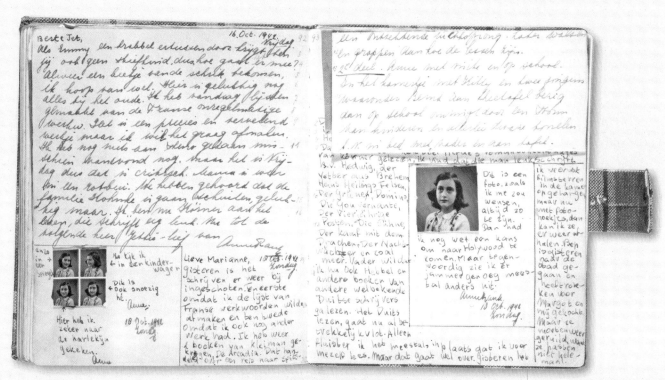

Otto Frank obtained his daughter Anne's diary after the Holocaust and had it published in 1947.

STUDENT DIARY ENTRY 37:

Dear Diary,

I'm beginning to realize that Anne Frank, Zlata Filipović, and I have a lot in common. We all seem to be trapped in some sort of a cage. Anne's cage was the secret **annex** she and her family hid in, and the attic where she spent most of her time. Zlata's cage was the basement she had to use for shelter, away from bombs. My cage is my own house.

Like Anne and Zlata, I have an enemy who is **gung-ho for dictatorship**: my father. He doesn't truly fit the role of a father in my perspective. James doesn't allow us to call him "dad" or "father" or any of those other sentimental, lovey-dovey names. He says the titles aren't his name so we can't call him that.

8 Relate Ideas
How does this diary entry show that Anne and Zlata's experiences are meaningful to the writer?

Monitor Comprehension

Explain
Do Ms. Gruwell's students relate to what they are reading? Give examples to support your answer.

In Other Words
annex addition to a building
gung-ho for dictatorship enthusiastic about giving orders and controlling other people

Unfortunately, I can't relate with Anne Frank and Zlata Filipović on the subject of their fathers. From what I've read, their fathers seemed to really love them. I can, however, **commiserate** with them on the situations they were forced to endure. For example, I can easily put James in Hitler's shoes, and our family in the roles of the Jews. Although not quite like the war Hitler started, the war in my house was also created by ignorance and stupidity. Like all wars, there is an enemy. There are innocent victims, destruction, senseless violence, displacement, and a winner and a loser. **9**

I've read about the monstrous things that were done in the concentration camps in World War II. I've read about how they would torture, starve, and mutilate people's bodies to something that was not recognizable as a human being. I watched my mother being beaten half to death by James and watched as blood and tears streamed down her face, which was also unrecognizable. I felt useless and scared, furious at the same time knowing that I could do nothing to help her. . . .

I can relate to Anne and Zlata. Like them, I have a diary. I write about how it feels to have disgust and hatred centered directly on you because of who you are. All I can do is wait for my mother to get rid of him. I'm surprised she hasn't already. She can be a strong woman if she **puts her mind to it**. I know that I will never let a man put his hands on me, won't ever tolerate that kind of abuse from anyone. I guess I'll have to wait for the war to end like Anne and Zlata did, except I won't die or get taken advantage of. I'm going to be strong. **10**

> I felt useless and scared, furious at the same time knowing that I could do nothing to help her. . . .

9 Relate Ideas
What part of Anne and Zlata's experiences can't this student relate to? Why?

10 Determine What's Important
For this student, what is important about keeping a diary? What was important about the experience? Write about it in your **Reading Journal**.

Key Vocabulary
commiserate *v.*, to share someone's unhappiness

In Other Words
puts her mind to it decides that she wants to

STUDENT DIARY ENTRY 38:

Dear Diary,

We've been talking about the war in Bosnia and how similar some of the events are to the Holocaust. We have been reading about a young girl named Zlata, who many call the modern-day Anne Frank. Zlata and I seem to have a lot in common because while Zlata was living through a war in Sarajevo, I was living through a different kind of war—the L.A. riots. Ironically, Zlata and I were both eleven years old when our city was under siege. I can understand how afraid and scared she was to see her city go up in flames, because my city was on fire, too.

The problem in Sarajevo began when a sniper fired a gun into a crowd at a peace rally. People panicked and war broke out. In L.A., several policemen beat on a man named Rodney King and had to go to trial. The "not guilty" verdict caused people to go crazy. People started looting and fighting.

Zlata and I both had to hide for our safety. This made us very frightened. Zlata was trapped in her basement while she heard bombs going off and people screaming. I was trapped inside my church while people were shooting, breaking windows, and screaming for their lives.

Zlata and I lost our childhood innocence because we were denied the right to do childlike things, like go to school, talk on the phone, and just play outside. The buildings were burning and people got beaten up just because of the color of their skin, their religion, or **ethnicity**. Unfortunately, we both had to suffer because of other people's ignorance and destruction.

Finally, the United Nations walked the streets of Bosnia trying to keep the peace. After days of chaos, the National Guard became the peacekeepers in L.A. Even though the United Nations and the National Guard were very successful at stopping the violence, the intolerance is still there.

I can't believe that someone I don't even know, who lives thousands of miles away, could have so much in common with me.

11 Relate ideas/
Determine What's
Important
What about Zlata's
story is most
important to this
student? Write
about it in your
Reading Journal.

Monitor Comprehension

Compare
Do the students who
wrote diary entries
37 and 38 find the
same things to be
important? Give
examples.

Key Vocabulary
● **ethnicity** *n.*, racial background

Historical Background
Adolf Hitler (1889–1945) was the leader of the Nazi Party and the head of Germany from 1933 to 1945. His anti-Jewish feelings led to the tragic events of the Holocaust.

STUDENT DIARY ENTRY 41:

Dear Diary,

   When we began our lesson about the importance of racial tolerance, I had no idea that that lesson would be a life-altering experience. After reading *Night* and *Anne Frank: The Diary of a Young Girl*, I guess you could say I knew about the Holocaust, but I was not prepared for what I was going to be faced with today.

12 Determine What's Important Do you think it is important to include one of Zlata's diary entries in this selection? Why or why not?

from Zlata's Diary **12**

Sunday, May 2, 1993

Dear Mimmy,

   Do you remember May 2, 1992, the worst day in this misery of a life? I often say that maybe it wasn't the most awful day, but it was the first of the most awful days, and so I think of it as the worst. I'll never forget the stench of the cellar, the hunger, the shattering of glass, the horrible shelling. We went for twelve hours without food or water, but the worst thing was the fear, huddling in the corner of the cellar, and the uncertainty of what was going to happen. Not understanding what was happening. It gives me the shivers just to think about it.

   It's been a year since then, a year in which every day has been May 2. But here I am still alive and healthy, my family is alive and well, sometimes we have electricity, water, and gas, and we get the odd scrap of food. KEEP GOING. But for how long, does anyone really know?

   Zlata

Ms. Gruwell had been talking for a long time about bringing in a Holocaust survivor named Gerda Seifer. Well today, we actually met her. Like Anne, she is Jewish and was born in Poland and she didn't meet Hitler's standards of purity either. During World War II, Gerda's parents made her go into hiding with a Catholic family. She was forced to live in a basement where she could barely stand up. She could hear the SS soldiers marching outside, waiting for their next victim. She is the only survivor in her family. Luckily, she was spared from a camp.

Just as Anne was trapped, Gerda was trapped. Neither Gerda nor Anne could lead normal teenage lives. They lost their innocence due to uncontrollable circumstances. Whenever they ventured outdoors they faced the possibility of being captured by the Gestapo. Jewish people had to wear a yellow Star of David, which distinguished them from others. They were forced to attend special schools isolated from other children. They were ridiculed and tormented throughout the war.

Unfortunately, I know exactly what it feels like to not be able to go outside, not because of the Gestapo, but because of gangs. When I walk outside, I constantly glance from side to side watching those standing around me. Since I feel out of place, I often put on a facade so that I fit in. Maybe if I look and act like I belong they will not confront me. It is disrespectful to look a gang member in the eye. Imagine what would happen if a prisoner in a concentration camp insulted a Gestapo—they would get killed instantly. After the stories I'd heard from Gerda, I can guarantee that I won't repeat the mistakes of others.

It amazed me how I could **empathize** not only with Anne Frank, but also with a Holocaust survivor. I'm glad I had the opportunity to hear about the past through Gerda. She is living proof of history. This experience will help me pass on the message of tolerance that Anne died for and that Gerda survived for. 🔢

13 Determine What's Important
What do you think is the most important part of this diary entry?

Monitor Comprehension

Paraphrase
In your own words, describe how this student relates to Anne Frank and Gerda Seifer.

Key Vocabulary
empathize *v.*, to understand someone's feelings

Historical Background
SS soldiers were members of the Nazi military. The SS included the **Gestapo,** or Hitler's secret police.

STUDENT DIARY ENTRY 75:

Dear Diary,

I feel like I finally have a purpose in this class and in life.

That purpose is to make a difference and **stand up for a cause**.

Ms. G showed us a video during Black History Month about a group of Civil Rights activists in the 1960s who were inspired by Rosa Parks. They decided to challenge **segregation** in the South. Rather than boycott buses, they took their challenge a step farther. They **integrated** their bus and traveled from Washington, D.C., through the deep South. **14**

There were seven whites and six blacks on the bus, most of them college students. They were called the Freedom Riders, and their goal was to change segregated interstate travel, along with everyone's life, forever. The Freedom Riders had faith that what they were doing was right, and they wanted the world to know that change was necessary and that being tolerant of each other is good. . . .

Even though they didn't expect a warm welcome, no one was to be seen at the station, not even the attendants. All of a sudden, Ku Klux Klan members were everywhere. Hundreds of them surrounded the bus, some carried bats or metal poles, and others held vicious German shepherds, growling and ready to attack these unarmed people. The mob was just waiting to get their hands on the riders. The Freedom Riders were **barricaded** on the bus. . . .

By choice, the seating arrangement on the bus was integrated: Blacks sat by whites, and vice versa. They were breaking a law that had been established in the South. This was unheard of! Jim Zwerg, a white man, stood up from the back of the bus. He wanted to be the first person to step off, even though he knew at the other side of the door was **a mob of bigots drooling for a victim**.

14 Relate Ideas
How does this student feel after seeing the video? How can you tell?

Key Vocabulary

segregation *n.*, separation of people by race
- **integrate** *v.*, to support the mixing of people of all races

In Other Words

stand up for a cause work to support something you believe in
barricaded trapped
a mob of bigots drooling for a victim a group of racist people waiting to attack someone

What was he thinking? He felt this was his chance to fight back, nonviolently, and show his feelings to others. These strong feelings put his life at risk. Jim took that first step off of the bus, and the mob pulled him into their grasp. It was as if he had been swallowed up and disappeared, like bees on honey. Jim was almost beaten to death. He suffered a cracked skull from being hit with an iron pipe, a broken leg, and many cuts and bruises. During the moments the mob was beating on him, the other Freedom Riders got a chance to run for shelter.

15 **Text Features**
Why do you think it is important to include some information on the Freedom Riders in this selection?

Who Were the Original Freedom Riders? **15**

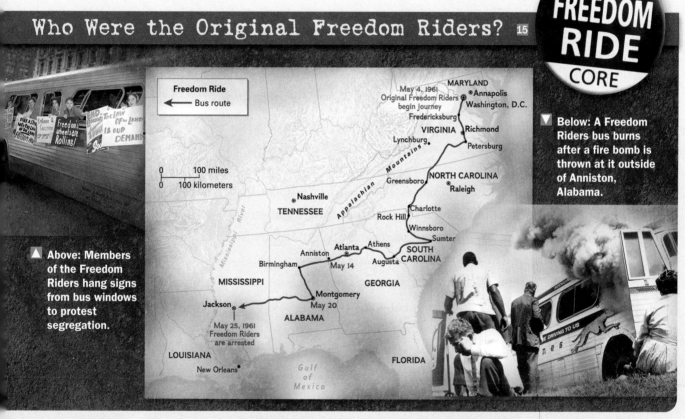

Freedom Ride
← Bus route

0 ——— 100 miles
0 ——— 100 kilometers

MARYLAND
May 4, 1961
Original Freedom Riders ⊕ Annapolis
begin journey   Washington, D.C.
Fredericksburg
VIRGINIA   Richmond
Lynchburg,   Petersburg

NORTH CAROLINA
Greensboro   Raleigh

Nashville
TENNESSEE

Charlotte
Rock Hill   Winnsboro
Sumter

Atlanta   Athens
Anniston   SOUTH
Birmingham   May 14   Augusta   CAROLINA

MISSISSIPPI   GEORGIA

Jackson   Montgomery
May 20
May 25, 1961   ALABAMA
Freedom Riders
are arrested

LOUISIANA   FLORIDA
New Orleans   Gulf of Mexico

FREEDOM RIDE CORE

▼ Below: A Freedom Riders bus burns after a fire bomb is thrown at it outside of Anniston, Alabama.

▲ Above: Members of the Freedom Riders hang signs from bus windows to protest segregation.

🔺 Understand the Map Approximately how many miles did the original Freedom Riders travel from start to finish? How long did their journey take?

Monitor Comprehension

Describe
What kind of person is Jim Zwerg? Give two examples from the text to support your description.

I was impressed that Jim made a choice to be on that bus when he didn't have to. After all, he was white and could sit wherever he wanted and risked everything when he didn't have to. He wanted to fight for others who didn't have the same privileges or rights as he did. . . . People gave those riders a chance to get off the bus, and they didn't, and I'm going to face intolerance head-on as well. **16**

16 Relate Ideas
What fact about Jim is most important to this student?

The way I feel about segregation in school is the way Jim must have felt about segregation in the sixties. I want people to interact with different cultures and races. I don't want segregation like you see in class or in the school quad. The way Jim must have felt when he stepped off the bus is probably the same way I felt those first couple of days in the class. I remember feeling scared, like a wimp.

> He wanted to fight for others who didn't have the same privileges or rights as he did. . . .

I was the only white student in the class. I felt helpless. But after I stayed in the class and **toughed it out**, a lot more white students transferred in, just like more people joined the Freedom Rider movement after Jim's first step.

At the end of the video, a fellow classmate asked the question, "They fought racism by riding the bus?" That was it! The bells were ringing, the sirens were sounding. It hit me! The Freedom Riders fought intolerance by riding a bus and pushing racial limits in the deep South. Then somebody suggested that we name ourselves the Freedom Writers, in honor of the Freedom Riders. Why not? It's perfect! But **those are huge shoes to fill**, so if we're going to take their name, we better take their courage and conviction. It's one thing to ride a bus, but they eventually had to get off and **face the music**. **17**

17 Relate Ideas
Why do you think the student wrote this paragraph?

In Other Words
toughed it out lived through a difficult time with courage
those are huge shoes to fill it's a big responsibility
face the music deal with a difficult situation

So, it's one thing for us to write diaries like Anne and Zlata, but if we want to be like the Freedom Riders, we need to take that extra step. Just like Anne's story made it out of the attic and Zlata's out of the basement, I hope our stories make it out of Room 203. Now when I write, I'll remember Jim's work and what he risked his life for. Like him, I am willing to step forward, unafraid of who or what lies ahead. After all, history tells me that I am not alone. **18**

18 Determine What's Important
What important piece of self-knowledge can you tell this student gained? How do you know this?

The Freedom Writers won several awards, including the Spirit of Anne Frank Award, for their efforts to promote tolerance.

All 150 Freedom Writers graduated from high school and went on to attend college. Erin Gruwell is now president of the Freedom Writers Foundation, a nonprofit organization that provides scholarships for students in need and promotes inclusiveness in education. She and The Freedom Writers regularly talk to audiences nationwide about the importance of tolerance and to share their belief that "voices can be heard, change is possible, and . . . words have the power to affect people throughout the world." **19** ❖

19 Text Features
In what way does the Epilogue tie together the students' diary-writing experiences?

ANALYZE The Freedom Writers Diary

1. **Explain** Why did the students decide to call themselves The Freedom Writers? Be sure to cite evidence from the text

2. **Vocabulary** How might learning to **empathize** require people to challenge expectations of themselves and others?

3. **Relate ideas** Think of three experiences that student writers shared in "The Freedom Writers Diary." For each one, tell what personal feelings the writer shared along with the facts.

4. **Focus Strategy Determine What's Important** Talk with a partner about the strategies you used to decide which ideas in "The Freedom Writers Diary" are important. Then compare **Reading Journals**. Tell why you chose the ideas you did.

🔄 Return to the Text
Reread and Write On page 196 a student asks, "Why should I read books about people who don't look like me?" How would you answer that question? Reread the selection to get examples, and explain your ideas in a paragraph.

Dreams

by Langston Hughes

Hold fast to dreams
For if dreams die
Life is a broken-winged bird
That cannot fly.

5   Hold fast to dreams
For when dreams go
Life is a barren field
Frozen with snow.

About the Poet

Langston Hughes (1902–1967) is one of the most important writers of the Harlem Renaissance, a movement in the 1920s that celebrated African American culture. A big fan of jazz music, Hughes incorporated elements of it into his writing.

BEFORE READING Strength, Courage, and Wisdom

song lyrics by India Arie

Reading Strategies

- Plan and Monitor
- ▶ **Determine Importance**
- Make Inferences
- Ask Questions
- Make Connections
- Synthesize
- Visualize

Analyze Style: Word Choice

Song lyrics are words set to music and sung. Song lyrics often have the same elements as poems. Here are some examples:

- **word choices** decisions about which words best fit the singer's ideas and the structure of the writing
- **repetition** repeated words *say the same thing over again*
- **rhyme** repeated sounds *words the sound alike*
- **stanza** a group of lines that form a unit (In a song, a stanza is called a **verse.**) *a group of line paragraph.*
- **chorus** a repeated stanza or verse *a repeated stanza.*

Look Into the Text

Many songs use rhyme.

> Behind my pride there lives a me that knows humility.
> Inside my voice there is a soul, and in my soul, there is a voice.
> But I've been too afraid to make a choice.
> Cause I'm scared of the things that I might be missing,
> Running too fast to stop and listen.
>
> *Chorus*
> Strength, courage, and wisdom.
> It's been inside of me all along.
> Strength, courage, and wisdom
> Inside of me.

Sometimes lines in a chorus are **repeated**.

Some word choices are made for **rhyme** and to give the song a certain rhythm. Others set the tone of the song—that is, they express the singer's attitude.

Focus Strategy ▶ Determine Importance

Songwriters emphasize important ideas through word choice and often through repetition and rhyme. When you read song lyrics, think about the words and phrases and the important ideas that they are meant to express.

HOW TO DETERMINE WHAT'S IMPORTANT

Focus Strategy

1. **Reread** the song lyrics above.

2. **Choose** a part of the song that catches your attention. Think about the lyrics.

3. **Write** the idea that the lyrics express in a **Reading Journal**.

Reading Journal

Song Lyric	The Idea
• Strength, courage, and wisdom (twice in the Chorus)	• The repetition of these positive words suggests that the singer feels a sense of power in her life.

Connect Across Texts

The students in "The Freedom Writers Diary" learned to **empathize** with people who stood up for human rights. In this song, the singer realizes that she needs to stand up for her convictions.

Strength, Courage, and Wisdom

by India Arie

Verse 1

Inside my head there lives a dream that I want to see in the sun.
Behind my eyes there lives a me that I've been hiding for much too long.
'Cause I've been too afraid to let it show
'Cause I'm scared of the judgment that may follow,
Always putting off my living for tomorrow. **1**

Pre-Chorus

It's time to step out on faith. I've gotta show my faith.
It's been elusive for so long, but freedom is mine today.
I've gotta step out on faith. It's time to show my faith.
Procrastination had me down, but look what I have found.
I found

Chorus

Strength, courage, and wisdom.
It's been inside of me all along.
Strength, courage, and wisdom
Inside of me. **2**

Verse 2

Behind my pride there lives a me that knows humility.
Inside my voice there is a soul, and in my soul, there is a voice.
But I've been too afraid to make a choice.
'Cause I'm scared of the things that I might be missing,
Running too fast to stop and listen.

1 Word Choice
How would you describe the tone, or singer's attitude, in this verse? What word choices make you think so?

2 Determine What's Important
Think about the lyrics in the Chorus. What important idea do they express?

India Arie performs at a festival in Colorado.

In Other Words
It's been elusive It's been hard to find

[Repeat Pre-Chorus]

[Repeat Chorus]

Bridge
I close my eyes and I think of all the things that I want to see.
'Cause I know now that I've opened up my heart
I know that anything I want can be.
So let it be. So let it be.
So let it be. So let it be. **3**

Strength, courage, and wisdom.
It's been inside of me all along.
Strength, courage, and wisdom.
It's been inside of me all along.
Strength, courage, and wisdom
Inside of me. **4**

3 Word Choice
What does the singer mean by "So let it be"? Why does she repeat that statement?

4 Determine What's Important
What has the singer learned about herself? How do you know this?

ANALYZE Strength, Courage, and Wisdom

1. **Explain** How does the singer challenge her own expectations about strength, courage, and wisdom? Where does the speaker find strength, courage, and wisdom? Why does it take her so long to find these things? Be sure to cite evidence from the text.

2. **Vocabulary** What **perception** of herself does India Arie describe in her song?

3. **Analyze Style: Word Choice** What does Arie mean when she sings, "I've opened up my heart"? Why do you think she chose those words to express her thoughts?

4. **Focus Strategy Determine What's Important** Discuss with a partner the details or lines that most powerfully express what the song is about. Explain how you determined this.

Return to the Text
Reread and Write Reread your favorite lines from the song. Write a diary entry telling why you think they are meaningful to listeners.

About the Songwriter
India Arie (1975–) is a singer and songwriter whose work often deals with issues of self-acceptance and empowerment. Her albums *Acoustic Soul* (2001) and *Voyage to India* (2002) have sold more than six million copies and have received eleven Grammy nominations.

EQ How Do People Challenge Expectations?

Reading
Critical Thinking

1. **Analyze** Reread the **Quickwrite** you wrote for the Prepare to Read activity on page 188. How do you think The Freedom Writers or India Arie would respond to the same statements? Explain.

2. **Interpret** In "The Freedom Writers Diary," a student says, "We all seem to be trapped in some sort of cage." What does this student mean? Give examples from both texts to support your answer.

EQ 3. **Compare** What do you think is the most important lesson that The Freedom Writers learned about challenging expectations? Is that lesson similar to or different from the ideas in "Strength, Courage, and Wisdom"? Explain.

4. **Speculate** People often make resolutions, or promises to themselves, about what they will do in the future. Do you think The Freedom Writers will stick to their resolutions? What about the singer in "Strength, Courage, and Wisdom"? Explain.

EQ 5. **Draw Conclusions** The selections in this unit focus on people who have overcome obstacles and challenged expectations. Do you think this is possible for everyone? Support your answer with examples from the texts you just read.

Writing
Write About Literature

Advice Letter It is Ms. Gruwell's first day as an English teacher. How do you think she feels? What advice from "Strength, Courage, and Wisdom" would you give to her? Go back to both texts to get ideas and write a short letter to her.

Vocabulary
Key Vocabulary Review

Oral Review Work with a partner. Use these words to complete the paragraph.

alienation	ethnicity	segregation
commiserate	integrate	tolerance
empathize	perception	

Today I saw a movie about __(1)__, or respect for different beliefs and ways of life. Before I saw the movie, my __(2)__ was that in the U.S. a student's race or __(3)__ has never mattered. From the movie, I learned that U.S. schools once practiced __(4)__ and separated African American students from white students. The movie had an interview with one of the first African American students to attend and __(5)__ an all-white school. She said she was scared when a crowd of angry white parents shouted at her. I could __(6)__ and feel her fear. It took her a long time to overcome her feelings of __(7)__. I felt the pain behind her words. I can __(8)__ with anyone who is alone and scared.

Writing Application In your opinion, how important is **tolerance** for other people? State your ideas in a paragraph. Use at least three Key Vocabulary words.

Fluency
Read with Ease: Intonation

Assess your reading fluency with the passage in the Reading Handbook, p. 804. Then complete the self-check below.

1. My intonation did/did not sound natural.

2. My words correct per minute: _____.

Grammar

Use Verbs to Talk About the Present

The verb **have** has two forms in the **present**.

> I **have** courage. You **have** courage, too.
> He **has** strength. She **has** wisdom.

The verb **be** has three forms in the **present**.

> I **am** brave. She **is** brave, too. We **are** both brave.

Use **am**, **is**, or **are**, plus a **main verb** that ends with **-ing** to tell about something that is in the process of happening.

> I **am** **reading** a diary about the war.
> My friend **is** **reading** a diary, too.
> The diaries **are** **giving** us a new viewpoint.

Oral Practice (1–5) With a partner, say five sentences in the present about "The Freedom Writers Diary." Choose from each column. You can use words more than once.

Example: Ms. Gruwell is teaching the class.

Ms. Gruwell	have	diary entries.
The students	has	the class.
I	is teaching	tolerant.
They	are writing	courage.
We	am	hope.

Written Practice (6–10) Rewrite the journal entry below. Fix the verbs. Add two more sentences using present tense.

> In our class, one student be complaining a lot. So our teacher are having us keep journals. We is writing something every day.

Language Development

Elaborate in a Description

Group Share Name a person in "The Freedom Writers Diary" and describe something about him or her. Have your group elaborate on your description by telling more about this person's life, problems, or opinions.

Literary Analysis

Analyze Point of View

The entries in "The Freedom Writers Diary" are written in the **first-person point of view**. In this point of view, a person or character uses pronouns like *I*, *my*, and *me* to describe what he or she did, thought, or felt.

Ms. Gruwell uses the first person in her diary:

> Tomorrow morning, <u>my</u> journey as an English teacher officially begins. <u>I</u> wonder what <u>my</u> students will think of <u>me</u>?

In the **third-person point of view**, a person or character uses pronouns like *she*, *he*, and *they* to describe what someone else did or thought. Here is Ms. Gruwell's entry rewritten in the third person:

> Tomorrow morning, <u>her</u> journey as an English teacher officially begins. <u>She</u> wonders what <u>her</u> students will think of <u>her</u>.

Which point of view sounds more personal? Why? How does first-person point of view make the writing seem more credible, or believable?

Now, choose one of the student diary entries from "The Freedom Writers Diary" and rewrite it in the third person.

Context Clues: Examples

To figure out the meaning of an unfamiliar word, look for clues in nearby words and sentences. One helpful kind of context clue is an example. Look for these words that signal an example: *like*, *such as*, *for example*, *include*, and *including*.

Define the underlined word in each sentence by using context clues.

1. The store sells kitchen gadgets, such as bottle openers, measuring cups, and bowls.
2. The museum has many Native American artifacts, such as arrowheads, beads, and clay pots.
3. Ruminants include cows, sheep, goats, deer, and other hooved animals that digest their food in two steps.
4. Conifers, such as spruce, pine, and fir, grow here.

Panel Discussion

Social Studies: Tolerance With a group, present a panel discussion on the topic of **tolerance** .

1. **Choose Roles** Select a moderator. A moderator defines the topic, explains why it is important, and asks each panel member a question.

2. **Plan** Together, discuss why it is important to talk about tolerance in school. Write down your ideas. Then write a question or two about tolerance that you think your audience would like to know about.

3. **Present the Discussion** Use your class as your audience. The moderator begins the discussion by defining the topic and its importance. He or she then asks the questions, and each group member answers at least once.

📖 **Language and Learning Handbook,** p. 750

Write an Explanation

A test may ask you to explain your ideas about a topic. The prompt often states the topic and asks you to respond to it.

1. **Unpack the Prompt** Read the prompt and underline the key words.

> **Writing Prompt**
> Whom do you admire the most? The person could be someone you know or someone famous who you wish to be like. Write an essay telling why you admire the person.

2. **Plan Your Response** Answer the question that the prompt asks: Whom do you admire the most? Once you decide, brainstorm the reasons.

3. **Draft** When you are explaining something, organize your essay. Add at least three reasons from your brainstorming list.

The person I admire the most is [insert the name of the person]. There are several reasons I admire this person. First of all, this person [tell the most important reason you admire him/her]. Secondly, [tell the second most important reason]. Furthermore, [give one more reason].

In conclusion, [summarize why this person is so important to you and the reasons why you admire him/her].

4. **Check Your Work** Reread your essay. Ask:
   - Does my essay address the writing prompt?
   - Do I give examples to support my ideas?
   - Are all present tense verbs formed correctly?

📖 **Writing Handbook,** p. 832

from The Cruelest Journey

by Kira Salak

1   In the beginning, my journeys feel at best **ludicrous**, at worst insane. This one is no exception. The idea is to paddle nearly 600 miles on the Niger River in a kayak, alone, from the Malian town of Old Ségou to Timbuktu. And now, at the very hour when I have decided to leave, a thunderstorm bursts open the skies, sending down **apocalyptic** rain, washing away the very ground beneath my feet. It is the rainy season in Mali, for which there can be no comparison in the world. Lightning pierces trees, slices across houses. Thunder racks the skies and pounds the earth like **mortar fire**, and every living thing huddles in **tenuous** shelter, expecting the world to end. Which it doesn't. At least not this time. So that we all give a collective sigh to the salvation of the passing storm as it rumbles its way east, and I **survey** the river I'm to leave on this morning. Rain or no rain, today is the day for the journey to begin. And no one, not even the oldest in the village, can say for certain whether I'll get to the end.

2   "Let's do it," I say, leaving the shelter of an **adobe** hut. My guide from town, Modibo, points to the north, to further storms. He says he will pray

Remi Benali, 2003.

Kira Salak paddles down the Niger River.

In Other Words

ludicrous foolish
apocalyptic powerful and intense
mortar fire bombs
tenuous fragile, weak
survey look over, study
adobe clay

Geographical Background

Timbuktu is in the African country of Mali. From 1400 to 1600, it was a key trading post and center of learning. The Niger River flows south of Timbuktu.

Timbuktu, MALI
Niger River
AFRICA

for me. It's the best he can do. To his knowledge, no man has ever completed such a trip, though a few have tried. And certainly no woman has done such a thing. This morning he took me aside and told me he thinks I'm crazy, which I understood as concern and thanked him. He told me that the people of Old Ségou think I'm crazy too, and that only uncanny good luck will keep me safe.

3   Still, when a person tells me I can't do something, I'll want to do it all the more. It may be a failing of mine. I carry my inflatable kayak through the narrow passageways of Old Ségou, past the small adobe huts melting in the rains,

> **This morning he took me aside and told me he thinks I'm crazy...**

past the huddling goats and smoke of cooking fires, people peering out at me from the dark entranceways. It is a **labyrinth** of ancient homes, built and rebuilt after each storm, plastered with the very earth people walk upon. Old Ségou must look much the same as it did in Scottish explorer Mungo Park's time when, exactly 206 years ago to the day, he left on the first of his two river journeys down the Niger to Timbuktu, the first such trip by a Westerner. It is no coincidence that I've planned to leave on the same day and from the same spot. Park is my benefactor of sorts, my guarantee. If he could travel down the Niger, then so can I. And it is all the guarantee I have for this trip—that an obsessed nineteenth-century adventurer did what I would like to do. Of course Park also died on this river, but I've so far managed to overlook that.

4   Hobbled donkeys cower under a new onslaught of rain, ears back, necks craned. Little naked children dare each other to touch me, and I make it easy for them, stopping and holding out my arm. They stroke my white skin as if it were velvet, using only the pads of their fingers, then stare at their hands for wet paint.

5   Thunder again. More rain falls. I stop on the shore, near a centuries-old kapok tree under which I imagine Park once took shade. I open my bag, spread out my little red kayak, and start to pump it up. A couple of women nearby, with colorful cloth wraps called *pagnes* tied tightly about their breasts, gaze at me cryptically, as if to ask: *Who are you and what do you think you're doing?* The Niger churns and slaps the shore, in a **surly** mood. I don't pretend to know what I'm doing. Just one thing at a time now, kayak inflated, kayak loaded with my gear. Paddles fitted together and ready. Modibo is standing on the shore, watching me.

In Other Words
labyrinth maze, network
surly annoyed, unfriendly

6   "I'll pray for you," he reminds me.

7   I balance my gear, adjust the straps, get in. And, finally, **irrevocably**, I paddle away.

> ## Already, I fear the irrationality of my journey...

8   When Mungo Park left on his second trip, he never admitted that he was scared. It is what fascinates me about his writing—his insistence on maintaining an illusion that all was well, even as he began a journey that he knew from previous experience could only beget tragedy. Hostile peoples, unknown rapids, malarial fevers. Hippos and crocodiles. The giant Lake Debo to cross, like being set adrift on an inland sea, no sight of land, no way of knowing where the river starts again. Forty of his forty-four men dead from sickness, Park himself afflicted with dysentery when he left on this ill-fated trip. And it can **boggle** the mind, what drives some people to risk their lives for the mute promises of success. It boggles my mind, at least, as I am caught up in the same affliction. Already, I fear the irrationality of my journey, the relentless stubbornness that drives me on.

9   The storm erupts in a new overture. Torrential rains. Waves higher than my kayak, trying to **capsize** me. But my boat is self-bailing and I stay afloat. The wind drives the current in reverse, tearing and ripping at the shores, sending spray into my face. I paddle madly, crashing and driving forward. I travel inch by inch, or so it seems, arm muscles smarting and rebelling against this journey.

10   A popping feeling now and a screech of pain. My right arm lurches from a ripped muscle. But this is no time and place for such an injury, and I won't tolerate it, stuck as I am in a storm. I try to get used to the **metronome-like** pulses of pain as I fight the river. There is only one direction to go: forward.

11   I wonder what we look for when we embark on these kinds of trips. There is the pat answer that you tell the people you don't know: that you're interested in seeing a place, learning about its people. But then the trip begins and the hardship comes, and hardship is more honest: it tells us that we don't have enough patience yet, nor humility, nor gratitude. And we thought that we had. Hardship brings us closer to truth, and thus is more difficult to bear, but from it alone comes **compassion**. And I've told the

In Other Words
irrevocably permanently
boggle confuse, puzzle
capsize overturn
metronome-like regular
compassion concern for others

world that it can do what it wants with me if only, by the end, I have learned something more. A **bargain**, then. The journey, my teacher.

12   And where is the river of just this morning, with its whitecaps that would have liked to drown me, with its current flowing backward against the wind? Gone to this: a river of smoothest glass, a placidity unbroken by wave or eddy, with islands of lush greenery awaiting me like distant **Xanadus**.

13   I barely travel at one mile an hour, the river preferring—as I do—to loiter in the sun. I lean down in my seat and hang my feet over the sides of the kayak. I eat turkey jerky and wrap up my injured arm, part of which has swollen to the size of a grapefruit. I'm not worried about the injury anymore. I'm not worried about anything. I know this feeling won't last, but for now I wrap myself in it, feeling the rare peace. To reach a place of not worrying is a greater freedom than anything I could hope to find on one of these trips. It is my true Undiscovered Country.

14   The Somono fishermen, casting out their nets, puzzle over me as I float by.

15   "*Ça va, madame?*" they yell.

16   Each fisherman carries a young son perched in the back of his pointed canoe to do the paddling. The boys stare at me, transfixed; they have never seen such a thing. A white woman. Alone. In a red, inflatable boat. Using a two-sided paddle.

17   I'm an even greater novelty because Malian women don't paddle here, not ever. It is a man's job. So there is no good explanation for me, and the people want to understand. They want to see if I'm strong enough for it, or if I even know how to use a paddle. They want to determine how sturdy my boat is. They gather on the shore in front of their villages to watch me pass, the kids screaming and jumping in excitement, the women with hands to foreheads to shield the sun as they stare, men yelling out questions in Bambarra which by now I know to mean: "Where did you come from? Are you alone? Where's your husband?" And of course they will always ask: "Where are you going?"

18   "Timbuktu!" I yell out to the last question.

19   "*Tombouctou!?!*" they always repeat, just to be sure.

20   "*Awo*," I say in the Bambarra I've learned. "Yes." ❖

Remi Benali, 2003.

In Other Words
bargain agreement, deal
Xanadus grand, luxurious places
Ça va, madame? Is everything OK, ma'am?
 (in French)

AGAINST THE ODDS

EQ ESSENTIAL QUESTION:
How Do People Challenge Expectations?

myNGconnect.com
🔊 Download the rubric.

EDGE LIBRARY

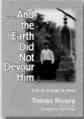

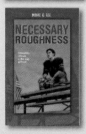

Present Your Project: Press Conference

It's time to hold your press conference about the Essential Question for this unit.

1 Review and Complete Your Plan

Consider these points as you complete your project:

- How will your press conference address the Essential Question?
- Which famous person will answer questions at the press conference?
- What questions should the reporters ask the person?

Work together to prepare the questions that will be asked and to plan the answers that will be given.

2 Hold the Press Conference

Follow the plan you made to hold the press conference in class. Consider taking additional questions from students outside your own group.

3 Evaluate the Press Conference

Use a rubric to evaluate each of the press conferences, including your own.

Reflect on Your Reading

Many of the people in this unit challenged expectations.

Think back on your reading of the unit selections, including your choice of Edge Library books. Then, discuss the following with a partner or in a small group.

Genre Focus Compare and contrast the elements of a short story with the features of a memoir. Give examples, using the selections in this unit.

Focus Strategy Choose one of the selections in the unit and summarize it for a partner. Ask the partner to evaluate whether you covered the most important details.

EQ Respond to the Essential Question

Throughout this unit, you have been thinking about how people challenge expectations. Discuss the Essential Question with a group. What have *you* decided? Support your response with evidence from your reading, discussions, research, and writing.

Write an Autobiographical Narrative

Writing Portfolio

Writing Mode
Narrative

Writing Trait Focus
Voice and Style

We all face challenges. The challenge may come from within, or we may confront obstacles in the world. For this project, you will write an autobiographical narrative about overcoming an obstacle.

Study Autobiographical Narratives

Autobiographical narratives are stories about events in your own life. Whenever you describe something that happened to you, such as overcoming a problem or challenge, you are telling an autobiographical narrative.

❶ Connect Writing to Your Life

You probably tell autobiographical narratives often. You might tell classmates what you did over the weekend. You might trade stories with your family about your day. This project builds on your personal storytelling skills.

❷ Understand the Form

Remember that you are not writing just for yourself. Because other people will read your narrative, be sure to adapt your voice to suit the expectations of your audience. For example, you would probably use a more informal voice if writing for elementary school students than you would if writing for a college admissions board.

Like all good stories, an autobiographical narrative has a beginning, a middle, and an end. When you write your narrative, be sure to:

Beginning
Start with an interesting background that identifies the obstacle, problem, or challenge that you face. In other words, establish the main point, or **controlling idea**, of your narrative.

Middle
Tell what happened in **chronological order**. Show how you responded to the challenge. Use lively dialogue and descriptive details to show how you felt and to re-create the experience for your readers. By bringing events to life, you give your audience insight into meeting challenges of their own.

End
Tell how your story turned out. Did you resolve the problem or not? What did you learn about yourself along the way? In writing the end of your narrative, consider what impression or idea you want to leave in the mind of your reader. The ending should also relate to your controlling idea.

Now look at these parts in action. Read an autobiographical narrative by a professional writer.

❸ Analyze a Professional Model

As you read, look for the three main parts of the story.

Facing Up to Stage Fright
by Martin Hakim

It's called "stage fright," and three years ago I discovered what it meant. I had strolled onto the stage all set for my audition. Only fifty teens a year get admitted to the Paul Robeson School of the Performing Arts, but I felt sure I'd be one of them. Yet, as I saw the teachers looking up at me with serious expressions, their pens poised over notepads like cobras ready to strike, I froze in panic and forgot how to perform.

I speak two languages, but in that moment I couldn't remember a syllable of either one. My throat tightened and my heart pounded.

"You may begin now, Martin," said Ms. Gupta, whose glasses perched on the end of her nose. I heard nervous laughter and turned red, realizing that it had come from me.

At first, the words came as slowly as ketchup dripping out of a bottle. Next, I mumbled a sentence. Suddenly, the words came pouring out in a rush, like crowds of busy people pushing their way out of a sports stadium. Finally, I bowed. It was over.

As I turned to leave, I saw looks of surprise, disappointment, and, worst of all, sympathy. That look—I'll never forget it!—really woke me up. No way was I walking out of there with people feeling sorry for me. Determined to show my best, I asked if I could do it over again.

"No problem," said Mr. McLean, as Ms. Gupta and the other teachers nodded agreement.

"Remember to breathe," added Ms. Gupta gently. *Remember to breathe.* That's what my teacher, Mrs. Rico, always said. Suddenly, Mrs. Rico's speaking tips came back to me. *Speak slowly and clearly. Use expression to show how your character feels. Vary the pitch and tone of your voice. And don't forget to breathe.*

So that's just what I did, and I even had fun up there. As I thanked the teachers, I felt new confidence. Not the kind that comes from winning, but something more lasting that comes from a willingness to try. I did not get admitted that summer, but I received a personal letter from Ms. Gupta praising my strengths, offering ideas for improvement, and encouraging me to try again next year. Did I? Yes, and I got in, too. But I will always remember—and be proud of—the day I overcame my fear.

The writer presents the **controlling idea**, or the kind of obstacle he faced.

The writer uses **sensory details** to show how it felt to face the challenge.

The writer tells what happened in **chronological order**.

Dialogue brings the scene to life.

What resulted when the writer faced the obstacle? Do you consider that failure or success?

▶ **Prompt** Write an autobiographical narrative about a challenge or obstacle you have faced. Be sure to:

- describe the obstacle and how you responded
- follow a sequence
- include dialogue and descriptive detail

✔ Prewrite

Now that you know the basics of autobiographical narratives, you are ready to plan one of your own. Making a Writing Plan will help you overcome "page fright," when you stare at a blank page and can't think of anything to say.

❶ Choose Your Topic

The following ideas will help you choose a topic:

- Consider a problem that you overcame. If you're proud of yourself for overcoming it, here is your chance to tell people about it.
- Pick an obstacle that you did not overcome. Here is your chance to explore your feelings about it. You can even explore ways to overcome it in the future.
- Brainstorm ideas with a friend or family member.

❷ Clarify the Audience, Controlling Idea, and Purpose

Decide on your audience. Who might be inspired by your narrative? Write down your ideas.

Then, think about the main point you want to get across about the personal challenge that you faced. What is your controlling idea? Jot it down.

Finally, think about your purpose, or reason, for writing. One purpose is to tell a story about yourself. What are some other purposes? Do you want to entertain your audience? Make them understand how you felt? Jot down your purpose.

❸ Gather Supporting Details

Next, gather details to elaborate on your effort to face a challenge. Relive the experience. Recall what happened and how you felt. Take notes.

Then, tell your story. Have your partner take notes and ask questions to:

- generate more details that are specific, important, and on target
- help you clarify your ideas
- fill in background information

> **Prewriting Tip**
>
> **Ask yourself these questions to find your controlling idea:**
>
> - Did I overcome my personal obstacle?
> - How did the challenge affect me?

❹ Organize the Details

Organize the details in chronological order, the order in which they happened. You might use a graphic organizer like a time line. Put the moment when you faced the personal obstacle in the middle. Then add events on the left and right in time order.

Technology Tip

You can find tools for making a time line and other graphic organizers on your computer by searching their names online.

Time Line

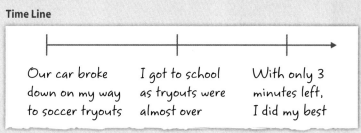

Our car broke down on my way to soccer tryouts

I got to school as tryouts were almost over

With only 3 minutes left, I did my best

❺ Finish Your Writing Plan

Use your prewriting ideas to make a Writing Plan like the student's plan below.

Writing Plan

Topic	travel delay as an obstacle
Audience	teacher, soccer coach, classmates
Controlling Idea	a good player never gives up
Purpose	to tell the story of meeting a challenge
Time Frame	start today; due on Friday

Beginning
1. Soccer is my life. I play it, watch it, read about it.
2. Soccer tryouts took place on my first day at a new school.
3. On the way to soccer tryouts, the family car broke down.
4. finally arrived; principal said tryouts were almost over

Middle
5. felt frustrated and wanted to give up
6. I ran to the sports field.
7. coach said there were 3 minutes left in the tryout game
8. I focused on the game, not the time.

End
9. I scored a goal.
10. I made the team.

Reflect on Your Writing Plan

▶ Do you have enough details for the beginning, the middle, and the end? Are you pleased with your topic and controlling idea? If not, now's the time to change them!

✔ Write a Draft

Now you are ready to write. Use your Writing Plan as a guide while you write your narrative. It's OK to make mistakes. You'll have chances to improve your draft.

❶ Keep Your Ideas Flowing

Sometimes writers get "stuck." They can't figure out what to say or how to say it. If you have trouble getting your ideas on paper, try these techniques:

- **Talk It Over** Tell someone what you want to say in your narrative. Together, explore ways to express it.

- **Change Your Plan** If your plan is not helping, change it. Brainstorm, list, and organize new details.

- **Skip Over the Hard Part** If you have trouble writing one part of your paper, skip to a part that is easier to write. It will then be easier to finish it.

- **Do a Focused Freewrite** Write continuously about your topic for about five minutes. During that time, do not stop writing. If you can't think of anything to say, then say that. Then, reread what you wrote. Underline ideas that you might be able to use in your paper. Study this example:

> It was an awful feeling. What am I going to say? <u>Fought back tears.</u> When the principal said I was too late, <u>I felt frustrated. Defeated.</u>

❷ Use Sensory Details and Images

How will you re-create the experience for your readers? Vivid description, including sensory details and images, helps "keep it real." Here's an example:

Without Description

> At first, I felt bad. Why run all the way out to the field for nothing? But a player never quits.

With Description

> At first, I felt frustrated and defeated. I clenched my fists at my sides, bit my lower lip, and fought back tears. Why run all the way out to the field just to humiliate myself? But a player never quits, not even in the final minutes of a game. I took a deep breath.

Technology Tip

Make your text double- or triple-spaced, or as your teacher directs. (Use the Paragraph feature from the Format menu to change line spacing.)

Print a copy of your draft to read later. The extra space between lines will give you room to mark changes.

Read this draft to see how the student used the Writing Plan to get ideas down on paper. As you will see, the student fixed the mistakes later.

Making the Goal

This is an autobiographical narrative and it is about a sport that is known as soccer. Soccer is my favorite sport. Soccer is my favorite thing in life. Mom and Dad got me a subscription to a magazine. It's all about you guessed it soccer. Therefore, it was a very difficult idea for me to believe when my dream of playing soccer in high school hit a big obstacle. On the way to tryouts the family car broke down.

It is necessary for me to explain that my family had just moved here from another city that perhaps some of you know. It was my first day at a new school. It was the only day of soccer tryouts. It was very early in the morning when we left. It was our plan to be at our new place before school began. If everything had gone perfectly, there would have been time for me to do what is required of us educationally, meet people, and even warm up before the tryouts.

"Oh, dear! I think your too late for tryouts," said principal Morgan, as I hastily signed in at the school office. She glanced up at the clock and shook her head. "Their almost finished, but you maybe check anyway."

"Sorry," I gasped, nearly out of breath. "Our car broke down. We waited too hours for a tow truck, and then another to for a rental car."

"I understand," said the principal picking up the telephone. "mrs. Kovad, will you escort Tina to the sports field to meet the teams?"

At first, I felt bad. Why run all the way out to the field for nothing? But a player never quits. Next, I decided to act as if it did not bother me. Finally, mrs. Kovad, whose the Assistant Principal, emerged from her office, and we hurried too the field.

"Are you Tina?" asked a sandy-haired man in a gruff voice. What a way to meet coach Turner! "We're almost done" he said. Then he grinned. "Think you show us you're soccer skills in just three minutes?"

I nodded—ran onto the field—found the Team Captain. By changing my nervous energy into enthusiasm, I kept my focus on the game, not the time. Suddenly, I kicked the ball into the net, scoring a goal. When the Team Captain and coach turner cheered in unison, I knew that I had made the team.

As I discovered that day, I love soccer so much that nothing not even time itself could stop me from achieving my goal!

Reflect on Your Draft

▶ Is your controlling idea clear? Do you have enough details, and are they in chronological order? Talk them over with a partner.

✔ Revise Your Draft

Your first draft is done. Now, polish it. Improve the voice and style, and your choice of supporting words and details. Make what was just OK into something much better.

❶ Revise for Voice and Style

A good autobiographical narrative has a **voice** that sounds real and gets readers involved in the story. Since your story is your own, the best voice for telling it is your own. Trying to sound different from the person you really are is usually a mistake. Be yourself.

Good writing also has **style**. That means that the words and sentences are appropriate to the purpose and the audience. The word choices are vivid and precise. As for the sentences, they don't all begin in the same way, have the same end punctuation, or run the same length. The writer varies the sentence length and structure, such as by using a longer sentence to discuss a complex idea, or a short sentence to emphasize a point.

TRY IT ▶ With a partner, evaluate the voice and style of the two drafts below. Which draft is more powerful and engaging? Explain.

Draft 1

This is an autobiographical narrative and it is about a sport that is known as soccer. Soccer is my favorite sport. Soccer is my favorite thing in life. Mom and Dad got me a subscription to a magazine. It's all about you guessed it soccer. Therefore, it was a very difficult idea for me to believe when my dream of playing soccer in high school hit a big obstacle.

Draft 2

Soccer is my life. I play soccer, go to soccer games, and watch soccer on television with Mom and Dad. They even got me a subscription to a magazine that's all about—you guessed it—soccer. So I couldn't believe it when my dream of playing soccer in high school hit a big obstacle.

Now use the rubric to evaluate the voice and style in your own draft. What score would you give your draft and why?

Voice and Style

	Does the writing have a clear voice and is it the best style for the type of writing?	Is the language interesting and are the words and sentences appropriate for the purpose, audience, and type of writing?
4 Wow!	The writing <u>fully</u> engages the reader with its individual voice. The writing style is best for the type of writing.	The words and sentences are interesting and appropriate to the purpose and audience. • The words are precise and engaging. • The sentences are varied and flow together smoothly.
3 Ahh.	<u>Most</u> of the writing engages the reader with an individual voice. The writing style is mostly best for the type of writing.	<u>Most</u> of the words and sentences are interesting and appropriate to the purpose and audience. • Most words are powerful and engaging. • Most sentences are varied and flow together.
2 Hmm.	<u>Some</u> of the writing engages the reader, but it has no individual voice and the style is not best for the writing type.	<u>Some</u> of the words and sentences are interesting and appropriate to the purpose and audience. • Some words are precise and engaging. • Some sentences are varied, but the flow could be smoother.
1 Huh?	The writing does <u>not</u> engage the reader.	<u>Few or none</u> of the words and sentences are appropriate to the purpose and audience. • The words are often vague and dull. • The sentences lack variety and do not flow together.

myNGconnect.com
- Rubric: Voice and Style
- Evaluate and practice scoring other student essays.

✔ Revise Your Draft, continued

❷ Revise Your Draft

You have now evaluated the voice and style of your own draft. If you scored 3 or lower, how can you improve your work? Use the checklist below to revise your draft.

Revision Checklist

Ask Yourself	Check It Out	How to Make It Better
Does the writing voice sound like me?	If your score is 3 or lower, revise.	☐ Read your narrative aloud. Listen for any words that do not sound natural. ☐ Write as you speak.
Does the tone stay the same?	If your score is 3 or lower, revise.	☐ Read your narrative aloud. Listen for changes in tone. ☐ Choose new words that make the tone consistent.
Does the style fit the audience?	If your score is 3 or lower, revise.	☐ Look for words that your audience may not relate to. ☐ Be sure sentences are varied. ☐ Check that sentence fragments, if any, are used sparingly and intentionally for effect.
Do I state the problem or challenge clearly in the introduction? Do I give enough background information?	Read your narrative to someone else. See if you provide enough detail for the person to understand the obstacle you faced.	☐ Provide more background information about the problem or challenge.
Do I end my narrative effectively and memorably?	Read the end of your narrative. Do you share what you learned from the experience, or clearly show how you resolved it?	☐ Decide what you want the reader to remember most about your experience and add this to the final paragraph.

❸ Conduct a Peer Conference

It helps to get a second opinion when you are revising your draft. Ask a partner to read your draft and look for the following:

- any part of the draft that is confusing
- any part where the voice and style seem weak
- anything that the person doesn't understand

Discuss your draft with your partner. Focus on the items in the Revision Checklist. Use your partner's comments to improve the voice and style of your narrative.

❹ Make Revisions

Read the revisions below and the peer-reviewer conversation on the right. Notice how the peer reviewer commented and asked questions. Notice how the writer used the comments and questions to revise.

Revised for Voice and Style

It is necessary for me to explain that my family had just moved here from ~~another city that perhaps some of you know.~~ St. Louis. It was my first day at a new high school, ~~It was~~ and the only day of soccer tryouts. ~~It was~~ We had left very early in the morning ~~when we left. It was our~~ plan~~ning~~ to be at our new ~~place~~ home before school began. If everything had gone perfectly, there would have been time for me to ~~do what is~~ find my classes ~~required of us educationally,~~ meet people, and even warm up before the tryouts.

Peer Conference

Reviewer's Comment:
This part doesn't sound like you. Since this is personal, can you use an informal voice for the whole thing?

Writer's Answer:
Definitely! I like to be direct, so I'll cut unnecessary words and use specific word choices.

Reviewer's Comment:
By the way, you're nice and clear about what was supposed to happen, but the repetitive sentences slow things down.

Writer's Answer: I agree. I'm going to vary the sentence structure—like we do when we're talking!

Reflect on Your Revisions

▶ Think about the results of your peer conference. What are some of your strengths as a writer? What are some things that give you trouble?

✔ Edit and Proofread Your Draft

Before you share your narrative, find and fix any mistakes.

❶ Capitalize Job Titles, Courtesy Titles, and Family Titles

Job titles should be capitalized when they come before a person's name. When they follow the person's name or the word *the*, they are not capitalized.

Principal Morgan	Dr. Morgan, the principal	Carlotta Mendez is the principal.

Family titles should be capitalized when they are used in place of a person's name. When they follow a pronoun, they are not capitalized.

I saw Mother standing in the hall.	My mother stood in the hall.

Courtesy titles, such as *Mr., Mrs.,* and *Ms.*, should always be capitalized.

> Ms. Johnson's lessons . . .   Mr. Gatti's reminders . . .

TRY IT ▶ Copy the sentence. Fix the capitalization errors. Use proofreader's marks.

> The Assistant Principal, mrs. Kovad, works with principal Morgan.

❷ Use the Dash Correctly

Use a dash or dashes to show a sudden break in a change in thought or speech.

> They got me a magazine that's all about—you guessed it—soccer.

Do not overuse dashes. For example, dashes should not be used in place of periods, commas, and other appropriate punctuation.

Incorrect	Correct
I nodded—ran onto the field—found the team captain. Nothing not even time itself could stop me.	I nodded, ran onto the field, and found the team captain. Nothing — not even time itself — could stop me.

TRY IT ▶ Copy the sentences. Insert or replace dashes as needed.

> 1. I think—you may be—too late—
> 2. Mr. Turner he's the soccer coach let me try out.

Proofreader's Marks

Use proofreader's marks to correct errors.

Capitalize:
This is coach Turner.

Do not capitalize:
Mr. Turner is the Coach.

Add a dash.
Suddenly, I saw it a soccer ball.

Replace dashes.
Next I took a deep breath.

Proofreading Tip

If you are unsure about how to use dashes correctly, refer to a style manual for more information and examples.

3 Check Your Spelling

Homonyms are words that sound alike but have different meanings and spellings. Spell these homonyms correctly when you edit.

Technology Tip

Most word-processing programs include a Spell-check feature and a Grammar feature. Always use these, but know their limits. Spell-checkers cannot find homonym errors.

Homonyms and Their Meanings	Examples
to (preposition) = toward, in the direction of	We hurried **to** the field.
two (noun) = one more than one	We waited **two** hours.
too (adverb) = also	I wanted to play soccer, **too**.
your (possessive adjective) = belonging to you	What are **your** skills?
you're (contraction) = you are	"**You're** late," she said.

TRY IT ▶ Copy the sentence. Find and fix the three homonym errors.

> When your playing soccer, you're enthusiasm spreads to the spectators, two.

4 Use the Verbs *Can, Could, May,* and *Might* Correctly

Use the verb *can*, *could*, *may*, or *might* with an action verb to express the ability to do something or the possibility that something may happen. Use *may* to emphasize that an action is permitted, or allowed. Use *can*, *could*, or *might* to indicate that something is possible.

Can, Could, May, Might	
I **can kick** the ball across the field.	Coach said, "You **may join** our team!"
I **could play** better if I practiced.	It **might rain** tomorrow.

TRY IT ▶ Copy the sentences. Find and fix the errors.

> 1. If the principal permits it, we leave school early.
> 2. It maybe snow tomorrow.
> 3. Now that our food is here, we eat.

📖 **Writing Handbook**, p. 850

Reflect on Your Corrections

▶ Give your paper a final check for correct grammar and punctuation.

❺ Edited Student Draft

Here's the student's draft, revised and edited. How did the writer improve it?

Making the Goal

Soccer is my life. I play soccer, go to soccer games, and watch soccer on television with Mom and Dad. They even got me a subscription to a magazine that's all about—you guessed it!—soccer. So I couldn't believe it when my dream of playing soccer in high school hit a big obstacle. On the way to tryouts, the family car broke down. But a good player never gives up. Even when the game seems lost.

My family had just moved here from St. Louis. It was my first day at a new high school and the only day of soccer tryouts. We had left very early in the morning, planning to be at our new home before classes began. If everything had gone perfectly, there would have been time for me to find my classes, meet people, and even warm up before the tryouts.

"Oh, dear! I think you're too late for tryouts," said Principal Morgan, as I hastily signed in at the school office. She glanced up at the clock and shook her head. "They're almost finished, but you might check anyway."

"Sorry," I gasped, nearly out of breath. "Our car broke down. We waited two hours for a tow truck, and then another two for a rental car."

"I understand," said the principal, picking up the telephone. "Mrs. Kovad, will you escort Tina to the sports field to meet the teams?"

At first, I felt so frustrated and defeated. I clenched my fists at my sides, bit my lower lip, and fought back tears. Why run all the way out to the field just to humiliate myself? But a player never quits, not even in the final minutes of a game. Next, I took a deep breath, determined to act as if it did not bother me. Finally, Mrs. Kovad, who's the assistant principal, emerged from her office, and we hurried to the field. By the time we got there, I didn't have to worry about warming up.

"Are you Tina?" asked a sandy-haired man in a gruff voice. What a way to meet Coach Turner! "We're almost done," he said. Then he grinned, "Think you can show us your soccer skills in just three minutes?"

I nodded, ran onto the field, and found the team captain. By changing my nervous energy into enthusiasm, I kept my focus on the game, not the time. Suddenly, I kicked the ball into the net, scoring a goal for our side. When the team captain and Coach Turner cheered in unison, I knew that I had made the team.

As I discovered that day, I love soccer so much that nothing—not even time itself—could stop me from achieving my goal!

The writer used **dashes** correctly.

The writer used a **sentence fragment** for effect.

The writer varied the sentence structure and used precise word choice to improve the style. The writer also consistently used an informal voice.

The writer used the **correct homonyms**. The writer also supplied a **verb** to replace *maybe check* with *might check*.

The writer fixed **capitalization errors**.

The writer added sensory details and images to engage the reader.

The writer added a missing **verb**.

The writer used **dashes** correctly.

✔ Publish and Present

You are now ready to publish and present your narrative. Print out a copy of it or write a clean copy by hand. Give your audience a chance to read or hear what you have to say. You may also want to present your work in a different way.

Alternative Presentations

Do a Reading Read your narrative aloud to your class. Make it come alive for your classmates by reading with expression.

1 Introduce your Narrative Tell your audience the subject. For example, you might say, "My narrative tells how I faced the challenge of _____ ."

2 Read Effectively Use your tone of voice to show how you felt, and speak at a pace that is comfortable for your audience. Don't hide your face behind the paper. Look over the paper at your audience to make eye contact from time to time. Does anyone look puzzled? If so, slow down.

3 Ask for Feedback When you are finished, thank your audience. Then ask for feedback:

- Was the beginning interesting? If not, how could I improve it?

- Was it easy to understand how I resolved the problem? If not, how could I make it clearer?

- Did the narrative feel complete? If not, what suggestions do you have?

Publish on the Internet With your teacher's supervision, reach a wider audience by publishing your narrative online. As a group, work with your teacher to research appropriate Web sites that publish student writing.

1 Find a Good Web Site Depending on school policy, you may also post your paper on the school's Web site, or another site.

2 Send Your Writing Follow the teacher's and the publisher's instructions for submitting your writing.

3 Ask for Feedback If there is a comment box, ask readers to share appropriate comments with you and your teacher on your work. Use readers' suggestions to improve your writing.

📖 **Writing Handbook**, p. 839

Reflect on Your Work

▶ Ask for and use feedback from your audience to evaluate your strengths as a writer.

- What parts of your narrative did your audience like?
- What parts of your narrative did your audience say need improvement?
- What would you like to do better the next time you write? Set a goal for your next writing project.

☑ Save a copy of your work in your portfolio.

EQ **ESSENTIAL QUESTION:**

What Tests a Person's Loyalty?

We are inevitably our brother's keeper because we are our brother's brother. Whatever affects one affects all indirectly.

—MARTIN LUTHER KING, JR.

No person is your friend who demands your silence, or denies your right to grow.

—ALICE WALKER

Critical Viewing ▶
On March 21, 1965, people marched from Selma to Montgomery, Alabama, to demonstrate against unfair voting laws for African Americans. What does this photo suggest about their loyalty to their country?

THE
TIES
THAT
BIND

EQ ESSENTIAL QUESTION:
What Tests a Person's Loyalty?

Study the Photos and Captions

We would all like to think we're loyal: faithful to our family, friends, school, community, and country. What happens, though, when our loyalty is tested? Imagine that your best friend is running for class president against a more qualified student. Who would you vote for?

Candidate 1
1. Two years experience on the student council
2. Captain of the speech and debate team
3. Active in community service
4. Gets along with all students

Candidate 2
1. New member of the student council
2. Captain of the basketball team
3. Speaks English and Spanish
4. Your best friend

Compare and Debate

1. Who is the better candidate for class president? Explain the reasons for your decision.

2. How do you decide between loyalties? How much should loyalty to your friend influence your vote?

Talk with a group. Explain your opinion and support your ideas with evidence from your own experience.

EQ ESSENTIAL QUESTION

In this unit, you will explore the **Essential Question** in class through reading, discussion, research, and writing. Keep thinking about the question outside of school, too.

① Plan a Project

Reality TV Show

In this unit, you'll role-play characters in a reality TV show. Choose the kind of show you would like to produce and the kind of characters you would like to play. To get started, watch a few different reality TV shows. Look for

- the tasks the characters must undertake
- the challenges to loyalty that they experience
- the personality traits the characters must have to win a contest.

Study Skills Start planning your reality TV show. Use the forms on myNGconnect.com to help plan your time and to prepare the content.

myNGconnect.com
- ▶ Planning forms
- ▶ Scheduler
- ▶ Reality show sites
- ▶ Contestant profiles
- ▶ Rubric

② Choose More to Read

These readings provide different answers to the Essential Question. Choose a book and online selections to read during the unit.

Two Badges
by Mona Ruiz with Geoff Boucher

Mona grew up on the gang-controlled streets of Santa Ana, California. She always wanted to become a police officer. But if she wore an officer's badge, she would betray her gang. Would Mona get a chance to choose her future? Or would the dangers of gang life decide for her?

▶ **NONFICTION**

Things Fall Apart
by Chinua Achebe

Okonkwo is a leader of the Ibo tribe. But an accident forces him and his family to leave their village for seven years. They return to find outsiders in their village teaching new ideas. Will Okonkwo and his tribesman stay loyal to their traditions or will their tribe fall apart?

▶ **NOVEL**

The Wave
by Todd Strasser

Teacher Ben Ross decides to try an experiment about power and discipline. His students form a group called The Wave. But the experiment turns into a nightmare. Doesn't anyone see how dangerous the group has become? Can anyone stop The Wave before it's too late?

▶ **NOVEL**

myNGconnect.com
- 🌐 Read real-life stories of teens who have faced a question of loyalty.
- 🌐 Take a loyalty quiz to find out what type of friend you are.
- 🌐 Watch movies about the bonds of loyalty between families and friends.

From the moment you begin reading, you get a sense of an author's style, or manner of writing. Try it. Read these sentences from two books and two stories, each written by a famous American author.

#1 from ***The Adventures of Huckleberry Finn,*** a novel by Mark Twain

You don't know about me, without you have read a book by the name of *The Adventures of Tom Sawyer,* but that ain't no matter.

#2 from **"A Day's Wait,"** a short story by Ernest Hemingway

"What's the matter, Schatz?"
"I've got a headache."
"You better go back to bed."
"No. I am all right."

#3 from **"Blues Ain't No Mockin Bird,"** a short story by Toni Cade Bambara

Me and Cathy look over toward the meadow where the men with the station wagon'd been roamin around all morning. The tall man with a huge camera lassoed to his shoulder was buzzin our way.

#4 from ***Absalom, Absalom,*** a novel by William Faulkner

From a little after two oclock until almost sundown of the long still hot weary dead September afternoon they sat in what Miss Coldfield still called the office because her father had called it that—a dim hot airless room with the blinds all closed and fastened for forty-three summers because when she was a girl someone had believed that light and moving air carried heat and that dark air was always cooler, and which (as the sun shone fuller and fuller on that side of the house) became latticed with yellow slashes full of dust motes which Quentin thought of as being flecks of the dead old dried paint itself blown inward from the scaling blinds as winds might have blown them.

Connect Reading to Your Life

Each of the following sentences comes later in one of the books or stories on page 238. Decide whether the sentence was written by Mark Twain, Ernest Hemingway, Toni Cade Bambara, or William Faulkner.

page 238

_____ The twins were danglin in the tire, lookin at Granny. Me and Cathy were waitin, too, cause Granny always got somethin to say.

_____ She had not seen him since the summer before although he had been home Christmas with Charles Bon, his friend from the university, and she had heard about the balls and parties at Sutpen's Hundred during the holidays, but she and her father had not gone out.

_____ Do you reckon _you_ can learn 'em anything?

_____ When the doctor came he took the boy's temperature. "What is it?" I asked him. "One hundred and two."

Focus Strategy ▶ Make Inferences

You were able to **infer**, or make a good guess about, which author wrote each sentence by focusing on the author's **style** . You probably noticed:

- the length of the sentences
- the choice of words and the **tone** , or the authors' feelings toward their topics
- a little about the plot, setting, or characters

You make inferences about style all the time. Imagine you're shopping for clothes. You look at clothes in store windows to decide which stores have clothes in your style.

■ Your Job as a Reader

One of your jobs as a reader is to pay attention to the author's style and to **evaluate** the effectiveness of the author's stylistic choices. After reading, ask yourself whether the author's style:

- drew you into the story
- created an interesting mood
- helped you appreciate the story as a whole, including its theme.

Elements of Literature
style _n._, distinct, individual way of writing
tone _n._, author's attitude toward the topic and characters

Academic Vocabulary
- **infer** _v._, to make a good guess based on evidence and knowledge
- **evaluate** _v._, to judge the worth or importance of something

Reading Strategies
- Plan and Monitor
- Determine Importance
▶ Make Inferences
- Ask Questions
- Make Connections
- Synthesize
- Visualize

■ Unpack the Thinking Process

Analyze Style

Style isn't a precise thing, but you can use tools to help you think about the ingredients of style:

Tone is all about the way the writing feels and sounds. What is the tone of #1 on page 238?

Tone Scale

serious/heavy   fun/lighthearted

All good writing uses a variety of sentences, but many writers choose a rhythm for their sentences. Short, choppy sentences can create tension or excitement, for example. How would you describe the sentence structure of #4 on page 238?

Sentence Structure Scale

simple   complex

Most writers love words and want to choose just the right word to convey what they want to say. How would you describe the words the author chose in #3 on page 238?

Word Choice Scale

casual   formal

Compare Authors

The easiest way to think about an author's style is to make comparisons. That is, you compare one author to another author. Compare Hemingway and Faulkner. Hemingway writes with short, straightforward sentences. These stand out when compared to a writer like Faulkner, who writes long, complicated sentences. Hemingway also uses simple, everyday vocabulary. This stands out because writers like Faulkner use more complicated words.

Compare One Author's Choices

Another way is to compare the stylistic choices the author made to the stylistic choices he or she could have made. Think about the choices that Mark Twain made when he wrote *The Adventures of Huckleberry Finn*. The most important choice that Twain made was to tell the story from Huck's point of view and to tell it in the language that a young boy of that time and place would have used.

Not everyone likes a writer's style! In 1885, when *The Adventures of Huckleberry Finn* was published, *The San Francisco Argonaut* newspaper wrote: "A remarkable feature is the variety of dialects spoken by the characters." In that same year, however, the *Boston Herald* newspaper wrote that the book was "pitched in but one key, and that is the key of a vulgar and abhorrent life."

■ Try an Experiment

One way to test your understanding of style is to write a **parody**. A parody is an imitation of a certain style, and it's usually very funny. To create a parody, match the tone, sentence structure, and type of words used in the original, but change the topic. Your audience should be able to "hear" the original style, but be surprised by the new, humorous topic. Here are some ideas for pieces of writing to parody:

- a children's book

> See Jane. See Jane run.
> Run, Jane, run.

- a fairy tale

> *Once upon a time, in a land far, far away...*

- a popular song
- one of the writers in this book

Collaborative Writing Work with a group. Choose a style that you know well, and create a parody. Perform it for the class. After each performance, have the audience guess the original. Then, everyone can discuss:

1. How is the tone of the parody like or unlike the original?
2. How are the sentence structure and word choice like those of the original?

Elements of Literature
parody *n.*, humorous imitation of a piece
of writing

Monitor Comprehension
1. ***Tone*** What is tone?
2. ***Style*** When is an author's style effective?

EQ What Tests a Person's Loyalty?
Find out how competition can test people's loyalty.

Make a Connection

Anticipation Guide Think about the importance of loyalty in your relationships with friends and family. Then tell whether you agree or disagree with these statements. After reading the selections, see if you still feel the same way.

ANTICIPATION GUIDE	Agree or Disagree
1. In any contest, you should always try your hardest to win.	_____
2. You can't be good friends with a person you compete against.	_____
3. It is more important to be loyal to someone than to be honest with them.	_____

Learn Key Vocabulary

Study the Words Pronounce each word and its meaning. You may also want to look up the definitions in the Glossary.

• Academic Vocabulary

Key Words	Examples
• **acknowledgment** (ik-**nah**-lij-munt) *noun* ▶ page 254	An **acknowledgment** is something done to express thanks. You make an **acknowledgment** of a gift you receive when you send a thank-you note for the gift.
devastating (**de**-vu-stāt-ing) *adjective* ▶ pages 248, 264	Something **devastating** is destructive and damaging. Many trees fell down on our street during last night's **devastating** storm. *Synonym:* harmful; *Antonym:* beneficial
dispel (di-**spel**) *verb* ▶ pages 255, 260	The crowd began to **dispel** after the football game ended. *Synonyms:* scatter, separate; *Antonyms:* gather, collect
evade (i-**vād**) *verb* ▶ page 257	If you **evade** something, you avoid it or escape it. Boxers **evade** punches by moving out of the way.
improvise (**im**-prah-vīz) *verb* ▶ pages 253, 265	When you **improvise** a speech or a performance, you make It up on the spur of the moment, without planning or preparing for it.
opponent (u-**pō**-nunt) *noun* ▶ pages 251, 267	Your **opponent** in a game is the person or team playing against you. *Synonym:* rival; *Antonym:* teammate
pensively (**pen**-siv-lē) *adverb* ▶ page 249	When people act **pensively**, they are quiet and thoughtful. *Synonyms:* seriously, thoughtfully; *Antonym:* thoughtlessly
surge (**surj**) *verb* ▶ page 259, 260	If something begins to **surge**, it is suddenly rising in strength. The soccer player's excitement began to **surge** after he scored the winning goal.

Practice the Words Work with a partner to write four sentences. Use at least two Key Vocabulary words in each sentence.

Example: My <u>opponent</u> won the debate because she <u>improvised</u> a great speech.

BEFORE READING **Amigo Brothers**

short story by Piri Thomas

Reading Strategies

· Plan and Monitor
· Determine Importance
▶ Make Inferences
· Ask Questions
· Make Connections
· Synthesize
· Visualize

Analyze Style: Language

Style is the way an author uses language to express ideas. Many factors influence an author's style, such as **word choice** and the length of sentences. An author's style may be formal, informal, or a combination of both. In the informal style of "Amigo Brothers," the word choice is casual and conversational. **Point of view**, or the perspective from which a story is told, also affects style. In "Amigo Brothers," Piri Thomas uses word choices and a third-person omniscient point of view (in which the narrator is not part of the story but knows how the characters feel) to help the audience understand the characters and the narrator of his story.

Look Into the Text

This is an example of third-person omniscient point of view.

> Each youngster had a dream of someday becoming lightweight champion of the world....
>
> One morning less than a week before their bout, they met as usual for their daily workout. They fooled around with a few jabs at the air, slapped skin, and then took off, running lightly along the dirty East River's edge....
>
> After a mile or so, Felix puffed and said, "Let's stop a while, bro. I think we both got something to say to each other."

The word choice reflects the informal style of everyday speech.

Which word tells you that the style is **informal**?

Focus Strategy ▶ Make Inferences

An **inference** is a reasonable conclusion. When you make inferences, you read between the lines of a story. You use important clues and details to figure out what the author suggests but does not say directly. You can use what you know about the world to make inferences about characters and events in stories.

HOW TO MAKE INFERENCES

Focus Strategy

1. As you read, jot down details in the text that help you understand story characters and their relationships.

2. Use your knowledge about people and their relationships as you read to make sense of the story.

3. Track your thoughts in a chart like the one below.

I Read	I Know	And So
"they met as usual"	My friends and I get together a lot.	Antonio and Felix are already friends.

Piri Thomas
(1928–2011)

I've read stories from wherever I could find a book to read.

Piri Thomas communicated his message of unity by performing dramatic poetry readings all across the United States.

In "Amigo Brothers," author **Piri Thomas** wrote about two friends, each with his own individual identity. Their strong identities come from Thomas's own struggle for identity growing up in a life ruled by poverty and racism.

Thomas was born to Cuban and Puerto Rican parents in New York's Spanish Harlem. He learned the pain of racism, as his dark skin drew insults from lighter-skinned people in his neighborhood. Thomas was an avid reader as a child, but as a young man he turned to crime. In the 1950s he served a six-year prison term for an attempted armed robbery.

Upon his release Thomas began to act on his belief that "the worst prison is the prison of the mind." He taught prisoners and young people to use writing to free themselves from lives of pain and desperation. He also began his own writing career. His classic 1967 autobiography *Down These Mean Streets* used the unique language of the streets to tell of his difficult upbringing and promote unity. He also wrote several books, along with many poems and newspaper articles, and he gave spoken-word poetry performances and lectures.

myNGconnect.com

🔍 Watch Piri Thomas perform several of his poems.
🔍 Explore Piri Thomas's East Harlem neighborhood today.

Amigo Brothers
by Piri **Thomas**

Comprehension Coach

Find out how two friends deal with the conflict between their drive to succeed and their loyalty to each other.

Antonio Cruz and Felix Varga were both seventeen years old. They were so together in friendship that they felt themselves to be brothers. **1** They had known each other since childhood, growing up on the lower east side of Manhattan in the same **tenement building** on Fifth Street between Avenue A and Avenue B.

Antonio was fair, lean, and lanky, while Felix was dark, short, and husky. Antonio's hair was always falling over his eyes, while Felix wore his black hair in a natural Afro style.

Each youngster had a dream of someday becoming lightweight champion of the world. Every chance they had the boys worked out, sometimes at the Boy's Club on 10th Street and Avenue A and sometimes at the pro's gym on 14th Street. Early morning sunrises would find them running along the East River Drive, wrapped in sweat shirts, short towels around their necks, and handkerchiefs **Apache style** around their foreheads.

While some youngsters were into street negatives, Antonio and Felix slept, ate, rapped, and dreamt positive. Between them, they had a collection of *Fight* magazines **second to none**, plus a scrapbook filled with torn tickets to every boxing match they had ever attended, and some clippings of their own. If asked a question about any given fighter, they would immediately **zip out from their memory banks** divisions, weights, records of fights, **knockouts**, technical knockouts, and **draws** or losses. **2**

Each had fought many bouts representing their community and had won two gold-plated medals plus a silver and bronze medallion. The difference was in their style. Antonio's lean form and long reach made him the better boxer, while Felix's short and muscular frame made him the better slugger. Whenever they had met in the ring for sparring sessions, it had always been **hot and heavy**.

1 Style: Language/ Point of View
Look at the second sentence. What does it tell you about the point of view of the story? Explain.

2 Style: Language
How do words and phrases that the narrator uses—for example, "street negatives," "rapped," and "zip out"—affect the style of this paragraph?

In Other Words
tenement building run-down apartments
Apache style folded like a headband
second to none better than any others
zip out from their memory banks remember

knockouts victories after an opponent is knocked down and can't get up in 10 seconds
draws ties, finishes with neither side winning
hot and heavy energetic and intense

Now, after a series of **elimination bouts**, they had been informed that they were to meet each other in the division finals that were scheduled for the seventh of August, two weeks away—the winner to represent the Boys Club in the Golden Gloves Championship Tournament.

The two boys continued to run together along the East River Drive. But even when joking with each other, they both **sensed a wall rising between them**. ■3

One morning less than a week before their bout, they met as usual for their daily workout. They fooled around with a few **jabs** at the air, slapped skin, and then took off, running lightly along the dirty East River's edge.

East River Sunset, 2002, Lawrence Kelsey. Oil on canvas, private collection.

3 Inferences/ Compare and Contrast
How are Antonio and Felix the same? How are they different? Jot down details on your chart to support your inferences about their similarities and differences.

◁ **Critical Viewing: Setting**
How does this painting compare to how you visualize the story's setting?

In Other Words
elimination bouts single matches in which each loser is removed from the competition
sensed a wall rising between them began to feel isolated from each other
jabs punches

Historical Background
The Golden Gloves Championship Tournament is an annual competition for amateur boxing. Some famous past winners include Muhammad Ali, George Foreman, and Oscar De La Hoya.

Antonio glanced at Felix who kept his eyes purposely straight ahead, pausing from time to time to do some fancy leg work while throwing one-twos followed by **upper cuts** to an imaginary jaw. Antonio then beat the air with a barrage of body blows and short **devastating** lefts with an overhand jaw-breaking right.

After a mile or so, Felix puffed and said, "Let's stop a while, bro. I think we both got something to say to each other." 4

Antonio nodded. It was not natural to be acting as though nothing unusual was happening when two **ace-boon buddies** were going to be blasting each other within a few short days.

They rested their elbows on the railing separating them from the river. Antonio wiped his face with his short towel. The sunrise was now creating day.

Felix leaned heavily on the river's railing and stared across to the shores of Brooklyn. Finally, he broke the silence.

"Man, I don't know how to come out with it."

Antonio helped. "It's about our fight, right?"

"Yeah, right." Felix's eyes squinted at the rising orange sun.

"I've been thinking about it too, *panín*. In fact, since we found out it was going to be me and you, I've been awake at night, pulling punches on you, trying not to hurt you."

"Same here. It ain't natural not to think about the fight. I mean, we both are *cheverote* fighters and we both want to win. But only one of us can win. There ain't no draws in the eliminations." 5

Felix tapped Antonio gently on the shoulder. "I don't mean to sound like I'm bragging, bro. But I wanna win, **fair and square**."

Antonio nodded quietly. "Yeah. We both know that in the ring the better man wins. Friend or no friend, brother or no . . . "

4 **Inferences**
What do you think the boys have to say to each other?

5 **Style: Language**
Dialogue is a conversation between characters. Which words or phrases make the dialogue in this paragraph informal?

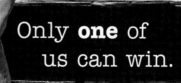

Only **one** of us can win.

Key Vocabulary
devastating *adj.*, destructive, very damaging

In Other Words
upper cuts powerful, upward punches
ace-boon buddies best friends
panín pal (in Spanish)
cheverote great (in Spanish)
fair and square without any advantages

Felix finished it for him. "Brother. Tony, let's promise something right here. Okay?"

"If it's fair, **hermano**, I'm for it." Antonio admired the courage of a tug boat pulling a barge five times its welterweight size. **6**

"It's fair, Tony. When we get into the ring, it's gotta be like we never met. We gotta be like two heavy strangers that want the same thing and only one can have it. You understand, don'tcha?"

"*Sí*, I know." Tony smiled. "No pulling punches. We go all the way."

"Yeah, that's right. Listen, Tony. Don't you think it's a good idea if we don't see each other until the day of the fight? I'm going to stay with my Aunt Lucy in the Bronx. I can use Gleason's Gym for working out. My manager says he got some **sparring** partners with more or less your style."

Tony scratched his nose **pensively**. "Yeah, it would be better for our heads." **7** He held out his hand, palm upward. "Deal?"

"Deal." Felix lightly slapped open skin.

"Ready for some more running?" Tony asked lamely.

"Naw, bro. Let's cut it here. You go on. I kinda like to get things together in my head."

"You ain't worried, are you?" Tony asked.

"No way, man." Felix laughed out loud. "I got too much smarts for that. I just think it's cooler if we split right here. After the fight, we can get it together again like nothing ever happened."

The **amigo** brothers were not ashamed to hug each other tightly.

"Guess you're right. Watch yourself, Felix. I hear there's some pretty heavy dudes up in the Bronx. **Suavecito**, okay?"

"Okay. You watch yourself too, **sabe**?"

Tony jogged away. Felix watched his friend disappear from view, throwing rights and lefts. Both fighters had a lot of **psyching up** to do before the big fight.

6 Inferences
What does Antonio's thought about the tug boat tell you about him?

7 Language
An **idiom** is an expression that has a different meaning from the meaning of its individual words. What does Antonio mean when he says that working out separately would be "better for our heads"?

Monitor Comprehension

Summarize
How do Antonio and Felix deal with the tension between them?

Key Vocabulary
pensively *adv.*, thoughtfully

In Other Words
hermano brother (in Spanish)
sparring boxing practice
amigo friend (in Spanish)
Suavecito Take it easy (Spanish slang)
sabe understand (in Spanish)
psyching up thinking and preparing

The days in training passed much too slowly. Although they kept out of each other's way, they were aware of each other's progress **via the ghetto grapevine**.

The evening before the big fight, Tony made his way to the roof of his tenement. In the quiet early dark, he peered over the ledge. Six stories below the lights of the city blinked and the sounds of cars mingled with the curses and the laughter of children in the street. He tried not to think of Felix, feeling he had succeeded in psyching his mind. But only in the ring would he really know. To spare Felix hurt, he would have to knock him out, early and quick.

Up in the South Bronx, Felix decided to take in a movie in an effort to keep Antonio's face away from his fists. The flick was *The Champion* with Kirk Douglas, the third time Felix was seeing it.

The champion was getting the daylights beat out of him. He was saved only by the sound of the bell.

Felix became the champ and Tony the challenger.

The movie audience was **going out of its head**. The champ hunched his shoulders grunting and sniffing red blood back into his broken nose. The challenger, confident that he had the championship **in the bag**, threw a left. The champ countered with a dynamite right. **8**

Felix's right arm felt the shock. Antonio's face, **superimposed on the screen**, was hit by the awesome force of the blow. Felix saw himself in the ring, blasting Antonio against the ropes. The champ had to be forcibly **restrained**. The challenger fell slowly to the canvas.

When Felix finally left the theatre, he had figured out how to psyche himself for tomorrow's fight. It was Felix the Champion vs. Antonio the Challenger. **9**

8 Style: Language
Which of the narrator's words and phrases help you visualize the movie scene?

9 Inferences
What do the details on this page suggest about Felix's personality? How does it compare with Antonio's personality?

In Other Words
via the ghetto grapevine through other people in the neighborhood
going out of its head shouting with excitement
in the bag easily won
superimposed on the screen seen in place of the movie actor's face
restrained held back

He walked up some dark streets, deserted except for small pockets of wary-looking kids wearing gang colors. Despite the fact that he was Puerto Rican like them, they eyed him as a stranger to their turf. Felix did a fast shuffle, **bobbing and weaving**, while letting loose a torrent of blows that would demolish whatever got in its way. It seemed to impress the brothers, who went about their own business.

Finding no takers, Felix decided **to split** to his aunt's. Walking the streets had not relaxed him, neither had the fight flick. All it had done was to **stir him up**. He let himself quietly into his Aunt Lucy's apartment and went straight to bed, falling into a fitful sleep with sounds of the gong for Round One.

> **He would have to knock him out, early and quick.**

Antonio was passing some heavy time on his rooftop. How would the fight tomorrow affect his relationship with Felix? After all, fighting was like any other profession. Friendship had nothing to do with it. A gnawing doubt crept in. He cut negative thinking real quick by doing some speedy fancy dance steps, bobbing and weaving like mercury. The night air was blurred with perpetual motions of left hooks and right crosses. Felix, his *amigo* brother, was not going to be Felix at all in the ring. Just an **opponent** with another face. Antonio went to sleep, hearing the opening bell for the first round. Like his friend in the South Bronx, he prayed for victory, via a quick clean knockout in the first round. **10**

Large posters plastered all over the walls of local shops announced the fight between Antonio Cruz and Felix Vargas as the main bout.

The fight had created great interest in the neighborhood. Antonio and Felix were well liked and respected. Each had his own loyal following.

10 Style: Language
The author mixes formal and informal language here. Which sentences sound most like everyday speech? Why?

Key Vocabulary
opponent *n.*, person who competes against you or takes the opposite side of an argument

In Other Words
bobbing and weaving bending and moving sideways
to split to leave, to go
stir him up make him feel anxious and restless

Antonio's fans had **unbridled** faith in his boxing skills. On the other side, Felix's admirers trusted in his dynamite-packed fists.

Felix had returned to his apartment early in the morning of August 7th and stayed there, hoping to avoid seeing Antonio. He turned the radio on to *salsa* **music sounds** and then tried to read while waiting for word from his manager. **11**

Jorge and Pedro, 2004, John Sonsini. Oil on canvas, 72x60, courtesy of the artist and Cheim & Read, New York.

▲ **Critical Viewing: Character** Who appears more relaxed, the figure on the left or right? What can you tell about them from the way they are standing?

11 Inferences
What can you infer about Felix at this point? What is his state of mind? Write the details on your chart.

Monitor Comprehension

Confirm Prediction
Was your prediction about Antonio and Felix accurate? If not, why? What happened that you did not expect?

In Other Words

unbridled complete
salsa **music sounds** Latin dance music

Will the boys become enemies or remain loyal friends?

The fight was scheduled to take place in Tompkins Square Park. It had been decided that the gymnasium of the Boys Club was not large enough to hold all the people who were sure to attend. In Tompkins Square Park, everyone who wanted could view the fight, whether from ringside or window fire escapes or tenement rooftops.

The morning of the fight Tompkins Square was a **beehive of activity** with numerous workers setting up the ring, the seats, and the guest speakers' stand. The scheduled bouts began shortly after noon and the park had begun filling up even earlier.

The local junior high school across from Tompkins Square Park served as the dressing room for all the fighters. Each was given a separate classroom with desk tops, covered with mats, serving as resting tables. Antonio thought he caught a glimpse of Felix waving to him from a room at the far end of the corridor. He waved back just in case it had been him. **12**

The fighters changed from their street clothes into fighting gear. Antonio wore white trunks, black socks, and black shoes. Felix wore sky blue trunks, red socks, and white boxing shoes. Each had dressing gowns to match their fighting trunks with their names neatly stitched on the back.

The loudspeakers blared into the open windows of the school. There were speeches by **dignitaries**, community leaders, and great boxers of yesteryear. Some were well prepared, some **improvised** on the spot. They all carried the same message of great pleasure and honor at being part of such a historic event. This great day was in the tradition of champions emerging from the streets of the lower east side. **13**

Interwoven with the speeches were the sounds of the other boxing events. After the sixth bout, Felix was much relieved when his trainer Charlie, said, "Time change. Quick knockout. This is it. We're on."

12 Inferences
What does Antonio's wave suggest about the way he feels about Felix and the fight?

13 Style: Language/ Inferences
What word choices indicate that the fight is a major event?

Key Vocabulary
improvise *v.*, to create without planning or preparation

In Other Words
beehive of activity very lively place
dignitaries important people
Interwoven with Mixed in with

Waiting time was over. Felix was **escorted** from the classroom by a dozen fans in white T-shirts with the word FELIX across their fronts.

Antonio was escorted down a different stairwell and guided through a roped-off path.

As the two climbed into the ring, the crowd exploded with a roar. Antonio and Felix both bowed gracefully and then raised their arms in **acknowledgment**.

Antonio tried to be cool, but even as the roar was **in its first birth**, he turned slowly to meet Felix's eyes looking directly into his. Felix nodded his head and Antonio responded. And both as one, just as quickly, turned away to face his own corner. **14**

Bong—bong—bong. The roar turned to stillness.

"Ladies and Gentlemen, *Señores y Señoras.*"

The announcer spoke slowly, pleased at his bilingual efforts.

"Now the moment we have all been waiting for— the main event between two fine young Puerto Rican fighters, products of our lower east side.

"In this corner, weighing 134 pounds, Felix Vargas. And in this corner, weighing 133 pounds, Antonio Cruz. The winner will represent the Boys Club in the tournament of champions, the Golden Gloves. There will be no draw. May the best man win."

The cheering of the crowd shook the window panes of the old buildings surrounding Tompkins Square Park. At the center of the ring, the referee was giving instructions to the youngsters.

"Keep your punches up. No low blows. No punching on the back of the head. Keep your heads up. Understand. Let's have a clean fight. Now shake hands and come out fighting." **15**

Both youngsters touched gloves and nodded. They turned and danced

> **The crowd exploded with a roar.**

14 Inferences
What do Antonio and Felix's actions just before the fight tell you about how they are feeling?

15 Style: Language
Reread the announcer's instructions with expression. What do you notice about the word choices and style here?

Key Vocabulary
- **acknowledgment** *n.*, something done to express thanks or recognition

In Other Words
escorted accompanied
in its first birth just beginning

quickly to their corners. Their head towels and dressing gowns were lifted neatly from their shoulders by their trainers' **nimble** fingers. Antonio crossed himself. Felix did the same.

BONG! BONG! ROUND ONE. Felix and Antonio turned and faced each other squarely in a fighting pose. Felix wasted no time. He came in fast, head low, half hunched toward his right shoulder, and lashed out with a straight left. He missed a right cross as Antonio slipped the punch and countered with one-two-three lefts that snapped Felix's head back, sending a mild shock coursing through him. If Felix had any small doubt about their friendship affecting their fight, it was being neatly **dispelled**.

Antonio danced, a joy to behold. His left hand was like a **piston** pumping jabs one right after another with seeming ease. Felix bobbed and weaved and never stopped boring in. He knew that at long range he was at a disadvantage. Antonio had too much reach on him. Only by coming in close could Felix hope to achieve the dreamed-of knockout.

Antonio knew the dynamite that was stored in his *amigo* brother's fist. He ducked a short right and missed a **left hook**. Felix trapped him against the ropes just long enough to pour some punishing rights and lefts to Antonio's hard midsection. Antonio slipped away from Felix, crashing two lefts to his head, which set Felix's right ear to ringing.

Bong! Both *amigos* froze a punch well on its way, sending up a roar of approval for **good sportsmanship**. [16]

Felix walked briskly back to his corner. His right ear had not stopped ringing. Antonio gracefully danced his way toward his stool none the worse, except for glowing glove burns, showing angry red against the whiteness of his midribs.

"Watch that right, Tony." His trainer talked into his ear. "Remember Felix always goes to the body. He'll want you to drop your hands for his overhand left or right. Got it?"

[16] **Inferences**
Has Antonio and Felix's friendship affected the fight so far? What details support your inference?

Key Vocabulary
dispel *v.*, to scatter, to separate, to drive away or vanish

In Other Words
nimble quick
piston sliding cylinder
left hook short power punch that swings from the left side to the center
good sportsmanship showing fairness and respect during competition

Antonio nodded, spraying water out between his teeth. He felt better as his sore midsection was being firmly rubbed.

Felix's corner was also busy.

"You gotta get in there, fella." Felix's trainer poured water over his curly Afro locks. "Get in there or he's gonna chop you up from way back."

Bong! Bong! Round two. Felix was off his stool and rushed Antonio like a bull, sending a hard right to his head. Beads of water exploded from Antonio's long hair.

Antonio, hurt, sent back **a blurring barrage** of lefts and rights that only meant pain to Felix, who returned with a short left to the head followed by a looping right to the body. Antonio countered with his own flurry, forcing Felix to give ground. But not for long.

Felix bobbed and weaved, bobbed and weaved, occasionally punching his two gloves together.

Antonio waited for the rush that was sure to come. Felix closed in, feinted with his left shoulder, and threw his right instead. 🔢17 Lights suddenly exploded inside Felix's head as Antonio slipped the blow and hit him with a pistonlike left, catching him flush on the point of his chin.

Bedlam broke loose as Felix's legs momentarily buckled. He fought off a series of rights and lefts and came back with a strong right that taught Antonio respect.

Antonio danced in carefully. He knew Felix had the habit of **playing possum when hurt**, to **sucker** an opponent within reach of the powerful bombs he carried in each fist.

A right to the head slowed Antonio's pretty dancing. He answered with his own left at Felix's right eye that began puffing up within three seconds.

Antonio, a bit too eager, moved in too close and Felix had him entangled into a rip-roaring, punching **toe-to-toe** slugfest that brought the whole Tompkins Square Park screaming to its feet.

In Other Words
a blurring barrage an overwhelming amount
Bedlam An uproar
playing possum when hurt pretending to be more hurt than he really is
sucker attract or draw in sneakily
toe-to-toe direct

Corrales-Castillo II, 2005, Richard T. Slone. Enamel and acrylic on canvas, collection of the artist.

▲ **Critical Viewing: Design** How does the artist's use of line and color re-create the energy and excitement of this famous boxing match?

Rights to the body. Lefts to the head. Neither fighter was **giving an inch**. Suddenly a short right caught Antonio squarely on the chin. His long legs **turned to jelly** and his arms flailed out desperately. 18 Felix, grunting like a bull, threw wild punches from every direction. Antonio, groggy, bobbed and weaved, **evading** most of the blows. Suddenly his head cleared. His left **flashed out** hard and straight, catching Felix on the bridge of his nose.

18 **Style: Language**
Notice the narrator's use of short, choppy sentence fragments. What effect do these sentence fragments produce?

Key Vocabulary
evade *v.*, to avoid, to escape

In Other Words
giving an inch going to quit
turned to jelly became very weak
flashed out extended quickly

Felix lashed back with a haymaker, right off the ghetto streets. At the same instant, his eye caught another left hook from Antonio. Felix swung out trying to clear the pain. Only the frenzied screaming of those along ringside let him know that he had dropped Antonio. Fighting off the growing haze, Antonio struggled to his feet, got up, ducked, and threw a smashing right that dropped Felix flat on his back. **19**

Felix got up as fast as he could in his own corner, **groggy but still game**. He didn't even hear the count. In a fog, he heard the roaring of the crowd, who seemed to have gone insane. His head cleared to hear the bell sound at the end of the round. He was damned glad. His trainer sat him down on the stool.

In his corner, Antonio was doing what all fighters do when they are hurt. They sit and smile at everyone.

The referee signaled the ring doctor to check the fighters out. He did so and then gave his okay. The cold water sponges brought clarity to both *amigo* brothers. They were rubbed until their circulation ran free.

> He heard the roaring of the crowd, who seemed to have gone **insane.**

Bong! Round three—the final round. Up to now it had been tic-tac-toe, pretty much even. But everyone knew there could be no draw and that this round would decide the winner.

This time, to Felix's surprise, it was Antonio who came out fast, charging across the ring. Felix braced himself but couldn't ward off the barrage of punches. Antonio drove Felix hard against the ropes. **20**

The crowd **ate it up**. Thus far the two had fought with *mucho corazón*. Felix tapped his gloves and commenced his attack anew. Antonio, **throwing boxer's caution to the winds**, jumped in to meet him.

19 Inferences
What clues help you infer whether or not Felix and Antonio each want to win?

20 Inferences
At this point in the match, which boxer seems more likely to win? Explain. Write the details that support your opinion on your chart.

In Other Words
groggy but still game light-headed but ready to continue
ate it up loved it
mucho corazón great courage or heart (in Spanish)

throwing boxer's caution to the winds forgetting about the safe way to box

Both pounded away. Neither gave an inch and neither fell to the canvas. Felix's left eye was tightly closed. **Claret** red blood poured from Antonio's nose. They fought toe-to-toe.

The sounds of their blows were loud in contrast to the silence of a crowd gone completely mute. **21**

Bong! Bong! Bong! The bell sounded over and over again. Felix and Antonio were past hearing. Their blows continued to pound on each other like hailstones.

Finally the referee and the two trainers pried Felix and Antonio apart. Cold water was poured over them to bring them back to their senses.

They looked around and then rushed toward each other. A cry of alarm **surged** through Tompkins Square Park. Was this a fight to the death instead of a boxing match?

The fear soon gave way to wave upon wave of cheering as the two *amigos* embraced.

No matter what the decision, they knew they would always be champions to each other.

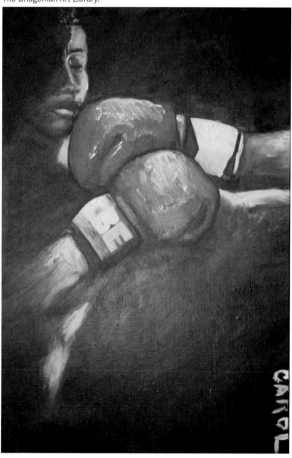

Boxer Right, Carol Tatham. Acrylic on canvas, private collection, The Bridgeman Art Library.

21 Inferences
For the first two rounds, the crowd has been cheering loudly. Why do you think the crowd is silent now?

◁ **Critical Viewing: Effect**
Compare this painting to the one on page 257. Describe how the moods of these two paintings are different.

Key Vocabulary
surge *v.*, to rise or increase suddenly

In Other Words
Claret Deep, dark

BONG! BONG! BONG! "Ladies and Gentlemen. *Señores* and *Señoras*. The winner and representative to the Golden Gloves Tournament of Champions is . . . "

The announcer turned to point to the winner and found himself alone. Arm in arm, the champions had already left the ring. **22** ❖

22 Style: Language/ Inferences
Why does the narrator say that *champions* (plural) left the ring when the match is meant to produce just one champion?

ANALYZE Amigo Brothers

1. **Recall and Interpret** What do you think helps the boys maintain their perpetual friendship? Be sure to cite evidence from the text.

2. **Vocabulary** At the end of the match, why does "a cry of alarm" **surge** through the crowd? How do the boys **dispel** the crowd's fear?

3. **Analyze Style: Language** Specific word choices help create the informal style of "Amigo Brothers." Work with a partner to choose a paragraph from the story that you find interesting. List the word choices and language that create the informal style. What feeling or effect does this language communicate? Share your findings with the class.

4. **Focus Strategy Make Inferences** Felix tells Antonio that when they get into the boxing ring, they need to act as if they have never met. Use what you know about friendships to make an inference about Felix. Why do you think Felix says this? What does it tell you about him?

Return to the Text
Reread and Write Did Antonio and Felix remain loyal to each other, or did their quest for a Golden Gloves championship divide their loyalty? Reread and write a paragraph, supporting your conclusion with at least two pieces of evidence from the text.

BEFORE READING **Lean on Me**

song lyrics by Bill Withers

Reading Strategies

· Plan and Monitor
· Determine Importance
▶ **Make Inferences**
· Ask Questions
· Make Connections
· Synthesize
· Visualize

Analyze Structure: Rhyme Scheme

A repeated sound at the end of two or more words is called a **rhyme**. In **end rhyme**, the sound occurs in words at the ends of lines. In **internal rhyme**, the sound occurs in words anywhere within a line. A pattern of rhyme, called a **rhyme scheme**, helps give structure to a poem or song. Songwriters structure their lyrics carefully, paying attention to both end rhyme and internal rhyme.

Look Into the Text

These lines have end rhyme.

Chorus

Lean on me when you're not strong,	a
And I'll be your friend;	b
I'll help you carry on,	c
For it won't be long	a
'Til I'm gonna need	d
Somebody to lean on.	c

The rhyming words create this rhyme scheme: abcadc.

Focus Strategy ▶ Make Inferences

Songwriters and other authors always have a purpose for writing but may not state directly what that point is. When you combine details from the text with your own experience, you can make an **inference** about an author's purpose.

HOW TO MAKE INFERENCES

Focus Strategy

1. As you read, think about the songwriter's purpose in writing the song. Notice details in the lines of the song.

2. Think about your own experiences. How does the song remind you of your own life?

3. Track your thoughts in a chart like the one below.

Details from the Song	What It Means to Me	What I Can Infer About the Songwriter's Purpose
"Lean on me"	I can count on this person for support.	The songwriter wants people to have someone for support.

Connect Across Texts

In "Amigo Brothers," Felix and Antonio's friendship is put to the test. In this song, read about the meaning of friendship during challenging times.

Lean on Me
by Bill Withers

Sometimes in our lives we all have pain,
We all have sorrow,
But if we are wise
We know that there's always tomorrow.

Chorus
Lean on me when you're not strong,
And I'll be your friend;
I'll help you carry on,
For it won't be long
'Til I'm gonna need
Somebody to lean on. **1**

Please swallow your pride
If I have things you need to borrow,
For no one can fill those of your needs
That you won't let show. **2**

Central Park Skate II, 2005, Joseph Holston. Oil on canvas, collection of the artist.

△ **Critical Viewing: Design** What connections can you make between the composition of these figures and the lyrics of this song?

In Other Words
Lean on rely on
swallow forget about, don't think about

You just call on me brother when you need a hand.

We all need somebody to lean on.

I just might have a problem that you'd understand.

We all need somebody to lean on.

[Chorus]

You just call on me brother when you need a hand.

We all need somebody to lean on.

I just might have a problem that you'd understand.

We all need somebody to lean on. **3**

If there is a load you have to bear

That you can't carry,

I'm right up the road.

I'll share your load

If you just call me.

1 Inferences
In the Chorus, who is invited to give and get support?

2 Inferences
What point is the songwriter trying to make about pride?

3 Structure: Rhyme Scheme
Reread this verse. Identify an example of end rhyme. Tell how you know. Then identify the rhyme scheme, which helps give this verse its structure.

About the Songwriter

Bill Withers (1938–) When singer Bill Withers couldn't find songs that expressed what he felt, he began writing his own. He says, "I write and sing about whatever I am able to understand and feel. I feel that it is healthier to look out at a world through a window than through a mirror." Withers has won several Grammy awards, and many popular artists, such as Will Smith and Mick Jagger, record his songs today.

The Power of Words

What started as a simple phrase grew into a number-one song. One day as singer/songwriter Bill Withers was playing around on a new piano, he came up with the words "lean on me." That called to mind his experiences growing up in a West Virginia coal mining town. When times were hard for someone in the community, everyone would lend a helping hand.

"You know, most songs are about romantic love, perhaps the most inconsistent kind there is. Well, there's another kind of love where people say, 'Hey, if there's anything I can do for you, let me know.' At the same time, they're smart enough to say, 'And if there's any way you can help me out, I'd sure appreciate it.'"

ANALYZE Lean on Me

1. **Explain** What does the singer urge the listener to do? Tell how you know. Be sure to cite evidence from the text.

2. **Vocabulary** How can friendship and loyalty make difficult times less **devastating** for a person?

3. **Analyze Structure: Rhyme Scheme** What are three examples of end rhyme in the song lyrics? What is the rhyme scheme of lines 11–14?

4. **Focus Strategy Make Inferences** Review the chart you created as you read the song lyrics. What inference can you make about the songwriter's purpose in the song? What overall message was he trying to communicate? Compare your interpretation with that of a partner.

Return to the Text

Reread and Write What do you think the songwriter is saying about loyalty? Write your opinion, using two details from the song to support your conclusion.

EQ What Tests a Person's Loyalty?

Critical Thinking

1. **Analyze** Complete the **Anticipation Guide** on page 242 again as if you were a character in the short story. Share your answers with a group and support your responses with evidence from the text.

2. **Compare** From which point of view are both "Amigo Brothers" and "Lean on Me" told? Compare the authors' purposes in using the particular points of view for each selection.

EQ 3. **Interpret** In "Amigo Brothers," why do you think the author ended the story the way he did? How did the outcome affect Antonio and Felix's friendship? Explain your answers.

4. **Speculate** Imagine that Antonio telephones Felix several hours after the fight. What do the boys say to each other?

EQ 5. **Evaluate** Which do you think presents a stronger challenge to loyalty—competition or pride? Why?

Write About Literature

Diary Entry Write a diary entry from the perspective of Antonio, Felix, or the singer of "Lean on Me." Use specific details from the appropriate text. Include thoughts or feelings the character or singer might have been experiencing, judging from the story's dialogue or the lines in the song.

Key Vocabulary Review

Oral Review Work with a partner. Use these words to complete the paragraph.

acknowledgment	evade	pensively
devastating	improvise	surge
dispel	opponent	

Loyalty is tested when a friend becomes an ___(1)___ in a competition. When faced with this new situation, we may have to think quickly and ___(2)___ a response. We may try to ___(3)___ the other person, but sooner or later we will have to face him or her. Talking openly is one of the best ways to ___(4)___, or clear away, any doubts we may have about the friendship. We may speak ___(5)___, in a serious, thoughtful manner. We may shake hands to give an ___(6)___ that the friendship is important to us. Refusing to talk at all could be ___(7)___ to the friendship and could cause bad feelings to ___(8)___. Even when on opposite sides, two people can maintain a good friendship.

Writing Application Write a paragraph about a time when you or a friend had to **improvise** a solution to a problem or challenge. Use at least three Key Vocabulary words.

Read with Ease: Intonation

Assess your reading fluency with the passage in the Reading Handbook, p. 805. Then complete the self-check below.

1. My intonation did/did not sound natural.

2. My words correct per minute: _____.

INTEGRATE THE LANGUAGE ARTS

Use Verb Tenses

Use the **present tense** to talk about an action that happens now or happens often. Use the **past tense** to talk about an action that already happened. If there is more than one verb in a sentence, use parallel structure: Put all the verbs in the same tense.

Felix **jabs** the air. Antonio **punched** the air.

The verbs **be** and **have** are irregular verbs. They have special forms to show the past tense. Find their past tense forms in the sentences below.

- **Present:** Antonio **is** lean and lanky, **has** long arms, and **is** a good boxer.

  Past: Felix **was** solid, **had** strong arms, and **was** also a good boxer.

  Past: They **were** both determined and **had** a plan for their training.

Oral Practice (1–4) With a partner, take turns answering each question. Use the past tense verb in parentheses.

1. What dream did Antonio and Felix have? (had)
2. Why did they work out? (worked)
3. How did they help each other? (helped)
4. Why did they stop training together? (stopped)

Written Practice (5–8) Rewrite the paragraph. Correct the underlined verbs.

Tony and Felix slapped skin, <u>laugh</u>, and hugged each other. Tony <u>jogs</u> away and threw jabs in the air. The night before the fight, Tony went to the roof, peered over the ledge, and <u>listens</u>. Meanwhile, Felix <u>watches</u> a movie and imagined being the champ.

Retell a Story

Pair Talk Who are the "Amigo Brothers"? What happens to them? Take turns retelling your favorite part of the story.

Word Choice in Description

Description is a detailed account of a scene, event, or character. By using words that appeal to the reader's senses, a writer helps the reader see, hear, smell, taste, or feel a story.

In "Amigo Brothers," the author gives his narrator descriptive words to tell about the setting, characters, and action. These words create images and add details. For example:

> Antonio was fair, lean, and lanky, while Felix was dark, short, and husky.

With descriptive words such as the adjectives <u>fair</u> and <u>dark</u>, the reader can picture what the characters look like.

The narrator also has colorful words that make the fight scene between Antonio and Felix come to life.

1. Review pages 256–260 and notice the adjectives, nouns, and verbs the author uses to describe the fight.

2. With a partner, pick a passage and find other descriptions that appeal to the senses. Track your findings in a chart like the one below. Note effective adjectives, nouns, or verbs.

3. What words helped you to imagine the scene? Imagine what that passage would be like without the descriptive words that create images and add details. Would you still be able to picture the scene?

Sense	Description

Evaluate Word Choice The theme of "Amigo Brothers" is the importance of friendship. How do the author's word choices for the narrator and for the characters' dialogue help you picture the characters and events so that you can appreciate the theme?

Word Families

A **word family** is a group of words with the same base word but different prefixes or suffixes. For example, the Key Vocabulary word **opponent** is part of a family that has as its base the word *oppose* (resist or stand against).

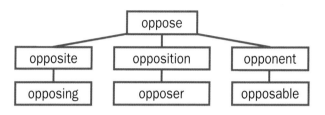

With a partner, use your understanding of the base word *oppose* and its prefixes or suffixes to define each of the words on the above chart.

Compare Themes

Compare Themes In literature, a **theme** is the central idea of the work—a message about life or human nature. Remember that a theme is not the same as the topic of the work. "Amigo Brothers" is about two friends and boxing, but what message about life, about friendship, is the author conveying?

With a partner, identify the theme of "Amigo Brothers." Give evidence from the text to support the theme. Use the title, the resolution of the story, and how the characters change during the story. Then compare the theme of "Amigo Brothers" with another story, movie, or TV show. How is the message, or theme, like and unlike "Amigo Brothers"?

▼ **Language and Learning Handbook**, p. 750

Write a Short Comparison Essay

A test may ask you to respond in writing to literature. The prompt often names a selection and asks you to think about some aspect of it.

❶ Unpack the Prompt Read the prompt and underline the key words.

> **Writing Prompt**
>
> Write an essay to compare a lesson you have learned in life to the lesson Antonio and Felix learned in "Amigo Brothers." Use examples from the story and your life for support.

❷ Prewrite Choose a life lesson to write about. Then compare it to the lesson learned by the Amigo Brothers. Use a **Venn Diagram** to help you plan.

Venn Diagram

My life lesson / Both / Amigo Brothers' lesson

❸ Draft When you compare, organize your essay like this. Add specific ideas from your diagram.

> **Essay Organizer**
>
> In "Amigo Brothers," Antonio and Felix learned [tell what the lesson was]. In my life, I have learned [tell what my lesson was].
>
> Our life lessons are alike because [tell how they are alike]. Antonio and Felix [give an example from the story]. I also [give an example from my life].
>
> However, our life lessons are different because [tell how they are different]. [give an example from the story], but [give an example from my life].
>
> In conclusion, [summarize the comparison].

❹ Edit and Proofread Reread your essay. Ask:

- Does my essay address the prompt?
- Do I give examples to support my ideas?
- Do I use verb tenses correctly?

▼ **Writing Handbook**, p. 832

1

2

3

At a Construction Site

People in the construction industry are responsible for building, maintaining, and improving structures. Construction projects include buildings, roads, bridges, tunnels, and other structures.

Jobs in the Construction Industry

Many career opportunities exist in the construction industry for people of different abilities and educational backgrounds.

Job	Responsibilities	Education/Training Required
Construction Worker 1	• Prepares construction sites • Controls traffic • Works to build and repair structures • Operates manual equipment	• On-the-job experience • Training at a vocational school or community college • Training in safety procedures
Construction Manager 2	• Plans and oversees projects, schedules, and budgets • Works with engineers and architects • Obtains permits and licenses • Hires, directs, and reviews workers	• Associate's degree in construction management or • College degree • Experience in construction industry
Architect 3	• Designs structures • Explains his or her ideas to clients and contractors • Studies job sites, costs, and other factors • Follows building codes	• College degree from a school of architecture • Three-year training period • Pass registration examination to be licensed

Research the Job Outlook

When you choose a career, consider what jobs will be available in the future. Analyze the job outlook for a position in the construction industry.

1. Prepare a four-column chart with the following headings: Job, Number of Employees in Industry, Earnings, and Job Outlook.

2. Consult the U.S. Department of Labor, Bureau of Labor Statistics Web site's Occupational Outlook Handbook.

3. Fill in the information about your chosen job in the chart. Work with a partner to determine if there is a positive or negative job outlook for your chosen careers. Save the information in a professional career portfolio.

myNGconnect.com

◉ Learn more about the construction industry.

◉ Download a form to evaluate whether you would like to work in this field.

Use What You Know

You can often understand words in other languages because they look similar to words you know. For example, the Spanish word *minuto* looks a lot like the English word *minute*. The two words mean the same thing. They are called **cognates**—words in different languages that are related.

Even in just one language, you can often recognize something familiar in an unfamiliar word. **Word families** are words that share the same root word. For example, you might not know the word *decidedly*. However, you probably know the root word *decide*. Once you have identified the familiar part, you can use your knowledge of other word parts, like prefixes and suffixes, to determine the word's meaning. You can use this strategy to help you understand all the words in a word family.

Sometimes the root word has a slightly different spelling, as in *decision*. The spelling changes are usually small though, so you can still recognize the word.

Use Word Families to Find Meaning

Work with another student to use familiar parts of words to figure out their meanings.

1. Copy the chart to the right onto a piece of paper.
2. Discuss what each word in the **decide** word family may mean.
3. Look up each word in the dictionary.
4. Think of other words in the *decide* word family and add them to the chart.

Words in the **Decide** Family
decided
decidedly
deciding
decision

Put the Strategy to Use

When you come to a word you don't know, use this strategy to figure out its meaning:

1. Look for a root word.
2. Identify the other part or parts of the word.
3. Figure out how the part you know fits with the other part or parts.
4. Take a guess at the word's meaning.

TRY IT▶ With a partner, make a list of as many words as you can think of from the word families below. Share and compare your list of words with the rest of the class.

develop   equal   favor   simple

📕 Reading Handbook,
p. 781

EQ ## What Tests a Person's Loyalty?
Consider whether loyalty is always the best policy.

Make a Connection

Quickwrite Sometimes loyalty means staying a fan of your favorite sports team even when they are losing. At other times loyalty means supporting someone in good times and bad. Should you always be loyal? Write about a situation that tested your loyalty to a friend or family member. What did you decide to do?

Learn Key Vocabulary

Study the Words Pronounce each word and learn its meaning. You may also want to look up definitions in the Glossary.

● Academic Vocabulary

Key Words	Examples
● **abstract** (**ab**-strakt) *noun* ▶ page 294	Something in the **abstract** is an idea that is not concrete or specific. In the **abstract**, loyalty is a good thing, but loyalty can be complicated in specific situations.
adhere (ad-**hear**) *verb* ▶ page 295	When you **adhere** to ideas, beliefs, and other concepts, you remain devoted to them or you keep doing or believing the same thing. To play fairly, everyone must **adhere** to the rules.
● **advocate** (**ad**-vu-kāt) *verb* ▶ page 294	When you **advocate** something, you speak in favor of it. Do you **advocate** wearing a helmet when riding a bicycle? *Synonyms:* support, favor; *Antonym:* oppose
deliberately (di-**li**-bah-rut-lē) *adverb* ▶ pages 286, 291	The field manager took his time, slowly and **deliberately** marking the baseball diamond with chalk. *Synonym:* purposefully; *Antonym:* accidentally
desolately (**de**-su-lut-lē) *adverb* ▶ page 284	I could tell how miserable she felt about the hard test when I saw her walk **desolately** out of the room. *Synonym:* sadly; *Antonym:* happily
dilemma (dah-**le**-mah) *noun* ▶ pages 294, 296..297	A **dilemma** is a situation that requires you to make a difficult choice. My **dilemma** was to finish my math homework or practice my speech. I didn't have time for both.
● **ethical** (**e**-thi-kul) 尊貴守法 *adjective* ▶ pages 295, 296	An **ethical** action respects rules of right and wrong. *Synonyms;* moral, decent; *Antonyms:* unethical, immoral
● **reinforce** (rē-un-**fors**) *verb* ▶ page 295	How can working with a tutor help **reinforce** a lesson you learned in class? *Synonyms:* strengthen, solidify

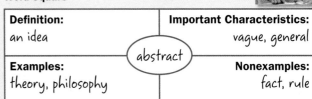

Practice the Words Work with a partner. Make a **Word Square** for each Key Vocabulary word.

Word Square

Definition: an idea	Important Characteristics: vague, general
Examples: theory, philosophy	Nonexamples: fact, rule

(*abstract*)

BEFORE READING My Brother's Keeper

short story by Jay Bennett

Reading Strategies

- Plan and Monitor
- Determine Importance
- ▶ **Make Inferences**
- Ask Questions
- Make Connections
- Synthesize
- Visualize

Analyze Style: Sentence Structure

An author's **sentence structure** helps create the style that's best for the story. For example, the author can write long or short sentences, or use **repetition** to emphasize words. He or she can also use **fragments**, or incomplete sentences. Each of these techniques helps create the story's overall feeling. Read the following passage aloud to hear the effect the author creates.

Look Into the Text

The writer uses short sentences and sentence fragments.

> Jamie was alone.
> And now the phone was ringing.
> He reached over to the night table and picked up the dark, gleaming receiver.
> The summer curtain rustled noiselessly.
> Then he heard the voice.
> "Jamie?"
> A slight chill went through him and he was silent.
> "Jamie?"
> It was his brother.
> His only brother.

Complex sentences create contrast.

Fragments create a choppy style and a feeling of tension.

What effect does the repetition of words create?

Focus Strategy ▶ Make Inferences

When you make **inferences**, you read between the lines of a text as well as use your personal experiences. An author may provide clues and details that help you figure out for yourself why characters act, speak, and feel as they do.

HOW TO MAKE INFERENCES

Focus Strategy

1. As you read, ask yourself how the details from the story connect with what you already know. What do you think these details suggest about the story's characters and their relationships?

2. Track your thoughts on a chart like the one on the right.

When I Read	I Already Know
"Jamie was alone" . . .	I feel scared when I'm home alone.
"A slight chill went through him and he was silent" . . .	A "slight chill" can be a sign of fear.
"It was his brother. His only brother."	I would be relieved to know the caller was a family member and not a stranger.

What I Can Infer: Jamie is entering a threatening situation that involves his brother.

Jay Bennett
(1912– 2009)

Jay Bennett wrote many television scripts, even an adaptation of Shakespeare's *Hamlet*.

Jay Bennett knew that to be human is sometimes to feel alone. "I speak to the loner in our society," he said. "There are so many loners, especially among the young."

In stories such as "My Brother's Keeper," Bennett wrote about loners who face difficult decisions. "The reader identifies with my 'loner' characters and enjoys the crisis of decision and at the same time feels his sensibilities open up," he explained. "The reader thinks and feels as he enjoys, and whether or not he knows it consciously, he has learned something about the world he is living in."

Bennett grew up in New York City. He had always dreamed of being a writer, but the hard times he lived in made getting any job difficult. For many years he held odd jobs and wrote in his free time. His breakthrough finally came when he sold a script for a radio drama. Eventually Bennett became a much sought-after scriptwriter and a successful novelist.

myNGconnect.com

🔊 Find out more about the American justice system.
🔊 Listen to a recording of a radio drama.

My Brother's Keeper
by Jay Bennett

Boy with Caution Tape, 2000, Sidney Goodman. Oil on canvas, courtesy of ACA Galleries, New York.

▲ **Critical Viewing: Effect** What feeling or mood does the painting create? What details does the artist use to create that mood?

D o you swear to tell the truth and nothing but the truth?"

The truth?

Nothing but the truth?

What is truth? **1**

1 Style: Sentence Structure
How do the short, repetitive questions in italics affect the style at the beginning of the story?

Jamie raised his hand, his right hand, in the hushed courtroom and as he did that, **his senses began to reel**, to reel back to the beginning.

The very beginning.

He had been sleeping, a restless sleep and then the clear ring of the telephone **cut into him**. His eyes slowly opened and he looked about the silent shadowy room, listening to the cold, insistent ring.

He was alone in the dark house.

Completely alone.

His uncle, with whom he lived, had gone off on a fishing trip near the state border. **2**

2 Inferences/ Language
How do you think Jamie is feeling as he wakes up? What words or phrases help create the mood?

"If the fishing is fine I'll stay awhile. If it's bad, real bad, I'll come on home. Anyway I'll be back before you go on to college."

Jamie nodded silently.

"I'll drive you up there. See you settled in."

"You don't have to, Harry. I'll manage."

"I know you can. But I want to do it."

Ted's away in his own fantasy world and I'm all you have left, Jamie thought.

"Okay," he said. "You'll take me up there."

The man smiled and started up the motor. Then he waved his lean, tanned hand and was gone.

Jamie was alone.

And now the phone was ringing.

In Other Words

his senses began to reel his mind began to spin

cut into him woke him up

Civics Background

In a United States courtroom, witnesses must first take an *oath*, or make a promise to tell the truth. After taking the oath, witnesses can then answer questions in a trial.

He reached over to the night table and picked up the dark, gleaming **receiver**.

The summer curtain **rustled noiselessly**.

Then he heard the voice.

"Jamie?"

A slight chill went through him and he was silent.

"Jamie?"

It was his brother.

His only brother.

"You alone?"

"Yes," Jamie said.

Outside in the distant night a dog began to bark.

A low **mournful** sound.

Jamie listened to it.

"Uncle Harry?"

"He's gone fishing."

"Where?"

"Upstate. Near the falls."

"Oh."

The barking had stopped and the silence of the long night flooded into the room.

And all the time Jamie waited. **3**

Waited.

For his older brother to tell him.

Then he heard it.

"I'm in trouble, Jamie."

> # A slight chill went through him and he was silent.

3 Inferences
How is Jamie feeling about getting the phone call? How do you know? Track your thoughts in your chart.

In Other Words
receiver earpiece of the phone
rustled noiselessly moved silently
mournful sad, desolate
Upstate. Near the falls. In the northern part of the state, close to the waterfalls.

And you need me **to bail you out**, Jamie thought bitterly.

"Trouble."

This time the voice was almost a whisper.

But Jamie heard it clearly.

His lips thinned into a straight line.

I'm your kid brother. Five long years younger than you are and all the time, all through the years I had to act like I was the older brother.

All the time. **4**

Jamie's hand tightened around the receiver.

"What have you done, Ted?"

"I want to come over and talk."

"You **slugged** somebody in a bar? A guy came over to get your autograph and he got nasty and you were with a girl and you . . . "

"It's not that," Ted cut in.

"Then what?"

"It . . . it's hard to explain."

Jamie's voice **grew harsh**.

"Nothing's hard to explain. Tell me now."

"Let me see you. I have to."

Jamie breathed out and looked over at the clock on the night table. The clock Ted had given him as a birthday present along with a thousand-dollar check. **5**

"It's three in the morning," he said. "Let it wait."

"It can't wait."

"What do you mean?"

"I'm coming over. Whether you want me or not. I need you."

There was a slight break in the voice.

And Jamie thought to himself **bleakly**, this time it must be bad.

Really bad.

4 Style: Sentence Structure
How does the repetition of "all" and "all the time" show how Jamie feels?

5 Inferences
What do Jamie's comments about an autograph tell you about Ted? What do the other details on this page tell you about Ted?

In Other Words
to bail you out to come to your rescue
slugged hit
grew harsh became angry
bleakly without hope

"Okay," he said. "Come on over."

"Thanks, Jamie."

Jamie was silent.

"I'll never forget it."

You will, Ted. You will.

You always do.

Then he slowly **put the receiver back onto its hook**.

He sat there in the dark, narrow room a long time, thinking, ever thinking.

His hand clenched into a tight fist.

Then after a while, the hand unclenched.

And lay hopelessly against Jamie's side. **6**

Man Overboard, 1906, Christian Krohg. Oil on canvas, National Museum, Stockholm, Sweden, The Bridgeman Art Library.

⚠ **Critical Viewing: Plot** How would you connect the situation in the painting with the situation in the story? Explain.

6 Inferences
What do Jamie's thoughts and his tightened fist suggest about Ted's past behavior? Write what you know about these details on your chart.

In Other Words
put the receiver back onto its hook
hung up the telephone

Monitor Comprehension

Explain
What does Ted want? Why might Jamie be reacting as he does?

He let the doorbell ring three times, then he slowly went down the carpeted stairs and walked slowly through the dimly lit corridor to the front door.

His brother stood big and large against the night.

A menacing figure.

But the face was pale and gentle and the eyes **haunting**.

"Jamie."

And his brother reached out with his large, muscular arms and drew him close.

So very close.

Jamie was tall but his head barely reached Ted's shoulder.

He felt a deep tremor of love for the big man and then the tremor was gone.

The bleak feeling was back within him.

"I need you. Need you a lot," Ted murmured.

Jamie slowly drew away.

"Let's go into the kitchen and have a cup of coffee, Ted. You look like you could use one."

"Sure. Whatever you say."

"Then we'll talk," Jamie said softly.

"Anything. Anything you say."

Then Ted followed his smaller brother into the neat, yellow kitchen, lifted a heavy wooden chair, swung it about, set it down without a sound and slid into it gracefully.

It was all done in one smooth, flowing motion.

And watching him, Jamie thought of the times he had watched Ted weave and run and evade tacklers with **an effortless grace**. **7**

The crowd in the packed stands roaring.

7 **Style: Sentence Structure**
Why does the author use longer sentences to describe Ted's movements? How does this contrast with how Ted speaks?

In Other Words
A menacing figure. A person who looks dangerous.
haunting unforgettable
an effortless grace easy movements

His teammates on the sidelines jumping with their hands raised high against a cold autumn sky.

And Jamie thought how on the football field Ted loomed large, so very large.

In full control of himself.

So very well put together.

So finely disciplined.

Rarely making a wrong move.

Every inch a rounded, mature man.

But once he stepped off the field and took off his uniform, he became a child.

A huge, gentle child.

Who got himself into **scrapes** and had to be bailed out.

Again and again. **8**

Jamie **lighted the jet** under the coffeepot.

"What's it this time?"

Ted looked at his brother's trim, straight back and didn't speak.

Jamie was tall and slender, his fine-featured face with the **ever-somber** look on it always made him appear older than his eighteen years.

Ted fondly called him "**Straight Arrow**."

"Tell me, Ted."

"I . . . I hit a man."

Jamie stared at the blue jet on the gas range.

His voice was low when he spoke.

"Another bar fight? You're not a drinker. How do you get into these things?" **9**

"No, Jamie," Ted murmured.

"Then what?"

"I was driving on Desmond Street and I . . . I hit a man."

8 Style: Sentence Structure
Notice the sentence structure in the last ten sentences. What effect does the structure create?

9 Inferences
Reread Jamie's questions on this page. What do they suggest about how he feels?

In Other Words
scrapes bad situations
lighted the jet turned on the gas
ever-somber always serious
Straight Arrow the person who always does the
  right thing

Jamie didn't turn.

"He was drunk and he walked in front of the car. It was very dark and nobody was around. You know how **deserted** Desmond Street is. You know, Jamie. You know. Dark and deserted and . . . and . . . " **10**

His voice trailed off into the silence.

Jamie's hands gripped the top of the white range.

The range was hot to the touch but he didn't feel it.

Then he heard his brother speak again.

"I was sober. Clean sober. It's the truth, Jamie. The truth."

"And?"

"I **panicked** and left him lying there."

Jamie swung about **sharply**.

His face white and tense.

His voice cold and harsh.

"What in the heck are you saying? What?"

The tears came into Ted's eyes.

His gentle blue eyes.

"I . . . I panicked."

Jamie came swiftly over to him.

"And you left him there?" he shouted.

His angry voice filled the narrow room.

Ted shivered.

His lips trembled.

"How? How could you do that?"

The big man looked up to him pleadingly.

When he spoke, his voice was low, very low.

As if he was talking to himself.

"I . . . **I lost my head.** . . . It wasn't my fault. He walked in front of the car. He was drunk. Drunk. Came out of the night. From nowhere. I wasn't

I panicked and left him lying there.

10 Style: Sentence Structure/ Inferences
How do you think Ted feels as he speaks in these broken sentences? Explain.

11 Inferences
Read to the end of the paragraph, at the top of page 281. Does this new information about the boys' parents change your understanding of Jamie and Ted? Explain.

In Other Words
deserted empty
panicked became filled with fear
sharply suddenly
I lost my head. I couldn't think clearly.

going fast. I wasn't. I **swear to you** on Dad and Mom's graves that I . . . " 11

Jamie fiercely cut into him.

"You left him lying in the street? In the street?"

"There was nobody around. Nobody saw it. That's all that was in my mind."

"And you drove off?"

"All I was thinking of was my career and nobody saw it. **I wasn't myself.** You know I'm not like that. You know it. I help everybody. Everybody. I haven't a mean feeling in my . . . I wasn't myself."

He hit his knee with his big hand again and again.

"I got scared. Scared. I wasn't myself. I wasn't."

Jamie reached down and fiercely grabbed him by his shirt.

"But he was a human being. Not a dog. You don't even leave a dog lying in the street and run off."

Fire and Destruction, 1985, Jüri Palm. Oil on canvas, Art Museum of Estonia, Tallinn, Estonia, The Bridgeman Art Library.

▲ **Critical Viewing: Plot** How does the title of this oil painting relate to what is happening in the story?

"It all happened so fast. I couldn't handle it. Just couldn't." 12

Jamie slowly let go of the shirt and drew back.

"Was he dead?"

And he felt inside of him the heavy beating of his heart while he waited for the answer.

12 **Style: Sentence Structure**
What do you notice about the author's style in Ted's speeches? Why do you think the author uses this style?

In Other Words
swear to you promise
I wasn't myself. I wasn't behaving as I normally would.

And also mixed within was an overwhelming pity for his lost brother.

Then he heard the words.

"No. Just hurt."

Jamie breathed out silently.

"Badly hurt?"

Ted shook his head and then ran his hand through his curly blond hair before answering.

"Just hurt."

"How do you know that?"

"I went back. Walked. And there was an ambulance there. I stood where nobody could see me."

"And?"

"I could **make out** what was happening."

"He was hurt enough to be taken to a hospital," Jamie said sharply.

"He was."

Jamie's voice rose.

"Why didn't you come out of the dark and go over there and **face it**?"

"I . . . I just couldn't."

"The truth. All you needed was to tell them the truth. The truth."

"Couldn't do it. Just . . . "

And Jamie, looking at him, knew that he couldn't.

You're lost, Ted.

Lost. **13**

Ever since Mom and Dad were killed in that crash.

You never got over it.

And you turned to me.

To me.

When Jamie spoke again, his voice was gentle.

"And then what did you do?"

13 Inferences
Use what you've read so far and what you know about the word *lost* to infer Jamie's opinion of Ted.

In Other Words
make out see
face it do or say something

"I went back to the car and drove away. Nobody saw me."

Jamie went over to the window and stared out into the night.

The dark, cloudless night.

He did it this time, Jamie thought.

He really did it.

Jamie heard his brother's voice **drift over** to him.

"I spoke to Carmody."

"Who is he?"

"The team's lawyer. He wants to talk to you."

"To me? Why?"

"He . . . he said he'd explain to you."

"Explain what to me?"

Ted looked at him and didn't answer.

"Tell me."

"I don't know. I really don't know." 14

"You do."

"I swear to you on Mom's . . . "

Jamie cut in **savagely**.

"Don't swear. Leave Mom and Dad out of this. Let them sleep in peace. Thank God, they're long dead. Dead and away from you." 15

"Jamie, please don't talk to me that way. Please don't do it."

"You make me."

He came over to the table and sat down heavily and then looked across it at the big man.

"I'm tired of you, Ted," he said.

"Please, Jamie. Don't say that."

And the desperate lost look in his brother's eyes pierced through him.

"Jamie, don't leave me alone."

Jamie looked away from him and out to the night.

14 Inferences
Do you believe Ted when he says he doesn't know what Carmody wants to speak to Jamie about? Explain.

15 Inferences
What does Jamie mean when he tells Ted that their parents are "Dead and away from you"? Use your chart to help you make the inference.

In Other Words
drift over come across the room
savagely with sudden anger

"I can't make it without you."

I know.

How well I know it.

"When does this Carmody want me to talk to him?"

"In the morning. Anytime you choose."

"Okay," Jamie murmured **desolately**. "I'll see him."

"Thanks."

That's all the big man said.

And Jamie knew that he was too full of emotion to say anymore.

"Get upstairs," Jamie suddenly shouted.

Ted looked fearfully at him and didn't speak.

"Get to bed and try to get some rest. You look **like a damned wreck**."

Ted slowly rose.

"Sure, Jamie. Sure."

Then Jamie watched him turn and go to the stairs.

Watched him as he swung on the second step, swung around, with that smooth, graceful motion, and then stood stock-still and stared **bewilderedly** about him as if he didn't know where he was.

"I'm sorry, Jamie," he said. "I always bring you trouble. I'm sorry."

Then Jamie watched him go up the steps and out of sight.

Jamie was now alone in the night-filled room.

Thinking.

Ever thinking.

The truth.

Nothing but the truth. **17**

I always bring you trouble. I'm sorry.

16 Language
How does the phrase "night-filled room" help you picture the setting and better understand Jamie's mood?

17 Style: Sentence Structure
Where in the story do these lines first occur? Why do you think they appear here, too?

Monitor Comprehension

Confirm Prediction
Was your prediction accurate? If not, what happened that you did not expect?

Key Vocabulary
desolately *adv.*, very sadly, miserably

In Other Words
like a damned wreck tired, upset
bewilderedly strangely and confusedly

Predict
What do you think the lawyer will say to Jamie?
How will Jamie react?

"**T**ed claims that nobody saw him. Nobody."

"That's right," Ted murmured.

The lawyer turned to him.

"But soon somebody will come forward and say that he or she did see you in the car. It's happened before in my practice. And I've been a lawyer a long, long time."

Jamie sat waiting.

Carmody spoke again.

"We must be ready."

Ready for what? Jamie thought bleakly.

They were sitting in the high-ceilinged, elaborately furnished office.

The three of them.

Carmody, Ted, and Jamie.

The door of the room was closed.

Tightly closed.

Carmody was a **lithe**, tanned man with dark alert eyes and a quiet, self-assured voice.

"So far the police have no clues. Not a one."

It's early, Jamie thought **somberly**.

"I have some good friends there who will tell me if they come up with any. Such as a license-plate number." 18

Carmody lit a cigarette and paused.

Then he turned to Jamie.

And quietly studied him.

He spoke.

"I understand that you were **valedictorian** in your graduating class."

"I was," Jamie said.

18 Inferences
Who do you think these "good friends" might be? What does this tell you about the lawyer?

In Other Words
lithe slender, thin
somberly sadly, seriously
valedictorian the student with the best grades

"And you've been accepted to a **very prestigious** college."

"Yale."

"He's getting a full scholarship. I told you that," Ted said proudly.

Carmody smiled.

"You did, Ted."

He puffed at his cigarette.

"There's not **a blemish on your record**, Jamie."

He pronounced the word "blemish" softly.

So very softly.

And Jamie knew instantly that he disliked the man.

Disliked him intensely. [19]

Carmody spoke again.

"Your brother needs your help. Needs it badly."

"What does he need?"

"For you to say that he was with you on the night of the accident."

Jamie stared silently at the man.

The room had grown still.

Very still.

Ted had risen from his chair, a wild, **anguished** look on his face.

Carmody's voice cut through the stillness.

"Ted was with you all night long. Every minute of it. Never leaving you."

Ted walked over to the lawyer.

"You didn't tell me that Jamie would have to do that."

"We've no choice."

Ted loomed over the man.

"But it's against all he stands for. I know him. I don't want it."

Carmody snuffed out his cigarette, slowly and **deliberately**.

"You'll do as I tell you." [20]

"No. I won't hold still for this."

[19] **Inferences**
Why does Jamie intensely dislike Carmody? Write the details on your chart that help you infer the reason.

[20] **Style: Sentence Structure/Inferences**
How does the sentence structure change as the lawyer talks to Jamie and then to Ted? What does this reveal about what Carmody thinks of them?

Key Vocabulary
deliberately *adv.*, on purpose

In Other Words
very prestigious top quality
a blemish on your record any evidence that you ever did anything wrong
anguished hurt, devastated

"You'll have to."

Ted pounded the desk with his big fist.

"No. No."

His face was pale and sweat glistened on his forehead.

"Keep quiet and sit down."

Ted's big hands began to tremble.

"Sit," Carmody commanded.

The big man slowly turned and went back to his seat. **21**

Carmody's voice when he spoke was precise and clean.

His eyes cold and **impassive**.

"Listen to me. There's a real world out there. So listen. The two of you."

He paused and then went on.

"Ted, you are one of the young stars of pro football today. You made three million dollars your first year. You will make much, much more as you play on. You are sure to become the club's most **valuable property**."

The real world, Jamie thought bitterly.

The real world has its own truth. **22**

But, dammit, I have my own.

My own.

Carmody was speaking.

" . . . Ted, you did a damn fool thing. I believe you. It was not your fault. You panicked. But you drove away and left a man lying on the street, not knowing whether he was dead or alive."

"Lost my head. Lost it," Ted murmured.

Your brother needs your help. Needs it badly.

21 Inferences
Why does the author repeat the word *big* in this scene? Who is more powerful, Ted or his lawyer? Explain.

22 Inferences/ Language
Use what you know about the term "real world" to explain this sentence.

In Other Words
impassive showing no emotion
valuable property important player

"I know and understand. But you're going to be **called into court**. And when that happens I want to be there at your side with **an airtight alibi**. And no matter what they come up with, that alibi will pull us through. Do you hear me?"

Ted bowed his head and covered his face with his hands. **23**

"I'll pull you through. I will."

Carmody turned to Jamie.

"You say you care for your brother."

"Yes."

"Then you must do this."

"Must?"

"Yes. I assure you that nothing will happen to you or him. Nothing."

"You know from experience?"

23 Inferences
What do the details from this sentence tell you about Ted's response to Carmody's plan?

Figure with Caution Tape, 2001, Sidney Goodman. Oil on canvas, courtesy of ACA Galleries, New York.

◀ Critical Viewing: Character
Whom do you think this figure more accurately represents: Jamie or Ted? Why?

In Other Words

called into court ordered to speak in court
an airtight alibi a believable claim that you were not at the place when the crime was committed

Carmody nodded.

"I know. Well, Jamie?"

Jamie looked away to Ted and didn't answer.

He heard Carmody's voice.

"If you're thinking of the man who was injured . . . ?"

"I am."

Carmody smiled.

"He's going to fully recover. And then he's going to be quietly well taken care of. It will turn out to be the best thing that has ever happened to him." **24**

He leaned forward to Jamie.

"Well?"

"Let's wait and see what happens," Jamie said.

"But we can **count on** you?"

Jamie looked from Carmody over to his brother.

Ted still sat there, his head bowed, his face still covered by his big hands.

Jamie turned back to the lawyer.

"You can count on me."

"After the crash, when I came to get the two of you and take you home with me . . . "

Uncle Harry paused and looked out over the lake and didn't speak for a while.

His lean, lined face was tight and sad.

Jamie waited for him to speak again.

"It just **tore my heart out**. I reached over to get his hand but he turned away from me and went to you. And he stood there looking down into your face and then he reached out to you and held you and cried. And all the while you stood there, holding him, your face tight and silent. Like you were a big man, sheltering him." **25**

24 Inferences
What do these new details add to your understanding of Carmody? Remember to track the details on your chart.

25 Style: Sentence Structure
How does the sentence structure change when Uncle Harry speaks? How does this help you compare Uncle Harry to the lawyer?

In Other Words
count on depend on, rely on
tore my heart out upset me

The sun was still high and the lake rippled, ripples of gold.

Uncle Harry cast his line out again.

"He needs you. He'll always need you."

Then he said, "I can't tell you what to do, Jamie. **It's your call.**"

"And you think it will work out like the lawyer says?"

Harry nodded.

"You'll end up in court in the witness chair. That's if you decide to go along with them."

"You can't help me decide?"

He shook his head.

"**I'd give my right arm** to help you decide. But I just can't. It's your call, Jamie. Yours alone." 26

He got up.

"I don't feel like fishing anymore. Let's pack up and go home."

He reeled in his line.

"It's getting cloudy anyway."

But the sun was shining.

Very brightly.

The voice **pierced** the dead silence of the courtroom.

"Do you swear to tell the truth and nothing but the truth?"

Jamie raised his right hand and looked over to where Ted sat.

The haunted, pleading look in Ted's eyes.

He knew that he would remember that look for the rest of his life.

I can't tell you what to do, Jamie. It's your call.

26 Inferences
Why does Uncle Harry tell Jamie it's Jamie's decision whether or not to tell the truth?

In Other Words

It's your call. You have to decide for yourself.
I'd give my right arm I'd do anything
pierced filled

But within he said:

I can't do it, Ted.

I just can't.

And Jamie knew that he could never again be **his brother's keeper**.

The tears came to his eyes.

And he bowed his head. 27 ❖

27 Style: Sentence Structure/ Inferences
How do the short sentences at the end of the story help express how Jamie feels about his decision?

ANALYZE My Brother's Keeper

1. **Explain** In the end, which value does Jamie uphold—truth or loyalty?

2. **Vocabulary** Do you think Jamie made his decision about what he would say quickly or **deliberately**? Support your answer with evidence from the text.

3. **Analyze Style: Sentence Structure** Find at least two examples of each of the following style features in the story. Write your examples on a chart like the sample shown. Explain how each affects the story.

Short Sentences/Fragments	Repetition
Example:	Example:
Effect:	Effect:

4. **Focus Strategy Make Inferences** Whose point of view is the story told from? What can you infer about the author's motivation for choosing this perspective? Tell a partner what inference you made and why.

🔁 Return to the Text

Reread and Write Jamie faces a difficult loyalty test. Reread the story, and identify parts that show this. Write a paragraph describing the difficulties of his test.

In Other Words
his brother's keeper his brother's protector

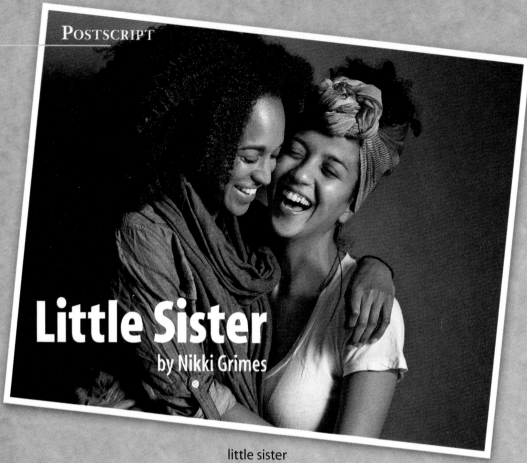

Little Sister
by Nikki Grimes

little sister
holds on tight.
My hands hurt
from all that squeezing,
5   but I don't mind.
She thinks no one will bother her
when I'm around,
and they won't
if I can help it.
10   And even when I can't,
I try
'cause she believes in me.

About the Poet

Nikki Grimes (1950–) is an author, poet, artist, and educator. She describes writing as her first love and poetry as her greatest pleasure. She says, "It seemed uncanny that words, spread across a page just so, had the power to transport me to another time and place."

BEFORE READING What Price Loyalty?

news commentary by Gerald Pomper

Reading Strategies

- Plan and Monitor
- Determine Importance
- ▶ **Make Inferences**
- Ask Questions
- Make Connections
- Synthesize
- Visualize

Determine Viewpoint

A **news commentary** is one person's interpretation of a current event or issue. Usually you will find the individual writer's **viewpoint**, or opinion, in a news commentary, even if he or she uses the pronoun *we*.

Look Into the Text

The use of *we* shows the author wants everyone to agree with him.

> We should be suspicious of glib claims of loyalty to principle. Instead, we need to consider the consequences of individual actions, public and private. One basic question to ask: How many people may be harmed by adhering to one form of loyalty or another?

The writer uses opinionated language such as *should* and *need* to express his viewpoint.

Focus Strategy ▶ Make Inferences

When reading a news commentary, you can make **inferences** about the writer's viewpoint. Look for clues and specific word choices to see how the writer supports his or her viewpoint. As you read, decide whether you agree or disagree with the writer.

HOW TO MAKE INFERENCES

Focus Strategy

1. As you read, think about the writer's purpose in writing the news commentary. For example, is it to persuade? If so, what does the writer want to persuade readers to think or do?

2. Track your thoughts about the writer's message using a chart like the one below.

What the Writer Says	What the Writer Means	Do I Agree with What the Writer Is Saying?
"We should be suspicious of glib claims of loyalty to principle." "We need to consider the consequences of individual actions, public and private."	Opinion: We should not just accept anything people say about loyalty. We need to think about the effects of what people do.	yes

What Price Loyalty?
by Gerald Pomper

Connect Across Texts

In "My Brother's Keeper," you read about a **dilemma** between family loyalty and telling the truth. In this news commentary, read about the role of loyalty in society.

Loyalty is in the news. But what does it mean?

Loyalty has been a concern throughout American history. The Declaration of Independence, remember, was an act of disloyalty toward the British Crown, and opponents of the rebellion called themselves "Loyalists." In the Civil War, Northerners **swore fealty to** the federal union, Southerners to their individual states.

In the **abstract**, loyalty is an unquestioned virtue; nobody **advocates** disloyalty. But it gets more complicated in the real world. **1** Because of their oaths to Adolf Hitler, the German General Staff ignored the Holocaust.

Dissenters such as Martin Luther King, Jr., have been accused of disloyalty because they disobeyed the law, even as they claimed a **higher allegiance to the nation's overriding principles**. Can it be, in the words of the late journalist Alan Barth, that "Loyalty in a free society depends upon the toleration of disloyalty"?

We in fact have many loyalties, each **commendable** in itself. We believe in loyalty to family, friends, employers

Martin Luther King, Jr., delivered his famous "I Have a Dream" speech in Washington, D.C. on August 28, 1963.

1 Inferences
What is the author's opinion about loyalty? Explain why you do or do not agree with it. Track your notes on your chart.

[Handwritten notes:] Loyalty is people believe in you and ~~they~~ follow you.
– MLK believed in equal rights for everyone, regardless of skin color.
– Adolf Hitler believed in killing people who were not "perfect"

Key Vocabulary

dilemma *n.*, situation that requires you to choose between two unfavorable options
- **abstract** *n.*, idea, nonreal situation
- **advocate** *v.*, to speak in favor of

In Other Words

swore fealty to promised to be loyal to
higher allegiance to the nation's overriding principles more important loyalty to the nation's basic beliefs
commendable worthy of praise

and employees, the institutions where we work, perhaps our political party, our country, our God, and our conscience. Often these loyalties **reinforce** each other. 2️⃣

But **ethical** problems arise when these loyalties conflict—as often happens. Should we protect a criminal relative? Should an employee stay with a failing corporation, or an employer keep his workers on the payroll even as profits fall?

These dilemmas are not resolved by the easy answer that we should always stick to our principles; each of the conflicting loyalties is, after all, a **statement of principle**. 3️⃣

Loyalty to friends, for example, is a good principle, but it can create problems. In 1950 during the Cold War, Secretary of State Dean Acheson said he refused to "turn my back" on Alger Hiss, even when his friend was revealed to be a Soviet spy.

Is such loyalty always commendable?

We should be suspicious of **glib claims of loyalty** to principle. Instead, we need to consider the consequences of individual actions,

public and private. One basic question to ask: How many people may be harmed by **adhering** to one form of loyalty or another?

We may get closer to resolving these conflicts if we recall a famous statement of loyalty—naval commander Stephen Decatur's toast, "Our country, right or wrong."

2️⃣ Determine Viewpoint
Why does the writer use the pronoun *we*? Why does he name examples of loyalty in this order?

3️⃣ Inferences
What is the writer's opinion about sticking to our principles? Do you agree? Explain.

Students recite the Pledge of Allegiance, which is a patriotic oath of loyalty to the United States.

Blind loyalty is not always a good thing depending on your leader.

Key Vocabulary
- **reinforce** *v.*, to strengthen
- **ethical** *adj.*, moral
  adhere *v.*, to stick with

In Other Words
statement of principle way of expressing what we truly believe
glib claims of loyalty casual statements about loyalty

Fifty-five years later, Carl Schurz, a United States general and United States senator, provided a better rule: "Our country, right or wrong. When right, to be kept right; when wrong, to be put right." That is appropriate conduct for thinking men and women in a free land. ▪4 ❖

4 Determine Viewpoint
How do the opinion words on this page affect the tone of the piece?

ANALYZE What Price Loyalty?

1. **Explain** How does the writer suggest we decide if our loyalty to someone or something is good or bad? What are the strengths and weaknesses of this approach?

2. **Vocabulary** How can a conflict of loyalties lead to **ethical dilemmas**? Give an example from the news commentary.

3. **Determine Viewpoint** Locate a passage where the writer chooses opinionated words. What viewpoint does the writer express in the passage? Give examples of ways the writer uses his knowledge of history to support his viewpoint.

4. **Focus Strategy Make Inferences** How does the writer feel about people who are disloyal? Explain to a partner how you used details from the selection to make this inference. Do you agree or disagree with the writer?

Return to the Text
Reread and Write The writer says there is "one basic question to ask" about loyalty. Reread to find this basic question. Write a paragraph to explain how you would apply this question to one of the situations described in the selection.

REFLECT AND ASSESS

▶ My Brother's Keeper
▶ Little Sister
▶ What Price Loyalty?

EQ What Tests a Person's Loyalty?

Reading
Critical Thinking

EQ 1. **Analyze** What values or qualities can create a **dilemma** with loyalty? Give examples from both texts.

2. **Interpret** Why does the author not tell you what Jamie said in the courtroom in "My Brother's Keeper"? Do you think he gave the alibi that Carmody wanted? Explain your conclusion using details from the selection.

3. **Compare** Which person mentioned in the news commentary is most like Jamie? Support your answer with evidence from both texts.

4. **Speculate** Imagine Ted and Jamie after the hearing. What do they say to each other? How might their lives change?

EQ 5. **Synthesize** When is it acceptable *not* to be loyal? Support your answer with at least two examples, along with details from both texts.

Writing
Write About Literature

Advice E-mail Imagine that you have an online advice column and that Jamie sends you an e-mail asking what he should do in his situation. What advice would you give him? Write the e-mail question from Jamie and then write an e-mail responding to his question. Use examples and details from both texts to support your response.

Vocabulary
Key Vocabulary Review

Oral Review Work with a partner. Use these words to complete the paragraph.

abstract	deliberately	ethical
adhere	desolately	reinforce
advocate	dilemmas	

In the ___abstract___(1) world of ideas, loyalty is an easy value to believe in. People who ~~reinforce~~ advocate (2) loyalty say that if we always ~~reinforce~~ adhere (3) to basic principles, we will _____(4), or strengthen, standards of good behavior. Dissenters oppose this idea and say that we must consider both sides carefully and ___deliberately___(5) before deciding what is the most ___desolately___(6) and moral thing to do. One thing is clear, we must think about our loyalties before they are tested. Otherwise, when difficult ___dilemmas___(7) occur, we may just respond ___(8) ethical___ to them, feeling too hopeless or confused to do the right thing.

Writing Application Think of a time when you or a friend faced a dilemma. How was this problem or conflict solved? Write a paragraph about it. Use at least three Key Vocabulary words.

Fluency
Read with Ease: Phrasing

Assess your reading fluency with the passage in the Reading Handbook, on p. 806. Then complete the self-check below.

1. I did/did not pause appropriately for punctuation and phrases.

2. My words correct per minute: _____.

Reflect and Assess **297**

INTEGRATE THE LANGUAGE ARTS

Use Verb Tenses

Writers need to change the tense of verbs to show shifts in time. Regular past tense verbs end in **-ed**. Irregular verbs have special forms to show the past tense. For example, the verb **do** is an irregular verb.

Present: Jamie **does** a lot for his brother.

Past: Ted **did** something wrong.

Here are some common irregular verbs.

Present	Past	Present	Past
am, is, are	was, were	know	knew
do, does	did	say	said
go, goes	went	see	saw
have, has	had	sleep	slept

Use the **future tense** to tell about an action that has not yet happened. Use **will** before the main verb to tell about the future. If you use more than one main verb in the same sentence, use **will** only before the first verb.

Present: Ted **talks** to Jamie, **explains** his situation, and **asks** for help.

Future: He **will tell** his story, **make** excuses, and **stammer**.

Oral Practice (1–5) With a partner, find an example of parallel structure with five verbs on page 278. Tell the tense of each verb.

Written Practice (6–8) Rewrite each sentence. Change the underlined verb to the tense in parentheses.

6. Uncle Harry <u>goes</u> on a fishing trip. (past)
7. Ted <u>got</u> into trouble. (future)
8. Jamie <u>will think</u> about his brother. (present)

Make Comparisons

Group Talk In "My Brother's Keeper," how are Jamie and his brother alike? How are they different? Discuss in a group and make a list of your best ideas.

Analyze Style

The way a writer uses language—word choice, sentence length—and the tone created by that language is called **style**. In "My Brother's Keeper," the author uses both dialogue and short sentences to tell the story. For example, Jamie asks his brother, "What have you done, Ted?" This simple, short question tells you that Jamie is upset with his brother. Would the effect be the same if the author had written, "Jamie asked his brother what he did"?

With a partner, pick a passage from the story to read aloud.

1. Analyze the dialogue. What does it reveal about the brothers' relationship?

2. What kind of a **mood**, or feeling, does the combination of short sentences and dialogue create?

3. How would the mood of the story change if the author had used less dialogue and longer descriptions?

Analyze Theme

Authors do not usually come right out and explain the **theme** of a story; they want readers to put clues together to arrive at the message about life or human nature.

With a partner, identify the theme of "My Brother's Keeper." Give evidence from the text as support. Think about:

- the title of the story
- the choices the characters make
- the way the story ends, or its resolution

Word Families

A huge number of English words are based on roots from Greek and Latin. You can learn one root, but then recognize many more words. For example, the root *punct* means "point or dot" and can be found in such words as *punctual, punctuation,* and *acupuncture.* These words are all part of the same word family.

Find as many words as you can for these common roots. Use a dictionary to confirm the word's meaning.

ROOT	MEANING	WORDS WITH THAT ROOT
1. *spir*	breath	
2. *typ*	print	
3. *cred*	believe	

Problem-Solution Report

Social Studies: The Faces of Loyalty Find out more about one of the people mentioned in "What Price Loyalty?" Research a dilemma that the person faced and how he resolved it.

myNGconnect.com

- 🔗 **Search the archive of a documentary TV program.**
- 🔗 **Review an online biographical dictionary.**
- 🔗 **Read news features in a national magazine.**

Write your research in a problem-solution report. Share it with your class.

📕 **Writing Handbook**, p. 832

Organization: Introductions

Readers usually decide if they want to continue reading a text based on the opening section. Use strong introductions to grab your readers' interest and to tell them the main ideas in your work.

1 Study the Models Read the introductions below from essays about the role of loyalty in everyday life. Which one makes you want to read further? Why?

Just OK

> Loyalty has had a large role in my relationship with my sister. In fact, it is one of the most important values in our relationship.

Much Better

> "I've got your back." I'll never forget when my sister spoke these words. In this brief statement, she expressed a deep loyalty to me at a time when other people turned away.

2 Plan Think about loyalty in your own relationships. Choose a quotation that you can use to develop your own introduction to a personal essay about loyalty. The quotation should express the importance of loyalty in family or true friendship. Jot down what it makes you think about.

3 Draft Now write a draft of your introductory paragraph. Be sure to include the quotation and the name of the speaker.

4 Edit and Proofread Reread your writing. Ask:
- Does my quotation relate to the topic?
- Will readers be interested in what I have to say?
- Do I use verb tenses correctly?

5 Publish Print out and share your paragraph with others.

📕 **Writing Handbook**, p. 832

DEBATE

When someone you care about does something wrong, should you report him or her? Hold a lively but respectful debate on this matter or another question about loyalty.

1. Plan Your Debate

Divide into teams of three or five people to argue the question and moderate.

- Assign one person to be the moderator, or the person who will lead the discussion and monitor the time.

- Brainstorm with team members their ideas about loyalty. The moderator can state the question as a "yes/no" question, such as "Should you turn in a friend who has broken the law?"

- Think about what the opposing team's opening statement might consist of. Write potential responses. Use facts and cite sources to strengthen each response.

Notice how this speaker uses note cards while staying connected to her audience.

2. Practice Your Debate

Each team should prepare to argue its side.

- Practice making the opening statement and get helpful suggestions from team members.
- Practice your counter argument. Anticipate the other team's response.
- The debate can follow this order, introduced by the moderator:
  - –opening statement by Team A
  - –response by Team B
  - –opening statement by Team B
  - –response by Team A

3. Hold Your Debate

Keep your debate focused and respectful by doing the following:

- Take notes during the other team's opening statement in order to prepare your response.
- Speak clearly and with the appropriate tone so that you can be understood.
- The person making the opening statement should glance at notes only occasionally.
- Maintain eye contact with your opponent. Eye contact shows that you are respectful of your opponent's views.

4. Discuss and Rate the Debate

Use the rubric to discuss and rate each team, including your own.

Debate Rubric

Scale	Content of Debate	Team's Preparation	Team's Performance
3 Great	• Led with an interesting, on-topic question • Made me really think about the issue and influenced my thinking	• Was well organized • Included strong evidence to support argument	• Spoke clearly and was easy to follow • Each team worked really well together
2 Good	• Led with a weak question • Made me think somewhat about the issue	• Was somewhat well organized • Included some evidence to support argument	• Spoke clearly most of the time and was usually easy to follow • Each team worked fairly well together
1 Needs Work	• Did not lead with an interesting question • Did not make me think about the issue	• Was not well organized • Did not include good support	• Was hard to hear and understand • Did not work well together

myNGconnect.com
🔊 Download the rubric.

DO IT ▶ **Now that you know how to debate, organize your group and do your best to prove your point!**

📖 Language and Learning Handbook, p. 750

EQ What Tests a Person's Loyalty?
Explore the ways loyalties may change over time.

Make a Connection

Discussion and Debate Imagine that a teenage boy wants to be a musician, but his parents want him to be a doctor. What should he do: be loyal to his parents' wishes or his own? Discuss your ideas in a small group.

Learn Key Vocabulary

Study the Words Pronounce each word and learn its meaning. You may also want to look up the definitions in the Glossary.

● Academic Vocabulary

Key Words	Examples
abolish (ah-**bah**-lish) *verb* ▶ page 329	When you **abolish** something, you do away with it or get rid of it. The principal decided to **abolish** the dress code and let students choose what to wear to school.
admonish (ad-**mah**-nish) *verb* ▶ page 308	To **admonish** someone is to gently but firmly tell the person that he or she has done something wrong. *Synonyms:* warn, scold; *Antonyms:* compliment, praise
● **coherent** (kō-**hir**-unt) *adjective* ▶ page 324	If something is **coherent**, it is orderly, logical, and easy to understand. *Synonym:* clear; *Antonym:* confusing
conscientious (kon-shē-**en**-shus) *adjective* ▶ pages 313, 325	When people are **conscientious** about their work, they are careful and responsible. Teresa is very **conscientious** because she completes her math homework every day.
● **controversial** (kahn-trah-**vur**-shul) *adjective* ▶ pages 327, 330	If something is **controversial**, people have very different opinions about it. Paul wants to see the **controversial** new movie that upset a lot of people.
naive (nah-**ēv**) *adjective* ▶ pages 310, 325	People who are **naive** are easily fooled because they do not have the knowledge they need to make good decisions. *Synonym:* simple; *Antonym:* sophisticated
● **pursue** (pur-**sü**) *verb* ▶ pages 317, 327, 331	To **pursue** something is to make an effort to do something. After high school, do you want to **pursue** a college degree? *Synonyms:* work toward, seek; *Antonyms:* give up, avoid
subdued (sub-**düd**) *adjective* ▶ page 320	People who are **subdued** are quiet and control their emotions. She was more **subdued** after the argument. *Antonyms:* lively, noisy

Practice the Words Work with a partner. Make a **Definition Map** for each Key Vocabulary word. Use a dictionary to find other forms of the word.

Definition Map

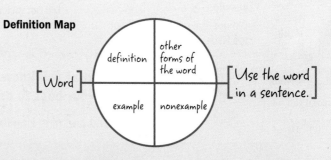

BEFORE READING The Hand of Fatima

short story by Elsa Marston

Reading Strategies

- Plan and Monitor
- Determine Importance
▶ **Make Inferences**
- Ask Questions
- Make Connections
- Synthesize
- Visualize

Analyze Viewpoint

Viewpoint refers to attitudes and opinions. Viewpoints in fiction include the attitudes that characters have toward each other and the attitude that the narrator displays. The author's word choices, descriptions, and even sentence structure reveal these attitudes and opinions. By focusing on the way that the author presents the characters and narrator, you can see the author's own attitude toward what he or she is writing about. This attitude helps achieve the author's purpose for writing, such as giving readers a personal sense of life in another culture.

Viewpoint: attitude and opinion of the characters; word choice.
Inference: form ideas. What the character says or thinks.

Look Into the Text

Long sentences emphasize how long Aneesi works.

> Aneesi paused outside the dining room. She had spent the long, hot summer morning helping Sitt Zeina prepare a lavish lunch, had waited on the guests without a single slip, and had just finished clearing the dessert dishes. She was tired and hungry, and her plastic sandals chafed from so much running back and forth. All she wanted right now was to sit down in the kitchen and enjoy the leftovers.
>
> But something had caught her attention. Holding the silver serving plates still half full of pastries, she lingered in the hallway to listen.
>
> Sitt Zeina was telling her husband, in no uncertain terms, "We must have that garden wall repaired, Yusuf. You know, where the old fig tree is pushing it over. You've put it off long enough, and costs are going up every day. Besides, there's a lot more we should do with the garden."

These precise descriptions show a sympathetic attitude.

What does the author's word choice say about Sitt Zeina's attitude toward her husband? What does it say about the author's attitude toward Sitt Zeina?

Focus Strategy ▶ Make Inferences

Every day we make **inferences**, or form ideas, about each other. Sometimes our inferences are right, but other times they are wrong. As you read, notice what the characters wonder, guess, and discover about each other. Their inferences can help you see how real people understand and misunderstand each other.

Focus Strategy

HOW TO MAKE INFERENCES

1. **Take notes** about the inferences that characters make about each other.

2. **List the event or statement** that a character uses as evidence to make the inference.

3. **Confirm** whether the character's inference is correct or incorrect.

Inference	Text Evidence	Correct or Incorrect?
Sitt Zeina thinks her husband doesn't care about the garden.	The old fig tree is pushing the wall over.	Correct. He has not repaired the wall yet.

Elsa Marston
(1944–)

Elsa Marston dreamed of being a trapeze performer, a concert pianist, a humanitarian worker, and an artist before she finally became a writer.

Growing up in Massachusetts, **Elsa Marston** dreamed of faraway places. "We often went to the Boston Museum of Fine Arts, where the ancient Egyptian rooms sparked my fascination," she explains. In the fourth grade, she even began writing a novel about a boy who lived in ancient Egypt, though she did not finish writing the story.

Later, Marston's interest in the culture of the Middle East grew. In college she studied international relations and Middle Eastern history. When she married a man from Lebanon, her connection to Middle Eastern culture became more personal because of regular visits to the area.

Marston often draws upon her experiences with the Middle East in her writing. The story "The Hand of Fatima" is from the collection *Figs and Fate: Stories About Growing Up in the Arab World Today* (2005). She also achieved her childhood dream of writing about a boy in ancient Egypt when her novel *The Ugly Goddess* was published in 2002.

Whether Marston writes about what the Middle East was like long ago or today, her goal is clear: "I want to share with young readers my own interest in those lands and peoples, and equally important, contribute to better understanding of the Arab/Muslim world."

myNGconnect.com

🔊 **Discover what Elsa Marston has to say about "The Hand of Fatima."**

🔊 **View photographs of Lebanon and Lebanese life.**

The Hand of Fatima

by Elsa Marston

▲ Critical Viewing: Design Why did the artist paint the woman in the shadow instead of in the light? What does this tell you about her?

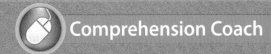

Comprehension Coach

Set a Purpose
Discover what happens when a teenager's loyalty to her family is tested.

Aneesi paused outside the dining room. She had spent the long, hot summer morning helping Sitt Zeina prepare a **lavish** lunch, had waited on the guests without **a single slip**, and had just finished clearing the dessert dishes. She was tired and hungry, and her plastic sandals **chafed** from so much running back and forth. All she wanted right now was to sit down in the kitchen and enjoy the leftovers.

But something had caught her attention. Holding the silver serving plates still half full of pastries, she lingered in the hallway to listen.

Sitt Zeina was telling her husband, in no uncertain terms, "We *must* have that garden wall repaired, Yusuf. You know, where the old fig tree is pushing it over. You've put it off long enough, and costs are going up every day. Besides, there's a lot more we should do with the garden."

Before Dr. Jubeili could answer, one of the guests broke in with a laugh. "What are you thinking of, Zeina? Big ideas for the Jubeili estate?"

"Oh, nothing too **extravagant**," she answered. "Just terraces for my roses, with good walls of well-fitted stones. There aren't many fine old villas like ours left close to Beirut—what with those dreadful apartment buildings springing up everywhere. We must make the most of this one."

Aneesi could hear Dr. Jubeili sigh. "Zeina, have you any idea what workers are getting paid these days? Stonemasons can charge whatever they want. Lebanese ones, that is. Syrian workers are cheaper—but just try to find one who knows how to do good stonework." **1**

A charge of excitement ran through Aneesi. *I know one, she thought—my father!*

A few days earlier, a letter had arrived from her older brother Hussein, who was at home in Syria. Papa needed more work, Hussein wrote. He had to borrow continually, just to feed the six people who depended on him. Hussein was thinking of quitting school so he could get a job.

1 Analyze Viewpoint
How would you describe Dr. Jubeili's opinion of the workers? Explain.

2 Inferences
What does Aneesi's excitement suggest about her feelings for her family?

In Other Words
lavish fancy
a single slip one mistake
chafed rubbed against her skin
Sitt Lady (in Arabic)
extravagant fancy, expensive

Geographical Background
Syria and Lebanon are neighboring countries located in the Middle East. Lebanon is west of Syria.

No, he mustn't! Aneesi was **dismayed at** the thought. After all, she had left school at twelve so that Hussein, being a boy and smart, could go on with his education. For two years she'd been sending home every bit of her earnings— and now Hussein was saying that her money and Papa's **miserable pay** still weren't enough. **3**

But there must be another solution. Maybe, Hussein wrote, their father could find work in Lebanon, where a few weeks' pay would feed a family for months in a Syrian village. What were the chances of Papa finding something in the town where Aneesi was living?

Door with Palm Trees, 2003, © Joseph Matar. Watercolor, courtesy of LebanonArt.com.

⚠ **Critical Viewing: Setting** How does the scene in this painting compare with your image of the story's setting? Explain.

In Other Words
dismayed at discouraged by
miserable pay tiny salary

Aneesi had delayed her answer to Hussein, afraid that her father didn't stand much chance of finding work in Lebanon. Many Syrian laborers, most of them young, strong men, came to Lebanon for manual day-by-day jobs. Competition was **keen**, and Papa was not **as hardy** as he had been. But he had something in his favor, at least: his skill as a stonemason.

And now, **out of the blue**, the Jubeilis were talking about hiring somebody to do stonework. What luck!

For a moment Aneesi recalled Sitt Zeina speaking to her—more than once, in fact—about not listening to the family's private conversations. It was an improper, low kind of behavior to "eavesdrop," as Sitt Zeina had put it. Aneesi had bristled inwardly at being **admonished**, but at least it was better than being thought of as too dull to care what people were saying, like a pet dog. **4** Besides, Aneesi found it hard to resist listening. With no family or friends of her own, what else could she do but share, in a secondhand way, the Jubeilis' family life? So now she'd eavesdropped again—but maybe this time Sitt Zeina would be glad of it.

Although almost too excited to eat, Aneesi soon felt hunger pangs again and settled down to a plate of leftovers. She was chewing the last piece of broiled chicken when Sitt Zeina came into the kitchen to prepare coffee. Swallowing quickly, Aneesi spoke up with **uncustomary** boldness. "Sitt Zeina, I couldn't help hearing something—I didn't mean to, but I was just leaving the dining room—"

"Yes? What is it, Aneesi? As you can see, I'm busy." **5**

"Well . . . are you going to mend the wall by the driveway?"

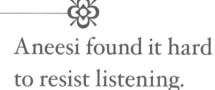

Aneesi found it hard to resist listening.

4 Inferences
What does Aneesi's reaction to the warning tell you about her character? Note your impression on your chart.

5 Analyze Viewpoint
What do you think the narrator thinks of Sitt Zeina? How do you know?

Key Vocabulary
admonish *v.*, to warn or scold

In Other Words
keen difficult, tough
as hardy as strong
out of the blue unexpectedly
uncustomary unusual

With raised eyebrows Sitt Zeina shot a disapproving look at Aneesi. Sitt Zeina was a tall, handsome woman with thick black hair worn loose to her shoulders. It made her look very young, except for the lines in her face that deepened when she **took on** serious matters. But rather than another lecture about proper behavior, she gave a dramatic sigh. "So you heard what we were saying about that wall. Why does it concern you?" **6**

"Because, Sitt Zeina, because I—I know a good worker you could hire."

"Really?"

"Yes. My father."

"But he's working in Syria."

"He could come, Sitt Zeina. He has done stonework, a lot of it, and he is very good. He learned from his father, who built our house. He built a wall all around the government building in the village—a nice wall, with places for flowers. He knows how to cut stone carefully and trim the pieces to fit, and everybody says he can be trusted to do his best."

Considering this news, Sitt Zeina frowned in thought. "I thought he had a different kind of job," she said.

"Yes, he drives a car for the government, but they don't pay much. If he comes here to work, they won't mind, I think, and will let him have the same job when he goes back. He is honest and good—you can count on him. And . . . " Aneesi paused, uncertain.

"And what?"

"He would not take very much. I mean, you would not have to pay him as much as a Lebanese worker."

"Hmmm." Sitt Zeina reached into the cupboard for the small coffee cups, then started heating finely ground coffee and water in a small pot. "Well, I don't know. I'll **take it up** with my husband."

6 Analyze Viewpoint
What is Sitt Zeina's attitude toward Aneesi? Which words and phrases reveal her viewpoint?

In Other Words
took on thought about
take it up discuss it

Monitor Comprehension

Explain
What are some of the ways that Aneesi tries to help her family?

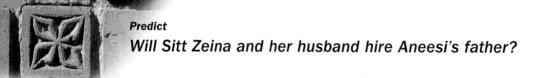

Predict

Will Sitt Zeina and her husband hire Aneesi's father?

As Aneesi went back to her work, washing the dishes and putting the kitchen in order, she tried to force herself to relax. She had done what she could, but hopes and doubts kept pricking at her. If only Dr. Jubeili would agree to hire her father, it would help the family so much! Hussein could stay in school—and she could be a daughter again for a while. Two weeks a year, all that her contract allowed, was such a tiny bit of time to spend with her family, to be a daughter. The rest of the year she was just a maid.

Just a maid. Even now Aneesi sometimes shuddered as she thought of the risk she'd taken in leaving home. Her parents had not wanted her to go, and there had been tearful, noisy scenes. In the end, though, the thought of the money she could earn **outweighed** their fears—and of course the agency had assured them she would be treated well. Just the same, how **naive** and trusting she'd been! She could so easily have been hired by a family who would have overworked her and crushed her spirit. But God had been merciful and had sent her to the Jubeili home. Once again, Aneesi gave thanks. **7**

The next morning, Sitt Zeina had news for Aneesi. Dr. Jubeili had agreed to give her father a chance. "We've been pleased with your work, Aneesi," she added, "and we know life is hard for your family. We hope this arrangement will work out well for all of us."

"Yes, of course!" Aneesi answered. "Thank you, Sitt Zeina. I think you will be satisfied." She wanted to skip, jump, and shout with happiness, but she kept her feet in place and her manner **composed**. A good maid knew how to behave. **8**

In any case, she had enough work to keep her from thinking too much about her father coming. Maya Jubeili soon reminded her of that. Maya was

7 **Analyze Viewpoint**
What do you think is the author's opinion of Aneesi? Why do you think so?

8 **Inferences**
What does Aneesi's reaction to Sitt Zeina's news tell you about their relationship?

Key Vocabulary
naive *adj.*, easily fooled because of a lack of experience

In Other Words
outweighed was more important than
composed calm

seventeen, romping through the summer before her last year of secondary school. She came and went in the house so quickly that she barely took time for anything except to tell Aneesi what to do next.

Now, in her usual manner, Maya came dashing into the kitchen, gave her mother a quick kiss on the cheek, then turned to Aneesi. "Wash my good black jeans today, Aneesi, will you? And anything else you find loose in my room. I want to wear the jeans tonight and they'll need to be ironed, so you'd better get busy. Oh, and do a better job ironing, Aneesi. There were wrinkles on the front of my pink silk blouse." 9

9 Inferences
What is Maya suggesting about Aneesi when she complains about her wrinkled blouse? Track the inference on your chart.

Aneesi managed to keep calm as she answered politely. "That blouse gets wrinkles from hanging in the closet, Sitt Maya."

"Well, whatever. Do something about it. I have to look nice, not like some old beggar woman." Maya whirled out of the kitchen and out of the house, off to meet friends at a café. Sitt Zeina shook her head but said nothing.

Aneesi left her work in the kitchen and went to Maya's room, where she collected the clothes draped on chairs and dropped in corners. Standing before the mirror, she held the black jeans up to her body for a moment, trying to imagine what she would look like in them. No, it wasn't even worth dreaming about. Maya's jeans fit like a second skin . . . a girl had to be **slim as an eel** to wear them. Aneesi's own **stocky shape** was doomed to baggy slacks.

She held the black jeans up to her body . . . to imagine what she would look like.

The sound of voices from the direction of the front door startled her. Maya was back for some reason, talking excitedly with her mother. A moment later she hurtled into the bedroom, closely followed by Sitt Zeina. Seeing the black jeans still in Aneesi's hands, she seized them.

In Other Words
slim as an eel very skinny
stocky shape heavier body

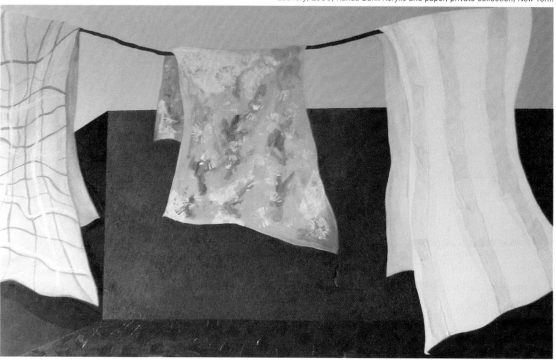

Laundry, 1996, Randa Baki. Acrylic and paper, private collection, New York.

▲ **Critical Viewing: Plot** What connection can you make between this image and the story?

"Here, I have to—" Maya jammed a hand into one pocket and then into the other. A smile of relief flashed over her face as she withdrew her hand and tossed the jeans back at Aneesi. "I've got them, Mama, everything's okay!"

"Really, Maya!" Sitt Zeina started to **chide** her but was too late. Maya, stuffing something in her purse, was already dashing out of the bedroom.

"That girl!" said Sitt Zeina, as the front door slammed shut once more. "She is so careless these days. So much money, just forgotten in her pocket!" Frowning in annoyance, she too, left the room, her **dignified** steps a contrast with Maya's headlong rush. Aneesi let out her breath in relief. 🔟

As she went on with her morning's work, Aneesi allowed her thoughts to run ahead to those happy days when she and Papa would be together and he could do work that he enjoyed and took pride in, while earning good money.

🔟 **Analyze Viewpoint** What words and phrases does the author use to show the difference between Maya and Sitt Zeina? What is the author's attitude toward these characters?

In Other Words
chide punish, scold
dignified slow and subdued

Oh, how lucky it was that she had eavesdropped on the Jubeilis' lunchtime conversation!

Then came a break that Aneesi looked forward to: her lesson with Iskandar, a few afternoons a week. She often wondered how Maya and her brother could be so different. Iskandar, serious and **conscientious**, was studying education at the American University of Beirut. Finding Aneesi intelligent, he had decided not only to help her with Arabic but to teach her some English.

Today Iskandar greeted her with a chuckle. "I hear my sister left a treasure in her jeans pocket for you to put through the wash."

"She found it, thanks to God," said Aneesi.

"That Maya . . . she's **got her head in the clouds** these days, and she thinks money **grows in the garden**, but she'll get better. Now, let's work."

After a while Iskandar put down the book they were reading together and sat back. "That's very good, Aneesi. You've got a quick mind. You shouldn't have to be a maid forever. I've been thinking . . . Know what you should do?"

She looked at him, hoping, and waited to hear more.

"Take **a commercial course** at the YWCA in Beirut, in a couple of years. Then you could get a real job. I mean—" Iskandar corrected himself—"this is a good job for you now, and you're a real help to Mama. But if you learn some office skills, then you can start to earn a lot more." 11

Aneesi smiled, quietly delighted. At last! This was the sort of thing she'd been hoping to hear. A job in an office someday, maybe as a secretary or even a manager, an important job with a good salary—the realization of her dreams. It was with this dream that she had left her family: to help them out and to gain a better life for herself.

Just the same, she **feigned a modest response to** Iskandar. 12 "Really, do you think I could? Oh yes, I'd like that. Thank you, Mr. Iskandar." She could hardly wait to tell her father what Mr. Iskandar had said. Papa would be so proud.

11 **Analyze Viewpoint**
What does Iskandar's advice tell you about his attitude toward Aneesi?

12 **Inferences**
What does Aneesi's response suggest about her relationship with Iskandar?

Monitor Comprehension

Confirm Prediction
Was your prediction correct? If so, what was the most important evidence you used? If not, what misled you?

Key Vocabulary
conscientious *adj.*, careful and responsible

In Other Words
got her head in the clouds not paying careful attention to what she does
grows in the garden is easy to get
a commercial course an educational program
feigned a modest response to pretended not to be excited with

After a day's ride from Syria in a battered old taxi, Aneesi's father arrived, tired and rumpled. Aneesi was thrilled to see him—and in the next instant, worried. He had grown so thin in the nine or ten months since she'd last been home. Was he really healthy? **13**

Anyway, she knew he would eat well here. The Jubeilis believed in good food and plenty of it, and they were generous to the people who worked for them. Papa could sleep in the space at the rear of the house where the garden tools were kept—Iskandar had helped Aneesi move things around to make room.

As soon as they were alone, on the terrace outside the tool room, Aneesi's father hugged her again. A feeling both happy and sad went through her as she smelled the familiar old Papa-smell of tobacco and garlic, the mothballs in which his suit was kept, and the **faint overlay** of soap. Then he stepped back to look at her. His **weathered** face took on a look of eager happiness, which had been hidden during the polite greetings with his new employers.

"Aneesi, I have news for you. Good news!"

Something about Hussein—he must have passed his exams with high scores! Aneesi smiled, eager to hear.

"I am so glad to tell you, daughter," her father went on. "There is a man from the village—a very good man—who has asked for you." He waited to see her reaction.

Aneesi's heart suddenly went cold. Her smile faded, and she sat down slowly on a white plastic chair by the door, unable to meet his eyes. **14**

"Papa . . ."

He continued in a lower voice. "Listen, my daughter. Let me tell you about him. He is the son of the postmaster. They are a good family, respected by everybody. Fareed is not too old—I think around thirty—and he has not

13 Inferences
After Aneesi first sees her father, she is worried. What does she think about him? How do you know? Write your thoughts on your chart.

14 Analyze Viewpoint
How does our view of Aneesi shift at this point of the story? What words does the author use to change our view?

In Other Words
faint overlay light, subtle scent
weathered old, wrinkled

been married before. He is educated, and he has a store in Safita, only half an hour from the village. Electrical things, a good business. He is kind and good-hearted, and not bad-looking."

Aneesi heard the words, but they meant nothing to her. After a moment she asked, "Why does he want me, Papa? Why doesn't he marry a nice woman in Safita?"

"He wants a girl from the village, my daughter. That is important to him. He does not have a cousin whom he wants to marry. And he knows our family. We are not well-off, but we are good people. He knows you are a good girl. And . . . "

Aneesi's father paused to look around for something to sit on, then lowered himself onto a pile of firewood that lay alongside the wall. "He knows you are smart. The teacher told him you were one of the best students he ever had. Yes, that teacher still talks about you."

> **Aneesi's heart suddenly went cold.**

A tiny flicker of warmth quickened in Aneesi as she recalled the teacher. He had been angry with her father for letting her leave school. Twice he had come to the house, and the two men had argued in loud voices. Hearing them, Aneesi had felt torn and had almost changed her mind. But it had been her own decision, after all, to work in Lebanon, her decision to help the family— and herself—in this way.

Now Aneesi looked up at her father, her eyes starting to fill with tears. "I am learning English, Papa. Mr. Iskandar is teaching me. He says I should—"

"That's good, daughter. Fareed Fakhoury will like that. He doesn't want a wife who can do nothing but cook." **15**

"Papa, I'm not even fifteen yet!"

15 Inferences
What does the dialogue between Aneesi and her father tell you about the nature of their conflict?

He made calming gestures with his large-knuckled hands. "Mr. Fareed is willing to wait, until you are sixteen or so. He knows you have to grow up a bit more."

The happiness had gone from her father's face, and it cut Aneesi to the heart to see the anxious look return to his eyes. If only it had been good news about Hussein that he brought, how she would have rejoiced with him! But for two years now she had been on her own, learning and growing. She was no longer a child who had to accept everything decided for her. Surely that meant something—surely her father could see she had changed. **16**

"Papa," she said, rubbing at her moist cheek, "I don't want to marry. Mr. Fareed may be a very good man, and I know you would not want me to marry somebody who wasn't. But I don't want it."

"Daughter, this is your chance! Any girl would envy you. And your family will benefit . . . you have to think of that, too, you know."

Another thought came to Aneesi, shading her voice with bitterness. "And you wouldn't have to worry about me any longer, would you?" What she meant was "my virtue," but she could not bring herself to say it.

Now it was her father's turn **to harden**. "My daughter, I cannot force you to marry a man you don't want. That is against the law, and it is not my way. But I require that you meet Fareed Fakhoury and decide after you have had a chance to get to know him. You will see, my daughter, that you would be stupid not to accept."

"Yes, Papa," whispered Aneesi, her heart heavy. She left him and returned to her work in the kitchen.

But her mind was turbulent. **17** She thought back to her first weeks in this new country, how hard it had been to learn new ways, to live with a different family . . . how **baffling** to bump into unfamiliar ideas and assumptions . . . how humiliating to make mistakes and blunders time after time. She had cried quietly so often at night in her bed, missing her home, where everything

16 Inferences
Which words and phrases tell you how Aneesi feels about her father's plans for her?

17 Access Vocabulary
What does *turbulent* mean? Use the rhythm of the next sentence and details in this paragraph to make an educated guess.

In Other Words
to harden to feel more strongly that he was right
baffling confusing

was simple and familiar. All that unhappiness, and everything she had learned since then—did it all count for nothing? Would she have to give up her hopes?

For most of July, Aneesi's father worked on the Jubeilis' garden walls. Dr. Jubeili hired a second worker, a muscular young man who could do most of the heavy lifting, and the two men made a good team. Madame Jubeili was so pleased with the walls that she made more and more elaborate plans for the terraces and rose gardens.

It made Aneesi happy to see her father content in his work. He looked healthier, and the lines of anxiety eased in his face. As the days passed and he said nothing more about the man who had "asked for her," Aneesi hoped that he had decided not to **pursue** the matter.

Then, as if to make life even better, Maya Jubeili went away to visit friends at a fashionable seaside resort. For a week, Aneesi would not have to worry about the constant demands and prodding, let alone the clothes strewn everywhere around the house.

One evening soon after Maya's departure, Aneesi's father came to her in the kitchen, his face crinkled in a happy smile. "Mr. Iskandar took me with him to Beirut this afternoon, my daughter, and I bought something for you. Hold out your hand."

Sweets? Or a fancy headband to control her curly hair? No. What Aneesi found in her palm, in a small plastic box, was a **charm of gold**, shaped like a hand with a turquoise in the center.

"The Hand of Fatima," said her father. "Not very big, but it will bring you good luck. It will protect you. Someday you will have much more gold— but this is a start." 18

"Papa . . . Papa, thank you!" For a moment Aneesi didn't know what more to say. She had never owned gold before, not even a tiny piece. Gold meant

18 Inferences
What does Aneesi's father mean when he says, "Someday you will have much more gold . . ."?

Key Vocabulary
- **pursue** v., to seek, to become involved in

In Other Words
charm of gold small piece of gold jewelry

Cultural Background
To some Muslims, **the Hand of Fatima** represents power and protection from evil. It is often worn on necklaces as a good-luck charm.

something that could always be counted on, especially for a woman. Then the inevitable question had to come out. "But . . . Papa, how could you pay for it? Something like this costs a lot."

"Yes, I know. But don't worry. Dr. Jubeili gave me my first pay today, and I wanted to do something nice for you. It is not so much. I am saving the rest of my pay, you can be sure."

Aneesi kissed him and went right to her little room next to the kitchen, where she tucked the gold charm into a safe place. But her heart was not completely happy. Could Papa really afford to buy gold for her? Wasn't it an extravagance? Or worse—a chill went through her—could it be a sort of bribe, to encourage her to look with favor on Mr. Fareed Fakhoury? Aneesi tried to bury that thought, but it lingered. **19**

A few days later, Maya came home from the seaside resort, suntanned, beautiful, and **sulky**. In the late afternoon she sat with her mother on the balcony, while Aneesi served them lemonade. A strange nervousness **seemed to underlie Maya's casual pose**, and Aneesi wondered whether anything had gone wrong during the visit.

"Did you get to all the **boutiques**, dear?" asked Sitt Zeina. "Silly question. Well, show me what you bought. What were the shoes like? Did you find a nice purse for your cousin's wedding?"

Maya appeared to examine her **manicure**. Then she said, bluntly, "No."

"Well, what happened? Didn't the stores have nice things?"

No answer came from Maya, who ordinarily would have given a complete inventory of every boutique she visited. Aneesi could feel Maya's gaze on her, but she kept busy setting down the glasses of lemonade, the sugar, napkins,

19 Analyze Viewpoint
What does Aneesi's concern about the gift tell you about her impression of her father?

In Other Words
sulky unhappy
seemed to underlie Maya's casual pose appeared to affect Maya, though she pretended to be relaxed
boutiques shops
manicure painted fingernails

and sweet biscuits. Curious about this unusual behavior, she wanted to hear more. [20]

Finally Maya said, "I didn't have enough money."

Sitt Zeina sat up straight. "Enough money? Of course you did! I know prices are high there, but I gave you two hundred-thousand-pound notes just before you left. That certainly should have been enough for a decent pair of shoes and a purse. Now, what happened?"

"I don't know, Mama. All I remember is . . . " Maya paused again.

There was no way Aneesi could stall any longer. She left the balcony but paused inside the sitting room, where she could still hear the conversation.

"*What*, Maya?"

"Well . . . this is what happened." Maya's voice dropped, and Aneesi strained to listen. "You gave me the money just before I left, remember? And Iskandar was waiting in the car and already getting impatient and honking the horn. And he knows it always rattles me when he does that—I hate it! So it wasn't my fault I got nervous, was it? And then I remembered I'd forgotten my cell phone, so I had to go back for it. But I didn't want to drag along my purse and that big box of sweets you made me take, so I set them down on the garden wall for just a minute, while—" Maya broke off the story. [21]

A moment later Aneesi heard Sitt Zeina call to her. "Aneesi! You have plenty to do in the kitchen. We'll call you if we need you."

So Aneesi heard no more, but what she had heard **disquieted her**. And that evening she knew that Dr. and Madame Jubeili were talking to her father, with Maya and Iskandar present. Aneesi had been told to stay in her room.

The next morning, everything happened so fast she could hardly **grasp** what was going on. Just the day before, she had been so happy to see her father working contentedly, pruning the old fig tree, repairing the wall for the rose garden. Now he was here in the kitchen with her, **distraught**. Worse, he

[20] **Inferences**
What clues tell you that something probably went wrong during Maya's vacation?

[21] **Analyze Viewpoint**
What do the word choice and descriptions reveal about the author's attitude toward Maya?

In Other Words
disquieted her made her feel anxious
grasp understand
distraught very upset

Economic Background
Money in Lebanon is calculated in **pounds**. The Lebanese pound (LBP) can be exchanged in paper notes or in coins. Currently, just over 1,500 LBPs are equivalent to one U.S. dollar.

was not wearing his work clothes but the shabby suit and frayed white shirt he'd had on when he first arrived.

He spoke briefly, in a **subdued**, hoarse voice. Aneesi could sense the effort with which he controlled himself.

"They are sending me away, my daughter. They say I stole. They think I took money from Sitt Maya's purse when she left it on the wall. I remember when it happened. I was working near there, and the boy was working in back of the house. I saw the purse. Of course I did not touch it. But Sitt Maya could not find the money when she looked in her purse, so they think I took it. And now they don't want me any more."

At that point Iskandar came out to the kitchen. Looking pained, he spoke curtly, "Sorry, we've got to hurry or you'll miss the bus to Damascus."

Unable to **utter** a word, Aneesi kissed her father goodbye. As soon as he had left, she sat down at the kitchen table and wept.

She tried to keep the little Hand of Fatima out of her thoughts, but **stealthily** it worked its way in. When had Papa bought it? Yes, just a day or two after Sitt Maya had gone away. Could he really . . . ? No, never! Impossible! 23 Still . . . With sudden passion, Aneesi hated the Hand of Fatima. And she hated herself more, for allowing such hateful thoughts into her head.

A Tramp, circa 1904–6, John Singer Sargent. Translucent watercolor and touches of opaque watercolor, Brooklyn Museum. ©Francis G. Mayer/Corbis

△ **Critical Viewing: Character** How would you describe this man? How does he compare to your image of Aneesi's father?

22 Analyze Viewpoint Read this paragraph out loud. Describe how the Jubeilis' opinion of Aneesi's father has changed.

23 Inferences How would you elaborate on the sentence "Could he really . . . ?" to show what Aneesi is thinking?

Monitor Comprehension

Confirm Prediction Did you correctly predict whether Aneesi would achieve her dream? If so, what evidence supported your prediction?

Key Vocabulary
subdued *adj.*, quiet, controlled

In Other Words
utter say
stealthily secretly

Predict

Will the Jubeilis prove to be right about Aneesi's father?

In the next day or two, no one said anything out of the ordinary to Aneesi. She went about her work as always, but unsmiling, with downcast eyes. She **took pains** to avoid even the smallest slip and said nothing except when spoken to. Maya avoided her, and Mr. Iskandar said he was too busy for lessons.

On the third day, Aneesi went to Maya's room to gather up the clothes for laundering. As she did so, an image slipped into her mind . . . the black jeans, hiding that money in the pocket, a few weeks back. And with that image came an **impelling thought**. What had Maya been wearing on her drive to the resort? Aneesi didn't know; she hadn't seen Maya leave. But her sudden, desperate **hunch** held the only possible hope.

In an increasing frenzy, she searched through all the jeans and shorts. Nothing. She found a jacket and a couple of shirts with pockets lying around the room. Nothing. Then she glanced at the open closet—but no, she couldn't search there. Clothes hanging in the closet were private. She looked behind chairs, under the bed. No clothes hiding there.

Finally Aneesi gave up in despair. Her eyes blurring with tears of frustration, she tried to get on with her work. She gathered up an armful of clothes and was about to carry them to the washing machine when she noticed something on the closet floor. A garment must have fallen from a hanger. Setting down her armload, Aneesi picked it up . . . a light cardigan sweater. Could Maya have been wearing that recently? Sometimes, even in midsummer, morning fog made the air cool.

In fumbling haste, Aneesi examined the sweater. Her heart suddenly seemed to pound as she found a small pocket. She stuck her fingers in— and they touched folded paper. Trembling, she drew it out. Two bank notes, two hundred thousand pounds. **24**

24 Analyze Viewpoint
How do the words and phrases "fumbling haste," "heart suddenly seemed to pound," and "trembling" change the way that we view Aneesi at this moment in the story?

In Other Words
took pains tried hard
impelling thought interesting idea
hunch feeling

For a minute or two, unable to take the next step, Aneesi sat on the edge of Maya's bed. Then she left the room to look for Sitt Zeina.

Elegantly dressed and ready to go down to Beirut, Sitt Zeina was checking her appearance at a mirror in the front hall. She turned with a frown of irritation. "What is it, girl? Can't you see, I'm—"

Still half in a daze, Aneesi held out the money and the cardigan sweater.

Sitt Zeina stared blankly at the bills. Then, backing up to a chair, she sat down heavily. "Oh, my God," she whispered. "The money was in Maya's pocket all the time. That careless girl, so careless with money . . . she took off the sweater and forgot all about it. And we accused the poor man. Oh, God forgive us." **25**

That evening the family gathered again in the sitting room. After a while, Aneesi was asked to join them. Maya sat with slumped shoulders, streaks of black mascara on her cheeks.

"I'm sorry, Aneesi." she mumbled. "I was in such a hurry . . . I didn't know what I was doing. I thought . . . "

"No, you didn't think!" growled her brother. "And you didn't know what you were doing. You never do, these days."

Sitt Zeina gave them both a warning look, then turned to Aneesi. "We are so very sorry, Aneesi," she said in a low voice. "We hope you and your father will forgive us."

Though **at a loss for words**, Aneesi lifted her head and tried to look Sitt Zeina in the eye. She nodded slightly.

With a cough, Sitt Zeina spoke **more diffidently**. "We appreciated his good work. He is a fine workman. Do . . . do you think he would come back?"

Dr. Jubeili broke in sharply. "Of course not! What do you think? The man has his pride." **26**

Aneesi could tell that the gruff voice covered his own regret and embarrassment. And she knew he was absolutely right.

25 **Analyze Viewpoint** Why does the author have Sitt Zeina react the way she does? How does she want us, as readers, to think about Sitt Zeina now?

26 **Inferences** How does Dr. Jubeili know whether Aneesi's father would work for his family again?

In Other Words
at a loss for words unable to say anything
more diffidently less confidently, timidly

But her own feelings were so mixed up she wondered how she could ever see her life clearly again. Now, remembering how she had yielded to even faint suspicions about her father, *she* felt like **the betrayer**. And no matter how unfair it was, she felt responsible. She had brought him here, to the place where he was forced to suffer such a harsh blow. It would have been better, she thought, if she had never overheard that conversation about stone walls. Now there was only one thing she could do.

"I must go to my father," she said. **27**

As soon as she could pack her things, Aneesi left the Jubeili home. Dr. Jubeili gave her the remaining pay for the days her father had worked, plus a large bonus. Aneesi was sure her father would accept it, pride or no pride.

Sitt Zeina said quietly, "You could come back, Aneesi, maybe later on, when you're ready." Aneesi thanked her and said nothing more.

Iskandar drove Aneesi to a nearby town where she could get the weekly taxi to Syria. Neither spoke on the way, but when they arrived and he had taken her suitcase from the car, he looked at her with concern. "Aneesi, I have a couple of books for you, an English grammar and a book of short

She wondered how she could ever see her life clearly again.

stories I think you'll like. Remember what I told you, Aneesi. You can do good things in life, important things. And . . . come back, if you possibly can."

"Thank you, I will," she said, aware that her answer would serve for everything he'd said. Then she climbed into the battered old taxi, and it got under way.

27 Inferences
Why do you think Aneesi believes she must take this action?

In Other Words
the betrayer the one who had turned against him

After a while Aneesi took the gold charm from her small purse, placed it on her palm, and studied it. What did it mean, the Hand of Fatima? Luck . . . protection? A token of her father's love, surely. But also, she feared, a claim for obedience.

No, it meant more—it must! The Hand of Fatima also stood for strength, power.

For the first time in days, Aneesi felt her heart quickening, her thoughts becoming **coherent**. She was headed, she knew, for the most difficult encounter of her young life: facing her father—and what he wanted for her. But even though she would probably stand alone, she would stand firm. The Hand would help her . . . a reminder that her fate must rest in her own hands. 28

Aneesi closed her fingers around the gold trinket. Then she turned to gaze out the grimy window of the taxi, as it hurtled on through stony hills punctuated with fig trees, pines, and raw new buildings. ❖

Lola, 1961, © Joseph Matar. Oil, courtesy of LebanonArt.com.

🔺 **Critical Viewing: Character** How would you describe the expression on this young woman's face? What qualities might she share with Aneesi?

28 **Inferences**
What has Aneesi decided to do? How can you tell?

Key Vocabulary
● **coherent** *adj.*, orderly, logical, and easy to understand

ANALYZE The Hand of Fatima

1. **Recall and Interpret** At the end of the story, Aneesi must make a choice about her work with the Jubeilis. Recall the situations that have tested Aneesi's loyalty and feelings. Be sure to cite evidence from the text.

2. **Vocabulary** Who is more **conscientious**, Aneesi or Maya? Who is more **naive**? Explain.

3. **Analyze Viewpoint** Does the author seem to like Aneesi? Does she seem to have empathy toward Aneesi? Describe the author's attitude toward Aneesi and tell how you determined this.

4. **Focus Strategy Make Inferences** Maya makes an inference about Aneesi's father. Why do Maya's parents believe her? Did you believe her? Explain.

Return to the Text

Reread and Write Do you think Aneesi should remain loyal to her family or her dream? Can she be loyal to both? Reread the story to find sentences that support your answer. Write your explanation.

BEFORE READING Old Ways, New World

news report by Joseph Berger

Reading Strategies

· Plan and Monitor
· Determine Importance
▶ **Make Inferences**
· Ask Questions
· Make Connections
· Synthesize
· Visualize

Determine Viewpoint

News reports provide facts about topics and events. A news report may also include the **viewpoints**, or opinions, of different people. However, reporters do not give their own viewpoint about a subject. They present the information in an objective, or unbiased, way. Good reporters want readers to make up their own minds about who or what may be right about an issue. For this reason, reporters try to mask their personal feelings so that their news reports do not favor one viewpoint over another.

Look Into the Text

The reporter gives factual details.

> Bodh Das, a physician from India, wanted his daughters to marry within his Hindu caste. His eldest daughter, Abha, returned to India in 1975 to wed a man she had never met from her father's Kayashta caste. Das's second daughter, Bibha, also married a Kayashta.
>
> But Rekha, who is the most Americanized of Das's three daughters, married a man outside her father's caste whom she met in school. **It was what Indians call "a love marriage"**: that is, a marriage that is not arranged by the parents.

Does the reporter express a viewpoint about the marriages?

Careful wording creates an objective presentation here.

Focus Strategy ▶ Make Inferences

When you make inferences, you can make up your own mind about topics and events. Putting the details in your own words helps you form your own opinions.

HOW TO MAKE INFERENCES

Focus Strategy

1. **Note factual details** and other people's opinions as you read "Old Ways, New World."

2. **Write the details and opinions** in your own words.

3. **Make inferences** about each person's opinion of arranged marriages as you read the news report. Make a chart like the one shown below to keep track of your ideas.

Factual Detail:	Others' Opinion:
My Own Words:	My Own Words:
What I Infer:	

Old Ways, NEW WORLD by Joseph Berger

Connect Across Texts

In "The Hand of Fatima," Aneesi is torn between loyalty to her family and her own dreams. As you read the following news report, consider how loyalty to family and culture might impact people's life decisions.

A Delicate Balance

For Afghan and Indian immigrants in the United States, dating and marriage present special challenges. Ashrat Khwajazadah and Naheed Mawjzada are in many ways modern American women, **spurning** the headscarves and modest outfits customarily worn by Afghan women.

Both in their early twenties, they have taken a route still **controversial** for Afghan women living in America: going to college to pursue professions. And both defy the ideal of **submissive** Afghan womanhood. Mawjzada speaks up forcefully when men talk politics at the dinner table.

But at the same time, neither woman has ever dated. Like most women in the Afghan community in New York, they are waiting for their parents to pick their spouses. **1**

Elsewhere in New York, Bodh Das, a physician from India, wanted his daughters to marry within his Hindu **caste**. His eldest daughter, Abha,

A young couple takes part in a traditional Hindu marriage ceremony in New York's Central Park.

1 Inferences
How do the women show their loyalty to their culture? How are they untraditional?

Key Vocabulary
- **controversial** *adj.*, causing disagreement

In Other Words
spurning rejecting
submissive quiet and obedient
caste society, social division

returned to India in 1975 to wed a man she had never met from her father's Kayashta caste. Das's second daughter, Bibha, also married a Kayashta.

But Rekha, who is the most Americanized of Das's three daughters, married a man outside her father's caste whom she met in school. It was what Indians call "a love marriage": that is, a marriage that is not arranged by the parents.

Indians and Afghans living in America, particularly women, must often **strike a delicate balance** as they grow up in a relatively

Ashrat Khwajazadah (right) and her sister Alliy both attend Queens College in New York.

Afghan women pray at their neighborhood mosque in New York.

freewheeling society, but with immigrant parents who are holding on to the customs of their homeland. The tension between immigrant parents and children today is no different from that experienced by the Irish, Italian, Jewish, and other immigrant groups of the nineteenth and twentieth centuries. Those newcomers also looked on with anger or resignation as their children gradually **adopted the prevailing culture**. 2

Among Afghans, no tradition is more ironclad than parents arranging their children's marriages. It is generally felt that if a daughter chooses her own husband, it damages her father's **stature in the community**.

2 **Determine Viewpoint**
How does the comparison between Afghans and other immigrants show the reporter's objectivity?

In Other Words
strike a delicate balance act with care
freewheeling society free world with few restrictions
adopted the prevailing culture became more like the dominant culture or mainstream society
stature in the community status or reputation among other Afghans

328 Unit 3 The Ties That Bind

"The girl is a trophy piece," says Mawjzada. "If the girl has a good reputation, the family has a good reputation."

Marriage customs for men are **more lenient**. Bashir Rahim, 29, says that if he meets a girl who interests him at a family gathering he will find out her address, then send his parents to her home to start a conversation about marriage. **3**

An Ancient
Hierarchy

India's caste system goes back thousands of years to the origins of Hinduism. At the top were the Brahmin scholars and priests;

Hariharan Janakiraman, 31, trusts his parents to find him a Brahmin wife.

at the bottom were the Dalit, or "untouchables." After India gained its independence from Britain in 1947, the legal forms of the caste system were **abolished**. But attitudes shaped by **an ancient and pervasive social system** don't change easily.

Some young people are still attached to the old ways. Hariharan Janakiraman, a 31-year-old software engineer, has agreed to let his parents find a Brahmin wife for him. They will consult his horoscope and that of his prospective bride. The young woman will then be asked to prepare some food and sing and dance to show that all her limbs work. If he were to marry a woman outside of his caste, says Janakiraman, "My uncle and aunt won't have a good impression of my parents, so I won't do that."

But sometimes an arranged marriage can be painful. Masuda Sultan, 26, grew up in New York and is now a graduate student at Harvard. When she was 15, her father arranged for her to marry a doctor twice her age. **4**

3 Inferences
What do Rahim's actions tell you about his loyalty to Afghan customs? Write the details on your chart.

4 Determine Viewpoint
How does the presentation in this paragraph show that this news report is unbiased?

Key Vocabulary
abolish *v.*, to do away with or get rid of

In Other Words
more lenient not as strict
an ancient and pervasive social system
  old and widespread traditions in society

Afghan or American?

"I actually thought it could work," recalls Sultan. "When your actions are limited and you're from a certain world and you respect your family, you go along with their wishes."

Sultan wanted to finish college before they began having children, and tensions with her husband became **irreconcilable**. After three years, they divorced, which is a rare and humiliating event in the Afghan community.

"The core issue was really a different philosophy of what it means to be Afghan and what it means to be American," says Sultan. "Ultimately I was being treated as a child and my role was set and I was being told what I could and couldn't do." **5** ❖

5 Inferences
What do the quotations tell you about the speaker's perspective on arranged marriages?

ANALYZE Old Ways, New World

1. **Recall and Interpret** What is the "delicate balance" that some of the Afghan and Indian immigrants featured in the story try to keep? Be sure to cite evidence from the text.

2. **Vocabulary** Why do you think arranged marriages are a **controversial** issue?

3. **Determine Viewpoint** Identify two instances when the reporter presents controversial information in an objective, neutral way. Do you think he remains neutral throughout the article? Explain.

4. **Focus Strategy Make Inferences** Refer to the inference chart you made as you read. What inferences did you make about each person's opinion of arranged marriage? Exchange your chart with a partner and compare notes.

⟲ Return to the Text
Reread and Write What factors might influence a person's loyalty to family and traditions? How might loyalties change? Reread to confirm. Then write a paragraph to explain.

In Other Words
irreconcilable impossible to repair

EQ What Tests a Person's Loyalty?

Critical Thinking

EQ **1. Interpret** Review your thoughts about the Make a Connection question on page 302. How do you think Aneesi ("The Hand of Fatima") would answer the question? How do you think Masuda Sultan ("Old Ways, New World") would answer it?

2. Analyze How might living away from home change a young person's beliefs and values? Give examples from both texts.

3. Compare How does the author's viewpoint in "The Hand of Fatima" differ from the author's viewpoint in the news report? How does each viewpoint support the purpose of the selection? Explain.

4. Speculate What will Aneesi say to persuade her family to let her make her own decisions about her life? Dramatize the scene in a small group.

EQ **5. Draw Conclusions** How can conflicting goals test a person's loyalty to family? Use details from both texts to support your conclusions.

Write About Literature

Comparison Paragraph From your reading, what are two ways that life in the Middle East appears to be like or unlike life in the United States? Write a paragraph in which you explain the similarities or differences, using examples from both texts.

Key Vocabulary Review

Oral Review Work with a partner. Use these words to complete the paragraph.

abolished	conscientious	pursue
admonishes	controversial	subdued
coherent	naive	

Making my choice to work toward or __(1)__ my college education far from home is a __(2)__ and difficult topic in my family because not everyone agrees. My family wants me to stay close to home and sometimes __(3)__ me for wanting to attend college so far away. I have to make a thoughtful and __(4)__ decision that everyone agrees with and that is not __(5)__ or too quickly decided upon. When I make my decision, I will go to a private and __(6)__ place where loud noises are __(7)__, like the library. Since I am a dedicated and __(8)__ student, I know that I will make the right choice and that my family will support me in whatever I choose.

Writing Application In a paragraph, explain one of your goals in life and ways you will **pursue** it. Use at least five Key Vocabulary words.

Read with Ease: Expression

Assess your reading fluency with the passage in the Reading Handbook, on p. 807. Then complete the self-check below.

1. My expression did/did not sound natural.

2. My words correct per minute: _____ .

Use Subject and Object Pronouns

Nouns can be a subject or an object in a sentence.

Aneesi washes the **dishes**.

subject   object

Pronouns can take the place of nouns. Use a **subject pronoun** to replace the subject. Use an **object pronoun** to replace the object.

Aneesi washes the **dishes**.

She washes **them**.

Subject Pronouns		Object Pronouns	
I	we	me	us
you	they	you	them
he, she, it		him, her, it	

Oral Practice (1–5) With a partner, read the sentences. Change the underlined words to correct pronouns.

1. <u>Aneesi</u> works for <u>Sitt Zeina</u>. (She/Her)
2. She misses <u>her mother and father</u>. (they/them)
3. Sitt Zeina needs to repair <u>a garden wall</u>. (it/them)
4. <u>Aneesi and he</u> need the work. (They/Them)
5. Aneesi talks to <u>Papa</u>. (he/him)

Written Practice (6–10) Rewrite to edit the paragraph. Fix the pronouns.

    Papa talked to she. Him wanted Aneesi to marry Fareed. Aneesi listened to he. Her did not want to marry Fareed. Her wanted to choose her own husband.

Compare and Contrast

Pair Talk Think about Aneesi and another character from "The Hand of Fatima" or another story. Explain their similarities and differences. Use words such as *like*, *unlike*, and *similar to*.

Symbolism

A **symbol** is a person, place, event, or object that represents something else. For example, a tiger might represent strength or power. A symbol can have more than one meaning and its meaning might change throughout a story. In "The Hand of Fatima," the gold charm is an important symbol.

Reread pages 317–324. Think about the importance of the gold charm as a symbol in this story. Work with a partner and answer the following questions:

1. What do you think the gold charm symbolizes when Aneesi first receives it from her father?
2. What does giving the gold charm to his daughter represent to the father?
3. How does the meaning of the symbol change after the Jubeili family assumes something about Aneesi's father?
4. The Hand of Fatima takes on a new meaning by the end of the story. What does it represent to Aneesi? Compare this with what it first represented for her.

Did you and your partner come up with the same interpretations? Discuss why or why not.

What does this symbol represent to you?

Word Families

Many English words have roots that come from Greek and Latin. Words with the same root can be considered part of the same word family. For example, the Latin root *spect* means "see" and is found in words such as *inspect, respect,* and *spectacular.*

Find as many words as you can for these common roots. Use a dictionary to confirm each word's meaning.

ROOT	MEANING	WORDS WITH THAT ROOT
1. *junct*	join	
2. *struct*	build	
3. *phon*	sound	

Oral Presentation

Social Studies: Family Traditions In "Old Ways, New World," you learned about the Afghan tradition of parents arranging marriages for their children. Conduct a research project to prepare a short presentation about other family or cultural traditions.

Interview classmates or people in your community who are from countries outside the United States or who have relatives from other countries. Ask them which traditions their cultures still practice in the United States and which traditions they do not follow in this country. Present your findings to the class.

▼ **Language and Learning Handbook,** p. 750

Write a Business Letter

There are several reasons you might write a business letter, including to apply for a job or to ask for information. Draft a business letter to apply for a job.

1 **Prewrite** Organize any notes or material you will need to compose the letter, such as the job advertisement you are responding to and the employer's contact information.

2 **Draft** A business letter should be concise. Make your point as quickly and clearly as possible.

3 **Revise** Make any necessary revisions. Does the letter clearly communicate what you want to say?

4 **Edit and Proofread** Edit any unclear sentences, and correct any mistakes in grammar, spelling, or punctuation.

5 **Send the Letter** Print out your letter to mail. Sign the letter at the bottom above your name.

▼ **Writing Handbook,** p. 832

Sample Business Letter

August 24, 2013 — date

John Green
123 Maryland Ave.
Columbia, MO 65201 — your contact information

Mr. Jim Travis
Larson Employment Agency
10010 W. Jefferson Ave.
St. Louis, MO 63106 — company contact information

Dear Mr. Travis,

I am writing in response to your agency's — body
advertisement requesting resumes. I have recently earned a bachelor's degree in communications. I would greatly appreciate your review of my resume, which I have enclosed.

I will contact you soon to see if you have had — closing
a chance to review my resume. Thank you.

Sincerely,

John Green

John Green

from Anthem

BY AYN RAND

1 Our name is Equality 7-2521, as it is written on the iron bracelet which all men wear on their left wrists with their names upon it. We are twenty-one years old. We are six feet tall, and this is a burden, for there are not many men who are six feet tall. Ever have the Teachers and the Leaders pointed to us and frowned and said:

2 "There is evil in your bones, Equality 7-2521, for your body has grown beyond the bodies of your brothers." But we cannot change our bones nor our body.

3 We were born with a **curse**. It has always driven us to thoughts which are forbidden. It has always given us wishes which men may not wish. We know that we are evil, but there is no will in us and no power to resist it. This is our wonder and our secret fear, that we know and do not resist.

4 We strive to be like all our brother men, for all men must be alike. Over the portals of the Palace of the World Council, there are words cut in the marble, which we repeat to ourselves whenever we **are tempted**:

5 *"WE ARE ONE IN ALL AND ALL IN ONE.
THERE ARE NO MEN BUT ONLY THE GREAT WE,
ONE, INDIVISIBLE AND FOREVER."*

Lecture, News, Advertising, for the Social Science Hall, "A Century of Progress" Exposition, Chicago, Illinois, 1933, Alfonso Iannelli. Scale model, The Wolfsonian-Florida International University, Miami Beach, Florida, The Mitchell Wolfson, Jr. Collection.

▲ **Critical Viewing: Character** How would you describe the people in this art? How are they like the people described in the story?

In Other Words
curse terrible problem
are tempted desire to do wrong

6 We repeat this to ourselves, but it helps us not.

7 These words were cut long ago. There is green mold in the grooves of the letters and yellow streaks on the marble, which come from more years than men could count. And these words are the truth, for they are written on the Palace of the World Council, and the World Council is the body of all truth. Thus has it been ever since the Great Rebirth, and farther back than that no memory can reach.

8 But we must never speak of the times before the Great Rebirth, else we are sentenced to three years in the Palace of Corrective Detention. It is only the Old Ones who whisper about it in the evenings, in the Home of the Useless. They whisper many strange things, of the towers which rose to the sky, in those Unmentionable Times, and of the wagons which moved without horses, and of the lights which burned without flame. But those times were evil. And those times passed away, when men saw the Great Truth which is this: that all men are one and that there is no will save the will of all men together.

9 All men are good and wise. It is only we, Equality 7-2521, we alone who were born with a curse. For we are not like our brothers. And

...we are not like our brothers.

as we look back upon our life, we see that it has **ever been thus** and that it has brought us step by step to our last, supreme **transgression**, our crime of crimes hidden here under the ground.

10 We remember the Home of the Infants where we lived **till** we were five years old, together with all the children of the City who had been born in the same year. The sleeping halls there were white and clean and bare of all things save one hundred beds. We were just like all our brothers then, save for the one transgression: we fought with our brothers. There are few offenses blacker than to fight with our brothers, at any age and for any cause whatsoever. The Council of the Home told us so, and of all the children of that year, we were locked in the cellar most often.

11 When we were five years old, we were sent to the Home of the Students, where there are ten wards, for our ten years of learning. Men must learn till they reach their fifteenth year. Then they go to work. In the Home of the Students we arose when the big bell rang in the tower and we went to our

In Other Words
ever been thus always been this way
transgression misbehavior
till until

beds when it rang again. Before we removed our **garments**, we stood in the great sleeping hall, and we raised our right arms, and we said all together with the three Teachers at the head:

12   "We are nothing. Mankind is all. By the grace of our brothers are we allowed our lives. We exist through, by and for our brothers who are the State. Amen."

13   Then we slept. The sleeping halls were white and clean and bare of all things save one hundred beds.

14   We, Equality 7-2521, were not happy in those years in the Home of the Students. It was not that the learning was too hard for us. It was that the learning was too easy. This is a great sin, to be **born with a head which is too quick**. It is not good to be different from our brothers, but it is evil to be superior to them. The Teachers told us so, and they frowned when they looked upon us. . . .

15   So we wished to be sent to the Home of the Scholars. We wished it so much that our hands trembled under the blankets in the night, and we bit our arm to stop that other pain which we could not endure. It was evil and we dared not face our brothers in the morning. For men may wish nothing for themselves. And we were punished when the Council of Vocations came to give us our life Mandates which tell those who reach their fifteenth year what their work is to be for the rest of their days.

16   The Council of Vocations came on the first day of spring, and they sat in the great hall. And we who were fifteen and all the Teachers came into the great hall. And the Council of Vocations sat on a high **dais**, and they had but two words to speak to each of the Students. They called the Students' names, and when the Students stepped before them, one after another, the Council said: "Carpenter" or "Doctor" or "Cook" or "Leader." Then each Student raised their right arm and said: "The will of our brothers be done."

17   Now if the Council has said "Carpenter" or "Cook," the Students so assigned go to work and they do not study any further. But if the Council has said "Leader," then those Students go into the Home of the Leaders, which is the greatest house in the City, for it has three stories. And there they study for many years, so that they may become candidates and be elected to the City Council and the State Council and the World Council—by a free and general vote of all men. But we wished not to be a Leader, even though it is a great honor. We wished to be a Scholar.

In Other Words
garments clothes
born with a head which is too quick too smart
dais stage

Pillars of the Game, 2000, Hugh Shurley. Photo collage © Hugh Shurley/Corbis.

⚠ **Critical Viewing: Effect** How would this painting be different if the artist had chosen to include all of the people shown?

18   So we awaited our turn in the great hall and then we heard the Council of Vocations call our name: "Equality 7-2521." We walked to the dais, and our legs did not tremble, and we looked up at the Council. There were five members of the Council, three of the male gender and two of the female. Their hair was white and their faces were cracked as the clay of a dry river bed. They were old. They seemed older than the marble of the Temple of the World Council. They sat before us and they did not move. And we saw no breath to stir the folds of their white **togas**. But we knew that they were alive, for a finger of the hand of the oldest rose, pointed to us, and fell down again. This was the only thing which moved, for the lips of the oldest did not move as they said: "Street Sweeper."

19   We felt the cords of our neck grow tight as our head rose higher to look upon the faces of the Council, and we were happy. We knew we had been **guilty**, but now we had a way to **atone** for it. We would accept our Life Mandate, and we would work for our brothers, gladly and willingly, and we would erase our sin against them, which they did not know,

We would accept our Life Mandate...

but we knew. So we were happy, and proud of ourselves and of our victory over ourselves. We raised our right arm and we spoke, and our voice was the clearest, the steadiest voice in the hall that day, and we said:

20   "The will of our brothers be done."

21   And we looked straight into the eyes of the Council, but their eyes were as cold blue glass buttons. ❖

In Other Words
togas robes
guilty to blame
atone make up

THE TIES
THAT BIND

 ESSENTIAL QUESTION:

What Tests a Person's Loyalty?

myNGconnect.com

🌐 Download the rubric.

Present Your Project: Reality TV Show

It's time to present your reality TV show about the Essential Question for this unit: What Tests a Person's Loyalty?

1 Review and Complete Your Plan

Consider these points as you complete your project:

- What format will your show use? How will it address the Essential Question?
- What situations will the characters face and what actions will they take? How will their loyalty to one another be tested?
- Will the situations and characters create interest for the viewers?

2 Hold the Press Conference

Make sure all the actors are prepared, and then present your reality TV show. Seat your audience so they can view your show.

3 Evaluate the Press Conference

Use the online rubric to evaluate each of the reality TV shows, including your own.

Reflect on Your Reading

Many of the characters in the stories in this unit learned about the test of loyalty.

Think back on your reading of the unit selections, including your choice of Edge Library books. Then, discuss the following with a partner or in a small group.

Genre Focus Compare and contrast the style of one short story with the style of another short story. Give examples, using the selections in this unit.

Focus Strategy With a partner, compare the kinds of relationships you read about in this unit. Then take a closer look at one of these relationships. Use details from the text to make inferences about the importance of loyalty in the relationship.

EQ Respond to the Essential Question

Throughout this unit, you have been thinking about what tests a person's loyalty. Discuss the Essential Question with a group. What have *you* decided? Support your response with evidence from your reading, discussions, research, and writing.

Write a Position Paper

What issues make you want to speak out? Present an argument about an issue that matters to you by writing a position paper.

Writing Mode
Argument

Writing Trait Focus
Development of Ideas

Study Position Papers

Position papers contain claims, or positions, on issues that have at least two sides. Writers of position papers want their readers to believe what they have to say, so they support their positions with reasons and evidence.

❶ Connect Writing to Your Life

You have probably stated your position on many topics. For example, you may have argued that one singer is better than another. Or maybe you have stated your beliefs about the environment, school rules, or driving laws. In each case, you probably stated your position and then gave reasons for it. You do the same thing when you write a position paper.

❷ Understand the Form

A good position paper is written with a formal tone and contains the following elements:

Introduction

Present the issue. Identify both sides. One side is your position, or claim. The other side is the opposing position, or counterclaim. Your position is the **controlling idea** of your paper.

Body

Explain why you believe your position.

Support

Provide **reasons** to support your position and **evidence** to support your reasons. Address the opposing position, or other side of the argument, and provide reasons that show why it is wrong.

Conclusion

Summarize your position in a memorable way.

Now look at these parts in action. Read a position paper by a professional writer.

❸ Analyze a Professional Model

As you read, look for the writer's position and supporting evidence.

Baseball: An American Tradition

by Mark Giddis

As baseball players' salaries rise and tickets to games cost more and more, many fans worry about the future of America's greatest pastime. Baseball has become too commercial to survive, they fear. It is true that baseball, like many other professional sports today, is as much about profits than play, but fans need not worry. The game has been around for more than a century, and it will be around for centuries to come. Baseball is an American tradition that will never die.

Baseball will survive because it is a game suited to a democracy. Almost anyone can play it. You do not have to be tall, strong, or fast to play baseball. Children grow up playing baseball. It is the game of choice at family gatherings. Workers form teams. Soldiers play baseball during breaks from battle. Sailors play baseball on the decks of ships. Baseball can be, and is, played by people of all ages and abilities.

Another reason that baseball will survive is that it binds us together. It unites us in victory and in defeat. Longtime baseball fan Bob Romano recalls sitting in the stadium, watching his city's team playing in the World Series: "We needed just one more out to win the game. The crowd held its breath. The pitch came. 'Strike 3!' the umpire shouted, and the crowd roared. Fans of all ages, colors, income levels, and beliefs hugged and shook each other's hands. 'We did it!' they cried. I thought, now that's the way it should be." That is the way it will stay, because people are drawn to things that unite them. Who can deny that baseball is one of those things?

Finally, baseball will survive because it is living history. It is a link between one generation and the next. Though players' salaries have soared and stadiums have changed, the enjoyment of watching a game is much the same today as it was in the past. Parents take their children to games for a day of fun in the sun. When the children grow up, they take their own children to the game.

Baseball is a deeply rooted part of our culture and always will be. Therefore, worried fans should relax, sit back, and enjoy the game. They might even try playing a little ball for themselves. After all, it is an American tradition.

The writer states the issue and his **position**, as well as an **opposing position**, in the introduction.

These **reasons** support the writer's position. Also, the writing has a formal style.

The writer uses **transition words** to connect ideas.

The writer addresses the **opposing position** and offers a response to it.

How does the writer summarize his position in a memorable way?

▶**Prompt** Write a position paper about an issue that affects your school or your community. Be sure to:

- state your position on the issue
- give reasons to support your position
- address the opposing position
- use a formal writing style
- end in a thought-provoking, memorable way

✔ Prewrite

Once you know the basics of position papers, plan one of your own. Planning, or prewriting, will make it easier for you to write later on. When you are finished prewriting, you will have a detailed Writing Plan to guide you as you write.

❶ Choose Your Topic

Think of an issue to write about. Here are some good ways to choose a topic:

- With a small group of students, brainstorm a list of issues that affect your school or community. Choose the issue that is most important to you.
- Skim the headlines of a school or community newspaper. What issues are in the news? Which could you write about?

❷ Clarify the Audience, Controlling Idea, and Purpose

Your teacher and classmates will probably be your main audience. Who else might be interested in reading your paper? Jot down your ideas.

What is your position on the situation you are writing about? Do you want to encourage it or stop it? In a sentence or two, state your position. That is your **controlling idea**.

Finally, think about your reason for writing. What do you want your audience to understand? Your answer will be your purpose for writing.

❸ Gather Your Support

Next, gather reasons to support your position. List every reason your position is credible. Then choose the reasons that would be most understandable to your audience. Also, think of reasons someone might not support your position and provide evidence to refute them, or prove them wrong. You may have to do some research to provide concrete, specific evidence. Remember, your purpose for writing is to make the audience understand and consider your position.

To make it easier to clarify your audience, ask yourself these questions:

- Who is affected by this issue?
- Who has the power to make things change in the way I want them to?

These people could be part of your audience.

❹ Organize the Details

Organize your position paper in a sustained and logical fashion. For example, you might present supporting information in order of importance, from least important to most important. That way the audience will remember your most important reason best. How can you tell which one is the most important? Decide which reason you have the most to say about.

❺ Finish Your Writing Plan

Make a Writing Plan like the one below. Include a simple outline or other graphic organizer to show which ideas will go in the introduction, the body, and the conclusion.

Writing Plan

Topic	keeping traditions alive
Audience	my teacher and all students
Controlling Idea	keeping cultural traditions alive is important
Purpose	to explain why cultural traditions are important
Time Frame	one week from today

I. Introduction

    A. Many young people don't want to keep cultural traditions.

    B. Keeping cultural traditions is important.

II. Body

    A. Cultural origins are a part of a person's identity.

    B. Culture and tradition help strengthen family relationships.

    C. Cultural traditions influence U.S. culture.

    D. Opposing position: Kids need to live in the present and learn about their new culture, not focus on their old one.

III. Conclusion

    A. Summarize position.

    B. End in a memorable way.

Reflect on Your Writing Plan

▶ Is your position clear? Do you have good reasons to support it? Have you included specific details that will be understandable to your audience?

✔ Write a Draft

Now you are ready to write. Use your Writing Plan as a guide while you write your position paper. It's OK to make mistakes. You'll have chances to improve your draft later. For now, just keep writing!

❶ Put Ideas into Words

Sometimes writers look at a blank page and freeze. They do not know how to put their ideas into words. If you have this trouble, try these techniques:

- **Talk to Your Audience** Tell your ideas to one of your classmates. Ask the person to take notes. Use the notes to get your ideas down on paper.

- **Picture Your Audience** Choose one real person who will read your paper. Picture this person in your mind. Begin writing to this person alone. If it helps, you might write in the form of a letter. Underline parts you can use in your draft.

- **Send Yourself an E-mail** If you are used to writing e-mails, begin your draft in an e-mail. It can be easier to write because it seems less permanent. Send yourself the e-mail. Underline text you think you might use; then cut and paste the text into a document.

❷ Use Evidence for Support

One way to make your audience believe your position is to provide precise and relevant evidence presented objectively, or fairly. Here are some kinds of evidence that you can use to support your position:

- **Facts** are statements that are proved to be true.

- **Examples** illustrate why your position is believable.

- **Analogies** allow you to compare your position to something the audience might better understand.

> **Technology Tip**
>
> As you write your draft, use boldface type for your position and for each reason. Then use regular type for your supporting details. You will quickly see which reasons need additional supporting evidence.

OK

> Your country of origin is part of your identity, it's part of what makes you unique. If this part of your identity is suppressed, your full potential won't be achieved.

Better

> Your country of origin is part of your identity, it's part of what makes you unique. If this part of your identity is suppressed, your full potential won't be achieved. This is what happened to Jenny Lin, a Chinese American aspiring artist at Central high school. "I kept trying to paint in what I believed was a modern style," she says. "I tried to strip any Chinese influence out of my work, and I ended up with paintings that had no depth or soul." It wasn't until she let herself keep the Chinese influence that vivid, moving pieces of work were created.

Read this draft to see how the student used the Writing Plan to get ideas down on paper. This first draft does not have to be perfect. As you'll see, the student fixed the mistakes later.

Keeping Traditions Alive

The United States is made up of many different cultures. When people from these cultures first arrived, the people worked hard to maintain the traditions of their homelands. However, each following generation embraced fewer and fewer of these traditions. Today, many of my friends are all trying so hard to be American that they're not keeping ties to their country of origin. Adapting to a new culture is important, however, retaining elements of the old one is equally important.

First, your country of origin is part of your identity, it's part of what makes you unique. If this part of your identity is suppressed, your full potential won't be achieved. This is what happened to Jenny Lin, a Chinese American aspiring artist at Central high school. "I kept trying to paint in what I believed was a modern style," she says. "I tried to strip any Chinese influence out of my work, and I ended up with paintings that had no depth or soul." It wasn't until she let herself keep the Chinese influence that vivid, moving pieces of work were created.

Culture and tradition help strengthen family relationships. Culture and tradition provide something that can be appreciated by different generations. Just think about how some teens can't seem to relate to their grandparents. A tradition would give them something in common.

Finally, preserving cultural traditions is important because these traditions influence U.S. culture. Billboard has a Top 100 chart for Latin music, and many songs by Latin performers also appear on the general Top 100 chart. According to the national retail federation, the Pan-African festival of Kwanzaa was celebrated by nearly 7 million Americans in 2006. This shows that it is possible to preserve one's heritage and be a part of American culture at the same time. Celebrating traditions, in fact, is one of the most "American" things a person can do.

People who make the past a part of the present help not only themselves but their entire community. When we share our knowledge, customs, and values with others, everyone benefits.

Reflect on ▶ Your Draft

Did you find it difficult to write your draft? If so, did you have trouble starting, deciding what to write, or putting your ideas into words? Learn from this experience. Think about what you might change next time.

✔ Revise Your Draft

Your first draft is done. Now, you need to polish it. Improve the development of ideas. Make something that was just OK into something much better.

❶ Revise for Development of Ideas

Good writing has **well-developed ideas** that flow clearly from one to the next. It doesn't just contain a list of ideas. A good writer **elaborates** on ideas by supporting them with specific details and connects the ideas and details with clear transitions.

In a position paper, a writer elaborates on his or her position by supporting it with reasons. The reasons are, in turn, supported by evidence.

Don't expect to fully develop all of your ideas in your first draft. As you read your draft, you may notice that some of your reasons need more support.

TRY IT ▶ With a partner, decide which reason in the draft below needs more evidence to support it. Discuss what kind of evidence the writer could add.

Student Draft

> First, your country of origin is part of your identity, it's part of what makes you unique. If this part of your identity is suppressed, your full potential won't be achieved. This is what happened to Jenny Lin, a Chinese American aspiring artist at Central high school. "I kept trying to paint in what I believed was a modern style," she says. "I tried to strip any Chinese influence out of my work, and I ended up with paintings that had no depth or soul." It wasn't until she let herself keep the Chinese influence that vivid, moving pieces of work were created.
>
> Culture and tradition help strengthen family relationships. Culture and tradition provide something that can be appreciated by different generations. Just think about how some teens can't seem to relate to their grandparents. A tradition would give them something in common.

Now use the rubric to evaluate the development of ideas in your own draft. What score do you give your draft and why?

Development of Ideas

	How thoughtful and interesting is the writing?	How well are the ideas or claims explained and supported?
4 Wow!	The writing engages the reader with meaningful ideas or claims and presents them in a way that is interesting and appropriate to the audience, purpose, and type of writing.	The ideas or claims are fully explained and supported. • The ideas or claims are well developed with important details, evidence, and/or description. • The writing feels complete, and the reader is satisfied.
3 Ahh.	<u>Most</u> of the writing engages the reader with meaningful ideas or claims and presents them in a way that is interesting and appropriate to the audience, purpose, and type of writing.	<u>Most</u> of the ideas or claims are explained and supported. • Most of the ideas or claims are developed with important details, evidence, and/or description. • The writing feels mostly complete, but the reader still has some questions.
2 Hmm.	<u>Some</u> of the writing engages the reader with meaningful ideas or claims and presents them in a way that is interesting and appropriate to the audience, purpose, and type of writing.	<u>Some</u> of the ideas or claims are explained and supported. • Only some of the ideas or claims are developed. Details, evidence, and/or description are limited or not relevant. • The writing leaves the reader with many questions.
1 Huh?	The writing does <u>not</u> engage the reader. It is not appropriate to the audience, purpose, and type of writing.	The ideas or claims are <u>not</u> explained or supported. The ideas or claims lack details, evidence, and/or description, and the writing leaves the reader unsatisfied.

myNGconnect.com

• Rubric: Development of Ideas
• Evaluate and practice scoring other student papers.

❷ Revise Your Draft

You've now evaluated the development of ideas in your own draft. If you scored 3 or lower, how can you improve your work? Use the checklist below to revise your draft.

Revision Checklist

Ask Yourself	Check It Out	How to Make It Better
Do I clearly state my position, as well as an opposing position, in the introduction?	If your score is 3 or lower, revise.	☐ If your paper does not have a controlling idea, add one. ☐ If you have not stated an opposing position, add it.
Do I develop at least two clear supporting reasons in my paper?	If your score is 3 or lower, revise.	☐ Add more reasons if you have just one.
Have I explained and supported my reasons well?	If your score is 3 or lower, revise.	☐ Add supporting evidence to develop each reason. ☐ If necessary, do some research to gather more supporting evidence.
Does my position paper have an introduction, a body, and a conclusion?	Draw a box around each part.	☐ Add any part that is missing.
Do I address both sides of the issue in the body?	Underline each side.	☐ Address the side of the issue that opposes your position.
Have I used a formal style and presented my claims objectively?	Look for informal language, including contractions.	☐ Replace informal language with more formal, less personal sounding language. Add academic terms. ☐ Spell out contractions.
Are my reasons strategically organized, with clear transitions between them?	Check to see that you listed your reasons in order of importance and used transitional words and phrases.	☐ Put your reasons in order from least to most important. ☐ Add transitional words and phrases, if necessary.
Is my conclusion memorable?	Ask a classmate to read your conclusion.	☐ Summarize your position. End your paper with a thought that will get your audience thinking.

📙 **Writing Handbook,** p. 832

❸ Conduct a Peer Conference

It helps to get a second opinion when you are revising your draft. Ask a partner to read your draft and look for the following:

- any part of the draft that is confusing
- any part where something seems to be missing or lacks support
- anything that the person doesn't understand

Then talk with your partner about the draft. Focus on the items in the Revision Checklist. Use your partner's comments to make your paper clearer, more complete, and easier to understand.

❹ Make Revisions

Look at the revisions below and the peer-reviewer conversation on the right. Notice how the peer reviewer commented and asked questions. Notice how the writer used the comments and questions to revise.

Revised for Development of Ideas

> Another benefit of   is that they
> ︿Culture and tradition︿help strengthen family relationships.
>
> Culture and tradition provide something that can be appreciated
>
> by different generations. ~~Just think about how some teens can't~~
>
> ~~seem to relate to their grandparents. A tradition would give them~~
>
> ~~something in common.~~ Robert Martinez, a senior at Central High,
>
> looks like a typical American teenager—baggy T-shirt, jeans, sneakers.
>
> However, in the evenings, he plays the vihuela, a five-string guitar, with
>
> his father and grandfather in a local mariachi band. "When I was
>
> younger, I couldn't relate to my grandfather at all," says Martinez.
>
> "When I learned how to play the guitar, we finally had something in
>
> common. He taught me mariachi style, and I hope to teach it to my kids
>
> one day."

Reflect on Your Revisions

▶ What did you learn from your peer conference? What parts of your paper did your partner suggest that you revise?

✔ Edit and Proofread Your Draft

You focus on ideas when you revise. Now is the time to find and fix mechanical mistakes, such as capital letters or punctuation.

❶ Capitalize the Names of Groups

Each main word in the name of a specific organization, business, or agency should begin with a capital letter.

Organization: Boy Scouts of America
Government Agency: Federal Bureau of Investigation (FBI)
Business: First Bank of Centreville

TRY IT ▶ Copy the sentences. Fix the capitalization errors. Use proofreader's marks.

> 1. This is what happened to Jenny Lin, a Chinese American aspiring artist at Central high school.
> 2. According to the national retail federation, Kwanzaa was celebrated by nearly 7 million Americans in 2006.

❷ Use Semicolons Correctly

Use a semicolon (;) to join two complete sentences that are closely related in theme or meaning. Using only a comma (without the conjunction *and*, *but*, or *or*) is incorrect and causes a run-on sentence. Also use a semicolon when you combine two sentences with the conjunctive adverb *however*.

Incorrect	Correct
I'm proud of my heritage, I love all the traditions.	I'm proud of my heritage; I love all the traditions.
I am American, however, I'm also Mexican.	I am American; **however,** I'm also Mexican.

TRY IT ▶ Copy the sentences. Add semicolons where needed.

> 1. Adapting to a new culture is important, however, retaining elements of the old one is just as important.
> 2. Your country of origin is part of your identity, it's part of what makes you unique.

Proofreading Tip

If you are unsure of whether to use a semicolon or a comma, look in a style manual for help.

❸ Use the Active Voice

Sentences can be written in two different ways: the active voice and the passive voice. In the active voice, the subject of the sentence performs the action; in the passive voice, the subject is acted upon.

Active	Ramón borrowed my Spanish guitar.
Passive	My Spanish guitar was borrowed by Ramón.

In general, it is better to write sentences in the active voice. Sentences in the passive voice are usually wordy and sound awkward. Too much use of the passive voice can make your paper sound dull and uninteresting.

TRY IT ▶ Copy the sentences. Rewrite them in the active voice.

> 1. If this part of your identity is suppressed, your full potential won't be achieved.
> 2. It wasn't until she let herself keep the Chinese influence that vivid, moving pieces of work were created.
> 3. The Pan-African festival of Kwanzaa was celebrated by nearly seven million Americans in 2006.

❹ Use Subject Pronouns Correctly

Subject pronouns can take the place of nouns in the subject of a sentence. They are *I, you, he, she, it, we,* and *they.* Using subject pronouns can help vary your writing, making it more interesting and less repetitive.

Repetitive	More Interesting
Nhia is from Laos. **Nhia** knows a lot about her Hmong heritage.	**Nhia** is from Laos. **She** knows a lot about her Hmong heritage.
The Hmong New Year is recognized with a big celebration. **The Hmong New Year** takes place in November or December.	**The Hmong New Year** is recognized with a big celebration. **It** takes place in November or December.

TRY IT ▶ Copy the sentences. Vary the writing by using pronouns.

> 1. When people from these cultures first arrived, the people worked hard to maintain the traditions of their homelands.
> 2. Culture and tradition help strengthen family relationships. Culture and tradition provide something that can be appreciated by different generations.

Reflect on Your Corrections

▶ Look back over your corrections. Do you see a pattern? Do you keep making the same kinds of errors? Make a note to watch for these errors in your writing.

Here's the student's draft, revised and edited. How did the writer improve it?

Keeping Traditions Alive

The United States is made up of many different cultures. When people from these cultures first arrived, they worked hard to maintain the traditions of their homelands. However, each following generation embraced fewer and fewer of these traditions. Today, many teanagers are more concerned with being American than keeping ties to their country of origin. Adapting to a new culture is important; however, retaining elements of the old one is equally important.

First, your country of origin is part of your identity; it is part of what makes you unique. If you try to suppress this part of your identity, you are not achieving your full potential. This is what happened to Jenny Lin, a Chinese American aspiring artist at Central High School. "I kept trying to paint in what I believed was a modern style," she says. "I tried so hard to strip any Chinese influence out of my work, and I ended up with paintings that had no depth or soul." It was not until she let herself keep the Chinese influence that she created vivid, moving pieces of work.

Another benefit of culture and tradition is that they help strengthen family relationships. They provide something that can be appreciated by different generations. Robert Martinez, a senior at Central High looks like a typical American teenager—baggy T-shirt, jeans, sneakers. However, in the evenings, he plays the vihuela, a five-string guitar, with his father and grandfather in a local mariachi band. "When I was younger, I couldn't relate to my grandfather at all," says Martinez. "When I learned how to play the guitar, we finally had something in common. He taught me mariachi style, and I hope to teach it to my kids one day."

Finally, preserving cultural traditions is important because they influence U.S. culture. Billboard has a Top 100 chart for Latin music, and many songs by Latin performers also appear on the general Top 100 chart. According to the National Retail Federation, nearly 7 million Americans celebrated the Pan-African festival of Kwanzaa in 2006. This shows that it is possible to preserve one's heritage and be a part of American culture at the same time. Celebrating traditions, in fact, is one of the most "American" things a person can do.

People who make the past a part of the present help not only themselves but their entire community. When we share our knowledge, customs, and values with others, everyone benefits.

The writer substituted a **subject pronoun** to make the writing less repetitive.

The writer rewrote the sentence in a less personal, more **formal style**.

The writer corrected the run-on sentence by using a **semicolon** instead of a comma. The writer also spelled out **contractions** and rewrote a sentence in the **active voice** to make it sound better.

The writer corrected the **capitalization error** and rewrote another sentence in the **active voice**.

The writer substituted a **subject pronoun** to make the writing less repetitive.

The writer corrected the **capitalization error** in the name of the organization and rewrote the sentence in the **active voice**.

✔ Publish and Present

You are now ready to publish and present your position paper. Print out your paper or write a clean copy by hand. You may also want to present your work in a different way.

Alternative Presentations

Send a Letter to the Editor Many newspapers and magazines publish letters from readers. Often, the body of such a letter is a position paper.

1 **Choose a Publication** Think about your topic and audience. What publication would be interested in your topic? What newspaper or magazine is your audience likely to read?

2 **Follow the Instructions** Send your paper electronically or by mail. Most publications provide instructions on how to submit editorials. Follow these directions.

3 **Ask for Feedback** If you send your position paper to an e-zine, ask your readers to e-mail you feedback. Use the feedback to improve your writing next time.

Make a Multimedia Presentation A multimedia presentation combines sights and sounds. Consider using a computer presentation program to add images and sound to your work.

1 **Select Types of Media** Decide what forms of media you will use. Will you read your paper aloud, record it, or display it in print?

2 **Collect Sights and Sounds** Search for media that will illustrate or add to your work. Find images, music, or sound effects. Be sure to give credit to the creator of any media you use in your presentation.

3 **Plan** Create a plan that shows what media is used and when. One way to write out your plan is to create a two-column chart. One column lists the images or sounds that will be used. The other column contains the script of what will be said.

4 **Practice** Try to put everything together before you give your presentation. Make sure, for example, that you know how to hook up the computer and projector. Ask a friend to operate the equipment as you present.

📖 **Language and Learning Handbook**, p. 750

Publishing Tip

As you collect sounds and images, save them in a file format that will take the least amount of space on your computer. MP3 is a good format for audio files, and JPEG or GIF is a good format for image files.

Reflect on Your Work

▶ Ask for and use feedback from your audience to evaluate your strengths as a writer.

- Did your audience clearly understand your position?
- Did your audience think you supported your position with strong reasons?
- What would you like to do better the next time you write? Set a goal for your next writing project.

 Save a copy of your work in your portfolio.

EQ ESSENTIAL QUESTION:

What Does It Really Mean to Communicate?

Words can be bullets or butterflies. The truth uplifts, while lies destroy.

—PIRI THOMAS

Only talk when it improves the silence.

—CHRIS MATTHEWS

Critical Viewing ▶
Three teens express their joy at the Holi Festival in Mathura, India. The ancient Hindu celebration corresponds with the arrival of spring, and people are encouraged to socialize and have fun. How might this celebration help people communicate?

EXPRESS
YOURSELF

EQ ESSENTIAL QUESTION:
What Does It Really Mean to Communicate?

Study the Cartoon

How do we communicate? What are possible barriers to communication? Study this cartoon:

Source: ©Kevin Fagan/United Features Syndicate, Inc.

Analyze and Debate

1. What is humorous about the communication in the cartoon? What does the cartoon imply about the family's ability to communicate?

2. The cartoon suggests that technology changes how we communicate. Do you think this is true? Is the change a positive or negative one?

Analyze and debate these questions with a partner. Explain your opinion and support your ideas with evidence and experience. Then listen carefully to your partner's opinion.

EQ ESSENTIAL QUESTION

In this unit, you will explore the **Essential Question** in class through reading, discussion, research, and writing. Keep thinking about the question outside of school, too.

① Plan a Project

Multimedia Presentation

In this unit, you'll be working with a group to create a multimedia presentation that addresses the Essential Question. Remember that *media* refers to any format of presenting information. To get started, look at various types of media. Think about

- which media you want to use in your presentation
- which media will best address the Essential Question
- how you want to combine the various media.

Study Skills Start planning your multimedia presentation. Use the forms on myNGconnect.com to plan your time and to prepare the content.

myNGconnect.com
- ▶ Planning forms
- ▶ Scheduler
- ▶ Rubric
- ▶ Examples of different media

② Choose More to Read

These readings provide different answers to the Essential Question. Choose a book and online selections to read during the unit.

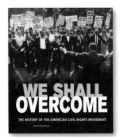

We Shall Overcome
by Reggie Finlayson

Until the 1960s, African Americans did not have equal rights in the United States. The civil rights movement changed that. People from all over the country united to voice their hatred of racism. Some even died for the cause. Would you speak out against injustice if it meant risking your life?

▶ NONFICTION

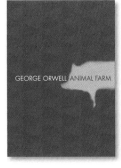

Animal Farm
by George Orwell

The animals of Manor Farm are overworked and underfed. So they decide to take over the farm. But when one of the pigs becomes the leader, the animals learn that equality is not what they expected. Soon the new society looks a lot like the one that they rebelled against.

▶ NOVEL

Code Talker
by Joseph Bruchac

Kii Yázhí's whole life changes when he is sent to school. Kii's name is changed to Ned and he is forbidden to speak the Navajo language. But years later, the Marines need help from Navajos. Can Ned forget the past and use his language to help win the war?

▶ NOVEL

myNGconnect.com
- ◉ See how people communicate through photo essays.
- ◉ Take a quiz to see how well you read body language.
- ◉ Learn useful phrases in a different language.

Writers of nonfiction texts organize information in certain ways. Different patterns of organization give you different understandings of the text.

DEMO TEXT #1

The human face conveys a variety of emotions through the movement of facial muscles. For example, a face communicates surprise when muscles lift the eyebrows and make the eyes wider than normal. Anger is communicated when muscles in the face pull the eyebrows together and tighten the skin around the eyes and eyelids. Happiness is communicated when muscles pull the lips upward and outward, creating a smile.

DEMO TEXT #2

I enjoy speaking in front of groups, but this hasn't always been the case. Like most people, the thought of public speaking made me nervous. Then, about two years ago, I joined a Toastmasters club in my town. We meet once a week to practice public speaking and to give one another suggestions and support. The result has been amazing. Because of Toastmasters, I am a confident and polished public speaker.

DEMO TEXT #3

It can be difficult to communicate in a language that you are still trying to learn. Often, you stumble over words, make mistakes, or hesitate to speak at all. But don't give up! If you can't think of the exact word for something, then use more familiar words to describe it (such as *small room with rain* for *shower*). Or, use pictures and gestures such as pointing.

■ Connect Reading to Your Life

Here are some possible titles for the Demo Texts you just read. With a partner, match each Demo Text with the best title.

Reading Strategies

- Plan and Monitor
- Determine Importance
- Make Inferences
▶ **Ask Questions**
- Make Connections
- Sythesize
- Visualize

> I think the title of #1 is "Muscles and Emotions."

> Yeah, me too. It tells what the text is about.

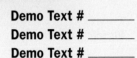

Demo Text # _____   How I Found My Voice
Demo Text # _____   Solutions for Language Learners
Demo Text # _____   Muscles and Emotions

Focus Strategy ▶ Ask Questions

To figure out which title went with which text, you probably asked yourself (and your partner) questions such as these: What is each text about? Which title sounds as if it goes with the text?

Experienced readers ask themselves all kinds of questions as they read. Some questions are about figuring out what is important. Other questions are to monitor, or check, comprehension. And still others are directed at the author.

Ask the Text	• Who...? • Where...? • Why...? • What...? • When...? • How...?
Ask Yourself	• What does this remind me of? • What do I already know about this? • What can I predict from what I've read so far? • Do I agree with this?
Ask the Author	• What are you saying or implying here? • What's your main point?

■ Your Job as a Reader

As you know, nonfiction texts describe, explain, and persuade. One of the best ways to read nonfiction—with all of its facts, details, and arguments—is to ask a lot of questions as you read. Your job as a reader is to question the text, question yourself, and question the author.

◼ Unpack the Thinking Process

Authors can organize their nonfiction texts in many ways. One of the secrets to reading nonfiction is to figure out how the authors put their ideas together. This will help you follow those ideas and evaluate whether they make sense.

Text Structures

A text structure is basically a pattern for ideas, and that pattern can be represented visually. An outline is a visual representation of ideas, for example. Here are some common text structures:

Text Structure	Purpose	Signal Words		Visual Representation
Cause and Effect	To show how something happened or came to be the way it is	as a result because since	if/then therefore consequently	Cause → Effect → Effect
Problem and Solution	To show how a problem or issue can be solved	if then or		**If** A **Then** B **or** C

Examples	To **illustrate** or describe examples of a particular main idea, or **thesis**	for example
		that is
		for instance
				I. Main Idea 1
				  a. Example 1
				  b. Example 2
				II. Main Idea 2
				  a. Example 1
				  b. Example 2

Chronological Order	To show the time order or **sequence** of events	afterward as soon as finally first, second, third following immediately initially later	meanwhile next, then not long after on (date) preceding until when	First Next Then Later

Academic Vocabulary

- **illustrate** *v.*, to explain;
  illustration *n.*, something that helps explain
- **thesis** *n.*, statement to be supported
- **sequence** *n.*, order or arrangement in which one thing follows another;
  sequential *adj.*, forming a sequence

■ Try an Experiment

With a group, decide which text structure is used in each demo text on page 358. Then, go on a scavenger hunt to find different examples of as many kinds of text structures as you can. Here's how:

1. Gather a variety of textbooks—science, social studies, math, and so on.

2. Skim the books to find an example of each kind of text structure.

Types of Text Structures	Book	Page
Cause and Effect		
Problem and Solution		
Examples		
Chronological Order		

3. Discuss why each text structure is suited to the **topic**.

4. Finally, share what you found with the rest of the class.

Monitor Comprehension

Text Structures
Describe four kinds of text structures.

EQ ## What Does It Really Mean to Communicate?
Discover the variety of ways people communicate.

Make a Connection

Anticipation Guide Think about the ways people communicate their ideas and feelings. Then tell whether you agree or disagree with these statements.

ANTICIPATION GUIDE	Agree or Disagree
1. Words are the best way to communicate.	_____
2. You cannot tell what someone is thinking by looking at him or her.	_____
3. *What* we communicate is not as important as *how* we communicate.	_____

Learn Key Vocabulary

Study the Words Pronounce each word and learn its meaning. You may also want to look up the definitions in the Glossary.

● Academic Vocabulary

Key Words	Examples
competent (**kom**-pu-tent) *adjective* ▶ pages 379, 380	**Competent** means capable and qualified. A **competent** worker has the necessary skills or knowledge to do a job well.
● **emphasis** (**em**-fu-sis) *noun* ▶ page 379	An **emphasis** is a type of special attention or importance. People sometimes use hand gestures to add **emphasis** to their words.
emulate (**em**-yū-lāt) *verb* ▶ page 380	To **emulate** is to do something or behave in the same way as someone else. *Synonyms:* imitate, copy; *Antonym:* differ
● **enhance** (in-**hants**) *verb* ▶ pages 366, 372, 380, 381	To **enhance** is to make better or improve. Good grades and extracurricular activities will **enhance** your chances of getting into college.
● **precision** (pri-**si**-zhun) *noun* ▶ page 366	**Precision** means exactness or accuracy. A good surgeon must operate with **precision** in order to fix tiny areas of the human body.
subtle (**su**-tul) *adjective* ▶ page 371	Something that is **subtle** is hard to notice. Painters can see **subtle** differences between similar colors.
● **vary** (**vair**-ē) *verb* ▶ pages 367, 383	To **vary** is to be different. Hairstyles **vary** among today's students. Some have very short hair; some have extremely long hair; and some even have no hair.
● **visualize** (**vi**-zhu-wu-līz) *verb* ▶ page 379	When you **visualize** something, you imagine what it looks like. I can **visualize** her face in my mind even though she's not here.

Practice the Words Work with a partner to write four sentences. Use at least two Key Vocabulary words in each sentence.

Example: We knew she was <u>competent</u> because of the <u>precision</u> she showed in her work.

Face Facts: The Science of Facial Expressions

magazine article by Mary Duenwald

Reading Strategies

· Plan and Monitor
· Determine Importance
· Make Inferences
▶ **Ask Questions**
· Make Connections
· Synthesize
· Visualize

Analyze Text Structure: Cause and Effect

Nonfiction texts often show cause-and-effect relationships between major events and ideas. A writer might discuss a **cause** and then examine its **effects**. Another writer might start with an effect and then explore what causes it. Words such as *because*, *since*, *as a result*, and *if/then* signal such relationships. One cause may have several effects, and an effect may become the cause of something else.

Look Into the Text

Signal words alert you to a cause-and-effect relationship.

Emotion usually leads to an expression, but studies have shown that the process can also work in reverse: **If** you force your face to look sad or angry, **then** the rest of your body will react as well, and you may involuntarily begin to feel those emotions. A look of anger will make your heart speed up and your blood vessels dilate until your skin turns red; a look of fear can make your hands cold and clammy and your hairs stand on end; a look of disgust can make you nauseated.

What effect happens due to the cause?

Focus Strategy ▶ Ask Questions

Good readers often stop while they are reading and ask themselves questions. Asking questions helps you think along with the author and check your understanding.

Focus Strategy

HOW TO SELF-QUESTION

1. Pause in your reading and ask yourself one of the "five *Ws* + *H*" questions (*who*? *what*? *when*? *where*? *why*? or *how*?) to check your understanding.

> My Question
> What happens when people force their facial expressions?

2. State each answer clearly in your own words.

> My Answer
> They begin to feel the same emotions throughout their body.

3. If you cannot answer your own question, go back and reread to find the answer.

Talking Without Words

What is communication? It's a letter, a phone call, shouting, waving, and nodding. Don't forget television, radio, books, and newspapers. The list is long—much longer than you might think.

People are not the only ones who communicate. Long before humans walked on Earth, animals had solved the problem of communication. They used sound, color, taste, smell, and movement to send messages to each other.

We may think of speech as our simplest communication skill, but the first humans could not talk. Instead they grunted and used gestures. Even when people learned to speak, they never lost these basic, "no-words" communications skills. The next time you have a face-to-face conversation, tune in to your animal side. You may express yourself better by punctuating your sentences with facial expressions and body language.

myNGconnect.com

⬤ **Learn more about how animals communicate.**
⬤ **Test your ability to read nonverbal communication.**

face facts

the science of facial expressions

BY MARY DUENWALD

 Comprehension Coach

Facial Expressions

Chances are, you're not very good at faking a smile. You can raise the corners of your lips into a neat grin—as one does for the camera—and you can probably tighten your eyelids a bit to **enhance** the effect. But unless you're amused, excited, grateful, relieved, or just plain happy, you probably can't pull your cheeks up and your eyebrows down to form a smile that looks **genuine**. No more than one in ten people can **voluntarily** control the outer orbicularis oculi, the muscles surrounding the eye sockets, with that much **precision**.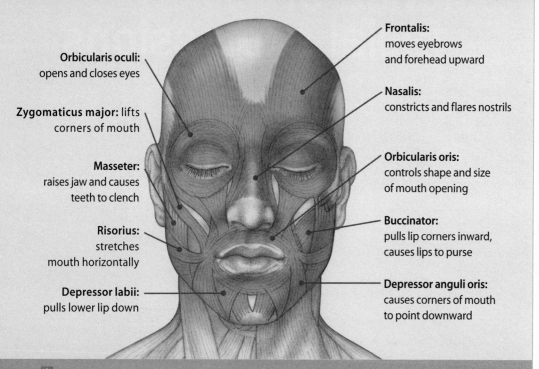

1 Ask Questions
Check your understanding by asking and answering a question about fake smiles.

Commonly Used Facial Muscles

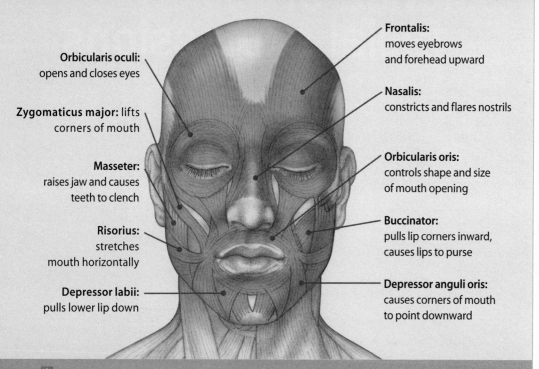

Orbicularis oculi: opens and closes eyes

Zygomaticus major: lifts corners of mouth

Masseter: raises jaw and causes teeth to clench

Risorius: stretches mouth horizontally

Depressor labii: pulls lower lip down

Frontalis: moves eyebrows and forehead upward

Nasalis: constricts and flares nostrils

Orbicularis oris: controls shape and size of mouth opening

Buccinator: pulls lip corners inward, causes lips to purse

Depressor anguli oris: causes corners of mouth to point downward

▲ Analyze the Diagram The diagram shows 10 of 43 facial muscles. Which muscles do you think you use when you smile? Which do you use when you frown?

Key Vocabulary
- **enhance** *v.*, to improve
- **precision** *n.*, accuracy

In Other Words
genuine real, sincere
voluntarily willingly

Paul Ekman has spent forty years watching thousands of people try. An **emeritus** professor of psychology at the University of California at San Francisco, Ekman is a world authority on facial expressions. He is also extraordinarily skilled at faking them. In the course of cataloging more than ten thousand human expressions, he has taught himself to flex each of his forty-three facial muscles individually. He can even wiggle his ears one at a time. "If only they had an Olympic event for facial athletes," he says. **2**

Ekman may never win a gold medal, but he has no shortage of admirers. In recent years, as the war on terrorism **has escalated**, he and his colleagues have taught hundreds of police officers, judges, airport security officers, and FBI and CIA agents **to size up** their suspects and to read clues in their facial expressions. He is now an adviser for the Department of Defense, which is developing computer technology that can scan and analyze facial movements on videotape. **3**

In Washington state, Yi Zhou and other researchers demonstrate facial scanning, a technology that can be used to check personal identity.

Global Expressions

Charles Darwin was convinced that facial expressions don't **vary** from culture to culture, but by the 1950s most social scientists had come to believe the opposite. To see who was right, Ekman traveled to the highlands of Papua New Guinea in 1967 and visited the Fore people, who had never been exposed to movies, television, magazines, or

2 Ask Questions
Check your understanding of Paul Ekman by asking and answering questions about him.

3 Ask Questions
What questions can you ask yourself about Ekman's accomplishments?

Key Vocabulary
● **vary** v., to differ

In Other Words
emeritus retired with distinction
has escalated has become more intense
to size up to evaluate

many outsiders. **4** When Ekman showed the Fore photographs of faces with various expressions, they interpreted them exactly as Westerners would. A sad face, for instance, made them wonder if the person's child had died.

Similar studies by other scientists have since shown that facial expressions across the globe fall roughly into seven categories: sadness, surprise, anger, **contempt**, disgust, fear, and happiness.

Whether faces can express any more than these seven emotions is a matter of some debate. There could be specific expressions for contentment, excitement, pride, relief, guilt, and shame, Ekman says, but they have yet **to be delineated**. Individual elements of each expression can occur in varying intensities or may be missing altogether. A look of mild surprise can be shown by the eyes alone, for instance, if the mouth doesn't move. Emotion usually leads to an expression, but studies have shown that the process can also work in reverse: If you force your face to look sad or angry, the rest of your body will react as well, and you may involuntarily begin to feel those emotions. A look of anger will make your heart speed up and your blood vessels dilate until your skin turns red; a look of fear can make your hands cold and clammy and your hairs stand on end; a look of disgust can make you **nauseated**.

These internal responses may last a full minute or more—far longer than the expressions themselves, which last no more than two or three seconds. When people try to hide their emotions, their expressions may flash for one-fifteenth to one-twentieth of a second—just long enough for others to see them. After that, people can wipe away their "microexpressions," as Ekman describes them. **5** What about a person's voice? It is much harder to remove all traces of feeling from the voice. That's why Ekman tells police to keep their suspects talking.

4 Cause and Effect
Why were the Fore a good subject for Ekman's study? What effect might their lack of exposure to modern media have had on the study?

5 Access Vocabulary
The prefix *micro-* means "very small." It comes from a Greek word meaning "small." Knowing this, how would you define the word *microexpressions*?

In Other Words
contempt disrespect
to be delineated to be identified
nauseated feel sick to your stomach

Science Background
Charles Darwin (1809–1882) was the English scientist who first described the theory of biological evolution. His ideas are often used to help understand which human traits are natural and which are caused by culture.

Categories of Facial Expressions

Expression		Description
Sadness		The eyelids **droop** as the inner corners of the brows rise and, in extreme sadness, draw together. The corners of the lips pull down, and the lower lip may push up in a pout.
Surprise		The upper eyelids and brows rise, and the jaw drops open.
Anger		The lower and upper eyelids tighten as the brows lower and draw together. Anger raises the upper eyelids. The jaw thrusts forward, the lips press together. The lower lip may push up.
Contempt		This is the only expression that appears on just one side of the face: One half of the upper lip tightens upward.
Disgust		The nose wrinkles and the upper lip rises while the lower lip **protrudes**.
Fear		The eyes widen and the upper lids rise, as in surprise, but the brows draw together.
Happiness		The corners of the mouth lift in a smile. As the eyelids tighten, the cheeks rise and the outside corners of the brows pull down. [6]

In Other Words
droop hang down
protrudes sticks out

[6] Ask Questions
Ask yourself questions that would improve your understanding of the categories of facial expressions.

Monitor Comprehension

Explain
Why is it important for police to keep their suspects talking? Explain your reasoning.

Expressional Analysis

Ekman's weeklong classes teach law enforcement officers not only to analyze expressions but also to interpret voices and gestures, ask questions, and **build a rapport** with suspects. He shows his students how to recognize the basic emotions and spot **asymmetries**—a crooked smile, for instance, or a half-closed eye—that are often a sign of conscious lying. The techniques work best when a suspect is telling a lie for the first time. "The more often you tell a lie, the more likely you will come to believe it is the truth," Ekman says. That's why it's important that police and security officers learn to spot a liar on first contact. "By the time something gets to court, the lie has been rehearsed." **7**

No matter how skilled a person becomes at reading the clues, it's always easier to recognize when someone is lying than when he is telling the truth. And some lies are easier to catch than others. A polite lie—when a person tells her host that dinner was delicious or remarks on how much he likes a friend's new suit—is harder to spot than one that is **laced with emotion**. When people lie about whether they believe in the death penalty, for instance, they are not so good at hiding their true feelings. **High-stakes lies**, including whether one is engaged in illegal activity, for instance, are likewise difficult **to cover up**.

7 Cause and Effect
What situation could result if a police officer doesn't notice that a suspect is lying?

The Science of Smiling

Which is real? Paul Ekman demonstrates a polite smile (left) and a true smile (right).

The computer system that Ekman is helping the Department of Defense develop will be able to read all ten thousand facial movements involved in emotion. The system is

In Other Words

build a rapport develop a good relationship
asymmetries things that do not appear equal or balanced
laced with emotion full of emotion
High-stakes lies Lies that have serious consequences
to cover up to hide

a few years from completion, but even if it's successful, Ekman would **put his money on** a human being if he had to choose between the two. "Human beings have a complex computer sitting up there in their brains," he says. "With enough training, humans can do very complex evaluations very quickly." They also don't have to wait for a suspect to be videotaped and thus get more time to practice lying.

When Ekman trains police and security officers, whether in person or with a version of his program on CD, it takes them only about an hour to learn to recognize microexpressions. But some are far more skilled than others. As a group, United States Secret Service agents tend to be better than average—a third of those Ekman tested could distinguish a lying face from a truthful one about 80 percent of the time. However, psychologists, police officers, CIA and FBI agents, lawyers, and students tend to do little better than **chance**.

Ekman's colleague Maureen O'Sullivan has found that a select few can become nearly 100 percent accurate at catching liars: Of the more than thirteen thousand people she has tested in the past ten years, thirty-one were "wizards," as she calls them. Wizards see the whole picture, not expression alone. "Some people, when they're lying, don't show anything on their faces," O'Sullivan explains. **8** Wizards tend to be unusually intelligent, but they also have plenty of practice and are eager to **hone their skill**. "You have to have the basic talent but also the motivation to work at the skill," she says. Although the majority of police officers are not that good at catching liars, her small group of wizards includes unusually **savvy** cops, as well as lawyers, dispute mediators, and therapists who have taken their natural people instincts far beyond the norm. **9**

Ekman's next challenge is to identify more specific expressions of anger. Are there **subtle** facial movements that separate, say, **aggression and petulance** or

8 Ask Questions
Ask yourself a question that would help build your understanding of this section.

9 Access Vocabulary
Some English words are actually shortened versions of longer words. What word do you think the term *norm* comes from? How does this help you figure out the meaning of the expression "beyond the norm"?

Key Vocabulary
  subtle *adj.*, hard to notice

In Other Words
  put his money on pick with absolute certainty
  chance random guessing
  hone their skill improve their ability
  savvy clever
  aggression and petulance angry and impatient behavior

rage and plain annoyance? Law enforcement agencies are eager for the answer—particularly if Ekman can identify any expressions or body language that signal a forthcoming attack. Even if they exist, Eckman probably won't publicize his findings—otherwise, criminals will just learn **to better mask their intentions**. "We will make this available for law enforcement and security agents alone," he says. **10** ❖

10 Cause and Effect
What might be the effect if Ekman publicizes all of his findings about facial expressions?

ANALYZE Face Facts: The Science of Facial Expressions

1. **Summarize** What factors influence a person's ability to tell if someone is lying?

2. **Vocabulary** How does understanding differences in facial expressions **enhance** people's ability to communicate? Give examples.

3. **Analyze Text Structure: Cause and Effect** How do you think Ekman's findings about facial expressions could affect our everyday lives? List three possible effects in a chart. Then discuss your effects with a partner. Explain your reasoning.

   | **Cause:** Understanding how to read facial expressions |
   | **Effect:** |

4. **Focus Strategy Ask Questions** Choose one passage in which you asked and answered a question. Explain to a partner how asking and answering the question helped you understand the text.

Return to the Text
Reread and Write How do you think Professor Ekman would answer the question "What does it really mean to communicate?" Reread the selection, noting specific ideas and information. Then write a paragraph that answers the question.

In Other Words
to better mask their intentions to become better at hiding what they plan to do

Face It

by Janet S. Wong

My nose belongs
to Guangdong, China—
short and round, a Jang
    family nose.

5 My eyes belong
to Alsace, France—
wide like Grandmother
    Hemmerling's.

But my mouth, my big-talking
10   mouth, belongs
to me, alone.

Maylene #2, 2004, Cristopher Nolasco. Mixed media on paper, collection of the artist.

▲ Critical Viewing: Character What does the expression on the young woman's face communicate?

About the Poet

Janet S. Wong wrote "Face It" about her son, whose face shows the influence of many different family members. She was a successful lawyer before deciding to dedicate herself to writing poetry.

BEFORE READING Silent Language

magazine article by Dr. Bruce Perry
and Charlotte Latvala

Reading Strategies

· Plan and Monitor
· Determine Importance
· Make Inferences
▶ **Ask Questions**
· Make Connections
· Synthesize
· Visualize

Analyze Text Structure: Problem and Solution

Nonfiction articles sometimes focus on a **problem** and a **solution**. This kind of structure is similar to a cause-and-effect structure. The writer describes a problem and then explores one or more possible solutions to it.

Look Into the Text

Avoiding Eye Contact

The authors call attention to a problem.

> **THE PROBLEM:** Refusing to meet someone's eyes says that you're unconfident, nervous, or, even worse—untrustworthy.

One solution is given.

> **HOW TO FIX IT:** Ease yourself in—practice maintaining eye contact for slightly longer periods of time. You might feel uncomfortable at first, notes communication specialist Debra Fine, author of *The Fine Art of Small Talk*. "One good trick is to look the person right between the eyes; somehow, this little shift will make you feel more comfortable and connected," she says.

What is a second possible solution?

Focus Strategy ▶ Ask Questions

As you read, you can ask yourself questions that deal with big topics. You can ask questions that lead to discussions about the answers. You can even ask questions that you cannot immediately answer.

HOW TO SELF-QUESTION

Focus Strategy

1. Read a passage, or even a single sentence.

> Refusing to meet someone's eyes says that you're unconfident, nervous, or, even worse—untrustworthy.

2. Ask yourself what bigger issues the sentence or passage raises.

> • Is this really true?
> • Do I agree with this?
> • Is this a reliable fact?
> • What does this say about communication?

3. Discuss your answers with classmates.

Connect Across Texts

"Face Facts" focuses on facial expressions. In *"Silent Language,"* discover what your body movements may communicate.

Silent Language

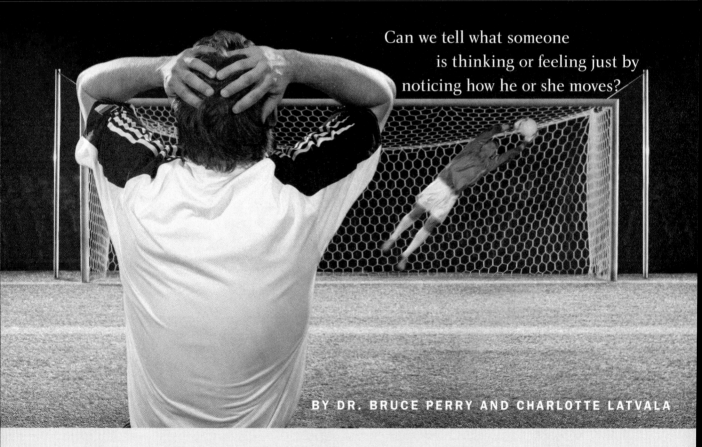

Can we tell what someone is thinking or feeling just by noticing how he or she moves?

BY DR. BRUCE PERRY AND CHARLOTTE LATVALA

Your posture, your gestures, and even where you direct your gaze reveal your level of interest and attention. What does the body language in this photo communicate?

READING THE SIGNS

We all read minds every day, and we read minds continuously. We're always trying to understand what our parents, teachers, friends, and classmates are thinking or feeling. So think for a moment and you'll realize you can often tell what's on—or in—the mind of someone else. You usually know when a person "likes" you or not; you know when a friend is **preoccupied**, sad, or angry. You can even tell if your parents are disappointed or proud.

We humans are specifically designed to read and respond to each other's **nonverbal cues**, with a special ability to judge safety-related signals: Is this a friend or **a foe**? Will this person hurt me or help me? **1**

1 Ask Questions
Ask a question to help you think about big issues regarding nonverbal cues.

In Other Words
preoccupied thinking about something else
nonverbal cues signals without words
a foe an enemy

Some people are better at "mind reading" than others. You can become better if you pay attention to body language, such as hand gestures and facial expressions. For example, when people are feeling uncomfortable, they may squirm, blush, bite their lip, pick at their fingernails, and have a hard time maintaining eye contact. When someone likes you, he or she may often look into your eyes, touch his or her hair, smile, or touch your arm when talking to you. You'll find the subtle cues a person gives off are somewhat unique—for one friend, you may find one nervous habit (fingernail biting) and with another friend a different cue (fidgety feet).

Try to pay attention to how you behave when you feel anxious, happy, interested, or bored. What signals do you give off? Watch, listen, and build up a catalog of experience and you'll become a better "mind reader." **2**

2 Problem
and Solution
If your problem
is that you're not
good at knowing
what someone
else is thinking,
what possible
solution do you
see in the text?

Is Your Body Language Holding You Back? **3**

You probably think a lot about what you say to others, but did you know that you also send some very strong messages without **uttering** a word? Your gestures and posture say more than you know. Indeed, body language is the single most important means of getting a point across, say experts. Below, you'll find help for some of the most common body language **goofs**.

3 Ask Questions
What is your
answer to this
question? Think
of a particular
experience where
body language
did not help you
communicate
something.

Avoiding Eye Contact

THE PROBLEM: Refusing to meet someone's eyes says that you're unconfident, nervous, or, even worse—untrustworthy.

HOW TO FIX IT: Ease yourself in—practice maintaining eye contact for slightly longer periods of time. You might feel uncomfortable at first, notes communication specialist Debra Fine, author of *The Fine Art of Small Talk*. "One good trick is to look the person right between the eyes; somehow, this little shift will make you feel more comfortable and connected," she says.

In Other Words
uttering saying
goofs mistakes

Crossing Your Arms and Legs

THE PROBLEM: This gesture says, "I'm closed to whatever you're saying," "I wish I weren't here," or "I'm protecting myself from something."

HOW TO FIX IT: Find something comfortable to do with your arms other than crossing them, says communication coach Carmine Gallo, author of *10 Simple Secrets of the World's Greatest Business Communicators*. Try putting one hand in your pocket to train your body to get used to a more open feeling. "Placing both hands in your pockets will make you look nervous or uninterested," Gallo says. "Plus, having the other hand free to gesture makes you seem more confident." **4** Holding something (a glass, a notebook) can also remind you not to cross your arms. And practice sitting with your arms relaxed, hands in lap, and legs side by side.

Looking Around the Room When You're in a Group of Three or More

THE PROBLEM: The conversation **steers away from** you and you think, This is a good time to check out what's happening around us. Well, guess what: "It comes across as **arrogant** or rude," says Fine. (Same goes for continually glancing at your cell phone.)

4 **Problem and Solution**
Experts are sometimes called in to solve problems. Do you think this expert's solution would work? Why or why not?

What do the eye contact and body language in these photos communicate to you?

In Other Words
steers away from is no longer about
arrogant self-important

How does the body language help you determine what's happening in this photo?

HOW TO FIX IT: Even if the subject matter drifts away from you, look interested—lean in or nod your head in agreement with the person speaking. Too bored to **even bother**? Excuse yourself politely and walk away. And if you're caught glancing around, you might simply say (with an apologetic smile), "Sorry, but I've got to keep my eye on the door; I'm waiting for a friend to arrive."

Slouching

THE PROBLEM: Poor posture almost shouts, "I'm not handling this well," "I don't feel **competent**," or "I'm depressed."

HOW TO FIX IT: Just force yourself to stand (and sit) up straight! "And while you do it, hold your head up and smile," says Fine. "**Visualize** how you look to others. It may seem stiff at first, but these behaviors will eventually become natural." Before social situations, she adds, remind yourself to sit tall and keep your chin up. Or, role-play the experience you're about to go through (job interview, teacher conference) with an **emphasis** on body language. **5** Regardless of which mental tricks you use, says Fine, once you improve your posture, "You'll feel more confident."

5 Problem and Solution
How many solutions does the article provide for the problem of slouching? What are they, and how do they differ?

Key Vocabulary
competent *adj.*, capable, qualified
• **visualize** *v.*, to imagine what something looks like
• **emphasis** *n.*, type of special attention

In Other Words
even bother do that

Twisting Your Jewelry, Playing with Your Hair

THE PROBLEM: You look nervous.

HOW TO FIX IT: Because these habits are **so ingrained**, we're often not aware of what we're doing. So, whenever you feel even a little nervous, **take a mental inventory of** what's going on with your body language. (Are your feet jiggling? Are you playing with your jewelry?) Every time you're tempted to start the **unflattering** habit, take a deep breath instead. Another trick, says Fine: "The next time you're in a group of people, focus on [those] who look self-confident and relaxed, and **emulate** their behavior. It'll make you aware of your nervous **mannerisms** and help you stop them." ❖

ANALYZE Silent Language

1. **Explain** How can body language communicate messages you do not mean to send? Give examples from the article.

2. **Vocabulary** According to the article, how can being **competent** in your knowledge of body language **enhance** your chances for success?

3. **Analyze Text Structure: Problem and Solution** With a partner or small group, think of one or two other types of body language that could communicate messages you do not mean to send. Think of solutions to correct the behavior and discuss why these solutions would work.

4. **Focus Strategy Ask Questions** Were you able to answer your questions after reading the selection? Discuss your questions about the bigger topics with a partner. Explain your answers or look for answers to your unanswered questions.

Return to the Text

Reread and Write Look back at the problems listed in the selection and choose one that you have experienced. Do you think the provided solution would help you communicate better? Write a short journal entry telling why or why not.

Key Vocabulary
emulate *v.*, to imitate

In Other Words
so ingrained so much a part of our daily lives
take a mental inventory of pay attention to
unflattering unattractive
mannerisms behaviors, habits

EQ What Does It Really Mean to Communicate?

Critical Thinking

1. **Analyze** Return to the **Anticipation Guide** you completed on page 362. Have any of your responses changed based on what you've read? Explain why or why not.

EQ 2. **Interpret** How does careful observation **enhance** communication? Use evidence from both texts to support your response.

3. **Compare** What do facial expressions and body language tell you about how people really communicate? How are they similar? How are they different? Use examples from the texts.

4. **Speculate** How could you benefit from what you learned in these texts about reading facial expressions and body language? Describe a real-life situation where this knowledge could be useful to you.

EQ 5. **Evaluate** Which idea about communication in these selections is most meaningful or useful to you? Explain.

Write About Literature

Evaluate Text Structure As you know, writers of nonfiction texts organize information in certain ways. The writers of "Face Facts" and "Silent Language" each used a different text structure to present information. Review the two selections. Choose the one that you think was better organized. Then write a paragraph identifying the text structure and describing why that structure was effective for the writer's topic.

Key Vocabulary Review

Oral Review Work with a partner. Use these words to complete the paragraph.

competent	enhance	vary
emphasis	precision	visualize
emulate	subtle	

Most people are __(1)__ at interpreting basic nonverbal signals. However, other signals are not obvious, so it takes work to __(2)__ this skill and to develop greater __(3)__ , or accuracy, in understanding what others are truly telling us. Some signals are very __(4)__ , or difficult to notice, and may __(5)__ from person to person. It can be difficult to know whether to place __(6)__ on a person's facial expressions or body language. To better control your own nonverbal communication, you can __(7)__ in your mind how you would like to appear to others. Also, you can study someone you like and __(8)__ their actions.

Writing Application Describe a situation when you might have to communicate without speaking or writing. Use at least four Key Vocabulary words.

Read with Ease: Intonation

Assess your reading fluency with the passage in the Reading Handbook, p. 808. Then complete the self-check below.

1. My intonation did/did not sound natural.

2. My words correct per minute: _____ .

Show Possession

Use **possessive words** to show who owns something.

	Possessive Nouns	Possessive Adjectives	Possessive Pronouns
One Owner	Paul's Debra's liar's country's	my your his, her, its	mine yours his, hers
More Than One Owner	liars' countries'	our your their	ours yours theirs

Study these examples.

Here is **Paul's** report on facial expressions. The research is **his**.

Look at the **boy's** face. **His** eyes are wide.

Liars' eyes may shift. **Their** eyes may look down.

These pictures show **your** expressions. That smile is certainly **yours**!

Oral Practice (1–5) With a partner, say each sentence with the correct possessive word.

1. We smile for the camera. Do (our/their) smiles look fake?
2. A man smiles. (His/Their) smile looks real.
3. I use the muscles in (my/mine) face to smile.
4. Some people hide (their/theirs) true feelings.
5. I am looking for your photo. Which one is (yours/ours)?

Written Practice (6–10) Rewrite the paragraph. Choose the correct possessive word. Add three more sentences about facial expressions. Use possessives correctly.

Paul Ekman trains police officers. (Its/His) program helps officers determine micro-expressions. Few people are 100 percent accurate at identifying liars. (Your/Their) success depends on practice.

Literary Paradox

An idea or statement that seems impossible but has an element of truth is called a **paradox**. The concept of speaking without making a sound, as presented in "Silent Language," is one example of a paradox:

> You probably think a lot about what you say to others, but did you know that you also send some very strong messages without uttering a word?

In this instance, the idea of speaking, which we associate with a person's voice, seems to contradict the idea of being silent. However, it is true that we can "speak" through facial expressions and body language.

Read each quotation below. Discuss with a partner how it is an example of a paradox. Remember, a paradox must seem logically impossible and must have an element of truth.

Quotations:

"Well, less is more, Lucrezia. . . ."
—Robert Browning, *The Faultless Painter*

"Cowards may die many times before their deaths."
—William Shakespeare, *Julius Caesar*

"It was the best of times, it was the worst of times."
—Charles Dickens, *A Tale of Two Cities*

Define and Explain

Pair Talk Find a science word in the selections. Tell what it means and explain more about it.

Vocabulary Study

Multiple-Meaning Words

Many multiple-meaning words have specialized meanings in different subject areas as the chart shows. Copy the chart. For each word below, look in a dictionary to find specialized definitions in two or more subject areas. Add them to your chart.

1. vary 2. charge 3. capacity 4. element

WORD	SOCIAL STUDIES	SCIENCE	MATH
ruler	a person who rules or governs	the primary planet of a zodiac sign	a strip of wood or other material marked off in units and used for measuring

Media Study

Analyze Nonverbal Communication

Media Interpretation Watch a television news program that contains interview segments. Take notes on the body language and facial expressions of both the interviewer and the interviewee.

Based on your reading, draw conclusions about:

- the attitude of the interviewee and the interviewer
- their rapport, or relationship
- the sincerity, or truthfulness, of the interviewee

Write a short paragraph in which you explain your overall interpretation of the interview.

◥ **Language and Learning Handbook**, p. 750

Writing on Demand

Write a Cause-and-Effect Essay

A test may ask you to write a cause and effect essay. A writing prompt may identify a cause and ask you to analyze its effects. Some prompts may identify effects and ask you to analyze their causes.

❶ **Unpack the Prompt** Read the prompt and underline the key words.

> **Writing Prompt**
>
> Your school changes to an earlier start time. Write an essay in which you identify and analyze the effects of this change. Think about the positive and negative effects on students, teachers, and parents.

❷ **Plan Your Response** Brainstorm possible effects:

Cause	Effects
earlier start time	

❸ **Draft** Organize your essay like this:

Essay Organizer

Recently, [state the event that is the cause]. This will affect people in many different ways.

[The cause] will affect students because [name the effect]. This is a [positive/negative] effect because [explain].

[The cause] will affect teachers because [effect]. This is a [positive/negative] effect because [explain].

[The cause] will affect parents because [effect]. This is a [positive/negative] effect because [explain].

In summary, [the cause] will affect people because [briefly restate the effects].

❹ **Check Your Work** Reread your essay. Ask:

- Does my essay address the prompt?
- Are all the effects described clearly?
- Do I form possessive nouns, pronouns, and adjectives correctly?

◥ **Writing Handbook**, p. 832

1

2

3

Inside a Police Department

People who work in law enforcement are responsible for protecting lives and property in their communities. A police department in a large city is often divided into areas called precincts.

Jobs in Law Enforcement

People who wish to work in law enforcement have a wide variety of career choices. Many opportunities exist for promotion and advancement.

Job	Responsibilities	Education/Training Required
Police Dispatcher 1	• Answers emergency calls and communicates requests for help • Sends officers where they are needed	• High school diploma • On-the-job training
Police Officer 2	• Enforces laws • Patrols a specific area and responds to calls for assistance • Maintains reports and records	• High school diploma • Pass physical exam and written test • Training period in police academy
Forensic Science Technician 3	• Collects and analyzes evidence from crime scenes • Performs tests on weapons and other evidence to determine what happened • Prepares reports about their findings	• Associate's degree in science technology or • College degree in chemistry, biology, or forensic science

Research a Career

There are many federal police agencies in charge of enforcing particular areas of law. Research one of these agencies to see what it would be like to work for them.

1. Visit the home page of one of these federal agencies: Environmental Protection Agency, Drug Enforcement Administration, Federal Bureau of Investigation.

2. Read what the agency does and what kind of laws they work to enforce. Visit their "Careers" link to find out what kind of jobs the agency offers. Choose one to read about.

3. Write a brief summary about the agency and the job you researched. Exchange your summary with a partner and discuss what it would be like to work for that agency. Save the information in a professional career portfolio.

myNGconnect.com

🔍 Learn more about law enforcement jobs.

🔍 Download a form to evaluate whether you would like to work in this field.

Access Words During Reading

When you read, you may not understand some parts of the text. Use this set of strategies to help you access the meaning.

Use Strategies During Reading

1. What unfamiliar word should I figure out in order to understand the selection?

2. Have I seen this word before? What do I know about it already?

Now do I understand the word well enough to continue?

3. Does this part of the selection help me understand the word? Do other parts of the selection help me understand the word?

Now do I understand the word well enough to continue?

4. Do any parts of the word help me understand it?

Now do I understand the word well enough to continue?

5. Who or what can help me understand the word right away?

If I still don't understand the word, I'll mark it and come back to it later.

Put the Strategy to Work

TRY IT ▶ Read the passage below and apply the five strategies above. Then answer this question: When we view a film, why don't we view each image separately?

▶ Films are made of single images played together so quickly that we can't see the spaces between each image. Our eyes retain the vision of each image long enough to make the transition to the next image seem smooth. We don't see the gap between the images because of persistence of vision, a fortuitous feature of human sight.

EQ ## What Does It Really Mean to Communicate?
Explore everyday challenges to communication.

Make a Connection

Quickwrite When is it hard for you to express yourself as you would like? Maybe you have trouble speaking before a large group of people or calling someone on the telephone for the first time. Write a paragraph about a time when it was hard for you to speak to a person or a group of people.

Learn Key Vocabulary

Study the Words Pronounce each word and learn its meaning. You may also want to look up the definitions in the Glossary.

• Academic Vocabulary

Key Words	Examples
abbreviated (u-**brē**-vē-ā-ted) *adjective* ▶ page 396	When something is **abbreviated**, it is made shorter. The governor had to give an **abbreviated** version of her speech in order to fit it into the evening newscast. *Synonym:* shortened; *Antonym:* lengthened
ambience (**am**-bē-ents) *noun* ▶ pages 403, 405	**Ambience** is the feeling or mood associated with a place or thing. The café owners played soft music and put fresh flowers on the tables to create a pleasant **ambience**.
articulate (ar-**ti**-kyü-let) *adjective* ▶ pages 396, 399	**Articulate** people express their ideas clearly and effectively when they speak. *Synonym:* well-spoken; *Antonym:* stammering
humiliation (hyū-mi-lē-**ā**-shun) *noun* ▶ page 403	**Humiliation** is a feeling of shame and embarrassment. Losing to the worst team in the conference was a great **humiliation** for us.
intimidating (in-**ti**-mu-dā-ting) *adjective* ▶ page 396	**Intimidating** situations make people feel nervous. She found it very **intimidating** to dance in front of a large audience. *Synonym:* frightening; *Antonym:* comforting
obligation (ah-blu-**gā**-shun) *noun* ▶ pages 402, 407	An **obligation** is a duty you have because your conscience, family, or society demands it. Everyone has an **obligation** to obey the law. *Synonym:* responsibility; *Antonym:* choice
stimulating (**stim**-yū-lā-ting) *adjective* ▶ page 394	If something is **stimulating**, it is interesting, exciting, or full of new ideas. *Synonym:* thought-provoking; *Antonym:* boring
surpass (sur-**pas**) *verb* ▶ page 399	To **surpass** someone or something is to become better or greater than it. Earth's population will **surpass** 9 billion by 2050.

Practice the Words With a partner, make an **Expanded Meaning Map** for each Key Vocabulary word.

Expanded Meaning Map

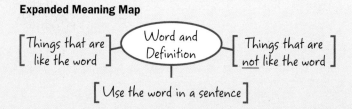

Before Reading They Speak for Success

news feature by Tom Seligson

Reading Strategies

· Plan and Monitor
· Determine Importance
· Make Inferences
▶ **Ask Questions**
· Make Connections
· Synthesize
· Visualize

Analyze Text Structure: Main Idea and Details

Nonfiction writers use various kinds of details to support, or to explain and clarify, main ideas. Often, those details take the form of **examples**. Writers may use signal words such as *for example* or *including* to introduce example details. Examples also may appear after a colon (:) or a dash (—), in a numbered or bulleted list, or in a text box.

Look Into the Text

The title helps you understand the topic.

What Is Forensics?

Today forensics is offered as a class or extracurricular activity at many high schools and colleges. Many students who participate enjoy the theatrical aspect or want to improve their public speaking skills. Members of a forensics team compete against others in one or more of the following areas:

The colon signals that examples follow.

How do the example details help you understand what forensics is?

- debate
- dramatic interpretation
- expository (informational) speech
- extemporaneous talk

Focus Strategy ▶ Ask Questions

You should answer questions that you ask yourself as you read. Sometimes the answers are right there on the page. Other times the answers are not directly stated but are in your head.

How To FIND QUESTION-ANSWER RELATIONSHIPS

Focus Strategy

1. **"Writer and Me" Strategy** If an answer is not directly stated, think about what you already know and what the author tells you. Then decide how these two parts fit together. Use a chart like the one shown to organize your thoughts.

2. **"On My Own" Strategy** If an answer is not in the book, think about experiences you or others have had. Make a new chart to organize your thoughts.

My Question	What happens at a forensics tournament?
What I Already Know	At a tournament, people perform before judges, as in a singing or dancing contest.
What the Author Tells Me	Forensics speakers compete in four types of speaking.
My Answer: How It Fits Together	At a forensics tournament, individual speakers perform, and judges award prizes in four different categories.

Can Public Speaking Prepare You for Your Dream Job?

For most Americans, NFL stands for the National Football League. For many students NFL also stands for the National Forensic League, an organization that promotes public speaking and debate through a nationwide network of tournaments. Every year, thousands of students compete and display their speaking skills. They also prepare themselves for a wide variety of professions. Here's how some students say that the NFL has helped them:

"The NFL has helped me because I'm more confident in myself than I've ever been. I used to sit in the corner and not say anything. The NFL experience has given me the confidence and experience to become a lawyer."
— Jessica from Minnesota

"I want to be a stage actress, doing Shakespeare in the Globe Theatre. NFL has helped me to overcome my stage fright and do something live instead of recorded. . . ."
— Anna from Missouri

"My dream profession is to be a hotel and restaurant manager. NFL has helped me by teaching me how to speak well, to be more of a people person."
— Nathan from New Mexico

"I long to become a professional baseball announcer. My NFL experience will help me use low-quality puns on the spot."
— Michael from Nebraska

myNGconnect.com

🔗 Read about the National Forensic League.
🔗 Watch and listen to speeches that changed the world.

THEY SPEAK FOR SUCCESS

by Tom Seligson

At Logan High School in Union City, California, students like Clayton Rogers (left) and Essay Gebreyesus Tsegay have become skilled speakers, thanks to the commitment of teacher Tommie Lindsey.

Comprehension Coach

Talking in Class

With banners draped on the walls and more trophies than you can count, Tommie Lindsey's classroom resembles a winning high school athletic department. At the front of the room stands Nico Parrilla, a **lanky** 16-year-old who has just delivered a twelve-minute **monologue** from a Whoopi Goldberg one-woman show. His classmates applaud, but Lindsey is not satisfied: "You're still making mistakes, Nico. You need to practice more." **1**

Welcome to Forensics Class at Logan High in Union City, California, twenty miles south of San Francisco. Here "forensics" does not refer to

1 Main Idea and Details
A nonfiction writer often uses an example to introduce a main idea in an interesting way. What does this example tell you about the standards Lindsey sets for his students? What does it suggest about what the main idea of the news article will be?

"I stress vocabulary development in my classes," says Lindsey. "I believe learning words and their meanings allows students to grow far beyond their expectations."

In Other Words
lanky tall and thin
monologue speech given by one person

criminal science but to the word's original meaning: competitive public speaking that includes dramatic presentations, **impromptu speeches, original oratory**, and traditional debate. Lindsey's students are black, white, Hispanic, and Filipino; freshmen, sophomores, juniors, and seniors. Some are honors students. Some are poor or even homeless.

"They all help each other," says their teacher. "They find refuge here. I've tried to create an environment where it's safe for them to stand up and speak in public." He knows it can be scary. "Speaking in public is as frightening to many people as coming down with cancer," says Lindsey, 53. "But I believe that getting good at it can be the key to success." And his students prove him right. While only 40 percent of Logan graduates go on to four-year colleges, **virtually** all of Lindsey's students do—but not before they show off their talents at tournaments across the country. **2**

"Forensics is usually a white, upper-middle-class activity," Lindsey says. "Not many poor kids or kids of color get involved. But we've been able to make people respect us." With many state and national honors, Lindsey's students certainly command respect. But

> Speaking in public is … frightening to many people.

the real rewards, they say, are not the trophies. "This class teaches how to **compose yourself** and not get nervous when you speak," says Gabriella Sierra, 15. "It gives confidence in everything you do." **3**

More than the curriculum, it is Lindsey who has changed his students' lives. "He's one of the few teachers I know who cares this much," says Justin Hinojoza, 17. "He spends hours and hours, evenings and weekends, working with us." When Justin's family didn't have money to buy the suit required for tournaments, Lindsey bought one for him. "And I'm not alone," Justin says.

In Other Words

impromptu speeches, original oratory unprepared speeches, a speech on a subject of the speaker's own choosing
virtually almost
compose yourself stay calm and relaxed

2 Ask Questions
Why might the ability to speak well be a key to success? Think about what you already know and what the writer tells you; then create a chart.

3 Ask Questions
Do you think the ability to speak well builds confidence? Think about your own experiences and then explain your reasoning.

Monitor Comprehension

Summarize
What are two benefits of taking a forensics class?

"He's done this for lots of us." One of nine kids raised by a single mother, Lindsey fondly remembers the teacher who bought him new clothes after he came to school in a torn shirt and jeans. "That made me want to be a teacher," he says. "I wanted to care for other people the way she cared for me." **4**

As a ninth-grader, Lindsey became a public speaker himself. Though his English teacher doubted his ability, Lindsey prepared a speech that earned him a standing ovation. "She was expecting me to fail, and I **turned the tables on her**," he says. "And we do that with our forensics program. When we started, a lot of people didn't believe our kids could do the things they do."

Lindsey's students have gone on to become doctors, lawyers, and teachers. "I was going through a tough time," says Robert Hawkins, now 21. "Mr. Lindsey helped me out. I asked how I could pay him back and he said, 'Just help someone the way I helped you.'" Hawkins is studying to be a teacher. But whatever field his students choose, "I want them to go back and be a voice in their communities," Lindsey says. **5**

Though his program struggles against **budget constraints**, Lindsey's work has not gone unnoticed: In September 2004, he received a MacArthur Fellowship, or "genius award." Of the twenty-three recipients of this award, he was the only high school teacher. "This amazing opportunity is here for us students," says Michael Joshi, 17, "and it wouldn't be if Mr. Lindsey didn't create it."

I want them to ... **be a voice** in their communities.

4 Ask Questions
What do you think makes Lindsey want to help his students? Think about what the author tells you as well as what you know about people.

5 Main Idea and Details
What example is given to clarify the main idea of this paragraph?

In Other Words
turned the tables on her did the opposite of what she expected me to do
budget constraints limits on available money

Cultural Background
A **MacArthur Fellowship** is an award of $500,000 given to a person who has shown unusual dedication to original work that benefits society. The MacArthur Foundation gives the award to about 20 people each year.

What Is Forensics?

Forensics is the art and study of different forms of public speaking. It dates back to the time of Ancient Greece when communication skills were recognized as necessary to being a good citizen. Most Ancient Greeks used forensics to defend themselves in court or to persuade their fellow citizens to take action.

Today forensics is offered as a class or extracurricular activity at many high schools and colleges. Many students who participate enjoy the theatrical aspect or want to improve their public speaking skills. Members of a forensics team compete against others in one or more of the following areas:

- debate
- dramatic interpretation
- expository (informational) speech
- **extemporaneous talk**

Winston Kwong, a student in Lindsey's class, uses expression and body language to make a point during his presentation.

In Other Words

extemporaneous talk a speech given without preparation or practice

Monitor Comprehension

Paraphrase
What does Lindsey mean when he says he wants his students to be "a voice in their communities"?

Tips For Successful Public Speaking

Know the room.
Be familiar with the place in which you will speak. Arrive early, walk around the speaking area, and practice using the microphone and any visual aids.

Know the audience.
Greet some of the audience as they arrive. It's easier to speak to a group of friends than to a group of strangers.

Visualize yourself giving your speech.
Imagine yourself speaking, your voice loud, clear, and assured.

Know your material.
If you're not familiar with your material or are uncomfortable with it, your nervousness will increase. Practice your speech and revise it if necessary.

Realize that people want you to succeed.
Audiences want you to be interesting, **stimulating**, informative, and entertaining.

Concentrate on the message.
Focus your attention away from your own anxieties and outwardly toward your message and your audience. Your nervousness will decrease.

Source: Toastmasters International

Key Vocabulary
stimulating *adj.*, interesting, exciting

Finding a Voice

In the book It Doesn't Take a Genius, *Tommie Lindsey's students talk about the effect his forensics classes had on their lives. Here are some of their stories.* **6**

The Art of Everyday Speech

Jamie Walker   Mr. Lindsey always stood in front of his class. I can't remember him ever sitting. In his hand was always a note, a piece of paper listing our competition dates, a film manuscript, or a play.

"Stand up straight," he would say. "Emphasize certain words in your speech and use hand gestures wisely. Pause for effect if need be."

I always loved the pauses. Mr. Lindsey taught us natural pauses and to be **cognizant of shifts in tonal quality**. Indeed, we might as well have been taking music or voice lessons in his class, for every aspect of our instrument had to be **honed** and trained. Reading stacks of plays and piles of film manuscripts in his office, we learned the rhythms of everyday speech, as well as the rhythms of our characters. We learned how they walked, talked, laughed, loved, and cried. **7** Indeed, we might not have known it at the time, but we were actually learning the rhythm of a strong work ethic— one that could only **yield fruitful results** with discipline, time, focus, and constant practice. Our teacher figured that if athletes, musicians, and ballplayers all practiced to hone and perfect their craft, then why shouldn't actors, orators, or public speakers?

> **We were actually learning the rhythm of a strong work ethic.**

6 **Main Idea and Details**
What words signal that the writer has chosen examples to support the idea that forensics classes have affected students' lives?

7 **Language**
A **metaphor** is a figure of speech that compares two seemingly unlike things. How is the word *instrument* used as a metaphor in this paragraph?

Monitor Comprehension

Summarize
What did this student learn from Mr. Lindsey?

In Other Words
cognizant of shifts in tonal quality aware of changes in the tone of a person's voice
honed improved
yield fruitful results produce good results

Overcoming Shyness

Jennifer Chang Kuo Today, I feel like a confident, happy, and successful woman—and an **articulate** one. But I can't say the same of myself when I started high school. I was painfully shy—so shy, I even **abhorred** speaking to store clerks or waitresses. I didn't want to speak in public and definitely didn't like it. My only reason for joining the forensics team was because my brother had joined the year before, and I could see the benefits it would bring to me.

My very first speech for the forensics team was meant to be five minutes long—an impromptu, in front of a class of less than fifteen people. It doesn't sound **intimidating**. It shouldn't be frightening. But it was. I remember standing there for what seemed like an eternity, with a thousand **abbreviated** thoughts swirling through my mind, unable to form words. I knew my knees were shaking, and my voice **was quivering**—I was unable to make eye contact with anyone. My very first speech was **an unmitigated disaster**. 🔲8

I was never one of the best speakers on the team. But over time, after hours and hours of work, long weekends, and many sweaty palms, I achieved an award of Outstanding Distinction from the National Forensic League. I must admit it was more from sheer stubbornness, time, and hard work rather than from talent. I knew which members of the team had talent—they were amazing. But for me, it was enough to **get by**. Today, my knees will still shake and my heart will still pound when I speak in public, but I can now project an image of calm and confidence. I have even been complimented on my public speaking. 🔲9

My very **first speech** was an unmitigated disaster.

🔲8 **Ask Questions**
What questions can you ask and answer to understand this student's experience?

🔲9 **Main Idea and Details**
What idea does this student want her experiences to illustrate?

Key Vocabulary
articulate *adj.*, able to speak clearly, effectively
intimidating *adj.*, frightening
abbreviated *adj.*, shortened

In Other Words
abhorred really hated
was quivering was shaking
an unmitigated disaster a complete failure
get by do the basic minimum

One Very Important Ingredient

Steve Kuo Mr. Lindsey taught me one of life's most important lessons during my freshman year of high school. This was after I had lost the regional Lions Club competition—one of the most devastating losses of a very young speech career. It was especially tough after talking to Mr. Lindsey and finding out why I had lost. He told me that my preparation and content were superior to that of my competitors but I was missing one very important ingredient: **poise**. The seven minutes that I had spent in front of the judges while giving my speech were well received, but the twenty minutes before and after the speech were disastrous. My head was facing the floor the entire time; my legs would not stop shaking beneath the table. I looked like a nervous freshman unprepared for the event. Mr. Lindsey taught me that being a winner is not only about being ready for the moment but being poised and composed throughout the entire process. He told me, "You are judged from the moment you step into a room, and it is up to you to show poise and confidence without having to **utter** a single word." 🔟

> You are **judged** from the moment you step into a room.

10 Ask Questions
What questions can you ask and answer to check your understanding of this student's experience?

In Other Words
poise confident behavior
utter speak

Monitor Comprehension

Describe
What elements are involved in being poised?

The Need to Communicate

Sharahn LaRue McClung The state finals, my senior year, my last chance to make a mark as a competitor, and I **was on a mission**. Though I had made steady progress since my first speech tournament, I had not yet won first place. Coming out of the semifinal round, I was seized by a competitive spirit and told myself that I was ready for anything and that trophy was mine.

In the final round, I found myself soaring along through my selection. I felt that the audience was with me. Then, that "anything" happened. Through a window in the back of the room a chicken emerged. Yes, a chicken. As the chicken pecked its way through the audience, chuckles erupted into laughter, glances dispersed downward, and I was **mortified**. Suddenly, all I wanted in this moment was for everyone to keep listening to my words. Slowly, I regained the eye contact and the attention of my audience. **11**

Then two minutes and thirty-five seconds later, a pizza delivery man interrupted with an obligatory "Thirty minutes or your pizza's free!" Again, I thought, "Listen to my words," and again, I pulled the distracted audience's gaze back to me. (I also attracted the focus of the confused delivery guy, who spent the better part of the round standing in the doorway, steaming pizza in hand.) The round ended and all I could think was, "Kiss the championship good-bye, and at least no one will remember the chicken." **12**

> I ... told myself that **I was ready** for anything and that trophy was mine.

Hours later, I sat on the bus, stunned for two reasons. One, I had already broken the little wreath off the top of my first-place trophy. And two, none of

11 Main Idea and Details
What idea does this former student's anecdote illustrate?

12 Ask Questions
How do you think this student felt at the end of the final round? Think about your own feelings and what the writer tells you.

In Other Words
was on a mission had a clear goal
mortified extremely embarrassed

my ballots mentioned anything about the chicken or the pizza. One judge's critique only had "I felt like you were talking only to me" written on it.

In *Respect for Acting*, the late Uta Hagen wrote, "When all the work is done, every artist wants to communicate, no matter how much he may speak of 'art for art's sake,'" or, in my case, competition for the sake of a trophy. **13** I never considered the simplicity of that statement. One want—I want them to listen to my words. One result—they listened. My need to compete was **surpassed** by my need to communicate, and everything else fell into place. ❖

13 Main Idea and Details
What idea does the quotation illustrate?

ANALYZE They Speak for Success

1. **Explain** What obstacles did Sharahn LaRue McClung have to overcome to win the state finals, and how did she overcome them? Give examples from the selection to support your answer.

2. **Vocabulary** List three ways that a person can become more **articulate** when speaking to or communicating with others.

3. **Analyze Text Structure: Main Idea and Details** Find an example that illustrates each of the following statements from the article. Put the examples in a chart.

Statement	Supporting Example
"[Mr. Lindsey is] one of the few teachers I know who cares...."	
Lindsey's work has not gone unnoticed.	

4. **Focus Strategy Ask Questions** Ask a partner a question about "They Speak for Success" that is not directly answered in the text. Have your partner answer the question. Then switch roles and repeat the activity.

◗ Return to the Text
Reread and Write Write a memo to persuade students to take a new forensics class. Give two examples from the selection to illustrate how participating in forensics can help students overcome everyday challenges to communication.

Key Vocabulary
surpass *v.*, to become greater or better than something else

BEFORE READING **Breaking the Ice**

humor column by Dave Barry

Reading Strategies

- Plan and Monitor
- Determine Importance
- Make Inferences
▶ **Ask Questions**
- Make Connections
- Synthesize
- Visualize

Analyze Humor

Authors write **humor** to entertain readers and make them laugh. Almost anything can be a subject for humor, and good humorists structure their writing so that a variety of audiences respond. Here are some common ways to structure writing to achieve humor.

- everyday situations
- impossible events
- odd or absurd comparisons
- exaggeration
- informal language
- unexpected statements

Look Into the Text

The comparison between the writer and a mother fish is silly and absurd.

> As a mature adult, I feel an obligation to help the younger generation, just as the mother fish guards her unhatched eggs, keeping her lonely vigil day after day, never leaving her post, not even to go to the bathroom, until her tiny babies emerge and she is able, at last, to eat them. "She may be your mom, but she's still a fish" is a wisdom nugget that I would pass along to any fish eggs reading this column.

Adults helping youth is an everyday situation.

An **impossible event** grows out of the absurd comparison.

Focus Strategy ▶ Ask Questions

Sometimes the answers to questions are stated word-for-word in the text you are reading. At other times, you need to put together information from several places in the text to get the answer.

HOW TO FIND QUESTION-ANSWER RELATIONSHIPS

Focus Strategy

1. **"Right There" Strategy**
   - Ask the question.
   - See if the words that answer the question are directly stated in one of the sentences.

Question	To whom does the writer give a "wisdom nugget"?
Answer Stated in Text	He gives it to any fish eggs reading his column.

2. **"Think and Search" Strategy**
   - Ask the question.
   - Find the words that answer the question in different sentences or paragraphs.
   - Put the information you have found together.

Question	How is the writer like a mother fish?
Gathered Information	A mother fish guards her eggs to protect them.
Answer from Gathered Information	The writer wants to protect the younger generation in the same way that a mother fish protects her eggs.

Connect Across Texts

In "They Speak for Success," students overcome challenges to communication. In "Breaking the Ice," Dave Barry recalls his toughest communication challenge—how to ask a girl out on a date.

Breaking the Ice

BY DAVE BARRY

As a mature adult, I feel an **obligation** to help the younger generation, just as the mother fish guards her unhatched eggs, keeping her lonely **vigil** day after day, never leaving her post, not even to go to the bathroom, until her tiny babies emerge and she is able, at last, to eat them. "She may be your mom, but she's still a fish" is a wisdom nugget that I would pass along to any fish eggs reading this column.

But today I want to talk about dating. This subject was raised in a letter to me from a young person named Eric Knott, who writes:

> *I have got a big problem. There's this girl in my English class who is really good-looking. However, I don't think she knows I exist. I want to ask her out, but I'm afraid she will say no, and I will be the freak of the week. What should I do?*

Eric, you have sent your question to the right mature adult, because as a young person I spent a lot of time thinking about this very problem. Starting in about eighth grade, my time was divided as follows:

- Academic Pursuits: 2 percent
- Zits: 16 percent
- Trying to Figure Out How to Ask Girls Out: 82 percent

I don't think
she knows I exist.

▬▬ ▬ ▬ ▬

The most sensible way to ask a girl out is to walk directly up to her on foot and say, "So, you want to go out? Or what?" I never did this. I knew, as Eric Knott knows, that there was always the possibility that the girl would say no, thereby leaving me with **no viable option** but to leave Harold C. Crittenden Junior High School forever and go into the woods and become a bark-eating **hermit** whose only companions would be the gentle and understanding woodland creatures. **1**

"Hey, ZITFACE!" the woodland creatures would shriek in cute little

1 Ask Questions
Why didn't the writer directly ask girls out? Gather information from the text to find the answer.

Key Vocabulary
obligation *n.*, duty, responsibility

In Other Words
vigil period of watching
no viable option no other choice
hermit person who lives away from society

Chip 'n' Dale voices while raining acorns down upon my head. "You wanna DATE? HAHAHAHAHAHA."

So the first rule of dating is: Never risk direct contact with the girl in question. Your role model should be the nuclear submarine, gliding silently beneath the ocean surface, tracking an enemy target that does not even begin to suspect that the submarine would like to date it. **2** I spent the vast majority of 1960 **keeping a girl named Judy under surveillance**, maintaining a minimum distance of fifty lockers to avoid the danger that I might somehow get into a conversation with her, which could have led to disaster.

JUDY: Hi.

ME: Hi.

JUDY: Just in case you have ever thought about having a date with me, the answer is no.

WOODLAND CREATURES: HAHAHAHAHA.

The only problem with the nuclear-submarine technique is that it's difficult to get a date with a girl who has never, technically, been asked. This is why you need Phil Grant. Phil was a friend of mine who had the ability to talk to girls. It was a mysterious superhuman power he had, comparable to X-ray vision. So, after several thousand hours of intense discussion and planning with me, Phil approached a girl he knew named Nancy, who approached a girl named Sandy, who was a direct personal friend of Judy's and who passed the word back to Phil via Nancy that Judy would be willing to go on a date with me. This procedure protected me from direct **humiliation** ... **3**

Thus it was that, finally, Judy and I went on an actual date, to see a movie in White Plains, New York. If I were to sum up the romantic **ambience** of this date in four words, those words would be: "My mother was driving." This made for an extremely quiet drive, because my mother, realizing that her presence

2 Humor
What odd comparison helps the writer structure this paragraph?

3 Humor/Language
Exaggeration is a figure of speech that makes something seem much larger or better than it really is. Where does the writer use exaggeration in this paragraph?

Key Vocabulary
humiliation *n.*, shame, embarrassment
ambience *n.*, feeling or mood of a place or thing

In Other Words
keeping a girl named Judy under surveillance watching a girl named Judy closely

was hideously embarrassing, had to pretend she wasn't there. If it had been legal, I think she would have got out and sprinted alongside the car, steering through the window. Judy and I, sitting in the back seat about seventy-five feet apart, were also silent, unable to communicate without the assistance of Phil, Nancy, and Sandy.

After what seemed like several years, we got to the movie theater, where my mother went off to sit in the Parents and **Lepers** Section. The movie was called *North to Alaska*, but I can tell you nothing else about it because I spent the whole time wondering whether it would be necessary to **amputate** my right arm, which was not getting any blood flow as a result of being perched for two hours like a **petrified** snake on the back of Judy's seat exactly one molecule away from physical contact.

After what seemed like several years, we got to the movie theater.

So it was definitely a fun first date, featuring all the relaxed spontaneity of a real-estate closing, and in later years I did regain some feeling in my arm. My point, Eric Knott, is that the key to successful dating is *self-confidence*. I bet that good-looking girl in your English class would LOVE to go out with you. But YOU have to make the first move. So just do it! Pick up that phone! Call Phil Grant. 4 ❖

4 **Ask Questions**
What questions can you ask to help gather the information needed to understand the last three paragraphs of this selection?

In Other Words
Lepers people who are shunned, or avoided, by the rest of society
amputate cut off
petrified stone-like and still

ANALYZE Breaking the Ice

1. **Interpret** Do you think the writer is being serious when he says that "it was definitely a fun first date"? What evidence in the text supports your response?

2. **Vocabulary** How would you describe the **ambience** of the writer's first date?

3. **Analyze Humor** With the help of a partner, find an example of each of the following elements of humor:

Element of Humor	Example in "Breaking the Ice"
Everyday situation	
Impossible event	
Odd or absurd comparison	
Exaggeration	
Informal language	
Unexpected statement	

4. **Focus Strategy Ask Questions** Write three "Think and Search" questions that someone could answer by reading the selection. Then ask a classmate to answer the questions. Check his or her answers.

Return to the Text

Reread and Write Reread to find examples of the challenges to communication when first dating. Look beyond the writer's humor to understand his message. Write a list of the challenges he presents.

About the Writer

Dave Barry (1947–) was a humorist for *The Miami Herald*, but his column was reprinted in many newspapers across the United States. He was also a member of the literary rock band The Rock Bottom Remainders, along with fellow authors Amy Tan and Stephen King.

For Better or For Worse® by Lynn Johnston

About the Cartoonist

Lynn Johnston (1947–   ) "I always knew I would be a cartoonist.I never expected to make my living as one!" says Lynn Johnston. She worked in an animation studio and then as a medical illustrator before developing a comic strip based on her own family. First published in 1978, "For Better or For Worse" now appears in over two thousand newspapers in Canada, the United States, and twenty other countries.

EQ ## What Does It Really Mean to Communicate?

Critical Thinking

1. **Analyze** What do the two selections say about the relationship between self-confidence and successful communication?

2. **Compare** The students in "They Speak for Success" and the narrator in "Breaking the Ice" both sometimes find it hard to communicate. Compare the difficulties they have.

3. **Interpret** In "Breaking the Ice," the narrator says, "As a mature adult, I feel an **obligation** to help the younger generation." Does he mean that? Does Mr. Lindsey in "They Speak for Success" feel a genuine duty to help young people? Explain.

4. **Assess** Both selections are about communication. Which selection would you recommend that other students at your school read and why?

EQ 5. **Speculate** How do you think the students in "They Speak for Success" would answer the Essential Question? How do you think the narrator in "Breaking the Ice" would answer it?

Write About Literature

Opinion Statement Which is more challenging—speaking formally to a group or talking seriously to someone on a first date? Write your opinion and support it with examples from both texts.

Key Vocabulary Review

Oral Review Work with a partner. Use these words to complete the paragraph.

abbreviated	humiliation	stimulating
ambience	intimidating	surpass
articulate	obligation	

Before radio, TV, and movies came along to __(1)__ it, public speaking was a popular form of entertainment. Festivals were held in barns and tents, and well-spoken, or __(2)__, speakers drew huge audiences. The __(3)__ was exciting, like a county fair. Some speeches were quite __(4)__ and to the point, but the more long-winded speakers felt they had an __(5)__ to speak for several hours. Debates on __(6)__ topics were also popular, with __(7)__ speakers who inspired fear in their opponents and tried to bring them down to defeat and even __(8)__. The most famous speakers went on tours the way rock stars do today!

Writing Application Write a paragraph about an obligation or a responsibility that you found challenging. Use at least four Key Vocabulary words.

Read with Ease: Expression

Assess your reading fluency with the passage in the Reading Handbook, p. 809. Then complete the self-check below.

1. My expression did/did not sound natural.

2. My words correct per minute: _____.

INTEGRATE THE LANGUAGE ARTS

Use Pronouns in Prepositional Phrases

Prepositions show how words relate. Some common prepositions are **about, for, from, in, on, to,** and **with**.

A **prepositional phrase** is a group of words that begins with a preposition and ends with a noun or an object pronoun. **Object pronouns** are **me, you, him, her, it, us,** and **them**.

> The class was **for the students**.

> The class was **for** them .

When a prepositional phrase ends with both a noun and an **object pronoun** , put the object pronoun last.

> Audiences listen to my teammates and me .

> Audiences take notice of our teacher and us .

Oral Practice (1–5) With a partner, say each sentence. Then say it again, replacing the underlined word or words with an object pronoun.

1. Students deliver monologues to judges.
2. Mr. Lindsey helps students with a competition.
3. Forensics students learn from Mr. Lindsey.
4. Forensics is a good experience for Jennifer.
5. I would like a forensics club for my classmates and me.

Written Practice (6–10) Rewrite to edit the paragraph. Fix three problems with prepositional phrases. Add two more sentences. Use prepositional phrases.

> Forensics was a competitive activity for us and the other teams. Students were nervous about impromptu speeches, but Sharahn and I had practiced for they. The audience looked friendly to she and I.

Flashback

In "Breaking the Ice," Dave Barry interrupts his response to the letter from Eric Knott to talk about an experience that occurred when he was a teenager. This type of interruption is called a **flashback**.

When you notice a flashback in a piece of writing, ask yourself why the author is interrupting the flow of the text. Here are some common reasons for using flashbacks:

- to give more information about a person, place, or event
- to relate a memory or dream
- to emphasize the importance of a story element by extending its presence backward in time

Reread "Breaking the Ice" and pay attention to the flashback. Ask yourself:

1. Who is the focus of the flashback?
2. How much earlier did the flashback occur?
3. Why do you think Dave Barry uses a flashback in his column?
4. What does the flashback add to the selection?

Recognize and Respond to Humor

Group Talk Read aloud a funny passage from "Breaking the Ice." Tell why you think it is funny.

Jargon

Every job or activity has special words and phrases that describe its materials, actions, or tools. Sports and subject areas, such as science, have their own special language, too. For example, in football, a touchdown is the scoring play a team makes. This specialized vocabulary is called **jargon**.

Jargon for a new activity, such as forensics, may be unfamiliar. Copy the chart. With a small group, find and define a few of the terms related to public speaking in "They Speak for Success." Use a dictionary to verify the terms. You may need to look up words in a two-word phrase separately.

JARGON	DEFINITION
original oratory	a speech on a subject of the speaker's own choosing

Short Public Speech

Social Studies: Popular Sayings With a small group, take turns giving a short speech that illustrates a popular saying.

1 **Prepare and Present** Illustrate a saying, such as "People in glass houses shouldn't throw stones," by using it appropriately in a situation. Explain how the example illustrates the saying. Deliver your speech with enthusiasm.

2 **Evaluate** Use this list to evaluate each speech in your group:

- The speaker stated the main idea directly.
- The speaker gave enough supporting details.
- The speaker spoke clearly.
- The example was appropriate.

🖱 **Language and Learning Handbook**, p. 750

Writing an Evaluation of a Speech

Writing an evaluation of a speech involves listening, observing, describing, and judging. Good evaluations give the reader accurate information about what the speaker said and how he or she presented it.

Watch and listen to a speech on TV or on the Internet. Write down the main ideas, supporting details, and any observations of the speaker's style.

Speaker's name and title: Mayor John Moore
Date: June 12, noon
Place: Central Fountain, City Center
Topic: Water Quality in Our City
Main idea: Tests prove our water quality is excellent.
Supporting details: 1 —new city report is just out,
2 —scientists agree on low level of pollution,
3 —citizens agree city water tastes good, too
Atmosphere: positive, friendly, like a holiday crowd
Speaker's style: confident, direct, articulate
Audience response: respect, applause, congratulations

1 **Prewrite** Organize your notes in these categories:

- Facts—Who is the speaker? Where and when is the speech given?
- Content—What is the main idea?
- Overall Effect—Is the speaker effective? Why or why not?

2 **Draft** Write a draft of your evaluation. Be sure to include the important details from your notes.

3 **Revise** Reread your evaluation. Ask:

- Does my evaluation clearly state my opinion of the speech?
- Did I give examples to support my reasons?

4 **Edit and Proofread** Ask yourself:

- Do I use prepositions correctly?
- Do I use the correct pronouns in prepositional phrases?

5 **Publish** Share your evaluation with a classmate.

🖱 **Writing Handbook**, p. 832

Panel Discussion

We all have different ideas about "what it really means to communicate." One helpful way to share different ideas is to organize a panel discussion in which each speaker, or panelist, expresses a different view on a given subject. Afterward, a moderator opens up the discussion to the audience. Here is how you can plan and conduct a panel discussion.

1 Plan Your Panel Discussion

Discuss the question "What does it really mean to communicate?" with a group of four or five people. Then, do the following:

- Have each panelist plan to discuss a different response to the question. For example, discuss body, written, and verbal language, or art and music.
- Decide on a moderator, the person who introduces each speaker and leads the discussion with the audience afterward.
- Create notes about the main idea, details, and examples that support each response.

2 Practice Your Panel Discussion

Cooperate with each other so that the discussion is polished and informative.

- Speak in a logical order. Communicate each panelist's idea to the audience in a way that makes sense as a whole.
- Become familiar with your notes so that you only look at them occasionally.
- Listen to the panel and offer helpful suggestions for improving content and speaking techniques.
- Have the moderator practice introducing each panelist, and thanking or concluding after each speaker.
- Write questions the audience might ask, so the moderator can practice leading the discussion afterward.

3 Hold Your Panel Discussion

Have the panelists sit at a long table facing the audience, with the moderator in the center. All panelists remain seated during their presentations. Be sure to:

- Make eye contact with audience members.
- Speak clearly and loudly enough so that the audience can understand you.
- Refer to your notes if needed, but use them as little as possible.
- Listen attentively to the other panelists when they are speaking.

④ Discuss and Rate the Panel Discussion

Use the rubric to discuss and rate the panels, including your own.

Panel Discussion Rubric

Scale	Content of Panel Discussion	Students' Preparation	Students' Performance
3 Great	• Thoroughly covered the topic with many good examples • Taught me something and made me think	• Seemed to know a lot about the topic • Divided the topic in an interesting and logical way	• Moderator and group worked well together • Handled all the questions and comments very well
2 Good	• Gave pretty good coverage to the topic with some good examples • Had some effect on my opinions	• Seemed fairly well-informed about the topic • Divided up the topic in a way that mostly made sense	• Moderator and group worked fairly well together • Responded to most questions and comments fairly well
1 Needs Work	• Gave only a little coverage to the topic • Did not make me think	• Did not seem familiar with the topic • Did not divide the topic well— presenters repeated information	• Moderator and group were not well coordinated • Did not respond to questions and comments well

DO IT ▶ Now that you know how to do a panel discussion, hold one for your classmates and keep it lively!

🔖 Language and Learning Handbook, p. 750

How can you effectively divide the topic between panelists?

myNGconnect.com
🔗 Download the rubric.

EQ What Does It Really Mean to Communicate?
Observe how people learn new forms of communication.

Make a Connection

Brainstorming What do you think of when you hear the word *language*? Work in a small group to brainstorm a list of thoughts. Then in your group, discuss each thought and the connection it has to the word *language*. See if you can develop additional ideas based on your discussion.

Learn Key Vocabulary

Study the Words Pronounce each word and learn its meaning. You may also want to look up the definitions in the Glossary.

● Academic Vocabulary

Key Words	Examples
accentuate (ik-**sen**-shü-wāt) *verb* ▶ pages 421, 427	To **accentuate** something is to make it more noticeable. Red lipstick can **accentuate** a woman's smile.
banish (**ba**-nish) *verb* ▶ page 424	To **banish** someone is to not allow him or her to stay or come into a particular place. Our mother will **banish** us to our rooms if we argue at the dinner table.
countenance (**kown**-tun-ents) *noun* ▶ pages 417, 426	Your **countenance** is the look on your face or your expression. People can often guess your feelings by looking at your **countenance**.
discerning (di-**sur**-ning) *adjective* ▶ page 417	Someone who is **discerning** can make good judgments about someone or something. Her **discerning** eye can easily spot imitation works of art.
disrespectful (dis-ri-**spekt**-ful) *adjective* ▶ page 418	To be **disrespectful** is to treat someone in an insulting way or without respect. You will receive a detention if you are **disrespectful** to your teacher.
enlist (in-**list**) *verb* ▶ pages 418, 422, 427	When you **enlist** someone, you persuade him or her to help and support you. Would you please **enlist** a friend to put up fliers about the meeting?
enumerate (i-**nü**-mu-rāt) *verb* ▶ pages 419, 422	To **enumerate** means to name or list things one by one. Can you **enumerate** all your favorite singers?
interminably (in-**tur**-mi-nu-blē) *adverb* ▶ page 421	**Interminably** means without ending. The road before us stretched on **interminably**.

Practice the Words Fill in a **Word Square** for each Key Vocabulary word.

Word Square

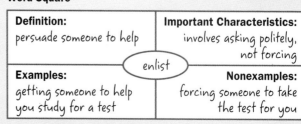

Definition: persuade someone to help	Important Characteristics: involves asking politely, not forcing
	enlist
Examples: getting someone to help you study for a test	Nonexamples: forcing someone to take the test for you

BEFORE READING My English

narrative nonfiction by Julia Alvarez

Reading Strategies

- Plan and Monitor
- Determine Importance
- Make Inferences
▶ Ask Questions
- Make Connections
- Synthesize
- Visualize

Analyze Text Structure: Chronological Order

Nonfiction writers make choices about how to organize and present information. In a nonfiction narrative, just as in a fiction narrative, the writer presents a series of events. **Chronological order**, or time order, is the sequence in which events take place. Words such as *before*, *during*, *after*, *first*, *last*, *next*, *then*, and *when* signal when a writer is using this text structure.

Look Into the Text

Signal words help show the order of events.

> When we arrived in New York, I was shocked. A country where everyone spoke English! ... It took some time before I understood that Americans were not necessarily a smarter, superior race.... Soon it wasn't so strange that everyone was speaking in English instead of Spanish.

Here the writer uses signal words to indicate a passing of time between events.

Focus Strategy ▶ Ask Questions

As you read, you can ask questions about the choices the author made to organize and present information. Asking these questions can help you better understand what you are reading. Questions can also help you evaluate how successful the author was in communicating his or her message.

HOW TO QUESTION THE AUTHOR

Focus Strategy

1. **Pause** in your reading and ask these questions:

   Questions
   - What is the author trying to say?
   - Why is the author telling me this?
   - How could the author have said it better?
   - Why does the author use this text structure?

2. **State** each answer clearly in your own words.

   Question
   - Why is the author telling me this?

   Answer
   - The author must be telling me this because it was a very emotional time for her.

3. If you cannot answer your own questions, reread the text and think about the reasons for the author's decisions.

Julia Alvarez
(1950–)

Learning English helped Alvarez develop as a writer.

During a life filled with many twists and turns, **Julia Alvarez** has had one constant—stories. "As a kid, I loved stories, hearing them, telling them," she recalls about the years she lived in the Dominican Republic. "Ours was an oral culture."

It wasn't until her family moved to New York City, when she was 10 years old, that she began to associate storytelling with writing. As Alvarez explains in "My English," learning a new language was one of the challenges of adapting to a new home, but one that brought great benefits, too.

"Having to learn a language, of course, really makes you pay attention to why people are saying things one way as opposed to another," she explains. "And that's what we do when we're writers."

Alvarez's approach to language has served her well. She has written seventeen books, including fiction, poetry, and essays. However, no matter how much Alvarez writes, her experience as an English language learner is one that she returns to again and again. To Alvarez, "[Writing is] a craft where you always have to keep a beginner's mind."

myNGconnect.com
- Visit the author's Web site.
- Watch a television interview with the author.

from

MY ENGLISH

by Julia Alvarez

With humor and insight, Julia Alvarez recalls how she left the Dominican Republic as a young person and "landed, not in the United States, but in the English language."

Comprehension Coach

Preview

Look at the first sentence of the selection and the photo. What is the setting of the narrative?

I began to learn more English at the Carol Morgan School in Santo Domingo. That is, when I had stopped **gawking**. The teacher and some of the American children had the strangest coloration: light hair, light eyes, light skin, as if Ursulina had soaked them in bleach too long, **to' deteñío**. I did have some blond cousins, but they had deeply tanned skin, and as they grew older, their hair darkened, so their earlier paleness seemed a phase of their acquiring normal color. Just as strange was the little girl in my reader who had a *cat* and a *dog*, that looked just like **un gatito y un perrito**. Her mami was *Mother* and her papi *Father*. **1** Why have a whole new language for school and for books with a teacher who could speak it teaching you double the amount of words you really needed?

Butter, butter, butter, butter. All day, one English word that had particularly struck me would go round and round in my mouth and weave through all the Spanish in my head until by the end of the day, the word did sound like just another Spanish word. And so I would say, "Mami, please pass **la mantequilla**." She would scowl and say in English, "I'm sorry, I don't understand. But would you be needing some butter on your bread?"

WHY MY PARENTS didn't first educate us in our native language by enrolling us in a Dominican school, I don't know. Part of it was that Mami's family had a tradition of sending the boys to the States to boarding school and college, and she had been one of the first girls to be allowed to join her brothers. At Abbot Academy, whose school song was our lullaby as babies ("Although Columbus and Cabot never heard of Abbot, it's quite the place for you and me"), she had become quite Americanized. **2** It was very important, she kept saying, that we learn our English. She always used the possessive pronoun: *your* English, an inheritance we had come

1 Ask Questions
What is the author trying to tell readers by putting some of the English words—but none of the Spanish words—in italics?

2 Chronological Order
How does the author interrupt the chronological order at this point in the narrative?

In Other Words
gawking staring
to' deteñío too long (in Dominican Spanish)
un gatito y un perrito a kitten and a puppy (in Spanish)
la mantequilla butter (in Spanish)

into and must wisely use. Unfortunately, my English became all mixed up with our Spanish.

Mix-up, or what's now called Spanglish, was the language we spoke for several years. There wasn't a sentence that wasn't **colonized by** an English word. At school, a Spanish word would suddenly slide into my English like someone butting into line. Teacher, whose face I was learning to read as **minutely** as my mother's, would scowl but no smile played on her lips. Her pale skin made her strange **countenance** hard to read, so that I often misjudged how much I could get away with. Whenever I made a mistake, Teacher would shake her head slowly, "In English, YU-LEE-AH, there's no such word as *columpio*. Do you mean a *swing*?"

I would bow my head, humiliated by the smiles and snickers of the American children around me. I grew insecure about Spanish. My native tongue was not quite as good as English, as if words like *columpio* were illegal immigrants trying to cross a border into another language. But Teacher's **discerning** grammar-and-vocabulary-patrol ears could tell and send them back. **3**

3 Language
A **simile** is a comparison of two unlike things that often uses the word *like* or *as*. What simile does the author use here and why?

The author grew up in Santo Domingo, the capital and largest city of the Dominican Republic.

Monitor Comprehension

Summarize
Summarize what happens to the writer as she learns more and more English.

Key Vocabulary
countenance *n.*, facial expression
discerning *adj.*, good at making judgments

In Other Words
colonized by mixed with
minutely closely, carefully
columpio swing (in Spanish)

SOON, I WAS **talking up an English storm**. "Did you eat English parrot?" my grandfather asked one Sunday. I had just **enlisted** yet one more patient servant to listen to my **rendition** of "Peter Piper picked a peck of pickled peppers" at breakneck pace. "Huh?" I asked impolitely in English, putting him in his place. *Cat got your tongue? No big deal! So there! Take that! Holy Toledo!* (Our teacher's favorite "curse word.") *Go jump in the lake! Really dumb. Golly. Gosh.* Slang, clichés, sayings, hot-shot language that our teacher called, **ponderously**, idiomatic expressions. Riddles, jokes, puns, conundrums. *What is yellow and goes click-click? Why did the chicken cross the road? See you later, alligator.* How wonderful to call someone an alligator and not be scolded for being **disrespectful**. In fact, they were supposed to say back, *In a while, crocodile.* **4**

There was also a neat little trick I wanted to try on an English-speaking adult at home. I had learned it from Elizabeth, my **smart-alecky** friend in fourth grade, whom I alternately worshiped and resented. I'd ask her a question that required an explanation, and she'd answer, "Because . . ." "Elizabeth, how come you didn't go to Isabel's birthday party?" "Because . . ." "Why didn't you put your name in your reader?" "Because . . ." I thought that such a cool way to get around having to come up with answers. So, I practiced saying it under my breath, planning for the day I could use it on an unsuspecting English-speaking adult.

ONE SUNDAY AT our extended family dinner, my grandfather sat down at the children's table to chat with us. **5** He was famous, in fact, for the way he could carry on adult conversations with his grandchildren. He often spoke to us in English so that we could practice speaking it outside the classroom. He **was a Cornell man**, a United Nations representative from our country.

4 Language
An **idiom** is an expression that does not mean what each word means individually. Look at the idioms the author includes in the narrative. What do they mean?

5 Chronological Order
Where does the author begin writing about a new event in the sequence? What words signal this shift?

Key Vocabulary
enlist *v.*, to convince someone to help
disrespectful *adj.*, insulting

In Other Words
talking up an English storm speaking English all the time
rendition version
ponderously very seriously
smart-alecky annoying
was a Cornell man attended Cornell University

He gave speeches in English. Perfect English, my mother's phrase. That Sunday, he asked me a question. I can't even remember what it was because I wasn't really listening but lying in wait for my chance. "Because . . . ," I answered him. Papito waited a second for the rest of my sentence and then gave me a thumbnail grammar lesson, "*Because* has to be followed by a clause."

"Why's that?" I asked, **nonplussed**.

"Because," he winked, "Just because."

A BEGINNING WORDSMITH, I had so much left to learn; sometimes it was disheartening. Once Tío Gus, the family **intellectual**, put a speck of salt on my grandparents' big dining table during Sunday dinner. He said, "Imagine this whole table is the human brain.

Then this teensy grain is all we ever use of our intelligence!" He **enumerated** geniuses who had perhaps used two grains, maybe three: Einstein, Michelangelo, da Vinci, Beethoven. We children believed him. It was the kind of impossible fact we **thrived on**, proving as it did that the world out there was not drastically different from the one we were making up in our heads.

A beginning wordsmith, I had so much left to learn; sometimes it was disheartening.

Later, at home, Mami said that you had to take what her younger brother said "with a grain of salt." I thought she was still referring to Tío Gus's demonstration, and I tried to puzzle out what she was saying. Finally, I asked what she meant. "Taking what someone says with a grain of salt is an idiomatic expression in English," she explained. It was **pure voodoo** is what it was— what later I learned poetry could also do: a grain of salt could symbolize both the human brain and a **condiment for human nonsense**. And it could be itself, too: a grain of salt to flavor a bland plate of American food. ▣

6 Ask Questions
What is the author trying to say here about words?

Monitor Comprehension

Confirm Prediction
Was your prediction accurate? If not, why? What happened that you did not expect?

Key Vocabulary
enumerate *v.*, to name one by one

In Other Words
nonplussed surprised
intellectual intelligent, well-educated person
thrived on enjoyed hearing
pure voodoo magical
condiment for human nonsense way to present foolish ideas

How do you predict the author will deal with a new situation?

WHEN WE ARRIVED in New York, I was shocked. A country where everyone spoke English! These people must be smarter, I thought. Maids, waiters, taxi drivers, doormen, bums on the street, all spoke this difficult language. It took some time before I understood that Americans were not necessarily a smarter, superior race. It was as natural for them to learn their **mother tongue** as it was for a little Dominican baby to learn Spanish. It came with "mother's milk," my mother explained, and for a while I thought a mother tongue was a mother tongue because you got it from your mother's breast, along with proteins and vitamins.

Soon it wasn't so strange that everyone was speaking in English instead of Spanish. I learned not to hear it as English, but as sense. I no longer **strained** to understand, I understood. I relaxed in this second language. Only when someone with a heavy southern or British accent spoke in a movie, or at church when the priest **droned his sermon**—only then did I experience that little catch of anxiety. I worried that I would not be able to understand, that I wouldn't be able to "keep up" with the voice speaking in this acquired language. **7** I would be like those people from the Bible we had studied in religion class, whom I imagined standing at the foot of an enormous tower that looked just like the skyscrapers around me. They had been punished for their pride by being made to speak different languages so that they didn't understand what anyone was saying.

7 Chronological Order/Ask Questions What does the author illustrate through chronological order?

At eight million, the population of New York City is four times that of Santo Domingo.

In Other Words
mother tongue first, or native, language
strained tried very hard
droned his sermon gave a long, boring religious speech

Cultural Background
The author refers to the **Tower of Babel** from the Bible's Book of Genesis. The Book says that all people once spoke the same language. When they began to build a tower to heaven, God stopped them by creating different languages so they could no longer communicate.

But at the foot of those towering New York skyscrapers, I began to understand more and more—not less and less—English. In sixth grade, I had one of the first in a lucky line of great English teachers who began to nurture in me a love of language, a love that had been there since my childhood of listening closely to words. ▪8 Sister Maria Generosa did not make our class **interminably** diagram sentences from a workbook or learn a **catechism** of grammar rules. Instead, she asked us to write little stories imagining we were snowflakes, birds, pianos, a stone in the pavement, a star in the sky. What would it feel like to be a flower with roots in the ground? If the clouds could talk, what would they say? She had an expressive, dreamy look that was **accentuated** by the **wimple** that framed her face.

I began to understand more and more—not less and less . . .

Supposing, just supposing . . . My mind would take off, soaring into possibilities, a flower with roots, a star in the sky, a cloud full of sad, sad, tears, a piano crying out each time its back was tapped, music only to our ears.

Sister Maria stood at the chalkboard. Her chalk was always snapping in two because she wrote with such energy, her whole **habit** shaking with the swing of her arm, her hand tap-tap-tapping on the board. "Here's a simple sentence: 'The snow fell.'" Sister pointed with her chalk, her eyebrows lifted, her wimple poked up. Sometimes I could see wisps of gray hair that strayed from under her headdress. "But watch what happens if we put an adverb at the beginning and a prepositional phrase at the end: 'Gently, the snow fell on the bare hills.'"

I thought about the snow. I saw how it might fall on the hills, tapping lightly on the bare branches of trees. Softly, it would fall on the cold, bare fields. On toys children had left out in the yard, and on cars and on little birds and on people out late walking on the streets. Sister Maria filled the chalkboard with snowy print, on and on, handling and shaping and moving the language,

8 Chronological Order/Language
Authors sometimes use **imagery** to clarify the sequence of events. What image does Alvarez use in this sentence to introduce a pattern of events?

Key Vocabulary
interminably *adv.*, endlessly
accentuate *v.*, to make more noticeable

In Other Words
catechism manual
wimple head covering
habit religious dress

scribbling all over the board until English, those verbal **gadgets**, those tricks and turns of phrases, those little fixed units and counters, became a charged, fluid mass that carried me in its great fluent waves, rolling and moving onward, to deposit me on the shores of my new homeland. I was no longer a foreigner with no ground to stand on. I had landed in the English language. **9** ❖

9 Ask Questions
Why does the author use the word *ground* to refer to the English language?

ANALYZE **My English**

1. **Explain** Did the author deal with her shock in the ways you predicted? If so, what in the narrative illustrated what you predicted? If not, explain what she did differently.

2. **Vocabulary Enumerate** at least three reasons the author came to love the English language.

3. **Analyze Text Structure: Chronological Order Enlist** the help of a partner and create a time line like the one below. Include at least five events from "My English." Place the events in chronological order.

   Time Line

   Event 1   Event 2   Event 3   Event 4   Event 5

4. **Focus Strategy Ask Questions** Write several questions for the author about choices she made when writing this narrative. Share your questions with a partner, and decide how the author probably would answer them.

⤺ Return to the Text
Reread and Write Reread to identify what the author discovers as she learns her new form of communication. Write a short journal entry describing Alvarez's discoveries in what could be her own words.

In Other Words
gadgets tools

How I Learned English

poem by Gregory Djanikian

Reading Strategies

· Plan and Monitor
· Determine Importance
· Make Inferences
▶ **Ask Questions**
· Make Connections
· Synthesize
· Visualize

Analyze Text Structure: Free Verse

Not all poetry has a specific rhythm and rhyme. **Free verse** is a style of poetry that doesn't follow any set pattern. This form is sometimes used when a poet is trying to tell a story with poetry.

In a free verse poem, the lines usually have different lengths. The poet may use line breaks to call attention to specific words or phrases. When you read a free verse poem, however, follow the punctuation marks instead of the line breaks. Then you will experience the narrative flow of the poem.

Look Into the Text

Punctuation tells you when to pause or stop.

> I watched it closing in
> Clean and untouched, transfixed
> By its easy arc before it hit
> My forehead with a thud.
>   I fell back,
> Dazed, clutching my brow,

The poet uses line breaks to separate specific details of the incident he's describing.

Focus Strategy ▶ Ask Questions

As you read a poem, question the poet. If you wonder why a poem looks the way it does, stop and ask this question: "Why did the poet decide to use this form instead of some other form?" Asking and answering questions will help you enjoy and understand the poem better.

HOW TO QUESTION THE AUTHOR

Focus Strategy

1. **Read** the poem excerpt above.

2. **Ask** your question.

3. **Think** about possible answers.

4. **Discuss** your answers with other classmates.

> Why does the poet put a long space before the short line "I fell back"?
>
> Maybe the poet is trying to show his dazed feeling after he gets hit in the head.

Connect Across Texts

In "My English," Julia Alvarez accentuates the variety of ways in which she made the English language her own. In this poem, the writer tells how he became more comfortable with English by playing baseball with friends.

How I Learned English

By Gregory Djanikian

It was in an empty lot
Ringed by elms and fir and honeysuckle.
Bill Corson was pitching in his buckskin jacket,
Chuck Keller, fat even as a boy, was on first,

5   His t-shirt riding up over his gut,
Ron O'Neill, Jim, Dennis, were talking it up
In the field, a blue sky above them
Tipped with cirrus.
        And there I was,

10 Just off the plane and plopped in the middle
Of Williamsport, Pa. and a neighborhood game,
Unnatural and without any moves,
My notions of baseball and America
Growing fuzzier each time I whiffed. **1**

15 So it was not impossible that I,
Banished to the outfield and daydreaming
Of water, or a hotel in the mountains,
Would suddenly find myself in the path

1 Access Vocabulary
Slang is a type of informal speech that consists of newly created words. Based on the context, what do you think the slang word *whiffed* means?

Key Vocabulary
  banish *v.*, send away

In Other Words
  without any moves not having baseball skills

Of a ball stung by Joe Barone.

20   I watched it closing in
Clean and untouched, transfixed
By its easy arc before it hit
My forehead with a thud.
          I fell back,

25   Dazed, clutching my brow,
Groaning, "Oh my shin, oh my shin,"
And everybody peeled away from me
And dropped from laughter, and there we were,
All of us writhing on the ground for one reason

30   Or another.
          Someone said "shin" again,
There was a wild stamping of hands on the ground,
A kicking of feet, and the fit
Of laughter overtook me too,

35   And that was important, as important
As Joe Barone asking me how I was
Through his tears, picking me up
And dusting me off with hands like swatters,
And though my head felt heavy,

40   I played on till dusk
Missing flies and pop-ups and grounders
And calling out in desperation things like
"Yours" and "take it," but doing all right,
Tugging at my cap in just the right way,

45   Crouching low, my feet set,
"Hum baby" sweetly on my lips.

2 **Ask Questions**
What does the speaker mean when he says that everyone's laughter was important?

In Other Words

transfixed frozen into one position
peeled away ran away suddenly
writhing twisting

Cultural Background

Williamsport, Pennsylvania, is the home of the Little League youth baseball program, which began in 1939. At the end of every summer, teams from around the world come to Williamsport to participate in the Little League World Series championship tournament.

ANALYZE How I Learned English

1. **Explain** How did the speaker and his friends react to his use of English? How did their reactions affect how he learned English? Be sure to cite examples from the text.

2. **Vocabulary** Describe the speaker's **countenance** after he is hit in the forehead by the ball.

3. **Analyze Text Structure: Free Verse** Read lines 24–30 aloud to a partner. Have your partner evaluate how you follow punctuation instead of line breaks. Then switch roles and repeat the activity. Tell which line ends with a full stop, which lines end with a slight pause, and which lines end with no pause at all.

4. **Focus Strategy Ask Questions** Why do you think Gregory Djanikian chose to write about this event in a poem rather than in a nonfiction narrative? Do you think the form is appropriate for communicating his story?

Return to the Text

Reread and Write Reread lines 39–46 of the poem. Write one paragraph telling how the speaker's actions illustrate his success at communicating.

About the Poet

Gregory Djanikian (1949–) moved to the United States from Egypt as a young boy. He quickly learned English, and went on to become a professor of creative writing. He has written four poetry collections, including *Falling Deeply into America* (1989), which includes "How I Learned English" and other poems that reflect on his experiences in a new land.

EQ What Does It Really Mean to Communicate?

Critical Thinking

1. **Analyze** Return to the brainstorming list on page 412 in which you associated thoughts with the word *language*. What new ideas would you now add to the list? Have any of your ideas changed? Tell why or why not.

EQ 2. **Compare** According to each author, what does it really mean to communicate?

3. **Interpret** Why does Gregory Djanikian call his poem "How I Learned English"? Could Julia Alvarez's narrative have the same title? Explain.

4. **Speculate** Do you think that most immigrant children in America have had different experiences from those of the authors of "My English" and "How I Learned English"? Explain your opinion.

EQ 5. **Evaluate** If you were telling a friend about these two selections, which event or idea about communication would you **accentuate**? Explain which event or idea made the greatest impression on you.

Write About Literature

Letter or E-mail Think about your experience learning a new language. Were you learning just a few words and phrases, or did you need to speak it every day? Using examples from both texts, write a letter or an e-mail to a partner in which you tell how your experience compared with those in "My English" and "How I Learned English." Then explain what you did to become successful in communicating.

Key Vocabulary Review

Oral Review Work with a partner. Use these words to complete the paragraph.

accentuated	**discerning**	**enumerated**
banish	**disrespectful**	**interminably**
countenance	**enlisted**	

When I moved to the United States, I thought I would struggle __(1)__ with learning English. I was afraid to speak because I might say something rude, or __(2)__. So I chose to __(3)__ myself from people's company. People could tell from my __(4)__ how alone I felt. But an amazing thing happened. I was __(5)__ to help put on a play! I was part of the stage crew, and the director __(6)__ my jobs: 1. move the sets; 2. make sound effects. I became a __(7)__ listener, paying attention to the actors' performances and the director's reactions. My drama experience __(8)__ the role of English in my life.

Writing Application Recall a time when you were **enlisted** to help a friend communicate with someone else. What did you do to help? Write a paragraph about the experience. Use at least three Key Vocabulary words.

Read with Ease: Phrasing

Assess your reading fluency with the passage in the Reading Handbook, p. 810. Then complete the self-check below.

1. I did/did not pause appropriately for punctuation and phrases.

2. My words correct per minute: _____ .

INTEGRATE THE LANGUAGE ARTS

Use the Correct Pronoun

The pronoun you use depends on the **noun** it refers to.

To choose the correct pronoun, ask yourself:

- Does the noun name a male or a female?
- Does the noun name one or more than one?
- Do you need a **subject pronoun** or an **object pronoun**?

Study these examples:

Julia speaks Spanish. **She** is learning English.

English is Julia's second language. **It** can be confusing.

Grandfather listens to **Julia**. **He** replies to **her**.

Papi knows **English**. **He** speaks **it** well.

Oral Practice (1–5) With a partner, take turns saying each pair of words below in sentences. Your sentences should tell about "My English."

Mami, she	English, it	children, them
Papi, him	language, your	

Written Practice (6–10) Rewrite the paragraph below. Choose the correct pronouns. Add two more sentences about Julia. Use pronouns.

Julia likes to have fun with language. (She/Her) mixes English and Spanish words in her sentences. (They/Them) are easy to understand if you are bilingual. Julia also writes stories. She likes to read (they/them) to her students.

Use Appropriate Language

Act It Out Make up a skit about Julia Alvarez talking with friends. Then act out a scene when you talk to your teacher. How does your language change?

Multiple Levels of Meaning

The English language has many words and sayings that can have more than one meaning depending upon the context in which they are used. For example, in "My English," a young Julia Alvarez discovers three possible meanings for the phrase "a grain of salt":

> … [A] grain of salt could symbolize both the human brain and a condiment for human nonsense. And it could be itself, too: a grain of salt to flavor a bland plate of American food.

With a partner, read the following examples of phrases that could have different meanings depending on the context in which they are used. Then write a brief explanation of the different levels of meaning for each phrase.

- … a sentence that wasn't colonized by the English language (p. 417)
- … talking up an English storm (p. 418)
- Cat got your tongue? (p. 418)
- Go jump in the lake! (p. 418)
- … shaping and moving the language … (p. 421)

Source: ©Mark Lynch/CartoonStock, Ltd.

Vocabulary Study

Content-Area Words

When you read about a topic related to science, math, social studies, or English, authors use **content-area words**. These words have specialized meanings in a specific subject area. For example, in "My English," words such as *vocabulary* and *idiomatic expressions* are content-area words used in an English or language arts class.

Copy the chart. With a partner, look in a dictionary to find the definition of the content-area words listed below. List also the content area that the word is used in.

WORD(S)	DEFINITION	CONTENT AREA
idiomatic expression	a saying that does not have literal meaning	English
logarithm		
recession		
condensation		

Listening / Speaking

Anecdote

Language Arts: Communicating Choose a partner and each tell an anecdote, or brief personal story, about how you learned the meaning of a certain English word or phrase.

1 **Prepare** Think of these questions as you choose your topic: Did you use a word incorrectly in a humorous way? Did someone you admire teach it to you?

2 **Present** Tell your anecdote briefly and clearly. Be sure the anecdote shows how you learned the correct meaning.

3 **Evaluate** Be sure your partner's anecdote was interesting or entertaining and gave enough background and details. Offer helpful feedback.

Writing Trait

Development of Ideas

When you write, you need to support ideas with specific details. Details help you elaborate and write more about the main topic. What do the details tell you in the paragraph below? Did the writer use details to elaborate?

Just OK

> Julia Alvarez strained to understand English. Then, she began to feel more confident. Julia finally began to embrace English words. She had a good teacher.

The paragraph tells about Julia Alvarez, but it doesn't explain how she felt or what she thought. The writer doesn't support the ideas with specific details. Read how the writer improved the paragraph:

Much Better

> Julia Alvarez was overwhelmed by all the speakers. She thought all of the native speakers were smarter than she was. Soon, Julia began to understand English everywhere she heard it. Eventually, she learned to love the way words could communicate images and feelings.

Now it's your turn to elaborate on ideas. Write a short paragraph describing a scene from nature. Remember:

- Use nouns that can be more specific.
- Describe the action precisely.
- Use adjectives to provide more detail and support ideas.

🔖 **Writing Handbook, p. 832**

from Txtng: The Gr8 Db8

BY DAVID CRYSTAL

1 A remarkable number of **doom-laden prophecies** arose during the opening years of the new millennium, all relating to the **linguistic evils** which would be unleashed by texting. The prophecies went something like this:

2 • Texting uses new and nonstandard **orthography**.

3 • This will **inevitably erode** children's ability to spell, punctuate, and capitalize correctly—an ability already thought to be poor.

4 • They will inevitably transfer these new habits into the rest of their schoolwork.

5 • This will inevitably give them poorer marks in examinations.

6 • A new generation of adults will inevitably grow up unable to write proper English.

7 • Eventually the language as a whole will inevitably decline.

8 Misinformation of this kind can be crushed only by solid research findings. And research is slowly beginning to show that texting actually benefits literacy skills. The studies are few, with small numbers of children,

In Other Words

doom-laden prophecies negative predictions
linguistic evils language-related problems
orthography spelling
inevitably erode surely harm

so we must be cautious; but a picture is emerging that texting does not harm writing ability and may even help it. Here are the findings of some recent studies:

> ...texting does not harm writing ability...

9
- Veenal Raval, a speech and language therapist working at the City University in London, compared group of 11- to 12-year-old texters with a similar group of non-texters. She found that neither group had noticeably worse spelling or grammar than the other, but that both groups made some errors. She also noted that **text abbreviations** did not appear in their written work.

10
- A team of Finnish researchers found that the informal style of texting was an important motivating factor, especially among teenage boys, and provided fresh opportunities for linguistic creativity.

11
- In a series of studies carried out in 2006-7, Beverly Plester, Clare Wood, and others from Coventry University found strong positive links between the use of text language and the skills underlying success in standard English in a group of pre-teenage children. The children were asked to compose text messages that they might write in a particular situation—such as texting a friend to say that they had missed their bus and they were going to be late. The more text abbreviations they used in their messages, the higher they scored on tests of reading and vocabulary. The children who were better at spelling and writing used the most texting abbreviations. Also interesting was the finding that the younger the children received their first phone, the higher their scores.

12
These results surprise some people. But why should one be surprised? Children could not be good at texting if they had not already developed considerable literacy awareness. Before you can write **abbreviated** forms effectively and play with them, you need to have a sense of how the sounds of your language relate to the letters. You need to know that there are such things as alternative spellings. You need to have a good visual memory and good **motor** skills. If you are aware that your texting behavior is different, you must have already **intuited** that there is such a thing as a standard. If you are

---

Key Vocabulary
abbreviated *adj.*, shortened

In Other Words
text abbreviations shortened versions of words
motor hand movement
intuited understood

using such abbreviations as *lol* ("laughing out loud") and *brb* ("be right back"), you must have developed a sensitivity to the communicative needs of your textees, because these forms show you are responding to them. If you are using *imho* ("in my humble opinion") or *afaik* ("as far as I know"), you must be aware of the possible effect your choice of language might have on them, because these forms show you are self-critical. Teenage texters are not stupid nor are they socially inept within their peer group. They know exactly what they are doing.

Teenage texters are not stupid...

13 Texting is one of the most **innovative linguistic phenomena** of modern times, and perhaps that is why it has generated such strong emotions—"a kind of laziness," "an affectation," "ridiculous." Yet all the evidence suggests that belief in an **impending** linguistic disaster is a consequence of a mythology largely created by the media. Children's use of text abbreviations has been **hugely exaggerated**, and the mobile phone companies have played a part in this by emphasizing their "cool" character, compiling dictionaries, and publishing usage guides—doubtless, thereby, motivating sales.

14 Texting has been blamed for all kinds of evils that it could not possibly have been responsible for. Virtually any piece of nonstandard English in schoolwork is now likely to be considered the result of texting, even if the evidence **is incontrovertible** that the nonstandardism has been around for generations. The other day I read about someone **condemning** *would of* (for *would have*) as a consequence of texting. That misspelling has been around for at least 200 years. You will find it in Keats. I have encountered similar misapprehensions in Japan, Finland, Sweden, and France, and it is probably present in every country where texting has become a feature of daily communication.

15 In a logical world, text messaging should not have survived. Imagine a pitch to a potential investor. "I have this great idea. A new way of person-to-person communication, using your phone. The users won't have a familiar keyboard. Their fingers will have trouble finding the keys. They will be able to send messages, but with no more than 160 characters at a time. The writing on the screens will be very small and difficult to read, especially if you have a visual handicap. The messages will arrive at any time, interrupting your daily

In Other Words
innovative linguistic phenomena creative language changes
impending upcoming
hugely exaggerated overstated
is incontrovertible clearly shows
condemning blaming

routine or your sleep. Oh, and every now and again you won't be able to send or receive anything because your battery will run out. Please invest in it." What would you have done?

16　　But, it was direct, avoiding the problem of tracking down someone over the phone. It was quick, avoiding the waiting time associated with letters and emails. It was focused, avoiding time-wasting small-talk. It was portable, allowing messages to be sent from virtually anywhere. It could even be done with one hand, making it usable while holding on to a roof-strap in a crowded bus. It was personal, allowing **intimacy** and secrecy, reminiscent of classroom notes under the desk. It was unnoticed in public settings, if the user turned off the ringtone. It allowed young people to overcome the spatial boundary of the home, allowing communication with the outside world without the knowledge of parents and siblings. It hugely empowered the deaf, the shared writing system reducing the gap between them and hearing people. And it was relatively cheap (though, given the quantity of messaging, some parents still had an unpleasant shock when their phone bill arrived). It wasn't surprising, therefore, that it soon became the preferred method of communication among teenagers. Youngsters valued its role both as a badge of identity, like accents and dialects, and as **a ludic linguistic pastime**. And in due course adults too came to value its discreetness and convenience. The interruption caused by the arrival of a text message is disregarded. To those who text, the beep heralding a new message invariably thrills, not pains.

17　　How long will it last? It is always difficult to predict the future, when it comes to technology. Perhaps it will remain as part of an increasingly sophisticated **battery** of communicative methods, to be used as circumstances require. Or perhaps in a generation's time texting will seem as **archaic** a method of communication as the typewriter or the telegram does today, and new styles will have emerged to replace it. For the moment, texting seems here to stay, though its linguistic character will undoubtedly alter as its use spreads among the older population.

18　　Some people dislike texting. Some are **bemused** by it. Some love it. I am fascinated by it, for it is the latest **manifestation** of the human ability to be linguistically creative and to adapt language to suit the demands of diverse settings. In texting we are seeing, in a small way, language in evolution. ❖

How long will it last?

In Other Words

intimacy a sense of closeness
a ludic linguistic pastime an activity that uses language and technology in simple ways
battery set

archaic old
bemused confused
manifestation expression

EXPRESS YOURSELF

EQ **ESSENTIAL QUESTION:**
What Does It Really Mean to Communicate?

myNGconnect.com
Download the rubric.

myNGconnect.com

EDGE LIBRARY

Present Your Project: Multimedia Presentation

It's time to complete your multimedia presentation about the Essential Question for this unit.

1 Review and Complete Your Plan

Consider these points as you complete your project:

- How will your presentation address the Essential Question?
- Which of the various media will you use?
- What is the most effective way to combine the media?

Divide up the following tasks:

- finding or creating images
- selecting appropriate literary excerpts or writing original texts
- locating any sound effects or recordings
- putting the different elements together

2 Present Your Presentation

Give your multimedia presentation. Each group member should have a chance to present. Stage the presentation in class.

3 Evaluate the Presentation

Use a rubric to evaluate each of the multimedia presentations, including your own.

Reflect on Your Reading

Think back on your reading of the unit selections, including your choice of Edge Library books. Then, discuss the following with a partner or in a small group.

Genre Focus Think about the structure of each selection in the unit. Consider whether a different text structure could be used with any one of the selections. Give examples of how this could happen.

Focus Strategy Using the same selection, exchange three or more of the questions you asked with a partner. Answer each other's questions, and then compare and contrast the kind of questions you asked.

EQ Respond to the Essential Question

Throughout this unit, you have been exploring the question "What does it really mean to communicate?" Discuss this with a group. What is *your* opinion? Support your response with evidence from your reading, discussions, research, and writing.

Write a Research Report

Uriting Portfolio

Writing Mode
Informative/Explanatory

Writing Trait Focus
Organization

How do you find out more about something that interests you? You research the topic, or gather information about it. Now's your chance to learn more about communication methods as you write a research report.

Study Research Reports

Research reports combine and synthesize information about a topic. In a research report, you combine and organize facts from various sources, put the information in your own words, and let readers know where you found it.

❶ Connect Writing to Your Life

How do you find the location of a new restaurant? You look it up on the Internet or in the phone book. How do you find a part-time job? You read the want ads in the paper or look for "now hiring" signs in store windows. All of these methods, no matter how simple, are a form of research. What other kinds of research do you perform in everyday life?

❷ Understand the Form

Like other kinds of informative/explanatory writing, a research report has an introduction, a body, and a conclusion. It is written with a formal, objective voice and often includes section headings, charts, or other graphic aids to present the information visually. An additional feature of a research report is the Works Cited section or page at the end. It includes the sources of information you cite, or use, in your report. A good research report must contain the following elements:

1. Thesis Statement	A **thesis statement** consists of one or two sentences that state the **controlling**, or main, **idea** that you will develop in your report. It should appear at the end of the introduction and be restated in the conclusion.
2. Supporting Information and Evidence	Supporting information and evidence come from your research on your topic and make up the body of the paper. They should both relate to the thesis statement and provide background or proof.
3. Conclusion	In the conclusion, you repeat your thesis statement and summarize your supporting ideas in an interesting way.
4. Citations	Citations are references to the sources from which you gathered your information and evidence. They appear with the supporting information and evidence you are citing, or using, in your paper.
5. Works Cited Page	This page appears after the conclusion. It is a list of all the sources you used to write your report. Use a style guide to learn how to format and arrange your sources.

Before you get started, you need to become familiar with the research process.

❸ Understand the Research Process

When you research a topic, you look for useful, accurate, and trustworthy information about it.

- **Decide What You Need to Know** What do you want to know about a topic? Make a list of questions that you would like to answer. Look at the most important words in your questions. Those are **key words** that you can use to find information.

- **Locate Resources** Find sources of information about your topic. Typical resources are print materials, such as books, magazines, and newspapers, and electronic media, such as documentaries or Web sites. Different types of resources will provide different information and perspectives on your topic.

- **Include Primary and Secondary Sources** There are two kinds of resources: primary and secondary sources. **Primary sources** give firsthand information about a topic. Some examples are historical documents, diaries, and letters. **Secondary sources** give explanations and interpretations of a topic. Some examples are encyclopedias, books, and journal articles.

- **Evaluate the Resources** Just because information you find seems interesting doesn't mean that it is valuable or significant. To check the validity of your resources, answer the questions below. The more you can answer with a "yes," the more likely that the resource is of value.

  1. Will this resource answer at least some of my questions?
  2. Does this resource explain my topic in ways that I can understand?
  3. Can I tell who the author is?
  4. Is the author an expert on my topic?
  5. Is the information up to date?
  6. Does the information contain specific data, facts, and ideas?
  7. Does the resource contain graphs, charts, or maps that I can use in my report?

- **Gather Information and Take Notes** Use tables of contents, indexes, and Internet search engines to locate your key words. This will help you save time as you look for information. While you read, jot down important ideas on note cards along with their sources.

◆ **Language and Learning Handbook**, p. 770–775

> ### Research Tip
>
> **Paraphrase**, or take notes in your own words, to avoid **plagiarizing**. This occurs when you use someone else's words or ideas without giving the person credit.

▶ **Prompt** Write a research report about an invention that has had an impact on how we communicate. Be sure to tell:

- what area of communication the invention is from
- how it came about or originated
- how it developed into what we know today
- how it has affected people's everyday lives

✔ Prewrite

Once you know the basics of research reports, you are ready to plan one of your own. Planning will make it easier for you to write later on.

❶ Choose Your Topic

Think of a communication invention that you want to learn more about.

- Pick a form of communicating that you enjoy using.
- Pick a form of communicating that puzzles or interests you.
- Explore how a type of communication has changed over time.

❷ Clarify the Audience, Thesis Statement, and Purpose

Your teacher and your classmates will probably be part of your audience. Who else would like to know about your topic? Jot down your ideas.

What aspect of your topic will you focus on? Write one or two sentences that summarize what your research will be about. These sentences will form your **thesis statement**.

Think about your purpose for writing. Is it to inform? Why else might you write about your topic? Write down your ideas.

❸ Do Your Research

Use questions to drive your research. How did the form of communication originate? How has it affected everyday life? Be sure to take detailed notes on note cards. Use a separate card for each piece of information. Remember to paraphrase, and use quotation marks if you write an exact quotation. Be sure you've written any technical terms correctly. Include the source information, too.

author	*Baker, Burton H.*
title	*The Gray Matter*
where and when published	*St. Joseph: Telepress, 2000*
paraphrased information	*Elisha Gray fought Alexander Graham Bell in court over invention of telephone.*

Prewriting Tip

Be sure that your topic isn't too broad, or general, to cover in a short report.

Also be sure that your topic will be of interest to your audience. Ask the question "Why should we care?" about your topic. If you can't come up with a reason, you might want to choose a different topic.

Prewriting Tip

Read your note cards carefully and pull out the ones that are closely related to your thesis statement.

Sort these note cards into groups based on common ideas. The idea for each group will become a main point in your research report.

4 Evaluate Your Sources

As you conduct your research and choose your sources, evaluate the credibility, or believability, of the source and what is said. To check the validity of your sources, consider the following:

- Is the source written by an authority on the topic?
- How recent is the information? Check the publication date to see if the source reflects the most current research on your topic.
- Is it a reliable resource? Some popular-interest magazines or Web sites may not be credible sources. More reliable sources include an approved encyclopedia, a scholarly Web site, or a respected newspaper or magazine.

Refer to the **Language and Learning Handbook** on pages 770–777 for information about evaluating and citing sources.

5 Finish Your Writing Plan

Choose a graphic organizer, such as an outline, to create a Writing Plan. Use your groupings to help organize your main points.

Writing Plan

Topic	the origins of the cell phone
Audience	my teacher and classmates
Thesis Statement	The development of the cell phone is as controversial as the device itself can be.
Purpose	to inform
Time Frame	two weeks from today

I. Introduction
    A. statistic from MIT survey
    B. story of cell phone full of controversy
II. Body
    A. story of Bell/Gray's invention
    B. story of Marconi/Tesla's work
    C. story of Cooper/Bell Lab's innovation
III. Conclusion
    A. restate thesis
    B. end with anecdote

Writing Handbook, p. 832

Technology Tip

Outlining software can help you organize information. Your word-processing program may have an outline feature. If not, look for outlining software on the Internet.

Reflect on Your Writing Plan

► Are your main points organized in a way that will make your report easy to understand? Do you have enough research to support your thesis statement?

✔ Write a Draft

Use your Writing Plan as a guide while you write your report. It's OK to make mistakes. You'll have chances to improve your draft later on.

❶ Keep Your Ideas Flowing

If you took good notes during your research, you have a head start on the writing. Use your notes to write your draft.

❷ Cite Your Sources

As you write, cite your sources. That is, tell where you got information, ideas, or words that are not your own. One way to cite sources is to indicate them in parentheses. This is called the parenthetical method. When you use this method, you put the author's name in parentheses after the information, along with the page number on which the information was found. Check with your teacher to find out what citation style you should use.

> His first success was the handheld radio (Oehmke 1).

After you finish writing, create your Works Cited list. Include all the sources that you cited in your paper. Sources are listed in alphabetical order by authors' last names.

📖 **Language and Learning Handbook**, p. 777

❸ Student Model

Read this draft to see how the student used the Writing Plan to get ideas down on paper. The student will fix any mistakes later on.

Drafting Tip

Some of your sources may not have a listed author. In this case, you should use part of the title in your parenthetical element. You can also use it when alphabetizing your Works Cited list at the end of your report.

In the Works Cited list, format the titles of books, journals, Web sites, and newspapers with underlining or italics. The MLA format (shown in the student model) uses underlining, but if you type your research paper, you may use italics instead, if your teacher allows it.

A History of the Cell Phone

Today, there is nothing strange about someone walking down the street talking on their cell phone. In a survey taken by MIT in 2004, this device was voted "the most hated invention we cannot live without (Oehmke 1)." Some people still have mixed feelings about the cell phone, and the story of its development is just as full of controversy as the device itself.

Alexander Graham Bell worked to develop a way to send the human voice over a wire, but he wasn't alone. Other scientists, such as Elisha Gray, were also working on the idea. Gray fought Bell in court to have himself recognized as the true inventor of the telephone (Baker 10). Unfortunately, he lost, but the controversy still exists.

Guglielmo Marconi made great strides in wireless communication, but he was not alone. One of the first people to dabble in the field was the Serbian American Nikola Tesla. When Marconi developed a working transmitter and receiver, he quickly patented his discoveries. However, his work depended on some of Tesla's earlier work. Tesla objected to Marconi's claim that he had invented radio. Eventually, the U.S. Patent Office declared that Tesla was the true inventor ("Marconi" 2).

In 1954, a small electronics company called Motorola hired an engineer to develop portable products named Martin Cooper. His first success was the handheld radio, which was soon used in police cruisers and taxicabs (Oehmke 1). They could not be used to make telephone calls, however. They only worked between the car and the police station or taxi office. They also had limited signal range.

Cooper soon realized the solution to the range problem. If many broadcasting stations were placed close to one another, a wireless phone would usually be within range of one of them. The area that a base station covered was called its cell. After setting up a group of cells, the next step was to link them to the telephone network. The only problem was that the idea of the cell had been developed by rival Bell Laboratories. (Oehmke 1)

However, Bell Labs was only interested in this stuff for use with car phones. Cooper believed that people would be more interested in handheld phones. On April 3, 1973, Cooper placed a base station on top of a New York City office building and dialed a number on a handset. The phone connected to the base station, which connected to the telephone network. It was the first cell phone call.

Though getting a lot of the credit, his work depended on the work of many others, including Bell, Gray, Marconi, Tesla, and of course Bell Laboratories. Who do you think was the recipient of that historic first cell phone call? It was Joe Engel, Bell Labs' head of research.

Works Cited

Baker, Burton H. The Gray Matter. St. Joseph: Telepress, 2000.

"Marconi, Guglielmo." Encyclopædia britannica. 2007. Encyclopædia
    Britannica Online. 26 Jan. 2007 <http://www.search.eb.com/eb/
    article-9050813>.

Oehmke, Ted. "Cell Phones Ruin the Opera? Meet the culprit." New York
    Times 6 Jan. 2000, late ed.: G1.

✔ Revise Your Draft

Your first draft is done. Now, you need to polish it. Check to see if you need to improve the organization.

❶ Revise for Organization

One thing that all good research reports have in common is **organization**. A well-organized report has a clear structure that is appropriate for the writer's purpose and easy for the reader to follow.

The paragraphs and sentences of a good research report are carefully organized as well. A good writer uses **transitions** to guide readers from one idea to the next. Transitions can be as simple as words such as *first*, *next*, and *finally*, or they can be entire sentences that tie one paragraph to the next.

TRY IT ▶ With a partner, discuss the organization of the draft below. Use the rubric to evaluate and score it.

Student Draft

> Alexander Graham Bell worked to develop a way to send the human voice over a wire, but he wasn't alone. Other scientists, such as Elisha Gray, were also working on the idea. Gray fought Bell in court to have himself recognized as the true inventor of the telephone (Baker 10). Unfortunately, he lost, but the controversy still exists.
>
> Guglielmo Marconi made great strides in wireless communication, but he was not alone. One of the first people to dabble in the field was the Serbian American Nikola Tesla. When Marconi developed a working transmitter and receiver, he quickly patented his discoveries. However, his work depended on some of Tesla's earlier work. Tesla objected to Marconi's claim that he had invented radio. Eventually, the U.S. Patent Office declared that Tesla was the true inventor ("Marconi" 2).
>
> In 1954, a small electronics company called Motorola hired an engineer to develop portable products named Martin Cooper. His first success was the handheld radio, which was soon used in police cruisers and taxicabs (Oehmke 1).

Writing Plan

Thesis Statement	The development of the cell phone is as controversial as the device itself can be.

Now use the rubric to evaluate the organization of your own draft. What score
do you give your draft and why?

Organization

myNGconnect.com
- Rubric: Organization
- Evaluate and practice scoring other student reports.

	Does the writing have a clear structure, and is it appropriate for the writer's audience, purpose, and type of writing?	How smoothly do the ideas flow together?
4 Wow!	**The writing has a structure that is <u>clear</u> and appropriate for the writer's audience, purpose, and type of writing.**	**The ideas progress in a smooth and orderly way.** • The introduction is strong. • The ideas flow well from paragraph to paragraph. • The ideas in each paragraph flow well from one sentence to the next. • Effective transitions connect ideas. • The conclusion is strong.
3 Ahh.	**The writing has a structure that is <u>generally</u> clear and appropriate for the writer's audience, purpose, and type of writing.**	**<u>Most</u> of the ideas progress in a smooth and orderly way.** • The introduction is adequate. • Most of the ideas flow well from paragraph to paragraph. • Most ideas in each paragraph flow from one sentence to the next. • Effective transitions connect most of the ideas. • The conclusion is adequate.
2 Hmm.	**The structure of the writing is <u>not</u> clear or <u>not</u> appropriate for the writer's audience, purpose, and type of writing.**	**<u>Some</u> of the ideas progress in a smooth and orderly way.** • The introduction is weak. • Some of the ideas flow well from paragraph to paragraph. • Some ideas in each paragraph flow from one sentence to the next. • Transitions connect some ideas. • The conclusion is weak.
1 Huh?	**The writing is not clear or organized.**	**<u>Few or none</u> of the ideas progress in a smooth and orderly way.**

❷ Revise Your Draft

You've now evaluated the organization of your own draft. If you scored 3 or lower, how can you improve your work? Use the checklist below to revise your draft.

Revision Checklist

Ask Yourself	Check It Out	How to Make It Better
Is my writing well organized to achieve my purpose?	If your score is 3 or lower, revise.	☐ If you are not clear about your purpose, state it in a sentence. ☐ If the overall organization does not fit your purpose, rearrange it. ☐ If the organization of a paragraph is not clear and effective, fix it.
Have I helped the reader follow the organization of ideas in my report?	If your score is 3 or lower, revise.	☐ Add information to fill any confusing gaps between ideas. ☐ Add headings and transitions to lead the reader from one idea to the next.
Does my report have an introduction, a body, and a conclusion?	Find and mark the boundaries between the parts.	☐ Add any part that is missing.
Have I explained and supported my thesis statement well?	Reread your thesis statement. Check to see if each body paragraph relates back to it.	☐ Look back at your note cards and see if there is any information you may have overlooked while writing your draft. ☐ If necessary, do more research to gather more information. ☐ Consider adding graphic aids such as charts and diagrams.
Have I used a formal voice and an objective tone?	**Look for informal language, slang, and contractions.**	☐ Replace slang with more formal language and academic vocabulary. ☐ Spell out contractions.
Do I cite everything that I need to cite in my report?	Reread your report to be sure that any ideas or words that are not your own are properly cited.	☐ Add citations where necessary, using the correct style according to MLA or another style guide.
Is every source that I cited included on a Works Cited list?	Compare your Works Cited list with your citations.	☐ Add any missing information.

❸ Conduct a Peer Conference

It helps to get a second opinion when you are revising your draft. Ask a partner to read your draft and look for the following:

- any part of the draft that is confusing
- any part where information seems to be missing
- anything that the person doesn't understand

Then talk with your partner about the draft. Focus on the items in the Revision Checklist. Use your partner's comments to make your report clearer, more complete, and easier to understand.

❹ Make Revisions

Look at the revisions below and the peer-reviewer conversation on the right. Notice how the peer reviewer commented and asked questions. Notice how the writer used the comments and questions to revise.

Revised for Organization

> The story begins with two other disputed inventions—the telephone and the radio. Alexander Graham Bell worked to develop a way to send the human voice over a wire, but he wasn't alone. Other scientists, such as Elisha Gray, were also working on the idea. Gray fought Bell in court to have himself recognized as the true inventor of the telephone (Baker 10). Unfortunately, he lost, but the controversy still exists.
>
> Nearly twenty years later, Guglielmo Marconi made great strides in wireless communication, but he also was not alone. One of the first people to dabble in the field was the Serbian American Nikola Tesla. When Marconi developed a working transmitter and receiver, he quickly patented his discoveries. However, his work depended on some of Tesla's earlier work. Tesla objected to Marconi's claim that he had invented radio. Eventually, the U.S. Patent Office declared that Tesla was the true inventor ("Marconi" 2).
>
> These two inventions are so important to the cell phone's history because a cell phone is technically a telephone with a small radio. Today it might seem simple to put these gadgets together, but back then, the size and bulk of both devices stood in the way. In 1954, a small electronics company called Motorola hired an engineer to develop portable products named Martin Cooper. His first success was the handheld radio, which was soon used in police cruisers and taxicabs (Oehmke 1).

Peer Conference

Reviewer's Comment: I'm not sure why you talk about Bell and Marconi. You never explain what they have to do with the cell phone.

Writer's Answer: I guess I do kind of jump from one idea to another. I will add some transitions to make my report flow better.

Reflect on Your Revisions

▶ Which revisions improved your paper the most? Take note of them. The next time you write, refer to your notes to remember which areas you most want to improve.

✔ Edit and Proofread Your Draft

Your revised report should now be complete. Before you share it with others, find and fix any mistakes that you made.

❶ Capitalize the Titles of Publications

Capitalize all main words in the titles of resources. Do not capitalize small words such as articles or prepositions. However, the first word in a title should always be capitalized, even if it's an article or preposition.

Book: *The History of Telecommunications*
Magazine: *Telcomm Monthly*
Newspaper: *The Washington Post*
Article: "Do You Hear Me?"

TRY IT ▶ Copy the titles. Fix the capitalization errors. Use proofreader's marks.

> 1. Encyclopædia britannica
> 2. "Cell Phones Ruin the Opera? Meet the culprit."

❷ Use Parentheses Correctly

Parentheses ( ) can be used to set off a sentence, phrase, or citation.

- If the words in parentheses interrupt the train of thought or are a citation, the end punctuation goes after the end parenthesis.

  Many households have cell phones instead of landlines (telephones connected to a wire line**).**

  One in eight households got rid of the landline in 2001 (Jones 1**).**

- When you are citing a direct quotation, the citation comes after the end quotation and before the end punctuation.

  He is "the greatest inventor on the planet" **(Smith 53).**

TRY IT ▶ Copy the sentences. Correct any errors with parentheses.

> 1. In a survey taken by MIT in 2004, this device was voted "the most hated invention we cannot live without (Oehmke 1)."
> 2. The only problem was that the idea of the cell had been developed by rival Bell Laboratories. (Oehmke 1)

Proofreading Tip

If you are unsure about whether a word in a title should be capitalized or not, look in a style manual to see if there is a similar example.

Proofreader's Marks

Use proofreader's marks to correct errors.

Capitalize:
An article in *popular science* discussed future cell phones.

Do not capitalize:
The book *The Future Of Communication* has a chapter on cell phones.

Add parentheses:
Cooper now wants to focus on the Internet (Oehmke1).

❸ Place Modifiers Correctly

A misplaced modifier is a modifier that is placed too far away from the word it describes. Modifiers should be placed as close as possible to the words they describe to avoid confusion.

Unclear	I returned the cell phone to the store **that was broken**.
Clear	I returned the cell phone **that was broken** to the store.

A dangling modifier is a modifier that doesn't have a word or phrase to modify, or it modifies the wrong word or phrase. Dangling modifiers usually come at the beginning of the sentence and start with a verb ending in –*ing*. In the first sentence below, the modifier is incorrect, or "dangling," because it suggests that her phone was driving.

Unclear	**While driving down the street**, her phone rang.
Clear	**While she was driving down the street**, her phone rang.

TRY IT ▶ Copy the sentences. Correct any misplaced or dangling modifiers.

> 1. A small electronics company called Motorola hired an engineer to develop portable products named Martin Cooper.
> 2. Though getting a lot of the credit, his work depended on the work of many others.

❹ Make Pronouns Agree with Their Antecedents

A pronoun takes the place of a noun. The pronoun you use depends on its antecedent, or the noun it replaces. To choose the correct pronoun, you must decide if the antecedent is male or female and if it's singular or plural.

A customer will buy a cell phone if **she (or he)** really needs one.
The **cell phone** is broken. **It** needs to be repaired.

In paragraphs and essays, the antecedent may not always appear in the same sentence as the pronoun. Check your work to be sure you are not switching from singular to plural pronouns, or vice versa, to describe the same antecedent.

TRY IT ▶ Copy the sentences. Correct any pronoun agreement errors.

> 1. Today, there is nothing strange about someone walking down the street talking on their cell phone.
> 2. His first success was the handheld radio. They could not be used to make telephone calls, however.

Reflect on Your Corrections

▶ Look back at any edits you made. Do you see a pattern? If there are things you keep missing, make a list of what to watch in your writing.

🕮 **Writing Handbook**, p. 876

5 Edited Student Draft

Here's the student's draft, revised and edited. How did the writer improve it?

A History of the Cell Phone

Today, there is nothing strange about someone walking down the street talking on his or her cell phone. In a survey taken by MIT in 2004, this device was voted "the most hated invention we cannot live without" (Oehmke 1). Some people still have mixed feelings about the cell phone, and the story of its development is just as full of controversy as the device itself.

A Contest from the Start

The story begins with two other disputed inventions—the telephone and the radio. Alexander Graham Bell worked to develop a way to send the human voice over a wire, but he was not alone. Other scientists, such as Elisha Gray, were also working on the idea. Gray fought Bell in court to have himself recognized as the true inventor of the telephone (Baker 10). Unfortunately, he lost, but the controversy still exists.

Nearly twenty years later, Guglielmo Marconi made great strides in wireless communication, but he also was not alone. One of the first people to dabble in the field was the Serbian American Nikola Tesla. When Marconi developed a working transmitter and receiver, he quickly patented his discoveries. However, his work depended on some of Tesla's earlier work. Tesla objected to Marconi's claim that he had invented radio. Eventually, the U.S. Patent Office declared that Tesla was the true inventor ("Marconi" 2).

Telephone Meets Radio

These two inventions are so important to the cell phone's history because a cell phone is technically a telephone with a small radio. Today it might seem simple to put these gadgets together, but back then, the size and bulk of both devices stood in the way. In 1954, a small electronics company called Motorola hired an engineer named Martin Cooper to develop portable products. His first success was the handheld radio, which was soon used in police cruisers and taxicabs (Oehmke 1). It could not be used to make telephone calls, however. It only worked between the car and the police station or taxi office. It also had limited signal range.

Cooper soon realized the solution to the range problem. If many broadcasting stations were placed close to one another, a wireless phone would usually be within range of one of them. The area that a base station covered was called its cell. After setting up a group of cells, the next step was to link them to the telephone network. The only problem was that the

The writer corrected the **pronoun agreement** error.

The writer correctly used quotation marks and end punctuation with **parentheses**.

The writer added **headings** and **transitions** to improve the organization and flow of the paper.

The writer spelled out a **contraction**.

The writer fixed the **misplaced modifier** by moving it closer to the word it modifies.

The writer corrected the **pronoun agreement** errors.

idea of the cell had been developed by rival Bell Laboratories (Oehmke 1).

However, Bell Labs was only interested in cellular technology for use with car phones. Cooper believed that people would be more interested in handheld phones. On April 3, 1973, Cooper placed a base station on top of a New York City office building and dialed a number on a handset. The phone connected to the base station, which connected to the telephone network. It was the first cell phone call.

Though Cooper gets a lot of the credit, his work depended on the work of many others, including Bell, Gray, Marconi, Tesla, and of course Bell Laboratories. Who do you think was the recipient of that historic first cell phone call? It was Joe Engel, Bell labs' head of research.

Works Cited

Baker, Burton H. The Gray Matter. St. Joseph: Telepress, 2000.

"Marconi, Guglielmo." Encyclopædia Britannica. 2007. Encyclopædia Britannica Online. 26 Jan. 2007 <http://www.search.eb.com/eb/article-9050813>.

Oehmke, Ted. "Cell Phones Ruin the Opera? Meet the Culprit." New York Times 6 Jan. 2000, late ed.: G1.

*The writer correctly used end punctuation with **parentheses** and replaced informal language with more **formal vocabulary**.*

*The writer corrected the **dangling modifier** by giving it a word to modify.*

*The writer corrected **capitalization** errors in the titles.*

✔ Publish and Present

You are now ready to publish and present your report. Print it out or write a clean copy by hand. You may also want to present your work in a different way.

Alternative Presentation

Deliver a Presentation Use information from your report to give a presentation on your topic.

1 Use presentation software to create a slide show.

2 Gather images such as graphs, tables, charts, and photographs to illustrate your presentation. If you need to create any graphics, use appropriate technology to ensure that they are accurate.

3 Use your report as a script as you present the slide show.

4 Lead a question-and-answer session about your presentation.

◆ **Language and Learning Handbook**, p. 750

Reflect on Your Work

▶ Ask for and use feedback from your audience to evaluate your strengths as a writer.

- Did your audience find your report to be interesting? What did they learn?

- What did your audience think was the strongest point of your report? What did they think was the weakest point?

- What would you like to do better the next time you write? Set a goal for your next writing project.

☑ Save a copy of your work in your portfolio.

UNIT 5 SHORT STORIES

EQ **ESSENTIAL QUESTION:**

What Do People Discover in a Moment of Truth?

You gain strength, courage, and confidence by every experience in which you really stop to look fear in the face. You must do the thing which you think you cannot do.

—ELEANOR ROOSEVELT

You have to trust your inner knowing. If you have a clear mind and an open heart, you won't have to search for direction. Direction will come to you.

—PHIL JACKSON

Critical Viewing ▷
Police officer Sarmin Tangadji was escorting photographers in Papua New Guinea, when they came upon a group of whale sharks. He got so excited about seeing the sharks up close that he just plunged into the water. What might be his moment of truth in this experience?

MOMENT OF
TRUTH

EQ ESSENTIAL QUESTION:
What Do People Discover in a Moment of Truth?

Study the Survey

In a moment of truth, people get to know things about themselves they may never have realized before. A moment of truth may reveal the values that are most important to you, such as truth, responsibility, or excellence. What might you discover about yourself—and others—in a moment of truth? Now, with your class, experience your own moment of truth.

What Do You Value Most?

Review this list of personal values. Select the six values that are most important to you.

Cooperation	Competition	Creativity	Kindness	Excellence
Fame	Helping Others	Honesty	Intelligence	Integrity
Loyalty	Popularity	Power	Responsibility	Security

Now that you have identified six, imagine that you could only have three values. Which three would you give up?

Now cross off two of your values. Which is the one value on the list that means the most to you?

Compare and Debate

1. What did you discover in your moment of truth? What did your classmates discover?

2. Why is that one value so important to you personally? How has this shown up in your life?

Discuss the survey with the class. Explain your opinions and support your ideas with an example from your own experiences.

EQ ESSENTIAL QUESTION

In this unit, you will explore the **Essential Question** in class through reading, discussion, research, and writing. Keep thinking about the question outside of school, too.

① Plan a Project

Skit

In this unit, you will perform a skit that addresses the Essential Question. To get started, choose a setting, create characters, and determine the plot. Read other scripts and notice how

- the characters are developed
- the setting is established
- the dialogue moves the action forward.

Study Skills Start planning your skit. Use the forms on www.myNGconnect.com to plan your time and to prepare the content.

www.myNGconnect.com
- ▶ Planning forms
- ▶ Scheduler
- ▶ Sample scripts
- ▶ Acting basics
- ▶ Rubric

② Choose More to Read

These readings provide different answers to the Essential Question. Choose a book and online selections to read during the unit.

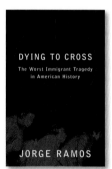

Dying to Cross
by Jorge Ramos

Imagine being trapped inside a hot truck for hours. On May 13, 2003, dozens of illegal immigrants lived this nightmare. How could this have happened? Jorge Ramos needed to find out. His book reveals the facts behind this tragedy. But can the whole truth ever be known?

▶ **NONFICTION**

The House of Dies Drear
by Virginia Hamilton

Thomas and his family move to a huge, historic house. Townspeople say the house is haunted. The family quickly discovers that someone does not want them there. Will the Small family discover the secrets of the house? Or will they be too scared to stay?

▶ **NOVEL**

Speak
by Laurie Halse Anderson

Melinda's first year of high school is a nightmare. Everyone hates her because of something that happened during the summer. But no one knows the truth. Melinda wants to forget that terrible night. Then something happens that makes Melinda end her silence.

▶ **NOVEL**

myNGconnect.com

- 🌐 Explore a survey about what other people around the world value most.
- 🌐 Read about what some people decided to do in a difficult situation.
- 🌐 Watch movies about a person's moment of truth and self-discovery.

Authors have all kinds of ways to speed up, slow down, and mix up time. Read "The Letter" and keep track of the story's shifts in time.

The Letter

Lia opened the mailbox slowly and there it was—the letter she'd been waiting for. "College of Musical Studies, New York" was embossed in gold on the outside. If she was accepted, her life would change forever. At 18, she'd be on her way to a career as a concert pianist. Who would have thought the daughter of a construction worker and a hotel maid would have such a chance? Lia shut her eyes and held the envelope tightly.

Her memory drifted back to her seventh birthday, to the sight of wrapping paper strewn everywhere. And the presents: a harmonica from her cousin, a book about musicians from her uncle, sheet music from her aunt. But nothing from her parents? Then Lia heard a delivery truck pull up to her family's home, and suddenly there it was, a piano of her very own!

"You've loved music since you were a baby," her father had said. "I'm going to work weekends to pay for this. But when I get home, you'll play me a song, won't you?"

The wind howled and Lia's fingers grew numb, but she didn't loosen her grip on the envelope. It was like that December day five years ago when she and her mother stood on Julia Saxson's porch. Ms. Saxson was the most accomplished pianist in the state. "Come in," Ms. Saxson said when Lia and her mother rang the doorbell. "Let's go to the music room."

The room held the biggest piano Lia had ever seen. "Would you play for me?" Ms. Saxson had asked her. Lia nodded. After only a few minutes, Ms. Saxson interrupted her. She offered to teach Lia for free.

Lia's neighbor and longtime friend Justin walked slowly up the street. He wondered what Lia was doing standing out in the cold. Last November, he had run to her aid. She was trying to get into the school auditorium to practice piano, but some mean kids blocked her way. And then Justin was there, and he made sure she got inside. "You don't have to worry about those jerks anymore, Lia," he had said.

"Well, are you going to open it?" asked Justin. Lia nodded and tore open the envelope. She turned to Justin and smiled. His face split into a grin. "Remember us folks back home when you're rich and famous," he joked.

"How could I ever forget?" she said.

College of Musical Studies, New York

Connect Reading to Your Life

Reading Strategies
- Plan and Monitor
- Determine Importance
- Make Inferences
- Ask Questions
- ▶ **Make Connections**
- Synthesize
- Visualize

Think about what just happened to Lia. Then think about what you know about:

- musicians
- families
- kids' behavior
- schools

Now, imagine something that you think is likely to have happened to Lia in the past—from getting the piano at age seven to taking the letter out of the mailbox at age eighteen. Come up with ideas by thinking about what you know of real life. With a partner, make a list of possible events. Then discuss how these ideas give you a better understanding of Lia in "The Letter."

1. Lia played piano at a piano recital.
2.
3.
4.

Focus Strategy ▶ Make Connections

When you try to understand how past events in a story lead to current situations, you're doing a kind of thinking you do all the time in your day-to-day life.

Think about the key **incidents** in your life—the kinds of incidents that would be worth writing about. It's likely that they came about as a result of a number of earlier incidents. When you think about those incidents, you may also think about influential events that led up to them. Recalling those memories can help you understand events in your own life—and events in the stories that you read.

Your Job as a Reader

Sometimes authors show us how one event leads to the next by starting at the beginning and moving straight through to the end. At other times, they use **flashbacks**, jumping from the present situation to the past events that led up to it. When you read a story with flashbacks, your job as a reader is to make sure you understand the time line of a story. When you're sure you do, you need to ask yourself why the events the author flashes back to are so important.

Elements of Literature
flashback *n.*, interruption in the action of a story to tell about an event that happened earlier

Academic Vocabulary
- **incident** *n.*, something that happens, event

■ Unpack the Thinking Process

Plot Structure

Almost all stories have a general pattern of events that make up the plot.

- Stories begin with **exposition**. You meet the characters and find out about the setting. Often, you get a sense of the problem they might face.
- Then the **conflict** develops. Complications occur, and the main character struggles.
- As the story continues, more events occur that make the conflict worse. These complications are part of the **rising action**.
- The conflict builds, and then something really important or exciting may happen. This event is the **climax**, or turning point, in the story.
- The remaining events are part of the **falling action** that leads to the **resolution**, in which the conflict ends or is resolved.

Plot Diagram

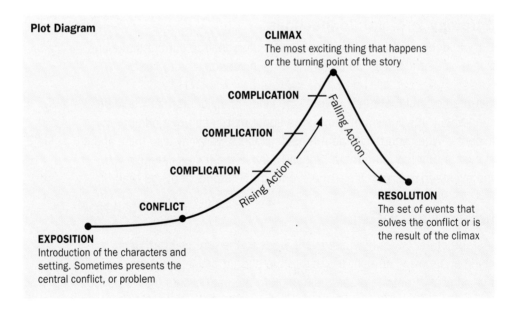

CLIMAX
The most exciting thing that happens or the turning point of the story

COMPLICATION

COMPLICATION

COMPLICATION

CONFLICT

Rising Action

Falling Action

RESOLUTION
The set of events that solves the conflict or is the result of the climax

EXPOSITION
Introduction of the characters and setting. Sometimes presents the central conflict, or problem

---

Elements of Literature

conflict *n.*, problem or struggle that drives a story's plot

rising action *n.*, events and complications that add to the conflict

climax *n.*, turning point, or most important event

falling action *n.*, events that lead to the resolution of the story

resolution *n.*, solution to the problem in a story

Plot Devices

Not all stories follow a straight line, and not all plot events occur at regular points in time. As an active reader, make sure you're clear about when story events occur in the time line. Often, authors announce shifts in time. In "The Letter," the narrator tells us about the change in time. You know from the first paragraph that Lia is eighteen, so when the narrator says, "Her memory drifted back to her seventh birthday," you know that the author is using a flashback.

If there is an abrupt shift in the setting, the characters, or the situation, the author is playing with the time of the story. For example, the fourth paragraph begins with wind howling. The previous scene ended with Lia and her parents in the house with the piano. These things don't go together, so the author must have interrupted the flow of time to return readers to the scene in the present.

Once you know that a flashback occurs, consider why the author chose to tell readers about that particular past event. Authors insert flashbacks because they think that the incident is crucially important. It's your job to figure out why. In "The Letter," each flashback tells us about people who went above and beyond the call of duty to help Lia out. The author could have given us flashbacks of Lia's practicing or of the wild applause that followed her first concert. The fact that the author made the choice to show us the people who helped Lia tells us that the author wants us to focus more on how people are connected than on how Lia's success is the result of her own talent and efforts.

■ Try an Experiment

One great way to understand what authors do is to be an author yourself. Choose one of the other characters in the story: Lia's mom or dad, Ms. Saxson, or Justin. Think about something in the past that would have influenced the character to be generous to Lia. Sketch out the incident in pictures or words.

Think, Pair, Share Then answer these questions with a partner:

1. How does the incident relate to your character's behavior toward Lia?
2. Are all the details in your description or picture relevant? Explain.

Monitor Comprehension

1. **Flashback** How do flashbacks help readers understand characters in stories?
2. **Plot** What is the resolution of the story "The Letter"?

EQ ## What Do People Discover in a Moment of Truth?
Find out how people's values differ.

Make a Connection

Anticipation Guide Think about how someone's personal values might differ from other people's values. Then tell whether you agree or disagree with these statements.

ANTICIPATION GUIDE

Agree or Disagree

1. Sometimes it's better to follow the rules rather than your own values. _____

2. It's OK to have different values from other people no matter what situation you are in. _____

3. It's more important to be true to yourself than to care for others. _____

Learn Key Vocabulary

Study the Words Pronounce each word and learn its meaning. You may also want to look up the definitions in the Glossary.

• Academic Vocabulary

Key Words	Examples
disarm (dis-**ahrm**) verb ▸ page 462	When you **disarm** someone, you win the person's approval and make him or her feel friendly toward you. *Synonym*: charm; *Antonym*: discourage
ensuing (en-**sü**-ing) adjective ▸ pages 465, 479	The **ensuing** years after the hurricane were spent cleaning up and rebuilding the city. *Synonyms*: following, resulting; *Antonyms*: earlier, beginning
harmonize (**hahr**-mu-nīz) verb ▸ pages 462, 477, 479	To **harmonize** is to be in agreement or go together well. The two singers **harmonize** their notes well in the song. *Synonym*: match; *Antonym*: differ
inquisitive (in-**kwi**-zu-tiv) adjective ▸ pages 463, 479	An **inquisitive** person asks questions and is eager for more information about something. *Synonym*: curious; *Antonym*: uninterested
• **integrity** (in-**te**-gru-tē) noun ▸ pages 472, 477	People who have a lot of **integrity** have a strong sense of right and wrong and are true to their values. A courtroom judge must have **integrity**.
irritating (**ir**-u-tāt-ing) adjective ▸ pages 469, 479, 531	Something that is **irritating** is annoying. The loud music that the teenagers enjoyed was quite **irritating** to their parents. *Synonym*: disturbing; *Antonym*: agreeable
melancholy (**me**-lun-kah-lē) noun ▸ pages 475, 476, 479	His **melancholy** was obvious, because he looked very sad and gloomy. *Synonyms*: sadness, gloom; *Antonyms*: cheerfulness, happiness
transaction (tran-**zak**-shun) noun ▸ pages 467, 479	A **transaction** is an action involving two or more people or things that influence or affect each other. In a business **transaction**, a customer gets products or services in exchange for money.

Practice the Words Work with a partner to write four sentences. Use at least two Key Vocabulary words in each sentence.

Example: The inquisitive child asked so many questions it was irritating.

short story by Toshio Mori

Analyze Structure: Plot

Plot is the sequence of events that give structure to a story. Each plot event reflects choices that the writer makes to create an overall effect.

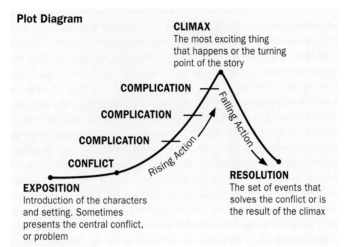

Plot Diagram

CLIMAX
The most exciting thing that happens or the turning point of the story

COMPLICATION

COMPLICATION

COMPLICATION

CONFLICT

Rising Action

Falling Action

EXPOSITION
Introduction of the characters and setting. Sometimes presents the central conflict, or problem

RESOLUTION
The set of events that solves the conflict or is the result of the climax

Look Into the Text

In this exposition, there are three characters.

What is the setting?

> He was a strange one to come to the shop and ask Mr. Sasaki for a job, but at the time I kept my mouth shut. There was something about this young man's appearance which I could not altogether harmonize with a job as a clerk in a flower shop.

The writer hints at a difficulty—perhaps a conflict—to come.

Focus Strategy ▶ Make Connections

When you read, make connections between the information you are reading and what you already know. Making connections helps you understand the characters and their actions. Good readers clarify texts by making connections to personal experiences, other texts, or bigger ideas in the world.

HOW TO MAKE CONNECTIONS

Focus Strategy

1. As you read, think of connections between events in the story and events from your own experiences.

2. Record the connections on your **Plot Diagram**.

3. How do your personal connections help clarify the text?

Exposition:

He was a strange one to come to the shop ... but at the time I kept my mouth shut.

This reminds me of when my brother applied for a job at the bookstore. He was really nervous when he spoke to the manager.

The Writer and His Experiences

Toshio Mori
(1910–1980)

Toshio Mori was the first Japanese American writer to be published in the United States.

Like the characters in "Say It with Flowers," Japanese American writer **Toshio Mori** worked in a California flower and plant nursery most of his life. In the evenings, after work, Mori devoted himself to his real passion—writing.

His hard work seemed about to pay off in 1941 when his first collection of short stories, *Yokohama, California*, was accepted for publication. But world events intervened. In December 1941, the United States declared war on Japan and entered World War II. In the months that followed, the U.S. government began placing thousands of Japanese Americans in relocation camps. Mori and his family were forced to live in the Topaz Relocation Center in Utah.

They returned to California in 1945 after the war ended, but *Yokohama, California* was not published until 1949. Mori continued to write but did not publish again until the 1970s, when a younger generation of writers rediscovered his stories. In Mori's work, they saw Japanese Americans woven into the fabric of American life, with the concerns typical of Americans everywhere. As Mori said, "I try to depict human beings, no matter what, living out their days as best they can, facing their human problems. Humanity transcends race at a certain point."

myNGconnect.com

🔵 Explore the history of WWII internment camps.
🔵 Find out about the history of Japanese Americans in California.

Say It with

Flowers

by Toshio Mori

Abundant Bouquet, 2001, Joan Son. Japanese papers, origami rose model by Pier Paulo Pessina, Italy.

▲ Critical Viewing: Design Origami is the Japanese art of folding paper. How do the details make this artwork like or unlike a painting?

Comprehension Coach

He was a strange one to come to the shop and ask Mr. Sasaki for a job, but at the time I kept my mouth shut. There was something about this young man's appearance which I could not altogether **harmonize** with a job as a clerk in a flower shop. I was a delivery boy for Mr. Sasaki then. I had seen clerks come and go, and although they were of various sorts of **temperaments** and conducts, all of them had the technique of **waiting on** the customers or acquired one eventually. You could never tell about a new one, however, and to be on the safe side I said nothing and watched our boss readily take on this young man. Anyhow we were glad to have **an extra hand**.

Mr. Sasaki undoubtedly remembered last year's **rush** when Tommy, Mr. Sasaki, and I had to do everything and **had our hands tied behind our backs** for having so many things to do at one time. He wanted to be ready this time. "Another clerk and we'll be all set for any kind of business," he used to tell us. When Teruo came around looking for a job, he got it, and Morning Glory Flower Shop was all set for the year as far as our boss was concerned. **1**

When Teruo reported for work the following morning, Mr. Sasaki left him in Tommy's hands. Tommy was our number one clerk for a long time.

"Tommy, teach him all you can," Mr. Sasaki said. "Teruo's going to be with us from now on."

"Sure," Tommy said.

"Tommy's a good florist. You watch and listen to him," the boss told the young man.

"All right, Mr. Sasaki," the young man said. He turned to us and said, "My name is Teruo." We shook hands.

We got to know one another pretty well after that. He was a quiet fellow with very little words for anybody, but his smile **disarmed** a person. **2**
We soon learned that he knew nothing about the florist business. He could

1 Structure: Plot
Which details in the exposition of the story indicate why Mr. Sasaki hires Teruo?

2 Make Connections
How is Teruo like or unlike people you have met in real life? How does that connection clarify your understanding of Teruo?

Key Vocabulary
harmonize v., to coordinate or go together well
disarm v., to win someone's trust and make the person friendly toward you

In Other Words
temperaments personalities
waiting on helping
an extra hand the help of another person
rush busy time
had our hands tied behind our backs were too busy to do our best work

identify a rose when he saw one, and gardenias and carnations, too; but other flowers and materials were new to him.

"You fellows teach me something about this business and I'll be grateful. I want to **start from the bottom**," Teruo said.

Tommy and I nodded. We were pretty sure by then he was all right. Tommy eagerly went about showing Teruo the florist game. Every morning for several days Tommy repeated the prices of the flowers for him. He told Teruo what to do on telephone orders, how to keep the greens fresh, how to make bouquets, corsages, and sprays. "You need a little more time to learn how to make big funeral pieces," Tommy said. "That'll come later."

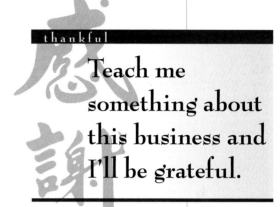

thankful

Teach me something about this business and I'll be grateful.

In a couple of weeks, Teruo was just as good a clerk as we had had in a long time. He was curious almost **to a fault** and was **a glutton for work**. ◼3 It was about this time our boss decided to move ahead his yearly business trip to Seattle. Undoubtedly he was satisfied with Teruo, and he knew we could get along without him for a while. He went off and left Tommy in full charge.

During Mr. Sasaki's absence I was often in the shop helping Tommy and Teruo with the customers and the orders. One day when Teruo learned that I once had worked in the nursery and had experience in flower growing, he became **inquisitive**.

"How do you tell when a flower is fresh or old?" he asked me. "I can't tell one from the other. All I do is follow your instructions and sell the ones you tell me to sell first, but I can't tell one from the other."

I laughed, "You don't need to know that, Teruo," I told him. "When the customers ask you whether the flowers are fresh, say yes firmly. 'Our flowers are always fresh, madam.'"

◼3 **Make Connections**
When have you felt as interested in an activity as Teruo is? Use your personal experiences to suggest reasons Teruo is willing to work so hard.

Key Vocabulary
inquisitive *adj.*, curious

In Other Words
start from the bottom learn each job in the shop
to a fault too much so
a glutton for work very eager to work hard

◀ **Critical Viewing:
Effect**
The young man in
this painting could
be going to or from
work. What mood,
or feeling, does the
painting convey to
you? Why?

Teruo picked up a vase of carnations. "These flowers came in four or five
days ago, didn't they?"

"You're right. Five days ago," I said.

"How long will they **keep** if a customer bought them today?" Teruo asked.

"I guess in this weather they'll hold a day or two," I said.

"Then they're old," Teruo almost gasped. "Why, we have fresh ones that last
a week or so in the shop."

"Sure, Teruo. And why should you worry about that?" Tommy said. "You
talk right to the customers, and they'll believe you. 'Our flowers are always
fresh? You bet they are! Just came in a little while ago from the market.'"

Teruo looked at us calmly. "That's a hard thing to say when you know
it isn't true."

"You've got to get it over with sooner or later," I told him. "Everybody has
to do it. You, too, unless you want to lose your job." **4**

4 **Structure: Plot**
What complication
does Teruo
encounter at this
point? Record it on
your **Plot Diagram**.
What difficulties
could it cause for
him?

Monitor Comprehension

In Other Words
keep last

Economic Background
Commercial floral businesses contribute more
than $19 billion to the national economy.
Today many people purchase cut flowers online,
spending more than $990 million a year.

Summarize
What happened during
the couple of weeks
after Teruo was hired?

"I don't think I can say it convincingly again," Teruo said. "I must've said yes forty times already when I didn't know any better. It'll be harder next time."

"You've said it forty times already, so why can't you say yes forty million times more? What's the difference? Remember, Teruo, it's your business to lie," Tommy said.

"I don't like it," Teruo said.

"Do we like it? Do you think we're any different from you?" Tommy asked Teruo. "You're just a **green** kid. You don't know any better, so I don't get **sore**, but you got to play the game when you're in it. You understand, don't you?" **5**

Teruo nodded. For a moment he stood and looked curiously at us for the first time and then went away to water the potted plants.

In the **ensuing** weeks we watched Teruo develop into a slick salesclerk, but for one thing. If a customer forgot to ask about the condition of the flowers, Teruo did splendidly. But if someone should mention about the freshness of the flowers, he wilted right in front of the customer's eyes. Sometimes he would sputter. On other occasions he would stand **gaping speechless**, without a **comeback**. Sometimes, looking embarrassedly at us, he would take the customers to the fresh flowers in the rear and complete the sale. **6**

"Don't do that any more, Teruo," Tommy warned him one afternoon after watching him repeatedly sell the fresh ones. "You know we got plenty of the old stuff in the front. We can't throw all that stuff away. First thing you know the boss'll start losing money and we'll all be thrown out."

"I wish I could sell like you," Teruo said. "Whenever they ask me, 'Is this fresh? How long will it keep?' I lose all sense about selling the stuff and begin to think of the difference between the fresh and the old stuff. Then the trouble begins."

5 Structure: Plot/Make Connections Which of the two salesclerks experiences conflict, and why? Explain how personal connections help you identify with Tommy's or Teruo's attitude.

6 Language/Make Connections When the author writes that Teruo *wilted*, what else does the word remind you of? What kind of personal connection could help you understand why Teruo reacts this way?

Key Vocabulary
ensuing *adj.*, following, resulting

In Other Words
green young and inexperienced
sore angry
gaping speechless with his mouth open, unable to talk
comeback quick reply

"Remember, the boss has to run the shop so he can keep it going," Tommy told him. "When he returns next week, you better not let him see you touch the fresh flowers in the rear."

On the day Mr. Sasaki came back to the shop, we saw something unusual. For the first time I watched Teruo sell old stuff to a customer. I heard the man **plainly** ask him if the flowers would keep good, and very clearly I heard Teruo reply, "Yes, sir. These **flowers'll** keep good." I looked at Tommy, and he winked back. When Teruo came back to make it into a bouquet, he looked as if he had just discovered a snail in his mouth. **7** Mr. Sasaki came back to the rear and

7 **Make Connections**
When have you been reluctant to do something? How does that memory help you understand this description of Teruo?

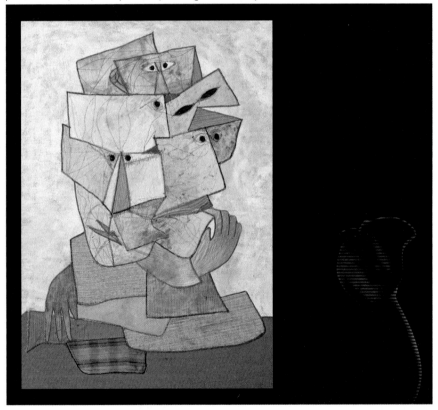

Composed Head, Bona (b. 1926). Tissue and oil on canvas, private collection, Paris, France/Peter Willi/The Bridgeman Art Library.

◄ **Critical Viewing: Conflict**
How does this image suggest conflict?

In Other Words
plainly clearly, directly
flowers'll flowers will

watched him make the bouquet. When Teruo went up front to complete the sale, Mr. Sasaki looked at Tommy and nodded approvingly.

When I went out to the truck to make my last delivery for the day, Teruo followed me. "Gee, I feel rotten," he said to me. "Those flowers I sold won't last longer than tomorrow. I feel lousy. I'm lousy. The people'll get to know my word pretty soon."

"Forget it," I said. "Quit worrying. What's the matter with you?" **8**

"I'm lousy," he said, and went back to the store.

Then one early morning the inevitable happened. While Teruo was selling the fresh flowers in the back to a customer, Mr. Sasaki came in quietly and watched the **transaction**. The boss didn't say anything at the time. All day Teruo looked sick. He didn't know whether to explain to the boss or shut up.

While Teruo was out to lunch, Mr. Sasaki called us aside. "How long has this been going on?" he asked us. He was pretty sore.

"He's been doing it off and on. We told him to quit it," Tommy said. "He says he feels rotten selling the old flowers."

"Old flowers!" snorted Mr. Sasaki. "I'll tell him plenty when he comes back. Old flowers! Maybe you can call them old at the **wholesale market**, but they're not old in a flower shop."

"He feels guilty fooling the customers," Tommy explained. **9**

The boss laughed impatiently. "That's no reason for a businessman."

When Teruo came back, he knew **what was up**. He looked at us for a moment and then went about cleaning the stems of the old flowers.

"Teruo," Mr. Sasaki called.

Teruo approached us as if **steeled** for an attack.

"You've been selling fresh flowers and leaving the old ones go to waste. I can't afford that, Teruo," Mr. Sasaki said. "Why don't

8 Make Connections
Recall a time when you were in a situation like that of the narrator. What would you have advised Teruo?

9 Structure: Plot
How does Tommy explain Teruo's motivation to Mr. Sasaki? What does this suggest about Tommy's role?

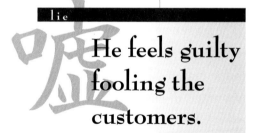

lie
嘘
He feels guilty fooling the customers.

Key Vocabulary
transaction *n.*, purchase by a shopper

In Other Words
wholesale market place where business owners can buy goods to resell to the public
what was up what would probably happen
steeled mentally prepared

you do as you're told? We all sell the flowers in the front. I tell you they're not old in a flower shop. Why can't you sell them?"

"I don't like it, Mr. Sasaki," Teruo said. "When the people ask me if they're fresh, I hate to answer. I feel rotten after selling the old ones."

"Look here, Teruo," Mr. Sasaki said. "I don't want to fire you. You're a good boy, and I know you need a job, but you've got to be a good clerk here or you're going out. Do you get me?"

"I get you," Teruo said.

In the morning we were all at the shop early. I had an eight o'clock delivery, and the others had to rush with a big funeral order. Teruo was there early. "Hello," he greeted us cheerfully, as we came in. He was unusually high-spirited, and I couldn't **account for** it. 🔟 He was there before us and had already filled out the eight o'clock package for me.

He was almost through with the funeral frame, padding it with wet moss and covering it all over with **brake fern**, when Tommy came in. When Mr. Sasaki arrived, Teruo waved his hand and cheerfully went about gathering the flowers for the funeral piece. As he **flitted here and there**, he seemed as if he had forgotten our presence, even the boss. He looked at each vase, sized up the flowers, and then cocked his head at the next one. He did this with great deliberation, as if he were the boss and the last word in the shop. That was all right, but when a customer soon after came in, he swiftly attended him as if he owned all the flowers in the world. When the man asked Teruo if he was getting fresh flowers, without **batting an eye** he escorted the customer into the rear and eventually showed and sold the fresh ones. He did it with so much grace, dignity, and swiftness that we stood around like his **stooges**. 🔟🔟 However, Mr. Sasaki went on with his work as if nothing had happened.

🔟 Access Vocabulary
What does *high-spirited* mean? Find a word in the same paragraph that is close in meaning.

🔟🔟 Structure: Plot
How do Teruo's actions complicate the situation for him and the other workers in the shop?

Monitor Comprehension

Confirm Prediction
Recall the prediction you made about Teruo. How did his actions confirm or challenge your ideas about him?

In Other Words
account for explain
brake fern large leafy plants
flitted here and there quickly moved from
  place to place

batting an eye pausing, hesitating
stooges lowly helpers

Along toward noon Teruo attended his second customer. He fairly ran to greet an old lady who wanted a cheap bouquet around fifty cents for a dinner table. This time he not only went back to the rear for the fresh ones but added three or four extras. To make it more **irritating** for the boss, who was watching every move, Teruo used an extra lot of **maidenhair** because the old lady was appreciative of his art of making bouquets. Tommy and I watched the boss **fuming** inside of his office.

When the old lady went out of the shop, Mr. Sasaki was furious. "You're a blockhead. You have no business sense. What are you doing here?" he said to Teruo. "Are you crazy?"

Teruo looked cheerful enough. "I'm not crazy, Mr. Sasaki," he said. "And I'm not dumb. I just like to do it that way, that's all."

. The boss turned to Tommy and me. "That boy's a **sap**," he said. "**He's got no head.**"

Teruo laughed and walked off to the front with a broom. Mr. Sasaki shook his head. "What's the matter with him? I can't understand him," he said. 🔢

While the boss was out to lunch, Teruo went **on a mad spree**. He waited on three customers at one time, ignoring our presence. It was amazing how he did it. He hurriedly took one customer's order and had him write a birthday greeting for it, jumped to the second customer's side and persuaded her to buy roses because they were the freshest of the lot. She wanted them delivered, so he jotted the address down on the sales book and leaped to the third customer.

"I want to buy that orchid in the window," she stated without deliberation.

"Do you have to have an orchid, madam?"

"No," she said. "But I want something nice for tonight's ball, and I think the orchid will match my dress. Why do you ask?"

🔢 **Make Connections**
How do your own experiences help you make sense of the conflicting moods of Teruo and Mr. Sasaki?

Key Vocabulary
irritating *adj.*, annoying

In Other Words
maidenhair delicate fern
fuming showing his anger
sap fool
He's got no head. He has no business sense.
on a mad spree through a period of rushed activity, as if he were crazy

Florist, 2004, Sara Nowen. Watercolor, collection of the artist.

◁ Critical Viewing: Plot
How would you connect the person and the situation in this image with the characters and events in the story?

"If I were you I wouldn't buy that orchid," he told her. "It won't keep. I could sell it to you and **make a profit**, but I don't want to do that and spoil your evening. Come to the back, madam, and I'll show you some of the nicest gardenias in the market today. We call them Belmont and they're fresh today."

He came to the rear with the lady. We watched him pick out three of the biggest gardenias and make them into a corsage. When the lady went out with her package, a little boy about eleven years old came in and wanted a twenty-five-cent bouquet for his mother's birthday. Teruo waited on the boy. He was out in the front, and we saw him pick out a dozen of the two-dollar-a-dozen roses and give them to the kid.

Tommy **nudged me**. "If he was the boss, he couldn't do those things," he said.

"In the first place," I said, "I don't think he could be a boss."

"What do you think?" Tommy said. "Is he crazy? Is he trying **to get himself fired**?"

"I don't know," I said. 🔢

When Mr. Sasaki returned, Teruo was waiting on another customer, a young lady.

🔢 Make Connections
Based on what you know, what do you think Teruo is really trying to do? Why do you think that is?

In Other Words
make a profit have money left after paying the costs of running a business
nudged me gave me a gentle push
to get himself fired to lose his job

"Did Teruo eat yet?" Mr. Sasaki asked Tommy.

"No, he won't go. He says he's not hungry today," Tommy said.

We watched Teruo talking to the young lady. The boss shook his head. Then it came. Teruo came back to the rear and picked out a dozen of the very fresh white roses and took them out to the lady.

"Aren't they lovely!" we heard her exclaim.

We watched him come back, take down a box, place several maidenhairs and **asparagus fern**, place the roses neatly inside, sprinkle a few drops, and then give it to her. We watched him thank her, and we noticed her smile and thanks. The girl walked out.

Mr. Sasaki ran excitedly to the front. "Teruo! She forgot to pay!"

Teruo stopped the boss on the way out. "Wait, Mr. Sasaki," he said. "I gave it to her."

"What!" the boss cried indignantly.

"She came in just to look around and see the flowers. She likes pretty roses. Don't you think she's wonderful?"

"What's the matter with you?" the boss said. "Are you crazy? What did she buy?"

"Nothing, I tell you," Teruo said. "I gave it to her because she admired it, and she's pretty enough to deserve beautiful things, and I liked her."

"You're fired! Get out!" Mr. Sasaki spluttered. "Don't come back to the store again."

"And I gave her fresh ones, too," Teruo said.

Mr. Sasaki rolled out several bills from his pocketbook. "Here's your **wages** for this week. Now get out," he said.

"I don't want it," Teruo said. "You keep it and buy some more flowers."

"Here, take it. Get out," Mr. Sasaki said. **14**

14 **Structure: Plot / Confirm Prediction**
When do you think the climax of the story occurs? How is it a moment of truth? Mark the event on your **Plot Diagram**. Now, recall the prediction you made about who would change— Teruo or Mr. Sasaki. How do the characters' actions confirm or challenge your prediction?

angry

What's the matter with you? . . . Are you crazy?

In Other Words
asparagus fern feathery plants
wages payment for doing the job

Teruo took the **bills** and rang up the cash register. "All right, I'll go now. I feel fine. I'm happy. Thanks to you." He waved his hand to Mr. Sasaki. **"No hard feelings."**

On the way out Teruo remembered our presence. He looked back.

"Goodbye. Good luck," he said cheerfully to Tommy and me.

He walked out of the shop with his shoulders straight, head high, and whistling. He did not come back to see us again. **15** ❖

15 Structure: Plot
How would Teruo and Mr. Sasaki each describe the way things worked out at the end? Is the resolution a happy ending for either of them? Explain.

ANALYZE **Say It with Flowers**

1. **Recall and Interpret** What decision does Teruo make? What do you think was the motivation for his action? Be sure to cite evidence from the text.

2. **Vocabulary** How does Teruo maintain his sense of **integrity** on the job?

3. **Analyze Structure: Plot** What do you think is the climax, or turning point, of the story? Support your answer with evidence from the text.

4. **Focus Strategy Make Connections** Choose one of the connections you recorded on your **Plot Diagram**. Describe the connection you made, and tell a partner how your previous experience helped you understand the event.

Return to the Text

Reread and Write Reread the story. Then write a letter to a future employer as if you are Teruo. In the letter, explain why you left the flower shop and why this new employer should hire you.

Key Vocabulary
• **integrity** *n.*, strong sense of right and wrong, honesty

In Other Words
bills paper money, dollars
No hard feelings. There's no anger about it.

BEFORE READING The Journey

poem by Mary Oliver

Reading Strategies

- Plan and Monitor
- Determine Importance
- Make Inferences
- Ask Questions
- ▶ **Make Connections**
- Synthesize
- Visualize

Analyze Language: Metaphor and Extended Metaphor

Figurative language is language that expresses ideas beyond the literal, or ordinary, meaning of words. One type of figurative language is a **metaphor**, in which a writer compares two unlike things by pointing out an important similarity between them. An **extended metaphor** is a comparison that is made throughout a whole work or a large part of it.

Look Into the Text

> One day you finally knew
> what you had to do, and began,
> though the voices around you
> kept shouting
> their bad advice—
> though the whole house
> began to tremble
> and you felt the old tug
> at your ankles.

This is the start of an extended metaphor.

What do you think the tug might be?

Personification gives human traits to things that are not human.

Focus Strategy ▶ Make Connections

When you make connections to a poem, you notice how certain details remind you of your own experiences or compare with your own way of looking at life. These connections make the text clearer and more personal for you.

HOW TO MAKE CONNECTIONS

Focus Strategy

1. As you read "The Journey," notice the details that stand out to you.

2. Reread the poem. Mark notes about the details on a self-stick note. Then make connections:
   - What does this detail make me think of?
   - What were my feelings when I read this part?
   - What other texts does this remind me of?

3. Reflect on how each connection helped you understand or appreciate the text.

> One day you
> finally knew
> what you had
> to do, and began,
> though the voices around you
> kept shouting their bad
> advice—

This reminds me of Teruo in "Say It with Flowers." He realized he had to do what was right for him.

Connect Across Texts

In "Say It with Flowers," Teruo's moment of truth leads him to decisive action. In this poem, the speaker also makes a decision.

The Journey
by Mary Oliver

The Ramble, 2005, Ross Penhall. Oil on canvas, courtesy of Caldwell Snyder Gallery, San Francisco, California.

◀ **Critical Viewing: Effect**
What mood does *The Ramble* create? If you were walking along this path, how would you feel?

One day you finally knew
what you had to do, and began,
though the voices around you
kept shouting

5   their bad advice—
though the whole house
began to tremble
and you felt the old tug
at your ankles.

10 "Mend my life!"
each voice cried.
But you didn't stop.
You knew what you had to do,
though the wind pried

15 with its stiff fingers **1**
at the very foundations—
though their melancholy
was terrible. **2**

It was already late

20 enough, and a wild night,
and the road full of fallen
branches and stones.
But little by little,
as you left their voices behind,

25 the stars began to burn
through the sheets of clouds, **3**
and there was a new voice,
which you slowly
recognized as your own,

30 that kept you company
as you strode deeper and deeper
into the world, **4**
determined to do
the only thing you could do—

35 determined to save
the only life you could save.

1 Language: Metaphor and Extended Metaphor
How does the speaker compare the wind to a person?

2 Make Connections
Recall a time when "you finally knew what you had to do." How did others react? How does remembering others' reactions help you understand this moment in the poem?

3 Make Connections
How does any experience you've had leaving voices behind make the poem more personal?

4 Language: Metaphor and Extended Metaphor
To stride means to walk by taking long steps. How might striding "deeper and deeper into the world" be a metaphor for a way of living?

Key Vocabulary
melancholy *n.*, sadness

In Other Words
"Mend my life!" "Rescue me!"

ANALYZE The Journey

1. **Recall and Interpret** What is the author comparing to "the sheets of clouds"? Which lines of the poem tell you this?

2. **Vocabulary** Whose **melancholy** is the speaker referring to? How do you know?

3. **Analyze Language: Metaphor and Extended Metaphor** Think about the poet's use of the words *voices* and *voice* (lines 3, 11, 24, and 27). How does the repetition of these words help create an extended metaphor in the poem?

4. **Focus Strategy Make Connections** Review the connections you made to the details of the poem. Which connections helped you understand the themes, or messages, of the poem? Share your ideas with a partner.

Return to the Text

Reread and Write What discovery does the speaker make in a moment of truth? Reread to find examples of what led to this discovery. Then write a paragraph to share your conclusion.

About the Poet

Mary Oliver (1935–) is a Pulitzer prize-winning poet. Growing up in Ohio, she spent much of her time observing and walking in nature. Her poems are inspired by images from her daily walks.

EQ What Do People Discover in a Moment of Truth?

Critical Thinking

EQ 1. Interpret What discoveries do Teruo and the speaker in "The Journey" make? How are those discoveries likely to change each of them? Refer to details in both texts.

2. Analyze Look again at the **Anticipation Guide** on page 458. How do the statements apply to the characters in the story and the speaker in the poem?

3. Compare In what ways are Teruo and the speaker in "The Journey" similar? In what ways are they different? Give examples from both texts.

4. Speculate Imagine that Teruo is the boss at another flower shop. What would he say to his employees? How successful would the flower shop be? Explain.

EQ 5. Synthesize Both Teruo and the speaker in the poem are expected to **harmonize** their values with other people's values. Think about your own ideas and values. Have you ever experienced a situation when your ideas were different from someone else's? What did you do?

Write About Literature

Personal Mission Statement Businesses or groups often have a mission statement that they use. This is a sentence that expresses the values of the group, such as "We are committed to making a positive difference in education." How might the characters in "Say It with Flowers" and the speaker in "The Journey" express their values? Reread the selections to determine the values each lives by. Then write a brief mission statement for each.

Key Vocabulary Review

Oral Review Work with a partner. Use these words to complete the paragraph.

disarm	inquisitive	melancholy
ensuing	integrity	transaction
harmonize	irritating	

The teacher assigned Maylin to be partners with Juan for a class project. Maylin's personality was more __(1)__ than Juan's. She asked a lot of questions. At first, Juan thought Maylin's questions could be __(2)__ and annoying, but both Maylin and Juan had too much __(3)__ and pride to stop working together. In the __(4)__ weeks, Juan and Maylin stopped arguing and agreed to __(5)__ their ideas for the project even though they had different views. The project became so interesting to work on that Maylin's creativity began to __(6)__ Juan. He felt __(7)__ and unhappy when the __(8)__ of their partnership ended.

Writing Application Think about a time when you had to consider your **integrity**. Write a paragraph telling about the situation. Use at least four Key Vocabulary words.

Read with Ease: Phrasing

Assess your reading fluency with the passage in the Reading Handbook, p. 811. Then complete the self-check below.

1. I did/did not pause appropriately for punctuation and phrases.

2. My words correct per minute: _____

Use Adjectives to Elaborate

Adjectives are describing words. Use adjectives to elaborate, or tell more, about people, places, and things.

Some adjectives describe the way someone or something looks, sounds, smells, tastes, or feels.

The flower shop sells **gorgeous**, **colorful** bouquets.

The flowers fill the shop with a **fragrant** scent.

Some flowers are **edible**. They taste **spicy**.

I touch the rose's **smooth**, **silky** petals.

The clerk feels **delighted** that we like his shop.

Use adjectives to make your writing more interesting. Choose lively, descriptive adjectives to elaborate. Which sentence provides the most detail?

I bought a rose.

I bought a **red** rose.

I bought a **deep**, **crimson** rose.

Oral Practice (1–5) With a partner, look at one of the illustrations in the selections you just read. Describe the art in five sentences. Use at least one adjective in each sentence to elaborate and add detail.

Written Practice (6–10) Rewrite the paragraph to add detail. Add adjectives that appeal to the senses.

The __(6)__ lady wants to buy a bouquet. The __(7)__ flowers are in the case. She picks some __(8)__ gardenias. They have a __(9)__ smell. The bouquet is __(10)__!

Evaluate

Group Talk In a group, evaluate the behavior of the characters in "Say It with Flowers." Did the characters do the right thing? Give your evaluation and support it with examples.

Compare Characters' Motivations

A good story has characters with rich, realistic personalities. Motivation is one aspect of a character's personality. **Character motivation** is the reason a character does what he or she does. Over the course of a story, the characters' motivations may become clearer, or even change.

In the beginning of "Say It with Flowers," Mr. Sasaki and Teruo are both motivated by what they think is best for the flower shop.

- Mr. Sasaki: "Another clerk and we'll be all set for any kind of business."
- Teruo: "You fellows teach me something about this business and I'll be grateful."

Over time, different motivations emerge for each character. Refer to the **Plot Diagram** you constructed for the story. Then discuss the following questions with a partner.

1. What early story events show the motivations for Teruo? For Mr. Sasaki? How do their motivations differ?
2. How does each character's motivation affect the climax of the story?
3. Is there another way that Teruo and Mr. Sasaki could have resolved their differences? How?

Synonyms

A **synonym** is a word or phrase that means about the same thing as another word. For example, the word *result* is a synonym for the word *consequence*. The word *deal* is a synonym for the word ***transaction*** .

Work with a partner. Use a thesaurus to find a synonym for each underlined word below.

1. The melancholy child looked out the window at the rainy weather.
2. Newspaper reporters must be inquisitive and persistent.
3. The ensuing show will be much more interesting than the one we're watching now.
4. My neighbor's dog's yapping is so irritating!
5. We get along well because our opinions always harmonize.

Public Service Announcement

Social Studies: Values Public service announcements, or PSAs, are commercial-length television pieces that promote strong values. In a small group, develop a PSA to deliver to the class.

1. **Choose a Value** What value would your group like to see more of or promote?
2. **Review** Watch and discuss a few TV PSAs.
3. **Write a Script** Develop a fifteen-second PSA for your value. Show your reasoning and give evidence for supporting the value.
4. **Discuss** Discuss the PSAs as a class. How effective are the reasoning and evidence in it?

📖 **Language and Learning Handbook**, p. 750

Write a Review

A review is a short essay in which a writer gives his or her opinion of a text or performance. Use the steps below to write a one-paragraph review of one of the selections from this unit.

1. **Prewrite** Choose the selection you're going to review. Then create a list of the things you think the author did and did not do well. Think about the details the author uses in the selection, and note the ones that stood out to you.
2. **Draft** Write a clear topic sentence that sums up your ideas about the story. Support it with examples from the text.
3. **Revise** What other ideas could you use to support your opinion? What ideas could you cut?
4. **Edit and Proofread** Check carefully for proper spelling, grammar, and punctuation.

5. **Publish** Print a copy of your paragraph and share it with the class.

Model

> I like the poem "The Journey" by Mary Oliver because she uses personal and detailed language. — **Topic sentence**
> I think the writer makes the poem feel like it is my story because she uses *you* throughout the poem. I also like the way the writer uses detailed language about nature. For example, "the wind pried," "a wild night," and — **Examples**
> "the stars began to burn." Through her use of personal and detailed language, I feel like I can relate to and understand the poem. — **Strong conclusion**

📖 **Writing Handbook**, p. 832

1

2

3

Inside a Pharmacy

In a pharmacy, pharmacists dispense prescription medications. A pharmacy may also have counters or shelves where medical supplies and nonprescription drugs are sold.

Jobs in a Pharmacy

Most pharmacy-related jobs require special training and certification. Some entry-level positions, such as a cashier, require no previous work experience.

Job	Responsibilities	Education/Training Required
Cashier **1**	• Receives money from customer purchases and makes correct change • Makes sure money in drawer matches sales receipts • May stock shelves with merchandise	• On-the-job training • Basic math skills
Pharmacy Technician **2**	• Assists pharmacist in filling prescriptions and pricing medications • Prepares insurance claim forms and may perform stock inventory	• Two years of college • Pharmacy technician program may be required • On-the-job training
Pharmacist **3**	• Distributes drugs prescribed by doctors • Provides information about medications • Keeps records of patients' prescriptions	• Degree from a college of pharmacy • License to practice pharmacy • Training in lab work and research

Fill out a Job Application

Practice filling out a job application for a part-time job as a cashier at a pharmacy.

1. Make sure you have all the required information you will need to fill out the application. You will need: personal contact information, social security number, names of three adult references, and your education and job history.

2. Fill out the application neatly, using blue or black ink.

3. Trade your completed application with a partner. Check each other's work for accuracy. Save the information in a professional career portfolio.

myNGconnect.com

🔊 Learn more about working in a pharmacy.

🔊 Download a form to evaluate whether you would like to work in this field.

🔊 Download a practice application form.

Make Word Connections

Imagine you see a magazine cover with a photo of a family and a headline that describes how happy the family is about moving into their *domicile*. You may not know the meaning of *domicile*, but you can guess that it means something relating to a place to live. But what if you really wanted to understand the meaning of the word?

When you learn a new word, like *domicile*, you can understand how it is different from similar words by relating it to its synonyms. You can find synonyms (and antonyms) in a print or digital **thesaurus**.

Explore Word Relationships

With a partner, read the Thesaurus Entry for *domicile*. Then answer the questions below.

1. What synonyms describe specific types of homes?

2. Which synonyms describe size?

3. Which synonyms show ownership?

4. Which synonyms refer to general types of homes?

5. Is *domicile* a general or specific type of home?

Thesaurus Entry

> **domicile** *They lived in a wooden domicile: n.* place to live; abode, apartment, castle, co-op, condo, condominium, crib, dwelling, home, house, legal residence, mansion, residence, roost

Put the Strategy to Use

When you learn a new word, relate it to others you know that are like it. You can then improve your understanding of the word, just as you did with *domicile*.

1. Determine the meaning of the word.

2. Relate it to other words that you know. Look it up in a thesaurus.

3. Group the synonyms according to what aspect of the word they describe.

4. Refine your understanding of the new word as a result of relating it to synonyms.

TRY IT ▶ Now work with a partner to refine your understanding of the word *hospitable*. Follow the steps above and describe how this strategy improved your understanding of the word *hospitable*.

☙ Reading Handbook, p. 781

EQ ## What Do People Discover in a Moment of Truth?
See how people decide what is right.

Make a Connection

Quickwrite In the following selections, the main characters struggle with their sense of responsibility and duty. They must decide what is the right thing to do. When have you had a moment of truth about doing the right thing? Write a paragraph describing the situation.

Learn Key Vocabulary

Pronounce each word and learn its meaning. You may also want to look up the definitions in the Glossary.

• Academic Vocabulary

Key Words	Examples
destiny (**des**-tu-nē) *noun* ▶ pages 492, 496, 499	**Destiny** is a predetermined course of events that are thought to be out of our own control. Lee believed it was his **destiny** to win the championship. *Synonym:* fate; *Antonym:* accident
indelible (in-**de**-lu-bul) *adjective* ▶ page 491	An **indelible** mark is one that is lasting and cannot be easily removed. The **indelible** ink stain ruined his new shirt. *Synonym:* permanent; *Antonym:* temporary
indifference (in-**di**-furns) *noun* ▶ page 487	When you are not interested in a situation, you may show **indifference**. She showed **indifference** to her grades by never doing homework. *Synonym:* disinterest; *Antonym:* care
inflexible (in-**flek**-su-bul) *adjective* ▶ page 488	An **inflexible** object cannot easily be bent out of shape. *Synonyms:* rigid, firm; *Antonyms:* bendable, soft
poised (poizd) *adjective* ▶ page 488	When something is **poised**, it is held ready to begin. The runners stood **poised**, waiting for the race to begin. *Synonyms:* ready, prepared
• **priority** (pri-**or**-u-tē) *noun* ▶ pages 493, 499	You give **priority** to a task or idea that is most important to you. Which takes **priority**, your loyalty to your family or to your friends? *Synonym:* importance; *Antonym:* unimportance
• **regime** (rā-**zhēm**) *noun* ▶ pages 487, 493	A **regime** is a group that controls a government. People who live in a country with harsh rulers may want a more democratic **regime**. *Synonyms:* leadership, government
virtue (**vur**-chü) *noun* ▶ pages 497, 498	Something that has **virtue** has benefits. Rain may spoil a picnic, but it has the **virtue** of making plants grow. *Synonym:* honor; *Antonym:* evil

Practice the Words Work with a partner and use the **Word Square** to practice using each Key Vocabulary word.

Word Square

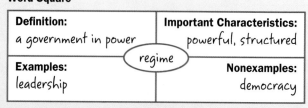

Definition: a government in power	Important Characteristics: powerful, structured
Examples: leadership	Nonexamples: democracy

regime

BEFORE READING Just Lather, That's All

short story by Hernando Téllez

Reading Strategies

- Plan and Monitor
- Determine Importance
- Make Inferences
- Ask Questions
- ▶ **Make Connections**
- Synthesize
- Visualize

Analyze Structure: Suspense

Suspense is the growing curiosity, tension, or excitement readers feel as they read. Authors might create suspense by putting characters in tense or risky situations. They also build suspense by providing just enough information to keep readers guessing as to what might happen next, slowly revealing one detail and then another.

Look Into the Text

The author doesn't tell the characters' names yet.

These clues about one of the characters reveal the tense situation.

> He said nothing when he entered. I was passing the best of my razors back and forth on a leather strop. When I recognized him I started to tremble. But he didn't notice. Hoping to conceal my emotion, I continued sharpening the razor. I tested it on the meat of my thumb, and then held it up to the light. At that moment he took off the bullet-studded belt and the gun holster that dangled from it. He hung it up on a wall hook and placed his military cap over it. Then he turned to me, loosening the knot of his tie, and said, "It's hot as hell. Give me a shave." He sat in the chair.

The author slowly reveals details about the characters and the setting.

What additional detail is uncovered in the dialogue?

Focus Strategy ▶ Make Connections

By making connections as you read, you build a better understanding of the story. With connections, you can explain story events in your own words.

Focus Strategy ▶ Make Connections

Focus Strategy

1. Copy the **Double-Entry Journal** below. Use it to keep track of details and events in the story, recording them in the journal as you read. Be sure to include the page number.

2. Use what you know to explain the events of the story in your own words.

Double-Entry Journal

Details and Events	My Explanation
1. "When I recognized him I started to tremble." page 486	The narrator is scared of the man who walks in.
2.	

Hernando Téllez
(1908–1966)

Téllez was known for capturing the history and the emotion of Colombia in his writing.

In the South American country of Colombia, the years between the late 1940s and early 1960s are known as *La Violencia*, or "the violent times," and with good reason. Hundreds of thousands of people died in a long period of conflict between political groups.

Hernando Téllez saw this situation first hand. He was born and lived in Bogotá, the capital of Colombia. He became a journalist at an early age and for many years wrote for several of Colombia's most popular publications. In the early 1940s, his writings about the country's political situation earned him a wide readership. Four years later he became a member of the Colombian Senate.

In 1950, Téllez published a collection of short stories called *Cenizas al viento*, or *Ashes to the Wind*. These stories deal with difficult choices people face and the moments of truth that occur in everyday life. He illustrates the struggle of making choices in his most famous story, "Just Lather, That's All." Téllez offers no easy answers, and the story endures today as a classic tale of conscience in politically uncertain times.

myNGconnect.com

- Discover important facts about Colombia.
- Listen to a radio program about *La Violencia* and its influence on Colombian writers.

Just Lather, That's All

by Hernando Téllez

Barber Shop, 2006, Michael and Tammy Rice. Digital photograph, Twisted Tree Photography.

▲ **Critical Viewing: Setting** Describe the details in the photograph. What are your impressions of the setting?

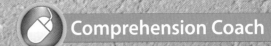
Comprehension Coach

He said nothing when he entered. I was passing the best of my razors back and forth on a **leather strop**. When I recognized him I started to tremble. **1** But he didn't notice. Hoping to conceal my emotion, I continued sharpening the razor. I tested it on **the meat** of my thumb, and then held it up to the light. At that moment he took off the bullet-studded belt and the gun **holster** that dangled from it. He hung it up on a wall hook and placed his military cap over it. Then he turned to me, loosening the knot of his tie, and said, "It's hot as hell. Give me a shave." He sat in the chair.

I estimated he had a four-day growth of beard. Four days had been taken up by the latest expedition in search of our rebel troops. His face seemed reddened, burned by the sun. Carefully, I began to prepare the soap. I cut off a few slices, dropped them into the cup, mixed in a bit of warm water, and began to stir with the brush. Immediately the foam began to rise.

"The other men in the group must have this much beard, too," he said. I continued stirring the lather.

"But we did all right, you know," he continued. "We got the main ones. We brought back some dead, and we've got some others still alive. But pretty soon they'll all be dead."

"How many did you catch?" I asked.

"Fourteen. We had to go pretty deep into the woods to find them. But we'll get even. Not one of them will come out of this alive. Not one." **2**

He leaned back on the chair when he saw me with the lather-covered brush in my hand.

1 Structure: Suspense
What feeling has the author created after the first three sentences? Tell how the author does this.

2 Structure: Suspense
What mood is created by the dialogue between the two men? What details contribute to this feeling?

In Other Words
leather strop thick leather band used for sharpening razors
the meat the soft, fleshy part
holster case or holder

I still had to put the sheet on him. No doubt about it, I was nervous. I took a sheet out of a drawer and knotted it around my customer's neck. He wouldn't stop talking. He probably thought that I was on the side of the current **regime**. 3

"The town must have learned a lesson from what we did the other day," he said.

"Yes," I replied, securing the knot at the base of his dark, sweaty neck.

"That was a **fine show**, eh?"

"Very good," I answered, turning back for the brush. The man closed his eyes with a gesture of fatigue and sat waiting for the cool **caress** of the soap. I had never had him so close to me. The day he ordered the whole town to file into the patio of the school to see the four rebels hanging there, I came face to face with him for an instant. But the sight of the **mutilated** bodies kept me from noticing the face of the man who had directed it all, the face I was now about to **take into my hands**.

It was not an unpleasant face, certainly. And the beard, which made him seem a bit older than he was, didn't look bad at all. His name was Torres. Captain Torres.

I began to apply the first layer of soap. With his eyes closed, he continued. "Without any effort I could go straight to sleep," he said, "but there's plenty to do this afternoon."

I stopped the lathering and asked with pretended **indifference**, "A **firing squad**?"

"Something like that, but a little slower."

I got on with the job of lathering his beard. My hands started trembling again. The man could not possibly realize it, which was lucky for me. But I wished that he had never come. Chances were good that one of our men had seen him enter. And with an enemy under my own roof, I felt responsible.

Not one of them will come out of this alive.

3 **Structure: Suspense**
What events has the author revealed so far in the story? What are you left wondering about?

Monitor Comprehension

Explain
What is the barber's reaction to Captain Torres? Why?

Key Vocabulary
- **regime** *n.*, government
  indifference *n.*, disinterest, lack of concern

In Other Words
fine show good performance
caress gentle touch
mutilated damaged
take into my hands be responsible for
firing squad group of soldiers set to kill a prisoner

I **would have to shave that beard like any other one,** carefully, gently, like that of any customer, taking pains to see that no single **pore emitted** a drop of blood. Making sure that the little tufts of hair did not lead the blade astray. Seeing that his skin ended up clean, soft, and healthy, so that I could pass the back of my hand over it without feeling a hair. Yes, I was secretly a rebel, but I was also a **conscientious** barber, and proud of my professional skills. And this four-day growth of beard was a **fitting challenge**. **4**

I took the razor, opened up the two protective arms, exposed the blade, and began the job, from one of the sideburns downward. The razor responded beautifully. His beard was **inflexible** and hard, not too long, but thick. Bit by bit the skin emerged. The razor rasped along, making its customary sound as **fluffs** of lather mixed with bits of hair gathered along the blade. **5** I paused a moment to clean it, then took up the strop again to sharpen the razor, because I'm a barber who does things properly.

The man, who had kept his eyes closed, opened them now, removed one of his hands from under the sheet, felt the spot on his face where the soap had been cleared off, and said, "Come to the school today at six o'clock."

"The same thing as the other day?" I asked horrified.

"It could be better," he replied.

"What do you plan to do?"

"I don't know yet. But we'll amuse ourselves."

Once more he leaned back and closed his eyes. I approached him with the razor **poised**.

"Do you plan to punish them all?" I asked **timidly**.

"All."

4 Structure:
Suspense
What do you discover about the barber? How does this discovery build suspense?

5 Access Vocabulary
What clues in this sentence help you understand the meaning of the word *rasped*?

Key Vocabulary
inflexible *adj.*, unbending, rigid, firm
poised *adj.*, held ready or in position

In Other Words
pore tiny opening or channel in the skin
emitted gave out
conscientious careful, thoughtful
fitting challenge good test of my skills
fluffs small, light piles
timidly shyly

The soap was drying on his face. I had to hurry. In the mirror I looked toward the street. It was the same as ever. There was the grocery store with two or three customers in it. I glanced at the clock. It was two-twenty in the afternoon.

The razor continued on its downward stroke. Now from the other sideburn down. A thick, blue beard. He should have let it grow like some poets or priests do. It would look good on him. A lot of people wouldn't recognize him. That would be just as well, I thought, as I attempted to cover the neck area smoothly. There, for sure, the razor had to be handled skillfully, since the hair, although softer, grew into little swirls. It was a curly beard. One of the tiny pores could be opened up and let out a tiny **pearl** of blood. A good barber like me takes pride in never allowing this to happen to a client. **6**

In the Barbershop, 1934, Ilya Bolotowsky. Smithsonian American Art Museum, Washington, D.C.

6 **Make Connections**
The narrator refers to himself as a *conscientious* and *good* barber. Note these details in your **Journal**, and explain why these details are important.

◁ **Critical Viewing: Setting**
How does this setting compare to the setting of the story?

In Other Words
pearl drop

And this was a very important client. How many of us had he ordered shot? How many of us had he ordered mutilated? It was better not to think about it. Torres did not know that I was his enemy. He did not know it, and neither did the others. It was a secret shared by very few, **precisely** so that I could inform the rebels what Torres was doing in the town and what he planned to do each time he went hunting for rebels. So it was going to be very difficult to explain that I had him right in my hands and let him go peacefully, alive, and with a clean shave.

The beard was now almost completely gone. He seemed younger, less burdened by years than when he had arrived. I suppose this always happens with men who visit barber shops. Under the stroke of my razor, Torres looked like a new man. After all, I am a good barber, the best in the town, if I say so myself. **7**

A little more lather here, under his chin, on his Adam's apple, on this big vein. How hot it is getting! Torres must be sweating as much as I. But he is not afraid. He is a calm man, who is not even thinking about what he was going to do with the prisoners that afternoon. I, on the other hand, shaving his skin with this razor but trying to avoid **drawing blood**, can't even think clearly.

Curse the hour he entered my shop! I'm a revolutionary but not a murderer. And how easy it would be to kill him. He deserves it. Or does he? No! Why should I make the sacrifice of becoming a murderer? What is gained by it? Nothing. Others come along and still others, and the first ones kill the second ones, and then these kill the next ones, and so on, until everything is a sea of blood. I could cut this throat like so—*zip! zip!* I wouldn't give him time to complain, and with his eyes closed he wouldn't see the shine of the razor or the **gleam** in my eyes. **8**

It was a secret shared by very few.

7 Make Connections
When have you read, seen, or heard about a character or real person like the narrator? How does this help you understand the narrator? Make notes in your **Journal**.

8 Language/ Structure: Suspense
The author uses *stream of consciousness*, writing that imitates a character's thought process. How is this writing different from the other paragraphs on the page?

Monitor Comprehension

Confirm Prediction
Did you predict the barber's reaction? Explain.

In Other Words
precisely exactly
drawing blood cutting the skin until it bleeds
Curse the hour I regret the time
gleam glow

But I'm trembling like a real murderer. Out of his neck a gush of blood would spout onto the sheet, on the chair, on my hands, on the floor. I would have to close the door. And the blood would keep inching along the floor, warm, **indelible**, uncontainable, until it reached the street, like a little red river. 9

9 Language
A **simile** compares two unlike things using the words *like* and *as*. Explain the simile in this paragraph.

Throes of Progress: Quiet Invasions, 2005, Jacqueline Moses. Oil and phototransfers on canvas, private collection.

⬛ Critical Viewing: Effect Think about the title and look closely at the details in this painting. What contrasts do you notice?

Key Vocabulary
  indelible *adj.*, lasting or permanent

I'm sure that one solid stroke, one deep **incision**, would prevent any pain. He wouldn't suffer. But what would I do with the body? Where would I hide it? I would have to flee, leave all I have behind, and seek shelter far, far away. But they would follow until they caught me.

"The murderer of Captain Torres!" they would say. "He slit his throat while he was shaving him. What a coward!"

But people on the other side of the conflict would say, "He is the **avenger of** our people. A name to remember. (And here they would mention my name.) He was the town barber. No one knew he was defending our cause."

And so, which will it be? Murderer or hero? My **destiny** depends on the edge of this blade. I can turn my hand a bit more, press a little harder on the razor, and sink it in. The skin would **give way** like silk, like rubber, like the leather strop. There is nothing more tender than human skin and the blood is always there, ready to pour forth. A blade like this cannot fail. It is my best. 🔟

But I don't want to be a murderer, no sir. You came to me for a shave. And I perform my work honorably. I don't want blood on my hands. Just lather, that's all. You are an executioner, and I am only a barber. Each person has **his own place in the scheme of things**. That's what is right. Each to his own place.

His chin was now clean and smooth. The man sat up and

Untitled, 1986, Jean-Charles Blais. Oil and collage on panel, Musée Cantini, Marseille, France, Giraudon/The Bridgeman Art Library.

🔟 **Make Connections**
Describe the barber's dilemma, or struggle. How does this relate to any other situations you have read about or seen?

◀ **Critical Viewing: Effect**
What does this image suggest about how the barber feels?

Key Vocabulary
destiny *n.*, predetermined course of events that are thought to be out of our own control, fate

In Other Words
incision thin cut
avenger of one who took revenge for
give way cut open easily
his own place in the scheme of things
a specific job to do for society

looked at himself in the mirror. He rubbed his hands over his skin and felt it fresh, like new.

"Thanks," he said. He gathered his belt, his pistol, and his cap. I must have been very pale; my shirt felt soaked. Torres finished adjusting his belt buckle and straightened his pistol in the holster. After automatically smoothing down his hair, he put on his cap. From his pants pocket, he took out several coins to pay for the shave. Then he turned to go. In the doorway, he paused for a moment. Turning to me, he said, "They told me that you would kill me. I came to find out. But it isn't easy to kill someone. You can take my word for it." **11** ❖

11 Structure: Suspense

Irony is when the opposite of a reader's expectations occurs. What is ironic about the story's ending?

ANALYZE Just Lather, That's All

1. **Explain** In the end, does the barber give greater **priority** to his political beliefs or his own sense of right and wrong? What reason does he give for his decision?

2. **Vocabulary** What kind of **regime** do you think the barber prefers in power?

3. **Analyze Structure: Suspense** At which points in the story did you feel the most tension or suspense? What details helped to build the suspense? List at least three events in the story that were suspenseful. Explain, using details from the story.

4. **Focus Strategy Make Connections** Review your **Double-Entry Journal**. Pick an event that you marked, and share your explanation of the event with a partner. Tell what connection you made to that event and how it helped you understand the story.

Return to the Text

Reread and Write Reread pages 491–493. Then write a paragraph from Captain Torres's point of view to show what his thoughts might have been in his moment of truth.

Key Vocabulary
• **priority** *n.*, importance

BEFORE READING **The Woman Who Was Death**

myth retold by Josepha Sherman

Reading Strategies

· Plan and Monitor
· Determine Importance
· Make Inferences
· Ask Questions
▶ **Make Connections**
· Synthesize
· Visualize

Analyze World Literature: Myth

A **myth** is a traditional story told to explain natural events, such as the creation of the world. These stories usually involve gods, goddesses, or heroes, and often draw attention to a life lesson. In a myth, nonhuman things may be personified, or given human qualities. The origins, or beginnings, of myths are usually unknown since the stories were told and retold over time, not written down. Myths are strongly linked to the values, beliefs, or experiences of a particular culture.

Most cultures have creation myths. Why do you think these stories are passed down over time?

Look Into the Text

In the day of the beginning, Lord Brahma created the earth and all that lived upon it: plant, animal, human.

One thing only did Brahma not create, and that was death. And so the created ones lived and thrived and multiplied till all the lands and seas were crowded. Famine came, and illness, yet there was no escape from pain. And the earth itself groaned beneath the weight of it.

What is personified in the last sentence?

Focus Strategy ▶ Make Connections

When you read a myth or other traditional literature, you use your personal experiences and what you already know to make the writing of the past more relevant.

HOW TO MAKE CONNECTIONS

Focus Strategy

1. As you read, mark the text of the myth with self-stick notes. Think about your experiences, other texts you've read, and what you know about the world to make connections. Use one note for each connection you make.

Famine came, and illness, yet there was no escape from pain.

This reminds me of an article I read about famine in Africa.

2. Use the connections to help you explain the ideas and main lesson in this myth and how they might apply to life today.

The connection helps me understand just how bad things might have been.

THE WOMAN WHO WAS DEATH

A Myth from India   RETOLD BY JOSEPHA SHERMAN

Connect Across Texts

In "Just Lather, That's All," the narrator must decide whether to take action. In this myth, a woman discovers the true purpose of her actions.

Lotus, 2000, Joel Nakamura. Acrylic on copper panel, private collection.

In the day of the beginning, Lord Brahma created the earth and all that lived upon it: plant, animal, human.

One thing only did Brahma not create, and that was death. And so the created ones lived and thrived and multiplied till all the lands and seas were crowded. **Famine** came, and illness, yet there was no escape from pain. And **the earth itself groaned beneath the weight upon it**. **1**

When Lord Brahma saw this suffering, he cried out in sorrow, and created from himself a woman, skin and hair

1 World Literature: Myth
Who do you think Lord Brahma is? What do his actions show you about the beliefs of the culture from which this myth comes?

◀ **Critical Viewing: Effect**
Do you think this painting captures the world as Lord Brahma initially created it? Explain.

In Other Words

Famine An extreme scarcity of food
the earth itself groaned beneath the weight upon it nature struggled to support so many living things

and eyes dark and beautiful as night, and said to her:

"Your name is Death. And your task shall be to destroy life." **2**

When the woman who was Death heard these words, she wept in horror. Not waiting to hear what else Lord Brahma might say, she **fled** from him.

But there was no escaping Lord Brahma. "You are Death," he told her. "The taking of life is your destiny."

Again she fled, weeping at these **bitter words**. Again Lord Brahma found her where she hid.

"I created you to be the destroyer of life," he told her. "It is as it must be."

A third time the woman who was Death fled, till she reached the very ends of creation. But there again, **on that very edge of emptiness**, Lord Brahma overtook her. And this time there was no place left to which Death could flee.

"O my lord, spare me!" she pleaded. "Why should I do this cruel thing? Why should I harm those who have done me no harm? I beg you, let me not be Death!" **3**

"Daughter," Lord Brahma said gently, his great, wise eyes warm with pity, "you have not heard me out. If there is life, there must be an end to life."

"But how cruel to—"

⬛ **Critical Viewing: Character** How does this sculpture of Brahma compare with your image of Lord Brahma in the myth?

2 **Myth**
How is death personified here? What does the fact that death is personified suggest about the beliefs of this culture?

3 **Make Connections**
Have you ever had to do something you didn't want to do but which you knew was right? Explain.

In Other Words
fled ran away
bitter words harsh statements
on that very edge of emptiness in that empty, open space

Untitled, 2004, Dewashish Das. Tempera on handmade paper, courtesy of Kala Fine Art, Austin, Texas.

⚠ **Critical Viewing: Character** What qualities might this woman have in common with the woman in the myth?

"Hush, daughter. Listen. Death shall not be evil, or cruel, or without **virtue**. Without death, there can be no peace, no rest for the suffering, the aged. Without death, there can be no rebirth. Daughter, death shall not be the destroyer of the world, but its protector." **4**

4 Make Connections
What other myth, story, or movie does this myth remind you of? Explain the connection.

Key Vocabulary
virtue *n.*, benefits

Cultural Background
Reincarnation, or rebirth, is a central idea in several Eastern religions. Some people believe that after death, a person takes on a new form of life determined by his or her behavior in the previous life.

When Death heard these words, she **pondered**. She dried her tears. And at last the woman called Death smiled a tender little smile, a mother's smile. She bowed low before Lord Brahma and went forth to **do his bidding**.

And so all things came in time to die, and to be reborn. Order was restored to the earth. ❖

ANALYZE The Woman Who Was Death

1. **Summarize** What events lead to the woman's moment of truth about the world? Be sure to provide evidence from the text.

2. **Vocabulary** Briefly describe the **virtue** that Lord Brahma connects to death.

3. **Analyze World Literature: Myth** What is the life lesson that this myth contains? Why do you think the story was told and retold over time?

4. **Focus Strategy Make Connections** Look at the connections you made when Lord Brahma confronts the woman. What did this remind you of? How did this connection help you understand the message of this myth? Share your response with a partner.

Return to the Text

Reread and Write How did the woman's feelings about her responsibility change from the beginning to the end of the myth? Reread and write a paragraph describing at least two ways she changed and what the turning point was.

In Other Words
pondered thought carefully
do his bidding follow his commands

EQ What Do People Discover in a Moment of Truth?

Critical Thinking

EQ 1. **Analyze** Reread the **Quickwrite** exercise you completed on page 482. How does what you discovered in your moment of truth compare with the discoveries of the characters in the texts? Discuss this with a partner.

EQ 2. **Compare** How do the barber in "Just Lather, That's All" and the woman in the myth come to realize their moment of truth? Compare how they react to their responsibility and what they do about it.

3. **Interpret** Do you think the barber made the right decision? Explain your answer and use details from the text, your experience, other texts, and your knowledge of the world to support your response.

4. **Speculate** How do you think the story would have ended if the barber acted on his other option?

5. **Evaluate** What other choices do you think the barber had? What other factors could have helped him make his decision? Tell your reasons for your answer.

Write About Literature

Opinion Statement Do you believe that people can influence their own **destiny**? Or do you think a person's fate is fixed and unable to be changed? Support your answer with evidence from both texts.

Key Vocabulary Review

Oral Review Work with a partner. Use these words to complete the paragraph.

destiny	inflexible	regime
indelible	poised	virtue
indifference	priority	

> Coach Riviera always said that __(1)__ or what is meant to happen in the future depends on effort and what __(2)__ you place on your goals. Some of the players showed __(3)__ and did not care when Coach Riviera spoke about the benefits and __(4)__ of teamwork in any __(5)__ or organization. Most players were __(6)__ for victory and were __(7)__ because they did not want to listen to change. When we won the championship, I realized that Coach Riviera's speeches had a lasting or __(8)__ effect on me. We cheered for one another but gave Coach Riviera the victory trophy because we realized that behind every good player is a good coach.

Writing Application How do you determine what gets **priority** in your life? Write a paragraph answering this question. Use at least three Key Vocabulary words.

Read with Ease: Intonation

Assess your reading fluency with the passage in the Reading Handbook, p. 812. Then complete the self-check below.

1. My intonation did/did not sound natural.

2. My words correct per minute: _____

Grammar

Use Adjectives Correctly

To compare two people, places, or things, add **-er** to one-syllable adjectives.

The barber is **mean**, but Captain Torres is **meaner**.

If a two-syllable adjective ends in a consonant + **y**, change **y** to **i** before you add **-er**.

The barber is **scary**, but Captain Torres is **scarier**.

To compare three or more people, places, or things, add **-est** to one-syllable adjectives.

The intruder is the **meanest** person in the story.

For adjectives of three or more syllables, use **more** instead of **-er** and **most** instead of **-est**.

Torres is **more dangerous** than the doctor.
In fact, Torres is the **most dangerous** man in town.

Most other two-syllable adjectives take **more** and **most**.

Torres is the **most vicious** man in town.

A few adjectives use special forms to compare.

A risk is **bad**, but a mistake is even **worse**. Lying about it is the **worst** thing you can do.

Oral Practice (1–5) With a partner, compare the barber, the rebels, and Captain Torres. Use adjectives like *mean*, *nervous*, and *honorable*.

Written Practice (6–10) Rewrite the paragraph. Fix five adjectives.

The soldiers come into town. Their captain, Torres, is most cold-hearted than any man in the army. He is the crueler man who has ever come to town. The rebels in the town are scared, but the townspeople are even most scared. The barber is the braver rebel of all the people. He gives Torres a shave. After Torres leaves the barbershop, everyone is much happiest than before.

Language Development

Clarify

Pair Talk State a viewpoint about the story to a partner. For example, tell whether you think the barber made the right decision. Then your partner asks a question to clarify your view: *So you think …?*

Research / Viewing

Illustrated Report

Social Studies: Colombia The setting for "Just Lather, That's All" is Colombia. Using library and Internet resources, research this South American country's geography, natural resources, and cultural traditions. Work with a group to create images and maps that show what you have learned. Assign each team member a topic to research.

myNGconnect.com

- Visit a United States government Web site about Colombia.
- View photos of Colombian architecture from the United Nations.

Write descriptive captions for the images you researched or drew. Collect each team member's work and then present your findings in a group report.

Language and Learning Handbook, p. 750

Old and new in Cartagena, Colombia

Synonyms and Antonyms in Analogies

A **synonym** is a word or phrase that means the same thing as another word. An **antonym** is the opposite. For example, *frightening* is a synonym for *scary*, and *comforting* is an antonym. Copy and complete the chart. Use a dictionary and a thesaurus to help you.

WORD	DEFINITION	SYNONYM	ANTONYM
menace	An annoying Person	Mean, bad bothersome	Nice. helpful. kind.
dangerous	Not safe, harm	Harm, hurt. damage	Safe. peace free
surprise	Pleasant shock	Unprepared unexpected	Prepared. Expected

Then complete the analogies:

1. *Dangerous* is to *safe* as *hazardous* is to _____.
2. *Surprise* is to *fright* as *calm* is to _____.

Understand Irony

Irony is a contrast between appearance and reality. When something is ironic, it is not what it seems to be. In *verbal irony*, a contrast exists between what is said and what is meant. Someone might say, "I just love this beautiful weather we're having!" when it is storming outside. In *situational irony*, there is a reversal between what we expect and what actually happens. In "The Woman Who Was Death," you would not expect death to be portrayed by a beautiful woman.

Answer these questions to uncover different points of irony in "Just Lather, That's All."

1. From the narrator's point of view, what is ironic about Captain Torres's situation as the captain sits down in the barber's chair for a shave?

2. What irony emerges at the very end of the story?

Voice and Style

Every author has a distinctive **style**, or way, of writing. An author's **voice** is his or her own way of using language to create a story's personality. In "Just Lather, That's All," the author uses a tense, suspenseful voice. He creates this style by using specific words and leaving out details that keep the reader guessing. Does the writer use a suspenseful style in the paragraph below?

Just OK

> I walked in and looked around for a place to sit. I thought I saw Marco across the room. He sure looked surprised to see me. I think I may have scared him because he looked like he was trembling. I'm not sure why he would be so nervous.

Phrases like "I thought" and "I'm not sure" don't create tension in the story. Here is how the writer improved the story's voice:

Much Better

> I walked straight into the room and knew exactly where I wanted to sit. Then I saw Marco across the room. I looked right into his eyes. I could see his fear, and he started to tremble. He practically jumped out of his seat. Good. He should be nervous.

Now it's your turn to use the appropriate voice. Write the opening paragraph of the story from Captain Torres's point of view. How would the style and voice of the story change?

After you rewrite the paragraph, check your work:

- Is the voice consistent throughout the paragraph?
- Did I keep the same ideas that were in the original story?
- What adjectives did I use to create the style?

Make more revisions if necessary.

❧ **Writing Handbook,** p. 832

EXTEMPORANEOUS Talk

An extemporaneous talk is the kind of speech that requires speakers to "think on their feet." That means that the speech allows a little time for research beforehand, and it requires the speaker to put together a clear set of ideas quickly and in an interesting way. Here's how to do it.

1. Plan Your Extemporaneous Talk

You will be given a specific topic based on the Essential Question for this unit: "What do people discover in a moment of truth?" You can do the following ahead of time:

- Think about moments of truth in your life, in history, in current events, and in the selections you have read in this unit.
- Brainstorm about what a "moment of truth" is and what your audience can learn from it.
- List reasons each of these was a moment of truth.

2. Research Your Extemporaneous Talk

Once you receive your topic, you have approximately 15 minutes to research it.

- Use encyclopedias, the Internet, and other resource materials to research the topic.
- Write down a few simple, brief ideas on note cards that will inform the audience about the topic that has been assigned to you.
- Create a clear, concise introduction that states the topic. Follow up with a strong conclusion that sums up your ideas.

3. Present Your Extemporaneous Talk

Make your extemporaneous talk successful by doing the following:

- Speak clearly and loudly so that the audience can understand everything you say.
- Make eye contact and use gestures in order to make your points.
- Remain relaxed and confident as you speak. Although speaking extemporaneously requires you to gather your ideas quickly, your delivery should be clear and controlled.

myNGconnect.com

🌐 **Download the rubric.**

4. Discuss and Rate the Extemporaneous Talk

Use the rubric to discuss and rate the extemporaneous talks, including your own.

Extemporaneous Talk Rubric

Scale	Content of Extemporaneous Talk	Student's Preparation	Student's Performance
3 Great	• Expressed a clear response to the topic or question • Included an excellent introduction, body, and conclusion	• Seemed to have thought carefully about the general topic • Research was careful and supported the topic well	• Was relaxed and maintained eye contact with the audience • Spoke clearly and loudly
2 Good	• Expressed a fairly clear response to the topic or question • Had a clear introduction, body, and conclusion	• Seemed to have given some thought to the general topic • Most research supported the topic	• Was somewhat relaxed and maintained eye contact with the audience a lot of the time • Could be heard most of the time but spoke somewhat quickly
1 Needs Work	• Didn't provide a clear response to the topic or question • Was missing one or more of the parts—introduction, body, and conclusion	• Did not seem to have thought at all about the topic • None of the research supported the topic	• Seemed very nervous and did not make eye contact with the audience • Could not be heard well and spoke too quickly

DO IT ▶ Now that you know what an extemporaneous talk is, research your topic and talk about it!

📖 Language and Learning Handbook, p. 750

How can you prepare for your extemporaneous talk?

EQ ## What Do People Discover in a Moment of Truth?
Learn how a moment of truth can change your life.

Make a Connection

Brainstorm With a partner, brainstorm how a family's life can change in a moment for better or for worse. List situations and how they might challenge or change a family.

Learn Key Vocabulary

Pronounce each word and learn its meaning. You may also want to look up the definitions in the Glossary.

● Academic Vocabulary

Key Words	Examples
accelerate (ik-**se**-lu-rāt) *verb* ▶ page 512	To **accelerate** is to move faster. Did the sled's speed **accelerate** as it neared the bottom of the hill? *Synonym:* increase; *Antonym:* decrease
commentary (**kahm**-un-tair-ē) *noun* ▶ page 526	A **commentary** is a series of explanations, interpretations, or opinions. After the gymnastics competition, two gymnasts gave a detailed **commentary** about the event.
● **conformist** (kun-**for**-mist) *noun* ▶ pages 508, 529	A person who follows the customs or rules of a group is a **conformist**. *Synonym:* follower; *Antonym:* rebel
● **contrary** (**kahn**-trair-ē) *adjective* ▶ pages 511, 521, 529	A **contrary** idea is the opposite of what is expected. Doing what you feel is right may be **contrary** to what is easiest. *Synonyms:* opposite, dissimilar; *Antonym:* similar
malleable (**mal**-e-uh-bul) *adjective* ▶ page 508	The clay is **malleable** and soft, so I can easily change its shape. *Synonyms:* bendable, adaptable; *Antonyms:* rigid, unyielding
revelation (re-vu-**lā**-shun) *noun* ▶ pages 525, 528, 529	A **revelation** is a sudden insight or discovery. In a time of crisis, we may have a revelation about what we are capable of. *Synonyms:* vision, clarification
saturate (**sa**-chu-rāt) *verb* ▶ page 526	To **saturate** is to fill completely. A day of rain will not just wet the lawn; it will **saturate** it. *Synonym:* soak; *Antonym:* dry out
● **temporary** (**tem**-puh-rair-ē) *adjective* ▶ page 516	Something that is **temporary** lasts for only a short time. Since he will only live here for the summer, he is looking for a **temporary** job. *Synonym:* short-lived; *Antonym:* permanent

Practice the Words Work with a partner. Make a **Definition Map** for each Key Vocabulary word. Use a dictionary to find other forms of the word.

Definition Map

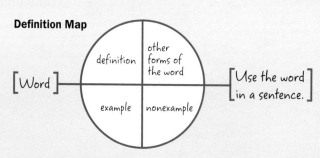

Reading Strategies
· Plan and Monitor
· Determine Importance
· Make Inferences
· Ask Questions
▶ **Make Connections**
· Synthesize
· Visualize

Analyze Structure: Foreshadowing

Foreshadowing is the author's use of clues or hints about events that will happen later in a story. An author may use dialogue, details, or a character's actions to foreshadow events. Foreshadowing often creates **suspense**, or a feeling of tension, curiosity, or excitement that makes a reader want to know what will happen next.

Look Into the Text

Details about a character suggest how he or she might act.

Dad stirred uneasily in his chair. "Aw, Dorothy," he mumbled. "Leave him be. He's a good kid."

"Or could be. *Maybe*," she threw back at him. "What he seems like to me is rock-bottom lazy. He sure is slow-moving, and could be he's slow in the head, too. Dumb."

How do you think Albert feels here?

Albert's eyes flickered at that word, but that's all. He just stood there and watched, eyes level.

"But I love him a lot," continued Mom, "and unlike you, I don't plan t'just sit around and watch him grow dumber. If it's the last thing I do, I'm gonna light a fire under his feet."

This dialogue foreshadows another event.

Focus Strategy ▶ Make Connections

When you make connections, you relate what you are reading to what you have experienced personally. By making these connections, you can clarify and understand the text better.

HOW TO MAKE CONNECTIONS

Focus Strategy

1. Make a chart like the one below to track details from the text.

2. Add the connection you made to the text. How did you relate to the event or character?

3. Then determine whether the connection you made was helpful or not. What new understanding did you gain?

Details from the Text	My Connection	Helpful?
1. "Leave him be. He's a good kid."	This reminds me of what a parent might say.	Yes, because I understand how sometimes parents might not agree. No, because I don't understand why the father is saying this.

Budge Wilson
(1927–)

Rebellion should be expected and often accepted during adolescence by one's family and peers.

Budge Wilson's stories have been published in ten countries and in seven languages.

Growing up in Nova Scotia, Canada, **Budge Wilson** wanted to become a writer someday. Before realizing her dream of writing, Wilson worked as a teacher, artist, and fitness instructor. She says, "When I did start to write, I found that I loved it more than any other thing I had tried to do."

Wilson's career paths mirror the difficult choices that some characters in her stories make, as they search for their identities and try to express themselves.

Wilson has worked with several literary organizations, sharing her experience as a writer. "As a result of doing this, I know that many children want to be writers when they grow up; and many of them have started to write excellent stories and poems. It is very exciting to see this happening—to see young people loving to read and to tell stories, and wanting to live a life that is based on the writing of books."

myNGconnect.com

◗ View photographs of Nova Scotia.
◗ Learn more about Budge Wilson.

Be-ers and Doers

by Budge Wilson

The Springhouse, 1944, Newell Convers Wyeth. Oil tempera, gesso on canvas, 36x48. Delaware Art Museum, Wilmington, Delaware. Special Purchase Fund, 1946, DAM 1946-1.

Critical Viewing Read the title of the story. How well does this painting connect to the title? Explain.

Comprehension Coach

Discover the different personalities in one family and each person's attitude toward life.

Mom was a little narrow wisp of a woman. You wouldn't have thought to look at her that she could move a card table; even for me it was sometimes hard to believe the ease with which she could shove around an entire family. Often I tried to explain her to myself. She had been brought up on the South Shore of Nova Scotia. I wondered sometimes if the scenery down there had rubbed off on her—all those granite rocks and fogs and screeching gulls, the slow, laboring springs, and the quick, grudging summers. And then the winters—grayer than doom, and endless. **1**

I was the oldest. I was around that house for five years before Maudie came along. They were peaceful, those five years, and even now it's easy to remember how everything seemed calm and simple. But now I know why. I was a **conformist** and **malleable** as early as three years old; I didn't **buck the system**. If Mom said, "Hurry, Adelaide!" I hurried. If she said to me, at five, "Fold that laundry, now, Adie, and **don't let no grass grow under your feet**," I folded it fast. So there were very few battles at first, and no major wars.

Dad, now, he was peaceful just by nature. If a tornado had come whirling in the front door and lifted the roof clear off its hinges, he probably would have just scratched the back of his neck and said, with a kind of slow surprise, "Well! Oho! Just think o' that!" He had been born in the Annapolis Valley, where the hills are round and gentle, and the summers sunlit and very warm.

"Look at your father!" Mom would say to us later. "He thinks that all he's gotta do is *be*. Well, bein' ain't good enough. You gotta *do*, too. Me, I'm a doer." All the time she was talking, she'd be knitting **up a storm**, or mixing dough, or pushing a mop—hands forever and ever on the move. **2**

Although Mom was fond of pointing out to us the things our father didn't do, he must have been doing something. Our farm was in the most fertile part of the Valley, and it's true that we had the kind of soil that seemed to make

1 Make Connections Describe someone you know whose personality seems influenced by where he or she is from. What qualities do both the person and the place share? Is the connection helpful in clarifying the mother's character? Jot your notes on your chart.

2 Structure: Foreshadowing How are the mother's and father's personalities different? What conflicts can you see arising because of their personalities?

Key Vocabulary
• **conformist** *n.*, follower
 malleable *adj.*, bendable, easy to influence

In Other Words
buck the system disobey the rules
don't let no grass grow under your feet don't be slow
up a storm a lot

Wisconsin Landscape, 1938–39, John Steuart Curry. Oil on canvas, George A. Hearn Fund, 1942, The Metropolitan Museum of Art, New York.

◀ Critical Viewing: Effect
What is the overall mood or atmosphere in this painting? What details create this mood?

things grow **all of their own accord**. Those beets and carrots and potatoes just **came pushing up into the sunshine** with an effortless grace, and they kept us well fed, with plenty left over to sell. But there was weeding and harvesting to do, and all those ten cows to milk—not to mention the thirty apple trees in our orchard to be cared for. I think maybe he just did his work so slowly and quietly that she found it hard to believe he was doing anything at all. Besides, on the South Shore, nothing ever grew without a struggle. And when Dad was through all his chores, or in between times, he liked to just sit on our old porch swing and watch the spring unfold or the summer blossom. And in the fall, he sat there smiling, admiring the rows of vegetables, the giant sunflowers, the golden leaves gathering in the trees of North Mountain. **3**

Maudie wasn't Maudie for the reasons a person is a Ginny or a Gertie or a Susie. She wasn't called Maudie because she was cute. She got that name because if you've got a terrible name like Maud, you have to do something to rescue it. She was called after Mom's Aunt Maud, who was **a miser** and had

3 Compare Across Texts
How is Dad's relationship to plants like Teruo's in "Say It with Flowers"?

In Other Words

all of their own accord completely on their own
came pushing up into the sunshine grew
a miser someone who is very stingy and not generous

Geographical Background
The eastern Canadian province of **Nova Scotia** is known for its rocky Atlantic coast and marine culture.

the whole Bank of Nova Scotia under her mattress. But she was a crabby old thing who just sat around living on her dead husband's stocks and bonds. A be-er, not a doer. Mom really scorned Aunt Maud and hated her name, but she had high hopes that our family would sometime cash in on that gold mine under the mattress. She hadn't counted on Aunt Maud going to Florida one winter and leaving her house in the care of a dear old friend. The dear old friend emptied the contents of the mattress, located Aunt Maud's three diamond rings, and took off for Mexico, leaving the pipes to freeze and the cat to die of starvation. After that, old Aunt Maud couldn't have cared less if everybody in the whole district had been named after her. She was that bitter.

Maudie was so like Mom that it was just as if she'd been cut out with a cookie cutter from the same dough. **Raced around at top speed** all through her growing-up time, full of projects and sports and hobbies and gossip and nerves. And mad at everyone who **sang a different tune**. **4**

But this story's not about Maudie. I guess you could say it's mostly about Albert.

Albert was the baby. I was eight years old when he was born, and I often felt like he was my own child. He was special to all of us, I guess, except maybe to Maudie, and when Mom saw him for the first time, I watched a slow soft tenderness in her face that was a rare thing for any of us to see. I was okay because I was cooperative, and I knew she loved me. Maudie was her clone, and almost like a piece of herself, so they admired one another, although they were too similar to be at peace for very long. But Albert was something different. Right away, I knew she was going to pour into Albert something that didn't reach the rest of us, except in part. As time went on, this scared me. **5** I could see that she'd made up her mind that Albert was going to be a perfect son. That meant, among other things, that he was going to be a fast-moving doer. And even when he was three or four, it wasn't hard for me to know that this wasn't going to be easy. Because Albert was a be-er. *Born* that way.

4 Make Connections
Which character do you most connect with in this story? Explain. On your chart, track your connections and how they affect your understanding of the story.

5 Structure: Foreshadowing
Why do you think the narrator was scared? What might this feeling foreshadow?

Monitor Comprehension

Explain
Who are the be-ers in the family? Who are the doers? Tell how you know.

In Other Words
Raced around at top speed Moved quickly
sang a different tune acted in another way

Will Albert become a "doer" or a "be-er"? Read on to find out.

As the years went by, people around Wilmot used to say, "Just look at that family of Hortons. Mrs. Horton made one child—Maudie. Then there's Adelaide, who's her own self. But Albert, now. Mr. Horton made him all by himself. They're alike as two pine needles." **6**

And just as nice, I could have added. But Mom wasn't either pleased or amused. "You're a bad **influence on** that boy, Stanley," she'd say to my dad. "How's he gonna get any ambition if all he sees is a father who can spend up to an hour leanin' on his hoe, starin' at the Mountain?" Mom had it all worked out that Albert was going to be a lawyer or a doctor or a Member of **Parliament**.

My dad didn't argue with her, or at least not in an angry way, "Aw, c'mon now, Dorothy," he might say to her, real slow. "The vegetables are comin' along jest fine. No need to shove them more than necessary. It does a man good to look at them hills. You wanta try it sometime. They tell you things."

"Nothin' *I* need t'hear," she'd huff, and disappear into the house, clattering pans, thumping the mop, scraping the kitchen table across the floor to get at more dust. And Albert would just watch it all, saying not a word, chewing on a piece of grass.

Mom really loved my dad, even though he drove her nearly crazy. Lots more went on than just nagging and complaining. If you looked really hard, you could see that. If it hadn't been for Albert and wanting him to be **a four-star** son, she mightn't have bothered to make Dad look so useless. Even so, when they sat on the swing together at night, you could feel their closeness. They didn't hold hands or anything. Her hands were always too busy embroidering, crocheting, mending something, or just swatting mosquitoes. But they liked to be together. **Personal chemistry**, I thought as I grew older, is a mysterious and **contrary** thing.

6 Make Connections
Which relatives in your family are you most like? In what ways? How does this help you understand the story?

Key Vocabulary
- **contrary** *adj.*, opposite

In Other Words
influence on example for
Parliament Canada's Congress
a four-star an excellent
Personal chemistry Attraction between two people

One day, Albert brought his report card home from school, and Mom looked at it hard and anxious, eyebrows knotted. "'Albert seems a nice child,'" she read aloud to all of us, more loudly than necessary, "'but his marks could be better. He spends too much time looking out the window, dreaming.'" She paused. No one spoke.

"Leanin' on his hoe," continued Mom **testily**. "Albert!" she snapped at him. "You **pull up your socks** by Easter or you're gonna be in deep trouble."

Dad stirred uneasily in his chair. "Aw, Dorothy," he mumbled. "Leave him be. He's a good kid."

"Or could be. *Maybe*," she threw back at him. "What he seems like to me is **rock-bottom lazy**. He sure is slow-moving, and could be he's slow in the head, too. Dumb."

Albert's eyes flickered at that word, but that's all. He just stood there and watched, eyes level.

"But I love him a lot," continued Mom, "and unlike you, I don't plan t'just sit around and watch him grow dumber. If it's the last thing I do, I'm gonna light a fire under his feet." **7**

Albert was twelve then, and the nagging began to **accelerate** in earnest.

"How come you got a low mark in your math test?"

"I don't like math. It seems like my head don't want it."

"But do you *work* at it?"

"Well, no. Not much. Can't see no sense in workin' hard at something I'll never use. I can add up our grocery bill. I pass. That's enough."

"Not for me, it ain't," she'd storm back at him. "No baseball practice for you until you get them **sums** perfect. Ask Maudie t'check them." Maudie used to **drum that arithmetic into him** night after night. She loved playing schoolteacher, and that's how she eventually ended up. And a cross one.

One thing Albert was good at, though, was English class. By the time he got to high school, he spent almost as much time reading as he did staring

7 Structure:
Foreshadowing
What do you think Albert's mother means by "light a fire under his feet"?

Key Vocabulary
accelerate *v.*, to increase, to move
  faster

In Other Words
testily impatiently, angrily
pull up your socks show better results
rock-bottom lazy naturally unwilling to work hard
sums addition or multiplication problems
drum that arithmetic into him test him in math

into space. His way of speaking changed. He stopped dropping his *g*'s. He said *isn't* instead of *ain't*. His tenses were **all neated up**. 8 He wasn't **putting on airs**. I just think that all those people in his books started being more real to him than his own neighbors. He loved animals, too. He made friends with the calves and even the cows. Mutt and Jeff, our two gray cats, slept on his bed every night. Often you could see him out in the fields, talking to our dog, while he was working.

"Always messin' around with animals," complained Mom. "Sometimes I think he's three parts woman and one part child. He's fifteen years old, and last week I caught him **bawlin'** in the hayloft after we had to shoot that male calf. Couldn't understand why y' can't go on feedin' an animal that'll never produce milk."

"Nothing wrong with liking animals," I argued. I was home for the weekend from my secretarial job in Wolfville.

"Talkin' to dogs and cryin' over cattle is not what I'd call a short-cut to success. And the cats spend so much time with him that they've forgotten why we brought them into the house in the first place. For mice."

"Maybe there's more to life than success or mice," I said. I was twenty-three now, and more interested in Albert than in conformity. 9

Mom made a "huh" sound through her nose. "Adelaide Horton," she said, "when you're my age, you'll understand more about success and mice than you do now. Or the lack of them." She turned on her heel and went back in the house. "And if you can't see," she said through the screen door, "why I don't want Albert to end up exactly like your father, then you've got even less sense than I thought you had. I don't want any son of mine goin' through life just satisfied to *be*." Then I could hear her banging around in the kitchen.

I'm gonna light a fire under his feet.

8 Language
How is Albert's new way of speaking different from the way his family speaks? Support your response with examples from the text to this point.

9 Structure: Foreshadowing
What does Adelaide and her mother's conversation hint at about future events and relationships in the story?

In Other Words
all neated up correctly used
putting on airs acting as if he thought he was better than others
bawlin' crying

Round Lake, Mud Bay, 1915, Thomas John Thomson. Oil on wood panel,
Art Gallery of Ontario, Toronto, Canada, The Bridgeman Art Library.

▲ **Critical Viewing: Setting** How does the scene in this painting compare with the one described in the story?

I looked off the **verandah** out at the front field, where Dad and Albert were raking up hay for the cattle, slowly, with lots of pauses for talk. All of a sudden they stopped, and Albert pointed up to the sky. It was fall, and four long wedges of geese were flying far above us, casting down their strange muffled cry. The sky was cornflower blue, and the wind was sending white clouds scudding across it. **10** My breath was caught with the beauty of it all, and as I looked at Dad and Albert, they threw away their rakes and lay down flat on their backs, right there in the front pasture, in order to **drink in** the sky. And after all the geese had passed over, they stayed like that for maybe twenty minutes more.

In Other Words
verandah porch
drink in appreciate

10 Access Vocabulary
What does the word *scudding* mean? Use the clues in the sentence to help you determine the meaning.

Monitor Comprehension

Confirm Prediction
Was your prediction about Albert correct? If so, how did you know? If not, what details misled you?

How will the family respond when it is time to take action?

We were all home for Christmas the year Albert turned eighteen. Maudie was having her Christmas break from teaching, and she was looking skinnier and more **tight-lipped** than I remembered her. I was there with my husband and my new baby, Jennifer, and Albert was even quieter than usual. But content, I thought. **Not making any waves.** Mom had intensified her big **campaign** to have him go to Acadia University in the fall. "Pre-law," she said, "or maybe teacher training. Anyways, you gotta go. A man has to be successful." She avoided my father's eyes. "In the fall," she said. "For sure."

"It's Christmas," said Dad, without anger. "Let's just be happy and forget all them plans for a few days." He was sitting at the kitchen table breaking up the bread slowly, slowly, for the turkey stuffing. He chuckled. "I've decided to be a doer this Christmas." 🔟

"And if the doin's bein' done at that speed," she said, taking the bowl from him, "we'll be eatin' Christmas dinner on New Year's Day." She started to break up the bread so quickly that you could hardly focus on her flying fingers.

Christmas came and went. It was a pleasant time. The food was good; Jennifer slept right through dinner and didn't cry all day. We listened to the Queen's Christmas message; we opened presents. Dad gave Mom a ring with a tiny sapphire in it, although she'd asked for a new vacuum cleaner. 🔢

"I like this better," she said, and looked as though she might cry.

"We'll get the vacuum cleaner in January," he said, "That's no kind of gift to get for Christmas. It's a work thing."

She looked as if she might say something, but she didn't.

It was on December 26th that it happened. That was the day of the fire.

It was a lazy day. We all got up late, except me, of course, who had to feed the baby at two and at six. But when we were all up, we just sort of

🔟 **Structure:**
Foreshadowing
What do you think the father's comments mean? How do his words foreshadow what might happen?

🔢 **Make Connections**
What connections can you make to how people in your community celebrate holidays like Christmas? How does this help you picture the scene? Add the connection to your chart.

In Other Words
tight-lipped tense, rigid
Not making any waves. Not causing any trouble.
campaign efforts

Cultural Background
The Queen's Christmas message is a holiday greeting from Queen Elizabeth II of England that is broadcast on British television and radio, as well as on the Internet, every Christmas.

lazed around in our dressing gowns, drinking coffee, admiring one anothers' presents, talking about old times, singing a carol or two around the old organ. Dad had that look on him that he used to get when all his children were in his house at the same time. Like he was in **temporary** possession of the best that life had to offer. Even Mom was softened up, and she sat by the grate fire and talked a bit, although there was still a lot of jumping up and down and rushing out to the kitchen to check the stove or cut up vegetables. Me, I think that on the day after Christmas you should just eat up leftovers and enjoy a **slow state of collapse**. But you can't blame a person for feeding you. It's handy to have a Martha or two around a house that's already equipped with three Marys. Albert was the best one to watch, though. To me, anyway. He was sitting on the floor in his striped pajamas, holding Jennifer, rocking her, and singing songs to her in a low, **crooning** voice. Tender, I thought, the way I like a man to be.

Albert had just put the baby back in her carriage when a giant spark flew out of the fireplace. It hit the old nylon carpet like **an incendiary** bomb, and the rug burst into flames. Mom started waving an old **afghan** over it, as though she was blowing out a match, but all she was doing was fanning the fire.

While most of us stood there in immovable 🔳**13** fear, Albert had already grabbed Jennifer, carriage and all, and rushed out to the barn with her. He was back in a flash, just in time to see Maudie's dressing gown catch fire. He pushed her down on the floor and lay on top of her to smother the flames, and then he was up on his feet again, taking charge.

"Those four buckets in the summer kitchen!" he yelled. "Start filling them!" He pointed to Mom and Dad, who obeyed him like he was a general and they were the privates. To my husband he roared, "Get out to th' barn and keep that baby warm!"

"And you!" He pointed to me. "Call the fire department. It's 825–3131." In the meantime, the smoke was starting to fill the room and we were all

13 Access Vocabulary
The prefix *im-* can mean "not." Use the prefix to help you determine what *immovable* means.

Key Vocabulary
- **temporary** *adj.*, lasting for a short time

In Other Words
lazed around sat quietly
slow state of collapse time of relaxation
crooning soft and sentimental
an incendiary a fire-producing
afghan blanket

coughing. Little spits of fire were crawling up the curtains, and Maudie was just standing there, shrieking.

Before Mom and Dad got back with the water, Albert was out in the back bedroom hauling up the carpet. Racing in with it over his shoulder, he bellowed, "Get out o' the way!" and we all moved. Then he slapped the carpet over the flames on the floor, and the fire just died **without so much as a protest**. Next he grabbed one of the big cushions off the sofa, and chased around after the little lapping flames on curtains and chairs and table runners, smothering them. When Mom and Dad appeared with a bucket in each hand, he shouted, "Stop! Don't use that stuff! No need t'have water damage, too!"

Then Albert was suddenly still, hands hanging at his sides with the fingers spread. He smiled shyly.

"It's out," he said.

I rushed up and hugged him, wailing like a baby, loving him, thanking him. For protecting Jennifer—from smoke, from fire, from cold, from heaven knows what. Everyone opened windows and doors, and before too long, even the smoke was gone. It smelled pretty awful, but no one cared.

When we all gathered again in the **parlor** to clear up the mess, and Jennifer was back in my bedroom asleep, Mom stood up and looked at Albert, her eyes ablaze with admiration—and with something else I couldn't put my finger on. 🔢14

"Albert!" she breathed, "We all thank you! You've saved the house, the baby, all of us, even our Christmas presents. I'm proud, proud, *proud* of you." 🔢15

Albert just stood there, smiling quietly, but very pale. His hands were getting red and sort of puckered looking.

Mom took a deep breath. "And *that*," she went on, "is what I've been looking for, all of your life. Some sort of a sign that you were one hundred percent alive. And now we all know you are. Maybe even **a lick** more alive than the

14 Structure: Foreshadowing
The fire is out, but Mom's eyes are described as "ablaze with admiration." What is the author indicating by these words?

15 Structure: Foreshadowing
What earlier statement about Albert by the mother foreshadows the event that just took place?

In Other Words
without so much as a protest suddenly and completely
parlor living room
a lick a little bit

Literary Background
Martha and Mary are friends of Jesus in the Christian Bible (Luke 10:38–42). Martha is the hard-working head of the household. Martha resents that her sister Mary chooses sitting to listen to Jesus over helping in the kitchen.

rest of us. So!" She folded her arms, and her eyes bored into him. "I'll have no more excuses from you now. No one who can put out a house fire single-handed and rescue a niece and a sister and organize us all into a fire **brigade** is gonna sit around for the rest of his life gatherin' dust. No siree! Or leanin' against no hoe. Why, you even had the fire department number tucked away in your head. Just imagine what you're gonna be able to do with them kind o' brains! I'll never, never rest until I see you educated and successful. Doin' what you was meant to do. I'm just proud of you, Albert. So terrible proud!" **16**

Members of the fire department were starting to arrive at the front door, but Albert ignored them. He was white now, like death, and he made a low and terrible sound. He didn't exactly pull his lips back from his teeth and growl, but the result was similar. It was like the sound a dog makes before he leaps for the throat. And what he said was "*You jest leave me be, woman!*"

We'd never heard words like this coming out of Albert, and the parlor was as still as night as we all listened.

"You ain't proud o' me, Mom," he whispered, all his beautiful grammar gone. "Yer jest proud o' what you want me t'be. And I got some news for you. Things I shoulda tole you **years gone by**. *I ain't gonna be what you want.*" His voice was starting to **quaver** now, and he was trembling all over. "*I'm gonna be me.* And it seems like if that's ever gonna happen, it'll have t'be in some other place. And I plan t'do somethin' about that before the day is out."

Then he shut his eyes and fainted right down onto the **charred** carpet. **17** The firemen carted him off to the hospital, where he was treated for shock and **second-degree burns**. He was there for three weeks.

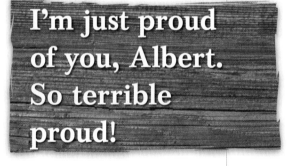

I'm just proud of you, Albert. So terrible proud!

In Other Words
brigade group or team
years gone by a long time ago
quaver shake, tremble
charred burnt
second-degree burns serious injury, burns from the fire

Predict

What will Albert's life be like now?

My dad died of a stroke when he was sixty-six. "Not enough exercise," said Mom, after she'd got over the worst part of her grief. "Too much sittin' around watchin' the lilacs grow. No way for his blood to circulate good." Me, I ask myself if he just piled up his silent tensions until he burst wide open. Maybe he wasn't all that calm and peaceful after all. Could be he was just waiting, like Albert, for the moment when it would all come pouring out. Perhaps that wasn't the way it was; but all the same, I wonder.

Mom's still going strong at eighty-eight. Unlike Dad's, her blood must circulate like a racing stream, what with all that rushing around; she continues to move as if she's being chased. She's still knitting and **preserving** and scrubbing and mending and preaching. She'll never get one of those tension diseases like angina or cancer or even arthritis, because she doesn't keep one single thing **bottled up** inside her for more than five minutes. Out it all comes like air out of a flat tire—with either a hiss or a bang.

Perhaps it wasn't growing up on the South Shore that made Mom the way she is. I live on that coast now, and I've learned that it's more than just gray and stormy. I know about the long sandy beaches and the peace that comes of a clear horizon. I've seen the razzle-dazzle colors of the low-lying scarlet bushes in the fall, blazing against the black of the spruce trees and the bluest sky in the world. I'm familiar with the way one single radiant summer day can make you forget a whole **fortnight** of fog—like birth after a long labor. You might say that the **breakers** out on the reefs are angry or full of threats. To me, though, those waves are leaping and dancing, wild with freedom and joyfulness. **18** But I think Mom was in a hurry from the moment she was born. I doubt if she ever stopped long enough to take notice of things like that.

Albert left home as soon as he got out of the hospital. He worked as

18 Make Connections
How do you relate to what the narrator says about where she lives? How well does the connection help you understand the narrator?

In Other Words
preserving preparing fruit for jams and jellies
bottled up tight
fortnight two weeks
breakers crashing waves

Critical Viewing: Title What might be a good title for this illustration? How does the story relate to your title?

a **stevedore** in Halifax for a number of years, and when he got enough money saved, he bought a little run-down house close to Digby, with a view of the Bay of Fundy. He's got a small chunk of land that's so black and rich that it doesn't take any pushing at all to make the flowers and vegetables grow. He has a cow and a beagle and four cats—and about five hundred books. He fixes lawn mowers and boat engines for the people in his area, and he

In Other Words
stevedore dockworker

Geographical Background
The tides, or rise and fall in the water level, in the **Bay of Fundy** are the highest in the world. During high tide, the water level may rise as much as 21 meters (70 feet).

putters away at his funny little house. He writes pieces for *The Digby Courier,* and *The Novascotian,* and last winter he confessed to me that he writes poetry. He's childless and wifeless, but he **has the time of day for** any kid who comes around to hear stories or to have a broken toy fixed. He keeps an old rocker out on the edge of the cliff, where he can sit and watch the tides of Fundy rise and fall. ⓳ ❖

⓳ **Make Inferences**
Do you think Albert is happy with the life he has chosen? What makes you think so?

ANALYZE Be-ers and Doers

1. **Recall and Interpret** What did Albert do after his confrontation with his mother? Do you think he did the right thing? Explain. Support your explanation with evidence from the text.

2. **Vocabulary** Why does Albert's mother find his actions so **contrary** to her own expectations for him? Do you think he is a be-er or a doer?

3. **Analyze Structure: Foreshadowing** What events or dialogue foreshadow Albert's actions in the end? Find two examples in the text.

4. **Focus Strategy Make Connections** What does Albert discover in a moment of truth? Refer to your connections chart and describe to a partner the connection you made to that moment. What aspect of the story did that connection help you understand better?

Return to the Text

Reread and Write Reread the story. Write a short news feature for *The Novascotian* as if you were a reporter reporting on the fire. Use details from the text to describe how the family's life changed after that event.

In Other Words
putters away casually busies himself
has the time of day for will spend time with

The Calling

by Luis J. Rodríguez

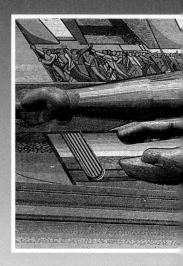

The calling came to me
while I languished
in my room; while I
whittled away my youth
5   in jail cells
and damp *barrio* fields.

It brought me to life,
out of captivity,
in a street-scarred
10 and tattooed place
I called body.

Until then I waited silently,
a deafening clamor in my head,
but voiceless to all around me;
15 hidden from America's eyes,
A brown boy without a name,

I would sing into a solitary
    tape recorder,
music never to be heard.
20 I would write my thoughts
in scrambled English;
I would take photos in my mind—
    plan out new parks;
    bushy green, concrete free.
25 New places to play
and think.

Waiting.
Then it came.
The calling.
30 It brought me out of my room.
It forced me to escape
night captors
in street prisons.

In Other Words
languished wasted away
whittled away lost bit by bit
barrio neighborhood (in Spanish)

The People for the University, the University for the People, David Alfaro Siqueiros (1896–1974). Mural, Universidad Nacional Autonoma de Mexico, Mexico City, Mexico.

▲ Critical Viewing: Theme What elements in this painting remind you of the theme of the poem?

It called me to war;
35 to be writer,
to be scientist
and march with the soldiers
  of change.

It called me from the shadows,
40 out of the wreckage,
of my *barrio*—from among those
who did not exist.

I waited all of 16 years
for this time.

45 Somehow, unexpected,
I was called.

About the Poet

Luis J. Rodríguez (1954–) is one of America's most famous poets, speakers, and educators. In 2001, the Dalai Lama, a world-respected spiritual leader, named him one of the world's "Unsung Heroes of Compassion."

BEFORE READING My Moment of Truth

magazine article by
Caroline V. Clarke and Sonja D. Brown

Reading Strategies

- Plan and Monitor
- Determine Importance
- Make Inferences
- Ask Questions
- ▶ **Make Connections**
- Synthesize
- Visualize

Determine Author's Purpose

The **author's purpose** is his or her reason for writing. An author may write to inform, entertain, inspire, reflect, or persuade. Details in a magazine article can give clues to the author's purpose. In the first paragraph of "My Moment of Truth," the authors say that moments of truth change us. These "turning points" hint that the authors' goal is to inspire others by showing several different perspectives.

Look Into the Text

Dominique Dawes: Olympic Gold Medalist, Motivational Speaker

> But one night, at home alone in Maryland, Dawes confronted a critical question for the first time. "I asked myself what I really wanted to do … At home alone that night, I finally realized, this is my life and I need to pave my own path."

The authors describe Dawes's turning point.

Wynton Marsalis: Jazz Musician, Artistic Director of "Jazz at Lincoln Center"

> "I played it again. I still didn't like it, but I kept playing it. There was something about it … something that compelled me to keep playing it … That's when I started to realize I wanted to be a jazz musician. I had always played, but now I wanted to be good."

How is Marsalis's perspective different from Dawes's?

Focus Strategy ▶ Make Connections

As you read, think about the different ways Dominique Dawes and Wynton Marsalis discovered what they wanted in life. Relate their experiences to your own. Think about how the connections give you a better understanding of the article.

HOW TO MAKE CONNECTIONS

Focus Strategy

1. Work with a partner to complete a connection chart as you read.

2. Compare your responses with those of your partner.

In the Article	My Connection
In a moment of truth, Dominique Dawes realized that _____	When I relate this to my own life, I understand that _____
In a moment of truth, Wynton Marsalis realized that _____	When I relate this to my own life, I understand that _____

Title: My Moment of Truth

My Moment of Truth

By Caroline V. Clarke, Sonja D. Brown, *Black Enterprise* magazine

Connect Across Texts

In "Be-ers and Doers," we see how a young man changes his life. The following article describes turning points in the lives of real people.

We all have them. Those moments that fundamentally change us. We may not always recognize them as they're happening, but we look back and they are crystal clear—the turning points that shape our lives, alter our direction, offer us a deeper understanding of who we are or want to become. Moments of truth often come **in the guise of** a challenge or even a crisis. Sometimes **no great strife** is involved at all. **Revelation** comes in all forms. But the result is always the same: We are molded by specific events and experiences. The lessons they teach help and heal us. They provide answers to questions we may not have even known we had. **1**

1 Author's Purpose
What is the authors' purpose in writing this article? How do you know?

DOMINIQUE DAWES
The Night I Found My Path

Dominique Dawes's young life has been a series of dazzling, dramatic highlights. She began taking gymnastics at age six and was competing by age ten. Just five years later, she burst onto the international scene in 1992, becoming the first African American gymnast to ever qualify and compete in the Olympic Games in Barcelona.

By the time she retired, following the 2000 Olympic Games in Sydney, Australia . . . she had

Dominique Dawes
Olympic Gold Medalist, Motivational Speaker

Key Vocabulary
revelation *n.*, sudden insight, discovery

In Other Words
in the guise of concealed as
no great strife no hardship

won more national championship medals than any other athlete—male or female—as well as four world championship medals, two Olympic bronze medals, and one gold. Perhaps because Dawes was **saturated** by the spotlight for so many years, her moment of truth came at a quiet time, **devoid of** drama, cameras, coaches, or fans. "There was no real single experience that brought me to that moment . . . I was working on my degree in communications from the University of Maryland, and I was doing a lot of [public] speaking, some gymnastics **commentary**, and some acting . . . I had been doing all of the things everyone around me kept telling me I'd be good at. But I was **somewhat on autopilot**. I was doing things to please other people, not because I really had a passion for them. I was almost a robot. Whatever people said was good for me, I'd just say, 'Okay. Fine. I'll do it.'"

But one night, at home alone in Maryland, Dawes confronted a critical question for the first time. "I asked myself what I really wanted to do. I felt almost like I was dreaming, I had never asked myself that. From the time I was young, I was guided in a very structured way. That was good for my gymnastics career. I needed it then. But when I retired, I kept waiting for someone to tell me what to do—like they always had. And they did. But a wonderful friend sat me down one day and made me realize that I wasn't happy doing those things. At home alone that night, I finally realized, this is my life and I need to pave my own path. I also came to the realization that the key to failure is trying to please everyone. I needed to figure out for myself what Dominique loves to do, wants to do, and is really good at. That was the beginning of my changing the way I thought about my life. . . . **2**

"When I finally retired (in 2000)—from gymnastics and from living for other people—I felt like I had a 1,000 pound weight lifted off me," she says. "That's how I feel now—like I have been totally freed! I'm free to do what I like, and what I want. This is the life that I want."

2 Make Connections
How have you or how has someone you know experienced a turning point in life? What was that like?

Key Vocabulary
saturate *v.*, to fill completely, to soak
commentary *n.*, series of interpretations, explanations, or opinions

In Other Words
devoid of free from, empty of any
somewhat on autopilot acting without careful thought, going through routines

WYNTON MARSALIS
The Summer I Discovered Coltrane

Listening to Wynton Marsalis play, one would think this Juilliard-trained, nine-time Grammy award-winning jazz and classical musician has loved jazz and classical music from the time he was able to hold a trumpet. Not so. "Mama took us to see classical orchestras play a few times, but I didn't know anything about classical music. I couldn't get into it. Daddy always played jazz, but I didn't like that either. I liked them [the musicians his father played with] but I didn't like the music. **3** And I didn't understand his dedication to it. The funk bands I knew used to **pack the house**; I played in a funk band when I was a teenager. But whenever daddy played, there would only be ten or fifteen people around.

"Jazz musicians were strange to me. I liked Earth, Wind & Fire, and Parliament; I was used to people in shiny suits and costumes and stuff. The people on the covers of my daddy's jazz albums looked funny to me. They were dressed normal and looked all serious."

Then one day when Marsalis was twelve years old, he came home from his summer job and decided to try something. "I came home from work one day and put on one of my daddy's John Coltrane records. I didn't like it." And for most of us, that would have been the end of it. Went there, tried that, didn't like it. But something was happening that Marsalis didn't quite understand. "I played it again. I still didn't like it, but I kept playing it. There was something about it, something about the sound that I couldn't get away from, something that compelled me to keep playing it and playing it and playing it. And then I started listening to other people. That's when I started to realize I wanted to be a jazz musician. I had always played,

Wynton
Marsalis
Jazz Musician, Artistic Director of "Jazz At Lincoln Center"

3 Make Connections
How has the music your parents or friends listen to affected your own musical tastes? How does this connection help you understand what Marsalis is saying?

In Other Words
pack the house play to large audiences

Cultural Background
Saxophonist **John Coltrane** (1926–1967) and trumpeter **Miles Davis** (1926–1991) were two of the most influential jazz musicians of the mid-1900s.

but now I wanted to be good. I wanted to play like 'trane, like Miles [Davis], and everybody else I was listening to. **4**

"[Jazz] helped me understand life and my place in it. Music is like that, it's spiritual. It goes beyond emotion; music can take you to a whole different **consciousness**. My whole approach to everything changed, not just playing." **5**

Now, almost thirty years and one Pulitzer Prize in Music later, Marsalis is jazz. He plays it, composes it, teaches it, and it's always in his head—at any moment he's liable to surprise you with a **riff** on his trumpet. . . . "I just want people to be aware of jazz, to make the music available through recordings and broadcasts . . . " ❖

4 Author's Purpose
How do Dawes and Marsalis respond to the influence of others? Why do you think the authors chose to write about these two people?

5 Make Connections
How has an interest of yours changed your life? Compare this to how music changed Marsalis's life.

ANALYZE **My Moment of Truth**

1. **Recall and Interpret** Do you agree with what the authors say about how a moment of truth occurs? Explain your answer.

2. **Vocabulary** How was Coltrane's music a **revelation** for Marsalis?

3. **Determine Author's Purpose** Which details in this magazine article gave you clues to the author's purpose for the article?

4. **Focus Strategy Make Connections** Have you ever had a "moment of truth"? Did it happen unexpectedly, or was it something you set out to discover? Describe your experience with a partner and tell how the connection helped you understand this selection.

Return to the Text

Reread and Write Suppose Dawes and Marsalis did not experience a moment of truth. What might their lives be like? Reread the selection for details that support your speculation. Then write comments Dawes and Marsalis might make about their lives.

In Other Words
consciousness understanding of the relationship between one's self and the world
riff short tune

EQ **What Do People Discover in a Moment of Truth?**

Critical Thinking

EQ 1. Analyze How did each character or person respond to a moment of truth? What common theme or message can you take away from these different experiences?

EQ 2. Compare What situations can create an opportunity for a moment of truth? How does Albert's experience compare with Dominique Dawes's and Wynton Marsalis's experiences?

3. Interpret What turning points did Albert, Dominique Dawes, and Wynton Marsalis experience? How do you think their lives have changed since then? What impact do you think their experience had on their families?

4. Speculate Imagine that Albert's parents' roles were reversed. How would the story be different? Would Albert have experienced his turning point differently? Explain.

5. Evaluate Is it better to be a **conformist** or to live **contrary** to what others expect? When might there be times when one way is better than another? Explain your answer and support it with evidence from both texts.

Write About Literature

Speech Should you be a *doer* or a *be-er*? Is it possible to be both? Write a paragraph to convince people why it is more important to be either a *doer* or a *be-er*. Make sure that your first sentence captures the attention of your listeners. Use details from both texts in your speech.

Key Vocabulary Review

Oral Review Work with a partner. Use these words to complete the paragraph.

accelerate	contrary	saturated
commentary	malleable	temporary
conformists	revelation	

A moment of truth can send your life in a direction that is __(1)__ to where you and others thought you were going. When we are young, our minds are more __(2)__ . We are __(3)__ by the opinions of others, like a wet sponge. We are __(4)__ who just obey the rules and listen to the __(5)__ of others. This is only a __(6)__ thing, however, since when we grow up we gain experience. We may have a sudden __(7)__ about our true calling. From that time on, we gain confidence and __(8)__ toward new goals.

Writing Application Write a paragraph on your personal goals, telling when you finally had the **revelation** that helped you realize what you want. Use at least three Key Vocabulary words.

Read with Ease: Expression

Assess your reading fluency with the passage in the Reading Handbook, p. 813. Then complete the self-check below.

1. My expression did/did not sound natural.

2. My words correct per minute: _____

INTEGRATE THE LANGUAGE ARTS

Use Adverbs Correctly

An **adverb** is a describing word. Adverbs often end in **-ly**. Use adverbs to tell *how*, *when*, or *where*. An adverb can describe a <u>verb</u>.

Mom <u>moves</u> **quickly** .

Father **usually** <u>looks</u> at the mountains for a long time.

An adverb can also describe an adjective or another adverb.

Dad is **not** <u>lazy</u>. He just works **really** slowly.

Some adverbs compare actions. Use **more** or **-er** to compare two actions. Use **most** or **-est** to compare three or more actions.

We moved **fast**, but Albert moved **faster**.

The fire spread **more quickly** than we thought.

Albert worked the **most confidently** of all of us.

Oral Practice (1–5) Choose from each column to make five sentences. Use words more than once.

Albert	moved	patiently
Dad	spoke	very loudly
Mom	complained	slowly

Written Practice (6–10) Rewrite the paragraph. Fix three adverbs. Add two more sentences about Albert. Use adverbs to compare.

Albert was a good observer. He watched things more careful than his mom. She usually moved quickest than Albert, but on the day of the fire, he ran more quickly of all. Albert...

Dialect

Writers use dialect to reveal things about their characters and establish the setting of a story. **Dialect** is a unique form of a language spoken by people in the same region or group. This includes changes in:

- the way characters pronounce words
- the vocabulary they use
- the way they spell words and structure sentences in English

In "Be-ers and Doers," Albert's mother says, "Well, bein' ain't good enough. You gotta *do*, too." Her dialect tells you something about her background.

Review the story "Be-ers and Doers" with a partner and look for examples of how the characters use dialect. Read the examples aloud. Notice how the text sounds, and think about what the dialect tells you about a character. Create a chart to track the examples you found. Be sure to include what these examples reveal about the characters.

Dialect	Meaning	Characterization

Verify Information

Pair Talk With a partner, take turns naming an instruction Albert gives when the fire breaks out. You can make it correct or incorrect. For example: *Albert told his sister to get the water.* Read the text to confirm your partner's information.

Synonyms and Antonyms in Analogies

A **synonym** is a word or phrase that means the same thing as another word. An **antonym** is the opposite. For example, *annoying* is a synonym for ***irritating*** and *soothing* is an antonym. Copy and complete the chart. Use a dictionary and a thesaurus to help you.

WORD	DEFINITION	SYNONYM	ANTONYM
joyous			
gigantic			

Then complete the analogies:

1. *Little* is to *big* as *tiny* is to _____.
2. *Joyous* is to *miserable* as *happy* is to _____.

Compare News Commentaries

Research Report News commentaries can be found in newspapers and on talk radio and the Internet. Some commentaries explain a person's opinion on an issue. Other commentaries explain or illustrate the facts behind a complicated subject in the news.

With a partner, find an example of each type of commentary, one that presents an opinion and one that presents the facts about a similar event. Answer these questions:

- Which commentary is more effective in helping you understand the issue or event?
- What tone does the person use? Is the language formal or more casual? How do the tone and language affect the credibility of the commentary?

Write an Analysis of an Issue

A test may ask you to write an analysis of an issue and explain your point of view on the subject.

1 **Unpack the Prompt** Underline key words that show what your response should include.

> **Writing Prompt**
> How should you make a decision in a moment of truth? Should you base major decisions on your own personal feelings or on the feelings of others, such as family members? Describe a person who you think made the right decision when facing a moment of truth.

2 **Prewriting** Decide your opinion on the issue. Use a chart to organize your ideas about a person who acted in a way that supports your opinion.

Name	Decision	Why It Was the Right Decision
Wynton Marsalis	to play jazz	Stayed true to himself even though funk music was more popular.

3 **Draft** Organize your analysis like this. Include specific ideas from your chart.

> **Analysis Organizer**
>
> To me, it is most important to follow [your own feelings/feelings of others] when facing a moment of truth. One person who followed [his/her feelings/feelings of others] is [person's name].
>
> [Person's name] made the right decision because [he/she] [example of why it was the right decision]. Furthermore, [he/she] [another example].
>
> In conclusion, I think you must base major decisions on [your own feelings/feelings of others]. I believe this because [explain why].

4 **Edit and Proofread** Reread your response. Ask:

- Does my response address the writing prompt?
- Did I give examples to support my opinion?
- Have I used adverbs correctly?

📖 **Writing Handbook**, p. 808

from
Black Boy

by Richard Wright

1   The school term ended. I was selected as **valedictorian** of my class and assigned to write a paper to be delivered at one of the public auditoriums. One morning the principal **summoned** me to his office.

2   "Well, Richard Wright, here's your speech," he said with smooth bluntness and shoved a stack of stapled sheets across his desk.

3   "What speech?" I asked as I picked up the papers.

4   "The speech you're to say the night of graduation," he said.

5   "But, professor, I've written my speech already," I said.

6   He laughed confidently, indulgently.

7   "Listen, boy, you're going to speak to both *white* and colored people that night. What can you alone think of saying to them? You have no experience . . ."

8   I burned.

9   "I know that I'm not educated, professor," I said. "But the people are coming to hear the students, and I won't make a speech that you've written."

Lynford, 1969, Karen Armitage. Oil on canvas, private collection, The Bridgeman Art Library.

⚠ **Critical Viewing: Subject** What can you know about this person, based on the details you see? What can you not know about him?

In Other Words
valedictorian the highest-ranking student
summoned called

Historical Background
Richard Wright wrote about society's poor treatment of African Americans. In his autobiography, *Black Boy*, he describes his experiences growing up in the U.S. in the 1910s and 20s.

10   He leaned back in his chair and looked at me in surprise.

11   "You're just a young, hotheaded fool," he said. He toyed with a pencil and looked up at me. "Suppose you don't graduate?"

12   "But I passed my examinations," I said.

13   "Look, mister," he shot at me, "I'm the man who says who passes at this school."

14   I was so astonished that my body **jerked**. I had gone to this school for two years and I had never suspected what kind of man the principal was; it simply had never occurred to me to wonder about him.

15   "Then I don't graduate," I said flatly.

16   I turned to leave.

17   "Say, you. Come here," he called.

18   I turned and faced him; he was smiling at me in a remote, superior sort of way.

19   "You know, I'm glad I talked to you," he said. "I was seriously thinking of placing you in the school system, teaching. But, now, I don't think that you'll fit."

20   He was tempting me, baiting me; this was the technique that **snared** black young minds into supporting the southern way of life.

21   "Look, professor, I may never get a chance to go to school again," I said. "But I like to do things right."

22   I went home, hurt but determined. I had been talking to **a "bought" man** and he had tried to "buy" me. I felt that I had been dealing with something unclean. That night Griggs, a boy who had gone through many classes with me, came to the house.

23   "Look, Dick, you're throwing away your future here in Jackson," he said. "Go to the principal, talk to him, take his speech and say it. I'm saying the one he wrote. So why can't you? What the hell? What can you lose?"

> I felt that I had been dealing with something unclean.

24   "No," I said.

In Other Words
jerked shook
snared tricked
a "bought" man someone who did things
    because others told him to

25   "Why?"

26   "I know only a hell of a little, but my speech is going to reflect that," I said.

27   "Then you're going to be **blacklisted for** teaching jobs," he said.

28   "Who the hell said I was going to teach?" I asked.

29   "God, but you've got a will," he said.

30   "It's not will. I just don't want to do things that way," I said.

31   He left. Two days later Uncle Tom came to me. I knew that the principal had called him in.

32   "I hear that the principal wants you to say a speech which you've rejected," he said.

> ## "I just don't want to do things that way."

33   "Yes, sir. That's right," I said.

34   "May I read the speech you've written?" he asked.

35   "Certainly," I said, giving him my manuscript.

36   "And may I see the one that the principal wrote?"

37   I gave him the principal's speech too. He went to his room and read them. I sat quiet, waiting. He returned.

38   "The principal's speech is the better speech," he said.

39   "I don't doubt it," I replied. "But why did they ask me to write a speech if I can't deliver it?"

40   "Would you let me work on your speech?" he asked.

41   "No, sir."

42   "Now, look, Richard, this is your future . . ."

43   "Uncle Tom, I don't care to discuss this with you," I said.

44   He stared at me, then left. The principal's speech was simpler and clearer than mine, but it did not say anything; mine was cloudy, but it said what I wanted to say. What could I do? I had **half a mind** not to show up at the graduation exercises. I was hating my environment more each day. As soon as school was over, I would get a job, save money, and leave.

In Other Words
blacklisted for not able to get
half a mind an idea

45   Griggs, who had accepted a speech written by the principal, came to my house each day and we went off into the woods to practice **orating**; day in and day out we spoke to the trees, to the creeks, frightening the birds, making the cows in the pastures stare at us in fear. I memorized my speech so thoroughly that I could have recited it in my sleep.

46   The news of my clash with the principal had spread through the class and the students became openly critical of me.

47   "Richard, you're a fool. You're throwing away every chance you've got. If they had known the kind of fool boy you are, they would never have made you valedictorian," they said.

48   I gritted my teeth and kept my mouth shut, but my **rage was mounting** by the hour. My classmates, motivated by a desire to "save" me, pestered me until I all but reached the breaking point. In the end the principal had to caution them to let me alone, for fear I would **throw up the sponge** and walk out.

49   On the night of graduation I was nervous and tense; I rose and faced the audience and my speech rolled out. When my voice stopped there was some applause. I did not care if they liked it or not; I was through. Immediately, even before I left the platform I tried to **shunt** all memory of the event from me. A few of my classmates managed to shake my hand as I pushed toward the door, seeking the street. Somebody invited me to a party and I did not accept. I did not want to see any of them again. I walked home saying to myself: The hell with it! With almost seventeen years of **baffled** living behind me, I faced the world in 1925. ❖

Graduation, 1948, Jacob Lawrence. Brush and black ink © 2013 The Jacob and Gwendolyn Lawrence Foundation, Seattle / Artists Rights Society (ARS), New York.

🔺 **Critical Viewing: Design** How does the artist use shape to differentiate the groups of people in this painting? What effect does this have?

In Other Words
orating speaking
rage was mounting anger was growing
throw up the sponge give up suddenly
shunt remove
baffled confused

MOMENT OF
TRUTH

EQ ESSENTIAL QUESTION:
What Do People Discover in a Moment of Truth?

myNGconnect.com

◆ Download the rubric.

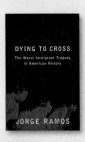

Present Your Project: Skit

It's time to present your skit about the Essential Question for this unit: What Do People Discover in a Moment of Truth?

1 Review and Complete Your Plan

Consider these points as you finish preparing your skit:

- How do your characters and plot address the Essential Question?
- Which group members will play which roles?
- What costumes and props will you need?

Practice your skit at least once before performing it for the class.

2 Present Your Skit

Perform your skit for an audience. Afterwards, invite audience members to tell you what they think about your skit.

3 Evaluate the Dramatization/Skit

Use the online rubric to evaluate each of the skits, including your own.

Reflect on Your Reading

Many of the characters and people in this unit made an important discovery about themselves in a moment of truth.

Think back on your reading of the unit selections, including your choice of Edge Library books. Then, discuss the following with a partner or in a small group.

Genre Focus Choose a selection from this unit. Name and give examples of the plot devices the author used in the story. If you were to rewrite the selection, would you choose the same plot device or a different one? Explain, giving examples.

Focus Strategy With a partner, compare and contrast the connections you each made to one of the unit selections. Discuss how your personal experiences and other reading affected your understanding and enjoyment of the text.

EQ Respond to the Essential Question

Throughout this unit, you have been thinking about what people discover in a moment of truth. Discuss the Essential Question with a group. What have *you* decided? Support your response with evidence from your reading, discussions, research, and writing.

Write a Literary Research Report

Writing Portfolio

Combining research with your own insights about something you've read is a great way to find out more about the literature that interests you. For this project, you will write a literary research report to examine an author's ideas, purpose, and style.

Study Literary Research Reports

Literary research reports combine and synthesize information from multiple sources about a literary topic. In a literary research report, you combine and organize facts from different sources with your own analysis.

❶ Connect Writing to Your Life

By now, you have read many short stories, novels, poems, and other works of literature. You also may have worked with classmates to gather information about authors and the background that shaped their ideas. Whenever you look beyond the text to find out more about it, you are conducting research.

❷ Understand the Form

A literary research report is primarily informative/explanatory writing, because it presents factual information and critics' published opinions on a specific literary work. It also includes your interpretation of the literature. A literary research report has an introduction, a body, and a conclusion, followed by a list of Works Cited. A good literary research report must contain the following elements:

Research Tip

When using multiple sources, identify discrepancies, or differences between important details.

For example, if one source says a poem was first published in 1923 and another source says it was 1926, check to see which date most sources report. If you cannot resolve a discrepancy, note this in your report.

1. Thesis Statement	A **thesis statement** consists of one or two sentences that state the **controlling**, or main, **idea** that you will develop in your report. It usually appears at the end of the introduction and is restated in the conclusion.
2. Supporting Information	Supporting information comes from research on your topic and makes up the body of the paper. It should relate to the thesis statement and provide background. Supporting information includes expert opinion, such as **literary criticism**, or published interpretation of literature and factual information, such as biographical details about the author.
3. Citations	Citations are references to the sources from which you gathered your information and evidence. They appear with the supporting information and evidence you are citing, or using, in your paper.
4. Conclusion	In the conclusion, you restate your thesis statement and briefly summarize your supporting ideas.
5. Works Cited Page	This page appears after the conclusion. It is a list of all the sources you used to write your report. Use a style guide to format and arrange your sources.

Now look at how these parts come together.

Read a literary research report by a professional writer.

❸ Analyze a Professional Model

As you read, look for the elements of the literary research report.

Family Conflict in Amy Tan's Short Story "Two Kinds"

by Irene Owens

Author Amy Tan believes that family relationships form the heart of her work (Shields 88). Her writing often explores conflict between Chinese immigrant parents and their children (Huntley 20). In the short story "Two Kinds," such family conflict leads to better understanding between a mother and her daughter.

Jing-mei's mother expects her daughter to follow Chinese ways. The mother's use of language reflects this conflict with her English-speaking, American-born daughter. In Tan's works, the difference in language "sharpens the edge of conflict between mothers and daughters" (Shields 91). Thus, the mother says to Jing-mei in Chinese: "Only one kind of daughter can live in this house. Obedient daughter!" Jing-mei replies in English, "Then I wish I wasn't your daughter."

Gradually, mother and daughter begin to see that two kinds of daughter can exist within the same person (Bloom 79). For example, Jing-mei eventually recognizes that "Pleading Child" and "Perfectly Contented" are "two halves of the same song."

Yet Jing-mei's new understanding occurs because her mother has also grown to understand her. For example, the mother offers the piano to Jing-mei on her thirtieth birthday, an act which transforms the piano from something forced upon Jing-mei as a child into a gift that the adult Jing-mei is free to enjoy.

Ultimately, the family conflict that drives "Two Kinds" results in greater family understanding.

Works Cited

Bloom, Harold, ed. <u>Amy Tan</u>. Philadelphia: Chelsea House, 2000.
Huntley, E. D. <u>Amy Tan: A Critical Companion</u>. Westport, CT: Greenwood Press, 1998.
Shields, Charles J. <u>Amy Tan</u>. Philadelphia: Chelsea House, 2002.

The writer states her **controlling idea**.

The writer supports her controlling idea with detailed examples, including accurate quotations from the text and literary criticism.

The writer **cites sources** by using the parenthetical method.

The writer provides a detailed **list of research materials**.

▶ **Prompt** Write a literary research report. Be sure to:

- identify the literary work's title, genre, and author
- introduce the topic and present a thesis statement about a significant aspect of the work
- provide supporting details from multiple sources, including the literary work itself
- restate your thesis statement in the conclusion

✔ Prewrite

Once you know what goes into a literary research report, plan one of your own. Begin by finding an interesting topic. As you work through the prewriting stage, you will focus your thoughts and make a Writing Plan.

❶ Choose Your Topic

These tips can help you find a topic:

- Choose a work of literature that is meaningful to you.
- What interests you about the work? What raised uncertainties or questions in your mind? Jot down your ideas and questions.
- Research answers to your questions. Find and read essays, books, and articles about the literary work you chose.

❷ Clarify the Audience, Thesis Statement, and Purpose

Your teacher and your classmates will probably be part of your audience. Who else would like to know about your topic? Jot down your ideas.

What aspect of your topic will you focus on? Write one or two sentences that summarize what your literary research will be about. These sentences will form your **thesis statement**.

Think about your purpose for writing. Is it to inform? Why else might you write about your topic? Write down your ideas.

❸ Do Your Research

When you research a literary topic, you look for detailed, accurate, and valid information about the author and his or her work. To get started, choose a graphic organizer to brainstorm what you already know about the work and include your thesis statement. What else will you need to find out in order to support your thesis statement? Jot down a list of questions. To find out more about the research process, see **Understand the Research Process** on page 437 as well as the **Language and Learning Handbook**, page 750.

Prewriting Tip

Choose a topic that is related to a poem, short story, novel, or play that you have read. You may want to compare and contrast two stories or a group of poems. Remember that in literary research

- the **primary source** is the literary work itself
- the **secondary sources** include critical, historical, and biographical texts and other resources.

Prewriting Tip

Prepare a working **bibliography**, or a list of available sources, to help you plan your research and get a head start on writing a Works Cited list. Ask a reference librarian or use an online search engine to locate

- books of literary criticism and other books, articles, and essays related to your topic
- *Reader's Guide to Periodical Literature*, an excellent guide to more contemporary, or recent, work
- Web sites by or about the author and his or her work.

❹ Organize the Details

In general, writers organize research reports either by order of importance or by chronological ideas. The student writer who researched Langston Hughes wanted to compare some of Hughes's earlier poetry with his later poetry. To do this, he first used a time line to track when each poem was first published. Then, he used a Venn diagram to compare and contrast details.

Langston Hughes's
Treatment of Dreams

earlier poetry
hopeful
powerful
alive
nurtured
protected

dreams

later poetry
neglected
deferred
drying up
explode
nearly extinct

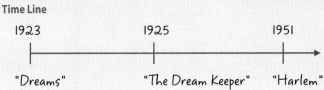

Time Line

1923 — "Dreams"
1925 — "The Dream Keeper"
1951 — "Harlem"

❺ Finish Your Writing Plan

Choose a graphic organizer, such as an outline, to create a Writing Plan.

Writing Plan

Topic	dreams in selected poems of Langston Hughes
Audience	my teacher, classmates, and other students
Thesis Statement	The treatment of dreams in some of Hughes's earlier poetry contrasts sharply with the treatment of dreams in a much later poem.
Purpose	to support an idea about a group of poems
Time Frame	start today; due in two weeks

I. Introduction
   A. introduce topic
   B. state thesis
II. Body
   A. earlier poems sound hopeful; speaker compares dreams to living things
      1. "Dreams," 1923
      2. "The Dream Keeper," 1925
   B. later poem "Harlem," 1951 sounds harsh; speaker describes dream as somewhat neglected, nearly extinct
III. Conclusion
   A. restate thesis
   B. summarize key points

🔖 **Writing Handbook**, p. 833

Prewriting Tip

Think about whether your audience will already have read the selection you choose to write about. If your audience does not know the work, you will need to give more background information.

Reflect on Your Writing Plan

▶ Have you organized the details in a way that suits your audience, controlling idea, and purpose? Talk them over with a partner.

✔ Write a Draft

Use your Writing Plan as a guide while you write your report. It's OK to make mistakes. You will have chances to improve your draft later on.

❶ Keep Your Ideas Flowing

If you took good notes during your research, you have a head start on the writing. Use your notes to write your draft.

❷ Cite Your Sources

As you write, cite your sources. That is, tell where you got information, ideas, or words that are not your own. One way to cite sources is to indicate them in parentheses. This is called the parenthetical method. When you use this method, you put the author's name in parentheses after the information, along with the page number on which the information was found. Check with your teacher to find out what citation style you should use.

> Some critics argue that "Hughes's bitter tone may actually be meant to provoke readers into keeping the dream of freedom alive," such as by supporting civil rights for all (McGrath 87).

After you finish writing, you are ready to create your Works Cited list. Include all the sources that you cited in your paper. Sources are listed in alphabetical order by authors' last names.

▼ **Language and Learning Handbook**, p. 777

❸ Student Model

Read this draft to see how the student used the Writing Plan to get ideas down on paper. This first draft does not have to be perfect. As you will see, the student fixed the mistakes later.

Dreams in the Poems of Langston Hughes

Langston Hughes was one of the most important writers and thinkers in the Harlem Renaissance. Hughes was a poet, a playwright, and liked jazz music. As a poet, "Hughes kept at the center of his art the hopes and dreams, as well as the actual lived conditions, of African Americans . . .". The treatment of dreams in Langston Hughes's earlier poetry contrasts sharply with the treatment of dreams in his later poetry. In Hughes's earlier poems, he presents dreams that are hopeful and alive, but in his later work, he doesn't.

For example, in the poem "Dreams," first published in 1923, Hughes urges the reader to "Hold fast to dreams." In this poem, Hughes compares dreams with a living thing. Hughes evokes dreams so real that people can hold them, nurturing them, and follow them to freedom.

Such hopeful dreams appear again in "The Dream Keeper," first published in 1925. In this poem, the speaker says, bring me all of your dreams, / You dreamers and promises to wrap . . . them / Away from the too-rough fingers / Of the world.

Many years later, however, Hughes presents dreams in a harsh light. "what happens to a dream deferred?" he asks in "Harlem [2]," published as part of Montage to a Dream Deferred in 1951. "Does it dry up / like a raisin in the sun? . . . /or does it explode?" In this poem, the dream is no longer a living, carefully tended being. Instead, the dream has become a mere thing, neglected and at risk of disappearing. Perhaps the dream will go slowly over a lifetime ("dry up," which reminds me of the words *give up*), or in a moment of outrage ("explode").

Some critics argue that Hughes's "Bitter tone may actually be meant to provoke readers into keeping the dream of freedom alive," such as by supporting civil rights for all (McGrath 87). I agree, because this poem is set up as questions the reader must answer. In 1963, four years before the poet's death, civil rights leader Dr. Martin Luther King, Jr. seemed to answer Hughes's questions when he gave his famous (and hopeful) "I Have a Dream" speech in Washington, D.C.

In summary, the earlier poems of Langston Hughes present dreams as hopeful and alive and his later works showed dreams that are somewhat neglected and nearly extinct. From these contrasting views, Hughes inspired fellow Americans to make the dream of freedom for all a reality.

Works Cited

Hughes, Langston. The Collected Poems of Langston Hughes. Ed. Arnold Rampersad. New York: Vintage Books, 1995.

McGrath, J.F. "He Dreamed a World." Journal of Literature. 12 Feb. 2006: 87.

Reflect on Your Draft

▶ Have you given detailed, accurate examples from the literary work and other sources to support your thesis statement? Talk them over with a partner.

✔ Revise Your Draft

Your first draft is done. Now, polish it. Improve the development of ideas. Make sure your writing is engaging and includes important and interesting details.

❶ Revise for Development of Ideas

In a good literary research report, the quality of the content is high. The writer presents **well-developed ideas**, both others' and his or her own. A good writer elaborates, or builds on, each significant idea by providing specific details for support. These include accurate quotations, helpful examples and descriptions, and clear references to cited sources of information. A well-developed research report also anticipates readers' concerns. For example, a literary report should include explanations of literary terms, stylistic devices, and other terms that may not be familiar to the audience. It should also be specific enough to make sense to readers who may not be familiar with the author and his or her work.

TRY IT ▶ With a partner, decide which ideas in the draft below need more explanation and support.

Student Draft

Langston Hughes was one of the most important writers and thinkers of the Harlem Renaissance. Hughes was a poet, a playwright, and liked jazz music. As a poet, "Hughes kept at the center of his art the hopes and dreams, as well as the actual lived conditions, of African Americans . . .". The treatment of dreams in Langston Hughes's earlier poetry contrasts sharply with the treatment of dreams in his later poetry. In Hughes's earlier poems, he presents dreams that are hopeful and alive, but in his later work, he doesn't.

For example, in the poem "Dreams," published in 1923, Hughes urges the reader to "Hold fast to dreams." In this poem, Hughes compares dreams with a living thing. Hughes evokes an image of dreams that are so real that people can hold them, nurturing them, and follow them to freedom.

Now use the rubric to evaluate the development of ideas in your own draft. What score do you give your draft and why?

Development of Ideas

	How thoughtful and interesting is the writing?	How well are the ideas or claims explained and supported?
4 Wow!	The writing engages the reader with meaningful ideas or claims and presents them in a way that is interesting and appropriate to the audience, purpose, and type of writing.	The ideas or claims are fully explained and supported. • The ideas or claims are well developed with important details, evidence, and/or description. • The writing feels complete, and the reader is satisfied.
3 Ahh.	<u>Most</u> of the writing engages the reader with meaningful ideas or claims and presents them in a way that is interesting and appropriate to the audience, purpose, and type of writing.	<u>Most</u> of the ideas or claims are explained and supported. • Most of the ideas or claims are developed with important details, evidence, and/or description. • The writing feels mostly complete, but the reader still has some questions.
2 Hmm.	<u>Some</u> of the writing engages the reader with meaningful ideas or claims and presents them in a way that is interesting and appropriate to the audience, purpose, and type of writing.	<u>Some</u> of the ideas or claims are explained and supported. • Only some of the ideas or claims are developed. Details, evidence, and/or description are limited or not relevant. • The writing leaves the reader with many questions.
1 Huh?	The writing does <u>not</u> engage the reader. It is not appropriate to the audience, purpose, and type of writing.	The ideas or claims are <u>not</u> explained or supported. • The ideas or claims lack details, evidence, and/or description, and the writing leaves the reader unsatisfied.

myNGconnect.com

◐ **Rubric: Development of Ideas**

◐ **Evaluate and practice scoring other student reports.**

❷ Revise Your Draft

You've now evaluated the development of ideas in your own draft. If you scored
3 or lower, use this checklist to improve your work and revise your draft.

Revision Checklist

Ask Yourself	Check It Out	How to Make It Better
Are the ideas in my literary research report clear?	If your score is 3 or lower, revise.	☐ If your report does not have a thesis statement, add one. ☐ Be sure that each body paragraph relates to the thesis. ☐ Make the main idea of each paragraph easy to identify. If necessary, add a topic sentence at the beginning of each body paragraph.
Have I explained and supported my ideas well? Have I cited multiple sources, including literary criticism and quotations from the literary work?	If your score is 3 or lower, revise.	☐ Look back at your notes and see if there is information you may have overlooked while writing your draft. ☐ If necessary, do more research to gather more supporting information, examples, and quotations.
Does my report reflect my own analysis of the literature?	Check to see that your main ideas come from your own thoughts and are not simply quotations from other people.	☐ Add a sentence to each body paragraph that clearly states your views.
Does my report have an introduction, a body, and a conclusion?	Find and mark the boundaries between the parts.	☐ Add any part that is missing.
Do I cite everything that I need to cite in my report? Do I accurately quote from the literary work?	Reread your report to be sure that any ideas or words that are not your own are properly cited.	☐ Add citations where necessary. ☐ Compare your quotations to the text.
Is every source that I cited included on a Works Cited list?	Compare your Works Cited list with your citations.	☐ Add any missing information. ☐ Check your citations for accuracy and proper format.

📖 **Language and Learning Handbook,** p. 750

❸ Conduct a Peer Conference

It helps to get a second opinion when you are revising your draft. Ask a partner to read your draft and look for the following:

- any part of the draft that is confusing
- any part where something seems to be missing
- anything that the person doesn't understand

Then talk with your partner about the draft. Focus on the items in the Revision Checklist. Use your partner's comments to make your report clearer, more complete, and easier to understand.

❹ Make Revisions

Look at the revisions below and the peer-reviewer conversation on the right. Notice how the peer reviewer commented and asked questions. Notice how the writer used the comments and questions to revise.

Revised for Development of Ideas

> Langston Hughes was one of the most important writers ∧an artistic movement in the 1920s that celebrated African American culture and thinkers of the Harlem Renaissance. Hughes was a poet, a
>
> playwright, and liked jazz music. As a poet, "Hughes kept at the
>
> center of his art the hopes and dreams, as well as the actual
>
> (Rampersad 5)
> lived conditions, of African Americans . . ."∧ The treatment of
>
> dreams in Langston Hughes's earlier poetry contrasts sharply
>
> with the treatment of dreams in his later poetry. In Hughes's
>
> earlier poems, he presents dreams that are hopeful and alive,
>
> but in his later work, he ~~doesn't.~~ presents a dream that is neglected
>
> and in danger of extinction.
>
> For example, in the poem "Dreams," first published in
>
> 1923, Hughes urges the reader to "hold fast to dreams." In this
>
> poem, Hughes compares dreams with a living thing. Hughes
>
> evokes an image of dreams that are so real that people can hold
>
> them, nurturing them, and follow them to freedom.
> / For if dreams die / Life is a broken-winged bird / That cannot fly.

Peer Conference

Reviewer's Comment:
What was the Harlem Renaissance? It sounds interesting.

Writer's Answer: Oh, I should explain that, because it helps show the significance of Hughes's work.

Reviewer's Comment:
I still have some unanswered questions. Who are you citing in the first paragraph? What living thing does Hughes compare dreams to? The brief quotation doesn't explain.

Writer's Answer: I see what you mean. I'll add specific details to support and clarify my ideas.

Reflect on Your Revisions

▶ Think about the results of your peer conference. What are some of your strengths as a writer? What things would you like to improve?

✔ Edit and Proofread Your Draft

When you have revised your draft, find and fix any mistakes that you made.

❶ Capitalize Quotations Correctly

When you are quoting only part of a sentence from a work of literature or criticism, you do not capitalize the first word of the quotation unless it is a proper noun or it is the first word of the entire sentence you are writing. With poetry, however, you should then follow the poet's capitalization for the rest of the quotation.

> In his later years, Hughes **"devoted** his life to teaching and lecturing."

> The speaker urges readers, **"Keep** dreams alive / **For** if dreams die / **Life** is a broken-winged bird / **That** cannot fly."

TRY IT ▶ Copy the sentences and fix the capitalization errors. Use proofreader's marks.

> 1. Hughes urges the reader to "Hold fast to dreams / for if dreams die / life is a broken-winged bird / that cannot fly."
> 2. "what happens to a dream deferred?" he asks in "harlem."
> 3. Hughes speaks of protecting dreams from "The too-rough fingers of the world."

❷ Use Quotation Marks Correctly

Put quotation marks (" ") around the exact phrase or sentence that you quote from a source. Do not use quotation marks if you are paraphrasing.

> Langston Hughes had an **"unrivaled command of the nuances of black urban culture."**

TRY IT ▶ Copy the sentences. Add quotation marks where necessary.

> 1. In this poem, the speaker says, Bring me all of your dreams, / You dreamers and promises to wrap . . . them / Away from the too-rough fingers / Of the world.
> 2. McGrath said, This poem is important.

Proofreader's Marks

Use proofreader's marks to correct errors.

Capitalize:
I read a̲ Guide to Lang̲ston Hughes.

Do not capitalize:
The poem is in the collection titled Poems F̸or Our Times

Add quotation marks:
˅"I like poetry,˅ she said.

Proofreading Tip

If you are unsure of when to use quotation marks or where to place them, look in a style manual for help and examples.

---

❸ Check for Parallel Structure

Combining shorter sentences into one longer sentence is a good way to add variety to your writing; however, you must be sure that similar elements in your sentences are parallel in form. For instance, if you have two or more ideas in the predicate, make sure they have the same word pattern.

Incorrect: Langston Hughes was a poet, a playwright, and liked jazz music.

Correct: Langston Hughes was **a poet**, **a playwright**, and **a jazz enthusiast**.

TRY IT ▶ Copy the sentence. Rewrite it so it has parallel structure.

> Hughes evokes dreams so real that people can hold them, nurturing them, and follow them to freedom.

❹ Use Adjectives and Adverbs Correctly

Use a comparative adjective to show how things are alike or different. Add *–er* to most adjectives followed by *than*. Use *more than* or *less than* with the adjective or adverb if it has three or more syllables.

Incorrect	Correct
This poem sounds more happy than that poem.	This poem sounds **happier than** that poem.
This poem is seriouser than that poem.	This poem is **more serious than** that poem.

Use an adverb instead of an adjective to modify a verb.

Incorrect	Correct
You can read this poem quick.	You can read this poem **quickly**.

TRY IT ▶ Copy the sentences. Correct any adjective or adverb errors.

> 1. The treatment of dreams in Hughes's earlier poetry contrasts sharp with the treatment of dreams in his later poetry.
> 2. Many years later, Hughes presents dreams in a more harsh light.

Reflect on Your Corrections

▶ Choose the paragraph from your report in which you made the most corrections. Read the original draft of that paragraph. Then read your edited version. Make a list of the changes that you made, and why.

❤ **Writing Handbook**, p. 832

5 Edited Student Draft

Here's the student's draft, revised and edited. How did the student improve it?

Dreams in the Poems of Langston Hughes

Langston Hughes was one of the most important writers and thinkers in the Harlem Renaissance, an artistic movement in the 1920s that celebrated African American culture ("Brief Guide"). He was a poet, a playwright, and a jazz enthusiast. As a poet, "Hughes kept at the center of his art the hopes and dreams, as well as the actual lived conditions, of African Americans . . ." (Rampersad 5). Yet, the treatment of dreams in Langston Hughes's earlier poetry contrasts sharply with the treatment of dreams in his later poetry. In Hughes's earlier poems, he presents dreams that are hopeful and alive, but in his later work, he presents a dream that is neglected and in danger of extinction.

For example, in the poem "Dreams," first published in 1923, Hughes urges the reader to "Hold fast to dreams / For if dreams die / Life is a broken-winged bird / That cannot fly." In this poem, Hughes compares dreams with a living thing, a bird. Hughes evokes dreams so real people can hold them, nurture them, and follow them to freedom.

Such hopeful dreams appear again in "The Dream Keeper," first published in 1925. In this poem, the speaker says, "Bring me all of your dreams, / You dreamers" and promises to "wrap . . . them / Away from the too-rough fingers / Of the world."

Many years later, however, Hughes presents dreams in a harsher light. "What happens to a dream deferred?" he asks in "Harlem [2]," published in 1951. "Does it dry up / like a raisin in the sun? . . . / Or does it explode?" In this poem, the dream is no longer a living, carefully tended being. Instead, the dream has become a mere thing, neglected and at risk of disappearing. Perhaps the dream will go slowly over a lifetime ("dry up," which reminds me of the words give up) or end in a moment of outrage ("explode").

Some critics argue that Hughes's "bitter tone may actually be meant to provoke readers into keeping the dream of freedom alive," such as by supporting civil rights for all (McGrath 87). I agree, because this poem is set up as questions the reader must answer. In 1963, four years before the poet's death, civil rights leader Dr. Martin Luther King, Jr. seemed to answer Hughes's questions when he gave his famous (and hopeful) "I Have a Dream" speech in Washington, D.C.

The writer added specific and accurate details to improve the development of ideas. The writer also used **parallel construction.**

The writer used **quotation marks** correctly.

The writer used **parallel construction** for similar elements in a sentence.

The writer fixed **capitalization errors.**

The writer used **adjectives and adverbs** correctly.

In summary, the earlier poems of Langston Hughes present dreams as hopeful and alive and his later works show dreams that are somewhat neglected and nearly extinct. From these contrasting views, Hughes inspired fellow Americans to make the dream of freedom for all a reality.

Works Cited

"Brief Guide to the Harlem Renaissance." Academy of American Poets. 2007 <http: www.poets.org/Harlem Renaissance>.

Hughes, Langston. The Collected Poems of Langston Hughes. Ed. Arnold Rampersad. New York: Vintage Books, 1995.

McGrath, J.F. "He Dreamed a World." Journal of Literature. 12 Feb. 2006: 87.

The writer used **parallel construction** for similar elements in a sentence.

The writer added a missing citation.

✔ Publish and Present

You are now ready to publish and present. Print out your report or write a clean copy by hand. You may also want to present your work a different way.

Develop a Multigenre Response With a group, present your report as part of a multigenre response. The multigenre response will consist of different types of writing, based on information in your report.

Plan Your Genres Divide a copy of your report into logical sections. With the group, decide which genres to use for each section. List them on a chart to help you keep track. Here's an example, based on the student's report.

Section I, Introduction	introduces Hughes, the Harlem Renaissance, and the thesis statement	• Kailah: write <u>letter</u> from Hughes's point of view • Maurice: <u>historical brochure</u> about Harlem in the 1920s • Carl: contrasting <u>poems</u> about dreams

Write Your Genres Present your genres in a binder beginning with the complete research report. Then, show Section 1 only of your report, followed by the genres. Repeat this process for each section.

Share Your Multigenre Response You can present your multigenre responses in a series of class readings, or donate a copy of your binder to the library.

🦋 **Writing Handbook**, pp. 838–839

Publishing Tip

With guidance from your reference librarian or teacher, find out about literary and creative writing journals that publish nonfiction by teens and other students of literature.

Reflect on Your Work

▶ Ask for and use feedback from your audience to evaluate your strengths as a writer.

• Did your audience find your report to be interesting? What did they learn?

• What did your audience think was the strongest point of your report? What did they think was the weakest point?

• What would you like to do better the next time you write? Set a goal for your next writing project.

 Save a copy of your work in your portfolio.

EQ ESSENTIAL QUESTION:

How Can We Balance Everyone's Rights?

People tend to forget their duties but remember their rights.

—INDIRA GANDHI

I believe that every right implies a responsibility; every opportunity, an obligation; every possession, a duty.

—JOHN D. ROCKEFELLER, JR.

Critical Viewing ▷
A young man speaks his mind at Speaker's Corner in Hyde Park, London, England. The law ensures that he can speak freely, no matter what he has to say. How does this demonstrate a balance between his rights and others'?

RIGHTS
AND RESPONSIBILITIES

EQ ESSENTIAL QUESTION:
How Can We Balance Everyone's Rights?

Study the Chart

The First Amendment to the United States Constitution guarantees some basic civil liberties. Among these are the three freedoms listed below: speech, the press, and religion. How do the responsibilities balance the rights in each case?

Freedoms	EVERYONE HAS THE RIGHT TO . . .	EVERYONE HAS A RESPONSIBILITY TO . . .
Freedom of Speech	express beliefs or opinions	avoid telling things that are not true or that might harm a person's ability to earn a living
Freedom of the Press	print all the news without government censorship or interference	strive to be accurate
Freedom of Religion	practice a religion of one's choice	avoid interfering with the rights of others or breaking the law

www.ccsu.edu/students/survival/images/rights.gif

Analyze and Debate

1. Imagine that you are sitting in a crowded movie theater when someone stands up and yells "Fire!" even though he knows there is no fire. Is this person balancing his rights with his responsibilities? Why or why not? What consequences could stem from his actions?

2. There have been many instances where a newspaper considers publishing an article that the government believes will reveal information that is important to our national security. Does the newspaper have a right to publish this type of article? Is the newspaper acting responsibly if it does? How can the paper balance the right to freedom of the press with the responsibility to protect national security?

Talk with a group. Explain your opinion and support your ideas with evidence from your knowledge and experience. Listen carefully to others' positions.

EQ ESSENTIAL QUESTION

In this unit, you will explore the **Essential Question** in class through reading, discussion, research, and writing. Keep thinking about the question outside of school, too.

1 Plan a Project

Political Campaign

In this unit, you'll be designing and carrying out a political campaign. Choose the kind of campaign you want to develop and issues you want to debate that address the Essential Question. To get started, look at past political ads, speeches, and Web sites. Look for

- the issues that cause the most debate
- what arguments the candidates use to persuade voters
- the types of media used in the campaign.

Study Skills Start planning your political campaign. Use the forms on myNGconnect.com to help plan your time and to prepare the content.

myNGconnect.com
- ▶ Planning forms
- ▶ Scheduler
- ▶ Sample political ads and speeches
- ▶ Cartoons and bumper stickers
- ▶ Rubric

2 Choose More to Read

These readings provide different answers to the Essential Question. Choose a book and online selections to read during the unit.

I Will Plant You a Lilac Tree
by Laura Hillman

It was the spring of 1942. Hannelore Wolff received news that her father had been killed and the rest of her family would be sent to a concentration camp. Hannelore could never have imagined the pain she would endure. But amidst the suffering, she found love and the will to survive.

▶ **NONFICTION**

The Autobiography of Miss Jane Pittman
by Ernest J. Gaines

Ticey is a slave girl who owns nothing. Maybe that is why she fights to take the name Jane. It tastes like freedom. But when Jane gets her freedom, it isn't what she thought it would be. Many things are taken from her. But there are some things that cannot be taken away.

▶ **NOVEL**

Monster
by Walter Dean Myers

Steve Harmon is 16 years old and on trial for murder. He must convince the jury that he is no murderer. But who is going to believe him when he looks like everybody else in jail? Will Steve receive a fair trial when he has already been labeled a monster?

▶ **NOVEL**

myNGconnect.com
- ◓ Read about the abuse of human rights around the world.
- ◓ Learn about landmark Supreme Court cases.

PERSUASIVE NONFICTION

Writers of persuasive nonfiction want to convince readers to agree with their position. Read these passages. Decide whether you think spending tax money on sports stadiums is a good idea.

DEMO TEXT #1

Taxpayers Unfairly Taking One for the Team

by Alejandra Ortiz, Citizens Against Useless Stadium Expense (CAUSE)

Since 1950, funding for new professional sports stadiums has come from taxes. Supporters of this practice claim that these buildings earn enough money to offset their cost, but the actual evidence does not support this. For example, Ray Hobbs, the author of a study on tax-generated sporting arenas, found that "the money gained by the community as a result of the new arena did not usually equal the cost in taxes used to build it."

The question at hand is simple: Are new sports stadiums worth the tax dollars they cost? The answer is even simpler: No. Using tax revenue to finance a new stadium will take money away from residents of our city. We should be using this money to build affordable housing, to improve our schools, or to build a new youth center. Wasting this money on an expensive sports stadium is the wrong thing to do.

DEMO TEXT #2

New Sports Stadium Is About Civic Pride

by Daniel Chu, City Sports and Tourism Board

All residents who love our city puff their chests out whenever the topic of our recent Super Bowl victory comes up. We all can remember where we watched that final game and were finally able to shout, "We're Number One!" What a party that was!

All of us, therefore, were shocked last year when the team's owner announced he would have to move the team to a different city unless a new stadium was built. It means that we might never have that amazing feeling again. It means that, every year, we would have to watch some other city feel the pride that could be ours.

While it's clear that a new stadium will earn millions for our city, this is about more than money. Using our tax dollars to build a new stadium would truly keep us together and make the city *ours*. Losing our team to another city would be a devastating loss.

Is it a good idea to spend tax money on a professional sports stadium?

■ Connect Reading to Your Life

What do you think about spending tax money on a new sports stadium? Should citizens support or oppose the idea? Take a vote.

Now, think about why you voted the way that you did. With a partner, list reasons for and against spending tax money on a new stadium.

New stadiums cost more money than they give back to the city.

People love to root for their city's sports teams.

Agree with Ms. Ortiz	Agree with Mr. Chu
I.	I.
2.	2.
3.	3.

Focus Strategy ▶ Synthesize

As you decided what you thought about spending tax dollars on a new sports stadium, you considered many different pieces of information. You thought about the excitement a professional sports team brings to a city, and you thought about the high cost of building a new stadium. You also probably thought about additional reasons based on your personal experience. You took all this information and used it to make your decision. That's synthesizing. When you synthesize, you put together ideas and events to form new overall understandings.

■ Your Job as a Reader

When you read persuasive nonfiction, you must remember that there are two sides to every argument. It is useful to read about both sides of an issue before making your decision. You can evaluate each writer's argument and combine the arguments to gain an even greater understanding of the issue. For example, you may agree that new stadiums are costly, but you still decide that the excitement generated by a professional sports team is worth the expense.

■ Unpack the Thinking Process

Whenever you are being persuasive, you are making an argument. Whether your arguments are formal (for example, writing an editorial about changing the school's dress code) or informal (such as talking your friends into going to the movies with you), they all need a certain structure.

The Structure of Arguments

At the heart of every argument is a **claim**. A claim is a statement that expresses the writer's position or main point. Good writers try to persuade readers to accept the claim by offering strong, relevant **evidence** and connecting that evidence to the claim by presenting reasons that make sense.

Claim	Reasons	Evidence
I believe that _____. The point you are trying to make (your position)	*Why do I say that?* A clear explanation of why the evidence supports the reasons, making the claim valid	*What's my proof?* • Facts • Statistics • Expert Opinions • Personal Experience

Responding to Counterclaims

Good writers know that people's opinions about a topic may differ. A **counterclaim** is what someone who disagrees with a writer's claim might say. In persuasive writing, the writer often includes one or more counterclaims and then explains why his or her own position is stronger.

Evaluate the Argument

Review the argument in each Demo Text. Ask yourself:

- **Reliability:** Is the evidence reliable—that is, does it come from a trustworthy source, and can it be checked? Is the evidence relevant to the topic?
- **Connection to Claim:** Does the writer present reasons that clearly explain how the evidence supports the claim?
- **Possible Counterclaims:** Does the writer consider other opinions and then defend against them?

Elements of Persuasion
claim *n.,* a statement defining an idea as true or false, right or wrong, good or bad

Academic Vocabulary
● **evidence** *n.,* ideas that support or prove a point

Identifying False Statements and Fallacious Reasoning

Remember that evidence may not always be accurate. Similarly, the writer may use methods that mislead the reader. Consider these questions:

- Why does the writer want me to agree with him or her?
- Is the writer's argument specific, or does it strike you as vague and unclear?
- Does the writer base the argument on specific facts, or does he or she rely heavily upon restating opinions or using highly emotional language?

■ Try an Experiment

Read this persuasive text.

DEMO TEXT #3

Give Teens a Break!

In all of the discussion about the new sports stadium, the focus has been on adult taxpayers, as if teenagers don't count. That thinking is bigoted. Every teenager loves sports, and teens are a vital part of our community. As our mayor herself has said, "Today's teens are tomorrow's leaders."

To help our local teens, I feel that the sports stadium should offer them a substantial discount on tickets to its athletic events. True, doing this may drive up the cost of the other tickets, but don't teens matter? Affordable tickets will allow teens a greater chance to socialize with friends and family and to get away from the pressures of everyday life. More important, teens will build their civic pride by following the home team in person.

So listen to your heart, not your wallet. You know that our teens deserve this.

—David Wilson
Youth Now

Think, Pair, Share To answer these questions, synthesize what you have read. Then compare answers with a partner. Include text evidence in your answers.

- What is the writer's claim?
- What counterclaims does he address? How does he defend against them?
- Does the writer mislead readers by making false statements or by using fallacious reasoning? Explain.

Evaluate As a class, decide whether the argument in Demo Text #3 is valid. If you agree that it is, discuss why. Otherwise, discuss how it could be more effective.

Monitor Comprehension

Persuasion What do readers need to consider as they read persuasive text? Explain.

EQ ## How Can We Balance Everyone's Rights?
Examine personal rights and privileges.

Make a Connection

Anticipation Guide Think about the positive and negative results of issuing a driver's license to someone who is 16 years old. Then tell whether you agree or disagree with each of these statements.

ANTICIPATION GUIDE	Agree or Disagree
1. Teens should not be allowed to drive until they pass a course in driver's education.	_____
2. Teens are safer drivers than adults.	_____
3. Parents should supervise teen drivers more closely.	_____

Learn Key Vocabulary

Study the Words Pronounce each word and learn its meaning. You may also want to look up the definitions in the Glossary.

● Academic Vocabulary

Key Words	Examples
● **consistently** (kun-**sis**-tent-lē) *adverb* ▶ page 565	The principal enforces school rules **consistently** so that all students are treated exactly the same way. *Synonym:* equally; *Antonym:* irregularly
excessive (ik-**se**-siv) *adjective* ▶ page 568	If something is **excessive**, it is more than the usual amount. It goes over usual limits. Tia's **excessive** spending caused her to run out of money quickly.
intrusion (in-**trü**-zhun) *noun* ▶ page 566	An **intrusion** occurs when people put themselves in situations or places where they have not been invited and are unwanted. It would be considered an **intrusion** if you walked through a doorway marked "No Entry."
precaution (pri-**kaw**-shun) *noun* ▶ pages 567, 577	A **precaution** is an action that a person takes to prevent possible danger or harm. Carlos sets his clock ten minutes early as a **precaution** against being late.
proficiency (pru-**fi**-shun-sē) *noun* ▶ pages 567, 577	Her **proficiency** in reading, writing, and speaking English is impressive; she almost never makes a mistake. *Synonym:* skillfulness; *Antonym:* inability
● **restrict** (ri-**strikt**) *verb* ▶ page 569	If you **restrict** something, you limit it. There are laws in many states that **restrict** 16-year-olds to working no more than three hours a day on school days.
● **transform** (trans-**form**) *verb* ▶ page 567	To **transform** is to change into something else. A caterpillar **transforms** into a butterfly when it emerges from a cocoon.
● **violate** (**vī**-u-lāt) *verb* ▶ pages 566, 576	If you drive faster than the speed limit, you **violate** the law and may get a ticket or fine. *Synonym:* break; *Antonym:* follow

Practice the Words Work with a partner to write four sentences. Use at least two Key Vocabulary words in each sentence.

Example: His <u>excessive</u> talking annoyed his teacher and was an <u>intrusion</u> on his classmates' time.

BEFORE READING Too Young to Drive?

editorial by Fred Bayles and
Maureen Downey

Reading Strategies

· Plan and Monitor
· Determine Importance
· Make Inferences
· Ask Questions
· Make Connections
▶ **Synthesize**
· Visualize

Evaluate Argument

A writer of **persuasive nonfiction** presents an **argument**, or claim, and then supports it with **evidence**, such as facts and expert opinions. Usually, the writer's argument takes one side of an issue. If the writer is *for* the issue, he or she takes the **pro** side. If the writer is *against* the issue, he or she takes the **con** side.

Read the following excerpt that shows one writer's argument for raising the driving age and another writer's argument against it.

Look Into the Text

The first writer's argument is on the con side of the issue.

Should the Driving Age Be Raised?
Author 1: NO! Driver's ed, not age, is key to road safety. Although the state requires that teens under 18 take driving classes before getting their licenses, it sets no specific curriculum standards.

Both writers support their argument with facts as evidence.

The word *should* is a signal that this is persuasive nonfiction.

Author 2: YES! Because immaturity fuels fatal crashes, Georgia should raise the driving age to 17 and permit age to 16. Sixteen-year-old drivers account for the highest percentages of crashes involving speeding, single vehicles, and driver error.

Focus Strategy ▶ Synthesize

Authors use persuasive nonfiction to convince you to believe or act in a certain way. When you **draw conclusions**, you develop judgments, or opinions, about the author's message. When you **synthesize**, you put together these conclusions and other ideas to form a new overall understanding.

HOW TO DRAW CONCLUSIONS

Focus Strategy

Use a chart to keep track of information.

1. Look for several facts or details the author provides about the topic.

2. Use logical reasoning and what you already know to develop a judgment, or opinion, about the facts that make sense.

3. As you continue reading, check to see if additional details cause you to rethink your conclusions.

Issue: Should the driving age be raised?

What I Already Know	What I Learned in the Text	→	My Conclusion
Some teens goof around and show off when driving.	16-year-old drivers have the highest percentage of crashes.	→	The driving age probably should be raised to an age when teens are more mature.

Teens at the Wheel

There is *some* good news for 16-year-old drivers. The number of fatal crashes among kids their age has declined in the United States, dropping 26 percent between 1993 and 2003, reports the Insurance Institute for Highway Safety.

The reason for the decline? Here it is, but it's bad news if you're a teen itching to get behind the wheel at night or with your friends in the car: Most of the fifty states have instituted graduated licensing, which restricts the freedoms of teenagers who are licensed drivers but do not have a full license. In many states, these young drivers are not allowed to drive at night and are prohibited from driving with other teens in a car. These rules have led to fewer teens being killed in car accidents.

Some say the great results with graduated licensing mean that society should take the next logical step: Ban driving by 16-year-olds altogether. So far, only New Jersey has done that. There, you have to be 17 to get a license.

Should other states follow New Jersey's lead and raise the driving age?

myNGconnect.com

🔊 Read a special report on teens at the wheel.
🔊 Learn safe driving tips and read about studies on teen driving.

TOO YOUNG TO DRIVE?

Comprehension Coach

Should the Driving Age Be Raised?

Driver's ed, not age, is key to road safety

FRED BAYLES, *The Boston Globe*

The latest fatal car crash involving a new teen driver has brought an understandable public outcry. The deaths of Andrea Goncalves, 17, and her 10-year-old brother Joshua add to a recent string of tragedies that have killed young drivers and their friends. Such stories **weigh heavily on** all parents as they hand the car keys over to their children.

But there is strong evidence the Massachusetts Legislature's rush to fix the problem is speeding off in the wrong direction.

Legislative leaders are pushing a bill to move up the legal driving age from $16\frac{1}{2}$ to $17\frac{1}{2}$. Other legislation would extend the period of time teens must drive with adult supervision before they can go solo or take their friends along.

The Legislature's sudden activism has been criticized by those who argue that experience, not age, is the key factor for safe driving. But this debate ignores some harsh truths about two critical failures by the state. The first is the woeful level of driver's education in Massachusetts. The second is evidence that the state's driver's exam is little more than **a formality**. 🔢1

Last fall, journalism graduate students in Boston University's Boston Statehouse Program conducted an examination of teen driving. They reviewed laws in other states, visited driving schools, interviewed driver's ed experts around the nation, and **polled** hundreds of teen drivers in the community.

Their findings, published in newspapers around the state, should **give pause to** those who think a year's delay in giving teens a license will cure a complex problem.

1 Evaluate Argument
What two arguments against raising the driving age does the writer introduce in this paragraph?

In Other Words
weigh heavily on deeply worry
a formality something you must do that has no importance or effect
polled questioned
give pause to cause second thoughts for

Among the findings:

1. Although the state requires that teens under 18 take driving classes before getting their licenses, it sets no specific curriculum standards. A majority of other states require driving instructors to take courses to prepare them to teach. Massachusetts instructors only need to have a safe driving record for certification.

2. Teens aren't being tested **consistently** or thoroughly.

   - Thirty-five percent of 459 high school seniors surveyed by the Statehouse Program said they were tested on seven or fewer of the twelve driving skills state police testers are supposed to check. Only 41 percent said they were tested on ten or more of the points.

   - Fifty-six percent of the students said their driver's test lasted ten minutes or less. Only 15 percent said the test took over twenty minutes.

   - Twenty-one percent said their driving school was either "fair" or "poor." Only 24 percent rated their driving school as "excellent." **2**

There is no question that instructors at many of the state's 215 driving schools take their responsibilities seriously. However, there also is no mechanism to screen the bad from the good. And there is much evidence of the bad.

A visit to one busy metro area school found some students asleep during class. Others stayed awake by text-messaging friends or reading magazines. Teens at other schools and concerned driving instructors confirm this was not unusual. Some schools, they say, are assembly lines that fill the required thirty hours of instruction with 30-year-old safety videos and simple recitation of the Registry's rules-of-the-road. **3**

Fixing driver's ed and **cracking down on** the testing system are essential steps forward, but other efforts are required. The Legislature should act on proposals that require more supervised experience behind the wheel.

2 Evaluate Argument What supporting evidence does the writer give to convince readers that teens "aren't being tested consistently or thoroughly"?

3 Evaluate Argument The writer says there is "much evidence" that many driving schools are bad. Do the examples in this paragraph convince you that he is right? Explain.

Key Vocabulary
- **consistently** *adv.*, equally

In Other Words
cracking down on improving, fixing

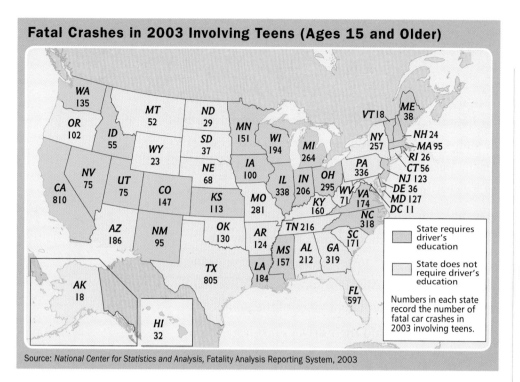

Fatal Crashes in 2003 Involving Teens (Ages 15 and Older)

WA 135
OR 102
ID 55
MT 52
ND 29
MN 151
WI 194
MI 264
ME 38
VT 18
NH 24
MA 95
NY 257
RI 26
CT 56
NJ 123
NV 75
UT 75
WY 23
SD 37
NE 68
IA 100
IL 338
IN 206
OH 295
PA 336
DE 36
MD 127
DC 11
CA 810
CO 147
KS 113
MO 281
KY 160
WV 71
VA 174
NC 318
AZ 186
NM 95
OK 130
AR 124
TN 216
SC 171
MS 157
AL 212
GA 319
AK 18
TX 805
LA 184
FL 597
HI 32

State requires driver's education

State does not require driver's education

Numbers in each state record the number of fatal car crashes in 2003 involving teens.

Source: *National Center for Statistics and Analysis*, Fatality Analysis Reporting System, 2003

◀ **Analyze the Map**
Does completion of a driver's ed course help to lower the number of crashes involving teens? Explain your reasoning.

National data suggest that teens become safer drivers if their first year behind the wheel is limited and supervised. There is no evidence, however, that having teens **cool their heels** until they are 17 will magically make them better, more mature drivers.

Also lost in the rush for a **quick fix** is the hard truth that parents must bear more responsibility. Many of the past year's fatal accidents involve recently licensed teens who have **violated** state law by driving after the midnight curfew for under-18 drivers or chauffeuring passengers under 18 within six months of getting a license.

Making parents **culpable** for such actions with stiff civil or even criminal penalties should be part of the legislative debate. Such tough love for parents should not be dismissed as more governmental **intrusion** into the family. A harsh fine **pales in comparison** to the life sentence of grief faced by the parent of a dead teen. **4**

4 Draw Conclusions
Do you think holding parents responsible for their teens' driving habits will reduce the number of deadly accidents? Why or why not?

Monitor Comprehension

Key Vocabulary
● **violate** *v.*, to break, not follow
intrusion *n.*, unwelcome interference

In Other Words
cool their heels wait patiently
quick fix fast and easy solution
culpable responsible
pales in comparison is very small compared to

Summarize
List three actions that the writer believes we should take to reduce unsafe driving among teens.

Should the Driving Age Be Raised?

Because immaturity fuels fatal crashes, Georgia should raise driving age to 17 and permit age to 16

YES!

MAUREEN DOWNEY, *The Atlanta Journal-Constitution*

The cause of most fatal car crashes involving teenagers is not **poor visibility** or road conditions. It's poor judgment.

The lack of experience and immaturity of young drivers leads them to be overrepresented in accident statistics: 16-year-old drivers account for the highest percentages of crashes involving speeding, single vehicles, and driver error.

Parents often overestimate their children's **proficiency** behind the wheel. After their teens pass driver's education and the on-road test, parents hand over the keys. Unfortunately, the evidence suggests that only one thing reliably **transforms** a teenager into a good driver—growing up. **5**

Driver education programs have been found to have little to no effect on reducing teen crashes. What does seem to work is limiting how early and how much teens can drive and how many passengers they can transport.

The older newly licensed drivers are, the less likely they are to crash, which is why Georgia ought to raise its driving age to 17 and its permit age to 16. Teen drivers should not be allowed to carry nonfamily members in the car during their first year. This **precaution** protects both them and their friends. In 2004, 62 percent of teenage passengers killed in crashes were traveling in cars driven by other teens.

Teens should be forbidden to use cell phones, a proven distraction to both children and adults. The state should also lower its midnight teen driving curfew to 9 p.m., as has neighboring North Carolina. **6**

5 Evaluate Argument
Analyze the writer's comments about parents. How does this reasoning support or weaken her argument?

6 Evaluate Argument
What examples of persuasive language does the writer use in this paragraph to support her argument?

Key Vocabulary
proficiency *n.*, skillfulness
• **transform** *v.*, to change
precaution *n.*, action to protect against harm

Teen Brains:
Still Under Construction

Researchers, such as Dr. Jay Giedd at the National Institutes of Health (NIH), have recently begun to understand the biological basis for teenagers' sometimes peculiar behavior.

Giedd, who studies brain development at NIH's National Institute of Mental Health, explained that scientists have only recently learned more about the path of brain growth. One important finding, he said, showed that the frontal cortex area—which governs judgment, decision-making, and **impulse control**—doesn't fully mature until around age 25.

"That really threw us," Giedd said. "We used to joke about having to be 25 to rent a car, but tons of industry data show that 24-year-olds are costing insurance companies more than 44-year-olds are." **7**

Source: *News In Health*, National Institutes of Health, September 2005

But none of these measures can replace **vigilant** parents, who have to understand that while their teen drivers may be confident about their driving skills, few are competent.

The reasons may rest in the research suggesting that the teenage brain is simply **not wired for** driving and that the impulse control and **risk assessment skills** needed to be a safe driver aren't developed until age 25.

Despite the advances in both car and road safety, teen deaths remain fairly constant. In 2004, drivers age 15 to 20 were involved in 7,898 fatalities, according to the National Highway Traffic Safety Administration. Too many Georgia children are among those fatalities.

Police blamed a recent crash that killed a high school senior on **excessive** speed and erratic driving. A day later, another high school student died when she turned left in the path of a dump truck.

7 Draw Conclusions
Combine what you already know with this information. What can you logically conclude about the role of brain development in driving?

Key Vocabulary
excessive *adj.*, more than the usual amount or limit

In Other Words
impulse control control of sudden, not-thought-out actions
vigilant watchful, careful
not wired for not naturally capable of
risk assessment skills judgment of danger

In February, a teenager died when the car he was riding in ran off a winding road near his school. Police charged the 16-year-old driver as a juvenile with **first-degree vehicular homicide**, reckless driving, two counts of serious injury by vehicle, and violation of his driver's license. DeKalb County has already had four teen driving deaths, including a 16-year-old who died on the first night of spring break. **8**

Parents have to start treating a driver's license as a first step in their child's driving education, not a final destination. ❖

8 Evaluate Argument
Does the evidence in this paragraph appeal mainly to the reader's sense of logic or sense of emotions? Explain.

ANALYZE Too Young to Drive?

1. **Explain** What does Fred Bayles think is the proper role of parents in the debate on teenage driving? How do you know this? Give examples from the text.

2. **Vocabulary** Why does Maureen Downey believe that Georgia should **restrict** issuing driver's licenses to people who are 17 years and older?

3. **Evaluate Argument** Find two examples of factual evidence used by each writer to support his or her argument. List your examples on a chart like the one below.

Fred Bayles	Maureen Downey

4. **Focus Strategy Draw Conclusions** Should the driving age be raised or should it stay the same? Support your conclusion with evidence from the selection and what you already know.

⤺ Return to the Text
Reread and Write Reread the selection. Then write a paragraph telling which writer balances people's personal rights and privileges better.

Key Vocabulary
• **restrict** *v.*, to limit

In Other Words
first-degree vehicular homicide causing a person's death by driving a car

BEFORE READING **Rules of the Road**

how-to article by Lynn Lucia

Reading Strategies

· Plan and Monitor
· Determine Importance
· Make Inferences
· Ask Questions
· Make Connections
▶ **Synthesize**
· Visualize

Analyze Development of Ideas

A **how-to article** describes a process or gives instructions about how to do something. In this type of writing, it is important to help the reader learn by highlighting important ideas—for example, through the use of heads to indicate subjects and subheads to indicate rules or tips. Then the writer usually follows up by giving more detailed instruction about how to follow the rule or apply the tip.

Look Into the Text

This head identifies the subject of the how-to article.

These sentences give more detailed how-to information.

How to Be a Safe Driver
Go slow near schools.

Watch for kids getting on and off school buses. When a bus stops in front of you and flashes its lights, you MUST stop. The flashing lights mean that students are getting on and off the bus and may be crossing the street.

Skim, or look ahead, for subheads that briefly state each step.

Focus Strategy ▶ Synthesize

A how-to article is meant to give you instructions one step or part at a time, but you still have to put all the parts together to understand fully how to do something.

HOW TO DRAW CONCLUSIONS

Focus Strategy

1. As you read a how-to article, take note of each instruction given by the writer.

> When a bus stops in front of you and flashes its lights, you MUST stop.

When a bus stops and flashes its lights, it means kids are getting off the bus and might run into the street. This instruction is a good tip for driving safely.

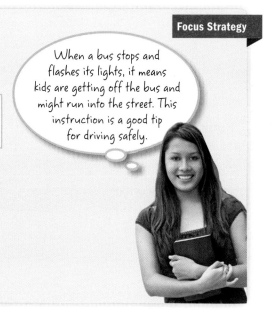

2. Combine all the instructions into a complete picture. Decide whether you have enough information and whether the information is reliable.

3. What does it all mean? Put ideas together and draw a conclusion about what you've learned.

Connect Across Texts

In "Too Young to Drive?" you read about different solutions to the problem of unsafe driving among teens. Now read the following how-to article for tips on safe driving.

Rules of the Road

by Lynn Lucia

So, you've mastered left-hand turns, parallel parking, and merging onto the freeway. Now all you need are the keys to the family car and you'll be fully able to take advantage of your vehicular independence . . .

Not so fast! Passing the driving test is only half the challenge. Becoming an experienced, safe driver is the other. Remember, driving isn't a right. It's a privilege that can be easily revoked if you don't play it safe.

In Other Words

your vehicular independence the freedom of being able to drive a car
revoked taken away, removed

The day Eddie Angert got his driver's license, he was **on top of the world**. "Getting my license was huge," says the 18-year-old senior from Oceanside, New York. **1** "Now I don't have to depend on my parents, or my friends' parents, to drive me anywhere." But within a year after getting his license, Eddie found out there's more to driving than turning on the ignition and stepping on the accelerator. "I got three traffic tickets at once," Eddie says. "I lost control of my car on a turn and a cop gave me tickets for **imprudent** speed, failure to keep right, and making an unsafe turn."

Eddie isn't alone in making mistakes behind the wheel. Teens ages 16 and 17 represent only about 2 percent of all drivers in the United States, but they are involved in nearly 11 percent of all motor-vehicle crashes.

Why are teen drivers so unreliable? They're inexperienced drivers, say transportation and driving safety experts. It takes at least five years of driving to make someone an experienced driver, says Edwin Bailey, a safety education officer in Amherst, New York. "You're not going to become proficient in driving unless you do it," Bailey says. "Get your parents to take you out to get that driving experience."

> ## It takes at least five years of driving to make someone an experienced driver.

Of course, getting that experience isn't easy. There's plenty to be concerned about while driving: your car, other cars on the road, traffic lights, road conditions, and bad weather. Below are tips from driving-school teachers, police officers, and department of motor vehicle officials on how to **steer clear of** trouble on the road. **2**

1 Language
An **idiom** is a word or phrase that has a meaning beyond its literal definition. What do you think the idiom *huge* means?

2 Analyze Development of Ideas
Does the author fully explain why teen drivers are unreliable? Support your conclusion.

How to Be a Safe Driver

Obey laws. Wear your seat belt. Seat belts save 9,500 lives per year according to the National Highway Traffic Safety Administration. Don't drink and drive. Do obey the posted speed limit. ▪3

▪3 Analyze Development of Ideas
How do the details in the paragraph expand on the tip in the subhead?

Cut down on distractions. Say your favorite tune is playing on the radio so you reach over and **blast the volume**. Bad idea. The noise reduces your ability to hear sirens coming from police cars, fire trucks, or ambulances, and honking horns from other cars and trucks. Don't chat on a cell phone while driving either; people who talk on phones while driving are four times more likely to have an accident.

Distractions such as loud music, cell phones, and rowdy friends are dangerous for the driver.

At a green light, accelerate gradually. If your car is the first vehicle at a red light, wait a few seconds after the light turns green before proceeding. Often, cars try to make it through an intersection during a yellow light. If you **gun your vehicle** immediately when a light turns green, you run the risk of crashing into an oncoming car.

In Other Words
blast the volume turn the sound up very loud
gun your vehicle make your car go very fast

Go slow near schools. Watch for kids getting on and off school buses. When a bus stops in front of you and flashes its lights, you MUST stop. The flashing lights mean that students are getting on and off the bus and may be crossing the street.

Many schools have crossing guards stationed nearby to warn drivers and protect pedestrians.

Look both ways before making a right-hand turn. You may think you only have to look to the left to watch for oncoming cars before you make a right-hand turn. But if you don't look to the right, you risk hitting **a pedestrian** who's crossing the street and who has the **right of way**.

Turn left at a light only when there's a green arrow. Sure it's legal to turn left at a green light that doesn't have a green arrow. But it's a dangerous move if **traffic is heavy**. A green arrow guarantees that you have the right of way. If you want to practice turning left at lights that don't have green arrows, make sure an experienced driver is with you. He or she can help you judge the flow of traffic. **4**

Don't rely only on mirrors when changing lanes. Looking in your car's rearview and sideview mirrors isn't enough to make sure that a car isn't too close to your vehicle. Those mirrors have blind spots—areas where cars are hidden from your vision. The only way to know for sure if it's safe to change lanes is to turn your head and see for yourself.

4 Draw Conclusions
Based on your own experience and what you're reading, are these safety tips valid and relevant? Explain your conclusion.

In Other Words
a pedestrian someone walking
right of way right to cross a street or intersection first
traffic is heavy there is a lot of traffic

Be careful in parking lots. Believe it or not, many accidents occur in parking lots. A common **collision** happens when cars parked across from each other are both backing out. Always back out slowly and check for cars and pedestrians crossing into your path.

5 Analyze Development of Ideas
How does the example help you understand the tip?

Don't assume what other drivers will do. Just because you're paying attention to the road and driving safely doesn't mean that other drivers are doing the same. For example, a car with a flashing turn signal may not, in fact, turn at all. The driver may change his or her mind about turning, or may not realize that the turn signal is on. 5

Be cautious in bad weather. Rain, snow, and ice make streets harder to drive on, so when roads are wet, slow down. A good rule is to double the space between you and the vehicle in front of you. This will give you more space to stop if you have to hit the brakes. Turn your headlights on anytime you need to turn your windshield wipers on. This will help you see other cars and other cars see you. Some states require that all vehicles turn on their lights during bad weather. ❖

Bad weather can seriously affect a driver's ability to see and to react.

In Other Words
collision crash

ANALYZE Rules of the Road

1. **Explain** Which tip in this how-to article offers the most helpful information? Explain your choice.

2. **Vocabulary** Do you think that talking on a cell phone while driving **violates** the public's right to safety? Why or why not?

3. **Analyze Development of Ideas** Why are subheads especially helpful in a how-to article?

4. **Focus Strategy Draw Conclusions** What conclusion do you draw about all the tips in this selection? Work with a partner and decide what they have in common and how relevant they are.

Return to the Text

Reread and Write How well do the tips in "Rules of the Road" promote teens' safety and driving privileges? Reread the selection and determine whether the tips apply to drivers in general or teen drivers in particular. Write a paragraph explaining your findings.

EQ How Can We Balance Everyone's Rights?

Reading
Critical Thinking

1. **Analyze** Reread the **Anticipation Guide** on page 560. After reading the selections, would you like to change any of your answers? Explain.

2. **Interpret** What are two **precautions** teen drivers should take, based on both of the articles? Use evidence from the selections to support your conclusions.

3. **Compare Across Texts** Which of the writers—Fred Bayles, Maureen Downey, or Lynn Lucia—depends most heavily on logical appeals as opposed to emotional appeals? Explain.

4. **Speculate** Bayless mentions that many students are not paying attention in driver's education classes. Imagine that you are a driver's ed teacher. What are some steps you might take to keep students interested and alert? Explain.

EQ 5. **Synthesize** How does the driving age affect the public's right to safety and adolescents' right to freedom? Does it favor one group's rights over the other? Explain. Support your answer with evidence from the texts.

Writing
Write About Literature

Analysis of Evidence In persuasive writing, supporting evidence is very important. Write two or three paragraphs in which you identify two types of supporting evidence used in each selection. Evaluate how these types of evidence are important.

Vocabulary
Key Vocabulary Review

Oral Review Work with a partner. Use these words to complete the paragraph.

consistently	precaution	transform
excessive	proficiency	violate
intrusion	restrict	

There are many ways we can __(1)__ our roads into safer places. First, every driver should have to take a yearly test to prove his or her __(2)__ in driving, and we should __(3)__ the driving privileges of anyone who does poorly on the test. You may think that a yearly test is unfair and __(4)__, but I believe it is a necessary __(5)__ that will prevent harm. The police should also enforce laws __(6)__ and fairly, so that all drivers are treated the same way. If an officer sees someone __(7)__ a traffic law, the officer should give the person a ticket rather than just a warning. This is not an unfair __(8)__ into the person's life. It is, instead, a lifesaver for all of us.

Writing Application Think of a sport, hobby, or skill in which you would like to achieve **proficiency**. Then write a paragraph telling why. Use at least four Key Vocabulary words.

Fluency
Read with Ease: Phrasing

Assess your reading fluency with the passage in the Reading Handbook, p. 814. Then complete the self-check below.

1. I did/did not pause appropriately for punctuation and phrases.

2. My words correct per minute: _____ .

INTEGRATE THE LANGUAGE ARTS

Vary Your Sentences

Writing that uses a variety of sentence patterns can be more interesting to read.

How can you vary your sentences.

- Use an **infinitive phrase**.

    To get a license takes weeks.

- Start some sentences with a **gerund**.

    Speeding is the cause of many accidents.

- Begin a sentence with a **prepositional phrase**.

    At the corner, turn left.

- Use parallel structure: **infinitives** with infinitives, **gerunds** with gerunds.

    I hope **to drive** well and **to stay** safe. **Voting** is a right, but **driving** is a privilege.

Oral Practice (1–5) With a partner, start a sentence with each group of words and then finish the sentence.

1. Using cell phones
2. One important class to take
3. To drive safely
4. Limiting the number of passengers
5. Passing the test and getting a license

Written Practice (6–10) Rewrite the paragraph below. Vary the sentence structure and use parallel structure.

You don't become a good driver just by passing the test and get your license. Experience counts, and there is plenty absorbing your attention and to distract you on the road. Think about the tips of experts on safe driving and how to stay out of trouble.

Bias

When you read a news article in the paper or online, you are given basic facts that tell about a process or event. In "Rules of the Road," for instance, the writer gives you some factual tips for driving safely.

However, when you read an editorial, such as "Too Young to Drive?" you are introduced to the writer's bias. **Bias** is a strong opinion that can occasionally be unreasonable and reveals an author's viewpoint. It can prevent a person from looking fairly at both sides of an issue.

To detect bias in a text, look for the following:

- explanation of only one side of an argument
- words and language structures that reveal feelings and emotions
- stereotypes, or simplified beliefs about a particular group of people

Think about and discuss the following questions in a small group:

1. In "Too Young to Drive?" what type of bias does Fred Bayles show? What words show his viewpoint? What other clues reveal his bias?

2. Does Maureen Downey show the same bias as Fred Bayles? How do you know this?

Express and Support Opinions

Group Talk You have read selections in which teen drivers are described as unreliable. Do you agree with that description? Justify your opinion with facts and evidence.

Denotation and Connotation

The words *cheap* and *economical* have the same direct meaning, or **denotation**. They both mean "inexpensive." However, *cheap* conveys a negative feeling, and *economical* conveys a positive one. These feelings are called **connotations** and can be negative, positive, or neutral. Determine the denotation of each row of words below, and then decide if each word's connotation is negative, positive, or neutral. Use a dictionary to help you.

1. busy   energetic   hyperactive
2. frustrating   challenging   difficult
3. tenacious   stubborn   persistent

Interview

Social Studies: Coming of Age How important is a driver's license to teenagers as a symbol of becoming adults? Interview your classmates to gather opinions on this subject.

1 **Prepare Interview Questions** Write at least three questions that will help your classmates think about what a driver's license means to them.

2 **Conduct the Interviews** When you ask your classmates the questions you have prepared, speak clearly and slowly. Then listen carefully. Take notes on what your classmates say.

Write a Short Persuasive Essay

A test may ask you to write a persuasive essay. The prompt often names the topic, or issue, and asks you to support it or argue against it.

1 **Unpack the Prompt** Read the prompt and underline the key words.

> **Writing Prompt**
>
> In "Too Young to Drive?" two opinion columnists argue different sides of the same issue. With whom do you agree? Write a persuasive essay stating and supporting your argument.

2 **Plan Your Response** Choose the pro or con side of the issue. Then fill out a map such as the one shown below.

Persuasion Map

My Argument → Reason 1 → Supporting Evidence
My Argument → Reason 2 → Supporting Evidence
My Argument → Reason 3 → Supporting Evidence

3 **Draft** When you draft, organize your supporting evidence in an order that makes sense. Use introductory words and phrases to tie ideas together.

Essay Organizer

> I believe that [state your argument].
> First, [state your first reason]. [State your supporting evidence].
> In addition, [state your second reason]. [State your supporting evidence].
> Finally, [state your third reason]. [State your supporting evidence].
> For these reasons, I urge you to [restate your argument].

4 **Check Your Work** Reread your essay. Ask:

- Does my essay address the writing prompt?
- Do I give reasons, examples, and other evidence to support my argument?
- Do I vary my sentences?

Writing Handbook, p. 832

1

2

3

Inside Public Transit

A public transit agency provides transportation services in a city or town. Most transportation authorities provide bus service. Some also provide train or subway services.

Jobs in Transportation

A public transit agency requires many workers. Drivers, schedulers, and managers work together to provide efficient service.

Job	Responsibilities	Education/Training Required
Bus Driver 1	• Collects fares • Drives a bus along a set route • Conducts routine daily maintenance checks	• High school diploma • Commercial driver's license • On-the-job training
Scheduler 2	• Analyzes data to schedule routes • Uses scheduling software • Assists scheduling supervisor	• College degree • Experience in transit operations
Community Transportation Manager 3	• Creates budgets • Manages transportation resources and operations • Brings in new customers through advertisements or promotions	• College degree in business-related field or certification by a transit industry organization • Experience supervising transit workers

Write a Business Memo

A memo is a written way to communicate inside an organization.

1. Imagine you are a scheduler for your local public transit agency. You would like to add a new bus route to the city's transportation schedule.

2. Write a business memo to your supervisor proposing this new route. Include reasons you think it would be a good idea. Remember to use a professional tone.

3. Share your memo with classmates, and see if they have any suggestions for improvement. Save the information in a professional career portfolio.

myNGconnect.com

🌐 **Learn more about community transportation authorities.**

🌐 **Download a form to evaluate whether you would like to work in this field.**

🌐 **Download a memo form.**

🔖 **Writing Handbook, p. 832**

Build Word Knowledge

Imagine three people describe you. The first says, "You are calm." The second says, "You are inactive." The third says, "You are lazy." Are they saying different things? *Calm*, *inactive*, and *lazy* all mean "not moving much." This is their *denotation*, their direct meaning. The words also convey feelings, their *connotations*. Connotations can be positive, negative, or neutral.

A **dictionary** is a good place to look up direct meanings of words and compare meanings. A **thesaurus** lists words that are similar to each other. It is a great tool for finding a word that conveys the connotation you want.

Positive	Neutral	Negative
calm	inactive	lazy

Identify Connotations

Turn the following insults into compliments by replacing the highlighted words with a word from the Word Bank that has the same direct meaning but communicates more positive or neutral feelings. Use a print or digital dictionary or thesaurus as needed.

1. You are **conceited**!
2. It was **reckless** of you to act that way.
3. You are acting **wild**.
4. You have a **weird** voice.
5. You are so **naïve**!

> **Word Bank**
>
> distinctive, innocent, proud, energetic, impulsive

Put the Strategy to Use

Use this strategy to expand your vocabulary with denotations and connotations.

1. If necessary, use a dictionary to look up a word.
2. Think of words that have the same denotation but different connotations. Use a thesaurus if you like.
3. Rewrite the sentence using the word you thought of or found in the thesaurus.
4. Write *positive*, *neutral*, or *negative* after the sentence to show how the word you chose affects the connotation of the sentence.

TRY IT▶ Use the word *proud* in a sentence. Follow the steps above and identify how your sentence affects the connotation of the word *proud*.

📖 Reading Handbook, p. 781

EQ How Can We Balance Everyone's Rights?
Decide how best to protect individual and public rights.

Make a Connection

Quickwrite Do you think all content on the Web should be free, or should people have to pay to use certain materials? Write down your thoughts in a short paragraph.

Learn Key Vocabulary

Study the Words Pronounce each word and learn its meaning. You may also want to look up the definitions in the Glossary.

● Academic Vocabulary

Key Words	Examples
● **access** (**ak**-ses) *verb* ▶ page 587	When you **access** something, you find and retrieve it. Type in your name and password to **access** your assignments on the school's computer network.
counterfeit (**kown**-tur-fit) *adjective* ▶ page 587	The salesperson was shocked to learn that the $20 bill was **counterfeit**. *Synonyms:* fake, phony; *Antonyms:* real, genuine
● **facilitate** (fu-**si**-lu-tāt) *verb* ▶ page 591	If you **facilitate** an action, you help to make it happen. You can **facilitate** your entry to the concert by having your ticket out and ready for the usher.
● **fundamental** (fun-du-**men**-tul) *adjective* ▶ pages 587, 592	Our **fundamental** rights are listed in the first ten amendments to the Constitution. *Synonyms:* basic, essential; *Antonyms:* secondary, minor
● **impact** (**im**-pakt) *noun* ▶ pages 586, 600, 601	An **impact** is an effect or influence on something. Computers have had a deep **impact** on everyday life by allowing us to access information quickly.
merit (**mer**-it) *noun* ▶ pages 591, 601	If the committee believes that the new project has **merit**, the members will vote to adopt it. *Synonyms:* worth, value; *Antonyms:* worthlessness, inferiority
repercussion (rē-pur-**ku**-shun) *noun* ▶ page 591	A **repercussion** is a negative effect of an action or event. At my high school, a **repercussion** of being late to class is detention.
verify (**ver**-i-fī) *verb* ▶ page 587	To **verify** something is to check whether it is correct or true. Please show your driver's license to **verify** your identity.

Practice the Words Work with a partner. For each Key Vocabulary word, complete a **Word Square**.

Word Square

Definition: a negative effect of an action or event	Important Characteristics: usually not intended or on purpose
Examples: getting a ticket for speeding	Non-examples: getting an A on an art project

repercussion

BEFORE READING **Piracy Bites!**

persuasive nonfiction by Reps. Lamar Smith
and Edolphus Towns

Reading Strategies

· Plan and Monitor
· Determine Importance
· Make Inferences
· Ask Questions
· Make Connections
▶ **Synthesize**
· Visualize

Evaluate Argument

When you **evaluate** an argument, you decide if the evidence a writer presents is credible and persuasive enough to support the writer's claim.

Look Into the Text

Piracy in Cyberspace
by Rep. Lamar Smith

The writer uses an analogy, or comparison.

Pirates still exist, but they aren't like the pirates of the past. The modern day thieves are engaged in the theft of intellectual property....

Intellectual property represents the largest single sector of the American economy, employing 4.3 million Americans.

This sentence gives a statistic to provide support for the claim.

Piracy Hurts Everyone Both Online and Offline
by Rep. Edolphus Towns

The writer gives an ethical reason, or a reason why the claim is the moral thing to do.

... The rush to make all content available online ... has real world consequences. These consequences ... affect small urban record stores, rural used booksellers, and other retailers.... These are small businesses that provide jobs in my community, ... and theft ... affects the ability of these small business owners to exist. I have a serious problem with that.

Notice the emotional language.

Focus Strategy ▶ Synthesize

When you read persuasive writing about a particular issue, it is a good idea to read the argument of more than one writer. You can evaluate each writer's argument and compare evidence across texts to gain a greater understanding of the issue.

HOW TO COMPARE EVIDENCE

Focus Strategy

Use a chart to compare both writers' evidence.

1. As you read, write examples of effective evidence provided by each writer.

2. Determine your own understanding based on your evaluation of both writers' works.

Types of Evidence	Rep. Smith	Rep. Towns
Facts / Statistics	4.3 million work in intellectual property	no statistics provided
Examples	modern pirates steal intellectual property	piracy affects small business

My understanding: Stealing intellectual property has become a serious crime.

Downloading Material from the Internet

With a world of music available at the click of a computer mouse, many people feel they have the right to download, copy, and share whatever they find online—without paying for it. But under copyright law, the person who creates the music owns the music, and taking it without paying for it is just a high-tech form of theft.

Illegal downloading has become a hot issue in the Internet age, and the question of how best to solve that problem is just as hotly debated. Now read what two congressional representatives say should be done about illegal downloading. Who do you think offers the more effective solution?

myNGconnect.com

🔊 Learn about recording artists' views on piracy.
🔊 Read about the consequences of movie piracy.

PIRACY BITES!

Speeches by Rep. Lamar Smith, R-Texas and Rep. Edolphus Towns, D-New York

Comprehension Coach

PIRACY IN CYBERSPACE

BY U.S. REPRESENTATIVE LAMAR SMITH, REPUBLICAN FROM TEXAS

Pirates were a major presence in the 17th and 18th centuries. These buccaneers **wreaked havoc** on the high seas by sailing the trade routes in search of vessels loaded with goods and merchandise to seize.

Stolen cargo at the hands of pirates not only created an economic loss for the merchant but also financed future illegal activities for the pirates who took it.

One could complete a transatlantic voyage today without ever spotting a pirate ship. Most people would say that pirates no longer exist, unless you count the Pirates of the Caribbean ride in Disneyland. Unfortunately, it isn't true.

Pirates still exist, but they aren't like the pirates of the past. These modern day thieves are engaged in the theft of **intellectual property**. And their **impact** is colossal. **1**

Intellectual property represents the largest single sector of the American economy, employing 4.3 million Americans.

The music industry estimates that annual sales of illegal compact discs approach 2 billion units—worth $4 to 5 billion. Globally, one in three recordings is a pirated copy. The motion picture industry faces huge losses, too. One million movie files are downloaded illegally on the Internet each day. Software manufacturers also **take a hit**. One out of every four copies of software used in the United States is an illegal copy, resulting in an annual loss to software makers of $2.6 billion. **2**

Pirates affect not only our economic security, they affect our national security. Their profits fund other illegal activities, including terrorism.

Terrorist organizations require considerable funds to maintain their worldwide activities and to purchase equipment, guns, and explosives. News stories reveal that terrorist organizations receive hundreds of millions of dollars through pirate operations. For example, police in Argentina and Paraguay uncovered a pirate CD business that has used their profits to **underwrite** terrorist activities.

1 Evaluate Argument
The speaker creates an analogy between pirates in the past and in the present. Does he convince you that the analogy is valid, or true? Explain.

2 Evaluate Argument
What kind of evidence is the speaker using to support his argument so far?

Key Vocabulary
- **impact** *n.*, effect, influence

In Other Words
wreaked havoc caused destruction
intellectual property someone's creation
take a hit suffer losses
underwrite pay for

Pirated goods have a large market. The Web is a virtual shopping mall of goods and services, both legal and illegal. But technological advances don't change the **fundamental** rules of right and wrong.

Colleges and universities are prime locations for illegal downloads. Students are both technologically **savvy** and primary consumers of music, video games, and movies. Forty percent of students surveyed at two public universities admitted to having pirated software.

Just because material is available in cyberspace doesn't make it legal to **access** it. Downloading a copyrighted song, video game, or movie from the Internet is the same as shoplifting a CD or DVD from a local store.

Under current law, we can prosecute someone for **trafficking in** fake labels for a computer program, but we cannot prosecute for faking the hologram that the software maker uses to **verify** that the software is genuine. We criminalize trafficking in **counterfeit** documentation and packaging of software programs, but not music and other products.

This week, I will introduce legislation to update and strengthen the federal criminal code, which currently makes it a crime to traffic in counterfeit labels or copies of certain forms of intellectual property, but not authentication features.

My legislation will also criminalize trafficking in counterfeit music, movies, and other audiovisual works, and it will give victims of intellectual property theft an opportunity to recover damages in federal court.

As we secure critical infrastructure from cyber attacks, we must not fail to secure copyrighted products from cyber theft, too. **3**

3 Evaluate Argument
What does the speaker want us to do or think about this issue?

SO I DOWNLOADED A FEW SONGS — SO WHAT?

Think again! Downloading illegal copies of music and movies carries some stiff penalties:

- up to ten years in prison
- thousands of dollars in fines
- hundreds of hours of community service

Monitor Comprehension

Evaluate
Which part of the author's argument did you find most effective? Which part did you find least effective? Explain.

Key Vocabulary
- **fundamental** *adj.*, basic
- **access** *v.*, to gain entry to
  verify *v.*, to check
  counterfeit *adj.*, fake, phony

In Other Words
savvy wise
trafficking in buying and selling

SPEAK OU
ON PIRACY

PIRACY FAQS

Q. What is piracy?

A. The general term *piracy* refers to the illegal copying and selling of sound and video recordings.

Q. How does it affect me?

A. Piracy drives up the price of legitimate recordings. The picture, sound, and packaging of pirated music and movies are also often of a poor quality, and the product cannot be returned.

Q. How can I tell if a CD or DVD is counterfeit or pirated?

A. Check these seven points:

- The packaging has blurry graphics and weak or bad color.
- The package or disc has misspelled words.
- The price is often way below retail value.
- You're buying it at a flea market, from a street vendor, at a **swap meet**, or in a concert parking lot.
- The record/studio label is missing or it's a company you've never heard of.
- It has cheaply made insert cards, often without **liner notes** or multiple folds.
- The sound quality is poor.

"When you make an illegal copy, you're stealing from the artist. It's that simple. Every single day we're out here pouring our hearts and souls into making music for everyone to enjoy. What if you didn't get paid for your job? Put yourself in our shoes!"

— Sean (Diddy) Combs, Multiplatinum Award-Winning Artist, Producer, Founder, and CEO of Bad Boy Entertainment
▼

In Other Words

FAQs Frequently Asked Questions
swap meet gathering to exchange used items
liner notes information about the songs and
   performers

"Making an album is a team effort, so when somebody pirates a record that not only affects the artist, but also the people who worked on it like coproducers, cowriters, and musicians. Say no to piracy."

◄ — Shakira, Grammy-Winning
Latin Pop Artist

"We really look at it as stealing, because, that's just it. To us it's black and white, either you pay for it or you don't. And you're not paying for it."

— Nelly, Multiplatinum ►
Hip-Hop Artist

"You might as well walk into a record store, put the CDs in your pocket, and walk out without paying for them."

◄ — Mark Knopfler,
Member of Dire Straits

Monitor Comprehension

Explain
Why do musicians oppose illegal downloading? How can it be prevented?

PIRACY HURTS EVERYONE [BOTH ONLINE AND OFFLINE]

BY U.S. REPRESENTATIVE EDOLPHUS TOWNS,
DEMOCRAT FROM NEW YORK

From the day that Gutenberg reproduced a book with his printing press, there has been a debate on copyright protections and what their reach should be.

I am of the opinion that content—offline and online—should be protected to the full power that the law allows. I have always been a strong proponent of technology and of the innovations that technology offers society. Technology and content are **the backbone of our economy** and will continue to be the engines that produce and distribute quality goods and services while creating high-paying jobs for workers.

But the rush to make all content available online to all consumers has real world consequences. These consequences not only affect consumer electronic and technology companies, artists, and large content companies but, more importantly, small urban record stores, rural used booksellers, and other retailers in congressional districts across the country. These are small businesses that provide jobs to people in my community, and theft—piracy is nothing but a fancy name for theft—affects the ability of these small business owners to exist. I have a serious problem with that. **4**

In addition, I believe that my colleagues and I must also be concerned about the long-term social effects of teaching our children that everything in life—if it happens to come online—is free. How can a parent be expected to teach a child the dignity of labor and the value of "an honest day's work for an honest day's pay" if the child or family members go online and steal other people's hard work? **5**

There are class issues in play here, too. If someone in a low-income community—who has no Internet or computer access—goes to a record

> ## "Piracy is nothing but a fancy name for theft."
> — U.S. REPRESENTATIVE EDOLPHUS TOWNS, D-NEW YORK

4 Evaluate Argument
What consequences does the speaker see for small businesses if piracy continues? How do these claims strengthen or weaken his argument?

5 Evaluate Argument
A speaker who uses an **ethical reason** addresses the audience's sense of right and wrong. What ethical reason does Rep. Towns use in this passage?

In Other Words
the backbone of our economy important businesses

Historical Background
Johannes Gutenberg (c.1397–1468) invented the modern printing press, which can reproduce texts in large numbers. His work led to important changes in publishing and communications.

store and steals a CD or DVD, he is fined and/or put in jail. If an affluent child with broadband access downloads (i.e., steals) ten CDs from online sharing services, there are no visible **repercussions** and parents often praise that child for being tech savvy. **6**

Luckily, I am not the only person who **sees inequity in this situation** and **takes issue with the plight of** local small businesses. There are many ideas floating around that attempt to provide a solution to this widespread problem.

While many legislative proposals have **merit**, I have three simple suggestions, which I would like to put forward—one for device manufacturers, one for content owners, and one for consumers.

To consumer electronics companies—stop advertising the notion that content is free and can be copied and distributed for the cost of a computer with burner functions. All fair use defenses or claims aside, if I put up a $10 million ad campaign behind a computer that copies DVDs and CDs, copyright piracy **is going to soar**.

When a person can purchase a computer and sell pirated music, books, or content for pennies on the dollar for what the local merchant in Brooklyn is selling it for or simply giving it away for free, we must act and act quickly because jobs and commerce are at stake. No one can compete with "free." If everyone could copy a computer purchased originally by a friend, manufacturers wouldn't be in business long.

To content companies—use all the self-help technological measures available to protect your products. I am pleased to know that more **encryption** technology is being developed, but as every smart businessman knows, the customer will only wait for so long before going to another outlet and, unfortunately, the other outlets are unlawfully giving your product away.

Further, develop your business models to get this content online in protected fashion. If Congress needs to help **facilitate** the necessary discussions, we will be more than happy to do so.

To consumers—remember that content is not always free to share or steal. Without profitable artists,

6 Evaluate Argument Does this contrast between low-income and affluent children seem true to you? Analyze how effective the speaker's argument is.

songwriters and, yes, content companies, there won't be any content left to enjoy. Remember that fair use does not mean, "Buy one get one free!"

I personally plan to redouble my efforts to focus these industries on the ultimate goal of resolving this issue without legislation that would **stifle innovation** or disrupt the distribution of content. **7**

We in Congress need to remember that while the large content and electronic companies get most of the **sound bites** in the piracy debate, it is the small business owners, songwriters and, in the end, consumers, who lose the most when content is stolen. I hope that my colleagues will join me in fighting for these people in the continuing debate on this issue. ❖

7 Compare Evidence
How do Rep. Towns's solutions to the problem compare with Rep. Smith's solutions?

ANALYZE Piracy Bites!

1. **Explain** What does Rep. Towns focus on in his argument against piracy? What is he most concerned about? Be sure to cite evidence from the text.

2. **Vocabulary** Do you agree that honesty is a **fundamental** issue in both representatives' arguments? Why or why not?

3. **Evaluate Argument** Who has the stronger argument against piracy—Rep. Smith or Rep. Towns? Explain the strengths and weaknesses of each.

4. **Focus Strategy Compare Evidence** What similar types of evidence do Rep. Smith and Rep. Towns use to support their proposals? How does this use of evidence affect your understanding of intellectual property theft? Explain.

Return to the Text

Reread and Write Reread the arguments. Then write a paragraph in which you either support new legislation, like Rep. Smith, or public cooperation, like Rep. Towns.

In Other Words

stifle innovation prevent the development of new technology
sound bites news coverage

POSTSCRIPT

by Dana Summers

© Dana Summers, *The Orlando Sentinal*, 2000.

Facts: reasearch

Feeling: appeal to your emotions

Head: logic. If then.

BEFORE READING Doonesbury on Downloading

editorial cartoon by Garry Trudeau

Reading Strategies

· Plan and Monitor
· Determine Importance
· Make Inferences
· Ask Questions
· Make Connections
▶ Synthesize
· Visualize

Analyze Central Idea

An **editorial cartoon** is intended to persuade the reader to think or act in a certain way about an issue, usually something current or in the news. The cartoonist has a central idea and develops that idea through choosing the order of events, the dialogue, and the details in the visuals. Editorial cartoonists hope to make their point more persuasive through the use of humor.

Look Into the Text

Speech balloons show who is speaking.

The editorial cartoonist uses humor to address a serious issue.

Focus Strategy ▶ Synthesize

When you **compare across texts**, you determine how the ideas in each text are the same and how they are different. To **synthesize**, you combine these ideas to form a new overall understanding of the issue.

HOW TO COMPARE EVIDENCE

Focus Strategy

1. As you read the cartoon, think about how it compares with the arguments in "Piracy Bites!" Use a chart like the one shown to keep track of your thoughts.

2. Evaluate the evidence and arguments for validity and relevance.

3. Form a new understanding of the issue by combining all three writers' ideas.

Trudeau's Ideas in "Doonesbury on Downloading"	Towns's and Smith's Ideas in "Piracy Bites!"
Dad doesn't agree with piracy.	Piracy is theft; it hurts owners of intellectual property.
Daughter thinks piracy is OK.	Lots of young people think everything on the Internet should be free.

My understanding of this issue: A generation gap exists in beliefs about intellectual property rights.

Connect Across Texts

In "Piracy Bites!" two Congressmen use persuasive language to argue against Internet piracy. Now see how a cartoonist uses a different method to present the same argument.

Doonesbury on Downloading

by Garry Trudeau

Over the years, readers have seen comic strip character Mike Doonesbury develop from a college student into a middle-aged parent. He and Alex, his daughter, disagree on many issues, including pirated music.

1 **Central Idea**
The third frame shows reactions instead of dialogue. What might each character be thinking? How might their thoughts point to a central idea for the cartoon?

Cultural Background

Beggars Banquet (1968) is an album by the Rolling Stones, one of the world's longest running, most popular rock bands.

2 **Compare Evidence**
How does Alex's argument here compare with the details you read in "Piracy Bites!"?

In Other Words
a looter's logic the way a thief thinks
set me straight on warn me about

3

3 Central Idea
How do Mike and Alex's viewpoints differ? What does that difference suggest about the central idea of the cartoon?

In Other Words
impounding taking away

4 Compare Evidence
How logical is Alex's argument here compared with the arguments in "Piracy Bites!"?

In Other Words
picking up sensing
Frankly Honestly

About the Cartoonist

Garry Trudeau (1948–   ) created Doonesbury when he was a college student. So far, his Doonesbury collections have sold over 7 million copies worldwide, and the cartoon appears in almost 1,400 newspapers. In 1975, he became the first comic strip artist to win a Pulitzer Prize for editorial cartooning. The Pulitzer Prize is considered the highest honor in the field of print journalism.

ANALYZE Doonesbury on Downloading

1. **Summarize** What are two arguments Alex uses to justify downloading music for free?

2. **Vocabulary** What is the **impact** of Alex's confession that she no longer pays for movies?

3. **Analyze Central Idea** What are two examples of humor in the editorial cartoon? How do they help clarify the cartoon's central idea?

4. **Focus Strategy Compare Evidence** When you compare evidence presented in this selection with evidence in "Piracy Bites!" what new understanding do you gain about Internet piracy? Explain.

Return to the Text

Reread and Write Reread the cartoon. Then write a paragraph explaining Garry Trudeau's views on balancing everyone's rights. Use evidence from the editorial cartoon to support your explanation.

EQ How Can We Balance Everyone's Rights?

Reading

Critical Thinking

1. **Compare** Reread the **Quickwrite** exercise you completed on page 582. After reading the selections, what revisions would you make to what you wrote? Discuss your reactions with a partner.

EQ 2. **Analyze** Do you think that downloading music for free is a "victimless" crime, or does it involve real costs and economic loss? Support your answer with examples from both the selections.

3. **Interpret** In his argument, Rep. Towns tells consumers to "remember that fair use does not mean, 'Buy one get one free!'" What does he mean?

4. **Speculate** Imagine that you are a successful pop singer and you learn from your recording company that sales of your recordings have dropped because of piracy. How would you explain your feelings about the situation to those who think musicians already make too much money?

EQ 5. **Synthesize** Do you believe that editorial cartoons can have as much of an **impact** as the speeches of politicians can on what people believe about people's rights? Support your answer with examples from the essays and the editorial cartoon.

Writing

Write About Literature

Letter Elected officials seek ideas from the public when considering new laws. Write a letter to a local representative expressing your opinions about file sharing. Support your opinions with evidence from both texts.

Vocabulary

Key Vocabulary Review

Oral Review Work with a partner. Use these words to complete the paragraph.

access	fundamental	repercussion
counterfeit	impact	verify
facilitate	merit	

Since the mid-1990s, the Internet has had a(n) __(1)__, or essential, __(2)__ on the ways people __(3)__, or get, information. Search engines greatly help, or __(4)__, the tasks of researchers, who are able to locate information easily and then __(5)__ its accuracy by consulting other Web sites. Now, however, the effect and __(6)__ of such a system is beginning to cause concerns. How accurate is information on the Web? Can we really tell whether something is genuine or __(7)__? The information on some sites, critics warn, may lack both __(8)__ and credibility.

Writing Application Think about what the idea of **merit** means to you. Then write a paragraph on this topic. Use at least three vocabulary words.

Fluency

Read with Ease: Expression

Assess your reading fluency with the passage in the Reading Handbook, p. 815. Then complete the self-check below.

1. My expression did/did not sound natural.

2. My words correct per minute: _____ .

Grammar

Use Compound Sentences

What is a **clause**? A clause is a group of words with a **subject** and a **verb**. An independent clause can stand alone as a sentence.

Most **people pay** for online music.

A **compound sentence** has two independent clauses. The clauses may be joined by a **conjunction** like **and**, **but**, and **or** with a comma (,) before the conjunction.

- Use **and** to join ideas that are alike.
- Use **but** to join ideas that are different.
- Use **or** to show a choice between two ideas.

Clauses may also be joined by a semicolon alone or with a semicolon, a conjunctive adverb, and a comma. *However* and *therefore* are common conjunctive adverbs.

- People can pay for music, **or** they may face a fine.
- Alex downloads for free; **however**, it isn't legal.
- It's not really fair; musicians lose money.

Oral Practice (1–5) Say five sentences about music piracy. Have a partner add an independent clause to make a compound sentence.

Written Practice (6–10) Rewrite the paragraph below. Use three different ways of combining sentences to create five compound sentences.

> Pirates exist today. They are not like pirates of the past. Today's pirates steal music and movies. They affect national security. Illegal music is available on the Web. It is for sale not for free. Laws need to change. Thieves should be punished. Look for signs of piracy. Help limit criminal activity.

Language Development

Persuade

Group Talk What do you think about music piracy? Take a position and convince others to agree. Support your position with strong reasons.

Literary Analysis

Faulty Persuasive Techniques

Writers use many techniques to persuade their readers. Some of these methods, however, are faulty. They may be unsupported by facts, not related to the issue, or simply not true. The following are some common faulty persuasive techniques:

- ***Ad hominem*** (Latin—"to attack the man") means to avoid discussion of an issue by attacking someone personally instead.

  Example: "Musicians are against file sharing because they're greedy!"

- **Circular reasoning** means to argue something is true by simply restating what you're arguing about.

  Example: "Instant messaging is a popular form of communication because lots of people do it."

- **Bandwagon appeals** argue that someone should do something because everyone else is.

  Example: "Everybody downloads free music from the Internet."

Review "Piracy Bites!" and "Doonesbury on Downloading." Find faulty modes of persuasion in the arguments. Write the text and the type of faulty persuasion.

" 'How I Spent My Summer Vacation,' by Lilia Anya, all rights reserved, which includes the right to reproduce this essay or portions thereof in any form whatsoever, including, but not limited to, novel, screenplay, musical, television miniseries, home video, and interactive CD-ROM."

Connotation

Connotations are the feelings conveyed by words. Connotations can be negative, as in the word *lazy*; positive, as in the word *calm*; or neutral, as in the word *inactive*. These words have similar **denotations**, or meanings, but they communicate very different feelings. Think of a word that has the opposite connotation from each word in the chart below.

POSITIVE	NEGATIVE
1. complex	_____
2. _____	boring
3. sensitive	_____

Oral Report

Social Studies: Copyright Law Using library and Internet resources, gather material for a short oral report on copyright law. In your report, you may want to cover some or all of the following topics:

- What are some examples of literary works that are still in copyright?
- What are "public domain" and "fair use"?
- How does an author obtain a copyright?
- What are some of the penalties for infringing, or violating, copyright?

After giving your report, listen to other reports.

🍂 **Language and Learning Handbook**, p. 750

Write a Position Statement

In a **position statement**, you form an opinion about an issue and support your position with evidence.

1 **Prewrite** Choose an issue that has more than one side. Write a topic sentence that states your position. Then list reasons and evidence to support it.

2 **Draft** Give your reasons in a logical order, such as most important to least important.

3 **Revise** Reread your statement. Ask yourself:

- Does my position statement clearly convey my stand on the issue?
- Do I give examples to support my ideas?
- Do I avoid faulty persuasive techniques?

4 **Edit and Proofread** Ask yourself:

- Do I use conjunctions correctly?
- Have I formed compound sentences correctly?
- Have I avoided using run-on sentences?

5 **Publish** Share your position statement with a partner.

🍂 **Writing Handbook**, p. 832

Model

> I believe the hours of operation of Town Park should be extended during the summer months. At this time, the park closes at 7:00 in the evening. This closing time makes sense for the winter months, when the days are shorter and visitors are fewer. However, during summer months, this closing time is too early for the people of my community. For example, last week my family held a birthday party for my aunt in the picnic area. At least four other families were holding picnics, too. Some guests to these parties did not arrive until well after 6:00. When park attendants began prompting people to leave, it was only 6:45, long before any of the parties showed any sign of slowing down. We all know that closing times are necessary for park maintenance and safety, but the enjoyment of the community the park serves should be considered as well.

Topic Sentence

Reason

Evidence

PERSUASIVE SPEECH

Would you like to be someone who makes things happen? Think about a project or activity that you would really like to see happen at your school or in your community. It could be something that meets an important need (such as a literacy center) or something that is just fun (like a dance club). Plan to give a persuasive speech that tells why your project is a good idea and convinces school or community leaders to make it a reality. Here is how to do it.

① SELECT YOUR SUBJECT AND FORM AN OPINION

Choose a project that you feel very strongly about as the subject for your persuasive speech. Keep these points in mind:

- You will be expressing an opinion. An opinion is one person's point of view about something.
- An opinion is different from a fact. A fact can be proved. Valid opinions are supported by facts, examples, and logic.
- Write your opinion in a sentence or two.

② PLAN YOUR SPEECH

Decide on the best facts and examples to support your opinion. Then decide on the order you will present these facts and examples in your speech.

- Choose background information that will help your audience see why your project is important.
- If you need to, do some extra research to find interesting facts and examples that people may not have heard before.
- Expect that some people will disagree with you. Think of ways to answer their objections respectfully.
- Present your ideas in an order that is easy to follow and convincing.
- Make graphics or find photos that support your opinion.

What about this speaker will help ensure that he is taken seriously?

myNGconnect.com
◐ **Download the rubric.**

③ PRACTICE YOUR SPEECH

Use your words, voice, and gestures to connect with your audience.

- Begin by clearly stating your opinion. Practice using persuasive words such as *must* and *should*.
- Use appropriate details and effective transitions.
- Find natural gestures to emphasize your ideas without using gestures too much.
- Display graphics and photos to illustrate your points and keep your audience engaged.
- End with a powerful conclusion.

④ GIVE YOUR SPEECH

Persuade your audience by using these techniques:

- Make eye contact with individuals in your audience.
- Stay as relaxed as possible and stay on topic.
- Speak clearly and loudly so that others can understand.
- Show that what you are saying is important to you by using a tone of voice that is convincing and confident.

⑤ DISCUSS AND RATE THE SPEECH

Use the rubric to discuss and rate the speeches, including your own.

PERSUASIVE SPEECH RUBRIC

Scale	Speech's Persuasiveness	Content of Speech	Speaker's Performance
3 Great	• Was powerful and effective • Made me care about the subject	• Used effective support • Order made sense all of the time	• Grabbed and held my attention • Was always easy to understand
2 Good	• Was interesting most of the time • Had some effect on my feelings	• Had a few good supporting facts • Order made sense most of the time	• Held my attention most of the time • Was usually easy to understand
1 Needs Work	• Was not very interesting • Did not make me care about the subject	• Support was weak or off the topic • Order made no sense	• Did not hold my attention • Was hard to hear or understand

DO IT ▶ Now that you know how to give a persuasive speech, persuade your audience that what you are saying is important!

🍃 Language and Learning Handbook, p. 750

EQ **How Can We Balance Everyone's Rights?**
Explore the struggle for human rights around the world.

Make a Connection

KWLS Chart Think about the following question: What do you know about human rights around the world?

List what you know in the first column of a **KWLS Chart**. In the second column, list what you would like to know about this topic. You will fill out the third and fourth columns after you've read the selections.

KWLS Chart

Topic: Human Rights Around the World

What I Know	What I Want to Know	What I Learned	What I Still Want to Learn

Learn Key Vocabulary

Study the Words Pronounce each word and learn its meaning. You may also want to look up the definitions in the Glossary.

● Academic Vocabulary

Key Words	Examples
apathetic (a-pu-**the**-tik) *adjective* ▶ pages 625, 629	If you are **apathetic**, you don't care or have any interest in something. *Synonyms:* uninterested, indifferent; *Antonyms:* interested, impassioned
● **distinction** (di-**stink**-shun) *noun* ▶ page 625	The main **distinction** between carrots and apples is that carrots are vegetables and apples are fruit. *Synonym:* difference; *Antonym:* similarity
emancipation (i-man-su-**pā**-shun) *noun* ▶ page 611	On January 1, 1863, President Abraham Lincoln ordered the **emancipation** of all slaves in the United States. *Synonym:* freedom; *Antonym:* enslavement
● **exploitation** (ek-sploi-**tā**-shun) *noun* ▶ pages 623	**Exploitation** is the act of using people in a selfish way by taking advantage of them. Laws prevent the **exploitation** of children by employers who would force them to work long hours.
inclination (in-klu-**nā**-shun) *noun* ▶ page 615	If you have an **inclination** for something, you have a liking for it. Her **inclination** for exercise led her to play soccer and tennis.
liberate (**li**-bu-rāt) *verb* ▶ page 611	To **liberate** is to set free. The soldiers opened the jail doors and **liberated** all the prisoners.
● **motivated** (**mō**-tu-vā-tid) *verb* ▶ pages 620, 627	To be **motivated** is to be very determined to do or achieve something. Kara was **motivated** to score a goal because her team was losing by only one point.
oppression (u-**pre**-shun) *noun* ▶ pages 611, 620, 623	**Oppression** occurs when one group treats another group unfairly and prevents them from having the same rights as everyone else. Slavery is a form of **oppression.**

Practice the Words Work with a partner to write four sentences. Use at least two Key Vocabulary words in each sentence.

Example: The apathetic man said he did not feel motivated to change the world.

BEFORE READING **Long Walk to Freedom**
autobiography by Nelson Mandela

Reading Strategies
· Plan and Monitor
· Determine Importance
· Make Inferences
· Ask Questions
· Make Connections
▶ **Synthesize**
· Visualize

Analyze Viewpoint: Word Choice

In his autobiography, Nelson Mandela repeats part of the speech he made when he became the first black president of South Africa. The purposes of the speech were to express his viewpoint and to make an argument that would persuade people to fight oppression and protect everyone's rights. To make his viewpoint clear and his argument effective, Mandela chose his words carefully:

- **emotion-filled words** to appeal to listeners' feelings
- **repetition of words** to emphasize key points
- **signal words** like *should* and *must* to emphasize the need for action

---

Look Into the Text

Emotion-filled words appeal to the audience's feelings.

>   …We thank all of our distinguished international guests for having come to take possession with the people of our country of what is, after all, a common victory for justice, for peace, for human dignity.
>   … Never, never, and never again shall it be that this beautiful land will again experience the oppression of one by another.…The sun shall never set on so glorious a human achievement.

Repetition emphasizes Mandela's viewpoint and argument.

This signal word is a form of the word *should*.

Focus Strategy ▶ Synthesize

Speech writers often use **generalizations** and persuade their audiences to form generalizations, too. When you form generalizations, you determine what multiple ideas and events have in common.

HOW TO FORM GENERALIZATIONS

Focus Strategy

1. **Take note of statements** by the author that seem to tie ideas together.

2. **Add examples** to the statements from your own knowledge and experience.

3. **Construct a sentence** that seems true for both the author's statements and your own examples.

> • Mandela states that gaining equal rights in "our country" (South Africa) is a glorious achievement.
> • The American Civil Rights Movement was also focused on gaining equal rights.
> **Generalization:** Many people in the world have struggled to gain equal rights.

Nelson Mandela
(1918–)

I never imagined the struggle would be either short or easy.

Nelson Mandela's life is proof of the power of one person to bring rights and freedom to many people.

Mandela was **44 years old** when he was sentenced to life imprisonment.

Mandela was born in a small South African village, the son of a Tembu tribal chief. He later left village life to study law and then worked with the African National Congress (ANC), a political party. His work with the ANC brought new strength to South Africa's nonwhite majority. It also brought him into conflict with the ruling white elite, a minority who enjoyed rights that they denied most other South Africans. In 1962, Mandela was imprisoned. Two years later he was given a life sentence.

Mandela continued his work for human rights from his prison cell on Robben Island. It was there, in 1974, that he secretly began writing the book *Long Walk to Freedom*.

When Mandela was finally released from prison in 1990, the world celebrated. In 1993, he and South Africa's white president, F.W. de Klerk, won the Nobel Peace Prize for their combined effort to end the country's policy of racial discrimination. A year later, Mandela, the former political prisoner, became president of South Africa.

myNGconnect.com

🔊 Listen to a reading from *Long Walk to Freedom*.
🔊 Read birthday messages people sent to Nelson Mandela when he turned 85.

People lined up for hours to vote in South Africa's first nonracial election in 1994.

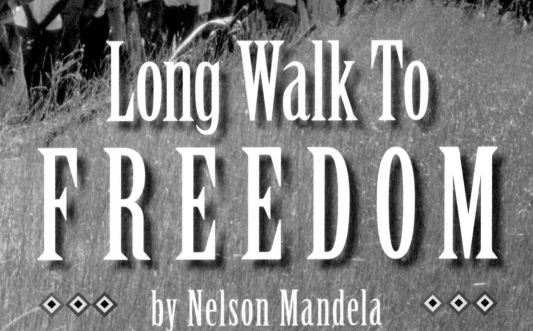

Long Walk To
FREEDOM

◆◇◆ ◆◇◆ by Nelson Mandela ◆◇◆ ◆◇◆

May 10, 1994, dawned bright and clear. For the past few days, I had been pleasantly besieged by arriving dignitaries and world leaders who were coming to pay their respects before the inauguration.

Read to discover why May 10, 1994, is an important day in world history.

THE INAUGURATION WOULD BE the largest gathering ever of international leaders on South African soil. The ceremonies took place in the lovely sandstone amphitheater formed by the Union Buildings in Pretoria. For decades, this had been the seat of **white supremacy**, and now it was the site of a rainbow gathering of different colors and nations for the installation of South Africa's first democratic, nonracial government. **1**

On that lovely autumn day I was accompanied by my daughter Zenani. On the podium, Mr. de Klerk was first sworn in as second deputy president. Then Thabo Mbeki was sworn in as first deputy president. When it was my turn, I pledged to obey and uphold the constitution and to devote myself to the well-being of the republic and its people. To the assembled guests and the watching world, I said:

> *Today, all of us do, by our presence here . . . confer glory and hope to newborn liberty. Out of the experience of an extraordinary human disaster that lasted too long, must be born a society of which all humanity will be proud.*

> *. . . We, who were outlaws not so long ago, have today been given the rare privilege to be host to the nations of the world on our own soil. We thank all of our distinguished international guests for having come to take possession with the people of our country of what is, after all, a common victory for justice, for peace, for **human dignity**.* **2**

Nelson Mandela takes the oath of office at his inauguration. Second Deputy President F.W. de Klerk stands next to him.

1 Word Choice
How does Mandela try to convince you of the importance of the inauguration?

2 Form Generalizations
What generalization does Mandela make in his speech?

A spectator climbs a tree for a better look at the inauguration ceremonies.

In Other Words
white supremacy belief that white people are better than people of other races
human dignity respect

Geographic Background
The Republic of South Africa is located at the southern tip of the African continent. It is often referred to as "The Rainbow Nation" because of its ethnically diverse population.

AFRICA

SOUTH AFRICA

*We have, at last, achieved our political **emancipation**. We pledge ourselves to **liberate** all our people from the continuing bondage of poverty, deprivation, suffering, gender, and other discrimination.*

*Never, never, and never again shall it be that this beautiful land will again experience the **oppression** of one by another. . . . The sun shall never set on so glorious a human achievement. Let freedom reign. God bless Africa!* **3**

3 Word Choice
Which words in these paragraphs seem emotional? What effect do you think they had on listeners, and why?

A few moments later we all lifted our eyes in awe as a spectacular array of South African jets, helicopters, and troop carriers roared in perfect formation over the Union Buildings. It was not only a display of pinpoint precision and military force, but a demonstration of the military's loyalty to democracy, to a new government that had been freely and fairly elected. Only moments before, the highest generals of the South African Defense Force and police, their chests bedecked with ribbons and medals from days gone by, saluted me and pledged their loyalty. I was not unmindful of the fact that not so many years before they

A choir wearing robes designed after the South African flag sings at the inauguration ceremonies.

would not have saluted but arrested me. Finally a chevron of Impala jets left a smoke trail of the black, red, green, blue, white, and gold of the new South African flag.

The day was symbolized for me by the playing of our two national anthems, and the vision of whites singing **"Nkosi Sikelel' iAfrika"** and blacks singing **"Die Stem,"** the old **anthem** of the republic. Although that day, neither group knew the lyrics of the anthem they once despised, they would soon know the words by heart.

Key Vocabulary
emancipation *n.*, act of freeing people from strict control
liberate *v.*, to set free
oppression *n.*, act of preventing people from having equal rights

In Other Words
"Nkosi Sikelel' iAfrika" God Bless Africa (in the Xhosa language)
"Die Stem [van Suid-Afrika]" The Call [of South Africa] (in the Afrikaans language)
anthem national song

Monitor Comprehension

Summarize
What important changes in South Africa's government did Mandela's election bring about?

Preview and Predict

Quickly look over the pictures, their captions, and the quotations. What do you predict this section will be about?

O N THE DAY OF THE INAUGURATION, I was overwhelmed with a sense of history. In the first decade of the twentieth century, a few years after the bitter Anglo-Boer War and before my own birth, the white-skinned peoples of South Africa **patched up their differences** and erected a system of racial domination against the dark-skinned peoples of their own land. The structure they created formed the basis of one of the harshest, most inhumane societies the world has ever known. Now, in the last decade of the twentieth century, and my own eighth decade as a man, that system had been overturned forever and replaced by one that recognized the rights and freedoms of all peoples regardless of the color of their skin. 🔲

That day had come about through the unimaginable sacrifices of thousands of my people, people whose suffering and courage can never be counted or repaid. I felt that day, as I have on so many other days, that I was simply the sum of all those African patriots who had gone before me. That long and noble line ended and now began again with me. I was pained that I was not able to thank them and that they were not able to see what their sacrifices **had wrought**.

The policy of apartheid created a deep and lasting wound in my country and my people. All of us will spend many years, if not generations, recovering from that profound hurt. But the decades of oppression and brutality had another, unintended effect, and that was that

> I was simply the sum of all those African patriots who had gone before me.
>

4 Word Choice
Think about the purpose for using words like *bitter* and *inhumane*. How are these words meant to make you feel about South Africa's old government?

In Other Words
patched up their differences ended their argument
had wrought had created

Historical Background
The **Anglo-Boer War** of 1899–1902 was fought between British colonists and the Boers (South Africans whose ancestors were Dutch colonists). Each side wanted total control of South Africa. Great Britain won the war and made a peace treaty with the Boers.

"From these comrades . . .
I learned the meaning of courage."

Oliver Tambo
Cofounded the Youth League of the African National Congress with Nelson Mandela

Chief Albert John Luthuli
First African awarded a Nobel Prize for peace (1960)

Yusuf Dadoo
Revolutionary leader of the South African Indian Congress

Walter Sisulu
Political mentor of Nelson Mandela

Bram Fischer
Defended members of the African National Congress

Robert Sobukwe
Founder of the Pan Africanist Congress

it produced the Oliver Tambos, the Walter Sisulus, the Chief Luthulis, the Yusuf Dadoos, the Bram Fischers, the Robert Sobukwes of our time—men of such extraordinary courage, wisdom, and generosity that their like may never be known again. Perhaps it requires such depth of oppression to create such heights of character. My country is rich in the minerals and gems that lie beneath its soil, but I have always known that its greatest wealth is its people, finer and truer than the purest diamonds. **5**

It is from these **comrades** in the struggle that I learned the meaning of courage. Time and again, I have seen men and women risk and give their lives for an idea. I have seen men stand up to attacks and torture without breaking, showing a strength and **resiliency** that defies the imagination. I learned that courage was not the absence of fear, but the triumph over it. I felt fear myself

5 Analogy
To what does Mandela compare his people? What effect does his analogy have on your feelings about the people?

In Other Words
comrades friends
resiliency toughness

Historical Background
Apartheid, which means "apartness" in the Afrikaans language, was a system of laws enacted by the white South African government to segregate South Africans by race and ethnicity. It was officially in effect from 1948 to 1994.

more times than I can remember, but I hid it behind a mask of boldness. The brave man is not he who does not feel afraid, but he who conquers that fear. **6**

I never lost hope that this great transformation would occur. Not only because of the great heroes I have already cited, but because of the courage of the ordinary men and women of my country. I always knew that deep down in every human heart, there is mercy and generosity. No one is born hating another person because of the color of his skin, or his background, or his religion. People must learn to hate, and if they can learn to hate, they can be taught to love, for love comes more naturally to the human heart than its opposite. Even in the grimmest times in prison, when my comrades and I were pushed to our limits, I would see a glimmer of humanity in one of the guards, perhaps just for a second, but it was enough to reassure me and keep me going. Man's goodness is a flame that can be hidden but never extinguished. **7**

> # I never lost hope that this great transformation would occur.
> ◆ ◆ ◆

We took up the struggle **with our eyes wide open**, under no illusion that the path would be an easy one. As a young man, when I joined the African National Congress, I saw the price my comrades paid for their beliefs, and it was high. For myself, I have never regretted my commitment to the struggle, and I was always prepared to face the hardships that affected me personally. But my family paid a terrible price, perhaps too dear a price for my commitment.

In life, every man has twin obligations—obligations to his family, to his parents, to his wife and children; and he has an obligation to his people, his community, his country. In a civil and humane society, each man is able to

6 Word Choice
In this paragraph, what word choices does Mandela use to inspire his audience?

7 Form Generalizations
The viewpoint expressed in this sentence ties together many ideas Mandela just expressed. What are those ideas?

In Other Words
with our eyes wide open fully aware of all the danger involved

fulfill those obligations according to his own **inclinations** and abilities. But in a country like South Africa, it was almost impossible for a man of my birth and color to fulfill both of those obligations. In South Africa, a man of color who attempted to live as a human being was punished and isolated. In South Africa, a man who tried to fulfill his duty to his people was inevitably ripped from his family and his home and was forced to live a life apart, a **twilight existence** of secrecy and rebellion. 8

I did not in the beginning choose to place my people above my family, but in attempting to serve my people, I found that I was prevented from fulfilling my obligations as a son, a brother, a father, and a husband.

In that way, my commitment to my people, to the millions of South Africans I would never know or meet, was at the expense of the people I knew best and loved most. It was as simple and yet as incomprehensible as the moment a small child asks her father, "Why can you not be with us?" And the father must utter the terrible words: "There are other children like you, a great many of them . . ." and then one's voice trails off.

8 **Word Choice**
What is the persuasive effect of the repetition of the phrase "in South Africa" in this paragraph?

Before 1994, the country's beaches were segregated. Many of the better beaches were off limits to black South Africans.

Monitor Comprehension

Confirm Prediction
How accurately did you predict what the section would be about? Explain.

Key Vocabulary
inclination *n.*, liking, preference

In Other Words
twilight existence hidden life

Preview

Read the first sentence of each paragraph in this section. Study the picture and caption. What is the section about?

I WAS NOT BORN WITH A HUNGER TO BE FREE. I was born free—free in every way that I could know. Free to run in the fields near my mother's hut, free to swim in the clear stream that ran through my village, free to roast **mealies** under the stars and ride the broad backs of slow-moving bulls. As long as I obeyed my father and abided by the customs of my tribe, I was not troubled by the laws of man or God. 9

It was only when I began to learn that my boyhood freedom was an illusion, when I discovered as a young man that my freedom had already been taken from me, that I began to hunger for it. At first, as a student, I wanted freedom only for myself, the **transitory** freedoms of being able to stay out at night, read what I pleased, and go where I chose. Later, as a young man in Johannesburg, I **yearned for** the basic and honorable freedoms of achieving my potential, of earning my keep, of marrying and having a family—the freedom not to be obstructed in a lawful life.

But then I slowly saw that not only was I not free, but my brothers and sisters were not free. I saw that it was not just my freedom that **was curtailed**, but the freedom of everyone who looked like I did. That is when I joined the African National Congress, and that is when the hunger for my own freedom became the greater hunger for the freedom of my people. It was this desire for the freedom of my people to live their lives with dignity and self-respect that animated my life, that transformed a frightened young man into a bold one, that drove a law-abiding attorney to become a criminal, that turned a family-loving husband into a man without a home, that forced a life-loving man to **live like a monk**. I am no more virtuous or self-sacrificing than the next man, but I found that I could not even enjoy the poor and limited freedoms I was allowed when I knew my people were not free. Freedom is indivisible; the chains on any one of my people were the chains on all of them, the chains on all of my people were the chains on me. 10

9 Word Choice
What word does Mandela repeat in this paragraph? What important idea in Mandela's argument does it emphasize?

10 Word Choice
What are the "chains" Mandela refers to?

In Other Words
mealies corn
transitory temporary
yearned for strongly wished for
was curtailed was limited
live like a monk lead a very simple life with only the basic necessities

It was during those long and lonely years that my hunger for the freedom of my own people became a hunger for the freedom of all people, white and black. I knew as well as I knew anything that the oppressor must be liberated just as surely as the oppressed. A man who takes away another man's freedom is a prisoner of hatred, he is locked behind the bars of prejudice and narrow-mindedness. I am not truly free if I am taking away someone else's freedom, just as surely as I am not free when my freedom is taken from me. The oppressed and the oppressor alike are robbed of their humanity. 🔢

When I walked out of prison, that was my mission, to liberate the oppressed and the oppressor both. Some say that has now been achieved. But I know that that is not the case. The truth is that we are not yet free; we have merely achieved the freedom to be free, the right not to be oppressed. We have not taken the final step of our journey, but the first step on a longer and even more difficult road. For to be free is not merely to cast off one's chains, but to live in a way that respects and enhances the freedom of others. The true test of our devotion to freedom is just beginning.

I have walked that long road to freedom. I have tried not to **falter**; I have made missteps along the way. But I have discovered the secret that after climbing a great hill, one only finds that there are many more hills to climb. I have taken a moment here to rest, to steal a view of the glorious vista that surrounds me, to look back on the distance I have come. But I can rest only for a moment, for with freedom come responsibilities, and I dare not linger, for my long walk is not yet ended.

🔢 **Form Generalizations**
What ideas presented earlier in the argument does this sentence tie together?

On the day he was released from prison, Mandela told fellow South Africans, "Our march to freedom is irreversible."

In Other Words
falter hesitate, stumble

Monitor Comprehension

Interpret
Why do you think Mandela says achieving freedom is a "long walk"?

CLOSE-UP: South African Independence

BY THE BEGINNING OF THE TWENTIETH CENTURY, many European countries had established colonies in Africa. European rulers enacted laws that took away the land of the native people and forced them to work in mines or on farms. Many native people were little more than slaves. They had no rights and no support.

After decades of this treatment, Africans wanted to regain their independence. This process was called decolonization. **12** It was complicated by the many divisions within the African societies. Many language groups, religions, and ethnic differences existed, and many different solutions were set forth. . . .

One of the most amazing examples of decolonization occurred in South Africa. Originally the Dutch colonized the region, which later passed to British control. In 1948, the British enacted strict laws separating blacks and whites, a policy known as apartheid.

Blacks, who made up the majority of the population, struggled against the unjust rules. Apartheid governed every part of life: where a person could live, what entrance to the train he or she could use, how or if he or she would be educated. Many blacks were killed or jailed as a result of uprisings. **13** Nelson Mandela, a black leader, was arrested in 1962 for resisting apartheid and

12 Access Vocabulary
Define *decolonization* by looking at the context and the parts of the word: *de-* means "undo"; a colony is a land ruled by another country; and *-ize* means "to become."

13 Word Choice
How are the victims of apartheid described here? What details in the description invite an emotional response?

THE HISTORY OF APARTHEID

C.E. = Common Era

300 C.E.	1652	1910	1912	1913	1948
South Africa is populated by black Khoisan and Bantu-speaking peoples	Dutch settlers (called Boers) establish Cape Town	Union of South Africa is formed by British and Dutch	African National Congress (ANC) is formed to protect black African interests	Native Land Act is passed to prevent blacks from owning land	Policy of apartheid is adopted when white Afrikaner National Party takes power

Source: *African National Congress*

ANC

sentenced to life in prison. For twenty-seven years he remained a prisoner who believed in the cause of freedom.

Sanctions were passed against South Africa. Many nations, including the United States, refused to trade with the country because of its human rights violations. In addition, violent protests within the nation were heightened in 1984. Indians and "colored" people, who were of mixed race, gained some civil rights while blacks were still excluded. Finally, the white rulers determined that all nonwhites should be allowed to vote. Nelson Mandela was freed from Robben Island Prison in 1990. Four years later, when the first democratic elections were held, Mandela became the first democratically elected president of South Africa.

Present-Day South Africa

▲ **Analyze the Map** How many capital cities does South Africa have? What are their names?

▼ **Interpret the Time Line** For how many years was apartheid an official policy in South Africa?

1962	1964	1989	1990	1991	1994
United Nations forms Special Committee Against Apartheid	Nelson Mandela is sentenced to life imprisonment for sabotage	F.W. de Klerk becomes president	Nelson Mandela is released after 27 years in prison	De Klerk repeals, or ends, apartheid laws	ANC wins first nonracial elections; Mandela becomes president

EPILOGUE

As president, Nelson Mandela worked to ease racial tension between blacks and whites and rebuild the reputation of South Africa in the international community.

When he retired from public office in 1999, Mandela remained involved with social and human rights organizations. In 2003, he lent his support to the 46664 Campaign, an AIDS awareness organization named after his prisoner number on Robben Island. He also established the Nelson Mandela Foundation to share his ideals and values with the rest of the world. ❖

ANALYZE Long Walk to Freedom

1. **Explain** What **motivated** Nelson Mandela to fight for freedom in South Africa? Give examples from the selection.

2. **Vocabulary** How did the **oppression** of people in South Africa affect Mandela's relationship with his family?

3. **Analyze Viewpoint: Word Choice** Copy a passage from the selection that inspires you. Underline words that appeal to the reader's emotions.

4. **Focus Strategy Form Generalizations** What is one generalization you formed based on what you read and your own experience or knowledge? Have a partner identify ideas that the generalization ties together.

Return to the Text

Reread and Write Imagine you are Mandela in prison. A comrade asks, "Why did you decide to struggle for human rights?" Reread to find at least two reasons in the text. Use the reasons to write a personal letter to your comrade.

The Art of Nelson Mandela

To Mandela, the lighthouse on Robben Island was a contradiction as both a beacon of hope and oppression.

The Window, 2003, Nelson Mandela

In 2003, Nelson Mandela returned to Robben Island, where he had been jailed for eighteen years for standing up against apartheid. He had come for a most extraordinary art exhibition—to show his own sketches of his life there. The drawings show various images of the island, such as a communal prison cell, the prison courtyard, and the guard tower.

"Today when I look at Robben Island," said Mandela, "I see it as a celebration of the struggle and a symbol of the finest qualities of the human spirit, rather than as a monument to the brutal tyranny and oppression of apartheid.

"It is true that Robben Island was once a place of darkness, but out of that darkness has come a wonderful brightness, a light so powerful that it could not be hidden behind prison walls . . . I have attempted to color the island sketches in ways that reflect the positive light in which I view it."

▲ This sketch depicts Table Mountain through Mandela's prison cell window. The imagined view represents freedom but in fact, Table Mountain was not visible from the window (as seen in the photo at left).

BEFORE READING **We Hold These Truths**

declarations by the Continental Congress and the Seneca Falls Convention

Reading Strategies

- Plan and Monitor
- Determine Importance
- Make Inferences
- Ask Questions
- Make Connections
▶ **Synthesize**
- Visualize

Relate Arguments

Different writers have different arguments about similar topics. A good way to understand these arguments is to relate them, or see how they are alike and different. Compare the reasons and evidence each author uses to support a claim. Notice how the authors introduce and structure their ideas. Pay attention to how the words they use appeal to readers' emotions and help support the claim.

Look Into the Text

The authors make a claim at the beginning of this text.

Authors make specific word choices to appeal to readers' emotions.

From The Declaration of Independence, 1776

…whenever any Form of Government becomes destructive of these ends, it is the Right of the People to alter or to abolish it, and to institute new Government… The history of the present King of Great Britain is a history of repeated injuries and usurpations…

From The Declaration of Sentiments, 1848

…Whenever any form of government becomes destructive of these ends, it is the right of those who suffer from it to refuse allegiance to it, and to insist upon the institution of a new government… The history of mankind is a history of repeated injuries and usurpations on the part of man toward woman…

Authors may purposefully adopt the structure or wording of an existing text to connect their argument to that text.

Focus Strategy ▶ Synthesize

When you read the two texts, synthesize the information by gathering ideas and details together and thinking about how they contribute to a broader idea.

HOW TO FORM GENERALIZATIONS

Focus Strategy

1. **Compare Texts** Think about the authors' claims in both texts. Pay attention to their reasons and evidence. Ask yourself what the arguments have in common.

2. **Add Your Knowledge** Are there other things you have read or experiences you have had that add to your understanding?

3. **Use General Terms** State a broad idea about the two texts. Begin your generalization with a signal word or phrase such as *In general* or *Overall*.

Overall, the authors believe an unjust government should be changed.

In general, the authors feel they have been treated unfairly.

Connect Across Texts

In "Long Walk to Freedom," you read about how South Africans overcame **exploitation** and **oppression** and demanded equal rights. Now travel to the United States and read how two other groups declared their rights.

WE HOLD THESE TRUTHS

In 1776, a group of men representing Great Britain's 13 North American colonies wrote one of history's most famous persuasive texts. In it, they outlined the British king's exploitation of the Colonies and declared their freedom from the oppression of his rule.

Seventy years later, another group made a similar declaration, this time demanding women's equality and rights, including the right to vote.

John Parrot/Stocktrek Images, after the painting by J.L.G. Ferris.

▲ Ben Franklin (left), John Adams, and Thomas Jefferson (standing) study a draft of the Declaration of Independence.

▲ Elizabeth Cady Stanton (seated) and Susan B. Anthony (standing) were leaders and partners in the fight for women's rights.

Key Vocabulary
- **exploitation** *n.*, selfish use of others for personal gain
- **oppression** *n.*, the act of preventing people from having equal rights

from THE DECLARATION OF INDEPENDENCE, 1776

...We hold these truths to be self-evident, that all men are created equal, that they are **endowed** by their Creator with certain **unalienable** Rights, that among these are Life, Liberty and the pursuit of Happiness.—That to secure these rights, Governments are instituted among Men, deriving their just powers from the **consent of** the governed, —That whenever any Form of Government becomes destructive of these ends, it is the Right of the People to alter or to **abolish** it, and to institute new Government, laying its foundation on such principles and organizing its powers in such form, as to them shall seem most likely to effect their Safety and Happiness....—Such has been the patient sufferance of these Colonies; and such is now the necessity which constrains them to alter their former Systems of Government. **1**

The history of the present King of Great Britain is a history of repeated injuries and **usurpations**, all having in direct object the establishment of **an absolute Tyranny** over these States. To prove this, let Facts be submitted to a candid world....

—He has kept among us, in times of peace, Standing Armies without the Consent of our legislatures....

—He has combined with others to subject us to a jurisdiction foreign to our constitution, and unacknowledged by our laws...

—For cutting off our Trade with all parts of the world...

—For depriving us in many cases, of the benefits of Trial by Jury...

—For taking away our Charters, abolishing our most valuable Laws, and altering fundamentally the Forms of our Governments... **2**

We, therefore...solemnly publish and declare, That these United Colonies are, and of Right ought to be Free and Independent States...

1 Argument
What reasons do the authors give to support their claim for changing the current government? What specific word choices help the authors support their claim?

2 Form Generalizations
What generalization can you make about the King of Great Britain, based on evidence from the text?

In Other Words

endowed given
unalienable guaranteed
consent of agreement by
abolish end
usurpations takeovers
an absolute Tyranny complete power

Historical Background
The authors used a writing style typical of the 1700s, which included capitalizing important nouns. The Declaration contained the first formal statement by a whole people of their right to a government of their choosing.

from THE DECLARATION OF SENTIMENTS, 1848

...We hold these truths to be self-evident: that all men and women are created equal; that they are endowed by their Creator with certain inalienable rights; that among these are life, liberty, and the pursuit of happiness; that to secure these rights governments are instituted, deriving their just powers from the consent of the governed. Whenever any form of government becomes destructive of these ends, it is the right of those who suffer from it to refuse **allegiance** to it, and to insist upon the institution of a new government, laying its foundation on such principles, and organizing its powers in such form, as to them shall seem most likely to effect their safety and happiness....Such has been the patient sufferance of the women under this government, and such is now the necessity which constrains them to demand the equal station to which they are entitled. **3**

The history of mankind is a history of repeated injuries and usurpations on the part of man toward woman, having in direct object the establishment of an absolute tyranny over her. To prove this, let facts be submitted to a candid world....

He has **compelled** her to submit to laws, in the formation of which she had no voice....

He has denied her the **facilities** for obtaining a thorough education, all colleges being closed against her....

He has endeavored, in every way that he could, to destroy her confidence in her own powers, to lessen her self-respect, and to make her willing to lead a dependent and **abject** life.

Now,...because women do feel themselves aggrieved, oppressed, and **fraudulently deprived of their most sacred** rights, we insist that they have immediate admission to all the rights and privileges which belong to them as citizens of the United States.... **4** ❖

3 Argument
What reasons do the authors give for changing the current government? How do their reasons relate to the reasons in the Declaration of Independence?

4 Form Generalizations
What generalization can you make about what the authors want, based on their reasons and evidence?

Key Vocabulary
• **distinction** *n.*, difference
apathetic *adj.*, indifferent, uninterested

In Other Words
allegiance loyalty
compelled forced
facilities opportunities
abject horrible
fraudulently deprived of their most sacred without their most important

Historical Background
In 1848, the U.S. drew big **distinctions** between men and women, and many were **apathetic** about women's rights. Women's rights activists held a meeting in Seneca Falls, New York. There they signed the **Declaration of Sentiments**.

ANALYZE We Hold These Truths

1. **Inference** Why did the authors of the Declaration of Sentiments base their document on the Declaration of Independence?

2. **Vocabulary** What is an example of **oppression** given by the authors of the Declaration of Independence? What is an example of oppression in the Declaration of Sentiments? Explain why each is an example of oppression.

3. **Relate Arguments** How are the two declarations alike? How are they different? Use the authors' claims, reasons, and evidence from both texts to explain your responses.

4. **Focus Strategy Form Generalizations** What generalization can you make about how the authors of the two declarations had been treated? Use evidence from each text to support your response.

Return to the Text

Reread and Write With a partner, choose one of the declarations and write a paragraph about how the authors' word choices support their claims and appeal to readers' emotions.

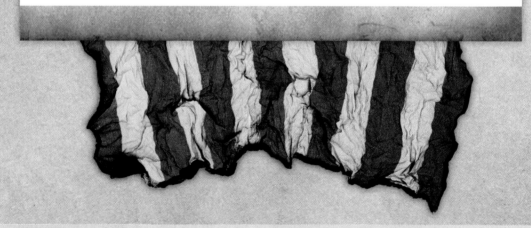

EQ How Can We Balance Everyone's Rights?

Critical Thinking

1. **Analyze** Look again at the **KWLS Chart** on page 606. After reading the selections, what did you learn about human rights around the world? What do you still need to learn? Revise and expand your chart.

EQ 2. **Compare** Compare Nelson Mandela's and the declarations writers' viewpoints about people's responsibility to make the world a better place. How are they similar or different? Give examples.

3. **Interpret** What do you think Mandela means when he says that the "long and noble line" of African patriots ended, then began again with him?

4. **Synthesize** Do you feel **motivated** to get involved in your community? What suggestions would these writers have for you?

EQ 5. **Evaluate** Based on your reading of the selections, do you think that the authors' concerns have been dealt with effectively? Explain.

Write About Literature

Letter to the Editor Write a letter to the editor of a newspaper in your area to share your opinion about a local or national issue that involves human rights, such as prisoner rights or immigrant rights. Use some of the same techniques that you see in Mandela's speech and the two declarations, such as repetition and emotional appeals, to convince readers they should support your point of view.

Key Vocabulary Review

Oral Review Work with a partner. Use these words to complete the paragraph.

apathetic	exploitation	motivated
distinction	inclination	oppression
emancipation	liberate	

Our history teacher works hard and is __(1)__ to provide us with a good education. She does not believe that teenagers are __(2)__ and do not care about the world around them. Instead, she thinks teens have a great __(3)__ to learn about world issues. She teaches us about __(4)__, or freedom, and the difficulties that result from __(5)__, or a lack of freedom. She makes a __(6)__ and helps us understand the difference between those who __(7)__ others and those who unfairly take advantage of others through __(8)__. Our teacher's lessons inspire me to make the world a better place.

Writing Application If you could fight for one cause, what would it be? What reasons would make you the most motivated? Write a paragraph in which you use at least four Key Vocabulary words.

Read with Ease: Intonation

Assess your reading fluency with the passage in the Reading Handbook, p. 816. Then complete the self-check below.

1. My intonation did/did not sound natural.

2. My words correct per minute: _____ .

INTEGRATE THE LANGUAGE ARTS

Use Complex Sentences

You can enhance your writing with **complex sentences**. A complex sentence has at least one independent clause and one dependent clause.

- An **independent clause** expresses a complete idea. It can stand alone as a sentence.

  Generations of black South Africans suffered .

- A **dependent clause** does not express a complete idea. It depends on the independent clause to make sense. A dependent clause cannot stand alone. Can the clause below stand alone?

  because of apartheid

- Subordinating conjunctions like **because**, **although**, **if**, and **since** start a dependent clause. If the dependent clause is at the beginning of the sentence, use a comma after it.

  Generations of black South Africans suffered **because** of apartheid. **Although** Nelson Mandela was treated harshly, he did not seek revenge.

  If people can be taught to hate, they can be taught to love. Conditions in South Africa have been slowly improving **since** the end of apartheid.

Oral Practice (1–3) Use the conjunction in parentheses to create a complex sentence.

1. The people chose their own leader. Elections had been fair and free. (because)
2. Life in South Africa was better. Change had not come quickly or easily. (although)
3. People treat each other fairly. They can live in harmony. (if)

Written Practice (4–10) Write a paragraph with complex sentences. Use seven subordinating conjunctions.

Rhetorical Devices

A **rhetorical device** is a tool that writers use to advance their viewpoint or their purpose for writing. In "Long Walk to Freedom," Nelson Mandela uses rhetorical devices to help make his point. The rhetorical devices that he uses include:

- **Parallelism** the pairing of words or phrases of equal importance and similar sound
- **Repetition** repeating a concept, phrase, or word in order to emphasize it
- **Alliteration** the repetition of consonant sounds in two or more words in the same sentence

Think about Mandela's argument in "Long Walk to Freedom" and the point he is trying to make. Then read these excerpts. Identify each as an example of parallelism, repetition, or alliteration.

1. [I]n attempting to serve my people, I found that I was prevented from fulfilling my obligations as a son, a brother, a father, and a husband.
2. It was this desire for the freedom of my people... that forced a life-loving man to live like a monk.
3. I was born free—free in every way that I could know. Free to run in the fields near my mother's hut, free to swim in the clear stream that ran through my village, free to roast mealies under the stars ...

Persuade

Pair Talk What arguments would you make to end an injustice you know about? Persuade a partner to agree with your opinion.

Denotation and Connotation

Recall that **denotations** are words' direct meanings, while **connotations** are the feelings that words convey. Two words, like *calm* and *lazy*, can have the same denotation but very different connotations.

Read the sentences below and think about the connotation of each underlined word. If it seems inappropriate, think of another word with the same denotation that fits the sentence better. (Hint: Three of the sentences need new words.)

1. I appreciate how much Ms. Novak cares about her students. She is really nosy.
2. Felipe is unique. I've never met anyone like him.
3. This place is so cozy that there's not enough room for us to move around.
4. Ana finds crossword puzzles frustrating. She really enjoys solving them.

Opinion Poll

Culture: Personal Motivation Design and conduct an opinion poll in which you research the most likely reasons for young people's activism.

1 Design the Poll In your planning, list issues that many young people are interested and involved in, such as immigration issues, environmental cleanup, or human rights. Identify the targets, or ideal participants, for your poll and write a set of questions.

2 Conduct the Poll You may choose to interview your respondents or you may ask them to write their answers on a survey form. After you conduct the poll, organize and review your results and present them to your class.

➥ **Language and Learning Handbook**, p. 750

Development of Ideas

When you develop ideas, you give reasons, facts, examples, and other kinds of supporting evidence to explain what you mean. The more you develop your ideas, the clearer they are to your reader. Read the following paragraph.

Just OK

> I think young people should get involved in their community. It's important not to be **apathetic**. Everybody can and should make a difference. That goes for young people just as much as it does for adults. Don't just sit around; get involved!

This paragraph does not contain any reasons to support the main idea. It simply repeats the writer's claim. Now read the next paragraph.

Much Better

> I think young people should get involved in their community. After all, young people live in their community, so they should want to make it as good to live in as possible. For example, they can reduce discrimination by insisting that their friends stop using stereotypical labels such as "nerd" or "loser."

The two paragraphs are almost the same length, but the second paragraph is clearer and more persuasive because it includes specific reasons to support the main idea, "I think young people should get involved in their community."

With a partner, further develop the second paragraph by adding two more reasons why young people should get involved.

➥ **Writing Handbook**, p. 832

FROM

What to the Slave Is the Fourth of July?

Frederick Douglass (1818–1895). Photograph ©Bettmann/CORBIS.

by Frederick Douglass

JULY 5, 1852

1   Mr. President, Friends and Fellow Citizens:

2   The papers and placards say that I am to deliver a Fourth [of] July oration. . . .

3   The fact is, ladies and gentlemen, the distance between this platform and the slave plantation, from which I escaped, is considerable—and the difficulties to be overcome in getting from **the latter to the former**, are by no means slight. . . .

4   So, fellow-citizens, pardon me, allow me to ask, why am I called upon to speak here to-day? What have I, or those I represent, to do with your national independence? Are the great principles of political freedom and of natural justice, embodied in that Declaration of Independence, extended to us? And am I, therefore, called upon to bring our humble offering to the national altar, and to confess the benefits and express **devout** gratitude for the blessings resulting from your independence to us?

5   Would to God, both for your sakes and ours, that an affirmative answer could be truthfully returned to these questions! Then would my task be light, and my burden easy and delightful. . . .

In Other Words

the latter to the former the slave plantation to the platform
devout sincere

Historical Background

Frederick Douglass was one of the most important human rights leaders of the 1800s. A former slave, Douglass wrote and spoke powerfully for the liberation of enslaved people, for women's rights, and for equal rights for all people.

6   But, such is not the state of the case. I say it with a sad sense of the disparity between us. I am not included within the **pale** of this glorious anniversary! Your high independence only reveals the immeasurable distance between us. The blessings in which you, this day, rejoice, are not enjoyed in common. The rich inheritance of justice, liberty, prosperity and independence, **bequeathed** by your fathers, is shared by you, not by me. The sunlight that brought life and healing to you, has brought stripes and death to me. This Fourth [of] July is yours, not mine. You may rejoice, I must mourn. To drag a man in **fetters** into the grand illuminated temple of liberty, and call upon him to join you in joyous anthems, **were inhuman mockery** and sacrilegious irony. Do you mean, citizens, to mock me, by asking me to speak to-day? . . .

7   Fellow-citizens, above your national, tumultuous joy, I hear the **mournful wail** of millions! Whose chains, heavy and grievous yesterday, are, to-day, rendered more intolerable by the **jubilee** shouts that reach them. If I do forget, if I do not faithfully remember those bleeding children of sorrow this day, "may my right hand forget her cunning, and may my tongue cleave to the roof of my mouth!" To forget them, to pass lightly over their wrongs, and to chime in with the popular theme, would be **treason** most scandalous and shocking, and would make me a **reproach** before God and the world. My subject, then, fellow-citizens, is American slavery. I shall see this day and its popular characteristics from the slave's point of view. Standing there identified with the American **bondman**, making his wrongs mine, I do not hesitate to declare, with all my soul, that the character and conduct of this nation never looked blacker to me than on this Fourth of July! . . .

8   But I **fancy** I hear some one of my audience say, "It is just in this circumstance that you and **your brother abolitionists** fail to make a favorable impression on the public mind. Would you argue more, and denounce less; would you persuade more, and rebuke less; your cause would be much more likely to succeed." But, I submit, where all is plain there is nothing to be argued. . . .

In Other Words

pale light
bequeathed given
fetters chains
were inhuman mockery is cruel teasing
mournful wail sad cry
jubilee joyful

treason disloyalty
reproach disgrace
bondman slave
fancy think
your brother abolitionists others who wish
    to free enslaved people

9   Would you have me argue that man is entitled to liberty? That he is the rightful owner of his own body? You have already declared it. Must I argue the wrongfulness of slavery? Is that a question for Republicans? Is it to be settled by the rules of logic and argumentation, as a matter **beset with** great difficulty, involving a doubtful application of the principle of justice, hard to be understood? How should I look to-day, in the presence of Americans, dividing and subdividing **a discourse**, to show that men have a natural right to freedom? Speaking of it relatively, and positively, negatively, and affirmatively. To do so, would be to make myself ridiculous, and to offer an insult to your understanding. There is not a man beneath the canopy of heaven, that does not know that slavery is wrong *for him.*

10   What, am I to argue that it is wrong to make men **brutes**, to rob them of their liberty, to work them without wages, to keep them **ignorant** of their relations to their fellow men, to beat them with sticks, to flay their flesh with the lash, to load their limbs with irons, to hunt them with dogs, to sell them at auction, to **sunder** their families, to knock out their teeth, to burn their flesh, to starve them into obedience and submission to their masters? Must I argue that a system thus marked with blood, and stained with pollution, is *wrong*? No! I will not. I have better employments for my time and strength than such arguments would imply.

11   What, then, remains to be argued? Is it that slavery is not divine; that God did not establish it; that our doctors of divinity are mistaken? There is **blasphemy** in the thought. That which is inhuman, cannot be **divine**! *Who* can reason on such a proposition? They that can, may; I cannot. The time for such argument is past.

12   At a time like this, **scorching irony**, not convincing argument, is needed. . . .

> **What, then, remains to be argued?**

13   What, to the American slave, is your Fourth of July? I answer: a day that reveals to him, more than all other days in the year, the gross injustice and cruelty to which he is the constant victim. To him, your celebration is a **sham**; your boasted liberty, an unholy license; your national greatness, swelling **vanity**; your sounds of rejoicing are empty and heartless; your

In Other Words
beset with of
a discourse an argument
brutes animals
ignorant unaware
sunder separate
blasphemy wickedness

divine godlike
scorching irony angry words
sham fake
vanity pride

denunciations of tyrants, **brass fronted impudence**; your shouts of liberty and equality, hollow mockery; your prayers and hymns, your sermons and thanksgivings, with all your religious parade and solemnity are, to him, mere bombast, fraud, deception, impiety, and hypocrisy—a thin veil to cover up crimes which would disgrace a nation of savages. There is not a nation on the earth guilty of practices more shocking and bloody than are the people of these United States, at this very hour. . . .

14　　Allow me to say, in conclusion, notwithstanding the dark picture I have this day presented of the state of the nation, I do not **despair of** this country. There are forces in operation which must inevitably work the downfall of slavery. "The arm of the Lord is not shortened," and the doom of slavery is certain. I, therefore, leave off where I began, with hope. While drawing encouragement from the Declaration of Independence, the great principles it contains, and the genius of American Institutions, my spirit is also cheered by the obvious tendencies of the age. Nations do not now stand in the same relation to each other that they did ages ago. No nation can now shut itself up from the surrounding world, and trot round in the same old path of its fathers without interference. . . . No abuse, no outrage whether in taste, sport, or **avarice**, can now hide itself from the **all-pervading light**. . . . ❖

▷ **Critical Viewing: Effect** What effect does a life-size sculpture have that a painting does not?

Frederick Douglass statue, Harlem, New York City, Randy Duchaine. Photograph ©Randy Duchaine/Alamy.

In Other Words

denunciations criticisms
brass fronted impudence showy confidence
despair of lose hope in
avarice greed
all-pervading light light that is everywhere

RIGHTS AND RESPONSIBILITIES

ESSENTIAL QUESTION:
How Can We Balance Everyone's Rights?

myNGconnect.com
Download the rubric.

EDGE LIBRARY

Present Your Project: Political Campaign

It's time to present your political campaign about the Essential Question for this unit.

1 Review and Complete Your Plan

Consider these points as you finish preparing your political campaign:

- What are your most important campaign issues? How do they deal with balancing people's rights?
- What persuasive techniques do you use in your campaign? Are any of them faulty?
- What type of voter does your campaign appeal to? Is that who you are trying to reach?

2 Present Your Political Campaign

Present your campaign. Show examples of your posters, pamphlets, or other campaign materials. Deliver any speeches you have written. Explain how your campaign will reach key supporters and sway undecided voters.

3 Evaluate the Political Campaigns

Use a rubric to evaluate each of the political campaigns, including your own.

Reflect on Your Reading

Many of the people in this unit face the challenge of balancing everyone's rights.

Think back on your reading of the unit selections, including your choice of Edge Library books. Then, discuss the following with a partner or in a small group.

Genre Focus Compare and contrast different persuasive elements and techniques. Are some types stronger than others? Are some less honest than others? Give examples, using the selections in this unit.

Focus Strategy With your partner or group, list some of the conclusions you drew about the unit selections. Write a brief statement to express what these ideas have in common.

Respond to the Essential Question

Throughout this unit, you have been thinking about how we can balance everyone's rights. Discuss the Essential Question with a group. What have *you* decided? Support your response with evidence from your reading, discussions, research, and writing.

Write a Persuasive Essay

Writing Mode
Argument

Writing Trait Focus
Focus and Unity

Persuasive messages are all around you. TV commercials try to get you to buy certain products. Political candidates try to convince you to vote for them. This project gives you a chance to see how convincing you can be as you write a persuasive essay.

Study Persuasive Essays

A persuasive essay, like other forms of argument, presents a position and anticipates readers' concerns and counterclaims. Unlike other types of argument, however, a persuasive essay uses strong language, emotional appeal, and other persuasive techniques to get the reader to take a particular action.

❶ Connect Writing to Your Life

You probably try to persuade other people often. You might persuade your friends to spend a Saturday playing sports outside instead of computer games inside. You might persuade family members to listen to your favorite music on a car trip. This project will help you build your persuasive powers.

❷ Understand the Form

The **controlling idea** of a persuasive essay is the argument, or **claim**. Usually, the claim is either *for* or *against* some type of issue. The claim is stated in the introduction and is supported by **reasons** and **evidence**. A strong persuasive essay must contain the following parts:

1. Claim	Introduce the issue by giving some background information. Then, state your opinion of the issue.
2. Reasons	List several reasons to support your claim. Why do you think your opinion is correct?
3. Evidence	Give facts, statistics, expert opinions, and examples that illustrate each reason. How do you prove that your reasons are good ones?
4. Counterclaim	Think of what people on the opposite side of the issue might say. Why might they think your claim is wrong or your reasons insufficient?
5. Rebuttal	Tell why the counterclaim is incorrect. What reasons can you give? What evidence can you show?
6. Call to Action	Restate your claim. What do you want your readers to do?

Now look at how these parts come together.
Read a persuasive essay by a professional writer.

❸ Analyze a Professional Model

As you read, look for the important parts of a persuasive essay.

Say "Yes" to Year-Round Schooling
by Dominique Washington

How would you like to improve your kids' education, use school buildings more efficiently, and save tax dollars? You can by supporting the school board's plan for year-round schools. The plan is simple. Students would still spend 180 days in school each year, but they would attend school in nine-week segments. After nine weeks of school, they would have three weeks off. This would be a big change, but year-round schooling offers so many benefits.

One benefit of year-round schooling is that it will help lessen overcrowding in our schools. With careful scheduling, a school built for 1,000 students can accommodate 1,300. All our schools have to do is stagger students' schedules so that at any given time, one group of students is on vacation.

This scheduling plan will also save us money. By making more efficient use of the buildings we have, we will not have to pay to build additions or new schools. Moreover, we will not be paying to maintain a mostly empty building over the summer.

The biggest benefit, however, is that year-round schooling will improve our students' ability to learn. Students remember information better when vacations are shorter. When students return to school, they haven't forgotten what they learned. Students can also cover more material because they do not spend as much time reviewing.

Now, I know that some of you have mixed feelings about year-round schooling. You may think that your children would hate it. But that has not been the case at schools that have adopted this plan. Teens say it is easier to work hard for nine weeks at a time rather than nine straight months. And they say it is easier to keep in touch with friends over shorter breaks.

When you look at all the advantages, I think you will agree. Year-round schooling is right for our teens. Vote for year-round schooling in the upcoming special election, and say "yes" to a better future for our students.

The writer gives background information about the issue and clearly states her **claim**.

The writer gives solid **reasons** to support her claim. Notice the use of statistics and examples as evidence.

The writer states a **counterclaim** and gives a rebuttal.

What is the writer's call to action?

▶ **Prompt** Write a persuasive essay on an issue about which you have strong feelings. Be sure to:

- tell what the issue is and state your claim
- give reasons and support them with evidence
- answer at least one opposing claim
- tell readers what action to take

✔ Prewrite

Now that you know the basics of a persuasive essay, you are ready to plan one of your own. A good Writing Plan will help you as you draft your essay.

❶ Choose Your Topic

Try these activities to help find and choose a topic:

- Complete this sentence five different ways: "The world (or our school or community) would be a better place if _____."
- Ask friends and family these questions: What is an important issue you care about? What change could you or I make to improve the world? What issues have you heard me talk about lately?

Technology Tip

Check out the key news stories on the Web sites of well-known news organizations or newspapers. This will give you a good idea of issues that are currently on the mind of the public.

❷ Clarify the Audience, Controlling Idea, and Purpose

Who are your readers? What background do they need to understand your topic? What opinions do they already have? List some ideas.

Then, write your argument, or **controlling idea**. Fit it into one of these sentences: "We should do X" or "We should not do Z."

Finally, think about your purpose. What do you want your audience to believe? What do you want to persuade your audience to do? Write down your ideas.

❸ Develop Reasons and Gather Evidence

Your next step is to think of reasons and gather evidence to support and develop your claim. Here are some helpful suggestions:

- Brainstorm a list of reasons you think your claim is right.
- Interview other students to explore commonly held beliefs. When students disagree, make careful note of their counterclaims and reasons.
- Research the topic. Note anything that can be used as evidence.

Prewriting Tip

Think about the following questions as you research evidence:

- Who wrote this evidence? What was his or her motivation?
- Will my audience think my sources are reliable?
- Is this information fact or opinion?

❹ Organize Your Reasons

Structure your reasons in a sustained and logical fashion to support your claim. For instance, you might build up to a strong finish by putting reasons in order of importance. Start with a good reason; then move to a better one. End with your best reason.

❺ Finish Your Writing Plan

Use your prewriting ideas to make a Writing Plan like the one below. Remember to organize your reasons and evidence in a logical fashion.

Prewriting Tip

Another good way to organize your reasons is the "sandwich method." Put your weakest reason second, and sandwich it between stronger reasons. That way, you begin and end on strong notes.

Writing Plan

Topic	teen curfew
Audience	other students and people of voting age
Claim	A teen curfew is unfair and unjust.
Purpose	to persuade voters to vote against the teen curfew proposal
Time Frame	one week from today
Reason 1 Teens have necessary reasons to be out after curfew.	**Evidence** Teens work, volunteer, and study late at night.
Reason 2 A curfew is a form of age discrimination.	**Evidence** People would never consider giving a curfew to adults.
Counterclaim	A curfew will lower the crime rate.
Rebuttal	No studies have proven this, and city statistics show that teens don't commit much crime to begin with.
Call to Action	Vote against the council's curfew proposal.

Reflect on Your Writing Plan

▶ Will your reasons be persuasive to your audience? Talk it over with a partner.

✔ Write a Draft

Now you are ready to write. Use your Writing Plan as a guide while you write your persuasive essay. You will have chances to improve your draft. Just keep writing!

❶ Use Persuasive Techniques

In a persuasive essay, you want to get your audience on your side, working toward your goal. There are three main techniques you can use to form a convincing argument:

- **Logical Appeal** This technique involves the use of evidence such as facts, statistics, and examples to support your claim.

    According to the Mesa Grande Police Department, only 3 percent of crimes committed by teens last year took place after 10 p.m.

- **Emotional Appeal** This technique involves the use of strong words that appeal to the audience's needs, values, and attitudes.

    "No taxation without representation!" Isn't that one of the main reasons for the Revolutionary War? Well, now the Mesa Grande City Council is acting just like the British!

- **Ethical Appeal** This technique involves convincing the audience that you are fair, honest, and well-informed about the issue.

    I know that council members believe a curfew will help keep teens out of trouble. They want to protect the youth in the community, and that is a good goal. But based on the evidence, a curfew is not a good idea.

❷ Wrap Up Loose Ends

Most writers begin a persuasive essay with an anecdote or quotation to grab the audience's attention. A good writer will tie this opening idea to the conclusion, too. This helps give the essay a sense of completeness.

Opening Idea

> "No taxation without representation!" That was one of the main reasons for the Revolutionary War.

Concluding Idea

> So please, on election day, I beg everyone of voting age to vote against the council's proposal. Do not let teens become victims of a law that they are not even allowed to vote on.

Technology Tip

Save your first draft under a file name that shows that it is a draft. You might use "persuasive01" to show that it is just the first version of the essay.

When you begin to revise, save the new version as "persuasive02." That way, as you revise, if you want to return to the draft version of the essay, it's easy to retrieve it.

Drafting Tip

In addition to these techniques, you can use various types of evidence to support your position.

- personal anecdote or experience
- case study—an analysis of the issue
- analogy—a comparison to something more understandable

❸ Student Model

Read this draft to see how the student used the Writing Plan to get ideas down on paper. The student will fix any mistakes later.

Teen Curfew Law Is Unfair

"No taxation without representation!" That was one of the main reasons for the Revolutionary War. Well, now the Mesa Grande City Council is acting just like the British and imposing a law on a group who has no say in the matter. The council hopes to have its way in this Fall's election. This means any citizen under the age of 18 will not be allowed to be out after 10 p.m. on weeknights and 11 p.m. on weekends. As a teenager in the community I am against this proposed curfew. I think that teen driving restrictions would make more sense.

Many teens have good reasons for being out after 10 or 11 p.m. Some work night jobs, such as babysitting. I hope to eventually get a nighttime job at the local pizza place. Others volunteer at places where they are needed at night, such as Mesa Grande Hospital. Many teens visit friends to study together. A curfew would prohibit teens from doing what they need to do to earn money, reach out to others, or get good grades.

Worse yet, a curfew is a form of age discrimination. It is unfair to punish all teens just because a small minority might be committing crimes late at night. How would most adults feel if they could be stopped and searched by a police officer just for being on the street? It makes teens feel like they are second-class citizens.

Many members of the community who support the curfew say it will lower the teen crime rate. However, most studies on curfews fail to show this. According to the Mesa Grande Police Department, only a small number of crimes committed by teens last year took place after 10 p.m., and the total number of teen crimes was not even a large amount of the total number of crimes. That means adults committed most of the crimes. Since the curfew would not apply to adults it would not reduce crime very much, would it?

I know that council members believe a curfew will help keep teens out of trouble. They want to protect the youth in the community, and that is a good goal. But based on the evidence, it is not a good idea. It would keep teens from worthwhile nighttime activities, punish good kids unfairly, and not reduce crime. So please, on election day, I beg everyone of voting age to vote against the council's proposal. Do not let teens become victims of a law that they are not even allowed to vote on.

Reflect on Your Draft

▶ Think about the process that you used to write your draft. What went smoothly? What went less smoothly? What have you learned that will make the process easier the next time you write?

✔ Revise Your Draft

Your first draft is done. Now, you need to polish it. Improve the focus and unity. Turn a good draft into a great essay.

❶ Revise for Focus and Unity

Good writing has a **focus**—it has a central, controlling idea. In a persuasive essay, the focus is the writer's claim.

Good writing also has **unity**—that means that all of the parts support the controlling idea. In a persuasive essay, the reasons, evidence, counterclaim, and rebuttal all relate to the writer's claim, and the claim is structured in a logical way with clear transitions.

Don't expect to have perfect focus and unity in your first draft. Every writer expects and needs to rewrite. Time spent revising helps you sharpen your focus. Cut out any word, sentence, or even paragraph that doesn't relate to your controlling idea.

TRY IT ▶ With a partner, discuss which parts of the draft below do not strongly support or relate to the writer's claim.

Writing Plan

Claim	A teen curfew is unfair and unjust.

Student Draft

> Many teens have good reasons for being out after 10 or 11 p.m. Some work night jobs, such as babysitting. I hope to eventually get a nighttime job at the local pizza place. Others volunteer at places where they are needed at night, such as Mesa Grande Hospital. Many teens visit friends to study together. A curfew would prohibit teens from doing what they need to do to earn money, reach out to others, or get good grades.

Now use the rubric to evaluate the focus and unity of your own draft. What score do you give your draft and why?

Focus and Unity

	How clearly does the writing present a central idea or claim?	How well does everything go together?
4 Wow!	The writing presents a <u>clear</u> central idea or claim about the topic.	**Everything in the writing goes together.** • The main idea of each paragraph goes with the central idea or claim of the paper. • The main idea and details within each paragraph are related. • The conclusion is about the central idea or claim.
3 Ahh.	The writing presents a <u>generally</u> clear central idea or claim about the topic.	**Most parts of the writing go together.** • The main idea of most paragraphs goes with the central idea or claim of the paper. • In most paragraphs, the main idea and details are related. • Most of the conclusion is about the central idea or claim.
2 Hmm.	The writing presents one topic, but the central idea or claim is <u>not</u> clear.	**Some parts of the writing go together.** • The main idea of some paragraphs goes with the central idea or claim of the paper. • In some paragraphs, the main idea and details are related. • Some of the conclusion is about the central idea or claim.
1 Huh?	The writing includes many topics and <u>does not</u> present one central idea or claim.	**The parts of the writing <u>do not</u> go together.** • Few paragraphs have a main idea, or the main idea does not go with the central idea or claim of the paper. • Few paragraphs contain a main idea and related details. • None of the conclusion is about the central idea or claim.

<u>myNGconnect.com</u>

- Rubric: Focus and Unity
- Evaluate and practice scoring other student essays.

✔ Revise Your Draft, continued

❷ Revise Your Draft

You have now evaluated the focus and unity of your own draft. If you scored a
3 or lower, how can you improve your work? Use the checklist below to revise
your draft.

Revision Checklist

Ask Yourself	Check It Out	How to Make It Better
Is my essay focused?	Underline your claim, or controlling idea. Check that it states your position on the issue.	☐ Add a controlling idea if you don't have one. ☐ Rewrite your controlling idea if it is not clear or if it covers more than one idea.
Is my essay unified?	Check every paragraph to be sure you stay on topic. Check the structure of your argument to see if it's logical.	☐ Cut or rewrite sections that do not support the claim. ☐ Reorganize your argument to make the structure more logical. ☐ Add transitional words to connect the sections.
Does my essay have an introduction, a body, and a conclusion?	Draw a box around each part.	☐ Add any part that is missing.
Do I provide enough background information on the issue?	Read your essay to someone else. See if the person understands the issue.	☐ Research more background information.
Do I support my claim with reasons and evidence?	Check to be sure you provide at least one type of evidence for each reason.	☐ Research the issue to find more evidence for your reasons.
Do I include at least one counterclaim and a rebuttal?	Underline parts where you gave the opinion of people who disagree with you. Also underline your response.	☐ Add the missing parts.
Did I include a call to action?	Read your conclusion. What does it tell the reader to do?	☐ Add a sentence that tells readers what action to take.

🔖 **Writing Handbook**, p. 832

❸ Conduct a Peer Conference

It is useful to get a second opinion when you are revising your draft. Ask a partner to read your draft and look for the following:

- any part of the draft that is confusing
- any ideas that need more support
- any information that seems off the topic
- any reasons that will not appeal to the audience

Then talk with your partner about the draft. Discuss the items in the Revision Checklist. Revise your essay based on your partner's comments.

❹ Make Revisions

Look at the revisions below and the peer-reviewer conversation on the right. Notice how the peer reviewer commented and asked questions. Notice how the writer used the comments and questions to revise.

Revised for Focus

> The council hopes to have its way in this Fall's election. This means any citizen under the age of 18 will not be allowed to be out after 10 p.m. on weeknights and 11 p.m. on weekends. As a teenager in the community I am against this proposed curfew. ~~I think that teen driving restrictions would make more sense.~~ I believe it is unfair and unjust.

Peer Conference

Reviewer's Comment: The last sentence is a whole new controlling idea that you don't even mention in the rest of the essay.

Writer's Answer: I'll replace that sentence with one that relates to the controlling idea.

Revised for Unity

> Many teens have good reasons for being out after 10 or 11 p.m. Some work night jobs, such as babysitting. ~~I hope to eventually get a nighttime job at the local pizza place.~~ Others volunteer at places where they are needed at night, such as Mesa Grande Hospital. Many teens visit friends to study together. A curfew would prohibit teens from doing what they need to do to earn money, reach out to others, or get good grades.

Reviewer's Comment: You went off track here. Where you want to get a job doesn't relate to your argument.

Writer's Answer: You're right. I'll delete that sentence.

Reflect on Your Revisions

▶ Think about the results of your peer conference. What did your partner like and dislike about your essay?

✔ Edit and Proofread Your Draft

Your revision should now be complete. Read it over one more time to fix any mistakes you might have missed.

❶ Capitalize the Names of Days, Months, and Holidays

The names of days, months, and holidays are capitalized because they are proper nouns. They name specific things. The seasons of the year are not capitalized. They are common nouns.

Capitalize	Do Not Capitalize
Monday	winter
November	autumn
Independence Day	summer

TRY IT ▶ Copy the sentences. Fix the capitalization errors. Use proofreader's marks.

> 1. A teen curfew law is on the ballot in this Fall's election.
> 2. On election day, I beg everyone to vote against the council's proposal.

❷ Use Commas with Introductory Phrases and Clauses

An introductory clause is a dependent clause that provides background information for the main part of the sentence. The comma goes at the end of the introductory clause.

If you don't leave now, you won't get home before curfew.

An introductory phrase also provides background information for the main part of the sentence, but it doesn't have both a subject and a verb. The comma goes at the end of the introductory phrase.

After the election, a new curfew was established for teens.

To avoid being out after curfew, we can't work later than 9 p.m.

TRY IT ▶ Copy the sentences. Add commas after introductory clauses or phrases.

> 1. As a teenager in the community I am against this proposed curfew.
> 2. Since the curfew would not apply to adults it would not reduce crime very much, would it?

Proofreading Tip

If you are unsure of where to place a comma, look in a style manual for help and examples.

❸ Use Precise Language

In a persuasive essay, you want to sound convincing. One way to do this is to use precise language. Check each sentence that contains supporting evidence in your essay. Can you:

- substitute a word or phrase with a word or phrase that is more specific?
- replace words like *few*, *many*, and *some* with specific amounts?
- add a word or phrase to provide more information about another word?

TRY IT ▸ Read the paragraph. Decide whether it contains precise language. If not, list ideas to tell how the paragraph could be improved.

> According to the Mesa Grande Police Department, only a small number of crimes committed by teens last year took place after 10 p.m., and the total number of teen crimes was not even a large amount of the total number of crimes.

❹ Build Effective Sentences

Sentence combining can add variety to the sentence length in your writing, but you must be sure to do it correctly. When you join two sentences with a subordinating conjunction, make sure the conjunction goes with the less important sentence. That way the less important sentence supports the main sentence instead of the other way around.

Incorrect: I was out after curfew because I got in trouble.

Correct: I got in trouble **because** I was out after curfew.

Another thing to check is that the structure of the new sentence is parallel. For instance, if you form a compound predicate with two or more ideas in it, make sure they have the same word pattern.

Incorrect: I like to volunteer at the animal shelter and studying with friends.

Correct: I like **to volunteer** at the animal shelter and **to study** with friends.

TRY IT ▸ Copy each pair of sentences. Combine one pair with a subordinating conjunction and the other pair by creating a compound predicate. Be sure to keep similar ideas parallel in form.

> 1. The council hopes to have its way in this fall's election. This means any citizen under the age of 18 will have a curfew.
> 2. A curfew would prohibit teens from doing what they need to do to earn money. It would also prevent teens from getting good grades.

Editing Tip

Subordinating conjunctions show the relationship between two clauses in a sentence.

- *because*—shows cause and effect
- *although*—shows contrast
- *if*—shows a conditional relationship

Reflect on Your Corrections

▶ Read your essay one more time to check for errors in grammar and punctuation. Make a list of problem areas so you can focus on them the next time you edit and proofread your writing.

5 Edited Student Draft

Here's the student's draft, revised and edited. How did the writer improve it?

Teen Curfew Law Is Unfair

"No taxation without representation!" That was one of the main reasons for the Revolutionary War. Well, now the Mesa Grande City Council is acting just like the British and imposing a law on a group who has no say in the matter. If the council has its way in this fall's election, any citizen under the age of 18 will not be allowed to be out after 10 p.m. on weeknights and 11 p.m. on weekends. As a teenager in the community, I am against this proposed curfew. I believe it is unfair and unjust.

Many teens have good reasons for being out after 10 or 11 p.m. Some work night jobs, such as babysitting. Others volunteer at places where they are needed at night, such as Mesa Grande Hospital. Many teens visit friends to study together. A curfew would prohibit teens from doing what they need to do to earn money, reach out to others, or get good grades.

Worse yet, a curfew is a form of age discrimination. It is unfair to punish all teens just because a small minority might be committing crimes late at night. How would most adults feel if they could be stopped and searched by a police officer just for being on the street? It makes teens feel like they are second-class citizens.

Many members of the community who support the curfew say it will lower the teen crime rate. However, most studies on curfews fail to show this. According to the Mesa Grande Police Department, only 3 percent of crimes committed by teens last year took place after 10 p.m. And the total number of teen crimes was only about 10 percent of the total number of crimes. That means adults committed 90 percent of the crimes. Since the curfew would not apply to adults, it would not reduce crime very much, would it?

I know that council members believe a curfew will help keep teens out of trouble. They want to protect the youth in the community, and that is a good goal. But based on the evidence, it is not a good idea. It would keep teens from worthwhile nighttime activities, punish good kids unfairly, and not reduce crime. So please, on Election Day, I beg everyone of voting age to vote against the council's proposal. Do not let teens become victims of a law that they are not even allowed to vote on.

The writer used a **subordinating conjunction** to show a conditional relationship and corrected the **capitalization** error.

The writer inserted a **comma** after the introductory phrase and improved the focus of the controlling idea.

The writer improved the unity of the paragraph by removing the sentence that didn't relate.

The writer used **precise language** by giving specific numbers instead of general amounts.

The writer inserted a **comma** after the introductory clause.

The writer corrected the **capitalization** error.

✔ Publish and Present

Print out your essay or write a clean copy by hand. Share your persuasive essay with others. You have something to say. You may also want to present your work in a different way.

Alternative Presentations

Publish in a Newspaper Submit your essay to a newspaper. Many papers publish short essays from readers. Your local paper or school paper might accept yours.

1 Find a Publication Look for papers in your school or community whose audience would be interested in your topic.

2 Check the Guidelines Many publications have guidelines for writers. Ask for them if you can't find any.

3 Send Your Work Mail or e-mail your work. Include a way for the publisher to contact you. Ask for feedback on your work.

Put on a Debate Debate the subject of your essay in front of an audience. You will need to cover both sides of the issue.

1 Adapt Your Essay Rewrite it so that two people can argue the points you've covered. Further develop the objections people might make to your claim. You will probably need to do additional research.

2 Choose Debaters Present your claims yourself. Ask a classmate to present the claims of people who disagree with you. You will each need to prepare an opening statement to present your argument. You will also have to prepare a rebuttal to the opposing argument.

3 Present the Debate Practice debating your topic with the classmate you've chosen. Then debate your topic for your class.

- Take notes while the opposing side is talking so you can address what has been said in your response.
- Speak clearly so the audience and your opponent can understand you.

Refer to the **Listening and Speaking Workshop** on page 604 and to the **Language and Learning Handbook** on page 750 for more information about speaking persuasively.

Publishing Tip

Include a cover letter when you submit your essay. Begin it with a highlight from the essay that will grab the publisher's attention. You want to stand out from any other submissions.

Reflect on Your Work

▶ Ask for and use feedback from your audience to evaluate your strengths as a writer.

- Did your audience come away with a clearer understanding of your claim?
- Did you get feedback from anywhere else that made you reconsider your claim?
- What did you learn that you can apply to other writing you do? Set a goal or two for yourself.

☑ **Save a copy of your work in your portfolio.**

EQ ESSENTIAL QUESTION:

What Deserves Our Care and Respect?

I am I plus my surroundings, and if I do not preserve the latter, I do not preserve myself.

—JOSÉ ORTEGA Y GASSET

Remember the earth whose skin you are. . .

—JOY HARJO

1. Explain:

   Example:

2. Explain:

   Example: We need to treat Earth like ourselves.

Critical Viewing ▷
Miners work day and night to extract coal from a mountaintop in West Virginia, United States. Coal is a major source of power for people throughout the world. What responsibilities do we have in using the earth's resources?

FOR WHAT IT'S WORTH

EQ **ESSENTIAL QUESTION:**
What Deserves Our Care and Respect?

Study the Cartoon
Do we respect and care for the earth? Is caring for the earth an important priority?
Study this cartoon:

Frank and Ernest by Bob Thaves originally published 6-11-2000.

Analyze and Debate

1. What does the cartoon imply about our relationship with the earth? Is it a positive or negative relationship?

2. Does the earth deserve our care and respect? What can we do to show respect?

3. What are other people, places, objects, or ideas that are worthy of our care and respect? Why?

Analyze and debate these questions with a partner. Explain your opinion, support your ideas with evidence, and listen carefully to your partner's arguments.

EQ **ESSENTIAL QUESTION**
In this unit, you will explore the **Essential Question** in class through reading, discussion, research, and writing. Keep thinking about the question outside of school, too.

① Plan a Project

Literary Anthology

In this unit, your class will create an anthology of literature that addresses the Essential Question. To get started, look at an anthology in your classroom or library to get ideas. Consider

- how you will address the ideas of care and respect
- whether you want to include fiction, nonfiction, poetry, and drama
- how you will obtain selections—from student writers? From the public domain?

myNGconnect.com
▶ Planning forms
▶ Scheduler
▶ Book outline
▶ Information on U.S. copyright law
▶ Rubric

Study Skills Start planning your anthology. Use the forms on myNGconnect.com to plan your time and to prepare the content.

② Choose More to Read

These readings provide different answers to the Essential Question. Choose a book and online selections to read during the unit.

Othello
by Julius Lester

Othello is a respected general who marries a Lord's daughter. But Iago has become fiercely jealous of Othello. Iago makes Othello doubt his new wife's faithfulness. Will Othello discover the truth, or will this powerful general lose everything he loves because of a lie?

▶ **NOVEL**

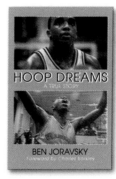

Hoop Dreams
by Ben Joravsky

William and Arthur have the potential to go to the NBA! The only trouble is that they live in one of the most dangerous neighborhoods in America. Will basketball be their ticket to a better life? Do William and Arthur have what it takes to get out of the projects and make it to the NBA?

▶ **NONFICTION**

Down Garrapata Road
by Anne Estevis

Chatita has a disastrous date, Paco learns about sacrifice, and Roberto risks his life for love. In this collection of stories, four families struggle with poverty, education, World War II, and the expectations of a changing world.

▶ **SHORT STORIES**

myNGconnect.com

🔖 Read environmental articles written and published by students.
🔖 Read real-life stories about what people did for love.

Plays are stories that actors perform for an audience. Read
this short script. Picture the details in your mind as you read.

Most Valuable Player

Act 1, Scene 2

[*A restaurant in a big city*]

Ms. Roan: Your son is quite gifted, Mr. Tran. Perhaps you were an athlete, too?

Mr. Tran: Chris, where are those napkins? We open soon, and it's going to be busy tonight. Do
you want more coffee, Ms. Roan? Chris, get Ms. Roan more coffee.

Chris: Can we just talk for a minute, Dad? This is important to me.

Mr. Tran: And this restaurant is important to me, Chris, and to our whole family.

Ms. Roan: I was hoping you'd see our school's offer to Chris as a blessing, Mr. Tran. College can
be quite expensive.

Mr. Tran: Yes, fancy schools can be quite expensive. But Chris can play football and study right
here, at a city school.

Chris: But Ms. Roan is with a great university, Dad. One of the best.

Ms. Roan: It's a full four-year scholarship. You wouldn't have to pay for a thing.

Mr. Tran: Oh, no. Just airfare and living expenses, and that's not
counting the money he'll lose by not working at the restaurant.
[*The phone rings*] One moment. Tran's Restaurant . . .

Chris: [*Approaches MS. ROAN'S table with coffee*] Ms. Roan, there's
something I should tell you.

Ms. Roan: That your father drives a hard bargain?

Chris: Yes. Well, no. It's more than that. He's sick.

Ms. Roan: I'm sorry. I didn't know.

Chris: That's just it. He doesn't want anybody to know. I only know
because I overheard him on the phone.

Ms. Roan: So this restaurant, your family, what will happen?

Chris: I'll run things, if I stay.

Ms. Roan: So four years away at school . . .

Chris: Is four years too long.
[*Lights down*]

Connect Reading to Your Life

Reading Strategies
- Plan and Monitor
- Determine Importance
- Make Inferences
- Ask Questions
- Make Connections
- Synthesize
▶ **Visualize**

Let your imagination go to work on "Most Valuable Player." Picture the characters, the setting, and the action. You may want to close your eyes.

- What do you think Ms. Roan, Mr. Tran, and Chris look like?
- Where does the action take place? What does the setting look like?
- What are some of the things Chris does for his job?

How did you answer these questions? The answers weren't in the text. You used your imagination to bring the scene to life. You staged the **drama** in the theater of your mind.

Focus Strategy ▶ Visualize

Imagine that you are sitting in a darkened movie theater as the movie begins. Some people in the seats behind you are having an argument. You cannot see them, but you can hear them. As you listen to their conversation, you begin to form ideas about them. In your mind, you create the following:

- what they look like
- their ages
- how they feel toward each other

You have no information except what they are saying. Your imagination creates a **mental** picture, or **image**, of the people. Reading drama requires you to use your imagination. When you read drama, you have only the characters' words to work with. From these words you can "see" what's going on.

Your Job as a Reader

Slow down as you read a play. Stop after a character speaks and let an impression form in your mind. How is the character saying the line? How does he or she look and move? What are the other characters doing? As you read, visualize the story.

- **Build the set**. Imagine it fully enough so that you can "walk around" on stage.
- **Choose the cast**. Select actors to play the characters in your mind. You might think of professional actors, or you might cast imaginary people.
- **Be the director**. Imagine how the actors move and speak.

Elements of Literature
drama *n.*, plays, or stories that are acted out, for theater, radio, and television

Academic Vocabulary
- **mental** *adj.*, existing in the mind
- **image** *n.*, picture

■ Unpack the Thinking Process

Onstage, actors make the characters in a drama real. They move, they speak, and they **interact** according to the script. They perform on a set that someone designed.

When you are reading a play, all you have is **dialogue**, the words the characters speak, and stage directions, or short descriptions of the set and the action to tell the story. From those words you learn everything the author has to say about the characters, setting, and plot.

Characters and Plot

At the heart of *any* story are characters and a **conflict**. The difference between short stories and plays is how much the author tells you. Look at the way a writer might introduce the conflict in a short story.

> Chris hurried up to Ms. Roan's table when Mr. Tran went to answer the phone. "There's something I should tell you," he whispered.
>
> Ms. Roan noticed the flash of pain on the boy's face. "What is it, Chris?" she asked.
>
> He poured coffee into Ms. Roan's cup, then sat down. After he explained that his father was ill, a silence fell over the table.

In the drama you learn about the conflict only through the characters' dialogue.

Setting and Stage Directions

If "Most Valuable Player" had been a short story, it might have started like this:

> Ms. Roan sat at a small table in a corner of Tran's Restaurant. She struggled to tell Mr. Tran about the scholarship her school wanted to offer his son, but his attention kept wandering away. His eyes darted around the room, making sure the restaurant was ready to open at five.

Notice how much the writer tells the reader about the setting and the characters' actions in the short story. The **playwright** leaves more to the reader's imagination.

Elements of Literature

dialogue *n.*, words that actors in a play speak
conflict *n.*, problem or struggle that drives a story's plot
playwright *n.*, person who writes a play

Academic Vocabulary

• **interact** *v.*, to be involved with people or things; **interactive** *adj.*, having to do with people or things that act upon one another

■ Try an Experiment

Drama is meant to be performed. When the actors portray the characters, they bring them to life. For many reasons, each performance is different. Maybe new actors **interpret** the characters differently or new sets change the look and feel of the play. Read the Demo Text below to yourself.

DEMO TEXT (continued)

Act 2, Scene 1

[*TRAN'S restaurant, a week later*]

Chris: Ms. Roan! It's good to see you again. How are you?

Ms. Roan: I'm fine, Chris. How are you doing? Did you have a chance to speak to your father again?

Mr. Tran: [*Yelling*] Chris! Table Four needs their check!

Chris: [*Leading MS. ROAN quickly to an empty table*] Please sit down, Ms. Roan. I'll tell you as soon as it slows down.

How do you think the play will end? In a group, create an ending for Act 2, Scene 1.

- Brainstorm possible endings. To get ideas flowing, read the roles of the characters and improvise. Take notes as you do.
- Choose the ending that the group likes best.
- Write a script for your ending, based on your notes.
- Assign roles and choose a director.
- Rehearse the complete scene and perform it for the class.

Discuss After each group has presented its scene, discuss the performances.

1. How were the various portrayals of the characters similar and different?

2. Which ending did you like best? Explain how the actors made that ending believable.

3. Describe the functions of the script, the actors, and the director.

4. How did reading the script to yourself differ from watching the performance?

Academic Vocabulary

- **interpret** *v.*, to express your understanding of something in a personal way; **interpretation** *n.*, act of expressing your personal understanding of something

Monitor Comprehension

Visualize Why do readers have to use their imaginations fully when they read drama?

Like drama, poetry is meant to be read aloud. Listen to the rhythm and the sounds of the words in this poem. Think about the mental images that the words and sounds create.

DEMO TEXT

I Wandered Lonely as a Cloud

by William Wordsworth (1815)

I wandered lonely as a cloud
That floats on high o'er vales and hills,
When all at once I saw a crowd,
A host of golden daffodils;
Beside the lake, beneath the trees,
Fluttering and dancing in the breeze.

Big Daffodils, 1990, John Newcomb/SuperStock. Casein on canvas.

■ Connect Reading to Your Life

You probably know many songs. Song lyrics, like poetry, say a lot in a few words. Song lyrics also follow patterns, just as many poems do. They have **verses**, lines that **rhyme**, and lines that repeat.

■ Your Job as a Reader

Slow down when you read a poem. Listen to the "music," or rhythm, of the words. See the images. *Feel* the emotions the poem makes you experience. Your job as a reader is to get involved in the poem.

Look at the image that accompanies the poem. Think about the words in the poem. Then look again at the picture of the daffodils. Compare the emotions and mental images that the poem and picture inspire. Discuss how the poem and picture are different.

Elements of Literature
verse *n.*, group of lines in a poem or a song
rhyme *n.*, repetition of the final sounds of words, as in the words *hide* and *side*

■ Unpack the Thinking Process

Experienced readers know that there are many **aspects** to poetry. Poems are not just words—those words are carefully chosen and arranged in a certain way.

Look at the Form

Poets choose different forms, or ways to organize their poems. Some poets divide poems into **stanzas** and follow patterns of line length and rhyme. For example, a sonnet is a poetic form that has fourteen lines and a certain **rhyme scheme** . Other poets choose a loose **structure**; the arrangement of the words follows the flow of their feelings and thoughts. **Free verse** is a form of poetry that has a loose structure.

Listen to the Sound

Appreciating the sounds in a poem helps you visualize the images and understand the meaning. Poets use rhythm and end rhyme to give their poems a musical quality. Another device is **assonance**, or the repetition of internal vowel sounds in words that are close to each other. In the Demo Text, notice the repetition of the long *o* sound, which expresses the sense of movement during a nature walk.

> I wandered lonely as a cloud
> That floats on high o'er vales and hills,
> When all at once I saw a crowd,
> A host of golden daffodils;

Visualize the Language

Poets want you to create full, vivid images in your mind. They use **imagery**, or language that helps you visualize how things look, smell, sound, taste, and feel. In the Demo Text, look at how Wordsworth used words that appeal to these senses:

Sight	Sound	Smell	Touch
cloud	fluttering	golden daffodils	breeze

■ Try an Experiment

Take turns reading the Demo Text with two or three classmates. Each of you should use a different rate of speed, pause in different places, and emphasize different words. How does each reading change the feel, images, and effect of the poem? Discuss which reading appeals to you most.

Monitor Comprehension

Poetry Describe three aspects of poetry.

Elements of Literature

stanza *n.*, section, or verse, of a poem

rhyme scheme *n.*, pattern of end rhymes used throughout a poem

free verse *n.*, form of poetry that does not have a fixed beat or pattern of rhyme

Academic Vocabulary

- **aspect** *n.*, part
- **structure** *n.*, way in which something is organized or put together

PREPARE TO READ

▶ **The Jewels of the Shrine**
▶ **Lineage**
▶ **Remembered**

EQ What Deserves Our Care and Respect?
See how people show what they respect.

Make a Connection

Think-Pair-Share Daniel Patrick Moynihan, a former United States senator, said, "The quality of civilization may be measured by how it cares for its elderly.... The future of a society may be forecast by how it cares for its young." Discuss with a partner the reasons you agree or disagree.

Learn Key Vocabulary

Study the Words Pronounce each word and learn its meaning. You may also want to look up the definitions in the Glossary.

• Academic Vocabulary

Key Words	Examples
• **compensate** (**kahm**-pun-sāt) *verb* ▶ pages 683, 697	To **compensate** is to pay someone for work performed. A parent may **compensate** a babysitter by writing him or her a check.
destitute (**des**-tah-tüt) *adjective* ▶ page 683	Someone who is **destitute** does not have any money or belongings. The **destitute** man could not afford to buy lunch. *Synonym:* penniless; *Antonym:* rich
impudently (**im**-pyu-dunt-lē) *adverb* ▶ page 670	A person who is behaving **impudently** is not showing respect for another person or idea. The girl behaved **impudently** when she refused to listen to her friend's opinion.
infuriate (in-**fyur**-ē-āt) *verb* ▶ page 669	To **infuriate** is to make someone very angry or impatient. The storm **infuriated** the travelers, who were stuck at the airport for two days. *Synonyms:* enrage, irritate
prophecy (**prah**-fu-sē) *noun* ▶ page 669	A **prophecy** is a prediction about something that will happen in the future. Many people have made **prophecies** about the end of the world, but they have never come true.
respectably (ri-**spek**-tah-blē) *adverb* ▶ pages 686, 690	To behave **respectably** is to act in a proper or correct way. She **respectably** listened to her grandfather's stories, though she had heard them often. *Synonyms:* properly, courteously; *Antonyms:* improperly, rudely
• **traditional** (tru-**di**-shu-nul) *adjective* ▶ pages 689, 697	The **traditional** way to do something is to do it the way it has been done for generations. We ate the **traditional** meal to celebrate the holiday. *Synonyms:* time-honored, customary

Practice the Words Work with a partner. Make a **Definition Map** for each Key Vocabulary word. Use a dictionary to find other forms of the word.

Definition Map

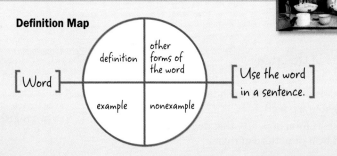

[Word]

definition | other forms of the word

example | nonexample

[Use the word in a sentence.]

BEFORE READING **The Jewels of the Shrine**

play by James Ene Henshaw

Reading Strategies

· Plan and Monitor
· Determine Importance
· Make Inferences
· Ask Questions
· Make Connections
· Synthesize
▶ Visualize

Analyze Structure: Script

Dramas are stories that are meant to be performed for an audience. A writer chooses dramatic elements that give structure to a **script**, or the text of the play. Here are some common elements that help to structure long and short plays:

- Long plays are divided into **acts**, or parts. The acts are divided into **scenes**. A new scene indicates a change in time or location.
- **Stage directions** give instructions to actors, directors, and stage crews.
- A **cast of characters** lists the name of each character and a brief description.
- Plays are mostly **dialogue**, or conversations between characters. Dialogue advances the plot and reveals information about the characters and the conflict.

Look Into the Text

Each scene takes place in a single setting. When and where does this scene occur?

Scene I. *The furniture consists of a wide bamboo bed, on which is spread a mat; a wooden chair; a low table; and a few odds and ends.* OKORIE, *an old man, is sitting at the edge of the bed. . . . On the wooden chair near the bed sits a* STRANGER, *a man of about forty-five years of age. It is evening.*

The dialogue reveals how the character feels.

OKORIE. I need help, Stranger, for although I have two grandsons, I am lonely and unhappy because they do not care for me. . . .

[*Exit* STRANGER. BASSI, *a beautiful woman of about thirty years, enters.*]

What instructions do these stage directions give, and to whom?

Focus Strategy ▶ Visualize

When you read a play, **visualize**, or mentally re-create, each scene. Visualizing the characters' actions, expressions, and surroundings helps you form emotional responses and deepen your understanding as you read.

HOW TO IDENTIFY EMOTIONAL RESPONSES

Focus Strategy

1. Use a chart like this one to take notes on the dialogue and stage directions that help you mentally re-create scenes.

2. Describe what you "see" and "hear" in your mind.

3. Combine the mental image with your personal experiences to identify how you feel. Note the specific words that led to your feelings.

Words or Phrases	I Visualize ...	I Feel ...
"I am lonely and unhappy because they do not care for me."	a scared, sad old man with a shaky voice.	sorry for Okorie. Thinking of a lonely, unhappy, and uncared-for grandfather makes me sad.

James Ene Henshaw
(1924–2007)

*The one single factor which urges me to write
... is the need to influence younger people
through the dramatic medium ...*

James Ene Henshaw was one of Nigeria's greatest playwrights, but he did not consider writing plays to be his profession.

Born in Calabar, Nigeria, Henshaw traveled to Ireland as a young man to study for a medical degree. While in Ireland, he began writing plays for an African student group that focused on the importance of African traditions and culture. He later returned to Nigeria and worked as a public health official while continuing to write plays.

"Writing plays has been a long-time hobby and comes as a welcome intrusion whenever opportunity occurs in the course of medical practice," he wrote. "I do not know how it happened . . . I just strayed into it. The profession itself gives one a lot of opportunity to observe and to interpret all kinds of human behavior and attitudes."

Henshaw's insight into human behavior is evident in his plays, many of which explore the difficult, but often humorous, situations that occur in the clash between society's traditional and modern values.

myNGconnect.com

◐ **Learn more about Nigeria and its people.**
◐ **View a time line of Nigerian history.**

THE JEWELS OF THE SHRINE

BY JAMES ENE HENSHAW

The Return of the Drummers, 2002, Jimoh Buraimoh. Bead painting, Museum of Modern African Art, UK.

▲ **Critical Viewing** Read the title of the painting. How do the shapes and colors suggest what's taking place?

**Read to discover why an old man is unhappy and what
he plans to do about it.**

CHARACTERS

What happened after their father dead.

OKORIE, an old man

AROB and **OJIMA**, Okorie's grandsons

BASSI, a woman

A STRANGER **1**

Act I

SETTING. *An imaginary village in* **Nigeria**. *All the scenes of this play take place in*
OKORIE'S *mud-walled house. The time is the present.*

Scene I. *The hall in* OKORIE'S *house. There are three doors. One leads directly into*
OKORIE'S *room. The two others are on either side of the hall. Of these, one leads to
his grandsons' apartment, while the other acts as a general exit.*

*The furniture consists of a wide bamboo bed, on which is spread a mat; a wooden
chair; a low table; and a few* **odds and ends**. OKORIE, *an old man, is sitting at the
edge of the bed. He holds a stout, rough walking-stick. On the wooden chair near the
bed sits a* STRANGER, *a man of about forty-five years of age. It is evening. The room
is rather dark, and a* **cloth-in-oil lantern** *hangs from a hook on the wall.* **2**

OKORIE. Believe me, Stranger, in my days things were different. It was a
happy thing to become an old man, because young people were taught to
respect elderly men.

STRANGER. Here in the village you should be happier. In the town where
I come from, a boy of ten riding a hired bicycle will knock down a man
of fifty years without **any feeling of pity**. You are lucky that you have
your grandchildren to help you. Many people in town have no one to
help them.

In Other Words

Nigeria a country in Africa
odds and ends small things
cloth-in-oil lantern hand-held lamp
  lit by oil
any feeling of pity caring or saying
  he is sorry

Cultural Background

In Nigeria and other West African countries,
butabu, or mud, has been used to construct
some of the most elaborate buildings, from
roundhouses to palaces. The tallest mud
building in Nigeria, the Goborau Minaret,
is 250 years old.

OKORIE. Look at me, Stranger, and tell me if these shabby clothes and this dirty beard show that I have good grandchildren. Believe me, Stranger, in my younger days things were different. Old men were happy. When they died, they were buried with honor. But in my case, Stranger, my old age has been unhappy. And my only fear now is that when I die, my grandsons will not **accord me the honor** due to my age. It will be a disgrace to me.

STRANGER. I will now go on my way, Okorie. May God help you.

OKORIE. I need help, Stranger, for although I have two grandsons, I am lonely and unhappy because they do not love or care for me. They tell me that I am from an older world. Farewell, Stranger. If you call again and I am alive, I will welcome you back. **3**

[*Exit* STRANGER. BASSI, *a beautiful woman of about thirty years, enters.*]

BASSI. Who was that man, Grandfather?

OKORIE. He was a stranger.

BASSI. I do not trust strangers. [*She points to* OKORIE.] What has happened, Grandfather? When I left you this afternoon, you were old, your mind was worried, and your eyes were swollen. Where now are the care, the sorrow, the tears in your eyes? You never smiled before, but now—

OKORIE. You know, woman, when I **worshipped at our forefathers' shrine**, I was happy. I knew what it was all about. It was my life. With my loving and helpful son, I thought that my old age would be as happy as that of my father before me. But death played me a trick. My son died and I was left to the mercy of his two sons. Unhappiness gripped my life. With all their education my grandsons lacked one thing—respect for age. But today the stranger who came here has once more brought happiness to me. Let me tell you this—

3 Structure: Script
What conflict does the dialogue between Okorie and the Stranger reveal? How might that conflict structure the story that this play tells?

In Other Words

accord me the honor give me the honorable funeral I deserve

worshipped at our forefathers' shrine prayed at the temple we built to honor the men who started this village

BASSI. It is enough, Grandfather. Long talks make you tired. Come, your food is now ready.

OKORIE. [*happily*] Woman, I cannot eat. When happiness fills your heart, you cannot eat.

[*Two voices are heard outside, laughing and swearing.*]

BASSI. Your grandchildren are coming back.

OKORIE. Don't call them my grandchildren. I am alone in this world. [4]

[*Door flings open. Two young men, about eighteen and twenty, enter the room. They are in shirts and trousers.*]

AROB. By our forefathers, Grandfather, you are still awake!

BASSI. Why should he not keep awake if he likes?

AROB. But Grandfather usually goes to bed **before the earliest chicken thinks of it**.

OJIMA. Our good Grandfather might be thinking of his youthful days, when all young men were fond of farming and all young women loved the kitchen. [5]

BASSI. Shame on both of you for talking to an old man like that. When you grow old, your own children will laugh and **jeer at you**. Come, Grandfather, and take your food.

[OKORIE *stands up with difficulty and limps with the aid of his stick through the exit, followed by* BASSI, *who* **casts a reproachful look on** *the two men before she leaves.*]

[4] **Identify Emotional Responses**
Visualize this conversation between Okorie and Bassi. What does Okorie tell Bassi about himself? How does this make you feel about him?

[5] **Structure: Script**
What information about Arob and Ojima does the writer suggest in this dialogue?

In Other Words
before the earliest chicken thinks of it when it is not yet dark outside
jeer at you say mean things to you
casts a reproachful look on looks angrily at

AROB. I wonder what Grandfather and the woman were talking about.

OJIMA. It must be the usual thing. We are bad boys. We have no regard for the memory of our father, and so on.

AROB. Our father left his responsibility to us. **Nature had arranged that he should bury Grandfather before thinking of himself.**

OJIMA. But would Grandfather listen to Nature when it comes to the matter of death? Everybody in his generation has died. But Grandfather has **made a bet with death**. And it seems that he will win. **6**

OKORIE. [*calling from offstage*] Bassi! Bassi! Where is that woman?

OJIMA. The old man is coming. Let us hide ourselves. [*Both rush under the bed.*]

OKORIE. [*comes in, limping on his stick as usual*] Bassi, where are you? Haven't I told that girl never—

BASSI. [*entering*] Don't shout so. It's not good for you.

OKORIE. Where are the two people?

BASSI. You mean your grandsons? They are not here. They must have gone into their room.

OKORIE. Bassi, I have a secret for you. [*He narrows his eyes.*] A big secret. [*His hands tremble.*] Can you keep a secret?

BASSI. Of course I can.

OKORIE. Listen, woman. My dear son died and left me to the mercy of his two sons. They are the worst grandsons in the land. They have sold all

Beadwork from Kenya

6 Identify Emotional Responses
Imagine listening to this conversation between Arob and Ojima. What does the writer reveal about their relationship with Okorie? How do you feel about this relationship?

In Other Words
Nature had arranged that he should bury Grandfather before thinking of himself. Grandfather should have died before our father.
made a bet with death planned to live forever

that their father left. They do not care for me. Now when I die, what will they do to me? Don't you think that they will abandon me in disgrace? An old man has a right to be properly cared for. And when he dies, he has a right to a good burial. But my grandchildren do not think of these things. **7**

BASSI. See how you tremble, Grandfather! I have told you not to think of such things.

OKORIE. Now, listen. You saw the stranger that came here. He gave me hope. But wait, look around, Bassi. Make sure that no one is listening to us.

BASSI. No one, Grandfather.

OKORIE. The stranger told me something. Have you ever heard of the Jewels of the Shrine?

BASSI. Real jewels?

OKORIE. Yes. Among the beads which my father got from the early white men were real jewels. When war broke out and **a great fever invaded all our lands**, my father **made a sacrifice in the village shrine**. He promised that if this village were spared, he would offer his costly jewels to the shrine. Death roamed through all the other villages, but not one person in this village died of the fever. My father kept his promise. In a big ceremony the jewels were placed on our shrine. But it was not for long. Some said they were stolen. But the stranger who came here knew where they were. He said that they were buried somewhere near the big oak tree on our farm. I must go out and dig for them. They can be sold for **fifty pounds** these days.

BASSI. But, Grandfather, it will kill you to go out in this cold and darkness. You must get someone to do it for you. You cannot lift a shovel. **8**

7 Identify Emotional Responses
Visualize this scene. What do you see and hear Okorie doing? How does this make you feel? Write your notes in your chart.

8 Structure: Script
What does the writer do in this dialogue between Okorie and Bassi to advance the plot?

In Other Words

a great fever invaded all our lands many people got very sick and died

made a sacrifice in the village shrine prayed to the village's gods and made a promise to them

fifty pounds a lot of money

OKORIE. [*infuriated*] So, you believe I am too old to lift a shovel. You, you, oh, I . . .

BASSI. [*coaxing him*] There now, young man, no temper. If you wish, I myself will dig up the whole farm for you. **9**

OKORIE. Every bit of it?

BASSI. Yes.

OKORIE. And hand over to me all that you will find?

BASSI. Yes.

OKORIE. And you will not tell my grandsons?

BASSI. No, Grandfather, I will not.

OKORIE. Swear, woman, swear by our fathers' shrine.

BASSI. I swear.

OKORIE. [*relaxing*] Now life is becoming worthwhile. Tell no one about it, woman. Begin digging tomorrow morning. Dig inch by inch until you bring out the jewels of our forefathers' shrine.

BASSI. I am tired, Grandfather. I must sleep now. Good night.

OKORIE. [*with feeling*] Good night. God and our fathers' spirits keep you. When dangerous bats alight on the roofs of wicked men, let them not trouble you in your sleep. When far-seeing owls hoot the menace of future days, let their evil **prophecies** keep off your path. **10** [BASSI *leaves.* OKORIE, *standing up and trembling, moves to a corner and brings out a small shovel. Struggling with his* **senile joints**, *he tries to imitate a young man*

9 Structure: Script
In creating this dialogue, what does the writer reveal about Okorie and Bassi's personalities and their relationship?

10 Identify Emotional Responses
As you read Okorie's blessing, visualize what he says. How do Okorie's words make you feel? What words led to your feelings?

Key Vocabulary
infuriate *v.*, to make extremely angry, to enrage
prophecy *n.*, statement of what someone believes will happen in the future, prediction

In Other Words
coaxing him trying to make him happy
senile joints arms and legs that are old, weak, and sore

digging.] Oh, who said I was old? After all, I am only eighty years. And I feel younger than most young men. Let me see how I can dig. [He tries to dig again.] Ah! I feel aches all over my hip. Maybe the soil here is too hard. I must rest now.

[*Carrying the shovel with him, he goes into his room. AROB and OJIMA crawl out from under the bed.*]

AROB. [*stretching his hip*] My hip, oh my hip!

OJIMA. My legs!

AROB. So there is a treasure in our farm! We must waste no time, we must begin digging soon.

OJIMA. Soon? We must begin tonight—now. The old man has taken one shovel. [*pointing to the corner*] There are two over there. [*They fetch two shovels from among the heap of things in a corner of the room.*] If we can only get the jewels, we can go and live in town and let the old man **manage as he can**. Let's move on.

[*As they are about to go out, each holding a shovel, OKORIE comes out with his own shovel. For a moment the three stare at each other in silence and surprise.*] ⑪

AROB. Now, Grandfather, where are you going with a shovel at this time of night?

OJIMA. [*impudently*] Yes, Grandfather, what is the idea?

OKORIE. I should ask you; this is my house. Why are you creeping about like thieves?

AROB. All right, Grandfather, we are going back to bed. ⑫

⑪ **Structure: Script**
Think about the dialogue and stage directions. What has the writer done with these elements to deepen the play's conflict?

⑫ **Identify Emotional Responses**
How do you react to Ojima and Arob's words and actions? Use your chart to track what you visualize and how you feel.

Key Vocabulary
  impudently *adv.*, in a disrespectful or bold way

In Other Words
  manage as he can take care of himself

Hidden Agenda, 1994, Jimoh Buraimoh. Bead painting, private collection.

◀ Critical Viewing:
Effect
Describe your
emotional
response to the
painting. What
details make you
feel as you do?

OKORIE. What are you doing with shovels? You were never fond
of farming.

OJIMA. We intend to go to the farm early in the morning.

OKORIE. But the harvest is over. When everybody in the village was digging out the crops, you were going around the town **with your hands in your pockets**. Now you say you are going to the farm.

OJIMA. Digging is good for the health, Grandfather.

OKORIE. [*re-entering his room*] Good night.

AROB and **OJIMA.** Good night, Grandfather.

[*They return to their room. After a short time* AROB *and* OJIMA *come out, each holding a shovel, and tiptoe out through the exit. Then, gently,* OKORIE *too comes out on his toes, and placing the shovel on his shoulder,* **warily** *leaves the hall.*] **13**

End of Scene I

13 Identify Emotional Responses
How do you visualize the end of this scene? What is your emotional response to each of these three characters at this point, and why?

In Other Words
with your hands in your pockets doing nothing instead of working
warily carefully and secretively

Monitor Comprehension

Explain
Why doesn't Okorie tell his grandsons about the jewels?

Will the grandsons treat Okorie with true respect? Why or why not?

Scene II. *The same, the following morning.* 🔢14

BASSI. [*knocking at* OKORIE'S *door; she is holding a shovel*] Grandfather, wake up. I am going to dig up the farm. You remember the treasure, don't you?

OKORIE. My grandsons were in this room somewhere. They heard what I told you about the Jewels of the Shrine.

BASSI. You are dreaming, Grandfather. Wake up! I must go to the farm quickly.

OKORIE. Yes, woman, I remember the jewels in the farm. But you are too late.

BASSI. [*excitedly*] Late? Have your grandsons discovered the treasure?

OKORIE. They have not, but I have discovered it myself.

BASSI. [*amazed*] You? [Okorie *nods his head with a smile on his face.*] Do you mean to say that you are now a rich man?

OKORIE. By our fathers' shrine, I am.

BASSI. So you went and worked at night. You should not have done it, even to **forestall your grandchildren**.

OKORIE. My grandsons would never have found it.

BASSI. But you said that they heard us talking of the treasure.

OKORIE. You see, I suspected that my grandsons were in this room. So I told you that the treasure was in the farm, but in actual fact it was in the

---

🔢14 **Structure: Script**
If you were watching the play, what changes would you expect to see onstage for Scene II? What details does the writer provide to suggest such changes?

In Other Words
By our fathers' shrine I promise
forestall your grandchildren make sure your grandchildren didn't find it

Cultural Background
About 60 percent of Nigeria's 137 million people make their living in agriculture. Nigeria is the world's largest producer of *cassava*, a root crop that is best known in the United States as an ingredient in tapioca pudding.

little garden behind this house, where the village shrine used to be. My grandsons traveled half a mile to the farm last night for nothing. **15**

BASSI. Then I am glad I did not waste my time.

OKORIE. [*with delight*] How my grandsons must have **toiled** in the night! [*He **is overcome with laughter**.*] My grandsons, they thought I would die in disgrace, **a pauper, unheard of**. No, not now. [*then boldly*] But those wicked children must change, or when I die, I shall not leave a penny for them.

BASSI. Oh, Grandfather, to think you are a rich man!

OKORIE. I shall send you to buy me new clothes. My grandsons will not know me again. Ha—ha—ha—ha! [OKORIE *and* BASSI *leave.* AROB *and* OJIMA *crawl out from under the bed, where for a second time they have hidden. They look rough, their feet dirty with sand and leaves. Each comes out with his shovel.*]

AROB. So the old man fooled us.

OJIMA. Well, he is now a rich man, and we must treat him with care.

AROB. We have no choice. He says that unless we change, he will not leave a penny to us.

[*A knock at the door.*]

15 Structure: Script
In these lines of dialogue, how does the writer change our understanding of the plot and of Okorie himself?

detail of *Baba Cheap Cheap*, 1998, Tyrone Geter. Oil on canvas, collection of the artist.

▲ Critical Viewing: Character How does this image compare to the way you visualize Okorie?

In Other Words
toiled worked so hard
is overcome with laughter cannot stop laughing
a pauper, unheard of poor and alone

AROB and **OJIMA.** Come in.

OKORIE. [*Comes in, and seeing them so rough and dirty, bursts out laughing; the others look surprised.*] Look how dirty you are, with shovels and all. "Gentlemen" like you should not touch shovels. You should wear white gloves and live in towns. But see, you look like two pigs. Ha—ha—ha—ha—ha! Oh what grandsons! How stupid they look! Ha—ha—ha! [AROB *and* OJIMA *are **dumbfounded**.*] I saw both of you a short while ago under the bed. I hope you now know that I have got the Jewels of the Shrine.

AROB. We, too, have something to tell you.

OKORIE. Yes, yes, "gentlemen." Come, tell me. [*He begins to move away.*] You must hurry up. I'm going to town to buy myself some new clothes and a pair of shoes.

AROB. New clothes?

OJIMA. And shoes?

OKORIE. Yes, grandsons, it is never too late to wear new clothes.

AROB. Let us go and buy them for you. It is too hard for you to—

OKORIE. If God does not think that I am yet old enough to be in the grave, I do not think I am too old to go to the market in town. I need some clothes and a comb to comb my beard. I am happy, grandchildren, very happy. [AROB *and* OJIMA *are dumbfounded.*] Now, "gentlemen," why don't you get drunk and shout at me as before? [*growing bolder*] Why not laugh at me as if I were nobody? You young **puppies**, I am now somebody, somebody.

OJIMA. You are a good man, Grandfather, and we like you. 🔢16

16 Structure: Script
What do you learn about Okorie, Arob, and Ojima from the dialogue and stage directions in this part of the script? Why do you think they behave this way?

In Other Words
dumbfounded amazed, surprised
puppies foolish boys

Cultural Background
Nigerian traditional clothing was made from dyed cloths. Nigerian women wore fabric wrapped around the head (*gele*), a blouse (*buba*) and a traditional dress (*kaba*). Men wore a long, wide robe (*agbada*), pants tied at the waist (*sokoto*) and a round cap (*fila*).

OKORIE. [*shouting excitedly*] Bassi! Bassi! Bassi! Where is that silly woman? Bassi, come and hear this. My grandchildren like me; I am now a good man. Ha—ha—ha—ha!

[*He limps into his room.* AROB *and* OJIMA *look at each other. It is obvious to them that the old man* **has all the cards** *now.*]

AROB. What has come over the old man?

OJIMA. Have you not heard that when people have money, it scratches them on the brain? That is what has happened to our grandfather now. **17**

AROB. He does not believe that we like him. How can we convince him?

OJIMA. You know what he likes most: someone to scratch his back. When he comes out, you will scratch his back, and I will use his big fan to fan at him.

AROB. Great idea. [OKORIE *coughs from the room.*] He is coming now.

OKORIE. [*comes in*] I am so tired.

AROB. You said you were going to the market, Grandfather.

OKORIE. You do well to remind me. I have sent Bassi to buy the things I want.

OJIMA. Grandfather, you look really tired. Lie down here. [OKORIE *lies down and uncovers his back.*] Grandfather, from now on, I shall give you all your breakfast and your midday meals.

AROB. [*jealously*] By our forefathers' shrine, Grandfather, I shall take care of your dinner and supply you with wine and clothing. **18**

17 **Language**
Money can't literally scratch someone's brain. Think about Okorie's behavior at this moment. What do you think this expression means?

18 **Structure: Script**
What does the writer's word choice in this stage direction suggest about Arob's motive for helping his grandfather?

In Other Words
has all the cards is the one who is in control

OKORIE. God bless you, little sons. That is how it should have been all the time. An old man has a right to live comfortably in his last days.

OJIMA. Grandfather, it is a very long time since we scratched your back.

AROB. Yes, it is a long time. We have not done it since we were infants. We want to do it now. It will remind us of our younger days, when it was a pleasure to scratch your back.

OKORIE. Scratch my back? Ha—ha—ha—ha. Oh, go on, go on; by our fathers' shrine you are now good men. I wonder what has happened to you.

OJIMA. It's you, Grandfather. You are such a nice man. As a younger man you must have looked very well. But in your old age you look simply wonderful.

AROB. That is right, Grandfather, and let us tell you again. Do not waste a penny of yours any more. We will keep you happy and satisfied to the last hour of your life. **19**

[OKORIE *appears pleased.* AROB *now begins to pick at, and scratch,* OKORIE'S *back.* OJIMA *kneels near the bed and begins to fan the old man. After a while a slow snore is heard. Then, as* AROB *warms up to his task,* OKORIE *jumps up.*]

OKORIE. Oh, that one hurts. Gently, children, gently.

[*He relaxes and soon begins to snore again.* OJIMA *and* AROB *gradually stand up.*]

AROB. The old **fogy** is asleep.

OJIMA. That was clever of us. I am sure he believes us now.

19 Identify Emotional Responses
Visualize this scene. What do you see and hear Arob, Ojima, and Okorie doing? Write the images in your chart. How do they make you feel?

In Other Words
fogy man

[*They leave. OKORIE opens an eye and peeps at them. Then he smiles and closes it again. BASSI enters, bringing some new clothes, a pair of shoes, a comb and brush, a tin of face powder, etc. She pushes OKORIE.*] [20]

BASSI. Wake up, Grandfather.

OKORIE. [*opening his eyes*] Who told you that I was asleep? Oh! You have brought the things. It is so long since I had a change of clothes. Go on, woman, and call those grandsons of mine. They must help me to put on my new clothes and shoes.

[*BASSI leaves. OKORIE begins to comb his hair and beard, which have not been touched for a long time. BASSI reenters with AROB and OJIMA. Helped by his grandsons and BASSI, OKORIE puts on his new clothes and shoes. He then sits on the bed and poses majestically like a chief.*]

End of Scene II

[20] **Structure: Script/ Identify Emotional Responses**
What important information does the writer reveal in these stage directions? As you visualize the action, how do you feel about Okorie?

Wooden comb from Nigeria

Monitor Comprehension

Confirm Prediction
Was your prediction valid? If not, why? What happened that surprised you?

Will Okorie's grandsons continue to take good care of him? Why or why not?

Act II

Scene III. *The same setting, a few months later.* OKORIE *is lying on the bed. He is well-dressed and looks happy, but it is easily seen that he is **nearing his end**. There is a knock at the door.* OKORIE *turns and looks at the door but cannot speak loudly. Another knock; the door opens, and the* STRANGER *enters.*

OKORIE. Welcome back, Stranger. You have come in time. Sit down. I will tell you **of my will**.

[*Door opens slowly.* BASSI *walks in.*]

BASSI. [*to* STRANGER] How is he?

STRANGER. Just holding on.

BASSI. Did he say anything?

STRANGER. He says that he wants to tell me about his will. **21** Call his grandsons.

[BASSI *leaves.*]

OKORIE. Stranger.

STRANGER. Yes, Grandfather.

OKORIE. Do you remember what I told you about my fears in life?

STRANGER. You were afraid your last days would be miserable and that you would not have a decent burial.

21 **Identify Emotional Responses** Using the stage directions and dialogue, how do you visualize this scene? How do you react to the idea that Okorie wants to tell the Stranger about his will?

In Other Words
nearing his end going to die soon
of my will who I want to have my house and money after I die
Just holding on. He is close to dying.

OKORIE. Now, Stranger, all that is past. Don't you see how happy I am? I have been very well cared for since I saw you last. My grandchildren have done everything for me, and I am sure they will bury me with great ceremony and rejoicing. I want you to be here when I am making my will. Bend to my ears; I will whisper something to you. [STRANGER *bends for a moment.* OKORIE *whispers. Then he speaks aloud.*] Is that clear, Stranger? **22**

STRANGER. It is clear.

OKORIE. Will you remember?

STRANGER. I will.

OKORIE. Do you promise?

STRANGER. I promise.

OKORIE. [*relaxing on his pillow*] There now. My end will be more cheerful than I ever expected.

[*A knock.*]

STRANGER. Come in.

[AROB, OJIMA, *and* BASSI *enter. The two men appear as sad as possible. They are surprised to meet the* STRANGER, *and stare at him for a moment.*]

OKORIE. [*with effort*] This man may be a stranger to you, but not to me. He is my friend. Arob, look how sad you are! Ojima, how tight your lips are with sorrow! Barely a short while ago you would not have cared whether I lived or died.

AROB. Don't speak like that, Grandfather. **23**

22 Structure: Script Why do you think the writer includes these stage directions? How do they affect our understanding of the plot?

23 Identify Emotional Responses Based on the stage directions and Okorie's comments, how do you feel about the grandsons at this moment? Why?

OKORIE. Why should I not? Remember, these are my last words on earth.

OJIMA. You **torture us**, Grandfather.

OKORIE. Since my son, your father, died, you have tortured me. But now you have changed, and it is good to forgive you both.

STRANGER. You wanted to make a will.

OKORIE. Oh, the will; the will is made.

AROB. Made? Where is it?

OKORIE. It is written out on paper.

[AROB *and* OJIMA *together.*]

AROB. Written?

OJIMA. What?

OKORIE. [*coolly*] Yes, someone wrote it for me soon after I had discovered the treasure.

AROB. Where is it, Grandfather?

OJIMA. Are you going to show us, Grandfather?

OKORIE. Yes, I will. Why not? But not now, not until I am dead. 24

AROB and **OJIMA.** What?

24 **Structure: Script/ Identify Emotional Responses**
What effect does this dialogue have on the grandsons? What effect does it have on you?

In Other Words
torture us are being mean and hurtful

Hidden Treasure, 1991, Emmanuel Ekong Ekefrey. Acrylic, Contemporary African Art Collection Limited/Corbis.

▲ **Critical Viewing: Title** The title of this work is *Hidden Treasure*. What story does it seem to tell? How does the painting's story relate to the play?

OKORIE. Listen here. The will is in a small box buried somewhere. The box also contains all my wealth. These are my wishes. Make my burial the best you can. Spend as much as is required, for you will be **compensated**. Do not forget that I am the oldest man in this village. An old man has a right to be decently buried. Remember, it was only after I had discovered the Jewels of the Shrine that you began to take good care of me. You should, by carrying out all my last wishes, **atone** for all those years when you left me poor, **destitute**, and miserable. [*to the* STRANGER, *in broken phrases*] Two weeks after my death, Stranger, you will come and unearth the box of my treasure. Open it **in the presence of** my grandsons. Read out the division of the property, and share it among them. Stranger, I have told you where the box containing the will is buried. That is all. May God . . . 25

AROB and **OJIMA.** [*rushing to him*] Grandfather, Grandfather—

STRANGER. Leave him in peace. [BASSI, *giving out a scream, rushes from the room.*] I must go now. Don't forget his will. Unless you bury him with great honor, you may not touch his property. 26

[*He leaves.*]

End of Scene III

25 **Structure: Script**
Think about the conflict. Why do you think the writer has Okorie give this speech?

26 **Inference**
What has happened to Okorie? How do you know?

Monitor Comprehension

Confirm Prediction
Did the grandsons act as you predicted? What confirmed or changed your ideas?

Key Vocabulary
- **compensate** *v.*, to be paid for work that was done
- **destitute** *adj.*, without money or possessions

In Other Words
atone make up, make amends
in the presence of when you are with

Predict

Will Okorie leave the Jewels of the Shrine to his grandsons?

Scene IV. *All in this scene are dressed in black. AROB, OJIMA, and BASSI are sitting around the table. There is one extra chair. The bed is still there, but the mat is taken off, leaving it bare. The shovel with which OKORIE dug out the treasure is lying on the bed as a sort of memorial.*

AROB. Thank God, today is here at last. When I get my own share, I will go and live in town.

OJIMA. If only that foolish stranger would turn up! Why a stranger should come into this house and—

BASSI. Remember, he was your grandfather's friend.

OJIMA. At last, poor Grandfather is gone. I wonder if he knew that we only **played up** just to get something from his will.

AROB. Well, it didn't matter to him. He believed us, and that is why he has left his property to us. A few months ago he would rather have thrown it all into the sea.

OJIMA. Who could have thought, considering the way we treated him, that the old man had such a kindly heart! **27**

[*There is a knock. All stand. STRANGER enters from OKORIE'S room. He is* **grim,** *dressed in black, and carries a small wooden box under his arm.*]

27 Identify Emotional Responses
How do you visualize this scene? How do the description and dialogue make you feel about the characters?

Ornamental box from Nigeria

In Other Words
played up pretended to care about him
grim serious

AROB. Stranger, how did you come out from Grandfather's room?

STRANGER. Let us not waste time on questions. This box was buried in the floor of your grandfather's room. [*He places the box on the table; AROB and OJIMA crowd together. STRANGER speaks **sternly**.*] Give me room, please. Your grandfather always wanted you to crowd around him. But no one would, until he was about to die. Step back, please. 28

[*Both AROB and OJIMA step back. OJIMA accidently steps on AROB.*]

AROB. [*to OJIMA*] Don't you step on me!

OJIMA. [*querulously*] Don't you shout at me!

[STRANGER *looks at both.*]

AROB. When I sat day and night watching Grandfather in his illness, you were away in town, dancing and getting drunk. Now you want to be the first to grab at everything.

OJIMA. You liar! It was I who took care of him.

AROB. You only took care of him when you knew that he **had come to some wealth**.

BASSI. Why can't both of you— 29

AROB. [*very sharply*] Keep out of this, woman. That pretender [*pointing to OJIMA*] wants to bring trouble today.

OJIMA. I, a pretender? What of you, who began to scratch the old man's back simply to get his money?

28 Structure: Script
What does the writer include in the dialogue and stage directions to suggest that the play's action is still rising?

29 Inference
What does Bassi's dialogue tell you about her feelings for Okorie and the grandsons?

In Other Words
sternly seriously
querulously aggressively
had come to some wealth became rich

AROB. How dare you insult me like that!

[*He throws out a blow.* OJIMA **parries**. *They fight and roll on the floor. The* STRANGER *looks on.*]

BASSI. Stranger, stop them. Stop them, or they will kill themselves. **30**

STRANGER. [*clapping his hands*] Are you ready to proceed with your grandfather's will, or should I wait till you are ready? [*They stop fighting and stand up,* **panting**.] Before I open this box, I want to know if all your grandfather's wishes have been kept. Was he buried with honor?

AROB. Yes, the greatest burial any old man has had in this village.

OJIMA. You may well answer, but I spent more money than you did.

AROB. No, you did not. I called the drummers and the dancers.

OJIMA. I arranged for the shooting of guns. I—

STRANGER. Please, brothers, wait. I ask you again. Was the old man **respectably** buried? **31**

BASSI. I can swear to that. His grandsons have sold practically all they have in order to give him a grand burial.

STRANGER. That is good. I shall now open the box.

[*There is silence. He opens the box and brings out a piece of paper.*]

AROB. [*in alarm*] Where are the jewels, the money, the treasure?

30 Structure: Script
What details does the writer include in the stage directions and dialogue to help you visualize the fight?

31 Identify Emotional Responses
Visualize what is happening at this moment. How do you feel when the Stranger interrupts Arob and Ojima? Why?

Key Vocabulary
respectably *adv.*, in a decent and moral way, properly

In Other Words
parries avoids or evades
panting breathing heavily

Rhythm in Blue, 2004, Mark Buku. Oil on canvas, courtesy of Novica.com.

▲ **Critical Viewing: Effect** What details help create the mood of this image? What line from the play goes with it the best?

STRANGER. Sh! Listen. This is the will. Perhaps it will tell us where to find everything. Listen to this.

AROB. But you cannot read. Give it to me.

OJIMA. Give it to me.

STRANGER. I can read. I am a schoolteacher.

AROB. Did you write this will for Grandfather? 32

32 **Identify Emotional Responses** Combine your mental image of this scene with what you know about this type of event. Use your chart to track what you visualize and how you feel.

Cultural Background

In traditional Nigerian culture, drumming and dancing play an important role in life events, such as birth ceremonies and planting season rituals. Drums are used for storytelling, and dancers interpret the story of the drums through motion.

STRANGER. Questions are useless at this time. I did not.

AROB. Stop talking, man. Read it.

STRANGER. [*reading*] Now, my grandsons, now that I have been respectably and honorably buried, as all grandsons should do to their grandfathers, I can tell you a few things. First of all, I have discovered no treasure at all. There was never anything like the Jewels of the Shrine. [AROB *makes a sound as if something had caught him in the throat.* OJIMA *sneezes violently.*] 33

There was no treasure hidden in the farm or anywhere else. I have had nothing in life, so I can only leave you nothing. The house which you now live in was my own. But I sold it some months ago and got a little money for what I needed. That money was my Jewels of the Shrine.

The house belongs now to the stranger who is reading this will to you. He shall take possession of this house two days after the will has been read. Hurry up, therefore, and pack out of this house. You young puppies, do you think I never knew that you had no

Hand and Egg, 2001, Emmanuel Atiamo Yeboa. Mixed media on canvas, courtesy of Novica.com.

▲ **Critical Viewing: Symbol** How might this image symbolize a character or an idea in the play?

33 **Structure: Script** Look that the details that the writer includes in these stage directions. How do Arob and Ojima react to the climax of the story? Why do you think the Stranger does not have the same reaction?

love for me, and that you were only playing up in order to get the money which you believed I had acquired?

When I was a child, one of my duties was to respect people who were older than myself. But you have thrown away our **traditional** love and respect for the elderly person. I shall make you pay for it.

Shame on you, young men, who believe that because you can read and write, you need not respect old age as your forefathers did! Shame on healthy young men like you, who let the land go to waste because they will not dirty their hands with work! **34**

OJIMA. [*furiously*] Stop it, Stranger, stop it, or I will kill you! **I am undone.** I have not got a penny left. I have used all I had to feed him and to bury him. But now I have not even got a roof to stay under. You **confounded** Stranger, how dare you buy this house?

STRANGER. Do you insult me in my house?

AROB. [*miserably*] The old cheat! He cheated us to the last. To think that I scratched his back only to be treated like this! We are now poorer than he had ever been.

OJIMA. It is a pity. It is a pity.

STRANGER. What is a pity?

OJIMA. It is a pity we cannot dig him up again.

[*Suddenly a hoarse, unearthly laugh is heard from somewhere. Everybody looks in a different direction. They listen. And then again . . .*]

34 Identify Emotional Responses
Imagine the sound of Okorie's words as the Stranger reads them aloud. What emotions do you feel, and why?

Key Vocabulary
- **traditional** *adj.*, long-established or time-honored act or belief

In Other Words
I am undone. My life is ruined.
confounded rotten, no good

VOICE. Ha—ha—ha—ha! [*They all look up.*] Ha—ha—ha—ha! [*The voice is unmistakably Grandfather OKORIE'S voice. Seized with terror, everybody except BASSI runs in confusion out of the room, stumbling over the table, box, and everything. As they run away, the voice continues.*] Ha—ha—ha—ha! [*BASSI, though frightened, boldly stands her ground. She is very curious to know whether someone has been playing them a trick. The voice grows louder.*] Ha—ha—ha—ha! [*BASSI, too, is terrorized, and runs in alarm off the stage.*] Ha—ha—ha—ha!!! 35

CURTAIN ❖

35 **Structure: Script**
What do you think the writer was trying to accomplish by ending the play with this voice?

ANALYZE The Jewels of the Shrine

1. **Explain** Does Okorie tell the truth about the jewels? Why or why not? What is he trying to teach his grandsons? Be sure to cite details from the text to support your answers.

2. **Vocabulary** How **respectably** do the grandsons treat their grandfather? Explain, using examples from the play.

3. **Analyze Structure: Script** In drama, writers choose dialogue details to reveal important information about the characters and the plot. Locate examples of dialogue from each scene that reveal information about the characters and the plot. Use a chart like this one to record the dialogue and what it reveals.

Character	Dialogue	What It Reveals
Arob	"We have no choice. [Okorie] says that unless we change, he will not leave a penny to us."	Arob cares more about money than about Okorie.

4. **Focus Strategy Identify Emotional Responses** Study the chart you used while reading the play to see which scene you responded to most. Discuss with a partner how you visualized the scene and why you responded as you did.

🔊 Return to the Text
Reread and Write The servant Bassi calls Okorie "Grandfather," too. How does she treat him? How fairly does Okorie treat her? Reread pp. 664–669 and 687–689. Then write a paragraph to explain whether each treats the other with the same care and respect.

Lineage

by Margaret Walker

My grandmothers were strong.
They followed plows and bent to toil.
They moved through fields sowing seed.
They touched earth and grain grew.
5 They were full of sturdiness and singing.
My grandmothers were strong.

My grandmothers are full of memories
Smelling of soap and onions and wet clay
With veins rolling roughly over quick hands
10 They have many clean words to say.
My grandmothers were strong.
Why am I not as they?

African Sunset, 2005, Angela Ferreira. Oil on canvas, collection of the artist.

🔺 **Critical Viewing: Setting** How would you describe the setting of this painting? What might it have in common with the poem?

About the Poet

Margaret Walker (1915–1998) developed an interest in her African American heritage at an early age. Her poem "For My People" won the Yale Series of Younger Poets Award, one of many poems that inspired several generations of readers.

poem by Naomi Shihab Nye

Reading Strategies

- Plan and Monitor
- Determine Importance
- Make Inferences
- Ask Questions
- Make Connections
- Synthesize
▶ **Visualize**

Analyze Word Choice

Poets create word images to help the reader picture and feel what the speaker experiences. **Imagery** can appeal to the senses of sight, hearing, smell, taste, and touch.

Look Into the Text

Literal imagery describes objects exactly as they appear.

> He wanted to be remembered so he gave people things they would remember him by. A large trunk, handmade of ash and cedar. A tool box with initials shaped of scraps. A tea kettle that would sing every morning,
> … the figs and berries that purpled his land.

Figurative imagery describes objects as if they were something else.

Words used in unconventional ways help create imagery.

Focus Strategy ▶ Visualize

As you read, let pictures develop in your mind, based on the text. Keep track of the images and your reactions in a chart like the one shown below.

HOW TO IDENTIFY EMOTIONAL RESPONSES

Focus Strategy

1. As you read, pay attention to the images in the poem and try to picture them in your mind. Use the words of the text and your own experiences to help you.

2. Think about words and phrases that help you visualize.

3. Think about what feelings these images bring to mind for you.

4. Go back to the text. What do you think the poet wants you to feel as you read? Describe whether your response is what the poet was aiming for.

What do you visualize?	What words and phrases help you visualize?	What do you feel? What does the poet want you to feel?	Does the poet succeed? Why or why not?
I hear a tea kettle boiling, smell wood, and imagine touching the initials on the tool box.	a tea kettle that would sing, ash and cedar, initials shaped of scraps	I feel empathy. The poet wants the reader to feel empathy for the man.	Yes, because I understand the man's happiness in his everyday life.

Remembered

by Naomi Shihab Nye

Creative Lifeline, 2005, Laura Lein-Svencner. Assemblage, collection of the artist.

▲ **Critical Viewing: Design** What kind of person might have such objects? Does this assemblage, or grouping of objects, seem like art to you? Why or why not?

He wanted to be remembered so he gave people things
they would remember him by. A large trunk, handmade of
ash and cedar. A tool box with initials shaped of scraps.
A tea kettle that would sing every morning,
5 antique glass jars to fill with crackers, noodles, beans.
A whole family of jams he made himself from the figs and berries
that purpled his land. **1**

He gave these things unexpectedly. You went to see him
and came home loaded. You said "Thank you" till your lips
10 grew heavy with gratitude and swelled shut.
Walking with him across the acres of piney forest,
you noticed the way he talked to everything, a puddle, a stump,
the same way he talked to you.
"I declare you do look purty sittin' there in that field
15 reflectin' the light like some kind of mirror, you know what?"
As if objects could listen.
As if earth had a memory too.

At night we propped our feet by the fireplace
and laughed and showed photographs and the fire remembered
20 all the crackling music it knew. The night remembered
how to be dark and the forest remembered how to be mysterious
and in bed, the quilts remembered how to tuck up under our chins.
Sleeping in that house was like falling down a deep well,
rocking in a bucket all night long. **2**

1 Identify Emotional Responses
What words and phrases help you visualize this scene? How do you think the poet wants you to feel about the old man's gifts?

2 Word Choice
How would you describe the imagery in lines 18–24? How does it appeal to your senses?

In Other Words
A whole family Different kinds
loaded carrying a lot of gifts

25   In the mornings we'd stagger away from an unforgettable breakfast
of biscuits—he'd lead us into the next room
ready to show us something or curl another story into our ear.
He scrawled the episodes out in elaborate longhand
and gave them to a farmer's wife to type. **3**

30   Stories about a little boy and a grandfather,
chickens and prayer tents, butter beans and lightning.
He was the little boy.
Some days his brain could travel backwards easier than it could
sit in a chair, right there.

35   When we left he'd say "Don't forget me! You won't forget me now,
will you?" as if our remembering could lengthen his life.
I wanted to assure him, there will always be a cabin in our blood
only you live in. But the need for remembrance silenced me,
a ringing rising up out of the soil's centuries, the ones
40   who plowed this land, whose names we do not know. **4**

3 Word Choice
Notice the verbs in lines 25–29. What do they show you about the speaker's experience?

4 Identify Emotional Responses
Compare the last two stanzas. How does what you visualize change? How do you feel about this change?

In Other Words
stagger away walk slowly, feeling full
could travel backwards would remember things
cabin in our blood place in our memory
plowed farmed

ANALYZE Remembered

1. **Explain** The word "But" starts the last sentence and signals that a change is coming. What changes in the last three lines of the poem?

2. **Vocabulary** How are the man's **traditional** ways reflected in the poem?

3. **Analyze Word Choice** From the poem, give examples of word choices that create powerful images—one image that appeals to the sense of sight and one image that appeals to the sense of hearing. Explain what effect you think they have on the poem.

4. **Focus Strategy Identify Emotional Responses** Which words or phrases helped you visualize the old man? What emotions did these words and phrases evoke?

Return to the Text

Reread and Write What do you think the speaker cares about and respects most in life? Reread the poem to find specific details that support your answer. Then write a paragraph as if you were the speaker explaining your answer.

About the Poet

Naomi Shihab Nye (1952–) began writing poems when she was six years old and was published at age seven. A Palestinian American poet born in Missouri, she advises young writers: "Read, read, and then read some more. Always read. Find the voices that speak most to *you*."

EQ What Deserves Our Care and Respect?

Critical Thinking

EQ 1. **Analyze** What do Ojima and Arob in "The Jewels of the Shrine" care about and respect? Do they care about and respect the same things as the speaker in "Remembered"? Explain.

2. **Compare** How do Okorie and the old man in the poem differ in their ideas of respect and in their attempts to be respected and remembered?

3. **Interpret** What is the theme of "The Jewels of the Shrine"? Is the theme of "Remembered" the same? Why or why not?

4. **Speculate** Based on their experiences, how do you think Ojima, Arob, and the speaker in "Remembered" will behave when they are older? What do you think they will value? How do you think they will treat their families and grandchildren?

EQ 5. **Evaluate** Do you believe that elderly people and **traditional** ways deserve your care and respect? Support your answer with examples from both texts.

Write About Literature

Analysis There is an old saying that "actions speak louder than words." How might this saying apply to the two selections? Write your ideas in a paragraph. Support them with examples from both texts.

Key Vocabulary Review

Oral Review Work with a partner. Use these words to complete the paragraph.

compensated	infuriated	traditional
destitute	prophecy	
impudently	respectably	

> Paul's kind grandfather made a _(1)_ at Paul's birth that Paul would be _(2)_ with a large fortune in the future. In order for this to happen, Paul's grandfather told Paul to act _(3)_ toward his elders and to honor their _(4)_ customs. He reminded Paul never to speak _(5)_ with people even if he felt _(6)_. So, Paul always helped those who were _(7)_ and cared for his elders. By helping others, Paul also respected himself and became a successful person.

Writing Application Do you think that children should be **compensated** for doing chores around the house? Write a paragraph giving your opinion. Use at least three Key Vocabulary words.

Read with Ease: Expression

Assess your reading fluency with the passage in the Reading Handbook, p. 817. Then complete the self-check below.

1. My expression did/did not sound natural.

2. My words correct per minute: _____ .

Write in the Present Perfect Tense

You can make your writing more specific when you use the correct verb tense. The **present perfect tense** of a verb can show action that happened at some point in the past.

The old man **has looked** for his grandsons.

Present perfect tense can also describe an action that began in the past and is still happening now.

So far, his grandsons **have ignored** his wishes.

To form the present perfect tense, use **have** or **has** plus the **past participle** of the main verb. For most verbs, add **-ed** to form the past participle.

Bassi **has helped** the old man.

Irregular verbs have special past participle forms.

Present	Past	Present Perfect
go	went	have gone, has gone
know	knew	have known, has known
bring	brought	have brought, has brought

Oral Practice (1–5) Choose from each column to make five sentences. Use words more than once.

The grandsons The Stranger Okorie	have has	lacked brought gone known	respect. happiness. a secret. to the shrine.

Written Practice (6–10) Choose the correct form of the verb and rewrite the paragraph. Add two more sentences about Okorie. Use present perfect verbs.

A stranger (have come/has come) to visit Okorie. Okorie (have shared/has shared) his worries with the stranger. Arob and Ojima (have gone/have went) to dig up the jewels. Bassi…

Character Foils

A **character foil** is a character whose traits contrast with those of the main character. For example, if the main character is nervous and unsure, the character foil may be brave and decisive.

• A character foil is a static character—he or she does not change during the story.

• The differences between the characters help the reader recognize the main character's traits.

Which character in "The Jewels of the Shrine" could be the foil to Okorie? Why? Work with a partner to identify the character foil and discuss the following:

1. What are the character foil's traits?
2. How do they contrast with Okorie's traits?
3. How do they help you understand Okorie?

Dialogue and Character Traits

Conversation between two or more characters is called **dialogue**. In plays, most of the story depends on dialogue. You get to know the characters' traits by what they say.

For example, in "The Jewels of the Shrine," you can tell right away how Okorie feels about his grandsons: "… tell me if these shabby clothes and this dirty beard show that I have good grandchildren."

1. Review the dialogue for Arob and Ojima.
2. Identify three lines of dialogue that show what they are like.

Justify

Group Talk How do you think elders should be treated? Use what you know to justify your belief.

Idioms

When you talk to friends and family, you might use common phrases and expressions—or idioms. **Idioms** are expressions that do not have a literal meaning. In "The Jewels of the Shrine," Okorie tells Bassi, "By our fathers' shrine, I am." Okorie does not mean that he is standing next to a shrine. He means that he is telling the truth. Writers often use idioms in dialogue to make characters more realistic or to express the character's personality.

With a partner, determine what each idiom below means. Rewrite the sentences using the literal meaning.

1. I'm **dying to** see that new movie.
2. **Get a load of** that bike!
3. Are you **pulling my leg**?

Dramatic Reading

Give a dramatic reading from "Remembered" or "The Jewels of the Shrine."

1 **Choose** Select a passage, such as the speaker's introduction of the man (p. 694, lines 1–17) or Okorie's story about the jewels (p. 668).

2 **Mark Up a Copy of the Text** Consider what the character feels and does. Then decide what tone of voice, gestures, and facial expressions to use.

3 **Rehearse** Practice reading the selection and using the appropriate feeling and facial expressions. Don't forget to make eye contact.

4 **Perform** Present your speech to a small group, and ask for feedback.

🐦 **Language and Learning Handbook**, p. 750

Write a Character Sketch

Write a short sketch, or description, that would help an actor perform one of the characters in "The Jewels of the Shrine."

1 **Choose a Character** Decide which character is most vivid and interesting to you.

2 **Plan** Reread the script for details that tell how the character looks, acts, and speaks. Make a chart like the one below.

Character: Okorie
Physical appearance: uses a walking stick; has a long beard and dirty clothes; is very old
How he feels: lonely, disrespected by his grandsons; misses the way the village used to be
How he acts: clever and tricky
What he says: "My grandsons lacked one thing—respect for age."

---

3 **Draft** Use the paragraph below to help you write your sketch.

In the play "The Jewels of the Shrine," Okorie is an old man who wears dirty clothes and uses a walking stick. He feels lonely and disrespected by his grandsons. He explains this to a stranger: "With all their education my grandsons lacked one thing—respect for age." Okorie is also clever, and he comes up with a plan to get the respect he believes he deserves.

---

4 **Edit and Proofread** Read your sketch and ask:

- Did I identify and support several traits?
- Did I include dialogue?
- Did I use active verbs to describe the character?

5 **Publish** Share your character sketch with your teacher and classmates.

🐦 **Writing Handbook**, p. 832

1

2

3

Inside a Bank

Banks protect customers' money and valuables. They also provide loans, financial services, and insurance services. There are several types of banks, including commercial banks, savings banks, credit unions, and Federal Reserve banks. Each type of bank is different in the number and kinds of services they provide.

Jobs in the Banking Industry

Many different jobs are available for people interested in a career in banking. Most banks offer opportunities for training and advancement.

Job	Responsibilities	Education/Training Required
Teller **1**	• Accepts deposits, cashes checks, handles withdrawals and other transactions • Counts cash, sorts checks and deposit slips, and balances accounts	• Training in business or accounting desirable • On-the-job training
Auditor **2**	• Checks accuracy of financial statements • Reviews how the bank conducts business • Ensures regulations are followed	• College degree in accounting or related field • Must pass a certification test
Bank Manager **3**	• Oversees bank branch and departments • Hires employees • Resolves customers' problems • Ensures good service is provided	• College degree in finance, accounting, or business administration • Substantial banking experience

Conduct Online Research

Research banking institutions online to find how they are alike and different.

1. Choose two types of banks from the following list: commercial bank, savings bank, credit union, or Federal Reserve bank.

2. Conduct online research to find out what services both types of banks offer.

3. Create a Venn diagram. Label each side of the diagram with one of the banks you chose. Label the middle section "Both." List the different services both banks offer under the correct label. If both banks offer the same service, write it under "Both."

4. Share your Venn diagram with a classmate and compare your findings. Save the information in a professional career portfolio.

myNGconnect.com
- Learn more about the banking industry.
- Download a form to evaluate whether you would like to work in this field.

Language and Learning Handbook, p. 750

Interpret Non-Literal Language

Read the following sentences. Think about the meaning of the highlighted phrases.

Robert and Lupe lost their homework, so they are both **in the same boat**.

When Albert really wants something, he can be **as stubborn as a mule**.

The owl's eyes were searchlights, scanning the forest floor for prey.

Each of these is an example of non-literal, or figurative, language. The first sentence contains an **idiom**, the second contains a **simile**, and the third contains a **metaphor**.

An **idiom** is a common expression that does not match the literal meaning of its words. For example, "in the same boat" means "dealing with the same problems."

A **simile** compares two things using the words *as* or *like*. The two things being compared, like Albert and a mule, may not actually be similar.

A **metaphor** is a figurative phrase that suggests that two things are similar. For example, the owl's eyes were doing something similar to what searchlights do.

Understand Figurative Language

Work with a partner. Identify each highlighted phrase as an idiom, a simile, or a metaphor. Then match it with its meaning in the box to the right.

1. The happy baby's eyes **sparkled like stars**.

2. There's more to it, but that's the story **in a nutshell**.

3. She **ran out of steam** just before the finish line.

4. The movie star was surrounded by **a sea** of photographers.

A. Became tired
B. As a brief summary
C. Shined brightly
D. Too many to count

Put the Strategy to Use

Use the strategy to figure out the meanings of figurative expressions.

1. Identify clues in the context around the phrase.

2. Form a mental picture of the phrase.

3. Guess the meaning from the context clues and your mental picture.

TRY IT ▶ Use the strategy to identify and figure out the figurative expressions in the sentences below. (Hint: There are five.)

▶ Lia's father stood up like a rocket when he saw her poor math grade. "But, Dad," she cried, "Algebra is a bear! I'm up to my eyeballs in homework." After they had a heart-to-heart about the importance of school, Lia promised to start hitting the books.

EQ **What Deserves Our Care and Respect?**
Consider love's importance to people.

Make a Connection

Brainstorm and Debate People have certain basic needs in order to live, like food and water. But can people live without love? With a group, make a list of what people can and cannot live without. Which list is love on? Discuss the importance of love, and whether or not you could live without the love of your family and friends.

Learn Key Vocabulary

Study the Words Pronounce each word and learn its meaning. You may also want to look up the definitions in the Glossary.

● Academic Vocabulary

Key Words	Examples
● **attitude** (a-tu-tüd) *noun* ▸ pages 707, 720, 721	Your **attitude** is the way you think or feel about things based on your experiences and beliefs. He had a positive **attitude** toward math because he enjoyed working with numbers. *Synonyms:* outlook, point of view
dense (dens) *adjective* ▸ page 717	When something is **dense**, its parts are crowded closely together. We could barely see the deer hidden in the **dense** forest. *Synonyms:* crowded, thick; *Antonyms:* bare, sparse
envious (en-vē-us) *adjective* ▸ page 706	If you are **envious** of someone, you wish you had someone else's belongings, character traits, or luck. She was **envious** of her sister's curly hair. *Synonym:* jealous
feud (fyūd) *noun* ▸ page 715	A **feud** is a long-lasting conflict between families or groups of people. No one could remember how the **feud** between the Smiths and Joneses had started.
fractured (frak-churd) *adjective* ▸ page 717	Something that is **fractured** is broken or cracked. He **fractured** his arm when he fell out of the tree.
● **mature** (mu-**choor**) *adjective* ▸ page 717	When something is **mature**, it is fully developed and complete in its natural growth. A **mature** person acts like an adult. *Synonym:* grown-up; *Antonym:* childish
perfection (pur-**fek**-shun) *noun* ▸ page 710	**Perfection** is the quality of being without faults. Professional athletes practice daily to try to achieve **perfection**. *Synonym:* excellence; *Antonym:* imperfection
resolution (re-zu-lü-shun) *noun* ▸ page 717	A **resolution** is a strong decision to do or not to do something. Since her goal was to graduate with honors this year, she made a **resolution** to get better grades. *Synonyms:* promise, determination

Practice the Words Work with a partner. Make a **Word Square** for each Key Vocabulary word.

Word Square

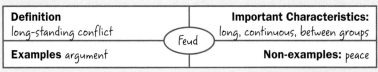

Definition long-standing conflict	Feud	Important Characteristics: long, continuous, between groups
Examples argument		**Non-examples:** peace

BEFORE READING Romeo and Juliet

play by William Shakespeare

Reading Strategies

· Plan and Monitor
· Determine Importance
· Make Inferences
· Ask Questions
· Make Connections
· Synthesize
▶ **Visualize**

Analyze Structure: Blank Verse

Like modern drama, William Shakespeare's plays did not include narration and were meant to be performed for an audience. Unlike today's drama, much of the dialogue in "Romeo and Juliet" is written in **blank verse**. Blank verse is unrhymed poetry in which each line has ten syllables and five stressed beats. Every second syllable is stressed. This **meter** is called iambic pentameter.

- Shakespeare and other sixteenth-century playwrights used blank verse to show that a character was of high rank.

- In blank verse, an idea may continue past the end of a line. Be sure to read sentence by sentence, not line by line.

Look Into the Text

Capulet's orchard. Enter Romeo.

ROMEO. He jests at scars that never felt a wound.

But soft, what light through yonder window breaks?
It is the East, and Juliet is the sun.
Arise, fair sun, and kill the envious moon,
Who is already sick and pale with grief
That thou, her maid, art far more fair than she.

Read Romeo's lines aloud. Hear the pattern of unstressed syllable followed by stressed syllable.

Imagery describes Juliet's beauty. In what way might Juliet be like the sun?

Focus Strategy ▶ Visualize

In order to **visualize**, look for descriptive words and phrases that help you form images of the characters, the setting, and the action. Creating a mental picture or drawing can help you understand the imagery and what you are reading.

HOW TO FORM MENTAL IMAGES

Focus Strategy

1. **Look for Clues** Notice details and descriptions that appeal to your senses. Picture in your mind the objects, people, and places described.

2. **Draw What You See** Think about the mental image the words create, and draw a sketch of how you visualize the scene.

Imagery	What I Visualize
Arise, fair sun, and kill the envious moon, Who is already sick and pale with grief...	

William Shakespeare
(1564–1616)

All the world's a stage
And all the men and women
merely players . . .

Shakespeare's plays have inspired hundreds of movies.

There are perhaps no more important influences on English literature than the Bible and the writings of **William Shakespeare**. His thirty-six plays—histories, tragedies, and comedies—are still performed and admired throughout the world. And yet, as one critic remarked, "A remarkable thing about Shakespeare is that he really is very good in spite of all the people who say he is very good."

William Shakespeare was born in the small town of Stratford-upon-Avon, England, and seems to have had a typical childhood. He attended school, following which he married and had children. By 1594 he was working as an actor and playwright at the Globe, which was then the best theater in London.

This was also about the time he wrote *Romeo and Juliet,* perhaps the best-known love story of all time. As with many of his plays, Shakespeare based the plot on the works of others, but he brought his own unique gift for characterization and language to this story of young "star-crossed" lovers. The following years would bring classics such as *Hamlet, King Lear*, and *A Midsummer Night's Dream*, as well as over 150 poems.

In the end, perhaps the best summary of Shakespeare's work came from his contemporary and fellow playwright, Ben Jonson: "He was not of an age, but for all time."

myNGconnect.com

◗ Visit the Web site of a television series about **William Shakespeare**.
◗ Review other plays by **William Shakespeare**.

Romeo and Juliet

BY WILLIAM SHAKESPEARE

The Montague and Capulet families had been enemies for as long as anyone in the land could remember. Then a Montague boy and a Capulet girl fell in love. Would their love prove stronger than their families' hatred?

 Comprehension Coach

The story of Romeo and Juliet is one of William Shakespeare's most popular plays. It centers on two families who have become enemies. When Romeo, a Montague, and Juliet, a Capulet, fall in love, their relationship could unite the families—or make the long-standing conflict between the families even worse. The young couple must decide what they respect and care about most, a decision that could have terrible consequences.

As Act 2, Scene 2 begins, Juliet is on her balcony, talking to herself about Romeo. Meanwhile, Romeo walks by and sees Juliet standing there. This selection gives you two versions of a scene from the play. The pages on the left present Shakespeare's original text, written in 16th century English. The pages on the right restate the text in modern English.

SHAKESPEARE'S VERSION

Act 2, Scene 2

Capulet's orchard. Enter Romeo.

ROMEO. He jests at scars that never felt a wound.

[*Enter* Juliet *above.*]

But soft, what light through yonder window breaks?
It is the East, and Juliet is the sun. **1**
5   Arise, fair sun, and kill the envious moon,
Who is already sick and pale with grief
That thou, her maid, art far more fair than she.
Be not her maid since she is **envious**.
Her vestal livery is but sick and green,
10   And none but fools do wear it. Cast it off.

1 Form Mental Images
What imagery helps you visualize both the setting and Juliet? Jot down notes in your chart, and draw a sketch of what you see.

Key Vocabulary
envious *adj.*, feeling or showing resentful longing for someone's wealth, traits, or luck; jealous

Cultural Background
In Shakespeare's time, family members and friends used the pronouns *thou* and *thee* to refer to each other rather than the pronoun *you*.

Modern Version

Act 2, Scene 2

ROMEO. Mercutio makes fun of love's scars: He's never felt love's wound.

[*He sees* Juliet *at the window of Capulet's house.*]

But quiet! What's that light shining through the window over there? It's like I'm looking east, and Juliet is the sun. Juliet, my beautiful sun, rise and shine; your brightness will make the moon disappear! That moon is like a woman who's sick with jealousy because she knows you're prettier than she is. Don't be the moon's maid if that's her **attitude**. Besides, the moonlight is like an ugly green outfit. Only clowns dress like that. Don't put it on! **2**

2 Structure: Blank Verse/Compare Across Texts
Read the two versions of the speech aloud. How is Shakespeare's version different? Which seems more effective? Explain.

Key Vocabulary
• **attitude** *n.*, set way of thinking or believing that can often be seen in someone's behavior, point of view

Literary Background
Mercutio is Romeo's relative and friend. Earlier, Romeo fell in love with Juliet at a ball, and Mercutio made fun of Romeo's feelings and his desire to see Juliet again.

SHAKESPEARE'S VERSION

It is my lady. O, it is my love!
O, that she knew she were!
She speaks, yet she says nothing. What of that?
Her eye discourses; I will answer it.

15   I am too bold. 'Tis not to me she speaks.
Two of the fairest stars in all the heaven,
Having some business, do entreat her eyes
To twinkle in their spheres till they return.
What if her eyes were there, they in her head?

20   The brightness of her cheek would shame those stars
As daylight doth a lamp; her eyes in heaven
Would through the airy region stream so bright
That birds would sing and think it were not night.
See how she leans her cheek upon her hand.

25   O, that I were a glove upon that hand,
That I might touch that cheek! **3**

JULIET. Ay me!

ROMEO. She speaks.
O, speak again, bright angel, for thou art

30   As glorious to this night, being o'er my head,
As is a winged messenger of heaven
Unto the white-upturned wondering eyes
Of mortals that fall back to gaze on him
When he bestrides the lazy puffing clouds

35   And sails upon the bosom of the air. **4**

3 Form Mental Images Identify Shakespeare's use of details and descriptions that appeal to your senses. How do they help you visualize Juliet?

4 Structure: Blank Verse Does it matter whether you read Romeo's speech in complete sentences or line by line? Explain.

Cultural Background

Shakespearean Pronunciation In blank verse, each line has ten syllables. To make the rhythm regular, Shakespearean actors often pronounce an -ed ending as its own syllable. Other words are shortened in order to remove syllables, such as "o'er" instead of "over."

MODERN VERSION

[Juliet walks onto the balcony.]

It's the woman I love! If only she knew it! Her lips are moving, but I don't hear her saying anything. No problem. That look in her eye says it all, so I'll just talk to her eyes.

[Romeo opens his mouth to address her, but his courage fails.]

I'm too confident. It's not me she's talking to, but the stars. Two of the most beautiful stars in the sky have asked her eyes to take their place for a while. What if Juliet's eyes and the stars have changed places? The glow of Juliet's cheeks would make those stars look dim, the way daylight outshines a lamp. Her eyes, sparkling so brightly in heaven, would make birds sing, because they'd think it was the dawn of a new day. See how she rests her cheek on her hand! I wish I were a glove on that hand, so I could touch her cheek!

JULIET. *[sighing heavily]* Oh, dear!

ROMEO. She just said something. Keep talking, bright angel! You're a wonderful sight, standing up there above me, like an angel who suddenly appears on a cloud to ordinary people.

SHAKESPEARE'S VERSION

JULIET. O Romeo, Romeo, wherefore art thou Romeo?
Deny thy father and refuse thy name;
Or, if thou wilt not, be but sworn my love,
And I'll no longer be a Capulet. **5**

40   **ROMEO.** Shall I hear more, or shall I speak at this?

JULIET. 'Tis but thy name that is my enemy.
Thou art thyself, though not a Montague.
What's Montague? It is nor hand, nor foot,
Nor arm, nor face, nor any other part
45   Belonging to a man. O, be some other name!
What's in a name? That which we call a rose
By any other word would smell as sweet.
So Romeo would, were he not Romeo called,
Retain that dear **perfection** which he owes
50   Without that title. Romeo, doff thy name,
And for thy name, which is no part of thee,
Take all myself.

ROMEO. I take thee at thy word. **6**
Call me but love, and I'll be new baptized.
55   Henceforth I never will be Romeo.

JULIET. What man art thou that, thus bescreened in night,
So stumblest on my counsel? **7**

ROMEO. By a name
I know not how to tell thee who I am.
60   My name, dear saint, is hateful to myself

---

5 Structure: **Blank Verse** How does the modern version help you understand what Juliet asks Romeo? How does the blank verse affect the way Juliet conveys what she wants Romeo to do?

6 Structure: **Blank Verse** Reread lines 52–53. Compare them with lines 26–28. Why do you think Shakespeare sometimes splits the iambic pentameter between two characters?

7 Form Mental Images How does Juliet's question suggest her facial expression and body language? Describe how you visualize the scene in lines 56–57.

Key Vocabulary
perfection *n.*, condition or quality of being without faults, excellence

Modern Version

JULIET. Oh, Romeo, Romeo! Why are you "Romeo"? Tell your father you want to change your name. Or, if you won't, then swear you love me, and I'll stop using the name Capulet.

ROMEO. [*to himself*] Hmm . . . should I keep listening, or say something now?

JULIET. It's just your name that's my enemy, not you. You'd be the same person, even if your last name weren't Montague. After all, what is a "Montague"? It's not a hand, or a foot, or an arm, or a face, or any other part of a person. Why can't you have another name? What's in a name? Even if we called a rose something else, it would still smell as sweet. So if Romeo weren't called Romeo, he'd still be perfect! Romeo, give up your name and take all of me instead!

ROMEO. [*to* Juliet *now*] I'll take you at your word. Call me "Love," as if I'd just been baptized and given a name. From now on, I'm done with the name "Romeo."

JULIET. [*startled*] Who is that hiding in the darkness, spying on me?

ROMEO. I don't know how to reply without using a name, and I hate my name because it's your enemy. If my name were written on a piece of paper, I'd tear it up.

Cultural Background

In **Shakespeare's Globe Theatre,** two large columns supported a roof—called the "heavens"—over the back of the stage. Because few stage sets or props were used, Juliet would stand in this upper section, while Romeo hid behind one of the columns.

SHAKESPEARE'S VERSION

Because it is an enemy to thee.
Had I it written, I would tear the word.

JULIET. My ears have yet not drunk a hundred words
Of thy tongue's uttering, yet I know the sound.
65   Art thou not Romeo, and a Montague?

ROMEO. Neither, fair maid, if either thee dislike.

JULIET. How cam'st thou hither, tell me, and wherefore?
The orchard walls are high and hard to climb,
And the place death, considering who thou art,
70   If any of my kinsmen find thee here.

ROMEO. With love's light wings did I o'erperch these walls,
For stony limits cannot hold love out,
And what love can do, that dares love attempt.
Therefore thy kinsmen are no stop to me. **8**

75 **JULIET.** If they do see thee, they will murder thee.

ROMEO. Alack, there lies more peril in thine eye
Than twenty of their swords. Look thou but sweet,
And I am proof against their enmity.

JULIET. I would not for the world they saw thee here. **9**

8 Form Mental Images
How do the descriptive words in this dialogue help you understand Romeo's feelings for Juliet?

9 Language
Hyperbole is an overstatement used for emphasis. What is the hyperbole here? What is the purpose of this exaggeration?

MODERN VERSION

JULIET. As soon as you started to speak, I recognized your voice. Aren't you Romeo, a Montague?

ROMEO. Neither one, if you dislike it.

JULIET. How did you get here, and why? The walls around the orchard are high and hard to climb. Considering who you are, this place could mean death for you if any of my relatives catch you here.

ROMEO. Love gave me wings to fly over these walls. Stone walls can't keep love out. Whatever love can do, love dares to try. So your relatives can't stop me.

JULIET. But if they see you, they'll kill you.

ROMEO. There's more danger in your eyes than in twenty of their swords. One sweet look from you, and I'll be safe from their hate. **10**

JULIET. I wouldn't want them to catch you here for anything in the world.

10 Form Mental Images
Reread Romeo's lines in Shakespeare's version. What mental image did you form as you read these lines? How do they compare to the mental image you formed as you read the modern text?

Shakespeare's Version

80   **ROMEO.** I have night's cloak to hide me from their eyes,
        And but thou love me, let them find me here.
        My life were better ended by their hate
        Than death prorogued, wanting of thy love. **11** ❖

11 Form Mental Images
How do you visualize Romeo as he speaks these lines?

MODERN VERSION

ROMEO. Oh, I'm all right, I've got night's darkness to hide me. And if you love me, I don't care if they find me. I'd rather my life was ended by their hate than have to live without your love. ❖

ANALYZE Romeo and Juliet

1. **Explain** How do Romeo and Juliet feel about each other and their families? What do they each consider to be important? How can you tell? Cite details from the text.

2. **Vocabulary** Romeo's family and Juliet's family have been fighting for a long time. How have this **feud** and hatred between the families affected Romeo and Juliet?

3. **Analyze Structure: Blank Verse** Reread the first two pages of Shakespeare's version and the modern version aloud. How are the two versions different? How does Shakespeare's use of blank verse and imagery affect the way you visualize the scene and the characters?

4. **Focus Strategy Form Mental Images** Reread p. 712. Working with a partner, identify the words and phrases that appeal to your senses. Make a sketch of how you visualize both the setting and Romeo and Juliet.

Return to the Text
Reread and Write Imagine that Romeo and Juliet had a chance to explain to their parents how much they care about each other. Reread the scene. Then write a paragraph explaining what Romeo and Juliet could say to convince their parents that they really care about each other. Include details from the text to support your explanation.

Key Vocabulary
feud *n.*, long-standing quarrel or hostility between two families or groups

screenplay by Ernest Lehman

Reading Strategies

· Plan and Monitor
· Determine Importance
· Make Inferences
· Ask Questions
· Make Connections
· Synthesize
▶ **Visualize**

Relate a Story to Its Source

Sometimes authors may draw on another story, or source, to create something new. They may use a theme, character, or idea from the source, or they may follow the source's plot in a new setting with new characters.

Knowing when an author is drawing from a source helps you understand and analyze what you are reading. Think about the scene you just read in *Romeo and Juliet* as you read this text from the screenplay *West Side Story*.

Look Into the Text

What scene in *Romeo and Juliet* does this stage direction remind you of?

[*Maria HEARS A VOICE calling to her from outside her open window, which leads to a fire escape.*]

54. EXT. BACK ALLEY AND FIRE ESCAPE

[*Tony is standing in the alley, looking about, not sure which window is Maria's.*]

TONY. [*calling*] Maria …

[*She appears on the fire escape, moves forward, sees Tony.*]

Based on what you know about *Romeo and Juliet*, why might Tony be looking for Maria?

Focus Strategy ▶ Visualize

Forming mental images as you read can help you compare what you are reading to the source that inspired it. This will help you see what the author has done to transform the source into something original.

HOW TO FORM MENTAL IMAGES

Focus Strategy

1. **Identify the Source** Ask yourself where you have read something like this before.

2. **Recall and Compare Mental Images** Recall details from the original work. As you read, note how the story elements are similar to and different from the original.

3. **Explain What Ideas the Author Is Expressing** In what ways has the author transformed, or changed, places or settings? How do these changes affect the story?

Tony and Maria remind me of Romeo and Juliet. In the play, Juliet is standing on a balcony. In this version, Maria is standing on the fire escape of an apartment building. This makes me picture a modern city. I think the author wanted to create a modern version of the story.

Connect Across Texts

West Side Story is a musical based on Shakespeare's play *Romeo and Juliet*.

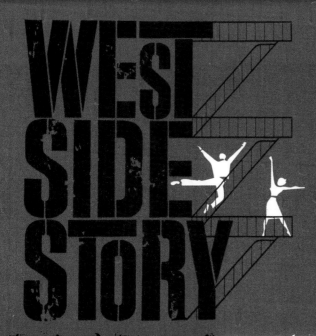

WEST SIDE STORY

by Ernest Lehman

Film logo, 1961, Saul Bass. © Pictorial Press Ltd / Alamy.

In *West Side Story*, Maria is the sister of gang leader Bernardo. She falls in love with Tony, who is from a rival gang. Tony and Maria's **resolution** to be together causes both gangs to hate each other even more, so Maria and Tony are forced to make a **mature** decision. They must try to heal the **fractured** relationship between the gangs and bring peace before it is too late. Instead of a balcony, this scene takes place on a fire escape among **dense** apartment buildings.

[*Maria HEARS A VOICE calling to her from outside her open window, which leads to a fire escape.*]

54. EXT. BACK ALLEY AND FIRE ESCAPE

[*Tony is standing in the alley, looking about, not sure which window is Maria's.*]

TONY. [*calling*] Maria … **1**

[*She appears on the fire escape, moves forward, sees Tony.*]

1 Form Mental Images
How do you imagine Tony sounds when he is calling Maria? Compare this to how Romeo responded to seeing Juliet on the balcony.

Key Vocabulary

resolution *n.*, strong decision to do or not do something

● **mature** *adj.*, fully developed, grown-up, adult

fractured *adj.*, broken

dense *adj.*, closely crowded together, thick

Technical Background

Screenplays are scripts for movies. Like scripts for plays, screenplays include dialogue, stage directions, and scenes. Each new scene begins with a number and a description of the scene's location. "EXT." stands for "EXTERIOR," meaning that the scene takes place outdoors.

MARIA. Quiet! If Bernardo—

TONY. Come down.

MARIA. [*turning*] My father and mother will wake up—

TONY. Just for a minute.

MARIA. [*smiles*] A minute is not enough.

TONY. [*smiles*] For an hour, then.

MARIA. I cannot.

TONY. Forever.

From the film *West Side Story*, 1961. Getty Images.

MARIA'S FATHER'S VOICE. [*from the apartment*] Maria?

MARIA. [*turning*] **Momentito**, Papa... [*to Tony*] Now see what you've done ... ▨2

TONY. [*climbing up*] *Momentito*, Maria.

55. CLOSER ANGLE - THE FIRE ESCAPE

MARIA. **Callate!** [*She reaches out her hand to stop him.*]

TONY. [*grabbing her hand*] [*He is at her side now.*]

MARIA. It is dangerous. If Bernardo knew—

TONY. We'll *let* him know. I am not "one of them," Maria.

MARIA. But you are not one of *us*, and I am not one of you. ▨3

TONY. To me, you're all the beautiful—

▨2 **Relate to Source**
Using details from the text, explain how the writer has transformed the character of Juliet into Maria. Why do you think he made these choices?

▨3 **Relate to Source**
Review pages 710–711. How is Maria's dialogue different from Juliet's?

In Other Words
Momentito One moment (in Spanish)
Callate! Be quiet! (in Spanish)

Historical Background
West Side Story had its first success in 1957 as a Broadway musical play. In 1961, it was released as a film starring Richard Beymar (as Tony) and Natalie Wood (as Maria). This excerpt is illustrated with images from that film.

[*She covers his mouth with her hand as:*]

MARIA'S FATHER'S VOICE. *Maruca!*

MARIA. *Si, yo vengo*, Papa.

[*They move towards the farther side of the fire escape, away from the window.*]

TONY. *Maruca?*

MARIA. His pet name for me.

TONY. I like him. He'll like me.

MARIA. No. He is like Bernardo: afraid. [*suddenly laughing*] Imagine being afraid of you!

TONY. Ya see?

From the film West Side Story, 1961. © John Springer Collection / CORBIS.

MARIA. [*touching his face*] I see you.

TONY. See only me.

MARIA. [*sings*] Only you, you're the only thing I'll see forever. In my eyes, in my words and in everything I do, Nothing else but you Ever!

TONY. [*sings*] And there's nothing for me but Maria, Every sight that I see is Maria. Always you, every thought I'll ever know, Everywhere I go, you'll be. **4**

MARIA. All the world is only you and me!

[*And now, through "special effects," the buildings, the sky, the very night seems to take on a magical quality.*]

TONY. Tonight, tonight, It all began tonight, I saw you and the world went away.

MARIA. Tonight, tonight, There's only you tonight, What you are, what you do, what you say.

4 Relate to Source Review pages 712–713. What part of the dialogue do you think inspired this song? Compare the meaning in each version.

In Other Words
Si, yo vengo Yes, I'm coming (in Spanish)

TONY. Today, all day I had the feeling
   A miracle would happen—
   I know now I was right.

BOTH. For here you are
   And what was just a
   world is a star
   Tonight!

[*As the scene fades back to "reality":*] **5**

MARIA'S FATHER'S VOICE. [*from
   inside*] *Maruca!*

MARIA. I cannot stay. Go quickly!

TONY. I'm not afraid.

MARIA. Please.

TONY. [*kissing her*] Good night.

MARIA. *Buenas noches.*

TONY. I love you.

MARIA. Yes, yes. Hurry. ❖

5 Form Mental
Images
Describe what the
setting looked like
before and after it
faded to "reality."
Why did it change?

ANALYZE West Side Story

1. **Explain** What does Tony mean when he tells Maria that he is not "one of them"? Explain what Maria is worried about.

2. **Vocabulary** What does Maria think her father's **attitude** toward Tony will be? Does Tony agree with Maria? Use text evidence to support your ideas.

3. **Relate a Story to Its Source** Explain how *West Side Story* both draws from and creates something new from *Romeo and Juliet*.

4. **Focus Strategy Form Mental Images** Work with a partner to identify two moments from *Romeo and Juliet* that create mental images. Describe how these moments are represented in *West Side Story*. Then explain how these changes affect the story.

↩ Return to the Text
Reread and Write Compare Romeo's last lines on pages 714–715 with Tony's lines on this page. How are the characters alike? How are they different? Include details from the text.

In Other Words
Buenas noches Good night (in Spanish)

EQ What Deserves Our Care and Respect?

Critical Thinking

EQ 1. Analyze Think about your responses to the **Brainstorm and Debate** activity on page 702. Pick Romeo and Juliet or Tony and Maria. How would the couple you chose respond to what you wrote? Explain.

2. Compare *Romeo and Juliet* draws attention to feuding families. *West Side Story* draws attention to rival gangs. Compare this element in the two stories. How do you think the difference affects the young lovers in the stories?

3. Interpret Juliet tells Romeo that if he promises to love her, she will give up the name "Capulet." What does she mean? Do you think that Maria would be willing to do the same thing? Why or why not?

4. Speculate How do you think the parents of Romeo, Juliet, Tony, and Maria would define the word *love*? How would Romeo, Juliet, Tony, and Maria themselves define the word?

EQ 5. Synthesize How important do you think love is to people? Use evidence from the play and the screenplay to support your answer.

Write About Literature

Literary Response Shakespeare's original play and the screenplay are written in distinct and different styles. Which style do you think speaks more clearly and sincerely about love? Write a short response to evaluate the styles. Explain your reasoning, using specific details from the texts in your response.

Key Vocabulary Review

Oral Review Work with a partner. Use these words to complete the paragraph.

attitude	feud	perfection
dense	fractured	resolution
envious	mature	

Love can make people do silly things. My brother once walked two miles in a __(1)__ snowstorm just to see his girlfriend. To him, she was flawless and absolute __(2)__ . Unfortunately, he slipped on the sidewalk in front of her house and ended up with a __(3)__ foot. His __(4)__ toward her changed when she started dating his best friend because he had a car. My brother could not afford a car, so he was __(5)__ of his friend and upset with him for going out with his girlfriend. My brother made a firm __(6)__ never to speak to the friend again, and a __(7)__ developed between them. Years later, when my brother was more __(8)__ , he called his old friend and apologized.

Writing Application What is your **attitude** toward love? Write a paragraph. Use at least three of the Key Vocabulary words.

Read with Ease: Intonation

Assess your reading fluency with the passage in the Reading Handbook, p. 818. Then complete the self-check below.

1. My intonation did/did not sound natural.

2. My words correct per minute: _____ .

INTEGRATE THE LANGUAGE ARTS

Write with the Perfect Tenses

When you write, choose the verb tense that best expresses your meaning. The **perfect tenses** have special uses.

Use the **present perfect tense** to tell about an action that happened at some point in the past or began in the past and is still happening now.

> Romeo and Juliet **have shared** their thoughts.

> Romeo **has loved** Juliet from the moment he saw her.

Use the **past perfect tense** to write about an action that happened before some other action in the past.

> Before the young lovers met, their two families **had fought** for years.

Use the **future perfect tense** to tell about an action that will be completed at an exact time in the future.

By the time the scene on the balcony ends, Romeo **will have declared** his love for Juliet.

Oral Practice (1–5) With a partner, use these verbs in sentences to tell about the balcony scene.

has compared	had named	will have become
have spoken	has found	

Written Practice (6–10) Rewrite the paragraph using the correct verb. Add three more sentences.

> For a long time, we (had wanted/will have wanted) to see this scene from the play. After Romeo (has hidden/had hidden), he watched for Juliet.

Negotiate

Role Play Act out a scene between Romeo and Juliet in which the two come to an agreement about telling their parents about their relationship.

Literary Criticism

Literary criticism is the interpretation and evaluation of literary works. There are many ways to critique a work, but here are several important ones:

- **biographical approach**: the critic looks at how the author's life affected the work
- **aesthetic approach**: the critic focuses on what makes a work appealing to the reader
- **historical approach**: the critic explains how the time period in which the work was written affected the work

Historical Approach The late sixteenth century in England—the Elizabethan period—was a time of peace. Queen Elizabeth I ruled for more than 40 years—almost all of Shakespeare's life. Poets and writers flourished. There was also terrible poverty as well as great inequality among classes of people and between men and women. Critic David Bevington reminds readers that in the late sixteenth century, only males were allowed to act onstage. He comments, "It is amazing that in a period of theatrical history when only men and boys occupied the stage...Juliet has...the best speeches in the play."

Learn more about the time when Shakespeare lived.

myNGconnect.com

- Find out about the Elizabethan period.
- See paintings of the time.

Then write a short critique of "Romeo and Juliet," telling how you think the time period affected this work. Consider:

- the relationship between the families
- the topic of young love
- the figurative language

Figurative Language: Simile

Shakespeare uses a lot of figurative language. For example, Romeo says, "The brightness of her cheek would shame those stars as daylight doth a lamp." Here, Romeo compares how the glow of Juliet's cheeks makes the stars look dim at night, just as daylight makes a lamp look dim. A simpler kind of figurative language is the **simile**, which compares two unlike things using the words *like* or *as*.

Read the following sentences. Identify the simile and then determine the meaning of each sentence.

1. The snow fell like small white feathers.
2. The lake was as smooth as silk.

Parody

A **parody** is a humorous work that imitates a more serious work. Many parodies of the balcony scene in "Romeo and Juliet" have been created for TV comedies and comic strips. In small groups, choose a story or song lyrics and create a parody in the same form as the original. Be sure your parody

- focuses on humor
- contains words and images that mock the original style
- maintains obvious connections to the original
- is creative and shows imagination.

♥ **Writing Handbook**, p. 832

Write a Literary Critique

Sometimes a test may ask you to write a critical analysis of a work of literature. For example, you might be asked to interpret "Romeo and Juliet" from an aesthetic approach. The prompt will give you a specific concept to analyze.

1 Unpack the Prompt Read the prompt and underline the key words.

> **Writing Prompt**
>
> In Act 2, Scene 2 of "Romeo and Juliet," how does Shakespeare's imagery of light and darkness contribute to its meaning? Use specific examples from the play to support your answer.

2 Plan Your Response Locate references to light and darkness in the play. Write down your examples in a two-column chart.

Light	Darkness
"Juliet is the sun."	The scene takes place at night.
Juliet is a "bright angel."	Romeo says, "I have night's cloak to hide me."

3 Draft Organize your critical analysis like this. Add specific ideas from your chart.

> **Essay Organizer**
>
> The imagery of light and darkness in the famous balcony scene of "Romeo and Juliet" contributes to the idea that [state the overall meaning of the imagery].
>
> Romeo makes many references to light and darkness. For example, in [state the line number(s)], he says, [quote an example from the play.]
>
> Juliet also invokes imagery of light and darkness. For example, in [state the line number(s)], she says, [quote an example from the play.]

4 Edit and Proofread Reread your analysis. Ask:

- Did I address the writing prompt?
- Did I give examples to support my answer?
- Did I use verb tenses correctly?

♥ **Writing Handbook**, p. 832

Dramatization

Drama really brings human relationships to life. Choose a short story about a relationship that involves respect and caring, and work with other students to present it as a dramatization. Here is how to do it:

1. Plan Your Dramatization

Find a story you like about a caring relationship. Then do the following:

- Select a scene with good dialogue (conversation between characters) and clear conflict (struggle of some kind).
- Rewrite the scene in dramatic form:

  –rewrite conversations into dramatic dialogue, deleting the "he said/she said" tags.

  –summarize the story's narration and turn it into stage directions, telling performers how to speak and move.
- Decide who will play which characters.
- Choose props, such as chairs, tables, telephones, and costumes, that are appropriate to the setting.

2. Practice Your Dramatization

Rehearse your scene several times. Ask some friends to watch.

- Memorize your lines (or at least be very familiar with them).
- Think about your character's personality, voice, and motives (reasons for taking action and saying each line).
- Look for connections with the other characters in the scene.
- Stay within the time limit.
- Get helpful suggestions from your listeners and incorporate them.

3. Present Your Dramatization

Make your dramatization powerful by doing the following:

- Remember what your character wants to get from the scene and do what you can to get it.
- Try to act in a way that shows your character's personality.
- Stay relaxed.
- Speak clearly and loudly so the audience can understand you.

myNGconnect.com

🔊 **Download the rubric.**

4. Discuss and Rate the Dramatization

Use the rubric to discuss and rate the dramatizations, including your own.

Dramatization Rubric

Scale	Content of Dramatization	Students' Preparation	Students' Performance
3 Great	• Scene chosen had powerful dialogue • Scene chosen had a powerful conflict	• Seemed to understand the scene well • Had effective set, costumes, and prop items	• Actors behaved naturally and with good emotions • Actors had memorized most of their lines
2 Good	• Scene chosen had some good dialogue • Scene chosen had some conflict	• Seemed to have given some thought to the scene • Set, costumes, and prop items were not effective	• Actors seemed reasonably natural with some emotion • Actors had memorized some of their lines
1 Needs Work	• Scene chosen had little or no meaningful dialogue • Scene chosen did not have any conflict	• Did not seem to have a good understanding of the scene • Did not include a set, costumes, or prop items	• Actors were stiff and unbelievable and did not convey emotions • Actors read all their lines directly from the script

DO IT ▶ Now that you know how to dramatize a short story, present your story, and give it your best performance!

📖 Language and Learning Handbook, p. 750

How are these students using props and nonverbal communication to dramatize the scene?

EQ ## What Deserves Our Care and Respect?
Examine how well people treat the earth.

Make a Connection

Anticipation Guide Think about the ways that people use natural resources like water, trees, and oil. Discuss with a partner whether you agree or disagree with these statements.

STATEMENTS	Agree or Disagree
1. Human beings take the resources of the earth for granted.	_____
2. Earth is like a loving, nurturing mother.	_____
3. We should protect the earth even if it means we're inconvenienced.	_____

Learn Key Vocabulary

Study the Words Pronounce each word and learn its meaning. You may also want to look up the definitions in the Glossary.

● Academic Vocabulary

Key Words	Examples
commercial (ku-**mur**-shul) *adjective* ▶ pages 732, 743	Something that is **commercial** has to do with the buying and selling of products and services. A **commercial** building is one used for offices or stores.
endure (in-**dyūr**) *verb* ▶ page 730	To **endure** means to last, or survive, in spite of difficult conditions. Mountains have **endured** centuries of wind, rain, sun, and snow.
essence (**e**-sens) *noun* ▶ pages 739, 742, 745	The **essence** of something is its most important quality. Her smile is the **essence** of her personality.
industrial (in-**dus**-trē-ul) *adjective* ▶ page 732	An **industrial** building is one that is used for processing, packing, shipping, or manufacturing products. An automobile plant is one example of an **industrial** building.
perish (**pair**-ish) *verb* ▶ pages 734, 737	To **perish** means to die. If we continue to pollute the air and water, many plants and animals will **perish**.
● **resolve** (ri-**zolv**) *noun* ▶ page 740	Your **resolve** is your will and determination to do something. Her **resolve** to get good grades helped her earn a college scholarship.
suffice (su-**fīs**) *verb* ▶ page 736	To **suffice** means to satisfy, or to be enough. Just a small helping of potatoes will **suffice**, thank you. I am not very hungry.
tremulous (**trem**-yu-lus) *adjective* ▶ page 734	**Tremulous** means timid or fearful. The **tremulous** child clung to his mother whenever a stranger approached.

Practice the Words With a partner, write as many sentences as you can with two Key Vocabulary words per sentence.

Example: A small office in an old commercial building suffered for the private detective.

BEFORE READING Poems for the Earth

poems by Pat Mora, Margaret Tsuda,
Sara Teasdale, and Robert Frost

Reading Strategies

· Plan and Monitor
· Determine Importance
· Make Inferences
· Ask Questions
· Make Connections
· Synthesize
▶ **Visualize**

Compare Representations: Poetry and Art

Throughout this book, you have seen subjects represented primarily through the **medium of words**—for example, in stories and articles. Subjects also can be represented through **visual media**—for example, in paintings, photographs, and sculpture. Even when the subject is the same, its impact will differ because of choices the writer or artist makes. Those choices may mean including, omitting, or emphasizing certain details.

Look Into the Text

The poet's words emphasize cactus plants and rain.

Compare details from the poem to details in the painting.

I say feed me.
She serves red prickly pear on a
    spiked cactus.
I say tease me.
She sprinkles raindrops in my face.

Orange Light on the Four Peaks, 2003, Stephen Morath. Acrylic on canvas, collection of the artist.

The painter's artwork emphasizes cactus plants but does not include rain.

Focus Strategy ▶ Visualize

Poets often use language to evoke sensory images in your mind. Note that these "images" are not just visual. A sensory image can appeal to any of the senses.

HOW TO FORM SENSORY IMAGES

Focus Strategy

You can use a chart like the one below to take notes.

1. **Look for Details** Notice words and phrases in a poem that appeal to your senses.

2. **Use Your Imagination** Picture in your mind the objects, animals, and places that are described. Use your own experiences to help you imagine the details.

My Response to the Text	
I see... rain falling, swallows flying, frogs in the pond, flowering plum trees	**I smell...** the damp smell of the wet ground
	I taste... wild plums
I hear... rain falling softly, frogs chanting and splashing, swallows calling out	**I feel...** the wet rain on my skin

A Sense of Nature

In a world that bombards you with electronic images and information, nature brings you back to your senses—sight, hearing, smell, touch, and taste.

Wherever you live, nature is there: in the sight of geese flying south against a winter sunset; the sound of your heartbeat; the scent of orange blossoms at a city park; the crunch and tartness of an apple; the rough bark of an oak tree that you pass on your way to school.

In every age and culture, poets have captured the ordinary wonder of the natural world, using the power of imagery. You can tap into this power, too. Just fire up your senses and pay extra attention to familiar places.

• **Hearing** Use your hearing to scan your surroundings. Even in a city filled with traffic noise, you can hear the sound of nature in the patter of rain and the whistling of the wind.

• **Sight** What plants, animals, landforms, and weather are part of your everyday world? Even if you swear you can't draw, sketch images that catch your eye. The simple act of drawing will reveal details you never noticed before.

• **Touch and Smell** Did you ever notice the scent of a freshly mowed lawn, run your fingers under a cooling stream, or realize that a skunk must have visited your backyard during the night? The contrasting textures and subtle (or not so subtle!) scents of the natural world are everywhere.

Some people become so fascinated by nature that they write about it, photograph it, paint it, or spend their lives studying it. The next time nature signals for attention, how will *you* respond?

myNGconnect.com

🔊 View a video interview with poet and author Pat Mora.
🔊 Listen to tips on how to read poetry aloud.

Poems
for the
Earth

MI MADRE
by Pat Mora

I say feed me.
She serves red prickly pear on a spiked cactus.

I say tease me.
She sprinkles raindrops in my face.

5   I say frighten me.
She shouts thunder, flashes lightning.

I say comfort me.
She invites me to lay on her firm body. **1**

I say heal me.
10   She gives me *manzanilla, orégano, dormilón.*

I say caress me.
She strokes my skin with her warm breath.

I say make me beautiful.
She offers turquoise for my fingers, a pink blossom for my hair.

15   I say sing to me.
She chants lonely women's songs. **2**

I say teach me.
She endures: glaring heat
          numbing cold
20   frightening dryness.

She: the desert
She: strong mother.

1 Word Choice
How does the poet's use of repetition and rhythm affect the sound of the poem?

2 Form Sensory Images
Which words appeal to your senses? What do these words help you see and feel?

Key Vocabulary
endure *v.*, to survive

In Other Words
Mi Madre My Mother (in Spanish)
manzanilla, orégano, dormilón an herb for soothing, an herb for cooking, and an herb for sleeping (in Spanish)

Orange Light on the Four Peaks, 2003, Stephen Morath. Acrylic on canvas, collection of the artist.

3 Representations: Poetry and Art In addition to the cactus, what details from the poem do you sense in the painting? How does the impact of the painting differ from the impact of the poem?

About the Poet

Pat Mora (1942–) is an influential writer of both children's and adult literature who is committed to linking languages and cultures. A native of El Paso, Texas, Mora's writing often focuses on the theme of feeling alienated by living near borders. She is also an educator and the founder of Children's Day/Book Day, an annual family reading event.

HARD QUESTIONS

by Margaret Tsuda

Why not mark out the land
into neat rectangles
squares and clover leafs?

Put on them cubes of
5   varying sizes
according to use—
dwellings
    singles/multiples
complexes
10   commercial/industrial.

Bale them together with
bands of roads.

What if a child shall cry
"I have never known spring!
15 I have never seen autumn!"

What if a man shall say
"I have never heard
silence fraught with living as
in swamp or forest!"
20 What if the eye shall never see
marsh birds and muskrats? **4**

Does not the heart need
wildness?
Does not the thought need
25 something
to rest upon
not self-made by man,
a bosom
not his own? **5**

4 Form Sensory Images
Note the difference between the images in the second and fourth stanzas. How do these images deepen your understanding of the poem?

5 Structure
What form is this poem written in?

Key Vocabulary
commercial *adj.*, having to do with buying and selling goods and services
industrial *adj.*, having to do with manufacturing

In Other Words
dwellings houses
complexes groups of buildings
Bale Tie
fraught filled
bosom place of comfort and security

Down Eighteenth Street, 1980, Wayne Thiebaud. Oil and charcoal on canvas, gift of Edward R. Downe, Jr., 1979, Hirshhorn Museum and Sculpture Garden, Washington, D.C.

6 Representations: Poetry and Art Examine the shapes in this painting. Which objects are made with lines and angles? Which are made with curves? How do the images in the visual medium of this painting compare to the images in the verbal medium of the poem?

About the Poet

The poetry of **Margaret Tsuda (1921–)** is only part of her lifelong interest in the arts. She studied art and art history in college and also worked as a textile designer. An accomplished painter living in New York, Tsuda provided her own illustrations for her two poetry collections, *Urban River* and *Cry Love Aloud*.

There Will Come Soft Rains

by Sara Teasdale

There will come soft rains and the smell of the ground,
And swallows circling with their shimmering sound;

And frogs in the pools singing at night,
And wild plum trees in tremulous white;

5   Robins will wear their feathery fire
Whistling their whims on a low fence-wire; **7**

And not one will know of the war, not one
Will care at last when it is done.

Not one would mind, neither bird nor tree
10 If mankind perished utterly; **8**

And Spring herself, when she woke at dawn,
Would scarcely know that we were gone.

7 Form Sensory Images
Identify words and phrases in the previous three stanzas that appeal to the five senses. What feelings do these images evoke?

8 Tone
How do stanzas 4 and 5 differ from stanzas 1–3 in terms of the speaker's tone, or feeling?

Key Vocabulary
tremulous *adj.*, timid, fearful
perish *v.*, to die

In Other Words
whims wishes, desires
utterly completely
scarcely hardly, barely

Forest, 2004, Yvette Molina. Oil on aluminum, courtesy of Ruth Bachofner Gallery, Santa Monica, California.

9 **Representations: Poetry and Art** What aspect of the poem does this painting emphasize? How does the impact of this painting compare to the impact of the poem?

About the Poet

Sara Teasdale (1884–1933) was born in St. Louis, Missouri, and moved to New York City in the early 1900s. Her work is known for its traditional verse forms and strong focus on language and emotion.

Fire and Ice
by Robert Frost

Some say the world will end in fire,
Some say in ice. **10**
From what I've tasted of desire
I hold with those who favor fire.
5 But if it had to perish twice,
I think I know enough of hate
To say that for destruction ice
Is also great
And would suffice. **11**

Snow Storm, Maurice de Vlaminck (1876–1958). Musée des Beaux-Arts, Lyon, France.

10 Form Sensory Images
How does visualizing the world ending in fire or ice add to your understanding of this poem?

11 Rhyme Scheme
What is the effect of the rhyme scheme and rhythm? How well do you think both elements go along with the poem's message?

12 Representations: Poetry and Art
Describe this painting by using words from the poem.

Key Vocabulary
suffice *v.*, to satisfy

About the Poet

Robert Frost (1874–1963) is one of the most widely read and celebrated poets in American history. Much of his inspiration came from his love of country life in New England. He won four Pulitzer Prizes and read one of his poems at the inauguration of President John F. Kennedy. He believed a poem "begins in delight and ends in wisdom."

ANALYZE Poems for the Earth

1. **Explain** How does each speaker view the relationship between humans and nature? Be sure to cite examples from the poems.

2. **Vocabulary** Why do you think the speaker in "There Will Come Soft Rains" feels that nature would not care if humans **perished**? Which poem suggests that nature would care? Explain.

3. **Compare Representations: Poetry and Art** Which of the four images best suits the poem it accompanies? Explain your opinion to a partner.

4. **Focus Strategy Form Sensory Images** Describe a sensory image that stays in your mind after reading the four poems. Refer to specific words and phrases in the poem that help you form this image.

Return to the Text

Reread and Write According to the four speakers, what deserves our care and respect? Write a paragraph in which you summarize each speaker's answer to the question.

I Was Born Today/ Touching the Earth

poem by Amado Nervo and essay
by bell hooks

Analyze Structure and Style

The writer's **style** includes every choice he or she makes about language, form, and content. A writer has to consider special style elements, including the following:

- Should the poem have a regular rhyme scheme and rhythm, or should it be written in free verse? How would each choice affect the poem?
- How long should the poem be? How many lines and stanzas should it contain?
- What is the best way to organize the poem to communicate its message?
- Would it be more effective to write in a form other than poetry?

Look Into the Text

How can you tell that the poet chooses to write free verse?

> Every day that dawns, you must say to yourself,
> "I was born today!
> The world is new to me.
> This light that I behold
> Strikes my unclouded eyes for the first time."

The poet directly addresses the reader.

Focus Strategy ▶ Visualize

Remember that sensory images can appeal to any or all of the five senses. You can read a poem slowly, noting the images that form in your mind as you read.

HOW TO FORM SENSORY IMAGES

Focus Strategy

1. **Identify Sensory Language** Find the lines from the poem that appeal to your senses.

2. **Make a Chart** Using a chart like the one shown, record those lines and describe the sensory images.

Lines from the Poem	Sensory Images
"The world is new to me."	person looking around at a place he has never seen before; feeling a sense of wonder
"This light that I behold / Strikes my unclouded eyes for the first time."	bright sunlight dazzling the eyes, warmth of sun on the face

Connect Across Texts

In the last section, four poets commented on the tension between humankind and nature. Read the following poem and the essay passage to see another side of the bond between Earth and us.

I Was Born Today

by Amado Nervo

Every day that dawns, you must say to
    yourself,
"I was born today!
The world is new to me.
5 This light that I behold
Strikes my unclouded eyes for the
    first time;
The rain that scatters its crystal drops
Is my baptism! **1**

10 "Then let us live a pure life,
A shining life!
Already, yesterday is lost. Was it bad?
    Was it beautiful?
. . . Let it be forgotten.
15 And of that yesterday let there remain
    only the essence,
The precious gold of what I loved
    and suffered
As I walk along the road . . .

1 Form Sensory Images
Which senses do the descriptive details appeal to? How do the images help you visualize a new world and birth?

Light Spark, 2003, Johannes Seewald. Photography, collection of the artist.

▲ Crit
pho
the p

Key Vocabulary
essence *n.*, quality that determines
  someone or something's character

In Other Words
my baptism a new beginning

Key Vocabulary
• **resolve** *n.*, determin
  something

20　"Today, every moment shall bring

　　feelings of well being and cheer.

　　And the reason for my existence.

　　My most urgent resolve

　　Will be to spread happiness all over

25　　the world,

　　To pour the wine of goodness into the

　　eager mouths around me . . . [2]

　　"My only peace will be the peace of others;

　　Their dreams, my dreams;

30　Their joy, my joy;

　　My crystal tear,

　　The tear that trembles on the eyelash

　　of another;

　　My heartbeat,

35　The beat of every heart that throbs

　　Throughout worlds without end!"

　　Every day that dawns, you must say to

　　yourself,

　　"I was born today!" [3]

[2] **Structure and Style**
How do you think the poet's use of free verse adds to the mood and main idea of the poem?

[3] **Structure and Style**
Why do you think the poet ends the poem by repeating its first three lines?

About the Poet

Amado Nervo (1870–1919) is considered one of Mexico's most important and influential poets of the 19th and 20th centuries. Although he left the priesthood to become a writer, his poems are often spiritual and focus on living in a changing world. His wife's death inspired his most famous work, *La Amada Inmóvil (The Motionless One)*, which was published in 1922.

In Other Words

tion to do　　**for my existence** that I am alive

Touching the Earth
by bell hooks

When we love the earth, we are able to love ourselves more fully. I believe this. The ancestors taught me it was so.

As a child I loved playing in dirt, in that rich Kentucky soil, that was a source of life. Before I understood anything about the pain and **exploitation** of the southern system of sharecropping, I understood that grown-up black folks loved the land. I could stand with my grandfather Daddy Jerry and look out at fields of growing vegetables, tomatoes, corn, collards, and know that this was his handiwork. I could see the look of pride on his face as I expressed wonder and awe at the magic of growing things. **4**

I knew that my grandmother Baba's backyard garden would yield beans, sweet potatoes, cabbage, and yellow squash, that she too would walk with pride among the rows and rows of growing vegetables showing us what the earth will give when tended lovingly. **5** ❖

Preparing Broad Beans, Felicity House. Pastel on paper, private collection, The Bridgeman Art Library.

▲ Critical Viewing: Design How do you think Baba would respond to this painting? Explain.

4 Structure and Style
How is reading this selection different from reading a poem? What effect does it have on you?

5 Form Sensory Images
Which of the five senses do the images in this selection most appeal to? Explain.

In Other Words
exploitation abuse

Historical Background
The system of **sharecropping** developed in the southern U.S. after the Civil War. Freed slaves farmed their former owners' land in exchange for a share of the crops. Many sharecroppers were treated poorly, and most lived in poverty, unable to buy their own land.

ANALYZE I Was Born Today/Touching the Earth

1. **Explain** Why does the speaker of "I Was Born Today" urge the reader to see the world fresh and new every morning and to forget about yesterday? Be sure to include evidence from the poem in your answer.

2. **Vocabulary** Choose a partner. Discuss what each of you thinks is the **essence** of both speakers' relationships with the earth.

3. **Analyze Structure and Style** Describe the differences between the forms and styles of the poem and the essay. Describe the effect that each text has on you.

4. **Focus Strategy Form Sensory Images** Describe a striking picture that you imagined as you read either "I Was Born Today" or "Touching the Earth." Mention specific details that inspired the image.

Return to the Text

Reread and Write Did either selection change what you think deserves our care and respect? Why or why not? Write a journal entry about the effect of these selections on your thinking. Use details from the selections in your response.

EQ ## What Deserves Our Care and Respect?

Critical Thinking

1. **Analyze** Return to the **Anticipation Guide** you completed on page 726. Have your ideas about the relationship between people and the earth changed? Discuss your ideas with a partner.

2. **Compare** Which of the six writers seems to share your feelings about nature and the earth? Explain, using specific examples from the poems or the essay.

3. **Interpret** "Touching the Earth" is the only prose selection in this section. Did you respond to it in the same way as you responded to the poems? Explain similarities and differences between the two genres.

4. **Speculate** Suppose that either bell hooks or Amado Nervo had a conversation with one of the other poets in this section. What would the two writers say to each other about humankind and the earth?

EQ 5. **Synthesize** Much of human progress has depended on our using the earth's resources, such as wood, water, and petroleum. Consider what each of the poets would say about this kind of progress. Do you agree?

Key Vocabulary Review

Oral Review Work with a partner. Use these words to complete the paragraph.

commercial	industrial	suffice
endure	perish	tremulous
essence	resolve	

What is the __(1)__, or soul, of a neighborhood? I think a good neighborhood needs houses, parks, schools, __(2)__ buildings for stores and businesses, and __(3)__ buildings for factories. If a community has all of these things, it can __(4)__ for a long time. Without businesses, parks, and good schools, a neighborhood can quickly __(5)__ and will no longer __(6)__ or satisfy the needs of the people who live there. Community members who feel __(7)__ about changes in their neighborhood could __(8)__ to participate in groups that make positive decisions about the neighborhood's future.

Writing Application What is your opinion of **commercial** development where there used to be forests or parkland? Write a paragraph describing your views. Use at least five Key Vocabulary words.

Write About Literature

Analysis of an Issue How important is the earth to human beings? Do we treat it with care and respect? Write a short essay in which you analyze human beings' treatment of the earth. Use quotations from the poems or the essay to illustrate your ideas.

Read with Ease: Phrasing

Assess your reading fluency with the passage in the Reading Handbook, p. 819. Then complete the self-check below.

1. I did/did not pause appropriately for punctuation and phrases.

2. My words correct per minute: _____.

Grammar

Enrich Your Sentences

One longer sentence with a **participial phrase** or an **absolute** can be more interesting than two short sentences.

> Mora describes each of the desert's gifts. She uses repetitive phrasing.

Remember, a **participle** is a verb form that usually ends with -**ing** or -**ed**.

> **Using repetitive phrasing**, Mora describes each of the desert's gifts.

An **absolute** is a sentence-like phrase that has a subject and a participle.

> **Her phrases tumbling repetitively**, Mora describes the desert's gifts.

Oral Practice (1–5) Add -**ed** or -**ing** to the word in parentheses to make a participle or to complete an absolute. Then say each sentence, adding the word in the blank.

1. Poems can turn into pictures _____ by beautiful words. (paint)
2. _____ about nature, some poets celebrate the beauty of our world. (write)
3. Pat Mora writes about the desert, _____ with life. (fill)
4. Many poems use the same phrase, _____ to make its message stronger. (repeat)
5. Their hearts _____ with awe, poets use words to express nature's beauty. (flood)

Written Practice (6–10) Combine the sentences using participial phrases or absolutes.

> Poets combine sound and meaning in poems. They listen for the sounds of words. In one poem, Teasdale describes frogs. The frogs are singing at night. In "Fire and Ice," Frost uses end rhymes. He arranges them in a pattern. Nervo writes poems that are like songs. He celebrates life. Poets always have their fingers poised and ready. They wait for inspiration.

Literary Analysis/Research

Literary Criticism

As you know, literary criticism is the interpretation and evaluation of literary works. One way to critique a poem is to study the poet and his or her life. Take, for example, Robert Frost.

For much of his adult life, Frost worked as a farmer, a teacher, and a poet in rural New England. His poetry is filled with images like fields and trees that reflect this peaceful and picturesque landscape.

This seemingly happy life was marred by tragedy, however. In 1900, his first-born son died of cholera. Then in the 1930s, Frost experienced a series of terrible events. In 1934, his favorite child, a daughter, died a long, slow death from fever. Four years later his wife Elinor died suddenly of a heart attack, and in 1940, a son committed suicide.

After this sad period in his life, Frost published a volume of poetry titled *A Witness Tree*. Here is what the critic William H. Pritchard said about the book:

"A number of poems in *A Witness Tree* undoubtedly derived their dark tone from the family tragedies suffered over the decade..."

Now you try it. Learn more about the life of one of the poets in this unit.

myNGconnect.com

- Naomi Shihab Nye
- Sara Teasdale
- Pat Mora
- bell hooks

Then write a short critique of the poem you just read (or any of that poet's work), using the poet's life to interpret and evaluate the work.

Language Development

Use Appropriate Language

Formal Introductions Pretend the poets are coming to your school. Introduce one at an assembly.

Figurative Language: Metaphor

A **metaphor** is a figurative phrase that suggests that two things are similar. An author uses metaphor to make a direct comparison between two unlike things without using the word *like* or *as*. In the poem "I Was Born Today," the speaker compares the rain to his baptism when he states: *"The rain that scatters its crystal drops is my baptism!"*

Work with a partner. Read the following sentences, and identify the metaphor used in each sentence. Think about what is being compared and then rewrite each sentence replacing the metaphor with its literal meaning.

1. The band's music is a breath of fresh air.
2. He was showered with gifts at his sixteenth birthday party.
3. The teacher read over our research papers with an eagle eye.

Rhythm and Line Length

Poets often use rhythm to reinforce the poem's meaning. A poem's rhythm comes from the pattern of strong and weak beats in each line, along with the length of a line and how it breaks. Not all poems have a strict rhythm or similar line lengths. In free verse, for instance, the line lengths vary, which gives it a more natural sound and rhythm.

Sara Teasdale wrote "There Will Come Soft Rains" as a series of rhyming **couplets**, or pairs of lines. Work with a partner to rewrite the poem in free verse. You will need to add, change, or delete words to do this, but the poem's **essence** should stay the same.

Voice and Style

A writer's **style** is more than *what* the writer says, it is also the *way* he or she says something. The writer's **voice** is the way the work "sounds" in the reader's mind. Style and voice are created using word choice, figurative language and imagery, tone or attitude toward the subject, and sentence length and structure.

Just OK

> Baseball is my favorite sport. I like to watch the pitchers to see how they will try to get the batters out. Some people think the game is slow and boring, but it's really exciting.

Much Better

> Baseball is a mental and physical test of wills. The battle begins with pitcher and batter, each staring down the other, as still as statues. Suddenly, they spring into action. The baseball rockets across the field like a cannonball as a hushed crowd waits for the crack of the bat.

The second paragraph uses imagery and figurative language to paint a picture of the game. The reader can "hear" the writer's passion for the game and begin to believe that baseball is the best game.

Write a paragraph about something you enjoy. Use your voice and style to bring your subject to life and let the reader "hear" why you enjoy it.

🕭 **Writing Handbook,** p. 832

Wild Geese

by Mary Oliver

You do not have to be good.
You do not have to walk on your knees
for a hundred miles through the desert, repenting.
You only have to let the soft animal of your body
5   love what it loves.
Tell me about despair, yours, and I will tell you mine.
Meanwhile the world goes on.
Meanwhile the sun and the clear pebbles of the rain
are moving across the landscapes,
10   over the prairies and deep trees,
the mountains and the rivers.
Meanwhile the wild geese, high in the clean blue air,
are heading home again.
Whoever you are, no matter how lonely,
15   the world offers itself to your imagination,
calls to you like the wild geese, harsh and exciting—
over and over announcing your place
in the family of things.

In Other Words
repenting feeling sorry, regretting
despair sadness, hopelessness

Like You

by Roque Dalton
translated by Jack Hirschman

Handwritten annotations:

T. Like, love.

C. Love the sweet smell of things, the sky, blue landscape of spring.
A: positive. the love of nature
S: And : But
T: Love of the nature
T: Nature belongs to everyone and we must love it.

Like you I
love love, life, the sweet smell
of things, the sky-blue
landscape of January days.

5 And my blood boils up
and I laugh through eyes
that have known the buds of tears.

I believe the world is beautiful
and that poetry, like bread, is for everyone.

10 And that my veins don't end in me
but in the unanimous blood
of those who struggle for life,
love,
little things,
15 landscape and bread,
the poetry of everyone.

Arbol con Luces 1, Judy Paul. Mixed media on birch panel.

In Other Words
unanimous shared

FOR WHAT IT'S WORTH

EQ ESSENTIAL QUESTION:

What Deserves Our Care and Respect?

myNGconnect.com

◐ **Download the rubric.**

EDGE LIBRARY

Present Your Project: Literary Anthology

It's time to compile and publish your literary anthology that addresses the Essential Question for this unit.

1 Review and Complete Your Plan

Consider these points as you complete your project:

- How will your anthology address the Essential Question?
- What type of illustrations will your anthology have?
- How many selections will you include and how long will each selection be?

2 Publish

Assemble and publish your anthology. Follow the plan you made to divide up the tasks. Consider placing the anthology in your school library.

3 Evaluate the Literary Anthology

Use a rubric to evaluate the literary anthology your class compiled and published.

Reflect on Your Reading

Think back on your reading of the unit selections, including your choice of Edge Library books. Then, discuss the following with a partner or in a small group.

Genre Focus   Compare and contrast the main elements of prose (fiction and nonfiction), drama, and poetry. How are they similar? How are they different? Are they interchangeable? Take one or two selections from this unit and explore how they could be written in a different form (i.e., a poem written as prose, or prose written as drama).

Focus Strategy   You visualized many images in this unit. Which image do you remember most vividly? Read aloud the text that inspired the image and tell why that image was the most memorable for you.

EQ Respond to the Essential Question

Throughout this unit, you have been exploring the question "What deserves our care and respect?" Discuss this with a group. What is *your* opinion? Support your response with evidence from your reading, discussions, research, and writing.

RESOURCES

LANGUAGE AND LEARNING HANDBOOK

Strategies for Learning and Developing Language

Listening & Speaking

Viewing & Representing

Technology and Media

Research

Test-Taking Strategies

Strategies for
Learning and Developing Language

How Do I *Learn* Language?

1 Listen actively and try out language.

What to Do	Examples
Listen to others and use their language.	**You hear:** "When did our teacher say that the assignment is due?" **You say:** "Our teacher said that the assignment is due May 1."
Listen to yourself to perfect pronunciation of new words.	**You say:** "I see the word *privacy*. *Privacy* has a long *i* sound. Let me practice the long i sound to make sure I'm saying the word correctly."
Incorporate language chunks into your speech.	**You hear:** "Send me an e-mail or a text message on my cell." **You think:** I know what an e-mail is. So a text message must be an e-mail that you send on a phone. **You say:** "I'll e-mail you. I don't think I can send text messages on my cell."
Make connections across content areas. Use the language you learn in one subject area in other subject areas and outside of school.	**You read this in science class:** Studies show that each person in the U.S. produces more than 4 pounds of garbage each day. We don't have enough landfill space. Recycling is essential. **You write this in your reading journal:** Maybe I'll do my persuasive paper for English class on recycling. I have strong feelings about why it is good to recycle. **At home, you might say:** Mom, did you recycle the empty cans and bottles?
Take risks. Use words or phrases you know and use them in another way.	**All of these statements mean the same thing:** My teacher helps me push my thinking. My teacher helps me stretch my mind to see different viewpoints. Before I make a decision, my teacher suggests I role-play different choices in my imagination.
Memorize new words. They will help you build the background knowledge you need to understand more difficult language.	**Make flash cards:** Flash cards are a great way to memorize new words, phrases, or expressions. Write the English meaning on one side of a note card and the meaning in your language on the other side. Look at the words or phrases in your language and try to say the English meaning. Flip the card over to check your answer.

2 **Ask for help, feedback, and clarification.**

What to Do	Examples
Ask questions about how to use language.	*Did I say that right?* *Did I use that word the right way?* *Which is right: "brang" or "brought"?*
Use your native language or English to ask for clarification. Use what you learned to correct your mistakes.	**You say:** "Wait! Could you go over that point again, a little more slowly, please?" **Other examples:** "Does 'have a heart' mean 'to be kind'?" "Is 'paper' another word for 'essay'?"
Use context clues to confirm your understanding of difficult words.	**You hear:** "The team united, or came together, after they lost the game." **You think:** "I hear the word *or* after the word *united*, so *united* must mean 'came together.'"

3 **Use nonverbal clues.**

What to Do	Examples
Use gestures and mime to show an idea.	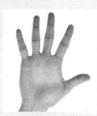 *I will hold up five fingers to show that I need five minutes.*
Look for nonverbal clues.	 *María invited me to a concert where her favorite band will be playing. They are electrifying!* *Electrifying must mean "good." She looks good.*
Identify and respond appropriately to nonverbal and verbal clues.	*Let's give him a hand.* *Everyone is clapping. "Give him a hand" must mean to clap for him. I should clap for him, too.*

What to Do	Examples
Test hypotheses about how language works.	**You can try out what you learned:** I can add -ation to the verb observe to get the noun observation. So maybe I can make a noun by adding -ation to some verbs that end in -e. Let's see. Prepare and preparation. Yes, that is right! Compare and comparation. That doesn't sound correct. I will see what the dictionary says ... Now I understand—it's comparison.
Use spell-checkers, dictionaries, and other available reference aids, such as the Internet.	**You just finished your draft of an essay, so you think:** *Now I'll use spell-check to see what words I need to fix.*
Use prior knowledge.	You can figure out unfamiliar words by looking for or remembering words you do know or experiences you've learned about previously. Use this prior knowledge to figure out new words. **Example:** We felt embarrassed for Tom when he behaved like a clown. I know the word "clown." Maybe "embarrassed" means the way I feel when one of my friends starts acting like a clown.
Use contrastive analysis to compare how your language works to how English works.	**You hear:** "She is a doctor." **You think:** *In English, an article, such as a or an, is used before the title of a job. In my native language, no article is used: "She is doctor."*
Use semantic mapping to determine the relationship between the meanings of words.	jogging tennis football water exercising weightlifting swimming goggles pool **You think:** Where should I place the word ball? It can attach to football or tennis because both activities use a kind of ball.
Use imagery.	Use descriptive language to form a picture in your imagination in order to figure out a word you don't know. You can draw pictures of what you imagined to remind you of the meaning of the word. Say the words while looking at the pictures to make connections.

5 **Monitor and evaluate your learning.**

What to Do	Examples
Self-monitor and self-assess language use.	Did I use the correct verb form to tell what my plans are for the future? Was it all right to use informal language only? Did I use transitions to show how my ideas were connected?
Take notes about language.	Active Voice Compared to Passive Voice • I should write most sentences in active voice. This is the most common way to construct sentences. The "doer," or actor, of the verb in the sentence should be the subject. **Incorrect**: The race was won by Jon. **Correct**: Jon won the race.
Use visuals to construct or clarify meaning.	This paragraph is confusing. Maybe I can use a graphic organizer to organize the main ideas.
Review.	Do I understand everything that was taught? I should review my notes and graphic organizers.

How Do I *Use* Language?

Sometimes you use language to clarify ideas or to find out about something. Other times you will want to share information.

How to Ask Questions

Ask about **a person**: *Who* is the girl in the photograph?

Ask about **a place**: *Where* are the people standing?

Ask about **a thing**: *What* is she holding?

Ask about **a time**: *When* do you think Anna plays tennis?

Ask about **reasons**: *Why* is the woman interviewing Anna?

How to Express Feelings

Name **an event**: I won the game.

Name **a feeling**: I was so happy when I won the game.

Tell **more**: I held the trophy over my head with pride!

Use the **subjunctive mood**: If you weren't here, I would be concerned.

How to Express Likes and Dislikes

Tell what you think: I like this painting. I think this painting is creative. In my opinion, this is a great painting.

How to Express Ideas, Needs, Intentions, and Opinions

Use words that **express your needs**: I need (require, must have) something to eat.

Be specific about **what you need**: I need a fire extinguisher now!

Elaborate on **why you need** something: I need some tape because I need to attach these two pieces of paper.

Use words that **signal your intentions**: I plan (intend, expect) to arrive at 6:00 p.m.

Use words that **tell your opinions**: I believe (think) the movie is great.

How to Give Oral Directions

Tell the first thing to do: Go to the board.

Tell the next step. Use a time order word: Now pick up the chalk.

Tell another step. Use another time order word: Next, write your name.

Tell the last thing to do: Go back to your seat.

Receive feedback on directions: Ask listeners if they were able to follow the directions. Repeat directions as needed.

How to Give Directions

Give information: The meeting begins at 3:15 p.m. at the library on Main Street.

Give one step directions: Go south on Ridge Road, then turn left on Main Street.

Provide directions to peers: The meeting is at the library on Main Street. It is on the same block as the school where last week's football game was held.

How to Give and Respond to Requests and Commands

Make polite requests: Could you please give me a pen? May I read aloud?

Respond to a request: Of course. You're welcome.

Make a polite command: Please listen carefully.

Make a strong command: Do not follow me!

Respond to a command: Of course. Certainly.

How to Engage in Conversation and Small Talk

Engage in small talk: How are you today? Nice weather we're having, isn't it?

Use social courtesies: May I borrow your pen, please? Thank you.

Ask and answer questions: Do you play baseball? Yes, I do.

Use verbal cues to show that you are listening: Uh-huh. Yes, I see. OK.

Use nonverbal language skills: For example, nod your head, smile at something funny, or make eye contact.

How to Tell an Original Story

Give the main idea of the story first: I want to tell you about my trip to Chicago.

Tell the important events of the story: I visited my cousin at her office. She showed me what her job is like.

Use transition words: First, I got off the bus. Then, I walked down into a tall, modern building.

Give details to make the story interesting: It was very cold that day. I remember I was wearing a big, warm jacket.

Retell a story: Maria said she was on her way to the library when she noticed something strange. Someone was following her.

How to Describe

Be specific by using descriptive words or phrases: I like the actor with the bright red hair.

Use descriptive imagery when possible: The room was as dark as a mountain cave. The butterfly floated gracefully through the air.

Describe a favorite activity: Playing volleyball is exciting and competitive.

Describe people: Marta has long, brown hair. She is wearing a blue t-shirt.

Describe places: The building on the corner had its windows covered with wood, and its yard was filled with trash.

Describe things: My house is large and brown. It looks like a barn.

Describe events: The jazz band is playing in the auditorium tonight.

Describe ideas: We plan to have a car wash next Saturday.

Describe feelings: I was bored, but happy.

Describe experiences: Playing guitar is relaxing for me.

Describe immediate surroundings: There are 28 desks in my English classroom.

Describe wishes using the subjunctive mood: I wish that my brother were nicer to me.

How to Elaborate an Idea

Give examples to support your ideas: All students should participate in an activity to fully experience their high school years. For example, people could join the chess club, a sports team, or the school band.

Give details about your ideas: I want to organize a group trip to the museum. We can take the city bus there. We will bring our own lunches to save money. There are many new, exciting exhibits to see at the museum.

Be as specific as possible: It takes several years of school to become a lawyer. First, you have to get a college degree. Then, you need to go to law school. Getting a law degree usually takes about three years.

How to Ask for and Give Information

Use polite requests to ask for information: Can you please tell me your name again?

Give the exact information someone is asking for: To get to the bus stop, walk down this street, then turn left at Carter Avenue.

How to Recognize, Express, and Respond Appropriately to Humor

Listen and watch for clues: For example, a change in a person's voice or facial expression might mean that the person is joking or using humor. Also, watch for more obvious clues such as smiling and laughing.

Use verbal or nonverbal responses to recognize humor: A smile or a nod of the head is a good nonverbal response to humor. You might also respond by saying, "I get it!" or "That's funny!"

Watch others to see how they react: If other people are responding to a humorous situation, then it is usually appropriate to respond to the humor, too.

How to Make Comparisons

Use compare and contrast words: The eagle is a majestic animal. Similarly, many people love dolphins. On the contrary, rats are pests and have few admirers.

Explain with details: The first math problem was difficult. But the second math problem was much more difficult. It required students to read a graph with data.

How to Define and Explain

Give a clear definition: A peacock is a large bird that is known for its colorful feathers.

Give details or examples to clarify: The large tail feathers of the male peacock are often bright green, gold, and blue.

Use a logical order for explanations: The house needs to be cleaned. First, pick up all of the toys and clothes and put them away. Then, vacuum and mop the floors.

Use graphic organizers to help explain: See the Index of Graphic Organizers on p. 772 for graphic organizers you can use to explain and define words and ideas.

How to Clarify Information

Restate your words with new words: The job is a volunteer position. In other words, you do not receive payment for doing the work.

Define some confusing words: Math class is intriguing, meaning it is very interesting.

Use synonyms and antonyms: The information in the memo is confidential, or secret. It is not public information, or common knowledge.

How to Verify and Confirm Information

Ask for repetition: Could you repeat that, please? Would you rephrase that for me?

Restate what you just heard: So, you're saying that it is OK to wear jeans to school?

How to Express Doubts, Wishes, and Possibilities

Understand the subjective mood: Verbs in the subjunctive mood describe doubts, wishes, and possibilities.

Use the subjunctive mood correctly:

- In the present tense, third-person singular verbs in the subjunctive mood do not have the usual -s or -es ending: She demands that he *play* outside.

- In present tense, the subjunctive mood of *be* is *be* (instead of *is* or *are*): She insists that the boys be quiet.

- In past tense, the subjunctive mood of *be* is *were*, regardless of the subject: If she *were* kinder, the boys might listen to her.

How to Understand Basic Expressions

Consider the social context:
This video game is so cool!
It's rather cool out today. It's 55 degrees.

Consider the language context: Turn right on Maple Street. The gas station will be just ahead on the left.

How to Justify with Reasons

State your claim clearly: I should be the class president.

Support your claim with evidence: This year I created a scholarship drive, organized career night, and spoke up for students at a school board meeting.

Give clear reasons that connect the evidence and your claim: My actions show that I can be a strong class president.

Combine your sentences to make the logic clear: I should be voted president of our class because I have worked hard to give students new opportunities this year.

How to Persuade or Convince

Use persuasive words: You can be a positive force in your community.

Give suggestions to others: You should listen to what the people in your community believe. You ought to consider all options available.

Give strong support for your persuasive idea: Everyone should ride his or her bicycle to work or school. It will lessen pollution and give people daily exercise.

How to Negotiate

Show that you know both sides of an issue: I see your point about the need for a new parking lot, but a park and soccer field would be more useful.

Use persuasive language: I believe you will agree with me if you consider these facts.

Clearly state your goals: We want to raise $2,000 by April and donate the money to the park fund.

How to Adjust Communication for Your Audience, Purpose, Occasion, and Task

Make sure your language is appropriate for your audience and the situation: You should choose a formal or informal manner of speaking depending on whom you are speaking to and the situation.

If you are addressing your teacher, an employer, or another adult, you might speak in this manner:

Excuse me, Mr. Johnson. May we please talk about my research paper?

If you are speaking to a friend, you can be less formal:

Hey Bob, can we talk about my research paper?

If you do not know whether a situation will call for formal or informal language, ask your teacher to help you.

Focus on your purpose: I want to make it very clear to you why that behavior could be hazardous to your health.

How to Engage in an Academic Discussion

Use formal speech: Please review the information at your convenience.

Refer to evidence: In the article we read, the author says that only 40 percent of newspapers have minorities as editors.

Ask questions: Why do you think that? What other options are there? What might have caused that?

Involve others: What do you think?

Express respect for what others say: I understand your opinion. Thank you for sharing that information.

Clarify and verify what others say: Can you explain that in another way? What evidence supports that opinion?

How to Express Social Courtesies

Listen politely and show interest: Yes, I see. Oh, what a good idea!

Wait your turn to speak: May I ask a question? I would just like to say that I disagree.

Use polite terms: Please. Thank you. That was nice of you. You are so welcome.

Use informal language when interacting with friends and family: Hi! How's it going? Thanks! No problem. Bye!

How to Conduct a Transaction or Business Deal

Clearly state numbers, dollar amounts, and other important details: Yes, I would like three textbooks. I cannot spend more than $50.

Be polite and professional: Thank you for your time. I appreciate your help.

Consider the context of the situation: Consider where you are and what is going on. For example, you can infer that when you are asked for your identification at a bank, the teller means your driver's license rather than a school ID.

How to Demonstrate and Interpret Nonverbal Communication

Watch for and use gestures, eye contact, or other visual or nonverbal communication.
Some examples include the following:

- waving to say "hello" or "good-bye"
- direct eye contact to show attention
- nodding to show understanding or approval
- using hands to show a number or a sign, like "stop"
- winking or smiling to show you are joking

Look for clues by combining verbal and nonverbal communication. You can often guess what someone means by watching how they communicate nonverbally while they speak. For example, you will have an easier time understanding someone's directions by watching where he or she points.

Listening and Speaking

Listening

Good listeners are able to learn new information and avoid confusion.

How to Listen Actively and Respectfully

- Set a purpose and prepare for listening.
- Pay close attention to the speaker. Demonstrate appropriate body language by sitting up straight and looking at the speaker as you listen.
- Connect texts or ideas that you are hearing to personal knowledge and experience—this will help you understand.
- Don't interrupt, unless you need to ask the speaker to speak more loudly.
- When the speaker is finished, ask him or her to explain things you did not understand. If the speaker did not talk enough about a topic, ask him or her to tell you more about it.

How to Overcome Barriers to Listening

- Pay close attention to the speaker.
- Try to ignore other noises or distractions around you.
- Politely ask any other people who are talking to be quiet.
- Close the classroom door or any windows if outdoor noises are distracting.
- Raise your hand, and ask the speaker to speak louder if necessary.
- Take notes on the topic being discussed. This will help you stay focused and self-monitor what you hear and track your understanding.
- In your notes, summarize the speaker's main idea and details. Were they effective enough to keep you interested? Was the speech's main idea easy to understand? Did the supporting ideas confirm the speech's main idea?

How to Use Choral Reading and Readers Theater

Choral Reading is a group activity that involves people reading a selection aloud, together. Readers Theater takes a story and treats it like a play. Students are assigned to read different parts, such as the narrator or a character.

During Choral Reading

- Listen carefully to how other readers pronounce words and phrases.
- Listen to how the intonation of the words changes.
- Listen to hear if your pitch and pronunciation sound like everyone else's.

During Readers Theater

- Listen to how different characters have different voices and expressions.
- Watch the speakers for gestures or acting.
- If you are the one who narrates or reads the stage directions, focus on describing where the action takes place.

Speaking

Speaking is saying aloud what you are thinking. Good speakers choose their words and use language effectively. They also choose an appropriate organizational strategy for their ideas. You may be required to speak in class during a discussion or when giving a presentation. Always speak responsibly and ethically. When you speak ethically, you are careful not to offend or upset anyone who is listening to you.

How to Manage Discussions and Presentations

To be a good speaker, you need to effectively share your ideas in class, in a group, or with a partner. There will be times when it is necessary to have a conference with your teacher or another student. In any discussion, whether it is formal or informal, there are things you can do to make it a productive meeting. Discussions are good ways to find information, check your understanding, and share ideas.

- In discussions, make positive comments about the ideas of others. Connect your ideas to what others say.

> Interesting point! That is a good idea. Thank you for sharing your opinion.

> I agree that people should recycle and I also think we should focus on saving water.

- Think about the topic that is being discussed. Give ideas about that topic, and exclude nonessential information.

> He is talking about how climate and weather are different in other parts of the world.

> There are many tropical climates near the equator.

- Ask questions if you need more information.
- Ask questions to verify or challenge ideas.

> Can you please repeat that? I do not understand. Can you explain that again?

> Can you give me evidence to support that idea? I respect your opinion but I think the character was shy, not scared.

- Anticipate, recognize, and adjust to listeners' needs and concerns.

> He looks confused. I should stop and explain that concept again.

How to Give Presentations

Choose an interesting topic that will engage listeners' attention. You may make a speech, share a poem, or give a performance or report to share your ideas. Be sure to justify your choice of performance technique. That is, does it fit your purpose and audience?

Use an engaging and effective introduction and conclusion. Keep your audience interested by changing your tone and volume and by using varied sentence structure to emphasize meaning. Speak using standard English grammar and syntax. It is fine to make your audience laugh, but be careful to use effective and appropriate humor that does not upset or offend your listeners. Use audience feedback to improve future presentations.

- Change your rate and volume for your audience or purpose. Be sure to speak with appropriate pitch, stress, intonation, and enunciation.

> I will be speaking about how dangerous chemicals are in the chemistry lab. I should use a serious tone during the presentation.

- Use body language such as gestures, facial expressions, and posture while you are speaking to show what you mean.

> I want to show how tall and wide a hockey goal is. I'll use my hands.

- Occasionally make eye contact with specific audience members.

> I do not want to appear nervous or unprepared. If I make eye contact with my audience, my presentation will be natural and relaxed.

How to Overcome Anxiety

Some people get a bit nervous or anxious about speaking in front of others. There are simple ways you can avoid this.

- **Be prepared**. If you plan your presentation well, you can be confident that you will speak well. Practice presenting in front of a mirror or a family member.

- **Use notes**. Use notes, graphic aids, and props as memory aids and to support the message. Notes can guide your speech or presentation. You can refer to the notes if you get confused or forget a topic you want to discuss. See the example on the right for the type of information you can keep track of in notes.

Civil Wars Around the World
— Mexico, 1857–1861
— U.S., 1861–1865
— Greece, 1946–1949
— Yugoslavia, 1991–2001

How to Self-Monitor

Monitoring is watching or noticing what is happening as you speak. It is important to monitor your audience's reactions, so you can adjust your presentation if necessary. If possible, tape your speech so you can listen to it before you give it. Analyze the tape to discover anything that might be confusing or inappropriate for the listeners. Use a rubric to prepare, critique, and improve your speech. Create a scoring guide that you can use to self-monitor. For sample rubrics and scoring guides, see page 796–798 and 840–848.

How to Use Rhetorical Devices

Rhetorical devices are ways to use language to make your presentation more interesting, engaging, or effective. Look at the examples below. Then produce one or two examples of your own.

Rhetorical Device	Example
Alliteration: The repetition of the same consonant sounds at the beginning of words.	Pablo prefers pecan pie.
Allusion: A form of literary language in which one text makes the reader think about another text that was written before it.	When Hannah wrote in her essay that vanity was the main character's weak point, or "Achilles' heel," her teacher understood that Hannah was referring to a character in a Greek myth.
Analogy: A way of illustrating or explaining a thing or an idea by comparing it with a more familiar thing or idea.	*Blogs* are to the *Internet* as *journals* are to *paper*.
Irony: When you say one thing, but want the listeners to understand something different. You may say the opposite of what is really true.	Your friend says to you after you trip and fall, "Today must be your lucky day!"
Mood: The attitude or feeling of your presentation. You create this for your listeners with the words you choose.	Slowly the car approached. It rolled to a stop, and a strange looking character stepped out of the back seat.
Quotation: Repeating the exact words of someone using quotation marks.	As Franklin D. Roosevelt said, "The only thing we have to fear is fear itself."
Pun: A humorous use of words that have more than one meaning.	To write with a broken pencil is *point*-less.
Parallelism: Similarity of structure in a pair or series of related words, phrases, or sentences.	We can change our school. We can make a difference. We can do this together.
Repetition: Repeating words, phrases, or ideas. Using this device shows your listeners that you believe the idea is very important.	All people are entitled to freedom. Freedom is something everyone deserves. Freedom will make the world a better place.
Tone: A speaker's attitude toward the topic, audience, or self.	I am definitely not in favor of a shorter lunch period.

Viewing and Representing

Monitoring Your Understanding of Visuals

You encounter visual elements constantly–in print, on TV, on the Internet, and in movies. How can you make sure you accurately understand and interpret what you see? Does the visual enhance your understanding of the oral presentation? Use the following strategies to self-monitor, or check that you understand, what you are viewing.

How to View and Look for Details

Study the image below. Ask these kinds of questions:

- Who or what does the image show? Are there other details that answer *when*, *where*, *why*, or *how* questions about the image?

- How does the image make me feel? Do I enjoy looking at it? Does it worry me, make me laugh, or give me a good or bad feeling?

- What do the details and elements (such as shape, color, and size of the image) add to the meaning?

How to Respond to and Interpret Visuals and Informational Graphics

When you view visuals and informational graphics, think about why they are included and what information they provide. Informational graphics often present facts or statistics. For example, you will sometimes see illustrations or informational graphics used in an oral presentation. Ask yourself:

- What message or information is the visual showing?

- Why did the artist, designer, or illustrator create and include the visual?

- Does the visual represent information accurately and fairly? What information did the creator choose to include or leave out? Why?

How to Self-Correct Your Thoughts as You View

Examine your understanding of visuals to correct any faulty thinking. Always question the validity and accuracy of visuals.

- Be aware of racial, cultural, and gender stereotyping. A **stereotype** is a general opinion that is not always true. A stereotype does not look at the differences between individual people or things. For example, "All cats are lazy." This is a stereotype because although some cats are lazy, some are very active.

- Look again at the image or graphic for more information and details that may change your understanding and for things you did not notice at first.

- Watch for **bias**. Is the writer or creator presenting information that is slanted or manipulated to show a particular point of view?

How to Understand Different Kinds of Visuals

It is important to be familiar with the different kinds of visuals that illustrate ideas for a text or spoken presentation. You will be expected to respond to and interpret these different visuals. Some examples are maps, charts, graphs, photographs, illustrations, and other artwork. As you look at a visual, decide what it is telling you. Visuals should help you better understand the information, especially if the language is elaborate or complex.

Map

A map is a visual layout of a specific location. Maps are an excellent way to gain more information about an idea presented in text.

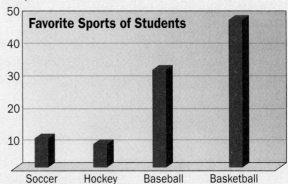

Graphic Displays

A chart or a graph can show comparisons or provide information more clearly than if the same statistics were only presented in a text. Be sure to evaluate the credibility of the source of the data.

Chart

Number of Endangered Species in the United States	
Classification	Number of Species
Mammals	70
Birds	76
Reptiles	13
Fish	74
Insects	47

Graph

Favorite Sports of Students

Photographs, Illustrations, Video, Sound, and Artwork

Photographs, illustrations, and other artwork can have a variety of purposes:

- to share an opinion
- to elicit, or draw out, emotions
- to make people think
- to entertain

Multimedia resources include sound, motion, special effects, audio, and visuals. Use what you see and hear. Think about how the creator of a video or media presentation uses music or effects to make a point. Animations and other interactive media change based on what you click or touch.

Using Visuals and Multimedia in Writing and Presenting

Here are some key points to keep in mind when you choose to represent your ideas by using a visual or other media.

Representing Your Ideas Through Visuals

Using visuals in your writing and oral presentations can help you make your point more clearly. Choose visuals that match your purpose and your topic. Strong visuals will make a strong impression. Music and sound effects in multimedia presentations also impact tone and can be used to emphasize ideas or information. For example, if you choose to illustrate a poem about nature, include a picture that will help readers picture the place or feel the mood of the poem.

How Key Elements of Design Create Meaning and Influence the Message

Different visuals share information in different ways.

- If your goal is to entertain, choose a humorous picture.

Source: ©Terry Warner/Cartoon Stock, Ltd.

"Is this seat taken?"

- If your goal is to inform, use a visual that gives additional information about your topic or clarifies the information in some way. See the Index of Graphic Organizers on page 934 for ideas of ways to share information in graphic form.

How Wild Tigers Affect the Environment

small animals eat the vegetation

tigers eat the small animals reducing their number

vegetation thrives

- If your goal is to persuade, or to make people feel or think a certain way, you may want to choose a visual that will appeal to emotions.

- If you use a visual from another source, be sure to identify the source.

Source: ©Jeff Rotman/Getty Images.

The Effects of Visual Arts on Mood

When you choose a visual to represent information in an essay or an oral presentation, make sure it is a visual that your particular audience will understand. A complex graph may not work well if your viewers do not know a lot about your topic. Creating a simple visual is especially important if you have an elaborate presentation. Your audience should be able to use the visual to make sense of the presentation. Make sure it is a visual you would want to view yourself.

In addition, consider the mood that you want the visual to create. The mood should be appropriate to your purpose and audience, such as a classroom of students listening to your oral presentation. If the mood of a presentation or essay is serious, do not use humorous or distracting visuals. For example, if you are giving a presentation on the United States government, you might display a graphic showing the legislative, executive, and judicial branches of government.

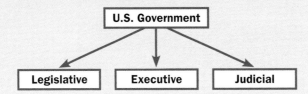

Interpreting and Analyzing Media

Media is the term used to describe the many forms of technology used today to provide communication to a large number of people. As you view media around you, such as the Internet, television, movies, magazines, and newspapers, make sure you remember the key points that are presented. What information is being presented in the visuals that are used? How is it presented? Make decisions about the information you are presented with by the media.

The information and visuals presented may be trustworthy, or they may be suspicious. In today's world, we are surrounded by images and information that we need to analyze and make decisions about. Keep in mind that visual media can easily influence our cultural and social expectations because it is much more visual than traditional texts. Be aware that you can make judgments and decisions while viewing the images and form your own opinions about the information they present.

Sometimes, the same event can be interpreted differently, based on the way the event is covered and the medium in which it is shown. Find a news event discussed in a newspaper and the same event on the Internet or TV. Then compare what is similar and what is different.

- What is the message?
- How do I know it is believable or valid?
- What information is included and what is left out?
- Is the information objective, or is it biased?

Technology and Media

How to Use Technology to Communicate

This section provides examples of the technology used today to communicate in school, in the workplace, and with friends and family.

Cell Phone

A **cell phone** does not need a wire connection to a phone network. It can be used anywhere there is a wireless phone network signal. It is completely portable. Cell phones can allow you to send text messages, connect to the Internet, play music, take photos, and make phone calls.

Personal Computer

A **personal computer** is an electronic tool that helps you create, save, and use information. You can also use a computer to communicate with e-mail, browse the Internet, work with digital photos or movies, or listen to music.

A **desktop computer** is not portable. It has several parts, including a monitor, a mouse, a keyboard, and a CD drive.

A **laptop computer** is smaller than a desktop computer. It is designed to be portable. A laptop computer usually fits in a travel case.

stylus

A **tablet computer** is typically even smaller than a laptop computer. You can use your fingers or a stylus pen to make most tablet computers work.

How to Select and Use Media to Research Information

Modern technology allows us to access a wide range of information. The Internet is a popular source for research and finding information for academic, professional, and personal reasons. Another source for research is your local library. It contains databases where you can gain access to many forms of print and nonprint resources, including audio and video recordings and many other sources of information.

The Internet

The **Internet** is an international network, or connection, of computers that share information with each other. The **World Wide Web** is a part of the Internet that allows you to find, read, and organize information. Using the Web is a fast way to get the most current information about many topics.

Any series of words or phrases can be typed into the "search" section of a search engine, and multiple Web sites with those words will be listed for you to investigate. Once you are at a Web site, you can perform a word or phrase search of the page you are on. This will help direct you to the information you are researching.

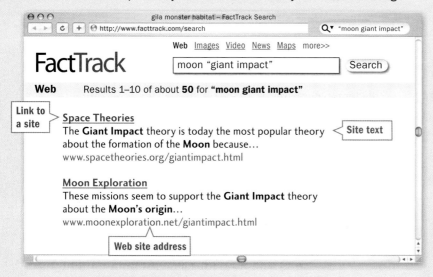

Other Sources of Information

There are many other reliable print and nonprint sources of information to use in your research. For example:

- magazines
- newspapers
- professional or scholarly journal articles
- experts
- political speeches
- press conferences

Most of the information from these sources is also available on the Internet. You should be careful to evaluate and choose the best sources for this information. It is important to double-check the source. Does the source show a bias? Is the source from a professor or from an anonymous blog post?

How to Evaluate the Quality of Information

There is so much information available on the Internet it can be hard to comprehend. It is important to be sure that the information you use as support or evidence is reliable and can be trusted. Use the following checklist as a guideline to decide if a Web page you are reading is reliable and a credible source.

Checklist to Determine Reliable Web Sites

☑ The information is from a well-known and trusted source. For example, Web sites that end in ".edu" are part of an educational institution and usually can be trusted. Other cues for reliable Web sites are sites that end in ".org" for "organization" or ".gov" for "government."

☑ The people who write or are quoted on the Web site are experts, not just everyday people expressing ideas or opinions.

☑ The Web site gives evidence, not just opinions.

☑ The Web site is free of grammatical and spelling errors. This is often a hint that the site was carefully constructed and will not have factual errors.

☑ The Web site is not trying to sell a product or persuade people. It is trying to provide accurate information.

If you are uncertain about the quality of a Web site, contact your teacher for advice.

How to Organize and Discuss Information From Various Media

Devise a system to organize the information you find from various forms of media, such as newspapers, books, and the Internet. You can make photocopies of important newspaper and magazine articles or pages from books and keep them in labeled folders. Web pages can be printed out or bookmarked on your computer for reference. You can discuss the information you find from various media with your classmates or teachers to evaluate its reliability. In fact, explaining aloud what you've gathered from a variety of media is one way to better understand the information. It will also help you to learn how to use specific language and vocabulary related to certain types of media.

How to Analyze and Interpret Information from Various Media

You should always try to analyze and interpret the information you find from various media sources. Many times the same event can be interpreted differently depending on the medium in which it is presented. Ask yourself if the source is reliable or if the information you find shows any bias or opinion. Some writers may only mention facts that support their ideas or opinions and not mention details that are not supportive of their arguments. Find an event that is covered both in your local newspaper and on television. Compare the differences between the coverage in the two media. Do you notice a difference in bias or opinion? Comparing two sources of information about the same topic may help you see that one is more biased than the other. It can help you see ways that different people present similar information.

How to Use Technology to Create Final Products

Technology allows people to create interesting final products to share information. Once you become comfortable with the appropriate equipment and software, there are many ways to create, change, and individualize your work using technology. Here are two examples of products that can be made with technology today.

Electronic Media

Electronic media, or a **word-processing document**, allows you to create and save written work. You can use it to:

- store ideas, plans, and essays
- write drafts of your work
- revise, edit, and proofread your writing
- format, publish, and share your work

There are many different kinds of word-processing programs. If you are not familiar with word-processing programs, talk to your teacher about learning one that will work well for you in class. Review or learn the following basic steps:

1 Start a File or Document Open a new document, and choose a place to save it.

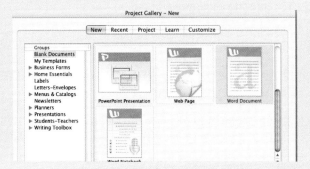

2 Type and Format Your Work Review how to do basic tasks, such as change a font, highlight words in color, and make type bold or underlined.

3 Save and Share Your Work Continually click the Save icon on the toolbar to ensure your work is not lost by computer error. Once you have a finished document, talk to your teacher about printing or using e-mail options.

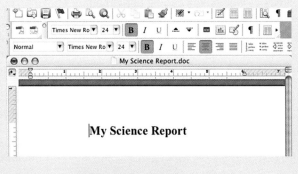

Multimedia Presentation

A **multimedia presentation** allows your audience to read, see, and hear your work. You may choose to include visuals, videos, photographs, or audio recordings in your presentation to make the information more interesting for your audience. Be sure to carefully plan and practice your presentation. This will help you avoid errors during your presentation.

What Is Research?

Research is collecting information about a specific subject. When you research, you are trying to find the answer to a question.

How to Use the Research Process

When you research, you search for information about a specific topic. You can use the information you find to write a story, an article, or a research report.

Choose and Narrow Your Topic

The best way to choose your research topic is to think of something you want to learn more about and that interests you. Make sure your teacher approves your topic. Pick a topic that is not too general. A specific topic is easier to research and write about. It also is more interesting to read about in a report.

Discover What Is Known and What Needs to Be Learned

Get to know your topic. Are there recent articles or reports in the news that relate to your topic? What are researchers and scientists currently working on that relates to the topic?

Formulate Research Questions

What do you know about your topic? What do you want to learn? Write down some questions about your topic that you want to find the answers to. Look at the most important words in your questions, or the key words. These are the words that will be the focus of your research.

> Is there life on Mars?
> Is water or oxygen found on Mars?
> Can life forms live on the surface of Mars?
> What have space missions to Mars discovered about possible life there?

Narrowing the Topic

> Outer Space: This is a very large topic. There are too many things to research in outer space, such as planets, stars, and meteors. There is too much information to cover in one report.

↓

> Planets: This topic is better, but it is still too large. There are many planets in our solar system. It is best to pick a specific planet, and decide on one thing you want to learn about that planet.

↓

> Life on Mars: This topic is more specific than researching the entire planet of Mars. The research can focus just on whether or not plants and animals exist on Mars, or if they ever existed there in the past.

Choose Appropriate Resources to Support Your Topic

Resources can be people you interview, such as experts or teachers. Textbooks, magazines, newspapers, videos, photographs, and the Internet are also resources. The four main types of resources are:

- print
- electronic
- audio visual
- graphic aids

Create a rubric to rate the reliability of your sources. Rate each source on a scale of 1 to 4; 4 is the most reliable, 1 is the least reliable. If you are unsure of the reliability of your sources, ask your teacher, your parents, or a partner.

Gather Information

You may need to survey, skim, or scan a variety of sources to pick the best ones. Use the research questions you formulated to guide your reading.

To Skim   Read the title to see if the article is useful for your topic. Read the beginning sentences of the main paragraphs, or any subheads. See if the article may give details about your topic. Read the last paragraph. At the end, there is usually a conclusion that will summarize the main points of the article.

To Scan   Look for key words or details. They may be underlined or in bold type. This will tell you if the article will discuss your topic.

Take Notes

As you read, take notes. You will gather the specific information you need from each source. For each resource:

1. Include the key words or important phrases about your topic.

2. Write down the source to record where you found the facts.
   - For a book, list the title, author, page number, publisher, and year of publication.
   - For a magazine or newspaper article, list the name, date, volume, and issue number of the source. Also list the title of the article and the author.
   - For an Internet site, list the Web address, the name of the site, the author (if there is one listed), and the date of the latest site update.

3. List the details and facts that are important to your topic. Be certain to summarize or paraphrase the information in your own words. If you use exact words from a source, you must put the words in quotation marks and note the page you copied it from. If you exactly copy someone else's words, you will be plagiarizing. **Plagiarism** is illegal and can be punished by law.

Notecard for a book

Is there life on Mars?
Mars by Seymour Simon, page 27
—Viking spacecraft supposed to find out if
there's life
—Some think experiments showed there isn't

Organize Information from Multiple Sources

After you have taken notes from several sources, **organize** them to see what information is the most important. See how the information from different sources is related.

One of the best ways to organize your information is to use a graphic organizer called an outline. You can also organize your information by using technology. For example, you could type up your notes and save them in a word processing document. It also allows you to choose which data (like dates or times), facts, or ideas are the most relevant.

Analyze, Evaluate, and Use Information

Review your rubric that showed which sources were the most reliable. After you check the reliability, usefulness, relevance, and accuracy of the information, **analyze** and **evaluate** the information. All resources are either primary or secondary sources. A **primary source** is an account of an event by someone who was actually there. A primary source might be a journal, letter, or photograph. A **secondary source** is an account of an event by someone who was not present at the event but that describes the event for other people. A secondary source could be a textbook or an article.

Primary Sources	Secondary Sources
• a soldier's journal	• a book about World War I
• a photograph of a volcano erupting	• a documentary that tells the story of the day a volcano erupted

Synthesize Information from Multiple Sources

Convert your data into graphic aids. Make an outline to **synthesize**, or organize and summarize, your research findings and draw conclusions. Doing this will allow you to identify complexities and discrepancies. You can also use your outline and notes to organize your Works Cited page at the end of your paper. Include the author, title, and page number or Web address.

How to Make an Outline:

1. Put all your notes that have the same keywords or phrases together.

2. Make the first question from your notes into a main idea statement. This will be Roman numeral I.

3. Each of your key research questions will be a Roman numeral heading.

4. Find details that explain each main idea statement. Each important detail about that idea should go below it, and be listed with capital letters.

5. More specific details can be listed with numbers under each capital letter detail.

6. Give your outline a title. This title should state the overall or main idea. It may be a good title to use for your report.

Sample Outline

The Mystery of Life on Mars
  I. Life on Mars
    A. How Mars is like Earth
      1. Volcanoes
      2. Giant canyons
    B. Fact-finding missions
      1. Viking
      2. Pathfinder
  II. Signs of life on Mars
    A. Studied by David McKay's team
    B. Meteorite
      1. Might contain bacteria fossils
      2. Found in Antarctica
      3. Probably from Mars
  III. Continued search for life on Mars
    A. Look underground
    B. More study
      1. Mission planned for future
      2. Gases in atmosphere
      3. What rocks are made of.

Design and Write a Research Report

Before you write, ask your teacher to show you which style guide to use. Follow the style guide to learn the proper formatting of the paper. It will also show you how to format your sources into a works cited page. Use the following techniques to complete your research paper.

Write the Title and Introduction

Copy the **title** from your outline. You can make it more interesting if you want. Make sure it gives the main idea of your topic. Next you should write an interesting **introduction** that will explain what the rest of your report will be about. Write an introduction that will get your readers' attention.

Outline

The Mystery of Life on Mars

Title and Introduction

The Mystery of Life on Mars
Perhaps you have heard stories about life on other planets. Or perhaps, you may have only thought about life here on Earth. I am going to explore the research on the planet Mars and discuss with you the studies that have been done to see if there is life on "the red planet."

Write the Body

The body is the main portion of your report. Use your main ideas to write topic sentences for each paragraph. Then use your research details to write sentences about each topic.

Outline

I. Life on Mars
   A. How Mars is like Earth
      1. Volcanoes
      2. Giant canyons

Topic Sentence and Detail

People have always wondered if there is life on other planets, especially Mars. Because Mars is similar to Earth with features like volcanoes and giant canyons, it seems possible that there is life on Mars.

Write the Conclusion

Write about the main ideas of your report in the **conclusion**. This will summarize your report. You can also include an interesting fact or opinion to end your report. This will keep your audience thinking after they have finished reading. For example, "I believe that with all the research still being done on Mars, perhaps in the near future, we will learn more about life on that mysterious planet."

Design Your Report: Graphic and Multimedia Aids

After you write your report, you should consider its **design**, or how it will look on a printed page. This includes choosing the font of the text and deciding whether you will use **graphic aids** to make the information in your report easier to understand or more interesting. Do you want to include illustrations or photographs? Does your audience need a time line or diagram to understand the text better? Is there a video or audio file that might support your ideas? Choose visuals or media that will make your presentation more effective.

Integrate Quotations and Citations

Adding **quotations** and including **citations** are important ways of sharing the information you find during your research. Any words that are not your own must be in quotation marks and the source must be given in the running text in order to avoid plagiarism. If you use an idea that is not your own, even if you paraphrase it in your own words, you must **cite** the source for that information.

To cite a source means to list the information of your source. This helps you to properly note where you found your information. Citing allows other readers to look at the source, too. Use the citation style your teacher tells you to use. Two commonly used citation styles were developed by the Modern Language Association (MLA) and the American Psychological Association (APA). Both of these associations publish style manuals that can help you write research papers. They are available at **www.mla.org** and **www.apastyle.org**.

A common way to cite is to use the MLA style for author and page citation. List the author and the page number of your source right after you use the words or idea of that author. The author's name should be either in the sentence itself or in parentheses following the quotation or paraphrase. The page number(s) should always appear in parentheses, not in the text of your sentence. For example:

> The writer T. S. Eliot has said that poetry expresses an "overflow of powerful feelings" (263).

> Poetry expresses an "overflow of powerful feelings" (Eliot 263).

At the end of your report create a separate **"Works Cited"** page.

> Works Cited
>
> Ackroyd, Peter. *T. S. Eliot: A Life.* London: Simon and Schuster, 1985.
>
> Vendler, Helen. "T. S. Eliot." *Time* 8 June 1998. 70–72.
>
> "T. S. Eliot." *Microsoft Encarta Online Encyclopedia.* 2006.
>
> <http://encarta.msn.com>

Evaluate Your Research Report and Draw Conclusions

After you complete your research report, you should **evaluate** it, or check its quality. Ask questions about how well you did each step of the report. Look at the paper overall. Does it accomplish what you want it to do? Do you have to do more research or adjust your main idea to achieve the goal of your paper? This will help you to decide if the end product is presented correctly.

Checklist to Evaluate

- ☑ The title tells what the report is about.
- ☑ The introduction is interesting, gets the attention of the reader, and gives the main idea of the report.
- ☑ The body gives the facts you found.
- ☑ Each paragraph covers a specific topic from your outline.
- ☑ Each topic in the body paragraphs is connected to the main idea.
- ☑ Other sentences give specific details about the topic.
- ☑ The conclusion is a summary of the most important information on your topic.
- ☑ The conclusion is interesting for the reader.
- ☑ The paper is formatted according to the style guide used.
- ☑ All sources are properly formatted per the style guide used.

Share Your Report

Publish your report. You can choose different media for publishing. You can print the final report in paper, put it online, create a poster or display of your final paper, or attach it to an email and send it to trusted friends or adults. Be sure to check your school's Acceptable Use Policy before posting your work.

Questions for Further Study

Now that you have finished the report, you may have questions based on the conclusions you drew. You can consider these questions as other research ideas for the future.

During Your Research

I see that there were space missions to Mars such as the Viking. How are those machines created? Who designs them? I would like to know more about space technology.

Now

Maybe my next research report will be about space technology. I could study who designs the machines that go into space and how they work.

Test-Taking Strategies

What Are Test-Taking Strategies?

Test-taking strategies are skills to help you effectively complete a test. These strategies will help you to show what you know on a test without making mistakes.

What to Do Before a Test

Use the following strategies to help you prepare for a test.

- Find out if the test will be multiple-choice, short answers, or essay. Noting the format will allow you to select an appropriate strategy.
- Ask your teacher for practice tests or examples to try before the test day.
- Carefully study the material that will be on the test.
- Make sure you get a good night of rest before a test. This will help you focus.
- Eat a nutritious meal before the test. This will give you energy to get through the test.

What to Do During a Test

Use the following strategies as you complete the test.

Relax: Relax and think carefully during the test. If you feel stressed, take a few deep breaths. Remind yourself that you are prepared.

Plan Your Time: Survey the test to estimate difficulty and plan time. See what questions you can answer easily. Do not work on one question for too long because you might not have enough time to finish the test if you only focus on one question.

Read: Read the directions for each section of the test. Then, read each question carefully. Underline key words in the directions and questions to focus on the most important information. Be certain that you are doing what the question asks. For example, if a question says to "describe," give more than a definition. You may need to give specific details.

Clarify: Tests ask logical questions. If something seems strange, reread the directions, question, or passage to clarify information. Think about words carefully to be certain you understand their meaning. Use typographic and visual clues to find meaning.

Mark Answers: Carefully mark your answers on the test and check for legibility. This can affect your test grade! Be sure to use the correct writing utensil. For example, some multiple choice tests require the use of a #2 pencil.

Check Completeness: Check to make sure all questions are answered (if there is no penalty for guessing). Always reread your answers or answer choices, if you have time. Finish any questions you may not have finished before.

You think:

> This question is difficult. I cannot answer this right now.

Then you decide:

> I will return to this question later. I will answer the questions I do know first.

Tips for Objective Tests

Use the following strategies to help you complete objective tests.

Easy First: Answer the easy questions first. Leave the most difficult ones for last.

Narrow the Choices: If you are uncertain of an answer, determine which choices are definitely not correct. Choose the two that are closest to correct. This will narrow your number of answers to choose from to only two.

Rephrase Questions and Answer Them Mentally: Try to put the question in your own words and think about how you will answer. Then, look at the answer choices to see which one matches your own answer the best.

Make Changes If Needed: Ask yourself if you answered each question correctly. Check your work by reading through the test a second time. Change your answer only if the question was initially misunderstood.

Shuttle Among the Passage, the Question, the Choices: Read the passage, the questions, and the choices until you fully understand what is being asked.

Tips for Essay Tests

Use the following strategies to help you complete essay tests.

Outline: Make an outline of your answer before you write. This way, you can make sure you discuss all the important points of your essay.

Plan: Plan the time for your essay. Know how long you have to write your essay. Mark on your outline how long you plan to spend writing each section of your essay.

Write: Only include information in your essay that you know is accurate and is about your topic. If you are uncertain if it is factual or important, do not include it. Use a topic sentence and supporting details for each paragraph.

Proofread: Carefully proofread your writing. Check for grammar, punctuation, and capitalization. Most importantly, make sure all parts of your essay can be read clearly.

Tips for Online Tests

Use the following strategies to help you complete tests on a computer.

- Find out how the test is designed—Can you go back to questions you have already answered? Can you change your answers? Is there a time limit? Is there a glossary? Audio? Some tests will show you this information on the introduction screen. You can also ask your teacher.

- Find out if this is an adaptive test. When you take adaptive tests, the questions get harder or easier based on whether you are getting answers correct or incorrect. So when you take an adaptive test, take your time and be careful as you answer the first several questions.

- Have a pencil and paper in addition to your computer test. Use your paper to jot down an idea or organize your thoughts with a graphic organizer.

READING HANDBOOK

Reading Strategies

Reading Fluency

Study Skills and Strategies

Vocabulary

What Are Reading Strategies?

Reading strategies are hints or techniques you can use to help you become a better reader. They help you interact with the text and take control of your own reading comprehension. Reading strategies can be used before, during, and after you read.

Plan and Monitor

Before you read, plan how to approach the selection by using prereading strategies. **Preview** the selection to see what it is about and try to make a prediction about its content. Keep in mind that English is read from left to right, and that text moves from the top of the page to the bottom. **Set a purpose** for reading, or decide why you will read the selection. You might want or need to adjust your purpose for reading as you read. Monitor your reading to check how well you understand and remember what you read.

How to Select and Use Prereading Strategies	
Title:	Surfing the Pipeline
Author:	Christina Rodriguez
Preview the Text	• Look at the title: Surfing the Pipeline. • Look at the organization of the text, including any chapter titles, heads, and subheads. • Look at any photos and captions. • Think about what the selection is about.
Activate Prior Knowledge	• I know many people surf in the ocean on surfboards. • I've seen a film about people trying to surf on huge waves in California.
Ask Questions	• What is the pipeline? • Where is the pipeline? • Who surfs the pipeline? • Why do people try to surf the pipeline?
Set a Purpose for Reading	• I want to read to find out how people surf the pipeline.

How to Make and Confirm Predictions

Making **predictions** about a selection will help you understand and remember what you read. As you preview a selection, **ask questions** and think about any **prior knowledge** you have about the subject. If you do not learn enough additional information from these steps, read the first few paragraphs of the selection.

Think about the events taking place, and then predict what will happen next. If you are reading fiction or drama, you can use what you know about common plot patterns to help you predict what may happen in the story. After you read each section, confirm your predictions, or see if they were correct. Sometimes you will need to revise your predictions for the next section based on what you read.

Preview to Anticipate Read the title. Think about what the selection will be about as you read the first few paragraphs. Look for clues about the selection's content.

Make and Confirm Predictions As you read, predict what will happen next in the selection based on text evidence or personal experience. Take notes while you are reading, and use a **Prediction Chart** to record your ideas. As you continue to read the selection, confirm your predictions. If a prediction is incorrect, revise it.

Surfing the Pipeline

There Uli was, standing on the white, sandy shores of Oahu, Hawaii. Right in front of her was the famous Banzai Pipeline—one of the most difficult and dangerous places to surf in the world. Uli looked out and saw twelve-foot waves crashing toward her.

Uli had been waiting for this day for a long time. She was ready.

Uli grabbed her surfboard and entered the water. The waves were fierce and strong that morning. It took all of Uli's energy to swim out to the surfing location. Uli could see rocks sticking up through the water. She finally found the perfect starting point and waited anxiously to begin surfing.

Prediction Chart

Prediction	Did It Happen?	Evidence
Uli is going to surf at the Banzai Pipeline.	Not yet, but she will soon.	She is at the starting point to begin surfing. (text evidence)
Surfing the Banzai Pipeline will be hard for Uli.	Not yet, but it will soon.	New activities are always hard when I try them for the first time. (personal experience)

How to Monitor Your Reading

When you **monitor your reading**, you are checking to make sure you understand the information you read. You can check your understanding by keeping track of your thinking while reading. Pause while reading to think about images you may be creating in your mind, connections you are making between words or topics within the text, or problems you are having with understanding the text. When you read something that doesn't make sense to you, use these monitoring strategies to help you.

Strategy	How to Use It	Example Text
Reread to Clarify Ideas	Reread silently the passage you do not understand. Then reread the passage aloud. Continue rereading until you feel more confident about your understanding of the passage.	I will silently reread the first paragraph. Then I will read it aloud. The paragraph is more understandable now.
Use Resources to Clarify Vocabulary	Look up confusing words in a dictionary or thesaurus, or ask a classmate for help.	"… dangerous places to surf …" I'm not sure what "surf" means. I'll look it up.
Read On and Use Context Clues to Clarify Ideas and Vocabulary	Read past the part of the text where you are confused. What does the rest of the information tell you? Are there nearby words or phrases, context clues or visuals that help you understand?	"… looked out and saw twelve-foot waves …" Maybe "surf" means riding ocean waves.
Adjust Your Reading Rate	Read slowly when something is confusing or difficult. Keep in mind that English is read from left to right and that text runs down the page from the top. If you are having a difficult time understanding what you're reading, first make sure that you're reading it in the right order.	"Right in front of her was the famous Banzai Pipeline …" I've never heard of the Banzai Pipeline. I'll read slower to find out what it is.
Adjust Your Purpose for Reading	Think of the purpose you set for reading before you started to read. Have you found a new purpose, or reason to read? If so, adjust your purpose and read on.	I originally wanted to read to find out how people surf the pipeline. Now I want to read to see if Uli actually does it.

How to Use Graphic Organizers

Before you read, you can use graphic organizers to prepare for better comprehension. For example, use a **KWL Chart** to record your prior knowledge about the topic.

KWL Chart

WHAT I <u>K</u>NOW	WHAT I <u>WANT</u> TO KNOW	WHAT I <u>L</u>EARNED

As you read, use a variety of graphic organizers such as diagrams and charts to help keep track of your thinking. Take notes about any ideas or vocabulary that confuse you. Writing down ideas keeps you actively involved in your reading. It also can help clear up any confusion you may have about information in a selection.

Use graphic organizers to capture your thoughts and to help you remember information based on how it was described in the text or based on the text structure. Here are some more examples of graphic organizers:

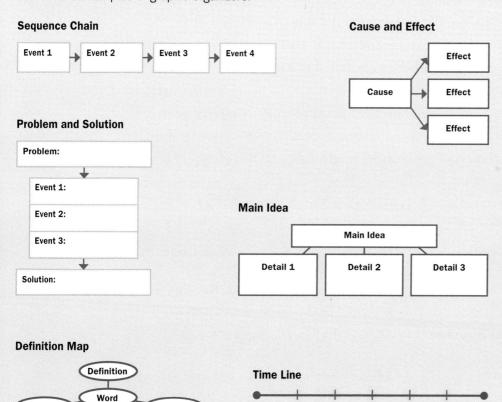

Sequence Chain

Event 1 → Event 2 → Event 3 → Event 4

Cause and Effect

Cause → Effect, Effect, Effect

Problem and Solution

Problem: → Event 1: → Event 2: → Event 3: → Solution:

Main Idea

Main Idea → Detail 1, Detail 2, Detail 3

Definition Map

Definition, Word, Example, Example

Time Line

For more graphic organizers, see the Index of Graphic Organizers on page 934.

Determine Importance

Determining importance is a reading strategy you can use to find the most important details or ideas in a selection. A good way to think about what is important in the selections you read is to **summarize**. When you summarize, you state the main idea and only the most important details in a selection, usually in a sentence or two. To summarize, identify the topic of a paragraph or selection, find the main idea and the most important details, and put them in your own words.

Stated Main Ideas

The main idea of a selection is the most important point a writer wants to relate to readers. Writers often state the main idea in a topic sentence near the beginning of a selection.

What's in a Name?

All college sports teams have special names. Many of these names are common, such as the Bears or the Tigers. However, more teams should have names that are unique and express the school's individuality. The University of Arkansas team names are Razorbacks and Lady Razorbacks. Virginia Tech athletes are called Hokies. Purdue has the Boilermakers. My favorite is the University of California at Santa Cruz's Banana Slugs and Lady Slugs. Slugs are unusual creatures. They have soft, slimy bodies and enjoy moist environments. These unique names make the college sports world a more interesting and fun place.

How to Identify Stated Main Ideas	
What is the paragraph about?	• names of college teams
Look for supporting details.	• Some teams have unique names like Razorbacks, Hokies, Boilermakers, and Lady Slugs. • The author feels these names make the college sports world more fun.
Eliminate unnecessary information or details.	• Slugs are slimy and enjoy moist environments.
Summarize the main idea.	• Unique sports team names are better and more fun than common names.

Implied Main Ideas

Sometimes a main idea is implied, or not directly stated. Readers have to figure out the main idea by studying all of the details in a selection.

The Future of Humankind

Many people agree that space exploration is important. However, when government spending is discussed, many people insist there are problems on Earth that need attention and money first. Don't they realize that the future of the human race depends on space exploration? Someday, the Earth's resources may run out. Paying for more exploration will allow us to learn more about space and how we can better care for our planet.

How to Identify Implied Main Ideas	
What is the paragraph about?	• space exploration
Find and list details.	• Many people feel other issues are more important than space exploration. • Our future depends on exploration.
What message is the author trying to convey?	• If we explore space now, we can better take care of ourselves and Earth.
Summarize the implied main idea.	• Space exploration should be paid for because it is just as important as any other issue. We could die without it.

Personal Relevance

An additional way to determine importance while reading a selection is to look for details that have personal relevance to you. These details may be important to you because they remind you of someone or something in your own life. For example, you might relate to "What's in a Name?" because you have a favorite sports team name. You might understand the main point that the writer is trying to make because you might agree that sports team names should be unique.

Make Connections

Making connections is a reading strategy you can use to better understand or enjoy the information presented in a selection.

As you read, think about what the information reminds you of. Have you seen or heard something like this before? Have you read or experienced something like this? Thinking about what you already know helps you make a connection to the new information.

Type of Connection	Description	Example
Text to Self	A connection between the text you are reading and something that has happened in your own life. A text-to-self connection can also be a feeling, such as happiness or excitement, that you feel as you are reading.	This part of the story reminds me of the first time I drove a car. My dad showed me how to turn and stop. I remember how scared I was. Thinking about this memory helps me better understand how the character is feeling as he learns how to drive.
Text to Text	A connection between the text you are reading and another selection you have read, a film you have seen, or a song you have heard. Sometimes the text you are reading might have a similar theme, or message, to something you've read, seen, or heard before. A text may also belong to a genre, such as mystery or biography, that you are familiar with.	This part of the news article reminds me of a movie I saw about space. Astronauts were taking a trip to the moon, but their spaceship lost all power. I can think about the movie as I read about the most recent space shuttle mission.
Text to World	A connection between something you read in the text and something that is happening or has happened in the world. You might also make a connection with the time period or era that a selection takes place in, such as the Great Depression or the 1980s. The setting may also be familiar.	This part of the text reminds me of presidential elections. I remember candidates giving speeches to tell why they should be president. Thinking about this helps me understand why the characters in the selection give speeches.

Use a chart like the one below to help make and record text-to-self, text-to-text, or text-to-world connections as you read.

Make Connections Chart

The text says ...	This reminds me of ...	This helps me because ...

Make Inferences

Making inferences is a reading strategy in which you make educated guesses about the text's content based on experiences that you've had in everyday life or on facts or details that you read.

Sometimes people call making inferences "reading between the lines." This means looking at *how* the text was written along with what is being discussed. When you "read between the lines," you pay attention to the writer's tone, voice, use of punctuation, or emphasis on certain words. Writers can also use irony, dialogue, or descriptions to infer messages.

When you add your prior knowledge or personal experiences to what you are reading, you can make inferences by reading all the clues and making your best guesses.

How to Make Inferences Using Your Own Experience

Read the following paragraph and chart to learn how to make an inference using your own experiences.

The Waiting

Rain pounded against the windows as Sarah stomped up and down the stairs. She only stopped going up and down to check the time on the clock downstairs every five minutes. She had been dressed and ready to go for more than an hour! Sarah had spent weeks picking out her dress and shoes, and she had even paid $50 to have her hair styled. She threw the flower she had so excitedly bought yesterday in the corner beside the camera. Sarah wondered, "Where is he? Will I have to go alone tonight?"

Inferences Based on Your Own Experience	
You read	Sarah had been dressed and ready to go somewhere for more than an hour. She spent a lot of time selecting her dress and shoes. She threw her flower in the corner by the camera.
You know	I know that people spend a lot of time choosing special outfits for events like dances, weddings, or parties. I know that my parents took a photo of me and my date for the prom last year. My date and I both had flowers for our outfits that night.
You infer	Sarah had a date to a special event that night. She was upset because she cared a lot about the event she was going to and didn't want to be late or go alone.

How to Make Inferences Using Text Evidence

Read the following paragraph and chart to learn how to make an inference by using clues that appear in the text.

The Waiting

Rain pounded against the windows as Sarah stomped up and down the stairs. She only stopped going up and down to check the time on the clock downstairs every five minutes. She had been dressed and ready to go for more than an hour! Sarah had spent weeks picking out her dress and shoes, and she had even paid $50 to have her hair styled. She threw the flower she had so excitedly bought yesterday in the corner beside the camera. Sarah wondered, "Where is he? Will I have to go alone tonight?"

Inferences Based on Text Evidence	
You read	Sarah had been dressed and ready to go somewhere for more than an hour. She spent a lot of time selecting her dress and shoes. She threw her flower in the corner by the camera.
You infer	Sarah had plans to go somewhere special that evening and was waiting for her date. She cared a lot about the event she was going to. Someone is late, and she is angry at him.

Ask Questions

You can **ask questions** to learn new information, to clarify, and to understand or figure out what is important in a selection. Asking questions of yourself and the author while reading can help you locate information you might otherwise miss.

How to Self-Question

Ask yourself questions to understand something that is confusing, keep track of what is happening, or think about what you know.

Ask and Write Questions Use a question word such as *Who, What, When, Where, Why,* or *How* to write your questions.

Examples: How can I figure out what this word means? What are the characters doing? Why is this important? Do I agree with this?

Answer the Questions and Follow Up Use the text, photographs, or other visuals to answer your questions. Write your answer next to the question. Include the page number where you found the answer.

How to Question the Author

Sometimes, you may have questions about what the author is trying to tell you in a selection. Write these types of questions, and then try to answer them by reading the text. The answers to these questions are known as "author and you" answers.

Questions to Ask the Author

- What is the author trying to say here?
- What is the author talking about?
- Does the author explain his or her ideas clearly?
- Does the author support his or her ideas or opinions with facts?

How to Find Question-Answer Relationships

Where you find the answers to your questions is very important. Sometimes the answers are located right in the text. Other times, your questions require you to use ideas and information that are not in the text. Some questions can be answered by using your background knowledge on a topic. Read the chart to learn about question-answer relationships.

Type of Answer	How to Find the Answers
"Right There"	Sometimes you can simply point to the text and say that an answer to one of your questions is "right there."
"Think and Search"	Look back at the selection. Find the information the question is asking about. Think about how the information fits together to answer the question.
"Author and You"	Use ideas and information that are not stated directly in the text. Think about what you have read, and create your own ideas or opinions based on what you know about the author.
"On Your Own"	Use your feelings, what you already know, and your own experiences to find these answers.

Synthesize

When you **synthesize**, you gather your thoughts about what you have read to draw conclusions, make generalizations, and compare the information to information you've read in other texts. You form new overall understandings by putting together ideas and events.

How to Draw Conclusions

Reading is like putting a puzzle together. There are many different parts that come together to make up the whole selection. Synthesizing is the process of putting the pieces together while we read. We combine new information with what we already know to create an original idea or to form new understandings.

Read this passage and the text that follows to help you understand how to synthesize what you read.

Distracted Drivers

Cell phone use in cars has steadily risen in the past decade. Studies from the Departments of Highway Safety show that the more distracted drivers are, the more likely they are to be in an accident. Lawmakers in some states have successfully passed laws requiring drivers to use hands-free accessories while a vehicle is moving. This means they may use an earpiece or a speaker-phone device but not hold the phone in their hands. Many people feel that talking on cell phones is not the only distracting activity that should be illegal for drivers.

Use text evidence from the selection and your own experience to draw conclusions as you read.

Drawing Conclusions	
Look for Details	The more distracted a driver is, the more likely he or she is to be involved in an accident. Cell phones are distracting.
Think About What You Know	I know people who have been in car accidents while talking on their cell phones.
Decide What You Believe	Lawmakers should continue to work on laws to stop drivers from being distracted.

How to Make Generalizations

Generalizations are broad statements that apply to a group of people, a set of ideas, or the way things happen. You can make generalizations as you read, using experience and text evidence from a selection to help you.

- **Take notes about the facts or opinions** Look for the overall theme or message of the selection.
- **Add examples** Think about what you know about the topic from your own knowledge and experience.
- **Construct a generalization** Write a statement that combines the author's statements and your own.

  Example: *Using a cell phone while driving can make you have an accident.*

How to Compare Across Texts

Comparing two or more texts helps you combine ideas, develop judgments, and draw conclusions. Read the following paragraph, and think about how it connects to the paragraph on page 630.

Graduated Driver's License Programs

More and more states are creating graduated driver's license (GDL) laws. Studies show that these programs help teen driver accidents and deaths to decline. The programs differ from state to state, but most GDL programs require an adult with a valid driver's license to be present when a teen is driving, and a teen driver must enroll in a certified driver's education and training course. Each state has various restrictions for teen drivers and punishments for when those restrictions are ignored.

Think About Something You Have Already Read In "Distracted Drivers," you read that cell phones are distracting to drivers and that many people feel it should be illegal to use one while driving.

Think About What You Are Reading Right Now Many states have graduated driver's license programs. Accidents involving teen drivers have declined.

Compare Across Texts and Draw Conclusions Both articles are about laws related to driving. Lawmakers hope that all of the laws they pass related to driving will create safer driving conditions for everyone.

Comparing across texts can help you foster an argument or advance an opinion. Having multiple opinions and facts from different sources makes your argument or opinion more credible.

Visualize

When you **visualize**, you use your imagination to better understand what the author is describing. While reading, create an image or picture in your mind that represents what you are reading about. Look for words that tell how things look, sound, smell, taste, and feel.

My Favorite Car Is a Truck

My name is Stephen, and today was a magical day. I've been working hard and saving money all summer. I finally have enough money for a down payment on a new car. Today my father took me to a car dealership to pick out my car. I immediately found my favorite vehicle. It was a red, shiny pickup truck with gleaming wheels. I climbed inside and looked around. The brown seats were sparkling clean, and the truck still had that new car smell inside the cab. I put the key in the ignition and turned it on. The quiet hum of the engine made me so happy. After a long test-drive, my father and I agreed this was the truck for me.

How to Visualize Using Sketches

- **Read the Text** Look for words that help create pictures in your mind about the characters, setting, and events.
- **Picture the Information in Your Mind** Stop and focus on the descriptive words. Create pictures in your mind using these words.
- **Draw the Events** Sketch pictures to show what is happening. You could draw Stephen climbing inside the pickup truck.

How to Visualize Using Senses

- **Look for Words** Find adjectives and sensory words: smell, look, sound, taste, and feel. Stephen uses the words *red, shiny, with gleaming wheels; brown seats, sparkling clean; new car smell;* and *quiet hum of the engine* to talk about the truck.
- **Create a Picture in Your Mind of the Scene** What do you hear, feel, see, smell, and taste? Examine how these details improve your understanding.

  I smell: new car smell   **I hear:** engine humming

  I see: red, shiny truck   **I feel:** texture of the seats, the key

How to Recognize Emotional Responses

Do any of the words in the selection make you feel certain emotions? Asking yourself how you feel when you read can help you remember the information.

Example: I feel excited for the main character because I know what it's like to pick out something new.

Reading Fluency

What Is Reading Fluency?

Reading fluency is the ability to read smoothly and expressively with clear understanding. Fluent readers are able to better understand and enjoy what they read. Use the strategies that follow to build your fluency in these four key areas:

- accuracy and rate
- phrasing
- intonation
- expression

How to Improve Accuracy and Rate

Accuracy is the correctness of your reading. Rate is the speed of your reading.

How to read accurately:

- Use correct pronunciation.
- Emphasize correct syllables.

How to read with proper rate:

- Match your reading speed to what you are reading. For example, if you are reading an exciting story, read slightly faster. If you are reading a sad story, read slightly slower.
- Recognize and use punctuation.

Test your accuracy and rate:

- Choose a text you are familiar with, and practice reading it aloud or silently multiple times.
- Ask a friend to use a watch or clock to time you while you read a passage.
- Ask a friend or family member to read a passage for you, so you know what it should sound like.

Use the formula below to measure a reader's accuracy and rate while reading aloud. For passages to practice with, see **Reading Fluency Practice**, pp. 799–819.

Accuracy and Rate Formula

$$\underset{\substack{\text{words read} \\ \text{in one minute}}}{\underline{}} \quad - \quad \underset{\text{number of errors}}{\underline{}} \quad = \quad \underset{\substack{\text{words correct per minute} \\ \text{(wcpm)}}}{\underline{}}$$

How to Improve Intonation

Intonation is the rise and fall in the tone of your voice as you read aloud. It means the highness or lowness of the sound.

How to read with proper intonation:

- Change the sound of your voice to match what you are reading.
- Make your voice flow, or sound smooth, while you read.
- Make sure you are pronouncing words correctly.
- Raise the sound of your voice for words that should be stressed, or emphasized.
- Use visual clues. (see box below)

Visual Clue and Meaning	Example	How to Read It
Italics: draw attention to a word to show special importance	She is *smart*.	Emphasize "smart."
Dash: shows a quick break in a sentence	She is—smart.	Pause before saying "smart."
Exclamation: can represent energy, excitement, or anger	She is smart!	Make your voice louder at the end of the sentence.
All capital letters: can represent strong emphasis, or yelling	SHE IS SMART.	Emphasize the whole sentence.
Bold facing: draws attention to a word to show importance	She is **smart**.	Emphasize "smart."
Question mark: shows curiosity or confusion	She is smart?	Raise the pitch of your voice slightly at the end of the sentence.

Use the rubric below to measure how well a reader uses intonation while reading aloud. For intonation passages, see **Reading Fluency Practice**, pp. 799–819.

Intonation Rubric

1	2	3
The reader's tone does not change. The reading all sounds the same.	The reader's tone changes sometimes to match what is being read.	The reader's tone always changes to match what is being read.

How to Improve Phrasing

Phrasing is how you use your voice to group words together.

How to read with proper phrasing:

- Don't read too quickly or too slowly.
- Pause for key words within the text.
- Make sure your sentences sound smooth, not choppy.
- Make sure you sound like you are reading a sentence instead of a list.
- Use punctuation to tell you when to stop, pause, or emphasize. (see box below)

Punctuation	How to Use It
. period	stop at the end of the sentence
, comma	pause within the sentence
! exclamation point	emphasize the sentence and pause at the end
? question mark	emphasize the end of the sentence and pause at the end
; semicolon	pause within the sentence between two related thoughts
: colon	pause within the sentence before giving an example or explanation

One way to practice phrasing is to copy a passage, then place a slash (/), or pause mark, within a sentence where there should be a pause. One slash (/) means a short pause. Two slashes (//) mean a longer pause, such as a pause at the end of a sentence.

Read aloud the passage below, pausing at each pause mark. Then try reading the passage again without any pauses. Compare how you sound each time.

> There are many ways to get involved / in your school and community. // Joining a club / or trying out for a sports team / are a few of the options. // Volunteer work can also be very rewarding. // You can volunteer at community centers, / nursing homes, / or animal shelters. //

Use the rubric below to measure how well a reader uses phrasing while reading aloud. For phrasing passages, see **Reading Fluency Practice**, pp. 799–819.

Phrasing Rubric		
1	**2**	**3**
Reading is choppy. There are few pauses for punctuation.	Reading is mostly smooth. There are some pauses for punctuation.	Reading is very smooth. Punctuation is being used properly.

How to Improve Expression

Expression in reading is how you use your voice to express feeling.

How to read with proper expression:

- Match the sound of your voice to what you are reading. For example, read louder and faster to show strong feeling. Read slower and quieter to show sadness or seriousness.
- Match the sound of your voice to the genre. For example, read a fun, fictional story using a fun, friendly voice. Read an informative, nonfiction article using an even tone and a more serious voice.
- Avoid speaking in monotone, or using only one tone in your voice.
- Pause for emphasis and exaggerate letter sounds to match the mood or theme of what you are reading.

Practice incorrect expression by reading this sentence without changing the tone of your voice: *I am so excited!* Now read the sentence again with proper expression: *I am so excited!* The way you use your voice while reading can help you to better understand what is happening in the text.

For additional practice, read the sentences below aloud with and without changing your expression. Compare how you sound each time.

- I am very sad.
- That was the most *boring* movie I have ever seen.
- We won the game!

Use the rubric below to measure how well a reader uses expression while reading aloud. For expression passages, see **Reading Fluency Practice**, pp. 799–819.

Expression Rubric		
1	**2**	**3**
The reader sounds monotone. The reader's voice does not match the subject of what is being read.	The reader is making some tone changes. Sometimes, the reader's voice matches what is being read.	The reader is using proper tones and pauses. The reader's voice matches what is being read.

Reading Fluency Practice

Practice Phrasing: "Who We Really Are"

Phrasing is how you use your voice to group words together. Use this passage to practice reading with proper phrasing. Print a copy of this passage from myNGconnect.com to help you monitor your progress. To use a Phrasing Rubric, see page 797.

Tamisha's box includes a picture of her smiling at the center, her braces still on. On the left side of the installation there's a cluster of photographs from her childhood; on the right, pictures of her now, with her family and friends.

"We're invisible to the media and just about everybody else out there," writes Delpheanea, 16. No matter, she does well for herself and lists, beside her picture, a long group of positive accomplishments. She gets good grades, she's engaged, and she's only been late to class twice this year. And she also has, if she does say so herself, a beautiful smile.

"This group is a gateway to freedom, a way to express yourself without someone judging," another sheet reads. "Our hope for the show is to be a messenger, to tell people about ourselves and what we do, to tell our stories. We hope you will get to know who we really are."

From "Who We Really Are," page 29

Practice Expression: "Two Kinds"

Expression in reading is how you use your voice to express feeling. Use this passage to practice reading with proper expression. Print a copy of this passage from myNGconnect.com to help you monitor your progress. To use an Expression Rubric, see page 798.

When my turn came, I was very confident. I remember my childish excitement. It was as if I knew, without a doubt, that the prodigy side of me really did exist. I had no fear whatsoever, no nervousness. I remember thinking to myself, This is it! This is it! I looked out over the audience, at my mother's blank face, my father's yawn, Auntie Lindo's stiff-lipped smile, Waverly's sulky expression. I had on a white dress layered with sheets of lace, and a pink bow in my Peter Pan haircut. As I sat down I envisioned people jumping to their feet and Ed Sullivan rushing up to introduce me to everyone on TV.

And I started to play. It was so beautiful. I was so caught up in how lovely I looked that at first I didn't worry how I would sound. So it was a surprise to me when I hit the first wrong note and I realized something didn't sound quite right. And then I hit another and another followed that. A chill started at the top of my head and began to trickle down. Yet I couldn't stop playing, as though my hands were bewitched. I kept thinking my fingers would adjust themselves back, like a train switching to the right track. I played this strange jumble through two repeats, the sour notes staying with me all the way to the end.

From "Two Kinds," page 41

Practice Intonation: "Skins"

Intonation is the rise and fall in the pitch or tone of your voice as you read aloud. Use this passage to practice reading with proper intonation. Print a copy of this passage from myNGconnect.com to help you monitor your progress. To use an Intonation Rubric, see page 796.

Randolph and his twin sisters were not smiling as they stood in the entrance to the school cafeteria that first day. People mumbled "Scuse me" as they slipped by, but no one made eye contact. No one shook hands. Maybe it was because no one knew what to say. Our images of African American teenagers up here in the sticks are what we get from TV, where rappers and gang-bangers predominate. What would the proper greeting be? "Yo, dog, whazzup?" or just a normal North Country "Hiya." Despite the fact that the White kids wore clothes so top-of-the-line that they might have been fashion models, everyone was avoiding them. It was obviously making Randolph and his sisters feel like four-day-old road kill.

It made me want to yell, "What's wrong with everyone!"

I didn't, though. Instead I walked across the room, sort of in their direction, with my lunch tray in my hand.

From "Skins," page 73

Practice Phrasing: "La Vida Robot"

Phrasing is how you use your voice to group words together. Use this passage to practice reading with proper phrasing. Print a copy of this passage from myNGconnect.com to help you monitor your progress. To use a Phrasing Rubric, see page 797.

Carl Hayden Community High School doesn't have a swimming pool, so one weekend in May, after about six weeks of work in the classroom, the team took Stinky to a scuba training pool in downtown Phoenix for its baptism. Luis hefted the machine up and gently placed it in the water. They powered it up. Cristian had hacked together off-the-shelf joysticks, a motherboard, motors, and an array of onboard finger-sized video cameras, which now sent flickering images to black-and-white monitors on a folding picnic table. Using five small electric trolling motors, the robot could spin and tilt in any direction. To move smoothly, two drivers had to coordinate their commands. The first thing they did was smash the robot into a wall.

"This is good, this is good," Oscar kept repeating, buying himself a few seconds to come up with a positive spin. "Did you see how hard it hit the wall? This thing's got power. Once we figure out how to drive it, we'll be the fastest team there."

From "La Vida Robot," page 131

Practice Expression: "My Left Foot"

Expression in reading is how you use your voice to express feeling. Use this passage to practice reading with proper expression. To use an Expression Rubric, see page 798.

"Try again, Chris," she whispered in my ear.

Again.

I did. I stiffened my body and put my left foot out again, for the third time. I drew one side of the letter. I drew half the other side. Then the stick of chalk broke and I was left with a stump. I wanted to fling it away and give up. Then I felt my mother's hand on my shoulder. I tried once more. Out went my foot. I shook, I sweated and strained every muscle. My hands were so tightly clenched that my fingernails bit into the flesh. I set my teeth so hard that I nearly pierced my lower lip. Everything in the room swam till the faces around me were mere patches of white. But—I drew it—*the letter* "A." There it was on the floor before me. Shaky, with awkward, wobbly sides and a very uneven center line. But it *was* the letter "A." I looked up. I saw my mother's face for a moment, tears on her cheeks. Then my father stooped down and hoisted me on to his shoulder.

I had done it!

From "My Left Foot," page 165

Practice Intonation: "The Freedom Writers Diary"

Intonation is the rise and fall in the pitch or tone of your voice as you read aloud. Use this passage to practice reading with proper intonation. Print a copy of this passage from myNGconnect.com to help you monitor your progress. To use an Intonation Rubric, see page 796.

At the end of the video, a fellow classmate asked the question, "They fought racism by riding the bus?" That was it! The bells were ringing, the sirens were sounding. It hit me! The Freedom Riders fought intolerance by riding a bus and pushing racial limits in the deep South. Then somebody suggested that we name ourselves the Freedom Writers, in honor of the Freedom Riders. Why not? It's perfect! But those are huge shoes to fill, so if we're going to take their name, we better take their courage and conviction. It's one thing to ride a bus, but they eventually had to get off and face the music.

So, it's one thing for us to write diaries like Anne and Zlata, but if we want to be like the Freedom Riders, we need to take that extra step. Just like Anne's story made it out of the attic and Zlata's out of the basement, I hope our stories make it out of Room 203. Now when I write, I'll remember Jim's work and what he risked his life for. Like him, I am willing to step forward, unafraid of who or what lies ahead. After all, history tells me that I am not alone.

From "The Freedom Writers Diary," page 191

Practice Intonation: "Amigo Brothers"

Intonation is the rise and fall in the pitch or tone of your voice as you read aloud. Use this passage to practice reading with proper intonation. Print a copy of this passage from myNGconnect.com to help you monitor your progress. To use an Intonation Rubric, see page 796.

After a mile or so, Felix puffed and said, "Let's stop a while, bro. I think we both got something to say to each other."

Antonio nodded. It was not natural to be acting as though nothing unusual was happening when two ace-boon buddies were going to be blasting each other within a few short days.

They rested their elbows on the railing separating them from the river. Antonio wiped his face with his short towel. The sunrise was now creating day.

Felix leaned heavily on the river's railing and stared across to the shores of Brooklyn. Finally, he broke the silence.

"Man, I don't know how to come out with it."

Antonio helped. "It's about our fight, right?"

"Yeah, right." Felix's eyes squinted at the rising orange sun.

"I've been thinking about it too, *panín*. In fact, since we found out it was going to be me and you, I've been awake at night, pulling punches on you, trying not to hurt you."

"Same here. It ain't natural not to think about the fight. I mean, we both are *cheverote* fighters and we both want to win. But only one of us can win."

From "Amigo Brothers," page 245

Practice Phrasing: "My Brother's Keeper"

Phrasing is how you use your voice to group words together. Use this passage to practice reading with proper phrasing. Print a copy of this passage from myNGconnect.com to help you monitor your progress. To use a Phrasing Rubric, see page 797.

Jamie was tall but his head barely reached Ted's shoulder.

He felt a deep tremor of love for the big man and then the tremor was gone.

The bleak feeling was back within him.

"I need you. Need you a lot," Ted murmured.

Jamie slowly drew away.

"Let's go into the kitchen and have a cup of coffee, Ted. You look like you could use one."

"Sure. Whatever you say."

"Then we'll talk," Jamie said softly.

"Anything. Anything you say."

Then Ted followed his smaller brother into the neat, yellow kitchen, lifted a heavy wooden chair, swung it about, set it down without a sound and slid into it gracefully.

It was all done in one smooth, flowing motion.

And watching him, Jamie thought of the times he had watched Ted weave and run and evade tacklers with an effortless grace.

From "My Brother's Keeper," page 273

Practice Expression: "The Hand of Fatima"

Expression in reading is how you use your voice to express feeling. Use this passage to practice reading with proper expression. Print a copy of this passage from myNGconnect.com to help you monitor your progress. To use an Expression Rubric, see page 798.

Sitt Zeina was telling her husband, in no uncertain terms, "We *must* have that garden wall repaired, Yusuf. You know, where the old fig tree is pushing it over. You've put it off long enough, and costs are going up every day. Besides, there's a lot more we should do with the garden."

Before Dr. Jubeili could answer, one of the guests broke in with a laugh. "What are you thinking of, Zeina? Big ideas for the Jubeili estate?"

"Oh, nothing too extravagant," she answered. "Just terraces for my roses, with good walls of well-fitted stones. There aren't many fine old villas like ours left close to Beirut—what with those dreadful apartment buildings springing up everywhere. We must make the most of this one."

Aneesi could hear Dr. Jubeili sigh. "Zeina, have you any idea what workers are getting paid these days? Stonemasons can charge whatever they want. Lebanese ones, that is. Syrian workers are cheaper—but just try to find one who knows how to do good stonework."

From "The Hand of Fatima," page 305

Practice Intonation: "Silent Language"

Intonation is the rise and fall in the pitch or tone of your voice as you read aloud. Use this passage to practice reading with proper intonation. Print a copy of this passage from myNGconnect.com to help you monitor your progress. To use an Intonation Rubric, see page 796.

Crossing Your Arms and Legs

THE PROBLEM: This gesture says, "I'm closed to whatever you're saying," "I wish I weren't here," or "I'm protecting myself from something."

HOW TO FIX IT: Find something comfortable to do with your arms other than crossing them, says communication coach Carmine Gallo, author of *10 Simple Secrets of the World's Greatest Business Communicators*. Try putting one hand in your pocket to train your body to get used to a more open feeling. "Placing both hands in your pockets will make you look nervous or uninterested," Gallo says. "Plus, having the other hand free to gesture makes you seem more confident." Holding something (a glass, a notebook) can also remind you not to cross your arms. And practice sitting with your arms relaxed, hands in lap, and legs side by side.

From "Silent Language," page 375

Practice Expression: "Breaking the Ice"

Expression in reading is how you use your voice to express feeling. Use this passage to practice reading with proper expression. Print a copy of this passage from myNGconnect.com to help you monitor your progress. To use an Expression Rubric, see page 798.

Thus it was that, finally, Judy and I went on an actual date, to see a movie in White Plains, New York. If I were to sum up the romantic ambience of this date in four words, those words would be: "My mother was driving." This made for an extremely quiet drive, because my mother, realizing that her presence was hideously embarrassing, had to pretend she wasn't there. If it had been legal, I think she would have got out and sprinted alongside the car, steering through the window. Judy and I, sitting in the back seat about seventy-five feet apart, were also silent, unable to communicate without the assistance of Phil, Nancy, and Sandy.

After what seemed like several years, we got to the movie theater, where my mother went off to sit in the Parents and Lepers Section. The movie was called *North to Alaska*, but I can tell you nothing else about it because I spent the whole time wondering whether it would be necessary to amputate my right arm, which was not getting any blood flow as a result of being perched for two hours like a petrified snake on the back of Judy's seat exactly one molecule away from physical contact.

From "Breaking the Ice," page 401

Practice Phrasing: "How I Learned English"

Phrasing is how you use your voice to group words together. Use this passage to practice reading with proper phrasing. Print a copy of this passage from myNGconnect.com to help you monitor your progress. To use a Phrasing Rubric, see page 797.

> And there I was,
> Just off the plane and plopped in the middle
> Of Williamsport, Pa. and a neighborhood game,
> Unnatural and without any moves,
> My notions of baseball and America
> Growing fuzzier each time I whiffed.
> So it was not impossible that I,
> Banished to the outfield and daydreaming
> Of water, or a hotel in the mountains,
> Would suddenly find myself in the path
> Of a ball stung by Joe Barone.
> I watched it closing in
> Clean and untouched, transfixed
> By its easy arc before it hit
> My forehead with a thud.
>   I fell back,
> Dazed, clutching my brow,
> Groaning, "Oh my shin, oh my shin,"
> And everybody peeled away from me
> And dropped from laughter, and there we were,
> All of us writhing on the ground for one reason
> Or another.

From "How I Learned English," page 424

Practice Phrasing: "Say It with Flowers"

Phrasing is how you use your voice to group words together. Use this passage to practice reading with proper phrasing. Print a copy of this passage from myNGconnect.com to help you monitor your progress. To use a Phrasing Rubric, see page 797.

He was a strange one to come to the shop and ask Mr. Sasaki for a job, but at the time I kept my mouth shut. There was something about this young man's appearance which I could not altogether harmonize with a job as a clerk in a flower shop. I was a delivery boy for Mr. Sasaki then. I had seen clerks come and go, and although they were of various sorts of temperaments and conducts, all of them had the technique of waiting on the customers or acquired one eventually. You could never tell about a new one, however, and to be on the safe side I said nothing and watched our boss readily take on this young man. Anyhow we were glad to have an extra hand.

Mr. Sasaki undoubtedly remembered last year's rush when Tommy, Mr. Sasaki, and I had to do everything and had our hands tied behind our backs for having so many things to do at one time. He wanted to be ready this time. "Another clerk and we'll be all set for any kind of business," he used to tell us. When Teruo came around looking for a job, he got it, and Morning Glory Flower Shop was all set for the year as far as our boss was concerned.

From "Say It with Flowers," page 461

Practice Intonation: "Just Lather, That's All"

Intonation is the rise and fall in the pitch or tone of your voice as you read aloud. Use this passage to practice reading with proper intonation. Print a copy of this passage from myNGconnect.com to help you monitor your progress. To use an Intonation Rubric, see page 796.

I took the razor, opened up the two protective arms, exposed the blade, and began the job, from one of the sideburns downward. The razor responded beautifully. His beard was inflexible and hard, not too long, but thick. Bit by bit the skin emerged. The razor rasped along, making its customary sound as fluffs of lather mixed with bits of hair gathered along the blade. I paused a moment to clean it, then took up the strop again to sharpen the razor, because I'm a barber who does things properly.

The man, who had kept his eyes closed, opened them now, removed one of his hands from under the sheet, felt the spot on his face where the soap had been cleared off, and said, "Come to the school today at six o'clock."

"The same thing as the other day?" I asked horrified.

"It could be better," he replied.

"What do you plan to do?"

"I don't know yet. But we'll amuse ourselves."

Once more he leaned back and closed his eyes. I approached him with the razor poised.

"Do you plan to punish them all?" I asked timidly.

"All."

From "Just Lather, That's All," page 485

Practice Expression: "Be-ers and Doers"

Expression in reading is how you use your voice to express feeling. Use this passage to practice reading with proper expression. Print a copy of this passage from myNGconnect.com to help you monitor your progress. To use an Expression Rubric, see page 798.

We were all home for Christmas the year Albert turned eighteen. Maudie was having her Christmas break from teaching, and she was looking skinnier and more tight-lipped than I remembered her. I was there with my husband and my new baby, Jennifer, and Albert was even quieter than usual. But content, I thought. Not making any waves. Mom had intensified her big campaign to have him go to Acadia University in the fall. "Pre-law," she said, "or maybe teacher training. Anyways, you gotta go. A man has to be successful." She avoided my father's eyes. "In the fall," she said. "For sure."

"It's Christmas," said Dad, without anger. "Let's just be happy and forget all them plans for a few days." He was sitting at the kitchen table breaking up the bread slowly, slowly, for the turkey stuffing. He chuckled. "I've decided to be a doer this Christmas."

"And if the doin's bein' done at that speed," she said, taking the bowl from him, "we'll be eatin' Christmas dinner on New Year's Day." She started to break up the bread so quickly that you could hardly focus on her flying fingers.

From "Be-ers and Doers," page 507

Practice Phrasing: "Too Young to Drive?"

Phrasing is how you use your voice to group words together. Use this passage to practice reading with proper phrasing. Print a copy of this passage from myNGconnect.com to help you monitor your progress. To use a Phrasing Rubric, see page 797.

The cause of most fatal car crashes involving teenagers is not poor visibility or road conditions. It's poor judgment.

The lack of experience and immaturity of young drivers leads them to be overrepresented in accident statistics: 16-year-old drivers account for the highest percentages of crashes involving speeding, single vehicles, and driver error.

Parents often overestimate their children's proficiency behind the wheel. After their teens pass driver's education and the on-road test, parents hand over the keys. Unfortunately, the evidence suggests that only one thing reliably transforms a teenager into a good driver— growing up.

Driver education programs have been found to have little to no effect on reducing teen crashes. What does seem to work is limiting how early and how much teens can drive and how many passengers they can transport.

The older newly licensed drivers are, the less likely they are to crash, which is why Georgia ought to raise its driving age to 17 and its permit age to 16. Teen drivers should not be allowed to carry nonfamily members in the car during their first year. This precaution protects both them and their friends. In 2004, 62 percent of teenage passengers killed in crashes were traveling in cars driven by other teens.

From "Too Young to Drive?" page 562

Practice Expression: "Piracy Bites!"

Expression in reading is how you use your voice to express feeling. Use this passage to practice reading with proper expression. Print a copy of this passage from myNGconnect.com to help you monitor your progress. To use an Expression Rubric, see page 798.

Pirates were a major presence in the 17th and 18th centuries. These buccaneers wreaked havoc on the high seas by sailing the trade routes in search of vessels loaded with goods and merchandise to seize.

Stolen cargo at the hands of pirates not only created an economic loss for the merchant but also financed future illegal activities for the pirates who took it.

One could complete a transatlantic voyage today without ever spotting a pirate ship. Most people would say that pirates no longer exist, unless you count the Pirates of the Caribbean ride in Disneyland. Unfortunately, it isn't true.

Pirates still exist, but they aren't like the pirates of the past. These modern day thieves are engaged in the theft of intellectual property. And their impact is colossal.

From "Piracy Bites!," page 586

Practice Intonation: "Long Walk to Freedom"

Intonation is the rise and fall in the pitch or tone of your voice as you read aloud. Use this passage to practice reading with proper intonation. Print a copy of this passage from myNGconnect.com to help you monitor your progress. To use an Intonation Rubric, see page 796.

Today, all of us do, by our presence here . . . confer glory and hope to newborn liberty. Out of the experience of an extraordinary human disaster that lasted too long, must be born a society of which all humanity will be proud.

. . . We, who were outlaws not so long ago, have today been given the rare privilege to be host to the nations of the world on our own soil. We thank all of our distinguished international guests for having come to take possession with the people of our country of what is, after all, a common victory for justice, for peace, for human dignity.

We have, at last, achieved our political emancipation. We pledge ourselves to liberate all our people from the continuing bondage of poverty, deprivation, suffering, gender, and other discrimination.

Never, never, and never again shall it be that this beautiful land will again experience the oppression of one by another. . . . The sun shall never set on so glorious a human achievement. Let freedom reign. God bless Africa!

From "Long Walk to Freedom," page 609

Practice Expression: "The Jewels of the Shrine"

Expression in reading is how you use your voice to express feeling. Use this passage to practice reading with proper expression. Print a copy of this passage from myNGconnect.com to help you monitor your progress. To use an Expression Rubric, see page 798.

STRANGER. Let us not waste time on questions. This box was buried in the floor of your grandfather's room. [*He places the box on the table*; AROB *and* OJIMA *crowd together.* STRANGER *speaks sternly.*] Give me room, please. Your grandfather always wanted you to crowd around him. But no one would, until he was about to die. Step back, please.

[*Both* AROB *and* OJIMA *step back.* OJIMA *accidently steps on* AROB.]

AROB. [*to* OJIMA] Don't you step on me!

OJIMA. [*querulously*] Don't you shout at me!

[STRANGER *looks at both.*]

AROB. When I sat day and night watching Grandfather in his illness, you were away in town, dancing and getting drunk. Now you want to be the first to grab at everything.

OJIMA. You liar! It was I who took care of him.

AROB. You only took care of him when you knew that he had come to some wealth.

BASSI. Why can't both of you—

AROB. [*very sharply*] Keep out of this, woman. That pretender [*pointing to* OJIMA] wants to bring trouble today.

OJIMA. I, a pretender? What of you, who began to scratch the old man's back simply to get his money?

AROB. How dare you insult me like that!

From "The Jewels of the Shrine," page 663

Practice Intonation: "Romeo and Juliet"

Intonation is the rise and fall in the pitch or tone of your voice as you read aloud. Use this passage to practice reading with proper intonation. Print a copy of this passage from myNGconnect.com to help you monitor your progress. To use an Intonation Rubric, see page 796.

Romeo. Mercutio makes fun of love's scars: He's never felt love's wound.

[*He sees* Juliet *at the window of Capulet's house.*]

But quiet! What's that light shining through the window over there? It's like I'm looking east, and Juliet is the sun. Juliet, my beautiful sun, rise and shine; your brightness will make the moon disappear! That moon is like a woman who's sick with jealousy because she knows you're prettier than she is. Don't be the moon's maid if that's her attitude. Besides, the moonlight is like an ugly green outfit. Only clowns dress like that. Don't put it on!

[*Juliet walks onto the balcony.*]

It's the woman I love! If only she knew it! Her lips are moving, but I don't hear her saying anything. No problem. That look in her eye says it all, so I'll just talk to her eyes.

[*Romeo opens his mouth to address her, but his courage fails.*]

I'm too confident. It's not me she's talking to, but the stars. Two of the most beautiful stars in the sky have asked her eyes to take their place for a while. What if Juliet's eyes and the stars have changed places? The glow of Juliet's cheeks would make those stars look dim, the way daylight outshines a lamp. Her eyes, sparkling so brightly in heaven, would make birds sing, because they'd think it was the dawn of a new day. See how she rests her cheek on her hand! I wish I were a glove on that hand, so I could touch her cheek!

From "Romeo and Juliet" page 705

Practice Phrasing: "Hard Questions"

Phrasing is how you use your voice to group words together. Use this passage to practice reading with proper phrasing. Print a copy of this passage from myNGconnect.com to help you monitor your progress. To use a Phrasing Rubric, see page 797.

Why not mark out the land
into neat rectangles
squares and clover leafs?

Put on them cubes of
5   varying sizes
according to use—
dwellings
    singles/multiples
complexes
10   commercial/industrial.

Bale them together with
bands of roads.

What if a child shall cry
"I have never known spring!
15   I have never seen autumn!"

What if a man shall say
"I have never heard
silence fraught with living as
in swamp or forest!"
20   What if the eye shall never see
marsh birds and muskrats?

Does not the heart need
wildness?
Does not the thought need
25   something
to rest upon
not self-made by man,
a bosom
not his own?

From "Poems for the Earth" page 729

Study Skills and Strategies

Before You Study

Studying can be difficult, especially when you are distracted or have many subjects you need to study all at the same time. There are several ways to prepare to study, including creating a routine and establishing a productive study environment. You can also make studying easier by studying subjects in a specific order and creating a schedule.

How to Create and Maintain a Study Routine

Before you begin studying, create a routine.

- Study at the same time and place for each session.
- Mark the study time in your calendar as an appointment, like going to the doctor. For example, *Tuesday: 3:30–4:30: Study English.*
- Set small, specific goals for each study session.
- Pay attention to what works best for you and repeat that method.
- Give yourself a small reward when you are finished. For example, call a friend or listen to your favorite music.

How to Create a Productive Study Environment

Setting up a study area will help you follow your routine. Find an area where you are comfortable that you can claim as your own.

Set Up Your Workplace
• Make sure your area is quiet or has background noise, depending on which you prefer.
• Make sure you have enough light—get an extra lamp if your area is too dark.
• Have everything you need for studying available beforehand.
• Designate certain places for each necessary item. Don't waste valuable time looking for books, notes, writing materials, self-stick notes, or information.
• After you have assembled the items you need, put them where you can easily access them.
• Keep a calendar and a watch or clock in your study area to help you stay focused on your available time and on your priorities.
• Keep your study area clean.

How to Create an Efficient Study Order

Creating priorities for study time will help you complete your tasks in an efficient order. Making a list of the things you need to do can help you organize your priorities. Look at the chart to understand how to create an efficient order for your study time.

Study Order Tips	
Label Your Assignments by Priority	• **Urgent** Must be done immediately • **Important** Must be done soon • **Upcoming** Must be done in the near future
Make a List	• List the things you have to do in order of importance. • Once you complete a task, cross it off your list.
Stay Organized	• Keep your list nearby to record new tasks or updates.

How to Complete Tasks on Schedule

A good schedule can help you stay focused and complete assignments on time. Create a schedule or purchase a day planner and record homework due dates, quizzes, and tests.

Think about events that might affect your schedule, such as appointments or extracurricular activities. You may need to postpone or cancel other plans to help you stay on schedule. If you are concerned about missing a date, circle the task.

	Weekly Schedule				
Subject	**Monday**	**Tuesday**	**Wednesday**	**Thursday**	**Friday**
Math	Chapter 6: Problems 1-10	None	Chapter 6: Problems 11-20	None	Chapter 7: Problems 1-15
Science	Study for Test	Review for Test	Test	Read Chapter 8	None
History	None	Read Chapter 11	Read Chapter 12	Study for Quiz	Quiz: Chapters 11 and 12
English	Read Chapter 3	Read Chapter 4 Study for Quiz	Quiz: Chapters 3 and 4	Read Chapter 5	None

While You Study

There are many different ways to study. Talk with classmates and your teachers to learn new study techniques and strategies that might work for you, too. No matter which study strategies you use, you should use a variety, such as writing and using graphic organizers, until you figure out which strategies work best for you.

How to Use Writing as a Study Tool

Use writing as a tool to assist you:

- Write your own questions about the topic, and practice answering them.
- Condense your classroom notes onto note cards or into charts for easier reviewing.
- Create an outline from your notes, and then write a summary of the information.
- Write notes on self-stick notes as you read. Later, attach the self-stick notes in an organized manner to a sheet of notebook paper for at-a-glance study.

How to Use Graphic Organizers as a Study Tool

Graphic organizers are effective study tools. For example, a time line can be used to organize the events covered in a nonfiction selection. A word web can be used to learn new vocabulary words. See the Index of Graphic Organizers on page Index 1 for more examples of graphic organizers you can use as study tools.

How to Review

It is very important to review material. The best time to review is right after you have finished reading something for the first time. Reviewing gives you an opportunity to figure out anything you do not understand and to better remember information in the future.

Review Effectively

- When you read something new, review the information on the same day.
- Reread information to measure what you have learned.
- Go over notes in detail to clarify information you may have missed or don't understand. Combine your notes with any outlines or study guides that you have about the topic.
- Write down any new questions you may have.
- Plan a time to review each day. This will help you learn to review information regularly as part of your daily study schedule.

How to Use a Learning Log and Set Goals

You can use learning logs to record what you have learned, what you found interesting, and questions you have about the text. The purpose of a learning log is to think about your understanding of the material and to clarify your knowledge for further study. Use the **What parts am I struggling with?** and **What will I do next?** columns in the learning log to set future learning goals.

Learning Log			
Title of Selection:			
Dates and page numbers	What have I learned?	What parts am I struggling with?	What will I do next?

How to Seek Help

There will be times when you don't understand certain information, even after studying and careful note taking. You will need to seek help to understand the information. Make a list of the topics or problems that you don't understand. Include the page numbers where they are located in your textbooks. Make a chart that lists people and places you can seek help from. Then use these resources to help clarify confusing information.

Resources for Help

People: teachers, parents, siblings, classmates, librarians, tutors

Places: libraries, museums, study centers, school

Reference Sources: dictionaries, thesauruses, encyclopedias, atlases, newspapers, magazines, Web sites, television programs

How to Make Words Your Own Routine

When you cook, you follow the steps of a recipe. This helps you make the food correctly. When you read, there are also steps you can follow to learn new words. The following steps will help you practice the words in different ways and make the words your own.

Learning a Word

Follow these steps to add new words to your vocabulary.

1. **Pronounce the Word** Write and say the word one syllable at a time.
   - **realize**: re-a-lize
   - Think about what looks familiar in the word. For example, *real* is part of *realize*.
2. **Study Examples** When you are given examples, read them carefully and think about how and why the word is being used.
   - **Example**: *Marietta did not **realize** that Lupe was so busy.* What does this sentence tell you about Marietta and Lupe?
   - Look for more examples to study in books or magazines.
3. **Elaborate** Create new sentences to check your understanding of the word.
   - Finish these sentence frames for practice:
   - I **realized** I was happy when _____.
   - Steve's mom **realized** he was growing up when _____.
   - How did your teacher **realize** that you _____?
4. **Practice the Words** Use the new word to write sentences.
   - Use the word in many different ways. This will help you remember the word and understand its meaning.

How to Relate Words

A good way to build your vocabulary is to **relate new words** to words or concepts you already know. Think about how the new word is similar to or different from words you are already familiar with. You can also create a **semantic map** to help you study the new word.

Semantic Map

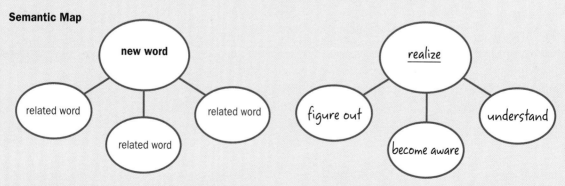

How to Use Context to Understand Words

Context is the surrounding text near a word or phrase that helps explain the meaning of the word or phrase.

Unfamiliar Words

Context clues are hints in a sentence or paragraph that can help define unknown or unfamiliar words. Context clues can include synonyms, antonyms, explanations, definitions, examples, sensory images, or punctuation, such as commas and dashes.

- **Example**: *My fascination with* celestial bodies—*such as* **stars**, **planets**, *and* **moons**—*made me want to buy a* **telescope**. The words *stars*, *planets*, and *moons* are clues that tell me *celestial bodies* are objects in the universe. The word *telescope* tells me I can see these objects from Earth, probably at night.

Multiple-Meaning Words

Some words have different meanings depending on how they are used in a sentence. Check what context the words are used in to help determine which meaning is correct in the material you are reading. Substitute each meaning you know in the context of the sentence until you find the use that makes the best sense.

- **Example**: *Please sign your name before entering the museum.* The word *sign* has more than one meaning. Which meaning is correct in this sentence? *Sign* can mean "to write" or it can mean "something that hangs on a wall to provide information." The first meaning is correct.

Figurative Language

Figurative language is a tool that writers use to help you visualize or relate to what is happening in a selection. This type of language is nonliteral because it does not mean exactly what it looks like it says, or it is using a special meaning. Idioms, similes, and metaphors are common types of nonliteral, or figurative language. It is helpful to use mental images or context clues to better understand what you are reading.

Idioms

An **idiom** is a phrase or an expression that can only be understood as a complete sentence or phrase. The individual words have separate meanings and they will not make sense if they are thought of literally. Read the words before or after the idiom to figure out the meaning. Remember to think about an idiom as a group of words, not as individual words.

- **Example**: Don't *bite off more than you can chew* or you will never finish the job. This is an idiom used to advise people against agreeing to do more work than they are capable of doing. It is not a phrase about biting or chewing.

Similes and Metaphors

Similes use *like* or *as* to compare two things.

- **Example**: *The willow tree's branches are like silken thread.* This simile is comparing a tree's branches to silk thread. Think about the things that are being compared and what they each mean. Silk is very soft and smooth. The simile means the willow's branches are also very soft and smooth.

Metaphors compare two things without using *like* or *as.*

- **Example**: *The night sky is a black curtain.* This metaphor compares the night sky to a black curtain. A black curtain would block out light from coming in a window. This metaphor means the night sky is very dark.

- **Example**: *The company planned an advertising blitz to promote its new product.* The word *blitz* comes from the German word *blitzkrieg,* which refers to the bombing of London, England, by Germany during World War II. The term *advertising blitz,* therefore, is a metaphor that expresses the way advertisements will overwhelm the public.

You can also use sensory images to learn new words by asking yourself or others: What does it look like? Feel like? Sound like?

Technical and Specialized Language

Technical, or specialized, language provides important information about a topic. Many words in English have an everyday meaning and a special meaning in a career field. For example, the word *shift* can mean "to move something from one place to another." In the workplace, however, *shift* can mean "a time period for work."

Example: *Be sure to clean your mouse regularly to make the cursor move smoothly on the computer monitor.*

- Read the sentence to determine the specialized subject.
- Identify technical vocabulary: *mouse, cursor, computer monitor.*
- Use context clues to help you figure out the meaning of the technical language, or jargon.

Denotation and Connotation

Denotation is the actual meaning of a word that you would find in a dictionary. For example, if you looked up the word *snake* in the dictionary, you could find that one of its meanings is "a limbless scaled reptile with a long tapering body."

Connotation is the suggested meaning of the word in addition to its literal meaning. Connotations can be positive or negative. For example, the word *snake* can be used in a positive or negative way.

- **Example**: *Jenny was caught sneaking around Maria's locker. She wanted to steal Maria's homework and copy Maria's answers. Nobody could believe that Jenny would be such a snake.*

By using the context of the paragraph (*sneaking around, steal*), you can understand that the connotation of *snake* in this usage is negative.

Analogies

An **analogy** is a comparison. Think of analogies as word problems. To solve the analogy, figure out what the connection is. Use context to see how the word pairs are related.

- **Example**: *Hard* is to *rocks* as *soft* is to _____. *Hard* describes the feeling of *rocks*. Rocks are hard. What does *soft* describe the feeling of? *Hard* is to *rocks* as *soft* is to *blankets*.

Use the relationships between words in an analogy to infer the meaning of an unfamiliar word. For example, in the analogy "*sparse* is to *meager* as *quarrel* is to *argue*," you can infer that *sparse* and *meager* mean the same thing.

Allusions

An **allusion** is a reference to another text. If you know or can find out about the source that the writer is alluding to, you can better understand the word or phrase.

- **Example**: "It took a herculean effort, but she finally made it to graduation." *Herculean* refers to a character from Greek mythology named Hercules. He fought monsters and faced many dangers. So the character must have faced challenges too.

How to Analyze Word Parts

Each piece in a puzzle fits together to make a picture. Words have pieces that come together, too. Analyzing the parts, or structures, of words will help you learn the meaning of entire words. Use a print or electronic dictionary to confirm your word analysis.

Compound Words

Compound words are made when two separate words are combined to make a new word. To learn the meaning of a compound word, study its parts individually. For example, *doghouse* is one word made from two smaller words, *dog* and *house*. Since you know that *dog* is an animal and *house* is a structure where people live, you can figure out that *doghouse* means a house for a dog.

Greek and Latin Roots

Many words in the English language derived from, or came from, other languages, especially Greek and Latin. It is helpful to know the **origins**, or **roots**, of English words. You may be able to figure out the meaning of an unknown word if you know the meaning of its root. Roots can form many different words and can't be broken into smaller parts. The chart below has examples of roots.

Root Chart		
Root	**Meaning**	**English Example**
crit (Greek)	to judge	*Criticize* means "to find fault." *Critique* means "an act of judgment."
mal (Latin)	bad	*Malady* means "an illness." *Malice* means "desire to harm another."

Prefixes and Suffixes

If you know common roots, **prefixes**, and **suffixes**, you can figure out the meanings of many words. The chart below shows how to analyze the word *constellation*.

Word Part	Definition	Example
Root	The main part of a word	*stella* means "star"
Prefix	A word part placed in front of the root to create a new meaning	*con-* means "together"
Suffix	A word part placed after the root to create a new meaning	*-tion* means "the act of"
Example: A *constellation* is a group of stars.		

Inflected Forms

An **inflection** is a change in the form of a word to show its usage. You can learn new words by analyzing what type of inflection is being used.

Inflection	Meaning	Examples
-er	more	cold**er**, fast**er**
-ed	in the past	call**ed**, talk**ed**
-s	plural	pen**s**, dog**s**

Word Families

A word family is a group of words that all share the same root but have different forms. For example, look at the word family for *success*: success**ful**, success**fully**, **un**success**ful**, **un**success**fully**. If you know the meaning of the root word *success*, you can use what you know to help you understand the rest of the meanings in the word family.

Cognates and False Cognates

Cognates are words that come from two different languages but that are very similar because they share root origins. Cognates have similar spellings and meanings. For example, the English word *artist* and the Spanish word *artista* both mean "a person who creates art."

False cognates seem like they share a meaning but they do not. For example, the English word *rope* means "a cord to tie things with," but the Spanish word *ropa* means "clothing."

How to Use Cognates to Determine Word Meaning

- Think about what the word means in the language you are most familiar with.
- Substitute the meaning of the word with your language's definition.
- If your language's definition does not make sense, you may be using a false cognate. Try to learn the word using a different resource.

Foreign Words in English

Some foreign words come directly into English, without changes in spelling. For example, the French phrase *avant-garde*, referring to a cutting-edge movement in art or music, is often used in English. Use a print or online dictionary to identify other foreign words in English.

How to Use a Reference

Dictionary

A dictionary lists words with correct spellings, pronunciations, meanings, and uses. It can be used to find the denotation, or exact meaning, of a word. Sometimes a dictionary definition may be helpful in determining the connotation, or feelings associated with a word.

- Read all the definitions of the new word to find the use and meaning you need. Use the dictionary's key to understand any abbreviations or symbols.
- Go back to the selection and reread the paragraph. Substitute the meaning you found for the original word. Check to make sure it is the correct use of the word.

fraud·u·lent

(frȯ' jə lənt), *adj.*: based on or done by fraud or trickery; deceitful. [ME *fraude* fr. L *fraud-*] –fraud'u·lent·ness, *n.* –fraud'u·lent·ly, *adv.*

	Key
ME	Middle English (an old version of English)
L	Latin
fr.	from
ȯ	pronounced like the *a* in *saw*
ə	pronounced like *uh*
'	accented syllable

Thesaurus

A thesaurus lists words with their synonyms and antonyms. Use a thesaurus to confirm word meanings.

- Try to identify a familiar word from the synonyms listed for the new word.
- Go back to the selection and reread the paragraph. Substitute the synonym you chose for the original word. Keep trying synonyms until the words make sense.

Glossary

A glossary is like a dictionary but only defines words found in a specific book.

- Check to see whether there is a glossary at the end of the book you are reading.
- Read the definition of the new word in the glossary.
- Reread the sentence and substitute the definition for the word.

Technology

The Internet links computers and information sites electronically.

Web Sites to Use for Vocabulary Support

- myNGConnect.com This Web site has links to reference sources.
- m-w.com The Merriam-Webster Dictionary Web site includes a dictionary, a thesaurus, Spanish-English translation, and word activities.

Practice Your Vocabulary

When you are trying to learn something new, like a musical instrument, you practice. The more you practice, the better you become. Practicing vocabulary words is an important step in learning new words.

Memorize New Words

- Read the word and its definition silently and aloud.
- Cover the definition and try to restate the word's meaning.
- Write words on one side of index cards and their meanings on the opposite sides to make flashcards. Have someone show you the words, and try to recite their definitions from memory.
- Ask yourself questions using the definition and the word.
- Think of clues or mental images to associate with the new word to help you better remember its definition. You can also use real images to help you remember. For example, look around the classroom. Point to an object and say what it is. Use this to describe the entire classroom.

Review New Words

- Reread the definition of each word.
- Create sentences expressing the correct meaning of each word.
- Make lists of new words with their definitions in a notebook to periodically review.
- Study each word until you are confident you understand its meaning and how to use the word properly.

Word Awareness

It is important to choose the right words in order to clearly say what you mean. You need to be aware of different kinds of words and how they work. For example, remember that some words have multiple meanings. If you are not aware of this as you read, you might use the wrong meaning or misunderstand a sentence.

Synonyms and Antonyms

Synonyms are words that have the same or similar meanings.

- Think of a different word that has the same meaning of the word you want to use. For example, synonyms for the word *loud* include *noisy* and *roaring*.
- Use a thesaurus when trying to identify synonyms.

Antonyms are words that have opposite meanings.

- Think of words that are the exact opposite of the word you want to use. For example, antonyms for the word *break* include *fix* and *repair*.
- Remember that antonyms are usually listed at the end of an entry for a word in a thesaurus.

Homonyms and Homophones

Homonyms are words that are spelled the same but have different meanings.

- **Example**: *I* rose *out of my chair to pick the* rose *from the top of the bush*. In this sentence, *rose* has two meanings. One *rose* is a verb (past tense of *rise*), and the other *rose* is a noun (a type of flower). Using context clues, you can see that *out of my chair* signals that "the past tense of rise" comes at the beginning of the sentence. You can then conclude that "the flower" is the second *rose*.

Homophones are words that sound the same but have different meanings and spellings.

- **Example**: *The wind* blew *the clouds across the* blue *sky*. *Blew* and *blue* sound alike, but they are spelled differently. *Blew* is a verb (the past tense of *blow*), and *blue* is an adjective (a color). Using context clues, you can see that *the clouds* signals that "the past tense of blow" comes at the beginning of the sentence. You can then conclude that "a color" is the second *blue*.

When you hear a homonym or a homophone read aloud, it is easy to become confused. Visualizing the word can help you figure out its correct meaning and spelling.

Phrasal Verbs, or Two-Word Verbs

Phrasal verbs combine a particle such as *out*, *up*, or *on* with a verb. These phrases are often idiomatic because the two words on their own mean something different than the phrase.

- **Example**: *I* brought up *my fight with Leon during dinner*. *Brought* is the past tense of *bring*, and *up* is a direction. But when the words are combined in the context shown in the sample sentence, they mean "mentioned." *I mentioned my fight with Leon during dinner.*

You may be able to find some phrasal verbs in a dictionary. If you do not understand a certain phrase, ask for help or look for English usage resources in the library.

Slang

Slang is language that is informal and specific to certain groups.

- Slang words are created and used in place of standard terms. Popular culture and the media heavily impact slang words and usage.
- Learning when to use slang is important. Slang is OK for casual situations, but not for more formal ones, like school discussions, writing, or presentations.
- If you become familiar with common slang words and phrases, it may help you to better understand everyday conversations. Special dictionaries for slang can help you learn more terms.

Dialect and Regionalism

A **dialect** is a way people in a specific region or area use a language.

- People in different locations often have different ways to express or pronounce words from the same language.
- If you are unfamiliar with a dialect, try to find out more about the way local people use their language. You can use the Internet or library resources to study dialects.

WRITING HANDBOOK

The Writing Process

What Is the Writing Process?

Writing is like anything else—if you want to do it well, you have to work at it. This work doesn't happen all at once, though. Good writers often follow a series of steps called the Writing Process. This process helps the writer break the writing into manageable tasks.

Prewrite

Prewriting is what you do before you write. In this step, you gather ideas, choose your topic, make a plan, and gather details.

❶ Gather Ideas

Great writing ideas are all around you. What interests do you have that other people might want to read about? Think about recent events or things you've read or seen. Brainstorm ideas with your classmates, teachers, and family. Then record your ideas in an "idea bank," such as a notebook, journal, or **word processing** file. Add to your idea bank regularly and draw from it whenever you are given a writing assignment.

❷ Choose Your Topic

Your teacher may give you a topic to write about, or you may have to choose one for yourself. Find several suitable topics in your idea bank; then ask these questions:

* What do I know about this topic?
* Who might want to read about this topic and why?
* Which topic do I feel most strongly about?
* Which topic best fits the assignment?
* What important question can I ask about the topic?

> Writing Ideas
> visiting my family in Mexico
> ✔ my first job
> teens and peer pressure

❸ Make a Plan

Create a Writing Plan to focus and organize your ideas.

Writing Plan
Topic: What will I write about?
my first job
Purpose: Why am I writing?
to share a lesson with others
Audience: Who will read this?
my teacher and classmates
Form: What form works best for my topic, audience, and purpose?
autobiographical narrative
Controlling Idea: What is this mainly about?
learning to do things for myself
Voice/Tone: What attitude and feeling do I want my writing to express?
serious, with a little humor

❹ Gather Details

A 5Ws and H chart will help you gather details for many kinds of writing assignments.

5Ws and H Chart	
Who?	my dad, my boss, and I
What?	first job
Where?	Garcia's Restaurant
When?	last summer to now
Why?	spending money, save for college
How?	fill out application, use bus to get to and from my job

❺ Research

Some writing forms and topics require research. Use these resources to find out more about your topic:

- **Internet** Develop a list of terms to enter into a search engine. Use sites that end in .edu or .gov for the most reliable information. For more on Internet research, see p. 608.

- **Library** Search the library's catalog and databases for books and articles about your topic. Ask a librarian for help.

- **Interview** You may want to interview a person who has knowledge about your topic. Prepare questions ahead of time and take notes on the responses.

❻ Get Organized

Review your details and choose a way to organize your writing. Use an appropriate graphic organizer such as a topic outline to show the main idea and details of your paragraphs in order. List your main ideas next to the roman numerals. List any supporting details underneath the main ideas, next to the capital letters.

Topic Outline

My First Job
  I. Introduction: I joined the workforce.
     A. Many teens work.
     B. Work taught me responsibility.
  II. Body: I looked for and got a job.
     A. I searched want ads.
     B. I applied for jobs.
     C. I interviewed.
  III. Body: I learned the job.
     A. My first day was hard.
     B. I improved over time.
  IV. Conclusion: I learned a lesson.
     A. I earned money for college.
     B. I learned responsibility.

For another sample outline, see **Language and Learning Handbook**, page 641.

Draft

The drafting stage is when you put your Writing Plan into action. Don't worry about making things perfect at this point. Drafts are meant to be changed. Instead, concentrate on writing out your ideas in complete sentences and paragraphs. The following ideas will help you organize your main idea and supporting details into a draft.

❶ Remember Purpose, Form, and Audience

Remember, you already made many important decisions about your work during the prewriting stage. Return to your Writing Plan often. Remind yourself of your purpose, form, and controlling idea as you organize your paragraphs. Think carefully about your audience, voice, and tone as you choose words and craft sentences.

❷ Introduce the Controlling Idea and Use Literary Devices

Your first paragraph should introduce your controlling idea and draw readers into your work. You can use any of the following literary devices to begin your paper in a clear and interesting way. Each device is an example of a **topic sentence**, which lets readers know what the text will be about.

- **Position Statement**: *Few things teach responsibility better than a part-time job.*

- **Question**: *Do you remember your first paycheck?*

- **Quotation**: *My dad always says, "If you really want something, you'll work for it."*

- **Statistic**: *In July 2006, almost 22 million teens in the United States held a job. I was one of them. It was my first job.*

The controlling idea is the main thing you are writing about, or the idea you want to express. It is more specific than the topic. The topic is the general area or subject of your writing. For example, if the topic of an article is baseball, the controlling idea could be learning how to hit home runs.

❸ Work Collaboratively

Involve other people in the writing of your draft early and often. Teachers, classmates, and family members can help you improve what you have written and determine what needs to be done. Listen carefully to what they have to say, and take notes on their suggestions.

❹ Use Technology to Draft

Continue writing until you have a complete draft. You can write your draft with a pen and paper or with a **word processor**. In either case, be sure to save a copy of your work.

Draft

My First Job

In July 2006, almost 22 million teens in the United States held a job (Bureau of Labor Statistics). I was one of them. It was my first job. That summer I learned lessons about responsibility that will last me the rest of my life.

The first thing I learned is that knowing how to find, apply for, and interview for a job is as important as knowing how to do the job itself. I searched the want ads in our local newspaper and on the Internet. In fact, I even filled out and submitted applications for several places online. I was sure to fill out each application as completely and honestly as possible. This work proved useful when two restaurants asked me to interview for busboy, or assistant server, positions. I dressed neatly and gave myself plenty of time to make it to the interviews on schedule. When I met the managers, I shook their hands, then listened closely to their questions before responding.

Revise

After you have written a draft, you need to revise it, or make changes. Revision is what takes your writing from good to great.

❶ Revise for Traits of Good Writing

Focus and Unity

- ☑ Do you have a clearly stated controlling idea or opinion?
- ☑ Is your controlling idea supported?
- ☑ Do your ideas and details flow logically?

Organization

- ☑ Do you have a title and an introductory paragraph?
- ☑ Do you transition between ideas?
- ☑ Are your ideas in a sensible order?
- ☑ Do you have a conclusion or ending?
- ☑ Does the organization match your purpose and audience?

Development of Ideas

- ☑ Are your ideas meaningful?
- ☑ Are your details vivid?
- ☑ Do your details answer questions that readers may have about the topic?
- ☑ Have you addressed purpose, audience, and genre to improve subtlety of meaning?

Voice and Style

- ☑ Is your writing unique and engaging?
- ☑ Are most of your sentences in active voice?
- ☑ Do the style and language used match your purpose and audience?
- ☑ Do you use figurative language to address purpose, audience, and genre?

Written Conventions

- ☑ Are your spelling, punctuation, capitalization, grammar, and usage correct?

See pages 706–715 for more information.

The Writing Process

Revise, continued

❷ Use Technology

The word processing software found on most computers will help you develop and make changes to your work quickly and easily. Here are some hints to help you get the most out of your computer:

- Save your work often. This will prevent the loss of your work in case of a computer malfunction.

- Create a "scrap file" of sentences and paragraphs you deleted as you revised. This deleted material may contain other ideas and details you can use in later writing.

- Think about how you will move your document from computer to computer. For example, if you e-mail yourself a copy, make sure the next computer you plan to use has Internet access.

❸ Hold a Peer Conference

Work with your classmates to improve each other's work.

Peer Review Guidelines

As Writer ...

- Read your draft aloud or supply copies for each member of your group.

- Ask for help on specific points related to the traits of good writing.

- Listen carefully and take notes on your reviewers' comments.

As Reviewer ...

- Read or listen to the complete writing. Take notes as you read or listen.

- Compliment the strong parts of the draft before you criticize weak points.

- Offer specific suggestions.

Edit and Proofread

After you have revised your draft for content, organization, and wording, it is time to check it for mistakes.

❶ Take Your Time

Successful editing and proofreading require attention to detail. The following hints will help you do your best work:

- Use a printed copy of your work. Text looks different on paper than on a computer screen. Many people catch more mistakes when they edit a printed version of their work.

- Set your work aside for a while. Your review may be more effective if you are rested.

- Read line by line. Use a ruler or piece of paper to cover the lines below the one you are reading. This will help you concentrate on the text in front of you.

❷ Check Your Sentences

Make sure your sentences are clear, complete, and correct. Ask yourself:

- Did I include a subject and a predicate in each sentence?

- Did I break up run-on sentences?

- Did I use a variety of sentence structures to keep my writing interesting?

- Did I combine short sentences, when possible, to create longer sentences?

- Did I use the active voice in most of my sentences?

❸ Check for Mistakes

Proofread to find errors in capitalization, punctuation, grammar, and spelling. Look especially for:

- capital letters, end marks, apostrophes, and quotation marks

- subject-verb agreement

- misspelled words

❹ Use Reference Tools

Reference tools are an important part of every writer's tool kit. Dictionaries, thesauruses, and electronic sources such as Web sites and the spell-checking features of most word processing programs are all reference tools available to the good writer. When in doubt, check different versions of several sources.

Use a **dictionary** to check the meaning and spelling of your words.

> I worked **diligently** that summer.
> *Is that spelled correctly?*

Use a **thesaurus** to find words that are livelier or more appropriate for your audience.

> I worked ~~diligently~~ **hard** that summer.
> *Maybe this word is clearer to my audience.*

Use a **grammar handbook** to fix sentences and punctuation errors.

> We ~~was~~ **were** cleaning the grill.
> *That's the correct verb.*

Use a **style guide** or **style manual**, which is a publication containing rules and suggestions about grammar, writing, and publishing, for help in **citing** your sources. When you use information and ideas from other authors, you need to give them credit for their work. **Plagiarism** is using someone's words or ideas without giving the person credit. When you reword another author's ideas, you still have to give the author credit for his or her ideas.

> In July 2006, almost 22 million teens in the United States held a job. (Bureau of Labor Statistics)
> *Now the statistic is properly cited, according to the method I found in the style guide.*

❺ Mark Your Changes

Use proofreader's marks to show changes on a printout of your draft. Then make changes to your word processed document.

> ¶ The first thing I learned is that knowing ~~how~~ how to find, apply for, and interview for a job is as important as knowing how to do the job itself. I searched the want ads in our local newspaper and on the Internet. In fact, I even filled out and submitted applications for several places online. I was sure to fill out each application as completely and honestly as possible. I dressed neatly and gave myself plenty of time to make it to the interviews on schedule. This work proved useful when two restaurants asked me to interview for busboy, or assistant server, positions. when I met the Managers, I shook their hands, then listened closely to their questions before responding.

Proofreader's Marks

ϱ	Delete
∧	Add text
⤳	Move to here
⊙	Add period
⌄	Add comma
≡	Capitalize
/	Make lowercase
¶	Start new paragraph

Publish and Evaluate

You've made it! You're now ready for the last step in the Writing Process. First, prepare your final document for your readers. Then, reflect back on what you've done well and what you could do better next time.

❶ Print Your Work

The final version of your work should be neat and easy to read. It should be visually appealing. You can increase the visual impact of the final version of your work by using different font types and sizes, headings, bullet points, or even diagrams and charts as a way to present data. Use the information below to format your document for final publication. Then print out and make copies of your work to share with others. Be sure to keep a copy for yourself.

1 inch top margin

Header with author, class, date

Sam Rodriguez

English 103

October 13, 2007

Centered/ boldfaced title; set in a different font from main text

My First Job

In July 2006, almost 22 million teens in the United States held a job (Bureau of Labor Statistics). I was one of them. It was my first job. That summer I learned lessons about responsibility that will last me the rest of my life.

The first thing I learned is that knowing how to find, apply for, and interview for a job is as important as knowing how to do the job itself. I searched the want ads in our local newspaper and on the Internet. In fact, I even filled out and submitted applications for several places online. I carefully filled out each application as completely and honestly as possible.

This work proved useful when two restaurants asked me to interview for busboy, or assistant server, positions. I dressed neatly and gave myself plenty of time to make it to the interviews on schedule. When I met the managers, I shook their hands, then listened closely to their questions before responding.

1

1 inch bottom margin

1.25 inch left margin

Page number centered, 0.5 inch from bottom

1.25 inch right margin

❷ Publish Your Work

Take your work beyond the classroom and share it in new ways.

- Save examples of your writing in a portfolio. This will allow you to see the improvement in your writing over time. Organize your portfolio by date or form. Each time you add pieces to your portfolio, take some time to self-reflect and compare the new piece to your older work.

Portfolio Review

- ☑ How does this writing compare to other work I've done?
- ☑ What traits am I getting better at?
- ☑ What traits do I need to work on?
- ☑ What is my style? What kinds of sentences and words do I often use?
- ☑ What makes me a super writer?

- Expand your work by making it into a poster or other visual display, such as a video or a Web site. What images best express your ideas? How will the text appear?

- Many newspapers and Web sites publish teen writing. Ask a teacher or librarian for examples, or research them yourself. For writers, there are few things more satisfying than sharing their ideas with as wide an audience as possible.

❸ Evaluate Your Work

Now that you have completed your work, look to see what you can improve.

- Use rubrics to evaluate the quality and effectiveness of your writing. Rubrics contain criteria for evaluating your work. Review the rubrics on pages 706–715.

- Discuss your work with your teacher and classmates, then ask yourself:

What did I do well?

I added some description. My details were sequential and organized.

What are some weaknesses that I could improve on easily?

It lacks uniqueness. I need to vary my sentence structures.

How will I make sure I improve on those weaker areas?

I could pick topics that I feel strongly about. During revision I can check my sentence structure.

What are some weaknesses that may take time to improve?

Expanding my ideas, making my voice more mature.

- Set goals based on your evaluation. Make a list of goals; cross them out as you accomplish them. Then set new goals.

Goals to Improve My Writing
1. ~~I am going to use more descriptive sentences in my next narrative piece.~~
2. I am going to check all my sentence beginnings and make sure they are different.
3. I am going to add more "important" facts to my expository nonfiction pieces.

Writing Traits

What Are Writing Traits?

Writing traits are the characteristics of good writing. Use the traits and writing examples on the following pages to plan, evaluate, and improve your writing.

Focus and Unity

All the ideas in a piece of writing should be related, or go together well. **Focus** your writing by selecting a single central or **controlling idea**. Then give your work **unity** by relating each main idea and detail to that controlling idea. Use the rubric below to help maintain focus and unity in your writing.

Focus and Unity

	How clearly does the writing present a central idea or claim?	How well does everything go together?
4 Wow!	The writing expresses a <u>clear</u> central idea or claim about the topic.	<u>Everything</u> in the writing goes together. • The main idea of each paragraph goes with the central idea or claim of the paper. • The main idea and details within each paragraph are related. • The conclusion is about the central idea or claim.
3 Ahh.	The writing expresses a <u>generally</u> clear central idea or claim about the topic.	<u>Most</u> parts of the writing go together. • The main idea of most paragraphs goes with the central idea or claim of the paper. • In most paragraphs, the main idea and details are related. • Most of the conclusion is about the central idea or claim.
2 Hmm.	The writing includes a topic, but the central idea or claim is <u>not</u> clear.	<u>Some</u> parts of the writing go together. • The main idea of some paragraphs goes with the central idea or claim of the paper. • In some paragraphs, the main idea and details are related. • Some of the conclusion is about the central idea or claim.
1 Huh?	The writing includes many topics and <u>does not</u> express one central idea or claim.	The parts of the writing <u>do not</u> go together. • Few paragraphs have a main idea, or the main idea does not go with the central idea or claim of the paper. • Few paragraphs contain a main idea and related details • None of the conclusion is about the central idea or claim.

Focus and Unity: Strong Example, score of 3 or 4

"Mother to Son"—An Amazing Poem

Nobody writes poetry like Langston Hughes. In the poem "Mother to Son," he shows why he is such an amazing poet. He is a master of theme, rhythm, and figurative language.

The theme of "Mother to Son" is about life's difficulties and the need to keep going. The voice in the poem is that of a mother. She talks about how her life has been such a struggle. The mother shares with her son that he is going to go through some tough times, too, but he has to stay strong and focused when life is hard.

Langston Hughes is also great at creating rhythm with words. His poems read like songs in your head, and "Mother to Son" is no different. He uses quick, short lines with repetitive beginnings to make the poem very rhythmic. Hughes also creates rhythm by adding just a couple of lines that rhyme.

This poem is all about figurative language. The poem really is one big metaphor. The mother compares her life to a rough, worn-out staircase. The metaphor helps me to picture what the mother means about life being difficult sometimes. It also symbolizes that in order to get somewhere, you have to keep trying and working until you get to where you want to be.

Langston Hughes is an amazing poet. He is able to write poems that affect me by making them about something I can relate to and by making them rhythmic and creative.

The beginning states the controlling idea.

The main idea of each paragraph is about the controlling idea.

Details support the main idea.

The end connects to the beginning.

Focus and Unity: Weak Example, score of 1 or 2

An Amazing Poem

The narrator of the poem is that of a mother. She talks about how her life has been such a struggle. The mother shares with her son that he is going to go through some tough times, too, but he has to stay strong and focused when life is hard.

Langston Hughes is a great poet. His poems have theme, figurative language, and rhythm. This poem is all about figurative language. The poem really is one big metaphor. The mother compares her life to a rough, worn-out staircase. The metaphor helps me to picture what the mother means about life being difficult sometimes. It also symbolizes that in order to get somewhere you have to keep trying and working until you get to where you want to be.

He uses quick, short lines with repetitive beginnings to make the poem very rhythmic. Hughes also creates rhythm by adding just a couple of lines that rhyme.

Langston Hughes is an amazing poet.

The controlling idea is unclear.

The paragraphs have no clear main idea.

The conclusion is vague and abrupt.

Organization

Having a clear central idea and supporting details is important, but in order for your audience to understand your ideas, make sure your writing is organized. Good **organization** helps readers move through your writing easily. In a well-organized work, all paragraphs work together to fulfill the author's purpose clearly and smoothly.

Organization

Scale	Does the writing have a clear and appropriate structure?	How smoothly do the ideas flow together?
4 Wow!	The writing has a structure that is <u>clear</u> and appropriate for the writer's audience, purpose, and type of writing.	**The ideas progress in a smooth and orderly way.** • The introduction is strong. • The ideas flow well from paragraph to paragraph. • The ideas in each paragraph flow well from one sentence to the next. • Effective transitions connect ideas. • The conclusion is strong.
3 Ahh.	The writing has a structure that is <u>generally</u> clear and appropriate for the writer's audience, purpose, and type of writing.	<u>Most</u> **of the ideas progress in a smooth and orderly way.** • The introduction is adequate. • Most of the ideas flow well from paragraph to paragraph. • Most ideas in each paragraph flow from one sentence to the next. • Effective transitions connect most of the ideas. • The conclusion is adequate.
2 Hmm.	The structure of the writing is <u>not</u> clear or <u>not</u> appropriate for the writer's audience, purpose, and type of writing.	<u>Some</u> **of the ideas progress in a smooth and orderly way.** • The introduction is weak. • Some of the ideas flow well from paragraph to paragraph. • Some ideas in each paragraph flow from one sentence to the next. • Transitions connect some ideas. • The conclusion is weak.
1 Huh?	The writing is not clear or organized.	<u>Few or none</u> **of the ideas progress in a smooth and orderly way.**

Common patterns of organization include:

- **chronological order**, in which details are told in time order
- **compare and contrast**, in which similarities and differences between two or more things are discussed
- **problem-solution**, in which a problem is discussed first and then one or more solutions are presented
- **order of importance**, in which the writer presents the strongest arguments first and last, and presents weaker arguments in the middle.

Organization: Strong Example, score of 3 or 4

> ### Say No to Raising the Legal Driving Age
>
> For teens in the United States, receiving a driver's license at age sixteen is an important part of growing up. However, some states are considering raising the legal driving age to eighteen years old. I believe that this idea would negatively affect teens and parents.
>
> One reason teens need to be able to drive at the age of sixteen is so they can get a job. Many teens need to get jobs to have money for food, clothes, and entertainment. Often, a teen who has a job must have a car and be able to drive it to work.
>
> Teens also want to be able to date and do other social activities on their own. Teens need the opportunity to be responsible and feel trusted. Being able to drive at sixteen helps teens earn this trust.
>
> Perhaps most importantly, teen students have to be able to drive to and from school. A lot of parents and guardians go to work before school starts and have to work until after school is out. The only way for some students to get to school or get to school events and practices is to drive. Without driver's licenses, students may end up missing a lot of school and school activities.
>
> While there may be some good reasons why the legal driving age should be raised, it is important to teens and parents that it stays the same. Sixteen-year-olds need to be able to drive to work, to social events, and to school functions.

The beginning makes the purpose clear: to persuade.

There are effective transitions between paragraphs.

Details support the main idea.

Each paragraph gives reasons that support the author's opinion.

Organization: Weak Example, score of 1 or 2

> ### Teens and Driving
>
> Can you imagine having your mom drive you to your high school graduation or to prom? How would you feel if you couldn't get a job? Many states want to make eighteen the legal driving age.
>
> Many teens do not reach age eighteen until after they have been graduated from high school. It wouldn't be fun waiting until eighteen before you could drive. My friends and I drove once when we were fifteen. Many kids need to work to earn money. It would be difficult to get a job if the legal driving age was eighteen.
>
> Students need to be able to drive to school. If the driving age is eighteen, lots of kids will have to take the bus. My friends and I rode the bus for many years. There are thousands of students who have to ride the bus each year.
>
> Can you imagine going on a date with your parents in the front seat? My mom drove me to a dance once, and I was so embarrassed. Students need to be able to go on dates.
>
> The legal driving age needs to stay the same so teens can drive to school, work, and on dates.

The purpose is not clear.

Paragraphs lack transitions.

The details here do not support the author's opinion.

Development of Ideas

Good ideas are important, but so are the details that describe the ideas. Details develop your ideas, or help your reader to understand them. They also make your writing much more interesting to read. When you are writing, there may be many ideas to choose from, so consider which ideas are most important to your audience and support your purpose for writing.

Development of Ideas

Scale	How thoughtful and interesting is the writing?	How well are the ideas or claims explained and supported?
4 Wow!	The writing engages the reader with meaningful ideas or claims and presents them in a way that is interesting and appropriate to the audience, purpose, and type of writing.	**The ideas or claims are fully explained and supported.** • The ideas or claims are well developed with important details, evidence, and/or description. • The writing feels complete, and the reader is satisfied.
3 Ahh.	<u>Most</u> of the writing engages the reader with meaningful ideas or claims and presents them in a way that is interesting and appropriate to the audience, purpose, and type of writing.	<u>Most</u> of the ideas or claims are explained and supported. • Most of the ideas or claims are developed with important details, evidence, and/or description. • The writing feels mostly complete, but the reader still has some questions.
2 Hmm.	<u>Some</u> of the writing engages the reader with meaningful ideas or claims and presents them in a way that is interesting and appropriate to the audience, purpose, and type of writing.	<u>Some</u> of the ideas or claims are explained and supported. • Only some of the ideas or claims are developed. Details, evidence, and/or description are limited or not relevant. • The writing leaves the reader with many questions.
1 Huh?	The writing does <u>not</u> engage the reader. It is not appropriate to the audience, purpose, and type of writing.	**The ideas or claims are <u>not</u> explained or supported.** The ideas or claims lack details, evidence, and/or description, and the writing leaves the reader unsatisfied.

Development of Ideas: Strong Example, score of 3 or 4

> ### Parent-for-a-Day
>
> Have you ever wondered what it would be like if we could change places with our parents just for the day? I have, and there are a few things I would like to do.
>
> No school! Making my parents go to school for me would be the first thing I would do as parent for the day. Oh, what fun to be the one to tell my parents to "wake up, eat your breakfast, get to school!" Off they would go to sit in classrooms while I headed to the park for a long game of soccer.
>
> No chores! When my parents got home from school, they would take out the trash, they would do the dishes, and they would clean the house. Meanwhile, I would sit in front of the television and watch my favorite shows.
>
> No bedtime! The last and best part of being a parent for the day is that there would be no bedtime. I would stay up until the wee hours of the morning watching television and finishing my favorite mystery novel.
>
> I have my "parent-for-a-day" all planned out, but the hardest part remains. I still need to convince my parents it is a good idea.

The writer asks a question to engage the audience.

Each paragraph explains and supports the main idea.

The end returns to the topic in a new way.

Development of Ideas: Weak Example, score of 1 or 2

> ### Parent-for-a-Day
>
> Have you ever wondered what it would be like if we could change places with our parents just for the day?
>
> No school! Making my parents go to school for me would be the first thing I would do as parent for the day.
>
> No chores! When my parents got home from school, I would make them do all the chores.
>
> No bedtime! The last and best part of being a parent for the day is that there would be no bedtime.
>
> Now I just need to talk my parents into the idea.

Paragraphs offer little explanation or support.

The ending is abrupt.

Voice and Style

Voice and **style** in writing contribute to communicating the meaning of writing. These qualities make each writer and piece of writing unique.

- **Voice** in writing is the quality that makes the words sound as if they are being spoken by someone. Voice communicates the author's or speaker's attitude.
- **Style** is the characteristic way a writer expresses his or her ideas. Part of that style is the author's **tone**, or attitude toward his or her subject as reflected in word choice. Tone, word choice, and sentence structure are all parts of a writer's style.

Matching Voice and Style to Audience

Because writing is intended to communicate, it is important to match voice and style to the audience. A serious subject may require a serious tone. The intended audience may also dictate whether you can use informal English. If the audience is your classmates, you might be able to use informal or casual English as you would in everyday conversation. If your audience is your teacher or other adults, use formal English in your writing. Whoever the audience, choose vivid words, and vary your sentence patterns.

Voice and Style

Scale	Does the writing have a clear voice and is it the best style for the type of writing?	Is the language interesting and are the words and sentences appropriate for the purpose, audience, and type of writing?
4 Wow!	The writing <u>fully</u> engages the reader with its individual voice. The writing style is best for the type of writing.	The words and sentences are interesting and appropriate to the purpose and audience. • The words are precise and engaging. • The sentences are varied and flow together smoothly.
3 Ahh.	<u>Most</u> of the writing engages the reader with an individual voice. The writing style is mostly best for the type of writing	<u>Most</u> of the words and sentences are interesting and appropriate to the purpose and audience. • Most words are precise and engaging. • Most sentences are varied and flow together.
2 Hmm.	<u>Some</u> of the writing engages the reader, but it has no individual voice and the style is not best for the writing type.	<u>Some</u> of the words and sentences are interesting and appropriate to the purpose and audience. • Some words are precise and engaging. • Some sentences are varied, but the flow could be smoother.
1 Huh?	The writing does <u>not</u> engage the reader.	<u>Few or none</u> of the words and sentences are appropriate to the purpose and audience. • The words are often vague and dull. • The sentences lack variety and do not flow together.

Voice and Style: Strong Example, score of 3 or 4

Dried Up

Some people are meant to make speeches, and others are meant to listen. I learned the hard way that I am definitely a listener.

I have always been comfortable speaking out in class, so when my friend Heather joined the speech team, I decided to give it a try. This kind of activity looks great on college applications, I figured. Moreover, how hard could it be?

I learned just how hard on the afternoon of the regional speech competition. Preparation certainly wasn't a problem. I had spent hours crafting my words. Each of us had rehearsed time and time again in front of our coach and each other. The rhythm and accents of my speech had been drilled into my mind and body.

When I stepped on stage, however, all that preparation dried up under the hot lights. My mouth felt as if it were filled with cotton, and I thought even the packed auditorium could hear my dry bones tremble. As I began to speak, my voice creaked like a rusty door.

I would like to say that I overcame that rough start, but I barely recall giving the rest of my speech. I slouched off stage and took my seat to the sound of weak applause, eager to take my place as the quietest, most intent listener in the room.

The voice is light-hearted and clear.

The sentence lengths are varied.

Vivid verbs and modifiers make the scene seem real and exciting.

Voice and Style: Weak Example, score of 1 or 2

A Bad Day

It was one of the worst days of my life. I tried to give a speech in front of a lot of people and ended up a failure.

This is what happened. My friend was part of the speech team. She talked me into trying out. I thought that it would be easy and it was, at least in front of my classmates.

At our first competition, I sat waiting until the judge called my name. I went on stage, and I could see a lot of people in the audience. I couldn't move, and then I almost passed out. The speech didn't go well at all.

It was an embarrassing moment, but I am glad I at least tried.

The voice is flat and lifeless.

Sentences have little variety.

Words are general and uninteresting.

Written Conventions

You want readers to focus on your ideas, but errors can make it hard to understand what you mean. Good writers pay attention to **written conventions**, that is, the accepted methods and rules for grammar, punctuation, spelling, and capitalization that are commonly used to write English.

Written Conventions Rubric

Scale	Grammar: Are the sentences grammatically correct?	Mechanics and Spelling: Are there errors in spelling, punctuation, or capitalization that affect understanding?
4 Wow!	The writing contains grammatically correct sentences throughout.	There are few or no mistakes in spelling, punctuation, or capitalization.
3 Looks Good.	Most of the sentences contain proper grammar.	There are mistakes in spelling, punctuation, or capitalization, but they do not affect understanding.
2 Hmm.	Some of the sentences contain grammar errors.	There are some mistakes in spelling, punctuation, and capitalization that affect understanding.
1 Huh?	Many sentences contain grammar errors.	There are many mistakes in spelling, punctuation, and capitalization that make the writing difficult to understand.

Written conventions also include using **complete sentences**, **organization**, and **text features** that people understand. Complete sentences have a subject and a predicate and express a complete thought. For more help with written conventions, see Grammar, Usage, Mechanics, and Spelling on page 738.

Written Conventions: Strong Example, score of 3 or 4

A True Hispanic Hero

There are many Hispanic heroes, but my favorite is Miriam Colon Valle. With hard work and a strong belief in herself and her profession, she has become a role model for all.

Early Years

Miriam Colon Valle grew up in Puerto Rico in the 1940s. She participated in drama in high school, and her teacher saw that she had a lot of talent. Valle was then asked to take part in the drama program at the University of Puerto Rico. Her work at the university earned her scholarships that allowed her to attend the Lee Strasberg Acting Studio in the United States.

Rise to Stardom

In the United States, Valle worked hard. She played roles in more than thirty movies; one of her most famous was as the mother of Al Pacino in the movie *Scarface*. Valle was also on television shows, such as the soap opera *The Guiding Light*.

Valle also loved the theater. In the 1950s she started her own theater group. She also acted in numerous Broadway productions. Her drive to help other Hispanic actors and to share theater with poor people inspired her to start the Puerto Rican Traveling Theater.

Because of her love for acting and her love for Hispanic culture and theater, she was awarded a Lifetime Achievement Award in Theater. Miriam Colon Valle is an inspiration to Hispanics and people of all races.

Grammar is correct throughout.

Heads separate sections and give information.

Readers can easily understand the sequence of events.

Names and titles are properly formatted.

Punctuation occurs in the proper places throughout.

Written Conventions: Weak Example, score of 1 or 2

A true Hispanic Hero

There are many hispanic heroes. My favorite is Miriam Colon Valle. She is a role model for evrybody.

Miriam Colon Valle grew up in puerto rico in the 1940s she participated in drama in high school. Valle then taken part in the drama program at the "university of puerto rico." Her work at the university lead her to The United States eventually.

Valle also loved the theater. In the 1950s she started her own theater group. She also acted in a bunch of Broadway productions. She also started the Puerto Rican Traveling Theater. She was awarded a "Lifetime Achievement Award in Theater." Because of her love for acting and her love for hispanic culture and theater. Miriam Colon Valle is an inspiration to hispanics and people of all races.

In The United States, Valle worked hard. She played roles in more than thirty movies. Valle was also on television shows. Including the soap opera The Guiding Light.

There are many misspellings.

Names and titles are not properly capitalized or formatted.

Poor organization and lack of heads make it difficult to follow information.

Sentences are incorrectly punctuated or too long.

Writing Purposes, Modes, and Forms

There are many **forms** of writing, which appear in a number of **modes**, or types, based on the author's purpose and audience. Some writing is meant strictly to inform; other writing is meant to entertain. Other writing forms are intended to persuade or convince readers or listeners to act in certain ways or change their opinions or beliefs. Writing forms can often be categorized into more than one mode.

Writing Modes

A writing mode, or type, is defined by its purpose. Most of your writing tasks will occur in one of the modes described below.

Write to Inform or Explain

The purpose of **expository writing** is to present information or explanations about a topic. Many academic writing forms, such as research papers and literary response papers, are expository. Expository texts usually include a strong controlling idea or thesis in the first paragraph. Each of the body paragraphs presents a main idea and details related to the controlling idea. The final paragraph, or conclusion, restates, or sums up, the controlling idea.

Write Narratives

The purpose of **narrative writing** is to tell readers something they can follow in story form. Narratives can be fiction or nonfiction. They are often used for entertainment or to explain something that really happened. They offer a way of making sense of the world by ordering events into a clear beginning, middle, and end. Strong characters and interesting settings are usually key parts of narrative fiction. Most short stories are narratives, as are autobiographical and biographical essays.

Write Arguments

You can argue to defend your own ideas or opinions or you can try to influence the thinking or actions of other people. When you try to convince others, it's called **persuasive writing**. All arguments include a claim. A claim clearly states the writer's idea or opinion. Good arguments include evidence like facts, statistics, expert opinions, or personal experiences. Clear explanations, or reasons, connect evidence to claims. The reasons may appeal to the reader's emotions, ethics (sense of right and wrong), or to logic and understanding of facts. Persuasive texts should have an appropriate voice and tone for the intended audience, clear organization of ideas, and strong supporting details.

Common Academic Writing Forms

The following pages explain the most common writing forms you will use in school. You may be asked to write, read, evaluate, and respond to any of these forms while you are a student.

Cause-and-Effect Essay

A **cause-and-effect essay** traces the relationship between events. A cause is the reason something happens. An effect is the result of that cause.

Use a graphic organizer like the one below to develop your cause-and-effect essays.

Single Cause/Multiple Effects

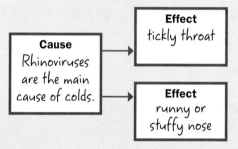

Multiple Causes/Single Effect

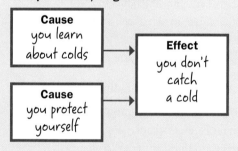

Check your essay for the following:

- A clear statement of the relationship that is being analyzed and discussed.

Causes and Effects of Colds

Cold season is almost here. It's a good time to review the causes and symptoms, or effects, of colds. The more you know, the better prepared you will be to protect yourself from catching a cold.

- A clear main idea for each paragraph.
- Appropriate supporting details.
- Signal words like *if/then* and *because*.

Most colds are caused by rhinoviruses. There are more than one hundred kinds of these tiny, disease-causing organisms. If a rhinovirus infects the lining of your nose or throat, then you have a cold.

The first effects of a cold are a tickling feeling in the throat and a runny or stuffy nose. Other symptoms include sneezing, headaches, and achiness.

A severe cold may cause further effects. For example, the cold sufferer may develop a low-grade temperature, or fever. If his or her chest becomes congested, then the person may also develop a cough.

College Entry Essay

If you apply to a college or university, you may be asked to submit an **entrance essay** as part of the application. A college entrance essay is a kind of **reflective essay**, in which a person tells stories about their experiences. Your essay should do more than introduce who you are to the college board. It should detail specific events in your life and how these events impacted you. Choose words that show your personality, point out your skills and talents, and outline your future plans. A good college entrance essay should explain how your unique talents and personality will make you a successful student.

A college may provide you with a topic to write about, or it may ask you to select your own topic.

Use the graphic organizer below to develop your college entry essay.

College Entry Essay Overview

> **Beginning**
>
> Introduce yourself by writing in your own conversational tone. Get the reader interested with a good story or description. You might also present your controlling idea here.

> **Middle**
>
> Develop your main ideas with clearly organized supporting details. These details should help readers understand how your experiences have helped you grow as a person. Focus on how one or a few experiences helped you grow in one very important way.

> **End**
>
> Lead the reader back to the controlling idea. Leave a lasting, positive impression with a strong ending that tells who you are and why you should be accepted at the college.

Check your college entry essay for the following elements:

- clear focus on your own experience
- a personal voice and tone
- interesting details
- correct grammar, spelling, and punctuation

"Travel broadens the mind," my dad always says just before our summer road trip. Every June, he piles Mom, me, my sisters, and our dog into the car, and away we go. Though I used to dread our trips, I now realize how much I have gained from them. Our road trips have broadened my mind in many ways.

Comparison-Contrast Essay

A **comparison-contrast essay** tells how things are similar and different. Comparisons show how two or more things are alike. Contrasts show how they differ.

Use a Venn diagram to collect information for your comparison-contrast essay. List characteristics of each thing being described. Then, in the center, list the characteristics they share.

Venn Diagram

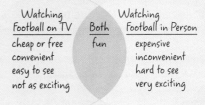

Watching Football on TV
cheap or free
convenient
easy to see
not as exciting

Both
fun

Watching Football in Person
expensive
inconvenient
hard to see
very exciting

Check your essay for the following:

- A clear statement of what is being compared and contrasted
- A clear main idea for each paragraph
- Appropriate supporting details
- Signal words like *both/and*, *similar*, and *like* for comparisons; signal words like *but*, *however*, and *on the other hand* for contrasts

At Home or at the Stadium?

If you really like football, you probably watch it on TV every chance you get. You may even go to the stadium to see your home team play. Though both ways of watching football are fun, there are some important differences between the two.

The first big difference is cost. Watching a football game on TV costs little or nothing. If the game is on network TV, it's free. If the game is on cable, it may be included in the cable package. But a ticket to a professional football game is expensive. The average price for a ticket to an NFL game is $50.

Descriptive Essay

A **descriptive essay** provides the reader with a strong impression of a setting, event, person, animal, or object. The essay may contain many different sensory details, but all the details should work together to support the author's controlling idea.

Use a details web to gather and organize sensory details for your descriptive essay.

Details Web

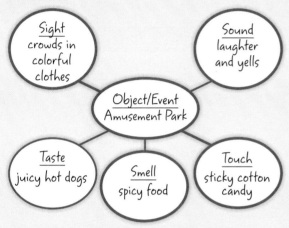

Check your descriptive essay for the following elements:

- a controlling idea that presents a single, strong impression that appeals to the five senses
- Information about how the subject affects more than one of the senses
- Vivid verbs, adjectives, and adverbs
- Clear organization of information, using a pattern such as spatial order (describing items from left to right, top to bottom, etc.)
- A unique style and appropriate tone for the audience

An Amusing Mixture

When summer vacation starts, I want to go to Alman's Amusement Park. Of course, I enjoy the thrilling rides there. But I enjoy the mixture of sights, sounds, smells, tastes, and feelings even more.

As I stroll past the Tilt-A-Whirl, I always see a blur of colors. People in bright summer clothes madly twirl, staining the sky with swirls of red, blue, green, and yellow. I hear the kids laughing and giggling, and I want to stop and watch. But I can't. The tempting scent of spicy food is in the air. I follow my nose to the Food Court for a juicy hot dog.

How-To Essay

A **how-to essay** explains a process. This kind of essay is also known as a process description or a technical document. A how-to essay describes the equipment, materials, and steps needed to complete a task. It answers any possible questions readers might have in order to make the process clear. The essay also often explains why the process is worth doing.

Use the chart below to collect information for your how-to essay.

How-To Planner

Task: Making a grilled cheese sandwich

Materials:	Steps:
2 slices rye bread	First, butter one side of each piece of bread.
1 tablespoon butter	Next, place the cheese between the bread.
1, one ounce slice sharp cheddar cheese	Next, fry the sandwich until brown.
1 slice tomato	Then, add the tomato to the sandwich.
1 nonstick frying pan	Finally, serve the sandwich with chips.

Writing Purposes, Modes, and Forms

Common Academic Writing Forms, continued

Check your **how-to essay** for the following elements:

- a clear statement of the process
- a complete list of materials and equipment needed to complete the process
- chronological organization of steps
- signal words such as *first*, *next*, and *then*
- complete description of the actions to take during each step
- benefits of performing the process

Deluxe Grilled Cheese Sandwich

A grilled cheese sandwich is delicious and easy to make. Try this simple but yummy recipe. All you need are two pieces of rye bread, a tablespoon of butter, a one-ounce slice of sharp cheddar cheese, a slice of tomato, and a nonstick frying pan.

First, spread half a tablespoon of butter on one side of each slice of bread. Be sure to spread the butter evenly, from corner to corner, so that the sandwich browns evenly when you fry it.

Next, place the unbuttered sides of the bread slices together. Put the piece of cheese inside the slices to form a sandwich. Make sure that the cheese slice is not larger than the bread. If it is, trim the cheese so that it fits inside the bread. Otherwise, when the cheese melts it will drip over the sides of the bread.

Literary Response Essay

In a **literary response essay**, you present your reactions to and analysis of a text. In an analysis, you look at elements that make up the text. For an analysis of fiction, for example, you might look at characters and conflict. For an analysis of nonfiction, you might look at word choice and meaning.

Use a graphic organizer like the one below to collect information and organize your literary response essay.

Literary Response Essay
Text Title: "Gettysburg Address"
Author: Abraham Lincoln
Date Written: November, 1863
Publishing Information: first published in newspapers
My Overall Impression of the Text: powerful speech!
Main Idea 1 about Text: nation founded on equality   Supporting Detail: "soldiers gave their lives" for this
Main Idea 2 about Text: other founding principles   Supporting Detail: "of the people, by the people, for the people"
My Responses to Main Idea 1: Soldiers' sacrifices keep us free.
My Responses to Main Idea 2: I, too, have responsibilities to my country.

The text a writer responds to is called *a source text*. Read the source text below. Then note how the reader responded to it.

The Gettysburg Address
By Abraham Lincoln

Four score and seven years ago our fathers brought forth on this continent a new nation, conceived in liberty, and dedicated to the proposition that all men are created equal.

Now we are engaged in a great civil war, testing whether that nation, or any nation so conceived and so dedicated, can long endure. We are met on a great battle-field of that war. We have come to dedicate a portion of that field as a final resting place for those who here gave their lives that this nation might live. It is altogether fitting and proper that we should do this.

But, in a larger sense, we can not dedicate—we can not consecrate—we can not hallow—this ground. The brave men, living and dead, who struggled here, have consecrated it, far above our poor power to add or detract.... It is rather for us to be here dedicated to the great task remaining before us—that from these honored dead we take increased devotion to that cause for which they gave the last full measure of devotion— that we here highly resolve that these dead shall not have died in vain—that this nation, under God, shall have a new birth of freedom—and that government of the people, by the people, for the people, shall not perish from the earth.

The Message of Gettysburg

In 1863, President Abraham Lincoln traveled to Pennsylvania. The occasion was the dedication of a cemetery for the soldiers who had died at the Battle of Gettysburg. Lincoln's brief comments are today known as "The Gettysburg Address," and they present a new vision of the founding principles of the United States.

Lincoln begins his speech by noting that our nation was founded on the idea of equality just eighty-seven years prior to his speech. He then notes that the men buried at Gettysburg "gave their lives that this nation might live." This point makes me think of all the wars since then and the ways that soldiers' sacrifices allow me to enjoy the benefits of a democratic society.

Most powerfully, Lincoln ends his speech by restating the founding principles of the Declaration of Independence and the U.S. Constitution. Ours is a government "of the people, by the people, for the people." It was the brave sacrifice of those people and the ones who died at Gettysburg that Lincoln so beautifully honors in his speech. It reminds me that I have responsibilities to be a part of the government that so many have fought to keep alive.

In the introductory paragraph, identify the author and date.

State controlling idea of the text.

Include quotations from the text.

Describe reaction to a main idea.

Describe reaction to a main idea.

Narratives

Narratives can be either fiction or nonfiction. Fiction narratives tell stories featuring characters, settings, and plots. The forms of nonfiction narrative include:

- autobiographical essays/personal essays
- biographical essays
- diary or journal entries

Personal Essay or Autobiographical Narrative

In a personal essay, a writer describes events that he or she actually experienced. The purpose is often to entertain readers or to teach them.

Personal/Autobiographical Narrative Overview

> **Beginning**
> Introduce the people, setting, and situation. State why the event or experience was important.

> **Middle**
> Give details about what happened in the order that it happened. Share your thoughts and feelings. Use lively details and dialogue.

> **End**
> Explain how the action came to an end or the problem was solved. Summarize why the event or experience was important.

Personal Narrative Model

> ### A Hard Lesson Learned
>
> When Marie invited me to her birthday party, I was thrilled. She was the most popular girl in school. My best friend said, "Why do you want to go? Marie is not nice. She doesn't know how to be a friend." I wish I had listened, because my friend was right. The best I can say about my time with Marie is that it taught me a hard but valuable lesson about friendship.

Journal or Diary Entry

Journal entries are the least formal kind of nonfiction narrative. They are often used to record events from a person's life, but they can also be used as learning tools, such as when a person documents a research process or traces thoughts about something over time.

Journal Entry Model

> January 4, 2007
>   I went to the library today to research my paper about hip-hop music. I was worried that I wouldn't find anything, but then I remembered a tip my teacher gave me: ask a librarian! So I did, and he was very helpful. We found three books, six magazine articles, and even a documentary film. I'm glad I thought to ask. It definitely made doing the assignment easier for me.

Short Story or Novel

Short stories and **novels** are common forms of narrative fiction. Novels are typically longer than short stories, with more developed characters and plots. Both of these forms usually include descriptive elements, such as figurative language and vivid word choice.

Plot Diagram for Fiction

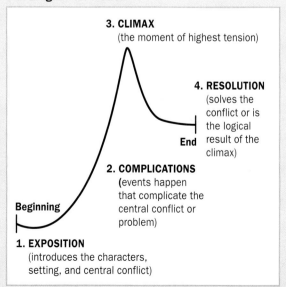

3. CLIMAX (the moment of highest tension)

4. RESOLUTION (solves the conflict or is the logical result of the climax)

End

2. COMPLICATIONS (events happen that complicate the central conflict or problem)

Beginning

1. EXPOSITION (introduces the characters, setting, and central conflict)

Using Persuasive Strategies

Good persuasive essays demonstrate effective use of persuasive strategies. Use persuasive strategies, such as appeals, to support your opinions. Note in the following examples how the writer's opinion statement changes depending on the appeal chosen.

Persuasive Essay

In a **persuasive essay**, you try to convince readers to agree with you or take a particular action. TV commercials, magazine ads, newspaper editorials, and campaign speeches are all kinds of persuasive media that begin as persuasive writing.

Persuasive Essay Planner

OPINION STATEMENT	I BELIEVE THAT WE SHOULD … KEEP OUR CATS INDOORS
Reason 1:	It's safe for the cat.
Evidence:	Many cats catch diseases outdoors.
Reason 2:	It's safer for wildlife.
Evidence:	Many animals are killed by outdoor cats each year.
Reason 3:	Cats lead happy lives indoors.
Evidence:	Experts say house cats are content.
Counter-argument	Cats like to be outside. However, they don't need to be.

Start a persuasive essay by stating an issue in a way that will make the audience care about it. Then state your opinion about the issue.

Keep Cats Indoors!

According to the American Bird Conservancy, pet cats kill thousands of birds each year. Now, I love cats. In fact, I own one. But I never let him go outdoors unless he is in his cat carrier. If you are a true animal lover, you will keep your cat indoors, too.

Support your opinion with reasons, evidence, and other appeals.

- An ethical appeal is directed at the reader's sense of right and wrong.

It's just plain wrong to let your cat hunt and hurt other animals. Birds, rabbits, and other wildlife animals have the right to live just as your cat does.

- A logical appeal is directed at the reader's common sense.

The fact is that it is dangerous for your cat to be outdoors. Your pet may be hit by a car. It may catch a serious disease from an infected animal. It may be chased by a dog or other larger animal.

- An emotional appeal is directed at the reader's feelings.

Do you really want your cat to be lost? Picture how cold, lonely, scared, and hungry your pet might become while it is looking for your home.

Now picture what it is like for a bird or a rabbit to be chased by a cat. Can you feel the terror of these little animals?

Additional things to remember:

- A personal anecdote, case study, or analogy validates your opinion.
- Think of questions or concerns your reader might have and address them.

Writing Purposes, Modes, and Forms

Common Academic Writing Forms, continued

Position Paper

In a **position paper**, you state your opinion, or position, on an issue that has at least two sides to it. You also give reasons and evidence to support your position. The purpose of position papers is to persuade, or convince, your readers to agree with you.

Unlike a persuasive essay, a position paper does not necessarily include a call to action. A position paper also does not necessarily contain counter-arguments. The main purpose of a position paper is to state and support an opinion.

Position Paper Overview

Beginning

Introduce the issue. Show readers why they should care about it; then state your position, the controlling idea of the paper.

Middle

Support your position with reasons that will convince your audience. Organize the reasons strategically. Use transitions to help readers move smoothly from one reason to another.

End

Restate your position in a memorable way.

Check your position paper for the following elements:

- an attention-grabbing introduction with a clear statement of opinion
- supporting reasons with evidence for each reason
- clear organization and transition words, such as *first*, *next*, and *most important*

Play Your Way to Good Health

Recently, I joined the swim team. I had never been particularly interested in sports before. However, I have always been interested in having good health and making new friends. I received these benefits and many more from being on the swim team. Therefore, I think that all students should become involved in sports.

The first big benefit of becoming involved in a sport is that it will improve your health.

Persuasive Speech

A **persuasive speech** tries to convince the audience to take an action or believe something.

Persuasive Speech Overview

Beginning

Introduce the topic. Get listeners' attention. You might tell a story from your own experience or describe a case study of someone else's experience. Give necessary background information. End by stating your opinion. It is your controlling idea.

Middle

Support your position. Give reasons readers or listeners should agree with you. Also use ethical or emotional appeals when appropriate. Then state at least one possible objection, or counterargument, to your opinion and respond to it respectfully.

End

Sum up your reasons and give a call to action. Tell readers what action you want them to take or what belief you want them to have.

Check your persuasive speech for the following elements:

- An attention-grabbing introduction with a clear statement of opinion.
- Paragraphs organized by reason.
- Strong appeals appropriate to the topic and audience.
- A counterargument with reasons and evidence against that argument.
- A summary of your opinion and a call to action.
- Respectful tone throughout.

Watch Educational Television

Can watching TV actually be good for you? Surprisingly, a recent university study suggests that it can. However, there's a catch. You have to watch educational TV, like nature shows and history programs. According to the study, watching shows like these can help improve your scores on standardized tests. Based on this study, I urge you to examine your TV habits and, if necessary, form a new habit: watching educational TV.

Though you may not at first believe it, watching educational TV shows can be fun. They can make a dry subject come alive for you. And when that happens, you learn and remember more. Let me give you an example. I had a hard time remembering anything I read about World War II. For me, the war happened so long ago that it did not seem real or interesting. When I watched a Public Broadcasting System series about the war, however, I began to feel differently. The subject became interesting to me when I watched and listened to interviews with people who lived through World War II. After watching the series, I reread my history book, and it made a lot more sense to me.

Problem-Solution Essay

A **problem-solution essay** informs readers about a problem and suggests one or more ways to solve it. A problem-solution essay has five main parts:

Problem-Solution Essay Planner

1. PROBLEM	Clearly state the problem. Where does it take place? When does it happen? Why does it matter?
2. CAUSES	Why does the problem happen? Who or what is to blame?
3. EFFECTS	Who is affected? How?
4. SOLUTIONS	Think about possible solutions. What has already been done? Has it helped? Think of new solutions. What are the benefits and risks of each idea?
5. CONCLUSION	Which solution is best? What makes it best? How could it be carried out? What do you want your reader or listener to understand? What do you want your reader or listener to do?

Reduce, Reuse, and Recycle

The United States is running out of land—land for landfills, that is. Landfills are where trash is taken and buried after workers collect it from homes or businesses and haul it away. Our landfill system is a good one. Or it would be, if we did not generate so much trash. Unfortunately, the average American throws away more than four pounds of paper, packaging, meal scraps, and other kinds of garbage each day. Multiply four pounds by the number of Americans, and you can see why we have a problem. Fortunately, there are simple solutions that anyone can put into effect. They are the "Three *Rs*": Reduce, Reuse, and Recycle.

Summary or Abstract

A **summary** is a brief restatement of the main points of a text or visual medium, such as plays or books. An **abstract** is a summary of a research report that appears before the report. It tells the reader what your report is about. Begin a summary by giving information about the original work. Then present the main ideas and the most important supporting details. Use quotations and proper citation when necessary. (For sample citations, see the model research report on pp. 727–728.)

Summary Model

> William Shakespeare wrote the tragic play *Hamlet* in about 1600. Since then, it has become one of the most famous plays in the English language.
>
> As the play opens, Hamlet, the Prince of Denmark, is visited by the ghost of his father, the king. The king's ghost tells Hamlet that the king was murdered, and Hamlet decides to find out by whom. He suspects that his uncle Claudius, who has married his mother and taken over the role of king, is the murderer.
>
> Hamlet's behavior grows stranger over the course of the play, as he is tormented by the idea of his father's murder and his mother's betrayal. He decides to create a play that he believes will show that Claudius is guilty. When Claudius does indeed show himself to be guilty, Hamlet's words and actions grow increasingly violent.
>
> In the end, Hamlet, his mother, and Claudius are all killed during a duel. An invading army stumbles upon the bloody scene, and Hamlet is carried away to be buried.

Research Reports

A **research report** is a presentation of information about a topic. In a research report, you combine and organize facts from different sources of information. You put the information in your own words and let your readers know where you found the information you cite, or use, in your report.

Research reports are typically researched, written, and cited using either the Modern Language Association (MLA) style or the American Psychological Association (APA) style. The style is often determined by the subject matter.

To learn more about research, see the **Language and Learning Handbook**, pp. 639–644.

Analysis of an Issue

To write an **analysis of an issue**, research a controversial situation—one that has at least two sides to it. Then use the information to write a report that answers the question *How?* or *Why?* In an analysis, the writer's personal opinion does not need to be included. The purpose of the analysis is to inform and explain, not to persuade.

Use the following graphic organizer to organize your report.

Issue Analysis Overview

Beginning
Start with an interesting fact or idea about the issue. Make readers care about it. Give background if necessary. Then state your controlling idea.

Middle
Analyze the issue. Take it apart, and examine each part. Answer the question *How?* or *Why?*

End
Sum up the results of your analysis. You might state the importance, or significance, of what you discovered. Or you might restate your controlling idea in an interesting way.

Works Cited
List the sources of information you used.

The following pages show a Research Report with citations done in MLA style.

J. Smith
Mrs. Walker
English 100
January 10, 2013

An Analysis of the Global Warming Debate

The issue of global warming has divided the scientific community. Some scientists believe that carbon dioxide and other greenhouse gases are warming Earth, causing dangerous changes in the climate. Other scientists disagree. They believe that there is no proof of global warming or its effects on the climate. Is global warming real? And if it is, should we be worried about it?

The theory of global warming is not new. It was first proposed in 1896 by Svante Arrhenius, a Swedish scientist. He said that people were unknowingly causing Earth's temperature to rise. The rise, he believed, was caused by people releasing carbon dioxide into the atmosphere when they burned coal and other carbon-based fuels. The carbon dioxide, he believed, raised Earth's temperature (Maslin 24).

Over the years, other scientists further developed Arrhenius's theory, which has evolved into a scientific model called the "greenhouse effect." According to the effect, Earth's atmosphere is like the glass in a greenhouse. Glass lets sunlight in and re-reflects it, bouncing heat from sunrays back into the house and trapping it there. Similarly, carbon dioxide and other greenhouse gases re-reflect rays from the sun, trapping heat in the atmosphere around Earth.

The greenhouse effect is a natural process that protects us and our planet. Without the greenhouse effect, it would not be warm enough on Earth for plants and animals to live (Fridell 25). However, many scientists believe that problems occur when the level of greenhouse gases rises, causing the amount of heat energy trapped around Earth also to rise. This process, it is believed, may cause Earth to become warmer than it has ever been.

Most scientists believe that this temperature change has already happened. For example, scientists at the U.S. Environmental Protection Agency (EPA) say that over the past century Earth's surface temperature has increased about 1.4 degrees F ("Basic Information"). The EPA believes that the rise has been caused by carbon dioxide produced by the burning of gasoline, oil, and coal.

Does such a small rise in temperature really matter? Many scientists believe it does. They think that the higher surface temperature of Earth is causing dangerous changes to our planet. Temperature changes will result in changes in rainfall patterns like drought and flooding. As ice in the north and south poles melts, global sea levels will rise. People living near

WRITING HANDBOOK

This section gives the name of the writer, the name of the writer's teacher, the name of the class, and the date.

The introductory paragraph is clear and effective and states the controlling idea.

The analysis focuses on these controlling ideas.

Parenthetical citations like this one tell readers where the student found information.

Background helps readers understand the issue.

The student uses a variety of sentence structures.

The student develops the analysis by explaining a main viewpoint on global warming.

Smith 2

the ocean may lose land or experience more severe storms. People and animals will be impacted. ("Global Warming"). These changes will impact citizens across the globe, including people in the United States (Karl, J.M. et al).

Kerry Emanuel, a scientist at the Massachusetts Institute of Technology (MIT) is a strong believer in global warming. He thinks that global warming has caused hurricanes to be more powerful and destructive. After studying about 5,000 hurricanes, he found that storms increased in intensity during the same period that Earth's temperature began to rise. The number of big storms has increased since 1923 (Tollefson 2012). Emanuel believes that warmer ocean temperatures are to blame for the increase in storms' destructive power (Kluger 92).

Not all scientists agree that global warming is causing climate changes. Physicist S. Fred Singer is representative of this group. In an interview for the Public Broadcasting System (PBS), Singer said that "whether or not human beings can produce a global climate change is an important question [that] is not at all settled. It can only be settled by actual measurements, data. And the data are ambiguous.... Since 1979, our best measurements show that the climate has been cooling just slightly. Certainly, it has not been warming" ("What's up?"). Singer bases his conclusion on measurements from weather satellites, which he believes to be more accurate than measurements from ground-based thermometers.

Dr. Richard Lindzen, a scientist at MIT, shares Singer's doubts about global warming and climate change. According to Dr. Lindzen, rises in Earth's temperature and carbon dioxide levels "neither constitute support for alarm nor establish man's responsibility for the small amount of global warming that has occurred" (Lindzen). He believes that the computer models on which global warming forecasts have been made are flawed and incorrect.

> The student develops the analysis by explaining a different main viewpoint on global warming.

Why, then, do so many scientists believe in global warming? Lindzen believes the answer has more to do with money than with science. He believes that government money is more often given to scientists whose work appears to predict and prevent disasters than to scientists whose work does not predict gloom and doom. Lindzen feels that because these kinds of projects tend to attract funding, some scientists have exaggerated the effects of global warming to get government grants (Lindzen).

> The student answers the question *Why?*

And so the debate continues. Perhaps this is for the best. As James Hansen of the National Aeronautics and Space Administration (NASA) put it, "Science thrives on repeated challenges . . . and there is even special pleasure in trying to find something wrong with well-accepted theory. Such challenges eventually strengthen our understanding of the subject" (Hansen).

> In the conclusion, the student effectively sums up the report.

Works Cited

"Basic Information." *Climate Change.* 14 Dec. 2006. U.S. Environmental
    Protection Agency. 5 Jan. 2007
    <http://www.epa.gov/climatechange/basicinfo.html>.

Fridell, Ron. *Global Warming.* New York: Franklin Watts, 2002.

"Global Warming: A Way Forwrad: Facing Climate Change." National
    Geographic. Video and Audio. 30 Nov. 2012.
    <http://video.nationalgeographic.com/video/environment/
    global-warming-environment/way-forward-climate/>.

Hansen, James. "The Global Warming Debate." Education. Jan. 1999. NASA
    Goddard Institute for Space Studies. 7 Jan. 2007
    <http://www.giss.nasa.gov/edu/gwdebate>.

Karl, T.R, Melillo, J.M, and Peterson T.C. *U.S. Global Change Research Program.*
    2009. Global climate change impacts in the United States. Cambridge:
    Cambridge University Press, 2009.

Kluger, Jeffrey. "The Man Who Saw Katrina Coming." *Time* 8 May 2006: 92.

Lindzen, Richard. "Climate of Fear." Opinion Journal from the Wall Street
    Journal Editorial Page. 12 April 2006. WSJ.com. 2 Jan. 2007
    <http://www.opinionjournal.com/extra/?id=110008220&mod=RSS_O>.

Maslin, Mark. *Global Warming: A Very Short Introduction.* Oxford: Oxford
    University Press, 2004.

Tollefson, J. "Hurricane Sandy Spins Up Climate Change Discussion."
    Nature. October 2012.
    <http://www.nature.com/news/hurricane-sandy-spins-up-climate-
    discussion-1.11706>. Accessed November 23, 2012.

"What's up with the Weather?" NOVA Frontline. 2000. WGBH/NOVA/
    FRONTLINE. 4 Jan. 2007
    <http://www.pbs.org/wgbh/warming>.

The student lists all the sources of information cited in the research report.

Career and Workplace Communication

In the world of work, there are expectations about the form and style of written communications. The following writing forms will help you at your workplace.

Business Letter

Business letters serve many purposes. You might write a business letter to make a request or to register a complaint with a business or other organization. The example below is a cover letter, a type of business letter in which the sender introduces himself or herself to an employer and states his or her qualifications for a job. Business letters should be typed on a computer or other word processor and should sound and look professional. Follow the business letter format below, and always check your letters carefully for grammatical or spelling errors.

Adam Russell
1297 Newport Ave.
Chicago, IL 79910
(555) 212-9402
May 18, 2013

Ms. Carlita Ortiz
Ortiz Corner Grocery
2480 North Lincoln Ave.
Chicago, IL 79919

Dear Ms. Ortiz:

I recently read in the *Chicago Tribune* that you are taking applications for the position of full-time checkout clerk. I am very interested in interviewing for this position.

I worked for supermarkets for the previous two summers in similar positions, first at Green Grocers and then at The Grainery Foods. My managers always gave me good performance reviews, and I truly enjoy the work.

I currently attend Julius Jones High School, but I am available for work in the evenings and will be available in the summer after June 10, 2013. I can be reached after 4 p.m. on weekdays. I look forward to hearing from you about this opportunity and thank you for your consideration.

Sincerely,

Adam Russell

Adam Russell

Insert contact information for yourself followed by the person you are writing to.

Insert a space between the date and the contact information.

Use a formal greeting, addressing a specific person. Use formal titles and last names to show respect in business letters.

Do not indent paragraphs.

Use single-spaced paragraphs. Separate paragraphs with an extra space.

Always thank recipients for their attention.

Include a traditional closing with a handwritten and typed signature.

Résumé

A résumé is a document that describes your qualifications for a job. A well-written résumé includes the kind of information a potential employer would like to know about you. Examples include previous work experience, skills, and achievements. It is very important that résumés be free of errors, so that the employer can see that you would take a job seriously and pay attention to detail. Use the format below to set apart your résumé from all the résumés of other applicants.

Adam Russell

1297 Newport Ave.

Chicago, IL 79910

(555) 212-9402

Objective

To obtain full-time, seasonal work in the food service industry.

Work History

2012, Grainery Foods

Full-time checkout and stock clerk at a busy supermarket

- Used a standard register and invoice-tracking equipment

- Trained new employees

- Met and exceeded cash handling accuracy reviews

2011, Green Grocers

Full-time retail assistant at a local outdoor market

- Set up and closed market stalls

- Supervised volunteer staff

- Assisted customers with pricing and selection

Education

Currently enrolled at Julius Jones High School.

Awards

Student of the Month, April 2013.

References

Available upon request.

Include your contact information clearly at the top of the page.

Use boldface type, italics, or underlining to make important information or headings stand out.

List your experience, starting with your most recent job.

Use bullet points to draw attention to specific skills or responsibilities.

Include information about your education and any information that would show what you have done well in the past.

Keep a list of 3 to 5 references available. Check with your references before you give their names out.

Job Application

Many jobs require you to fill out an **application**. Follow the instructions closely and write as neatly as possible or type the information. You will often need to provide reference information for your work ability or character. It is important to have personal identification with you when completing job applications. Ask a manager if you have any questions.

Please type or print neatly.

Today's Date: 5 / 1 / 13

First Name: _____ Adam _____   Last Name: _____ Russell _____

Address: _____ 1297 Newport Ave. _____

City: Chicago   State: IL   Zip: 79910

Phone: (555) 212-9402   Birth date: 7 / 20 / 99

Sex: M ☑ F ☐

Follow instructions.

Education

High School Name: _____ Currently attending Julius Jones High School. _____

Employment History (List each job, starting with most recent.)

1. Employer: _____ The Grainery Foods _____   Phone: (555) 436-0090

   Dates: 5/2013 – 9/2013   Position: _____ Full-time checkout and stock clerk _____

   Duties: _____ Check out orders and stock inventory. _____

Provide complete and accurate information.

References

1. Name: _____ Consuela Ybarra _____   Relationship: _____ supervisor _____

   Company: _____ The Grainery Foods _____

   Address: _____ 123 Main Street, Chicago _____   Phone: (555) 436-0092

2. Name: _____ Roman Hrbanski _____   Relationship: _____ teacher/coach _____

   Company: _____ Julius Jones High School _____

   Address: _____ 321 N. Elm Street, Chicago _____   Phone: (555) 233-0765

Provide contact information for people who can tell the employer that you are a good and dependable worker.

Business Memo

A memo, or memorandum, provides employees with information concerning the business or organization.

Date: June 28, 2013
From: Carlita Ortiz, General Manager
To: All Full-Time and Part-Time Staff
Re: Independence Day Sale Hours

Please remember that all employees scheduled to work the morning of Sunday, July 1, should report at 7:00 A.M., one hour earlier than usual, as we will need special help setting up the Independence Day Sale.

Thank you for your attention.

Give information regarding date, sender, recipients, and the topic.

State the purpose of the memo and any supporting information.

Be short and specific.

Creative Writing

Your imagination is the most important tool in building the forms of creative writing. Some of these forms, such as plays and some kinds of poetry, have set structures. Others, such as parody, are defined by their purpose rather than their structure. Creative writing allows you to describe people, things, and events in new and interesting ways.

To learn more about these forms, see the **Literary Terms**.

Poetry

Poetry is a literary form in which special emphasis is given to ideas through the use of style and rhythm. In poetry, lines of text are called verses, and groups of verses are called stanzas. Rhyme and other sound effects within and among lines and words are popular elements of poetic style.

Some poems are written in conventional poetic forms. The number of lines, rhythm, and rhyme patterns are defined by the form. Other poems have a style all their own. These are called free verse:

> **Friendship**
>
> To never judge
> To accept your true self
> Through all your faults
> Still loyal and caring.
> That is the making,
> An act of giving and taking,
> of what we call a true friend.

Song Lyrics

A **song lyric** is text set to music and meant to be sung. Like lyric poetry, song lyrics often express personal feelings using rhythm and sound effects. These effects provide musical qualities similar to those often found in lyric poetry. In fact, the word *lyric* comes from the ancient Greek word for *lyre*, a musical instrument with strings.

Parody

A **parody** makes fun of, imitates, or exaggerates another creation or work. The parody can be sarcastic, and it is often used to make a point in a funny way. A parody can be in any form, from plays to essays to poems.

> **Twinkle, Twinkle?**
>
> Twinkle, twinkle unseen star,
> Covered in our smog you are.
> Up above our town once bright,
> Now we cannot see your light.

Play/Skit

A **play** is a narrative that is meant to be performed before an audience. The text of a play consists of dialogue spoken by the characters and brief descriptions of sets, lighting, stage movements, and vocal tone. A **skit** is a very short play:

> **James.** You mean I won? [*grabbing Paula's hands*]
>
> **Paula.** Yes, you did. You won the Battle of the Singers competition!
>
> **James.** [*shocked, then jumps, screaming and hooting*] I can't believe it!

Poster

A **poster** is used to get people's attention and give information in a visually appealing way. Posters should have the following:

- a purpose: What do you want people to know or think?
- attention-grabbing colors or pictures
- a large heading that tells people what the poster is about
- large print so people can read the poster from a distance
- just enough details to convey your message

Electronic Communication

More and more, people are writing to each other using electronic forms of communication. Computers and portable devices, such as cell phones, offer a number of ways to research school assignments, conduct business, and keep in contact with friends and family. You need to protect your identity and stay safe online. Check your school's Acceptable Use Policy for guidance on how to protect your hardware and, more importantly, yourself.

E-mail

Electronic mail, or **e-mail**, allows users to exchange written messages and digital files over the Internet. Like traditional mail, e-mail requires an address to enable users to send and receive messages. This address is attached to an account that a user accesses through the Internet or through an e-mail software program. Keep the following rules in mind when writing e-mail:

- Carefully check the address of your recipient.
- Include the subject of the e-mail.
- Include a greeting.
- Be sure to supply enough background information to help the reader understand the topic and purpose of your e-mail.
- Unless you are writing to a peer, such as a friend or classmate, use a formal tone, proper punctuation, and grammar.
- Include a closing, and give your name.

From: student@studentweb.edu
To: n.patterson@njc.library.org
Subject: Library Books

Dear Ms. Patterson:

I have returned the books that you asked me about. I put the books in the return box. Please let me know if you don't receive them.

Thank you,
Jamie

Instant Messaging and Text Messaging

Instant messaging, or **IM**, allows two users to exchange messages instantly over the Internet. **Text messages** are sent over cell phone lines. Like e-mail, these messages require each user to have an account. Messaging is used most frequently by peers, so the writing style may be very casual. Abbreviations are often used to shorten the amount of time and space needed for the message.

Blogs

Web logs, or **blogs**, are Internet newsletters. Many individuals and organizations use blogs to communicate their ideas to a wide audience. Some blogs offer articles on a particular topic, much like a newspaper or magazine. Others are more like journals, with individuals documenting their interests or events from their lives. Most blogs are updated regularly.

Listserves

A **listserve** is an electronic forum in which users discuss and share information about a particular topic. Users sign up for the listserve, then post and respond to questions using their e-mail account. Many experts use listserves to exchange information with others in their field.

Message Boards

A **message board**, or **forum**, allows users to post thoughts and questions about a topic to a Web site and then see what others have to say about it. The site is usually organized by individual topics, called threads.

Social Media

There are many different kinds of tools and web sites that connect individuals to friends or groups. Individuals choose whether to subscribe, follow, or "like" an individual or group. This gives you access to that group. After you have access to a group, messages can be created or shared. You can join study groups, or connect with other readers or authors.

Media and Feature Writing

Many forms of **media and feature writing** are used in newspapers, magazines, radio, and television programs. Some of these forms are like narration because they tell a story. Other forms are types of persuasive writing. The most common forms are described below.

Advertisement

Advertisements, or **ads**, are meant to persuade readers to buy a product or service. Ad text should make an immediate impact on the reader and be easily remembered. Usually, advertisements appeal to people's emotions rather than to logic. Advertising messages are usually presented in visually interesting ways. Ads on TV may use visual techniques and background music to increase their effectiveness.

News Article and Feature Article

The purpose of a **news article** is to provide information. It should provide well-researched facts about a current event. It answers the questions: *Who? What? Where? When? Why?* and *How?* The first paragraph of a news article introduces the main facts, and the following paragraphs provide supporting details.

The purpose of a **feature article** is to provide information and points of view about something fun, entertaining, or important in people's daily lives. Feature articles are lively, fact-based discussions. Magazines contain many examples of feature writing, such as "Great Prom Ideas" or "The Year's Best Music." One characteristic of feature articles is a strong lead, or first paragraph, that draws readers into the piece.

Because they are based in fact, both news articles and feature articles can be considered narrative nonfiction.

Editorial/Letter to the Editor

Editorials are common features of most newspapers. These articles give newspaper staff writers the chance to voice their opinions on important issues. Many periodicals also publish letters to the editor, in which the public can voice opinions on a periodical's content or other topics of interest to its readers. When writing a letter to the editor, be sure to support your opinion with facts and evidence. Editorials and letters to the editor are usually persuasive in tone.

Critique or Review

A **critique**, or **review**, presents the author's opinion of a book, movie, or other work. The review usually includes a brief plot summary or description of the work of art. A critique does more than just summarize the main ideas of a work, however. Details about performances or the author's opinion of the quality of the work supports the author's opinion. In an effective review, the author's opinions about the work are always supported by specific details. The purpose of critiques and reviews is to help readers decide whether to experience the work for themselves.

Worth Seeing?

The Fellowship of the Ring is a movie version of the epic J. R. R. Tolkien novel about a mythical world threatened by the power of an evil ring. Director Peter Jackson uses beautiful computer graphics to show the struggle of a small group of adventurers who set out to destroy the ring. The rich characters, exciting action scenes, and incredible music make *The Fellowship of the Ring* a must-see for all fans of fantasy and adventure films.

Speech

A **speech** is a type of spoken message, often planned in advance and later delivered to a group of people. A speech can have many purposes:

- **to inform or explain,** as when a community leader speaks to a group of news reporters about a new neighborhood program

- **to argue,** as when a political candidate makes a speech on TV to convince people to vote for him or her

- **to tell a story** and build relationships, as when a business leader makes a humorous after-dinner speech at a business convention, or tells their life story to inspire others to reach success.

Before planning a speech, identify the occasion for speaking, the audience, and your purpose. These three elements will help you select an appropriate tone, words, and details. For example, if you are planning a speech about computers for the members of a computer club, you will not need to define computer terms for your audience. If you were to give the same speech to a general audience, however, you might need to define the terms because some members of the audience may not know what the words mean.

Computer Speech for Computer Club

I am here to give you tips on creating Web pages. I will speak to you about the asynchronous qualities of Ajax and the advantages and disadvantages of pulling content with it.

Computer Speech for General Audience

I am here to give you tips on creating Web pages. I will speak to you about Ajax, which stands for "Asynchronous JavaScript and XML." Simply put, Ajax is a way to put content on a Web page by using codes that pull information from a server for you.

Script or Transcript

A **nonfiction script** is the prewritten text for a presentation or broadcast program. Like a news story, a nonfiction script contains the five Ws, but no unnecessary details. A **transcript** is a written record of a live discussion or broadcast.

Scripts and transcripts usually follow the written conventions of plays. The names of the speakers are followed by their dialogue and brief descriptions of movement, visual material, and other information necessary to describe how the presentation should look when it happens or how it looked when it happened.

Transcript of WXQV TV Interview

MARCY RAY, INTERVIEWER: Coach, you must be very excited about the big win today. Can you describe your feelings for me and our viewers?

COACH: It's hard to put my feelings into words right now, Marcy. I guess what I'm feeling most is pride. The team worked so hard this year. Every one of those kids earned this win, and I'm very, very proud of the entire team.

[*Background cheers from team members*]

RAY: How will you and the team celebrate, Coach?

COACH: We won't be celebrating alone. This win belongs to the whole school. So there will be a celebration and ceremony in the school gym Monday morning at 9 a.m. Students, parents, faculty, staff— everyone in the school community— are invited.

Social Communication

The forms of **social communication** help people establish and maintain relationships with friends and family. When you communicate socially, always think about the occasion for writing and how well you know the recipients. For example, if the occasion is informal and you know the recipients well, your tone and word choice can be informal. However, if the occasion is formal and you are not well acquainted with the recipients, a formal tone and formal language are more appropriate.

Friendly Letter

Before the development of electronic forms of communication, **friendly letters** were the most common way of exchanging ideas with friends and family. Today, the conventions of friendly letters are still used to write e-mail messages. The extra time and effort it takes to write and mail a letter show the recipient how much you care. Use the following rules to develop your friendly letters.

- Friendly letters can be handwritten or typed.
- Include the date.
- Include a salutation, or greeting, such as "Dear Joe."
- Indent the paragraphs.
- End the letter with a complimentary closing like "Sincerely," and your signature.
- Be sure to include the proper address and postage on the envelope.

November 3, 2007
Dear Grandfather,

I want you to know how much we are all looking forward to your visit. It's been so long since we've seen you! Dad has already planned some special events for us, but I hope that we can go fishing.

Yours truly,
Carlos

Thank-You Letter

A **thank-you letter** is a brief, friendly letter in which the sender expresses appreciation for a gift or an act of kindness.

September 4, 2007
Dear Janita,

Thank you so much for your help on the school newsletter. Your attention to detail and hard work were a big part of our success.

Thanks again,
Mr. Hahn

Invitation

An **invitation** gives the date, time, place, and purpose of a social event. An invitation often includes an RSVP. This is an abbreviation of *répondez, s'il vous plaît,* a French phrase for "please respond." Including an RSVP can help you plan for the number of people attending your event.

Come One, Come All!

Come celebrate Crystal's
sixteenth birthday!

Where: Elm Park
1900 Elm Street

When: Friday, May 25
6:00–8:30 p.m.

RSVP: Please let Crystal know by Wednesday,
May 23, whether you can attend.

Grammar, Usage, Mechanics, and Spelling

Parts of Speech Overview

All the words in the English language can be put into one of eight groups. These groups are the eight **parts of speech**. You can tell a word's part of speech by looking at how it functions, or the way it is used, in a sentence. Knowing about the functions of words can help you become a better writer.

The Eight Parts of Speech	Examples
A **noun** names a person, place, thing, or idea.	**Erik Weihenmayer** climbed the highest **mountain** in the **world**. The **journey** up **Mount Everest** took **courage**.
A **pronoun** takes the place of a noun.	**He** made the journey even though **it** was dangerous.
An **adjective** describes a noun or a pronoun.	Erik is a **confident** climber. He is **strong**, too.
A **verb** can tell what the subject of a sentence does or has. A **verb** can also link a noun or an adjective in the predicate to the subject.	Erik also **skis** and **rides** a bike. He **has** many hobbies. Erik **is** an athlete. He **is** also blind.
An **adverb** describes a verb, an adjective, or another adverb.	Illness **slowly** took his eyesight, but it **never** affected his spirit. His accomplishments have made him **very** famous. He has been interviewed **so** often.
A **preposition** shows how two things or ideas are related. It introduces a prepositional phrase.	Erik speaks **to** people **around** the world. **In** his speeches, he talks **about** his life.
A **conjunction** connects words or groups of words.	Courage **and** skill have carried him far. He has one disability, **but** he has many abilities.
An **interjection** expresses strong feeling.	**Wow**! What an amazing person he is. **Hurray**! He reached the mountain top.

Grammar and Usage

Grammar and **usage** rules tell us how to correctly identify and use the parts of speech and types of sentences.

Nouns

A **noun** names a person, place, thing, or idea. There are different kinds of nouns.

Common and Proper Nouns	Examples
A **common noun** names a general person, place, thing, or idea.	A **teenager** sat by the **ocean** and read a **magazine**.
Capitalize a common noun only when it begins a sentence.	**Magazines** are the perfect thing to read at the beach.
A **proper noun** names a specific person, place, thing, or idea. Always capitalize a proper noun.	**Jessica** sat by the **Pacific Ocean** and read *Teen Talk Magazine*.

Count and Noncount Nouns	Examples
Count nouns name things that you can count. The singular form of a count noun names one thing. The plural form names more than one thing.	<table><tr><th>Singular</th><th>Plural</th></tr><tr><td>one desk</td><td>two desks</td></tr><tr><td>one book</td><td>many books</td></tr><tr><td>one teacher</td><td>several teachers</td></tr></table>
You can count some food items by using a measurement word like **cup**, **slice**, or **glass** followed by the word **of**. To show the plural form, make the measurement word plural.	Jessica drank **a glass of water** after school. Jessica drank **two glasses of water** while she was reading her book.
Noncount nouns name things that you cannot count. They can be divided into different categories.	

Activities and Sports:	baseball, camping, dancing, golf, singing, soccer
Category Nouns:	clothing, equipment, furniture, machinery, mail
Food:	bread, cereal, cheese, lettuce, meat, milk, soup, tea
Ideas and Feelings:	democracy, enthusiasm, freedom, honesty, health
Materials:	air, fuel, gasoline, metal, paper, water, dust, soil
Weather:	fog, hail, heat, rain, smog, snow, humidity, sunshine

Some nouns can be either count or noncount nouns. It depends on how the nouns are used.	Jessica has read the book two **times**. She is fascinated by the idea of traveling through **time**.

Plural Nouns	Examples
Plural nouns name more than one person, place, thing, or idea. Add **-s** to most count nouns to make them plural.	My favorite **guitar** was made in Spain, but I also like my two American **guitars**.

Other count nouns follow simple rules to form the plural.

Forming Noun Plurals

When a Noun Ends in:	Form the Plural by:	Examples
ch, **sh**, **s**, **x**, or **z**	adding **-es**	box—box**es** brush—brush**es**
a consonant + **y**	changing the **y** to **i** and adding **-es**	story—stor**ies**
a vowel + **y**	just adding **-s**	boy—boy**s**
f or **fe**	changing the **f** to **v** and adding **-es**, in most cases for some nouns that end in **f** or **fe**, just add **-s**	leaf—lea**ves** knife—kni**ves** cliff—cliff**s** safe—safe**s**
a vowel + **o**	adding **-s**	radio—radio**s** kangaroo—kangaroo**s**
a consonant + **o**	adding **-s**, in most cases; other times adding **-es** some nouns take either **-s** or **-es**	photo—photo**s** potato—potato**es** zero—zero**s**/zero**es**

A few count nouns are **irregular**. These nouns do not follow the rules to form the plural.

Forming Plurals of Irregular Count Nouns

For some irregular count nouns, change the spelling to form the plural.	one child many **children**	one man several **men**	one person a few **people**
	one foot many **feet**	one ox ten **oxen**	one woman most **women**
For other irregular count nouns, keep the same form for the singular and the plural.	one deer two **deer**	one fish many **fish**	one sheep twelve **sheep**

Possessive Nouns	Examples
Possessive nouns show ownership or relationship of persons, places, or things.	**Ted's** daughter made the guitar. The **guitar's** tone is beautiful.
Follow these rules to make a noun possessive: • Add **'s** to a singular noun or a plural noun that does not end in **s**. • If the owner's name ends in **s**, form the possessive by adding **'s** or just an apostrophe. Either is correct. • Add an apostrophe after the final **s** in a plural noun that ends in **s**.	When she plays the piano, it attracts **people's** attention. **Louis's** music is playful and funny. **Louis'** music is playful and funny. Three **musicians'** instruments were left on the bus.

Noun Phrases and Clauses	Examples
A **noun phrase** is made up of a noun and its modifiers. Modifiers are words that describe, such as adjectives. A **noun clause** is a group of words that functions as a noun and has a subject and a verb. It may begin with *that*, *how*, or a *wh-* word such as *why*, *what*, or *when*.	**The flying frog** does not actually fly. It glides on **special skin flaps.** Thailand is **a frog-friendly habitat.** **How any animal flies** is hard to understand. He explained **that it is called a flying frog.** Its name makes sense to **whoever sees it.**

Articles

An **article** is a word that helps identify a noun.

Articles	Examples
A, **an**, and **the** are **articles**. An article often comes before a count noun. Do not use the articles **a** or **an** before a noncount noun.	It is **an** amazing event when **a** flying frog glides in **the** forest.
A and **an** are **indefinite articles**. Use **a** or **an** before a noun that names a nonspecific thing.	**A flying frog** stretched its webbed feet. **An owl** watched from a nearby tree.
• Use **a** before a word that starts with a consonant sound.	a **f**oot a **r**ainforest a **p**ool a **u**nion (*u* is pronounced like *y*, a **n**est a consonant)
• Use **an** before a word that starts with a vowel sound.	an **e**gg an **a**nimal an **a**dult an **a**mount an **o**cean an **hou**r (The *h* is silent.)
The is a **definite article**. Use **the** before a noun that names a specific thing.	Leiopelmids are **the** oldest kind of frog in **the** world. They are survivors of **the** Jurassic period.

Pronouns

A **pronoun** is a word that takes the place of a noun. **Case** refers to the form that a pronoun takes to show how it is used in a sentence.

Subjective Case Pronouns	Examples
Use a **subject pronoun** as the subject of a sentence.	**Antonio** is looking forward to the homecoming dance. **He** is trying to decide what to wear. **Subject Pronouns**<table><tr><td>Singular</td><td>Plural</td></tr><tr><td>I</td><td>we</td></tr><tr><td>you</td><td>you</td></tr><tr><td>he, she, it</td><td>they</td></tr></table>
The pronoun **it** can be used as a **subject** to refer to a noun. **But**: The pronoun **it** can be the subject without referring to a specific noun.	The **dance** starts at 7:00. **It** ends at 10:00. **It** is important to arrive on time. **It** is fun to see your friends in formal clothes.

Objective Case Pronouns	Examples
Use an **object pronoun** after an **action verb**.	Tickets are on sale, so buy **them** now. **Object Pronouns**<table><tr><td>Singular</td><td>Plural</td></tr><tr><td>me</td><td>us</td></tr><tr><td>you</td><td>you</td></tr><tr><td>him, her, it</td><td>them</td></tr></table>
Use an **object pronoun** after a **preposition**.	Antonio invited Caryn. He ordered flowers for **her**.
Use **reciprocal pronouns** to show a two-way action between two or more people.	Mary and Juan tossed the ball to **each other**. Mary, Juan, and Lorenzo tested **one another** on the new math skills.

Possessive Words	Examples
A **possessive pronoun** tells who or what owns something.	**His** photograph of a tree won an award.
Possessive pronouns take the place of a **possessive noun and the person**, **place**, **or thing it owns**. Possessive pronouns always stand alone.	Which camera is Aleina's? The expensive camera is **hers**. **Mine** is a single-use, disposable camera.

Possessive Pronouns

Singular	Plural
mine	ours
yours	yours
his, hers	theirs

Some possessive words act as **adjectives**, so they are called **possessive adjectives**. Possessive adjectives always come before a noun.	Aleina's photographs are beautiful because of **her** eye for detail.

Possessive Adjectives

Singular	Plural
my	our
your	your
his, her, its	their

Demonstrative Words	Examples
A **demonstrative pronoun** points out a specific person, place, or thing. It can point to something near or far away.	**That** is a good photo of my grandparents. **These** are good photos, too.

Demonstrative Words

	Singular	Plural
Near	this	these
Far	that	those

A demonstrative word can **act as an adjective**, answering the question *Which one?* or *Which ones?*	**This** photo album has pictures of my family. **These** photographs are of my grandparents.

Indefinite Pronouns	Examples
Use an **indefinite pronoun** when you are not talking about a specific person, place, or thing.	**Someone** has to lose the game. **Nobody** knows who the winner will be.

Some Indefinite Pronouns

These **indefinite pronouns** are always singular and need a **singular verb**.	
another either nobody someone anybody everybody no one something anyone everyone nothing anything everything one each neither somebody	**Something is** happening on the playing field. We hope that **everything goes** well for our team.
These **indefinite pronouns** are always plural and need a **plural verb**. both few many several	**Many** of us **are** hopeful.
These **indefinite pronouns** can be either singular or plural. all any most none some Look at the phrase that follows the indefinite pronoun. If the noun or pronoun in the phrase is plural, use a **plural verb**. If the noun or pronoun is singular, use a **singular verb**.	**Most** of the players **are** tired. **Most** of the game **is** over.

Relative Pronouns	Examples
A **relative pronoun** introduces **a relative clause**. It connects, or relates, the clause to a word in the sentence. Relative pronouns are used in restrictive and nonrestrictive clauses.	**Relative Pronouns** who whoever whosoever whom whomever whomsoever whose which whichever what whatever whatsoever

Grammar Tip

In informal speech, it is acceptable to say "**Who** did you ask?" In formal writing, use the correct form, "**Whom** did you ask?"

Use **who**, **whom**, or **whose** for people. The pronouns **whoever**, **whomever**, **whosoever**, and **whomsoever** also refer to people.	The student **who** was injured is Joe. We play **whomever** we are scheduled to play.
Use **which**, **whichever**, **what**, **whatever**, and **whatsoever** for things.	Joe's wrist, **which** is sprained, will heal.
Use **that** for people or things.	The trainer **that** examined Joe's wrist is sure. The injury **that** Joe received is minor.

Reflexive and Intensive Pronouns	Examples
Reflexive and **intensive pronouns** refer to nouns or other pronouns in a sentence. These pronouns end with -**self** or -**selves**.	**I** will go to the store by **myself**.
Use a **reflexive pronoun** when the object **refers back to the subject**.	To surprise her technology teacher, **Kim** taught **herself** how to create a Web site on the computer.

Reflexive and Intensive Pronouns

Singular	Plural
myself	ourselves
yourself	yourselves
himself, herself, itself	themselves

Use an **intensive pronoun** when you want **to emphasize a noun or a pronoun** in a sentence.	The technology **teacher himself** learned some interesting techniques from Kim.

Agreement and Reference	Examples
When nouns and pronouns **agree**, they both refer to the same person, place, or thing. The **noun** is the **antecedent**, and the **pronoun** refers to it.	**Rafael and Felicia** visited a local college. **They** toured the campus. *antecedent pronoun*
A pronoun must agree (match) in **number** with the noun it refers to. • **Singular pronouns** refer to one person. • **Plural pronouns** refer to more than one person.	**Rafael** plays violin. **He** enjoyed the music school. **The teenagers** were impressed. **They** liked this college.
Pronouns and adjectives must agree in **gender** with the nouns they refer to. Use **she**, **her**, and **hers** to refer to females. Use **he**, **him**, and **his** to refer to males.	Felicia told **her** uncle about the college visit. **Her** uncle told **her** that **he** received **his** graduate degree from that school.

Editing Tip

Find each pronoun in your paper. Find the noun it is replacing. Do they match?

Adjectives

An **adjective** describes, or modifies, a noun or a pronoun. It can tell what kind, which one, how many, or how much.

Adjectives	Examples
Adjectives provide more detailed information about a noun. Usually, an adjective comes before the noun it describes.	Deserts have a **dry** climate.
But an adjective can also come after the noun.	The climate is also **hot**.

Adjectives That Compare	Examples
Comparative adjectives help show the similarities or differences between two nouns.	Deserts are **more fun** to study than forests are.
To form the comparative of one-syllable adjectives and two-syllable adjectives that end in a consonant + **y**, add -**er**, and use **than**. Use **more ... than** if the adjective has three or more syllables.	The Sechura Desert in South America is small**er than** the Kalahari Desert in Africa. Is that desert **more interesting than** this one?
Superlative adjectives help show how three or more nouns are alike or different.	Of the Sechura, Kalahari, and Sahara, which is the **largest**?
To form the superlative of one-syllable adjectives and two-syllable adjectives that end in a consonant + **y**, add -**est**. Use **most** if the adjective has three or more syllables.	Which of the three deserts is the **smallest**? I think the Sahara is the **most beautiful**.
Irregular adjectives form the comparative and superlative differently. good better best some more most bad worse worst little less least	I had the **best** time ever visiting the desert. But the desert heat is **worse** than city heat.
Some two-syllable adjectives form the comparative with either -**er** or **more** and superlative with either -**est** or **most**. **Do not form a double comparison by using both.**	Most desert animals are **more lively** at night than during the day. Most desert animals are **livelier** at night than during the day.

Adjective Phrases and Clauses	Examples
An **adjective phrase** is a group of words that work together to modify a noun or a pronoun. A phrase has no verb.	Plants **in the desert** have developed adaptations.
An **adjective clause** is also a group of words that work together to modify a noun or a pronoun. Unlike a phrase, however, a clause has both a subject and a verb.	Desert plants **that have long roots** tap into water deep in the earth.

Verbs

Every sentence has two parts: a subject and a predicate. The subject tells who or what the sentence is about. The predicate tells something about the subject. For example: The dancers / **performed** on stage.

The **verb** is the key word in the predicate because it tells what the subject does or has. Verbs can also link words.

Action Verbs	Examples
An **action verb** tells what the subject of a sentence does. Most verbs are action verbs.	Dancers **practice** for many hours. They **stretch** their muscles and **lift** weights.
Some **action verbs** tell about an action that you cannot see.	The dancers **recognize** the rewards that come from their hard work.

Linking Verbs	Examples
A **linking verb** connects, or links, the subject of a sentence to a word in the predicate.	**Linking Verbs**

Linking Verbs

Forms of the Verb *Be*

am	was
is	were
are	

Other Linking Verbs

appear	seem	become
feel	smell	taste
look		

The word in the predicate can describe the subject.	Their feet **are** calloused.
Or the word in the predicate can rename the subject.	These dancers **are** athletes.

Conditional Verbs	Examples
Conditional verbs show, in the present, how one event depends on another event in the future.	Dancers **should** stretch to prevent injuries. An injury **might** prevent a dancer from performing.

Some Conditional Verbs

| can | could | might | must |
| shall | should | will | would |

Sentences with conditional verbs often use **if** and **then** to show how two events are connected. Conditional verbs are sometimes called **modal verbs**.	**If** a principal dancer is unable to perform, **then** the understudy will perform the role.

Helping Verbs	Examples
Verb phrases have more than one verb: helping verbs and a main verb.	Ballet **is considered** a dramatic art form. helping verb main verb
The action word is called the **main verb**. It shows what the subject does, has, or is.	This dance form **has been evolving** over the years. helping verbs main verb
Any verbs that come before the main verb are the **helping verbs**.	Ballet **must have been** very different in the 1500s. helping verbs main verb
Helping verbs agree with the subject.	Baryshnikov **has performed** around the world. Many people **have praised** this famous dancer.
Adverbs can be in several places in a sentence. The adverb **not** always comes between the **helping verb** and the **main verb**.	If you **have** not **heard** of him, you can watch the film *Dancers* to see him perform. He sometimes **has danced** in films. Usually, he dances on stage.
In questions, the subject comes between the **helping verb** and the **main verb**.	**Have** you **heard** of Mikhail Baryshnikov?

Helping Verbs

Forms of the Verb *Be*		Forms of the Verb *Do*		Forms of the Verb *Have*	
am	was	do	did	have	had
is	were	does		has	
are					

Other Helping Verbs

To express ability: **can**, **could**	I **can** dance.
To express possibility: **may**, **might**, **could**	I **might** dance tonight.
To express necessity or desire: **must**, **would like**	I **must** dance more often. I **would like** to dance more often.
To express certainty: **will**, **shall**	I **will** dance more often.
To express obligation: **should**, **ought to**	I **should** practice more often. I **ought to** practice more often.

Verb Tense

The **tense** of a verb shows when an action happens.

Present Tense Verbs	Examples
The **present tense** of a verb tells about an action that happens now.	Greg **checks** his watch to see if it is time to leave. He **starts** work at 5:00 today.

Habitual Present Tense Verbs	Examples
The **habitual present tense** of a verb tells about an action that happens regularly or all the time.	Greg **works** at a pizza shop on Saturdays and Sundays. He **makes** pizzas and **washes** dishes.

Past Tense Verbs (Regular and Irregular)	Examples
The **past tense** of a verb tells about an action that happened earlier, or in the past.	Yesterday, Greg **worked** until the shop closed. He **made** 50 pizzas.
• The past tense form of **regular verbs** ends with -**ed**.	He **learned** how to make a stuffed-crust pizza. Then Greg **chopped** onions and peppers.
• **Irregular verbs** have **special forms** to show the past tense. For more irregular verbs, see the **Troubleshooting Guide**, page 773.	Greg **cut** the pizza. It **was** delicious. We **ate** all of it!

Some Irregular Verbs

Present Tense	Past Tense
cut	cut
is	was
eat	ate

Future Tense Verbs	Examples
The **future tense** of a verb tells about an action that will happen later, or in the future. To talk about the future, use:	Greg **will ride** the bus home after work tonight.
• the helping verb **will** plus a main verb.	Greg's mother **will drive** him to work tomorrow. On Friday, he **will get** his first paycheck.
• the phrase **am going to**, **is going to**, or **are going to** plus a **main verb**.	He **is going to take** a pizza home to his family. They **are going to eat** the pizza for dinner.

Perfect Tense Verbs

All verbs in the **perfect tenses**—**present**, **past**, and **future**—have a helping verb and a form of the main verb that is called the **past participle**.

Present Perfect Tense Verbs	Examples
For **regular verbs**, the past tense and the past participle end in -**ed**. To form the present perfect, use **has** or **have** with the past participle.	
Present Tense like	I **like** the Internet.
Past Tense liked	I **liked** the Internet.
Present Perfect has/have liked	I **have** always **liked** the Internet.
Irregular verbs have **special forms** for the past tense and past participle. Always use **has** or **have** with the past participle. See page 773.	
Present Tense know	I **know** a lot about the Internet.
Past Tense knew	I **knew** very little about the Internet last year.
Present Perfect has/have known	I **have known** about the Internet for a long time.
The **present perfect tense** of a verb can tell about an action that began in the past and is still going on.	The public **has used** the Internet since the 1980s. **Have** you **done** research on the Internet?

Past Perfect Tense Verbs	Examples
The **past perfect tense** of a verb tells about an action that was completed before some other action in the past. It uses the helping verb **had** and the past participle of the main verb.	Before the Internet became popular, people **had done** their research in the library.

Future Perfect Tense Verbs	Examples
The **future perfect tense** of a verb tells about an action that will be completed at a specific time in the future. It uses the helping verbs **will have** and the past participle of the main verb.	By the end of next year, 100,000 people **will have visited** our Web site.

Contractions

A **contraction** is a shortened form of a verb or verb and pronoun combination.

Contractions	Examples	
Use an **apostrophe** to show which letters have been left out of the contraction.	I would = I'd they are = they're	is not = isn't can not = can't
In contractions made up of a verb and the word **not**, the word **not** is usually shortened to **n't**.	I **can't** stop eating these cookies!	

Verb Forms

The **form** a verb takes changes depending on how it is used in a sentence, phrase, or clause.

Progressive Verbs	Examples
The **progressive verb** form tells about an action that occurs over a period of time.	
The **present progressive tense** of a verb tells about an action as it is happening.	They **are expecting** a big crowd for the fireworks show this evening.
• It uses the helping verb **am**, **is**, or **are**. The main verb ends in -**ing**.	**Are** you **expecting** the rain to end before the show starts?
The **past progressive tense** of a verb tells about an action that was happening over a period of time in the past.	They **were thinking** of canceling the fireworks.
• It uses the helping verb **was** or **were** and a main verb. The main verb ends in -**ing**.	A tornado **was heading** in this direction.
The **future progressive tense** of a verb tells about an action that will be happening over a period of time in the future.	The weather forecasters **will be watching** for the path of the tornado.
• It uses the helping verbs **will be** plus a main verb. The main verb ends in -**ing**.	I hope that they **will** not **be canceling** the show.

Transitive and Intransitive Verbs	Examples
Action verbs can be transitive or intransitive. A **transitive verb** needs an **object** to complete its meaning and to receive the action of the verb.	**Not complete:** **Complete:** Many cities **use** Many cities **use** fireworks.
The object can be a **direct object**. A direct object answers the question *Whom?* or *What?*	**Whom:** The noise **surprises** the audience. **What:** The people in the audience **cover** their ears.
An **intransitive verb** does not need an object to complete its meaning.	**Complete:** The people in our neighborhood **clap**. They **shout**. They **laugh**.
An **intransitive verb** may end the sentence, or it may be followed by other words that tell how, where, or when. These words are not objects since they do not receive the action of the verb.	The fireworks **glow** brightly. Then, slowly, they **disappear** in the sky. The show **ends** by midnight.

Active and Passive Voice	Examples
A verb is in **active voice** if the **subject** is doing the action.	Many cities **hold** fireworks displays for the Fourth of July.
A verb is in **passive voice** if the **subject** is not doing the action. A verb in passive voice always includes a form of the verb **be**, plus the past participle of the main verb. Use active voice to emphasize the subject. Use passive voice to put less emphasis on the subject, such as when: • the object, or receiver of the action, is more important than the doer • you don't know who the doer is • you don't want to name the doer or place blame	Fireworks displays **are held** by many cities for the Fourth of July. Our celebration **was held** after the winds died down. The fireworks **were made** in the U.S. The start time **is listed** incorrectly in the newspaper.

Two-Word Verbs

A **two-word verb** is a verb followed by a preposition. The meaning of the two-word verb is different from the meaning of the verb by itself.

Some Two-Word Verbs

Verb	Meaning	Example
break **break down** **break up**	to split into pieces to stop working to end to come apart	I didn't **break** the window with the ball. Did the car **break down** again? The party will **break up** before midnight. The ice on the lake will **break up** in the spring.
bring **bring up**	to carry something with you to suggest to raise children	**Bring** your book to class. She **brings up** good ideas at every meeting. **Bring up** your children to be good citizens.
check **check in** **check up** **check off** **check out**	to make sure you are right to stay in touch with someone to see if everything is okay to mark off a list to look at something carefully	We can **check** our answers at the back of the book. I **check in** with my mom at work. The nurse **checks up** on the patient every hour. Look at your list and **check off** the girls' names. Hey, Marisa, **check out** my new bike!

Two-Word Verbs, continued

Verb	Meaning	Example
fill	to place as much as can be held	**Fill** the pail with water.
fill in	to color or shade in a space	Please **fill in** the circle.
fill out	to complete	Marcos **fills out** a form to order a book.
get	to go after something	I'll **get** some milk at the store.
	to receive	I often **get** letters from my pen pal.
get ahead	to go beyond what is expected	She worked hard to **get ahead** in math class.
get along	to be on good terms with	Do you **get along** with your sister?
get out	to leave	Let's **get out** of the kitchen.
get over	to feel better	I hope you'll **get over** the flu soon.
get through	to finish	I can **get through** this book tonight.
give	to hand something to someone	We **give** presents to the children.
give out	to stop working	If she runs ten miles, her energy will **give out**.
give up	to quit	I'm going to **give up** eating candy.
go	to move from place to place	Did you **go** to the mall on Saturday?
go on	to continue	Why do the boys **go on** playing after the bell rings?
go out	to go someplace special	Let's **go out** to lunch on Saturday.
look	to see or watch	Don't **look** directly at the sun.
look over	to review	She **looks over** her test before finishing.
look up	to hunt for and find	We **look up** information on the Internet.
pick	to choose	I'd **pick** Lin for class president.
pick on	to bother or tease	My older brothers always **pick on** me.
pick up	to go faster	Business **picks up** in the summer.
	to gather or collect	**Pick up** your clothes!
run	to move quickly	Juan will **run** in a marathon.
run into	to see someone unexpectedly	Did you **run into** Chris at the store?
run out	to suddenly have nothing left	The cafeteria always **runs out** of nachos.
stand	to be on one's feet	I have to **stand** in line to buy tickets.
stand for	to represent	A heart **stands for** love.
stand out	to be easier to see	You'll **stand out** with that orange cap.
turn	to change direction	We **turn** right at the next corner.
turn up	to raise the volume	Please **turn up** the radio.
turn in	to give back	You didn't **turn in** the homework yesterday.
turn off	to make something stop	Please **turn off** the radio.

Forms of Irregular Verbs

Irregular verbs form the past tense and the past participle in a different way than regular verbs. These verb forms have to be memorized.

Some Irregular Verbs

Irregular Verb	Past Tense	Past Participle	Irregular Verb	Past Tense	Past Participle
be: am, is be: are	was were	been been	eat	ate	eaten
beat	beat	beaten	fall (*intr.*)	fell	fallen
become	became	become	feed	fed	fed
begin	began	begun	feel	felt	felt
bend	bent	bent	fight	fought	fought
bind	bound	bound	find	found	found
bite	bit	bitten	fly	flew	flown
blow	blew	blown	forget	forgot	forgotten
break	broke	broken	forgive	forgave	forgiven
bring	brought	brought	freeze	froze	frozen
build	built	built	get	got	got, gotten
burst	burst	burst	give	gave	given
buy	bought	bought	go	went	gone
catch	caught	caught	grow	grew	grown
choose	chose	chosen	have	had	had
come	came	come	hear	heard	heard
cost	cost	cost	hide	hid	hidden
creep	crept	crept	hit	hit	hit
cut	cut	cut	hold	held	held
dig	dug	dug	hurt	hurt	hurt
do	did	done	keep	kept	kept
draw	drew	drawn	know	knew	known
dream	dreamed, dreamt	dreamed, dreamt	lay (*tr.*)	laid	laid
drink	drank	drunk	lead	led	led
drive	drove	driven	leave	left	left

Irregular Verb	Past Tense	Past Participle
lend	lent	lent
lie (*intr.*)	lay	lain
let	let	let
light	lit	lit
lose	lost	lost
make	made	made
mean	meant	meant
meet	met	met
pay	paid	paid
prove	proved	proved, proven
put	put	put
quit	quit	quit
read	read	read
ride	rode	ridden
ring	rang	rung
rise (*intr.*)	rose	risen
run	ran	run
say	said	said
see	saw	seen
seek	sought	sought
sell	sold	sold
send	sent	sent
set	set	set
shake	shook	shaken
show	showed	shown
shrink	shrank	shrunk
shut	shut	shut

Irregular Verb	Past Tense	Past Participle
sing	sang	sung
sink	sank	sunk
sit	sat	sat
sleep (*intr.*)	slept	slept
slide	slid	slid
speak	spoke	spoken
spend	spent	spent
stand	stood	stood
steal	stole	stolen
stick	stuck	stuck
sting	stung	stung
strike	struck	struck
swear	swore	sworn
swim	swam	swum
swing	swung	swung
take	took	taken
teach	taught	taught
tear	tore	torn
tell	told	told
think	thought	thought
throw	threw	thrown
understand	understood	understood
wake	woke, waked	woken, waked
wear	wore	worn
weep	wept	wept
win	won	won
write	wrote	written

Verbals

A **verbal** is a word made from a verb but used as another part of speech.

Gerunds	Examples
A **gerund** is a verb form that ends in -**ing** and that is used as a noun. Like all nouns, a gerund can be the subject of a sentence or an object.	**Cooking** is Mr. Jimenez's favorite hobby. *subject* Mr. Jimenez truly enjoys **cooking**. *direct object* Mr. Jimenez is very talented at **cooking**. *object of preposition*

Infinitives	Examples
An **infinitive** is a verb form that begins with **to**. It can be used as a noun, an adjective, or an adverb.	Mr. Jimenez likes **to cook**. *noun* Mr. Jimenez's beef tamales are a sight **to see**. *adjective* Mr. Jimenez cooks **to relax**. *adverb*

Participial Phrases	Examples
A **participle** is a verb form that is used as an adjective. For regular verbs, it ends in -**ing** or -**ed**. Irregular verbs take the past participle form.	His **sizzling** fajitas taste delicious. Mr. Jimenez also makes tasty **frozen** desserts.
A **participial phrase** begins with a participle. Place the phrase next to the noun it describes.	**Standing by the grill**, he cooked meat. **Not**: He cooked meat, standing by the grill.

Absolutes

An **absolute** is a sentence-like phrase. It is usually formed with a subject and a participle.

Absolutes	Examples
An **absolute** modifies all the remaining parts of the sentence.	**More guests having arrived,** Mr. Jimenez added burgers to the grill.
Use a comma to set off the **absolute** from the rest of the sentence.	Mr. Jimenez, **his plans for a good party accomplished**, smiled broadly.

A phrase that utilizes a gerund, an infinitive, a participle, or an absolute is known as a **verbal phrase**.

Adverbs

An **adverb** describes a verb, an adjective, or another adverb.

Adverbs	Examples
Adverbs answer one of the following questions: • How? • Where? • When? • How often?	**Carefully** aim the ball. Kick the ball **here**. Try again **later** to make a goal. Cathy **usually** scores.
Adverbs that tell how often usually come before the main verb or after a form of **be**. Other adverbs often come after the verb.	Our team **always wins**. The whole team **plays well**.
An adverb can strengthen the meaning of an **adjective** or another **adverb**.	Gina is **really good** at soccer. She plays **very well**.

> ### Grammar Tip
> Use an adjective, rather than an adverb, after a linking verb.
> *My teacher **is** fairly.*

Adverbs That Compare	Examples
Some **adverbs** compare actions. Add -**er** to compare the actions of two people. Add -**est** to compare the actions of three or more people.	Gina runs **fast**. Gina runs **faster** than Maria. Gina runs **the fastest** of all the players.
If the adverb ends in -**ly**, use **more** or **less** to compare two actions.	Gina aims **more carefully** than Jen. Jen aims **less carefully** than Gina.
Use **the most** or **the least** to compare three or more actions.	Gina aims **the most carefully** of all the players. Jen aims **the least carefully** of all the players.

Adverbial Phrases and Clauses	Examples
An **adverb phrase** is a prepositional phrase that modifies a verb, an adjective, or another adverb.	When Gina kicked the ball, it **went into the net**. The coach was **happy about the score**. Gina plays **best under pressure**.
An **adverb clause** has a subject and a verb. It modifies an independent main clause and cannot stand alone. Adverb clauses can tell when, why, or where.	**After the team won**, the coach praised the players. Everyone was muddy **because it had rained**. Soccer is popular **wherever there are fields available**.

Prepositions

A **preposition** comes at the beginning of a prepositional phrase. **Prepositional phrases** add details to sentences.

Uses of Prepositions	Examples
Some prepositions show **location**.	The Chávez Community Center is **by my house**. The pool is **behind the building**.
Some prepositions show **time**.	The Teen Club's party will start **after lunch**.
Some prepositions show **direction**.	Go **through the building** and **around the fountain** to get **to the pool**. The snack bar is **down the hall**.
Some prepositions have **multiple uses**.	We might see Joshua **at the party**. Meet me **at my house**. Come **at noon**.

Prepositional Phrases	Examples
A **prepositional phrase** starts with a preposition and ends with a noun or a pronoun. It includes all the words in between. The noun or pronoun is the **object of the preposition**.	I live **near the Chávez Community Center**. *object of preposition* Tom wants to walk there **with you and me**. *objects of preposition*
Prepositional phrases are often consecutive.	The Community Center is **up the street** and **on the right**.

Some Prepositions

Location		Time	Direction	Other Prepositions	
above	near	after	across	about	for
behind	next to	before	around	against	from
below	off	during	down	along	of
beside	on	till	into	among	to
between	out	until	out of	as	with
by	outside		through	at	without
in	over		toward	except	
inside	under		up		

Conjunctions and Interjections

A **conjunction** connects words or groups of words. An **interjection** expresses strong feeling or emotion.

Conjunctions	Examples
A **coordinating conjunction** connects words, phrases, or clauses.	
To show similarity: **and**	Irena **and** Irving are twins.
To show difference: **but**, **yet**	I know Irena, **but** I do not know Irving.
To show choice: **or**	They will celebrate their birthday Friday **or** Saturday night.
To show cause/effect: **so**, **for**	I have a cold, **so** I cannot go to the party.
To put negative ideas together: **nor**	My mother will not let me go, **nor** will my father.
Correlative conjunctions are used in pairs. The pair connects phrases or words.	**Some Correlative Conjunctions** both … and not only … but also either … or whether … or neither … nor
A **subordinating conjunction** introduces a **dependent clause** in a complex sentence. It connects the **dependent clause** to the main clause.	**Some Subordinating Conjunctions** after · before · till although · if · until as · in order that · when as if · since · where as long as · so that · while because · though
A **conjunctive adverb** joins two independent clauses. Use a semicolon before the conjunction and a comma after it.	**Some Conjunctive Adverbs** besides · meanwhile · then consequently · moreover · therefore however · nevertheless · thus

> **Grammar Tip**
>
> When you use paired words, make sure you use both words in the sentence. Don't leave one out!

Interjections	Examples
An **interjection** shows emotion. If an interjection stands alone, follow it with an exclamation point.	**Help!** **Oops!** **Oh boy!**
An interjection used in a sentence can be followed by a comma or an exclamation mark. Use a comma after a weak interjection. Use an exclamation mark after a strong interjection.	**Oh**, it's a baby panda! **Hooray!** The baby panda has survived!

Sentences

A **sentence** is a group of words that expresses a complete thought. Every sentence has a subject (a main idea) and a predicate that describes what the main idea is, has, or does. Sentences can be classified according to their function and structure.

Sentence Types	Examples
A **declarative sentence** makes a statement. It ends with a period.	The football game was on Friday. The coach made an important announcement.
An **interrogative sentence** asks a question. It ends with a question mark.	Who heard the announcement? What did the coach say?
An **exclamatory sentence** shows surprise or strong emotion. It ends with an exclamation point.	That's fantastic news! I can't believe it!
An **imperative sentence** gives a command. • An imperative sentence usually begins with a verb and ends with a period. • If an imperative sentence shows strong emotion, it ends with an exclamation point.	Give the team my congratulations. **Be** on time. Beat the opponent!

> **Grammar Tip**
>
> Use **please** to make a command more polite:
>
> *Please call me if you have any questions.*

Negative Sentences	Examples
A **negative sentence** uses a **negative word** to say "no."	The game in Hawaii was **not** boring! **Nobody** in our town missed it on TV. Our team **never** played better.

Negative Words			
no	none	no one	not
nowhere	never	nobody	nothing

Use only one negative word in a sentence. Using two negatives in one sentence is called a **double negative**. Two negatives cancel each other out. **I did not see no one**, means **I saw someone**.	The other team could not do ~~nothing~~ right. _anything_ Their team never scored ~~no~~ points. _any_

Conditional Sentences	Examples
Conditional sentences tell how one action depends on another. These sentences often use conditional or modal verbs, such as **can**, **will**, **could**, **would**, or **might**. Sometimes a conditional sentence tells about an imaginary condition and its imaginary result.	**If** our team returns today, **then** we **will** have a party. **Unless** it rains, we **can** have the party outside. If my dog **could talk**, he **would tell** me his thoughts.

Sentence Structure

Phrases	Examples
A **phrase** is a group of related words that does not have both a subject and a verb. English can have noun phrases, verb phrases, adjective phrases, adverb phrases, prepositional phrases, and more.	The football team has won many games in overtime. *noun phrase* *verb phrase* *noun phrase* *prepositional phrase*

Clauses	Examples
A **clause** is a group of words that has both a **subject** and a **predicate**. A clause can be a complete sentence.	California's population / grew during the 1840s. *subject* *predicate*
An **independent clause** can stand alone as a complete sentence.	California's population / increased. *subject* *predicate*
A **dependent clause** cannot stand alone as a complete sentence.	**because** gold / was found there during that time
An **adjective clause** gives more details about the noun or pronoun that it describes.	The news **that gold had been found** spread fast.
An **adverb clause** can tell when, where, or why.	**When someone found gold**, people celebrated.
A **noun clause** can function as a subject, a direct object, or an object of a preposition.	The reporter knew **why the miners were celebrating.**
A **nonrestrictive clause** is a clause that adds non-essential detail to your sentence. Set it off with commas.	The miners, **who were happy to hear the news,** leaped for joy.

Simple Sentences	Examples
A **simple sentence** is one independent clause with a subject and a predicate. It has no dependent clauses.	Supplies / were scarce. The miners / needed goods and services.

Compound Sentences	Examples
When you join two independent clauses, you make a **compound sentence**.	
Use a comma and a **coordinating conjunction** or a **semicolon** to join independent clauses.	People opened stores, **but** supplies were scarce.
Or use a **conjunctive adverb** with a semicolon before it and a comma after it.	People opened stores; supplies slowly arrived. Miners made money; **however**, merchants made more money.

Complex Sentences	Examples
To make a **complex sentence**, join an independent clause with one or more dependent clauses.	Many writers visited camps **where miners worked**. *independent* *dependent*
If the dependent clause comes first, put a **comma** after it.	**While the writers were there**, they wrote stories about the miners.
Use a comma or commas to separate the nonrestrictive clause from the rest of the sentence.	The writers, **who were from California,** lived in the same tents as the miners.

Compound-Complex Sentences	Examples
You can make a **compound-complex sentence** by joining two or more independent clauses and one or more dependent clauses.	Many miners never found gold, **but** they stayed in California **because they found other jobs there**. *dependent*

Properly Placed Modifiers and Clauses	Examples
Place **modifiers** as closely as possible to the word or words that they describe. The meaning of a clause may be unclear if a modifier is not placed properly.	Unclear: Some miners **only** found fool's gold. (Does *only* describe *found* or *fool's gold*?) Clear: Some miners found **only** fool's gold.
A **misplaced clause** may make a sentence unclear and accidentally funny.	Unclear: I read that miners traveled by mule **when I studied American history**. (Did the miners travel while you studied?)
When the clause is placed properly, it makes the meaning of the sentence clear.	Clear: **When I studied American history**, I read that miners traveled by mule.
A **misplaced modifier** is a phrase placed too far away from the word or words it describes.	Unclear: The stream rushed past the miners, **splashing wildly**. (Did the miners or the stream splash wildly?)
Correct a misplaced modifier by placing it closer to the word or words it describes.	Clear: **Splashing wildly**, the stream rushed past the miners.
A **dangling modifier** occurs when you accidentally forget to include the word being described.	**Standing in rushing streams**, the search for gold was dangerous. (Who stood in the streams?)
Correct a dangling modifier by adding the missing word being described, adding words to the modifier, or rewording the sentence.	The search for gold was dangerous for **miners** standing in rushing streams.

Parenthetical Phrases and Appositives	Examples
A **parenthetical phrase** adds nonessential information to a sentence. You can leave out a nonessential phrase without changing the meaning of the sentence. Use commas to set off a nonessential phrase.	Most miners did not, **in fact**, find gold. Gold, **every miner's dream**, lay deeply buried.
An **appositive phrase** renames the noun next to it. An appositive phrase usually comes after the noun or pronoun it refers to. Use commas to set off an appositive.	James Marshall, **a mill worker**, started the Gold Rush when he found gold nuggets in 1848.

Clauses with Missing Words	Examples
In an **elliptical clause**, a word or words are left out to shorten a sentence and avoid repetition. You can tell what word is missing by reading the rest of the sentence.	Henry found six nuggets; **James**, **eight**. (You can tell that the missing word is "found.")
You may also combine two or more sentences that are similar and include related information. Some words, usually any pronouns that refer back to the subject, can be left out of the combined sentence. This is called **structural omission**.	James counted his gold nuggets. He put them away. He counted them again later.
In this example, the three sentences are combined, using commas and the conjunction **and**. The pronoun *he* is omitted from the final two sentences.	James counted his gold nuggets, put them away, **and** counted them again later.

Restrictive Relative Clauses	Examples
A **restrictive relative clause** is a clause that begins with a relative pronoun, such as **who**, **whom**, **which**, or **that**. You cannot remove the clause without changing its meaning. Do not use commas.	Only people **who have a ticket** can come in. The man **who found the dog** received a reward.

Coordination and Subordination	Examples
Use **coordination** to join clauses of equal weight, or importance.	Gold was often found next to streams, **and** it was also found deep beneath the earth.
Use **subordination** to join clauses of unequal weight, or importance.	The miners were called '49ers. *main idea*
Put the main idea in the main clause and the less important detail in the dependent clause.	Many miners arrived in 1849. *less important detail* The miners were called '49ers because many miners arrived in 1849.

Subjects and Predicates

A **subject** tells who or what the sentence is about. A **predicate** tells something about the subject.

Complete and Simple Subjects	Examples
The **complete subject** includes all the words in the subject.	**Many people** visit our national parks. **My favorite parks** are in the West.
The **simple subject** is the most important word in the complete subject.	Many <u>people</u> visit our national parks. My favorite <u>parks</u> are in the West.

Understood Subject	Examples
When you give a command, you do not state the subject. The subject **you** is understood in an imperative sentence.	Watch the geysers erupt. Soak in the hot springs. See a petrified tree.

It as the Subject	Examples
As the subject of a sentence, the pronoun *it* may refer to a specific noun. Or *it* can be the subject without referring to a specific noun.	See that **stone structure**? **It** is a natural bridge. **It** is amazing to see the natural wonders in these parks.

Complete and Simple Predicate	Examples
The predicate of a sentence tells what the subject is, has, or does. The **complete predicate** includes all the words in the predicate.	People **explore caves in Yellowstone Park**. Many flowers **grow wild throughout the park**. Some people **climb the unusual rock formations**.
The **simple predicate** is the **verb**. It is the most important word in the predicate.	People <u>explore</u> caves in Yellowstone Park. Many flowers <u>grow</u> wild throughout the park. Some people <u>climb</u> the unusual rock formations.

Compound Subject	Examples
A **compound subject** is two or more simple subjects joined by **and** or **or**.	<u>Yosemite</u> and <u>Yellowstone</u> are both in the West. Either <u>spring or fall</u> is a good time to visit.

Compound Predicate	Examples
A **compound predicate** has two or more verbs joined by **and** or **or**.	At Yosemite, some people **fish and swim**. My family **hikes** to the river **or stays** in the cabin. I **have seen** the falls **and have ridden** the trails.

Complete Sentences and Fragments

A **complete sentence** has both a **subject** and a **predicate** and expresses a complete thought. A **fragment** is written like a sentence but is not a complete thought.

Sentences and Fragments	Examples
Begin a complete sentence with a capital letter, and end it with a period or other end mark.	These parks / have many tourist attractions. subject predicate
A **fragment** is a sentence part that is incorrectly used as a complete sentence. For example, the fragment may be missing a subject. Add a subject to correct the problem.	**Incorrect:** Fun to visit because they have many attractions. **Correct:** Parks are fun to visit because they have many attractions.
Writers sometimes use fragments on purpose to emphasize an idea or for another effect.	I did not camp in bear country. **No way. Too dangerous**.

Subject-Verb Agreement

The number of a subject and the number of a verb must agree.

Subject-Verb Agreement	Examples
Use a **singular subject** with a **singular verb**.	Another popular **park is** the Grand Canyon.
Use a **plural subject** with a **plural verb**.	We **were amazed** by the colors of its cliffs.
If the simple subjects in a **compound subject** are connected by **and**, use a plural verb. If the compound subject is connected by **or**, look at the last simple subject. If it is singular, use a **singular verb**. If it is plural, use a **plural verb**.	A **mule** and a **guide are** available for a trip down the canyon. These **rafts or** this **boat is** the best way to go. This **boat or** these **rafts are** the best way to go.
The **subject** and **verb** must agree, even when other words come between them.	The **bikers** in the park **are looking** for animals.
The **subject** and **verb** must agree even if the subject comes after the verb.	There **are** other amazing **parks** in Arizona. Here **is** a **list** of them.

Editing Tip

Read your writing aloud to find mistakes in subject-verb agreement.

Grammar Tip

Subjects and verbs are not in prepositional phrases. Drop these phrases to find the subject and verb more easily.

Parallel Structure

A sentence is **parallel** when all of its parts have the same form.

Parallel Structure	Examples
The parts of a sentence must be **parallel**. Words, phrases, or clauses in a sentence that do the same job should have the same form.	They went hik**ing**, raft**ing**, and horseback rid**ing**. I know **that we must be** in shape to hike the Canyon, **that we have to carry** plenty of water, and **that we need to take and eat** salty snacks.

Mechanics

Proper use of capital letters and correct punctuation is important to effective writing.

Capitalization

Knowing when to use capital letters is an important part of clear writing.

First Word in a Sentence	Examples
Capitalize the first word in a sentence.	**We** are studying the Lewis and Clark Expedition.

In Direct Quotations	Examples
Capitalize the first word in a **direct quotation**.	Clark said, "**There is great joy in camp**." "**We are in view of the ocean**," he said. "**It's the Pacific Ocean**," he added.

In Letters	Examples
Capitalize the first word used in the **greeting** or in the **closing** of a letter.	**D**ear Kim, **Y**our friend,

In Titles of Works	Examples
All important words in a **title** begin with a capital letter. Articles (**a, an, the**), short conjunctions (**and, but, or, so**), and short prepositions (**at, for, from, in, of, with**, etc.) are not capitalized unless they are the first or last word in the title.	**book:** *The Longest Journey* **poem:** "Leaves of Grass" **magazine:** *Flora and Fauna of Arizona* **newspaper:** *The Denver Post* **song:** "Star-Spangled Banner" **game:** Exploration! **TV series:** "The Gilmore Girls" **movie:** *The Lion King*

Pronoun *I*	Examples
Capitalize the pronoun *I* no matter where it is located in a sentence.	**I** was amazed when **I** learned that Lewis and Clark's expedition was over 8,000 miles.

Proper Nouns and Adjectives	Examples
Common nouns name a general person, place, thing, or idea.	**Common Noun**: **t**eam
Proper nouns name a particular person, place, thing, or idea.	**Proper Noun**: **C**orps of **D**estiny
All the important words in a **proper noun** start with a capital letter.	

Proper Nouns and Adjectives, continued	Examples
Proper nouns include the following: • names of people and their titles	**S**tephanie **E**ddins **C**aptain **M**eriwether **L**ewis
Do not capitalize a title if it is used without a name.	The **captain's** co-leader on the expedition was William Clark.
• family titles like *Mom* and *Dad* when they are used as names.	"William Clark is one of our ancestors," **Mom** said.
	I asked my **mom** whose side of the family he was on, hers or my **dad's**.
• names of organizations	United Nations History Club Wildlife Society
• names of languages and religions	Spanish Christianity
• months, days, special days, and holidays	April Sunday Thanksgiving
Names of geographic places are proper nouns. Capitalize street, city, and state names in mailing addresses.	**Cities and States**: Dallas, Texas **Streets and Roads**: Main Avenue **Bodies of Water**: Pacific Ocean **Countries**: Ecuador **Landforms**: Sahara Desert **Continents**: North America **Public Spaces**: Muir Camp **Buildings, Ships, and Monuments**: *Titanic* **Planets and Heavenly Bodies**: Neptune
A **proper adjective** is formed from a **proper noun**. Capitalize proper adjectives.	Napoleon Bonaparte was from **Europe**. He was a **European** leader in the 1800s.

> **Grammar Tip**
>
> If the family title is preceded by a possessive pronoun, always use lower case.

Abbreviations of Proper Nouns

Abbreviations of geographic places are also capitalized.

Geographic Abbreviations

Words Used in Addresses				Some State Names Used in Mailing Addresses			
Avenue	Ave.	Highway	Hwy.	California	CA	Michigan	MI
Boulevard	Blvd.	Lane	Ln.	Florida	FL	Ohio	OH
Court	Ct.	Place	Pl.	Georgia	GA	Texas	TX
Drive	Dr.	Street	St.	Illinois	IL	Virginia	VA

Abbreviations of Personal Titles		
Capitalize abbreviations for a personal title. Follow the same rules for capitalizing a personal title.		
Mr. . . . . Mister	**Mrs.** . . . . . . Mistress	**Dr.** . . . . Doctor
Jr. . . . . Junior	**Capt.** . . . . . Captain	**Sen.** . . . . . . Senator

Punctuation

Punctuation marks are used to emphasize or clarify meanings.

Apostrophe	Examples
Use an **apostrophe** to punctuate a **possessive noun**. If there is one owner, add **'s** to the owner's name. If the owner's name ends in s, it is correct to add **'s** or just the apostrophe. If there is more than one owner, add **'** if the plural noun ends in **s**. Add **'s** if it does not end in **s**.	Mrs. Ramos**'s** sons live in New Mexico. Mrs. Ramos**'** sons live in New Mexico. Her sons**'** birthdays are both in January. She sends cards for her children**'s** birthdays.
Use an **apostrophe** to replace the letters left out of a contraction.	could ~~not~~ = couldn**'t** he ~~would~~ = he**'d**

> **Grammar Tip**
>
> Never use an apostrophe to form a plural—only to show possession or contraction.

End Marks	Examples
Use a **period** at the end of a statement or a polite command. Use a period after an indirect question. An indirect question tells about a question you asked.	Georgia read the paper to her mom. Tell me if there are any interesting articles. She asked if there were any articles about the new restaurant on Stone Street near their house.
Use a **question mark** at the end of a question. Use a question mark after a tag question that comes at the end of a statement.	What kind of food do they serve**?** The food is good, isn't it**?**
Use an **exclamation point** after an interjection. Use an exclamation point at the end of a sentence to show you feel strongly about something.	Wow**!** The chicken parmesan is delicious**!**

Comma	Examples
Use a **comma**:	
• before the **coordinating conjunction** in a compound sentence	Soccer is a relatively new sport in the United States, **but** it has been popular in England for a long time.
• to set off words that interrupt a sentence, such as an **appositive phrase** or a **nonrestrictive clause** that is not needed to identify the word it describes	Mr. Okada, **the soccer coach,** had the team practice skills like passing, **for example,** for the first hour. Passing, **which is my favorite skill,** was fun.
• to separate three or more items in a **series**	Shooting, passing, and dribbling are important skills.
• between two or more adjectives that tell equally about the same noun	The midfielder's quick, unpredictable passes made him the team's star player.
• after an **introductory phrase or clause**	**In the last game,** he made several goals.
• to separate a **nonrestrictive phrase** or **clause**, or a **nonrestrictive relative clause.**	The cook, **who used to be a teacher,** made enough soup to feed all of us.
• before someone's exact words and after them if the sentence continues	Mr. Okada said, "Meet the ball after it bounces," as we practiced our half-volleys.
• before and after a **nonrestrictive clause**	At the end of practice, **before anyone left,** Mr. Okada handed out revised game schedules.
• to set off a short phrase at the beginning of a sentence	**At last**, we could go home.
• to separate contrasting phrases	I like to watch movies, **not plays**.
Use a comma in these places in a letter:	
• between the city and the state	Milpas, AK
• between the date and the year	July 3, 2008
• after the greeting of a personal letter	Dear Mr. Okada,
• after the closing of a letter	Sincerely,

Dash	Examples
Use a **dash** to show a break in an idea or the tone in a sentence.	Water—a valuable resource—is often taken for granted.
Or use a dash to emphasize a word, a series of words, a phrase, or a clause.	It is easy to conserve water—wash full loads of laundry, use water-saving devices, fix leaky faucets.

Ellipsis	Examples
Use an **ellipsis** to show that you have left out words.	A recent survey documented **...** water usage.
Or use an ellipsis to show an idea that trails off.	The survey reported the amount of water wasted **...**

Hyphen	Examples
Use a **hyphen** to:	
• connect words in a number and in a fraction	**One-third** of the people wasted water every day.
• join some words to make a compound word	A **15-year-old boy** and his **great-grandmother** have started an awareness campaign.
• connect a letter to a word	They designed a **T-shirt** for their campaign.
• divide words at the end of a line. Always divide the word between two syllables.	Please join us in our awareness cam-paign.

Italics and Underlining	Examples
When you are using a computer, use **italics** for the names of:	
• magazines and newspapers	I like to read *Time Magazine* and the *Daily News*.
• books	They help me understand our history book, *The U.S. Story*.
• plays	Did you see the play *Abraham Lincoln in Illinois*?
• movies	It was made into the movie *Young Abe*.
• musicals	The musical *Oklahoma!* is about Southwest pioneers.
• music albums	*Greatest Hits from Musicals* is my favorite album.
• TV series	Do you like the singers on the TV show *American Idol*?
If you are using handwriting, underline.	

Parentheses	Examples
Use **parentheses** around extra information in a sentence.	The new story (in the evening paper) is very interesting.

Quotation Marks	Examples
Use **quotation marks** to show:	
• a speaker's exact words	"Listen to this!" Jim said.
• the exact words quoted from a book or other printed material	The announcement in the paper was: "The writer Josie Ramón will be at Milpas Library on Friday."
• the title of a song, poem, short story, magazine article, or newspaper article	Her famous poem "Speaking" appeared in the magazine article "How to Talk to Your Teen."
• the title of a chapter from a book	She'll be reading "Getting Along," a chapter from her new book.
• words used in a special way	We will be "all ears" at the reading.

Grammar Tip

Always put **periods** and **commas** inside quotation marks.

Semicolon	Examples
Use a **semicolon**:	
• to separate two simple sentences used together without a conjunction	A group of Jim's classmates plan to attend the reading; he hopes to join them.
• before a **conjunctive adverb** that joins two simple sentences. Use a comma after the adverb.	Jim wanted to finish reading Josie Ramón's book this evening; **however,** he forgot it at school.
• to separate a group of words in a series if the words in the series already have commas	After school, Jim has to study French, health, and math; walk, feed, and brush the dog; and eat dinner.

Colon	Examples
Use a **colon**:	
• after the greeting in a business letter	Dear Sir or Madam**:**
• to separate hours and minutes	The restaurant is open until 11:30 p.m.

• to start a list	If you decide to hold your banquet here, we can:
	  1. Provide a private room
	  2. Offer a special menu
	  3. Supply free coffee and lemonade.

• to set off a quotation	According to the review in *The Gazette:* El Gato Azul is *the* best place for tapas.
• to set off a list in running text	Among their best tapas are: fried goat cheese, caprece, and crab quesadilla.
• after a signal word like "the following" or "these"	Be sure to try these: black bean cakes, wontons con queso, and calamari frita.

Spelling

Correct spelling is important for clarity.

How to Be a Better Speller
To learn a new word: • Study the word and look up its meaning. • Say the word aloud. Listen as you repeat it. • Picture how the word looks. • Spell the word aloud several times. • Write the word several times for practice. • Use the word often in writing until you are sure of its spelling. • Keep a notebook of words that are hard for you to spell. • Use a dictionary to check your spelling.
Knowing spelling rules can help you when you get confused. Use the rules shown in the boxes to help improve your spelling.

Memorize Reliable Generalizations	Examples
Always put a **u** after a **q**.	The **qu**ick but **qu**iet **qu**arterback asked **qu**antities of **qu**estions. *Exceptions*: Iraq Iraqi
Use **i** before **e** except after **c**.	The f**ie**rce rec**ei**ver was ready to catch the ball. *Exceptions*: • **ei**ther, h**ei**ght, th**ei**r, w**ei**rd, s**ei**ze • w**ei**gh, n**ei**ghbor (and other words where **ei** has the long **a** sound)

Spell Correctly	Examples
If a word ends in a consonant plus **y**, change the **y** to **i** before you add -**es**, -**ed**, -**er**, or -**est**.	The coach was the happ**iest** when his players tried their best.
For words that end in a vowel plus **y**, just add -**s** or -**ed**.	For five days before the game, the team sta**yed** at practice an extra 30 minutes.
If you add -**ing** to a verb that ends in -**y**, do not change the **y** to **i**.	The players learned a lot from stud**ying** the videos of their games.

Troubleshooting Guide

In this section you will find helpful solutions to common problems with grammer, usage, and sentences. There is also an alphabetical list of words that are often misused in English. Use these to help improve your writing skills.

Grammar and Usage: Problems and Solutions

Use these solutions to fix grammar and usage problems.

Problems with Nouns

Problem: The sentence has the wrong plural form of an irregular noun.	**Incorrect:** Many deers live there.
Solution: Rewrite the sentence using the correct plural form. (Check a dictionary.)	**Correct:** Many deer live there.
Problem: The noun should be possessive, but it is not.	**Incorrect:** The beginning should capture the readers interest.
Solution: Add an apostrophe to make the noun possessive.	**Correct:** The beginning should capture the readers' interest.

Problems with Pronouns

Problem: The pronoun does not agree in number or gender with the noun it refers to.	**Incorrect:** Mary called Robert, but they did not answer him.
Solution: Match a pronoun's number and gender to the number and gender of the noun it is replacing.	**Correct:** Mary called Robert, but he did not answer her.
Problem: A pronoun does not agree in number with the indefinite pronoun it refers to.	**Incorrect:** Everyone brought their book to class.
Solution: Make the pronoun and the word it refers to agree in number, so that both are singular or plural.	**Correct:** Everyone brought his or her book to class. All the students brought their books to class.
Problem: A reciprocal pronoun does not agree with the number of nouns it refers to.	**Incorrect:** The three boys gave presents to each other.
Solution: Use *each other* when referring to two people, and use *one another* when referring to more than two people.	**Correct:** The three boys gave presents to one another.

Problems with Pronouns, continued

Problem: It is hard to tell which noun in a compound subject is referred to or replaced. **Solution:** Replace the unclear pronoun with the noun it refers to.	**Incorrect:** Ana and Dawn own a car, but only she drives it. **Correct:** Ana and Dawn own a car, but only Dawn drives it.
Problem: It is unclear which antecedent a pronoun refers to. **Solution:** Rewrite the sentence to make it clearer.	**Incorrect:** The kitten's mother scratched its ear. **Correct:** The mother cat scratched her kitten's ear.
Problem: The object pronoun *them* is used as a demonstrative adjective. **Solution:** Replace *them* with the correct demonstrative adjectives.	**Incorrect:** Were any of them packages delivered? **Correct:** Were any of those packages delivered?
Problem: An object pronoun is used in a compound subject. *Remember that subjects do actions and objects receive actions.* **Solution:** Replace the object pronoun with a subject pronoun.	**Incorrect:** My brother and me rebuild car engines. **Correct:** My brother and I rebuild car engines.
Problem: A subject pronoun is used in a compound object. **Solution:** Replace the subject pronoun with an object pronoun.	**Incorrect:** Leticia asked my brother and I to fix her car. **Correct:** Leticia asked my brother and me to fix her car.
Problem: A subject pronoun is used as the object of a preposition. **Solution:** Replace the subject pronoun with an object pronoun.	**Incorrect:** Give your timesheet to Colin or I. **Correct:** Give your timesheet to Colin or me.
Problem: The subject pronoun *who* is used as an object. **Solution:** Replace *who* with the object pronoun *whom*.	**Incorrect:** Who am I speaking to? **Correct:** Whom am I speaking to?
Problem: The object pronoun *whom* is used as a subject. **Solution:** Replace *whom* with the subject pronoun *who*.	**Incorrect:** Whom shall I say is calling? **Correct:** Who shall I say is calling?

Problems with Verbs

Problem: In a sentence with two verbs, the tense of the second verb doesn't match the first. **Solution:** Keep the verb tense the same unless there is a change in time, such as from past to present.	**Incorrect:** Yesterday, Alberto called me and says he has tickets for the game. **Correct:** Yesterday, Alberto called me and said he had tickets for the game.
Problem: The -ed ending is missing from a regular past-tense verb. **Solution:** Add the -ed ending.	**Incorrect:** This morning, I ask my brother to go with us. **Correct:** This morning, I asked my brother to go with us.
Problem: The wrong form of an irregular verb is used. **Solution:** Replace the wrong form with the correct one. (Check a dictionary.)	**Incorrect:** We brang our portable TV to the game. **Correct:** We brought our portable TV to the game.
Problem: The participle form is used when the past-tense form is required. **Solution:** Replace the wrong form with the correct one. (Check a dictionary.)	**Incorrect:** After the game, we run over to Marcia's house. **Correct:** After the game, we ran over to Marcia's house.
Problem: The passive voice is overused. **Solution:** Put the sentence in the active voice so that the subject does the action instead of receiving it.	**Poor:** A new activity schedule will be created by the camp counselors. Several fun activities are being considered by the counselors. **Better:** The camp counselors are creating a new activity schedule. The counselors are considering several fun activities.
Problem: The sentence has a split infinitive. **Solution:** Rewrite the sentence to keep the infinitive as a single unit.	**Poor:** The boy wanted to slowly walk to school. **Better:** The boy wanted to walk to school slowly.

Problems with Adjectives

Problem:	Incorrect:
The sentence contains a double comparison, using both an -er ending and the word *more*, for example.	Joseph is more older than he looks.
Solution: Delete the incorrect comparative form.	**Correct:** Joseph is older than he looks.

Problem:	Incorrect:
The wrong form of an irregular adjective appears in a sentence that makes a comparison.	Cal feels worser since he ran out of medicine.
Solution: Replace the wrong form with the correct one. (Check a dictionary.)	**Correct:** Cal feels worse since he ran out of medicine.

Problem:	Incorrect:
The wrong demonstrative adjective is used.	That car here is really fast. This car there is not as fast.
Solution: Use *this* or the plural *these* for things that are near or "here." Use *that* or the plural *those* for things that are farther away or "there."	**Correct:** This car here is really fast. That car there is not as fast.

Problem:	Incorrect:
The adjective *good* is used to modify a verb.	Julia did good on her test.
Solution: Rewrite the sentence using the adverb *well*, or add a noun for the adjective to describe.	**Correct:** Julia did well on her test. Julia did a good job on her test.

Problems with Adverbs

Problem:	Incorrect:
An adverb is used to modify a noun or pronoun after the linking verb *feel*.	I feel badly about the mistake.
Solution: Rewrite the sentence using an adjective.	**Correct:** I feel bad about the mistake.

Problem:	Incorrect:
An adverb is used but does not modify anything in the sentence.	Hopefully, I didn't make too many mistakes on the test.
Solution: Rewrite the sentence changing the adverb to a verb.	**Correct:** I hope I didn't make too many mistakes on the test.

Problem:	Incorrect:
Two negative words are used to express one idea.	We don't have no aspirin.
Solution: Change one negative word to a positive word.	**Correct:** We don't have any aspirin.

Sentences: Problems and Solutions

Some problems with sentences in English are the result of missing parts of speech or incorrect punctuation. Two common problems are sentence fragments and run on sentences.

Problems with Sentence Fragments

Problem: An infinitive phrase is punctuated as a complete sentence.	**Incorrect:** To show students alternative ways to learn.
Solution: Add a complete sentence to the phrase.	**Correct:** To show students alternative ways to learn, Mr. Harris organized the trip.
Problem: A clause starting with a relative pronoun is punctuated as a complete sentence.	**Incorrect:** Who might be interested in going on the trip.
Solution: Add a subject and predicate to the sentence.	**Correct:** Anyone who might be interested in going on the trip should see Mr. Harris.
Problem: A participial phrase is punctuated as a complete sentence.	**Incorrect:** When traveling overseas.
Solution: Add a sentence to the participial phrase.	**Correct:** When traveling overseas, always try to speak to people in their native language.

Problems with Run On Sentences

Problem: Two main clauses are separated by a comma. This is known as a comma splice.	**Incorrect:** Many music students fail to practice regularly, this is frustrating for teachers.
Solution: Add a semicolon between the clauses.	**Correct:** Many music students fail to practice regularly; this is frustrating for teachers.
Problem: Two or more main clauses are run together with no punctuation. This is known as a fused sentence.	**Incorrect:** I started playing guitar when I was twelve I thought I was great I knew very little.
Solution: Change one of the clauses into a subordinate clause. Rewrite the sentence as two sentences.	**Correct:** I thought I was great when I started playing guitar at age twelve. I knew very little!
Problem: Two or more main clauses are joined with a conjunction, but without a comma.	**Incorrect:** I continued to take lessons and I realized that I had much to learn to become a good guitarist.
Solution: Use a comma after the first main clause and before the conjunction.	**Correct:** I continued to take lessons, and I realized that I had much to learn to become a good guitarist.

Words Often Confused

This section will help you to choose between words that are often confused.

a lot, allot

A lot means "many" and is always written as two words, never as one word. *Allot* means "to assign."

I have **a lot** of friends who like to run.

We are **allotted** 30 minutes for lunch.

a while, awhile

The two-word form *a while* is a noun phrase and is often preceded by the prepositions *after*, *for*, or *in*. The one-word form *awhile* is an adverb and cannot be used with a preposition.

Let's stop here for **a while**.

Let's stop here **awhile**.

accept, except

Accept is a verb that means "to receive." *Except* can be a verb meaning "to leave out" or a preposition meaning "excluding."

I **accept** everything you say, **except** your point about music.

advice, advise

Advice is a noun that means "ideas about how to solve a problem." *Advise* is a verb and means "to give advice."

I will give you **advice** about your problem today, but do not ask me to **advise** you again tomorrow.

affect, effect

Affect is a verb. It means "to cause a change in" or "to influence." *Effect* as a verb means "to bring about." As a noun, *effect* means "a result."

The sunshine will **affect** my plants.

The governor is working to **effect** change.

The rain had no **effect** on our spirits.

aren't

Ain't is not used in formal English. Use the correct form of the verb *be* with the word *not*: *is not*, *isn't*; *are not*, or *aren't*.

We **are not going to sing** in front of you.

I **am not going to practice** today.

all ready, already

Use the two-word form, *all ready*, to mean "completely finished." Use the one-word form, *already*, to mean "before."

We waited an hour for dinner to be **all ready**.

It is a good thing I have **already** eaten today.

all right

The expression *all right* means "OK" and should be written as two words. The one-word form, *alright*, is not used in formal writing.

I hope it is **all right** that I am early.

all together, altogether

The two-word form, *all together*, means "in a group." The one-word form, *altogether*, means "completely."

It is **altogether** wrong that we will not be **all together** this holiday.

among, between

Use *among* when comparing more than two people or things. Use *between* when comparing a person or thing with one other person, thing, or group.

You are **among** friends.

We will split the money **between** Sal and Jess.

amount of, number of

Amount of is used with nouns that cannot be counted. *Number of* is used with nouns that can be counted.

The **amount of** pollution in the air is increasing.

A record **number of** people attended the game.

assure, ensure, insure

Assure means "to make feel better." *Ensure* means "to guarantee." *Insure* means "to cover financially."

I **assure** you that he is OK.

I will personally **ensure** his safety.

If the car is **insured,** the insurance company will pay to fix the damage.

being as, being that

Neither of these is used in formal English. Use *because* or *since* instead.

I went home early **because** I was sick.

beside, besides

Beside means "next to." *Besides* means "plus" or "in addition to."

Located **beside** the cafeteria is a vending machine.

Besides being the fastest runner, she is also the nicest team member.

bring, take

Bring means "to carry closer." *Take* means "to grasp." *Take* is often used with the preposition *away* to mean "carry away from."

Please **bring** the dictionary to me and **take** the thesaurus from my desk.

bust, busted

Neither of these is used in formal English. Use *broke* or *broken* instead.

I **broke** the vase by accident.

The **broken** vase cannot be fixed.

can't; hardly; scarcely

Do not use *can't* with *hardly* or *scarcely*. That would be a double negative. Use only *can't*, or use *can* plus a negative word.

I **can't** get my work done in time.

I **can scarcely** get my work done in time.

capital, capitol

A *capital* is a place where a government is located. A *capitol* is an actual government building.

The **capital** of the U.S. is Washington, D.C.

The senate met at the **capitol** to vote.

cite, site, sight

To *cite* means "to quote a source." A *site* is "a place." *Sight* can mean "the ability to see" or it can mean "something that can be seen."

Be sure to **cite** all your sources.

My brother works on a construction **site**.

Dan went to the eye doctor to have his **sight** checked.

The sunset last night was a beautiful **sight**.

complement, compliment

Complement means "something that completes" or "to complete." *Compliment* means "something nice someone says about another person" or "to praise."

The colors you picked really **complement** each other.

I would like to **compliment** you on your new shoes.

could have, should have, would have, might have

Be sure to use "have," not "of," with words like *could*, *should*, *would*, and *might*.

I **would have** gone, but I didn't feel well.

council, counsel

A *council* is a group that gives advice. To *counsel* is to give advice to someone.

The city **council** met to discuss traffic issues.

Mom, please **counsel** me on how to handle this situation.

coup d'état, coup de grâce

A *coup d'état* ("stroke of state") usually refers to the overthrow of a government. A coup de *grâce* ("stroke, or blow, or mercy") refers to a final action that brings victory.

different from, different than

Different from is preferred in formal English and is used when the comparison is between two persons or things. *Different than*, when used, is used with full clauses.

My interest in music is **different from** my friend's.

Movies today are **different than** they used to be in the 1950s.

each other, one another

Each other refers to two people. *One another* refers to more than two people.

Mika and I gave **each other** presents for Christmas.

The five of us looked out for **one another** on the field trip.

farther, further

Farther refers to a physical distance. *Further* refers to time or amount.

If you go down the road a little **farther**, you will see the sign.

We will discuss this **further** at lunch.

fewer, less

Fewer refers to things that can be counted individually. *Less* refers to things that cannot be counted individually.

The farm had **fewer** animals than the zoo, so it was **less** fun to visit.

good, well

The adjective *good* means "kind." The adjective *well* means "healthy." The adverb *well* means "ably."

She is a **good** person.

I am glad to see that you are **well** again after that illness.

You have performed **well**.

immigrate to, emigrate from

Immigrate to means "to move to a country." *Emigrate from* means "to leave a country."

I **immigrated to** America in 2001 from Panama.

I **emigrated from** El Salvador because of the war.

it's, its

It's is a contraction of *it is*. *Its* is a possessive word meaning "belonging to it."

It's going to be a hot day.

The dog drank all of **its** water already.

kind of, sort of

These words mean "a type of." In formal English, do not use them to mean "partly." Use *somewhat* or *rather* instead.

The peanut is actually a **kind of** bean.

I feel **rather** silly in this outfit.

lay, lie

Lay means "to put in a place." It is used to describe what people do with objects. *Lie* means "to recline." People can *lie* down, but they *lay* down objects. Do not confuse this use of *lie* with the noun that means "an untruth."

I will **lay** the book on this desk for you.

She **lay** the baby in his crib.

I'm tired and am going to **lie** on the couch.

If you **lie** in court, you will be punished.

learn, teach

To *learn* is "to receive information." To *teach* is "to give information."

If we want to **learn**, we have to listen.

She will **teach** us how to drive.

leave (alone), let

Leave alone means "not to disturb someone." *Let* means "to allow or permit."

Leave her **alone**, and she will be fine.

Let them go.

like, as

Like can be used either as a preposition or as a verb meaning "to care about something." *As* is a conjunction and should be used to introduce a subordinate clause.

She sometimes acts **like** a princess. But I still **like** her.

She acts **as** if she owns the school.

loose, lose

Loose can be used as an adverb or adjective meaning "free" or "not securely attached." The verb *lose* means "to misplace" or "not to win."

I let the dog **loose** and he is missing.

Did you **lose** your homework?

Did they **lose** the game by many points?

passed, past

Passed is a verb that means "moved ahead of" or "succeeded." *Past* is a noun that means "the time before the present."

The car **passed** us quickly.

I **passed** my English test.

Poor grades are in the **past** now.

precede, proceed

Precede means "to come before." *Proceed* means "to go forward."

> Prewriting **precedes** drafting in the writing process.

> Turn left; then **proceed** down the next street.

principal, principle

A *principal* is "a person of authority." Principal can also mean "main." A *principle* is "a general truth or belief."

> The **principal** of our school makes an announcement every morning.

> The **principal** ingredient in baking is flour.

> The essay was based on the **principles** of effective persuasion.

raise, rise

The verb *raise* takes an object and means "to lift" or "to be brought up." The verb *rise* means "to lift oneself up." People can *rise*, but objects are *raised*.

> **Raise** the curtain for the play.

> She **raises** baby rabbits on her farm.

> I **rise** from bed every morning at six.

real, really

Real means "actual." It is an adjective used to describe nouns. *Really* means "actually" or "truly." It is an adverb used to describe verbs, adjectives, or other adverbs.

> The diamond was **real**.

> The diamond was **really** beautiful.

set, sit

The verb *set* usually means "to put something down." The verb *sit* means "to go into a seated position."

> I **set** the box on the ground.

> Please **sit** while we talk.

than, then

Than is used to compare things. *Then* means "next" and is used to tell when something took place.

> She likes fiction more **than** nonfiction.

> First, we will go to town; **then** we will go home.

they're, their, there

They're is the contraction of *they are*. *Their* is the possessive form of the pronoun *they*. *There* is used to indicate location.

> **They're** all on vacation this week.

> I want to use **their** office.

> The library is right over **there**.

> **There** are several books I want to read.

this, these, that, those

This indicates something specific that is near someone. *These* is the plural form. *That* indicates something specific that is farther from someone. *Those* is the plural form of *that*.

> **This** book in my hand belongs to me. **These** pens are also mine.

> **That** book is his. **Those** notes are his, too.

where

Do not use *at* or *to* after *where*. Simply use *where*.

> The restaurant is **where** I am right now.

> **Where** is Ernesto?

who, whom

Who is a subject. *Whom* is an object.

> **Who** is going to finish first?

> My grandmother is a woman to **whom** I owe many thanks.

who's, whose

Who's is a contraction of *who is*. *Whose* is the possessive form of *who*.

> **Who's** coming to our dinner party?

> **Whose** car is parked in the garage?

Grammar Tip

If you can replace *who* or *whom* with *he*, *she*, or *they*, use *who*. If you can replace the word with *him*, *her*, or *them*, use *whom*.

you're, your

You're is a contraction of *you are*. *Your* is a possessive adjective meaning "belonging to you."

> **You're** going to be late if you don't hurry.

> Is that **your** backpack under the couch?

Literary Terms

A

Alliteration The repetition of the same sounds (usually consonants) at the beginning of words that are close together. *Example:* Molly makes magnificent mousse, though Pablo prefers pecan pie.

> *See also* **Assonance; Consonance; Repetition**

Allusion A key form of literary language, in which one text makes the reader think about another text that was written before it. Allusion can also mean a reference to a person, place, thing, or event that is not specifically named. *Example:* When Hannah wrote in her short story that vanity was the talented main character's "Achilles heel," her teacher understood that Hannah was referring to a character in a Greek myth. So, she suspected that the vanity of the main character in Hannah's short story would prove to be the character's greatest weakness.

> *See also* **Connotation; Literature; Poetry**

Analogy A way of illustrating a thing or an idea by comparing it with a more familiar thing or idea. *Example: Blogs* are to the *Internet* as *journals* are to *paper*.

> *See also* **Illustration; Metaphor; Rhetorical device; Simile**

Antagonist A major character who opposes the main character, or protagonist, in a fictional narrative or a play. *Example:* In many fairy tales, a wolf is the antagonist.

> *See also* **Protagonist**

Argument A type of writing or speaking that supports a position or attempts to convince the reader or listener. Arguments include a claim that is supported by reasons and evidence.

> *See also* **Claim; Reason; Evidence**

Article A short piece of nonfiction writing on a specific topic. Articles usually appear in newspapers and magazines.

> *See also* **Nonfiction; Topic**

Assonance The repetition of the same or similar vowel sounds between consonants in words that are close together. *Example:* The expression, "mad as a hatter."

> *See also* **Alliteration; Consonance; Repetition**

Autobiography The story of a person's life, written by that person. *Example:* Mahatma Gandhi wrote an autobiography titled *Gandhi: An Autobiography: The Story of My Experiments With Truth*.

> *See also* **Biography; Diary; Journal; Memoir; Narration; Personal narrative**

B

Biography The story of a person's life, written by another person.

> *See also* **Autobiography; Narration**

Blank verse A form of unrhymed verse in which each line normally has 10 syllables divided into five pairs of one unstressed and one stressed syllable. Of all verse forms, blank verse comes closest to the natural rhythms of English speech. Consequently, it has been used more often, in more ways than any other verse form in English. *Example:* Today she darts from the room with delight./Bizarre she does seem, like a haughty queen./I long to make her hot cinnamon tea/ One day, she will love me as I do her./

> *See also* **Meter; Rhyme; Stress; Verse**

C

Character A person, an animal, or an imaginary creature in a work of fiction.

> *See also* **Characterization; Character traits; Fiction**

Characterization The way a writer creates and develops a character. Writers use a variety of ways to bring a character to life: through descriptions of the character's appearance, thoughts, feelings, and actions; through the character's words; and through the words or thoughts of other characters.

> *See also* **Character; Character traits; Dynamic character; Motive; Point of view; Short story; Static character**

Character traits The special qualities of personality that writers give their characters.

> *See also* **Character; Characterization**

Claim A statement that clearly identifies an author's ideas or opinion.

> *See also* **Argument, Reason, Evidence**

Climax The turning point or most important event in a plot.

> *See also* **Falling action; Plot; Rising action**

Comedy A play or a fictional story written mainly to amuse an audience. Most comedies end happily for the leading characters.

> *See also* **Drama; Narration; Play**

Complication See **Rising action**

Conflict The main problem faced by the protagonist in a story or play. The protagonist may be involved in a struggle against nature, another character (usually the *antagonist*), or society. The struggle may also be between two elements in the protagonist's mind.

> *See also* **Plot**

Connotation The feelings suggested by a word or phrase, apart from its dictionary meaning. *Example:* The terms "used car" and "previously owned vehicle" have different connotations. To most people, the phrase "previously owned vehicle" sounds better than "used car."

> *See also* **Denotation; Poetry**

Consonance The repetition of the same or similar consonant sounds that come after different vowel sounds in words that are close together. *Example:* Sid did bid on a squid, he did.

> *See also* **Alliteration; Assonance; Repetition**

D

Denotation The dictionary meaning of a word or phrase. Denotation is especially important in functional texts and other types of nonfiction used to communicate information precisely.

> *See also* **Connotation; Functional text; Nonfiction**

Description Writing that creates a "picture" of a person, place, or thing—often using language that appeals to the five senses: sight, hearing, touch, smell, and taste. *Example:* The bright, hot sun beat down on Earth's surface. Where once a vibrant lake cooled the skin of hippos and zebras, only thin, dry cracks remained, reaching across the land like an old man's fingers, as far as the eye could see. The smell of herds was gone, and only silence filled the space.

> *See also* **Imagery**

Dialect A form of a language commonly spoken in a certain place or by a certain group of people—especially a form that differs from the one most widely accepted. Dialect includes special words or phrases as well as particular pronunciations and grammar. Writers use dialect to help make their characters and settings lively and realistic. *Example:* While someone from the southern United States might say "ya'll" when referring to several friends, someone from the Northeast or Midwest might say "you guys."

> *See also* **Diction; Jargon**

Dialogue What characters say to each other. Writers use dialogue to develop characters, move the plot forward, and add interest. In most writing, dialogue is set off by quotation marks; in play scripts, however, dialogue appears without quotation marks.

Diary A book written by a person about his or her own life as it is happening. Unlike an autobiography, a diary is not usually meant to be published. It is made up of entries that are written shortly after events occur. The person writing a diary often expresses feelings and opinions about what has happened.

> *See also* **Autobiography; Journal**

Drama A kind of writing, in verse or prose, in which a plot unfolds in the words and actions of characters performed by actors. Two major genres of drama are comedy and tragedy.

> *See also* **Comedy; Genre; Play; Plot; Tragedy**

Dramatic conventions The usual ways of making drama seem real. Dramatic conventions include imagining that actors really are the characters they pretend to be and that a stage really is the place it represents.

Dynamic character A character who changes because of actions and experiences.

> See also **Character; Static character**

E

Editorial An article in a newspaper or magazine that gives the opinions of the editors or publishers. *Example:* Rather than just reporting the facts, a newspaper editorial might argue that the city government should not clear preserved woodlands in order to build a shopping mall.

Electronic text Writing that a computer can store or display on a computer screen. Forms of electronic text include *Web sites* (groupings of World Wide Web pages that usually contain hyperlinks), *blogs* (Web logs—sites maintained by an individual or organization that contain various kinds of informal writing, such as diaries, opinion pieces, and stories), and *e-mail*.

Epic A long, fictional, narrative poem, written in a lofty style, that celebrates the great deeds of one or more heroes or heroines. *Example:* Homer's *The Odyssey* is a famous epic poem of over 12,000 lines. The hero, Odysseus, spends ten years overcoming various obstacles in order to return home to his wife and son after the end of the Trojan War.

> See also **Fiction; Hero** or **Heroine; Poetry**

Essay A short piece of nonfiction, normally in prose, that discusses a single topic without claiming to do so thoroughly. Its purpose may be to inform, entertain, or persuade.

> See also **Exposition; Nonfiction; Persuasion; Photo-essay; Review; Topic**

Evidence Information provided to support a claim. Facts, statistics, and quotes from experts are commonly used as evidence.

> See also **Argument; Claim; Reasons**

Exposition The rising action of a story in which characters and the problems they face are introduced.

> See also **Description; Functional text; Narration; Persuasion; Rising action**

F

Fable A brief fictional narrative that teaches a lesson about life. Many fables have animals instead of humans as characters. Fables often end with a short, witty statement of their lesson. *Example:* "The Tortoise and the Hare" is a famous fable in which a boastful, quick-moving hare challenges a slow-moving tortoise to a race. Because the overconfident hare takes a nap during the race, the tortoise wins. The moral of the fable is that slow and steady wins the race.

> See also **Fiction; Folk tale; Narration**

Falling action The actions and events in a plot that happen after the climax. Usually, the major problem is solved in some way, so the remaining events serve to bring the story to an end.

> See also **Climax; Conflict; Plot, Rising action**

Fantasy Fiction in which imaginary worlds differ from the "real" world outside the text. Fairy tales, science fiction, and fables are examples of fantasy.

> See also **Fable; Fiction; Science fiction**

Fiction Narrative writing about imaginary people, places, things, or events.

> See also **Fable; Fantasy; Folk tale; Historical fiction; Myth; Narration; Nonfiction; Novel; Realistic fiction; Science fiction; Short story; Tall tale**

Figurative language The use of a word or phrase to say one thing and mean another. Figurative language is especially important in literature and poetry because it gives writers a more effective way of expressing what they mean than using direct, literal language. *Example:* Upon receiving her monthly bills, Victoria complained that she was "drowning in debt."

> See also **Hyperbole; Idiom; Imagery; Irony; Literature; Metaphor; Personification; Poetry; Simile; Symbol**

Flashback An interruption in the action of a narrative to tell about something that happened earlier. It is often used to give the reader background information about a character or situation.

> See also **Character; Narration**

Folk literature The collection of a people's literary works shared mainly orally rather than in writing. Such works include spells, songs, ballads (songs that tell a story), jokes, riddles, proverbs, nursery rhymes, and folk tales.

> See also **Folk tale; Folklore; Literature; Song lyrics**

Folk tale A short, fictional narrative shared orally rather than in writing, and thus partly changed through its retellings before being written down. Folk tales include myths, legends, fables, tall tales, ghost stories, and fairy tales.

> See also **Fable; Folk literature; Myth; Tall tale**

Folklore The collection of a people's beliefs, customs, rituals, spells, songs, sayings, and stories as shared mainly orally rather than in writing.

> See also **Folk literature; Folk tale**

Foreshadowing A hint that a writer gives about an event that will happen later in a story. *Example:* In a story about a teenage girl who starts getting into trouble, an early scene may show her friend stealing earrings from a jewelry store. Later the girl herself begins stealing. Based on the earlier scene, the reader might guess this is what the girl would do.

Free verse Writing that is free of meter, and thus not really verse at all. It is closer to rhythmic prose or speech. But like verse, and unlike prose or speech, it is arranged in lines, which divide the text into units of rhythm. Free verse may be rhymed or unrhymed.

> See also **Meter; Prose; Rhyme; Rhythm; Verse**

Functional text Writing in which the main purpose is to communicate the information people need to accomplish tasks in everyday life. *Examples:* résumés, business letters, instruction manuals, and the help systems of word-processing programs.

G

Genre A type or class of literary works grouped according to form, style, and/or topic. Major genres include fictional narrative prose (such as short stories and most novels), nonfiction narrative prose (such as autobiographies, historical accounts, and memoirs), drama (such as comedies and tragedies), verse (such as lyrics and epics), and the essay.

> See also **Essay; Fiction; Literature; Narration; Nonfiction; Prose; Style; Topic; Verse**

H

Haiku A form of short, unrhymed poetry that expresses a moment of sudden, intensely felt awareness. The words in haiku focus on what can be seen, smelled, tasted, touched, or heard. The haiku was invented in Japan, and it traditionally consists of 17 syllables in three lines of 5, 7, and 5 syllables. *Example:*

Gold, red leaves rustle
A baby cries somewhere near
Blue sky fades to gray.

> See also **Imagery; Lyric; Poetry**

Hero or **Heroine** In myths and legends, a man or woman of great courage and strength who is celebrated for his or her daring feats; also, any protagonist, or main character.

> See also **Myth; Protagonist**

Historical account A piece of nonfiction writing about something that happened in the past.

> See also **Memoir; Nonfiction**

Historical fiction Fiction based on events that actually happened or on people who actually lived. It may be written from the point of view of a "real" or an imaginary character, and it usually includes invented dialogue.

> See also **Fiction**

Humor A type of writing meant to be funny in a good-natured way. It often makes what characters look like, say, or do seem serious to them but ridiculous to the reader.

> See also **Parody**

Hyperbole Figurative language that exaggerates, often to the point of being funny, to emphasize something. *Example:* When his mother asked how long he had waited for the school bus that morning, Jeremy grinned and said, "Oh, not long. Only about a million years."

See *also* **Figurative language; Tall tale**

I

Idiom A phrase or expression that means something different from the word or words' dictionary meanings. Idioms cannot be translated word for word into another language because an idiom's meaning is not the same as that of the individual words that make it up. *Example:* "Mind your p's and q's" in English means to be careful, thoughtful, and behave properly.

Illustration Writing that uses examples to support a main idea. Illustration is often used to help the reader understand general, abstract, or complex ideas.

Imagery Figurative language that communicates sensory experience. Imagery can help the reader imagine how people, places, and things look, sound, taste, smell, and feel. It can also make the reader think about emotions and ideas that commonly go with certain sensations. Because imagery appeals to the senses, it is sometimes called *sensory language*.

See *also* **Description; Figurative language; Symbol**

Interview A discussion between two or more people in which questions are asked and answered so that the interviewer can get information. The record of such a discussion is also called an interview.

Irony A type of figurative language that takes three forms: (1) *verbal irony* means the opposite of what is said, or it means both what is said and the opposite of what is said, at once; (2) *dramatic irony* (a) contrasts what a speaker or character says with what the writer means or thinks, or (b) in a story, presents a speech or an action that means more to the audience than to the character who speaks or performs it, because the audience knows something the character does not; (3)

situational irony (a) contrasts an actual situation with what would seem appropriate, or (b) contrasts what one expects with what actually happens. *Examples:* 1. Verbal Irony: After having her car towed, getting drenched in a thunderstorm, and losing her wallet, Kate told her friend, "Let me tell you, today has been a real picnic."
2. Dramatic Irony: In the final scene of William Shakespeare's play *Romeo and Juliet*, Romeo finds Juliet drugged. While the audience knows that she is still alive, Romeo presumes that she is dead and decides to kill himself. Juliet shortly thereafter awakes and, upon finding Romeo dead, kills herself.
3. Situational Irony: In O. Henry's short story "The Gift of the Magi," a husband and wife each want to buy a Christmas present for the other. The wife buys her husband a chain for his watch; the husband buys the wife combs for her hair. To get enough money to buy these gifts, the wife cuts and sells her hair, and the husband sells his watch.

See *also* **Figurative language**

J

Jargon Specialized language used by people to describe things that are specific to their group or subject. *Example: Mouse* in a computer class means "part of a computer system," not "a rodent."

See *also* **Dialect; Diction**

Journal A personal record, similar to a diary. It may include accounts of actual events, stories, poems, sketches, thoughts, essays, a collection of interesting information, or just about anything the writer wishes to include.

See *also* **Diary**

L

Literature A body of written works in prose or verse.

See *also* **Functional text; Poetry; Prose; Verse**

Literary criticism The careful study and discussion of works of literature, mainly to understand them and judge their effectiveness.

See *also* **Literature**

Lyric One of the main types of poetry. Lyrics tend to be short and songlike, and express the state of mind—or the process of observing, thinking, and feeling—of a single "speaker."

 See also **Haiku; Poetry; Song lyrics; Sonnet**

M

Memoir A written account of people the author has known and events he or she has witnessed. *Example:* Elie Wiesel's novel *Night* is a memoir. It documents his personal experiences in a concentration camp during World War II.

 See also **Autobiography; Historical account**

Metaphor A type of figurative language that compares two unlike things by saying that one thing is the other thing. *Example:* Dhara says her grandfather can be a real mule when he doesn't get enough sleep.

 See also **Figurative language; Simile; Symbol**

Meter The patterning of language into regularly repeating units of rhythm. Language patterned in this way is called *verse*. Most verse in English has been written in one of two main types of meter: (1) *accentual*, which depends on the number of stressed syllables in a line; (2) *accentual-syllabic*, which depends on the number of stressed and unstressed syllables in a line. By varying the rhythm within a meter, the writer can heighten the reader's attention to what is going on in the verse and reinforce meaning.

 See also **Poetry; Rhythm; Stress; Verse**

Mood The overall feeling or atmosphere a writer creates in a piece of writing.

 See also **Tone**

Motive The reason a character has for his or her thoughts, feelings, actions, or words. *Example:* Maria's motive for bringing cookies to her new neighbors was to learn what they were like.

 See also **Characterization**

Myth A fictional narrative, often a folk tale, that tells of supernatural events as a way of explaining natural events and their relation to human life. Myths commonly involve gods, goddesses, monsters, and superhuman heroes or heroines.

 See also **Folk tale; Hero** or **Heroine**

N

Narration The telling of events (a story), mostly through explanation and description, rather than through dialogue.

 See also **Narrator; Point of view; Story**

Narrative Writing that gives an account of a set of real or imaginary events (the story), which the writer selects and arranges in a particular order (the plot). Narrative writing includes nonfiction works such as news articles, autobiographies, and historical accounts, as well as fictional works such as short stories, novels, and epics.

 See also **Autobiography; Fiction; Historical account; Narrator; Nonfiction; Plot; Story**

Narrator Someone who gives an account of events. In fiction, the narrator is the teller of a story (as opposed to the real author, who invented the narrator as well as the story). Narrators differ in how much they participate in a story's events. In a first-person narrative, the narrator is the "I" telling the story. In a third-person narrative, the narrator is not directly involved in the events and refers to characters by name or as *he, she, it,* or *they.* Narrators also differ in how much they know and how much they can be trusted by the reader.

 See also **Character; Narration; Point of view; Voice**

Nonfiction Written works about events or things that are not imaginary; writing other than fiction.

 See also **Autobiography; Biography; Diary; Encyclopedia; Essay; Fiction; Historical account; Journal; Memoir; Personal narrative; Photo-essay; Report; Textbook**

Novel A long, fictional narrative, usually in prose. Its length enables it to have more characters, a more complicated plot, and a more fully developed setting than shorter works of fiction.

 See also **Character; Fiction; Narration; Plot; Prose; Setting; Short story**

O

Onomatopoeia The use of words that imitate the sounds they refer to. *Examples: buzz, slam, hiss*

P

Paradox A statement or an expression that seems to contradict itself but may, when thought about further, begin to make sense and seem true. Paradox can shock the reader into attention, thus underscoring the truth of what is being said. *Example:* The Time Paradox: A man travels back in time and kills his grandfather. The paradox is that if he killed his grandfather, the man himself never would have been born.

Parody A piece of writing meant to amuse by imitating the style or features of another (usually serious) piece. It makes fun of the original by taking the elements it imitates to extreme or ridiculous lengths or by applying them to a lowly or comically inappropriate subject. *Example:* In 1729, Jonathan Swift wrote a pamphlet titled "A Modest Proposal." In it, he outrageously recommends that the poor sell their children as food to the wealthy in order to make money. "A Modest Proposal" is a parody of similar pamphlets distributed by the wealthy business class, whose practices, Swift believed, neglected human costs and made it difficult for the poor to overcome poverty.

    See also **Genre; Humor; Style**

Personal narrative An account of a certain event or set of events in a person's life, written by that person.

    See also **Autobiography; Narration**

Personification Figurative language that describes animals, things, or ideas as having human traits. *Examples:* in the movie *Babe* and in the book *Charlotte's Web*, the animals are all personified

    See also **Figurative language**

Persuasion Writing that attempts to get someone to do or agree to something by appealing to logic or emotion. Persuasive writing is used in advertisements, editorials, sermons, and political speeches.

    See also **Description; Editorial; Exposition; Narration; Rhetorical device**

Photo-essay A short nonfiction piece made up of photographs and captions. The photographs are as important as the words in giving information to the reader.

    See also **Essay; Nonfiction**

Play A work of drama, especially one written to be performed on a stage. *Example:* Lorraine Hansberry's *A Raisin in the Sun*

    See also **Drama**

Plot The pattern of events and situations in a story or play. Plot is usually divided into four main parts: *conflict* (or *problem*), *rising action* (or *exposition* or *complication*), *climax*, and *falling action* (or *resolution*).

    See also **Climax; Conflict; Drama; Falling action; Fiction; Narration; Rising action; Story**

Poetry A form of literary expression that uses line breaks for emphasis. Poems often use connotation, imagery, metaphor, symbol, paradox, irony, allusion, repetition, and rhythm. Word patterns in poetry include rhythm or meter, and often rhyme and alliteration. The three main types of poetry are narrative, dramatic, and lyric.

    See also **Alliteration; Connotation; Figurative language; Literature; Lyric; Meter; Narration; Repetition; Rhyme; Rhythm; Verse**

Point of view The position from which the events of a story seem to be observed and told. A first-person point of view tells the story through what the narrator knows, experiences, concludes, or can find out by talking to other characters. A third-person point of view may be *omniscient*, giving the narrator unlimited knowledge of things, events, and characters, including characters' hidden thoughts and feelings. Or it may be *limited* to what one or a few characters know and experience. *Example* of First-Person Point of View: I'm really hungry right now, and I can't wait to eat my lunch. *Example* of Third-Person Limited Point of View: Olivia is really hungry right now and she wants to eat her lunch. *Example* of Third-Person Omniscient Point of View: Olivia is really hungry right now and she wants to eat her lunch. The other students are thinking about their weekend plans. The teacher is wondering how she will finish the lesson before the bell rings.

    See also **Character; Fiction; Narration; Narrator; Voice**

Prose A form of writing in which the rhythm is less regular than that of verse and more like that of ordinary speech.

See also **Rhythm; Verse**

Protagonist The main character in a fictional narrative or a play. He or she may be competing with an antagonist; sometimes called the hero or heroine. *Example:* Although the Tin Man, the Cowardly Lion, and the Scarecrow are important characters in *The Wizard of Oz*, Dorothy is the protagonist.

See also **Antagonist; Hero** or **Heroine**

Pun An expression, used for emphasis or humor, in which two distinct meanings are suggested by one word or by two similar-sounding words. *Example:* The following joke uses a pun on the way that the word "lettuce" sounds similar to "let us":

Q: Knock, knock.   **A**: Who's there?
Q: Lettuce.   **A**: Lettuce who?
Q: Lettuce in, it's cold out here!

See also **Humor**

R

Realistic fiction Fiction in which detailed handling of imaginary settings, characters, and events produces a lifelike illusion of a "real" world. *Example:* Although Upton Sinclair's *The Jungle* is a work of fiction, the author's graphic, detailed descriptions of the slaughterhouse workers' daily lives led to real changes in the meat packing industry.

See also **Fiction**

Reason A logical explanation that connects a piece of evidence to a writer or speaker's claim.

See also **Argument; Claim; Evidence**

Refrain A line, group of lines, or part of a line repeated (sometimes with slight changes) at various points in poetry or song.

See also **Poetry; Repetition; Song lyrics**

Repetition The repeating of individual vowels and consonants, syllables, words, phrases, lines, or groups of lines. Repetition can be used because it sounds pleasant, to emphasize the words in which it occurs, or to help tie the parts of a text into one structure. It is especially important in creating the musical quality of poetry, where it can take such forms as alliteration, assonance, consonance, rhyme, and refrain.

See also **Alliteration; Assonance; Consonance; Poetry; Refrain; Rhyme**

Report A usually short piece of nonfiction writing on a particular topic. It differs from an essay in that it normally states only facts and does not directly express the writer's opinions.

See also **Essay; Nonfiction; Topic**

Resolution See **Falling action**

Review An essay describing a work or performance and judging its effectiveness.

See also **Description; Essay**

Rhetorical device A use of language that differs from ordinary use in order to emphasize a point. It achieves its effects mainly by arranging words in a special way rather than by changing the meaning of the words themselves. Rhetorical devices include *analogy*, *antithesis* (placing words in contrast with one another), *anaphora* (repeating the same word or phrase in a series of lines, clauses, or sentences), the *rhetorical question* (asking a question not to request information, but to make a point more forcefully than simply stating it would do), and *apostrophe* (directly addressing an absent person, nonhuman, or an idea).

See also **Analogy; Figurative language**

Rhyme The repetition of ending sounds in different words. Rhymes usually come at the end of lines of verse, but they may also occur within a line. If rhymed sounds are exactly the same, they make a *perfect rhyme*. If the endings of rhyming words are spelled the same but sound different, they make an *eye rhyme*. And if the last stressed vowels of rhyming words are only similar but the rhyming consonants are the same (or nearly so), the words make a *partial rhyme* (also called *slant rhyme*, *near rhyme*, or *imperfect rhyme*). *Examples:* The words "look" and "brook" and "shook" are perfect rhymes. The words "slaughter" and "laughter" are an eye rhyme. The words "ought" and "fault" form a partial rhyme.

See also **Poetry; Repetition; Rhyme scheme; Stress; Verse**

Rhyme scheme The pattern of rhymed line endings in a work of verse or a stanza. It can be represented by giving a certain letter of the alphabet to each line ending on the same rhyme. *Example:* Because the end word of every other line rhymes in the following poem, the rhyme scheme is *abab*:

Winter night falls quick (a)
The pink sky gone, blackness overhead (b)
Looks like the snow will stick (a)
Down the street and up the hill I tread (b)

> *See also* **Rhyme; Stanza; Verse**

Rhythm The natural rise and fall, or "beat," of language. In English it involves a back-and-forth movement between stressed and unstressed syllables. Rhythm is present in all language, including ordinary speech and prose, but it is most obvious in verse.

> *See also* **Meter; Prose; Stress; Verse**

Rising action The part of a plot that presents actions or events that lead to the climax.

> *See also* **Climax; Conflict; Exposition; Falling action; Plot**

S

Science fiction A genre of fantasy writing based on real or imaginary scientific discoveries. It often takes place in the future.

> *See also* **Fantasy; Fiction**

Script The text of a play, radio or television broadcast, or movie.

Setting The time and place in which the events of a story occur.

> *See also* **Drama; Narration**

Short story A brief, fictional narrative in prose. Like the novel, it organizes the action, thought, and dialogue of its characters into a plot. But it tends to focus on fewer characters and to center on a single event, which reveals as much as possible about the protagonist's life and the traits that set him or her apart.

> *See also* **Character; Fiction; Narration; Novel; Plot; Prose; Protagonist; Story**

Simile A type of figurative language that compares two unlike things by using a word or phrase such as *like, as, than, similar to, resembles,*

or *seems. Examples:* The tall, slim man had arms as willowy as a tree's branches. The woman's temper is like an unpredictable volcano.

> *See also* **Figurative language; Metaphor**

Song lyrics Words meant to be sung. Lyrics have been created for many types of songs, including love songs, religious songs, work songs, sea chanties, and children's game songs. Lyrics for many songs were shared orally for generations before being written down. Not all song lyrics are lyrical like poems; some are the words to songs that tell a story. Not all poems called songs were written to be sung.

> *See also* **Folk literature; Lyric; Narration; Poetry; Refrain**

Sonnet A major form of poetry made up of 14 rhyming lines of equal length. Most sonnets in English take one of two basic patterns: (1) The Italian, or Petrarchan, sonnet consists of two parts: a group of eight lines rhyming *abbaabba*, followed by a group of six lines usually rhyming *cdecde*; (2) The English, or Shakespearean, sonnet is divided into three groups of four lines rhyming *abab cdcd efef* and a pair rhyming *gg*.

> *See also* **Lyric; Meter; Rhyme; Rhyme scheme; Verse**

Speech A message on a specific topic, spoken before an audience; also, spoken (not written) language.

Stanza A group of lines that forms a section of a poem and has the same pattern (including line lengths, meter, and usually rhyme scheme) as other sections of the same poem. In printed poems, stanzas are separated from each other by a space.

> *See also* **Meter; Rhyme scheme; Verse**

Static character A character who changes little, if at all. Things happen *to*, rather than *within*, him or her. *Example:* In Charles Dickens's novel *Great Expectations*, Joe Gargery is a static character. He is a poor, uneducated blacksmith who endures the cruelty of his wife and Pip, the main character. Throughout the novel, Joe remains humble, loyal, and supportive of those he loves.

> *See also* **Character; Characterization; Dynamic character**

Story A series of events (actual or imaginary) that can be selected and arranged in a certain order to form a narrative or dramatic plot. It is the raw material from which the finished plot is built. Although there are technical differences, the word *story* is sometimes used in place of *narrative*.

    See *also* **Drama; Narration; Plot**

Stress The force with which a syllable is spoken compared with neighboring syllables in a line of verse. A stressed syllable is spoken more forcefully than an unstressed one.

    See *also* **Meter; Rhythm; Verse**

Style The way a writer uses language to express the feelings or thoughts he or she wants to convey. Just as no two people are alike, no two styles are exactly alike. A writer's style results from his or her choices of vocabulary, sentence structure and variety, imagery, figurative language, rhythm, repetition, and other resources.

    See *also* **Diction; Figurative language; Genre; Imagery; Parody; Repetition; Rhythm; Voice**

Suspense A feeling of curiosity, tension, or excitement a narrative creates in the reader about what will happen next. Mystery novels, like horror movies, are often full of suspense.

    See *also* **Narration**

Symbol A word or phrase that serves as an image of some person, place, thing, or action but that also calls to mind some other, usually broader, idea or range of ideas. *Example:* An author might describe doves flying high in the sky to symbolize a peaceful setting.

    See *also* **Figurative language; Imagery**

T

Tall tale A kind of folk tale that wildly exaggerates a character's strength and ability, usually for comic effect. *Example:* Stories about Paul Bunyan, the enormous lumberjack whose footprints created Minnesota's 10,000 lakes, are considered tall tales.

    See *also* **Hyperbole**

Textbook A book prepared for use in schools for the study of a subject.

Theme The underlying message or main idea of a piece of writing. It expresses a broader meaning than the topic of the piece.

    See *also* **Topic**

Tone A writer's or speaker's attitude toward his or her topic or audience or toward him- or herself. A writer's tone may be positive, negative, or neutral. The words the writer chooses, the sentence structure, and the overall pattern of words convey the intended tone.

    See *also* **Connotation; Figurative language; Literature; Mood; Rhythm; Topic**

Topic What or who is being discussed in a piece of writing; the subject of the piece.

    See *also* **Theme**

Tragedy A play or a fictional narrative about the disastrous downfall of the protagonist, usually because of a flaw in his or her moral character. Though brought to ruin, the protagonist comes to understand the meaning of his or her actions and to accept the consequences. *Example:* William Shakespeare's play *Hamlet* is about the downfall and eventual death of the protagonist, Hamlet, so it is considered a tragedy.

    See *also* **Drama; Narration; Protagonist**

V

Verse Language that differs from prose and ordinary speech by being arranged in regular units of rhythm called *meter*. The meter, in turn, occurs within a larger unit of rhythm and meaning: the *line*. In written verse, unlike written prose, the writer rather than the printer decides where one line ends and the next begins. Not all poetry is written in verse (poetry can even be written in prose), and not all verse is poetry (even skillfully written verse can be ineffective in communicating experience).

    See *also* **Blank verse; Free verse; Meter; Poetry; Prose; Rhythm; Sonnet**

Voice The specific group of traits conveyed by the narrator or "speaker" in a literary work.

    See *also* **Narrator**

Vocabulary Glossary

The definitions in this glossary are for words as they are used in the selections in this book. Use the Pronunciation Key below to help you use each word's pronunciation. Then read about the parts of an entry.

Pronunciation Key

Symbols for Consonant Sounds

b	box	**p**	pan
ch	chick	**r**	ring
d	dog	**s**	bus
f	fish	**sh**	fish
g	girl	**t**	hat
h	hat	**th**	earth
j	jar	**th**	father
k	cake	**v**	vase
ks	box	**w**	window
kw	queen	**wh**	whale
l	bell	**y**	yarn
m	mouse	**z**	zipper
n	pan	**zh**	treasure
ng	ring		

Symbols for Short Vowel Sounds

a	hat
e	bell
i	chick
o	box
u	bus

Symbols for Long Vowel Sounds

ā	cake
ē	key
ī	bike
ō	goat
yū	mule

Symbols for R-controlled Sounds

ar	barn
air	chair
ear	ear
īr	fire
or	corn
ur	girl

Symbols for Variant Vowel Sounds

ah	father
aw	ball
oi	boy
ow	mouse
oo	book
ü	fruit

Miscellaneous Symbols

shun	fraction
chun	question
zhun	division

Academic Vocabulary

Certain words in this glossary have a red dot indicating that they are academic vocabulary words. These are the words that are necessary for you to learn in order to understand the concepts being taught in school.

Parts of an Entry

The **entry** shows how the word is spelled and how it is broken into syllables.

The **pronunciation** shows you how to say the word.

part of speech
n. for noun
v. for verb
adj. for adjective
adv. for adverb.

The red dot signals that a word is an **academic vocabulary** word. Not all words have a red dot.

• **af·firm** (u-**furm**) *v.* showing, saying, or proving that something is true. *My decision to volunteer at the hospital was **affirmed** when I saw how happy the patients were because of my visit.*

The **definition** gives the meaning of the word.

The **sample sentence** uses the word in a way that shows its meaning.

A

abbreviated (u-**brē**-vē-ā-ted) *adj.* shortened. *The governor had to give an **abbreviated** version of her speech in order to fit it into the evening newscast.*

abolish (ah-**bah**-lish) *v.* to do away with or get rid of. *The principal decided to **abolish** the dress code and let students choose what to wear to school.*

• **abstract** (**ab**-strakt) *n.* an idea that is not concrete or specific. *In the **abstract**, loyalty is a good thing, but loyalty can be complicated in specific situations.*

accelerate (ik-**se**-lu-rāt) *v.* to increase, to move faster. *Did the sled's speed **accelerate** as it neared the bottom of the hill?*

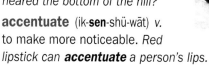

accentuate (ik-**sen**-shü-wāt) *v.* to make more noticeable. *Red lipstick can **accentuate** a person's lips.*

• **access** (**ak**-ses) *v.* to gain entry to. *Type your name and password to **access** your grades on the school's computer network.*

accusation (ak-yū-**zā**-shun) *n.* saying that another person has done something wrong. *Has anyone ever made an **accusation** about you by saying that you cheated on a test?*

• **acknowledgment** (ik-**nah**-lij-munt) *n.* something done to express thanks or recognition. *You make an **acknowledgment** of a gift you receive when you send a thank-you note for the gift.*

adhere (ad-**hir**) *v.* to stick with, to keep. *To play fairly, everyone must **adhere** to the rules.*

admonish (ad-**mah**-nish) *v.* to warn or scold. *My mother **admonished** me for going out before I made my bed.*

• **advocate** (**ad**-vu-kāt) *v.* to speak in favor of. *Do you **advocate** wearing a helmet when riding a bicycle?*

alienation (ā-lē-e-**nā**-shun) *n.* the feeling of being separate. *After going away to school, he felt a sense of **alienation**.*

ambience (**am**-bē-ents) *n.* feeling or mood of a place or thing. *The café owners played soft music and put fresh flowers on the table to create a pleasant **ambience**.*

ambitious (am-**bi**-shus) *adj.* having a strong desire for success. *An **ambitious** person works hard to achieve big goals.*

apathetic (a-pu-**the**-tik) *adj.* indifferent, uninterested. *Sometimes citizens seem **apathetic** and do not take time to vote.*

articulate (ar-**ti**-kyü-let) *adj.* able to speak clearly, effectively. *When giving a presentation, it is important to be **articulate**.*

assert (uh-**sert**) *v.* to insist on, to state strongly and clearly. *When they chose Eric over me, I had to **assert** myself.*

• **attitude** (**a**-tu-tüd) *n.* set way of thinking or believing that can often be seen in someone's behavior, point of view. *He had a positive **attitude** toward math because he enjoyed working with numbers.*

authenticity (aw-then-**ti**-su-tē) *n.* realness, genuineness. *The jeweler checked the **authenticity** of the stone to see whether it was a diamond or just glass.*

B

banish (**ba**-nish) *v.* to send away. *My mother will **banish** us to our rooms if we argue at the dinner table.*

C

characterize (**ker**-ik-tu-rīz) *v.* to describe the quality or character of a person. *How would you **characterize** your best friend?*

• **coherent** (kō-**hir**-unt) *adj.* orderly, logical, and easy to understand. *The math lesson was much more **coherent** after I studied.*

commentary (kam-un-**ter**-ē) *n.* series of interpretations, explanations, or opinions. *After the gymnastics competition, two gymnasts gave a detailed **commentary** about the event.*

commercial (ku-**mer**-shul) *adj.* having to do with buying and selling goods and services. *A **commercial** building is one used for offices or stores.*

commiserate (ku-**mi**-zu-rāt) *v.* to share someone's unhappiness. *I **commiserate** with friends who have a lot of homework.*

compel (kum-**pel**) *v.* to urge forcefully, to cause to do. *If you are **compelled** to do something, you feel you must do it.*

• **compensate** (**kahm**-pun-sāt) *v.* to be paid for work that was done. *Parents sometimes **compensate** their children for mowing the lawn or taking out the garbage.*

competent (**kom**-pu-tent) *adj.* capable, qualified. *A **competent** worker has the necessary skills or knowledge to do a job well.*

• **conformist** (kun-**for**-mist) *n.* a follower. *When he started dressing and talking like us, he became a **conformist**.*

conscientious (kon-shē-**en**-shus) *adj.* careful and responsible. *Teresa is very **conscientious** because she completes her math homework every day.*

• **consequence** (**kon**-su-kwens) *n.* result, effect. *If you never study, you may have to face a **consequence**, such as bad grades.*

• **consistently** (kun-**sis**-tent-lē) *adv.* equally. *The principal enforces school rules **consistently**, so that all students are treated exactly the same way.*

contemplate (**kon**-tem-plāt) *v.* to think carefully about. *You should **contemplate** every move in a game of chess.*

contend (kun-**tend**) *v.* to argue. *Many people **contend** that chicken soup is a cure for the common cold.*

• **contrary** (**kahn**-trer-ē) *adj.* opposite. *Doing what you feel is right may be **contrary** to what is easiest.*

• **controversial** (kahn-trah-**vur**-shul) *adj.* causing disagreement. *The **controversial** new movie upset a lot of people.*

conviction (kun-**vik**-shun) *n.* strong belief. *It is an American **conviction** that people should be allowed to choose their government's leaders.*

countenance (**kown**-tun-ents) *n.* facial expression. *Everyone could see his sad **countenance**.*

counterfeit (**kown**-ter-fit) *adj.* fake, phony. *The salesperson was shocked to learn that the $20 bill was **counterfeit**.*

D

deliberately (di-**li**-bah-rut-lē) *adv.* on purpose. *The field manager took his time, slowly and **deliberately** marking the baseball diamond with chalk.*

dense (**dens**) *adj.* closely crowded together, thick. *We could barely see the deer hidden in the **dense** forest.*

designate (**de**-zig-nāt) *v.* to point out, show. *Signs **designate** the names of streets and highways.*

desolately (**de**-su-lut-lē) *adv.* very sadly; miserably. *I could tell how upset she felt about the hard test when I saw her walk **desolately** out of the room.*

destiny (**des**-tu-nē) *n.* a predetermined course of events that are thought to be out of our own control; fate. *Lee believed it was his **destiny** to win the championship.*

destitute (**des**-tah-tüt) *adj.* without money or possessions. *The **destitute** man could not afford to eat lunch.*

devastating (**de**-vu-stāt-ing) *adj.* destructive, very damaging. *Many trees fell down on our street during last night's **devastating** storm.*

dictate (**dik**-tāt) *v.* to control, determine. *The school board can **dictate** what we're allowed to wear to school.*

dilemma (dah-**le**-mah) *n.* situation that requires you to choose between two unfavorable options. *My **dilemma** was whether to finish my math homework or practice my speech. I didn't have time for both.*

disarm (dis-**ahrm**) *v.* to win someone's trust and make the person friendly toward you. *My smile **disarmed** his bad mood.*

discerning (di-**sur**-ning) *adj.* good at making judgments. *The jury made **discerning** decisions about the evidence presented in the trial.*

disciplined (**di**-su-plund) *adj.* self-controlled. *Tomas is very **disciplined** with his paycheck. He always saves 75 percent.*

discordant (dis-**kord**-nt) *adj.* sounding harsh and unpleasant. *I cover my ears when I hear **discordant** music.*

- **discriminate** (dis-**kri**-mu-nāt) *v.* to treat differently because of prejudice. *The freshmen were **discriminated** against just because they were the youngest students in school.*

dispel (di-**spel**) *v.* to separate, to scatter, to spread out. *The crowd began to **dispel** after the football game ended.*

disrespectful (dis-ri-**spekt**-ful) *adj.* insulting. *The joke was very **disrespectful.***

- **distinction** (di-**stink**-shun) *n.* difference. *The main **distinction** between carrots and apples is that carrots are vegetables and apples are fruit.*

E

- **eliminate** (i-**li**-mu-nāt) *v.* to remove, to get rid of. *He used extra soap to **eliminate** the stain.*

emancipation (i-man-su-**pā**-shun) *n.* the act of freeing people from strict control. *On January 1, 1863, President Abraham Lincoln ordered the **emancipation** of all slaves in the United States.*

empathize (**em**-pu-thīz) *v.* to understand someone's feelings. *I broke my arm last year, so I can **empathize** with what she's experiencing with her broken arm.*

- **emphasis** (**em**-fu-sis) *n.* type of special attention. *People sometimes use hand gestures to add **emphasis** to their words.*

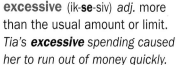

emulate (**em**-yū-lāt) *v.* to imitate. *I try to **emulate** my heroes.*

endeavor (in-**de**-vur) *n.* a serious effort or try. *Training for a marathon is her greatest **endeavor** so far.*

endure (in-**dyūr**) *v.* to survive. *Mountains have **endured** centuries of wind, rain, sun, and snow.*

- **enhance** (in-**hants**) *v.* to improve. *Good grades and extracurricular activities will **enhance** your chances of getting into college.*

enlist (in-**list**) *v.* to convince someone to help. *He **enlisted** our help with the project.*

ensuing (en-**sü**-ing) *adj.* following, resulting. *The **ensuing** years after the hurricane were spent cleaning up and rebuilding the city.*

enumerate (i-**nü**-mu-rāt) *v.* to name one by one. *He **enumerated** all the reasons he didn't want to do the yard work.*

envious (**en**-vē-us) *adj.* feeling or showing resentful longing of someone's wealth, traits, or luck; jealous. *She was **envious** of her older sister's curly hair and wished that her own hair wasn't straight.*

essence (**e**-sens) *n.* quality that determines someone or something's character. *Her smile is the **essence** of her personality.*

- **ethical** (**e**-thi-kul) *adj.* moral. *An **ethical** action respects rules of right and wrong.*

- **ethnicity** (eth-**ni**-se-tē) *n.* racial background. *Her **ethnicity** is Mexican because she was born in Mexico.*

evade (i-**vād**) *v.* to avoid, to escape. *Boxers **evade** punches by moving out of the way.*

excessive (ik-**se**-siv) *adj.* more than the usual amount or limit. *Tia's **excessive** spending caused her to run out of money quickly.*

expectation (ek-spek-**tā**-shun) *n.* a belief that something will happen. *Some students have the **expectation** that they will do well in every class.*

- **exploitation** (ek-sploi-**tā**-shun) *n.* selfish use of others for personal gain. *Laws prevent the **exploitation** of children by employers who would force them to work long hours.*

F

- **facilitate** (fu-**si**-lu-tāt) *v.* to make easier. *You can **facilitate** your entry to the concert by having your ticket out and ready for the usher.*

feud (**fyūd**) *n.* long-standing quarrel or hostility between two families or groups. *The **feud** between the Smiths and the Joneses had lasted for so many years, no one could remember why they didn't like each other.*

fractured (**frak**-churd) *adj.* broken. *He **fractured** his arm when he fell out of the tree.*

- **fundamental** (fun-du-**men**-tul) *adj.* basic. *Our **fundamental** rights are listed in the first ten Amendments to the Constitution.*

H

harmonize (**hahr**-mu-nīz) *v.* to coordinate or go together well. *The two singers **harmonize** their notes well in the song.*

humiliation (hyū-mi-lē-**ā**-shun) *n.* shame and embarrassment. *Losing to the worst team in the state was a great **humiliation** for us.*

I

• **impact** (**im**-pakt) *n.* effect, influence. *Computers have had a deep **impact** on everyday life by allowing us to access information quickly.*

• **implement** (**im**-plu-ment) *v.* to perform, to do. *The mayor decided to **implement** the city evacuation plan as the hurricane moved closer.*

improvise (**im**-prah-vīz) *v.* to create without planning or preparation. *When you **improvise** a speech or a performance, you make it up without planning or preparing for it.*

impudently (**im**-pyu-dunt-lē) *adv.* in a disrespectful or bold way. *The girl behaved **impudently** when she refused to listen to her friend's opinion.*

• **inclination** (in-klu-**nā**-shun) *n.* liking, preference. *Her **inclination** for exercise led her to play soccer and tennis.*

indelible (in-**de**-lu-bul) *adj.* lasting or permanent. *The **indelible** ink stain ruined his new shirt.*

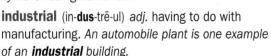

indifference (in-**di**-furns) *n.* disinterest, lack of concern. *She showed **indifference** to her grades by never doing homework.*

industrial (in-**dus**-trē-ul) *adj.* having to do with manufacturing. *An automobile plant is one example of an **industrial** building.*

• **inevitable** (in-**ev**-e-tuh-bul) *adj.* sure to happen, unavoidable. *It is **inevitable** that you will get wet if you walk in the rain without an umbrella or raincoat.*

inflexible (in-**flek**-su-bul) *adj.* unbending, rigid, firm. *When it came to house rules, she was **inflexible**.*

infuriate (in-**fyur**-ē-āt) *v.* to make extremely angry, to enrage. *His mean joke **infuriated** me.*

• **innovative** (**i**-ne-vā-tiv) *adj.* new, original. *Good companies ask designers to create **innovative** products that no other company has made.*

inquisitive (in-**kwi**-zu-tiv) *adj.* curious. *An **inquisitive** person asks questions and is eager for more information about something.*

• **integrate** (**in**-tu-grāt) *v.* to mix people of all races. *Because of the civil rights movement, a very important decision was made to **integrate** schools and other public places.*

integrity (in-**te**-gru-tē) *n.* a strong sense of right and wrong, honesty. *A courtroom judge must have **integrity**.*

• **intensity** (in-**ten**-su-tē) *n.* a lot of feeling or strength. *The woman's **intensity** on the basketball court made her a good player.*

interminably (in-**tur**-mi-nu-blē) *adv.* endlessly. *The class seemed **interminably** long.*

intimidating (in-**ti**-mu-dā-ting) *adj.* worried, not confident. *She found it very **intimidating** to dance in front of a large audience.*

intrusion (in-**trü**-zhun) *n.* unwelcome interference. *It would be considered an **intrusion** if you walked through a doorway marked "no entry."*

irritating (**ir**-u-tāt-ing) *adj.* annoying. *The loud music that the teenagers enjoyed was quite **irritating** to their parents.*

L

liberate (**li**-bu-rāt) *v.* to set free. *The soldiers opened the jail doors and **liberated** all the prisoners.*

lucid (**lü**-sid) *adj.* sensible and sane. *Sometimes the man talks crazy, but today he is **lucid** and sensible.*

M

malleable (**mal**-e-ah-bul) *adj.* bendable, easy to influence. *The clay is **malleable** and soft, so I can easily change its shape.*

mature (mu-**choor**) *adj.* fully developed, grown up, adult. *A **mature** person acts like an adult.*

melancholy (**me**-lun-kah-lē) *n.* sadness. *His* **melancholy** *was obvious, because he looked very sad and gloomy.*

merit (**mer**-it) *n.* worth, value. *If the committee believes that the new project has* **merit**, *the members will vote to adopt it.*

momentous (mō-**men**-tus) *adj.* very important. *Most people believe that getting married is a* **momentous** *event.*

• **motivated** (**mō**-tu-vā-tid) *adj.* inspired, determined. *Kara was* **motivated** *to score a goal because her team was losing by only one point.*

N

naive (nah-**ēv**) *adj.* easily fooled because of a lack of experience. *People who are* **naive** *trust almost everyone.*

O

obligation (ah-blu-**gā**-shun) *n.* duty, responsibility. *Everyone has an* **obligation** *to obey the law.*

obscure (ob-**skyur**) *v.* to conceal or hide. *The tall building across the street* **obscured** *the view outside my window.*

opponent (u-**pō**-nunt) *n.* a person who competes against you or takes the opposite side of the argument. *Your* **opponent** *in a game is the person or team playing against you.*

oppression (u-**pre**-shun) *n.* the act of preventing people from having equal rights. *Slavery is a form of* **oppression**.

P

pathetic (pu-**the**-tik) *adj.* pitiful, sad. *The person who has a* **pathetic** *look on her face appears to be miserable.*

pensively (**pen**-siv-lē) *adv.* quietly and thoughtfully. *He spoke* **pensively** *when giving his opinion in front of the class.*

• **perception** (pur-**sep**-shun) *n.* observation or feeling about something. *My* **perception** *of the study guide is that it is really helpful.*

perfection (pur-**fek**-shun) *n.* condition or quality of being without faults, excellence. *Professional athletes practice daily to try to achieve* **perfection** *in order to be the best.*

perish (**per**-ish) *v.* to die. *If we continue to pollute the air and water, many plants and animals will* **perish**.

perpetually (pur-**pe**-chü-we-lē) *adv.* always. *Someone who is* **perpetually** *late is always late.*

• **perspective** (pur-**spek**-tiv) *n.* point of view. *From your* **perspective**, *was the movie good or boring?*

poised (**poizd**) *adj.* held ready or in position. *The runners stood* **poised**, *waiting for the race to begin.*

• **potential** (pu-**ten**-shul) *n.* natural ability. *Ramon has the* **potential** *to be a great musician, but he needs to practice more often.*

precaution (pri-**kaw**-shun) *n.* action to protect against harm. *Carlos sets his clock ten minutes early as a* **precaution** *against being late.*

• **precision** (pri-**si**-zhun) *n.* accuracy. *A good surgeon must operate with* **precision** *in order to fix tiny areas of the human body.*

• **predominate** (pri-**dah**-mu-nāt) *v.* to be the stronger force, to have controlling power. *If one group of people* **predominates** *over another, it is more powerful than the other group.*

pretense (**prē**-tens) *n.* make-believe, pretending. *The fighter looked confident at the beginning of the fight, but that was just a* **pretense**. *He was actually afraid.*

priority (prī-**or**-u-tē) *n.* importance. *Which takes* **priority**, *your loyalty to your family or to your friends?*

procrastinate (prō-**kras**-te-nāt) *v.* to delay doing something. *If your homework is due Monday, don't* **procrastinate** *until Sunday.*

prodigy (**prah**-du-jē) *n.* unusually talented child, child genius. *Wolfgang Amadeus Mozart, a* **prodigy**, *wrote a musical symphony when he was eight years old.*

proficiency (pru-**fi**-shun-sē) *n.* skillfulness. *Her* **proficiency** *in reading, writing, and speaking English is impressive; she almost never makes a mistake.*

profound (prō-**fownd**) *adj.* filled with deep meaning. *Poems sometimes express* **profound** *truths.*

prophecy (**prah**-fu-sē) *n.* statement of what someone believes will happen in the future, prediction. *Many people have made **prophecies** about the end of the world, but they have never come true.*

• **pursue** (pur-**sü**) *v.* to seek, to become involved in. *After high school, do you want to **pursue** a college degree?*

R

racism (**rā**-si-zum) *n.* ill treatment of people on the basis of ancestry. *For a long time, because of **racism**, African Americans were denied the right to vote.*

• **regime** (rā-**zhēm**) *n.* a government. *People who live in a country with harsh rules may want a more democratic **regime**.*

• **reinforce** (rē-un-**fors**) *v.* to strengthen. *How can working with a partner help **reinforce** a lesson you learned in class?*

repercussion (rē-pur-**ku**-shun) *n.* unwanted negative effect. *At my high school, a **repercussion** of being late to class is detention.*

reproach (ri-**prōch**) *n.* blame. *A person who is beyond **reproach** cannot be criticized for anything.*

resolution (re-zu-**lü**-shun) *n.* strong decision to do or not to do something. *Since her goal was to graduate with honors this year, she made a **resolution** to get better grades.*

• **resolve** (ri-**zolv**) *n.* determination to do something. *Her **resolve** to get good grades helped her earn a college scholarship.*

respectably (ri-**spek**-tah-blē) *adv.* in a decent and moral way, properly. *She **respectably** listened to her grandfather's stories, though she had heard them often.*

• **restrict** (ri-**strikt**) *v.* to limit. *There are laws in many states that **restrict** 16-year-olds to working no more than three hours a day on school days.*

revelation (re-vu-**lā**-shun) *n.* sudden insight, discovery. *In a time of crisis, we may have a **revelation** about what we are capable of.*

S

saturate (**sa**-chu-rāt) *v.* to fill completely, to soak. *A day of rain will not just wet the lawn; it will **saturate** it.*

segregation (se-gri-**gā**-shun) *n.* separation of some people from others because of race. *He opposed the idea of **segregation**.*

spontaneously (spon-**tā**-nē-us-lē) *adv.* suddenly and without a plan. *Al **spontaneously** decided to go camping over the weekend.*

stigmatize (**stig**-mah-tīz) *v.* to label or mark as bad. *I try not to **stigmatize** people for what they may have done in the past.*

stimulating (**stim**-yū-lā-ting) *adj.* interesting, exciting. *The lecture in class was **stimulating**.*

subdued (sub-**düd**) *adj.* quiet, controlled. *She was more **subdued** after the argument.*

subtle (**su**-tul) *adj.* hard to notice. *Painters can see **subtle** differences between similar colors.*

suffice (su-**fīs**) *v.* to satisfy. *Just a small helping of potatoes will **suffice**, thank you. I am not hungry.*

surge (**surj**) *v.* to rise or increase suddenly. *He had a **surge** of support after making the speech.*

surpass (sur-**pas**) *v.* to become greater or better than something else. *Earth's population will **surpass** 9 billion by 2050.*

T

temporary (**tem**-pah-rer-ē) *adj.* lasting for a short time. *Since he will only live here for the summer, he is looking for a **temporary** job.*

• **tension** (**ten**-shun) *n.* stress, strain, or anxiety. *Did your **tension** go away when you turned in your term paper?*

tolerance (**to**-lu-runs) *n.* respect for different beliefs and ways of life. *Our government has a **tolerance** for all religions.*

• **traditional** (tru-**di**-shu-nul) *adj.* long-established or time-honored act or belief. *We ate the **traditional** meal, as my grandparents and great-grandparents had done, to celebrate the holiday.*

transaction (tran-**zak**-shun) *n.* purchase by a shopper. *In a business **transaction**, a customer gets products or services in exchange for money.*

• **transform** (trans-**form**) *v.* to change. *A caterpillar **transforms** into a butterfly when it comes out of a cocoon.*

transition (tran-**zi**-shun) *n.* a slow change. *The **transition** from the teenage years to adulthood can be both difficult and joyful.*

tremulous (**trem**-yu-lus) *adj.* timid, fearful. *The **tremulous** child clung to his mother whenever a stranger approached.*

V

• **vary** (**ver**-ē) *v.* to differ. *Hairstyles **vary** among today's students. Some have very short hair; some have extremely long hair; and some even have no hair.*

verify (**ver**-i-fī) *v.* to check. *Please show your driver's license to **verify** your identity.*

• **violate** (**vī**-u-lāt) *v.* to break, to not follow. *If you drive faster than the speed limit, you **violate** the law and may get a ticket or fine.*

virtue (**vur**-chü) *n.* positive points, benefits. *Rain may spoil a picnic, but it has the **virtue** of making plants grow.*

• **visualize** (**vi**-zhu-wu-līz) *v.* to imagine what something looks like. *I can **visualize** her face in my imagination even though she's not here.*

Beginning-Middle-End

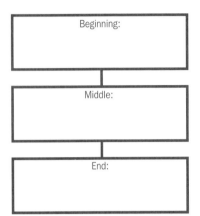

Character-Setting-Plot

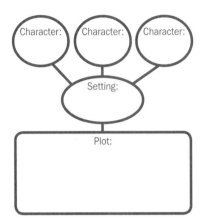

Character Description

Character	What the Character Does	What This Shows About the Character

Goal-and-Outcome

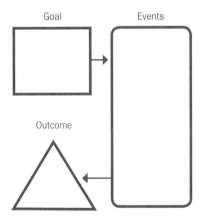

Problem-and-Solution

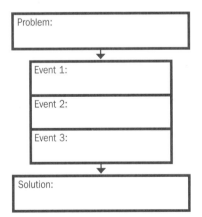

Cause-and-Effect Chart

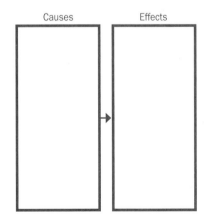

Cycle Diagram

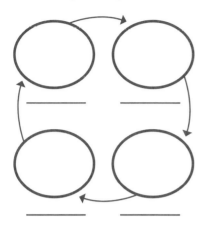

Sequence Chain

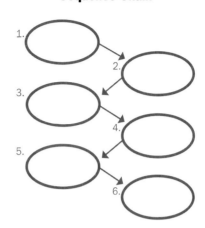

Time Line

Main-Idea Diagram

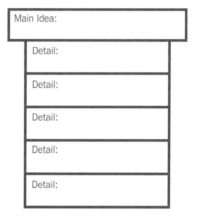

Idea Web

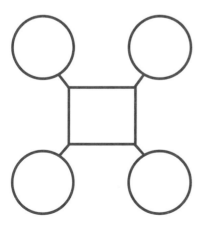

Topic Triangle

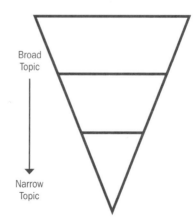

Venn Diagram

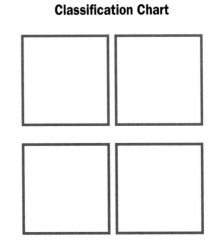

Classification Chart

Five-Ws Chart

What?
Who?
Where?
When?
Why?

KWL Chart

K What Do I **K**now?	W What Do I **W**ant to Learn?	L What Did I **L**earn?

Table

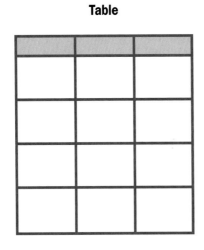

Outline

I. _____

   A. _____

   B. _____

II. _____

   A. _____

   B. _____

III. _____

   A. _____

   B. _____

Graph

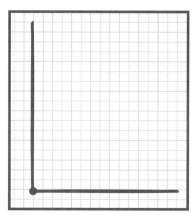

T Chart

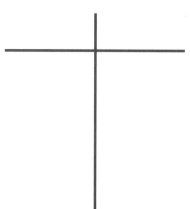

Word Map

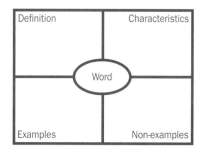

Common Core State Standards

UNIT 1: Double Take

SE Pages	Lesson	Code	Standards Text
0–1	Discuss the Essential Question	SL.9-10.1.b	Work with peers to set rules for collegial discussions and decision-making, clear goals and deadlines, and individual roles as needed.
		SL.9-10.3	Evaluate a speaker's point of view, reasoning, and use of evidence and rhetoric, identifying any fallacious reasoning or exaggerated or distorted evidence.
2	Analyze and Debate	SL.9-10.4	Present information, findings, and supporting evidence clearly, concisely, and logically such that listeners can follow the line of reasoning and the organization, development, substance, and style are appropriate to purpose, audience, and task.
3	Plan a Project	SL.9-10.1.b	Work with peers to set rules for collegial discussions and decision-making, clear goals and deadlines, and individual roles as needed.
3	Choose More to Read	RL.9-10.10	By the end of grade 10, read and comprehend literature, including stories, dramas, and poems, at the high end of the grades 9–10 text complexity band independently and proficiently.
		RI.9-10.10	By the end of grade 10, read and comprehend literary nonfiction at the high end of the grades 9–10 text complexity band independently and proficiently.
4–5	How to Read Using Reading Strategies	RI.9-10.10	By the end of grade 10, read and comprehend literary nonfiction at the high end of the grades 9–10 text complexity band independently and proficiently.
		L.9-10.6	Acquire and use accurately general academic and domain-specific words and phrases, sufficient for reading, writing, speaking, and listening at the college and career readiness level; demonstrate independence in gathering vocabulary knowledge when considering a word or phrase important to comprehension or expression.
6–9	How to Read Short Stories	RL.9-10.1	Cite strong and thorough textual evidence to support analysis of what the text says explicitly as well as inferences drawn from the text.
		RI.9-10.10	By the end of grade 10, read and comprehend literary nonfiction at the high end of the grades 9–10 text complexity band independently and proficiently.
		SL.9-10.1.a	Come to discussions prepared, having read and researched material under study; explicitly draw on that preparation by referring to evidence from texts and other research on the topic or issue to stimulate a thoughtful, well-reasoned exchange of ideas.
		L.9-10.6	Acquire and use accurately general academic and domain-specific words and phrases, sufficient for reading, writing, speaking, and listening at the college and career readiness level; demonstrate independence in gathering vocabulary knowledge when considering a word or phrase important to comprehension or expression.

Cluster 1

10	Prepare to Read	RI.9-10.4	Determine the meaning of words and phrases as they are used in a text, including figurative, connotative, and technical meanings; analyze the cumulative impact of specific word choices on meaning and tone.
		SL.9-10.1	Initiate and participate effectively in a range of collaborative discussions (one-on-one, in groups, and teacher-led) with diverse partners on grades 9–10 topics, texts, and issues, building on others' ideas and expressing their own clearly and persuasively.

Cluster 1, continued

SE Pages	Lesson	Code	Standards Text
10	**Prepare to Read** continued	L.9-10.4.c	Consult general and specialized reference materials, both print and digital, to find the pronunciation of a word or determine or clarify its precise meaning, its part of speech, or its etymology.
		L.9-10.6	Acquire and use accurately general academic and domain-specific words and phrases, sufficient for reading, writing, speaking, and listening at the college and career readiness level; demonstrate independence in gathering vocabulary knowledge when considering a word or phrase important to comprehension or expression.
11	**Before Reading: The Moustache**	RL.9-10.3	Analyze how complex characters develop over the course of a text, interact with other characters, and advance the plot or develop the theme.
		RL.9-10.10	By the end of grade 10, read and comprehend literature, including stories, dramas, and poems, at the high end of the grades 9–10 text complexity band independently and proficiently.
12–26	**Read The Moustache**	RL.9-10.1	Cite strong and thorough textual evidence to support analysis of what the text says explicitly as well as inferences drawn from the text.
		RL.9-10.3	Analyze how complex characters develop over the course of a text, interact with other characters, and advance the plot or develop the theme.
		RL.9-10.7	Analyze the representation of a subject or a key scene in two different artistic mediums, including what is emphasized or absent in each treatment.
		RL.9-10.10	By the end of grade 10, read and comprehend literature, including stories, dramas, and poems, at the high end of the grades 9–10 text complexity band independently and proficiently.
		W.9-10.3	Write narratives to develop real or imagined experiences or events using effective technique, well-chosen details, and well-structured event sequences.
		W.9-10.10	Write routinely over extended time frames (time for research, reflection, and revision) and shorter time frames (a single sitting or a day or two) for a range of tasks, purposes, and audiences.
		L.9-10.1.a	Use parallel structure.
		L.9-10.1.b	Use various types of phrases (noun, verb, adjectival, adverbial, participial, prepositional, absolute) and clauses (independent, dependent; noun, relative, adverbial) to convey specific meanings and add variety and interest to writing or presentations.
		L.9-10.2	Demonstrate command of the conventions of standard English capitalization, punctuation, and spelling when writing.
		L.9-10.5.a	Interpret figures of speech in context and analyze their role in the text.
		L.9-10.6	Acquire and use accurately general academic and domain-specific words and phrases, sufficient for reading, writing, speaking, and listening at the college and career readiness level; demonstrate independence in gathering vocabulary knowledge when considering a word or phrase important to comprehension or expression.

Common Core State Standards, continued

Cluster 1, continued

SE Pages	Lesson	Code	Standards Text
27	**Postscript: Grandmother**	RL.9-10.1	Cite strong and thorough textual evidence to support analysis of what the text says explicitly as well as inferences drawn from the text.
		SL.9-10.6	Adapt speech to a variety of contexts and tasks, demonstrating command of formal English when indicated or appropriate.
		L.9-10.5	Demonstrate understanding of figurative language, word relationships, and nuances in word meanings.
28	**Before Reading: Who We Really Are**	RI.9-10.5	Analyze in detail how an author's ideas or claims are developed and refined by particular sentences, paragraphs, or larger portions of a text.
		RI.9-10.10	By the end of grade 10, read and comprehend literary nonfiction at the high end of the grades 9-10 text complexity band independently and proficiently.
29–32	**Read Who We Really Are**	RI.9-10.1	Cite strong and thorough textual evidence to support analysis of what the text says explicitly as well as inferences drawn from the text.
		RI.9-10.2	Determine a central idea of a text and analyze its development over the course of the text, including how it emerges and is shaped and refined by specific details; provide an objective summary of the text.
		RI.9-10.5	Analyze in detail how an author's ideas or claims are developed and refined by particular sentences, paragraphs, or larger portions of a text.
		RI.9-10.10	By the end of grade 10, read and comprehend literary nonfiction at the high end of the grades 9-10 text complexity band independently and proficiently.
		W.9-10.9.b	Apply grades 9-10 Reading standards to literary nonfiction.
		W.9-10.10	Write routinely over extended time frames (time for research, reflection, and revision) and shorter time frames (a single sitting or a day or two) for a range of tasks, purposes, and audiences.
		L.9-10.1.b	Use various types of phrases (noun, verb, adjectival, adverbial, participial, prepositional, absolute) and clauses (independent, dependent; noun, relative, adverbial) to convey specific meanings and add variety and interest to writing or presentations.
		L.9-10.6	Acquire and use accurately general academic and domain-specific words and phrases, sufficient for reading, writing, speaking, and listening at the college and career readiness level; demonstrate independence in gathering vocabulary knowledge when considering a word or phrase important to comprehension or expression.
33	**Reflect and Assess Critical Thinking**	RL.9-10.3	Analyze how complex characters develop over the course of a text, interact with other characters, and advance the plot or develop the theme.
		RL.9-10.10	By the end of grade 10, read and comprehend literature, including stories, dramas, and poems, at the high end of the grades 9-10 text complexity band independently and proficiently.
		RI.9-10.10	By the end of grade 10, read and comprehend literary nonfiction at the high end of the grades 9-10 text complexity band independently and proficiently.
		SL.9-10.6	Adapt speech to a variety of contexts and tasks, demonstrating command of formal English when indicated or appropriate.

Cluster 1, continued

SE Pages	Lesson	Code	Standards Text
33	**Reflect and Assess** continued **Write About Literature**	W.9-10.1	Write arguments to support claims in an analysis of substantive topics or texts, using valid reasoning and relevant and sufficient evidence.
	Key Vocabulary Review	L.9-10.6	Acquire and use accurately general academic and domain-specific words and phrases, sufficient for reading, writing, speaking, and listening at the college and career readiness level; demonstrate independence in gathering vocabulary knowledge when considering a word or phrase important to comprehension or expression.
	Read with Ease: Phrasing	RI.9-10.10	By the end of grade 10, read and comprehend literary nonfiction at the high end of the grades 9–10 text complexity band independently and proficiently.
34	**Grammar: Write Complete Sentences**	L.9-10.1.b	Use various types of phrases (noun, verb, adjectival, adverbial, participial, prepositional, absolute) and clauses (independent, dependent; noun, relative, adverbial) to convey specific meanings and add variety and interest to writing or presentations.
34	**Language Development: Express Ideas and Opinions**	SL.9-10.1.a	Come to discussions prepared, having read and researched material under study; explicitly draw on that preparation by referring to evidence from texts and other research on the topic or issue to stimulate a thoughtful, well-reasoned exchange of ideas.
34	**Literary Analysis: Analyze Setting**	RL.9-10.3	Analyze how complex characters develop over the course of a text, interact with other characters, and advance the plot or develop the theme.
35	**Vocabulary Study: Prefixes**	L.9-10.4.b	Identify and correctly use patterns of word changes that indicate different meanings or parts of speech.
		L.9-10.4.d	Verify the preliminary determination of the meaning of a word or phrase.
35	**Writing on Demand: Write an Opinion Paragraph**	W.9-10.1	Write arguments to support claims in an analysis of substantive topics or texts, using valid reasoning and relevant and sufficient evidence.
		W.9-10.4	Produce clear and coherent writing in which the development, organization, and style are appropriate to task, purpose, and audience.
		W.9-10.5	Develop and strengthen writing as needed by planning, revising, editing, rewriting, or trying a new approach, focusing on addressing what is most significant for a specific purpose and audience.
35	**Research/Writing: Written Report**	W.9-10.2	Write informative/explanatory texts to examine and convey complex ideas, concepts, and information clearly and accurately through the effective selection, organization, and analysis of content.
		W.9-10.8	Gather relevant information from multiple authoritative print and digital sources, using advanced searches effectively; assess the usefulness of each source in answering the research question; integrate information into the text selectively to maintain the flow of ideas, avoiding plagiarism and following a standard format for citation.
36	**Workplace Workshop: Inside a Hospital**	W.9-10.7	Conduct short as well as more sustained research projects to answer a question (including a self-generated question) or solve a problem; narrow or broaden the inquiry when appropriate; synthesize multiple sources on the subject, demonstrating understanding of the subject under investigation.
		L.9-10.6	Acquire and use accurately general academic and domain-specific words and phrases, sufficient for reading, writing, speaking, and listening at the college and career readiness level; demonstrate independence in gathering vocabulary knowledge when considering a word or phrase important to comprehension or expression.

Common Core State Standards, continued

Cluster 1, continued

SE Pages	Lesson	Code	Standards Text
37	Vocabulary Workshop: Use Word Parts	L.9-10.4.b	Identify and correctly use patterns of word changes that indicate different meanings or parts of speech.
		L.9-10.4.c	Consult general and specialized reference materials, both print and digital, to find the pronunciation of a word or determine or clarify its precise meaning, its part of speech, or its etymology.
		L.9-10.4.d	Verify the preliminary determination of the meaning of a word or phrase.

Cluster 2

SE Pages	Lesson	Code	Standards Text
38	Prepare to Read	RI.9-10.4	Determine the meaning of words and phrases as they are used in a text, including figurative, connotative, and technical meanings; analyze the cumulative impact of specific word choices on meaning and tone.
		SL.9-10.1	Initiate and participate effectively in a range of collaborative discussions (one-on-one, in groups, and teacher-led) with diverse partners on grades 9-10 topics, texts, and issues, building on others' ideas and expressing their own clearly and persuasively.
		L.9-10.6	Acquire and use accurately general academic and domain-specific words and phrases, sufficient for reading, writing, speaking, and listening at the college and career readiness level; demonstrate independence in gathering vocabulary knowledge when considering a word or phrase important to comprehension or expression.
39	Before Reading: Two Kinds	RL.9-10.3	Analyze how complex characters develop over the course of a text, interact with other characters, and advance the plot or develop the theme.
		RL.9-10.10	By the end of grade 10, read and comprehend literature, including stories, dramas, and poems, at the high end of the grades 9-10 text complexity band independently and proficiently.
40–58	Read Two Kinds	RL.9-10.1	Cite strong and thorough textual evidence to support analysis of what the text says explicitly as well as inferences drawn from the text.
		RL.9-10.2	Determine a theme or central idea of a text and analyze in detail its development over the course of the text, including how it emerges and is shaped and refined by specific details; provide an objective summary of the text.
		RL.9-10.3	Analyze how complex characters develop over the course of a text, interact with other characters, and advance the plot or develop the theme.
		RL.9-10.4	Determine the meaning of words and phrases as they are used in the text, including figurative and connotative meanings; analyze the cumulative impact of specific word choices on meaning and tone.
		RL.9-10.7	Analyze the representation of a subject or a key scene in two different artistic mediums, including what is emphasized or absent in each treatment.
		RL.9-10.10	By the end of grade 10, read and comprehend literature, including stories, dramas, and poems, at the high end of the grades 9-10 text complexity band independently and proficiently.
		W.9-10.4	Produce clear and coherent writing in which the development, organization, and style are appropriate to task, purpose, and audience.

Cluster 2, continued

SE Pages	Lesson	Code	Standards Text
40–58	**Read Two Kinds** continued	W.9-10.9.a	Apply grades 9–10 Reading standards to literature.
		W.9-10.10	Write routinely over extended time frames (time for research, reflection, and revision) and shorter time frames (a single sitting or a day or two) for a range of tasks, purposes, and audiences.
		L.9-10.1	Demonstrate command of the conventions of standard English grammar and usage when writing or speaking.
		L.9-10.2.c	Spell correctly.
		L.9-10.6	Acquire and use accurately general academic and domain-specific words and phrases, sufficient for reading, writing, speaking, and listening at the college and career readiness level; demonstrate independence in gathering vocabulary knowledge when considering a word or phrase important to comprehension or expression.
59	**Postscript: Why the Violin is Better**	RL.9-10.1	Cite strong and thorough textual evidence to support analysis of what the text says explicitly as well as inferences drawn from the text.
		RL.9-10.3	Analyze how complex characters develop over the course of a text, interact with other characters, and advance the plot or develop the theme.
		SL.9-10.6	Adapt speech to a variety of contexts and tasks, demonstrating command of formal English when indicated or appropriate.
60	**Before Reading: Novel Musician**	RI.9-10.5	Analyze in detail how an author's ideas or claims are developed and refined by particular sentences, paragraphs, or larger portions of a text.
		RI.9-10.10	By the end of grade 10, read and comprehend literary nonfiction at the high end of the grades 9–10 text complexity band independently and proficiently.
61–64	**Read Novel Musician**	RI.9-10.1	Cite strong and thorough textual evidence to support analysis of what the text says explicitly as well as inferences drawn from the text.
		RI.9-10.3	Analyze how the author unfolds an analysis or series of ideas or events, including the order in which the points are made, how they are introduced and developed, and the connections that are drawn between them.
		RI.9-10.4	Determine the meaning of words and phrases as they are used in a text, including figurative, connotative, and technical meanings; analyze the cumulative impact of specific word choices on meaning and tone.
		RI.9-10.5	Analyze in detail how an author's ideas or claims are developed and refined by particular sentences, paragraphs, or larger portions of a text.
		RI.9-10.10	By the end of grade 10, read and comprehend literary nonfiction at the high end of the grades 9–10 text complexity band independently and proficiently.
		W.9-10.2	Write informative/explanatory texts to examine and convey complex ideas, concepts, and information clearly and accurately through the effective selection, organization, and analysis of content.

Common Core State Standards, continued

SE Pages	Lesson	Code	Standards Text
61–64	**Read Novel Musician** continued	W.9-10.10	Write routinely over extended time frames (time for research, reflection, and revision) and shorter time frames (a single sitting or a day or two) for a range of tasks, purposes, and audiences.
		L.9-10.1.b	Use various types of phrases (noun, verb, adjectival, adverbial, participial, prepositional, absolute) and clauses (independent, dependent; noun, relative, adverbial) to convey specific meanings and add variety and interest to writing or presentations.
		L.9-10.6	Acquire and use accurately general academic and domain-specific words and phrases, sufficient for reading, writing, speaking, and listening at the college and career readiness level; demonstrate independence in gathering vocabulary knowledge when considering a word or phrase important to comprehension or expression.
65	**Reflect and Assess Critical Thinking**	RL.9-10.1	Cite strong and thorough textual evidence to support analysis of what the text says explicitly as well as inferences drawn from the text.
		RL.9-10.3	Analyze how complex characters develop over the course of a text, interact with other characters, and advance the plot or develop the theme.
		RL.9-10.10	By the end of grade 10, read and comprehend literature, including stories, dramas, and poems, at the high end of the grades 9–10 text complexity band independently and proficiently.
		RI.9-10.1	Cite strong and thorough textual evidence to support analysis of what the text says explicitly as well as inferences drawn from the text.
		RI.9-10.6	Determine an author's point of view or purpose in a text and analyze how an author uses rhetoric to advance that point of view or purpose.
		RI.9-10.10	By the end of grade 10, read and comprehend literary nonfiction at the high end of the grades 9–10 text complexity band independently and proficiently.
	Write About Literature	W.9-10.1	Write arguments to support claims in an analysis of substantive topics or texts, using valid reasoning and relevant and sufficient evidence.
	Key Vocabulary Review	L.9-10.6	Acquire and use accurately general academic and domain-specific words and phrases, sufficient for reading, writing, speaking, and listening at the college and career readiness level; demonstrate independence in gathering vocabulary knowledge when considering a word or phrase important to comprehension or expression.
	Read with Ease: Expression	RI.9-10.10	By the end of grade 10, read and comprehend literary nonfiction at the high end of the grades 9–10 text complexity band independently and proficiently.
66	**Grammar: Make Subjects and Verbs Agree**	L.9-10.1.b	Use various types of phrases (noun, verb, adjectival, adverbial, participial, prepositional, absolute) and clauses (independent, dependent; noun, relative, adverbial) to convey specific meanings and add variety and interest to writing or presentations.
66	**Language Development: Ask for and Give Information**	SL.9-10.1.a	Come to discussions prepared, having read and researched material under study; explicitly draw on that preparation by referring to evidence from texts and other research on the topic or issue to stimulate a thoughtful, well-reasoned exchange of ideas.
66	**Literary Analysis: Analyze Characters and Plot**	RL.9-10.3	Analyze how complex characters develop over the course of a text, interact with other characters, and advance the plot or develop the theme.

Cluster 2, continued

SE Pages	Lesson	Code	Standards Text
67	**Vocabulary Study: Suffixes**	L.9-10.4.b	Identify and correctly use patterns of word changes that indicate different meanings or parts of speech.
67	**Writing: Writing a Narrative Paragraph**	W.9-10.3.a	Engage and orient the reader by setting out a problem, situation, or observation, establishing one or multiple point(s) of view, and introducing a narrator and/or characters; create a smooth progression of experiences or events.
		W.9-10.3.d	Use precise words and phrases, telling details, and sensory language to convey a vivid picture of the experiences, events, setting, and/or characters.
		W.9-10.5	Develop and strengthen writing as needed by planning, revising, editing, rewriting, or trying a new approach, focusing on addressing what is most significant for a specific purpose and audience.
67	**Listening/Speaking: Interview**	W.9-10.2	Write informative/explanatory texts to examine and convey complex ideas, concepts, and information clearly and accurately through the effective selection, organization, and analysis of content.
68–69	**Listening and Speaking Workshop: Oral Interpretation of Literature**	SL.9-10.3	Evaluate a speaker's point of view, reasoning, and use of evidence and rhetoric, identifying any fallacious reasoning or exaggerated or distorted evidence.
		SL.9-10.6	Adapt speech to a variety of contexts and tasks, demonstrating command of formal English when indicated or appropriate.
		L.9-10.3	Apply knowledge of language to understand how language functions in different contexts, to make effective choices for meaning or style, and to comprehend more fully when reading or listening.

Cluster 3

SE Pages	Lesson	Code	Standards Text
70	**Prepare to Read**	RI.9-10.4	Determine the meaning of words and phrases as they are used in a text, including figurative, connotative, and technical meanings; analyze the cumulative impact of specific word choices on meaning and tone.
		SL.9-10.1	Initiate and participate effectively in a range of collaborative discussions (one-on-one, in groups, and teacher-led) with diverse partners on grades 9–10 topics, texts, and issues, building on others' ideas and expressing their own clearly and persuasively.
		L.9-10.6	Acquire and use accurately general academic and domain-specific words and phrases, sufficient for reading, writing, speaking, and listening at the college and career readiness level; demonstrate independence in gathering vocabulary knowledge when considering a word or phrase important to comprehension or expression.
71	**Before Reading: Skins**	RL.9-10.2	Determine a theme or central idea of a text and analyze in detail its development over the course of the text, including how it emerges and is shaped and refined by specific details; provide an objective summary of the text.
		RL.9-10.4	Determine the meaning of words and phrases as they are used in the text, including figurative and connotative meanings; analyze the cumulative impact of specific word choices on meaning and tone.

Common Core State Standards, continued

Cluster 3, continued

SE Pages	Lesson	Code	Standards Text
72–91	Read Skins	RL.9-10.1	Cite strong and thorough textual evidence to support analysis of what the text says explicitly as well as inferences drawn from the text.
		RL.9-10.2	Determine a theme or central idea of a text and analyze in detail its development over the course of the text, including how it emerges and is shaped and refined by specific details; provide an objective summary of the text.
		RL.9-10.3	Analyze how complex characters develop over the course of a text, interact with other characters, and advance the plot or develop the theme.
		RL.9-10.4	Determine the meaning of words and phrases as they are used in the text, including figurative and connotative meanings; analyze the cumulative impact of specific word choices on meaning and tone.
		RL.9-10.5	Analyze how an author's choices concerning how to structure a text, order events within it, and manipulate time.
		RL.9-10.7	Analyze the representation of a subject or a key scene in two different artistic mediums, including what is emphasized or absent in each treatment.
		RL.9-10.10	By the end of grade 10, read and comprehend literature, including stories, dramas, and poems, at the high end of the grades 9–10 text complexity band independently and proficiently.
		W.9-10.2	Write informative/explanatory texts to examine and convey complex ideas, concepts, and information clearly and accurately through the effective selection, organization, and analysis of content.
		W.9-10.9.a	Apply grades 9–10 Reading standards to literature.
		W.9-10.10	Write routinely over extended time frames (time for research, reflection, and revision) and shorter time frames (a single sitting or a day or two) for a range of tasks, purposes, and audiences.
		L.9-10.1	Demonstrate command of the conventions of standard English grammar and usage when writing or speaking.
		L.9-10.6	Acquire and use accurately general academic and domain-specific words and phrases, sufficient for reading, writing, speaking, and listening at the college and career readiness level; demonstrate independence in gathering vocabulary knowledge when considering a word or phrase important to comprehension or expression.
92–93	Postscript: One	RL.9-10.2	Determine a theme or central idea of a text and analyze in detail its development over the course of the text, including how it emerges and is shaped and refined by specific details; provide an objective summary of the text.
		SL.9-10.6	Adapt speech to a variety of contexts and tasks, demonstrating command of formal English when indicated or appropriate.
		L.9-10.5	Demonstrate understanding of figurative language, word relationships, and nuances in word meanings.

Cluster 3, continued

SE Pages	Lesson	Code	Standards Text
94	**Before Reading: Nicole**	RI.9-10.4	Determine the meaning of words and phrases as they are used in a text, including figurative, connotative, and technical meanings; analyze the cumulative impact of specific word choices on meaning and tone.
		RI.9-10.6	Determine an author's point of view or purpose in a text and analyze how an author uses rhetoric to advance that point of view or purpose.
95–98	**Read Nicole**	RL.9-10.1	Cite strong and thorough textual evidence to support analysis of what the text says explicitly as well as inferences drawn from the text.
		RI.9-10.1	Cite strong and thorough textual evidence to support analysis of what the text says explicitly as well as inferences drawn from the text.
		RI.9-10.2	Determine a central idea of a text and analyze its development over the course of the text, including how it emerges and is shaped and refined by specific details; provide an objective summary of the text.
		RI.9-10.4	Determine the meaning of words and phrases as they are used in a text, including figurative, connotative, and technical meanings; analyze the cumulative impact of specific word choices on meaning and tone.
		RI.9-10.6	Determine an author's point of view or purpose in a text and analyze how an author uses rhetoric to advance that point of view or purpose.
		RI.9-10.10	By the end of grade 10, read and comprehend literary nonfiction at the high end of the grades 9-10 text complexity band independently and proficiently.
		W.9-10.1	Write arguments to support claims in an analysis of substantive topics or texts, using valid reasoning and relevant and sufficient evidence.
		W.9-10.9.b	Apply grades 9-10 Reading standards to literary nonfiction.
		W.9-10.10	Write routinely over extended time frames (time for research, reflection, and revision) and shorter time frames (a single sitting or a day or two) for a range of tasks, purposes, and audiences.
		SL.9-10.1	Initiate and participate effectively in a range of collaborative discussions (one-on-one, in groups, and teacher-led) with diverse partners on grades 9–10 topics, texts, and issues, building on others' ideas and expressing their own clearly and persuasively.
		L.9-10.1	Demonstrate command of the conventions of standard English grammar and usage when writing or speaking.
		L.9-10.4.d	Verify the preliminary determination of the meaning of a word or phrase.
		L.9-10.6	Acquire and use accurately general academic and domain-specific words and phrases, sufficient for reading, writing, speaking, and listening at the college and career readiness level; demonstrate independence in gathering vocabulary knowledge when considering a word or phrase important to comprehension or expression.

Common Core State Standards, continued

Cluster 3, continued

SE Pages	Lesson	Code	Standards Text
99	**Reflect and Assess Critical Thinking**	RL.9-10.1	Cite strong and thorough textual evidence to support analysis of what the text says explicitly as well as inferences drawn from the text.
		RL.9-10.2	Determine a theme or central idea of a text and analyze in detail its development over the course of the text, including how it emerges and is shaped and refined by specific details; provide an objective summary of the text.
		RL.9-10.3	Analyze how complex characters develop over the course of a text, interact with other characters, and advance the plot or develop the theme.
		RL.9-10.10	By the end of grade 10, read and comprehend literature, including stories, dramas, and poems, at the high end of the grades 9–10 text complexity band independently and proficiently.
		RI.9-10.1	Cite strong and thorough textual evidence to support analysis of what the text says explicitly as well as inferences drawn from the text.
		RI.9-10.2	Determine a central idea of a text and analyze its development over the course of the text, including how it emerges and is shaped and refined by specific details; provide an objective summary of the text.
		RI.9-10.10	By the end of grade 10, read and comprehend literary nonfiction at the high end of the grades 9–10 text complexity band independently and proficiently.
	Write About Literature	W.9-10.2	Write informative/explanatory texts to examine and convey complex ideas, concepts, and information clearly and accurately through the effective selection, organization, and analysis of content.
	Key Vocabulary Review	L.9-10.6	Acquire and use accurately general academic and domain-specific words and phrases, sufficient for reading, writing, speaking, and listening at the college and career readiness level; demonstrate independence in gathering vocabulary knowledge when considering a word or phrase important to comprehension or expression.
	Read with Ease: Intonation	RL.9-10.10	By the end of grade 10, read and comprehend literature, including stories, dramas, and poems, at the high end of the grades 9–10 text complexity band independently and proficiently.
100	**Grammar: Fix Sentence Fragments**	L.9-10.1	Demonstrate command of the conventions of standard English grammar and usage when writing or speaking.
100	**Language Development: Engage in Discussion**	SL.9-10.1	Initiate and participate effectively in a range of collaborative discussions (one-on-one, in groups, and teacher-led) with diverse partners on grades 9–10 topics, texts, and issues, building on others' ideas and expressing their own clearly and persuasively.
100	**Literary Analysis: Characters: Static and Dynamic**	RL.9-10.3	Analyze how complex characters develop over the course of a text, interact with other characters, and advance the plot or develop the theme.
101	**Vocabulary Study: Greek and Latin Roots**	L.9-10.4.b	Identify and correctly use patterns of word changes that indicate different meanings or parts of speech.
101	**Writing Trait: Focus and Unity**	W.9-10.5	Develop and strengthen writing as needed by planning, revising, editing, rewriting, or trying a new approach, focusing on addressing what is most significant for a specific purpose and audience.

Cluster 3, continued

SE Pages	Lesson	Code	Standards Text
101	**Research/Speaking: Oral Report**	W.9-10.7	Conduct short as well as more sustained research projects to answer a question (including a self-generated question) or solve a problem; narrow or broaden the inquiry when appropriate; synthesize multiple sources on the subject, demonstrating understanding of the subject under investigation.
		W.9-10.8	Gather relevant information from multiple authoritative print and digital sources, using advanced searches effectively; assess the usefulness of each source in answering the research question; integrate information into the text selectively to maintain the flow of ideas, avoiding plagiarism and following a standard format for citation.

Close Reading

SE Pages	Lesson	Code	Standards Text
102–103	**Read Yes**	RL.9-10.10	By the end of grade 10, read and comprehend literature, including stories, dramas, and poems, at the high end of the grades 9–10 text complexity band independently and proficiently.

Unit Wrap-Up

SE Pages	Lesson	Code	Standards Text
104	**Unit Wrap-Up Present Your Project**	SL.9-10.5	Make strategic use of digital media in presentations to enhance understanding of findings, reasoning, and evidence and to add interest.
	Reflect on Your Reading	SL.9-10.1.a	Come to discussions prepared, having read and researched material under study; explicitly draw on that preparation by referring to evidence from texts and other research on the topic or issue to stimulate a thoughtful, well-reasoned exchange of ideas.
	Respond to the Essential Question	SL.9-10.1.a	Come to discussions prepared, having read and researched material under study; explicitly draw on that preparation by referring to evidence from texts and other research on the topic or issue to stimulate a thoughtful, well-reasoned exchange of ideas.

Writing Project: Short Story

SE Pages	Lesson	Code	Standards Text
105–109	**Study Short Stories and Prewrite**	W.9-10.3.c	Use a variety of techniques to sequence events so that they build on one another to create a coherent whole.
		W.9-10.5	Develop and strengthen writing as needed by planning, revising, editing, rewriting, or trying a new approach, focusing on addressing what is most significant for a specific purpose and audience.
110–111	**Short Story: Draft**	W.9-10.3.a	Engage and orient the reader by setting out a problem, situation, or observation, establishing one or multiple point(s) of view, and introducing a narrator and/or characters; create a smooth progression of experiences or events.
		W.9-10.3.d	Use precise words and phrases, telling details, and sensory language to convey a vivid picture of the experiences, events, setting, and/or characters.
		W.9-10.4	Produce clear and coherent writing in which the development, organization, and style are appropriate to task, purpose, and audience.
		W.9-10.5	Develop and strengthen writing as needed by planning, revising, editing, rewriting, or trying a new approach, focusing on addressing what is most significant for a specific purpose and audience.

Common Core State Standards, continued

Student Handbooks, continued			
Writing Project: Short Story, continued			
SE Pages	**Lesson**	**Code**	**Standards Text**
110–111	**Short Story: Draft** continued	W.9-10.6	Use technology, including the Internet, to produce, publish, and update individual or shared writing products, taking advantage of technology's capacity to link to other information and to display information flexibly and dynamically.
112–115	**Short Story: Revise Trait: Focus and Unity**	W.9-10.5	Develop and strengthen writing as needed by planning, revising, editing, rewriting, or trying a new approach, focusing on addressing what is most significant for a specific purpose and audience.
		SL.9-10.1.d	Respond thoughtfully to diverse perspectives, summarize points of agreement and disagreement, and, when warranted, qualify or justify their own views and understanding and make new connections in light of the evidence and reasoning presented.
116–118	**Short Story: Edit and Proofread** **Capitalization: Proper Nouns and Adjectives** **Serial Commas** **Spelling** **Run-on Sentences**	W.9-10.3.a	Engage and orient the reader by setting out a problem, situation, or observation, establishing one or multiple point(s) of view, and introducing a narrator and/or characters; create a smooth progression of experiences or events.
		W.9-10.3.b	Use narrative techniques, such as dialogue, pacing, description, reflection, and multiple plot lines, to develop experiences, events, and/or characters.
		W.9-10.3.c	Use a variety of techniques to sequence events so that they build on one another to create a coherent whole.
		W.9-10.3.d	Use precise words and phrases, telling details, and sensory language to convey a vivid picture of the experiences, events, setting, and/or characters.
		W.9-10.3.e	Provide a conclusion that follows from and reflects on what is experienced, observed, or resolved over the course of the narrative.
		W.9-10.5	Develop and strengthen writing as needed by planning, revising, editing, rewriting, or trying a new approach, focusing on addressing what is most significant for a specific purpose and audience.
		W.9-10.6	Use technology, including the Internet, to produce, publish, and update individual or shared writing products, taking advantage of technology's capacity to link to other information and to display information flexibly and dynamically.
		SL.9-10.1.d	Respond thoughtfully to diverse perspectives, summarize points of agreement and disagreement, and, when warranted, qualify or justify their own views and understanding and make new connections in light of the evidence and reasoning presented.
		L.9-10.1	Demonstrate command of the conventions of standard English grammar and usage when writing or speaking.
		L.9-10.2	Demonstrate command of the conventions of standard English capitalization, punctuation, and spelling when writing.
		L.9-10.2.a	Use a semicolon (and perhaps a conjunctive adverb) to link two or more closely related independent clauses.
		L.9-10.2.c	Spell correctly.
		L.9-10.3	Apply knowledge of language to understand how language functions in different contexts, to make effective choices for meaning or style, and to comprehend more fully when reading or listening.

Writing Project: Short Story, continued

SE Pages	Lesson	Code	Standards Text
116–118	Short Story: Edit and Proofread Capitalization: Proper Nouns and Adjectives Serial Commas Spelling Run-on Sentences continued	L.9-10.3.a	Write and edit work so that it conforms to the guidelines in a style manual appropriate for the discipline and writing type.
119	Short Story: Publish and Present	W.9-10.4	Produce clear and coherent writing in which the development, organization, and style are appropriate to task, purpose, and audience.
		W.9-10.6	Use technology, including the Internet, to produce, publish, and update individual or shared writing products, taking advantage of technology's capacity to link to other information and to display information flexibly and dynamically.
		SL.9-10.5	Make strategic use of digital media in presentations to enhance understanding of findings, reasoning, and evidence and to add interest.
		SL.9-10.6	Adapt speech to a variety of contexts and tasks, demonstrating command of formal English when indicated or appropriate.

UNIT 2: Against the Odds

SE Pages	Lesson	Code	Standards Text
120–121	Discuss the Essential Question	SL.9-10.1.b	Work with peers to set rules for collegial discussions and decision-making, clear goals and deadlines, and individual roles as needed.
		SL.9-10.3	Evaluate a speaker's point of view, reasoning, and use of evidence and rhetoric, identifying any fallacious reasoning or exaggerated or distorted evidence.
122	Analyze and Speculate	SL.9-10.4	Present information, findings, and supporting evidence clearly, concisely, and logically such that listeners can follow the line of reasoning and the organization, development, substance, and style are appropriate to purpose, audience, and task.
123	Plan a Project	SL.9-10.1.b	Work with peers to set rules for collegial discussions and decision-making, clear goals and deadlines, and individual roles as needed.
123	Choose More to Read	RL.9-10.10	By the end of grade 10, read and comprehend literature, including stories, dramas, and poems, at the high end of the grades 9–10 text complexity band independently and proficiently.
		RI.9-10.10	By the end of grade 10, read and comprehend literary nonfiction at the high end of the grades 9–10 text complexity band independently and proficiently.
124–127	How to Read Nonfiction	RI.9-10.2	Determine a central idea of a text and analyze its development over the course of the text, including how it emerges and is shaped and refined by specific details; provide an objective summary of the text.
		RI.9-10.3	Analyze how the author unfolds an analysis or series of ideas or events, including the order in which the points are made, how they are introduced and developed, and the connections that are drawn between them.

Common Core State Standards, continued

UNIT 2: Against the Odds, continued

SE Pages	Lesson	Code	Standards Text
124–127	**How to Read Nonfiction** continued	RI.9-10.10	By the end of grade 10, read and comprehend literary nonfiction at the high end of the grades 9–10 text complexity band independently and proficiently.
		SL.9-10.1.a	Come to discussions prepared, having read and researched material under study; explicitly draw on that preparation by referring to evidence from texts and other research on the topic or issue to stimulate a thoughtful, well-reasoned exchange of ideas.
		L.9-10.6	Acquire and use accurately general academic and domain-specific words and phrases, sufficient for reading, writing, speaking, and listening at the college and career readiness level; demonstrate independence in gathering vocabulary knowledge when considering a word or phrase important to comprehension or expression.

Cluster 1

SE Pages	Lesson	Code	Standards Text
128	**Prepare to Read**	RI.9-10.4	Determine the meaning of words and phrases as they are used in a text, including figurative, connotative, and technical meanings; analyze the cumulative impact of specific word choices on meaning and tone.
		SL.9-10.1	Initiate and participate effectively in a range of collaborative discussions (one-on-one, in groups, and teacher-led) with diverse partners on grades 9–10 topics, texts, and issues, building on others' ideas and expressing their own clearly and persuasively.
		L.9-10.6	Acquire and use accurately general academic and domain-specific words and phrases, sufficient for reading, writing, speaking, and listening at the college and career readiness level; demonstrate independence in gathering vocabulary knowledge when considering a word or phrase important to comprehension or expression.
129	**Before Reading: La Vida Robot**	RI.9-10.2	Determine a central idea of a text and analyze its development over the course of the text, including how it emerges and is shaped and refined by specific details; provide an objective summary of the text.
		RI.9-10.7	Analyze various accounts of a subject told in different mediums, determining which details are emphasized in each account.
130–152	**Read La Vida Robot**	RI.9-10.1	Cite strong and thorough textual evidence to support analysis of what the text says explicitly as well as inferences drawn from the text.
		RI.9-10.2	Determine a central idea of a text and analyze its development over the course of the text, including how it emerges and is shaped and refined by specific details; provide an objective summary of the text.
		RI.9-10.4	Determine the meaning of words and phrases as they are used in a text, including figurative, connotative, and technical meanings; analyze the cumulative impact of specific word choices on meaning and tone.
		RI.9-10.7	Analyze various accounts of a subject told in different mediums, determining which details are emphasized in each account.
		RI.9-10.10	By the end of grade 10, read and comprehend literary nonfiction at the high end of the grades 9–10 text complexity band independently and proficiently.
		W.9-10.2	Write informative/explanatory texts to examine and convey complex ideas, concepts, and information clearly and accurately through the effective selection, organization, and analysis of content.

Cluster 1, continued

SE Pages	Lesson	Code	Standards Text
130–152	**Read La Vida Robot** continued	W.9-10.9.b	Apply grades 9–10 Reading standards to literary nonfiction.
		W.9-10.10	Write routinely over extended time frames (time for research, reflection, and revision) and shorter time frames (a single sitting or a day or two) for a range of tasks, purposes, and audiences.
		L.9-10.1.b	Use various types of phrases (noun, verb, adjectival, adverbial, participial, prepositional, absolute) and clauses (independent, dependent; noun, relative, adverbial) to convey specific meanings and add variety and interest to writing or presentations.
		L.9-10.4.b	Identify and correctly use patterns of word changes that indicate different meanings or parts of speech.
		L.9-10.6	Acquire and use accurately general academic and domain-specific words and phrases, sufficient for reading, writing, speaking, and listening at the college and career readiness level; demonstrate independence in gathering vocabulary knowledge when considering a word or phrase important to comprehension or expression.
153	**Before Reading: Reading, Writing, and... Recreation?**	RI.9-10.2	Determine a central idea of a text and analyze its development over the course of the text, including how it emerges and is shaped and refined by specific details; provide an objective summary of the text.
		RI.9-10.3	Analyze how the author unfolds an analysis or series of ideas or events, including the order in which the points are made, how they are introduced and developed, and the connections that are drawn between them.
154–156	**Read Reading, Writing, and... Recreation?**	RI.9-10.1	Cite strong and thorough textual evidence to support analysis of what the text says explicitly as well as inferences drawn from the text.
		RI.9-10.2	Determine a central idea of a text and analyze its development over the course of the text, including how it emerges and is shaped and refined by specific details; provide an objective summary of the text.
		RI.9-10.3	Analyze how the author unfolds an analysis or series of ideas or events, including the order in which the points are made, how they are introduced and developed, and the connections that are drawn between them.
		RI.9-10.5	Analyze in detail how an author's ideas or claims are developed and refined by particular sentences, paragraphs, or larger portions of a text.
		RI.9-10.10	By the end of grade 10, read and comprehend literary nonfiction at the high end of the grades 9–10 text complexity band independently and proficiently.
		W.9-10.9.b	Apply grades 9–10 Reading standards to literary nonfiction.
		W.9-10.10	Write routinely over extended time frames (time for research, reflection, and revision) and shorter time frames (a single sitting or a day or two) for a range of tasks, purposes, and audiences.
		L.9-10.6	Acquire and use accurately general academic and domain-specific words and phrases, sufficient for reading, writing, speaking, and listening at the college and career readiness level; demonstrate independence in gathering vocabulary knowledge when considering a word or phrase important to comprehension or expression.

Common Core State Standards, continued

Cluster 1, continued

SE Pages	Lesson	Code	Standards Text
157	**Reflect and Assess** **Critical Thinking**	RI.9-10.2	Determine a central idea of a text and analyze its development over the course of the text, including how it emerges and is shaped and refined by specific details; provide an objective summary of the text.
		RI.9-10.10	By the end of grade 10, read and comprehend literary nonfiction at the high end of the grades 9–10 text complexity band independently and proficiently.
	Write About Literature	W.9-10.1	Write arguments to support claims in an analysis of substantive topics or texts, using valid reasoning and relevant and sufficient evidence.
	Key Vocabulary Review	L.9-10.6	Acquire and use accurately general academic and domain-specific words and phrases, sufficient for reading, writing, speaking, and listening at the college and career readiness level; demonstrate independence in gathering vocabulary knowledge when considering a word or phrase important to comprehension or expression.
	Read with Ease: Phrasing	RI.9-10.10	By the end of grade 10, read and comprehend literary nonfiction at the high end of the grades 9–10 text complexity band independently and proficiently.
158	**Grammar: Use Subject** **Pronouns**	L.9-10.1	Demonstrate command of the conventions of standard English grammar and usage when writing or speaking.
158	**Language Development:** **Describe a Process**	SL.9-10.4	Present information, findings, and supporting evidence clearly, concisely, and logically such that listeners can follow the line of reasoning and the organization, development, substance, and style are appropriate to purpose, audience, and task.
158	**Literary Analysis: Analogy** **and Allusion**	RI.9-10.4	Determine the meaning of words and phrases as they are used in a text, including figurative, connotative, and technical meanings; analyze the cumulative impact of specific word choices on meaning and tone.
158	**Listening/Speaking:** **Technology Demonstration**	SL.9-10.4	Present information, findings, and supporting evidence clearly, concisely, and logically such that listeners can follow the line of reasoning and the organization, development, substance, and style are appropriate to purpose, audience, and task.
159	**Vocabulary Study: Context** **Clues: Definitions**	L.9-10.4.a	Use context as a clue to the meaning of a word or phrase.
159	**Writing: Write a News** **Feature**	W.9-10.2	Write informative/explanatory texts to examine and convey complex ideas, concepts, and information clearly and accurately through the effective selection, organization, and analysis of content.
		W.9-10.5	Develop and strengthen writing as needed by planning, revising, editing, rewriting, or trying a new approach, focusing on addressing what is most significant for a specific purpose and audience.
160	**Workplace Workshop:** **Inside a Veterinary Clinic**	W.9-10.7	Conduct short as well as more sustained research projects to answer a question (including a self-generated question) or solve a problem; narrow or broaden the inquiry when appropriate; synthesize multiple sources on the subject, demonstrating understanding of the subject under investigation.
		W.9-10.10	Write routinely over extended time frames (time for research, reflection, and revision) and shorter time frames (a single sitting or a day or two) for a range of tasks, purposes, and audiences.

Cluster 1, continued

SE Pages	Lesson	Code	Standards Text
160	**Workplace Workshop: Inside a Veterinary Clinic** continued	L.9-10.6	Acquire and use accurately general academic and domain-specific words and phrases, sufficient for reading, writing, speaking, and listening at the college and career readiness level; demonstrate independence in gathering vocabulary knowledge when considering a word or phrase important to comprehension or expression.
161	**Vocabulary Workshop: Use Context Clues**	L.9-10.4.a	Use context as a clue to the meaning of a word or phrase.
		L.9-10.4.c	Consult general and specialized reference materials, both print and digital, to find the pronunciation of a word or determine or clarify its precise meaning, its part of speech, or its etymology.
		L.9-10.4.d	Verify the preliminary determination of the meaning of a word or phrase.

Cluster 2

162	**Prepare to Read**	RI.9-10.4	Determine the meaning of words and phrases as they are used in a text, including figurative, connotative, and technical meanings; analyze the cumulative impact of specific word choices on meaning and tone.
		SL.9-10.1	Initiate and participate effectively in a range of collaborative discussions (one-on-one, in groups, and teacher-led) with diverse partners on grades 9–10 topics, texts, and issues, building on others' ideas and expressing their own clearly and persuasively.
		L.9-10.6	Acquire and use accurately general academic and domain-specific words and phrases, sufficient for reading, writing, speaking, and listening at the college and career readiness level; demonstrate independence in gathering vocabulary knowledge when considering a word or phrase important to comprehension or expression.
163	**Before Reading: My Left Foot**	RI.9-10.2	Determine a central idea of a text and analyze its development over the course of the text, including how it emerges and is shaped and refined by specific details; provide an objective summary of the text.
		RI.9-10.3	Analyze how the author unfolds an analysis or series of ideas or events, including the order in which the points are made, how they are introduced and developed, and the connections that are drawn between them.
164–176	**Read My Left Foot**	RI.9-10.1	Cite strong and thorough textual evidence to support analysis of what the text says explicitly as well as inferences drawn from the text.
		RI.9-10.2	Determine a central idea of a text and analyze its development over the course of the text, including how it emerges and is shaped and refined by specific details; provide an objective summary of the text.
		RI.9-10.3	Analyze how the author unfolds an analysis or series of ideas or events, including the order in which the points are made, how they are introduced and developed, and the connections that are drawn between them.
		RI.9-10.4	Determine the meaning of words and phrases as they are used in a text, including figurative, connotative, and technical meanings; analyze the cumulative impact of specific word choices on meaning and tone.
		RI.9-10.5	Analyze in detail how an author's ideas or claims are developed and refined by particular sentences, paragraphs, or larger portions of a text.

Common Core State Standards, continued

Cluster 2, continued

SE Pages	Lesson	Code	Standards Text
164–176	**Read My Left Foot** continued	RI.9-10.10	By the end of grade 10, read and comprehend literary nonfiction at the high end of the grades 9–10 text complexity band independently and proficiently.
		W.9-10.9.b	Apply grades 9–10 Reading standards to literary nonfiction.
		W.9-10.10	Write routinely over extended time frames (time for research, reflection, and revision) and shorter time frames (a single sitting or a day or two) for a range of tasks, purposes, and audiences.
		L.9-10.1	Demonstrate command of the conventions of standard English grammar and usage when writing or speaking.
		L.9-10.2.c	Spell correctly.
		L.9-10.4.b	Identify and correctly use patterns of word changes that indicate different meanings or parts of speech.
		L.9-10.6	Acquire and use accurately general academic and domain-specific words and phrases, sufficient for reading, writing, speaking, and listening at the college and career readiness level; demonstrate independence in gathering vocabulary knowledge when considering a word or phrase important to comprehension or expression.
177	**Before Reading: Success Is a Mind-Set**	RI.9-10.2	Determine a central idea of a text and analyze its development over the course of the text, including how it emerges and is shaped and refined by specific details; provide an objective summary of the text.
		RI.9-10.3	Analyze how the author unfolds an analysis or series of ideas or events, including the order in which the points are made, how they are introduced and developed, and the connections that are drawn between them.
178–182	**Read Success Is a Mind-Set**	RI.9-10.1	Cite strong and thorough textual evidence to support analysis of what the text says explicitly as well as inferences drawn from the text.
		RI.9-10.2	Determine a central idea of a text and analyze its development over the course of the text, including how it emerges and is shaped and refined by specific details; provide an objective summary of the text.
		RI.9-10.3	Analyze how the author unfolds an analysis or series of ideas or events, including the order in which the points are made, how they are introduced and developed, and the connections that are drawn between them.
		RI.9-10.4	Determine the meaning of words and phrases as they are used in a text, including figurative, connotative, and technical meanings; analyze the cumulative impact of specific word choices on meaning and tone.
		RI.9-10.5	Analyze in detail how an author's ideas or claims are developed and refined by particular sentences, paragraphs, or larger portions of a text.
		RI.9-10.10	By the end of grade 10, read and comprehend literary nonfiction at the high end of the grades 9–10 text complexity band independently and proficiently.
		W.9-10.1	Write arguments to support claims in an analysis of substantive topics or texts, using valid reasoning and relevant and sufficient evidence.

Cluster 2, continued

SE Pages	Lesson	Code	Standards Text
178–182	**Read Success Is a Mind-Set** continued	W.9-10.9.b	Apply grades 9–10 Reading standards to literary nonfiction.
		W.9-10.10	Write routinely over extended time frames (time for research, reflection, and revision) and shorter time frames (a single sitting or a day or two) for a range of tasks, purposes, and audiences.
		L.9-10.1.b	Use various types of phrases (noun, verb, adjectival, adverbial, participial, prepositional, absolute) and clauses (independent, dependent; noun, relative, adverbial) to convey specific meanings and add variety and interest to writing or presentations.
		L.9-10.4	Determine or clarify the meaning of unknown and multiple-meaning words and phrases based on grades 9–10 reading and content, choosing flexibly from a range of strategies.
		L.9-10.6	Acquire and use accurately general academic and domain-specific words and phrases, sufficient for reading, writing, speaking, and listening at the college and career readiness level; demonstrate independence in gathering vocabulary knowledge when considering a word or phrase important to comprehension or expression.
183	**Reflect and Assess Critical Thinking**	RI.9-10.1	Cite strong and thorough textual evidence to support analysis of what the text says explicitly as well as inferences drawn from the text.
		RI.9-10.2	Determine a central idea of a text and analyze its development over the course of the text, including how it emerges and is shaped and refined by specific details; provide an objective summary of the text.
		RI.9-10.4	Determine the meaning of words and phrases as they are used in a text, including figurative, connotative, and technical meanings; analyze the cumulative impact of specific word choices on meaning and tone.
		RI.9-10.10	By the end of grade 10, read and comprehend literary nonfiction at the high end of the grades 9–10 text complexity band independently and proficiently.
	Write About Literature	W.9-10.1	Write arguments to support claims in an analysis of substantive topics or texts, using valid reasoning and relevant and sufficient evidence.
	Key Vocabulary Review	L.9-10.6	Acquire and use accurately general academic and domain-specific words and phrases, sufficient for reading, writing, speaking, and listening at the college and career readiness level; demonstrate independence in gathering vocabulary knowledge when considering a word or phrase important to comprehension or expression.
	Read with Ease: Expression	RI.9-10.10	By the end of grade 10, read and comprehend literary nonfiction at the high end of the grades 9–10 text complexity band independently and proficiently.
184	**Grammar: Use Action Verbs in the Present Tense**	L.9-10.1.b	Use various types of phrases (noun, verb, adjectival, adverbial, participial, prepositional, absolute) and clauses (independent, dependent; noun, relative, adverbial) to convey specific meanings and add variety and interest to writing or presentations.
184	**Language Development: Describe People and Actions**	SL.9-10.1.a	Come to discussions prepared, having read and researched material under study; explicitly draw on that preparation by referring to evidence from texts and other research on the topic or issue to stimulate a thoughtful, well-reasoned exchange of ideas.

Common Core State Standards, continued

Cluster 2, continued

SE Pages	Lesson	Code	Standards Text
184	**Literary Analysis: Author's Purpose, Text Structure, and Point of View**	RI.9-10.3	Analyze how the author unfolds an analysis or series of ideas or events, including the order in which the points are made, how they are introduced and developed, and the connections that are drawn between them.
		RI.9-10.6	Determine an author's point of view or purpose in a text and analyze how an author uses rhetoric to advance that point of view or purpose.
185	**Vocabulary Study: Context Clues: Multiple-Meaning Words**	L.9-10.3	Apply knowledge of language to understand how language functions in different contexts, to make effective choices for meaning or style, and to comprehend more fully when reading or listening.
		L.9-10.4.a	Use context as a clue to the meaning of a word or phrase.
185	**Writing Trait: Voice and Style**	W.9-10.2	Write informative/explanatory texts to examine and convey complex ideas, concepts, and information clearly and accurately through the effective selection, organization, and analysis of content.
		W.9-10.5	Develop and strengthen writing as needed by planning, revising, editing, rewriting, or trying a new approach, focusing on addressing what is most significant for a specific purpose and audience.
185	**Research/Writing: Summary of Events**	W.9-10.2	Write informative/explanatory texts to examine and convey complex ideas, concepts, and information clearly and accurately through the effective selection, organization, and analysis of content.
		W.9-10.7	Conduct short as well as more sustained research projects to answer a question (including a self-generated question) or solve a problem; narrow or broaden the inquiry when appropriate; synthesize multiple sources on the subject, demonstrating understanding of the subject under investigation.
		W.9-10.9	Draw evidence from literary or informational texts to support analysis, reflection, and research.
186–187	**Listening and Speaking Workshop: Narrative Presentation**	SL.9-10.3	Evaluate a speaker's point of view, reasoning, and use of evidence and rhetoric, identifying any fallacious reasoning or exaggerated or distorted evidence.
		SL.9-10.4	Present information, findings, and supporting evidence clearly, concisely, and logically such that listeners can follow the line of reasoning and the organization, development, substance, and style are appropriate to purpose, audience, and task.
		L.9-10.3	Apply knowledge of language to understand how language functions in different contexts, to make effective choices for meaning or style, and to comprehend more fully when reading or listening.

Cluster 3

SE Pages	Lesson	Code	Standards Text
188	**Prepare to Read**	RI.9-10.4	Determine the meaning of words and phrases as they are used in a text, including figurative, connotative, and technical meanings; analyze the cumulative impact of specific word choices on meaning and tone.
		SL.9-10.1	Initiate and participate effectively in a range of collaborative discussions (one-on-one, in groups, and teacher-led) with diverse partners on grades 9–10 topics, texts, and issues, building on others' ideas and expressing their own clearly and persuasively.

Cluster 3, continued

SE Pages	Lesson	Code	Standards Text
188	**Prepare to Read** continued	L.9-10.6	Acquire and use accurately general academic and domain-specific words and phrases, sufficient for reading, writing, speaking, and listening at the college and career readiness level; demonstrate independence in gathering vocabulary knowledge when considering a word or phrase important to comprehension or expression.
189	**Before Reading: The Freedom Writers Diary**	RI.9-10.2	Determine a central idea of a text and analyze its development over the course of the text, including how it emerges and is shaped and refined by specific details; provide an objective summary of the text.
		RI.9-10.3	Analyze how the author unfolds an analysis or series of ideas or events, including the order in which the points are made, how they are introduced and developed, and the connections that are drawn between them.
190–206	**Read The Freedom Writers Diary**	RI.9-10.1	Cite strong and thorough textual evidence to support analysis of what the text says explicitly as well as inferences drawn from the text.
		RI.9-10.2	Determine a central idea of a text and analyze its development over the course of the text, including how it emerges and is shaped and refined by specific details; provide an objective summary of the text.
		RI.9-10.3	Analyze how the author unfolds an analysis or series of ideas or events, including the order in which the points are made, how they are introduced and developed, and the connections that are drawn between them.
		RI.9-10.5	Analyze in detail how an author's ideas or claims are developed and refined by particular sentences, paragraphs, or larger portions of a text.
		RI.9-10.6	Determine an author's point of view or purpose in a text and analyze how an author uses rhetoric to advance that point of view or purpose.
		RI.9-10.7	Analyze various accounts of a subject told in different mediums, determining which details are emphasized in each account.
		RI.9-10.10	By the end of grade 10, read and comprehend literary nonfiction at the high end of the grades 9–10 text complexity band independently and proficiently.
		W.9-10.1	Write arguments to support claims in an analysis of substantive topics or texts, using valid reasoning and relevant and sufficient evidence.
		W.9-10.9.b	Apply grades 9–10 Reading standards to literary nonfiction.
		W.9-10.10	Write routinely over extended time frames (time for research, reflection, and revision) and shorter time frames (a single sitting or a day or two) for a range of tasks, purposes, and audiences.
		L.9-10.1.b	Use various types of phrases (noun, verb, adjectival, adverbial, participial, prepositional, absolute) and clauses (independent, dependent; noun, relative, adverbial) to convey specific meanings and add variety and interest to writing or presentations.
		L.9-10.4.b	Identify and correctly use patterns of word changes that indicate different meanings or parts of speech.
		L.9-10.4.d	Verify the preliminary determination of the meaning of a word or phrase.

Common Core State Standards, continued

Student Handbooks, continued			
Cluster 3, continued			
SE Pages	Lesson	Code	Standards Text
190–206	**Read The Freedom Writers Diary** continued	L.9-10.6	Acquire and use accurately general academic and domain-specific words and phrases, sufficient for reading, writing, speaking, and listening at the college and career readiness level; demonstrate independence in gathering vocabulary knowledge when considering a word or phrase important to comprehension or expression.
207	**Postscript: Dreams**	RL.9-10.1	Cite strong and thorough textual evidence to support analysis of what the text says explicitly as well as inferences drawn from the text.
		RL.9-10.4	Determine the meaning of words and phrases as they are used in the text, including figurative and connotative meanings; analyze the cumulative impact of specific word choices on meaning and tone.
		RI.9-10.1	Cite strong and thorough textual evidence to support analysis of what the text says explicitly as well as inferences drawn from the text.
		SL.9-10.6	Adapt speech to a variety of contexts and tasks, demonstrating command of formal English when indicated or appropriate.
208	**Before Reading: Strength, Courage, and Wisdom**	RL.9-10.2	Determine a theme or central idea of a text and analyze in detail its development over the course of the text, including how it emerges and is shaped and refined by specific details; provide an objective summary of the text.
		RL.9-10.4	Determine the meaning of words and phrases as they are used in the text, including figurative and connotative meanings; analyze the cumulative impact of specific word choices on meaning and tone.
209-210	**Read Strength, Courage, and Wisdom**	RL.9-10.1	Cite strong and thorough textual evidence to support analysis of what the text says explicitly as well as inferences drawn from the text.
		RL.9-10.2	Determine a theme or central idea of a text and analyze in detail its development over the course of the text, including how it emerges and is shaped and refined by specific details; provide an objective summary of the text.
		RL.9-10.4	Determine the meaning of words and phrases as they are used in the text, including figurative and connotative meanings; analyze the cumulative impact of specific word choices on meaning and tone.
		RL.9-10.10	By the end of grade 10, read and comprehend literature, including stories, dramas, and poems, at the high end of the grades 9–10 text complexity band independently and proficiently.
		RI.9-10.2	Determine a central idea of a text and analyze its development over the course of the text, including how it emerges and is shaped and refined by specific details; provide an objective summary of the text.
		W.9-10.9.a	Apply grades 9–10 Reading standards to literature.
		W.9-10.10	Write routinely over extended time frames (time for research, reflection, and revision) and shorter time frames (a single sitting or a day or two) for a range of tasks, purposes, and audiences.
		L.9-10.6	Acquire and use accurately general academic and domain-specific words and phrases, sufficient for reading, writing, speaking, and listening at the college and career readiness level; demonstrate independence in gathering vocabulary knowledge when considering a word or phrase important to comprehension or expression.

Cluster 3, continued

SE Pages	Lesson	Code	Standards Text
211	**Reflect and Assess Critical Thinking**	RL.9-10.1	Cite strong and thorough textual evidence to support analysis of what the text says explicitly as well as inferences drawn from the text.
		RL.9-10.2	Determine a theme or central idea of a text and analyze in detail its development over the course of the text, including how it emerges and is shaped and refined by specific details; provide an objective summary of the text.
		RL.9-10.4	Determine the meaning of words and phrases as they are used in the text, including figurative and connotative meanings; analyze the cumulative impact of specific word choices on meaning and tone.
		RL.9-10.10	By the end of grade 10, read and comprehend literature, including stories, dramas, and poems, at the high end of the grades 9–10 text complexity band independently and proficiently.
		RI.9-10.1	Cite strong and thorough textual evidence to support analysis of what the text says explicitly as well as inferences drawn from the text.
		RI.9-10.2	Determine a central idea of a text and analyze its development over the course of the text, including how it emerges and is shaped and refined by specific details; provide an objective summary of the text.
		RI.9-10.4	Determine the meaning of words and phrases as they are used in a text, including figurative, connotative, and technical meanings; analyze the cumulative impact of specific word choices on meaning and tone.
		RI.9-10.10	By the end of grade 10, read and comprehend literary nonfiction at the high end of the grades 9–10 text complexity band independently and proficiently.
		SL.9-10.6	Adapt speech to a variety of contexts and tasks, demonstrating command of formal English when indicated or appropriate.
	Write About Literature	W.9-10.1	Write arguments to support claims in an analysis of substantive topics or texts, using valid reasoning and relevant and sufficient evidence.
	Key Vocabulary Review	L.9-10.6	Acquire and use accurately general academic and domain-specific words and phrases, sufficient for reading, writing, speaking, and listening at the college and career readiness level; demonstrate independence in gathering vocabulary knowledge when considering a word or phrase important to comprehension or expression.
	Read with Ease: Intonation	RI.9-10.10	By the end of grade 10, read and comprehend literary nonfiction at the high end of the grades 9–10 text complexity band independently and proficiently.
212	**Grammar: Use Verbs to Talk About the Present**	L.9-10.1.b	Use various types of phrases (noun, verb, adjectival, adverbial, participial, prepositional, absolute) and clauses (independent, dependent; noun, relative, adverbial) to convey specific meanings and add variety and interest to writing or presentations.
212	**Language Development: Elaborate in a Description**	SL.9-10.1.a	Come to discussions prepared, having read and researched material under study; explicitly draw on that preparation by referring to evidence from texts and other research on the topic or issue to stimulate a thoughtful, well-reasoned exchange of ideas.
212	**Literary Analysis: Analyze Point of View**	RI.9-10.10	By the end of grade 10, read and comprehend literary nonfiction at the high end of the grades 9–10 text complexity band independently and proficiently.

Common Core State Standards, continued

Cluster 3, continued

SE Pages	Lesson	Code	Standards Text
213	Vocabulary Study: Context Clues: Examples	L.9-10.4.a	Use context as a clue to the meaning of a word or phrase.
213	Writing on Demand: Write an Explanation	W.9-10.1	Write arguments to support claims in an analysis of substantive topics or texts, using valid reasoning and relevant and sufficient evidence.
		W.9-10.5	Develop and strengthen writing as needed by planning, revising, editing, rewriting, or trying a new approach, focusing on addressing what is most significant for a specific purpose and audience.
213	Listening/Speaking: Panel Discussion	SL.9-10.1.b	Work with peers to set rules for collegial discussions and decision-making, clear goals and deadlines, and individual roles as needed.
		SL.9-10.6	Adapt speech to a variety of contexts and tasks, demonstrating command of formal English when indicated or appropriate.

Close Reading

SE Pages	Lesson	Code	Standards Text
214-217	Read The Cruelest Journey	RI.9-10.10	By the end of grade 10, read and comprehend literary nonfiction at the high end of the grades 9-10 text complexity band independently and proficiently.

Unit Wrap-Up

SE Pages	Lesson	Code	Standards Text
218	Unit Wrap-Up Present Your Project	SL.9-10.3	Evaluate a speaker's point of view, reasoning, and use of evidence and rhetoric, identifying any fallacious reasoning or exaggerated or distorted evidence.
		SL.9-10.6	Adapt speech to a variety of contexts and tasks, demonstrating command of formal English when indicated or appropriate.
	Reflect on Your Reading	SL.9-10.1	Initiate and participate effectively in a range of collaborative discussions (one-on-one, in groups, and teacher-led) with diverse partners on grades 9-10 topics, texts, and issues, building on others' ideas and expressing their own clearly and persuasively.
	Respond to the Essential Question	SL.9-10.1	Initiate and participate effectively in a range of collaborative discussions (one-on-one, in groups, and teacher-led) with diverse partners on grades 9-10 topics, texts, and issues, building on others' ideas and expressing their own clearly and persuasively.

Writing Project: Autobiographical Narrative

SE Pages	Lesson	Code	Standards Text
219-223	Study Autobiographical Narratives and Prewrite	W.9-10.5	Develop and strengthen writing as needed by planning, revising, editing, rewriting, or trying a new approach, focusing on addressing what is most significant for a specific purpose and audience.
		W.9-10.3.c	Use a variety of techniques to sequence events so that they build on one another to create a coherent whole.
224-225	Autobiographical Narrative: Draft	W.9-10.3.d	Use precise words and phrases, telling details, and sensory language to convey a vivid picture of the experiences, events, setting, and/or characters.
		W.9-10.4	Produce clear and coherent writing in which the development, organization, and style are appropriate to task, purpose, and audience.
		W.9-10.6	Use technology, including the Internet, to produce, publish, and update individual or shared writing products, taking advantage of technology's capacity to link to other information and to display information flexibly and dynamically.

Writing Project: Autobiographical Narrative, continued

SE Pages	Lesson	Code	Standards Text
226-229	**Autobiographical Narrative: Revise Trait: Voice and Style**	W.9-10.3.a	Engage and orient the reader by setting out a problem, situation, or observation, establishing one or multiple point(s) of view, and introducing a narrator and/or characters; create a smooth progression of experiences or events.
		W.9-10.3.e	Provide a conclusion that follows from and reflects on what is experienced, observed, or resolved over the course of the narrative.
		W.9-10.4	Produce clear and coherent writing in which the development, organization, and style are appropriate to task, purpose, and audience.
		W.9-10.5	Develop and strengthen writing as needed by planning, revising, editing, rewriting, or trying a new approach, focusing on addressing what is most significant for a specific purpose and audience.
		SL.9-10.1	Initiate and participate effectively in a range of collaborative discussions (one-on-one, in groups, and teacher-led) with diverse partners on grades 9–10 topics, texts, and issues, building on others' ideas and expressing their own clearly and persuasively.
		SL.9-10.1.d	Respond thoughtfully to diverse perspectives, summarize points of agreement and disagreement, and, when warranted, qualify or justify their own views and understanding and make new connections in light of the evidence and reasoning presented.
		L.9-10.1.b	Demonstrate command of the conventions of standard English grammar and usage when writing or speaking. Use various types of phrases (noun, verb, adjectival, adverbial, participial, prepositional, absolute) and clauses (independent, dependent; noun, relative, adverbial) to convey specific meanings and add variety and interest to writing or presentations.
230-232	**Autobiographical Narrative: Edit and Proofread Capitalization: Titles Dashes Spelling Verbs *Can, Could, May,* and *Might***	L.9-10.2.c	Spell correctly.
		L.9-10.3.a	Write and edit work so that it conforms to the guidelines in a style manual appropriate for the discipline and writing type.
233	**Autobiographical Narrative: Publish and Present**	W.9-10.6	Use technology, including the Internet, to produce, publish, and update individual or shared writing products, taking advantage of technology's capacity to link to other information and to display information flexibly and dynamically.
		SL.9-10.1.d	Respond thoughtfully to diverse perspectives, summarize points of agreement and disagreement, and, when warranted, qualify or justify their own views and understanding and make new connections in light of the evidence and reasoning presented.
		SL.9-10.6	Adapt speech to a variety of contexts and tasks, demonstrating command of formal English when indicated or appropriate.

UNIT 3: The Ties That Bind

SE Pages	Lesson	Code	Standards Text
234–235	**Discuss the Essential Question**	SL.9-10.1.b	Work with peers to set rules for collegial discussions and decision-making, clear goals and deadlines, and individual roles as needed.
		SL.9-10.3	Evaluate a speaker's point of view, reasoning, and use of evidence and rhetoric, identifying any fallacious reasoning or exaggerated or distorted evidence.

Common Core State Standards, continued

UNIT 3: The Ties That Bind, continued

SE Pages	Lesson	Code	Standards Text
236	**Compare and Debate**	SL.9-10.4	Present information, findings, and supporting evidence clearly, concisely, and logically such that listeners can follow the line of reasoning and the organization, development, substance, and style are appropriate to purpose, audience, and task.
237	**Plan a Project**	SL.9-10.1.b	Work with peers to set rules for collegial discussions and decision-making, clear goals and deadlines, and individual roles as needed.
237	**Choose More to Read**	RL.9-10.10	By the end of grade 10, read and comprehend literature, including stories, dramas, and poems, at the high end of the grades 9–10 text complexity band independently and proficiently.
		RI.9-10.10	By the end of grade 10, read and comprehend literary nonfiction at the high end of the grades 9–10 text complexity band independently and proficiently.
238–241	**How to Read Short Stories**	RL.9-10.1	Cite strong and thorough textual evidence to support analysis of what the text says explicitly as well as inferences drawn from the text.
		RL.9-10.4	Determine the meaning of words and phrases as they are used in a text, including figurative, connotative, and technical meanings; analyze the cumulative impact of specific word choices on meaning and tone.
		RL.9-10.5	Analyze how an author's choices concerning how to structure a text, order events within it, and manipulate time create such effects as mystery, tension or surprise.
		RL.9-10.10	By the end of grade 10, read and comprehend literature, including stories, dramas, and poems, at the high end of the grades 9–10 text complexity band independently and proficiently.
		W.9-10.10	Write routinely over extended time frames (time for research, reflection, and revision) and shorter time frames (a single sitting or a day or two) for a range of tasks, purposes, and audiences.
		L.9-10.6	Acquire and use accurately general academic and domain-specific words and phrases, sufficient for reading, writing, speaking, and listening at the college and career readiness level; demonstrate independence in gathering vocabulary knowledge when considering a word or phrase important to comprehension or expression.
Cluster 1			
242	**Prepare to Read**	RI.9-10.4	Determine the meaning of words and phrases as they are used in a text, including figurative, connotative, and technical meanings; analyze the cumulative impact of specific word choices on meaning and tone.
		SL.9-10.1	Initiate and participate effectively in a range of collaborative discussions (one-on-one, in groups, and teacher-led) with diverse partners on grades 9–10 topics, texts, and issues, building on others' ideas and expressing their own clearly and persuasively.
		L.9-10.6	Acquire and use accurately general academic and domain-specific words and phrases, sufficient for reading, writing, speaking, and listening at the college and career readiness level; demonstrate independence in gathering vocabulary knowledge when considering a word or phrase important to comprehension or expression.

Cluster 1, continued

SE Pages	Lesson	Code	Standards Text
243	**Before Reading: Amigo Brothers**	RL.9-10.1	Cite strong and thorough textual evidence to support analysis of what the text says explicitly as well as inferences drawn from the text.
		RL.9-10.4	Determine the meaning of words and phrases as they are used in a text, including figurative, connotative, and technical meanings; analyze the cumulative impact of specific word choices on meaning and tone.
244–260	**Read Amigo Brothers**	RL.9-10.1	Cite strong and thorough textual evidence to support analysis of what the text says explicitly as well as inferences drawn from the text.
		RL.9-10.2	Determine a theme or central idea of a text and analyze in detail its development over the course of the text, including how it emerges and is shaped and refined by specific details; provide an objective summary of the text.
		RL.9-10.4	Determine the meaning of words and phrases as they are used in a text, including figurative, connotative, and technical meanings; analyze the cumulative impact of specific word choices on meaning and tone.
		RL.9-10.7	Analyze the representation of a subject or a key scene in two different artistic mediums, including what is emphasized or absent in each treatment.
		RL.9-10.10	By the end of grade 10, read and comprehend literature, including stories, dramas, and poems, at the high end of the grades 9–10 text complexity band independently and proficiently.
		W.9-10.1	Write arguments to support claims in an analysis of substantive topics or texts, using valid reasoning and relevant and sufficient evidence.
		W.9-10.9.b	Apply grades 9–10 Reading standards to literary nonfiction.
		W.9-10.10	Write routinely over extended time frames (time for research, reflection, and revision) and shorter time frames (a single sitting or a day or two) for a range of tasks, purposes, and audiences.
		L.9-10.1.a	Use parallel structure.
		L.9-10.2.c	Spell correctly.
		L.9-10.4.a	Use context as a clue to the meaning of a word or phrase.
		L.9-10.5.a	Interpret figures of speech in context and analyze their role in the text.
		L.9-10.6	Acquire and use accurately general academic and domain-specific words and phrases, sufficient for reading, writing, speaking, and listening at the college and career readiness level; demonstrate independence in gathering vocabulary knowledge when considering a word or phrase important to comprehension or expression.
261	**Before Reading: Lean on Me**	RL.9-10.1	Cite strong and thorough textual evidence to support analysis of what the text says explicitly as well as inferences drawn from the text.
		RL.9-10.5	Analyze how an author's choices concerning how to structure a text, order events within it, and manipulate time create such effects as mystery, tension or surprise.

Common Core State Standards, continued

Cluster 1, continued

SE Pages	Lesson	Code	Standards Text
262–264	**Read Lean on Me**	RL.9-10.1	Cite strong and thorough textual evidence to support analysis of what the text says explicitly as well as inferences drawn from the text.
		RL.9-10.5	Analyze how an author's choices concerning how to structure a text, order events within it, and manipulate time create such effects as mystery, tension or surprise.
		RL.9-10.7	Analyze the representation of a subject or a key scene in two different artistic mediums, including what is emphasized or absent in each treatment.
		RL.9-10.10	By the end of grade 10, read and comprehend literature, including stories, dramas, and poems, at the high end of the grades 9–10 text complexity band independently and proficiently.
		W.9-10.1	Write arguments to support claims in an analysis of substantive topics or texts, using valid reasoning and relevant and sufficient evidence.
		W.9-10.10	Write routinely over extended time frames (time for research, reflection, and revision) and shorter time frames (a single sitting or a day or two) for a range of tasks, purposes, and audiences.
		L.9-10.6	Acquire and use accurately general academic and domain-specific words and phrases, sufficient for reading, writing, speaking, and listening at the college and career readiness level; demonstrate independence in gathering vocabulary knowledge when considering a word or phrase important to comprehension or expression.
265	**Reflect and Assess Critical Thinking**	RL.9-10.1	Cite strong and thorough textual evidence to support analysis of what the text says explicitly as well as inferences drawn from the text.
		RL.9-10.5	Analyze how an author's choices concerning how to structure a text, order events within it, and manipulate time create such effects as mystery, tension or surprise.
		RL.9-10.10	By the end of grade 10, read and comprehend literature, including stories, dramas, and poems, at the high end of the grades 9–10 text complexity band independently and proficiently.
		SL.9-10.1.a	Come to discussions prepared, having read and researched material under study; explicitly draw on that preparation by referring to evidence from texts and other research on the topic or issue to stimulate a thoughtful, well-reasoned exchange of ideas.
	Write About Literature	W.9-10.3	Write narratives to develop real or imagined experiences or events using effective technique, well-chosen details, and well-structured event sequences.
	Key Vocabulary Review	L.9-10.6	Acquire and use accurately general academic and domain-specific words and phrases, sufficient for reading, writing, speaking, and listening at the college and career readiness level; demonstrate independence in gathering vocabulary knowledge when considering a word or phrase important to comprehension or expression.
	Read with Ease: Intonation	RL.9-10.10	By the end of grade 10, read and comprehend literature, including stories, dramas, and poems, at the high end of the grades 9–10 text complexity band independently and proficiently.
266	**Grammar: Use Verb Tenses**	L.9-10.1.a	Use parallel structure.

Cluster 1, continued

SE Pages	Lesson	Code	Standards Text
266	**Language Development: Retell a Story**	SL.9-10.1.a	Come to discussions prepared, having read and researched material under study; explicitly draw on that preparation by referring to evidence from texts and other research on the topic or issue to stimulate a thoughtful, well-reasoned exchange of ideas.
266	**Literary Analysis: Word Choice in Description**	RL.9-10.4	Determine the meaning of words and phrases as they are used in a text, including figurative, connotative, and technical meanings; analyze the cumulative impact of specific word choices on meaning and tone.
267	**Vocabulary Study: Word Families**	L.9-10.4.b	Identify and correctly use patterns of word changes that indicate different meanings or parts of speech.
		L.9-10.4.c	Consult general and specialized reference materials, both print and digital, to find the pronunciation of a word or determine or clarify its precise meaning, its part of speech, or its etymology.
267	**Writing on Demand: Write a Short Comparison Essay**	W.9-10.2	Write informative/explanatory texts to examine and convey complex ideas, concepts, and information clearly and accurately through the effective selection, organization, and analysis of content.
		W.9-10.5	Develop and strengthen writing as needed by planning, revising, editing, rewriting, or trying a new approach, focusing on addressing what is most significant for a specific purpose and audience.
267	**Listening/Speaking: Compare Themes**	RL.9-10.2	Determine a theme or central idea of a text and analyze in detail its development over the course of the text, including how it emerges and is shaped and refined by specific details; provide an objective summary of the text.
268	**Workplace Workshop: At a Construction Site**	W.9-10.7	Conduct short as well as more sustained research projects to answer a question (including a self-generated question) or solve a problem; narrow or broaden the inquiry when appropriate; synthesize multiple sources on the subject, demonstrating understanding of the subject under investigation.
		W.9-10.10	Write routinely over extended time frames (time for research, reflection, and revision) and shorter time frames (a single sitting or a day or two) for a range of tasks, purposes, and audiences.
269	**Vocabulary Workshop: Use What You Know**	L.9-10.4.b	Identify and correctly use patterns of word changes that indicate different meanings or parts of speech.
		L.9-10.4.c	Consult general and specialized reference materials, both print and digital, to find the pronunciation of a word or determine or clarify its precise meaning, its part of speech, or its etymology.
		L.9-10.4.d	Verify the preliminary determination of the meaning of a word or phrase.

Common Core State Standards, continued

Cluster 2

SE Pages	Lesson	Code	Standards Text
270	**Prepare to Read**	RI.9-10.4	Determine the meaning of words and phrases as they are used in a text, including figurative, connotative, and technical meanings; analyze the cumulative impact of specific word choices on meaning and tone.
		SL.9-10.1	Initiate and participate effectively in a range of collaborative discussions (one-on-one, in groups, and teacher-led) with diverse partners on grades 9–10 topics, texts, and issues, building on others' ideas and expressing their own clearly and persuasively.
		L.9-10.6	Acquire and use accurately general academic and domain-specific words and phrases, sufficient for reading, writing, speaking, and listening at the college and career readiness level; demonstrate independence in gathering vocabulary knowledge when considering a word or phrase important to comprehension or expression.
271	**Before Reading: My Brother's Keeper**	RL.9-10.1	Cite strong and thorough textual evidence to support analysis of what the text says explicitly as well as inferences drawn from the text.
		RL.9-10.5	Analyze how an author's choices concerning how to structure a text, order events within it, and manipulate time create such effects as mystery, tension or surprise.
272–291	**Read My Brother's Keeper**	RL.9-10.1	Cite strong and thorough textual evidence to support analysis of what the text says explicitly as well as inferences drawn from the text.
		RL.9-10.3	Analyze how complex characters develop over the course of a text, interact with other characters, and advance the plot or develop the theme.
		RL.9-10.5	Analyze how an author's choices concerning how to structure a text, order events within it, and manipulate time create such effects as mystery, tension or surprise.
		RL.9-10.7	Analyze the representation of a subject or a key scene in two different artistic mediums, including what is emphasized or absent in each treatment.
		RL.9-10.10	By the end of grade 10, read and comprehend literature, including stories, dramas, and poems, at the high end of the grades 9–10 text complexity band independently and proficiently.
		W.9-10.1	Write arguments to support claims in an analysis of substantive topics or texts, using valid reasoning and relevant and sufficient evidence.
		W.9-10.10	Write routinely over extended time frames (time for research, reflection, and revision) and shorter time frames (a single sitting or a day or two) for a range of tasks, purposes, and audiences.
		SL.9-10.1.d	Respond thoughtfully to diverse perspectives, summarize points of agreement and disagreement, and, when warranted, qualify or justify their own views and understanding and make new connections in light of the evidence and reasoning presented.
		L.9-10.1.a	Use parallel structure.
		L.9-10.1.b	Use various types of phrases (noun, verb, adjectival, adverbial, participial, prepositional, absolute) and clauses (independent, dependent; noun, relative, adverbial) to convey specific meanings and add variety and interest to writing or presentations.
		L.9-10.2.c	Spell correctly.

Cluster 2, continued

SE Pages	Lesson	Code	Standards Text
272–291	**Read My Brother's Keeper** continued	L.9-10.3	Apply knowledge of language to understand how language functions in different contexts, to make effective choices for meaning or style, and to comprehend more fully when reading or listening.
		L.9-10.5	Demonstrate understanding of figurative language, word relationships, and nuances in word meanings.
		L.9-10.6	Acquire and use accurately general academic and domain-specific words and phrases, sufficient for reading, writing, speaking, and listening at the college and career readiness level; demonstrate independence in gathering vocabulary knowledge when considering a word or phrase important to comprehension or expression.
292	**Postscript: Little Sister**	RL.9-10.1	Cite strong and thorough textual evidence to support analysis of what the text says explicitly as well as inferences drawn from the text.
		SL.9-10.6	Adapt speech to a variety of contexts and tasks, demonstrating command of formal English when indicated or appropriate.
293	**Before Reading: What Price Loyalty?**	RI.9-10.1	Cite strong and thorough textual evidence to support analysis of what the text says explicitly as well as inferences drawn from the text.
		RI.9-10.6	Determine an author's point of view or purpose in a text and analyze how an author uses rhetoric to advance that point of view or purpose.
294–296	**Read What Price Loyalty?**	RI.9-10.1	Cite strong and thorough textual evidence to support analysis of what the text says explicitly as well as inferences drawn from the text.
		RI.9-10.6	Determine an author's point of view or purpose in a text and analyze how an author uses rhetoric to advance that point of view or purpose.
		RI.9-10.10	By the end of grade 10, read and comprehend literary nonfiction at the high end of the grades 9–10 text complexity band independently and proficiently.
		W.9-10.9.b	Apply grades 9–10 Reading standards to literary nonfiction.
		W.9-10.10	Write routinely over extended time frames (time for research, reflection, and revision) and shorter time frames (a single sitting or a day or two) for a range of tasks, purposes, and audiences.
		L.9-10.5	Demonstrate understanding of figurative language, word relationships, and nuances in word meanings.
		L.9-10.6	Acquire and use accurately general academic and domain-specific words and phrases, sufficient for reading, writing, speaking, and listening at the college and career readiness level; demonstrate independence in gathering vocabulary knowledge when considering a word or phrase important to comprehension or expression.

Common Core State Standards, continued

Cluster 2, continued

SE Pages	Lesson	Code	Standards Text
297	**Reflect and Assess Critical Thinking**	RL.9-10.1	Cite strong and thorough textual evidence to support analysis of what the text says explicitly as well as inferences drawn from the text.
		RL.9-10.10	By the end of grade 10, read and comprehend literature, including stories, dramas, and poems, at the high end of the grades 9–10 text complexity band independently and proficiently.
		RI.9-10.1	Cite strong and thorough textual evidence to support analysis of what the text says explicitly as well as inferences drawn from the text.
	Write About Literature	W.9-10.3	Write narratives to develop real or imagined experiences or events using effective technique, well-chosen details, and well-structured event sequences.
	Key Vocabulary Review	L.9-10.6	Acquire and use accurately general academic and domain-specific words and phrases, sufficient for reading, writing, speaking, and listening at the college and career readiness level; demonstrate independence in gathering vocabulary knowledge when considering a word or phrase important to comprehension or expression.
	Read with Ease: Phrasing	RL.9-10.10	By the end of grade 10, read and comprehend literature, including stories, dramas, and poems, at the high end of the grades 9–10 text complexity band independently and proficiently.
298	**Grammar: Use Verb Tenses**	L.9-10.1.a	Use parallel structure.
		L.9-10.1.b	Use various types of phrases (noun, verb, adjectival, adverbial, participial, prepositional, absolute) and clauses (independent, dependent; noun, relative, adverbial) to convey specific meanings and add variety and interest to writing or presentations.
298	**Language Development: Make Comparisons**	SL.9-10.1.a	Come to discussions prepared, having read and researched material under study; explicitly draw on that preparation by referring to evidence from texts and other research on the topic or issue to stimulate a thoughtful, well-reasoned exchange of ideas.
298	**Literary Analysis: Analyze Style**	RL.9-10.2	Determine a theme or central idea of a text and analyze in detail its development over the course of the text, including how it emerges and is shaped and refined by specific details; provide an objective summary of the text.
		RL.9-10.4	Determine the meaning of words and phrases as they are used in the text, including figurative and connotative meanings; analyze the cumulative impact of specific word choices on meaning and tone.
		RL.9-10.5	Analyze how an author's choices concerning how to structure a text, order events within it, and manipulate time create such effects as mystery, tension, or surprise.
299	**Vocabulary Study: Word Families**	L.9-10.4.d	Verify the preliminary determination of the meaning of a word or phrase.
299	**Writing Trait: Organization: Introductions**	W.9-10.2.a	Introduce a topic; organize complex ideas, concepts, and information to make important connections and distinctions; include formatting, graphics, and multimedia when useful to aiding comprehension.
		W.9-10.5	Develop and strengthen writing as needed by planning, revising, editing, rewriting, or trying a new approach, focusing on addressing what is most significant for a specific purpose and audience.

Cluster 2, continued

SE Pages	Lesson	Code	Standards Text
299	**Research/Writing: Problem-Solution Report**	W.9-10.7	Conduct short as well as more sustained research projects to answer a question (including a self-generated question) or solve a problem; narrow or broaden the inquiry when appropriate; synthesize multiple sources on the subject, demonstrating understanding of the subject under investigation.
300–301	**Listening and Speaking Workshop: Debate**	SL.9-10.1.a	Come to discussions prepared, having read and researched material under study; explicitly draw on that preparation by referring to evidence from texts and other research on the topic or issue to stimulate a thoughtful, well-reasoned exchange of ideas.
		SL.9-10.1.b	Work with peers to set rules for collegial discussions and decision-making, clear goals and deadlines, and individual roles as needed.
		SL.9-10.1.c	Propel conversations by posing and responding to questions that relate the current discussion to broader themes or larger ideas; actively incorporate others into the discussion; and clarify, verify, or challenge ideas and conclusions.
		SL.9-10.1.d	Respond thoughtfully to diverse perspectives, summarize points of agreement and disagreement, and, when warranted, qualify or justify their own views and understanding and make new connections in light of the evidence and reasoning presented
		SL.9-10.3	Evaluate a speaker's point of view, reasoning, and use of evidence and rhetoric, identifying any fallacious reasoning or exaggerated or distorted evidence.
		SL.9-10.4	Present information, findings, and supporting evidence clearly, concisely, and logically such that listeners can follow the line of reasoning and the organization, development, substance, and style are appropriate to purpose, audience, and task.
		L.9-10.3	Apply knowledge of language to understand how language functions in different contexts, to make effective choices for meaning or style, and to comprehend more fully when reading or listening.

Cluster 3

SE Pages	Lesson	Code	Standards Text
302	**Prepare to Read**	RI.9-10.4	Determine the meaning of words and phrases as they are used in a text, including figurative, connotative, and technical meanings; analyze the cumulative impact of specific word choices on meaning and tone.
		SL.9-10.1	Initiate and participate effectively in a range of collaborative discussions (one-on-one, in groups, and teacher-led) with diverse partners on grades 9–10 topics, texts, and issues, building on others' ideas and expressing their own clearly and persuasively
		L.9-10.6	Acquire and use accurately general academic and domain-specific words and phrases, sufficient for reading, writing, speaking, and listening at the college and career readiness level; demonstrate independence in gathering vocabulary knowledge when considering a word or phrase important to comprehension or expression.
303	**Before Reading: The Hand of Fatima**	RL.9-10.1	Cite strong and thorough textual evidence to support analysis of what the text says explicitly as well as inferences drawn from the text.
		RL.9-10.6	Analyze a particular point of view or cultural experience reflected in a work of literature from outside the United States, drawing on a wide reading of world literature.

Common Core State Standards, continued

Cluster 3, continued

SE Pages	Lesson	Code	Standards Text
304–325	**Read The Hand of Fatima**	RL.9-10.1	Cite strong and thorough textual evidence to support analysis of what the text says explicitly as well as inferences drawn from the text.
		RL.9-10.2	Determine a theme or central idea of a text and analyze in detail its development over the course of the text, including how it emerges and is shaped and refined by specific details; provide an objective summary of the text.
		RL.9-10.3	Analyze how complex characters develop over the course of a text, interact with other characters, and advance the plot or develop the theme.
		RL.9-10.6	Analyze a particular point of view or cultural experience reflected in a work of literature from outside the United States, drawing on a wide reading of world literature.
		RL.9-10.7	Analyze the representation of a subject or a key scene in two different artistic mediums, including what is emphasized or absent in each treatment.
		RL.9-10.10	By the end of grade 10, read and comprehend literature, including stories, dramas, and poems, at the high end of the grades 9–10 text complexity band independently and proficiently.
		W.9-10.1	Write arguments to support claims in an analysis of substantive topics or texts, using valid reasoning and relevant and sufficient evidence.
		W.9-10.9.a	Apply grades 9–10 Reading standards to literature.
		W.9-10.10	Write routinely over extended time frames (time for research, reflection, and revision) and shorter time frames (a single sitting or a day or two) for a range of tasks, purposes, and audiences.
		L.9-10.1	Demonstrate command of the conventions of standard English grammar and usage when writing or speaking.
		L.9-10.4.a	Use context as a clue to the meaning of a word or phrase.
		L.9-10.6	Acquire and use accurately general academic and domain-specific words and phrases, sufficient for reading, writing, speaking, and listening at the college and career readiness level; demonstrate independence in gathering vocabulary knowledge when considering a word or phrase important to comprehension or expression.
326	**Before Reading: Old Ways, New World**	RI.9-10.1	Cite strong and thorough textual evidence to support analysis of what the text says explicitly as well as inferences drawn from the text.
		RI.9-10.6	Determine an author's point of view or purpose in a text and analyze how an author uses rhetoric to advance that point of view or purpose.
327–330	**Read Old Ways, New World**	RI.9-10.1	Cite strong and thorough textual evidence to support analysis of what the text says explicitly as well as inferences drawn from the text.
		RI.9-10.5	Analyze in detail how an author's ideas or claims are developed and refined by particular sentences, paragraphs, or larger portions of a text.

Cluster 3, continued

SE Pages	Lesson	Code	Standards Text
327–330	**Read Old Ways, New World** continued	RI.9-10.6	Determine an author's point of view or purpose in a text and analyze how an author uses rhetoric to advance that point of view or purpose.
		RI.9-10.10	By the end of grade 10, read and comprehend literary nonfiction at the high end of the grades 9–10 text complexity band independently and proficiently.
		W.9-10.9.b	Apply grades 9–10 Reading standards to literary nonfiction.
		W.9-10.10	Write routinely over extended time frames (time for research, reflection, and revision) and shorter time frames (a single sitting or a day or two) for a range of tasks, purposes, and audiences.
		L.9-10.1	Demonstrate command of the conventions of standard English grammar and usage when writing or speaking.
		L.9-10.6	Acquire and use accurately general academic and domain-specific words and phrases, sufficient for reading, writing, speaking, and listening at the college and career readiness level; demonstrate independence in gathering vocabulary knowledge when considering a word or phrase important to comprehension or expression.
331	**Reflect and Assess Critical Thinking**	RL.9-10.1	Cite strong and thorough textual evidence to support analysis of what the text says explicitly as well as inferences drawn from the text.
		RL.9-10.2	Determine a theme or central idea of a text and analyze in detail its development over the course of the text, including how it emerges and is shaped and refined by specific details; provide an objective summary of the text.
		RL.9-10.6	Analyze a particular point of view or cultural experience reflected in a work of literature from outside the United States, drawing on a wide reading of world literature.
		RL.9-10.10	By the end of grade 10, read and comprehend literature, including stories, dramas, and poems, at the high end of the grades 9–10 text complexity band independently and proficiently.
		RI.9-10.1	Cite strong and thorough textual evidence to support analysis of what the text says explicitly as well as inferences drawn from the text.
		RI.9-10.2	Determine a central idea of a text and analyze its development over the course of the text, including how it emerges and is shaped and refined by specific details; provide an objective summary of the text.
		RI.9-10.6	Determine an author's point of view or purpose in a text and analyze how an author uses rhetoric to advance that point of view or purpose.
		RI.9-10.10	By the end of grade 10, read and comprehend literary nonfiction at the high end of the grades 9–10 text complexity band independently and proficiently.
	Write About Literature	W.9-10.2	Write informative/explanatory texts to examine and convey complex ideas, concepts, and information clearly and accurately through the effective selection, organization, and analysis of content.

Common Core State Standards, continued

Cluster 3, continued

SE Pages	Lesson	Code	Standards Text
331	**Reflect and Assess** continued **Key Vocabulary Review**	L.9-10.6	Acquire and use accurately general academic and domain-specific words and phrases, sufficient for reading, writing, speaking, and listening at the college and career readiness level; demonstrate independence in gathering vocabulary knowledge when considering a word or phrase important to comprehension or expression.
	Read with Ease: Expression	RL.9-10.10	By the end of grade 10, read and comprehend literature, including stories, dramas, and poems, at the high end of the grades 9–10 text complexity band independently and proficiently.
332	**Grammar: Use Subject and Object Pronouns**	L.9-10.1	Demonstrate command of the conventions of standard English grammar and usage when writing or speaking.
332	**Language Development: Compare and Contrast**	SL.9-10.1.a	Come to discussions prepared, having read and researched material under study; explicitly draw on that preparation by referring to evidence from texts and other research on the topic or issue to stimulate a thoughtful, well-reasoned exchange of ideas.
332	**Literary Analysis: Symbolism**	RL.9-10.4	Determine the meaning of words and phrases as they are used in the text, including figurative and connotative meanings; analyze the cumulative impact of specific word choices on meaning and tone.
333	**Vocabulary Study: Word Families**	L.9-10.4.b	Identify and correctly use patterns of word changes that indicate different meanings or parts of speech.
		L.9-10.4.c	Consult general and specialized reference materials, both print and digital, to find the pronunciation of a word or determine or clarify its precise meaning, its part of speech, or its etymology.
333	**Writing: Write a Business Letter**	W.9-10.5	Develop and strengthen writing as needed by planning, revising, editing, rewriting, or trying a new approach, focusing on addressing what is most significant for a specific purpose and audience.
333	**Research/Listening and Speaking: Oral Presentation**	W.9-10.7	Conduct short as well as more sustained research projects to answer a question (including a self-generated question) or solve a problem; narrow or broaden the inquiry when appropriate; synthesize multiple sources on the subject, demonstrating understanding of the subject under investigation.
		SL.9-10.6	Adapt speech to a variety of contexts and tasks, demonstrating command of formal English when indicated or appropriate.

Close Reading

SE Pages	Lesson	Code	Standards Text
334–337	**Read Anthem**	RL.9-10.10	By the end of grade 10, read and comprehend literature, including stories, dramas, and poems, at the high end of the grades 9–10 text complexity band independently and proficiently.

Unit Wrap-Up

SE Pages	Lesson	Code	Standards Text
338	**Unit Wrap-Up** **Present Your Project**	SL.9-10.4	Present information, findings, and supporting evidence clearly, concisely, and logically such that listeners can follow the line of reasoning and the organization, development, substance, and style are appropriate to purpose, audience, and task.

Unit Wrap-Up, continued

SE Pages	Lesson	Code	Standards Text
338	**Unit Wrap-Up** continued **Reflect on Your Reading**	SL.9-10.1.a	Come to discussions prepared, having read and researched material under study; explicitly draw on that preparation by referring to evidence from texts and other research on the topic or issue to stimulate a thoughtful, well-reasoned exchange of ideas.
	Respond to the Essential Question	SL.9-10.1.a	Come to discussions prepared, having read and researched material under study; explicitly draw on that preparation by referring to evidence from texts and other research on the topic or issue to stimulate a thoughtful, well-reasoned exchange of ideas.

Writing Project: Position Papers

SE Pages	Lesson	Code	Standards Text
339–343	**Study a Position Paper and Prewrite**	W.9-10.1.a	Introduce precise claim(s), distinguish the claim(s) from alternate or opposing claims, and create an organization that establishes clear relationships among claim(s), counterclaims, reasons, and evidence.
		W.9-10.1.b	Develop claim(s) and counterclaims fairly, supplying evidence for each while pointing out the strengths and limitations of both in a manner that anticipates the audience's knowledge level and concerns.
		W.9-10.5	Develop and strengthen writing as needed by planning, revising, editing, rewriting, or trying a new approach, focusing on addressing what is most significant for a specific purpose and audience.
344–345	**Position Paper: Draft**	W.9-10.1.a	Introduce precise claim(s), distinguish the claim(s) from alternate or opposing claims, and create an organization that establishes clear relationships among claim(s), counterclaims, reasons, and evidence.
		W.9-10.1.b	Develop claim(s) and counterclaims fairly, supplying evidence for each while pointing out the strengths and limitations of both in a manner that anticipates the audience's knowledge level and concerns.
		W.9-10.4	Produce clear and coherent writing in which the development, organization, and style are appropriate to task, purpose, and audience.
		W.9-10.6	Use technology, including the Internet, to produce, publish, and update individual or shared writing products, taking advantage of technology's capacity to link to other information and to display information flexibly and dynamically.
		W.9-10.7	Conduct short as well as more sustained research projects to answer a question (including a self-generated question) or solve a problem; narrow or broaden the inquiry when appropriate; synthesize multiple sources on the subject, demonstrating understanding of the subject under investigation.
		W.9-10.8	Gather relevant information from multiple authoritative print and digital sources, using advanced searches effectively; assess the usefulness of each source in answering the research question; integrate information into the text selectively to maintain the flow of ideas, avoiding plagiarism and following a standard format for citation.

Common Core State Standards, continued

Student Handbooks, continued		

Writing Project: Position Papers

SE Pages Lesson	Code	Standards Text
346–349 Position Paper: Revise Trait: Development of Ideas	W.9-10.1.a	Introduce precise claim(s), distinguish the claim(s) from alternate or opposing claims, and create an organization that establishes clear relationships among claim(s), counterclaims, reasons, and evidence.
	W.9-10.1.b	Develop claim(s) and counterclaims fairly, supplying evidence for each while pointing out the strengths and limitations of both in a manner that anticipates the audience's knowledge level and concerns.
	W.9-10.1.c	Use words, phrases, and clauses to link the major sections of the text, create cohesion, and clarify the relationships between claim(s) and reasons, between reasons and evidence, and between claim(s) and counterclaims.
	W.9-10.1.d	Establish and maintain a formal style and objective tone while attending to the norms and conventions of the discipline in which they are writing.
	W.9-10.1.e	Provide a concluding statement or section that follows from and supports the argument presented.
	W.9-10.4	Produce clear and coherent writing in which the development, organization, and style are appropriate to task, purpose, and audience.
	W.9-10.5	Develop and strengthen writing as needed by planning, revising, editing, rewriting, or trying a new approach, focusing on addressing what is most significant for a specific purpose and audience.
	SL.9-10.1.d	Respond thoughtfully to diverse perspectives, summarize points of agreement and disagreement, and, when warranted, qualify or justify their own views and understanding and make new connections in light of the evidence and reasoning presented.
350–352 Position Paper: Edit and Proofread **Capitalize the Names of Groups** **Use Semicolons Correctly** **Use the Active Voice** **Use Subject Pronouns Correctly**	L.9-10.1	Demonstrate command of the conventions of standard English grammar and usage when writing or speaking.
	L.9-10.2.a	Use a semicolon (and perhaps a conjunctive adverb) to link two or more closely related independent clauses.
	L.9-10.3.a	Write and edit work so that it conforms to the guidelines in a style manual appropriate for the discipline and writing type.
353 Position Paper: Publish and Present	W.9-10.5	Develop and strengthen writing as needed by planning, revising, editing, rewriting, or trying a new approach, focusing on addressing what is most significant for a specific purpose and audience.
	W.9-10.6	Use technology, including the Internet, to produce, publish, and update individual or shared writing products, taking advantage of technology's capacity to link to other information and to display information flexibly and dynamically.
	SL.9-10.5	Make strategic use of digital media in presentations to enhance understanding of findings, reasoning, and evidence and to add interest.

UNIT 4: Express Yourself

SE Pages	Lesson	Code	Standards Text
354–355	**Discuss the Essential Question**	SL.9-10.1.b	Work with peers to set rules for collegial discussions and decision-making, clear goals and deadlines, and individual roles as needed
		SL.9-10.3	Evaluate a speaker's point of view, reasoning, and use of evidence and rhetoric, identifying any fallacious reasoning or exaggerated or distorted evidence.
356	**Analyze and Debate**	SL.9-10.4	Present information, findings, and supporting evidence clearly, concisely, and logically such that listeners can follow the line of reasoning and the organization, development, substance, and style are appropriate to purpose, audience, and task.
357	**Plan a Project**	SL.9-10.1.b	Work with peers to set rules for collegial discussions and decision-making, clear goals and deadlines, and individual roles as needed.
357	**Choose More to Read**	RL.9-10.10	By the end of grade 10, read and comprehend literature, including stories, dramas, and poems, at the high end of the grades 9–10 text complexity band independently and proficiently.
		RI.9-10.10	By the end of grade 10, read and comprehend literary nonfiction at the high end of the grades 9–10 text complexity band independently and proficiently.
358–361	**How to Read Nonfiction**	RI.9-10.1	Cite strong and thorough textual evidence to support analysis of what the text says explicitly as well as inferences drawn from the text.
		RI.9-10.5	Analyze in detail how an author's ideas or claims are developed and refined by particular sentences, paragraphs, or larger portions of a text.
		RI.9-10.10	By the end of grade 10, read and comprehend literary nonfiction at the high end of the grades 9–10 text complexity band independently and proficiently.
		SL.9-10.1	Initiate and participate effectively in a range of collaborative discussions (one-on-one, in groups, and teacher-led) with diverse partners on grades 9–10 topics, texts, and issues, building on others' ideas and expressing their own clearly and persuasively.
		L.9-10.6	Acquire and use accurately general academic and domain-specific words and phrases, sufficient for reading, writing, speaking, and listening at the college and career readiness level; demonstrate independence in gathering vocabulary knowledge when considering a word or phrase important to comprehension or expression.

Cluster 1

SE Pages	Lesson	Code	Standards Text
362	**Prepare to Read**	RI.9-10.4	Determine the meaning of words and phrases as they are used in a text, including figurative, connotative, and technical meanings; analyze the cumulative impact of specific word choices on meaning and tone.
		SL.9-10.1	Initiate and participate effectively in a range of collaborative discussions (one-on-one, in groups, and teacher-led) with diverse partners on grades 9–10 topics, texts, and issues, building on others' ideas and expressing their own clearly and persuasively.
		L.9-10.6	Acquire and use accurately general academic and domain-specific words and phrases, sufficient for reading, writing, speaking, and listening at the college and career readiness level; demonstrate independence in gathering vocabulary knowledge when considering a word or phrase important to comprehension or expression.

Common Core State Standards, continued

Cluster 1, continued

SE Pages Lesson	Code	Standards Text
363 **Before Reading: Face Facts: The Science of Facial Expressions**	RI.9-10.5	Analyze in detail how an author's ideas or claims are developed and refined by particular sentences, paragraphs, or larger portions of a text.
	RI.9-10.10	By the end of grade 10, read and comprehend literary nonfiction at the high end of the grades 9–10 text complexity band independently and proficiently.
364–372 Read Face Facts: The Science of Facial Expressions	RI.9-10.1	Cite strong and thorough textual evidence to support analysis of what the text says explicitly as well as inferences drawn from the text.
	RI.9-10.2	Determine a central idea of a text and analyze its development over the course of the text, including how it emerges and is shaped and refined by specific details; provide an objective summary of the text.
	RI.9-10.5	Analyze in detail how an author's ideas or claims are developed and refined by particular sentences, paragraphs, or larger portions of a text.
	RI.9-10.7	Analyze various accounts of a subject told in different mediums, determining which details are emphasized in each account.
	RI.9-10.10	By the end of grade 10, read and comprehend literary nonfiction at the high end of the grades 9–10 text complexity band independently and proficiently.
	W.9-10.1	Write arguments to support claims in an analysis of substantive topics or texts, using valid reasoning and relevant and sufficient evidence.
	W.9-10.9.b	Apply grades 9–10 Reading standards to literary nonfiction.
	W.9-10.10	Write routinely over extended time frames (time for research, reflection, and revision) and shorter time frames (a single sitting or a day or two) for a range of tasks, purposes, and audiences.
	L.9-10.1.b	Use various types of phrases (noun, verb, adjectival, adverbial, participial, prepositional, absolute) and clauses (independent, dependent; noun, relative, adverbial) to convey specific meanings and add variety and interest to writing or presentations.
	L.9-10.2.c	Spell correctly.
	L.9-10.4.b	Identify and correctly use patterns of word changes that indicate different meanings or parts of speech.
	L.9-10.6	Acquire and use accurately general academic and domain-specific words and phrases, sufficient for reading, writing, speaking, and listening at the college and career readiness level; demonstrate independence in gathering vocabulary knowledge when considering a word or phrase important to comprehension or expression.
373 Postscript: Face It	RL.9-10.1	Cite strong and thorough textual evidence to support analysis of what the text says explicitly as well as inferences drawn from the text.
	RL.9-10.4	Determine the meaning of words and phrases as they are used in the text, including figurative and connotative meanings; analyze the cumulative impact of specific word choices on meaning and tone.
	RI.9-10.1	Cite strong and thorough textual evidence to support analysis of what the text says explicitly as well as inferences drawn from the text.

Cluster 1, continued

SE Pages	Lesson	Code	Standards Text
373	Postscript: Face It continued	SL.9-10.6	Adapt speech to a variety of contexts and tasks, demonstrating command of formal English when indicated or appropriate.
374	Before Reading: Silent Language	RI.9-10.5	Analyze in detail how an author's ideas or claims are developed and refined by particular sentences, paragraphs, or larger portions of a text.
		RI.9-10.10	By the end of grade 10, read and comprehend literary nonfiction at the high end of the grades 9–10 text complexity band independently and proficiently.
375–380	Read Silent Language	RI.9-10.1	Cite strong and thorough textual evidence to support analysis of what the text says explicitly as well as inferences drawn from the text.
		RI.9-10.5	Analyze in detail how an author's ideas or claims are developed and refined by particular sentences, paragraphs, or larger portions of a text.
		RI.9-10.10	By the end of grade 10, read and comprehend literary nonfiction at the high end of the grades 9–10 text complexity band independently and proficiently.
		W.9-10.1	Write arguments to support claims in an analysis of substantive topics or texts, using valid reasoning and relevant and sufficient evidence.
		W.9-10.9.b	Apply grades 9–10 Reading standards to literary nonfiction.
		W.9-10.10	Write routinely over extended time frames (time for research, reflection, and revision) and shorter time frames (a single sitting or a day or two) for a range of tasks, purposes, and audiences.
		L.9-10.1	Demonstrate command of the conventions of standard English grammar and usage when writing or speaking.
		L.9-10.6	Acquire and use accurately general academic and domain-specific words and phrases, sufficient for reading, writing, speaking, and listening at the college and career readiness level; demonstrate independence in gathering vocabulary knowledge when considering a word or phrase important to comprehension or expression.
381	Reflect and Assess Critical Thinking	RI.9-10.1	Cite strong and thorough textual evidence to support analysis of what the text says explicitly as well as inferences drawn from the text.
		RI.9-10.10	By the end of grade 10, read and comprehend literary nonfiction at the high end of the grades 9–10 text complexity band independently and proficiently.
	Write About Literature	W.9-10.1	Write arguments to support claims in an analysis of substantive topics or texts, using valid reasoning and relevant and sufficient evidence.
	Key Vocabulary Review	L.9-10.6	Acquire and use accurately general academic and domain-specific words and phrases, sufficient for reading, writing, speaking, and listening at the college and career readiness level; demonstrate independence in gathering vocabulary knowledge when considering a word or phrase important to comprehension or expression.
	Read with Ease: Intonation	RI.9-10.10	By the end of grade 10, read and comprehend literary nonfiction at the high end of the grades 9–10 text complexity band independently and proficiently.

Common Core State Standards, continued

Cluster 1, continued

SE Pages	Lesson	Code	Standards Text
382 Grammar: Show Possession		L.9-10.1.b	Use various types of phrases (noun, verb, adjectival, adverbial, participial, prepositional, absolute) and clauses (independent, dependent; noun, relative, adverbial) to convey specific meanings and add variety and interest to writing or presentations.
382	Literary Analysis: Literary Paradox	SL.9-10.1.a	Come to discussions prepared, having read and researched material under study; explicitly draw on that preparation by referring to evidence from texts and other research on the topic or issue to stimulate a thoughtful, well-reasoned exchange of ideas.
382	Language Development: Define and Explain	RL.9-10.4	Determine the meaning of words and phrases as they are used in the text, including figurative and connotative meanings; analyze the cumulative impact of specific word choices on meaning and tone.
383	Vocabulary Study: Multiple-Meaning Words	L.9-10.4.c	Consult general and specialized reference materials, both print and digital, to find the pronunciation of a word or determine or clarify its precise meaning, its part of speech, or its etymology.
383 Writing on Demand: Write a Cause-and-Effect Essay		W.9-10.1	Write arguments to support claims in an analysis of substantive topics or texts, using valid reasoning and relevant and sufficient evidence.
		W.9-10.5	Develop and strengthen writing as needed by planning, revising, editing, rewriting, or trying a new approach, focusing on addressing what is most significant for a specific purpose and audience.
383	Media Study: Analyze Nonverbal Communication	W.9-10.2	Write informative/explanatory texts to examine and convey complex ideas, concepts, and information clearly and accurately through the effective selection, organization, and analysis of content.
384	Workplace Workshop: Inside a Police Department	W.9-10.7	Conduct short as well as more sustained research projects to answer a question (including a self-generated question) or solve a problem; narrow or broaden the inquiry when appropriate; synthesize multiple sources on the subject, demonstrating understanding of the subject under investigation.
		W.9-10.10	Write routinely over extended time frames (time for research, reflection, and revision) and shorter time frames (a single sitting or a day or two) for a range of tasks, purposes, and audiences.
		L.9-10.6	Acquire and use accurately general academic and domain-specific words and phrases, sufficient for reading, writing, speaking, and listening at the college and career readiness level; demonstrate independence in gathering vocabulary knowledge when considering a word or phrase important to comprehension or expression.
385	Vocabulary Workshop: Access Words During Reading	L.9-10.4	Determine or clarify the meaning of unknown and multiple-meaning words and phrases based on grades 9–10 reading and content, choosing flexibly from a range of strategies.

Cluster 2

386	Prepare to Read	RI.9-10.4	Determine the meaning of words and phrases as they are used in a text, including figurative, connotative, and technical meanings; analyze the cumulative impact of specific word choices on meaning and tone.
		SL.9-10.1	Initiate and participate effectively in a range of collaborative discussions (one-on-one, in groups, and teacher-led) with diverse partners on grades 9–10 topics, texts, and issues, building on others' ideas and expressing their own clearly and persuasively.

Cluster 2, continued

SE Pages	Lesson	Code	Standards Text
386	**Prepare to Read** continued	L.9-10.6	Acquire and use accurately general academic and domain-specific words and phrases, sufficient for reading, writing, speaking, and listening at the college and career readiness level; demonstrate independence in gathering vocabulary knowledge when considering a word or phrase important to comprehension or expression.
387	**Before Reading: They Speak for Success**	RI.9-10.1	Cite strong and thorough textual evidence to support analysis of what the text says explicitly as well as inferences drawn from the text.
		RI.9-10.5	Analyze in detail how an author's ideas or claims are developed and refined by particular sentences, paragraphs, or larger portions of a text.
388–399	**Read They Speak for Success**	RI.9-10.1	Cite strong and thorough textual evidence to support analysis of what the text says explicitly as well as inferences drawn from the text.
		RI.9-10.2	Determine a central idea of a text and analyze its development over the course of the text, including how it emerges and is shaped and refined by specific details; provide an objective summary of the text.
		RI.9-10.4	Determine the meaning of words and phrases as they are used in a text, including figurative, connotative, and technical meanings; analyze the cumulative impact of specific word choices on meaning and tone.
		RI.9-10.5	Analyze in detail how an author's ideas or claims are developed and refined by particular sentences, paragraphs, or larger portions of a text.
		RI.9-10.10	By the end of grade 10, read and comprehend literary nonfiction at the high end of the grades 9-10 text complexity band independently and proficiently.
		W.9-10.1	Write arguments to support claims in an analysis of substantive topics or texts, using valid reasoning and relevant and sufficient evidence.
		W.9-10.9.b	Apply grades 9-10 Reading standards to literary nonfiction.
		W.9-10.10	Write routinely over extended time frames (time for research, reflection, and revision) and shorter time frames (a single sitting or a day or two) for a range of tasks, purposes, and audiences.
		SL.9-10.1	Initiate and participate effectively in a range of collaborative discussions (one-on-one, in groups, and teacher-led) with diverse partners on grades 9-10 topics, texts, and issues, building on others' ideas and expressing their own clearly and persuasively.
		L.9-10.1.b	Use various types of phrases (noun, verb, adjectival, adverbial, participial, prepositional, absolute) and clauses (independent, dependent; noun, relative, adverbial) to convey specific meanings and add variety and interest to writing or presentations.
		L.9-10.4.a	Use context as a clue to the meaning of a word or phrase.
		L.9-10.6	Acquire and use accurately general academic and domain-specific words and phrases, sufficient for reading, writing, speaking, and listening at the college and career readiness level; demonstrate independence in gathering vocabulary knowledge when considering a word or phrase important to comprehension or expression.

Common Core State Standards, continued

Cluster 2, continued

SE Pages	Lesson	Code	Standards Text
400	**Before Reading: Breaking the Ice**	RI.9-10.1	Cite strong and thorough textual evidence to support analysis of what the text says explicitly as well as inferences drawn from the text.
		RI.9-10.5	Analyze in detail how an author's ideas or claims are developed and refined by particular sentences, paragraphs, or larger portions of a text.
401–405	**Read Breaking the Ice**	RI.9-10.1	Cite strong and thorough textual evidence to support analysis of what the text says explicitly as well as inferences drawn from the text.
		RI.9-10.5	Analyze in detail how an author's ideas or claims are developed and refined by particular sentences, paragraphs, or larger portions of a text.
		RI.9-10.10	By the end of grade 10, read and comprehend literary nonfiction at the high end of the grades 9-10 text complexity band independently and proficiently.
		W.9-10.1	Write arguments to support claims in an analysis of substantive topics or texts, using valid reasoning and relevant and sufficient evidence.
		W.9-10.9.b	Apply grades 9-10 Reading standards to literary nonfiction.
		W.9-10.10	Write routinely over extended time frames (time for research, reflection, and revision) and shorter time frames (a single sitting or a day or two) for a range of tasks, purposes, and audiences.
		L.9-10.1.b	Use various types of phrases (noun, verb, adjectival, adverbial, participial, prepositional, absolute) and clauses (independent, dependent; noun, relative, adverbial) to convey specific meanings and add variety and interest to writing or presentations.
		L.9-10.6	Acquire and use accurately general academic and domain-specific words and phrases, sufficient for reading, writing, speaking, and listening at the college and career readiness level; demonstrate independence in gathering vocabulary knowledge when considering a word or phrase important to comprehension or expression.
406	**Postscript: Comic**	RI.9-10.1	Cite strong and thorough textual evidence to support analysis of what the text says explicitly as well as inferences drawn from the text.
		RI.9-10.4	Determine the meaning of words and phrases as they are used in a text, including figurative, connotative, and technical meanings; analyze the cumulative impact of specific word choices on meaning and tone.
407	**Reflect and Assess Critical Thinking**	RI.9-10.2	Determine a central idea of a text and analyze its development over the course of the text, including how it emerges and is shaped and refined by specific details; provide an objective summary of the text.
		RI.9-10.3	Analyze how the author unfolds an analysis or series of ideas or events, including the order in which the points are made, how they are introduced and developed, and the connections that are drawn between them.
		RI.9-10.10	By the end of grade 10, read and comprehend literary nonfiction at the high end of the grades 9-10 text complexity band independently and proficiently.
	Write About Literature	W.9-10.1	Write arguments to support claims in an analysis of substantive topics or texts, using valid reasoning and relevant and sufficient evidence.

Cluster 2, continued

SE Pages	Lesson	Code	Standards Text
407	**Reflect and Assess** continued **Key Vocabulary Review**	L.9-10.6	Acquire and use accurately general academic and domain-specific words and phrases, sufficient for reading, writing, speaking, and listening at the college and career readiness level; demonstrate independence in gathering vocabulary knowledge when considering a word or phrase important to comprehension or expression.
	Read with Ease: Expression	RI.9-10.10	By the end of grade 10, read and comprehend literary nonfiction at the high end of the grades 9–10 text complexity band independently and proficiently.
408	**Grammar: Use Pronouns in Prepositional Phrases**	L.9-10.1.b	Use various types of phrases (noun, verb, adjectival, adverbial, participial, prepositional, absolute) and clauses (independent, dependent; noun, relative, adverbial) to convey specific meanings and add variety and interest to writing or presentations.
408	**Literary Analysis: Flashback**	RI.9-10.5	Analyze in detail how an author's ideas or claims are developed and refined by particular sentences, paragraphs, or larger portions of a text.
408	**Language Development: Humor**	SL.9-10.1.a	Come to discussions prepared, having read and researched material under study; explicitly draw on that preparation by referring to evidence from texts and other research on the topic or issue to stimulate a thoughtful, well-reasoned exchange of ideas.
409	**Vocabulary Study: Jargon**	L.9-10.4.d	Verify the preliminary determination of the meaning of a word or phrase.
409	**Writing: Writing an Evaluation of a Speech**	W.9-10.1	Write arguments to support claims in an analysis of substantive topics or texts, using valid reasoning and relevant and sufficient evidence.
		W.9-10.5	Develop and strengthen writing as needed by planning, revising, editing, rewriting, or trying a new approach, focusing on addressing what is most significant for a specific purpose and audience.
		SL.9-10.3	Evaluate a speaker's point of view, reasoning, and use of evidence and rhetoric, identifying any fallacious reasoning or exaggerated or distorted evidence.
409	**Listening/Speaking: Short Public Speech**	SL.9-10.3	Evaluate a speaker's point of view, reasoning, and use of evidence and rhetoric, identifying any fallacious reasoning or exaggerated or distorted evidence.
		SL.9-10.4	Present information, findings, and supporting evidence clearly, concisely, and logically such that listeners can follow the line of reasoning and the organization, development, substance, and style are appropriate to purpose, audience, and task.
410–411	**Listening and Speaking Workshop: Panel Discussion**	SL.9-10.1.a	Come to discussions prepared, having read and researched material under study; explicitly draw on that preparation by referring to evidence from texts and other research on the topic or issue to stimulate a thoughtful, well-reasoned exchange of ideas.
		SL.9-10.1.b	Work with peers to set rules for collegial discussions and decision-making, clear goals and deadlines, and individual roles as needed.
		SL.9-10.1.c	Propel conversations by posing and responding to questions that relate the current discussion to broader themes or larger ideas; actively incorporate others into the discussion; and clarify, verify, or challenge ideas and conclusions.
		SL.9-10-1.d	Respond thoughtfully to diverse perspectives, summarize points of agreement and disagreement, and, when warranted, qualify or justify their own views and understanding and make new connections in light of the evidence and reasoning presented.

Common Core State Standards **983**

Common Core State Standards, continued

Cluster 2, continued

SE Pages	Lesson	Code	Standards Text
410–411	**Listening and Speaking Workshop: Panel Discussion** continued	SL.9-10.3	Evaluate a speaker's point of view, reasoning, and use of evidence and rhetoric, identifying any fallacious reasoning or exaggerated or distorted evidence.
		SL.9-10.4	Present information, findings, and supporting evidence clearly, concisely, and logically such that listeners can follow the line of reasoning and the organization, development, substance, and style are appropriate to purpose, audience, and task.
		SL.9-10.6	Adapt speech to a variety of contexts and tasks, demonstrating command of formal English when indicated or appropriate.
		L.9-10.3	Apply knowledge of language to understand how language functions in different contexts, to make effective choices for meaning or style, and to comprehend more fully when reading or listening.

Cluster 3

SE Pages	Lesson	Code	Standards Text
	Prepare to Read	RI.9-10.4	Determine the meaning of words and phrases as they are used in a text, including figurative, connotative, and technical meanings; analyze the cumulative impact of specific word choices on meaning and tone.
		SL.9-10.1	Initiate and participate effectively in a range of collaborative discussions (one-on-one, in groups, and teacher-led) with diverse partners on grades 9–10 topics, texts, and issues, building on others' ideas and expressing their own clearly and persuasively.
		L.9-10.6	Acquire and use accurately general academic and domain-specific words and phrases, sufficient for reading, writing, speaking, and listening at the college and career readiness level; demonstrate independence in gathering vocabulary knowledge when considering a word or phrase important to comprehension or expression.
413	**Before Reading: My English**	RI.9-10.1	Cite strong and thorough textual evidence to support analysis of what the text says explicitly as well as inferences drawn from the text.
		RI.9-10.5	Analyze in detail how an author's ideas or claims are developed and refined by particular sentences, paragraphs, or larger portions of a text.
414–422	**Read My English**	RI.9-10.1	Cite strong and thorough textual evidence to support analysis of what the text says explicitly as well as inferences drawn from the text.
		RI.9-10.2	Determine a central idea of a text and analyze its development over the course of the text, including how it emerges and is shaped and refined by specific details; provide an objective summary of the text.
		RI.9-10.4	Determine the meaning of words and phrases as they are used in a text, including figurative, connotative, and technical meanings; analyze the cumulative impact of specific word choices on meaning and tone.
		RI.9-10.5	Analyze in detail how an author's ideas or claims are developed and refined by particular sentences, paragraphs, or larger portions of a text.
		RI.9-10.10	By the end of grade 10, read and comprehend literary nonfiction at the high end of the grades 9–10 text complexity band independently and proficiently.
		W.9-10.1	Write arguments to support claims in an analysis of substantive topics or texts, using valid reasoning and relevant and sufficient evidence.

Cluster 3, continued

SE Pages	Lesson	Code	Standards Text
414–422	**Read My English** continued	W.9-10.9.b	Apply grades 9–10 Reading standards to literary nonfiction.
		W.9-10.10	Write routinely over extended time frames (time for research, reflection, and revision) and shorter time frames (a single sitting or a day or two) for a range of tasks, purposes, and audiences.
		L.9-10.1.b	Use various types of phrases (noun, verb, adjectival, adverbial, participial, prepositional, absolute) and clauses (independent, dependent; noun, relative, adverbial) to convey specific meanings and add variety and interest to writing or presentations.
		L.9-10.4	Determine or clarify the meaning of unknown and multiple-meaning words and phrases based on grades 9–10 reading and content, choosing flexibly from a range of strategies.
		L.9-10.6	Acquire and use accurately general academic and domain-specific words and phrases, sufficient for reading, writing, speaking, and listening at the college and career readiness level; demonstrate independence in gathering vocabulary knowledge when considering a word or phrase important to comprehension or expression.
423	**Before Reading: How I Learned English**	RI.9-10.1	Cite strong and thorough textual evidence to support analysis of what the text says explicitly as well as inferences drawn from the text.
		RI.9-10.5	Analyze in detail how an author's ideas or claims are developed and refined by particular sentences, paragraphs, or larger portions of a text.
424–426	**Read How I Learned English**	RL.9-10.1	Cite strong and thorough textual evidence to support analysis of what the text says explicitly as well as inferences drawn from the text.
		RL.9-10.5	Analyze how an author's choices concerning how to structure a text, order events within it, and manipulate time create such effects as mystery, tension, or surprise.
		RL.9-10.10	By the end of grade 10, read and comprehend literature, including stories, dramas, and poems, at the high end of the grades 9–10 text complexity band independently and proficiently.
		W.9-10.1	Write arguments to support claims in an analysis of substantive topics or texts, using valid reasoning and relevant and sufficient evidence.
		W.9-10.9.b	Apply grades 9–10 Reading standards to literary nonfiction.
		W.9-10.10	Write routinely over extended time frames (time for research, reflection, and revision) and shorter time frames (a single sitting or a day or two) for a range of tasks, purposes, and audiences.
		L.9-10.1	Demonstrate command of the conventions of standard English grammar and usage when writing or speaking.
		L.9-10.4	Determine or clarify the meaning of unknown and multiple-meaning words and phrases based on grades 9–10 reading and content, choosing flexibly from a range of strategies.
		L.9-10.6	Acquire and use accurately general academic and domain-specific words and phrases, sufficient for reading, writing, speaking, and listening at the college and career readiness level; demonstrate independence in gathering vocabulary knowledge when considering a word or phrase important to comprehension or expression.

Common Core State Standards, continued

SE Pages	Lesson	Code	Standards Text
427	**Reflect and Assess Critical Thinking**	RL.9-10.2	Determine a theme or central idea of a text and analyze in detail its development over the course of the text, including how it emerges and is shaped and refined by specific details; provide an objective summary of the text.
		RL.9-10.10	By the end of grade 10, read and comprehend literature, including stories, dramas, and poems, at the high end of the grades 9–10 text complexity band independently and proficiently.
		RI.9-10.2	Determine a central idea of a text and analyze its development over the course of the text, including how it emerges and is shaped and refined by specific details; provide an objective summary of the text.
		RI.9-10.10	By the end of grade 10, read and comprehend literary nonfiction at the high end of the grades 9–10 text complexity band independently and proficiently.
		SL.9-10.1	Initiate and participate effectively in a range of collaborative discussions (one-on-one, in groups, and teacher-led) with diverse partners on grades 9–10 topics, texts, and issues, building on others' ideas and expressing their own clearly and persuasively.
	Write About Literature	W.9-10.3	Write narratives to develop real or imagined experiences or events using effective technique, well-chosen details, and well-structured event sequences.
	Key Vocabulary Review	L.9-10.6	Acquire and use accurately general academic and domain-specific words and phrases, sufficient for reading, writing, speaking, and listening at the college and career readiness level; demonstrate independence in gathering vocabulary knowledge when considering a word or phrase important to comprehension or expression.
	Read with Ease: Phrasing	RL.9-10.10	By the end of grade 10, read and comprehend literature, including stories, dramas, and poems, at the high end of the grades 9–10 text complexity band independently and proficiently.
428	**Grammar: Use the Correct Pronoun**	L.9-10.1	Demonstrate command of the conventions of standard English grammar and usage when writing or speaking.
428	**Language Development: Use Appropriate Language**	SL.9-10.6	Adapt speech to a variety of contexts and tasks, demonstrating command of formal English when indicated or appropriate.
428	**Literary Analysis: Multiple Levels of Meaning**	RI.9-10.4	Determine the meaning of words and phrases as they are used in a text, including figurative, connotative, and technical meanings; analyze the cumulative impact of specific word choices on meaning and tone.
429	**Vocabulary Study: Content-Area Words**	L.9-10.4.c	Consult general and specialized reference materials, both print and digital, to find the pronunciation of a word or determine or clarify its precise meaning, its part of speech, or its etymology.
429	**Writing Trait: Development of Ideas**	W.9-10.2	Write informative/explanatory texts to examine and convey complex ideas, concepts, and information clearly and accurately through the effective selection, organization, and analysis of content.
429	**Listening/Speaking: Anecdote**	SL.9-10.6	Adapt speech to a variety of contexts and tasks, demonstrating command of formal English when indicated or appropriate.

Close Reading

SE Pages	Lesson	Code	Standards Text
430–433	**Read Txtng: The Gr8 Db8**	RI.9-10.10	By the end of grade 10, read and comprehend literary nonfiction at the high end of the grades 9–10 text complexity band independently and proficiently.

Unit Wrap-Up

SE Pages	Lesson	Code	Standards Text
434	**Unit Wrap-Up Present Your Project**	SL.9-10.2	Integrate multiple sources of information presented in diverse media or formats evaluating the credibility and accuracy of each source.
		SL.9-10.4	Present information, findings, and supporting evidence clearly, concisely, and logically such that listeners can follow the line of reasoning and the organization, development, substance, and style are appropriate to purpose, audience, and task.
		SL.9-10.5	Make strategic use of digital media in presentations to enhance understanding of findings, reasoning, and evidence and to add interest.
	Reflect on Your Reading	SL.9-10.1	Initiate and participate effectively in a range of collaborative discussions (one-on-one, in groups, and teacher-led) with diverse partners on grades 9–10 topics, texts, and issues, building on others' ideas and expressing their own clearly and persuasively.

Writing Project: Research Report

SE Pages	Lesson	Code	Standards Text
435–439	**Study Research Reports and Prewrite**	W.9-10.2.a	Introduce a topic; organize complex ideas, concepts, and information to make important connections and distinctions; include formatting, graphics, and multimedia when useful to aiding comprehension.
		W.9-10.5	Develop and strengthen writing as needed by planning, revising, editing, rewriting, or trying a new approach, focusing on addressing what is most significant for a specific purpose and audience.
		W.9-10.6	Use technology, including the Internet, to produce, publish, and update individual or shared writing products, taking advantage of technology's capacity to link to other information and to display information flexibly and dynamically.
		W.9-10.7	Conduct short as well as more sustained research projects to answer a question (including a self-generated question) or solve a problem; narrow or broaden the inquiry when appropriate; synthesize multiple sources on the subject, demonstrating understanding of the subject under investigation.
		W.9-10.8	Gather relevant information from multiple authoritative print and digital sources, using advanced searches effectively; assess the usefulness of each source in answering the research question; integrate information into the text selectively to maintain the flow of ideas, avoiding plagiarism and following a standard format for citation.
440–441	**Research Report: Draft**	W.9-10.2	Write informative/explanatory texts to examine and convey complex ideas, concepts, and information clearly and accurately through the effective selection, organization, and analysis of content.
		W.9-10.4	Produce clear and coherent writing in which the development, organization, and style are appropriate to task, purpose, and audience.
		L.9-10.3.a	Write and edit work so that it conforms to the guidelines in a style manual appropriate for the discipline and writing type.

Common Core State Standards, continued

Writing Project: Research Report, continued

SE Pages	Lesson	Code	Standards Text
442–445	Research Report: Revise Trait: Organization	W.9-10.2.a	Introduce a topic; organize complex ideas, concepts, and information to make important connections and distinctions; include formatting, graphics, and multimedia when useful to aiding comprehension.
		W.9-10.2.b	Develop the topic with well-chosen, relevant, and sufficient facts, extended definitions, concrete details, quotations, or other information and examples appropriate to the audience's knowledge of the topic.
		W.9-10.2.c	Use appropriate and varied transitions to link the major sections of the text, create cohesion, and clarify the relationships among complex ideas and concepts.
		W.9-10.2.d	Use precise language and domain-specific vocabulary to manage the complexity of the topic.
		W.9-10.2.e	Establish and maintain a formal style and objective tone while attending to the norms and conventions of the discipline in which they are writing.
		W.9-10.2.f	Provide a concluding statement or section that follows from and supports the information or explanation presented
		W.9-10.4	Produce clear and coherent writing in which the development, organization, and style are appropriate to task, purpose, and audience.
		W.9-10.5	Develop and strengthen writing as needed by planning, revising, editing, rewriting, or trying a new approach, focusing on addressing what is most significant for a specific purpose and audience.
		W.9-10.7	Conduct short as well as more sustained research projects to answer a question (including a self-generated question) or solve a problem; narrow or broaden the inquiry when appropriate; synthesize multiple sources on the subject, demonstrating understanding of the subject under investigation.
		SL.9-10.1	Initiate and participate effectively in a range of collaborative discussions (one-on-one, in groups, and teacher-led) with diverse partners on grades 9–10 topics, texts, and issues, building on others' ideas and expressing their own clearly and persuasively.
		SL.9-10.1.d	Respond thoughtfully to diverse perspectives, summarize points of agreement and disagreement, and, when warranted, qualify or justify their own views and understanding and make new connections in light of the evidence and reasoning presented.
446–449	Research Report: Edit and Proofread Capitalization: Titles of Publications Parentheses Modifiers Pronoun Agreement	L.9-10.1	Demonstrate command of the conventions of standard English grammar and usage when writing or speaking.
		L.9-10.2	Demonstrate command of the conventions of standard English capitalization, punctuation, and spelling when writing.
		L.9-10.3.a	Write and edit work so that it conforms to the guidelines in a style manual appropriate for the discipline and writing type.

Writing Project: Research Report, continued

SE Pages	Lesson	Code	Standards Text
449	Research Report: Publish and Present	W.9-10.2.a	Introduce a topic; organize complex ideas, concepts, and information to make important connections and distinctions; include formatting, graphics, and multimedia when useful to aiding comprehension.
		W.9-10.6	Use technology, including the Internet, to produce, publish, and update individual or shared writing products, taking advantage of technology's capacity to link to other information and to display information flexibly and dynamically.
		SL.9-10.1.c	Propel conversations by posing and responding to questions that relate the current discussion to broader themes or larger ideas; actively incorporate others into the discussion; and clarify, verify, or challenge ideas and conclusions.
		SL.9-10.3	Evaluate a speaker's point of view, reasoning, and use of evidence and rhetoric, identifying any fallacious reasoning or exaggerated or distorted evidence.
		SL.9-10.4	Present information, findings, and supporting evidence clearly, concisely, and logically such that listeners can follow the line of reasoning and the organization, development, substance, and style are appropriate to purpose, audience, and task.
		SL.9-10.5	Make strategic use of digital media in presentations to enhance understanding of findings, reasoning, and evidence and to add interest.

UNIT 5: Moment of Truth

SE Pages	Lesson	Code	Standards Text
450–451	Discuss the Essential Question	SL.9-10.1.b	Work with peers to set rules for collegial discussions and decision-making, clear goals and deadlines, and individual roles as needed
		SL.9-10.3	Evaluate a speaker's point of view, reasoning, and use of evidence and rhetoric, identifying any fallacious reasoning or exaggerated or distorted evidence.
452	Compare and Debate	SL.9-10.4	Present information, findings, and supporting evidence clearly, concisely, and logically such that listeners can follow the line of reasoning and the organization, development, substance, and style are appropriate to purpose, audience, and task.
453	Plan a Project	SL.9-10.1.b	Work with peers to set rules for collegial discussions and decision-making, clear goals and deadlines, and individual roles as needed.
453	Choose More to Read	RL.9-10.10	By the end of grade 10, read and comprehend literature, including stories, dramas, and poems, at the high end of the grades 9–10 text complexity band independently and proficiently.
		RI.9-10.10	By the end of grade 10, read and comprehend literary nonfiction at the high end of the grades 9–10 text complexity band independently and proficiently.
454–457	How to Read Short Stories	RL.9-10.1	Cite strong and thorough textual evidence to support analysis of what the text says explicitly as well as inferences drawn from the text.
		RL.9-10.5	Analyze how an author's choices concerning how to structure a text, order events within it, and manipulate time create such effects as mystery, tension, or surprise.
		RL.9-10.10	By the end of grade 10, read and comprehend literature, including stories, dramas, and poems, at the high end of the grades 9–10 text complexity band independently and proficiently.

Common Core State Standards, continued

UNIT 5: Moment of Truth, continued

SE Pages	Lesson	Code	Standards Text
454–457	**How to Read Short Stories** continued	SL.9-10.1.a	Come to discussions prepared, having read and researched material under study; explicitly draw on that preparation by referring to evidence from texts and other research on the topic or issue to stimulate a thoughtful, well-reasoned exchange of ideas.
		L.9-10.6	Acquire and use accurately general academic and domain-specific words and phrases, sufficient for reading, writing, speaking, and listening at the college and career readiness level; demonstrate independence in gathering vocabulary knowledge when considering a word or phrase important to comprehension or expression.
Cluster 1			
458	**Prepare to Read**	RI.9-10.4	Determine the meaning of words and phrases as they are used in a text, including figurative, connotative, and technical meanings; analyze the cumulative impact of specific word choices on meaning and tone.
		SL.9-10.1	Initiate and participate effectively in a range of collaborative discussions (one-on-one, in groups, and teacher-led) with diverse partners on grades 9–10 topics, texts, and issues, building on others' ideas and expressing their own clearly and persuasively.
		L.9-10.6	Acquire and use accurately general academic and domain-specific words and phrases, sufficient for reading, writing, speaking, and listening at the college and career readiness level; demonstrate independence in gathering vocabulary knowledge when considering a word or phrase important to comprehension or expression.
459	**Before Reading: Say It with Flowers**	RL.9-10.5	Analyze how an author's choices concerning how to structure a text, order events within it, and manipulate time create such effects as mystery, tension, or surprise.
		RL.9-10.10	By the end of grade 10, read and comprehend literature, including stories, dramas, and poems, at the high end of the grades 9–10 text complexity band independently and proficiently.
460–472	**Read Say It with Flowers**	RL.9-10.1	Cite strong and thorough textual evidence to support analysis of what the text says explicitly as well as inferences drawn from the text.
		RL.9-10.2	Determine a theme or central idea of a text and analyze in detail its development over the course of the text, including how it emerges and is shaped and refined by specific details; provide an objective summary of the text.
		RL.9-10.3	Analyze how complex characters develop over the course of a text, interact with other characters, and advance the plot or develop the theme.
		RL.9-10.5	Analyze how an author's choices concerning how to structure a text, order events within it, and manipulate time create such effects as mystery, tension, or surprise.
		RL.9-10.7	Analyze the representation of a subject or a key scene in two different artistic mediums, including what is emphasized or absent in each treatment.
		RL.9-10.10	By the end of grade 10, read and comprehend literature, including stories, dramas, and poems, at the high end of the grades 9–10 text complexity band independently and proficiently.
		W.9-10.3	Write narratives to develop real or imagined experiences or events using effective technique, well-chosen details, and well-structured event sequences.
		W.9-10.9	Draw evidence from literary or informational texts to support analysis, reflection, and research.

Cluster 1, continued

SE Pages	Lesson	Code	Standards Text
460–472	**Read Say It with Flowers** continued	W.9-10.9.a	Apply grades 9–10 Reading standards to literature.
		W.9-10.10	Write routinely over extended time frames (time for research, reflection, and revision) and shorter time frames (a single sitting or a day or two) for a range of tasks, purposes, and audiences.
		L.9-10.1.b	Use various types of phrases (noun, verb, adjectival, adverbial, participial, prepositional, absolute) and clauses (independent, dependent; noun, relative, adverbial) to convey specific meanings and add variety and interest to writing or presentations.
		L.9-10.4.a	Use context as a clue to the meaning of a word or phrase.
		L.9-10.4.d	Verify the preliminary determination of the meaning of a word or phrase.
		L.9-10.6	Acquire and use accurately general academic and domain-specific words and phrases, sufficient for reading, writing, speaking, and listening at the college and career readiness level; demonstrate independence in gathering vocabulary knowledge when considering a word or phrase important to comprehension or expression.
473	**Before Reading: The Journey**	RL.9-10.4	Determine the meaning of words and phrases as they are used in the text, including figurative and connotative meanings; analyze the cumulative impact of specific word choices on meaning and tone.
		RL.9-10.10	By the end of grade 10, read and comprehend literature, including stories, dramas, and poems, at the high end of the grades 9–10 text complexity band independently and proficiently.
		L.9-10.5.a	Interpret figures of speech in context and analyze their role in the text.
474–476	**Read The Journey**	RL.9-10.1	Cite strong and thorough textual evidence to support analysis of what the text says explicitly as well as inferences drawn from the text.
		RL.9-10.4	Determine the meaning of words and phrases as they are used in the text, including figurative and connotative meanings; analyze the cumulative impact of specific word choices on meaning and tone.
		RL.9-10.10	By the end of grade 10, read and comprehend literature, including stories, dramas, and poems, at the high end of the grades 9–10 text complexity band independently and proficiently.
		W.9-10.1	Write arguments to support claims in an analysis of substantive topics or texts, using valid reasoning and relevant and sufficient evidence.
		W.9-10.10	Write routinely over extended time frames (time for research, reflection, and revision) and shorter time frames (a single sitting or a day or two) for a range of tasks, purposes, and audiences.
		L.9-10.5.a	Interpret figures of speech in context and analyze their role in the text.
		L.9-10.6	Acquire and use accurately general academic and domain-specific words and phrases, sufficient for reading, writing, speaking, and listening at the college and career readiness level; demonstrate independence in gathering vocabulary knowledge when considering a word or phrase important to comprehension or expression.

Common Core State Standards, continued

Cluster 1, continued

SE Pages	Lesson	Code	Standards Text
477	**Reflect and Assess Critical Thinking**	RL.9-10.1	Cite strong and thorough textual evidence to support analysis of what the text says explicitly as well as inferences drawn from the text.
		RL.9-10.3	Analyze how complex characters develop over the course of a text, interact with other characters, and advance the plot or develop the theme.
		RL.9-10.10	By the end of grade 10, read and comprehend literature, including stories, dramas, and poems, at the high end of the grades 9–10 text complexity band independently and proficiently.
		SL.9-10.1.a	Come to discussions prepared, having read and researched material under study; explicitly draw on that preparation by referring to evidence from texts and other research on the topic or issue to stimulate a thoughtful, well-reasoned exchange of ideas.
	Write About Literature	W.9-10.3	Write narratives to develop real or imagined experiences or events using effective technique, well-chosen details, and well-structured event sequences.
	Key Vocabulary Review	L.9-10.6	Acquire and use accurately general academic and domain-specific words and phrases, sufficient for reading, writing, speaking, and listening at the college and career readiness level; demonstrate independence in gathering vocabulary knowledge when considering a word or phrase important to comprehension or expression.
	Read with Ease: Phrasing	RL.9-10.10	By the end of grade 10, read and comprehend literature, including stories, dramas, and poems, at the high end of the grades 9–10 text complexity band independently and proficiently.
478	**Grammar: Use Adjectives to Elaborate**	L.9-10.1.b	Use various types of phrases (noun, verb, adjectival, adverbial, participial, prepositional, absolute) and clauses (independent, dependent; noun, relative, adverbial) to convey specific meanings and add variety and interest to writing or presentations.
478	**Language Development: Evaluate**	SL.9-10.1.a	Come to discussions prepared, having read and researched material under study; explicitly draw on that preparation by referring to evidence from texts and other research on the topic or issue to stimulate a thoughtful, well-reasoned exchange of ideas.
478	**Literary Analysis: Compare Characters' Motivations**	RL.9-10.3	Analyze how complex characters develop over the course of a text, interact with other characters, and advance the plot or develop the theme.
479	**Vocabulary Study: Synonyms**	L.9-10.4.c	Consult general and specialized reference materials, both print and digital, to find the pronunciation of a word or determine or clarify its precise meaning, its part of speech, or its etymology.
		L.9-10.5	Demonstrate understanding of figurative language, word relationships, and nuances in word meanings.
479	**Writing: Write a Review**	W.9-10.1	Write arguments to support claims in an analysis of substantive topics or texts, using valid reasoning and relevant and sufficient evidence.
		W.9-10.5	Develop and strengthen writing as needed by planning, revising, editing, rewriting, or trying a new approach, focusing on addressing what is most significant for a specific purpose and audience.
479	**Listening/Speaking: Announcement**	SL.9-10.3	Evaluate a speaker's point of view, reasoning, and use of evidence and rhetoric, identifying any fallacious reasoning or exaggerated or distorted evidence.

Cluster 1, continued

SE Pages	Lesson	Code	Standards Text
480	**Workplace Workshop: Inside a Pharmacy**	W.9-10.2	Write informative/explanatory texts to examine and convey complex ideas, concepts, and information clearly and accurately through the effective selection, organization, and analysis of content.
		W.9-10.10	Write routinely over extended time frames (time for research, reflection, and revision) and shorter time frames (a single sitting or a day or two) for a range of tasks, purposes, and audiences.
481	**Vocabulary Workshop: Make Word Connections**	L.9-10.4.c	Consult general and specialized reference materials, both print and digital, to find the pronunciation of a word or determine or clarify its precise meaning, its part of speech, or its etymology.
		L.9-10.5	Demonstrate understanding of figurative language, word relationships, and nuances in word meanings.

Cluster 2

SE Pages	Lesson	Code	Standards Text
482	**Prepare to Read**	RI.9-10.4	Determine the meaning of words and phrases as they are used in a text, including figurative, connotative, and technical meanings; analyze the cumulative impact of specific word choices on meaning and tone .
		SL.9-10.1	Initiate and participate effectively in a range of collaborative discussions (one-on-one, in groups, and teacher-led) with diverse partners on grades 9-10 topics, texts, and issues, building on others' ideas and expressing their own clearly and persuasively.
		L.9-10.6	Acquire and use accurately general academic and domain-specific words and phrases, sufficient for reading, writing, speaking, and listening at the college and career readiness level; demonstrate independence in gathering vocabulary knowledge when considering a word or phrase important to comprehension or expression.
483	**Before Reading: Just Lather, That's All**	RL.9-10.5	Analyze how an author's choices concerning how to structure a text, order events within it, and manipulate time create such effects as mystery, tension, or surprise.
		RL.9-10.10	By the end of grade 10, read and comprehend literature, including stories, dramas, and poems, at the high end of the grades 9–10 text complexity band independently and proficiently.
484–493	**Read Just Lather, That's All**	RL.9-10.1	Cite strong and thorough textual evidence to support analysis of what the text says explicitly as well as inferences drawn from the text.
		RL.9-10.5	Analyze how an author's choices concerning how to structure a text, order events within it, and manipulate time create such effects as mystery, tension, or surprise.
		RL.9-10.7	Analyze the representation of a subject or a key scene in two different artistic mediums, including what is emphasized or absent in each treatment.
		RL.9-10.10	By the end of grade 10, read and comprehend literature, including stories, dramas, and poems, at the high end of the grades 9–10 text complexity band independently and proficiently.
		W.9-10.3	Write narratives to develop real or imagined experiences or events using effective technique, well-chosen details, and well-structured event sequences.
		W.9-10.9.a	Apply grades 9-10 Reading standards to literature.

Common Core State Standards, continued

Cluster 2, continued

SE Pages	Lesson	Code	Standards Text
484–493	**Read Just Lather, That's All** continued	W.9-10.10	Write routinely over extended time frames (time for research, reflection, and revision) and shorter time frames (a single sitting or a day or two) for a range of tasks, purposes, and audiences.
		L.9-10.1.b	Use various types of phrases (noun, verb, adjectival, adverbial, participial, prepositional, absolute) and clauses (independent, dependent; noun, relative, adverbial) to convey specific meanings and add variety and interest to writing or presentations.
		L.9-10.2.c	Spell correctly.
		L.9-10.4.a	Use context as a clue to the meaning of a word or phrase.
		L.9-10.5	Demonstrate understanding of figurative language, word relationships, and nuances in word meanings.
		L.9-10.6	Acquire and use accurately general academic and domain-specific words and phrases, sufficient for reading, writing, speaking, and listening at the college and career readiness level; demonstrate independence in gathering vocabulary knowledge when considering a word or phrase important to comprehension or expression.
494	**Before Reading: The Woman Who Was Death**	RL.9-10.6	Analyze a particular point of view or cultural experience reflected in a work of literature from outside the United States, drawing on a wide reading of world literature.
		RL.9-10.10	By the end of grade 10, read and comprehend literature, including stories, dramas, and poems, at the high end of the grades 9–10 text complexity band independently and proficiently.
495–498	**Read The Woman Who Was Death**	RL.9-10.1	Cite strong and thorough textual evidence to support analysis of what the text says explicitly as well as inferences drawn from the text.
		RL.9-10.2	Determine a theme or central idea of a text and analyze in detail its development over the course of the text, including how it emerges and is shaped and refined by specific details; provide an objective summary of the text.
		RL.9-10.6	Analyze a particular point of view or cultural experience reflected in a work of literature from outside the United States, drawing on a wide reading of world literature.
		RL.9-10.7	Analyze the representation of a subject or a key scene in two different artistic mediums, including what is emphasized or absent in each treatment.
		RL.9-10.10	By the end of grade 10, read and comprehend literature, including stories, dramas, and poems, at the high end of the grades 9–10 text complexity band independently and proficiently.
		W.9-10.1	Write arguments to support claims in an analysis of substantive topics or texts, using valid reasoning and relevant and sufficient evidence.
		W.9-10.9.a	Apply grades 9–10 Reading standards to literature.
		W.9-10.10	Write routinely over extended time frames (time for research, reflection, and revision) and shorter time frames (a single sitting or a day or two) for a range of tasks, purposes, and audiences.

Cluster 2, continued

SE Pages	Lesson	Code	Standards Text
495–498	**Read The Woman Who Was Death** continued	L.9-10.1.b	Use various types of phrases (noun, verb, adjectival, adverbial, participial, prepositional, absolute) and clauses (independent, dependent; noun, relative, adverbial) to convey specific meanings and add variety and interest to writing or presentations.
		L.9-10.6	Acquire and use accurately general academic and domain-specific words and phrases, sufficient for reading, writing, speaking, and listening at the college and career readiness level; demonstrate independence in gathering vocabulary knowledge when considering a word or phrase important to comprehension or expression.
499	**Reflect and Assess Critical Thinking**	RL.9-10.2	Determine a theme or central idea of a text and analyze in detail its development over the course of the text, including how it emerges and is shaped and refined by specific details; provide an objective summary of the text.
		RL.9-10.10	By the end of grade 10, read and comprehend literature, including stories, dramas, and poems, at the high end of the grades 9–10 text complexity band independently and proficiently.
		SL.9-10.1	Initiate and participate effectively in a range of collaborative discussions (one-on-one, in groups, and teacher-led) with diverse partners on grades 9–10 topics, texts, and issues, building on others' ideas and expressing their own clearly and persuasively.
	Write About Literature	W.9-10.1	Write arguments to support claims in an analysis of substantive topics or texts, using valid reasoning and relevant and sufficient evidence.
	Key Vocabulary Review	L.9-10.6	Acquire and use accurately general academic and domain-specific words and phrases, sufficient for reading, writing, speaking, and listening at the college and career readiness level; demonstrate independence in gathering vocabulary knowledge when considering a word or phrase important to comprehension or expression.
	Read with Ease: Intonation	RL.9-10.10	By the end of grade 10, read and comprehend literature, including stories, dramas, and poems, at the high end of the grades 9–10 text complexity band independently and proficiently.
500	**Grammar: Use Adjectives Correctly**	L.9-10.1.b	Use various types of phrases (noun, verb, adjectival, adverbial, participial, prepositional, absolute) and clauses (independent, dependent; noun, relative, adverbial) to convey specific meanings and add variety and interest to writing or presentations.
500	**Language Development: Clarify**	SL.9-10.1.c	Propel conversations by posing and responding to questions that relate the current discussion to broader themes or larger ideas; actively incorporate others into the discussion; and clarify, verify, or challenge ideas and conclusions.
500	**Research/Viewing: Illustrated Report**	W.9-10.7	Conduct short as well as more sustained research projects to answer a question (including a self-generated question) or solve a problem; narrow or broaden the inquiry when appropriate; synthesize multiple sources on the subject, demonstrating understanding of the subject under investigation.
501	**Vocabulary Study: Synonyms and Antonyms in Analogies**	L.9-10.4.c	Consult general and specialized reference materials, both print and digital, to find the pronunciation of a word or determine or clarify its precise meaning, its part of speech, or its etymology.
		L.9-10.5	Demonstrate understanding of figurative language, word relationships, and nuances in word meanings.

Common Core State Standards, continued

Cluster 2, continued

SE Pages	Lesson	Code	Standards Text
501	Vocabulary Study: Synonyms and Antonyms in Analogies continued **Writing Trait: Voice and Style**	W.9-10.4	Produce clear and coherent writing in which the development, organization, and style are appropriate to task, purpose, and audience.
		L.9-10.3	Apply knowledge of language to understand how language functions in different contexts, to make effective choices for meaning or style, and to comprehend more fully when reading or listening.
501	**Literary Analysis: Understand Irony**	RL.9-10.4	Determine the meaning of words and phrases as they are used in the text, including figurative and connotative meanings; analyze the cumulative impact of specific word choices on meaning and tone.
502–503	**Listening and Speaking Workshop: Extemporaneous Talk**	W.9-10.7	Conduct short as well as more sustained research projects to answer a question (including a self-generated question) or solve a problem; narrow or broaden the inquiry when appropriate; synthesize multiple sources on the subject, demonstrating understanding of the subject under investigation.
		SL.9-10.1.c	Propel conversations by posing and responding to questions that relate the current discussion to broader themes or larger ideas; actively incorporate others into the discussion; and clarify, verify, or challenge ideas and conclusions.
		SL.9-10.2	Integrate multiple sources of information presented in diverse media or formats evaluating the credibility and accuracy of each source.
		SL.9-10.3	Evaluate a speaker's point of view, reasoning, and use of evidence and rhetoric, identifying any fallacious reasoning or exaggerated or distorted evidence.
		SL.9-10.4	Present information, findings, and supporting evidence clearly, concisely, and logically such that listeners can follow the line of reasoning and the organization, development, substance, and style are appropriate to purpose, audience, and task.
		L.9-10.3	Apply knowledge of language to understand how language functions in different contexts, to make effective choices for meaning or style, and to comprehend more fully when reading or listening.

Cluster 3

SE Pages	Lesson	Code	Standards Text
504	**Prepare to Read**	RI.9-10.4	Determine the meaning of words and phrases as they are used in a text, including figurative, connotative, and technical meanings; analyze the cumulative impact of specific word choices on meaning and tone.
		SL.9-10.1	Initiate and participate effectively in a range of collaborative discussions (one-on-one, in groups, and teacher-led) with diverse partners on grades 9–10 topics, texts, and issues, building on others' ideas and expressing their own clearly and persuasively.
		L.9-10.6	Acquire and use accurately general academic and domain-specific words and phrases, sufficient for reading, writing, speaking, and listening at the college and career readiness level; demonstrate independence in gathering vocabulary knowledge when considering a word or phrase important to comprehension or expression.
505	**Before Reading: Be-ers and Doers**	RL.9-10.5	Analyze how an author's choices concerning how to structure a text, order events within it, and manipulate time create such effects as mystery, tension, or surprise.
		RL.9-10.10	By the end of grade 10, read and comprehend literature, including stories, dramas, and poems, at the high end of the grades 9–10 text complexity band independently and proficiently.

Cluster 3, continued

SE Pages	Lesson	Code	Standards Text
506–521	**Read Be-ers and Doers**	RL.9-10.1	Cite strong and thorough textual evidence to support analysis of what the text says explicitly as well as inferences drawn from the text.
		RL.9-10.3	Analyze how complex characters develop over the course of a text, interact with other characters, and advance the plot or develop the theme.
		RL.9-10.4	Determine the meaning of words and phrases as they are used in the text, including figurative and connotative meanings; analyze the cumulative impact of specific word choices on meaning and tone.
		RL.9-10.5	Analyze how an author's choices concerning how to structure a text, order events within it, and manipulate time create such effects as mystery, tension, or surprise.
		RL.9-10.7	Analyze the representation of a subject or a key scene in two different artistic mediums, including what is emphasized or absent in each treatment.
		RL.9-10.10	By the end of grade 10, read and comprehend literature, including stories, dramas, and poems, at the high end of the grades 9–10 text complexity band independently and proficiently.
		W.9-10.1	Write arguments to support claims in an analysis of substantive topics or texts, using valid reasoning and relevant and sufficient evidence.
		W.9-10.3	Write narratives to develop real or imagined experiences or events using effective technique, well-chosen details, and well-structured event sequences.
		W.9-10.9.a	Apply grades 9–10 Reading standards to literature.
		W.9-10.10	Write routinely over extended time frames (time for research, reflection, and revision) and shorter time frames (a single sitting or a day or two) for a range of tasks, purposes, and audiences.
		SL.9-10.1.a	Come to discussions prepared, having read and researched material under study; explicitly draw on that preparation by referring to evidence from texts and other research on the topic or issue to stimulate a thoughtful, well-reasoned exchange of ideas.
		SL.9-10.1.d	Respond thoughtfully to diverse perspectives, summarize points of agreement and disagreement, and, when warranted, qualify or justify their own views and understanding and make new connections in light of the evidence and reasoning presented.
		L.9-10.1.b	Use various types of phrases (noun, verb, adjectival, adverbial, participial, prepositional, absolute) and clauses (independent, dependent; noun, relative, adverbial) to convey specific meanings and add variety and interest to writing or presentations.
		L.9-10.2.c	Spell correctly.
		L.9-10.4.b	Identify and correctly use patterns of word changes that indicate different meanings or parts of speech.
		L.9-10.6	Acquire and use accurately general academic and domain-specific words and phrases, sufficient for reading, writing, speaking, and listening at the college and career readiness level; demonstrate independence in gathering vocabulary knowledge when considering a word or phrase important to comprehension or expression.

Common Core State Standards, continued

Cluster 3, continued

SE Pages	Lesson	Code	Standards Text
522–523	**Postscript: The Calling**	RL.9-10.1	Cite strong and thorough textual evidence to support analysis of what the text says explicitly as well as inferences drawn from the text.
		RL.9-10.7	Analyze the representation of a subject or a key scene in two different artistic mediums, including what is emphasized or absent in each treatment.
		RL.9-10.10	By the end of grade 10, read and comprehend literature, including stories, dramas, and poems, at the high end of the grades 9–10 text complexity band independently and proficiently.
		SL.9-10.6	Adapt speech to a variety of contexts and tasks, demonstrating command of formal English when indicated or appropriate.
		L.9-10.6	Acquire and use accurately general academic and domain-specific words and phrases, sufficient for reading, writing, speaking, and listening at the college and career readiness level; demonstrate independence in gathering vocabulary knowledge when considering a word or phrase important to comprehension or expression.
524	**Before Reading: My Moment of Truth**	RI.9-10.2	Determine a central idea of a text and analyze its development over the course of the text, including how it emerges and is shaped and refined by specific details; provide an objective summary of the text.
		RI.9-10.6	Determine an author's point of view or purpose in a text and analyze how an author uses rhetoric to advance that point of view or purpose.
		RI.9-10.10	By the end of grade 10, read and comprehend literary nonfiction at the high end of the grades 9–10 text complexity band independently and proficiently.
525–528	**Read My Moment of Truth**	RI.9-10.6	Determine an author's point of view or purpose in a text and analyze how an author uses rhetoric to advance that point of view or purpose.
		RI.9-10.10	By the end of grade 10, read and comprehend literary nonfiction at the high end of the grades 9–10 text complexity band independently and proficiently.
		W.9-10.1	Write arguments to support claims in an analysis of substantive topics or texts, using valid reasoning and relevant and sufficient evidence.
		W.9-10.9.b	Apply grades 9–10 Reading standards to literary nonfiction.
		W.9-10.10	Write routinely over extended time frames (time for research, reflection, and revision) and shorter time frames (a single sitting or a day or two) for a range of tasks, purposes, and audiences.
		L.9-10.1.b	Use various types of phrases (noun, verb, adjectival, adverbial, participial, prepositional, absolute) and clauses (independent, dependent; noun, relative, adverbial) to convey specific meanings and add variety and interest to writing or presentations.
		L.9-10.6	Acquire and use accurately general academic and domain-specific words and phrases, sufficient for reading, writing, speaking, and listening at the college and career readiness level; demonstrate independence in gathering vocabulary knowledge when considering a word or phrase important to comprehension or expression.

Cluster 3, continued

SE Pages	Lesson	Code	Standards Text
529	**Reflect and Assess Critical Thinking**	RL.9-10.1	Cite strong and thorough textual evidence to support analysis of what the text says explicitly as well as inferences drawn from the text.
		RL.9-10.2	Determine a theme or central idea of a text and analyze in detail its development over the course of the text, including how it emerges and is shaped and refined by specific details; provide an objective summary of the text.
		RL.9-10.10	By the end of grade 10, read and comprehend literature, including stories, dramas, and poems, at the high end of the grades 9–10 text complexity band independently and proficiently.
		RI.9-10.1	Cite strong and thorough textual evidence to support analysis of what the text says explicitly as well as inferences drawn from the text.
		RI.9-10.2	Determine a central idea of a text and analyze its development over the course of the text, including how it emerges and is shaped and refined by specific details; provide an objective summary of the text.
		RI.9-10.10	By the end of grade 10, read and comprehend literary nonfiction at the high end of the grades 9–10 text complexity band independently and proficiently.
	Write About Literature	W.9-10.1	Write arguments to support claims in an analysis of substantive topics or texts, using valid reasoning and relevant and sufficient evidence.
		SL.9-10.6	Adapt speech to a variety of contexts and tasks, demonstrating command of formal English when indicated or appropriate.
	Key Vocabulary Review	L.9-10.6	Acquire and use accurately general academic and domain-specific words and phrases, sufficient for reading, writing, speaking, and listening at the college and career readiness level; demonstrate independence in gathering vocabulary knowledge when considering a word or phrase important to comprehension or expression.
	Read with Ease: Expression	RL.9-10.10	By the end of grade 10, read and comprehend literature, including stories, dramas, and poems, at the high end of the grades 9–10 text complexity band independently and proficiently.
530	**Grammar: Use Adverbs Correctly**	L.9-10.1.b	Use various types of phrases (noun, verb, adjectival, adverbial, participial, prepositional, absolute) and clauses (independent, dependent; noun, relative, adverbial) to convey specific meanings and add variety and interest to writing or presentations.
530	**Literary Analysis: Dialect**	RL.9-10.4	Determine the meaning of words and phrases as they are used in the text, including figurative and connotative meanings; analyze the cumulative impact of specific word choices on meaning and tone.
530	**Language Development: Verify Information**	SL.9-10.1.c	Propel conversations by posing and responding to questions that relate the current discussion to broader themes or larger ideas; actively incorporate others into the discussion; and clarify, verify, or challenge ideas and conclusions.
531	**Vocabulary Study: Synonyms and Antonyms in Analogies**	L.9-10.4.c	Consult general and specialized reference materials, both print and digital, to find the pronunciation of a word or determine or clarify its precise meaning, its part of speech, or its etymology.
		L.9-10.5	Demonstrate understanding of figurative language, word relationships, and nuances in word meanings.

Common Core State Standards, continued

Student Handbooks, continued

Cluster 3, continued

SE Pages	Lesson	Code	Standards Text
531	**Writing on Demand: Write and Analysis of an Issue**	W.9-10.1	Write arguments to support claims in an analysis of substantive topics or texts, using valid reasoning and relevant and sufficient evidence.
		W.9-10.4	Produce clear and coherent writing in which the development, organization, and style are appropriate to task, purpose, and audience.
531	**Media Study: Compare News Commentaries**	RL.9-10.7	Analyze the representation of a subject or a key scene in two different artistic mediums, including what is emphasized or absent in each treatment.
		W.9-10.8	Gather relevant information from multiple authoritative print and digital sources, using advanced searches effectively; assess the usefulness of each source in answering the research question; integrate information into the text selectively to maintain the flow of ideas, avoiding plagiarism and following a standard format for citation.

Close Reading

SE Pages	Lesson	Code	Standards Text
532–535	**Read Black Boy**	RI.9-10.10	By the end of grade 10, read and comprehend literary nonfiction at the high end of the grades 9–10 text complexity band independently and proficiently.

Unit Wrap-Up

SE Pages	Lesson	Code	Standards Text
536	**Unit Wrap-Up Present Your Project**	SL.9-10.6	Adapt speech to a variety of contexts and tasks, demonstrating command of formal English when indicated or appropriate.
	Reflect on Your Reading	SL.9-10.1	Initiate and participate effectively in a range of collaborative discussions (one-on-one, in groups, and teacher-led) with diverse partners on grades 9–10 topics, texts, and issues, building on others' ideas and expressing their own clearly and persuasively.
		SL.9-10.1.a	Come to discussions prepared, having read and researched material under study; explicitly draw on that preparation by referring to evidence from texts and other research on the topic or issue to stimulate a thoughtful, well-reasoned exchange of ideas.
	Respond to the Essential Question	SL.9-10.1.a	Come to discussions prepared, having read and researched material under study; explicitly draw on that preparation by referring to evidence from texts and other research on the topic or issue to stimulate a thoughtful, well-reasoned exchange of ideas.

Writing Project: Literary Research Report

SE Pages	Lesson	Code	Standards Text
537–541	**Study Literary Research Reports and Prewrite**	W.9-10.2.a	Introduce a topic; organize complex ideas, concepts, and information to make important connections and distinctions; include formatting, graphics, and multimedia when useful to aiding comprehension.
		W.9-10.5	Develop and strengthen writing as needed by planning, revising, editing, rewriting, or trying a new approach, focusing on addressing what is most significant for a specific purpose and audience.
		W.9-10.7	Conduct short as well as more sustained research projects to answer a question (including a self-generated question) or solve a problem; narrow or broaden the inquiry when appropriate; synthesize multiple sources on the subject, demonstrating understanding of the subject under investigation.
		W.9-10.8	Gather relevant information from multiple authoritative print and digital sources, using advanced searches effectively; assess the usefulness of each source in answering the research question; integrate information into the text selectively to maintain the flow of ideas, avoiding plagiarism and following a standard format for citation.

Writing Project: Literary Research Report, continued

SE Pages	Lesson	Code	Standards Text
542–543	Literary Research Report: Draft	W.9-10.2	Write informative/explanatory texts to examine and convey complex ideas, concepts, and information clearly and accurately through the effective selection, organization, and analysis of content.
		W.9-10.4	Produce clear and coherent writing in which the development, organization, and style are appropriate to task, purpose, and audience.
		W.9-10.6	Use technology, including the Internet, to produce, publish, and update individual or shared writing products, taking advantage of technology's capacity to link to other information and to display information flexibly and dynamically.
		L.9-10.3.a	Write and edit work so that it conforms to the guidelines in a style manual appropriate for the discipline and writing type.
544–547	Literary Research Report: Revise Trait: Development of Ideas	W.9-10.2.a	Introduce a topic; organize complex ideas, concepts, and information to make important connections and distinctions; include formatting, graphics, and multimedia when useful to aiding comprehension.
		W.9-10.2.b	Develop the topic with well-chosen, relevant, and sufficient facts, extended definitions, concrete details, quotations, or other information and examples appropriate to the audience's knowledge of the topic.
		W.9-10.5	Develop and strengthen writing as needed by planning, revising, editing, rewriting, or trying a new approach, focusing on addressing what is most significant for a specific purpose and audience.
		W.9-10.7	Conduct short as well as more sustained research projects to answer a question (including a self-generated question) or solve a problem; narrow or broaden the inquiry when appropriate; synthesize multiple sources on the subject, demonstrating understanding of the subject under investigation.
		SL.9-10.1.d	Respond thoughtfully to diverse perspectives, summarize points of agreement and disagreement, and, when warranted, qualify or justify their own views and understanding and make new connections in light of the evidence and reasoning presented.
548–551 Literary Research Report: Edit and Proofread Capitalization: Quotations Quotation Marks Parallel Structure Adjectives and Adverbs		L.9-10.1.a	Use parallel structure.
		L.9-10.2	Demonstrate command of the conventions of standard English capitalization, punctuation, and spelling when writing.
		L.9-10.3.a	Write and edit work so that it conforms to the guidelines in a style manual appropriate for the discipline and writing type.
551	Literary Research Report: Publish and Present	SL.9-10.1	Initiate and participate effectively in a range of collaborative discussions (one-on-one, in groups, and teacher-led) with diverse partners on grades 9–10 topics, texts, and issues, building on others' ideas and expressing their own clearly and persuasively.
		SL.9-10.4	Present information, findings, and supporting evidence clearly, concisely, and logically such that listeners can follow the line of reasoning and the organization, development, substance, and style are appropriate to purpose, audience, and task.
		SL.9-10.6	Adapt speech to a variety of contexts and tasks, demonstrating command of formal English when indicated or appropriate.

Common Core State Standards, continued

Student Handbooks, continued

UNIT 6: Rights and Responsibilities

SE Pages	Lesson	Code	Standards Text
552–553	**Discuss the Essential Question**	SL.9-10.1.b	Work with peers to set rules for collegial discussions and decision-making, clear goals and deadlines, and individual roles as needed
		SL.9-10.3	Evaluate a speaker's point of view, reasoning, and use of evidence and rhetoric, identifying any fallacious reasoning or exaggerated or distorted evidence.
554	**Analyze and Debate**	SL.9-10.4	Present information, findings, and supporting evidence clearly, concisely, and logically such that listeners can follow the line of reasoning and the organization, development, substance, and style are appropriate to purpose, audience, and task.
555	**Plan a Project**	SL.9-10.1.b	Work with peers to set rules for collegial discussions and decision-making (e.g., informal consensus, taking votes on key issues, presentation of alternate views), clear goals and deadlines, and individual roles as needed.
555	**Choose More to Read**	RL.9-10.10	By the end of grade 10, read and comprehend literature, including stories, dramas, and poems, at the high end of the grades 9–10 text complexity band independently and proficiently.
		RI.9-10.10	By the end of grade 10, read and comprehend literary nonfiction at the high end of the grades 9–10 text complexity band independently and proficiently.
556–559	**How to Read Persuasive Nonfiction**	RI.9-10.1	Cite strong and thorough textual evidence to support analysis of what the text says explicitly as well as inferences drawn from the text.
		RI.9-10.8	Delineate and evaluate the argument and specific claims in a text, assessing whether the reasoning is valid and the evidence is relevant and sufficient; identify false statements and fallacious reasoning.
		L.9-10.6	Acquire and use accurately general academic and domain-specific words and phrases, sufficient for reading, writing, speaking, and listening at the college and career readiness level; demonstrate independence in gathering vocabulary knowledge when considering a word or phrase important to comprehension or expression.

Cluster 1

SE Pages	Lesson	Code	Standards Text
560	**Prepare to Read**	RI.9-10.4	Determine the meaning of words and phrases as they are used in a text, including figurative, connotative, and technical meanings; analyze the cumulative impact of specific word choices on meaning and tone.
		SL.9-10.1	Initiate and participate effectively in a range of collaborative discussions (one-on-one, in groups, and teacher-led) with diverse partners on grades 9–10 topics, texts, and issues, building on others' ideas and expressing their own clearly and persuasively.
		L.9-10.6	Acquire and use accurately general academic and domain-specific words and phrases, sufficient for reading, writing, speaking, and listening at the college and career readiness level; demonstrate independence in gathering vocabulary knowledge when considering a word or phrase important to comprehension or expression.
561	**Before Reading: Too Young to Drive?**	RI.9-10.8	Delineate and evaluate the argument and specific claims in a text, assessing whether the reasoning is valid and the evidence is relevant and sufficient; identify false statements and fallacious reasoning.

SE Pages	Lesson	Code	Standards Text
562–569	Read Too Young to Drive?	RI.9-10.1	Cite strong and thorough textual evidence to support analysis of what the text says explicitly as well as inferences drawn from the text.
		RI.9-10.2	Determine a central idea of a text and analyze its development over the course of the text, including how it emerges and is shaped and refined by specific details; provide an objective summary of the text.
		RI.9-10.8	Delineate and evaluate the argument and specific claims in a text, assessing whether the reasoning is valid and the evidence is relevant and sufficient; identify false statements and fallacious reasoning.
		RI.9-10.10	By the end of grade 10, read and comprehend literary nonfiction at the high end of the grades 9–10 text complexity band independently and proficiently.
		W.9-10.1	Write arguments to support claims in an analysis of substantive topics or texts, using valid reasoning and relevant and sufficient evidence.
		W.9-10.9.b	Apply grades 9–10 Reading standards to literary nonfiction.
		W.9-10.10	Write routinely over extended time frames (time for research, reflection, and revision) and shorter time frames (a single sitting or a day or two) for a range of tasks, purposes, and audiences.
		L.9-10.1.b	Use various types of phrases (noun, verb, adjectival, adverbial, participial, prepositional, absolute) and clauses (independent, dependent; noun, relative, adverbial) to convey specific meanings and add variety and interest to writing or presentations.
		L.9-10.6	Acquire and use accurately general academic and domain-specific words and phrases, sufficient for reading, writing, speaking, and listening at the college and career readiness level; demonstrate independence in gathering vocabulary knowledge when considering a word or phrase important to comprehension or expression.
570	Before Reading: Rules of the Road	RI.9-10.3	Analyze how the author unfolds an analysis or series of ideas or events, including the order in which the points are made, how they are introduced and developed, and the connections that are drawn between them.
		RI.9-10.10	By the end of grade 10, read and comprehend literary nonfiction at the high end of the grades 9–10 text complexity band independently and proficiently.
571–576	Read Rules of the Road	RI.9-10.3	Analyze how the author unfolds an analysis or series of ideas or events, including the order in which the points are made, how they are introduced and developed, and the connections that are drawn between them.
		RI.9-10.7	Analyze various accounts of a subject told in different mediums, determining which details are emphasized in each account.
		RI.9-10.10	By the end of grade 10, read and comprehend literary nonfiction at the high end of the grades 9–10 text complexity band independently and proficiently.
		W.9-10.1	Write arguments to support claims in an analysis of substantive topics or texts, using valid reasoning and relevant and sufficient evidence.
		W.9-10.9.b	Apply grades 9–10 Reading standards to literary nonfiction.

Common Core State Standards, continued

Cluster 1, continued

SE Pages	Lesson	Code	Standards Text
571–576	**Read Rules of the Road** continued	W.9-10.10	Write routinely over extended time frames (time for research, reflection, and revision) and shorter time frames (a single sitting or a day or two) for a range of tasks, purposes, and audiences.
		L.9-10.1.a	Use parallel structure.
		L.9-10.1.b	Use various types of phrases (noun, verb, adjectival, adverbial, participial, prepositional, absolute) and clauses (independent, dependent; noun, relative, adverbial) to convey specific meanings and add variety and interest to writing or presentations.
		L.9-10.4	Determine or clarify the meaning of unknown and multiple-meaning words and phrases based on grades 9–10 reading and content, choosing flexibly from a range of strategies.
		L.9-10.5.a	Interpret figures of speech in context and analyze their role in the text.
		L.9-10.6	Acquire and use accurately general academic and domain-specific words and phrases, sufficient for reading, writing, speaking, and listening at the college and career readiness level; demonstrate independence in gathering vocabulary knowledge when considering a word or phrase important to comprehension or expression.
577	**Reflect and Assess Critical Thinking**	RI.9-10.1	Cite strong and thorough textual evidence to support analysis of what the text says explicitly as well as inferences drawn from the text.
		RI.9-10.8	Delineate and evaluate the argument and specific claims in a text, assessing whether the reasoning is valid and the evidence is relevant and sufficient; identify false statements and fallacious reasoning.
	Write About Literature	RI.9-10.10	By the end of grade 10, read and comprehend literary nonfiction at the high end of the grades 9–10 text complexity band independently and proficiently.
		W.9-10.1	Write arguments to support claims in an analysis of substantive topics or texts, using valid reasoning and relevant and sufficient evidence.
	Key Vocabulary Review	L.9-10.6	Acquire and use accurately general academic and domain-specific words and phrases, sufficient for reading, writing, speaking, and listening at the college and career readiness level; demonstrate independence in gathering vocabulary knowledge when considering a word or phrase important to comprehension or expression.
	Read with Ease: Phrasing	RI.9-10.10	By the end of grade 10, read and comprehend literary nonfiction at the high end of the grades 9–10 text complexity band independently and proficiently.
578	**Grammar: Vary Your Sentences**	L.9-10.1.a	Use parallel structure.
		L.9-10.1.b	Use various types of phrases (noun, verb, adjectival, adverbial, participial, prepositional, absolute) and clauses (independent, dependent; noun, relative, adverbial) to convey specific meanings and add variety and interest to writing or presentations.
578	**Literary Analysis: Bias**	RI.9-10.6	Determine an author's point of view or purpose in a text and analyze how an author uses rhetoric to advance that point of view or purpose.
		RI.9-10.8	Delineate and evaluate the argument and specific claims in a text, assessing whether the reasoning is valid and the evidence is relevant and sufficient; identify false statements and fallacious reasoning.

Cluster 1, continued

SE Pages	Lesson	Code	Standards Text
578	Language Development: Support Opinions	SL.9-10.4	Present information, findings, and supporting evidence clearly, concisely, and logically such that listeners can follow the line of reasoning and the organization, development, substance, and style are appropriate to purpose, audience, and task.
579	Vocabulary Study: Denotation and Connotation	L.9-10.4.c	Consult general and specialized reference materials, both print and digital, to find the pronunciation of a word or determine or clarify its precise meaning, its part of speech, or its etymology.
		L.9-10.5.b	Analyze nuances in the meaning of words with similar denotations.
579	Writing on Demand: Write a Short Persuasive Essay	W.9-10.1	Write arguments to support claims in an analysis of substantive topics or texts, using valid reasoning and relevant and sufficient evidence.
		W.9-10.4	Produce clear and coherent writing in which the development, organization, and style are appropriate to task, purpose, and audience.
579	Listening/Speaking: Interview	SL.9-10.6	Adapt speech to a variety of contexts and tasks, demonstrating command of formal English when indicated or appropriate.
580	Workplace Workshop: Inside Public Transit	W.9-10.1.d	Establish and maintain a formal style and objective tone while attending to the norms and conventions of the discipline in which they are writing.
		W.9-10.10	Write routinely over extended time frames (time for research, reflection, and revision) and shorter time frames (a single sitting or a day or two) for a range of tasks, purposes, and audiences.
581	Vocabulary Workshop: Build Word Knowledge	L.9-10.4.c	Consult general and specialized reference materials, both print and digital, to find the pronunciation of a word or determine or clarify its precise meaning, its part of speech, or its etymology.
		L.9-10.5.b	Analyze nuances in the meaning of words with similar denotations.

Cluster 2

SE Pages	Lesson	Code	Standards Text
582	Prepare to Read	RI.9-10.4	Determine the meaning of words and phrases as they are used in a text, including figurative, connotative, and technical meanings; analyze the cumulative impact of specific word choices on meaning and tone.
		SL.9-10.1	Initiate and participate effectively in a range of collaborative discussions (one-on-one, in groups, and teacher-led) with diverse partners on grades 9–10 topics, texts, and issues, building on others' ideas and expressing their own clearly and persuasively.
		L.9-10.6	Acquire and use accurately general academic and domain-specific words and phrases, sufficient for reading, writing, speaking, and listening at the college and career readiness level; demonstrate independence in gathering vocabulary knowledge when considering a word or phrase important to comprehension or expression.
583	Before Reading: Piracy Bites!	RI.9-10.8	Delineate and evaluate the argument and specific claims in a text, assessing whether the reasoning is valid and the evidence is relevant and sufficient; identify false statements and fallacious reasoning.

Common Core State Standards, continued

Cluster 2, continued

SE Pages	Lesson	Code	Standards Text
584–592	**Read Piracy Bites!**	RI.9-10.1	Cite strong and thorough textual evidence to support analysis of what the text says explicitly as well as inferences drawn from the text.
		RI.9-10.8	Delineate and evaluate the argument and specific claims in a text, assessing whether the reasoning is valid and the evidence is relevant and sufficient; identify false statements and fallacious reasoning.
		RI.9-10.10	By the end of grade 10, read and comprehend literary nonfiction at the high end of the grades 9–10 text complexity band independently and proficiently.
		W.9-10.1	Write arguments to support claims in an analysis of substantive topics or texts, using valid reasoning and relevant and sufficient evidence.
		W.9-10.9.b	Apply grades 9–10 Reading standards to literary nonfiction.
		W.9-10.10	Write routinely over extended time frames (time for research, reflection, and revision) and shorter time frames (a single sitting or a day or two) for a range of tasks, purposes, and audiences.
		L.9-10.1.b	Use various types of phrases (noun, verb, adjectival, adverbial, participial, prepositional, absolute) and clauses (independent, dependent; noun, relative, adverbial) to convey specific meanings and add variety and interest to writing or presentations.
		L.9-10.6	Acquire and use accurately general academic and domain-specific words and phrases, sufficient for reading, writing, speaking, and listening at the college and career readiness level; demonstrate independence in gathering vocabulary knowledge when considering a word or phrase important to comprehension or expression.
593	**Postscript: Comic**	RI.9-10.1	Cite strong and thorough textual evidence to support analysis of what the text says explicitly as well as inferences drawn from the text.
		RI.9-10.8	Delineate and evaluate the argument and specific claims in a text, assessing whether the reasoning is valid and the evidence is relevant and sufficient; identify false statements and fallacious reasoning.
594	**Before Reading: Doonesbury on Downloading**	RL.9-10.2	Determine a theme or central idea of a text and analyze in detail its development over the course of the text, including how it emerges and is shaped and refined by specific details; provide an objective summary of the text.
		RL.9-10.10	By the end of grade 10, read and comprehend literature, including stories, dramas, and poems, at the high end of the grades 9–10 text complexity band independently and proficiently.
595–600	**Read Doonesbury on Downloading**	RL.9-10.1	Cite strong and thorough textual evidence to support analysis of what the text says explicitly as well as inferences drawn from the text.
		RL.9-10.2	Determine a theme or central idea of a text and analyze in detail its development over the course of the text, including how it emerges and is shaped and refined by specific details; provide an objective summary of the text.
		RL.9-10.10	By the end of grade 10, read and comprehend literature, including stories, dramas, and poems, at the high end of the grades 9–10 text complexity band independently and proficiently.

Cluster 2, continued

SE Pages	Lesson	Code	Standards Text
595–600	**Read Doonesbury on Downloading** continued	RI.9-10.10	By the end of grade 10, read and comprehend literary nonfiction at the high end of the grades 9–10 text complexity band independently and proficiently.
		W.9-10.1	Write arguments to support claims in an analysis of substantive topics or texts, using valid reasoning and relevant and sufficient evidence.
		W.9-10.9.a	Apply grades 9–10 Reading standards to literature.
		W.9-10.10	Write routinely over extended time frames (time for research, reflection, and revision) and shorter time frames (a single sitting or a day or two) for a range of tasks, purposes, and audiences.
		L.9-10.1.b	Use various types of phrases (noun, verb, adjectival, adverbial, participial, prepositional, absolute) and clauses (independent, dependent; noun, relative, adverbial) to convey specific meanings and add variety and interest to writing or presentations.
		L.9-10.2.a	Use a semicolon (and perhaps a conjunctive adverb) to link two or more closely related independent clauses.
		L.9-10.6	Acquire and use accurately general academic and domain-specific words and phrases, sufficient for reading, writing, speaking, and listening at the college and career readiness level; demonstrate independence in gathering vocabulary knowledge when considering a word or phrase important to comprehension or expression.
601	**Reflect and Assess Critical Thinking**	RL.9-10.10	By the end of grade 10, read and comprehend literature, including stories, dramas, and poems, at the high end of the grades 9–10 text complexity band independently and proficiently.
		RI.9-10.10	By the end of grade 10, read and comprehend literary nonfiction at the high end of the grades 9–10 text complexity band independently and proficiently.
		SL.9-10.1	Initiate and participate effectively in a range of collaborative discussions (one-on-one, in groups, and teacher-led) with diverse partners on grades 9–10 topics, texts, and issues, building on others' ideas and expressing their own clearly and persuasively.
	Write About Literature	W.9-10.1	Write arguments to support claims in an analysis of substantive topics or texts, using valid reasoning and relevant and sufficient evidence.
	Key Vocabulary Review	L.9-10.6	Acquire and use accurately general academic and domain-specific words and phrases, sufficient for reading, writing, speaking, and listening at the college and career readiness level; demonstrate independence in gathering vocabulary knowledge when considering a word or phrase important to comprehension or expression.
	Read with Ease: Expression	RI.9-10.10	By the end of grade 10, read and comprehend literary nonfiction at the high end of the grades 9–10 text complexity band independently and proficiently.
602	**Grammar: Use Compound Sentences**	L.9-10.1.b	Use various types of phrases (noun, verb, adjectival, adverbial, participial, prepositional, absolute) and clauses (independent, dependent; noun, relative, adverbial) to convey specific meanings and add variety and interest to writing or presentations.
		L.9-10.2.a	Use a semicolon (and perhaps a conjunctive adverb) to link two or more closely related independent clauses.

Common Core State Standards, continued

Cluster 2, continued

SE Pages	Lesson	Code	Standards Text
602	Language Development: Persuade	SL.9-10.4	Present information, findings, and supporting evidence clearly, concisely, and logically such that listeners can follow the line of reasoning and the organization, development, substance, and style are appropriate to purpose, audience, and task.
602	Literary Analysis: Faulty Persuasive Techniques	RI.9-10.8	Delineate and evaluate the argument and specific claims in a text, assessing whether the reasoning is valid and the evidence is relevant and sufficient; identify false statements and fallacious reasoning.
603	Vocabulary Study: Connotation	L.9-10.5	Demonstrate understanding of figurative language, word relationships, and nuances in word meanings.
603	Writing: Write a Position Statement	W.9-10.1	Write arguments to support claims in an analysis of substantive topics or texts, using valid reasoning and relevant and sufficient evidence.
		W.9-10.5	Develop and strengthen writing as needed by planning, revising, editing, rewriting, or trying a new approach, focusing on addressing what is most significant for a specific purpose and audience.
603	Listening/Speaking: Oral Report	W.9-10.7	Conduct short as well as more sustained research projects to answer a question (including a self-generated question) or solve a problem; narrow or broaden the inquiry when appropriate; synthesize multiple sources on the subject, demonstrating understanding of the subject under investigation.
		SL.9-10.4	Present information, findings, and supporting evidence clearly, concisely, and logically such that listeners can follow the line of reasoning and the organization, development, substance, and style are appropriate to purpose, audience, and task.
604–605	Listening and Speaking Workshop: Persuasive Speech	SL.9-10.3	Evaluate a speaker's point of view, reasoning, and use of evidence and rhetoric, identifying any fallacious reasoning or exaggerated or distorted evidence.
		SL.9-10.4	Present information, findings, and supporting evidence clearly, concisely, and logically such that listeners can follow the line of reasoning and the organization, development, substance, and style are appropriate to purpose, audience, and task.
		SL.9-10.5	Make strategic use of digital media in presentations to enhance understanding of findings, reasoning, and evidence and to add interest.
		SL.9-10.6	Adapt speech to a variety of contexts and tasks, demonstrating command of formal English when indicated or appropriate.
		L.9-10.3	Apply knowledge of language to understand how language functions in different contexts, to make effective choices for meaning or style, and to comprehend more fully when reading or listening.

Cluster 3

SE Pages	Lesson	Code	Standards Text
606	Prepare to Read	RI.9-10.4	Determine the meaning of words and phrases as they are used in a text, including figurative, connotative, and technical meanings; analyze the cumulative impact of specific word choices on meaning and tone.
		SL.9-10.1	Initiate and participate effectively in a range of collaborative discussions (one-on-one, in groups, and teacher-led) with diverse partners on grades 9–10 topics, texts, and issues, building on others' ideas and expressing their own clearly and persuasively.

Cluster 3, continued

SE Pages	Lesson	Code	Standards Text
606	**Prepare to Read** continued	L.9-10.6	Acquire and use accurately general academic and domain-specific words and phrases, sufficient for reading, writing, speaking, and listening at the college and career readiness level; demonstrate independence in gathering vocabulary knowledge when considering a word or phrase important to comprehension or expression.
607	**Before Reading: Long Walk to Freedom**	RI.9-10.4	Determine the meaning of words and phrases as they are used in a text, including figurative, connotative, and technical meanings; analyze the cumulative impact of specific word choices on meaning and tone.
		RI.9-10.6	Determine an author's point of view or purpose in a text and analyze how an author uses rhetoric to advance that point of view or purpose.
		RI.9-10.10	By the end of grade 10, read and comprehend literary nonfiction at the high end of the grades 9–10 text complexity band independently and proficiently.
608–620	**Read Long Walk to Freedom**	RI.9-10.1	Cite strong and thorough textual evidence to support analysis of what the text says explicitly as well as inferences drawn from the text.
		RI.9-10.2	Determine a central idea of a text and analyze its development over the course of the text, including how it emerges and is shaped and refined by specific details; provide an objective summary of the text.
		RI.9-10.4	Determine the meaning of words and phrases as they are used in a text, including figurative, connotative, and technical meanings; analyze the cumulative impact of specific word choices on meaning and tone.
		RI.9-10.5	Analyze in detail how an author's ideas or claims are developed and refined by particular sentences, paragraphs, or larger portions of a text.
		RI.9-10.6	Determine an author's point of view or purpose in a text and analyze how an author uses rhetoric to advance that point of view or purpose.
		RI.9-10.7	Analyze various accounts of a subject told in different mediums, determining which details are emphasized in each account.
		RI.9-10.10	By the end of grade 10, read and comprehend literary nonfiction at the high end of the grades 9–10 text complexity band independently and proficiently.
		W.9-10.1	Write arguments to support claims in an analysis of substantive topics or texts, using valid reasoning and relevant and sufficient evidence.
		W.9-10.9.b	Apply grades 9–10 Reading standards to literary nonfiction.
		W.9-10.10	Write routinely over extended time frames (time for research, reflection, and revision) and shorter time frames (a single sitting or a day or two) for a range of tasks, purposes, and audiences.
		SL.9-10.1.a	Come to discussions prepared, having read and researched material under study; explicitly draw on that preparation by referring to evidence from texts and other research on the topic or issue to stimulate a thoughtful, well-reasoned exchange of ideas.
		L.9-10.1.b	Use various types of phrases (noun, verb, adjectival, adverbial, participial, prepositional, absolute) and clauses (independent, dependent; noun, relative, adverbial) to convey specific meanings and add variety and interest to writing or presentations.

Common Core State Standards, continued

Cluster 3, continued

SE Pages	Lesson	Code	Standards Text
608–620	Read Long Walk to Freedom continued	L.9-10.4.b	Identify and correctly use patterns of word changes that indicate different meanings or parts of speech.
		L.9-10.4.c	Consult general and specialized reference materials, both print and digital, to find the pronunciation of a word or determine or clarify its precise meaning, its part of speech, or its etymology.
		L.9-10.5.b	Analyze nuances in the meaning of words with similar denotations.
		L.9-10.6	Acquire and use accurately general academic and domain-specific words and phrases, sufficient for reading, writing, speaking, and listening at the college and career readiness level; demonstrate independence in gathering vocabulary knowledge when considering a word or phrase important to comprehension or expression.
621	Postscript: The Art of Nelson Mandela	RI.9-10.2	Determine a central idea of a text and analyze its development over the course of the text, including how it emerges and is shaped and refined by specific details; provide an objective summary of the text.
622	Before Reading: We Hold These Truths	RI.9-10.9	Analyze seminal U.S. documents of historical and literary significance, including how they address related themes and concepts.
		RI.9-10.10	By the end of grade 10, read and comprehend literary nonfiction at the high end of the grades 9–10 text complexity band independently and proficiently.
623–626	Read We Hold These Truths	RI.9-10.6	Determine an author's point of view or purpose in a text and analyze how an author uses rhetoric to advance that point of view or purpose.
		RI.9-10.9	Analyze seminal U.S. documents of historical and literary significance, including how they address related themes and concepts.
		RI.9-10.10	By the end of grade 10, read and comprehend literary nonfiction at the high end of the grades 9–10 text complexity band independently and proficiently.
		W.9-10.1	Write arguments to support claims in an analysis of substantive topics or texts, using valid reasoning and relevant and sufficient evidence.
		W.9-10.9	Draw evidence from literary or informational texts to support analysis, reflection, and research.
		W.9-10.9.b	Apply grades 9–10 Reading standards to literary nonfiction.
		W.9-10.10	Write routinely over extended time frames (time for research, reflection, and revision) and shorter time frames (a single sitting or a day or two) for a range of tasks, purposes, and audiences.
		L.9-10.1.b	Use various types of phrases (noun, verb, adjectival, adverbial, participial, prepositional, absolute) and clauses (independent, dependent; noun, relative, adverbial) to convey specific meanings and add variety and interest to writing or presentations.
		L.9-10.2.a	Use a semicolon (and perhaps a conjunctive adverb) to link two or more closely related independent clauses.
		L.9-10.5	Demonstrate understanding of figurative language, word relationships, and nuances in word meanings.

Cluster 3, continued

SE Pages	Lesson	Code	Standards Text
623–626	Read We Hold These Truths continued	L.9-10.6	Acquire and use accurately general academic and domain-specific words and phrases, sufficient for reading, writing, speaking, and listening at the college and career readiness level; demonstrate independence in gathering vocabulary knowledge when considering a word or phrase important to comprehension or expression.
627	Reflect and Assess Critical Thinking	RI.9-10.1	Cite strong and thorough textual evidence to support analysis of what the text says explicitly as well as inferences drawn from the text.
		RI.9-10.10	By the end of grade 10, read and comprehend literary nonfiction at the high end of the grades 9–10 text complexity band independently and proficiently.
		SL.9-10.1	Initiate and participate effectively in a range of collaborative discussions (one-on-one, in groups, and teacher-led) with diverse partners on grades 9–10 topics, texts, and issues, building on others' ideas and expressing their own clearly and persuasively.
	Write About Literature	W.9-10.1	Write arguments to support claims in an analysis of substantive topics or texts, using valid reasoning and relevant and sufficient evidence.
	Key Vocabulary Review	L.9-10.6	Acquire and use accurately general academic and domain-specific words and phrases, sufficient for reading, writing, speaking, and listening at the college and career readiness level; demonstrate independence in gathering vocabulary knowledge when considering a word or phrase important to comprehension or expression.
	Read with Ease: Intonation	RI.9-10.10	By the end of grade 10, read and comprehend literary nonfiction at the high end of the grades 9–10 text complexity band independently and proficiently.
628	Grammar: Use Complex Sentences	L.9-10.1.b	Use various types of phrases (noun, verb, adjectival, adverbial, participial, prepositional, absolute) and clauses (independent, dependent; noun, relative, adverbial) to convey specific meanings and add variety and interest to writing or presentations.
628	Literary Analysis: Rhetorical Devices	RI.9-10.6	Determine an author's point of view or purpose in a text and analyze how an author uses rhetoric to advance that point of view or purpose.
628	Language Development: Persuade	SL.9-10.4	Present information, findings, and supporting evidence clearly, concisely, and logically such that listeners can follow the line of reasoning and the organization, development, substance, and style are appropriate to purpose, audience, and task.
629	Vocabulary Study: Denotation and Connotation	L.9-10.5.b	Analyze nuances in the meaning of words with similar denotations.
629	Writing Trait: Development of Ideas	W.9-10.5	Develop and strengthen writing as needed by planning, revising, editing, rewriting, or trying a new approach, focusing on addressing what is most significant for a specific purpose and audience.
629	Research/Speaking: Opinion Poll	W.9-10.7	Conduct short as well as more sustained research projects to answer a question (including a self-generated question) or solve a problem; narrow or broaden the inquiry when appropriate; synthesize multiple sources on the subject, demonstrating understanding of the subject under investigation.
		SL.9-10.6	Adapt speech to a variety of contexts and tasks, demonstrating command of formal English when indicated or appropriate.

Common Core State Standards, continued

Close Reading

SE Pages	Lesson	Code	Standards Text
630–633	**Read What to the Slave Is the Fourth of July?**	RI.9-10.10	By the end of grade 10, read and comprehend literary nonfiction at the high end of the grades 9–10 text complexity band independently and proficiently.

Unit Wrap-Up

SE Pages	Lesson	Code	Standards Text
634	**Unit Wrap-Up Present Your Project**	SL.9-10.3	Evaluate a speaker's point of view, reasoning, and use of evidence and rhetoric, identifying any fallacious reasoning or exaggerated or distorted evidence.
		SL.9-10.4	Present information, findings, and supporting evidence clearly, concisely, and logically such that listeners can follow the line of reasoning and the organization, development, substance, and style are appropriate to purpose, audience, and task.
	Reflect on Your Reading	SL.9-10.1	Initiate and participate effectively in a range of collaborative discussions (one-on-one, in groups, and teacher-led) with diverse partners on grades 9–10 topics, texts, and issues, building on others' ideas and expressing their own clearly and persuasively.
		SL.9-10.1.a	Come to discussions prepared, having read and researched material under study; explicitly draw on that preparation by referring to evidence from texts and other research on the topic or issue to stimulate a thoughtful, well-reasoned exchange of ideas.
	Respond to the Essential Question	SL.9-10.1.a	Come to discussions prepared, having read and researched material under study; explicitly draw on that preparation by referring to evidence from texts and other research on the topic or issue to stimulate a thoughtful, well-reasoned exchange of ideas.

Writing Project: Persuasive Essay

SE Pages	Lesson	Code	Standards Text
635–639	**Study Persuasive Essays and Prewrite**	W.9-10.1.a	Introduce precise claim(s), distinguish the claim(s) from alternate or opposing claims, and create an organization that establishes clear relationships among claim(s), counterclaims, reasons, and evidence.
		W.9-10.1.b	Develop claim(s) and counterclaims fairly, supplying evidence for each while pointing out the strengths and limitations of both in a manner that anticipates the audience's knowledge level and concerns.
		W.9-10.5	Develop and strengthen writing as needed by planning, revising, editing, rewriting, or trying a new approach, focusing on addressing what is most significant for a specific purpose and audience.
		W.9-10.6	Use technology, including the Internet, to produce, publish, and update individual or shared writing products, taking advantage of technology's capacity to link to other information and to display information flexibly and dynamically.
		W.9-10.7	Conduct short as well as more sustained research projects to answer a question (including a self-generated question) or solve a problem; narrow or broaden the inquiry when appropriate; synthesize multiple sources on the subject, demonstrating understanding of the subject under investigation.
		W.9-10.8	Gather relevant information from multiple authoritative print and digital sources, using advanced searches effectively; assess the usefulness of each source in answering the research question; integrate information into the text selectively to maintain the flow of ideas, avoiding plagiarism and following a standard format for citation.

Writing Project: Persuasive Essay, continued

SE Pages	Lesson	Code	Standards Text
640–641	**Persuasive Essay: Draft**	W.9-10.1	Write arguments to support claims in an analysis of substantive topics or texts, using valid reasoning and relevant and sufficient evidence.
		W.9-10.1.e	Provide a concluding statement or section that follows from and supports the argument presented.
		W.9-10.4	Produce clear and coherent writing in which the development, organization, and style are appropriate to task, purpose, and audience.
642–645	**Persuasive Essay: Revise** **Trait: Focus and Unity**	W.9-10.1.a	Introduce precise claim(s), distinguish the claim(s) from alternate or opposing claims, and create an organization that establishes clear relationships among claim(s), counterclaims, reasons, and evidence.
		W.9-10.1.b	Develop claim(s) and counterclaims fairly, supplying evidence for each while pointing out the strengths and limitations of both in a manner that anticipates the audience's knowledge level and concerns.
		W.9-10.1.c	Use words, phrases, and clauses to link the major sections of the text, create cohesion, and clarify the relationships between claim(s) and reasons, between reasons and evidence, and between claim(s) and counterclaims.
		W.9-10.1.e	Provide a concluding statement or section that follows from and supports the argument presented.
		W.9-10.4	Produce clear and coherent writing in which the development, organization, and style are appropriate to task, purpose, and audience.
		W.9-10.5	Develop and strengthen writing as needed by planning, revising, editing, rewriting, or trying a new approach, focusing on addressing what is most significant for a specific purpose and audience.
		SL.9-10.1	Initiate and participate effectively in a range of collaborative discussions (one-on-one, in groups, and teacher-led) with diverse partners on grades 9–10 topics, texts, and issues, building on others' ideas and expressing their own clearly and persuasively.
		SL.9-10.1.d	Respond thoughtfully to diverse perspectives, summarize points of agreement and disagreement, and, when warranted, qualify or justify their own views and understanding and make new connections in light of the evidence and reasoning presented.
646–648	**Persuasive Essay: Edit and Proofread** **Capitalization: Names of Days, Months, and Holidays** **Commas with Introductory Phrases and Clauses** **Precise Language** **Effective Sentences**	L.9-10.1.b	Use various types of phrases (noun, verb, adjectival, adverbial, participial, prepositional, absolute) and clauses (independent, dependent; noun, relative, adverbial) to convey specific meanings and add variety and interest to writing or presentations.
		L.9-10.2	Demonstrate command of the conventions of standard English capitalization, punctuation, and spelling when writing.
		L.9-10.3	Apply knowledge of language to understand how language functions in different contexts, to make effective choices for meaning or style, and to comprehend more fully when reading or listening.
		L.9-10.3.a	Write and edit work so that it conforms to the guidelines in a style manual appropriate for the discipline and writing type.

Common Core State Standards, continued

Writing Project: Persuasive Essay, continued

SE Pages	Lesson	Code	Standards Text
646–648	Persuasive Essay: Edit and Proofread Capitalization: Names of Days, Months, and Holidays Commas with Introductory Phrases and Clauses Precise Language Effective Sentences continued	L.9-10.6	Acquire and use accurately general academic and domain-specific words and phrases, sufficient for reading, writing, speaking, and listening at the college and career readiness level; demonstrate independence in gathering vocabulary knowledge when considering a word or phrase important to comprehension or expression.
649	Persuasive Essay: Publish and Present	W.9-10.5	Develop and strengthen writing as needed by planning, revising, editing, rewriting, or trying a new approach, focusing on addressing what is most significant for a specific purpose and audience.
		W.9-10.6	Use technology, including the Internet, to produce, publish, and update individual or shared writing products, taking advantage of technology's capacity to link to other information and to display information flexibly and dynamically.
		SL.9-10.1.a	Come to discussions prepared, having read and researched material under study; explicitly draw on that preparation by referring to evidence from texts and other research on the topic or issue to stimulate a thoughtful, well-reasoned exchange of ideas.
		SL.9-10.1.d	Respond thoughtfully to diverse perspectives, summarize points of agreement and disagreement, and, when warranted, qualify or justify their own views and understanding and make new connections in light of the evidence and reasoning presented.
		SL.9-10.3	Evaluate a speaker's point of view, reasoning, and use of evidence and rhetoric, identifying any fallacious reasoning or exaggerated or distorted evidence.

UNIT 7: For What It's Worth

SE Pages	Lesson	Code	Standards Text
650–651	Discuss the Essential Question	SL.9-10.1.b	Work with peers to set rules for collegial discussions and decision-making, clear goals and deadlines, and individual roles as needed.
		SL.9-10.3	Evaluate a speaker's point of view, reasoning, and use of evidence and rhetoric, identifying any fallacious reasoning or exaggerated or distorted evidence.
652	Analyze and Debate	SL.9-10.4	Present information, findings, and supporting evidence clearly, concisely, and logically such that listeners can follow the line of reasoning and the organization, development, substance, and style are appropriate to purpose, audience, and task.
653	Plan a Project	SL.9-10.1.b	Work with peers to set rules for collegial discussions and decision-making, clear goals and deadlines, and individual roles as needed.
653	Choose More to Read	RL.9-10.10	By the end of grade 10, read and comprehend literature, including stories, dramas, and poems, at the high end of the grades 9–10 text complexity band independently and proficiently.
		RI.9-10.10	By the end of grade 10, read and comprehend literary nonfiction at the high end of the grades 9–10 text complexity band independently and proficiently.
654–657	How to Read Drama	RL.9-10.1	Cite strong and thorough textual evidence to support analysis of what the text says explicitly as well as inferences drawn from the text.

UNIT 7: For What It's Worth, continued

SE Pages	Lesson	Code	Standards Text
654–657	**How to Read Drama** continued	RL.9-10.4	Determine the meaning of words and phrases as they are used in the text, including figurative and connotative meanings; analyze the cumulative impact of specific word choices on meaning and tone.
		RL.9-10.7	Analyze the representation of a subject or a key scene in two different artistic mediums, including what is emphasized or absent in each treatment.
		SL.9-10.1	Initiate and participate effectively in a range of collaborative discussions (one-on-one, in groups, and teacher-led) with diverse partners on grades 9–10 topics, texts, and issues, building on others' ideas and expressing their own clearly and persuasively.
658–659	**How to Read Poetry**	SL.9-10.4	Present information, findings, and supporting evidence clearly, concisely, and logically such that listeners can follow the line of reasoning and the organization, development, substance, and style are appropriate to purpose, audience, and task.
		L.9-10.6	Acquire and use accurately general academic and domain-specific words and phrases, sufficient for reading, writing, speaking, and listening at the college and career readiness level; demonstrate independence in gathering vocabulary knowledge when considering a word or phrase important to comprehension or expression.

Cluster 1

SE Pages	Lesson	Code	Standards Text
660	**Prepare to Read**	RI.9-10.4	Determine the meaning of words and phrases as they are used in a text, including figurative, connotative, and technical meanings; analyze the cumulative impact of specific word choices on meaning and tone.
		L.9-10.6	Acquire and use accurately general academic and domain-specific words and phrases, sufficient for reading, writing, speaking, and listening at the college and career readiness level; demonstrate independence in gathering vocabulary knowledge when considering a word or phrase important to comprehension or expression.
661	**Before Reading: The Jewels of the Shrine**	RL.9-10.4	Determine the meaning of words and phrases as they are used in the text, including figurative and connotative meanings; analyze the cumulative impact of specific word choices on meaning and tone.
		RL.9-10.5	Analyze how an author's choices concerning how to structure a text, order events within it, and manipulate time create such effects as mystery, tension, or surprise.
662–690	**Read The Jewels of the Shrine**	RL.9-10.1	Cite strong and thorough textual evidence to support analysis of what the text says explicitly as well as inferences drawn from the text.
		RL.9-10.4	Determine the meaning of words and phrases as they are used in the text, including figurative and connotative meanings; analyze the cumulative impact of specific word choices on meaning and tone.
		RL.9-10.5	Analyze how an author's choices concerning how to structure a text, order events within it, and manipulate time create such effects as mystery, tension, or surprise.
		RL.9-10.7	Analyze the representation of a subject or a key scene in two different artistic mediums, including what is emphasized or absent in each treatment.
		RL.9-10.10	By the end of grade 10, read and comprehend literature, including stories, dramas, and poems, at the high end of the grades 9–10 text complexity band independently and proficiently.

Common Core State Standards, continued

Cluster 1, continued

SE Pages	Lesson	Code	Standards Text
662–690	**Read The Jewels of the Shrine** continued	W.9-10.1	Write arguments to support claims in an analysis of substantive topics or texts, using valid reasoning and relevant and sufficient evidence.
		W.9-10.9.a	Apply grades 9–10 Reading standards to literature.
		W.9-10.10	Write routinely over extended time frames (time for research, reflection, and revision) and shorter time frames (a single sitting or a day or two) for a range of tasks, purposes, and audiences.
		SL.9-10.1.a	Come to discussions prepared, having read and researched material under study; explicitly draw on that preparation by referring to evidence from texts and other research on the topic or issue to stimulate a thoughtful, well-reasoned exchange of ideas.
		SL.9-10.6	Adapt speech to a variety of contexts and tasks, demonstrating command of formal English when indicated or appropriate.
		L.9-10.1.b	Use various types of phrases (noun, verb, adjectival, adverbial, participial, prepositional, absolute) and clauses (independent, dependent; noun, relative, adverbial) to convey specific meanings and add variety and interest to writing or presentations.
		L.9-10.5.a	Interpret figures of speech in context and analyze their role in the text.
		L.9-10.6	Acquire and use accurately general academic and domain-specific words and phrases, sufficient for reading, writing, speaking, and listening at the college and career readiness level; demonstrate independence in gathering vocabulary knowledge when considering a word or phrase important to comprehension or expression.
691	**Postscript: Lineage**	RL.9-10.2	Determine a theme or central idea of a text and analyze in detail its development over the course of the text, including how it emerges and is shaped and refined by specific details; provide an objective summary of the text.
		RL.9-10.7	Analyze the representation of a subject or a key scene in two different artistic mediums, including what is emphasized or absent in each treatment.
		RL.9-10.10	By the end of grade 10, read and comprehend literature, including stories, dramas, and poems, at the high end of the grades 9–10 text complexity band independently and proficiently.
		SL.9-10.6	Adapt speech to a variety of contexts and tasks, demonstrating command of formal English when indicated or appropriate.
692	**Before Reading: Remembered**	RL.9-10.4	Determine the meaning of words and phrases as they are used in the text, including figurative and connotative meanings; analyze the cumulative impact of specific word choices on meaning and tone.
693–696	**Read Remembered**	RL.9-10.1	Cite strong and thorough textual evidence to support analysis of what the text says explicitly as well as inferences drawn from the text.
		RL.9-10.2	Determine a theme or central idea of a text and analyze in detail its development over the course of the text, including how it emerges and is shaped and refined by specific details; provide an objective summary of the text.
		RL.9-10.4	Determine the meaning of words and phrases as they are used in the text, including figurative and connotative meanings; analyze the cumulative impact of specific word choices on meaning and tone.

Cluster 1, continued

SE Pages	Lesson	Code	Standards Text
693–696	**Read Remembered** continued	RL.9-10.10	By the end of grade 10, read and comprehend literature, including stories, dramas, and poems, at the high end of the grades 9–10 text complexity band independently and proficiently.
		W.9-10.1	Write arguments to support claims in an analysis of substantive topics or texts, using valid reasoning and relevant and sufficient evidence.
		W.9-10.9.a	Apply grades 9–10 Reading standards to literature.
		W.9-10.10	Write routinely over extended time frames (time for research, reflection, and revision) and shorter time frames (a single sitting or a day or two) for a range of tasks, purposes, and audiences.
		L.9-10.1.b	Use various types of phrases (noun, verb, adjectival, adverbial, participial, prepositional, absolute) and clauses (independent, dependent; noun, relative, adverbial) to convey specific meanings and add variety and interest to writing or presentations.
		L.9-10.2.c	Spell correctly.
		L.9-10.6	Acquire and use accurately general academic and domain-specific words and phrases, sufficient for reading, writing, speaking, and listening at the college and career readiness level; demonstrate independence in gathering vocabulary knowledge when considering a word or phrase important to comprehension or expression.
697	**Reflect and Assess Critical Thinking**	RL.9-10.1	Cite strong and thorough textual evidence to support analysis of what the text says explicitly as well as inferences drawn from the text.
		RL.9-10.2	Determine a theme or central idea of a text and analyze in detail its development over the course of the text, including how it emerges and is shaped and refined by specific details; provide an objective summary of the text.
	Write About Literature	RL.9-10.10	By the end of grade 10, read and comprehend literature, including stories, dramas, and poems, at the high end of the grades 9–10 text complexity band independently and proficiently.
		W.9-10.1	Write arguments to support claims in an analysis of substantive topics or texts, using valid reasoning and relevant and sufficient evidence.
	Key Vocabulary Review	L.9-10.6	Acquire and use accurately general academic and domain-specific words and phrases, sufficient for reading, writing, speaking, and listening at the college and career readiness level; demonstrate independence in gathering vocabulary knowledge when considering a word or phrase important to comprehension or expression.
	Read with Ease: Expression	RL.9-10.10	By the end of grade 10, read and comprehend literature, including stories, dramas, and poems, at the high end of the grades 9–10 text complexity band independently and proficiently.
698	**Grammar: Write in the Present Perfect Tense**	L.9-10.1.b	Use various types of phrases (noun, verb, adjectival, adverbial, participial, prepositional, absolute) and clauses (independent, dependent; noun, relative, adverbial) to convey specific meanings and add variety and interest to writing or presentations.
		L.9-10.2.c	Spell correctly.
698	**Literary Analysis: Character Foils**	RL.9-10.3	Analyze how complex characters develop over the course of a text, interact with other characters, and advance the plot or develop the theme.

Common Core State Standards, continued

Cluster 1, continued

SE Pages	Lesson	Code	Standards Text
698	Literary Analysis: Dialogue and Character Traits	RL.9-10.3	Analyze how complex characters develop over the course of a text, interact with other characters, and advance the plot or develop the theme.
698	Language Development: Justify	SL.9-10.4	Present information, findings, and supporting evidence clearly, concisely, and logically such that listeners can follow the line of reasoning and the organization, development, substance, and style are appropriate to purpose, audience, and task.
699	Vocabulary Study: Idioms	L.9-10.5.a	Interpret figures of speech in context and analyze their role in the text.
699	Writing: Write a Character Sketch	W.9-10.2	Write informative/explanatory texts to examine and convey complex ideas, concepts, and information clearly and accurately through the effective selection, organization, and analysis of content.
		W.9-10.5	Develop and strengthen writing as needed by planning, revising, editing, rewriting, or trying a new approach, focusing on addressing what is most significant for a specific purpose and audience.
699	Listening/Speaking: Dramatic Reading	RL.9-10.7	Analyze the representation of a subject or a key scene in two different artistic mediums, including what is emphasized or absent in each treatment.
		SL.9-10.6	Adapt speech to a variety of contexts and tasks, demonstrating command of formal English when indicated or appropriate.
700	Workplace Workshop: Inside a Bank	W.9-10.7	Conduct short as well as more sustained research projects to answer a question (including a self-generated question) or solve a problem; narrow or broaden the inquiry when appropriate; synthesize multiple sources on the subject, demonstrating understanding of the subject under investigation.
		W.9-10.8	Gather relevant information from multiple authoritative print and digital sources, using advanced searches effectively; assess the usefulness of each source in answering the research question; integrate information into the text selectively to maintain the flow of ideas, avoiding plagiarism and following a standard format for citation.
		L.9-10.6	Acquire and use accurately general academic and domain-specific words and phrases, sufficient for reading, writing, speaking, and listening at the college and career readiness level; demonstrate independence in gathering vocabulary knowledge when considering a word or phrase important to comprehension or expression.
701	Vocabulary Workshop: Interpret Non-Literal Language	L.9-10.4.a	Use context as a clue to the meaning of a word or phrase.
		L.9-10.5.a	Interpret figures of speech in context and analyze their role in the text.

Cluster 2

SE Pages	Lesson	Code	Standards Text
702	Prepare to Read	RI.9-10.4	Determine the meaning of words and phrases as they are used in a text, including figurative, connotative, and technical meanings; analyze the cumulative impact of specific word choices on meaning and tone.
		L.9-10.6	Acquire and use accurately general academic and domain-specific words and phrases, sufficient for reading, writing, speaking, and listening at the college and career readiness level; demonstrate independence in gathering vocabulary knowledge when considering a word or phrase important to comprehension or expression.

Cluster 2, continued

SE Pages	Lesson	Code	Standards Text
703	**Before Reading: Romeo and Juliet**	RL.9-10.4	Determine the meaning of words and phrases as they are used in the text, including figurative and connotative meanings; analyze the cumulative impact of specific word choices on meaning and tone.
		RL.9-10.5	Analyze how an author's choices concerning how to structure a text, order events within it, and manipulate time create such effects as mystery, tension, or surprise.
704–715	**Read Romeo and Juliet**	RL.9-10.1	Cite strong and thorough textual evidence to support analysis of what the text says explicitly as well as inferences drawn from the text.
		RL.9-10.4	Determine the meaning of words and phrases as they are used in the text, including figurative and connotative meanings; analyze the cumulative impact of specific word choices on meaning and tone.
		RL.9-10.5	Analyze how an author's choices concerning how to structure a text, order events within it, and manipulate time create such effects as mystery, tension, or surprise.
		RL.9-10.10	By the end of grade 10, read and comprehend literature, including stories, dramas, and poems, at the high end of the grades 9–10 text complexity band independently and proficiently.
		W.9-10.1	Write arguments to support claims in an analysis of substantive topics or texts, using valid reasoning and relevant and sufficient evidence.
		W.9-10.9.a	Apply grades 9–10 Reading standards to literature.
		W.9-10.10	Write routinely over extended time frames (time for research, reflection, and revision) and shorter time frames (a single sitting or a day or two) for a range of tasks, purposes, and audiences.
		L.9-10.1.b	Use various types of phrases (noun, verb, adjectival, adverbial, participial, prepositional, absolute) and clauses (independent, dependent; noun, relative, adverbial) to convey specific meanings and add variety and interest to writing or presentations.
		L.9-10.3	Apply knowledge of language to understand how language functions in different contexts, to make effective choices for meaning or style, and to comprehend more fully when reading or listening.
		L.9-10.4	Determine or clarify the meaning of unknown and multiple-meaning words and phrases based on grades 9–10 reading and content, choosing flexibly from a range of strategies.
		L.9-10.5	Demonstrate understanding of figurative language, word relationships, and nuances in word meanings
		L.9-10.6	Acquire and use accurately general academic and domain-specific words and phrases, sufficient for reading, writing, speaking, and listening at the college and career readiness level; demonstrate independence in gathering vocabulary knowledge when considering a word or phrase important to comprehension or expression.
716	**Before Reading: West Side Story**	RL.9-10.4	Determine the meaning of words and phrases as they are used in the text, including figurative and connotative meanings; analyze the cumulative impact of specific word choices on meaning and tone.
		RL.9-10.9	Analyze how an author draws on and transforms source material in a specific work.

Common Core State Standards, continued

Cluster 2, continued

SE Pages	Lesson	Code	Standards Text
717–720	**Read West Side Story**	RL.9-10.1	Cite strong and thorough textual evidence to support analysis of what the text says explicitly as well as inferences drawn from the text.
		RL.9-10.4	Determine the meaning of words and phrases as they are used in the text, including figurative and connotative meanings; analyze the cumulative impact of specific word choices on meaning and tone.
		RL.9-10.9	Analyze how an author draws on and transforms source material in a specific work.
		RL.9-10.10	By the end of grade 10, read and comprehend literature, including stories, dramas, and poems, at the high end of the grades 9–10 text complexity band independently and proficiently.
		W.9-10.1	Write arguments to support claims in an analysis of substantive topics or texts, using valid reasoning and relevant and sufficient evidence.
		W.9-10.9.a	Apply grades 9–10 Reading standards to literature.
		W.9-10.10	Write routinely over extended time frames (time for research, reflection, and revision) and shorter time frames (a single sitting or a day or two) for a range of tasks, purposes, and audiences.
		L.9-10.1.b	Use various types of phrases (noun, verb, adjectival, adverbial, participial, prepositional, absolute) and clauses (independent, dependent; noun, relative, adverbial) to convey specific meanings and add variety and interest to writing or presentations.
		L.9-10.6	Acquire and use accurately general academic and domain-specific words and phrases, sufficient for reading, writing, speaking, and listening at the college and career readiness level; demonstrate independence in gathering vocabulary knowledge when considering a word or phrase important to comprehension or expression.
721	**Reflect and Assess Critical Thinking**	RL.9-10.1	Cite strong and thorough textual evidence to support analysis of what the text says explicitly as well as inferences drawn from the text.
		RL.9-10.2	Determine a theme or central idea of a text and analyze in detail its development over the course of the text, including how it emerges and is shaped and refined by specific details; provide an objective summary of the text.
		RL.9-10.3	Analyze how complex characters develop over the course of a text, interact with other characters, and advance the plot or develop the theme.
		RL.9-10.10	By the end of grade 10, read and comprehend literature, including stories, dramas, and poems, at the high end of the grades 9–10 text complexity band independently and proficiently.
	Write About Literature	W.9-10.1	Write arguments to support claims in an analysis of substantive topics or texts, using valid reasoning and relevant and sufficient evidence.
		W.9-10.9.a	Apply grades 9–10 Reading standards to literature.
	Key Vocabulary Review	L.9-10.6	Acquire and use accurately general academic and domain-specific words and phrases, sufficient for reading, writing, speaking, and listening at the college and career readiness level; demonstrate independence in gathering vocabulary knowledge when considering a word or phrase important to comprehension or expression.

Cluster 2, continued

SE Pages	Lesson	Code	Standards Text
721	Reflect and Assess continued Read with Ease: Intonation	RL.9-10.10	By the end of grade 10, read and comprehend literature, including stories, dramas, and poems, at the high end of the grades 9–10 text complexity band independently and proficiently.
722	Grammar: Write with the Perfect Tenses	L.9-10.1.b	Use various types of phrases (noun, verb, adjectival, adverbial, participial, prepositional, absolute) and clauses (independent, dependent; noun, relative, adverbial) to convey specific meanings and add variety and interest to writing or presentations.
722	Language Development: Negotiate	SL.9-10.6	Adapt speech to a variety of contexts and tasks, demonstrating command of formal English when indicated or appropriate.
722	Literary Research: Literary Criticism	RL.9-10.10	By the end of grade 10, read and comprehend literature, including stories, dramas, and poems, at the high end of the grades 9–10 text complexity band independently and proficiently.
723	Vocabulary Study: Figurative Language: Simile	L.9-10.5	Demonstrate understanding of figurative language, word relationships, and nuances in word meanings.
723	Writing on Demand: Write a Literary Critique	W.9-10.1	Write arguments to support claims in an analysis of substantive topics or texts, using valid reasoning and relevant and sufficient evidence.
		W.9-10.5	Develop and strengthen writing as needed by planning, revising, editing, rewriting, or trying a new approach, focusing on addressing what is most significant for a specific purpose and audience.
723	Literary Analysis: Parody	W.9-10.3	Write narratives to develop real or imagined experiences or events using effective technique, well-chosen details, and well-structured event sequences.
724–725	Listening and Speaking Workshop: Dramatization	SL.9-10.1.b	Work with peers to set rules for collegial discussions and decision-making (e.g., informal consensus, taking votes on key issues, presentation of alternate views), clear goals and deadlines, and individual roles as needed.
		SL.9-10.3	Evaluate a speaker's point of view, reasoning, and use of evidence and rhetoric, identifying any fallacious reasoning or exaggerated or distorted evidence.
		SL.9-10.6	Adapt speech to a variety of contexts and tasks, demonstrating command of formal English when indicated or appropriate.
		L.9-10.3	Apply knowledge of language to understand how language functions in different contexts, to make effective choices for meaning or style, and to comprehend more fully when reading or listening.

Cluster 3

SE Pages	Lesson	Code	Standards Text
726	Prepare to Read	RI.9-10.4	Determine the meaning of words and phrases as they are used in a text, including figurative, connotative, and technical meanings; analyze the cumulative impact of specific word choices on meaning and tone.
		SL.9-10.1	Initiate and participate effectively in a range of collaborative discussions (one-on-one, in groups, and teacher-led) with diverse partners on grades 9–10 topics, texts, and issues, building on others' ideas and expressing their own clearly and persuasively.

Common Core State Standards, continued

SE Pages	Lesson	Code	Standards Text
726	**Prepare to Read** continued	L.9-10.6	Acquire and use accurately general academic and domain-specific words and phrases, sufficient for reading, writing, speaking, and listening at the college and career readiness level; demonstrate independence in gathering vocabulary knowledge when considering a word or phrase important to comprehension or expression.
727	**Before Reading: Poems for the Earth**	RL.9-10.4	Determine the meaning of words and phrases as they are used in the text, including figurative and connotative meanings; analyze the cumulative impact of specific word choices on meaning and tone.
		RL.9-10.7	Analyze the representation of a subject or a key scene in two different artistic mediums, including what is emphasized or absent in each treatment.
728–737	**Read Poems for the Earth**	RL.9-10.1	Cite strong and thorough textual evidence to support analysis of what the text says explicitly as well as inferences drawn from the text.
		RL.9-10.4	Determine the meaning of words and phrases as they are used in the text, including figurative and connotative meanings; analyze the cumulative impact of specific word choices on meaning and tone.
		RL.9-10.5	Analyze how an author's choices concerning how to structure a text, order events within it, and manipulate time create such effects as mystery, tension, or surprise.
		RL.9-10.7	Analyze the representation of a subject or a key scene in two different artistic mediums, including what is emphasized or absent in each treatment.
		RL.9-10.10	By the end of grade 10, read and comprehend literature, including stories, dramas, and poems, at the high end of the grades 9–10 text complexity band independently and proficiently.
		W.9-10.1	Write arguments to support claims in an analysis of substantive topics or texts, using valid reasoning and relevant and sufficient evidence.
		W.9-10.9.a	Apply grades 9–10 Reading standards to literature.
		W.9-10.10	Write routinely over extended time frames (time for research, reflection, and revision) and shorter time frames (a single sitting or a day or two) for a range of tasks, purposes, and audiences.
		L.9-10.1.b	Use various types of phrases (noun, verb, adjectival, adverbial, participial, prepositional, absolute) and clauses (independent, dependent; noun, relative, adverbial) to convey specific meanings and add variety and interest to writing or presentations.
		L.9-10.6	Acquire and use accurately general academic and domain-specific words and phrases, sufficient for reading, writing, speaking, and listening at the college and career readiness level; demonstrate independence in gathering vocabulary knowledge when considering a word or phrase important to comprehension or expression.
738	**Before Reading: I Was Born Today/ Touching the Earth**	RL.9-10.4	Determine the meaning of words and phrases as they are used in the text, including figurative and connotative meanings; analyze the cumulative impact of specific word choices on meaning and tone.
		RL.9-10.5	Analyze how an author's choices concerning how to structure a text, order events within it, and manipulate time create such effects as mystery, tension, or surprise.

Cluster 3, continued

SE Pages	Lesson	Code	Standards Text
739–742	**Read I Was Born Today/ Touching the Earth**	RL.9-10.1	Cite strong and thorough textual evidence to support analysis of what the text says explicitly as well as inferences drawn from the text.
		RL.9-10.2	Determine a theme or central idea of a text and analyze in detail its development over the course of the text, including how it emerges and is shaped and refined by specific details; provide an objective summary of the text.
		RL.9-10.4	Determine the meaning of words and phrases as they are used in the text, including figurative and connotative meanings; analyze the cumulative impact of specific word choices on meaning and tone.
		RL.9-10.5	Analyze how an author's choices concerning how to structure a text, order events within it, and manipulate time create such effects as mystery, tension, or surprise.
		RL.9-10.7	Analyze the representation of a subject or a key scene in two different artistic mediums, including what is emphasized or absent in each treatment.
		RL.9-10.10	By the end of grade 10, read and comprehend literature, including stories, dramas, and poems, at the high end of the grades 9–10 text complexity band independently and proficiently.
		W.9-10.1	Write arguments to support claims in an analysis of substantive topics or texts, using valid reasoning and relevant and sufficient evidence.
		W.9-10.9.a	Apply grades 9–10 Reading standards to literature.
		W.9-10.10	Write routinely over extended time frames (time for research, reflection, and revision) and shorter time frames (a single sitting or a day or two) for a range of tasks, purposes, and audiences.
		L.9-10.1.b	Use various types of phrases (noun, verb, adjectival, adverbial, participial, prepositional, absolute) and clauses (independent, dependent; noun, relative, adverbial) to convey specific meanings and add variety and interest to writing or presentations.
		L.9-10.6	Acquire and use accurately general academic and domain-specific words and phrases, sufficient for reading, writing, speaking, and listening at the college and career readiness level; demonstrate independence in gathering vocabulary knowledge when considering a word or phrase important to comprehension or expression.
743	**Reflect and Assess Critical Thinking**	RL.9-10.1	Cite strong and thorough textual evidence to support analysis of what the text says explicitly as well as inferences drawn from the text.
		RL.9-10.10	By the end of grade 10, read and comprehend literature, including stories, dramas, and poems, at the high end of the grades 9–10 text complexity band independently and proficiently.
		SL.9-10.1.a	Come to discussions prepared, having read and researched material under study; explicitly draw on that preparation by referring to evidence from texts and other research on the topic or issue to stimulate a thoughtful, well-reasoned exchange of ideas.
	Write About Literature	W.9-10.1	Write arguments to support claims in an analysis of substantive topics or texts, using valid reasoning and relevant and sufficient evidence.
		W.9-10.9.a	Apply grades 9–10 Reading standards to literature.

Common Core State Standards, continued

Cluster 3, continued

SE Pages	Lesson	Code	Standards Text
743	**Reflect and Assess** continued **Key Vocabulary Review**	L.9-10.6	Acquire and use accurately general academic and domain-specific words and phrases, sufficient for reading, writing, speaking, and listening at the college and career readiness level; demonstrate independence in gathering vocabulary knowledge when considering a word or phrase important to comprehension or expression.
	Read with Ease: Phrasing	RL.9-10.10	By the end of grade 10, read and comprehend literature, including stories, dramas, and poems, at the high end of the grades 9–10 text complexity band independently and proficiently.
744	**Grammar: Enrich Your Sentences**	L.9-10.1.b	Use various types of phrases (noun, verb, adjectival, adverbial, participial, prepositional, absolute) and clauses (independent, dependent; noun, relative, adverbial) to convey specific meanings and add variety and interest to writing or presentations.
744	**Literary Analysis/ Research: Literary Criticism**	RL.9-10.10	By the end of grade 10, read and comprehend literature, including stories, dramas, and poems, at the high end of the grades 9–10 text complexity band independently and proficiently.
744	**Language Development: Use Appropriate Language**	SL.9-10.6	Adapt speech to a variety of contexts and tasks, demonstrating command of formal English when indicated or appropriate.
745	**Vocabulary Study: Figurative Language: Metaphor**	L.9-10.5	Demonstrate understanding of figurative language, word relationships, and nuances in word meanings.
745	**Writing Trait: Voice and Style**	W.9-10.2	Write informative/explanatory texts to examine and convey complex ideas, concepts, and information clearly and accurately through the effective selection, organization, and analysis of content.
		W.9-10.4	Produce clear and coherent writing in which the development, organization, and style are appropriate to task, purpose, and audience.
		L.9-10.3	Apply knowledge of language to understand how language functions in different contexts, to make effective choices for meaning or style, and to comprehend more fully when reading or listening.
745	**Literary Analysis: Rhythm/Line Length**	RL.9-10.5	Analyze how an author's choices concerning how to structure a text, order events within it, and manipulate time create such effects as mystery, tension, or surprise.
Close Reading			
746–747	**Read Wild Geese/ Like You**	RL.9-10.10	By the end of grade 10, read and comprehend literature, including stories, dramas, and poems, at the high end of the grades 9–10 text complexity band independently and proficiently.
Unit Wrap-Up			
748	**Unit Wrap-Up Present Your Project**	W.9-10.8	Gather relevant information from multiple authoritative print and digital sources, using advanced searches effectively; assess the usefulness of each source in answering the research question; integrate information into the text selectively to maintain the flow of ideas, avoiding plagiarism and following a standard format for citation.
	Reflect on Your Reading	SL.9-10.1.a	Come to discussions prepared, having read and researched material under study; explicitly draw on that preparation by referring to evidence from texts and other research on the topic or issue to stimulate a thoughtful, well-reasoned exchange of ideas.

Unit Wrap-Up, continued

SE Pages	Lesson	Code	Standards Text
748	**Respond to the Essential Question**	SL.9-10.1.a	Come to discussions prepared, having read and researched material under study; explicitly draw on that preparation by referring to evidence from texts and other research on the topic or issue to stimulate a thoughtful, well-reasoned exchange of ideas.

Language and Learning Handbook

SE Pages	Lesson	Code	Standards Text
751–760	**Strategies for Learning and Developing Language**	SL.9-10.1.c	Propel conversations by posing and responding to questions that relate the current discussion to broader themes or larger ideas; actively incorporate others into the discussion; and clarify, verify, or challenge ideas and conclusions.
		SL.9-10.3	Evaluate a speaker's point of view, reasoning, and use of evidence and rhetoric, identifying any fallacious reasoning or exaggerated or distorted evidence.
		SL.9-10.4	Present information, findings, and supporting evidence clearly, concisely, and logically such that listeners can follow the line of reasoning and the organization, development, substance, and style are appropriate to purpose, audience, and task.
		SL.9-10.6	Adapt speech to a variety of contexts and tasks, demonstrating command of formal English when indicated or appropriate.
		L.9-10.1	Demonstrate command of the conventions of standard English grammar and usage when writing or speaking.
		L.9-10.4	Determine or clarify the meaning of unknown and multiple-meaning words and phrases based on grades 9–10 reading and content, choosing flexibly from a range of strategies.
		L.9-10.4.c	Consult general and specialized reference materials, both print and digital, to find the pronunciation of a word or determine or clarify its precise meaning, its part of speech, or its etymology.
		L.9-10.5.a	Interpret figures of speech in context and analyze their role in the text.
		L.9-10.6	Acquire and use accurately general academic and domain-specific words and phrases, sufficient for reading, writing, speaking, and listening at the college and career readiness level; demonstrate independence in gathering vocabulary knowledge when considering a word or phrase important to comprehension or expression.
761–764	**Listening and Speaking**	SL.9-10.1	Initiate and participate effectively in a range of collaborative discussions (one-on-one, in groups, and teacher-led) with diverse partners on grades 9–10 topics, texts, and issues, building on others' ideas and expressing their own clearly and persuasively.
		SL.9-10.1.c	Propel conversations by posing and responding to questions that relate the current discussion to broader themes or larger ideas; actively incorporate others into the discussion; and clarify, verify, or challenge ideas and conclusions.
		SL.9-10.1.d	Respond thoughtfully to diverse perspectives, summarize points of agreement and disagreement, and, when warranted, qualify or justify their own views and understanding and make new connections in light of the evidence and reasoning presented.
		L.9-10.1.a	Use parallel structure.
		L.9-10.5	Demonstrate understanding of figurative language, word relationships, and nuances in word meanings.

Common Core State Standards, continued

Language and Learning Handbook, continued

SE Pages	Lesson	Code	Standards Text
765–768	**Viewing and Representing**	RI.9-10.7	Analyze various accounts of a subject told in different mediums, determining which details are emphasized in each account.
		W.9-10.8	Gather relevant information from multiple authoritative print and digital sources, using advanced searches effectively; assess the usefulness of each source in answering the research question; integrate information into the text selectively to maintain the flow of ideas, avoiding plagiarism and following a standard format for citation.
		SL.9-10.2	Integrate multiple sources of information presented in diverse media or formats evaluating the credibility and accuracy of each source.
		SL.9-10.5	Make strategic use of digital media in presentations to enhance understanding of findings, reasoning, and evidence and to add interest.
769–772	**Technology and Media**	W.9-10.6	Use technology, including the Internet, to produce, publish, and update individual or shared writing products, taking advantage of technology's capacity to link to other information and to display information flexibly and dynamically.
		SL.9-10.5	Make strategic use of digital media in presentations to enhance understanding of findings, reasoning, and evidence and to add interest.
773–778	**Research**	W.9-10.7	Conduct short as well as more sustained research projects to answer a question (including a self-generated question) or solve a problem; narrow or broaden the inquiry when appropriate; synthesize multiple sources on the subject, demonstrating understanding of the subject under investigation.
		W.9-10.8	Gather relevant information from multiple authoritative print and digital sources, using advanced searches effectively; assess the usefulness of each source in answering the research question; integrate information into the text selectively to maintain the flow of ideas, avoiding plagiarism and following a standard format for citation.
		L.9-10.3.a	Write and edit work so that it conforms to the guidelines in a style manual appropriate for the discipline and writing type.

Reading Handbook

SE Pages	Lesson	Code	Standards Text
782–794	**Reading Strategies**	RL.9-10.1	Cite strong and thorough textual evidence to support analysis of what the text says explicitly as well as inferences drawn from the text.
		RL.9-10.10	By the end of grade 10, read and comprehend literature, including stories, dramas, and poems, at the high end of the grades 9–10 text complexity band independently and proficiently.
		RI.9-10.1	Cite strong and thorough textual evidence to support analysis of what the text says explicitly as well as inferences drawn from the text.
795–819	**Reading Fluency**	RL.9-10.10	By the end of grade 10, read and comprehend literature, including stories, dramas, and poems, at the high end of the grades 9–10 text complexity band independently and proficiently.
		RI.9-10.10	By the end of grade 10, read and comprehend literary nonfiction at the high end of the grades 9–10 text complexity band independently and proficiently.

Reading Handbook, continued

SE Pages	Lesson	Code	Standards Text
820–823	**Study Skills and Strategies**	SL.9-10.1.a	Come to discussions prepared, having read and researched material under study; explicitly draw on that preparation by referring to evidence from texts and other research on the topic or issue to stimulate a thoughtful, well-reasoned exchange of ideas.
		SL.9-10.2	Integrate multiple sources of information presented in diverse media or formats evaluating the credibility and accuracy of each source.
824–831	**Vocabulary**	L.9-10.4	Determine or clarify the meaning of unknown and multiple-meaning words and phrases based on grades 9–10 reading and content, choosing flexibly from a range of strategies.
		L.9-10.4.a	Use context as a clue to the meaning of a word or phrase.
		L.9-10.4.b	Identify and correctly use patterns of word changes that indicate different meanings or parts of speech.
		L.9-10.4.c	Consult general and specialized reference materials, both print and digital, to find the pronunciation of a word or determine or clarify its precise meaning, its part of speech, or its etymology.
		L.9-10.4.d	Verify the preliminary determination of the meaning of a word or phrase.
		L.9-10.5	Demonstrate understanding of figurative language, word relationships, and nuances in word meanings.
		L.9-10.6	Acquire and use accurately general academic and domain-specific words and phrases, sufficient for reading, writing, speaking, and listening at the college and career readiness level; demonstrate independence in gathering vocabulary knowledge when considering a word or phrase important to comprehension or expression.

Writing Handbook

SE Pages	Lesson	Code	Standards Text
833–839	**The Writing Process**	W.9-10.4	Produce clear and coherent writing in which the development, organization, and style are appropriate to task, purpose, and audience.
		W.9-10.6	Use technology, including the Internet, to produce, publish, and update individual or shared writing products, taking advantage of technology's capacity to link to other information and to display information flexibly and dynamically.
840–849	**Writing Traits**	RI.9-10.10	By the end of grade 10, read and comprehend literary nonfiction at the high end of the grades 9–10 text complexity band independently and proficiently.
		W.9-10.1.c	Use words, phrases, and clauses to link the major sections of the text, create cohesion, and clarify the relationships between claim(s) and reasons, between reasons and evidence, and between claim(s) and counterclaims.
		W.9-10.2.c	Use appropriate and varied transitions to link the major sections of the text, create cohesion, and clarify the relationships among complex ideas and concepts.
		W.9-10.2.e	Establish and maintain a formal style and objective tone while attending to the norms and conventions of the discipline in which they are writing.
		W.9-10.2.f	Provide a concluding statement or section that follows from and supports the information or explanation presented.

Common Core State Standards, continued

Writing Handbook, continued

SE Pages	Lesson	Code	Standards Text
840–849	**Writing Traits** continued	W.9-10.3.d	Use precise words and phrases, telling details, and sensory language to convey a vivid picture of the experiences, events, setting, and/or characters.
		W.9-10.4	Produce clear and coherent writing in which the development, organization, and style are appropriate to task, purpose, and audience.
		L.9-10.1	Demonstrate command of the conventions of standard English grammar and usage when writing or speaking.
850–871	**Writing Purposes, Modes, and Forms**	W.9-10.1	Write arguments to support claims in an analysis of substantive topics or texts, using valid reasoning and relevant and sufficient evidence.
		W.9-10.4	Produce clear and coherent writing in which the development, organization, and style are appropriate to task, purpose, and audience.
		W.9-10.5	Develop and strengthen writing as needed by planning, revising, editing, rewriting, or trying a new approach, focusing on addressing what is most significant for a specific purpose and audience.
		W.9-10.6	Use technology, including the Internet, to produce, publish, and update individual or shared writing products, taking advantage of technology's capacity to link to other information and to display information flexibly and dynamically.
		SL.9-10.2	Integrate multiple sources of information presented in diverse media or formats evaluating the credibility and accuracy of each source.
		L.9-10.3.a	Write and edit work so that it conforms to the guidelines in a style manual appropriate for the discipline and writing type.
872–906	**Grammar, Usage, Mechanics, and Spelling**	L.9-10.1	Demonstrate command of the conventions of standard English grammar and usage when writing or speaking.
		L.9-10.1.a	Use parallel structure.
		L.9-10.1.b	Use various types of phrases (noun, verb, adjectival, adverbial, participial, prepositional, absolute) and clauses (independent, dependent; noun, relative, adverbial) to convey specific meanings and add variety and interest to writing or presentations.
		L.9-10.2	Demonstrate command of the conventions of standard English capitalization, punctuation, and spelling when writing.
		L.9-10.2.a	Use a semicolon (and perhaps a conjunctive adverb) to link two or more closely related independent clauses.
		L.9-10.2.b	Use a colon to introduce a list or quotation.
		L.9-10.2.c	Spell correctly.

Writing Handbook, continued

SE Pages	Lesson	Code	Standards Text
872–906	**Grammar, Usage, Mechanics, and Spelling** continued	L.9-10.3	Apply knowledge of language to understand how language functions in different contexts, to make effective choices for meaning or style, and to comprehend more fully when reading or listening.
907–915	**Troubleshooting Guide**	L.9-10.1	Demonstrate command of the conventions of standard English grammar and usage when writing or speaking.
		L.9-10.3	Apply knowledge of language to understand how language functions in different contexts, to make effective choices for meaning or style, and to comprehend more fully when reading or listening.

INDEX OF SKILLS

Informative writing *see Genre; Writing modes; Writing forms*

Interior monologue 106, 107, 118

Interjections 872, 893, 902

Internal conflict 8, 11

Internal rhyme 261

Interview 67, 94, 177–182, 579, 629, 834, 920

Intonation *see Reading fluency*

Introduction 299, 340, 640, 776

Irony 493, 501, 764, 920

Italics 797, 904

J

Jargon 409, 920

Job application 480, 866

Journal or diary entry 483, 489, 493, 856, 920

K

Key vocabulary 10, 15, 19, 22, 29, 38, 42, 43, 45, 47, 49, 55, 56, 70, 78, 83, 85, 95, 97, 128, 134, 135, 139, 143, 146, 148, 155, 162, 167, 168, 174, 179, 181, 182, 188, 192, 193, 194, 198, 199, 201, 202, 242, 248, 249, 251, 254, 255, 257, 259, 270, 284, 286, 294, 295, 302, 308, 310, 313, 317, 320, 324, 327, 329, 362, 366, 367, 371, 379, 380, 386, 394, 396, 399, 402, 403, 412, 417, 418, 419, 421, 424, 431, 458, 462, 463, 465, 467, 469, 472, 475, 482, 487, 488, 491, 492, 493, 497, 503, 504, 508, 511, 512, 516, 525, 526, 560, 565, 566, 567, 568, 569, 582, 586, 587, 591, 606, 611, 615, 623, 625, 660, 669, 670, 683, 686, 689, 702, 706, 707, 710, 715, 717, 726, 730, 732, 734, 736, 739, 740

  review 33, 65, 99, 157, 183, 211, 265, 297, 331, 381, 407, 427, 477, 499, 529, 577, 601, 627, 697, 721, 743

L

Language 764

  analysis of 419

  appropriate language, use 428, 744

  emotion-filled words 607

  emotive 631

  evaluate and analyze 711

  formal and informal 243, 251, 449

  hyperbole 400, 403, 712, 920

  narrator's style 250, 254, 257, 260

  strategies for learning 751–754

  see also Dialogue; Figurative language; Irony; Specialized language

Language and learning handbook 751–780

Language development 755–760

  ask questions 755

  clarify 500

  compare and contrast 332

  define and explain 382, 758

  describe 158, 184, 756

  elaborate 212, 757

  engage in discussion 100, 760

  evaluate 478

  express and support opinions 578

  express ideas and opinions 34

  make comparisons 298, 758

  negotiate 722, 759

  persuade 602, 628, 759

  recognize and respond to humor 408, 757

  retell a story 266

  use appropriate language 428, 744

  verify information 530, 758

Letters 333, 353, 427, 601, 627, 864, 869, 871, 900, 903, 905

Library resources 36, 834

Listening and speaking workshop

  debate 300–301

  dramatization 724–725

  extemporaneous talk 502–503

  narrative presentation 186–187

  oral interpretation 68–69

  panel discussion 410–411

  persuasive speech 604–605

Listening strategies

  actively and respectfully 761

  listen attentively 410

  note taking 60, 67, 301

  overcome barriers 761

  self-monitor 764

Literal imagery 692

Literary background 517, 707

Literary criticism/critique 538, 722, 723, 744, 920

  see also Reviews

Literary devices and elements 8, 39, 43, 45, 46, 49, 51, 52, 56, 57, 66, 106, 107, 184, 208, 221, 228, 241, 261, 263, 264, 274, 360, 408, 413, 416, 418, 420–423, 455–457, 459, 471, 483, 486–488, 490, 493, 505, 583, 603, 637, 640, 656, 658, 659, 723, 736, 738, 834, 842, 867, 916, 917, 921–925

  see also Author's viewpoint; Autobiography; Biography; Characters/characterization; Conflict; Dialogue; Drama; Narrator's point of view; Plot; Poems/poetry; Quotations; Setting; Style; Theme; Tone; Viewpoint

Literary paradox 382

Literary research report 537–551

Literary response 721, 854–855

Literary terms 916–924

Logical appeal 640, 857

Logical fallacies 559, 602

M

Magazine article 365–372, 375–380, 524, 525–528

  author's purpose 524, 525

  cause and effect structure 363, 368, 370, 372

  problem and solution structure 374, 377, 378, 379, 380

Main idea and details

  identify 127, 129, 132, 134, 136, 139, 143, 146, 147, 148, 149, 150, 152, 786, 787

  relate 128, 153, 155, 156

Main idea and details (text structure) 387, 390, 392, 395, 398, 399

Map 142, 203, 566, 619, 766

Media

  analyze 768

  compare news commentaries 531

  feature writing and 869–870

  as information source 770–771

  interpret and analyze 383, 768

  interpret information from 771

  multimedia presentation 158, 353, 357, 434, 449, 767, 772, 777

  public service announcement 479

Mental images

  compare 716

  form 404, 655, 703, 706, 708, 710, 712, 713, 714, 715, 716, 720, 794

  see also Visualize

Metaphor 395, 465, 473, 475, 476, 701, 723, 745, 826, 921

Meter 703, 921

Modifiers

  dangling 447, 449, 896

  misplaced 447, 448

  see also Adjectives; Adverbs

suspense 483, 486, 487, 488, 490, 493, 925

Theme 106, 107, 925

  analyze 298

  compare 267

  critical viewing 78, 90, 523

  of short stories 71, 75, 76, 78, 79, 82, 83, 86, 88, 90, 91, 108

Thesaurus 479, 481, 531, 581, 829, 837

Thesis 360

Thesis statement 436, 438, 442, 538, 540

Thesis tip 436

Thinking process 8–9, 125, 240–241, 360, 456–457, 558–559, 656, 659

Time line 184, 223, 422, 541, 618–619, 785

Time-order words 189

Titles 71, 520

  capitalization 446, 900

  italic or underlining of 904

  quotation marks 905

Tone 240, 241, 734, 764, 925

Topic 387, 925

  choose 108, 222, 342, 438, 540, 638, 773, 833

  narrow 438, 773

Topic sentence 776, 834

Tragedy 925

Transcript 870

Transition words and phrases 341, 442, 448

Troubleshooting guide 907–914

Turning point *see Climax*

U

Unfamiliar words 825

Unit project

  literary anthology 653, 748

  multimedia presentation 357, 434

  political campaign 555, 634

  press conference 123, 218

  reality TV show 237, 338

  skit 453, 536

  video or sound recording 3, 104

V

Verbals

  gerund 578, 890

  infinitive 578, 890

  participial phrase 890

Verbs 184, 212, 231–232, 266, 298, 351–352, 578, 602, 698, 722, 744, 831, 872, 878, 881, 881–883, 882, 883, 885, 885–890, 886, 886–887, 888–889, 890, 894, 899, 909

Verify information 530, 758

Verses 658, 925

Viewing

  effects of visuals on mood 768

  illustrated report 500

  interpret and analyze media 768

  monitor understanding of visuals 765

  respond to and interpret visuals and informational graphics 765

  self-control thoughts 765

  understand different kinds of visuals 766

  view and look for details 765

  see also Critical viewing

Viewpoint 922

  author's purpose determining 184

  first-person 94, 163, 184, 212

  of editorial 578

  of news commentary 293

  of news reports 326, 328, 329, 330

  of oral history 94, 97, 98

  of personal narrative 94

  of short stories 246, 303, 306, 308, 309, 310, 312, 313, 314, 318, 319, 320, 321, 322, 325

  style created by 243

  third-person 212

  third-person omniscient narrator 243

  word choice 607, 620

  see also Author's viewpoint

Visual analysis *see Critical viewing*

Visualize 4, 655, 657, 659, 661, 692, 703, 716, 727, 738, 748, 794

  see also Emotional responses, identify; Mental images, form; Sensory images, identify

Visuals

  construct and clarify meaning 754

  effects of 767–768

  graphic displays 766

  map 766

  monitor understanding of 765

  photos, illustrations, videos, artwork 766

  respond to and interpret 765

  self-correcting thoughts concerning 765

  use in writing and presentations 767, 777

  see also Critical viewing

Vocabulary 26, 32, 58, 64, 91, 98, 152, 156, 176, 182, 206, 210, 260, 264, 291, 296, 325, 330, 372, 380, 399, 405, 422, 426, 472, 476, 493, 498, 521, 528, 569, 576, 592, 600, 620, 626, 690, 696, 715, 720, 737, 742

  access vocabulary 15, 135, 137, 170, 196, 256, 316, 368, 371, 424, 468, 488, 514, 516, 618

  allusions 827

  analogies 827

  analyze word parts 827–829

  clarify vocabulary 71, 75, 76, 79, 81, 84, 94, 95, 97, 98, 784

  connotation and denotation 579, 603, 629, 826

  content-area words 429

  context clues 159, 185, 213, 825–826

  definitions 159

  dialect and regionalism 831

  examples 213

  figurative language 723, 745, 825–826

  Greek, Latin roots 101

  idioms 699, 825

  jargon 409

  metaphor 745

  multiple-meaning words 185, 383, 825

  phrasal (two-word) verbs 831

  prefixes 35

  relate words 824

  simile 723

  slang 832

  specialized vocabulary 826

  suffixes 67

  synonyms 479

  synonyms and antonyms in analogies 501, 531

  use reference materials 829

  word awareness 830

  word families 267, 299, 333, 818

  see also Academic vocabulary; Key vocabulary; Vocabulary workshop

Vocabulary routine 824, 830

Vocabulary Workshop

  access vocabulary 385

  build word knowledge 581

  cognates 269

  context clues 161

  interpret non-literal language 701

INDEX OF AUTHORS AND TITLES

INDEX OF ART AND ARTISTS

Acknowledgments, continued from page ii

TEXT

Alfred Publishing Co., Inc.: "Strength, Courage and Wisdom," words and music by India Arie © 2006 WB Music Corp. and Gold & Iron Music Publishing. Lyrics recorded by permission of Alfred Publishing Co., Inc. All Rights Reserved.

Arte Publico Press: "Mi Madre" by Pat Mora from *Chants*. Copyright © 1985 by Pat Mora. Recorded with permission by Arte Público Press-University of Houston.

The Atlanta-Journal Constitution: "Stall Teen Motorists" by Maureen Downey from *The Atlanta Journal-Constitution*, April 24, 2006. Copyright © 2006 by The Atlanta Journal-Constitution. Recorded with permission from The Atlanta Journal-Constitution.

Fred Bayles: "Drivers Ed, Not Age, Is Key to Road Safety" by Fred Bayles from *The Boston Globe*, March 30, 2006. Copyright © 2006 by Fred Bayles. Recorded by permission of Fred Bayles.

Steven Bennett: "My Brother's Keeper" by Jay Bennett from *From One Experience to Another*. Copyright © by Jay Bennett. Recorded by permission of Steven Bennett.

Susan Bergholz Literary Services: "My English" by Julia Alvarez from *Something to Declare*, published by Plume, an imprint of Penguin Group (USA), in 1999 and in hardcover by Algonquin Books of Chapel Hill. Originally published by Brujulla/Compass, fall, 1992. Copyright © 1998 by Julia Alvarez. Recorded by permission of Susan Bergholz Literary Services, New York. All rights reserved.

Black Enterprise Magazine: "My Moment of Truth" by Caroline V. Clarke and Sonja D. Brown, July 2003 issue of Black Enterprise. Reprinted by permission.

Indiana University Press: "The Hand of Fatima" from *Figs and Fate: Stories about Growing Up in the Arab World Today* by Elsa Marston. Copyright © by Elsa Marston. Recorded by permission of Indiana University Press.

Curtis Brown: "Little Sister" by Nikki Grimes from *Something on My Mind*, published by Dial Books for Young Readers. Copyright © 1978 by Nikki Grimes. Reprinted by permission of Curtis Brown, Ltd.

Cartoon Bank: Cartoon by Charles Barsotti from cartoonbank.com. Copyright © 1998 by the New Yorker Collection. Reprinted by permission of Cartoon Bank. All rights reserved.

"How I Spent My Summer Vacation" by Mort Gerber from the New Yorker. Copyright © 1988 by the New Yorker Collection. All Rights Reserved. © 1993 by the New Yorker Collection Reprinted by permission of the Cartoon Bank. All Rights Reserved.

Caxton Printers: "Say It with Flowers" by Toshio Mori in Yokohama, California. Copyright © 1949 by the Caxton Printers, Ltd. Used by permission.

The Courier-Journal: "Extracurricular activities part of high school experience" by Nancy C. Rodriguez from the *Courier-Journal*, July 31, 2005. Copyright © by Gannett. All rights reserved. Used by permission and protected by the Copyright Laws of the United States. The printing, copying, redistribution, or retransmission of this Content without express written permission is prohibited.

Joshua Davis: "Beat MIT, Go Directly to College" from Wired.com, June 2005 and "La Vida Robot" from Wired.com, April 2005 by Joshua Davis Copyright © 2005 by Joshua Davis. Reprinted by permission of Joshua Davis, author of the book *The Underdog: Seeking the Meaning of Life in the World's Most Outlandish Competitions.*

Sandra Dijkstra Agency and Amy Tan: "Two Kinds" by Amy Tan from *The Joy Luck Club*. Copyright © 1989 by Amy Tan. Reprinted by permission of and the Sandra Dijkstra Literary Agency and the author.

Gregory Djanikian: "How I Learned English" from *Falling Deeply Into America* by Gregory Djanikian. Copyright © 1984 by Gregory Djanikian. Recorded by permission of the author.

Mary Duenwald: "The Physiology of...Facial Expressions" by Mary Duenwald from *Discover*, June 2005. Copyright © 2005 by Mary Duenwald. Used by permission of the author.

Paul Ekman: Photographs from "The Physiology of Facial Expressions" courtesy of the Paul Ekman Group LLC.

Fitzhenry & Whiteside Publishers: "Be-ers and Doers" from *The Leaving* by Budge Wilson. Text copyright © 1990 by Budge Wilson. Reprinted by permission of Fitzhenry & Whiteside Publishers.

Randy Glasbergen: "It's a special program..." cartoon © Randy Glasbergen, www.glasbergen.com. Used by permission.

Grove/Atlantic: "The Journey" from Dream Work by Mary Oliver. Copyright © 1986 by Mary Oliver. Reprinted by permission of Grove/Atlantic, Inc. Any third party use of material outside of this publication is prohibited.

Erin Gruwell Education Project: "The Freedom Writers Diary. Used by permission of Freedom Writers Foundation and Erin Gruwell.

HarperCollins Publishers: Excerpts from Black Boy by Richard Wright. Copyright 1937, 1942, 1944, 1945 by Richard Wright; renewed © 1973 by Ellen Wright. Used by permissions of HarperCollins Publishers.

Hewitt Associates: "Success is a Mind Set" from Hewitt, October 2005. Used with permission of Hewitt Associates LLC.

Henry Holt: "Fire and Ice" by Robert Frost from *Poetry of Robert Frost*, edited by Edward Connery. Copyright © 1987 by Henry Holt and Company, Inc. Used with permission of Henry Holt and Company, Inc.

The Hill: "Piracy hurts everyone both online and offline" by Rep. Ed Towns. First appeared in *The Hill*, July 27, 2006. Reprinted by permission of The Hill.

Barbara Kouts Agency: "Skins" by Joseph Bruchac from Face Relations. Copyright © 2004 by Joseph Bruchac. Reprinted by permission of the Barbara Kouts Literary Agency.

Charlotte Latvala: "Is your body language holding you back?" by Charlotte Latvala from *Redbook*, March 2006. Copyright © 2006 by Charlotte Latvala. Used by permission of the author.

Hal Leonard: "Lean on Me" by Bill Withers. Copyright © 1972, renewed, Interior Music Corporation. Used by Permission of the Hal Leonard Corp. All Rights Reserved.

Little, Brown and Co. Inc.: Excerpt from *Long Walk to Freedom* by Nelson Mandela. Copyright © 1994, 1995 by Nelson Rolihlahla Mandela. Used by permission of Little, Brown and Co., Inc.

McGraw-Hill: "Independence Movements in Africa" from *Contemporary's World History* by Matthew T. Downey. Copyright © 2006 by Wright Group/McGraw-Hill. Reprinted by permission of the McGraw-Hill Companies.

Excerpts from *It Doesn't Take a Genius: Five Truths to Inspire Success in Every Student* by Randall Mc-Cutcheon & Tommie Lindsey. Copyright © 2006 by McGraw Hill. Reprinted by permission of the McGraw-Hill Companies.

M. E. Sharpe: "The Woman Who Was Death" by Josepha Sherman from *Mythology for Storytellers*. Copyright © 2003 by M. E. Sharpe. Used by permission of M. E. Sharpe.

National Geographic Society: Excerpt from *The Cruelest Journey* by Kira Silak. Copyright © 2005 the National Geographic Society. Recorded by permission of the National Geographic Society. All rights reserved.

Northwestern University Press: "Like You" by Roque Dalton, from *Poetry Like Bread: Poets of the Political Imagination*, edited by Martin Espada, translated by Jack Hirschman. Copyright (c) 2000, Curbstone Press. Used by permission of Northwestern University Press.

Naomi Shihab Nye: "Remembered" by Naomi Shihab Nye from *Words Under Words*. Copyright © 2006 by Naomi Shihab Nye. Used by permission of the author.

Oxford University Press: Excerpt from *Txting: The GR8 DB8* by David Crystal. Copyright © 2008 by David Crystal. Used by permission of Oxford University Press.

Penguin Group: "Sunday, May 2, 1993," by Zlata Filipovic from *Zlata's Diary*, translated by Christina Pribichevich-Zoric, Copyright © 1994 by Editions Robert Laffont/Fixot. Used by permission of Viking Penguin, a division of Penguin Group (USA) Inc.

"Two Kinds," from *The Joy Luck Club* by Amy Tan. Copyright © 1989 by Amy Tan. Used by permission of G.P. Putnam's Sons, a division of Penguin Group (USA) Inc.

"One" from *When I Dance* by James Berry. Copyright © 1998 by James Berry. UK: Penguin Books, 1998. Reprinted by permission of Penguin, a division of Penguin Group (USA) Inc.

"Why the Violin Is Better" by Hal Sirowitz from *Identity Lessons* edited by Maria Mazziotti Gillan and Jennifer Gillan. Copyright © 1999 by Hal Sirowitz. Used by permission of Penguin, a division of Penguin Group (USA) Inc.

Gerald M. Pomper: From "What price loyalty?" by Gerald M. Pomper from the *Star-Ledger*, August 14, 2005. Copyright © 2005 by Gerald M. Pomper. Gerald M. Pomper is Board of Governors Professor of Political Science (Emeritus) at Rutgers University and author of *On Ordinary Heroes and American Democracy*. published by Paradigm Publishers. Used by permission.

Random House: "Breaking the Ice," by Dave Barry from *Dave Barry is Not Making This Up*. Copyright © 1994 by Dave Barry. Used by permission of Crown Publishers, a division of Random House, Inc.

Excerpt from the *Freedom Writers Diary* by the Freedom Writers with Erin Gruwell. Copyright © 1999 by the Tolerance Education Foundation. Used by permission of Freedom Writers Foundation and Erin Gruwell, and by permission of Doubleday, a division of Random House, Inc.

New York. **253** Allsport Concepts/Getty Images; Allsport Concepts/Getty Images. **257** Corrales-Castillo II, 2005, Richard T. Stone. Enamel and acrylic on canvas, collection of the artist. **259** Boxer Right, Carol Tatham. Acrylic on canvas, private collection. The Bridgeman Art Library. **262** Central Park Skate II, 2005, Joseph Holston. Oil on canvas, collection of the artist. **263** Getty Images. **267** Ted S. Warren. **268** bikeriderlondon/Shutterstock; Dennis MacDonald/PhotoEdit, Inc; Cindy Charles/PhotoEdit, Inc. **271** Boy with Caution Tape, 2000, Sidney Goodman. Oil on canvas, courtesy of ACA Galleries, New York. **272** Jay Bennett. **273** Boy with Caution Tape, 2000, Sidney Goodman. Oil on canvas, courtesy of ACA Galleries, New York. **274** Kristi J. Black/CORBIS. **277** Man Overboard, 1906, Christian Krohg. Oil on canvas, National Museum, Stockholm, Sweden, The Bridgeman Art Gallery. **278** Kristi J. Black/CORBIS. **281** Fire and Destruction, 1985, Jüri Palm. Oil on canvas, Art Museum of Estonia, Talinn, Estonia, The Bridgeman Art Gallery. **285** Kristi J. Black/CORBIS. **288** Figure with Caution Tape, 2001, Sidney Goodman. Oil on canvas, courtesy of ACA Galleries, New York. **292** Granger Wootz/CORBIS; Copyright 2007 by Nikki Grimes. Photo by Steve Elliott. First appeared in National Geographic Learning Edge, published by Cengage Learning. Reprinted by permission of Curtis Brown, Ltd. **294** Jeff Greenberg/PhotoEdit Inc.; Bettman/CORBIS. **300–301** Stewart Cohen/Getty Images. **302** Stewart Cohen/Getty Images; Westend61/CORBIS; Michael N. Paras/SuperStock. **303** Dream, 2000, Safwan Dahoul. Oil on canvas, private collection. **304** Elsa Marston/Ric Cradick. **305** Digital Image [year] Museum Associates/LACMA. Licensed by Art Resource, NY. **306** Reprinted by permission of Curtis Brown, Ltd. **307** Door with Palm Trees, 2003, Joseph Matar. Watercolor, courtesy of LebanonArt.com. **310** Madrasha Sharabiya/AKG Images. **312** Laundry, 1996, Randa Baki. Acrylic on paper, private collection, New York. **314** Madrasha Sharabiya/AKG Images. **318** Robert Harding Picture Library/SuperStock. **320** John Singer Sargent/Francis G. Mayer/CORBIS. **321** Madrasha Sharabiya/AKG Images. **324** Lola, 1961, Joseph Matar. Oil. Courtesy of LebanonArt.com. **327** Najlah Feanny/CORBIS. **328** National Geographic Maps. **332** MarciSchauer/Shutterstock. **334** The Wolfsonian-Florida International University. **334–337** The Wolfsonian-Florida International University. **337** Hugh Shurley/CORBIS. **339** Blend Images/Alamy. **340** Ty Allison/Taxi/Getty Images. **345** IMAGEMORE Co, Ltd/Imagemore/Getty Images. **354–355** Poras Chaudhary/The Image Bank/Getty Images. **356** Source: Kevin Fagan/United Features Syndicate, Inc. **357** Suzanne Dechillo/The New York Times/Redux. **358** Comstock/Getty Images. **359** Brand X Pictures/PunchStock. **359** Randy Faris/CORBIS. **361** Bomshtein/Shutterstock. **362** DigitalVision/PunchStock; Photodisc Green/Getty Images. **363** Bob Krist/CORBIS. **364** Photodisc Green/Getty Images. **366** Christy Krames. **368** Richard Milner/Handout/epa. **369** Hulton Archive/Getty Images; For Better or For Worse 1990 Lynn Johnston Productions, Dist by Universal Press Syndicate. Reprinted with permission. All rights reserved.; Universal Press Syndicate. **373** Maylene #2, 2004, Cristopher Nolasco. Mixed media on paper, collection of the artist; Anne Lindsay Photography. **375** M.Thomsen/zefa/CORBIS. **376** Purestock/Getty

Images. **378** Stockbyte/Getty Images; ©Photodisc/Alamy. **379** Nancy Ney/Digital Vision/Getty Images. **384** Jeff Greenberg/PhotoEdit, Inc.; Bob Dammearich/PhotoEdit, Inc.; Park Street/PhotoEdit, Inc. **386** Richard Schultz/CORBIS. **387** CRAIG LEE/San Francisco Chronicle/CORBIS. **388** Mango Productions; Virgo Productions/zefa. **389** CRAIG LEE/San Francisco Chronicle/CORBIS. **390** Igor Djurovic/iStockphoto; Coach Tommie Lindsey and the James Logan Forensics Team of Union City, California. **393** CRAIG LEE/San Francisco Chronicle/CORBIS. **395** CRAIG LEE/San Francisco Chronicle/CORBIS. **405** Presselect/Alamy. **411** Purestock/Alamy. **412** Brooke Fasani/CORBIS. **412** Herbert Spichtinger/zefa/CORBIS. **413** Brigitte Sporrer/zefa/CORBIS; Harold Sund/Riser/Getty Images; Craig Tuttle/CORBIS. **414** Erika Larsen 2004/Redux; Harold Sund/Riser/Getty Images. **415** Brigitte Sporrer/zefa/CORBIS. **416** Henri Silberman/Picture Quest/Jupiter Images; Craig Tuttle/CORBIS. **417** National Geographic Maps; Alfredo Maiquez/Getty Images. **418** Henri Silberman/Picture Quest/Jupiter Images; Craig Tuttle/CORBIS. **419** Brigitte Sporrer/zefa. **420** Henri Silberman/Picture Quest/Jupiter Images; James Lemas/Index Stock; Craig Tuttle/CORBIS; Brigitte Sporrer/zefa/CORBIS. **424–425** Randy Faris/CORBIS. **425** John Martin/Illustration Source. **426** Jesse Blatt, 2006; Randy Faris/CORBIS. **428** Source: Mark Lynch/CartoonStock, Ltd. **430** Jude Buffum. **430–433** Jude Buffum. **436** John Still/Photonica/Getty Images; Stuart Gregory/Photodisc Red/Getty Images; George Doyle/StockByte/Getty Images; Don Hammond/Design Pics/CORBIS; magus/Alamy. **441** David Young-Wolff/PhotoEdit, Inc. **442** Ariel Skelley/CORBIS; Mary Evans Picture Library/Alamy; Mary Evans Picture Library/Alamy. **443** Lawrence Manning/CORBIS; Benoit Chartron/iStockphoto; V&A Images/Alamy. **450–451** Michael AW. **457** Photodisc/PunchStock. **458** Tyler Olson/Shutterstock. **459** Abundant Bouquet, 2001, Joan Son, Japanese papers, origami rose model by Pier Paulo Pessina, Italy; Suzanne Tucker/Shutterstock. **460** courtesy of Caxton Press. **460–461** The Image Bank/Getty Images. **461** ABUNDANT BOUQUET, 2001, by Joan Son, all Japanese papers. Origami butterfly design is by Michael LaFosse. Origami rose design is by Pier-Paolo Pessina. **462** Creatas Images/Jupiter Images; The Image Bank/Getty Images. **464** MUNI Nap, 2001, Anna L. Conti. Acrylic on canvas, private collection, Atherton, California. **465** Creatas Images/Jupiter Images; The Image Bank/Getty. **466** Composed Head, Bona (b. 1926). Tissue and oil on canvas, private collection, Paris, France/Peter Will/The Bridgeman Art Library. **469** Creatas Images/Jupiter Images; The Image Bank/Getty. **470** Michele Constantini/Photo Alto/Jupiter Images; Florist, 2004, Sara Nowen. Watercolor. Collection of the artist. **474–475** Image 100/CORBIS. **474** The Ramble, 2005, Ross Penhall. Oil on canvas, courtesy of Caldwell Snyder Gallery, San Francisco, California. **476** Image 100/CORBIS; Frederick M. Brown/Getty Images. **478** Andrew Fox/CORBIS. **480** Pauline St. Denis/CORBIS. **480** Tom Grill/Getty Images. **480** Rick Gomez/CORBIS. **482** Mike Watson. **483** Barber shop, 2006, Michael and Tammy Rice. Digital photograph, Twisted Tree Photography. **484–485** Craig Aurness/CORBIS. **484–485** German Telez. **485** Barber shop, 2006, Michael and Tammy Rice. Digital photograph, Twisted Tree Photography. **486** Stockbyte Silver/Getty Images. **486** Image 100/CORBIS. **487**

Photowood Inc/CORBIS. **488** Image 100/CORBIS. **489** Bolotowsky, Ilya (1907–1981) VAGA, NY In the Barber Shop, 1934. Smithsonian American Art Museum, Washington, DC/Art Resource, NY. **490** Photowood Inc/CORBIS. **491** Image 100/CORBIS; In the Barber Shop, 1934. Smithsonian American Art Museum, Washington, DC/Art Resource, NY. **492** Untitled, Jean-Charles Blais. Oil and collage on panel, Musee Cantini, Marseille, France, Giraudon/The Bridgeman Art Library. **495** Paul Seheult/Eye Ubiquitous/CORBIS; Lotus, 2000, Joel Nakamura, Acrylic on copper panel, private collection. **496** Idol of the god Brahma, bronze, Dinodia Bombay. India/The Bridgeman Art Library. **497** Untitled, 2004, Dewashish Das, Tempera on handmade paper, courtesy of Kala Fine Art Gallery, Austin Texas. **500** Dave G. Houser/CORBIS. **502–503** Comstock. **504** Brian Balley; Thirteen/Shutterstock. **505** The Springhouse, 1944, Newell Convers Wyeth, Oil tempera, gesso on canvas, 36x48. Delaware Art Museum, Wilmington, Delaware, Special Purchase Fund, 1946, DAM 1946-1. **506** The Halifax Herald Limited. **506–507** Jason Witherspoon/Design Pics. **507** The Springhouse, 1944 (gesso on canvas), Wyeth, Newell Convers (1882-1945)/Delaware Art Museum, Wilmington, USA/The Bridgeman Art Library. **508** Jason Sohn/Visions of America. **509** Yuri Samsonov/Shutterstock; Curry, John Steuart (1897-1946) Wisconsin Landscape. 1938-39. Oil on canvas, 42 x 84 in. (106.7 x 213.4 cm). George A. Hearn Fund, 1942 (42.154). Image copyright The Metropolitan Museum of Art. Image source: Art Resource, NY. **511** Jason Sohn/Visions of America. **513** Jason Witherspoon/Design Pics/CORBIS. **514** Round Lake, Mud Bay, 1915, Thomas John Thomson. Oil on Wood panel, Art Gallery of Ontario, Toronto, Canada. The Bridgeman Art Library. **515** Jason Sohn/Visions of America. **518** Jason Witherspoon/Design Pics/CORBIS. **519** Jason Sohn/Visions of America. **520** Connie Hayes/SIS Illustration/Veer. **522–523** Siqueiros, David Alfaro (1896-1974) ARS SEF/Art Resource, NY on page: 2013 Artists Rights Society (ARS), New York/SOMAAP, Mexico City. **523** Mugshot Photography. **525** Ales Fevzer. **527** Fabrice Coffrini/epa. **532** Lynford, 1969, Armitage, Karen (Contemporary Artist)/Private Collection/The Bridgeman Art Library; Hulton Archive/Stringer/GettyImages. **532–535** Ekely/Vetta/GettyImages. **535** Jacob Lawrence Foundation/Art Institute of Chicago/ARS. **537** Hulton Archive/Getty Images; Image Source/Getty Images; Silvia Koner/CORBIS; CORBIS; arvin Koner/CORBIS. **538** Hulton Archive/Getty Images. **543** Arnold Newman/Liaison Agency. **544–545** Time & Life Pictures/Getty Images. **552–553** Will & Deni McIntyre/CORBIS; Self Determination, 2004, Jirra Lulla Harvey Kalinya Communications. **556** Sandy Felsenthal/CORBIS. **557** Dana White/PhotoEdit, Inc. **557** Tony Freeman/PhotoEdit, Inc. **560** Douglas Kirkland/CORBIS; Watchtheworld/Shutterstock. **561** Ariel Skelley/CORBIS. **562–563** Ariel Skelley/CORBIS. **564** timqup/Shutterstock. **566** National Geographic Maps. **568** The Image Bank/Getty Images. **571** Silvia Otte/Photonica/Getty Images. **573** Doug Menuez/Photodisc Green/Getty Images. **574** Terry Vine/Stone/Getty Images. **575** Stockbyte Silver/Stockbyte/Getty Images. **580** Comstock/Thinkstock; bikeriderlondon/Shutterstock; Design Pics. Inc/Alamy. **582** CORBIS; Hero Images/CORBIS. **584–585** Juice Images/Getty Images. **586** Chuck Kennedy/Newscom. **588** Christ Carlson/AP/World Wide Images. **589** 2006 AFP/Getty Images; Rune

Acknowledgments, continued

Hellestad/CORBIS; Mark Shenley/Camera Press/Retna Ltd. **590** Roll Call Photos/Newscom. **593** Donna Summers, The Orlando Sentinel, 2000. **594** Gary Trudeau/Universal Press Syndicate. **595** Gary Trudeau/Universal Press Syndicate. **596** Gary Trudeau/Universal Press Syndicate. **597** Gary Trudeau/Universal Press Syndicate. **598** Gary Trudeau/Universal Press Syndicate. **599** Gary Trudeau/Universal Press Syndicate. **600** Universal Press Syndicate. **604–605** Tony Freeman/Photo Edit, Inc. **606** Repak De Choudhuri/CORBIS. **607** Peter Turnley/CORBIS. **608–609** Peter Turnley/CORBIS. **609** Reuters/CORBIS. **610** National Geographic Maps; Louise Gubb/CORBIS SABA/CORBIS; David Turnley/CORBIS. **611** David Turnley/CORBIS. **613** Jurgen Schadeberg/Hulton Archive/Getty Images; Viktoriya Field/Shutterstock; David Turnley; Bettman; Bettman. **613** Peter Turnley/CORBIS. **615** AP Images. **617** David Turnley/CORBIS. **618** African National Congress. **619** National Geographic Maps; National Geographic Maps; Antoine Gyori/CORBIS Sygma; Peter Probst/Alamy. **621** Robben Island, 2003, Nelson Mandela Louise Gubb/CORBIS SABA; The Window, 2003, Nelson Mandela Louise Gubb/CORBIS SABA; Louise Grubb/CORBIS. **623** Martin Paul/Photolibrary/Getty Images; Universal Images Group/Getty Images; Library of Congress Prints and Photographs. **625** Bob Daemmerich/CORBIS. **630** Bettmann/CORBIS. **633** Randy Duchaine/Alamy. **635** Mary Kate Denny/PhotoEdit; Dynamic Graphics Group/Alamy. **636** Marmaduke St. John/Alamy. **641** Ariel Skelley/CORBIS. **642** Chuck Savage/CORBIS. **650–651** Tree of Life, 1995, Alfredo Arreguin. Oil on Canvas, collection of the artist; J Henry Fair. **654** Hans Neleman. **655** Viktoriya Field/Shutterstock. **656** Blend Images/Alamy. **658** SuperStock. **660** Christopher Boswell/Shutterstock; Paul Barton/CORBIS. **661** The Return of the Drummers, 2002, Jimoh Buraimoh, Bead Painting, Museum of Modern African Art, UK. **663** The Return of the Drummers, 2002, Jimoh Buraimoh, Bead Painting, Museum of Modern African Art, UK. **664** A. Piatosa/Travel-Images.com; Christine Osborne/CORBIS. **667** Tom Cockrem/Lonely Planet Images/Getty Images. **668** Richard T. Nowitz/CORBIS. **671** Hidden Agenda, 1994, Jimoh Buraimoh, Bead painting, private collection. **673** Christine Osborne/CORBIS. **674** Baba Cheap Cheap, 1998, Tyrone Geter. Oil on canvas, collection of the artist. **679** Christine Osborne/CORBIS. **682** Hidden Treasure, 1991, EmmanuealEkong Ekefrey. Acyrilic, Contemporary African Art Collection Limited, CORBIS. **684** Christine Osborne/CORBIS. **687** Rhythm in Blue, 2004, Mark Buku. Oil on canvas, courtesy of Novica.com. **688** Hand and Egg, 2001, Emmanuel Atiamo Yeboa. Mixed media on canvas, courtesy of Novica.com. **691** African Sunset, 2005, Angela Ferriera. Oil on canvas, collection of the artist; Courtesy of the Margaret Walker Center, Jackson State University. **693** Creative Lifeline, 2005, Laura Lein Svencner, Assemblage, collection of the artist; Envision/CORBIS. **694–695** Envision/CORBIS. **695** Danny Lehman/CORBIS. **696** Ha Lam; Envision/CORBIS. **700** Brand X Pictures/PunchStock; Jose Luiz Peleaz, Inc./CORBIS. **702** Petrov Anton/Shutterstock; Russell Illig/Getty Images. **703** Mike Elliott/Shutterstock; Royal Shakespeare Company. **705** Royal Shakespeare Company. **707** Royal Shakespeare Company. **714** Royal Shakespeare Company. **717** Pictorial Press Ltd/Alamy; CORBIS. **718** Archive Photos/Moviepix/Getty Images. **719** John Springer Collection/CORBIS. **720** Envision. **724–725** Liz Garza Wiliams. **727** Richard Hamilton Smith/CORBIS. **729** Richard Hamilton Smith/CORBIS. **733** Down Eighteenth Street, 1980, Wayne Thiebaud. Oil and charcoal on canvas, gift of Edward R. Downe Jr., 1979, Hirschhorn Museum and Sculpture Garden, Washington, D.C. , Art © Wayne Thiebaud/Licensed by VAGA, New York, NY. **733** forARTSake. **735** The Yale Collection of American Literature, Beinecke Rare Book and Manuscript Library, Yale University; Forest, 2004, Yvette Molina. Oil on aluminum, courtesy of Ruth Bachofner Gallery, Santa Monica, California. **736** Snow, Storm, Tree, Winter Landscape Vlaminck, Maurice de (1876–1958) ARS, NY Snow Storm. Inv. 1935–29. Photo: René-Gabriel Ojéda. RMN-Grand Palais/Art Resource, NY ON PAGE: 2013 Artists Rights Society (ARS), New York/ADAGP, Paris. **737** CORBIS. **739** Light Spark, 2003, www.u-see.de. **739–740** Sam Diephuis/zefa. **741** Image 100/CORBIS; Preparing broad beans, Felicity House. Pastel on paper, private collection, The Bridgeman Art Library. **742** Librado Romero/The New York Times/Redux Pictures; Image 100/CORBIS. **746–747** Judy Paul. **752** Barna Tanko/Shutterstock; Jose Luis Pelaez, Inc./Blend Images/CORBIS. **756** Tim O'Hara/CORBIS. **757** Zero Creatives/Getty Images. **760** OLJ Studio/Shutterstock. **765** Arthur Tilley/Getty Images. **766** Scala/Art Resources; Jennifer Thermes/Getty Images; Claude Monet/Getty Images. **767** Jeff Rotman/Getty Images; Darwin Wiggett/AllCanada-Photos.com/CORBIS. **768** Skylines/Shutterstock; Hiroshi Higuchi/Getty Images; Flying Colours/Getty Images. **769** EDHAR/Shutterstock; Maksim Kabadou/Shutterstock; Igor Klimov/Shutterstock. **770** Bomshtein/Shutterstock. **772** Apple Computers; Terry Warner/Cartoon Stock Ltd; Apple Computers; Apple Computers. **927** Briann Balley/CORBIS; Nance Trueworthy/Getty Images. **929** Bob Krist/CORBIS; Eric Cahan/CORBIS. **930** Alan Abramowitz/Getty Images; Stockbyte/SuperStock; Pure Stock/Punchstock

ILLUSTRATION CREDITS

Michael Aki: **42** (bird), **46** (carp), **54** (snake); Henry Balaney: **203** (button); Steve Bjorkman: **401** (teen); Jude Buffum: **430–433** (texting). Peter Fasolino: **655–656** (four drawings in thought balloons); Dale Glasgow: **31** (education chart), **144–145** (robot tasks); Lauren Keswick: **366** (facial muscles); Christy Krames: **180** (nervous system, nerve cell); National Geographic maps: **142** (ROV competition map), **566** (U.S. map), **619** (South Africa map).

ALL MAPS: © NATIONAL GEOGRAPHIC MAPS